lonely pk

Eastern USA

| | New York, New Jersey & Pennsylvania p54 | New England p164 |

ND

MN

WI

MI

SD

Great Lakes p510

NE

IA

PA

NJ

DE

OH

IL

IN

WV

VA

Washington, DC & the Capital Region p248

MO

KY

KS

TN

NC

SC

OK

AR

The South p326

MS

AL

GA

TX

LA

Florida p452

ME

VT

NH

MA

NY

CT

RI

MD

FL

THIS EDITION WRITTEN AND RESEARCHED BY

Karla Zimmerman,

Amy C...   ...rg,

Paula...   ...g,

PLAN YOUR TRIP

JEREMY WOODHOUSE / GETTY IMAGES ©

BLUE RIDGE PARKWAY P319

RAY LASKOWITZ / GETTY IMAGES ©

EASTERN & SOUTHERN
USA CUISINE P278

ON THE ROAD

Contents

SPECIAL FEATURES

Welcome to Eastern USA

Flanked by mega-cities New York City and Chicago; landscaped with dune-backed beaches, smoky mountains and gator swamps; and steeped in musical roots, the East rolls out a sweet trip.

Mighty Metropolises

New York, New York is 'top of the heap,' as Frank Sinatra famously crooned. Brimming with 8.3 million people, the megalopolis looms like an alien mothership over the East, offering a mind-blowing array of culture, cuisine and entertainment. Cloud-poking Chicago, power-brokering Washington, DC, and fiery, Latin-fused Miami rise up close on its heels as other one-of-a-kind cityscapes. Look deeper to find the captivating old quarters of New Orleans, still ascending from waterlogged ashes, and raw-edged Detroit, where young DIY devotees are flocking to transform the abandoned city.

Beaches & Back Roads

The East Coast is where America gets its beach on, from the wild dunes and whale-rich waters of Cape Cod to the taffy-shop-lined boardwalks of Ocean City or the coral reefs of the Florida Keys. Inland, nature puts on a show in the swampy Florida Everglades, wolf-howling Boundary Waters, mist-tipped Appalachian Mountains and New England's forests, which blaze red, orange and yellow each autumn. Slowpoke byways unfurl throughout so you can soak up the landscapes, from historic Civil War battlefields to kitschy roadside attractions.

Chowhounds' Smorgasbord

Good eatin' reaches epic proportions here: hulking steamed lobsters with melted butter in Maine's seafood shacks, bagels and lox in Manhattan's delis, saucy barbecue ribs in Memphis' roadhouses, butter-smothered biscuits in North Carolina's diners, hot-spiced gumbo in New Orleans' cafes...and for dessert, thick slices of berry pie in the Midwest's supper clubs. You'll certainly work up a thirst – which you can slake with the region's sweet white wines, microbrewed beers and home-grown bourbon.

Cultural Cradle

The museums here are the nation's greatest hits – the Smithsonian, housing everything but the kitchen sink; the Metropolitan Museum of Art, a city-state of treasures; and the Art Institute of Chicago, hanging Impressionists by the roomful. Explore the roots of the blues, jazz and rock and roll at musical meccas such as Memphis' Sun Studio, where Elvis got his groove on; Cleveland's Rock and Roll Hall of Fame, for artifacts like Jimi Hendrix' Stratocaster; and the juke joints of Clarksdale, where blues slide guitar first pierced the air. For sky-high designs, Chicago and New York are drawing boards for the modern era's great architects.

Why I Love Eastern USA

By Karla Zimmerman, Author

I love the big city/rural mash-up in the eastern part of the country. You can be surrounded by skyscrapers in Chicago for breakfast, then two hours later be driving beside clip-clopping horses and buggies in Indiana's Amish country. You can be in the corridors of power in Washington, DC's Capitol for lunch, then hiking mountains in Virginia's dreamy Shenandoah National Park 90 minutes later. Throughout the region the music rocks, exquisite beers flow, and back-road diners, rib joints and lobster shacks tempt you into yet another slice of pie. Mmm, pie...

For more about our authors, see page 672

For more about our authors, see page 672

Above: Times Square (p73), Manhattan, NYC

Eastern USA

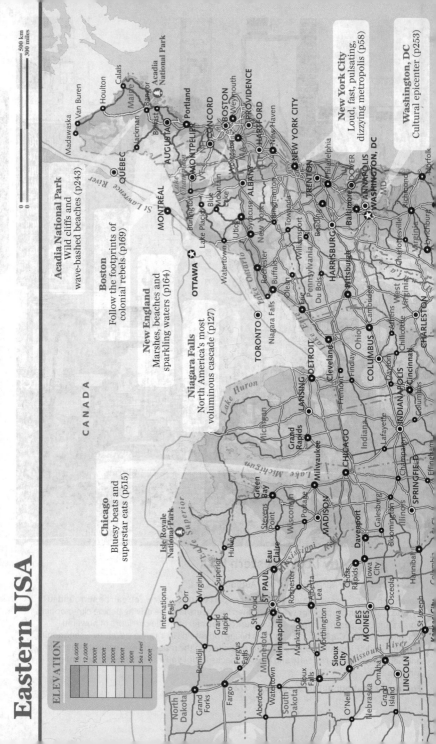

Acadia National Park
Wild cliffs and wave-bashed beaches (p243)

Boston
Follow the footprints of colonial rebels (p169)

New England
Marshes, beaches and sparkling waters (p164)

Niagara Falls
North America's most voluminous cascade (p127)

Chicago
Bluesy beats and superstar eats (p515)

New York City
Loud, fast, pulsating, dizzying metropolis (p58)

Washington, DC
Cultural epicenter (p253)

ELEVATION
16,000ft
12,000ft
9000ft
5000ft
2000ft
1000ft
500ft
Sea Level
-500ft

500 km
300 miles

CANADA

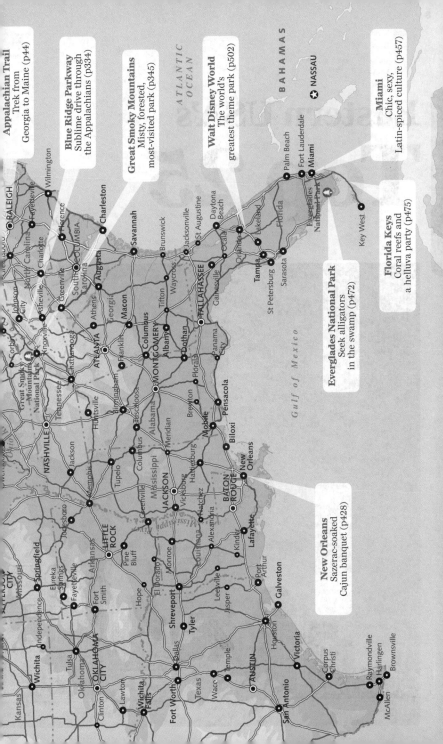

Appalachian Trail
Trek from
Georgia to Maine (p44)

Blue Ridge Parkway
Sublime drive through
the Appalachians (p334)

Great Smoky Mountains
Misty, forested,
most-visited park (p345)

Walt Disney World
The world's
greatest theme park (p502)

Miami
Chic, sexy,
Latin-spiced culture (p457)

Everglades National Park
Seek alligators
in the swamp (p472)

Florida Keys
Coral reefs and
a helluva party (p475)

New Orleans
Sazerac-soaked
Cajun banquet (p428)

ATLANTIC
OCEAN

BAHAMAS

★ NASSAU

Gulf of Mexico

Eastern USA's
Top 25

New York City

1 Home to striving artists, hedge-fund moguls and immigrants from every corner of the globe, New York City (p58) is constantly reinventing itself. It remains one of the world centers of fashion, theater, food, music, publishing, advertising and finance. A staggering number of museums, parks and ethnic neighborhoods are scattered through the five boroughs. Do as every New Yorker does: hit the streets. Every block reflects the character and history of this dizzying kaleidoscope, and on even a short walk you can cross continents. Below left: Lower Manhattan skyline with One World Trade Center (p61)

National Mall

2 Nearly two miles long and lined with iconic monuments and hallowed marble buildings, the National Mall is the epicenter of political and cultural life in Washington, DC (p253). In the summer, massive music and food festivals are staged here, while year-round visitors wander the halls of America's finest museums lining the green. For exploring American history, there's no better place to ruminate, whether tracing your hand along the Vietnam War Memorial or ascending the steps of the Lincoln Memorial, where Martin Luther King Jr gave his famous 'I Have a Dream' speech. Below: Washington Monument (p261)

SYLVAIN SONNET / GETTY IMAGES ©

ALTRENDO IMAGES / GETTY IMAGES ©

2

Chicago

3 The Windy City will blow you away with its architecture, lakefront beaches and world-class museums. But its true mojo is its blend of high culture and earthy pleasures. Is there another metropolis that dresses its Picasso sculpture in local sports-team gear? Where residents queue for hot dogs as equally as for North America's top restaurant? Winters are long, but come summer, Chicago (p515) fetes the warm days with a huge array of food and music festivals along its waterfront. Below: Crown Fountain by Jaume Plensa, Millennium Park

New England in Fall

4 It's an event that approaches epic proportions in New England (p164): watching the leaves change color. You can do it anywhere – all you need is one brilliant tree. But if you're most people, you want *lots* of trees. From the Litchfield Hills in Connecticut and the Berkshires in Massachusetts to the Green Mountains in Vermont, entire hillsides blaze in brilliant crimsons, oranges and yellows. Covered bridges and white-steeple churches with abundant maple trees put Vermont and New Hampshire at the forefront of leaf-peeping heaven.

LAURI PATTERSON / GETTY IMAGES ©

FLASH PARKER / GETTY IMAGES ©

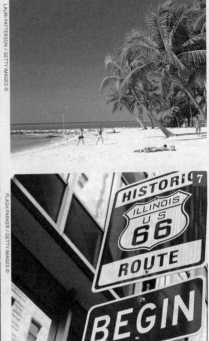

Walt Disney World

5 Want to set the bar high? Call yourself 'The Happiest Place on Earth.' Walt Disney World (p502) does, and then pulls out all the stops to deliver the exhilarating sensation that you are the most important character in the show. Despite all the frantic rides, entertainment and nostalgia, the magic is watching your own child swell with belief after they have made Goofy laugh, been curtsied to by Cinderella, guarded the galaxy with Buzz Lightyear, and battled Darth Maul like your very own Jedi knight.

Florida Keys

6 This island chain drifts as far south as you can get in continental USA. Except for drinking and partying, people come to the Keys (p475) to fish, snorkel, dive, kayak, hike, cycle, fish some more, snorkel again and swim with dolphins. North America's best coral reefs percolate under the jade-green water and provide brag-worthy expeditions. Then there's Key West, the gloriously unkempt, bawdy, freak-loving exclamation point at the end of the line. Hippies, fire-jugglers, artists and other free spirits converge on its carnival atmosphere after dark. Top right: Key West (p479)

Route 66

7 Known as the Mother Road, this fragile ribbon of concrete was the USA's original road trip, launched in 1926. It begins in Chicago, and the 300-mile stretch onward through Illinois (p540) offers classic, time-warped touring. Fork into thick slabs of pie in small-town diners; snap photos of roadside attractions like the Gemini Giant, a sky-high fiberglass spaceman; and motor on past neon signs, drive-in movie theaters and other Americana. From here it's 2100 miles more to the end of the route in Los Angeles. Above: Route 66 sign (p521), Chicago

Civil War Sites

8 Sites scatter over swaths of eastern USA, from Pennsylvania to Louisiana. Renowned places to connect with some of America's darkest hours are at Antietam, Maryland (site of the bloodiest day in American history, where 23,000 soldiers died); Gettysburg, Pennsylvania (the battlefield and cemetery, where President Lincoln delivered his 'Four score...' address); and Vicksburg, Mississippi (a must for history buffs, with a 16-mile driving tour through the areas General Grant besieged for 47 days). In summer, many sites host battle re-enactments. Below left: Gettysburg Monument

Boston

9 From cobbled colonial lanes to crazed sports fans, Boston (p169) brews a colorful scene. It is arguably the USA's most historic city – site of the Boston Tea Party, Paul Revere's ride and the first battle of the Revolutionary War – all of which you can trace on the 2.5-mile, red-brick Freedom Trail. Harvard University's campus lets you be a little rebellious yourself at its edgy music clubs. Boston's oyster houses, cafes and trattorias (especially thick in the Italian North End) fortify you for the evening's exploits. Below right: Harvard University rowing crew, Cambridge (p177)

ALLAN MONTAINE / GETTY IMAGES ©

Niagara Falls

10 Crowded? Cheesy? Well, yes. Niagara is short, too – it barely cracks the top 500 waterfalls worldwide for height. But c'mon, when those great muscular bands of water arch over the precipice like liquid glass and roar into the void below, and when you sail toward it in a misty little boat, Niagara Falls (p127) impresses big time. In terms of sheer volume, nowhere in North America beats its thundering cascade, with more than one million bathtubs of water plummeting over the edge every second.

Blue Ridge Parkway

11 In the southern Appalachian Mountains of Virginia and North Carolina, you can take in sublime sunsets, watch for wildlife and lose all sense of the present while staring off at the vast wilderness surrounding this 469-mile roadway (p35). Hikes take you deeper into nature, from easy trails along lakes to challenging scrambles up to eagles'-nest heights. Camp or spend the night at forest lodges, and don't miss the bluegrass and mountain music scene of nearby towns such as Asheville, North Carolina and Floyd in Virginia.

RAY LASKOWITZ / GETTY IMAGES ©

Musical Roots

12 Name the genre, and it probably began here. The Mississippi Delta birthed the blues, while New Orleans opened the door to jazz. Rock and roll arrived the day Elvis Presley walked into Sun Studio (p360) in Memphis. And country made its way from fiddle-and-banjo Appalachian hamlets to Nashville's Grand Ole Opry (p369). The Mississippi River took the music north, where Chicago and Detroit riffed into the electric blues and Motown sound, respectively. It all translates into great live music wherever you are in the region. Above: Trumpeter, New Orleans

New Orleans

13 Reborn after Hurricane Katrina in 2005, New Orleans (p428) is back. Caribbean-colonial architecture, Creole cuisine and a riotous air of celebration seem more alluring than ever in the Big Easy. Nights are spent catching Dixieland jazz, blues and rock amid bouncing live-music joints, and the city's riotous annual festivals (Mardi Gras, Jazz Fest) are famous the world over. 'Nola' is also a food-loving town that celebrates its myriad culinary influences. Feast on lip-smacking jambalaya, soft-shelled crab and Louisiana *cochon* (pulled pork) before hitting the bar scene on Frenchman St. Top right: Jambalaya

Antebellum South

14 Steeped in history and regional pride, the Antebellum South is about grand homes and cotton plantations, moss-draped trees and azalea-choked gardens. Absorb the vibe in Charleston (p348), with strolling, admiring the architecture and lingering over dinners on the verandah. Fall under the spell of Savannah's live oaks, shady boulevards, seafood and humid nights. Or ogle the mansions of genteel Natchez (p420), the oldest town on the Mississippi River – you'd be hard-pressed to see more sweeping staircases per square mile anywhere else. Above: Antebellum mansion, Selma (p412), Alabama

Miami

15 Miami (p457) seems to have it all. Beyond the stunning beaches and Art Deco Historic District, there's culture at every turn. In cigar-filled dance halls, Havana expats dance to *son* and boleros; in exclusive nightclubs stiletto-heeled, fiery-eyed Brazilian models shake to Latin hip-hop; and in the park old men clack dominoes. To top it off, street vendors and restaurants dish out flavors from the Caribbean, Cuba, Argentina and Spain. Below: Calle Ocho Festival, Carnaval Miami (p464)

Boardwalk Empire

16 Strolling along the East Coast's beach boardwalk is a rite of passage, be it in Ocean City, Maryland; Rehoboth Beach, Delaware; Virginia Beach, Virginia; or Atlantic City, New Jersey. It doesn't matter where. The point is to enjoy the all-star roster of summer indulgence that inevitably lines the walkway: funnel cakes, go-karts, pizza shacks, saltwater taffy shops. Parents push strollers, tots lick ice-cream cones, and teenagers check each other out. Don't get so caught up you forget to take in the sea views! Bottom: Rehoboth Beach (p296)

MARK NEWMAN / GETTY IMAGES ©

Appalachian Trail

17 The country's longest footpath (p44) is over 2100 miles long, crosses six national parks and slices through 14 states from Georgia to Maine. Deep woods, alpine peaks, cow-dotted farms and foraging bears are all part of the landscape. It's estimated that two to three million people trek a portion of the trail every year, inhaling the fresh air and admiring the spectacular scenery. Fewer than 600 hikers persevere all the way through. Got six months and fortitude to spare? The reward is sublime – true for shorter stretches, too.

Mississippi River

18 As Old Man River traces through the country from its Northwoods beginning in Minnesota to its palmetto-fringed end in Louisiana, it meanders past eagles' nests and juke joints, pine forests and plantations. Covering more than 2000 miles, it churns through major cities like Minneapolis, Memphis and New Orleans. There are still riverboats, as in Mark Twain's heyday, but they're more likely to be casinos or tour vessels now. Road trippers heed the call of the mythic Great River Road as it edges the waterway throughout its duration.

New England Coastline

19 Summer in New England (p164) can get quite humid, so the region's population flocks to the coast for cool ocean breezes. In Massachusetts, great beaches ring Martha's Vineyard, the area's largest island. At nearby Cape Cod National Seashore, salt marshes and wild dunes dot the landscape, while humpback whales spout majestically offshore. Unspoiled Block Island offers simple pleasures such as rolling farms, uncrowded beaches and quiet hiking and cycling trails. Top right: Portland Head Light (p238)

DON JOHNSTON / GETTY IMAGES ©

Everglades National Park

20 The Everglades (p472) unnerve. They don't reach majestically skyward or fill your heart with the aching beauty of a glacier-carved valley. They ooze, flat and watery, a river of grass mottled by hammocks, cypress domes and mangroves. You can't hike them, not really. To properly explore the Everglades – and meet its prehistoric residents – you must leave the safety of land. Push a canoe off a muddy bank, tamp down your fear, and explore the waterways on the Everglades' own, unforgettable terms.

Awesome Art

21 Start with the big guns: New York's Metropolitan Museum of Art (p77) and the Art Institute of Chicago (p517), both behemoths you could spend days at. Pittsburgh has the Andy Warhol Museum (p156), an eerie funhouse of bizarre films and pop art, while the mind-blowing Dalí Museum (p495), designed by HOK architects, adds a surreal splash to St Petersburg, Florida. Out of town, jet setters head to the hills of New York's Lower Hudson Valley (p116) for the hulking mod pieces at Storm King Art Center and Dia Beacon. Top: Dalí Museum

Great Smoky Mountains

22 Named for the heather-colored mist that hangs over the peaks, the Smokies comprise a national park that receives more visitors than any other. The pocket of deep Appalachian woods straddles Tennessee and North Carolina, protecting forested ridges where bears, deer, elk, wild turkeys and over 1600 kinds of flowers find sanctuary. Nearly 10 million people a year come to hike, camp, ride horses, cycle, raft and fish, though it's easy to lose the crowds if you're willing to walk or paddle. Bottom: Mountain Farm Museum (p346)

MARK NEWMAN / GETTY IMAGES ©

DAVID SUCSY / GETTY IMAGES ©

Amish Country

23 Life slows way down in the Amish communities of northeast Ohio (p557), southeast Pennsylvania (p152) and northern Indiana (p551) – the USA's three largest Amish clusters. Little boys in straw hats steer horse-drawn buggies, long-bearded men hand-plow the tidy fields, and demurely dressed women and girls carry shoofly pies to market. The 'Plain People,' as they're known, are a centuries-old sect who live a simple life without electricity, telephones or motorized vehicles. Berlin in Ohio, Lancaster in Pennsylvania, and Middlebury in Indiana, are good places to see the clock turned back.

Acadia National Park

24 Acadia National Park (p243) is where the mountains meet the sea. Miles of rocky coastline and even more miles of hiking and biking trails make this wonderland Maine's most popular destination, and deservedly so. The high point (literally) is Cadillac Mountain, the 1530ft peak that can be accessed by foot, bicycle or vehicle; early risers can catch the country's first sunrise from this celebrated summit. Later in the day, after working up an appetite on the trails and beaches, indulge in tea and popovers at Jordan Pond.

Great Lakes

25 Together, the five Great Lakes (p510) – Superior, Michigan, Huron, Ontario and Erie – that extend across the region's north possess about 20% of the earth's fresh water and 95% of America's. They offer miles of beaches, dunes, resort towns and lighthouse-dotted scenery. Add in wave-bashed cliffs, islands freckling the shore, and freighters chugging in to busy ports, and you can see how the region earned its 'Third Coast' nickname. Anglers, kayakers and even surfers will find their sweet spot here. Above: Marblehead Lighthouse, Lake Erie

Need to Know

For more information, see Survival Guide (p642)

Currency
US dollar ($)

Language
English

Visas
Visitors from Canada, the UK, Australia, New Zealand, Japan and many EU countries do not need visas for less than 90 days. Other nations, see http://travel.state.gov.

Money
ATMs widely available. Credits cards accepted at most hotels, restaurants and shops.

Cell Phones
Foreign phones operating on tri- or quad-band frequencies will work in the USA. Or purchase inexpensive cell phones with a pay-as-you-go plan here.

Time
Eastern Standard Time (GMT minus five hours): NYC, New England, Florida; Central Standard Time (GMT minus six hours): Chicago, New Orleans

When to Go

Boston
GO Apr–Oct

New York City
GO May–Sep

Chicago
GO May–Sep

Washington, DC
GO Mar–Apr & Sep–Oct

New Orleans
GO Feb–May

Miami
GO Dec–Apr

Tropical climate
Dry climate
Warm to hot summers, mild winters
Mild to hot summers, cold winters

High Season
(Jun–Aug)

➡ Warm, sunny days across the region

➡ Accommodation prices peak (30% up on average)

➡ Big outdoor music festivals abound: Milwaukee's Summerfest, Newport's Folk Fest, Chicago's Lollapalooza etc

Shoulder
(Oct, Apr & May)

➡ Milder temperatures; can be rainy

➡ Wildflowers bloom, especially in May

➡ Fall foliage areas (ie New England, Blue Ridge Parkway) remain busy

Low Season
(Nov–Mar)

➡ Dark, wintry days, with snowfall in the north

➡ Lowest prices for accommodation (aside from ski resorts and warmer getaway destinations like Florida, for which it's peak season)

➡ Attractions keep shorter hours or close for the winter

Websites

Festivals.com (www.festivals.com) Find America's best celebrations for live music, food, drink and dance.

Lonely Planet (www.lonelyplanet.com/usa) Destination information, hotel bookings, travel forum, photos.

National Park Service (www.nps.gov) Gateway to America's greatest natural treasures: its national parks.

New York Times Travel (http://travel.nytimes.com) Travel news, practical advice and engaging features.

Roadside America (www.roadsideamerica.com) For all things weird and wacky.

Important Numbers

To call any regular number, dial 1, followed by the area code and the seven-digit number.

USA country code	☑1
International access code	☑011
Emergency	☑911
Directory assistance	☑411
International directory assistance	☑00

Exchange Rates

Australia	A$1	$0.97
Canada	C$1	$0.97
Europe	€1	$1.37
Japan	¥100	$1.02
New Zealand	NZ$1	$0.85
UK	UK£1	$1.61

For current exchange rates see www.xe.com.

Daily Costs

Budget:
Less than $100

➡ Dorm beds: $20–30; campgrounds: around $15–30; budget motels: from $60

➡ Lunch from a cafe or food truck: $5–8

➡ Travel on public transit: $2–3

Midrange:
$150–250

➡ Double room in midrange hotel: $100–200

➡ Midrange restaurant dinner: $50–80 for two

➡ Car hire: from $30 per day

Top End:
More than $250

➡ Room in a top hotel/resort: from $250

➡ Dining in top restaurants: $60–100 per person

➡ Big nights out (plays, concerts): $60–200

Opening Hours

Opening hours vary throughout the year. We've provided high-season opening hours; hours will generally decrease in the shoulder and low seasons.

Banks 8:30am–4:30pm Monday to Friday

Bars 5pm–midnight Sunday to Thursday, to 2am Friday & Saturday

Nightclubs 10pm–3am Thursday to Saturday

Shopping malls 9am–9pm

Stores 9am–6pm Monday to Saturday, noon–5pm Sunday

Supermarkets 8am–8pm, some open 24hr

Arriving in Eastern USA

JFK, New York (p110) From JFK take the AirTrain to Jamaica Station and then LIRR to Penn Station, which costs $12 to $15 (45 minutes). A taxi to Manhattan costs $52, plus toll and tip (45 to 90 minutes).

Chicago O'Hare (p538) The Blue Line El train ($5) runs 24/7. Trains depart every 10 minutes or so; they reach the downtown area in 40 minutes. Airport Express shuttle vans cost $32 (40 to 60 minutes); taxis cost around $50 (25 to 50 minutes).

Miami International (p468) SuperShuttle to South Beach for $21 (50 to 90 minutes); taxi to Miami Beach for $34 (40 to 60 minutes). Take the Metrorail to downtown (Government Center) for $2 (15 minutes).

Getting Around

Car Driving is the main way to access the region. In big cities (New York, Chicago) it can be a hassle, though, with traffic gridlock and hefty parking fees (upward of $40 per day). Car rentals are available in every town.

Train Outside the Boston-to-Washington, DC corridor, train travel is mostly for scenic journeys. Amtrak (www.amtrak.com) is the national carrier.

Bus Short-haul carriers such as Megabus (www.megabus.com/us) and Bolt Bus (www.boltbus.com) are popular for getting between main cities (eg New York to DC) – this is typically the cheapest way to travel. Tickets must be purchased online in advance.

For much more on **getting around**, see p653

If You Like...

Big Cities

The East's big cities are a dominant feature of the region, and endlessly culturally diverse.

New York City You can't get bigger than NYC – 8.3 million people strong, loud, fast, pulsing with energy, symphonic and always evolving. (p58)

Chicago The Midwest's metropolis is a cultural stew of skyscrapers, public art, vast museums, indie clubs and a delirious number of eats. (p515)

Baltimore The gritty port city has morphed into a hip beauty, sporting world-class museums, trendy shops and boutique hotels. (p283)

Philadelphia History is everywhere in the USA's first capital, but Philly's urbane side comes out in its energetic food, music and arts scenes. (p136)

Detroit A case study of how cities rise and fall, and maybe – just maybe – rise again. (p564)

National Parks

Great Smoky Mountains Heather-colored mist clings to the peaks, while black bears, elk and wild turkeys prowl the USA's most-visited park. (p345)

Acadia Maine's unspoiled wilderness offers surging coastal mountains, towering sea cliffs, surf-pounded beaches and quiet ponds. (p243)

Shenandoah Spectacular vistas unfurl along the Blue Ridge Mountains, with great hiking and camping, including along the Appalachian Trail. (p315)

Everglades South Florida's watery wonderland is home to snaggle-toothed crocodiles, stealthy panthers, pink flamingos and mellow manatees. (p472)

Isle Royale Floating in Lake Superior's midst, it's devoid of roads, cars and crowds, giving wolves and moose room to roam. (p580)

Fabulous Food

Maine lobster, Philly cheesesteaks, Memphis barbecue, Wisconsin cheddar – you'll need to loosen the belt wherever you are in the East.

New Orleans Hot-spiced gumbo, fresh-shucked oysters and bourbon-soaked bread pudding highlight the Creole menu in America's most food-centric city. (p428)

New York City Whether you crave steak *frites*, linguini con vongole, sushi, chicken tikka masala or gourmet hot dogs, globe-trotting Gotham has you covered. (p58)

Chicago The Windy City plates an unapologetically rich clash of high gastronomy and comfort food, plus neighborhoods packed with many and varied ethnic eats. (p515)

Durham Rich in cafes and farm-to-table storefront joints, this North Carolina burg has been dubbed 'the South's tastiest town.' (p339)

Madison, WI An impressive locavore scene has cooked here for 30-plus years, along with food trucks and one of the nation's hugest farmers markets. (p585)

IF YOU LIKE... WINE

Swirl a glass in Virginia's vineyards. The state is now the USA's fifth-biggest wine producer. You can even sample wines grown on Thomas Jefferson's estate. (p303)

(Top) Art Deco Historic District (p457), Miami
(Bottom) National Air & Space Museum (p257), Washington, DC

Architecture

Chicago Birthplace of the skyscraper, Chicago has magnificent works by many of the great 20th-century architects. (p515)

Fallingwater This Frank Lloyd Wright masterpiece blends into the forested landscape and the waterfall over which the house is built. (p162)

Miami Miami's Art Deco Historic District is a Technicolor dream come to life. (p457)

Taliesin Another one for Frank Lloyd Wright fans: Taliesin was the site of his home and influential school in Spring Green, Wisconsin. (p588)

Columbus Believe it: there's big architecture in small Columbus, Indiana – thanks to the town's forward-thinking industrialists. (p558)

Museums

Smithsonian Institution The nation's premier treasure chest is actually a group of 19 museums. Best of all, they're all free. (p256)

Metropolitan Museum of Art The top-draw attraction in NYC is like a cultural city-state, boasting a trove of two million artworks. (p77)

Art Institute of Chicago The nation's second-largest art museum (after the Met) hangs masterpieces aplenty, especially impressionist paintings. (p517)

Andy Warhol Museum The big-spectacled King of Pop Art bestowed Pittsburgh with far-out works. (p156)

Salvador Dalí Museum A magnificent collection of the Surrealist's oil paintings makes its odd home in St Petersburg, Florida. (p495)

Theme Parks

Walt Disney World Plunge in the fairytale world of the 'Happiest Place on Earth' and get swept up in miles of nostalgia and thrill rides. (p502)

Dollywood A paean to the much-loved country singer Dolly Parton, with Appalachian-themed rides and attractions in the hills of Tennessee. (p381)

Cedar Point Masochists line up for the corkscrewing GateKeeper (new in 2013) at this Valhalla of roller coasters in Ohio. (p556)

Universal Orlando Resort Famed home of Universal Studios and the new Wizarding World of Harry Potter. (p499)

Outdoor Activities

Appalachian Trail Even if you choose not to walk all 2100 miles, hop on for a day hike to experience the sublime scenery; 14 states provide access. (p44)

Boundary Waters Canoe deep into Minnesota's northern wilderness to camp under the stars and perhaps glimpse the aurora borealis. (p605)

New River Gorge National River Legendary white water froths in West Virginia, ripping through a primeval forest gorge that's utterly Eden-like. (p325)

Long Island Surf's up in New York, from Montauk's waves to Nassau County's Long Beach, the newest stop on surfing's pro tour. (p112)

Stowe Mountain Vermont invented snowboarding. The state's premier crag is *the* place to shred. (p222)

History

The north has Colonial and Revolutionary hot spots, while the mid-Atlantic and south hold the majority of Civil War battlefields.

Independence National Historic Park Highlights include the Liberty Bell and Independence Hall, where America's founders signed the Constitution. (p138)

Boston's Freedom Trail Visit Paul Revere's home, an 18th-century graveyard and 14 other Revolutionary War sites along the 2.5-mile path. (p179)

Henry Ford Museum/Greenfield Village It holds history's greatest hits: the bus Rosa Parks sat in, the Wright Brothers' airplane workshop and more. (p571)

Washington, DC See the sites where Lincoln was assassinated, Martin Luther King Jr gave his most famous speech and Nixon's presidency was undone. (p253)

Vicksburg The Mississippi bluffs that General Grant besieged for 47 days are ground zero for Civil War enthusiasts. (p418)

Nightlife

New Orleans Go beyond Bourbon St into the neighborhoods where Sazerac swirls in glasses and jazz, Dixieland and zydeco spill from clubs. (p442)

New York City As Sinatra sang, it's the city that doesn't sleep, with bars and clubs throughout town staying open til 4am nightly. (p102)

Athens, Georgia The compact little college town boasts a mighty music scene that launched the B-52s and REM. (p559)

Minneapolis Everyone's in a band here, and there are bars and banged-up clubs aplenty to let them plug into. (p597)

Memphis Party on Beale St, a round-the-clock fiesta of bars, to-go beer counters and live, fret-bending blues. (p366)

Offbeat America

Foamhenge A magnificent homage to Styrofoam, this Stonehenge redux is done to scale and is appropriately tranquil around sunset. (p319)

NashTrash Tours Nashville's tall-haired 'Jugg Sisters' take visitors on a deliciously tacky journey through the city's spicier side. (p372)

Spam Museum Try your hand at canning the sweet pork magic in Austin, Minnesota, the blue-tinned meat's revered birthplace. (p602)

Key West Cemetery Wander the gothic labyrinth full of colorful epitaphs, such as 'I told you I was sick.' (p480)

American Visionary Art Museum Peruse outsider art (including pieces created by the clinically insane) at this Baltimore curiosity. (p285)

IF YOU LIKE... OLD-SCHOOL DINERS

Tuck into thick pancakes at Arcade, a classic Memphis diner that Elvis used to frequent. (p365)

Snowboarding, Killington (p221), Vermont

Theater

New York City and Chicago are the stars, while smaller cities such as Minneapolis give voice to emerging talents.

Broadway Theater District It doesn't get more iconic than the bright lights and glittering marquees along a certain street in Midtown Manhattan. (p107)

Steppenwolf Theatre John Malkovich, Gary Sinise and other now-famous actors launched Chicago's scene here nearly four decades ago. (p536)

Guthrie Theater Minneapolis has so many theaters it's nicknamed 'the Mini Apple.'

The uber-cool Guthrie leads the pack. (p598)

American Players Theatre It stages Shakespeare and other classics outdoors amid the woodlands of Spring Green, Wisconsin. (p588)

Grand Ole Opry There's more than country music under the lights – it's a full-fledged, foot-stompin' variety show. (p376)

Beaches

South Beach The world-famous strand is less about wave-frolicking than taking in the parade of people on Miami's favorite playground. (p457)

Cape Cod National Seashore Massive sand dunes, picturesque lighthouses and cool forests invite endless exploring on the Massachusetts cape. (p193)

Montauk At the eastern tip of Long Island, windswept Montauk has pretty seascapes, beach camping and a still-functioning 18th-century lighthouse. (p115)

Michigan's Gold Coast Endless stretches of sand, dunes, wineries, orchards and B&B-filled towns blanket the state's western shoreline. (p574)

Outer Banks North Carolina's isolated barrier islands offer everything from popular beaches to remote strands where wild ponies run free. (p331)

Month by Month

January

The New Year starts off with a shiver as snowfall blankets large swaths of the northern regions. Ski resorts kick into high gear, while sun-lovers seek refuge in warmer climes (especially Florida).

Mummers Parade

Philadelphia's biggest event is this brilliant parade (www.mummers.com) on New Year's Day, for which local clubs spend months creating costumes and mobile scenery in order to win top honors. String bands and clowns add cheer.

Chinese New Year

In late January or early February, you'll find colorful celebrations and feasting anywhere there's a Chinatown. NYC and Chicago each ring in the occasion with a parade, floats, firecrackers, bands and plenty of merriment.

St Paul Winter Carnival

Is it cold in Minnesota in late January? You betcha. That doesn't stop denizens from bundling up in parkas and snow boots to partake in 10 days of ice sculptures, ice skating and ice fishing (www.winter-carnival.com).

February

Despite indulging in winter mountain getaways, many Americans dread February for its long, dark nights and frozen days. For foreign visitors, this can be the cheapest time to travel, with ultra-discount rates for flights and hotels.

Mardi Gras

Held in late February or early March (on the day before Ash Wednesday), Mardi Gras (Fat Tuesday) is the finale of Carnival. New Orleans' hedonistic celebrations (www.mardigrasneworleans.com) are legendary as colorful parades, masquerade balls and plenty of feasting rule the day.

March

The first blossoms of spring arrive – at least in the south (the north still shivers in the chill). In New England's mountains, it's still ski season. Meanwhile, the Spring Break masses descend on Florida.

Baseball Spring Training

Throughout March, Florida hosts MLB's spring training 'Grapefruit League' (www.floridagrapefruitleague.com): 15 pro baseball teams train and play exhibition games, drawing fans to the Orlando, Tampa Bay and southeast areas.

St Patrick's Day

On the 17th, the patron saint of Ireland is honored with brass bands and ever-flowing pints of Guinness. Huge parades occur in New York, Boston and Chicago (which goes all-out by dyeing the Chicago River green).

National Cherry Blossom Festival

The brilliant blooms of Japanese cherry blossoms around DC's Tidal Basin are celebrated with concerts, parades, taiko drumming, kite-flying and 90 other events during the five-week fest (www.nationalcherry-blossomfestival.org). More than one million people go each year, so don't forget to book ahead.

🥢 Maple Syrup Tasting

Vermont's maple syrup producers invite the public to their 'sugarhouses' to see the sweet stuff being made during the Vermont Maple Open House Weekend (www.vermontmaple.org) in late March. Maine producers do the same on the last Sunday of the month.

April

The weather is warming up, but April can still be unpredictable, with chilly weather mixed with a few teasingly warm days up north. Down south, it's a fine time to travel.

🏃 Boston Marathon

At the country's oldest marathon (www.baa.org), tens of thousands of spectators watch runners cross the finish line at Copley Sq on Patriots' Day, a Massachusetts holiday held on the third Monday of April.

☆ New Orleans Jazz Fest

The Big Easy hosts the country's best jazz jam (www.nojazzfest.com) for 10 days in late April with top-notch horn blowers and ivory ticklers. Almost better than the music is the food: soft-shell crab po' boys, Cajun rice with pork sausage and white-chocolate bread pudding.

☆ Tribeca Film Festival

Robert De Niro co-organizes this NYC soiree (www.tribecafilm.com) showcasing documentaries and narrative features, held during 12 days in late April. It has quickly risen in stature since its 2002 inception.

May

May is true spring and one of the loveliest times to travel in the region, with blooming wildflowers and mostly mild sunny weather. Summer crowds and high prices have yet to arrive.

☆ Kentucky Derby

On the first Saturday of the month, a who's who of upper-crust America puts on their pinstripe suits and most flamboyant hats and descends on Louisville for the horse race known as the 'greatest two minutes in sports' (www.kentucky-derby.com).

☆ Movement Electronic Music Festival

The world's largest electronic music festival (www.movement.us) packs Detroit's Hart Plaza over Memorial Day weekend. You'll find both up-and-comers and the big names in the biz, such as Fatboy Slim, Carl Craig and Felix da Housecat, at the dance-loving extravaganza.

June

Summer is here. Americans spend more time at outdoor cafes and restaurants, and head to the shore or to national parks. School is out; vacationers fill the highways and resorts, bringing higher prices.

☆ Chicago Blues Festival

It's the globe's biggest free blues fest (www.chicagobluesfestival.us), with four days of the electrified music that made Chicago famous. More than a half-million people unfurl blankets by the multiple stages that take over Grant Park in early June.

☆ Bonnaroo Music & Arts Fest

Set in Tennessee's heartland on a 700-acre farm, this sprawling music fest (www.bonnaroo.com) showcases big-name rock, soul, country and more over four days in mid-June.

☆ Mermaid Parade

In Brooklyn, NYC, Coney Island celebrates summer's steamy arrival with a kitsch-loving parade (www.coneyisland.com), complete with skimpily attired mermaids and horn-blowing mermen.

☆ CMA Music Festival

Legions of country music fans don their cowboy boots and unite in Nashville for the chance to hear the genre's top crooners. Over 400 artists perform at stages on Riverfront Park and LP Field (www.cmaworld.com).

☆ Summerfest

Milwaukee lets loose with a heckuva music fest (www.summerfest.com) for 11 days in late June/early July, with hundreds of big-name rock, blues, jazz, country and alternative bands swarming 10 lakefront stages. Local beer, brats and cheese accompany the proceedings.

July

With summer in full swing, Americans break out the backyard barbecues or head for the beach. The prices are high and the crowds can be fierce, but it's one of the liveliest times to visit.

☆ Independence Day

The nation celebrates its birthday with a fireworks-filled bang on the 4th. In Philadelphia, descendents of the Declaration of Independence signatories ring the Liberty Bell. Chicago, Boston, New York and Washington, DC are also great spots to enjoy the fun.

☆ National Black Arts Festival

Artists converge on Atlanta for this 10-day event (www. nbaf.org) celebrating African American music, theater, literature and film. Maya Angelou, Wynton Marsalis, Spike Lee and Youssou N'Dour are among those who've performed here.

☆ Newport Folk Festival

Newport, Rhode Island, a summer haunt of the well-heeled, hosts this high-energy music fest (www. newportfolk.org) in late July. Top folk artists take to the storied stage, best remembered as the venue where Bob Dylan went electric.

(Top) Cherry blossoms in season, Washington, DC
(Bottom) Mardi Gras celebrations, New Orleans

August

Expect blasting heat in August, with temperatures and humidity less bearable the further south you go. You'll find people-packed beaches, high prices and empty cities on weekends, when residents escape to the nearest waterfront.

☆ Lollapalooza

This massive rock fest (www.lollapalooza.com) in Chicago is a raucous event, with 130 bands – including many A-listers – spilling off eight stages in Grant Park the first weekend in August.

✖ Maine Lobster Festival

If you love lobster like Maine loves lobster, indulge in this feeding frenzy (www.mainelobsterfestival. com) held in Rockland in early August. King Neptune and the Sea Goddess oversee a week full of events and, of course, as much crustacean as you can eat.

September

With the end of summer, cooler days arrive, making for pleasant outings region-wide. The kids are back in school, and concert halls, gallery spaces and performing-arts venues kick off a new season.

☆ New York Film Festival

One of several big film fests in NYC, this one features world premieres from all over, plus Q&As with indie and mainstream directors alike. The Lincoln Center (www.filmlinc.com) hosts.

October

Temperatures are falling as autumn brings fiery colors to northern climes. It's high season where the leaves are most brilliant (New England); elsewhere expect lower prices and fewer crowds.

✻ Fantasy Fest

Key West's answer to Mardi Gras brings more than 100,000 revelers to the subtropical enclave on the week leading up to Halloween. Expect parades, colorful floats, costume parties, the selecting of a conch king and queen and plenty of alcohol-fueled merriment (www.fantasyfest.net).

✻ Halloween

It's not just for kids; adults celebrate Halloween at masquerade parties. In NYC, you can don a costume and join the Halloween parade up Sixth Ave. Chicago does a cultural take with skeleton-rich Day of the Dead events at the National Museum of Mexican Art.

November

No matter where you go, this is generally low season, with cold winds discouraging visitors. Prices are lower (although airfares skyrocket around Thanksgiving). There's much happening culturally in the main cities.

✖ Thanksgiving

On the fourth Thursday of November, Americans gather with family and friends over daylong feasts of roast turkey, sweet potatoes, cranberry sauce, wine, pumpkin pie and loads of other dishes. New York City hosts a huge parade, and there's pro football on TV.

December

Winter arrives, though skiing conditions in the East usually aren't ideal until January. Christmas lights and holiday fairs make the region come alive during the festive season.

✻ Art Basel

This massive arts fest (www. artbaselmiamibeach.com) has four days of cutting-edge art, film, architecture and design. More than 250 major galleries from across the globe come to the event, with works by some 2000 artists, plus much hobnobbing with a glitterati crowd in Miami Beach.

✻ New Year's Eve

Americans are of two minds when it comes to ringing in the New Year. Some join festive crowds to celebrate; others plot a getaway to escape the mayhem. Whichever you choose, plan well in advance. Expect high prices (especially in NYC).

Itineraries

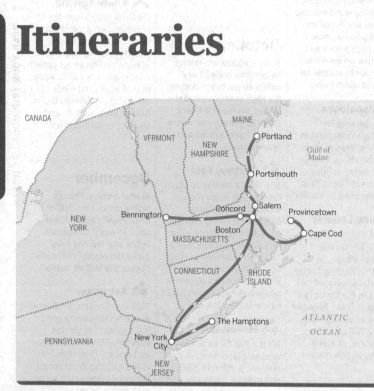

2 WEEKS Best of the Northeast

The great dynamo of art, fashion and culture, **New York City** is America at her most urbane. Spend three days blending touristy must-dos – Top of the Rock viewpoint, Upper East Side art museums, Central Park rambling – with vibrant nightlife and dining adventures, perhaps in the East Village. After big-city culture, catch your breath at the pretty beaches and enticing charms of the **Hamptons** on Long Island. Back in NYC, catch the train to **Boston**, for two days visiting historic sights, dining in the North End and pub-hopping in Cambridge. Rent a car and drive to **Cape Cod**, with its idyllic dunes, forests and pretty shores. Leave time for **Provincetown**, the Cape's liveliest settlement. Then set off for a three-day jaunt taking in New England's back roads, covered bridges, picturesque towns and beautiful scenery, staying at heritage B&Bs en route. Highlights include **Salem** and **Concord** in Massachusetts; **Bennington**, Vermont; and **Portsmouth**, New Hampshire. If time allows, head onward to Maine for lobster feasts amid beautifully rugged coastline – **Portland** is a fine place to start.

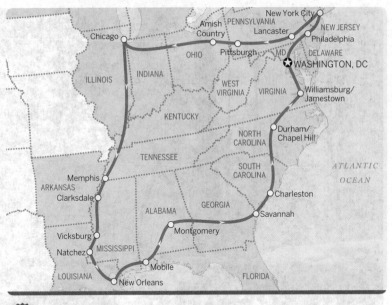

1 MONTH Eastern Grand Tour

This road trip loops around the East through towns big and small. Start in **New York City** (but hire a car cheaper in New Jersey) and hit the road for week one. Head west toward **Lancaster** to explore the idyllic back roads of Pennsylvania Dutch Country. Next is **Pittsburgh**, a surprising town of picturesque bridges and cutting-edge museums. Enter Ohio by interstate, but quickly step back in time amid the horses, buggies and byways of **Amish Country**. See the skyscrapers rising on the horizon? That's big-shouldered **Chicago**. Hang out for a few days to marvel at famous artworks and steely architecture, and chow through the city's celebrated restaurant scene.

For week two, motor south from Chicago on old Route 66, at least for a few time-warped, pie-filled miles. **Memphis** is the next destination, a mecca for Elvis fans, barbecue connoisseurs, civil-rights students and blues-music buffs alike. Follow the Great River Road south from here through juke-jointed **Clarksdale**, the Civil War battlegrounds of **Vicksburg** and the antebellum mansions of **Natchez**. It's not far now to **New Orleans**, where – Hurricane Katrina be damned – you can still hear live jazz, consult with a voodoo priestess or even ride a steamboat on the Mississippi River.

Begin journeying back east for week three. Wheel along the Gulf Coast to the azalea-lined boulevards of **Mobile**, then inland to **Montgomery**, where museums honor civil-rights pioneers like Rosa Parks, who refused to give up her seat to a white man on a city bus. Fall under the spell of **Savannah**'s live oaks and **Charleston**'s pastel architecture and decadent food. Take your pick of **Durham** or **Chapel Hill**, side-by-side university towns offering groovy nightlife.

Begin week four brushing up on your history in Virginia. Visit **Jamestown**, where Pocahontas helped the New World's first English settlement survive, then wander through the 18th century at nearby **Williamsburg**. A pair of big cities completes the route: **Washington, DC**, is a museum free-for-all, while **Philadelphia** fires up the Liberty Bell, Ben Franklin and the mighty, meaty cheesesteak. Finally, it's back to the neon lights of NYC.

Above: Shenandoah
National Park (p315)

Left: City skyline,
Boston (p169)

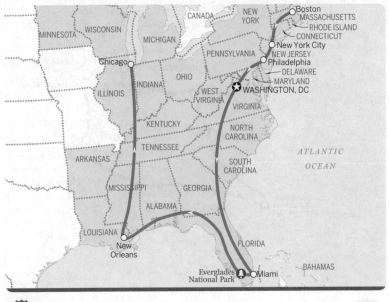

Bright Lights, Big Cities

For big, brawny, bold metropolises, the East is your place. Begin with a few days in history-rich **Boston**. Walk the Freedom Trail past Paul Revere's house. Hang out in Harvard Sq's cafes and bookshops, and chow down in North End trattorias and oyster houses. Then catch the train to **New York City**. With four days, you can indulge in iconic Manhattan and beyond. Stroll Central Park, walk the canyons of Wall St, go bohemian in Greenwich Village and catch a ferry to the Statue of Liberty. For a more local scene, join residents on the High Line, in NoLita's stylish shops and in Brooklyn's cool cafes.

Next hop a train to **Philadelphia**, which is practically down the block from NYC. Philly was the birthplace of American independence, and has the Liberty Bell and Declaration of Independence artifacts to prove it. Spend a few days touring the historic sites and indulging in foodie neighborhoods like Manayunk. Don't leave the northeast without spending a few days in **Washington, DC**, a quick trip by bus or train. Beyond the staggering number of free museums and monuments – the Air and Space Museum and Lincoln Memorial among them – the US capital has rich dining and drinking scenes in Georgetown, Dupont Circle and along U St. Who knows what politico might be swirling a Scotch next to you?

It's a long haul to **Miami** (flying is the easy way to go), so allocate four days to get your money's worth exploring the exotic museums and galleries, the art-deco district, Little Havana and sexy, sultry South Beach. For a change of pace, day-trip to the **Everglades** and commune with alligators. Keep the Southern thing going in jazz-loving **New Orleans**, with a soundtrack of smokin'-hot funk/brass bands and the sizzle of Cajun and Creole food. Three days of heavy eating with locals in Uptown, the Central Business District, Faubourg Marigny and the Bywater should do it.

Last, but not least, **Chicago** leaps up; the *City of New Orleans* train is a scenic way to arrive. Bike to the beach, see mod art in Millennium Park and plug into the blues. Chicago rocks, like the rest of the East's big cities.

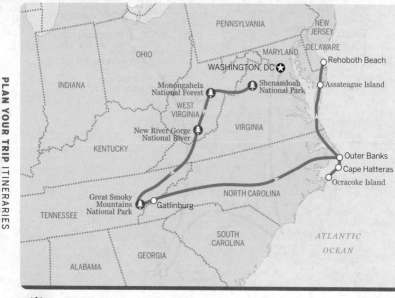

2 WEEKS The Great Outdoors

This trip is for those who like their nature ancient and wild. **Shenandoah National Park** rolls out the welcome mat: this sliver of gorgeousness straddles the Blue Ridge Mountains, so-named for their color when glimpsed in the hazy cerulean distance. Besides scenic drives, hiking is the big to-do here. Five hundred miles of paths – including 100 miles of the Appalachian Trail – wind by spring wildflowers, summer waterfalls and fiery autumn leaves. More activities await a few hours west at **Monongahela National Forest**, where you can strap on ropes for Seneca Rocks or a bicycle helmet for the Greenbrier River Trail. Adventure-sports enthusiasts will find their wet-and-wild bliss nearby at **New River Gorge National River**. Outfitters provide white-water rafting gear for the infamous Class V rapids.

Next up: **Great Smoky Mountains National Park**. Though it's the USA's most popular patch of parkland, you can leave most of the crowds behind if you're willing to hike or paddle (studies have shown that 95% of tourists here never venture more than 100 yards from their cars!). After a day spent in the wilderness surrounded by lush, heather-colored peaks, there's nothing quite like arriving in **Gatlinburg**, the park's kitschy base. Prepare for fudge shops, *Ripley's Believe It or Not* oddities and moonshine distilleries.

So goes the first week. Now it's time to fuel up for the twisty drive through the mountains and across to the coast, where the **Outer Banks** pay off big. Laid-back beach towns full of locally owned ice-cream shops and mom-and-pop motels dot the windswept barrier islands. Check out **Cape Hatteras**, with its unspoiled dunes, marshes and woodlands, or catch the ferry to remote **Ocracoke Island**, where the wild ponies run. Speaking of which: more wild horses roam **Assateague Island**, which floats to the north between Virginia and Maryland. It too offers brilliant, secluded beaches and a landscape ripe for birding, kayaking, crabbing and fishing.

Still craving surf and sand? Family-friendly, gay-friendly **Rehoboth Beach** bestows traditional gingerbread houses, kiddie amusements and a big ol' boardwalk along the oceanfront.

Road Trips & Scenic Drives

There's no better way to experience the region than on a classic four-wheeled journey. Dawdle in diners along the Lincoln Highway. Marvel at mansions on the Natchez Trace. Climb through the Appalachians on the Blue Ridge Parkway. Explore Highway 1's beaches. Or swing into bluesy joints along the Great River Road.

Blue Ridge Parkway

Snaking through the Appalachian Mountains of Virginia and North Carolina, the parkway (p319) immerses road trippers in glorious highlands scenery, with plenty of pull-offs for vista-gaping, hiking and Southern hospitality.

Why Go

Although it skirts dozens of small towns and a few metropolitan areas, the Blue Ridge Parkway feels far removed from modern-day America. Here, rustic log cabins with creaky rocking chairs on the front porches still dot the hillsides, while signs for folk-art shops and live-bluegrass-music joints entice travelers onto meandering side roads. Log-cabin diners dish up heaping piles of buckwheat pancakes with blackberry preserves and a side of country ham.

When you need to work off all that good Southern cooking, over 100 hiking trails can be accessed along the Blue Ridge Parkway, from gentle nature walks to rough-and-ready tramps along the legendary Appalachian Trail. Go canoeing, kayaking or inner-tubing along rushing rivers, or dangle a fishing line over the side of a rowboat on petite lakes.

Best Experiences

Beaches
See dazzling coastal scenery on Florida's Highway 1.

Oddball Sights
Discover goofball roadside attractions on Route 66 and the Lincoln Highway.

Scenery
Watch dramatic sunsets over the Appalachian Mountains on the Blue Ridge Parkway.

Music
Listen to blues at a Memphis juke joint on the Great River Road, or crazy fiddling at a Galax mountain music hall on the Blue Ridge Parkway.

Food
Fork into Nashville's chicken and biscuits on the Natchez Trace, or New Orleans' famed Creole fare.

History
Explore Gettysburg on the Lincoln Highway, or 450-year-old St Augustine on Florida Highway 1.

Pop Culture
Visit the Tupelo house where Elvis Presley grew up on the Natchez Trace Parkway.

Road Trips & Scenic Drives

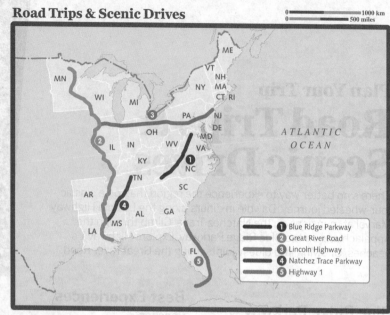

1	Blue Ridge Parkway
2	Great River Road
3	Lincoln Highway
4	Natchez Trace Parkway
5	Highway 1

The Route

The bucolic byway connects Virginia's Shenandoah National Park with Great Smoky Mountains National Park, straddling the North Carolina–Tennessee border. Towns along the way include Boone and Asheville in North Carolina and Galax and Roanoke in Virginia, with Charlottesville, VA, also a short drive away. Bigger cities within range of the parkway include Washington, DC (140 miles), and Richmond, VA (95 miles).

Many road trippers also add **Skyline Drive** (p316) onto their Blue Ridge route. The bendy, 105-mile Skyline connects to the parkway's northern end and ups the scenic ante by doling out mind-blowing mountain vistas on its ramble through Shenandoah National Park. One caveat: you will have to pay a $15 fee to travel the road – this is not a toll, but rather the park's admission charge.

When to Go

April through October, when visitor facilities are open (many close during winter) is best. May is best for wildflowers. Leaf-peepers pour in during October. Expect big crowds if you go during the summer or early fall.

Resources

Blue Ridge Parkway (www.blueridgeparkway.org) Maps, activities and places to stay along the way. Also offers the free *Blue Ridge Parkway Travel Planner* to download.

Hiking the Blue Ridge Parkway (Randy Johnson; 2003) In-depth trail descriptions, topographic maps and other essential info for hikes both short and long.

Skyline Drive (www.visitskylinedrive.org) Lodging, hiking and wildlife along the picturesque addendum to the parkway.

Time & Mileage

➡ Time: At least two days, but allow five days to do it right. It's slow going on the steep, curvy roads, plus you'll want to pit-stop for hiking, eating and sightseeing.

➡ Mileage: 469 miles.

➡ Start/End: Front Royal, VA/Cherokee, NC.

Great River Road

The epic roadway (p589) edges the Mississippi River from its headwaters in northern Minnesota's pine forests all the way south to its endpoint in New Orleans. For a look at America across cultural divides – north/south, urban/rural, Baptist/bohemian – this is the road trip to make.

Why Go

The sweeping scenery awes as you meander alongside America's longest river, from the rolling plains of the north down to the sun-baked cotton fields of the Mississippi Delta. Wind-hewn bluffs, dense forests, flower-filled meadows and steamy swamps are all part of the backdrop – along with smokestacks, riverboat casinos and urban sprawl: this is the good, the bad and the ugly of life on the Mississippi.

Small towns provide a glimpse into varying facets of American culture: there's Brainerd, MN, as seen in the Coen brothers' film *Fargo;* La Crosse, WI, where the world's largest six-pack pops its top; and Nauvoo, IL, a pilgrimage site for Mormons, complete with gleaming white temple.

The southern section of the route traces American musical history, from rock and roll in Memphis to blues in the Mississippi Delta to jazz in New Orleans. You won't go hungry either, with retro Midwestern diners, Southern barbecue joints and smokehouses, and Cajun taverns and dance halls in Louisiana.

The Route

Despite the name, the Great River Road is not a single highway, but a series of linked federal, state and county roads that follow the Mississippi River as it flows through 10 different states. The one constant wherever you are is the green paddle-wheel sign that marks the way. Major urban areas that provide easy access to the road include New Orleans, Memphis, St Louis and Minneapolis.

When to Go

May to October is best, for snow-free weather in the northern states.

Resources

Mississippi River Travel (www.experience mississippiriver.com) Great resource for history, outdoor recreation and live music in all 10 River Road states.

National Scenic Byways (www.fhwa.dot.gov/byways/byways/2279) Turn-by-turn directions.

Time & Mileage

➡ Time: Six days to drive the road from north to south; 10 days enables a more comfortable, realistic pace.

➡ Mileage: About 2000 miles.

➡ Start/End: Itasca State Park, MN/New Orleans, LA.

Lincoln Highway

Begun in 1913 and paved to completion by 1925, America's first transcontinental roadway rambles from New York City to San Francisco. Its 1000-mile eastern portion traces a distinctive path through the nation's heartland, leaving giant coffee-pot statues, fried-chicken diners, jellybean murals and other Americana in its wake.

DOWNLOADS: BLUEGRASS SOUNDS

➡ 'Blue Moon of Kentucky' – Bill Monroe and the Blue Grass Boys
➡ 'Foggy Mountain Breakdown' – Earl Scruggs
➡ 'Orange Blossom Special' – Rouse Brothers
➡ 'Rocky Top' – Osborne Brothers
➡ 'Windy Mountain' – Lonesome Pine Fiddlers
➡ 'Flame of Love' – Jim and Jesse
➡ 'I'm a Man of Constant Sorrow' – Stanley Brothers
➡ 'Every Time You Say Goodbye' – Alison Krauss and Union Station
➡ 'Like a Hurricane' – The Dillards

ADVANCE PLANNING

➡ Join an automobile club (p655) that provides 24-hour emergency roadside assistance and discounts on lodging and attractions.

➡ Some international automobile associations have reciprocal agreements with US clubs, so check first and bring your member card from home.

➡ International travelers might want to review the USA's road rules (p656) and common road hazards (p656).

➡ Make sure your vehicle has a spare tire, tool kit (eg jack, jumper cables, ice scraper, tire pressure gauge) and emergency equipment (eg flashers).

➡ Bring good maps, especially if you're touring off-road or away from highways. Don't rely solely on a GPS unit – it can malfunction, and in remote areas it may not even work.

➡ Always carry your driver's license (p655) and proof of insurance (p655).

Why Go

The Lincoln Highway is authentic road tripping, sans much of the hype and commercialization of other famous byways. While the route navigates some of the East's prominent cities – NYC and Philadelphia among them – it also steers well off the tourist path in genuine back-road style. You'll tick off seven states along the way: New York, New Jersey, Pennsylvania, West Virginia, Ohio, Indiana and Illinois.

The Route

Between New York City and Fulton, IL, the roadway cuts across the middle Atlantic and Midwestern regions. Note that the Lincoln Highway doesn't appear on most maps, because it's no longer an official road, but rather a patchwork of federal and state highways.

The journey begins at Times Sq, where the bright lights of Broadway provide an epic send-off. From there it's on to New Jersey and Princeton, the natty Ivy League university town. Pennsylvania rolls up next, offering the Liberty Bell and Independence Hall in Philadelphia; quilts and clip-clopping horses in the Amish communities near Lancaster; the Civil War super-site of Gettysburg; and river-tastic, Pop Art–rich Pittsburgh. Cornfields and haunted prisons flash by in Ohio. Indiana's pit stops include more Amish areas and the town of South Bend, home to the football-crazed university of Notre Dame. In Illinois, the route swipes Chicago's suburbs, then sets a course through small farming communities pressed flat against the horizon. After that, the Lincoln Highway heads over the Mississippi River and onward west to San Francisco.

Cities that provide easy access to the road include New York City, Philadelphia, Pittsburgh and Chicago.

When to Go

April through October is best, when the weather is snow-free and attractions are open (many shut down between November and March).

Resources

Lincoln Highway Association (www.lincolnhighwayassoc.org) Lots of free info online. It also sells turn-by-turn directions that are the definitive source for navigating the road.

The Lincoln Highway (Michael Wallis; 2007) Coffee-table book filled with gorgeous photos and the lowdown on route hot-spots.

Time & Mileage

➡ Time: 2½ days without stopping much, but four or five days lets you soak up the highway's essence.

➡ Mileage: About 1000 miles for the eastern portion.

➡ Start/End: NYC/Fulton, IL (for eastern portion).

Above: Fort Lauderdale
(p469), Florida

Right: Notre Dame
football stadium
(p550), South Bend,
Indiana

BILL GROVE / GETTY IMAGES ©

ROUTE 66

For a classic American road trip, nothing beats good ol' Route 66. Nicknamed the 'Mother Road' by novelist John Steinbeck, this string of small-town main streets and country byways first connected big-shouldered Chicago with the waving palm trees of Los Angeles in 1926.

Most of the Mother Road unfurls through the western part of the country, but Illinois' 300-mile portion offers classic, time-warped moseying. Fork into thick slabs of pie in neon-lit diners; snap photos of roadside attractions like the Gemini Giant, a sky-high fiberglass spaceman; and motor on past drive-in movie theaters, mom-and-pop motels and other Americana.

Road trippers with a couple of extra weeks to spare can keep on truckin' all the way to the Pacific. The route's remaining 2100 miles wind by singular sensations such as frozen custard stands in Missouri, a totem-pole park in Oklahoma, a barbed-wire museum in Texas, the Grand Canyon in Arizona and wild and crazy Santa Monica Pier in California. See **Historic Route 66** (www.historic66.com) for more.

Natchez Trace Parkway

With emerald mounds, jade swamps, hiking trails, opulent mansions, riverside saloons and layer upon layer of American history, the Natchez Trace Parkway (p377) is the richest drive in the South.

Why Go

Think about this as you set out: you'll be following the same path as a who's who of historic figures, including Andrew Jackson (7th president of the US and face of the $20 bill), Jefferson Davis (president of the Confederacy), James Audubon (naturalist and painter), Meriwether Lewis (famous explorer who died on the Trace in 1809), Ulysses S Grant (18th president of the US) and – wait for it – a young Elvis Presley. The drive meanders by various cultural and historic sites that let you learn more about each man.

The Route

Nashville is the easiest place to access the parkway, and for country-music fans and wannabe songwriters all over the world, a trip to the city is the ultimate pilgrimage, with boot-stomping honky-tonks, the Country Music Hall of Fame and a sweet historic district to explore. There's also good eatin' at local cafeterias, the ultimate way to indulge in everything from barbecue chicken and pig's feet to turnip greens and baked apples.

About 10 miles beyond Nashville, the road swings by one of the Civil War's bloodiest battlefields at Franklin, where 20,000 Confederates and 17,000 Union soldiers fought on November 30, 1864. Further along are confederate gravesites for unknown soldiers. Several centuries-old indigenous burial mounds likewise rise up along the way. Emerald Mound, near Natchez, is one of the nation's largest, and the massive grassy pyramid still buzzes with ancient energy.

Other highlights en route include the town of Tupelo – where you can visit the humble house where Elvis grew up, learned to play the guitar and dreamed big – and tree-shaded, milky-green Cypress Swamp, filled with alligators. Natchez itself is a living antebellum museum, all sweeping spiral staircases, chandeliers and thick column houses.

When to Go

April to June and September to November are best. Summer can be hotter than hot.

Resources

Natchez Trace Parkway (www.nps.gov/natr) Park-service website that provides road construction updates, plus information on local activities and historic sites.

Natchez Trace Compact (www.scenictrace.com) State tourism bureaus of Tennessee, Alabama and Mississippi band together to offer route itineraries, maps and event info.

Time & Mileage

➡ Time: Three days, though you could do it in two. Travel times aren't exactly speedy on the two-lane road.

➡ Mileage: 444 miles.

➡ Start/End: Nashville, TN/Natchez, MS.

Florida Highway 1

The coast-hugging thoroughfare features miles and miles of beaches interspersed with fascinating historical sights, from the USA's oldest city to sobering slavery exhibits to NASA rockets. Glittering Miami provides the big finale.

Why Go

For quintessential Florida sights and experiences, Highway 1 spanning the Atlantic shoreline is it: Palm Beach's mansions, Ft Lauderdale's yachts, Miami's domino-clacking Cuban enclave of Little Havana all pop up along the way. Pristine, windswept beaches harboring endangered birds and manatees? They're here (at Canaveral National Seashore). Beaches

known for hard-partying nightlife and NASCAR racing? Also here (at Daytona). Delicious seafood shacks and pastel-hued waterfront hotels are everywhere.

The Route

Begin in Florida's northeastern tip at Amelia Island, an upper-class beach-resort town since the 1890s. From there the road drifts south, past cultural parks and plantations where you can see how slaves lived. Pull over in venerable St Augustine, founded in 1565, to seek out Ponce de Leon's fountain of youth and the Pirate Museum. Lighthouses, unspoiled strands of sand and surfing hot spots flash by. Moving on you'll come to the Kennedy Space Center, where shuttles used to launch into the stratosphere. After that, art-filled West Palm Beach appears among a slew of well-heeled towns. Highway 1 then saves the best for last: Miami. The sexy city offers eye candy galore, from mural-splashed neighborhoods to the world's largest art-deco district to the young and glamorous locals preening around South Beach.

But let's back up a bit and cover a few basics. The road is actually called Highway A1A (not to be confused with US 1, the

OTHER GREAT ROAD TRIPS

ROUTE	STATE	START/END	SIGHTS & ACTIVITIES	BEST TIMES
Route 28	NY	Stony Hollow/Arkville	Catskills mountains, lakes, rivers; hiking, leaf-peeping, tubing	May–Sep
Old Kings Highway	MA	Sagamore/Provincetown	Historic districts, period homes, coastal scenery	Apr–Oct
Highway 13	WI	Bayfield/Superior	Lakeside beaches, forests, farmlands; nature walks	May–Sep
Highway 61	MN	Duluth/Canadian Border	State parks, waterfalls, quaint towns; hiking	May–Sep
VT 100	VT	Stamford/Newport	Rolling pastures, green mountains; hiking, skiing	Jun–Sep
Kancamagus Highway	VT	Conway/Lincoln	Craggy mountains, streams, waterfalls; camping, hiking, swimming	May–Sep
Highway 12	NC	Corolla/Sealevel	Beaches, lighthouses, ferry rides, Wright Brothers launching site	Apr–Oct
Overseas Highway	FL	Key Largo/Key West	Beaches, protected coral reefs, plates of conch fritters, key lime pie	Dec–Apr

larger, faster version that runs parallel). A1A is not continuous – there are a few towns where you have to detour onto other roads before picking up A1A again. Should you want more road-tripping after Miami, hop on US 1, which becomes the scenic Overseas Highway at Key Largo and dips south to Key West – a fine way to keep the party going.

When to Go

November to April is the best time, when it's warm but not too hot.

Resources

Florida Scenic Highways (www.floridasce-nichighways.com) Info for specially designated parts of the highway near St Augustine and Ft Lauderdale.

Highway A1A: Florida at the Edge (Herbert L Hiller; 2007) Part travel guide, part history about the cities and towns along the way.

Time & Mileage

➡ Time: Six days to take in the sights.

➡ Mileage: 475 miles.

➡ Start/End: Amelia Island/Miami.

Plan Your Trip
Outdoors

Smoky mountains, wave-bashed beaches, coral reefs, river-cut gorges: the eastern USA has no shortage of spectacular settings for a bit of adventure. No matter what your weakness – hiking, cycling, kayaking, rafting, surfing, diving or skiing – you'll find world-class places to commune with the great outdoors.

Hiking & Trekking

Almost anywhere you go, great hiking and backpacking are within easy striking distance. National parks are ideal for short and long hikes. Beyond them, you'll find troves of state-maintained footpaths. There's no limit to the terrain you can explore, from the dogwood-choked Wild Azalea Trail in Louisiana to the multistate **North Country National Scenic Trail** (www.nps.gov/noco), winding across rugged landscapes from New York to Minnesota.

Resources

Survive Outdoors (www.surviveoutdoors.com) Dispenses safety and first-aid tips, plus helpful photos of dangerous critters.

Wilderness Survival (Gregory Davenport; 2006) Easily the best book on surviving nearly every contingency.

American Hiking Society (www.americanhiking. org) Links to 'volunteer vacations' building trails.

Backpacker (www.backpacker.com) Premier national magazine for backpackers, from novices to experts.

Rails-to-Trails Conservancy (www.railstotrails. org) Converts abandoned railroad corridors into hiking and biking trails; publishes free trail reviews at www.traillink.com.

Best Outdoors

Best Hiking

Appalachian Trail, Shenandoah National Park, VA; Great Smoky Mountains National Park, NC & TN; Adirondack wilderness, NY

Best Cycling

Cherohala Skyway, NC & TN (on-road); Chequamegon National Forest, WI (off-road); Minneapolis, MN (city riding)

Best Paddling

Boundary Waters, MN (canoeing); New River Gorge National River (white-water rafting); Apostle Islands, WI (kayaking); Pictured Rocks, MI (kayaking)

Best Surfing

Cocoa Beach, FL; Long Island, NY; Coast Guard Beach, MA

Best Diving

Florida Keys (coral garden); Cape Hatteras, NC (Civil War shipwrecks); Dry Tortugas, FL (sea turtles); Crystal River, FL (manatees)

Best Wildlife-Watching

Baxter State Park, ME (moose); Provincetown, MA (whales); Florida Everglades (alligators, manatees, sea turtles); Wabasha, MN (eagles)

THE APPALACHIAN TRAIL

Completed in 1937, the country's longest footpath is 2180 miles, crossing six national parks, traversing eight national forests and hitting 14 states from Georgia to Maine. Misty mountains, deep woods, flowery pastures and bear sightings are the rewards. Each year, roughly 2500 hardy souls attempt to hike the entire trail – only one in four makes it all the way through. But don't let that discourage you. It's estimated that two to three million people trek a portion of the Appalachian Trail annually, thanks to easy-to-access day hikes up and down its length.

Practicalities

➡ Most through-hikers start at Springer Mountain in northern Georgia and finish at Mt Katahdin in Maine's Baxter State Park. They begin in March or April and finish six months later. Baxter closes for the season on October 15, so hikers must arrive before then.

➡ Hiking the route in reverse (from Maine to Georgia) is also possible, but cold weather in the north dictates you start later (in June) when the blackflies are ravenous and the trails are wet and muddy. Either way, hikers hit the weather gamut from snow to steamy humidity.

➡ Campsites, lean-tos and huts are the usual lodging options. Most hikers spend about $1000 per month for food and the occasional night in a motel or lodge, plus supplies and replacement gear.

Short Hikes & Resources

➡ If you're short on time, gorgeous and accessible areas to get a piece of the trail include **Shenandoah National Park** (www.nps.gov/shen) in Virginia and Harpers Ferry in West Virginia, which is also the trail headquarters (and a short Amtrak train ride from Washington, DC).

➡ The **Appalachian Trail Conservancy** (www.appalachiantrail.org) has the lowdown on all things AT: official maps and guidebooks, an online database of day hikes organized by state, terrain descriptions by state, trail updates, hiker profiles etc. It's a fantastic resource.

➡ Humorist Bill Bryson's *A Walk in the Woods* (1998) is a great recreational read about the trail.

Cycling

Cycling's popularity increases by the day, with cities (including New York and Chicago) adding more cycle lanes, and a growing number of greenways striping the countryside. You'll find die-hards in every town, and outfitters offering guided trips for all levels and durations. The Cherohala Skyway – 51 glorious miles of undulating road and Great Smoky Mountain views straddling Tennessee and North Carolina – is often cited as one the region's must-rides.

Mountain bikers should steer for Wisconsin's Chequamegon National Forest, revered for its bad-ass trails and grueling **Fat Tire Festival** (www.cheqfattire.com) in September.

Resources

Bicycling magazine (www.bicycling.com) Has information on city rides, off-road trails and much in between.

Kayaking & Canoeing

Paddlers will find their bliss in the eastern USA. Rentals and instruction are yours for the asking. Kayaking hot spots include Wisconsin's Apostle Islands National Lakeshore, for gliding through arches and sea caves on Lake Superior; Michigan's Pictured Rocks National Lakeshore, to paddle by wildly colored cliffs on Lake Superior; and Maine's Penobscot Bay, to poke around the briny waters and spruce-fringed islets.

Canoeing is downright legendary here, including the 12,000 miles of wet and wild routes in Minnesota's Boundary Waters and Alabama's Bartram Canoe Trail, with 300,000 acres of marshy delta bayous, lakes and rivers.

Resources

American Canoe Association (www.american canoe.org) Has a water trails database for canoeing and kayaking, as well as information on local paddling clubs and courses.

White-Water Rafting

East of the Mississippi, West Virginia has an arsenal of famous white water. First, there's the New River Gorge National River, which, despite its name, is one of the oldest rivers in the world. Slicing from North Carolina into West Virginia, it cuts a deep gorge, known as the Grand Canyon of the East, producing frothy rapids in its wake.

Then there's the Gauley, arguably among the world's finest white water. Revered for its ultra-steep and turbulent chutes, the venerable Appalachian river is a watery roller coaster, dropping more than 668ft and churning up 100-plus rapids in a mere 28 miles. Six more rivers, all in the same neighborhood, offer training grounds for less-experienced river rats.

Resources

American Whitewater (www.americanwhite water.org) Works to preserve America's wild rivers; has links to local rafting clubs.

Surfing

The Atlantic states harbor some terrific and unexpected surfing spots – especially if you're after more moderate swells. The warmest waters are off Florida's Gulf Coast. Top spots to hang 10:

➡ **Cocoa Beach and Melbourne Beach, FL** Small crowds and mellow waves make it a paradise for beginners and longboarders. Just south is the Inlet, known for consistent surf and crowds to match.

➡ **Long Island, NY** More than a dozen surfing areas dot the area, from Montauk's oft-packed Ditch Plains to Nassau County's Long Beach, with its 3-mile stretch of curling waves.

➡ **Coast Guard Beach, Eastham, MA** Part of the Cape Cod National Seashore, this family-friendly beach is known for its consistent shortboard/longboard swell all summer long.

Resources

Surfer (www.surfermag.com) Has travel reports covering the Eastern seaboard and just about every break in the USA.

Diving

Florida has the lion's share of great diving, with more than 1000 miles of coastline subdivided into 20 unique undersea areas. There are hundreds of sites and countless dive shops offering equipment and guided excursions. South of West Palm Beach, you'll find clear waters and fantastic year-round

TIPS FOR VISITING NATIONAL PARKS

Park entrance fees vary, from nothing at all to $25 per vehicle. The 'America the Beautiful' annual pass ($80; http://store.usgs.gov/pass), which allows admission for four adults and all children under 16 years old to all federal recreational lands for 12 calendar months, is sold at park entrances and visitor centers. Lifetime senior-citizen passes ($10) are also available.

Park lodges and campgrounds book up far in advance; for summer vacations, reserve six months to one year ahead. Some parks offer first-come, first-served campgrounds – for these, try to arrive between 10am and noon, when other campers may be checking out. For overnight backpacking and some day hikes, you'll need a wilderness permit; the number of permits is often subject to quotas, so apply far in advance (up to six months before your trip, depending on park regulations).

diving with ample reefs. In the Panhandle you can scuba in the calm and balmy waters of the Gulf of Mexico, off Pensacola and Destin are fabulous wreck dives, and you can dive with manatees near Crystal River.

The Florida Keys are the crown jewel. Expect a brilliant mix of marine habitats, North America's only living coral garden and the occasional shipwreck. Key Largo is home to the John Pennekamp Coral Reef State Park and more than 200 miles of underwater idyll. The expansive reefs around Dry Tortugas National Park swarm with barracuda, sea turtles and a couple of hundred sunken ships.

Other popular places to submerge in the eastern waters include North Carolina's Cape Hatteras National Seashore, where you can explore Civil War wrecks and encounter tiger sand sharks, and Lake Ouachita, Arkansas' largest lake, known for its pristine mountain waters and 16-mile water-based trail.

Resources

Scuba Diving (www.scubadiving.com) Provides the latest on diving destinations in the US and abroad.

Skiing & Winter Sports

Vermont's first-rate Stowe Mountain offers sweet slopes – freeze your tail off on the lifts, but thaw out nicely après-ski in timbered bars with local brews. In Lake Placid, New York, you can luge or bobsled at old Olympic facilities. Snowmobiles rev in northern Wisconsin, Michigan and Minnesota; in Minnesota, Voyageurs National Park hosts lots of wintry action on its frozen waterways.

Resources

Ski Resorts Guide (www.skiresortsguide.com) Provides lodging info, downloadable trail maps and more.

Plan Your Trip

Travel with Children

From north to south, you'll find superb attractions for all ages: bucket-and-spade fun at the beach, amusement parks, zoos, eye-popping aquariums and natural-history exhibits, hands-on science museums, camping adventures, battlefields, leisurely bike rides through the countryside and plenty of other activities likely to wow young ones.

Eastern USA for Kids

Dining with Children

The local restaurant industry seems built on family-style service: children are not just accepted at most places, but are often encouraged by special children's menus with smaller portions and lower prices. In some restaurants children under a certain age even eat for free. Restaurants usually provide high chairs and booster seats. Some restaurants may also offer children crayons and puzzles, and occasionally live performances by cartoonlike characters.

Restaurants without children's menus don't necessarily discourage kids, though higher-end restaurants might; even at the nicer places, however, if you show up early enough (right at dinnertime opening hours, often 5pm or 6pm), you can usually eat without too much stress – and you'll likely be joined by other foodies with kids. You can ask if the kitchen will make a smaller order of a dish, or if they will split a normal-size main dish between two plates for the kids. Chinese, Mexican and Italian restaurants seem to be the best bet for finicky young eaters.

Farmers markets are growing in popularity in the region, and every sizable

Best Regions for Kids

New York, New Jersey & Pennsylvania

New York City offers adventures such as row-boating in Central Park and kid-friendly museums. Head to the Jersey shore for boardwalk fun and to Pennsylvania for Amish Country horse-and-buggy rides.

New England

Boston's waterfront is a gateway to adventure with an aquarium, an 18th-century warship and whale-watching cruises. Plimoth Plantation, with its recreated Wampanoag and Pilgrim villages, is good family fun.

Washington, DC & the Capital Region

Washington has unrivaled allure for families with free museums, a panda-loving zoo and boundless green spaces. Virginia's Williamsburg is a slice of 18th-century America with costumed interpreters and fanciful activities.

Florida

Orlando's Walt Disney World is well worth planning a vacation around. Afterwards, hit the state's beautiful beaches.

town has at least one a week. This is a good place to assemble a first-rate picnic, sample the local specialties and support independent growers in the process. After getting your stash, head to the nearest park or waterfront.

Accommodations

Motels and hotels typically have rooms with two beds, which are ideal for families. Some also have roll-away beds or cribs that can be brought into the room for an extra charge – but keep in mind these are usually portable cribs, which not all children sleep well in. Some hotels offer 'kids stay free' programs for children up to 12 or sometimes 18 years old. Be wary of B&Bs, as many don't allow children; inquire before reserving.

Babysitting

Resort hotels may have on-call babysitting services; otherwise, ask the front-desk staff or concierge to help you make arrangements. Always ask if babysitters are licensed and insured, what they charge per hour per child, whether there's a minimum fee, and if they charge extra for transportation or meals. Most tourist bureaus list local resources for childcare and recreation facilities, medical services and so on.

Driving & Flying

Every car-rental agency should be able to provide an appropriate child seat, since these are required in every state, but you need to request it when booking; expect to pay around $13 more per day.

Domestic airlines don't charge for children under two years of age. Those two years and up must have a seat, and discounts are unlikely. Rarely, some resort areas (like Disneyland) offer a 'kids fly free' promotion. Amtrak and other train operators run similar deals (with kids up to age 15 riding free) on various routes.

Discounts for Children

Child concessions often apply for tours, admission fees and transport, with some discounts as high as 50% off the adult rate. However, the definition of 'child' can vary from under 12 to under 16 years. Unlike in Europe, few popular sights have discount rates for families; those that do will help you save a few dollars compared to buying individual tickets. Most sights give free admission to children under two years.

Children's Highlights

Outdoor Adventure

➡ Kayak, canoe or join guided walks in the **Florida Everglades** (p472).

➡ Go white-water rafting in **New River Gorge** (p325), a national park in West Virginia.

➡ Spot humpbacks on a **whale-watching tour** (p195) out of Provincetown, Massachusetts.

➡ Take an underground tour through **Mammoth Cave National Park** (p388) in central Kentucky.

Theme Parks & Zoos

➡ Immerse yourselves in the king of them all: **Walt Disney World** (p502), where four action-packed parks spread across 20,000 Florida acres.

➡ Hop the subway from Manhattan to one of the USA's best zoos at **Bronx Wildlife Conservation Park** (p86), NYC.

➡ Drive among 900 wild creatures roaming the **Lion Country Safari** (p471) in West Palm Beach, FL.

➡ Splash it up at 20-plus water parks and water-skiing thrill shows at **Wisconsin Dells** (p586).

➡ **Northern Ohio's Cedar Point** (p556) has some of the planet's wildest roller coasters, plus a mile-long beachfront and a water park.

➡ **Six Flags** (www.sixflags.com) is one of America's favorite amusement parks, with nine locations in the eastern USA.

Traveling in Time

➡ Don 18th-century garb and mingle with costumed interpreters in the history-rich settings of **Plymouth** (p188), **Williamsburg** (p307), **Yorktown** (p309) or **Jamestown** (p309).

➡ Plug your ears as soldiers in 19th-century costumes fire muskets and cannons at **Fort Mackinac** (p578), MI.

➡ Go on a walking tour of Boston's **Freedom Trail** (p179) with Ben Franklin (or at least his 21st-century look-alike).

➡ Explore a log cabin like the one Abraham Lincoln grew up in at the **Lincoln Presidential Museum** (p543) in Springfield, IL.

Rainy-Day Activities

➡ Inspire budding aviators at Washington, DC's **National Air & Space Museum** (p257) with rockets, spacecraft, old-fashioned biplanes and ride simulators.

➡ Discover the massive planetarium, immense dinosaur skeletons and 30 million other artifacts at New York's **American Museum of Natural History** (p77).

➡ Roam three stories of adventure and (cleverly disguised) learning, including an Egyptian tomb, farmers market, train, art studio and physics stations at Baltimore's **Port Discovery** (p286) museum.

➡ Geek out at Chicago's **Museum of Science & Industry** (p526), the largest science center in the western hemisphere, where you'll find attractions such as a fairy castle, baby chicks and mock tornadoes.

Eating

➡ Get messy eating scrumptious Maryland blue crabs at open-air restaurants along **Chesapeake Bay** (p289).

➡ Lick at the delicious source at **Ben & Jerry's Ice Cream Factory** (p222) in northern Vermont.

➡ Heft a slice of deep-dish pizza (and scrawl your name on the wall) at **Gino's East** (p531) in Chicago.

Planning

To find family-oriented sights and activities, accommodations, restaurants and entertainment among our reviews, just look for the child-friendly icon (⊞).

When to Go

➡ Peak travel season is June to August, when schools are out and the weather is warmest. Expect high prices and abundant crowds – meaning long lines at amusement and water parks, fully booked resorts and traffic on the roads; book in advance for popular destinations.

➡ High season for winter resorts (in the Catskills and White Mountains) runs from January to March.

Need to Know

➡ Many public toilets have a baby-changing table (sometimes in men's toilets, too), and gender-neutral 'family' facilities appear in airports.

➡ Medical services and facilities in America are of a high standard.

➡ Items such as baby food, formula and disposable nappies (diapers) are widely available.

➡ Single parents or guardians traveling with anyone under 18 should carry proof of legal custody or a notarized letter from the nonaccompanying parent(s) authorizing the trip. This isn't required, but it can help avoid potential problems entering the USA.

Resources

For more information and advice, check out Lonely Planet's *Travel with Children*. For outdoor advice, read *Kids in the Wild: a Family Guide to Outdoor Recreation* by Cindy Ross and Todd Gladfelter, and Alice Cary's *Parents' Guide to Hiking & Camping*.

Baby's Away (www.babysaway.com) Rents cribs, high chairs, car seats, strollers and even toys at locations across the country.

Family Travel Files (www.thefamilytravelfiles.com) Readymade vacation ideas, destination profiles and travel tips.

Kids.gov (www.kids.gov) Enormous, eclectic national resource; download songs and activities or even link to the CIA Kids' Page.

Travel Babees (www.travelbabees.com) Reputable nationwide baby-gear rental outfit.

Regions at a Glance

New York City is the East's hub. More than eight million inhabitants live in this mega-city, a world center for fashion, food, arts and finance. The crowd thins out in neighboring New Jersey and Pennsylvania, where beaches, mountains and literal horse-and-buggy hamlets join the landscape. New England arches north to rocky shores, clapboard fishing villages and Ivy League universities.

The Capital Region begins the march south through voluptuous valleys and a slew of historic sites. By the time you reach the true South, the pace has slowed, pecan pie tempts on the table and bluesy tunes drift from juke joints. Surreal Florida brings on mermaids, manatees, Mickey Mouse and Miami, while the sensible Great Lakes region prefers burgers and beer with its natural attractions.

New York, New Jersey & Pennsylvania

Arts
History
Outdoors

Culture Spot

Home to the Met, MoMA and Broadway – and that's just New York City. Buffalo, Philadelphia and Pittsburgh have also world-renowned cultural institutions, as well as bohemian enclaves with live music scenes.

A Living Past

From preserved Gilded Age mansions in the Hudson Valley to Independence National Historic Park in Philadelphia and sites dedicated to formative moments in the nation's founding, the region provides an interactive education.

Wild Outdoors

The outdoors lurks just beyond the city's gaze, with hiking in the Adirondack and Catskill mountains, rafting trips down the Delaware River, and ocean frolics along the Jersey Shore and Hamptons.

p54

New England

Seafood
History
Beaches

Land of Lobsters

New England is justifiably famous for its fresh seafood. Seaside eateries pepper the coast, where you can shuck and suck oysters, crack lobster claws and spoon into clam chowder while watching day-boats haul in the next meal's catch.

Colonial Tales

From the Pilgrims' landing in Plymouth and the witch hysteria in Salem to Paul Revere's revolutionary ride, New England has shaped American history.

Beachy Keen

Cape Cod, Martha's Vineyard and Block Island – New England is a summer mecca for sand and sea worshippers. The region's scores of beaches run the gamut from kid-friendly tidal flats to gnarly, open-ocean surf.

p164

Washington, DC & the Capital Region

Arts
History
Food

Museums & Music

Washington, DC has a superb collection of museums and galleries. You'll also find down-home mountain music on Virginia's Crooked Road and famous regional theaters and edgy art in Baltimore.

Times Past

For historical lore, Jamestown, Williamsburg and Yorktown offer windows into Colonial America, while Civil War battlefields stud the Virginia countryside. There are also fascinating presidential estates such as Mount Vernon and Monticello, plus history-rich charmers like Annapolis.

Culinary Delights

Decadent feasts await: Maryland blue crabs, oysters and seafood platters; international restaurants in DC; and farm-to-table dining rooms in Baltimore, Charlottesville, Staunton and Rehoboth.

p248

The South

Food
Music
Charm

Biscuits & Barbecue

Slow-cooked barbecue, fried chicken and catfish, butter-smothered biscuits, corn bread, grits and spicy Cajun-Creole dishes make the South a magnificent place to fill up a plate.

Country, Jazz & Blues

Nowhere on earth has a soundtrack as influential as the South. Head to music meccas for the authentic experience: country in Nashville, blues in Memphis and big-band jazz in New Orleans – with plenty of fusions and alternative sounds all across the region.

Southern Belles

Picture-book towns such as Charleston and Savannah have long captivated visitors with their historic tree-lined streets, antebellum architecture and friendly down-home welcome. Other charmers include Chapel Hill, Oxford, Chattanooga and Natchez.

p326

Florida

Culture
Wildlife
Beaches

Multifaceted

Florida has a complicated soul: it's the home of Miami's colorful art-deco district and Little Havana, plus historical attractions in St Augustine, theme parks in Orlando and museums and island heritage in Key West.

Wildlife-Watching

Immerse yourself in aquatic life on a snorkeling or diving trip. For bigger beasts, head off on a whale-watching cruise or try to spy alligators – along with egrets, eagles, manatees and other wildlife – on an Everglades excursion.

Shades of Sand

You'll find an array of sandy shores from steamy South Beach to upscale Palm Beach, island allure on Sanibel and Captiva, and panhandle rowdiness in Pensacola.

p452

Great Lakes

Food
Music
Roadside Oddities

Heartland Cuisine

From James Beard Award–winning restaurants in Chicago and Minneapolis to fresh-from-the-dairy milkshakes, the Midwest's farms, orchards and breweries satisfy the palate.

Rock & Roll

Home to the Rock and Roll Hall of Fame, blowout fests like Lollapalooza and thrashing clubs in all the cities, the Midwest knows how to turn up the volume.

Quirky Sights

A big ball of twine, a mustard museum, a cow-doo throwing contest: the quirks rise from the Midwest's backyards and back roads – wherever there are folks with passion, imagination and maybe a little too much time on their hands.

p510

On the Road

New York, New Jersey & Pennsylvania

Best Places to Eat

➡ Blue Hill at Stone Barns (p116)

➡ Hazelnut Kitchen (p121)

➡ Il Buco (p97)

➡ Anchor Bar (p126)

➡ Reading Terminal Market (p147)

Best Places to Stay

➡ Roxbury Motel (p119)

➡ Yotel (p92)

➡ Giacomo (p128)

➡ White Pine Camp (p122)

➡ Congress Hall (p139)

Why Go?

Where else could you visit an Amish family's farm, camp on a mountaintop, read the Declaration of Independence and view New York, New York from the 86th floor of an art-deco landmark – all in a few days? Even though it's the most densely populated part of the US, it's full of places where jaded city dwellers escape to seek simple lives, where artists retreat for inspiration, and where pretty houses line main streets in small towns set amid stunning scenery.

Urban adventures in NYC, historic and lively Philadelphia and river-rich Pittsburgh are a must. Miles and miles of glorious beaches are within reach, from glamorous Long Island to the Jersey Shore – the latter ranges from stately to kitschy. The mountain wilderness of the Adirondacks reaches skyward just a day's drive north of New York City, a journey that perfectly encapsulates this region's heady character.

When to Go
New York City

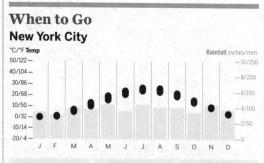

Oct–Nov Autumn in NYC brings cool temps, festivals, the marathon and gearing up for holiday season.

Feb Winter-sports buffs head to the mountains of the Adirondacks, Catskills and Poconos.

31 May–5 Sep Memorial Day through Labor Day is for beaches from Montauk to Cape May.

Transportation

The big cities all have airports, but New York's John F Kennedy is the region's major international gateway. Alternatives include Newark Liberty International Airport and LaGuardia, in Queens, with mostly domestic flights. Philadelphia and Pittsburgh also have international airports.

Greyhound buses serve main cities and towns, while Peter Pan Bus Lines and Adirondack Trailways are two regional bus lines. Amtrak provides rail services linking New York with much of New Jersey, as well as Philadelphia and Pittsburgh. Most popular day trips, at least from New York City, are easily accessible by one of the three commuter-rail lines. If you're driving, the main north–south highway is I-95.

NATIONAL & STATE PARKS

Parklands and recreation areas are in big supply here, as is wildlife, which is at first surprising to many who associate these states only with large urban areas. Black bears, bobcats and even elk can be found in forested parts of the states; more common are various species of deer. Falcons, eagles, hawks and migrating species of birds stop over in the region, some within only a few miles of New York City.

In New York alone, you'll find hundreds of state parks, ranging from waterfalls around Ithaca to wilderness in the Adirondacks. In New Jersey, float down the Delaware River, grab some sun at the Cape May beach and hike the forested Kittatinny Valley in the north. Pennsylvania includes a huge array of thick forests, rolling parklands and a significant portion of the Appalachian National Scenic Trail, a 2175-mile path that snakes its way from Maine to Georgia.

Top Five Scenic Drives

➡ **Catskills, New York – Platte Clove Rd to 214 to 28** This takes you past forested hills, rushing rivers and spectacular falls.

➡ **North Central, Pennsylvania – Rte 6** A drive through this rugged stretch of mountains and woodlands includes gushing creeks, wildlife and state forests.

➡ **Lake Cayuga, New York – Rte 80** Head north from Ithaca above the lake past dozens of wineries.

➡ **Delaware Water Gap, New Jersey – Old Mine Rd** One of the oldest roads in the US past beautiful vistas of the Delaware River and rural countryside.

➡ **PA Dutch Country – S Ronks Rd** This country lane takes you past bucolic farmland scenery between Strasburg and Bird-in-the-Hand.

THE WILD CENTER

Located in Tupper Lake, NY, the Wild Center (p124) is a jewel of a museum dedicated to the ecology of the Adirondacks. Interactive exhibits include a digitally rendered earth that displays thousands of science-related issues.

Fast Facts

➡ **Hub cities** New York City (population 8,245,000), Philadelphia (population 1,536,000)

➡ **Time zone** Eastern Standard

➡ **New York City subways** 24 hours a day

➡ **First oil well drilled** 1859, Titusville, PA

Did You Know?

From November to April harbor seals, as well as other seal species, migrate to the waters of the Jersey Shore, Long Island Sound and NYC, from Staten Island to beaches in the Bronx.

Resources

➡ **New York State Tourism** (www.iloveny.com) Info and maps available by phone.

➡ **New Jersey Travel & Tourism** (www.visitnj.org) Statewide tourism tips.

➡ **Pennsylvania Travel and Tourism** (www.visitpa.com) Maps, videos and suggested itineraries.

➡ **Gas Buddy** (www.gasbuddy.com) Find the cheapest places to grab gas.

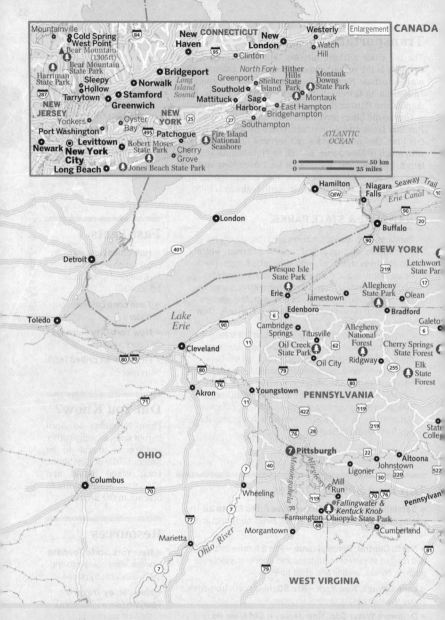

New York, New Jersey & Pennsylvania Highlights

1 Traveling round the world without ever leaving the kaleidoscope of neighborhoods and cultures that is **New York City** (p58).

2 Enjoying the kitsch and calm of the **Jersey Shore** (p130).

3 Absorbing the story of the birth of the nation in Philadelphia's **Independence National Historic Park** (p138).

4 Walking the densely forested paths of the unspoiled **Catskills** (p118).

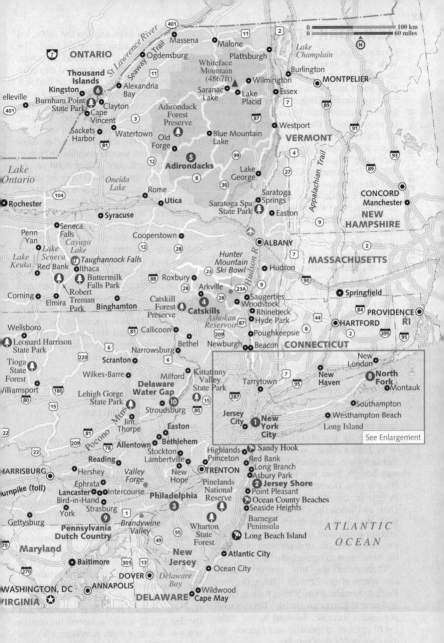

5 Exploring the impressive wilderness beauty of the **Adirondacks** (p122).

6 Camping along the shores of the St Lawrence River in the **Thousand Islands** (p95).

7 Catching big time sports at one of the riverside stadiums in **Pittsburgh** (p155).

8 Wine tasting on Long Island's **North Fork** (p115).

9 Cycling the back roads of **Pennsylvania Dutch Country** (p152).

10 Floating past bucolic scenery in the **Delaware Water Gap** (p129).

NEW YORK CITY

Loud and fast and pulsing with energy, New York City is symphonic, exhausting and always evolving. Maybe only a Walt Whitman poem cataloguing typical city scenes, from the humblest hole-in-the-wall to grand buildings, could begin to do the city justice. It remains one of the world centers of fashion, theater, food, music, publishing, advertising and finance. And as Groucho Marx once said, 'When it's 9:30 in New York, it's 1937 in Los Angeles.' Coming here for the first time from anywhere else is like stepping into a movie, one you've probably been unknowingly writing, one that contains all imagined possibilities. From the middle of Times Square to the most obscure corner of the Bronx, you'll find extremes. From Brooklyn's Russian enclave in Brighton Beach to the mini South America in Queens, virtually every country in the world has a bustling proxy community in the city. You can experience a little bit of everything on a visit here, as long as you take care to travel with a loose itinerary and an open mind.

History

After Henry Hudson first claimed this land in 1609 for his Dutch East India Company sponsors, he reported it to be 'as beautiful a land as one can hope to tread upon.' Soon after it was named 'Manhattan,' derived from local Munsee Native American words and meaning 'Island of Hills.'

By 1625 a colony, soon called New Amsterdam, was established, and the island was bought from the Munsee Indians by Peter Minuit. George Washington was sworn in here as the republic's first president in 1789, and when the Civil War broke out in 1861, New York City, which supplied a significant contingent of volunteers to defend the Union, became an organizing center for the movement to emancipate slaves.

Throughout the 19th century successive waves of immigrants – Irish, German, English, Scandinavian, Slavic, Italian, Greek and central European Jewish – led to a swift population increase, followed by the building of empires in industry and finance, and a golden age of skyscrapers.

After WWII New York City was the premier city in the world, but it suffered from a new phenomenon: 'white flight' to the suburbs. By the 1970s the graffiti-ridden subway system had become a symbol of New York's civic and economic decline. But NYC regained much of its swagger in the 1980s, led by colorful three-term mayor Ed Koch. The city elected its first African American mayor, David Dinkins, in 1989, but ousted him after a single term in favor of Republican Rudolph Giuliani (a 2008 primary candidate for US president). It was during Giuliani's reign that catastrophe struck on September 11, 2001, when the 110-story twin towers of the World Trade Center were struck by hijacked commercial airliners, became engulfed in balls of fire and then collapsed, killing 3000 people, the result of a now-infamous terrorist attack.

The billionaire Republican Mayor Michael Bloomberg, first elected in an atmosphere of turmoil and grief, came under early fire for his severe fiscal policies and draconian moves as head of the beleaguered public school system. Still, Bloomberg was elected to a second and a very controversial third term. Considered an independent political pragmatist, he's earned raves and criticism for his dual pursuit of environmental and development goals through a challenging period that has included the 'Global Financial Crisis' and Hurricane Sandy. It's anyone's guess who will rise to power once the Bloomberg days are over.

◉ Sights

◉ Lower Manhattan

★ **Brooklyn Bridge**   BRIDGE
(Map p62) Marianne Moore's description of the world's first suspension bridge – which inspired poets from Walt Whitman to Jack Kerouac even before its completion – as a 'climactic ornament, a double rainbow' is perhaps most evocative. Walking across the grand Brooklyn Bridge is a rite of passage for New Yorkers and visitors alike – with this in mind, walk no more than two abreast or else you're in danger of colliding with runners and speeding cyclists. With a span of 1596ft, it remains a compelling symbol of US achievement and a superbly graceful structure, despite the fact that its construction was plagued by budget overruns and the death of 20 workers. Among the casualties was designer John Roebling, who was knocked off a pier in 1869 while scouting a site for the western bridge tower and later died of tetanus poisoning. The bridge and the smooth pedestrian/cyclist path, beginning just east of City Hall, afford wonderful views of Lower Manhattan and Brooklyn

New York City

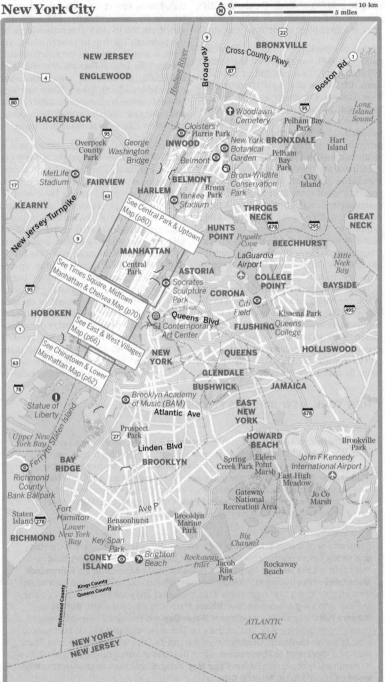

(despite ongoing repairs). On the Brooklyn side, the ever-expanding **Brooklyn Bridge Park** is a great place to continue your stroll.

Statue of Liberty MONUMENT
(☎877-523-9849; www.nps.gov/stli; Liberty Island; 🕐9:30am-5pm) In a city full of American icons, the Statue of Liberty is perhaps the most famous. Conceived as early as 1865 by French intellectual Edouard Laboulaye as a monument to the republican principals shared by France and the USA, it's still generally recognized as a symbol for the ideals of opportunity and freedom to many. French sculptor Frédéric-Auguste Bartholdi traveled to New York in 1871 to select the site, then spent more than 10 years in Paris designing and making the 151ft-tall figure *Liberty Enlightening the World*. It was then shipped to New York, erected on a small island in the harbor and unveiled in 1886. Structurally, it consists of an iron skeleton (designed by Gustave Eiffel) with a copper skin attached to it by metal bars.

The island suffered massive damage from Hurricane Sandy and only reopened to the public on July 4, 2013. Access to the crown is limited, however, so reservations are required as far in advance as possible (additional $3 admission). Keep in mind, there's no elevator and the climb from the base is equal to a 22-story building. Otherwise, a visit means you can wander the grounds, take in the small museum and enjoy the view from the 16-story observation deck in the pedestal. The trip to Liberty island, via ferry, is usually made in conjunction with nearby Ellis Island. **Ferries** (Map p62; ☎201-604-2800, 877-523-9849; www.statuecruises.com; adult/child $17/9; 🕐every 30min 9am-5pm, extended summer hr) leave from Battery Park and tickets include admission to both sights, and reservations can be made in advance.

Ellis Island LANDMARK, MUSEUM
(☎212-363-3200; www.nps.gov/elis; [S]1 to South Ferry, 4/5 to Bowling Green) Ellis Island is currently closed to visitors due to damage from Hurricane Sandy and as this book went to print there was no planned reopening date. Yet it remains one of New York's most iconic landmarks. The way-station from 1892 to 1954 for more than 12 million immigrants who were hoping to make new lives in the United States, Ellis Island conjures up the humble and sometimes miserable beginnings of the experience of coming to America – as well as the fulfillment of dreams. More than 3000 died in the island's hospital and more than two percent were denied admission. Before Hurricane Sandy wreaked havoc on the island, the handsome main building had been restored as the **Immigration Museum**, with fascinating exhibits

NEW YORK, NEW JERSEY & PENNSYLVANIA IN...

One Week

Start off with a gentle introduction in **Philadelphia**, birthplace of American independence. After a day touring the historic sites and a night sampling the hoppin' nightlife, head into New Jersey for a bucolic night in **Cape May**. Sample another beachtown like **Wildwood** or **Atlantic City** further north along the **Jersey Shore**, landing in **New York City** the following day. Spend the rest of your visit here, blending touristy must-dos – such as the **Top of the Rock** and **Central Park** – with vibrant nightlife and eclectic dining adventures, perhaps in the city's bustling **East Village**.

Two Weeks

Begin with several days in **New York City**, then a night or two somewhere in the **Hudson Valley**, before reaching the **Catskills**. After touring this bucolic region, head further north to **Lake George**, the gateway to the forested wilderness of the **Adirondack Mountains** where the outdoor-minded will have trouble leaving. Then loop back south through the Finger Lakes region with stops in wineries and waterfall-laden parks along the way, with a night in college-town **Ithaca**. From here you can head to **Buffalo** and **Niagara Falls** or south to the **Delaware Water Gap** and the quaint riverside towns of Pennsylvania and New York. The southern portion of Pennsylvania has loads of historic sites as well as **Lancaster County**, where you can stay on a working Amish farm. From here it's a short jaunt to **Philadelphia**, which deserves at least a couple of nights. Follow it up with a stay at a quaint B&B in **Cape May**, a day of boardwalk amusements in **Wildwood** and casino fun in **Atlantic City**.

and a film about immigrant experiences, the processing of immigrants and how the influx changed the USA.

National September 11 Memorial MEMORIAL
(Map p62; ☎ 212-266-5211; www.911memorial.org; 🕒 daily; [S] R to Cortlandt St) [FREE] After more than a decade of cost overruns, delays and politicking, the redevelopment of the World Trade Center site destroyed by the attacks of September 11, 2001, is finally coming to fruition. Half of the area's 16 acres is dedicated to honoring victims and preserving history, while the remaining space is occupied by office towers, a Santiago Calatrava–designed transport hub, museum and performing arts center – the last three not yet open. The focus of the moving memorial, which opened to the public on September 12, 2011, are the two large pools with cascading waterfalls set in the footprints of the north and south towers. Bronze parapets surrounding the pools are inscribed with the names of those killed in the attacks, and hundreds of swamp white-wood trees provide shade to the site. Visitor passes with a $2 service fee can be reserved through the memorial's website. The $3.2 billion One World Trade Center, formerly known as the Freedom Tower, has reached the 104th floor and the 408ft steel spire has been installed, making it at 1776ft the tallest building in the US. You can check progress on the site or reserve passes by visiting the **9/11 Memorial Preview Site** (Map p62; www.911memorial.org; 20 Vesey St; 🕒 9am-7pm Mon-Fri, 8am-7pm Sat & Sun) [FREE], which has exhibits and information on the rebuilding or go to www.wtcprogress.com.

Nearby is the **Tribute WTC Visitor Center** (Map p62; ☎ 866-737-1184; www.tributewtc.org; 120 Liberty St; adult/child $17/5; 🕒 10am-6pm Mon-Sat, to 5pm Sun; [S] E to World Trade Center, R/W to Cortland St), which provides exhibits, first-person testimony and **walking tours** of the site (adult/child $22/7, includes gallery admission, several tours from 11am to 3pm Sunday to Friday, and to 4pm Saturday).

Governor's Island National Monument PARK
(www.govisland.com; 🕒 10am-7pm Sat & Sun May 25-Sep 29) [FREE] Most New Yorkers have gazed out over this mysterious path of green in the harbor, less than half a mile from the southern tip of Manhattan, without a clue as to its purpose. Although it was once reserved only for the army or coast guard personnel who were based here, these days the general public can visit. The 22-acre Governor's Island National Monument is accessible by riding the **ferry** (Map p62; 🕒 10am, 11am, then every 30min) leaving from the Battery Marine Terminal next to the Staten Island Ferry Whitehall Terminal in lower Manhattan. Guided **walking tours**, 90 minutes long, are run by the park service; tickets are available first-come, first-served an hour in advance at the Battery Marine Terminal. Highlights include two 19th-century fortifications – Fort Jay and the three-tiered, sandstone Castle Williams – plus open lawns, massive shade trees and unsurpassed city views.

South Street Seaport NEIGHBORHOOD
(Map p62; ☎ 212-732-7678; www.southstreetseaport.com; 🕒 10am-9pm Mon-Sat, 11am-8pm Sun; [S] 2/3, 4/5, J/M/Z to Fulton St) This 11-block enclave of shops, piers and sights combines the best and worst in historic preservation. It's not on the radar for most New Yorkers, but tourists are drawn to the sea air, the nautical feel, the frequent street performers and the mobbed restaurants. Pier 17, a fairly mundane waterfront mall that was home to several floors of shops and restaurants, was slated to be demolished in October 2013 and replaced with a more contemporary light-filled shopping and entertainment complex. Preliminary plans call for the reopening some time in 2015.

The pedestrian malls, historic tall ships and riverside locale of this neighborhood create a lovely backdrop if you happen to be standing in line for discounted Broadway tickets at the downtown TKTS Booth.

Bowling Green Park PARK
(Map p62; cnr State & Whitehall Sts; [S] 4/5 to Bowling Green) At Bowling Green Park, British residents relaxed with quiet games in the late 17th century. The large **bronze bull** (Map p62) here is a tourist photo stop. The **National Museum of the American Indian** (Map p62; www.nmai.si.edu; 1 Bowling Green; 🕒 10am-5pm Fri-Wed, to 8pm Thu; [S] 4/5 to Bowling Green) [FREE], housed in the gorgeous and historic Alexander Hamilton US Customs House, has quite an extensive collection of Native American arts, crafts and exhibits, plus a library and a great gift shop.

Wall Street & The Financial District

Despite the worldwide economic crash of late 2007/early 2008 and the subsequent protests of Occupy Wall Street, the

Chinatown & Lower Manhattan

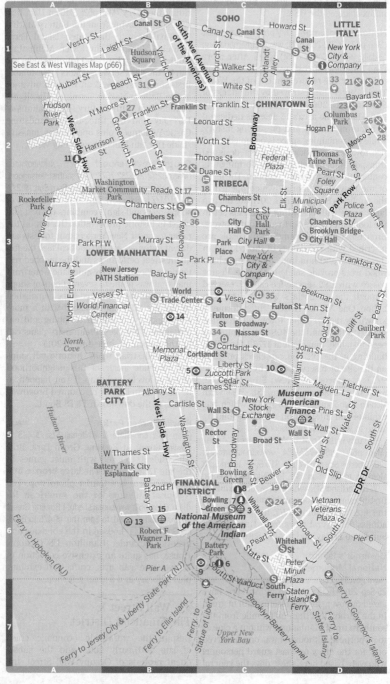

neighborhood and financial industry have rebounded. The etymological origin of **Wall Street**, both an actual street and the metaphorical home of US commerce, is the wooden barrier built by Dutch settlers in 1653 to protect Nieuw Amsterdam from Native Americans and the British. A comprehensive overview, warts and all, of the US economy is explained in fascinating up-to-date exhibits at the **Museum of American Finance** (Map p62; www.moaf.org; 48 Wall St btwn Pearl & William Sts; adult/child $8/free; ⏰10am-4pm Tue-Sat; [S] 2/3, 4/5 to Wall St), housed in the venerable former home of the Bank of New York. To get an up-close-and-personal view of what makes the world go round, sign up for an hour-plus tour of the **Federal Reserve** (Map p62; ☎212-825-6990; www.nps.gov/feha; 26 Wall St; ⏰9am-5pm) [FREE].

Battery Park & Around NEIGHBORHOOD

The southwestern tip of Manhattan Island has been extended with landfill over the years to form **Battery Park** (Map p62; www.nycgovparks.org; Broadway at Battery Pl; ⏰sunrise-1am; [S] 4/5 to Bowling Green, 1 to South Ferry), so named for the gun batteries that used to be housed at the bulkheads. **Castle Clinton** (Map p62; www.nps.gov/cacl; Battery Park; ⏰8:30am-5pm; [S] 1 to South Ferry; 4/5 to Bowling Green), a fortification built in 1811 to protect Manhattan from the British, was originally 900ft offshore but is now at the edge of Battery Park, with only its walls remaining. Come summertime, it's transformed into a gorgeous outdoor concert arena. The **Museum of Jewish Heritage** (Map p62; www.mjhnyc.org; 36 Battery Pl; adult/child $12/free, 4-8pm Wed free; ⏰10am-5:45pm Sun-Tue & Thu, to 8pm Wed, to 5pm Fri; [S] 4/5 to Bowling Green) depicts aspects of New York Jewish history and culture, and includes a holocaust memorial. Also worth a look, the **Skyscraper Museum** (Map p62; www.skyscraper.org; 39 Battery Pl; admission $5; ⏰noon-6pm Wed-Sun; [S] 4/5 to Bowling Green) housed in a ground-floor space of the Ritz-Carlton Hotel features rotating exhibits plus a permanent study of high-rise history. Finally, Battery Place is the start of the stunning **Hudson River Park** (Map p62; www.hudsonriverpark.org; Manhattan's west side from Battery Park to 59th St; [S] 1 to Franklin St, 1 to Canal St), which incorporates renovated piers, grassy spaces, gardens, basketball courts, a trapeze school, food concessions and, best of all, a ribbon of a cycle/skate/running path that stretches 5 miles up to 59th St.

Chinatown & Lower Manhattan

◎ Top Sights
1 Brooklyn Bridge F4
2 Museum of American Finance.............D5
3 National Museum of the
  American Indian...................................C6

◎ Sights
4 9/11 Memorial Preview Site..................C4
5 9/11 Tribute Center B4
6 Battery Park C6
7 Bowling Green Park................................C6
8 Bronze Bull C6
9 Castle Clinton C6
10 Federal Reserve C4
11 Hudson River Park..................................A2
12 Museum at Eldridge Street
   Synagogue..E1
13 Museum of Jewish Heritage.................B6
14 National September 11
   Memorial B4
15 Skyscraper Museum B6
16 South Street Seaport............................E4

◎ Sleeping
17 Cosmopolitan Hotel...............................B3
18 Duane Street Hotel................................C2

19 Wall Street Inn C6

⊗ Eating
20 Amazing 66 ....D1
21 Big Wong King..D1
22 Blaue Gans B2
23 Bo Ky Restaurant D2
24 Financier Patisserie...............................C6
25 Fraunces Tavern.....................................D6
26 Joe's Shanghai.......................................D2
27 Kutsher's Tribeca B2
28 Nom Wah Tea Parlor..............................D2
29 Original Chinatown Ice
   Cream Factory....................................D2
30 Ruben's Empanadas..............................D4

◎ Drinking & Nightlife
31 Brandy Library B1
32 Santos Party House C1
33 Whiskey Tavern D1

◎ Shopping
34 Century 21 ....C4
35 J&R Music & Computer
   World...C4
36 Philip Williams Posters B3

◎ Tribeca & SoHo

The 'TRIangle BElow CAnal St,' bordered roughly by Broadway to the east and Chambers St to the south, is the more downtown of these two sister 'hoods. It has old warehouses, very expensive loft apartments and chichi restaurants.

SoHo has nothing to do with its London counterpart, but instead, like Tribeca, takes its name from its geographical placement: SOuth of HOuston St. SoHo is filled with block upon block of cast-iron industrial buildings that date to the period just after the Civil War, when this was the city's leading commercial district. It had a Bohemian/artsy heyday that had ended by the 1980s, and now this super-gentrified area is a major shopping destination, home to chain stores and boutiques alike and to hordes of consumers, especially on weekends.

SoHo's hip cup overfloweth to the northern side of Houston St and the east side of Lafayette St, where two small areas, NoHo ('north of Houston') and NoLita ('north of Little Italy'), respectively, are known for excellent shopping – lots of small, independent and stylish clothing boutiques for women – and dining. Add them to SoHo and Tribeca

for a great experience of strolling, window-shopping and cafe-hopping, and you'll have quite a lovely afternoon.

◎ Chinatown & Little Italy

More than 150,000 Chinese-speaking residents live in cramped tenements and crowded apartments in Chinatown, the largest Chinese community that exists outside of Asia (though there are two other major Chinatowns in the city – Sunset Park in Brooklyn, and Flushing in Queens). In the 1990s, the neighborhood also attracted a growing number of Vietnamese immigrants, who set up their own shops and opened inexpensive restaurants; depending on what street you're on, you'll often notice more of a Vietnamese than Chinese presence.

The best reason to visit Chinatown is to experience a feast for the senses – it's the only spot in the city where you can simultaneously see whole roasted pigs hanging in butcher-shop windows, get whiffs of fresh fish and hear the twangs of Cantonese and Vietnamese rise over the calls of knock-off-Prada-bag hawkers on Canal St.

Whereas Little Italy, once a truly authentic pocket of Italian people, culture and eateries, is constantly shrinking (Chinatown keeps encroaching). Still, loyal Italian Americans, mostly from the suburbs, flock here to gather around red-and-white-checked tablecloths at one of a handful of longtime red-sauce restaurants. Join them for a stroll along Mulberry Street, and take a peek at the **Old St Patrick's Cathedral** (263 Mulberry St), which became the city's first Roman Catholic cathedral in 1809 and remained so until 1878, when its more famous uptown successor was completed. The former Ravenite Social Club, now a fancy shoe shop, is a reminder of the not-so-long-ago days when mobsters ran the neighborhood. Originally known as the Alto Knights Social Club, where big hitters like Lucky Luciano spent time, the Ravenite was a favorite hangout of John Gotti (and the FBI) before his arrest and life sentencing in 1992.

Museum of Chinese in America MUSEUM
(Map p66; ☎212-619-4785; www.mocanyc.org; 211-215 Centre St near Grand St; adult/child $10/free; 🕐11am-6pm Tue-Wed & Fri-Sun, to 9pm Thu; [S] N/Q/R/W, J/M/Z, 6 to Canal St) Strikingly designed and cutting-edge interactive exhibits trace the history and cultural impact of Chinese communities in the US. Lectures, film series and walking tours as well.

Lower East Side

First came the Jews, then the Latinos, followed by the hipsters and accompanying posers, frat boy bros, and the bridge and tunnel contingent. Today, this neighborhood, once the densest in the world, is focused on being cool – offering low-lit lounges, live-music clubs and trendy bistros. Luxury high-rise condominiums and boutique hotels coexist with public-housing projects (read Richard Price's novel *Lush Life* for entertaining insight into this class conflict). Nevertheless, 40% of residents are still immigrants and two-thirds speak a language other than English at home.

★Lower East Side Tenement Museum MUSEUM
(Map p66; ☎212-982-8420; www.tenement.org; 103 Orchard St; tours from $22; 🕐visitor center 10am-5:30pm, tours 10:15am-5pm) There's no museum in New York that humanizes the city's colorful past quite like this one. The neighborhood's heartbreaking but inspiring heritage is on full display in several recreations of turn-of-the-20th-century tenements. Always evolving and expanding, the museum has a variety of tours and talks. And while the main portion of your visit is the tenement tour, during which you'll have the opportunity to interact with a guide, don't forget to check out the one-of-a-kind visitor center unveiled at the end of 2011. The expansion has allowed for the addition of gallery space, an enlarged museum shop, a screening room that plays an original film and plenty of seminar space.

Museum at Eldridge Street Synagogue MUSEUM
(Map p62; ☎212-219-0302; www.eldridgestreet.org; 12 Eldridge St btwn Canal & Division Sts; adult/child $10/6; 🕐10am-5pm Sun-Thu, to 3pm Fri; [S] F to East Broadway) Built in 1887 with Moorish and Romanesque ornamental work, this synagogue attracted as many as 1000 worshippers on the High Holidays at the turn of the 20th century. But membership dwindled in the 1920s with restricted immigration laws, and by the 1950s the temple closed altogether. A 20-year restoration project was completed in 2007 and now the synagogue holds Friday-evening and Saturday-morning worship services, hosts weddings and offers **tours** (on the half-hour) of the building. Check out the massive circular **stained-glass window** above the ark (space where torahs are kept).

New Museum of Contemporary Art MUSEUM
(Map p66; ☎212-219-1222; www.newmuseum.org; 235 Bowery btwn Stanton & Rivington Sts; adult/child $14/free, 7-9pm Thu free; 🕐11am-6pm Wed & Fri-Sun, to 9pm Thu; [S] N/R to Prince St, F to 2nd Ave, J/Z to Bowery, 6 to Spring St) Housed in an architecturally ambitious building on a formerly gritty Bowery strip, this is the city's sole museum dedicated to contemporary art. There's the added treat of a city viewing platform, which provides a unique perspective on the constantly changing neighborhood landscape.

East Village

If you've been dreaming of those quintessential New York City moments – graffiti on crimson brick, punks and grannies walking side by side, and cute cafes with rickety tables spilling out onto the sidewalks – then the East Village is your Holy Grail. Stick to the area around Tompkins Square Park, and the lettered avenues (known as Alphabet City) to its east, for interesting little nooks

East & West Villages

in which to imbibe and ingest – as well as a collection of great little community gardens that provide leafy respites and sometimes even live performances.

Tompkins Square Park PARK

(Map p66; www.nycgovparks.org; E 7th & 10th Sts btwn Aves A & B; ⏰ 6am-midnight; Ⓢ 6 to Astor Pl) FREE This 10.5-acre park is like a friendly town square for locals, who gather for chess at concrete tables, picnics on the lawn on warm days and spontaneous guitar or drum jams on various grassy knolls. It's also the site of basketball courts, a fun-to-watch dog run (a fenced-in area where humans can unleash their canines), frequent summer concerts and an always-lively kids' playground. The annual Howl! Festival of East Village Arts brings Allen Ginsberg–inspired theater, music, film, dance and spoken-word events to the park and various neighborhood venues each September.

Astor Place & Around NEIGHBORHOOD

This square (Map p66; 8th St btwn Third & Fourth Aves; Ⓢ R/W to 8th St-NYU, 6 to Astor Pl) is named after the Astor family, who built an early New York fortune on beaver pelts and lived on Colonnade Row, just south of the square. The large, brownstone Cooper Union, the public college founded in 1859 by glue millionaire Peter Cooper, dominates the square – now more than ever – as the school now has its first new academic building in over 50 years, a striking, twisting, nine-story sculpture of glazed glass wrapped in perforated stainless steel (and LEED-certified, too) by architect Thom Mayne of Morphosis.

Russian & Turkish Baths BATHHOUSE

(Map p66; ☎ 212-674-9250; www.russianturkishbaths.com; 268 E 10th St btwn First Ave & Ave A; per visit $35; ⏰ noon-10pm Mon-Tue & Thu-Fri, 10am-10pm Wed, 9am-10pm Sat, 8am-10pm Sun; Ⓢ L to 1st Ave; 6 to Astor Pl) The historic bathhouse is a great place to work out your stress in one

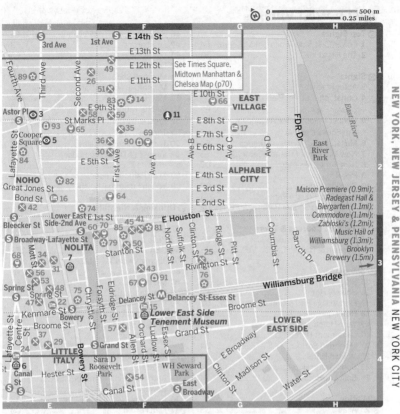

of the four hot rooms; traditional massages are also offered. It's authentic and somewhat grungy, and you're as likely to share a sauna with a downtown couple on a date, a well-known actor looking for a time-out or an actual Russian.

West Village & Greenwich Village

Once a symbol for all things artistic, outlandish and Bohemian, this storied and popular neighborhood – the birthplace of the gay-rights movement as well as former home of Beat poets and important artists – feels worlds away from busy Broadway and, in fact, almost European. Known by most visitors as 'Greenwich Village,' although that term is not used by locals (West Village encompasses Greenwich Village, which is the area immediately around Washington Square Park), it has narrow streets lined with well-groomed and high-priced real estate, as well as cafes and restaurants, making it an ideal place to wander.

Washington Square Park & Around PARK
This **park** (Map p66; Fifth Ave at Washington Sq N; ⓢA/C/E, B/D/F/V to W 4th St-Washington Sq, N/R/W to 8th St-NYU) began as a 'potter's field' – a burial ground for the penniless – and its status as a cemetery protected it from development. It is now a completely renovated and incredibly well-used park, especially on the weekend. Children use the playground, NYU students catch some rays and friends meet 'under the arch,' the renovated landmark on the park's northern edge, designed in 1889 by society architect Stanford White. Dominating a huge swath of property in the middle of the Village, New York University, one of the largest in the country, defines the area around the park and beyond, architecturally and demographically.

East & West Villages

Top Sights
1 Lower East Side Tenement Museum....F4
2 The High Line....B1

Sights
3 Astor Place....E1
4 Christopher Street Piers/Hudson River Park....B2
5 Cooper Union for the Advancement of Science and Art....E2
6 Museum of Chinese in America....E4
7 New Museum of Contemporary Art....E3
8 New York University....D2
9 Pier 45....B3
10 Sheridan Square....C2
11 Tompkins Square Park....F1
12 Washington Square Park....D2

Activities, Courses & Tours
13 Downtown Boathouse....B3
14 Russian & Turkish Baths....F1

Sleeping
15 Blue Moon Hotel....F3
16 Bowery Hotel....E2
17 East Village Bed & Coffee....G2
18 Hotel Gansevoort....B1
19 Jane Hotel....B1
20 Larchmont Hotel....D1
21 Mondrian SoHo....D4
22 Nolitan Hotel....E3
23 Soho Grand Hotel....D4
24 Solita SoHo....E4

Eating
25 Alias....G3
26 Angelica Kitchen....E1
27 Aroma Espresso Bar....D3
28 Babbo....C2
29 Bánh Mì Saigon Bakery....E4
30 Banjara....F2
31 BarBossa....E3
32 Bonsignour....B1
33 Boqueria Soho....D3
34 Café Gitane....E3
35 Caracas Arepa Bar....F2
36 Counter....F2
37 Da Nico....E4
38 Ditch Plains....C3
39 Dutch....D3
40 Fatty Crab....B1
41 Georgia's East Side BBQ....F3
42 Il Buco....E2
43 'Inoteca....F3
44 Joe's Pizza....C2
45 Katz's Delicatessen....F3
46 Kin Shop....C1
47 Lombardi's....E3
48 Lovely Day....E3
49 Luzzo's....F1
50 Meatball Shop....F3
51 Momofuku Noodle Bar....F1
52 Mooncake Foods....D4
53 Pinche Taqueria....E3
54 Prosperity Dumpling....F4
55 Tartine....B1
56 Torrisi Italian Specialties....E3
57 Vanessa's Dumpling House....F4
58 Veselka....E1
59 Xi'an Famous Foods....F1
60 Yonah Schimmel Knishery....E3

Drinking & Nightlife
61 124 Old Rabbit Club....D2
62 Bar Next Door....C2
63 Cielo....B1
64 DBA....F2
65 Jimmy's No 43....E2
66 Louis 649....G1
67 Mehanata....F3
68 Pravda....E3
69 Pyramid Club....F2
70 Sapphire....F3
71 SOBs....C3
72 Sway Lounge....C4

Entertainment
73 55 Bar....C2
74 Anthology Film Archives....E2
75 Bowery Ballroom....E3
76 Delancey....G3
77 Film Forum....C3
78 IFC Center....C2
Joe's Pub....(see 84)
79 Landmark Sunshine Cinema....F3
80 Le Poisson Rouge....D2
81 Mercury Lounge....F3
82 New York Theater Workshop....E2
83 PS 122....F1
84 Public Theater....E2
85 Rockwood Music Hall....F3
86 Smalls....C2
87 Village Lantern....D2
88 Village Vanguard....C1
89 Webster Hall....E1

Shopping
90 A-1 Records....F2
91 Economy Candy....F3
92 Strand Book Store....D1
93 Trash & Vaudeville....E2

Christopher Street Piers/Hudson River Park PIER, PARK
(Map p66; Christopher St & West Side Hwy; [S]1 to Christopher St-Sheridan Sq) Like so many places in the Village, the extreme west side was once a derelict eyesore used mostly as a cruising ground for quick, anonymous sex. Now it's a pretty waterside hangout, bisected

by the Hudson River Park's slender bike and jogging paths. It's still a place to cruise, just much less dangerous.

Sheridan Square & Around   NEIGHBORHOOD

The western edge of the Village is home to Sheridan Square (Map p66; Christopher St & Seventh Ave; **S** 1 to Christopher St-Sheridan Sq), a small, triangular park where life-sized white statues by George Segal honor the gay community and gay pride movement that began in the nearby renovated Stonewall Inn, sitting just across the street from the square. A block further east, an appropriately bent street is officially named Gay St. Although gay social scenes have in many ways moved further uptown to Chelsea, Christopher Street is still the center of gay life in the Village.

◉ Meatpacking District

Nestled between the far West Village and the southern border of Chelsea is the gentrified and now inappropriately named Meatpacking District. The neighborhood was once home to 250 slaughterhouses and was best known for its groups of tranny hookers, racy S&M sex clubs and, of course, its sides of beef. These days the hugely popular High Line park has only intensified an ever-increasing proliferation of trendy wine bars, eateries, nightclubs, high-end designer clothing stores, chic hotels and high-rent condos.

★ The High Line   OUTDOORS

(Map p66; ✆ 212-500-6035; www.thehighline.org; Gansevoort St; ◷ 7am-7pm; ▣ M11 to Washington St; M11, M14 to 9th Ave M23, M34 to 10th Ave, **S** L or A/C/E to 14th St-8th Ave, C/E to 23rd St-8th Ave) **FREE** With the completion of the High Line, a 30ft-high abandoned stretch of elevated railroad track has been transformed into a long ribbon of parkland. Spanning from Gansevoort St to W 34th St, there's finally some greenery amid the asphalt jungle. Only three stories above the streetscape, this thoughtfully and carefully designed mix of contemporary, industrial and natural elements is nevertheless a refuge and escape from the ordinary. A glass-front amphitheater with bleacher-like seating sits just above 10th Ave – bring some food and join local workers on their lunch break. Entrances are at Gansevoort, 14th, 16th, 18th, 20th and 30th Sts; elevator access at all but 18th St) The third and final phase will bend closer to the Hudson at 34th St but it's final status is dependent on the ongoing massive redevelopment of the adjoining Hudson Rail Yards. The Whitney Museum of American Art (long located on the Upper East Side), will relocate to its Renzo Piano–designed home situated between the High Line and the Hudson River in 2015.

◉ Chelsea

This 'hood is popular for two main attractions: one, the parade of gorgeous gay men (known affectionately as 'Chelsea boys') who roam Eighth Ave, darting from gyms to trendy happy hours; and two, it's one of the hubs of the city's art-gallery scene – it's currently home to nearly 200 modern-art exhibition spaces, most of which are clustered west of Tenth Ave. Find specific galleries at www.westchelseaarts.com.

Rubin Museum of Art   MUSEUM

(Map p70; ✆ 212-620-5000; www.rmanyc.org; 150 W 17th St at Seventh Ave; adult/child $10/free, 6-10pm Fri free; ◷ 11am-5pm Mon & Thu, to 7pm Wed, to 10pm Fri, to 6pm Sat & Sun; **S** 1 to 18th St) Dedicated to the art of the Himalayas and surrounding regions, this museum's impressive collections include embroidered textiles from China, metal sculptures from Tibet, intricate Bhutanese paintings, as well as ritual objects and dance masks from various Tibetan regions, spanning from the 2nd to the 19th centuries.

Chelsea Piers Complex   SPORTS

(Map p70; ✆ 212-336-6666; www.chelseapiers.com; Hudson River at end of W 23rd St; **S** C/E to 23rd St) A waterfront sports center that caters to the athlete in everyone. It's got a four-level driving range, indoor ice rink, jazzy bowling alley, Hoop City for basketball, a sailing school for kids, batting cages, a huge gym, indoor rock-climbing walls – the works.

◉ Flatiron District

The famous (and absolutely gorgeous) 1902 Flatiron Building (Map p70; Broadway cnr Fifth Ave & 23rd St; **S** N/R, 6 to 23rd St) has a distinctive triangular shape to match its site. New York's first iron-frame high-rise, and the world's tallest building until 1909. Its surrounding district is a fashionable area of boutiques, loft apartments and a burgeoning high-tech corridor, the city's answer to Silicon Valley. Peaceful Madison Square Park bordered by 23rd and 26th Sts, and Fifth and Madison Aves, has an active dog run, rotating outdoor sculptures, shaded

Times Square, Midtown Manhattan & Chelsea

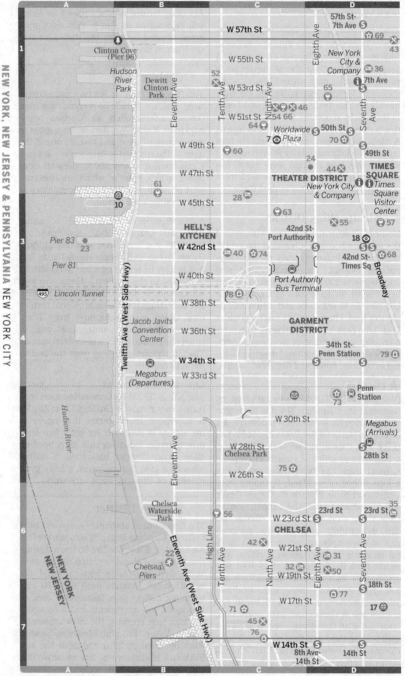

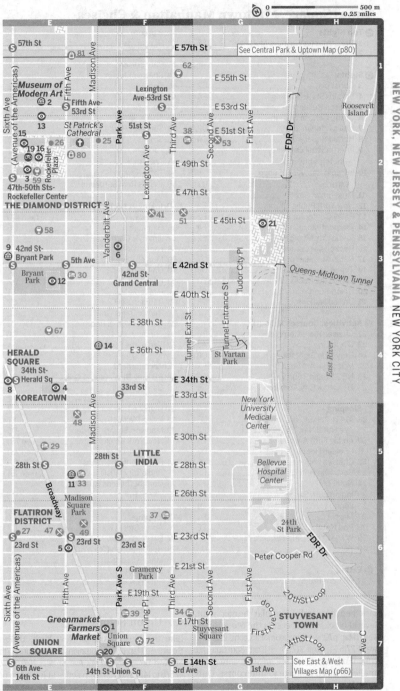

See Central Park & Uptown Map (p80)

57th St

E 57th St

Fifth Ave

Madison Ave

E 55th St

62

Lexington Ave-53rd St

E 53rd St

Museum of Modern Art

2

Fifth Ave-53rd St

13

51st St

Park Ave

Third Ave

Second Ave

First Ave

FDR Dr

Roosevelt Island

St Patrick's Cathedral

15

19 16

26

25

E 51st St

38

53

80

Rockefeller Plaza

3 59

47th-50th Sts-Rockefeller Center

THE DIAMOND DISTRICT

E 49th St

E 47th St

E 45th St

21

58

41

51

Vanderbilt Ave

9 42nd St-Bryant Park

5th Ave

6

Queens-Midtown Tunnel

Bryant Park

12

30

42nd St-Grand Central

E 42nd St

E 40th St

Tunnel Exit St

Tunnel Entrance St

Tudor City Pl

67

E 38th St

14

E 36th St

St Vartan Park

HERALD SQUARE

34th St-Herald Sq

8

E 34th St

E 33rd St

East River

4

KOREATOWN

33rd St

Madison Ave

New York University Medical Center

48

E 30th St

29

28th St

28th St

LITTLE INDIA

E 28th St

Bellevue Hospital Center

11 33

E 26th St

FLATIRON DISTRICT

Broadway

Madison Square Park

37

24th St Park

FDR Dr

27 47

49

E 23rd St

5

23rd St

23rd St

Peter Cooper Rd

Fifth Ave

Sixth Ave (Avenue of the Americas)

Gramercy Park

E 21st St

E 19th St

Park Ave S

Irving Pl

Third Ave

Second Ave

First Ave

20th St Loop

First Ave Loop

STUYVESANT TOWN

39

34

E 17th St

Greenmarket Farmers Market

1

Union Square

72

Stuyvesant Square

14th St Loop

Ave C

UNION SQUARE

20

6th Ave-14th St

E 14th St

14th St-Union Sq

3rd Ave

1st Ave

See East & West Villages Map (p66)

Times Square, Midtown Manhattan & Chelsea

Top Sights
1 Greenmarket Farmers Market........F7
2 Museum of Modern Art........E1

Sights
3 Christie's........E2
4 Empire State Building........E4
5 Flatiron Building........E6
6 Grand Central Station........F3
7 Hell's Kitchen........C2
8 Herald Square........E4
9 International Center of Photography........E3
10 Intrepid Sea, Air & Space Museum........B3
11 Museum of Sex........E5
12 New York Public Library........E3
13 Paley Center for Media........E2
14 Pierpont Morgan Library........F4
15 Radio City Music Hall........E2
16 Rockefeller Center........E2
17 Rubin Museum of Art........D7
18 Times Square........D3
19 Top of the Rock........E2
20 Union Square........F7
21 United Nations........G3

Activities, Courses & Tours
22 Chelsea Piers Complex........B6
23 Circle Line........A3
24 Gray Line Sightseeing........D2
25 Municipal Art Society........F2
26 NBC Studio Tours........E2
27 New York City Audubon........E6

Sleeping
28 414 Hotel........C3
29 Ace Hotel New York City........E5
30 Andaz Fifth Avenue........E3
31 Chelsea Hostel........D6
32 Chelsea Lodge........C6
33 Gershwin Hotel........E5
34 Hotel 17........F7
35 Inn on 23rd St........D6
36 London NYC........D1
37 Marcel........F6
38 Pod Hotel........F2
39 W New York Union Square........F7
40 Yotel........C3

Eating
41 99 Cent Pizza........F3
42 Blossom........C6
Breslin........(see 29)
43 Burger Joint........D1
44 Café Edison........D2
45 Chelsea Market........C7
46 Danji........C2
47 Eataly........E6
48 Hangawi........E5
49 Shake Shack........E6
50 Soccarat Paella Bar........D6
51 Sparks........F3
52 Taboon........C1
53 The Smith........G2
54 Totto Ramen........C2
55 Virgil's Real Barbecue........D3

Drinking & Nightlife
Birreria........(see 47)
56 Half King........C6
57 Jimmy's Corner........D3
58 Lantern's Keep........E3
59 Morrell Wine Bar & Café........E2
60 On the Rocks........C2
61 Pacha........B2
62 PJ Clarke's........F1
63 Réunion Surf........C3
64 Rudy's Bar & Grill........C2
65 Russian Vodka Room........D1
66 Therapy........C2
67 Top of the Strand........E4

Entertainment
68 BB King Blues Club & Grill........D3
69 Carnegie Hall........D1
70 Caroline's on Broadway........D2
71 Highline Ballroom........C7
72 Irving Plaza........F7
73 Madison Square Garden........D5
New York Knicks........(see 73)
New York Liberty........(see 73)
74 Playwrights Horizons........C3
Radio City Music Hall........(see 15)
75 Upright Citizens Brigade Theatre........C5

Shopping
76 Apple Store........C7
77 Barneys Co-op........D7
78 Hell's Kitchen Flea Market........C4
79 Macy's........D4
80 Saks Fifth Ave........E2
81 Tiffany & Co........E1

park benches and a popular burger joint. Several blocks to the east is the **Museum of Sex** (Map p70; www.museumofsex.com; 233 Fifth Ave at 27th St; adult $17.50; ⌚ 10am-8pm Sun-Thu, to 9pm Fri & Sat; [S] N/R to 23rd St), a somewhat intellectualized homage to intercourse. Only 18 and over admitted.

Union Square

Like the Noah's Ark of New York, **Union Square** (Map p70; www.unionsquarenyc.org; 17th St btwn Broadway & Park Ave S; [S] L, N/Q/R/W, 4/5/6 to 14th St-Union Sq) rescues at least two of every kind from the curling seas of concrete.

In fact, one would be hard-pressed to find a more eclectic cross-section of locals gathered in one public place. Here, amid the tapestry of stone steps and fenced-in foliage, it's not uncommon to find denizens of every ilk: suited businessfolk gulping fresh air during their lunch breaks, dreadlocked loiterers tapping beats on their tabla, skateboarding punks flipping tricks on the southeastern stairs, rowdy college kids guzzling student-priced eats, and throngs of protesting masses chanting fervently for various causes.

Gramercy Park, just to the northeast, is named after one of New York's loveliest parks; for residents only, though, and you need a key to get in!

★ Greenmarket Farmers Market — FOOD MARKET

(Map p70; ☎ 212-788-7476; www.grownyc.org; 17th St, btwn Broadway & Park Ave S; ⏲ 8am-6pm Mon, Wed, Fri & Sat) 🍃 On most days, Union Square's north end hosts the most popular of the nearly 50 greenmarkets throughout the five boroughs, where even celebrity chefs come for just-picked rarities including fiddlehead ferns, heirloom tomatoes and fresh curry leaves.

Midtown

The classic NYC fantasy – shiny skyscrapers, teeming mobs of worker bees, Fifth Ave store windows, taxi traffic – and some of the city's most popular attractions can be found here. Long ago when print ruled and newspaper and magazines were the cultural currency of the day, Midtown was actually also the literary district – the prime movers and shakers used to meet at the Algonquin Hotel. Major media companies such as the *New York Times* are still based here.

★ Museum of Modern Art — MUSEUM

(MoMA; Map p70; www.moma.org; 11 W 53rd St btwn Fifth & Sixth Aves, Midtown West; adult/child $25/free, 4-8pm Fri free; ⏲ 10:30am-5:30pm Sat-Thu, to 8pm Fri; [S] E/M to 5th Ave-53rd St) Superstar of the modern art scene, MoMA's booty makes many other collections look, well, endearing. You'll find more A-listers here than at an Oscars after party: Van Gogh, Matisse, Picasso, Warhol, Lichtenstein, Rothko, Pollock and Bourgeois. Since its founding in 1929, the museum has amassed over 150,000 artworks, documenting the emerging creative ideas and movements of the late 19th century through to those that dominate today. For art buffs, it's Valhalla. For the uninitiated, it's a thrilling crash course in all that is beautiful and addictive about art.

Times Square & Theater District — NEIGHBORHOOD

There are few images more universally iconic than the glittering orb dropping from **Times Square** (Map p70; www.timessquare.com; Broadway at Seventh Ave; [S] N/Q/R, S, 1/2/3, 7 to Times Sq-42nd St) on New Year's Eve – the first one descended 100 years ago. Smack in the middle of Midtown Manhattan, this area around the intersection of Broadway and Seventh Ave, with its gaudy billboards, glittery marquees and massive video screens, has become so intertwined with New York City in the minds of non–New Yorkers that regardless of how Disneyfied it has become, it's still considered quintessential New York. Once again 'the Crossroads of the World,' and unrecognizable from its '70s-era seediness of strip clubs, hookers and pickpockets, the square draws 35 million visitors annually. Massive chain and themed stores pull in folks, and multiplex theaters draw crowds with large screens and stadium seating. In an effort to make the area more pedestrian-friendly and diminish the perpetual gridlock, Broadway from 47th to 42nd St was turned into a vehicle-free zone.

The Times Square area is at least as famous as New York's official **Theater District**, with dozens of Broadway and off-Broadway theaters located in an area that stretches from 41st to 54th Sts, between Sixth and Ninth Aves. The Times Square branch of New York City & Company (p110) sits smack in the middle of this famous crossroads. Broadway, the road, once ran all the way to the state capitol in Albany.

Rockefeller Center — NOTABLE BUILDING

(Map p70; www.rockefellercenter.com; Fifth to Sixth Aves & 48th to 51st Sts; ⏲ 24hr, times vary for individual businesses; [S] B/D/F/M to 47th-50th Sts-Rockefeller Center) It was built during the height of the Great Depression in the 1930s, and construction of the 22-acre Rockefeller Center, including the landmark art-deco skyscraper gave jobs to 70,000 workers over nine years and was the first project to combine retail, entertainment and office space in what is often referred to as a 'city within a city.' The 360-degree views from the tri-level observation deck of the **Top of the Rock** (Map p70; www.topoftherocknyc.com; 30 Rockefeller Plaza at 49th St, entrance on W 50th St btwn Fifth

& Sixth Aves; adult/child $27/17, sunrise & sunset $40/22; ☉8:00am-midnight, last elevator at 11pm; S B/D/F/M to 47th-50th Sts-Rockefeller Center) are absolutely stunning and should not be missed; on a clear day you can see quite a distance across the river into New Jersey. In winter the ground floor outdoor space is abuzz with ice-skaters and Christmas-tree gawkers. Within the complex is the 1932, 6000-seat Radio City Music Hall (Map p70; www.radiocity.com; 1260 Sixth Ave at 51st St; tours adult/child $22.50/16; ☉tours 11am-3pm; S B/D/F/M to 47th-50th Sts-Rockefeller Center). To get an inside look at this former movie palace and protected landmark, which has been gorgeously restored in all its art-deco grandeur, join one of the frequent guided tours that leave the lobby every half-hour. Fans of the NBC TV show 30 Rock will recognize the 70-story GE Building as the network headquarters. Tours of the NBC studios (Map p70; ☏reservations 212-664-6298; www.nbcstudiotour.com; 30 Rockefeller Plaza at 49th St; tours adult/child $24/20, children under 6yr not admitted; ☉tours every 15mins 8:30am-5:30pm Mon-Thu, to 6:30pm Fri & Sat, to 4.30pm Sun; S B/D/F/M to 47th-50th Sts-Rockefeller Center) leave from the lobby of the GE Building every 15 minutes; note that children under six are not admitted. *The Today Show* broadcasts live 7am to 11am daily from a glass-enclosed street-level studio near the fountain.

New York Public Library   CULTURAL BUILDING
(Stephen A Schwarzman Building; Map p70; www.nypl.org; Fifth Ave at 42nd St; ☉10am-6pm Mon & Thu-Sat, to 8pm Tue & Wed, 1-5pm Sun, guided tours 11am & 2pm Mon-Sat, 2pm Sun; S B/D/F/M to 42nd St-Bryant Park, 7 to 5th Ave) Flanked by two huge marble lions nicknamed 'Patience' and 'Fortitude' by former mayor Fiorello La-Guardia, the stairway leading up to the New York Public Library is a grand entrance. The massive, superb beaux-arts building stands as testament to the value of learning and culture in the city, as well as to the wealth of the philanthropists who made its founding possible. A magnificent 3rd-floor reading room has a painted ceiling and bountiful natural light – rows of long wooden tables are occupied by students, writers and the general public working away at laptops. This, the main branch of the entire city library system, has galleries of manuscripts on display, as well as fascinating temporary exhibits. A controversial redesign of the building has been proposed. Immediately behind the library is beautifully maintained Bryant

Park, a grassy expanse furnished with tables and chairs, and even a lending library, chessboards and Ping Pong tables in warm weather, as well as an ice-skating rink in winter.

Empire State Building   NOTABLE BUILDING, LOOKOUT
(Map p70; www.esbnyc.com; 350 Fifth Ave at 34th St; 86th-floor observation deck adult/child $25/19, incl 102nd-floor observation deck $42/36; ☉8am-2am, last elevators up 1:15am; S B/D/F/M, N/Q/R to 34th St-Herald Sq) Catapulted to Hollywood stardom both as the planned meeting spot for Cary Grant and Deborah Kerr in *An Affair to Remember,* and the vertical perch that helped to topple King Kong, the classic Empire State Building is one of the most famous members of New York's skyline. It's a limestone classic built in just 410 days, or seven million man-hours, during the depths of the Depression at a cost of $41 million. On the site of the original Waldorf-Astoria Hotel, the 102-story, 1472ft (to the top of the antenna) Empire State Building opened in 1931 after 10 million bricks were laid, 6400 windows installed and 328,000 sq ft of marble laid. Today you can ride the elevator to observatories on the 86th and 102nd floors, but be prepared for crowds; try to come very early or very late (and purchase your tickets ahead of time, online or pony up for $50 'express passes') for an optimal experience.

Grand Central Station   NOTABLE BUILDING
(Map p70; www.grandcentralterminal.com; 42nd St at Park Ave) Built in 1913 as a prestigious terminal by New York Central and Hudson River Railroad, Grand Central Station is no longer a romantic place to begin a cross-country journey, as it's now the terminus for Metro North commuter trains to the northern suburbs and Connecticut. But even if you're not boarding a train to the 'burbs, it's worth exploring the grand, vaulted main concourse and gazing up at the restored ceiling, decorated with a star map that is actually a 'God's-eye' image of the night sky. There's a high-end food market and the lower level houses a truly excellent array of eateries, while the balcony has a cozy '20s-era salon kind of bar called the Campbell Apartment.

Fifth Avenue & Around   NEIGHBORHOOD
(725 Fifth Ave, at 56th St) Immortalized in both film and song, Fifth Ave first developed its high-class reputation in the early 20th century, when it was considered desirable for its 'country' air and open spaces. A series of mansions called Millionaire's Row extended

right up to 130th St, though most of the heirs to the millionaire mansions on Fifth Ave above 59th St sold them for demolition or converted them to the cultural institutions that now make up Museum Mile.

The avenue's Midtown stretch still boasts upmarket shops and hotels, including Trump Tower and the Plaza (cnr Fifth Ave and Central Park South). While a number of the more exclusive boutiques have migrated to Madison Ave – leaving outposts of Gap and H&M in their wake – several superstars still reign over Fifth Ave above 50th St, including the famous Tiffany & Co.

Pierpont Morgan Library MUSEUM

(Map p70; www.morganlibrary.org; 29 E 36th St at Madison Ave; adult/child $18/12; ⏲10:30am-5pm Tue-Thu, to 9pm Fri, 10am-6pm Sat, 11am-6pm Sun; [S] 6 to 33rd St) The beautifully renovated library is part of the 45-room mansion once owned by steel magnate JP Morgan. His collection features a phenomenal array of manuscripts, tapestries and books, a study filled with Italian Renaissance artwork, a marble rotunda and the three-tiered East Room main library.

United Nations NOTABLE BUILDING

(Map p70; ☎212-963-7539; www.un.org/tours; visitors' gate First Ave at 47th St; guided tour adult/child $16/9, children under 5yr not admitted; ⏲9:15am-4:15pm; [S] S, 4/5/6, 7 to Grand Central-42nd St) The UN is technically on a section of international territory overlooking the East River. Take a guided 45-minute tour (English language tours are frequent; limited tours in several other languages) of the facility and you'll get to see the General Assembly, where the annual fall convocation of member nations takes place, the Security Council Chamber (depending on schedules) and also the Economic & Social Council Chamber. There is a park to the south of the complex which is home to several sculptures with a peace theme. The visitors' gate entrance is at a temporary location until 2015, while the UN headquarters is undergoing renovation works; guided tours are slated to continue, but expect changes to access and tour availability.

Paley Center for Media CULTURAL BUILDING

(Map p70; www.paleycenter.org; 25 W 52nd St btwn Fifth & Sixth Aves; adult/child $10/5; ⏲noon-6pm Wed & Fri-Sun, to 8pm Thu; [S] E/M to 5th Ave-53rd St) TV fanatics who spent their childhood glued to the tube and proudly claim instant recall of all of Fonzi's *Happy Days* exploits can hold their heads high. This is the 'museum' for them. Search through a catalogue of more than 100,000 US TV and radio programs and advertisements and a click of the mouse will play your selection on one of the library's computer screens. A comfy theater shows some great specials on broadcasting history, and there are frequent events and screenings.

Intrepid Sea, Air & Space Museum MUSEUM

(Map p70; www.intrepidmuseum.org; Pier 86, Twelfth Ave at 46th St; adult/child $24/12; ⏲10am-5pm; 👪; 🚌M42 bus westbound, [S] A/C/E to 42nd St-Port Authority Bus Terminal) The USS *Intrepid,* a hulking aircraft carrier that survived both a WWII bomb and kamikaze attacks has been transformed into a military museum with high-tech exhibits and fighter planes and helicopters for view on the outdoor flight deck. The pier area contains the guided-missile submarine *Growler,* a decommissioned Concorde and, as of 2012, the *Enterprise* space shuttle.

International Center of Photography GALLERY

(ICP; Map p70; www.icp.org; 1133 Sixth Ave at 43rd St; adult/child $14/free, by donation Fri 5-8pm; ⏲10am-6pm Tue-Thu & Sat-Sun, to 8pm Fri; [S] B/D/F/M to 42nd St-Bryant Park) The city's most important showcase for major photographers, especially photojournalists. Its past exhibitions have included work by Henri Cartier-Bresson, Matthew Brady and Robert Capa.

Herald Square SQUARE

(Map p70; cnr Broadway, Sixth Ave & 34th St; [S] B/D/F/M, N/Q/R to 34th St-Herald Sq) This crowded convergence of Broadway, Sixth Ave and 34th St is best known as the home of **Macy's** department store, where you can still ride some of the remaining original wooden elevators to floors ranging from home furnishings to lingerie. But the busy square gets its name from a long-defunct newspaper, the *Herald,* and the small, leafy park here bustles during business hours. In order to cut down on some of the area gridlock, Broadway, from 33rd to 35th Sts has been turned into a pedestrian plaza.

West of Herald Sq, the **Garment District** has most of New York's fashion design offices, and while not much clothing is actually made here anymore, for anyone into pawing through dreamy selections of fabrics, buttons, sequins, lace and zippers it is the place to shop.

From 31st St to 36th St, between Broadway and Fifth Ave, **Koreatown** is an interesting and lively neighborhood with an ever-expanding number of good restaurants and authentic karaoke spots.

Hell's Kitchen NEIGHBORHOOD

(Clinton; Map p70) For years, the far west side of Midtown was a working-class district of tenements and food warehouses known as Hell's Kitchen – supposedly its name was muttered by a cop in reaction to a riot in the neighborhood in 1881. A 1990s economic boom seriously altered the character and developers reverted to using the cleaned-up name, Clinton, a moniker originating from the 1950s; locals are split on usage. New, primarily inexpensive ethnic restaurants exploded along Ninth and Tenth Aves between about 37th and 55th Sts. Thrift-store lovers should visit the **Hell's Kitchen Flea Market** (Map p70; ☎212-243-5343; 39th St btwn Ninth & Tenth Aves; ⏰7am-4pm Sat & Sun; [S] A/C/E to 42nd St), boasting 170 vendors of vintage clothing, antique jewelry, period furniture and more.

Museum of Arts & Design MUSEUM

(MAD; Map p80; www.madmuseum.org; 2 Columbus Circle btwn Eighth Ave & Broadway; adult/child $16/free; ⏰10am-6pm Tue-Wed & Sat-Sun, to 9pm Thu & Fri; [S] A/C, B/D, 1 to 59th St-Columbus Circle) On the southern side of the circle, exhibiting a diverse international collection of modern, folk, craft and fine-art pieces. The plush and trippy design of **Robert**, the 9th floor restaurant, complements fantastic views of Central Park.

SOLD!

Even if your idea of a significant art purchase is a Van Gogh postcard, the adrenalin-pumping thrill of an art auction combines the best of museum-going and high-end shopping. Both **Christie's** (Map p70; ☎212-636-2000; www.christies.com; 20 Rockefeller Plaza; [S] B/D/F/M to 47-50th Sts-Rockefeller Ctr) and **Sotheby's** (Map p80; ☎212-606-7000; www.sothebys.com; 1334 York Ave, at 72nd St; [S] 6 to 68th St-Hunter College), two of the city's and world's most prominent auction houses are open to the public. Whether it's a collection of Warhol canvases or old European masterworks, the prices remain generally stratospheric – keep your hands down or else your casual twitch will be taken for a bid and you could be on the hook for tens of millions of dollars.

Upper West Side

Shorthand for liberal, progressive and intellectual New York – think Woody Allen movies (although he lives on the Upper East Side) and *Seinfeld* – this neighborhood comprising the west side of Manhattan from Central Park to the Hudson River, and from Columbus Circle to 110th St, is no longer as colorful as it once was. Upper Broadway has been taken over by banks, pharmacies and national retail chain stores and many of the mom-and-pop shops and bookstores are long gone. You'll still find massive, ornate apartments and a diverse mix of stable, upwardly mobile folks (with many actors and classical musicians sprinkled throughout), and some lovely green spaces – **Riverside Park** stretches for 4 miles between W 72nd St and W 158th St along the Hudson River, and is a great place for strolling, running, cycling or simply gazing at the sun as it sets over the Hudson River.

★Central Park PARK

(Map p80; www.centralparknyc.org; 59th & 110th Sts btwn Central Park West & Fifth Ave; ⏰6am-1am; 👪) It's hard to imagine what the city would be like without this refuge from the claustrophobia, from the teeming sidewalks and clogged roadways. This enormous wonderland of a park, sitting right in the middle of Manhattan, provides oxygen, both metaphorical and actual, to its residents. The park's 843 acres were set aside in 1856 on the marshy northern fringe of the city. The landscaping (the first in a US public park), by Frederick Law Olmsted and Calvert Vaux, was innovative in its naturalistic style, with forested groves, meandering paths and informal ponds. Highlights include **Sheep Meadow** (mid-park from 66th to 69th Sts), where tens of thousands of people lounge and play on warm weather weekends; **Central Park Zoo** (Map p80; ☎212-861-6030; www.centralparkzoo.com; Central Park, 64th St at Fifth Ave; adult/child $12/7; ⏰10am-5:30pm Apr-Nov, to 4:30pm Nov-Apr; 👪; [S] N/Q/R to 5th Ave-59th St); and the **Ramble**, a rest stop for nearly 250 migratory species of birdlife – early morning is best for sightings. A favorite tourist activity is to rent a **horse-drawn carriage** (Map p80; at 59th St, Central Park South; 30min tour $50 plus generous tip) or hop in a pedicab (one hour tours $45); the latter congregate at Central Park West and 72nd St. For more information while you're strolling, visit the **Dairy Building visitor center** (Map p80; ☎212-794-6564; www.centralpark.org) in the southern section of the park.

★ **Lincoln Center** CULTURAL CENTER
(Map p80; ☎ 212-875-5456; www.lincolncenter.org; Columbus Ave btwn 62nd & 66th Sts; public plazas free, tours adults/child $15/8; ♿; [S] 1 to 66th St-Lincoln Center) The billion-dollar-plus redevelopment of the world's largest performing-arts center includes the dramatically redesigned Alice Tully Hall and other stunning venues surrounding a massive fountain; public spaces, including the roof lawn of the North Plaza (an upscale restaurant is underneath), have been upgraded. The lavishly designed **Metropolitan Opera House** (MET), the largest opera house in the world, seats 3900 people. Fascinating one-hour **tours** of the complex leave from the lobby of Avery Fisher Hall from 10:30am to 4:30pm daily; these vary from architectural to backstage tours. Free wi-fi is available on the property as well as at the **David Rubenstein Atrium** (Map p80; Broadway btwn 62nd & 63rd Sts; [S] 1 to 66th St-Lincoln Center), a modern public space featuring a lounge area, cafe, information desk, and ticket center offering day-of discounts to Lincoln Center performances.

★ **American Museum of Natural History** MUSEUM
(Map p80; ☎ 212-769-5100; www.amnh.org; Central Park West at 79th St; adult/child $19/10.50; ⏲ 10am-5:45pm, Rose Center to 8:45pm Fri, Butterfly Conservancy Oct-May; ♿; [S] B, C to 81st St-Museum of Natural History, 1 to 79th St) Founded in 1869, this museum includes more than 30 million artifacts, interactive exhibits and loads of taxidermy. It's most famous for its three large dinosaur halls, an enormous (fake) blue whale that hangs from the ceiling above the Hall of Ocean Life and the elaborate **Rose Center for Earth & Space**. Just gazing at its facade – a massive glass box that contains a silver globe, home to space-show theaters and the planetarium – is mesmerizing, especially at night, when all of its otherworldly features are aglow.

New-York Historical Society MUSEUM
(Map p80; www.nyhistory.org; 2 W 77th St at Central Park West; adult/child $15/5, by donation 6-8pm, library free; ⏲ 10am-6pm Tue-Thu & Sat, to 8pm Fri, 11am-5pm Sun; [S] B, C to 81st St-Museum of Natural History) This museum, founded in 1804 and widely credited with being the city's oldest, received a full-scale makeover in 2011. The quirky and wide-ranging collection, including a leg brace worn by President Franklin D Roosevelt and a 19th-century mechanical bank in which a political figure slips coins into his pocket, is now housed in a spruced-up contemporary exhibition space; there's an auditorium, a library and a restaurant as well.

Upper East Side

The Upper East Side (UES) is home to New York's greatest concentration of cultural centers, including the Metropolitan Museum of Art, and many refer to Fifth Ave above 57th St as Museum Mile. The real estate, at least along Fifth, Madison and Park Aves, is some of the most expensive in the world. Home to ladies who lunch as well as frat boys who drink, the neighborhood becomes decidedly less chichi the further east you go.

★ **Metropolitan Museum of Art** MUSEUM
(Map p80; ☎ 212-535-7710; www.metmuseum.org; 1000 Fifth Ave at 82nd St; suggested donation adult/child $25/free; ⏲ 10am-5:30pm Sun-Thu, to 9pm Fri & Sat; ♿; [S] 4/5/6 to 86th St) With more than five million visitors a year, the Met is New York's most popular single-site tourist attraction, with one of the richest coffers in the arts world. The Met is a self-contained cultural city-state, with two million individual objects in its collection and an annual budget of over $120 million; the revamped American galleries include everything from colonial portraiture to Hudson River School masterpieces. Other highlight rooms include ancient Egyptian Art, Arms and Armor, Modern Art, Greek and Roman Art, European Paintings and the gorgeous rooftop, which offers bar service and spectacular views throughout the summer. Note that the suggested donation (which is, truly, a *suggestion*) includes same-day admission to the Cloisters.

★ **Frick Collection** GALLERY
(Map p80; ☎ 212-288-0700; www.frick.org; 1 E 70th St at Fifth Ave; admission $18, by donation 11am-1pm Sun, children under 10 not admitted; ⏲ 10am-6pm Tue-Sat, 11am-5pm Sun; [S] 6 to 68th St-Hunter College) This spectacular art collection sits in a mansion built by Henry Clay Frick in 1914; it's a shame that the 2nd floor of the residence isn't open for viewing. The 12 richly furnished rooms on the ground floor display paintings by Titian, Vermeer, El Greco, Goya and other masters. Perhaps the best asset here is that it's rarely crowded, providing a welcome break from the swarms of gawkers at larger museums, especially on weekends.

Central Park

THE LUNGS OF NEW YORK

The rectangular patch of green that occupies Manhattan's heart began life in the mid-19th century as a swampy piece of land that was carefully bulldozed into the idyllic naturescape you see today. Since officially becoming Central Park, it has brought New Yorkers of all stripes together in interesting and unexpected ways. The park has served as a place for the rich to show off their fancy carriages (1860s), for the poor to enjoy free Sunday concerts (1880s) and for activists to hold be-ins against the Vietnam War (1960s). Since then, legions of locals – not to mention travelers from all kinds of faraway places – have poured in to stroll, picnic, sunbathe, play ball and catch free concerts and performances of works by Shakespeare.

The park's varied terrain offers a wonderland of experiences. There are quiet, woodsy knolls in the north. To the south is the

Loeb Boathouse
Perched on the shores of the Lake, the historic Loeb Boathouse is one of the city's best settings for an idyllic meal. You can also rent rowboats and bicycles and ride on a Venetian gondola.

Duke Ellington Circle

Harlem Meer

The Blockhouse

North Woods

97th St Transverse

Fifth Ave

86th St Transverse

The Great Lawn

Central Park West

Conservatory Garden
The only formal garden in Central Park is perhaps the most tranquil. On the northern end, chrysanthemums bloom in late October. To the south, the park's largest crab apple tree grows by the Burnett Fountain.

Jacqueline Kennedy Onassis Reservoir
This 106-acre body of water covers roughly an eighth of the park's territory. Its original purpose was to provide clean water for the city. Now it's a good spot to catch a glimpse of waterbirds.

Belvedere Castle
A so-called 'Victorian folly,' this Gothic-Romanesque castle serves no other purpose than to be a very dramatic lookout point. It was built by Central Park co-designer Calvert Vaux in 1869.

STEVEN GREATES / GETTY IMAGES ©

ANGUS OSBORN / GETTY IMAGES ©

reservoir, crowded with joggers. There are European gardens, a zoo and various bodies of water. For maximum flamboyance, hit the Sheep Meadow on a sunny day, when all of New York shows up to lounge.

Central Park is more than just a green space. It is New York City's backyard.

FACTS & FIGURES

» **Landscape architects** Frederick Law Olmsted and Calvert Vaux
» **Year that construction began** 1858
» **Acres** 843
» **On film** Hundreds of movies have been shot on location, from Depression-era blockbusters such as *Gold Diggers* (1933) to the monster-attack flick *Cloverfield*.

Conservatory Water
This pond is popular in the warmer months, when children sail their model boats across its surface. Conservatory Water was inspired by 19th-century Parisian model-boat ponds and figured prominently in EB White's classic book, *Stuart Little*.

Bethesda Fountain
This neoclassical fountain is one of New York's largest. It's capped by the *Angel of the Waters*, who is supported by four cherubim. The fountain was created by bohemian-feminist sculptor Emma Stebbins in 1868.

Metropolitan Museum of Art

Alice in Wonderland Statue

79th St Transverse

The Ramble

Delacorte Theater

The Lake

Fifth Ave

Central Park Zoo

65th St Transverse

Sheep Meadow

Columbus Center

Strawberry Fields
A simple mosaic memorial pays tribute to musician John Lennon, who was killed across the street outside the Dakota Building. Funded by Yoko Ono, its name is inspired by the Beatles song 'Strawberry Fields Forever.'

The Mall/ Literary Walk
A Parisian-style promenade – the only straight line in the park – is flanked by statues of literati on the southern end, including Robert Burns and Shakespeare. It is lined with rare North American elms.

Central Park & Uptown

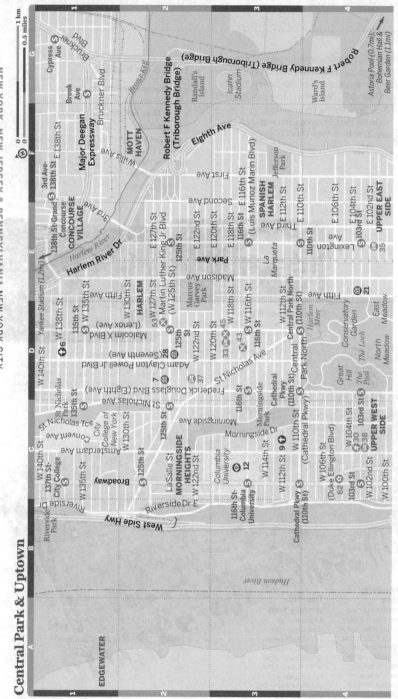

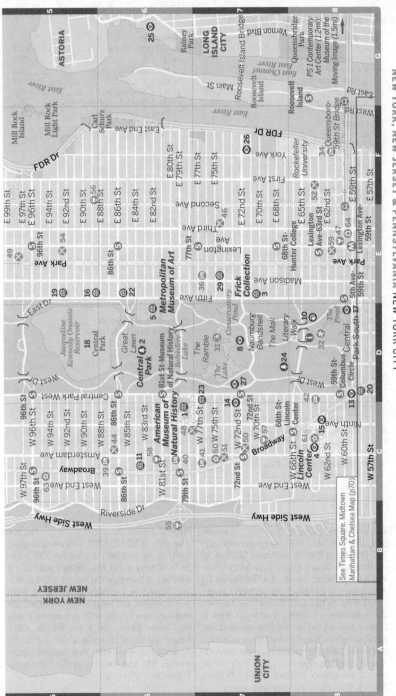

Central Park & Uptown

Top Sights

1 American Museum of Natural History C6
2 Central Park D6
3 Frick Collection E7
4 Lincoln Center C8
5 Metropolitan Museum of Art D6

Sights

6 Abyssinian Baptist Church D1
7 Apollo Theater D2
8 Bethesda Fountain D7
9 Cathedral Church of St John the Divine C3
10 Central Park Zoo D8
11 Children's Museum of Manhattan C6
12 Columbia University C3
13 Columbus Circle D8
14 Dakota Building C7
15 David Rubenstein Atrium C8
16 Guggenheim Museum E5
17 Horse-Drawn Carriages D8
18 Jacqueline Kennedy Onassis Reservoir D5
19 Jewish Museum E5
20 Museum of Arts & Design D8
21 Museum of the City of New York E4
22 Neue Galerie E6
23 New-York Historical Society D7
24 Sheep Meadow D7
25 Socrates Sculpture Park G6
26 Sotheby's F7
27 Strawberry Fields D7
28 Studio Museum in Harlem D2
29 Whitney Museum of American Art E7

Activities, Courses & Tours

30 Five Borough Bicycle Club C4
31 Loeb Boathouse D7
32 Wollman Skating Rink D8

Sleeping

33 102 Brownstone D3
34 Bentley F8
35 Bubba & Bean Lodges E4
36 Carlyle E7
37 Harlem Flophouse D2
38 Hostelling International New York C4
39 Jazz on Amsterdam Ave C6
40 Lucerne C6
41 On the Ave C7
42 YMCA D8

Eating

43 Amy Ruth's Restaurant D3
44 Barney Greengrass C6
45 Caffe Latte D3
46 Candle Cafe E7
47 David Burke Townhouse E8
48 Dovetail C6
49 Earl's Beer & Cheese E5
50 Gray's Papaya C7
51 Josie's Restaurant C7
52 Maya Mexican F8
53 Red Rooster D2
54 Sfoglia E5

Drinking & Nightlife

55 79th Street Boat Basin B6
56 Auction House F5
57 Barcibo Enoteca C7
Bemelmans Bar .... (see 36)
58 Dead Poet C6
59 Subway Inn E8

Entertainment

60 Beacon Theatre C7
61 Jazz at Lincoln Center C8
62 Smoke Jazz & Supper Club-Lounge C4
63 Symphony Space C5

Shopping

64 Bloomingdale's E8

Guggenheim Museum MUSEUM
(Map p80; ☎212-423-3500; www.guggenheim.org; 1071 Fifth Ave at 89th St; adult/child $22/free, by donation 5:45-7:45pm Sat; ⏰10am-5:45pm Sun-Wed & Fri, to 7:45pm Sat; 👪; [S] 4/5/6 to 86th St) A sculpture in its own right, architect Frank Lloyd Wright's building almost overshadows the collection of 20th century art that it houses. Completed in 1959, the inverted ziggurat structure was derided by some critics, but it was hailed by others as an architectural icon. Stroll its sweeping spiral staircase to view 20th-century masterpieces by Picasso, Pollock, Chagall, Kandinsky and others.

Neue Galerie MUSEUM
(Map p80; ☎212-628-6200; www.neuegalerie.org; 1048 Fifth Ave cnr E 86th St; admission $20, 6-8pm 1st Fri of every month free, children under 12 not admitted; ⏰11am-6pm Thu-Mon; [S] 4/5/6 to 86th St) Housed in a stately and elegant Fifth Ave mansion, the Neue showcases German and Austrian artists, with impressive works by Gustav Klimt and Egon Schiele. **Café Sabarsky** alone is worth a visit for its fin de siècle European vibe, rich desserts (apple strudel $8) and cabaret performances on Thursday nights ($45).

Whitney Museum of American Art MUSEUM
(Map p80; ☎212-570-3600; www.whitney.org; 945 Madison Ave cnr 75th St; adult/child $20/free; ⏲11am-6pm Wed, Thu, Sat & Sun, 1-9pm Fri; [S]6 to 77th St) One of the few museums that concentrates on American works of art, specializing in 20th-century and contemporary art, with works by Hopper, Pollock and Rothko, as well as special shows, such as the much-ballyhooed Biennial. In 2015, the Whitney is moving to Gansevoort St in the Meatpacking District.

Jewish Museum MUSEUM
(Map p80; ☎212-423-3200; www.jewishmuseum.org; 1109 Fifth Ave at 92nd St; adult/child $12/free, Sat free; ⏲11am-5:45pm Fri-Tue, to 8pm Thu; 👪; [S]6 to 96th St) This homage to Judaism primarily features artwork examining 4000 years of Jewish ceremony and culture; it also has a wide array of children's activities. The building, a gorgeous banker's mansion from 1908, houses more than 30,000 items of Judaica, as well as works of sculpture, paintings, decorative arts and photography.

Museum of the City of New York MUSEUM
(Map p80; ☎212-534-1672; www.mcny.org; 1220 Fifth Ave btwn 103rd & 104th Sts; suggested admission adult/child $10/free; ⏲10am-6pm; [S]6 to 103rd St) Traces the city's history from beaver trading to futures trading with various cultural exhibitions. An excellent bookstore for every NYC obsession.

👁 Morningside Heights

The Upper West Side's northern neighbor, comprises the area of Broadway and west up to about 125th St. Dominating the neighborhood is **Columbia University** (Map p80; www.columbia.edu; Broadway at 116th St, Morningside Heights; [S]1 to 116th St-Columbia University) [FREE], the highly regarded Ivy League college, which features a spacious, grassy central quadrangle.

Cathedral Church of St John the Divine CHURCH
(Map p80; ☎tours 212-932-7347; www.stjohndivine.org; 1047 Amsterdam Ave at W 112th St, Morningside Heights; admission by donation, tours $6, vertical tours $15; ⏲7:30am-6pm; 👪; [S]B, C, 1 to 110th St-Cathedral Pkwy) This storied Episcopal cathedral, the largest place of worship in the United States, commands attention with its ornate Byzantine-style facade, booming vintage organ and extravagantly scaled nave – twice as wide as Westminster Abbey in London. High Mass, held at 11am Sunday, often comes with sermons by well-known intellectuals.

👁 Harlem

The heart of African American culture has been beating in Harlem since its emergence as a black enclave in the 1920s. This neighborhood north of Central Park has been the setting for extraordinary accomplishments in art, music, dance, education and letters from the likes of Frederick Douglass, Paul Robeson, Thurgood Marshall, James Baldwin, Alvin Ailey, Billie Holiday, Jessie Jackson and many other African American luminaries. After steady decline from the 1960s to early '90s, Harlem is experiencing something of a second renaissance in the form of million-dollar brownstones and condos for sale next door to neglected tenement buildings and the presence of big box national chain stores all along 125th St.

For a traditional view of Harlem, visit on Sunday morning, when well-dressed locals flock to neighborhood churches. Just be respectful of the fact that these people are attending a religious service (rather than being on display for tourists). Unless you're invited by a member of a small congregation, stick to the bigger churches.

Apollo Theater HISTORIC BUILDING
(Map p80; ☎212-531-5305, tours 212-531-5337; www.apollotheater.org; 253 W 125th St at Frederick Douglass Blvd, Harlem; [S]A/C, B/D to 125th St) Not just a mythical legend but a living theater. Head here for high-profile concerts and its famous long-running amateur night, 'where stars are born and legends are made,' which takes place every Wednesday night.

Abyssinian Baptist Church CHURCH
(Map p80; www.abyssinian.org; 132 W 138th St btwn Adam Clayton Powell Jr & Malcolm X Blvds; 👪; [S]2/3 to 135th St) Has a superb choir and a charismatic pastor, Calvin O Butts, who welcomes tourists and prays for them. Sunday services start at 9am and 11am – the later one is *very* well attended.

Studio Museum in Harlem MUSEUM
(Map p80; ☎212-864-4500; www.studiomuseum.org; 144 W 125th St at Adam Clayton Powell Jr Blvd, Harlem; suggested donation $7; ⏲noon-9pm Thu & Fri, 10am-6pm Sat, noon-6pm Sun; 👪; [S]2/3 to 125th St) One of the premier showcases for African American artists; look for rotating exhibits from painters, sculptors, illustrators and other installation artists.

Washington Heights

Near the northern tip of Manhattan (above 155th St), Washington Heights takes its name from the first US president, who set up a Continental Army fort here during the Revolutionary War. An isolated spot until the end of the 19th century, it attracted New Yorkers sniffing out affordable rents. Still, this neighborhood manages to retain its Latino – mainly Dominican – flavor, and is an interesting mix of blocks that alternate between former downtowners and longtime residents who operate within a tight, warm community.

★Cloisters MUSEUM
(☎212-923-3700; www.metmuseum.org/cloisters; Fort Tryon Park, at 190th St; suggested admission adult/child $25/free; ⏲10am-5:30pm Sun-Thu, to 9pm Fri & Sat; [S] A to 190th St) Constructed in the 1930s using stones and fragments from several French and Spanish medieval monasteries, the romantic, castle-like creation houses medieval frescoes, tapestries, courtyards, gardens and paintings, and has commanding views of the Hudson. The walk from the subway stop to the museum through Fort Tryon Park offers stupendous **views** of the Hudson River; rock climbers head here for practice.

Brooklyn

Brooklyn is a world in and of itself; residents sometimes don't go into Manhattan for days or even weeks at a time. With 2.5 million people and growing, from well-to-do new parents seeking stately brownstones in Carroll Gardens to young band members wanting cheap rents near gigs in Williamsburg, this outer borough has long surpassed Manhattan in the cool and livability factors in many people's minds. From sandy beaches and breezy boardwalks at one end to foodie destinations at the other, and with a massive range of ethnic enclaves, world-class entertainment, stately architecture and endless shopping strips in between, Brooklyn is a rival to Manhattan's attractions. The **Brooklyn Tourism & Visitors Center** (☎718-802-3846; www.visitbrooklyn.org; 209 Joralemon St btwn Court St & Brooklyn Bridge Blvd; ⏲10am-6pm Mon-Fri; [S] 2/3, 4/5 to Borough Hall) 🌿, in Brooklyn Heights, is an informative place to begin.

★Coney Island & Brighton Beach NEIGHBORHOOD
About 50 minutes by subway from Midtown, this popular pair of beach neighborhoods makes for a great day trip. The wide sandy beach of **Coney Island** has retained its nostalgic and kitschy wood-plank boardwalk (partly destroyed and replaced after Hurricane Sandy) and famous 1927 Cyclone roller coaster, despite a sanitized makeover of the amusement park area including a handful of new adrenalin-pumping thrill rides. For better or worse, its slightly sleazy charm is a thing of the past and developers plan to transform the area into a sleek residential city complete with high-rise hotels. The **New York Aquarium** (www.nyaquarium.com; Surf Ave & W 8th St; adult/child $15/11, with 4-D theater show $19/15; ⏲10am-6pm Mon-Fri, to 7pm Sat & Sun May-Sep; 👪; [S] F, Q to W 8th St-NY Aquarium) is a big hit with kids, as is taking in an early evening baseball game at **Key Span Park**, the waterfront stadium for the minor league **Brooklyn Cyclones** (www.brooklyncyclones.com).

A five-minute stroll north along the boardwalk past handball courts where some of the best in the world compete brings you to **Brighton Beach** ('Little Odessa'), where old-timers play chess and locals enjoy pierogies (boiled dumplings filled with meat or vegetables) and vodka shots at several boardwalk eateries. Then head into the heart of the 'hood, busy Brighton Beach Ave, to hit the many Russian shops, bakeries and restaurants.

Williamsburg, Greenpoint & Bushwick NEIGHBORHOOD
There is a definite Williamsburg look: skinny jeans, multiple tattoos, a discreet body piercing, shaggy hair for men, maybe some kind of retro head covering for women. Denizens of this raggedy and rowdy neighborhood across the East River seem to have the time and money to slouch in cafes and party all night in bars; a fair share of older – early 30s – transplants from Manhattan and Europe qualify as elders. The main artery is **Bedford Ave** between N 10th St and Metropolitan Ave, where there are boutiques, cafes, bars and cheap eateries. But cool spots have also sprouted along N 6th St and Berry St, and perhaps a sign of the times is that the uber-hip consider Williamsburg over and have long-since moved on to colonizing next door **Greenpoint**, a traditionally Polish neighborhood as well as the former warehouse buildings further out in **Bushwick**. The **Brooklyn Brewery** (☎718-486-7422; www.brooklynbrewery.com; 79 N 11th St btwn Berry St & Wythe Ave; ⏲free tours on the hr 1-4pm Sat & Sun; [S] L to Bedford Ave) hosts weekend tours, special events and pub nights.

Park Slope & Prospect Heights NEIGHBORHOOD

The Park Slope neighborhood is known for its classic brownstones, tons of great eateries and boutiques and liberal-minded stroller-pushing couples who resemble those on the Upper West Side (but have a backyard attached to their apartment). The 585-acre **Prospect Park**, created in 1866, is considered the greatest achievement of landscape designers Olmsted and Vaux, who also designed Central Park. Next door is the excellent 52-acre **Brooklyn Botanic Garden** (www.bbg.org; 1000 Washington Ave at Crown St; adult/child $10/free, Tue & 10am-noon Sat free; ⏰8am-6pm Tue-Fri, 10am-6pm Sat & Sun mid-March–Oct, 8am-4:30pm Tue-Fri, 10am-4:30pm Sat & Sun Nov-Mar; 👪; [S] 2/3 to Eastern Pkwy-Brooklyn Museum), which features impressive cherry-tree blossoms in spring. Beside the garden is the **Brooklyn Museum** (☎718-638-5000; www.brooklynmuseum.org; 200 Eastern Pkwy; suggested admission $10; ⏰11am-6pm Wed, Sat & Sun, to 10pm Thu & Fri; [S] 2/3 to Eastern Pkwy-Brooklyn Museum) with comprehensive collections of African, Islamic and Asian art, plus the Elizabeth A Sackler Center for Feminist Art.

Brooklyn Heights & Downtown Brooklyn NEIGHBORHOOD

When Robert Fulton's steam ferries started regular services across the East River in the early 19th century, well-to-do Manhattanites began building stellar houses – Victorian Gothic, Romanesque, neo-Greco, Italianate and others – in Brooklyn Heights. Strolling along the tree-lined streets to gaze at them now is a lovely afternoon activity.

Follow **Montague St**, the Heights' main commercial avenue, down to the waterfront until you hit the **Brooklyn Heights Promenade**, which juts out over the Brooklyn–Queens Expwy to offer stunning views of Lower Manhattan. Underneath the expressway is the **Brooklyn Bridge Park**, an 85-acre development of landscaped green space and pathways, built on piers stretching from the Brooklyn Bridge south to Atlantic Ave.

The small but fascinating **New York Transit Museum** (☎718-694-1600; www.mta.info/mta/museum; Schermerhorn St at Boerum Pl; adult/child $7/5; ⏰10am-4pm Tue-Fri, 11am-5pm Sat & Sun; 👪; [S] 2/3, 4/5 to Borough Hall, R to Court St) has an amazing collection of original subway cars and transit memorabilia dating back more than a century. **Barclay's Center**, home to the NBA's New Jersey Nets, finally opened for the inaugural season in 2012, across the street from the Atlantic Center shopping mall in downtown Brooklyn.

Boerum Hill, Cobble Hill, Carroll Gardens & Red Hook NEIGHBORHOOD

These neighborhoods, home to a mix of families, mostly Italian, who have lived here for generations, and former Manhattanites looking for a real life after the city, are full of tree-lined streets with rows of attractively restored brownstones. **Smith St** and **Court St** are the two main arteries connecting to the most southerly area of the three, Carroll Gardens. The former is known as 'restaurant row,' while the latter has more of the

NEW YORK FOR CHILDREN

Contrary to popular belief, New York can be a pretty child-friendly city. Cutting-edge playgrounds have proliferated from Union Square to Battery Park and, of course, the city's major parks, including Central Park (check out Heckscher, Adventure and Ancient playgrounds), have them in abundance. There are at least as many attractions that will appeal to toddlers and tweens as there are for adults, from the two children's museums – **Children's Museum of Manhattan** (Map p80; www.cmom.org; 212 W 83rd St btwn Amsterdam Ave & Broadway; admission $11; ⏰10am-5pm Sun-Fri, to 7pm Sat; 👪; [S] B, C to 81st St-Museum of Natural History; 1 to 86th St) and the **Brooklyn Children's Museum** (www.brooklynkids.org; 145 Brooklyn Ave at St Marks Ave, Crown Heights; admission $9; ⏰10am-5pm, closed Mon; 👪; [S] C to Kingston-Throop Aves, 3 to Kingston Ave) – to the Central Park and Bronx zoos to the Coney Island aquarium. The boat ride to Lady Liberty or a Circle Line cruise offers the opportunity to chug around New York Harbor and the riverside Intrepid, Sea, Air & Space Museum has kid-friendly exhibits. Vintage carousels can be found in Bryant Park, Central Park and Brooklyn Bridge Park. Times Square's themed megastores and their neighboring kid-friendly restaurants are easy options. And of course delis and diners with quick sandwiches and extensive menus are everywhere. Check out the weekend Arts section of the *New York Times* for kid-themed events and performances.

old-school groceries, bakeries and red-sauce restaurants. Further west is Red Hook, a waterfront area with cobblestone streets and hulking industrial buildings. Though it's a bit of a hike from the subway line, the formerly gritty area is now home to a handful of bars and eateries, as well as a massive waterfront branch of Fairway (☑718-694-6868; 480-500 Van Brunt St, Red Hook; ⊙8am-10pm; ☑; ☑B61 to cnr Coffey & Van Brunt Sts, ☑F, G to Carroll St), a beloved gourmet grocery with breathtaking views of NY harbor.

Dumbo   NEIGHBORHOOD

Dumbo's nickname is an acronym for its location: 'Down Under the Manhattan–Brooklyn Bridge Overpass,' and while this north Brooklyn slice of waterfront used to be strictly for industry, it's now the domain of high-end condos, furniture shops and art galleries. Several highly regarded performing arts spaces are located in the cobblestone streets and the Empire-Fulton Ferry State Park hugs the waterfront and offers picture-postcard Manhattan views.

◉ The Bronx

This 42-sq-mile borough to the north of Manhattan has several claims to fame: the Yankees, fondly known as the Bronx Bombers, who can be seen in all their pinstriped glory at the new Yankee Stadium (☑718-508-3917, 718-293-6000; www.yankees.com; E 161st St at River Ave; tours $20; ⊙call for hrs; ☑B/D, 4 to 161st St-Yankee Stadium) in spring and summer; the 'real' Little Italy, namely Belmont (www.arthuravenuebronx.com), where bustling stretches of Arthur and Belmont Aves burst with Italian gourmet markets and eateries; and a super-sized attitude that's been mythologized in Hollywood movies from *The Godfather* to *Rumble in the Bronx*. But it's also got some cool surprises up its sleeve: a quarter of the Bronx is parkland, including the city beach of Pelham Bay Park. Also up in these parts is the magical City Island, a little slice of New England in the Bronx.

New York Botanical Garden   GARDENS

(www.nybg.org; Bronx River Pkwy & Fordham Rd; adult/child/senior & student $20/8/18, Wed & 10am-noon Sat free; ⊙10am-6pm Tue-Sun; ☑; ☑Metro-North to Botanical Garden) There are 250 acres, with old-growth forest, a wetlands trail, nearly 3000 roses and tens of thousands of newly planted azalea plants.

Bronx Wildlife Conservation Park   ZOO

(☑718-220-5100; www.bronxzoo.com; Bronx River Pkwy, at Fordham Rd; adult/child $15/11; ⊙10am-5pm Apr-Oct; ☑2 to Pelham Pkwy) Otherwise known as the Bronx Zoo, this is one of the biggest, best and most progressive zoos anywhere.

Woodlawn Cemetery   CEMETERY

(☑718-920-0500; www.thewoodlawncemetery.org; Webster Ave at E 233rd St; ⊙8:30am-5pm; ☑4 to Woodlawn) Famous, historic and fascinating, this 400-acre burial ground is the resting place of many notable Americans, including Irving Berlin and Herman Melville.

◉ Queens

There is no longer any typical Queens accent – think Archie and Edith Bunker in *All in the Family*. You're as likely to hear Bengali and Spanish – 170 languages are spoken – in this, the largest (282 sq miles) and most ethnically diverse county in the country. There are few of the tree-lined brownstone streets you find in Brooklyn, and the majority of the neighborhoods, architecturally speaking at least, do not befit this borough's grand name. However, because close to half its 2.3 million residents were born abroad, parts of Queens are endlessly reconstituting themselves, creating a vibrant and heady alternative universe to Manhattan. It's also home to two major airports, the Mets, a hip modern-art scene, miles of excellent beaches in the Rockaways and walking trails in the Gateway National Recreation Area (www.nps.gov/gate), and a wildlife refuge in Jamaica Bay, only minutes from JFK airport. The Queens Historical Society (☑718-939-0647; www.queenshistoricalsociety.org) offers tours through many areas of the massive borough.

Long Island City   NEIGHBORHOOD

(admission $15, open 2pm to 9pm; ☑G to 21st St) Neighboring Long Island City has several high-rise condominiums lining the riverfront with fantastic views of Manhattan. The area has also become a hub of art museums. PS 1 Contemporary Art Center (☑718-784-2084; www.ps1.org; 22-25 Jackson Ave, at 46th Ave; suggested donation $10; ⊙noon-6pm Thu-Mon) is dedicated solely to new, cutting-edge works. On Saturdays from early July through September, the center's outdoor courtyard is transformed into an installation art space and crammed with the highest concentration of hipsters this side of the Mississippi. If the weather is pleasant, don't miss the waterside Socrates Sculpture Park (Map p80; www.socratessculpturepark.org; Broadway at Vernon Blvd; ⊙10am-dusk; Ⓢ N/Q to Broadway) FREE with its outdoor exhibits of massive, climbable sculptures by greats including Mark di Suvero, who founded the space.

Astoria   NEIGHBORHOOD
Home to the largest Greek community outside of Greece, this is obviously the place to find amazing Greek bakeries, restaurants and gourmet shops, mainly along Broadway. An influx of Eastern European, Middle Eastern (Steinway Ave, known as 'Little Egypt,' is the place for falafel, kabobs and hookah pipes) and Latino immigrants have created a rich and diverse mix. Young Bohemian types have also migrated here, making the area Queens' answer to Williamsburg. A reminder that movie-making started in Astoria in the 1920s, the renovated American Museum of the Moving Image (www.movingimage.us; 35th Ave at 36th St, Astoria; adult/child $12/6, admission 4-8pm Fri free; ⊙10.30am-5pm Tue-Thu, to 8pm Fri, to 7pm Sat & Sun; Ⓢ M/R to Steinway St) exposes some of the mysteries of the craft with amazing exhibits and screenings in its ornate theater. In summer, cool off at the Astoria Pool (www.nycgovparks.org/parks/astoriapark; Astoria Park, cnr 19th St & 23rd Dr, Astoria; ⊙11am-7pm late Jun-early Sep; Ⓢ N/Q to Astoria Blvd), the city's largest and oldest. Much of the neighborhood, as well as curious Manhattanites, can be found at the Bohemian Hall & Beer Garden (www.bohemianhall.com; 29-19 24th Ave btwn 29th & 31st Sts, Astoria; Ⓢ N/Q to Astoria Blvd) during warm afternoons and evenings.

Flushing & Corona   NEIGHBORHOOD
The intersection of Main St and Roosevelt Ave, downtown Flushing, can feel like the Times Square of a city a world away from NYC. Immigrants from all over Asia, primarily Chinese and Korean, make up this neighborhood bursting at the seams with markets and restaurants filled with delicious and cheap delicacies. Flushing Meadows Corona Park, meanwhile, is the home of Citi Field, the USTA National Tennis Center (the US Open is held here every August) and many lakes, ball fields, bike paths and grassy expanses, and was used for the 1939 and 1964 World's Fairs, of which there are quite a few faded leftovers. Kids can learn about science and technology through fun hands-on exhibits at the New York Hall of Science (☏718-699-0005; www.nyhallsci.org; 47-01 111th St; adult/child $11/8, 2-5pm Fri Sep-Jun free; ⊙daily Apr-Aug, closed Mon Sep-Mar; Ⓢ 7 to 111th St); a quirky mini-golf course is on the site. Also within this massive park is the Queens Museum of Art (QMA; www.queensmuseum.org; Flushing Meadows Corona Park, Queens; suggested donation adult/child $5/free; ⊙noon-6pm Wed-Sun, to 8pm Fri Jul & Aug; Ⓢ 7 to 111th St).

Jackson Heights
Historic District   NEIGHBOURHOOD
(btwn Roosevelt & 34th Aves, from 70th to 90th Sts; Ⓢ E, F/V, R to Jackson Heights-Roosevelt Ave) A fascinating mix of Indian and South American (Roosevelt Ave) cultures, this is the place to purchase saris and 22-karat gold, dine on South Indian *masala dosas* – huge, paper-thin rice crepes folded around flavorful mixtures of masala potatoes, peas, cilantro and other earthy treats – and continue on with a plate of Colombian arepas (corn pancakes), a bite of Argentine empanadas and a cocktail at one of several Latin gay and lesbian bars, several of which line the main drag of Broadway.

⊙ Staten Island
While many New Yorkers will say that Staten Island has more in common with its neighbor, New Jersey, because of its suburban house and car cultures, there are compelling reasons to include this borough in your urban explorations. First and foremost is the Staten Island Ferry (Map p62; www.siferry.com; Whitehall Terminal at Whitehall & South Sts; ⊙24hr; Ⓢ 1 to South Ferry) FREE, which shuttles blasé commuters to work, while offering breathtaking views of the Statue of Liberty and the Manhattan skyline (the worlds' largest Ferris wheel is to be built amid a large shopping and retail complex near the ferry terminal). Not far from the ferry station on the Staten Island side is the Richmond County Bank Ballpark (75 Richmond Terrace, Staten Island), home to the minor-league Staten Island Yankees, as well as the hipper-than-ever neighborhood of St George.

🏃 Activities
Cycling
Hundreds of miles of designated cycling lanes have been added throughout the city by Mayor Bloomberg's very pro-cycling City Hall. And even more potentially momentous,

the Bloomberg administration launched Citi Bike (www.citibikenyc.com; 24hr/7 days $11/27), its long awaited and semi-contentious bike-sharing program – the largest in the country – in the summer of 2013. Hundreds of kiosks in Manhattan and parts of Brooklyn house the almost instantly iconic bright blue and very sturdy bicycles available for rides of 30-minutes or less. However, unless you're an experienced urban cyclist, pedaling through the streets can be a risky activity, as bike lanes are often blocked by trucks, taxis and double-parked cars. More than 28-miles, mostly riverfront, have been integrated into the Manhattan Waterfront Greenway, a patchwork of park pathways, overpasses and a few city streets that circle the entire island of Manhattan. The mostly uninterrupted 10-mile stretch from the GW Bridge to Battery Park, including Hudson River Park, is perhaps the most spectacular. Of course Central Park and Brooklyn's Prospect Park have lovely cycling paths.

For cycling tips and weekend trips, contact Five Borough Bicycle Club (Map p80; www.5bbc.org; 891 Amsterdam Ave at 103rd St; S 1 to 103rd St). Transportation Alternatives (www.transalt.org), a nonprofit bicycle-lobbying group, is also a good source of information. Gay cycling enthusiasts should check the website of Fast & Fabulous (www.fastnfab.org), a gay cycling club that organizes long weekend rides. For bike rentals (other than Citi Bike), try Central Park's Loeb Boathouse or locate a rental shop on the comprehensive website Bike New York (www.bikenewyork.org).

Water Sports

This is an island, after all, and as such there are plenty of opportunities for boating and kayaking. The Downtown Boathouse (Map p66; www.downtownboathouse.org; Pier 40, near Houston St; tours free; ⊙ 10am-6pm Sat & Sun, 5-7pm Thu Jun-Sep; S 1 to Houston St) offers free 20-minute kayaking (including equipment) in the protected embayment of the Hudson River. Other locations include Pier 96 and 72nd St.

In Central Park, Loeb Boathouse (Map p80; ☑ 212-517-2233; www.thecentralparkboathouse.com; Central Park btwn 74th & 75th Sts; boating per hr $12, bike rentals per hr $9-15; ⊙ 10am-dusk Apr-Nov; 🖬; S B, C to 72nd St, 6 to 77th St) rents rowboats for romantic trysts, and even fills Venice-style gondolas in summer ($30 for 30 minutes). For a sailing adventure,

hop aboard the *Schooner Adirondack* at Chelsea Piers.

Surfers may be surprised to find a tight group of wave worshippers within city limits, at Queens' Rockaway Beach at 90th St, where you can hang ten after only a 45-minute ride on the A train from Midtown.

ᑕ⅂ Tours

The following is a small sample:

Big Onion Walking Tours   WALKING TOUR
(☑ 888-606-9255; www.bigonion.com; tours $20) Popular and quirky guided tours specializing in ethnic and neighborhood tours.

Circle Line   BOAT TOUR
(Map p70; ☑ 212-563-3200; www.circleline42.com; Pier 83, W 42nd St; tickets from $29; S A/C/E to 42nd St-Port Authority Bus Terminal) Ferry boat tours, from semicircle to a full island cruise with guided commentary, as well as powerful speedboat trips (adult/child $27/21).

Gray Line Sightseeing   BUS TOUR
(Map p70; www.newyorksightseeing.com; 777 8th Ave; adult/child from $42/$32) Hop-on, hop-off double-decker multilingual guided bus tours of all the boroughs (except Staten Island).

Municipal Art Society   WALKING TOUR
(Map p70; ☑ 212-935-3960; www.mas.org; 111 W 57th St; tours $20; S F to 57th St) Various scheduled tours focusing on architecture and history, including daily 12:30pm tours of Grand Central Terminal.

New York City Audubon   WALKING TOUR
(Map p70; ☑ 212-691-7483; www.nycaudubon.org; 71 W 23rd St, Ste 1523; tours $8-100; S F/M to 23rd St) Expert instructors and guides lead trips including birding in Central Park and the Bronx and ecology cruises of the Jamaica Bay Wildlife Refuge.

NYC Gangster Tours   WALKING TOUR
(www.nycgangstertours.com; tours $25) Sure, it's a little schticky, but colorful and knowledgeable guides make these walking tours focusing on NYC's Italian, Chinese and Jewish mafia interesting and fun.

On Location Tours   TOUR
(☑ 212-209-3370; www.screentours.com; tours $15-45) *Gossip Girl* and *How I Met Your Mother* are on the list of tours as well as long-running ones that allow you to flesh out your Carrie Bradshaw or Tony Soprano fantasies.

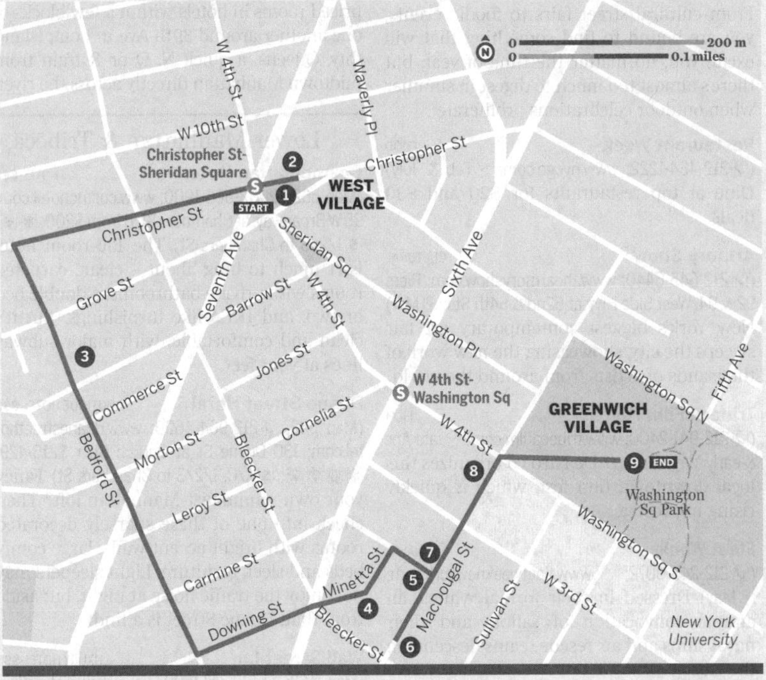

City Walk
Village Radicals

START CHRISTOPHER ST
END FIFTH AVE
LENGTH ½ MILE; 30 MINUTES

Greenwich Village has historically been a hotbed for upstarts, radicals, Bohemians, poets, folk singers, feminists and freedom-seeking gays and lesbians. Disembark the subway at Christopher St and stop at tiny [1] **Christopher Park**, where two life-sized statues of same-sex couples (Gay Liberation, 1992) stand guard. On its north side is the legendary [2] **Stonewall Inn**, where fed-up drag queens rioted for their civil rights in 1969, signaling the start of the gay revolution. Cross Seventh Ave South and continue west along Christopher St. Turn left onto quaint Bedford St; stop and peer into [3] **Chumley's**, the site of a prohibition-dodging socialist-run speakeasy (closed since 2007 but hopes to reopen in the future). Continue along Bedford St for several blocks, make a left on Downing St and cross Sixth Ave. Continue east on the crooked Minetta St, home to the unremarkable Panchito's Mexican Restaurant, which painted over the faded sign for the [4] **Fat Black Pussycat** – called the Commons in 1962, when a young Bob Dylan wrote and first performed 'Blowin' in the Wind' here. Turn right on Minetta Lane and right on MacDougal St to find the historic [5] **Minetta Tavern**, which opened as a speakeasy in 1922. Also on this block is the former site of the [6] **Folklore Center**, where Izzy Young established a hangout for folk artists including Dylan, who found his first audience at the music venue [7] **Cafe Wha?**. Continue back along MacDougal to the current Research Fellows & Scholars Office of the NYU School of Law, the former site of the [8] **Liberal Club**, a meeting place for free thinkers, including Jack London and Upton Sinclair, founded in 1913. Beyond here is the southwest entrance to [9] **Washington Square Park**, which has a long history as a magnet for radicals. Wrap up the tour by leaving the park at the iconic arch and head up Fifth Ave.

Festivals & Events

From cultural street fairs to foodie events, you are bound to find something that will excite you, no matter the time of year, but there's almost too much to digest in summer when outdoor celebrations proliferate.

Restaurant Week FOOD
(☎ 212-484-1222; www.nycgo.com; 🕒 Feb & July) Dine at top restaurants for $20 and $30 deals.

Armory Show CULTURAL
(☎ 212-645-6440; www.thearmoryshow.com; Piers 92 & 94, West Side Hwy at 52nd & 54th Sts; 🕒 Mar) New York's biggest contemporary art fair sweeps the city, showcasing the new work of thousands of artists from around the world.

Tribeca Film Festival FILM
(☎ 212-941-2400; www.tribecafilm.com; 🕒 late Apr & early May) Robert De Niro co-organizes this local downtown film fest, which is quickly rising in prestige.

Fleet Week NAVAL
(☎ 212-245-0072; www.fleetweeknewyork.com; 🕒 May) Dressed in their formal whites, an annual convocation of sailors and their naval ships and air rescue teams descend on the city.

Lesbian, Gay, Bisexual & Transgender Pride CULTURAL
(☎ 212-807-7433; www.nycpride.org; 🕒 Jun) Pride month, with a packed calendar of parties and events, culminates with a major march down Fifth Ave on the last Sunday of June.

Mermaid Parade CULTURAL
(www.coneyisland.com; 🕒 late Jun) Something of Mardi Gras on the boardwalk, this parade turns Surf Ave on Coney Island in Brooklyn into a free-expression zone that's fun, crazy and artistic.

New York Film Festival FILM
(www.filmlinc.com; 🕒 late Sep) Major world premieres from prominent directors at this Lincoln Center event.

Sleeping

Keep in mind that prices change depending on the value of the euro, yen and other worldwide currencies, as well as the general drift of the global economic climate, not to mention the day of the week and the season, with spring and fall being most expensive. Tax adds an additional 13.25% per night. A cluster of national chains, including Sheraton, Ramada and Holiday Inn, have affordably priced rooms in hotels within a few blocks of one another around 39th Ave in Long Island City, Queens, a quick N, Q or R train from midtown Manhattan directly across the river.

Lower Manhattan & Tribeca

Cosmopolitan Hotel HOTEL $$$
(Map p62; ☎ 212-566-1900; www.cosmohotel.com; 95 W Broadway, at Chambers St; d from $200; ❄📶; [S] 1/2/3 to Chambers St) The 130-room hotel isn't much to brag about – clean, carpeted rooms with private bathrooms, a double bed or two, and IKEA-like furnishings. But it's clean and comfortable, with major subway lines at your feet.

Duane Street Hotel BOUTIQUE HOTEL $$$
(Map p62; ☎ 212-964-4600; www.duanestreethotel.com; 130 Duane St at Church St; r $215-429; ❄@📶🐾; [S] A/C, 1/2/3 to Chambers St) Fancy your own minimalist Manhattan loft? Then check into one of these sparsely decorated rooms with bright accent walls, large comfy beds and sleek furniture. Light sleepers may not enjoy the traffic noise at night, but aside from that, Duane Street is a find.

Wall Street Inn LUXURY HOTEL $$$
(Map p62; ☎ 212-747-1500; www.thewallstreetinn.com; 9 S William St; r incl breakfast from $275; ❄@📶; [S] 2/3 to Wall St) Lehman Brothers, the failed bank, once occupied this classic limestone building and, while the mood of the hotel is very early American banker, there's little risk in a stay here. Old-fashioned and warm rather than stuffy, the rooms, with luxurious marble baths, are slightly overfurnished for their size.

SoHo

Mondrian SoHo HOTEL $$$
(Map p66; ☎ 212-389-1000; www.mondriansoho.com; 9 Crosby St btwn Howard & Grand Sts; r from $249; ❄@📶🐾; [S] 4/6, N/Q/R, J/Z to Canal St) The trademark Mondrian playfulness now inhabits over 250 rooms at this beautiful downtown property. The designs have dabbled with fairy-tale color schemes while tricking the senses with an eclectic assortment of oddly textured *objets d'art*.

Soho Grand Hotel BOUTIQUE HOTEL $$$
(Map p66; ☎ 212-965-3000; www.sohogrand.com; 310 W Broadway; d $195-450; ❄@📶🐾; [S] 6, N/Q/R, J to Canal St) The original boutique hotel of the 'hood still reigns, with its strik-

ing glass-and-cast-iron lobby stairway, and 367 rooms with cool, clean lines plus Frette linens, plasma flat-screen TVs and Kiehl's grooming products. The lobby's Grand Lounge buzzes with action.

Solita SoHo
HOTEL $$$
(Map p66; ☎ 212-925-3600; www.solitasohohotel. com; 159 Grand St, at Lafayette St; r from $220; ❋ 🛜; 🚇 6, N/Q/R, J to Canal St) Part of the Clarion chain, the Solita is a clean, functional alternative with boutique-style furnishings close to Little Italy, Chinatown, Soho and the Lower East Side. Lower winter rates.

🛏 Lower East Side, East Village & NoLita

Nolitan Hotel
HOTEL $$
(Map p66; ☎ 212-925-2555; www.nolitanhotel.com; 30 Kenmare St btwn Elizabeth & Mott Sts; r from $143; ❋ 🛜; 🚇 J to Bowery, 4/6 to Spring St, B/D to Grand St) Set behind a memorable facade of floating postive-negative Tetris bricks, the Nolitan is a great find. Tuck into a good book in the inviting lobby lounge, or head upstairs to your stylish pad, which feels like it's waiting to be photographed in the next CB2 catalog.

East Village Bed & Coffee
B&B $$
(Map p66; ☎ 212-533-4175; www.bedandcoffee.com; 110 Ave C btwn 7th & 8th Sts; s/d with shared bath from $125/130; ❋ 🛜; 🚇 F/V to Lower East Side-2nd Ave) This family home has been transformed into a quirky, arty, offbeat B&B with colorful, themed private rooms (one shared bathroom and kitchen per floor) and even free bikes. Dogs roam the 1st floor, but the upper ones are pet free and the owner can supply wonderful insider neighborhood tips.

Blue Moon Hotel
BOUTIQUE HOTEL $$$
(Map p66; ☎ 212-533-9080; www.bluemoon-nyc. com; 100 Orchard St btwn Broome & Delancey Sts; r from $250; ❋ 🛜; 🚇 F/V to Lower East Side-2nd Ave) You'd never guess that this quaint, welcoming brick guesthouse – full of festive colors – was once a foul tenement back in the day (the day being 1879). Except for a few ornate touches, like wrought-iron bed frames and detailed molding, Blue Moon's clean, spare rooms are entirely modern and comfortable.

Bowery Hotel
BOUTIQUE HOTEL $$$
(Map p66; ☎ 212-505-9100; www.theboweryhotel. com; 335 Bowery btwn 2nd & 3rd Sts; r from $325; ❋ @ 🛜; 🚇 F/V to Lower East Side-2nd Ave; 6 to Bleecker St) Perhaps as far as you can get from the Bowery's gritty flophouse history, this

stunningly stylish hotel is all 19th-century elegance. Rooms come equipped with lots of light and sleek furnishings mixed with antiques. The baroque-style lobby bar attracts the young and chic and on-site restaurant Gemma serves upscale Italian.

🛏 Chelsea, Meatpacking District & West (Greenwich) Village

Chelsea Hostel
HOSTEL $
(Map p70; ☎ 212-647-0010; www.chelseahostel. com; 251 W 20th St btwn Seventh & Eighth Aves; dm $38-68, s $70-95, d from $95; ❋ @ 🛜; 🚇 A/C/E, 1/2 to 23 St; 1/2 to 18 St) Walkable to the Village and Midtown, Chelsea Hostel capitalizes on its convenient location with somewhat steep prices, but it's kept clean (even a tad sterile at times) and there's access to common rooms and kitchens where other budget travelers often meet and hang.

Jane Hotel
HOTEL $
(Map p66; ☎ 212-924-6700; www.thejanenyc.com; 113 Jane St btwn Washington St & West Side Hwy; r with shared bath from $99; P ❋ 🛜; 🚇 L to 8th Ave, A/C/E to 14th St; 1/2 to Christopher St-Sheridan Sq) Originally built for sailors (obvious after one look at the cabin-sized rooms), the Jane became a temporary refuge for survivors of the *Titanic*, then a YMCA and a rock-and-roll venue. The single-bunk rooms feature flat-screen TVs and the communal showers are more than adequate.

Chelsea Lodge
HOTEL $$
(Map p70; ☎ 212-243-4499; www.chelsealodge. com; 318 W 20th St btwn Eighth & Ninth Aves; s/d from $118/128; ❋; 🚇 A/C/E to 14th St; 1 to 18th St) Housed in a landmark brownstone in Chelsea, the European-style, 20-room Chelsea Lodge is a super deal. Space is tight, so you won't get more than a bed, with a TV plopped on an old wooden cabinet. There are showers and sinks in rooms, but toilets are down the hall. Six suite rooms have private bathrooms, and two come with private garden access.

Inn on 23rd St
B&B $$
(Map p70; ☎ 212-463-0330; www.innon23rd.com; 131 W 23rd St btwn Sixth & Seventh Aves; r incl breakfast from $179; ❋ 🛜; 🚇 F/V, 1 to 23rd St) Housed in a lone 19th-century, five-story townhouse on busy 23rd St, this 14-room B&B is a Chelsea gem. The rooms are big and welcoming, with fanciful fabrics on big brass or poster beds and an ol' piano for you to play boogie-woogie on in the lounge, and a 2nd-floor, all-Victorian library that doubles as a breakfast room.

Larchmont Hotel HOTEL $$
(Map p66; ☎212-989-9333; www.larchmonthotel.com; 27 W 11th St, btwn Fifth & Sixth Aves; s/d with shared bath & breakfast from $90/119; ❄; [S]4/5/6, N/Q/R to 14th St-Union Sq) Housed in a prewar building that blends in with the other fine brownstones on the block, a stay at the Larchmont is about location. The carpeted rooms are basic and in need of updating, as are the communal baths, but it's not a bad deal for the price.

Ace Hotel New York City BOUTIQUE HOTEL $$$
(Map p70; ☎212-679-2222; www.acehotel.com/newyork; 20 W 29th St btwn Broadway & Fifth Ave; r from $249-549; ❄📶🐾; [S]N/R to 28th St) This outpost of a hip Pacific northwest chain is on the northern edge of Chelsea. Clever touches such as vintage turntables and handwritten welcome notes elevate the Ace beyond the standard. However, prison-issued bunk beds in one of the room styles are missteps. Juice, coffee and croissants are available in the morning.

Hotel Gansevoort LUXURY HOTEL $$$
(Map p66; ☎212-206-6700; www.hotelgansevoort.com; 18 Ninth Ave at 13th St; r from $325; ❄📶🏊🐾; [S]A/C/E, 1/2/3 to 14th St; L to 8th Ave) This 187-room luxury hotel in the trendy Meatpacking District has been a hit for its 400-thread-count linens, hypoallergenic down duvets, plasma TVs, chic basement spa and rooftop bar with fabulous views. Down-to-earth types, beware: it's on the nauseatingly trendy side of things.

Union Square, Flatiron District & Gramercy Park

Hotel 17 BUDGET HOTEL $$
(Map p70; ☎212-475-2845; www.hotel17ny.com; 225 E 17th St btwn Second & Third Aves; r $89-150; ❄📶; [S]N/Q/R/W, 4/5/6 to 14th St-Union Sq; L to 3rd Ave) Right off Stuyvesant Sq on a leafy residential block, this no-frills, eight-floor townhouse has relatively affordable prices. Rooms are small, with traditional, basic furnishings (gray carpet, chintzy bedspreads, burgundy blinds) and lack much natural light.

Gershwin Hotel HOTEL $$$
(Map p70; ☎212-545-8000; www.gershwinhotel.com; 7 E 27th St at Fifth Ave; r from $215; ❄@📶; [S]N/R, 6 to 28th St) This popular and funky spot is half youth hostel, half hotel, and buzzes with original pop art, touring bands and a young and artsy European clientele.

W New York Union Square HOTEL $$$
(Map p70; ☎888-625-5144, 212-253-9119; www.whotels.com; 201 Park Ave S at 17th St; r $389, ste from $625; ❄@📶🐾; [S]L, N/Q/R/W, 4/5/6 to 14th St-Union Sq) The ultra-hip W demands a black wardrobe and credit card. The standard rooms aren't big, but – set in a 1911, one-time insurance building – benefit from high ceilings, and are decked out with all the modern bells and whistles. The suites are spectacular.

Marcel BOUTIQUE HOTEL $$$
(Map p70; ☎212-696-3800; www.nychotels.com; 201 E 24th St, at Third Ave; d from $210; ❄@📶; [S]6 to 23rd St) Minimalist with earth-tone touches, this 97-room inn is a poor-man's chic boutique and that's not a bad thing. Modernist rooms on the avenue have great views, and the sleek lounge is a great place to unwind after a day of touring.

Midtown

★**Yotel** HOTEL $$
(Map p70; ☎646-449-7700; www.yotel.com; 570 Tenth Ave at 41st St; r from $150; ❄📶; [S]A/C/E to 42nd St-Port Authority Bus Terminal; 1/2/3, N/Q/R, S, 7 to Times Sq-42nd St) Part futuristic spaceport, part Austin Powers set, this uber-cool 669-room option bases its rooms on airplane classes. Small but cleverly configured, Premium cabins include automated adjustable beds, while all cabins feature floor-to-ceiling windows with killer views, slick bathrooms and iPod connectivity.

Pod Hotel HOTEL $$
(Map p70; ☎866-414-4617; www.thepodhotel.com; 230 E 51st St btwn Second & Third Aves; r from $145; ❄📶; [S]6 to 51st St; E, V to Lexington Ave-53rd St) A dream come true for folks who'd like to live inside their iPod – or at least curl up and sleep with it – this affordable hot spot has a range of room types, most barely big enough for the bed. 'Pods' have bright bedding, tight workspaces, flat-screen TVs, iPod docking stations and 'rain' showerheads.

Andaz Fifth Avenue BOUTIQUE HOTEL $$$
(Map p70; ☎212-601-1234; http://andaz.hyatt.com; 485 Fifth Ave at 41st St; d $355-595; ❄📶; [S]S, 4/5/6 to Grand Central-42nd St, 7 to 5th Ave) Uber-chic yet youthful and relaxed, the Andaz ditches stuffy reception desks for hip, mobile staff who check you in on tablets in the art-laced lobby. The hotel's 184 rooms are contemporary and sleek, with NYC-inspired details like 'Fashion District' rolling racks and subway-inspired lamps.

London NYC
LUXURY HOTEL $$$

(Map p70; 212-307-5000, 866-690-2029; www.thelondonnyc.com; 151 W 54th St btwn Sixth & Seventh Aves; ste from $389; ❉ 🔊; ⓢ B/D, E to 7th Ave) This luxe hotel salutes the British capital in sophisticated ways, including a Michelin-starred restaurant by Gordon Ramsay. But the real draw is the huge, plush rooms – all called suites, and all with separate bedroom and living area. In winter, online prices drop to the high $200s.

414 Hotel
HOTEL $$$

(Map p70; 212-399-0006; www.414hotel.com; 414 W 46th St btwn Ninth & Tenth Aves; r incl breakfast from $200; ❉ 🔊; ⓢ C/E to 50th St) Set up like a guesthouse, this affordable, friendly option offers 22 tidy and tastefully decorated rooms a couple of blocks west of Times Square. Rooms facing the leafy inner courtyard, which is a perfect spot to enjoy your complimentary breakfast, are the quietest.

Upper West Side

Hostelling International New York
HOSTEL $

(HI; Map p80; 212-932-2300; www.hinewyork.org; 891 Amsterdam Ave at 103rd St; dm $32-40, d from $135; ❉ 🔊; ⓢ 1 to 103rd St) It's got clean, safe and air-conditioned dorm rooms in a gorgeous landmark building, with a sprawling and shady patio and a super-friendly vibe.

Jazz on Amsterdam Ave
HOSTEL $

(Map p80; 646-490-7348; www.jazzhostels.com; 201 W 87th St at Amsterdam Ave; dm $44, r $100; ❉ 🔊; ⓢ 1 to 86th St) Only a short walk to Central Park, this hostel chain's Upper West Side branch has clean rooms, both private rooms and two- to six-bed dorms. Free wi-fi in the lobby. Other branches in Harlem and Chelsea.

YMCA
HOSTEL $$

(Map p80; 212-912-2600; www.ymca.com; 5 W 63rd St at Central Park West; r from $100; ❉ @; ⓢ A/B/C/D to 59th St-Columbus Circle) Just steps from Central Park, this grand art-deco building has several floors – 8th to the 13th – of basic, but clean, rooms. Guests have access to extensive, but old-school gym, racquet ball courts, pool and sauna. Wi-fi on the ground floor. Other locations on the Upper East Side and Harlem.

Lucerne
HOTEL $$$

(Map p80; 212-875-1000; www.thelucernehotel.com; 201 W 79th St cnr Amsterdam Ave; d $200-425, ste $400-625; ❉ 🔊 ♿; ⓢ B, C to 81st St) This unusual 1903 structure breaks away from beaux arts in favor of the baroque, with an ornately carved terracotta-colored facade. Inside is a stately 197-room hotel with nine types of guest rooms evoking a contemporary Victorian look. Think: flowered bedspreads, scrolled headboards and plush pillows with fringe.

On the Ave
BOUTIQUE HOTEL $$$

(Map p80; 212-362-1100; www.ontheave.com; 2178 Broadway at 77th St; r from $225; ❉ 🔊; ⓢ 1 to 77th St) A more welcoming feel and larger rooms make On the Ave a cut above the average sleek boutique hotel. And it's a good deal considering the high-concept design, stainless steel and marble baths, featherbeds, flat-screen TVs and original artwork.

Upper East Side

Bubba & Bean Lodges
B&B $$

(Map p80; 917-345-7914; www.bblodges.com; 1598 Lexington Ave btwn 101st & 102nd Sts; r from $180; ❉ 🔊; ⓢ 6 to 103rd St) Hardwood floors, crisp white walls and pretty navy bedspreads make the rooms at this nifty B&B feel spacious, modern and youthful. The rooms are really more like full apartments (some fit up to six people). Good winter rates.

Bentley
BOUTIQUE HOTEL $$$

(Map p80; 888-664-6835; www.nychotels.com; 500 E 62nd St, at York Ave; r from $200; ❉ 🔊; ⓢ N/Q/R to Lexington Ave/59th St) Featuring great East River views, the Bentley overlooks FDR Dr, as far east as you can go. Formerly an office building, the hotel has shed its utilitarian past in the form of chic boutique-hotel styling, a swanky lobby and sleek rooms.

★ Carlyle
LUXURY HOTEL $$$

(Map p80; 212-744-1600; www.thecarlyle.com; 35 E 76th St btwn Madison & Park Aves; r from $450; ❉ 🔊; ⓢ 6 to 77th St) This legendary New York classic, the epitome of old-fashioned luxury hosts foreign dignitaries and celebrities alike. Opulence reigns from the hushed lobby with glossy marble floors to framed English country scenes or Audubon prints in the rooms; some have terraces and baby grand pianos.

Harlem

102 Brownstone
HOTEL $$

(Map p80; 212-662-4223; www.102brownstone.com; 102 W 118th St btwn Malcolm X & Adam Clayton Powell Jr Blvds; r from $120; ❉ 🔊; ⓢ A/C, B, 2/3 to 116th St) A wonderfully redone Greek Revival row house on a beautiful residential street; room styles, all with plush bedding, range from Zen to classy boudoir.

710 Guest Suites APARTMENT $$
(☎212-491-5622; www.710guestsuites.com; 710 St Nicholas Ave at 146th St; ste from $174; ❄📶; [S]A/B/C/D to 145th St) Three fabulously chic suites with high ceilings, contemporary furnishings and wood floors in a brownstone. Three-night minimum and lower rates from January through March make this exceptionally good value. Located north of Central Park.

Harlem Flophouse GUESTHOUSE $$
(Map p80; ☎347-632-1960; www.harlemflophouse.com; 242 W 123rd St btwn Adam Clayton Powell Jr & Frederick Douglass Blvds, Harlem; r with shared bath from $125; ❄📶; [S]A/C, B/D, 2/3 to 124th St) The four attractive bedrooms have antique light fixtures, glossed-wood floors and big beds, plus classic tin-ceilings and wooden shutters. Cat on the premises.

Brooklyn

★ **New York Loft Hostel** HOSTEL $
(☎718-366-1351; www.nylofthostel.com; 249 Varet St btwn Bogart & White Sts, Bushwick; dm $50, r with/without bath $70/65; ❄@📶; [S]L to Morgan Ave) Live like a Williamsburg or more accurately Bushwick hipster in this renovated loft building. Brick walls, high ceilings, a beautiful kitchen and rooftop Jacuzzi make Manhattan hostels seem like tenements.

3B B&B $
(☎347-762-2632; www.3bbrooklyn.com; 136 Lawrence St; dm/r incl breakfast $60/150; ❄📶; [S]A/C/F/N/R to Jay St-Metro Tech) The 3rd floor of this downtown Brooklyn brownstone has been turned into a bright and contemporary four-room B&B.

Nu Hotel HOTEL $$$
(☎718-852-8585; www.nuhotelbrooklyn.com; 85 Smith St, Downtown Brooklyn; d incl breakfast from $300; ❄@📶; [S]F, G to Bergen St) This location, only blocks from Brooklyn Heights and a nexus of attractive brownstone neighborhoods, is absolutely ideal – except for the fact that it's across the street from the Brooklyn House of Detention. It has a chic minimalist vibe and the clean, all-white rooms are comfortable.

🍴 Eating

In a city with nearly 19,000 restaurants, and new ones opening every single day, where are you supposed to begin? From Little Albania to Little Uzbekistan, your choice of ethnic eats is only a short subway ride away. A hotbed of buzz-worthy culinary invention and trends like artisanal doughnuts, farm-to-table pork sandwiches and *haute cuisine* reinterpretations of fried chicken, pizza and good ol' burgers and fries, NYC's restaurant scene, like the city, is constantly reinventing itself. The latest foodie obsession is the flotilla of roving, tweeting food trucks, the 21st-century equivalent of the classic pushcart, selling gourmet cupcakes, dumplings and Jamaican curry goat and everything in between.

🍴 Lower Manhattan & Tribeca

Ruben's Empanadas ARGENTINE, FAST FOOD $
(Map p62; 64 Fulton St; empanadas $4; ⏲9am-7pm) Refuel with one of this Argentine chain's filling, greaseless empanadas in endless varieties, from chicken to apple or spicy tofu. Two other locations in the neighborhood.

Financier Patisserie BAKERY, SANDWICHES $
(Map p62; ☎212-334-5600; 62 Stone St at Mill Lane; mains $8; ⏲7am-8pm Mon-Fri, 8:30am-6:30pm Sat; 👪; [S]2/3, 4/5 to Wall St, J/Z to Broad St) There are now three Patisserie outposts in Lower Manhattan because nobody can get enough of the flaky, buttery croissants, almond, apricot and pear tarts, homemade soups and creamy quiches on the regular menu.

Fraunces Tavern AMERICAN $$
(Map p62; ☎212-968-1776; www.fraunces tavern.com; 54 Pearl St; mains $15-24; ⏲noon-5pm; [S]N/R to Whitehall) Can you really pass up a chance to eat where George Washington supped in 1762? Expect heaping portions of tavern stew, clam chowder and beef Wellington and, for dessert, bread pudding, spiked fig and apple tart or strawberry shortcake.

Blaue Gans GERMAN-AUSTRIAN $$$
(Map p62; ☎212-571-8880; www.kg-ny.com; 139 Duane St; mains $15-30; ⏲11am-midnight; 👪; [S]A/C, 1/2/3 to Chambers St) Step inside this homage to minimalist Austrian cuisine and dive into some delectable *kavalierspitz* (boiled beef with horseradish), various wursts and yummy fried schnitzels. Kids get their own menu, and non-Austrian foodies can try delicate fish dishes, spicy soups and pastas.

Kutsher's Tribeca
JEWISH $$$

(Map p62; 212-431-0606; www.kutsherstribeca.com; 186 Franklin St btwn Greenwich & Hudson Sts; mains $19-29; 11:45am-10pm Mon-Wed, to 11pm Thu-Sat, 10am-3pm Sun; S A/C/E to Canal St, 1 to Franklin St) Jewish comfort food gets a refreshing makeover here. Forget the starch and stodge: here you'll be grazing on crispy artichokes with lemon, garlic and Parmesan; borscht salad with marinated goat cheese; or latkes with local apple compote.

Chinatown, Little Italy & NoLita

Lovely Day
PAN-ASIAN $

(Map p66; 212-925-3310; 196 Elizabeth St, btwn Prince & Spring Sts; mains $9; 11am-11pm; S J/M/Z to Bowery St, 6 to Spring St) Everything is just precious inside this affordable and funky nook that serves lovingly prepared Thai-inflected food. Coconut-rich curries, noodle dishes, papaya salad and spicy tofu squares create a fascinating harmony with the soda shop–inspired decor.

Pinche Taqueria
MEXICAN $

(Map p66; 212-625-0090; www.pinchetaqueria.us; 227 Mott St, btwn Prince & Spring Sts; mains $4-9; 10:30am-11pm Sun-Thu, to 1am Fri & Sat; ; S 6 to Spring St) Dig into authentic Mexican tacos, tostadas, burritos, quesadillas and more, topped with fresh yuca (cassava)fries and guacamole, and wash it all down with *horchata* (a beverage made with rice, flavored with lime and cinnamon and sweetened with sugar). Crowded and upbeat, Pinche is a great find on a hot, hungry afternoon.

BarBossa
SOUTH AMERICAN $$

(Map p66; 212-625-2340; 232 Elizabeth St; mains $14; 11am-midnight; S 6 to Spring St) A breezy, wide-open front window and low-level bossa nova in the background give this cafe a sultry and jazzy feel that's complemented by a light, tropical cuisine, heavy on salads, delicious soups and a few hearty mains.

Café Gitane
MOROCCAN $$

(Map p66; 212-334-9552; www.cafegitanenyc.com; 242 Mott St; mains $12-18; 9am-midnight Sun-Thu, to 12:30am Fri & Sat; S N/R/W to Prince St) Clear the Gauloise smoke from your eyes and blink twice if you think you're in Paris. Label-conscious shoppers love this authentic bistro, with its dark, aromatic coffee and dishes such as yellowfin tuna seviche and spicy meatballs in tomato turmeric sauce.

Lombardi's
PIZZA $$

(Map p66; 212-941-7994; 32 Spring St btwn Mulberry & Mott Sts; 6-slice pizza $16.50; 11:30am-11pm Mon-Thu & Sun, to midnight Fri & Sat; S 6 to Spring St) The very first pizzeria in America was Lombardi's which opened here in 1905. It's justifiably proud of its New York style: thin crust and an even thinner layer of sauce – and slices that are triangular (unless they're Sicilian-style, in which case they're rectangular).

Da Nico
ITALIAN $$$

(Map p66; 212-343-1212; www.danicoristorante.com; 164 Mulberry St; mains $18-40; noon-11pm Sun-Thu, to midnight Fri & Sat; S J/M/Z N/Q/R/W, 6 to Canal St) If you're hell-bent on having a Little Italy dinner, Da Nico is a classic. It's family-run and traditional in feel and the extensive menu highlights both northern and southern Italian cuisine that's red-sauce predictable but delicious.

★ Torrisi Italian Specialties
ITALIAN $$$

(Map p66; 212-965-0955; www.torrisinyc.com; 250 Mulberry St btwn Spring & Prince Sts; prix fixe menu $65; 5:30-11pm Mon-Thu, from noon Fri-Sun; S N/R to Prince St; B/D/F, M to Broadway-Lafayette St; 4/6 to Spring St) Torrisi's tasting menu reads like an ode to Italy, with changes each week reflecting the whim of the owners (who also run popular Parm next door) and the seasonal rotation of fresh ingredients. Expect market produce and less-common items (such as rabbit and goat) spun into succulent platters.

Lower East Side

★ Katz's Delicatessen
DELI $

(Map p66; 212-254-2246; www.katzsdelicatessen.com; 205 E Houston St at Ludlow St; pastrami on rye $15, knockwurst $6; 8am-10:45pm Mon-Wed & Sun, to 2:45am Thu-Sat; S F/V to Lower East Side-2nd Ave) One of the few remaining

Jewish delicatessens in the city, Katz's attracts locals, tourists and celebrities whose photos line the walls. Massive pastrami, corned beef, brisket and tongue sandwiches are throwbacks, as is the payment system: hold on to the ticket you're handed when you walk in and pay cash only.

Yonah Schimmel Knishery
KNISHES $

(Map p66; ☎ 212-477-2858; 137 E Houston St, btwn Eldridge & Forsyth Sts; ◷ 9:30am-7pm; ☑ ; Ⓢ F/V to Lower East Side-2nd Ave) Originally selling from a pushcart on Coney Island c 1890, this family business sells potato, cheese, cabbage and kasha knishes from a mini storefront on the Lower East Side.

Meatball Shop
ITALIAN $

(Map p66; ☎ 212-982-8895; www.themeatballshop.com; 84 Stanton St btwn Allen & Orchard Sts; dishes from $9; ◷ noon-2am Mon-Wed, Sun, to 4am Thu-Sat; Ⓢ F to 2nd Ave; F to Delancey St; J/M/Z to Essex St) Masterfully executed meatball sandwiches have suddenly spiked in popularity,

and the Meatball Shop is riding the wave of success with moist incarnations of the traditional hero. Three other branches in the city.

Georgia's East Side BBQ
BBQ $

(Map p66; ☎ 212-253-6280; www.georgiaseast-sidebbq.com; 192 Orchard St btwn Houston & Stanton Sts; ◷ noon-11pm; Ⓢ F/V, M to Lower East Side-2nd Ave) Bring a big appetite to this little joint where the ribs are slow-cooked in beer then sizzled on the grill, the fried chicken is crisp and tender and there's no way you can eat all that sweet cornbread and decadent mac 'n' cheese. Cash only, and the bathroom is in the bar across the street.

Alias
MODERN AMERICAN $$

(Map p66; ☎ 212-505-5011; 76 Clinton St; ◷ 6-11pm Tue-Fri, 11am-11:30pm Sat, 10:30am-10:30pm Sun; Ⓢ F to Delancey St) Alias continues to deliver delicious, fresh food, heavy on seasonal ingredients, with dishes like Wild Alaskan black cod, maple syrup-drenched pears with ricotta and tomato-braised brisket.

EATING NYC: CHINATOWN

With hundreds of restaurants, from holes-in-the-wall to banquet-sized dining rooms, Chinatown is wonderful for exploring cheap eats on an empty stomach.

Amazing 66 (Map p62; 66 Mott St, at Canal St; mains $7; ◷ 11am-11pm; Ⓢ 6, J, N/Q to Canal St) Terrific Cantonese lunches.

Prosperity Dumpling (Map p66; ☎ 212-343-0683; 46 Eldridge St btwn Hester & Canal Sts; dumplings $1-5; ◷ Mon-Sun 7:30am-10pm; Ⓢ B/D to Grand St; F to East Broadway; J to Bowery) Among the best dumpling joints.

Vanessa's Dumpling House (Map p66; ☎ 212-625-8008; 118 Eldridge St btwn Grand & Broome Sts; dumplings $1-5; ◷ 7:30am-10:30pm; Ⓢ B/D to Grand St, J to Bowery, F to Delancey St) Great dumplings.

Big Wong King (Map p62; 67 Mott St, at Canal; mains $5-20; ◷ 7am-9:30pm; Ⓢ 6, J, N/Q to Canal St) Chopped meat over rice and reliable congee (sweet or savory soft rice soup).

Bo Ky Restaurant (Map p62; ☎ 212-406-2292; 80 Bayard St, btwn Mott & Mulberry Sts; ◷ breakfast, lunch & dinner; ☑ ; Ⓢ J, M, N, Q, R, W, Z, 6 to Canal St) Meat-studded soups, fish-infused flat noodles and curried rice dishes.

Banh Mi Saigon Bakery (Map p66; ☎ 212-941-1514; 198 Grand St btwn Mulberry & Mott Sts; mains $4-6; ◷ 10am-7pm Tue-Sun; Ⓢ J/M/Z, N/Q/R/W, 6 to Canal St) Some of the best Vietnamese sandwiches in town.

Joe's Shanghai (Map p62; ☎ 212-233-8888; www.joeshanghairestaurants.com; 9 Pell St btwn Bowery & Doyers St; mains $5-16; ◷ 11am-11pm Mon-Sun; Ⓢ J/Z, N/Q, 4/6 to Canal St, B/D to Grand St) Always busy and tourist-friendly. Does good noodle and soup dishes.

Nom Wah Tea Parlor (Map p62; 13 Doyers St; mains $4-9; ◷ 10:30am-9pm; Ⓢ 6, J, N/Q to Canal St) Looks like an old-school American diner, but is the oldest dim sum place in the city.

Original Chinatown Ice Cream Factory (Map p62; ☎ 212-608-4170; www.chinatown-icecreamfactory.com; 65 Bayard St; scoop $4; ◷ 11am-10pm; ☰ ; Ⓢ J/M, N/Q/R/W, 6 to Canal St) Overshadows the nearby Häagen-Dazs with its scoops of tea, ginger, passion fruit and lychee flavored sorbets.

'Inoteca ITALIAN $$

(Map p66; ☎212-614-0473; 98 Rivington St at Ludlow St; dishes $7-17; 🕒noon-1am; [S]F/V to Lower East Side-2nd Ave) It's worth joining the crowd waiting at the cramped bar of this airy, dark-wood-paneled corner haven to choose from *tramezzini* (small sandwiches on white or whole-wheat bread), panini and bruschetta options, all delicious and moderately priced. There's also a list of 200 wines, 25 by the glass.

🍴 SoHo & NoHo

Mooncake Foods ASIAN, SANDWICHES $

(Map p66; 28 Watts St, btwn Sullivan & Thompson Sts; mains $8; 🕒10am-11pm Mon-Fri, 9am-11pm Sat & Sun; [S]1 to Canal St) This unpretentious family-run restaurant serves some of the best sandwiches in the neighborhood. Try the smoked white-fish salad sandwich or Vietnamese pork meatball hero. Another location in Chelsea and uptown in Hell's Kitchen.

Aroma Espresso Bar CAFE $

(Map p66; ☎212-533-1094; 145 Greene St, at Houston St; sandwiches $8.50; 🕒7am-11pm; [S]B/D/F/V to Broadway-Lafayette St) An Israeli import to NYC, this sleek cafe chain has comfy and stylish seating and a menu bursting with fresh, tasty, affordable fare.

Boqueria Soho SPANISH TAPAS $$

(Map p66; ☎212-343-4255; 171 Spring St, btwn West Broadway & Thompson St; mains $13.50; 🕒lunch & dinner daily, brunch Sat & Sun; [S]C/E to Spring St) This expansive, welcoming tapas joint features classics as well as new twists on the expected, and you can watch them being assembled as you sip your unique beer-and-pear sangria and peer into the open kitchen.

Dutch AMERICAN $$$

(Map p66; ☎212-677-6200; www.thedutchnyc.com; 131 Sullivan St btwn Prince & Houston Sts; mains $16-48; 🕒11:30am-3pm Mon-Fri, 5:30pm-midnight Mon-Thu & Sun, 5:30pm-1am Fri & Sat, 10am-3pm Sat & Sun ; [S]A/C/E to Spring St, N/R to Prince St, 1/2 to Houston St) Oysters on ice and freshly baked homemade pies are the notable bookends of a meal – in the middle is fresh-from-the-farm cuisine, served in casseroles with the perfect amount of ceremony.

★Il Buco ITALIAN $$$

(Map p66; ☎212-533-1932; www.ilbuco.com; 47 Bond St btwn Bowery & Lafayette St; mains $21-32; 🕒noon-11pm Mon-Thu, to midnight Fri & Sat, 5-10:30pm Sun; [S]B/D/F/V to Broadway-Lafayette St; 6 to Bleecker St) This charming nook boasts hanging copper pots, kerosene lamps and antique furniture, plus a stunning menu and wine list. Sink your teeth into seasonal, ever-changing highlights such as white polenta with braised broccoli rabe and anchovies.

🍴 East Village

Every cuisine and style is represented in the East Village, though even the very best places are certainly more casual than stuffy. St Marks Place and around, from Third to Second Ave, has turned into a little Tokyo with loads of Japanese sushi and grill restaurants. Cookie-cutter Indian restaurants line Sixth St between First and Second Ave.

★Xi'an Famous Foods CHINESE $

(Map p66; 81 St Mark's Pl, at First Ave; mains $6; 🕒24hr; [S]6 to Astor Pl) This sliver of a restaurant, originally hailing from Flushing, Queens, has an an interesting menu specializing in spicy noodle and soup dishes. Two other locations in Chinatown.

Veselka UKRAINIAN $

(Map p66; ☎212-228-9682; www.veselka.com; 144 Second Ave at 9th St; mains $6-14; 🕒24hr; [S]L to 3rd Ave, 6 to Astor Pl) Generations of East Villagers have been coming to this bustling institution for blintzes and breakfast regardless of the hour.

Caracas Arepa Bar SOUTH AMERICAN $

(Map p66; ☎212-529-2314; www.caracasarepabar.com; 93 1/2 E 7th St btwn First Ave & Ave A; dishes $6-16; 🕒noon-11pm; 🌿; [S]6 to Astor Pl) Cram into this tiny joint and choose from 17 types of crispy, hot arepa (corn tortilla stuffed with veggies and meat), plus empanadas and daily specials like oxtail soup.

Luzzo's PIZZERIA $$

(Map p66; ☎212-473-7447; 211-213 First Ave btwn 12th & 13th Sts; pizzas $14-17; 🕒noon-11pm Tue-Sun, 5-11pm Mon; [S]L to 1st Ave) Fan-favorite Luzzo's occupies a thin sliver of real estate, which gets stuffed to the gills each evening as discerning diners feast on thin-crust pies, kissed with ripe tomatoes and cooked in a coal-fired oven.

Banjara INDIAN $$

(Map p66; ☎212-477-5956; 97 First Ave at 6th St; mains $12-18; 🕒noon-midnight; [S]L to 1st Ave) A little more upscale than some of the other options on the Indian restaurant row, Banjara has delicious, well-prepared Indian food without the headache-inducing Christmas lights that festoon many.

Angelica Kitchen VEGAN, CAFE $$
(Map p66; ☎212-228-2909; www.angelicakitchen.com; 300 E 12th St btwn First & Second Aves; dishes $14-20; ⏲11:30am-10:30pm; 🌱; [S] L to 1st Ave) This enduring herbivore classic has a calming vibe and enough creative options to make your head spin. Some dishes get too-cute names, but all do wonders with tofu, seitan (wheat gluten), spices and soy products, and sometimes an array of raw ingredients.

★ **Momofuku Noodle Bar** NOODLES $$
(Map p66; ☎212-777-7773; www.momofuku.com/noodle-bar/; 171 First Ave btwn 10th & 11th Sts; mains $16-25; ⏲noon-11pm Mon-Thu & Sun, to 2am Fri & Sat; [S] L to 1st Ave, 6 to Astor Pl) Ramen and steamed buns are the name of the game at this infinitely creative Japanese eatery, part of the growing David Chang empire. Seating is on stools at a long bar or at communal tables. Momofuku's famous steamed chicken and pork buns ($9 for two) are recommended.

🍴 Chelsea, Meatpacking District & West (Greenwich) Village

★ **Chelsea Market** MARKET $
(Map p70; www.chelseamarket.com; 75 9th Ave; ⏲7am-9pm Mon-Sat, 8am-8pm Sun; [S] A/C/E to 14th St) This former cookie factory has been turned into an 800ft-long shopping concourse that caters to foodies with boutique bakeries, gelato shops, ethnic eats and a food court for gourmands.

Joe's Pizza PIZZA $
(Map p66; ☎212-366-1182; www.joespizzanyc.com; 7 Carmine St btwn Sixth Ave & Bleecker St; slices from $2.75; ⏲10am-4:30am Mon-Sun; [S] A/C/E, B/D/F, M to W 4th St, 1/2 to Christopher St-Sheridan Sq, 1/2 to Houston St) Joe's is the Meryl Streep of pizza parlors, collecting dozens of awards and accolades over the last three decades. No-frills pies are served up indiscriminately to students, tourists and celebrities alike.

Bonsignour SANDWICHES $
(Map p66; ☎212-229-9700; 35 Jane St at Eighth Ave; mains $7-12; ⏲7:30am-10pm, to 8pm Sun; [S] L to 8th Ave; A/C/E, 1/2/3 to 14th St) Nestled on a quiet Village street, this sandwich shop offers dozens of delicious choices as well as salads, frittatas and a wonderful beef chili. Get a sandwich or a chicken curry salad to go and wander down the street to Abingdon Sq for al fresco dining.

Ditch Plains SEAFOOD $$
(Map p66; ☎212-633-0202; www.ditch-plains.com; 29 Bedford St; ⏲11am-midnight; 👪; [S] A/C/E, B/D/F to W 4th St, 1 to Houston St) The sleek, metallic interior with wood booths is an inviting place to inhale celeb chef Marc Murphy's glammed-up seafood-shack food: oysters, mussels, fish tacos, fried clams, po' boys and more feed the masses until 2am daily.

Fatty Crab ASIAN $$
(Map p66; ☎212-352-3590; www.fattycrab.com; 643 Hudson St btwn Gansevoort & Horatio Sts; mains $16-28; ⏲noon-midnight Mon-Wed, to 2am Thu & Fri, 11am-2am Sat, 11am-midnight Sun; [S] L to 8th Ave; A/C/E, 1/2/3 to 14th St) The Fatty folks have done it again with their small Malaysian-inspired joint. It's super hip and always teeming with locals who swing by in droves to devour fish curries and pork belly accompanied by a signature selection of cocktails.

Tartine FRENCH $$
(Map p66; ☎212-229-2611; www.tartinecafenyc.com; 253 W 11th St btwn 4th St & Waverly Pl; mains $10-24; ⏲9am-10:30pm Mon-Sat, to 10pm Sun; [S] 1/2/3 to 14th St, 1/2 to Christopher St-Sheridan Sq, L to 8th Ave) Tartine is the corner bistro of your Frenchified dreams: wobbly stacks of chairs and tables, pink steaks and escargot and a good-cop-bad-cop duo of waitresses who indiscriminately bounce dishes and diners around the teeny-tiny room. It's BYOB.

Kin Shop THAI $$
(Map p66; ☎212-675-4295; www.kinshopnyc.com; 469 Sixth Ave; mains $9-28; ⏲11:30am-3pm Mon-Sun, 5:30-11pm Mon-Thu, 5:30-11:30pm Fri & Sat, 5-10pm Sun; [S] L to 6th Ave; 1/2/3, F/M to 14th St) The second avatar of Top Chef winner Harold Dieterle (the first being Perilla – also a great find – nearby) is this Thai-inspired joint. Curry pastes are crushed in-house – a testament to the from-scratch methods used to craft every item on the colorful menu.

Soccarat Paella Bar SPANISH $$
(Map p70; ☎212-462-1000; www.soccaratpaelabar.com; 259 W 19th St, near Eighth Ave; mains $22; ⏲noon-11pm, to 4pm Sun; 🌱; [S] 1 to 18th St) A cozy, narrow room dominated by a glass-topped communal table, Soccarat is famous for its heavenly, saffron-scented paellas filled with veggies, seafood and/or meat. Tapas are served too, but nothing compares to the rice.

99

Babbo
ITALIAN $$$

(Map p66; ☎212-777-0303; www.babbonyc.com; 110 Waverly Pl; mains $19-29; ⏱11:30am-11:15pm, from 5pm Sun; ⓢC/E, B/D/F to W 4th St; 1 to Christopher St-Sheridan Sq) This two-level split townhouse might be the best in celebrity chef Mario Batali's empire. Whether you order mint love letters, lamb's brain *francobolli* (small, stuffed ravioli) or pig's foot *milanese,* you'll find Batali at the top of his innovative, eclectic game. Reservations are in order.

✕ Union Square & Flatiron District & Gramercy Park

Shake Shack
BURGERS $

(Map p70; ☎212-989-6600; www.shakeshack.com; cnr 23rd St & Madison Ave; hamburger from $4.50; ⏱11am-11pm; ⓢR/W to 23rd St) Tourists line up in droves for the hamburgers and shakes at this Madison Square Park counter-window-serving institution.

★Eataly
ITALIAN $$

(Map p70; www.eatalyny.com; 200 Fifth Ave at 23rd St; ⏱hours vary; ⓢF, N/R, 6 to 23rd St) The Macy's of food courts, celebrity-chef Mario Batali's NYC empire now has a footprint to match his ambitions. A number of specialty dining halls, all with a different focus (pizza, fish, vegetables, meat, pasta) and the *pièce de résistance,* a rooftop beer garden, not to mention a coffee shop, gelateria and grocery, would overwhelm even a blogging gourmand.

Breslin
MODERN AMERICAN $$

(Map p70; 16 West 29th St; mains $18; ⏱7am-midnight; ⓢN/R to 28th St) It might be hard to hear yourself think and the hipster overflow from the attached uber-trendy Ace Hotel can rub some the wrong way... However, what really matters is that the pub-influenced meat-heavy menu by widely celebrated chef April Bloomfield doesn't disappoint. No reservations, so expect a wait.

✕ Midtown

99 Cent Pizza
PIZZERIA $

(Map p70; 473 Lexington Ave; pizza slice $1; ⏱9:30am-4:30am; ⓢS, 4/5/6, 7 to Grand Central-42nd St) It's not gourmet and doesn't claim to be, but if you're craving a good slice with a nice balance of tangy tomato sauce and creamy cheese, this barebones joint won't disappoint.

★Burger Joint
BURGERS $

(Map p70; www.parkermeridien.com/eat4.php; Le Parker Meridien, 119 W 56th St; burgers $7; ⏱11am-11:30pm; ⓢF to 57th St) With only a small neon burger as your clue, this speakeasy burger hut loiters behind the curtain in the lobby of the Le Parker Meridien hotel. You'll find graffiti-strewn walls, retro booths and attitude-loaded staff slapping up beef-n-patty brilliance.

Totto Ramen
JAPANESE $

(Map p70; www.tottoramen.com; 366 W 52nd St; ramen $9.50-12.50; ⏱noon-midnight Mon-Sat, 4-11pm Sun; ⓢC/E to 50th St) Write your name and number of guests on the clipboard by the door and wait for your (cash-only) ramen revelation. Skip the chicken and go for the pork, which sings in dishes like miso ramen (with fermented soybean paste, egg, scallion, bean sprouts, onion and home-made chili paste).

Café Edison
DINER $

(Map p70; ☎212-840-5000; 228 W 47th St, btwn Broadway & Eighth Ave; mains from $6; ⏱6am-9:30pm Mon-Sat, to 7:30pm Sun; ⓢN/Q/R to 49th St) Where else can you get a bologna sandwich? This landmark New York spot has been in business since the 1930s, serving up American diner classics like grilled cheese, hot corned beef, open-faced turkey sandwiches and cheese blintzes. Cash only.

Hangawi
KOREAN $$

(Map p70; ☎212-213-0077; www.hangawirestaurant.com; 12 E 32nd St btwn Fifth & Madison Aves; mains $17-25; ⏱noon-10:15pm Mon-Sat, 5-9:30pm Sun; ⓢB/D/F/M, N/Q/R to 34th St-Herald Sq) Sublime, flesh-free Korean is the draw at high-achieving Hangawi. Leave your shoes at the entrance and slip into a soothing, zen-like space of meditative music, soft low seating and clean, complexly flavored dishes.

Virgil's Real Barbecue
AMERICAN $$

(Map p70; ☎212-921-9494; 152 W 44th St btwn Broadway & Eighth Ave; mains $14-25; ⏱11:30am-midnight; ⓢN/R, S, W, 1/2/3, 7 to Times Sq-42nd St) Menu items cover the entire BBQ map, with Oklahoma State Fair corndogs, pulled Carolina pork and smoked Maryland ham sandwiches, and platters of sliced Texas beef brisket and Georgia chicken-fried steak.

Danji
KOREAN $$

(Map p70; www.danjinyc.com; 346 W 52nd St; plates $7-20; ⏱noon-10:30pm Mon-Thu, to 11:30pm Fri, 5:30-11:30pm Sat; ⓢC/E to 50th St) Young-gun chef Hooni Kim has captured tastebuds with

NEW YORK, NEW JERSEY & PENNSYLVANIA NEW YORK CITY

his Michelin-starred Korean 'tapas' served in a snug-and-slinky contemporary space. The celebrity dish on the menu (divided into 'traditional' and 'modern' options) are the sliders, a duo of *bulgogi* beef and spiced pork belly served on butter-grilled buns.

The Smith AMERICAN $$
(Map p70; www.thesmithnyc.com; 956 Second Ave at 51st St; mains $17-29; ⏰ Mon-Wed 7:30am-midnight, Thu & Fri to 1am, Sat 10am-1am, Sun to midnight; [S] 6 to 51st St) The Smith has sexed-up dining in the eastern throws of Midtown with its industrial-chic interior, buzzing bar and well-executed brasserie grub. The emphasis is on regional produce, retro American and Italian-inspired flavors and slick, personable service.

Sparks STEAKHOUSE $$$
(Map p70; www.sparkssteakhouse.com; 210 E 46th St btwn Second & Third Aves, Midtown East; mains $40; ⏰ noon-midnight Mon-Fri, 5-11:30pm Sat; [S] S, 4/5/6, 7 to Grand Central-42nd St) Get an honest-to-goodness New York steakhouse experience at this classic joint, a former mob hangout that's been around for nearly 50 years and still packs 'em in for a juicy carnivorous feed.

Taboon MEDITERRANEAN $$$
(Map p70; ☎ 212-713-0271; 773 Tenth Ave; mains $25-32; ⏰ 5-11pm Mon-Sat, 11am-10pm Sun; [S] C/E to 50th St) A white-domed oven grabs the eye as you enter this airy, stone-floored and brick-walled eatery. The food is a fusion from both sides of the Mediterranean: shrimp in shredded pastry, haloumi salad, lamb kabobs and various grilled-fish dishes.

🍴 Upper West Side

★ **Gray's Papaya** HOT DOGS $
(Map p80; ☎ 212-799-0243; 2090 Broadway at 72nd St; hot dog $2; ⏰ 24hr; [S] A/B/C, 1/2/3 to 72nd St) It doesn't get more New York than bellying up to this classic stand-up joint in the wake of a beer bender. The lights are bright, the color palette is 1970s and the hot dogs are unpretentiously good.

Barney Greengrass DELI $$
(Map p80; www.barneygreengrass.com; 541 Amsterdam Ave at 86th St; mains $9-18, bagel with cream cheese $5; ⏰ 8:30am-4pm Tue-Fri, to 5pm Sat & Sun; 👪; [S] 1 to 86th St) Old-school Upper Westsiders and pilgrims from other neighborhoods crowd this century-old 'sturgeon king' on weekends. It serves a long list of traditional if pricey Jewish delicacies, from bagels and lox to sturgeon scrambled with eggs and onions.

Josie's Restaurant HEALTH FOOD $$
(Map p80; ☎ 212-769-1212; 300 Amsterdam Ave; mains $14-22; ⏰ 11:30am-10pm Mon-Fri, 4-10:30pm Sat & Sun; 🌿; [S] 1/2/3 to 72nd St) Organic fare (with its provenance listed on the menu) that satisfies vegans, vegetarians and meat eaters alike has kept Josie's around for more than a decade.

Dovetail MODERN AMERICAN $$$
(Map p80; ☎ 212-362-3800; www.dovetailnyc.com; 103 W 77th St cnr Columbus Ave; tasting menu $85, mains $36-58; ⏰ 5:30-10pm Mon-Sat, 11:30am-10pm Sun; 🌿; [S] A/C, B to 81st St-Museum of Natural History, 1 to 79th St) Everything about this Michelin-starred restaurant is simple, from the decor (exposed brick, bare tables) to the uncomplicated seasonal menus focused on bracingly fresh produce and quality meats (think: pistachio-crusted duck with sunchokes, dates and spinach).

🍴 Upper East Side

★ **Earl's Beer & Cheese** AMERICAN $
(Map p80; www.earlsny.com; 1259 Park Ave btwn 97th & 98th Sts; grilled cheese $6-8, mains $8-17; ⏰ 4pm-midnight Tue-Fri, 11am-midnight Sat & Sun; [S] 6 to 96th St) Chef Corey Cova's comfort food outpost channels a hipster hunting vibe. Basic grilled cheese is a paradigm shifter, served with pork belly, fried egg and kimchi. There is also mac 'n' cheese and waffles (with foie gras), none of it like anything you've ever eaten.

Maya Mexican MEXICAN $$
(Map p80; www.modernmexican.com; 1191 First Ave; mains $13-28; ⏰ 11:30am-10pm Mon-Fri, from 10:30am Sat & Sun; [S] 4/5/6 to 59th St) Renovated Maya's looks something akin to an 18th-century Mexican hacienda, and the decor complements the powerful, mole-infused dishes as well as corn masa with *oaxaca* cheese and *chile poblano rajas* and seviche halibut.

Candle Cafe VEGAN $$
(Map p80; ☎ 212-472-0970; www.candlecafe.com; 1307 Third Ave btwn 74th & 75th Sts; mains $15-20; ⏰ 11:30am-10:30pm Mon-Sat, to 9:30pm Sun; 🌿; [S] 6 to 77th St) The moneyed, yoga set piles into this attractive vegan cafe, which serves a long list of sandwiches, salads, comfort food and market-driven specials. The specialty here is the house-made seitan.

★Sfoglia ITALIAN $$$

(Map p80; ☎212-831-1402; 1402 Lexington Ave at E 92nd St; mains $26; ⏲noon-10pm Mon-Sat, from 5:30pm Sun; [S]6 to 96th St) A darling of the critics, Sfoglia brought its winning combo of fresh seafood and homemade Italian from Nantucket to New York. Innovative pairings like wild mussels with tomato, garlic, salami and fennel pollen.

David Burke Townhouse MODERN AMERICAN $$$

(Map p80; ☎212-813-2121; www.davidburketownhouse.com; 133 E 61St; mains $20-55; ⏲11:45am-10:30pm Mon-Sat, 10:30am-9pm Sun; [S]F to Lexington Ave-63rd St; N/R, W to Lexington Ave-59th St) Restaurateur Donatella Arpaia and partner David Burke have created a fashionable though stylish scene in an upper East Side townhouse. Food however is the focus, like salmon with warm potato knish, pretzel-crusted crabcake and yellowfin tuna on salt-rock.

Harlem

Caffe Latte CAFE $

(Map p80; ☎212-222-2241; www.ilcaffelatte.com; 189 Malcolm X Blvd, near 119th St; ⏲8am-10pm Mon-Fri; ✎👪; [S]2/3 to 116th St) Full of students, seniors, old Harlem and new Harlem, Caffe Latte is fast becoming the place to meet and hang in the 'hood. Breakfasts feature deep rich coffee, omelettes, granola, pancakes and more.

Amy Ruth's Restaurant SOUTHERN $$

(Map p80; www.amyruthsharlem.com; 113 W 116th St near Malcolm X Blvd, Harlem; chicken & waffles $10, mains $12-20; ⏲11:30am-11pm Mon, 8:30am-11pm Tue-Thu, 8:30am-5:30pm Fri-Sat, 7:30am-11pm Sun; [S]B, C, 2/3 to 116th St) Tourists flock here for the specialty waffles: choose from sweet (chocolate, strawberry, blueberry, smothered in sautéed apples) or savory (paired with fried chicken, rib-eye or catfish). Smoked ham, chicken and dumplings are favorites as well.

★Red Rooster MODERN AMERICAN $$$

(Map p80; www.redroosterharlem.com; 310 Malcolm X Blvd btwn 125th & 126th Sts, Harlem; dinner mains $16-35; ⏲11:30am-10:30pm Mon-Fri, 10am-11pm Sat & Sun; [S]2/3 to 125th St) Something of a pioneer, chef Marcus Samuelson's sophisticated uptown venture has a downtown bistro vibe, with a variety of Southern, soul and new American cooking such as blackened catfish and creative sandwiches. The front bar area and breakfast nook has pastries and coffee.

Brooklyn

Of course it's impossible to begin to do justice to Brooklyn's eating options – it's as much a foodie's paradise as Manhattan. Virtually every ethnic cuisine has a significant presence somewhere in this borough. As far as neighborhoods close to Manhattan go: Williamsburg is chockablock with eateries, as are Fifth and Seventh Aves in Park Slope. Smith St is 'Restaurant Row' in the Carroll Gardens and Cobble Hill neighborhoods. Atlantic Ave, near Court St, has a number of excellent Middle Eastern restaurants and grocery stores.

Tom's Restaurant DINER $

(☎718-636-9738; 782 Washington Ave at Sterling Pl, Prospect Heights; ⏲6am-4pm; [S]2/3 to Eastern Pkwy-Brooklyn Museum) Inspiration for the eponymously named Suzanne Vega song, this old-school soda fountain diner's specialty is its variety of pancakes (eg mango walnut). Coffee and cookies are served to those waiting in the line that invariably snakes out the door on weekend mornings.

Sahadi's SELF-CATERING $

(www.sahadis.com; 187 Atlantic Ave btwn Court & Clinton Sts, Boerum Hill; ⏲9am-7pm Mon-Sat; ✎; [S]2/3, 4/5 to Borough Hall) The smell of fresh-roasted coffee and spices greets you as you enter this beloved Middle Eastern delicacies shop. The olive bar boasts two-dozen options and enough breads, cheeses, nuts and hummus to fulfill the self-catering needs of a whole battalion.

Mile End DELI $

(www.mileendbrooklyn.com; 97A Hoyt St, Boerum Hill; sandwiches $8-12; ⏲8am-4pm Mon & Tue, 8am-11pm Wed-Sat, 10am-10pm Sun; [S]A/C/G to Hoyt Schermerhorn Sts) Mile End is small, like its portions, but big on flavors. Try a smoked beef brisket on rye with mustard ($12) – the bread is sticky soft and the meat will melt in your mouth. The only buzzkill is the extra $1.50 charge for a pickle.

Café Glechik RUSSIAN $$

(☎718-616-0766; 3159 Coney Island Ave, Brighton Beach; cabbage rolls $11, kabobs $11-15, dumplings $7-9; ⏲11am-11pm; [S]B, Q to Brighton Beach) The dishes to get are the dumplings: *pelmeni* and *vareniki* with a wide assortment of stuffings. (Sour-cherry *vareniki* are the jam!) You'll also find classics like borscht, kabobs and hyper-sweet compote drinks. Cash only.

Al Di Là Trattoria
ITALIAN **$$**

(www.aldilatrattoria.com; 248 5th Ave cnr Carroll St, Park Slope; ⊙noon-10:30pm Mon-Fri, 5:30-11pm Sat & Sun; **S** R to Union St) Run by a husband-and-wife team from northern Italy, this cheery Park Slope trattoria serves handmade pastas and belly-warming classics (braised rabbit with buttery polenta). There's an excellent brunch (duck confit hash!) and a long list of Italian wines.

Roberta's
PIZZA **$$**

(www.robertaspizza.com; 261 Moore St near Bogart St, Bushwick; individual pizza $9-17, mains $13-28; ⊙11am-midnight; ⊘; **S** L to Morgan Ave) This warehouse restaurant in Bushwick consistently produces some of the best pizza in New York. Service can be lackadaisical and the waits long, but the brick-oven pies are the right combination of chewy and fresh.

Prime Meats
GERMAN **$$**

(www.frankspm.com; 465 Court St cnr Luquer St, Carroll Gardens; mains $17-32; ⊙10am-midnight Mon-Wed, to 1am Thu & Fri, 8am-1am Sat, to midnight Sun; **S** F, G to Carroll St) A pre-fab vintage spot in Carroll Gardens comes with lots of old-world flavor. The menu is all late-19th-century German, focusing on house-cured butchered meats and items like slow-braised beef sauerbraten with red cabbage.

🍷 Drinking & Nightlife

Watering holes come in many forms in this city: sleek lounges, pumping clubs, cozy pubs and booze-soaked dives – no smoke, though, thanks to city law. The majority are open to 4am, though closing (and opening) times do vary; most nightclubs are open from 10pm. Here's a highly selective sampling.

🍸 Downtown

★ Birreria
BEER GARDEN

(Map p70; www.eatalyny.com; 200 Fifth Ave at 23rd St; ⊙11:30am-midnight Sun-Wed, to 1am Thu-Sat ; **S** F, N/R, 6 to 23rd St) The crown jewel of Italian gourmet market Eataly is its rooftop beer garden tucked betwixt the Flatiron's corporate towers. A beer menu of encyclopedic proportions offers drinkers some of the best brews on the planet. The signature pork shoulder is your frosty one's soul mate.

Brandy Library
BAR

(Map p62; www.brandylibrary.com; 25 N Moore St at Varick St; ⊙5pm-1am Sun-Wed, 4pm-2am Thu, 4pm-4am Fri & Sat; **S** 1 to Franklin St) When sipping means serious business, settle into this uber-luxe library, with soothing reading lamps and club chairs facing backlit, floor-to-ceiling, bottle-filled shelves. Go for top-shelf cognac, malt scotch or 90-year-old brandies (prices range from $9 to $340).

Pravda
COCKTAIL BAR

(Map p66; ☎212-226-4944; 281 Lafayette St btwn Prince & Houston Sts; **S** B/D/F/V to Broadway-Lafayette St) This subterranean bar heavy with Soviet-era nostalgia has red-leather banquettes and inviting armchairs. Enjoy blinis, handsomely made cocktails and a bit of eavesdropping on neighboring apparatchiks from the fashion or banking industry.

DBA
BAR

(Map p66; ☎212-475-5097; www.drinkgoodstuff. com; 41 First Ave btwn 2nd & 3rd Sts; ⊙1pm-4am; **S** F/V to Lower East Side-2nd Ave) There are over 200 beers here, plus 130 single-malt scotches and a few dozen tequilas. There's a tiny plastic-chair patio in back, but most action is near the taps.

SOBs
CLUB

(Map p66; ☎212-243-4940; www.sobs.com; 204 Varick St btwn King & Houston Sts; cover charge $10-20; ⊙6:30pm-3am; **S** 1 to Houston St) Brazilian bossa nova, samba and other Latin vibes draw a mix of those who know how to move smoothly and sensually and those who like to watch.

Whiskey Tavern
COCKTAIL BAR

(Map p62; ☎212-374-9119; 79 Baxter St btwn Bayard & Walker Sts; **S** J/M/Z, N/Q/R/W, 6 to Canal St) An odd interloper in the Chinatown scene, Whiskey Tavern nevertheless has earned many fans for its uber-friendly bartenders, casual ambience free of pretension, reasonably priced drinks and outdoor rear patio in warm weather.

Louis 649
BAR

(Map p66; ☎212-673-1190; www.louis649.com; 649 E 9th St, near Ave C; ⊙6pm-4am; **S** L to 1st Ave) Beloved by its patrons for the affordable prices and down-home, no-frills decor. Tuesday nights are free tasting nights, when the owner brings in a liquor specialist to talk about their brew and liberally pours free shots.

Jimmy's No 43
BAR

(Map p66; ☎212-982-3006; www.jimmysno43.com; 43 E 7th St btwn Third & Second Aves; ⊙noon-2am Mon-Thu & Sun, to 4am Fri & Sat; **S** N/R to 8th St-NYU, F to 2nd Ave, 4/6 to Astor Pl) Barrels and stag antlers line the walls of this basement beer hall. Select from over 50 imported favorites, to go with a round of delectable bar nibbles.

124 Old Rabbit Club BAR
(Map p66; ☎212-254-0575; 124 MacDougal St; ⓢA/C/E, B/D/F, M to W 4th St, 1/2 to Christopher St-Sheridan Sq, 1/2 to Houston St) You'll wanna pat yourself on the back when you find this speakeasy-style joint (hint: look for the '124' and ring the buzzer). Reward yourself with a quenching stout or one of the dozens of imported brews.

Half King PUB
(Map p70; ☎212-462-4300; www.thehalfking.com; 505 W 23rd St at Tenth Ave; ⊙11am-4am Mon-Fri, 9am-4am Sat & Sun; ⓢC/E to 23rd St) A unique marriage of cozy pub and sophisticated writers' lair, you'll often experience top-notch literary readings in this wood-accented, candlelit watering hole. During warm weather, there's also a front sidewalk cafe and backyard patio.

Bar Next Door BAR
(Map p66; ☎212-529-5945; 129 MacDougal St btwn W 3rd & W 4th Sts; ⊙6pm-2am Sun-Thu, to 3am Fri & Sat; ⓢA/C/E, B/D/F/V to W 4th St) The basement of this restored townhouse is all low ceilings, exposed brick and romantic lighting. You'll find mellow, live jazz nightly, as well as a tasty Italian menu at the restaurant next door, La Lanterna di Vittorio.

Pyramid Club CLUB
(Map p66; ☎212-228-4888; www.thepyramidclub. com; 101 Ave A; cover charge $5-10; ⊙11pm-4am Mon, 8:30pm-1am Tue & Sun, 9pm-4am Thu & Sat, 10pm-4am Fri; ⓢF/V to Lower East Side-2nd Ave) You'll find rather beat-up stools and sticky wooden floors, and if you like cheap drinks and sweaty, unselfconscious dancing to '80s tunes, then Thursdays are for you. Gay night is on Friday.

Sway Lounge CLUB
(Map p66; ☎212-620-5220; www.swaylounge.com; 305 Spring St; ⊙9pm-3am Mon & Thu; ⓢC/E to Spring St) Small, seductive and sleek with an elegant Moroccan decor, Sway's got a tough door policy, but there's room to dance to '80s on Thursday nights, rock and hip-hop Fridays, and DJs like Mark Ronson and DJ Herschel other nights.

Mehanata CLUB
(Map p66; ☎212-625-0981; www.mehanata.com; 113 Ludlow St; ⓢF, J/M/Z to Delancey St-Essex St) The 'Bulgarian Bar' is still gypsy heaven for East Euro–chic and indie-popsters. East Euro DJs spin some nights, and belly dancers and 'gypsy bands' take the small stage for jumping-in-place dancers.

Sapphire CLUB
(Map p66; ☎212-777-5153; www.sapphirenyc. com; 249 Eldridge St at E Houston St; admission $5; ⊙7pm-4am; ⓢF/V to Lower East Side-2nd Ave) This tiny, hoppin' venue has survived the crowds of the mid-'90s Ludlow St boom with its hip factor intact, and its $5 cover keeps snootiness at a minimum. The tightly packed dance floor gets lit with a mix of R&B, rap, disco and funk.

Santos Party House CLUB
(Map p62; ☎212-584-5492; www.santospartyhouse.com; 96 Lafayette St; cover $5-15; ⊙10pm-4am) Shaggy rocker Andrew WK created this bi-level 8000-sq-ft cavernous bare-bones dance club. Devoted to good times and good vibes, this place requires that you check your attitude at the door – funk to electronica, and WK spins some nights.

Cielo CLUB
(Map p66; ☎212-645-5700; www.cieloclub.com; 18 Little W 12th St; cover charge $15-25; ⊙10:30pm-5am Mon-Sat; ⓢA/C/E, L to 8th Ave-14th St) Known for its intimate space and kick-ass sound system, this space-age-looking Meatpacking District staple packs in a fashionable, multiculti crowd nightly for its blend of tribal, old-school house and soulful grooves.

Midtown

★Russian Vodka Room BAR
(Map p70; ☎212-307-5835; 265 W 52nd St, btwn Eighth Ave & Broadway; ⓢC/E to 50th St) Actual Russians aren't uncommon at this swanky and welcoming bar. The lighting is dark and the corner booths intimate, but more importantly the dozens of flavored vodkas, from cranberry to horseradish, are fun to experiment with.

Rudy's Bar & Grill BAR
(Map p70; 627 Ninth Ave; ⊙8am-4am; ⓢA/C/E to 42nd St-Port Authority Bus Terminal) This semi-dive bar – neighborhood newcomers and professional types rub beer-soaked shoulders with hard-core drinkers – is a good place for cheap beer and even greasy hot dogs, if you don't mind not being able to hear yourself think.

Lantern's Keep COCKTAIL BAR
(Map p70; ☎212-453-4287; www.thelanternskeep. com; Iroquois Hotel, 49 W 44th St; ⊙5pm-midnight Tue-Sat; ⓢB/D/F/M to 42nd St-Bryant Park) Cross the lobby of the Iroquois Hotel and slip into this dark, intimate cocktail salon. Its

specialty is pre-Prohibition libations, shaken and stirred by passionate, personable mixologists. Reservations recommended.

Top of the Strand
COCKTAIL BAR

(Map p70; www.topofthestrand.com; Strand Hotel, 33 W 37th St btwn Fifth & Sixth Aves; ♿; Ⓢ B/D/F/M to 34th St) For that 'Oh my God, I'm in New York' feeling, head to the Strand hotel's rooftop bar, order a martini (extra dirty) and drop your jaw (discreetly). Sporting slinky cabanas and a sliding glass roof, its view of the Empire State Building is unforgettable.

Pacha
CLUB

(Map p70; ☎ 212-209-7500; www.pachanyc.com; 618 W 46th St btwn Eleventh Ave & West Side Hwy; admission $20-40; Ⓢ A/C/E to 42nd St-Port Authority) A massive and spectacular place, this is 30,000 sq ft and four levels of glowing, sleek spaces and cozy seating nooks that rise up to surround the main dance-floor atrium. Big-name DJs are always on tap.

Morrell Wine Bar & Café
BAR, CAFE

(Map p70; ☎ 212-262-7700; 1 Rockefeller Plaza, W 48th St btwn Fifth & Sixth Aves; ⊘ 11:30am-11pm Mon-Sat, noon-6pm Sun; Ⓢ B/D/F/M to 47th-50th Sts-Rockefeller Center) The list of vinos at this pioneering wine bar is over 2000 long, with a whopping 150 available by the glass. And the airy, split-level room, right across from the famous skating rink, is equally as intoxicating.

Jimmy's Corner
BAR

(Map p70; 140 W 44th St btwn Sixth & Seventh Aves, Midtown West; ⊘ 10am-4am; Ⓢ N/Q/R, 1/2/3, 7 to 42nd St-Times Sq; B/D/F/M to 42nd St-Bryant Park) This skinny, welcoming, completely unpretentious dive off Times Square is run by an old boxing trainer – as if you wouldn't guess by all the framed photos of boxing greats. The jukebox covers Stax to Miles Davis.

PJ Clarke's
BAR

(Map p70; www.pjclarkes.com; 915 Third Ave at 55th St, Midtown East; Ⓢ E/M to Lexington Ave-53rd St) A bastion of old New York, this lovingly worn wooden saloon has been straddling the scene since 1884. Choose a jukebox tune, order a round of crab cakes, and settle in with a come-one-and-all crowd.

Réunion Surf
BAR

(Map p70; 357 W 44th St at Ninth Ave; ⊘ 5:30pm-2am, to 4am Thu-Sat) Swanky Tiki-themed bar and restaurant serving delicious French South Pacific cuisine, such as banana-leaf-steamed mahi mahi.

On the Rocks
COCKTAIL BAR

(Map p70; 696 Tenth Ave, btwn 48th & 49th Sts; ⊘ 5pm-4am) Whiskey nerds will delight at this cubbyhole-sized space.

Therapy
GAY

(Map p70; www.therapy-nyc.com; 348 W 52nd St btwn Eighth & Ninth Aves; Ⓢ C/E, 1 to 50th St) Multileveled, airy and sleekly contemporary, Therapy is a longstanding gay Hell's Kitchen hot spot. Theme nights abound, from stand-up comedy to musical shows.

🍸 Uptown

79th Street Boat Basin
BAR

(Map p80; W 79th St, in Riverside Park; ⊘ noon-11pm) A covered, open-sided party spot under the ancient arches of a park overpass, this is an Upper West Side favorite once spring hits. Order a pitcher, some snacks and enjoy the sunset view over the Hudson River.

Bemelmans Bar
LOUNGE

(Map p80; www.thecarlyle.com/dining/bemelmans_bar; Carlyle Hotel, 35 E 76th St at Madison Ave; ⊘ noon-2am Mon-Sat, to 12:30am Sun; Ⓢ 6 to 77th St) Waiters wear white jackets, a baby grand piano is always being played and Ludwig Bemelman's *Madeline* murals surround you. It's a classic spot for a serious cocktail.

Barcibo Enoteca
WINE BAR

(Map p80; www.barciboenoteca.com; 2020 Broadway cnr 69th St; ⊘ 4:30pm-2am; Ⓢ 1/2/3 to 72nd St) Just north of Lincoln Center, this casual chic marble-table spot is ideal for sipping, with a long list of vintages from all over Italy, including 40 different varieties sold by the glass.

Auction House
BAR

(Map p80; ☎ 212-427-4458; 300 E 89th St; ⊘ 7:30pm-4am; Ⓢ 4/5/6 to 86th St) Dark maroon doors lead into a sexy, candlelit hangout that's perfect for a relaxing drink. Victorian-style couches and fat, overstuffed easy chairs are strewn about the wood-floored rooms.

Subway Inn
BAR

(Map p80; 143 E 60th St btwn Lexington & Third Aves; Ⓢ 4/5/6 to 59th St; N/Q/R to Lexington Ave-59th St) An old-geezer watering hole with cheap drinks and loads of authenticity. The entire scene – from the vintage neon sign to the well-worn red booths – is truly reminiscent of bygone days.

Dead Poet BAR
(Map p80; www.thedeadpoet.com; 450 Amsterdam Ave btwn 81st & 82nd Sts; 🕑9am-4am Mon-Sat, noon-4am Sun; [S]1 to 79th St) This mahogany-paneled pub has been a neighborhood favorite for over a decade, with a mix of locals and students nursing pints of Guinness and cocktails named after dead poets.

Brooklyn

★**Commodore** BAR
(366 Metropolitan Ave cnr Havenmeyer St, Williamsburg; 🕑4pm-midnight Sun-Thu, to 1am Fri & Sat; [S]L to Lorimer St) This corner bar is a faux '70s recreation room with plenty of wood paneling and a few big booths to spread out in. Order a mint julep or a sloe gin fizz and play vintage arcade games for free.

61 Local BEER GARDEN
(www.61local.com; 61 Bergen St btwn Smith St & Boerum Pl, Cobble Hill; snacks $1-7, sandwiches $4-8; 🕑11am-midnight Sun-Thu, to 1am Fri & Sat; [S]F, G to Bergen) A roomy brick-and-wood hall in Cobble Hill manages to be both chic and warm, with large communal tables, a mellow vibe and a good selection of craft beers. There's a simple menu of charcuterie and other snacks.

Maison Premiere COCKTAIL BAR
(www.maisonpremiere.com; 298 Bedford Ave btwn 1st & Grand Sts, Williamsburg; 🕑4pm-4am Mon-Fri, noon-4am Sat & Sun; [S]L to Bedford Ave) This old-timey place features a chemistry lab–style bar full of syrups and essences and suspendered bartenders to mix them all up. The epic cocktail list includes more than 20 absinthe drinks and a raw bar provides a long list of snacks on the half shell.

Zabloski's BAR
(☎718-384-1903; 107 N 6th St btwn Berry St & Wythe Ave, Williamsburg; 🕑2pm-4am; [S]L to Bedford Ave) This welcoming brick-lined spot in Williamsburg has cheap beer, chill bartenders, a pinball machine, a dart board and a pool table. Snag the table by the roll-down gate during happy hour and watch the street come alive at night.

Union Hall BAR
(☎718-638-4400; 702 Union St btwn Fifth & Sixth Aves; 🕑4pm-4am Mon-Fri, noon-4am Sat & Sun; [S]M, R to Union St; 2/3 to Bergen St; F to 7th Ave) In Park Slope, head to this creatively idiosyncratic bar – leather chairs à la a snooty London social club, walls lined with bookshelves and two bocce courts, plus live music downstairs and an outdoor patio.

Weather Up COCKTAIL BAR
(589 Vanderbilt Ave btwn Bergen & Dean Sts; 🕑Tue-Sun; [S]2/3 to Bergen St; B, Q to 7th Ave) No signage marks the exterior of this dark and shadowy Prospect Heights cocktail-centric speakeasy-like neighborhood favorite.

Radegast Hall & Biergarten BEER GARDEN
(www.radegasthall.com; 113 N 3rd St at Berry St, Williamsburg; 🕑4pm-4am Mon-Fri, noon-4am Sat & Sun; [S]L to Bedford Ave) Rowdy Williamsburg spot with excellent veal schnitzel.

☆ Entertainment

Those with unlimited fuel and appetites can gorge themselves on a seemingly infinite number of entertainments – from Broadway shows to performance art in someone's Brooklyn living room, and everything in between. *New York* magazine and the weekend editions of the *New York Times* are great guides for what's on once you arrive.

Live Music

★**Joe's Pub** LIVE MUSIC
(Map p66; ☎212-539-8778; www.joespub.com; Public Theater, 425 Lafayette St btwn Astor Pl & 4th St; [S]R/W to 8th St-NYU; 6 to Astor Pl) Part cabaret theater, part rock and new-indie venue, this small and lovely supper club hosts a wonderful variety of styles, voices and talent.

Rockwood Music Hall LIVE MUSIC
(Map p66; ☎212-477-4155; www.rockwoodmusichall.com; 196 Allen St btwn Houston & Stanton Sts; [S]F/V to Lower East Side-2nd Ave) This breadbox-sized two-room concert space features a rapid-fire flow of bands and singer-songwriters, no cover, and a max of one hour per band.

55 Bar LIVE MUSIC
(Map p66; ☎212-929-9883; www.55bar.com; 55 Christopher St at Seventh Ave; cover charge $3-15, 2-drink minimum; 🕑1pm-4am; [S]1 to Christopher St-Sheridan Sq) This friendly basement dive is great for low-key shows without high cover. Regular performances twice nightly by quality artists-in-residence and some blues bands.

Bowery Ballroom LIVE MUSIC
(Map p66; ☎212-533-2111; www.boweryballroom.com; 6 Delancey St at Bowery St; 🕑performance times vary; [S]J/M/Z to Bowery St) This terrific, medium-sized venue has the perfect sound and feel for more blown-up indie-rock acts (The Shins, Stephen Malkmus, Patti Smith).

Le Poisson Rouge LIVE MUSIC
(Map p66; ☎212-505-3474; www.lepoissonrouge.com; 158 Bleecker St; [S] A/C/E, B/D/F/V to W 4th St-Washington Sq) This Bleecker St basement club is one of the premier venues for experimental contemporary, from classical to indie rock to electro-acoustic.

Mercury Lounge LIVE MUSIC
(Map p66; ☎212-260-4700; www.mercurylou ngenyc.com; 217 E Houston St btwn Essex & Ludlow Sts; cover charge $8-15; ⏲4pm-4am; [S] F/V to Lower East Side-2nd Ave) The Mercury dependably pulls in a cool new or cool comeback band everyone downtown wants to see.

Music Hall of Williamsburg LIVE MUSIC
(www.musichallofwilliamsburg.com; 66 N 6th St btwn Wythe & Kent Aves, Williamsburg; [S] L to Bedford Ave) This popular Williamsburg music venue is *the* place to see indie bands in Brooklyn. (For many groups traveling through New York, this is their one and only spot.)

BB King Blues Club & Grill BLUES, JAZZ
(Map p70; ☎212-997-4144; www.bbkingblues.com; 237 W 42nd St btwn Seventh & Eighth Aves; [S] N/R/W, 1/2/3, 7 to 42nd St-Times Sq) In the heart of Times Square offers old-school blues along with rock, folk and reggae acts.

Bargemusic CLASSICAL MUSIC
(www.bargemusic.org; Fulton Ferry Landing, Brooklyn Heights; tickets $35; 👪; [S] A/C to High St) Exceptionally talented classical musicians perform in this intimate space, a decommissioned barge docked under the Brooklyn Bridge.

Highline Ballroom LIVE MUSIC
(Map p70; ☎212-414-5994; 431 W 16th St, btwn Ninth & Tenth Aves) A classy Chelsea venue with an eclectic lineup, from Mandy Moore to Moby.

Beacon Theatre LIVE MUSIC
(Map p80; www.beacontheatre.com; 2124 Broadway btwn 74th & 75th Sts; [S] 1/2/3 to 72nd St) This Upper West Side venue hosts big acts in an environment that's more intimate than a big concert arena.

Radio City Music Hall CONCERT VENUE
(Map p70; ☎212-247-4777; www.radiocity.com; Sixth Ave, at W 50th St) The architecturally grand concert hall in Midtown hosts the likes of Barry Manilow and Cirque de Soleil and of course the famous Christmas spectacular.

Delancey LIVE MUSIC
(Map p66; ☎212-254-9920; www.thedelancey.com; 168 Delancey St at Clinton St; [S] F, J/M/Z to Delancey-Essex Sts) Great indie-band bookings.

Irving Plaza LIVE MUSIC
(Map p70; www.irvingplaza.com; 17 Irving Pl at 15th St; [S] L, N/Q/R/W, 4/5/6 to 14th St-Union Sq) A great in-between stage for quirky mainstream acts. There's a cozy floor around the stage, and good views from the mezzanine.

JAZZ

Second only to New Orleans, Harlem was an early home to a flourishing jazz scene and one of its principal beating hearts. The neighborhood fostered greats like Duke Ellington, Charlie Parker, John Coltrane and Thelonius Monk. From bebop to free improvisation, in classic art-deco clubs and at intimate jam sessions, Harlem and other important venues scattered throughout the city, especially around the Village, continue to foster old-timers and talented newcomers alike. Tune in to **WKCR** (89.9 FM) for jazz and especially from 8:20am to 9:30am Monday through Friday for Phil Schaap's 30-plus-year-old program in which he dazzles listeners with his encyclopedic knowledge and appreciation for the art form.

Smalls (Map p66; ☎212-252-5091; www.smallsjazzclub.com; 183 W 4th St; cover $20) is a subterranean jazz dungeon that rivals the world-famous **Village Vanguard** (Map p66; ☎212-255-4037; www.villagevanguard.com; 178 Seventh Ave at 11th St; [S] 1/2/3 to 14th St) in terms of sheer talent. Of course, the latter has hosted every major star of the past 50 years; there's a two-drink minimum and a serious no-talking policy.

Heading uptown, **Dizzy's Club Coca-Cola: Jazz at the Lincoln Center** (Map p80; ☎t212-258-9595; www.jazzatlincolncenter.org; Time Warner Center, Broadway at 60th St; [S] A/C, B/D, 1 to 59th St-Columbus Circle), one of Lincoln Center's three jazz venues, has stunning views overlooking Central Park and nightly shows featuring top lineups. Further north on the Upper West Side, check out the **Smoke Jazz & Supper Club-Lounge** (Map p80; ☎212-864-6662; www.smokejazz.com; 2751 Broadway, btwn W 105th & 106th Sts), which gets crowded on weekends.

Webster Hall CLUB
(Map p66; ☎212-353-1600; www.websterhall.com; 125 E 11th St, near Third Ave; ⏰10pm-4am Thu-Sat; [S]L, N/Q/R/W, 4/5/6 to 14th St-Union Sq) The granddaddy of dancehalls. You'll get cheap drinks, eager young things ready to dance and enough room to really work up a sweat.

Theater

In general, 'Broadway' productions are staged in the lavish, early-20th-century theaters surrounding Times Square. You'll choose your theater based on its production – *The Book of Mormon, Spider-Man: Turn off the Dark, Lion King*. Evening performances begin at 8pm.

'Off Broadway' simply refers to shows performed in smaller spaces (500 seats or fewer), which is why you'll find many just around the corner from Broadway venues, as well as elsewhere in town. 'Off-off Broadway' events include readings, experimental and cutting-edge performances and improvisations held in spaces with fewer than 100 seats; these venues are primarily downtown. Some of the world's best theater happens in these more intimate venues before moving to Broadway.

Choose from current shows by checking print publications, or a website such as **Theater Mania** (☎212-352-3101; www.theatermania.com). You can purchase tickets through **Telecharge** (☎212-239-6200; www.telecharge.com) and **Ticketmaster** (☎800-448-7849, 800-745-3000; www.ticketmaster.com) for standard ticket sales, or **TKTS ticket booths** (www.tdf.org/tkts; cnr Front & John Sts; ⏰11am-6pm Mon-Sat, to 4pm Sun; [S]A/C to Broadway-Nassau; 2/3, 4/5, J/Z to Fulton St) for same-day tickets to a selection of Broadway and off-Broadway musicals at up to 50% off regular prices.

★**Public Theater** THEATER
(Map p66; ☎212-539-8500; www.publictheater.org; 425 Lafayette St, btwn Astor Pl & E 4th St; [S]R/N to 8th Street, 6 to Astor Place)

St Ann's Warehouse THEATER
(☎718-254-8779; www.stannswarehouse.org; 29 Jay St, Dumbo; [S]A/C to High St)

PS 122 THEATER
(Map p66; ☎212-477-5288; www.ps122.org; 150 First Ave, at E 9th St)

Playwrights Horizons THEATER
(Map p70; ☎tickets 212-279-4200; www.playwrightshorizons.org; 416 W 42nd St btwn Ninth & Tenth Aves; [S]A/C/E to 42nd St-Port Authority Bus Terminal)

New York Theater Workshop THEATER
(Map p66; ☎212-460-5475; www.nytw.org; 79 E 4th St btwn Second & Third Aves; [S]F/V to Lower East Side-2nd Ave)

Comedy

From lowbrow prop comics to experimental conceptual humor, there's a venue for every taste and budget. More-established ones push the alcohol with drink minimums.

★**Upright Citizens Brigade Theatre** COMEDY
(Map p70; ☎212-366-9176; www.ucbtheatre.com; 307 W 26th St btwn Eighth & Ninth Aves; cover charge $5-8; [S]C/E to 23rd St) Improv venue featuring well-known, emerging and probably-won't-emerge comedians in a small basement theater nightly.

Village Lantern COMEDY
(Map p66; ☎212-260-7993; www.villagelantern.com; 167 Bleecker St; [S]A/B/C/D/F/M to W 4th St) Nightly alternative comedy underneath a bar of the same name.

Caroline's on Broadway COMEDY
(Map p70; ☎212-757-4100; www.carolines.com; 1626 Broadway at 50th St; [S]N/Q/R to 49th St, 1 to 50th St) One of the best-known places in the city, and host to the biggest names on the circuit.

Cinemas

Long lines in the evenings and on weekends are the norm. It's recommended that you call and buy your tickets in advance (unless it's midweek, midday or for a film that's been out for months already). Most cinemas are handled either through **Movie Fone** (☎212-777-3456; www.moviefone.com) or **Fandango** (www.fandango.com). You'll have to pay an extra $1.50 per ticket, but it's worth it. Large chain theaters with stadium seating are scattered throughout the city, including several in the Times Square and Union Sq areas. In summer free outdoor screenings blossom throughout the city on rooftops and in park spaces.

Film Forum CINEMA
(Map p66; ☎212-727-8110; www.filmforum.com; 209 W Houston St btwn Varick St & Sixth Ave; ⏰daily; 👪; [S]1 to Houston St) The long and narrow theaters can't dent cineasts love for this institution showing revivals, classics and documentaries.

IFC Center CINEMA
(Map p66; ☎212-924-7771; www.ifccenter.com; 323 Sixth Ave at 3rd St; [S]A/C/E, B/D/F/V to W 4th St-Washington Sq) Formerly the Waverly, this

three-screen art-house cinema shows new indies, cult classics and foreign films – and the popcorn is organic.

Landmark Sunshine Cinema CINEMA
(Map p66; ☎212-358-7709; www.landmarktheatres.com; 143 E Houston St at Forsyth St; [S] F/V to Lower East Side-2nd Ave) Housed in a former Yiddish theater; shows first-run indies.

Anthology Film Archives CINEMA
(Map p66; ☎212-505-5181; www.anthologyfilmarchives.org; 32 Second Ave at 2nd St; [S] F/V to Lower East Side-2nd Ave) Film studies majors head to this schoolhouse-like building for independent and avant-garde cinema.

Performing Arts

World-class performers and venues mean the city is a year-round mecca for arts lovers.

Every top-end genre has a stage at the massive Lincoln Center (p77) complex. Its Avery Fisher Hall is the showplace of the New York Philharmonic, while Alice Tully Hall houses the Chamber Music Society of Lincoln Center, and the New York State Theater is home to the New York City Ballet. Great drama is found at both the Mitzi E Newhouse and Vivian Beaumont theaters; and frequent concerts at the Juilliard School. But the biggest draw is the Metropolitan Opera House, home to the Metropolitan Opera and American Ballet Theater.

★**Carnegie Hall** LIVE MUSIC
(Map p70; ☎212-247-7800; www.carnegiehall.org; W 57th St & Seventh Ave; [S] N/Q/R to 57th St-7th Ave) Since 1891, the historic Carnegie Hall has hosted performances by the likes of Tchaikovsky, Mahler and Prokofiev, as well as Stevie Wonder, Sting and Tony Bennett. Today its three halls host visiting philharmonics, the New York Pops orchestra and various world-class musicians (mostly closed in July and August). Before or after a performance, check out the **Rose Museum** for a history of the institution.

★**Brooklyn Academy of Music** PERFORMING ARTS
(BAM; www.bam.org; 30 Lafayette Ave at Ashland Pl, Fort Greene; [S] D, N/R to Pacific St, B, Q, 2/3, 4/5 to Atlantic Ave) Sort of a Brooklyn version of the Lincoln Center – in its all-inclusiveness rather than its vibe, which is much edgier – the spectacular academy also hosts everything from modern dance to opera, cutting-edge theater and music concerts.

Symphony Space LIVE MUSIC
(Map p80; ☎212-864-5400; www.symphonyspace.org; 2537 Broadway btwn 94th & 95th Sts; 👪; [S] 1/2/3 to 96th St) A multigenre space with several facilities in one. This Upper West Side gem is home to many performance series as well as theater, cabaret, comedy, dance and world-music concerts throughout the week.

Sports

The uber-successful **New York Yankees** (☎718-293-6000, tickets 877-469-9849; www.yankees.com; tickets $20-300) play at **Yankee Stadium** (☎718-293-6000, tickets 877-469-9849; www.yankees.com; E 161st St at River Ave; tours $20; 👪; [S] B, D, 4 to 161st St-Yankee Stadium), while the more historically beleaguered **New York Mets** (www.mets.com; tickets $12-102) play at **Citi Field** (126th St, at Roosevelt Ave, Flushing, Queens; [S] 7 to Mets-Willets Pt).

For less-grand settings but no-less-pleasant outings, check out the minor-league **Staten Island Yankees** (☎718-720-9265; www.siyanks.com; tickets $12; 🕒 ticket office 9am-5pm Mon-Fri, 10am-3pm Sat) at **Richmond County Bank Ballpark** (75 Richmond Terrace, Staten Island; ⛴ Staten Island Ferry) or the **Brooklyn Cyclones** (☎718-449-8497; www.brooklyncyclones.com; tickets $8-16) at **MCU Park** (1904 Surf Ave & W 17th St, Coney Island; [S] D/F, N/Q to Coney Island-Stillwell Ave).

For basketball, you can get courtside with the NBA's **New York Knicks** (Map p70; ☎212-465-6073, tickets 866-858-0008; www.nyknicks.com; tickets $13-330) at **Madison Square Garden** (Map p70; www.thegarden.com; Seventh Ave btwn 31st & 33rd Sts; [S] 1/2/3 to 34th St-Penn Station), called the 'mecca of basketball.' Or check out the rejuvenated franchise of the **Brooklyn Nets** (www.nba.com/nets; tickets from $15), previously the New Jersey Nets, who played their inaugural season at the **Barclays Center** (www.barclayscenter.com; cnr Flatbush & Atlantic Aves, Prospect Heights; [S] B/D, N/Q/R, 2/3, 4/5 to Atlantic Ave) in downtown Brooklyn in 2012. Also playing at Madison Square Garden, the women's WNBA league team **New York Liberty** (Map p70; ☎212-564-9622, tickets 212-465-6073; www.nyliberty.com; tickets $10-85) provides a more laid-back time.

New York City's NFL (pro-football) teams, the **Giants** (www.giants.com) and **Jets** (www.newyorkjets.com), share **MetLife Stadium** in East Rutherford, New Jersey.

Shopping

While chain stores have proliferated, turning once-idiosyncratic blocks into versions of generic strip malls, NYC is still the best American city for shopping. It's not unusual for shops – especially downtown boutiques – to stay open until 10pm or 11pm.

Downtown

Lower Manhattan is where you'll find across-the-board bargains, as well as more of the small, stylish boutiques. Downtown's coolest offerings are in NoLita (just east of SoHo), the East Village and the Lower East Side. SoHo has more expensive and equally fashionable stores, while Broadway from Union Sq to Canal St is lined with big retailers like H&M and Urban Outfitters, as well as dozens of jeans and shoe stores. The streets of Chinatown are filled with knock-off designer handbags, jewelry, perfume and watches. For coveted designer labels stroll through the Meatpacking District around 14th St and Ninth Ave.

★**Strand Book Store** BOOKS
(Map p66; ☎212-473-1452; www.strandbooks.com; 828 Broadway at 12th St; 🕐9:30am-10:30pm Mon-Sat, 11am-10:30pm Sun; [S] L, N/Q/R/W, 4/5/6 to 14th St-Union Sq) The city's preeminent bibliophile warehouse, selling new and used books.

★**Century 21** FASHION
(Map p62; www.c21stores.com; 22 Cortlandt St btwn Church St & Broadway; 🕐7:45am-9pm Mon-Wed, to 9:30pm Thu & Fri, 10am-9pm Sat, 11am-8pm Sun; [S] A/C, J/Z, 2/3, 4/5 to Fulton St) A four-level department store loved by New Yorkers of every income. It's shorthand for designer bargains.

J&R Music & Computer World MUSIC
(Map p62; www.jr.com; 15-23 Park Row; [S] A/C, J/Z, M, 2/3, 4/5 to Fulton St-Broadway-Nassau St) Every electronic need, especially computer and camera related, can be satisfied here.

A-1 Records MUSIC
(Map p66; ☎212-473-2870; 439 E 6th St btwn First Ave & Ave A; 🕐1-9pm; [S] F/V to Lower East Side-2nd Ave) The East Village is home to New York's best selection of vinyl.

Economy Candy CANDY
(Map p66; ☎212-254-1531; www.economycandy.com; 108 Rivington St at Essex St; 🕐9am-6pm Sun-Fri, 10am-5pm Sat; [S] F, J/M/Z to Delancey St-Essex St) Bringing sweetness to the 'hood since 1937, this candy shop is stocked with floor-to-ceiling goods in package and bulk.

Trash & Vaudeville CLOTHING
(Map p66; 4 St Marks Pl; [S] 6 to Astor Pl) The capital of punk-rockerdom, Trash & Vaudeville was the veritable costume closet for singing celebs when the East Village played host to a much grittier scene.

Philip Williams Posters VINTAGE
(Map p62; www.postermuseum.com; 122 Chambers St btwn Church St & W Broadway; 🕐11am-7pm Tue-Sat; [S] A/C, 1/2/3 to Chambers St) You'll find over half a million posters in this cavernous treasure trove, from oversized French advertisements for perfume and cognac to Soviet film posters.

Apple Store COMPUTERS, ELECTRONICS
(Map p70; ☎212-444-3400; www.apple.com; 401 W 14th St at Ninth Ave; 🕐11am-8pm Mon-Fri, noon-7pm Sat & Sun; [S] A/C/E to 14th St, L to 8th Ave) Pilgrims flock here for shiny new gadgets.

Midtown & Uptown

Midtown's Fifth Ave and the Upper East Side's Madison Ave have the famous high-end fashion and clothing by international designers. Times Square has supersized chain stores. Chelsea has more unique boutiques, though like the Upper West Side it too has been colonized by banks, drugstores and big-box retailers.

Tiffany & Co JEWELRY, HOMEWARES
(Map p70; www.tiffany.com; 727 Fifth Ave; [S] F to 57th St) This famous jeweler, with the trademark clock-hoisting Atlas over the door, carries fine diamond rings, watches, necklaces etc, as well as crystal and glassware.

Saks Fifth Ave DEPARTMENT STORE
(Map p70; www.saksfifthavenue.com; 611 Fifth Ave at 50th St; [S] B/D/F/M to 47th-50th Sts-Rockefeller Center, E/M to 5th Ave-53rd St) Complete with beautiful vintage elevators, Saks' 10-floor flagship store fuses old-world glamour with solid service and must-have labels.

Macy's DEPARTMENT STORE
(Map p70; www.macys.com; 151 W 34th St at Broadway; [S] B/D/F/M, N/Q/R to 34th St-Herald Sq) The grande dame of Midtown department stores sells everything from jeans to kitchen appliances.

Bloomingdale's DEPARTMENT STORE
(Map p80; www.bloomingdales.com; 1000 Third Ave at E 59th St; 🕐10am-8:30pm Mon-Fri, to 7pm Sat, 11am-7pm Sun; 📶; [S] 4/5/6 to 59th St, N/Q/R to Lexington Ave-59th St) Uptown, the sprawling,

overwhelming Bloomingdale's is akin to the Metropolitan Museum of Art for shoppers.

Barneys Co-op FASHION, ACCESSORIES
(Map p70; ☎212-593-7800; 236 W 18th St; 🕐11am-8pm Mon-Fri, to 7pm Sat, noon-6pm Sun; [S]1 to 18th St) Offers hipper, less-expensive versions of high-end fashion.

Information

INTERNET ACCESS

It is rare to find accommodations in New York City that do not offer a way for guests to connect to the internet – a log-in fee is often required.

New York Public Library (☎212-930-0800; www.nypl.org/branch/local; E 42nd St, at Fifth Ave; [S]B, D, F or M to 42nd St-Bryant Park) offers free internet access for laptop toters and half-hour internet access via public terminals at almost all of its locations around the city.

Free wi-fi hotspots include Bryant Park, Battery Park, Tompkins Square Park and Union Square Park; other public areas with free wi-fi include Lincoln Center, Columbia University, South Street Seaport and Dumbo in Brooklyn and of course nearly 200 Starbucks scattered around the city.

Internet kiosks can also be found at **Staples** (www.staples.com) and **FedEx Kinko** (www.fedexkinkos.com) locations around the city.

MEDIA

Daily News (www.nydailynews.com) A daily tabloid, leans toward the sensational – archrival of the *New York Post*.

New York (www.newyorkmagazine.com) Weekly featuring nationally oriented reporting as well as NYC-centric news and listings for the arts and culture-oriented reader.

New York Post (www.nypost.com) Famous for spicy headlines, celebrity scandal-laden Page Six and good sports coverage.

New York Times (www.nytimes.com) The 'Gray Lady' is the newspaper of record for readers throughout the US.

NY1 (Time Warner Cable, Channel 1; www.ny1.com) This is the city's all-day news station on Time Warner cable's Channel 1.

Village Voice (www.villagevoice.com) The weekly tabloid is still a good resource for events, clubs and music listings.

WFUV-90.7FM The area's best alternative-music radio station is run by the Bronx's Fordham University.

WNYC 820am or 93.9FM National Public Radio's local affiliate.

MEDICAL SERVICES

Big retail pharmacies are everywhere, some with walk-in medical care; many stay open late.

New York County Medical Society (☎212-684-4670; www.nycms.org) Makes doctor referrals by phone, based on type of problem and language spoken.

New York University Langone Medical Center (☎212-263-7300; 550 First Ave; 🕐24hr)

Travel MD (☎212-737-1212; www.travelmd.com) A 24-hour house-call service for travelers and residents.

TELEPHONE

There are thousands of pay telephones lining the streets, but many are out of order. Manhattan's telephone area codes are ☎212, ☎646 and ☎917; in the four other boroughs they're ☎718, ☎347 and ☎929. You must dial ☎1 + the area code, even if you're calling from a borough that uses the same one you're calling to.

The city's ☎311 service allows you to dial from anywhere within the city for info or help with any city agency, from the parking-ticket bureau to the noise complaint department.

TOURIST INFORMATION

New York City & Company (Map p70; ☎212-484-1222; www.nycgo.com; 810 Seventh Ave, at 53rd St; 🕐8:30am-6pm Mon-Fri, 9am-5pm Sat & Sun; [S]B/D/E to 7th Ave) The official information service of the Convention & Visitors Bureau, it has helpful multilingual staff. Other branches include Chinatown (Map p62; cnr Canal, Walker & Baxter Sts; 🕐10am-6pm Mon-Fri, to 7pm Sat; [S]6/J/N/Q to Canal St); Lower Manhattan (Map p62; City Hall Park at Broadway; 🕐9am-6pm Mon-Fri, 10am-5pm Sat & Sun; [S]4/5/A/C to Fulton St); Times Square (Map p70; 1560 Broadway, btwn 46th & 47th Sts, Times Square; 🕐8am-8pm Mon-Sun; [S]N/Q/R to 49th St).

Getting There & Away

AIR

Three major airports serve New York City. The biggest is **John F Kennedy International Airport** (JFK; ☎718-244-4444; www.panynj.gov), in the borough of Queens, which is also home to **La-Guardia Airport** (LGA; www.panynj.gov/aviation/lgaframe). **Newark Liberty International Airport** (EWR; ☎973-961-6000; www.panynj.gov), across the Hudson River in Newark, NJ, is another option. When using online booking websites, search 'NYC' rather than a specific airport, which will allow most sites to search all three spots at once. **Long Island MacArthur Airport** (ISP; ☎631-467-3210; www.macarthurairport.com), in Islip, is a money-saving (though time-consuming) alternative, but may make sense if a visit to the Hamptons or other parts of Long Island are in your plans.

BUS

The massive and confusing **Port Authority Bus Terminal** (Map p70; ☎212-564-8484; www.

panynj.gov; 41st St at Eighth Ave; S A, C, E, N, Q, R, 1, 2, 3, & 7) is the gateway for buses into and out of Manhattan. Short Line (p118) runs numerous buses to towns in northern New Jersey and upstate New York, while **New Jersey Transit** (www.njtransit.state.nj.us) buses serve all of New Jersey.

A number of comfortable and reliably safe bus companies with Midtown locations, including **BoltBus** (☑ 877-265-8287; www.boltbus.com) and **Megabus** (☑ 877-462-6342; us.megabus.com), link NYC to Philadelphia ($10, two hours), Boston ($25, 4¼ hours) and Washington, DC ($25, 4½ hours); free wi-fi on board.

CAR & MOTORCYCLE

Note that renting a car in the city is expensive, starting at about $75 a day for a midsized car – before extra charges like the 13.25% tax and various insurance costs.

FERRY

Seastreak (www.seastreak.com) goes to Sandy Hook (return $45) in New Jersey and Martha's Vineyard (summer only; return $220) in Massachusetts from Pier 11 on the East River near Wall St and E 35th St. New York Waterway (p129) ferries leave from Pier 11 and the World Financial Center on the Hudson for Hoboken (one-way $7), Jersey City and other destinations.

TRAIN

Penn Station (33rd St, btwn Seventh & Eighth Aves; S 1/2/3/A/C/E to 34th St-Penn Station), not to be confused with the Penn Station in Newark, NJ, is the departure point for all **Amtrak** (☑ 800-872-7245; www.amtrak.com) trains, including the speedy Acela Express service to Boston (3¾ hours) and Washington, DC (two hours 52 minutes). Fares and durations vary based on the day and time you want to travel. Also arriving into Penn Station (NYC), as well as points in Brooklyn and Queens, is the **Long Island Rail Road** (LIRR; www.mta.nyc.ny.us/lirr), which serves several hundred-thousand commuters each day. New Jersey Transit (p129) also operates trains from Penn Station (NYC), with services to the suburbs and the Jersey Shore. Another option for getting into New Jersey, but strictly to points north of the city such as Hoboken and Newark, is the **New Jersey PATH** (☑ 800-234-7284; www.panynj.gov/path), which runs trains on a separate-fare system ($2.25) along the length of Sixth Ave, with stops at 34th, 23rd, 14th, 9th, and Christopher Sts and the World Trade Center station.

The only train line that departs from Grand Central Station, Park Ave at 42nd St, is the **Metro-North Railroad** (☑ 212-532-4900; www.mta.info/mnr), which serves the northern city suburbs, Connecticut and locations throughout the Hudson Valley.

❶ Getting Around

TO/FROM THE AIRPORT

All major airports have on-site car-rental agencies. It's a hassle to drive into NYC, though, and many folks take taxis, shelling out the $52 taxi flat rate (plus toll and tip) from JFK and Newark or a metered fare of about $25 to Midtown from LaGuardia.

A cheaper and pretty easy option to/from JFK is the AirTrain ($5 one way), which connects to subway lines into the city ($2.50; coming from the city, take the Far Rockaway-bound A train) or to the LIRR ($9.50 one way) at Jamaica Station in Queens (this is probably the quickest route to Penn Station in the city).

To/from Newark, the AirTrain links all terminals to a New Jersey Transit train station, which connects to Penn Station in NYC ($12.50 one way combined NJ Transit/Airtrain ticket).

For LaGuardia, a reliable option to consider if you allow plenty of time is the M60 bus ($2.50), which heads to/from Manhattan across 125th St in Harlem and makes stops along Broadway on the Upper West Side.

All three airports are also served by express buses ($16) and shuttle vans ($23); such companies include the **New York Airport Service Express Bus** (☑ 718-560-3915; www.nyairportservice.com; ⊙ every 20 or so min), which leaves every 20 or so minutes for Port Authority, Penn Station (NYC) and Grand Central Station; and **Super Shuttle Manhattan** (www.supershuttle.com), which picks you (and others) up anywhere, on demand, with a reservation.

BICYCLE

NYC has a new bike-sharing program, called Citi Bike (p88).

CAR & MOTORCYCLE

Even for the most spiritually centered, road rage is an inevitable by-product of driving within the city. Traffic and parking are always problematic and anxiety-provoking.

If you are driving out or in, however, know that the worst part is joining the masses as they try to squeeze through tunnels and over bridges to traverse the various waterways that surround Manhattan. Be aware of local laws, such as the fact that you can't make a right on red (like you can in the rest of the state) and also the fact that every other street is one way.

FERRY

The **East River Ferry** (www.eastriverferry.com) service (one way $4, every 20 minutes) connects spots in Brooklyn (Greenpoint, North and South Williamsburg and Dumbo) and Queens (Long Island City) with Manhattan (Pier 11 at Wall St and E 35th St). And **New York Water Taxi** (☑ 212-742-1969; www.nywatertaxi.com;

hop-on, hop-off service 1-day $26) has a fleet of zippy yellow boats that run along several different routes, including a hop-on, hop-off weekend service around Manhattan and Brooklyn.

PUBLIC TRANSPORTATION

The **Metropolitan Transport Authority** (MTA; ☑ 718-330-1234; www.mta.info) runs both the subway and bus systems. Depending on the train line, time of day and whether the door slams in your face or not, New York City's 100-year-old round-the-clock subway system (per ride $2.50) is your best friend or worst enemy. The 656-mile system can be intimidating at first, but regardless of its faults it's an incredible resource and achievement, linking the most disparate neighborhoods in a continually pulsating network. Maps should be available for the taking at every stop. To board, you must purchase a MetroCard, available at windows and self-serve machines, which accept change, dollars or credit/debit cards; purchasing many rides at once works out cheaper per trip.

If you're not in a big hurry, consider taking the bus (per ride $2.50). You get to see the world go by, they run 24/7 and they're easy to navigate – going crosstown at all the major street byways (14th, 23rd, 34th, 42nd, 72nd Sts and all the others that are two-way roads) and uptown or downtown, depending which avenue they serve. You can pay with a MetroCard or exact change but not bills. Transfers from one line to another are free, as are transfers to or from the subway.

TAXI

The classic NYC yellow cab is no longer a boxy gas-guzzling behemoth but rather a streamlined hybrid model, outfitted with mini-TVs and credit-card machines. No matter the make or year of the car, however, expect a herky-jerky, somewhat out-of-control ride. Current fares are $2.50 for the initial charge (first one-fifth mile), 50¢ each additional one-fifth mile, as well as per 60 seconds of being stopped in traffic, $1 peak surcharge (weekdays 4pm to 8pm), and 50¢ night surcharge (8pm to 6am daily). Tips are expected to be 10% to 15%; minivan cabs can hold five passengers. You can only hail a cab that has a lit light on its roof. Also know that it can be difficult to score a taxi in the rain, at rush hour and at around 4pm, when many drivers end their shifts.

NEW YORK STATE

There's upstate and downstate and never the twain shall meet. The two have about as much in common as NYC's Upper East Side and the Bronx. And yet everyone shares the same governor and dysfunctional legislature in the capital, Albany. While this incompatibility produces legislative gridlock and downright operatic drama, it's a blessing for those who cherish quiet and pastoral idylls as much as Lower East Side bars and the subway. Defined largely by its inland waterways – the Hudson River, the 524-mile Erie Canal connecting Albany to Buffalo, and the St Lawrence River – New York stretches to the Canadian border at world-famous Niagara Falls and under-the-radar Thousand Islands. Buffalo is a cheap foodies' paradise and wine aficionados can pick their favorite vintage from around the state, but especially in the Finger Lakes region close to the college town of Ithaca. From wilderness trails with backcountry camping to small-town Americana and miles and miles of sandy beaches, from the historic, grand estates and artists colonies in the Hudson Valley and Catskills to the rugged and remote Adirondacks, it's easy to understand why so many people leave the city, never to return.

❶ Information

New York State Office of Parks, Recreation and Historic Preservation (☑ 800-456-2267, 518-474-0456; www.nysparks.com) Camping, lodging and general info on all state parks. Reservations can be made up to nine months in advance.

511 New York: Traffic, Travel & Transit Info (www.511ny.org) Weather advisories, road information and more.

Uncork New York (☑ 585-394-3620; www. newyorkwines.org) One-stop shop for statewide wine info.

Long Island

Private-school blazers, nightmare commutes, strip malls colonized by national chains, cookie-cutter suburbia, moneyed resorts, windswept dunes and magnificent beaches – and those accents. Long Island, which accommodates the boroughs of Brooklyn and Queens, has all of these things, and that explains its somewhat complicated reputation. The site of small European whaling and fishing ports from as early as 1640, Levittown, just 25 miles east of Manhattan in Nassau County, is where builders first perfected the art of mass-producing homes. But visions of suburban dystopia aside, Long Island has wide ocean and bay beaches, important historic sites, renowned vineyards, rural regions and of course the Hamptons, in all their luxuriously sunbaked glory.

NEW YORK STATE FACTS

Nicknames Empire State, Excelsior State, Knickerbocker State

Population 19.6 million

Area 47,214 sq miles

Capital city Albany (population 98,000)

Other cities New York City (population 8,245,000)

Sales tax 4%, plus additional county and state taxes (total approximately 8%)

Birthplace of Poet Walt Whitman (1819–92), President Theodore Roosevelt (1858–1919), President Franklin D Roosevelt (1882–1945), first lady Eleanor Roosevelt (1884–1962), painter Edward Hopper (1882–1967), movie star Humphrey Bogart (1899–1957), comic Lucille Ball (1911–89), filmmaker Woody Allen (b 1935), actor Tom Cruise (b 1962), pro athlete Michael Jordan (b 1963), pop star Jennifer Lopez (b 1969)

Home of Six Nations of the Iroquois Confederacy, first US cattle ranch (1747, in Montauk, Long Island), US women's suffrage movement (1872), Erie Canal (1825)

Politics Popular Democratic governor Andrew Cuomo, NYC overwhelmingly Democratic, upstate more conservative

Famous for Niagara Falls (half of it), the Hamptons, wineries, Hudson River

Unusual river Genesee River is one of the few rivers in the world that flows south–north, from south central New York into Lake Ontario at Rochester

Driving distances NYC to Albany 160 miles, NYC to Buffalo 375 miles

ⓘ Getting There & Around

The most direct driving route is along the I-495, aka the LIE (Long Island Expwy), though be sure to avoid rush hour, when it's commuter hell. Once in the Hamptons, there is one main road to the end, Montauk Hwy. The **Long Island Rail Road** (LIRR; ☑718-217-5477; www.mta.info/lirr; one-way off-peak/peak $19.75/27) serves all regions of Long Island, including the Hamptons ($25 one way, two hours 45 minutes), from Penn Station (NYC), Brooklyn and Queens. The **Hampton Jitney** (☑212-362-8400; www.hamptonjitney.com; 1-way $25) and **Hampton Luxury Liner** (☑631-537-5800; www.hamptonluxuryliner.com; 1-way $40) bus services connect Manhattan's midtown and Upper East Side to various Hamptons villages; the former also has services to/from various spots in Brooklyn.

North Shore

Long Island's Gold Coast of the roaring 20s, of the Vanderbilts, Chryslers and Guggenheims, not to mention Gatsby, begins outside the suburban town of Port Washington. Castle Gould, the enormous turreted stable at the entrance to Sands Point Preserve (☑516-571-7900; www.sandspointpreserve.org; 127 Middleneck Rd; admission per car/walk-in $5/$2; ☺9am-4:30pm) and now a visitor center, was once owned by Howard Gould, the heir to a railroad fortune. The preserve's forested trails and beautiful sandy bayfront beach are worth a stroll and the 1923 mansion Falaise (www.sandspointpreserve.org; admission $10; ☺tours hourly noon-3pm Thu-Sun Jun-Oct) is intact and furnished and open to guided tours (hourly from noon to 3pm). Eastward is the bucolic town of Oyster Bay, home to Sagamore Hill (☑516-922-4788; www.nps.gov/sahi; adult/child $5/free; ☺9am-5pm Wed-Sun), a 23-room Victorian where Theodore Roosevelt and his wife raised six children and vacationed during his presidency. Spring and summer months mean long waits for guided tours. A nature trail leading from behind the excellent museum (admission free) ends at a picturesque waterfront beach. As of the summer of 2013, the guided tours of the home were suspended until a renovation and rehabilitation project is completed

South Shore

Despite the periodic roar of jets overhead, Long Beach, the closest beach to the city and most accessible by train, has a main town strip with ice-cream shops, bars and eateries, a lively surfers' scene and pale trendy city types mixing with suntanned locals.

On summer weekends the 6-mile stretch of pretty Jones Beach is a microcosm of the city's diversity, attracting surfers, wild city folk, local teens, nudists, staid families, gay and lesbian people and plenty of old-timers. The Long Island Rail Road (LIRR; ☑718-217-5477; www.mta.info/lirr) service to Wantagh has a bus connection to Jones Beach.

Further east, just off the southern shore, is a separate barrier island. Fire Island includes Fire Island National Seashore (☑631-289-4810; www.nps.gov/fiis) and several summer-only villages accessible by ferry from Long Island. The Fire Island Pines and Cherry Grove (both car-free) comprise a historic, gay bacchanalia that attracts men and women in droves from NYC, while villages on the west end cater to straight singles and families. There are limited places to stay, and booking in advance is strongly advised (check www.fireisland.com for accommodations information). Madison Fire Island (☑631-597-6061; www.themadisonfi.com; The Pines; r $200-775; ❋🖧🐕), the first and only boutique hotel here, rivals anything Manhattan has to offer in terms of amenities, but also has killer views from a rooftop deck and a gorgeous pool. At the eastern end of the island, the 1300-acre preserve of Otis Pike Fire Island High Dune Wilderness is a protected oasis of sand dunes that includes beach camping at Watch Hill (☑631-567-6664; www.watchhillfi.com; campsites $25; ☻early May-late Oct), though mosquitoes can be fierce and reservations are a must (Hurricane Sandy breached a nearby inlet so check on access routes). At the western end of Fire Island, Robert Moses State Park is the only spot accessible by car. Fire Island Ferries (☑631-665-3600; Bay Shore) runs services to Fire Island beaches and the national seashore; the terminals are close to LIRR stations at Bayshore, Sayville and Patchogue (round-trip adult/child $17/7.50, May to November).

The Hamptons

Attitudes about the Hamptons are as varied as the number of Maseratis and Land Rovers cruising the perfectly landscaped streets; however, no amount of attitudinizing can detract from the sheer beauty of the beaches and what's left of the picturesque farms and woodland. If you can bury the envy, a pleasurable day of sightseeing can be had simply driving past the homes of the extravagantly wealthy, ranging from cutting-edge modern-ist to faux-castle monstrosities. However, many summertime residents are partying the weekends away in much more modest group rentals and at the revolving doors of clubs. While each Hampton is not geographically far from every other, traffic can be a nightmare.

SOUTHAMPTON

Though the village of Southampton appears blemish-free, as if it has been Botoxed, it gets a face-lift at night when raucous clubgoers let their hair down. Its beaches are sweeping and gorgeous (only Coopers Beach (per day $40) and Road D (free) offer parking to non-residents May 31 to September 15). The Parrish Art Museum (☑631-283-2118; www.parrishart.org; 279 Montauk Hwy, Water Mill; adult/child $10/free; ☻11am-6pm Wed-Mon, to 8pm Fri) is an impressive regional institution. The town's colonial-era roots as a whaling and seafaring community are evident at Halsey House, the oldest residence in the Hamptons, and the nearby Southampton Historical Museum (☑631-283-2494; www.southamptonhistoricalmuseum.org; 17 Meeting House Ln; adult/child $4/free; ☻11am-4pm Tue-Sat). To learn more about an even earlier age of Long Island's history, head to the Shinnecock Nation Cultural Center & Museum (☑631-287-4923; www.shinnecock.com; 100 Montauk Hwy, Southampton; adult/child under 5 $10/free; ☻11am-5pm Thu-Sun) at the edge of the village. Run by the Native American group who live on an 800-acre peninsula that juts into the bay, the recently opened site allows Shinnecock members and visitors alike to experience a recreated Wikun (village) c 1640–1750 with guided tours, singing, dancing and demonstrations of traditional skills. For a quick and reasonable meal try Golden Pear (☑631-283-8900; www.goldenpear.com; 99 Main St; snacks & meals $6-18; ☻7:30am-5pm), which serves delicious soups, salads and wraps.

BRIDGEHAMPTON & SAG HARBOR

Moving east, Bridgehampton has a more modest-looking drag, but has its fair share of trendy boutiques and fine restaurants. The modest, low-slung Enclave Inn (☑631-537-2900; www.enclaveinn.com; 2668 Montauk Hwy, Bridgehampton; r from $199; ❋🖧), just a few blocks from the heart of the village, is one of the better value accommodations options; there are four other locations elsewhere in the Hamptons. Old-fashioned diner Candy Kitchen (☑646 537-9885; 2391 Montauk, Hwy, Bridgehampton; mains $5-12; ☻7am-9:30pm; 🖧)

has a luncheonette counter serving filling breakfasts, burgers and sandwiches.

Seven miles north, on Peconic Bay, is the lovely old whaling town of Sag Harbor; ferries to Shelter Island leave a few miles north of here. Check out Sag Harbor's Whaling & Historical Museum (631-725-0770; www.sagharborwhalingmuseum.org; 200 Main St; adult/child $6/2; 10am-5pm Mon-Sat, from 1pm Sun May 15 -Oct 1), or simply stroll up and down its narrow, Cape Cod–like streets. Get gourmet sustenance at Provisions (631-725-3636; cnr Bay & Division Sts; sandwiches $9; 8am-6pm), a natural foods market with delicious take-out wraps, burritos and sandwiches.

EAST HAMPTON

Don't be fooled by the oh-so-casual-looking summer attire, heavy on pastels and sweaters tied around the neck – the sunglasses alone are probably equal to a month's rent. Some of the highest-profile celebrities have homes here. Catch readings, theater and art exhibits at Guild Hall (631-324-0806; www.guildhall.org; 158 Main St). West of town on the way to Bridgehampton is the Townline BBQ (www.townlinebbq.com; 3593 Montauk Hwy; mains $9; 11:30am-10pm), a down-to-earth roadside restaurant churning out smoky ribs and barbecue sandwiches. Just to the east toward Amagansett is La Fondita (74 Montauk Hwy, Amagansett; mains $9; 11:30am-8pm Thu & Sun, to 9pm Fri & Sat), the place to go for reasonably priced Mexican fare. Nightclubs come and go with the seasons.

MONTAUK & AROUND

Once a sleepy and humble stepsister to the Hamptons, these days Montauk, at the far eastern end of Long Island, draws a fashionable, younger crowd and even a hipster subset to its beautiful beaches. Longtime residents, fishermen and territorial surfers round out a motley mix that makes the dining and bar scene more democratic compared to other Hamptons villages. At the very eastern, wind-whipped tip of the South Fork is Montauk Point State Park, with its impressive, 1796 Montauk Point Lighthouse (631-668-2544; www.montauklighthouse.com; adult/child $9/4; 10:30am-5:30pm, hours vary), the fourth oldest still-active lighthouse in the US. You can camp a few miles west of town at the dune-swept Hither Hills State Park (631-668-2554; www.nysparks.com; 164 Old Montauk Hwy), right on the beach; just reserve early during summer months. Several miles to the north is the Montauk

harbor, with dockside restaurants and hundreds of boats in the marinas.

You'll find a string of standard motels near the entrance to the town beach, including the Ocean Resort Inn (631-668-2300; www.oceanresortinn.com; 96 S Emerson Ave; r from $135, ste from $185;). A few miles west, just across the street from the beach, is Sunrise Guesthouse (631-668-7286; www.sunrisebnb.com; 681 Old Montauk Hwy; r $125-185;), a modest and comfortable B&B.

Two great places to wind down the day (from May to October) with drinks and hearty, fresh seafood are the roadside restaurants Clam Bar (631-267-6348; 2025 Montauk Hwy; mains $7-14; noon-8pm, weather permitting) and Lobster Roll (631-267-3740; 1980 Montauk Hwy; mains $10-12; 11:30am-10pm summer) aka 'Lunch,' now in its fifth decade, both on the highway between Amagansett and Montauk.

North Fork & Shelter Island

Mainly, the North Fork is known for its unspoiled farmland and wineries – there are close to 30 vineyards, clustered chiefly around the towns of Jamesport, Cutchogue and Southold – and the Long Island Wine Council (631-722-2220; www.liwines.com) provides details of the local wine trail, which runs along Rte 25 north of Peconic Bay. One of the nicer outdoor settings for a tasting is the Peconic Bay Winery (631-734-7361; www.peconicbaywinery.com; 31320 Main Rd, Cutchogue); this also means it's popular with bus and limo-loads of partiers. Beforehand, stop at popular Love Lane Kitchen (240 Love Lane; mains $9-28; 7am-9:30pm, Thu-Mon, 7am-4pm Tue & Wed) in Matituck for a meal, especially weekend brunch.

The main North Fork town and the place for ferries to Shelter Island, Greenport is a charming, laid-back place lined with restaurants and cafes, including family-owned Claudio's Clam Bar (www.claudios.com; 111 Main St; mains $15; 11:30am-9pm, closed Wed) with a wraparound deck perched over the marina. Or grab sandwiches for a picnic at the Harbor Front Park, where you can take a spin on the historic carousel.

Between the North and South Forks, Shelter Island, accessible by ferry from North Haven to the south and Greenport to the north (vehicle and driver $10, 10 minutes, every 15 to 20 minutes), is a low-key microcosm of beautiful Hamptons real estate with more of a traditional maritime New England atmosphere. And the Mashomack Nature Preserve (☏631-749-1001; www.nature.org; Rte 114; ☺9am-5pm Mar-Sep, to 4pm Oct-Feb), covering over 2000 acres of the southern part of the island is a great spot for hiking or kayaking (no cycling).

On Shelter Island, just down the road from Crescent Beach and nestled on a prime piece of property surrounded by woods fronting the bay, Pridwin Beach Hotel & Cottages (☏631-749-0476; www.pridwin. com; 81 Shore Rd, Shelter Island; r & cottages from $165-315; ✳☏) has standard hotel rooms as well as private water-view cottages, some in high-designer style.

Hudson Valley

Immediately north of New York City, green becomes the dominant color and the vistas of the Hudson River and the mountains breathe life into your urban-weary body. The region was home to the Hudson River School of painting in the 19th century and its history is preserved in the many grand estates and picturesque villages. The Lower Valley and Middle Valley are more populated and suburban, while the Upper Valley has a rural feel, with hills leading into the Catskills mountain region. For area-wide information, check out the Hudson Valley Network (www.hvnet.com).

Lower Hudson Valley

Several magnificent homes and gardens can be found near Tarrytown and Sleepy Hollow, on the east side of the Hudson. Kykuit, one of the properties of the Rockefeller family, has an impressive array of Asian and European artwork and immaculately kept gardens with breathtaking views. Lyndhurst is the estate of railroad tycoon Jay Gould and Sunnyside is the home of author Washington Irving. Go to the Historic Hudson Valley (www.hudsonvalley.org) website for info on these and other historic attractions. Nearby is the elegant country restaurant Blue Hill at Stone Barns (☏914-366-9600; www.bluehillfarm.com; 630 Bedford Rd, Pocantico Hills; 5-course meal $108, 8-courses $148; ☺5-10pm Wed-Thu, to 11pm Fri & Sat, 1-10pm Sun) ✿, a pillar of the farm-to-table movement and a locavore's dream.

A pristine forested wilderness with miles of hiking trails is just 40 miles north of New York City on the west side of the Hudson:

Harriman State Park (☏845-786-5003; http://nysparks.state.ny.us/parks) covers 72 sq miles and offers swimming, hiking and camping; adjacent Bear Mountain State Park (☏845-786-2701; http://nysparks.state. ny.us/parks; ☺8am-dusk) offers great views from its 1305ft peak, with the Manhattan skyline looming beyond the river and surrounding greenery; and there's a restaurant and lodging at the inn on Hessian Lake. In both parks there are several scenic roads snaking their way past secluded lakes with gorgeous vistas.

Not far to the north in Highland Falls and occupying one of the most breathtaking bends in the Hudson is West Point US Military Academy, open to visitors on guided tours (☏845-446-4724; www.westpoint-tours.com; adult/child $12/9). Next to the visitor center is a fascinating museum (open 10:30am-4:15pm; free admission) that traces the role of war and the military throughout human history. Nearby and west of Rte 9W, the Storm King Art Center (☏845-534-3115; www.stormking.org; Old Pleasant Hill Rd; admission $10; ☺Apr-Nov) is a 500-acre outdoor sculpture park with rolling hills that showcases stunning avant-garde sculpture by well-known artists; a free tram gives tours of the grounds.

At Beacon, a fairly nondescript town north of here, fashionable regulars of the international art scene stop for Dia Beacon (Beacon; ☏845-440-0100; www.diaart.org; adult $10; ☺11am-6pm Thu-Mon mid-Apr–mid-Oct, 11am-4pm Fri-Mon mid-Oct–mid-Apr), a gallery featuring a renowned collection from 1960 to the present, and huge sculptures and installation pieces. Stop by Hudson Beach Glass (www.hudsonbeachglass.com; 162 Main St, Beacon), a boutique-gallery where you can buy artfully designed, hand-crafted pieces or sign up for a class to learn how to do it yourself.

Middle & Upper Hudson Valley

On the western side of the Hudson is New Paltz, home of a campus of the State University of New York, natural food stores and a liberal ecofriendly vibe. In the distance behind the town, the ridge of the Shawangunk (Shon-gum or just the 'Gunks') mountains rises more than 2000ft above sea level. More than two-dozen miles of nature trails and some of the best rock climbing in the Eastern US is found in the Mohonk Mountain Preserve (☏845-255-0919; www.mohonk-preserve.org; day pass for hikers/climbers & cyclists $12/17). Nearby Minnewaska State Park Preserve has 12,000 acres of wild landscape, the centerpiece of which is a usually ice-cold mountain lake. Contact Alpine Endeavors (☑877-486-5769; www.alpineendeavors.com) for climbing instruction and equipment.

The iconic Mohonk Mountain House (☑845-255-1000; www.mohonk.com; 1000 Mountain Rest Rd; r $320-2500; ✲ 🕿 ✲ 🏄) looks like it's straight out of a fairy tale: a rustic castle perched magnificently over a dark lake. It's an all-inclusive resort where guests can gorge on elaborate five-course meals, stroll through gardens, hike miles of trails, canoe, swim etc. A luxury spa center is there to work out the kinks. Nonovernight guests can visit the grounds (adult/child per day $25/20, less on weekdays) – well worth the price of admission.

On the eastern side of the Hudson is Poughkeepsie (puh-kip-see), the largest town on the east bank. It's famous for Vassar, a private liberal-arts college that until 1969 only admitted women. Worth a stroll for its breathtaking views is the Walkway Over the Hudson (www.walkway.org; ☺7amsunset); formerly the Highland-Poughkeepsie railroad bridge, and since 2009 the world's longest pedestrian bridge and the state's newest park.

Just north of here is Hyde Park, long associated with the Roosevelts, a prominent family since the 19th century. The estate of 1520 acres, formerly a working farm, includes the newly renovated and expanded Franklin D Roosevelt Library & Museum (☑845-229-8114; www.fdrlibrary.marist.edu; 511 Albany Post Rd/Rte 9, Hyde Park; admission museum $7, museum & house $14; ☺9am-5pm), which details important achievements in FDR's presidency; a visit usually includes a guided tour of FDR's lifelong home where he delivered his fireside chats. First Lady Eleanor Roosevelt's peaceful cottage, Val-Kill (☑845-229-9115; www.nps.gov/elro; Albany Post Rd, Hyde Park; admission $8; ☺9am-5pm daily May-Oct, Thu-Mon Nov-Apr), was her retreat from Hyde Park, FDR's mother and FDR himself. Just north of here is the 54-room Vanderbilt Mansion (☑877-444-6777; www.nps.gov/vama; Rte 9, Hyde Park; adult/child $8/free; ☺9am-5pm), a Gilded Age spectacle of lavish beaux-arts design; nearly all of the original furnishings imported from European castles and villas remain in this country house – the smallest of any of the Vanderbilt mansions!

Hyde Park's famous Culinary Institute of America (☑845-471-6608; www.ciarestaurants.com; Hyde Park; ☺most restaurants 11:30am-1pm & 6-8pm) trains future chefs and can satisfy absolutely anyone's gastronomic cravings; the Apple Pie Café (mains $10; ☺7:30am-5pm), one of the five student-staffed eateries, looks out onto a tranquil courtyard and serves up gourmet sandwiches as well as specialty pastries. Tuck in for a good night's sleep at Journey Inn (☑845-229-8972; www.journeyinn.com; One Sherwood Pl, Poughkeepsie; r $130-190), a six-room B&B – including a Roosevelt Room, of course – right in the middle of Hyde Park's big estates.

Further north is Rhinebeck, with a charming main street, inns, farms and wineries. Three miles to the north, the Aerodrome Museum (☑845-752-3200; www.old-rhinebeck.org; 9 Norton Rd; adult/child Sat & Sun $20/5, Mon-Fri $10/3; ☺10am-5pm mid-Jun–mid-Oct) has a collection of pre-1930s planes and automobiles and air shows on weekends in the summer. The Bread Alone Bakery (45 E Market St; mains $9; ☺7am-7pm, 8am-3pm) serves lunch specialties such as brisket panini and spinach and feta quiche.

Continuing along 9G N you reach Hudson – a beautiful town with a hip, gay-friendly community of artists, writers and performers who fled the city. Warren St, the main road through town, is lined with antiques shops, high-end furniture stores, galleries and cafes. A few miles south of town is Olana (☑518-828-0135; www.olana.org; Rte 9G, Hudson; tour adult/child $12/free; ☺grounds 8am-sunset daily, tours 10am-5pm Tue-Sun), the fish-out-of-water Moorish-style home of Frederic Church, one of the primary artists of the Hudson River School of Painting. On a house tour you can appreciate the totality of Church's aesthetic vision, and view paintings from his collection. At the riverside end of Hudson, the whitewashed, cozy and affordable Front St Guesthouse (☑518-828-1635; www.frontstreetguesthouse.com; 20 S Front St, Hudson; r from $140; ✲ 🕿) has polished wood floors, high-end bedding and an accommodating owner who will quickly meet guests' needs. Helsinki (☑518-828-4800; www.helsinkihudson.com; 405 Columbia St, Hudson; mains $13-25), in a restored carriage house, has a restaurant serving locally sourced cuisine and a popular music venue showcasing rock, jazz and indie performers.

Catskills

American painters discovered this mountainous region rising west of the Hudson Valley in the mid-19th century. They celebrated its hidden mossy gorges and waterfalls as examples of sublime wilderness rivaling the Alps in Europe. Though the height and profile of its rounded peaks might have been exaggerated and romanticized, traveling through the Catskills it's still possible to glimpse the landscapes that beguiled these artists and inspires others today.

Despite the introduction of fine cuisine and cute boutiques in charming small towns, for some this bucolic region is still synonymous with Borscht-belt family resorts and the wise-cracking Jewish comedians and dance instructors *a la* Patrick Swayze in *Dirty Dancing* who entertained generations. While that era is long past, the Catskills have become a popular choice for sophisticated city dwellers seeking second-home getaways.

Having a car is near essential in these parts. Adirondack Trailways (☎800-776-7548; www.trailwaysny.com) operates daily buses from NYC to Kingston (one way $25.50, two hours), the Catskills' gateway town, as well as to Catskills and Woodstock (one way $28, 2½ hours). Shortline (☎201-529-3666, 800-631-8405; www.coachusa.com) has regular trips between NYC and Monticello (one way $30, two hours), the gateway to the southern Catskills. Buses leave from NYC's Port Authority. The commuter rail line Metro-North (☎212-532-4900, 800-638-7646; http://mta.info; one-way off-peak $9-16) makes stops through the Lower and Middle Hudson Valleys.

Woodstock & Around

Shorthand for free love, free expression and the political ferment of the 1960s, world-famous Woodstock today still wears its counterculture tie-dye in the form of healing centers, art galleries, cafes and an eclectic mix of aging hippies and young Phish-fan types. The famous 1969 Woodstock music festival, though, actually occurred in Bethel. Overlooking Woodstock's town square, actually in front of the bus stop, is the Village Green B&B (☎845-679-0313; www.villagegreenbb.com; 12 Tinker St; r incl breakfast $135; ❄ 🐾), a three-story Victorian with comfortable rooms. Housed in an elegantly restored farmhouse half a mile southeast of the town square, Cucina (☎845-679-9800; 109 Mill Hill Rd; mains $18; ⊙ 5am-late, from 11am Sat & Sun) does sophisticated seasonal Italian fare and thin-crust pizzas.

Saugerties, just 7 miles east of Woodstock, is not nearly as quaint and feels by comparison like the big city, but the Saugerties Lighthouse (☎845-247-0656; www.saugertieslighthouse.com; r $165-180) offers a truly romantic and unique place to lay your head. The picturesque 1869 landmark is located on a small island in the Esopus Creek, accessible by boat or more commonly by a half-mile trail from the parking lot. Rooms are booked far in advance, but a walk to the lighthouse is highly recommended regardless.

Finger Lakes Region

A bird's-eye view of this region of rolling hills and 11 long narrow lakes – the eponymous fingers – reveals an outdoor paradise stretching all the way from Albany to far western New York. Of course there's boating, fishing, cycling, hiking and cross-country skiing, but this is also the state's premier wine-growing region, with more than 65 vineyards, enough for the most discerning oenophile.

Ithaca & Around

An idyllic home for college students and older generations of hippies who cherish elements of the traditional collegiate lifestyle – laid-back vibe, cafe poetry readings, art-house cinemas, green quads, good eats – Ithaca is perched above Cayuga Lake. Besides being a destination in itself, it is also a convenient halfway point between New York City and Niagara Falls. For tourist information, head to the Visit Ithaca Information Center (☎607-272-1313; www.visitithaca.com; 904 E Shore Dr).

Founded in 1865, Cornell University boasts a lovely campus, mixing traditional and contemporary architecture, and sits high on a hill overlooking the picturesque town below. The modern Johnson Museum of Art (☎607-255-6464; www.museum.cornell.edu; University Ave; ⊙ 10am-5pm Tue-Sun) FREE, designed by IM Pei, has a major Asian collection, plus pre-Columbian, American and European exhibits. Just east of the center of the campus is Cornell Plantations (☎607-255-2400; www.cornellplantations.org; Plantations

SCENIC DRIVE: ROUTE 28 & AROUND

One sign that you've crossed into the Catskills is when the unending asphalt gives way to dense greenery crowding the snaking roadway as you exit the I-87 and turn onto Rte 28. As you drive through the heart of the region, the vistas open up and the mountains (around 35 peaks are above 3500ft) take on stunning coloring depending on the season and time of day. Esopus Creek winds its way through the area and Ashokan Reservoir is a nice place for a walk or drive. To the south of Rte 28, several roads wind their way up and over the high peaks in Catskill Park.

Emerson Spa Resort (☎877-688-2828; www.emersonresort.com; 5340 Rte 28, Mt Tremper; r at lodge/inn from $159/199; ❄@☎♨❁) 🖉 offers a full-service base for Catskills adventures whatever time of year. From luxurious Asian-inspired suites to rustic-chic rooms in the log-cabin-style lodge, Emerson aims to please; staff can help arrange trips from skiing to kayaking. The Phoenix restaurant (mains $15 to $30) is probably the best in the region and the Catamount, popular with locals, has pub fare (mains $10) including burgers and BBQ ribs, and live music and dancing Monday nights. The world's largest kaleidoscope and kaleidoscope boutique, selling sculpture-quality pieces, is attached, as well as a coffee-sandwich shop.

Only a few miles further west is the one-lane town of Phoenicia. It's a pleasant place to stop for a meal and a tube – Town Tinker Tube Rental (☎845-688-5553; www.towntinker.com; 10 Bridge St; tubes per day $15; ♿) can hook you up for repeated forays down the Esopus rapids. The refreshing water of Pine Hill Lake at nearby Belleayre Beach (☎845-254-5600; www.belleayre.com; ♿) is the summertime place to cool off (or ski in the winter). In nearby Arkville, you can take a scenic ride on the historic Delaware & Ulster Rail Line (☎845-586-3877; www.durr.org; Hwy 28; adult/child $12/7; ☉11am & 2pm, Sat & Sun Jun-Nov, additional trips Thu & Fri Jul-Sep; ♿). Less than a mile west of Phoenicia is the Phoenicia Lodge (☎845-688-7772; www.phoenicialodge.com; Rte 28; r from $80, ste from $130; ❄☎❁), a classic and affordable roadside motel.

From here you can carry on north on Rte 30 to the Roxbury Motel (☎607-326-7200; www.theroxburymotel.com; 2258 County Hwy 41; r incl breakfast Mon-Fri Jun-Oct $100-300; ❄☎), in the tiny village of the same name, a wonderfully creative gem of a place with luxuriously designed and whimsically named rooms, each inspired by a particular '60s or '70s TV show or film – think The Jetsons and Wizard of Oz. Wintertime (lower room rates) means huddling around the fire pit whereas warm weather means sunbathing and lounging near the gazebo and the small stream that runs along the property; any time is good for relaxing at the full-service spa.

In winter, skiers should head further north, where Rtes 23 and 23A lead you to Hunter Mountain Ski Bowl (☎518-263-4223; www.huntermtn.com), a year-round resort with challenging runs and a 1600ft vertical drop. Nearby is Kaaterskill Falls, the highest falls in New York and once popularized and idealized in paintings by Thomas Cole and Asher Durand. The most traveled trail starts near a horseshoe curve in Rte 23A; park the car in a turnout just up the road, cross to the other side and walk back down behind a guardrail. What you see from here is only Bastion Falls; it's a not very strenuous hike a little more than three-quarters of a mile up to the lower falls. Hotel Mountain Brook (☎518-589-6740; www.hotelmountainbrook.com; 57 Hill St; r Mon-Fri $150, Sat & Sun $200, all incl breakfast; ❄☎❁) in Tannersville is set on a hill and evokes an Adirondack 'great camp.' Check out Last Chance Cheese (6009 Main St, Tannersville; mains $9-20; ☉11am-midnight Fri-Sun), an independently minded Tannersville institution with an overstuffed counter displaying gourmet cheeses, chocolates, candies and three hundred varieties of beer.

Perhaps the most scenic drive in the region is the 7-mile stretch of Platte Clove Rd/Rte 16 (also signposted as 'Plattecove Mtn Rd') between Tannersville and Woodstock. It's white-knuckle driving through a narrow and steep valley with a 1200ft elevation change (sometimes no guardrail; no trucks or buses allowed; closed November to April).

Rd; ☉10am-5pm, closed Mon) 🌿**FREE**, an expertly curated herb and flower garden. Kids can go interactive-wild at the extremely hands-on Sciencenter (📞607-272-0600; www.sciencecenter.org; 601 First St; adult/child $8/6; ☉10am-5pm Tue-Sat, from noon Sun; 👪).

The area around Ithaca is known for its waterfalls, gorges and gorgeous parks. However, downtown has its very own natural feature: Cascadilla Gorge, which starts several blocks from Ithaca Commons and ends, after a steep and stunning vertical climb, at the Performing Arts Center of Cornell. Buttermilk Falls Park (📞607-273-5761; Rte 13) has something for everyone: a beach, cabins, fishing, hiking, recreational fields and camping. The big draw, however, is the waterfalls – more than 10 – some sending water tumbling as far as 500ft below into clear swimming pools. Robert Treman Park (📞607-273-3440; 105 Enfield Falls Rd), a few miles further out of town, has a gorge trail passing a stunning 12 waterfalls in under 3 miles. The two biggies you don't want to miss are Devil's Kitchen and Lucifer Falls. Eight miles north on Rte 89, the spectacular Taughannock Falls spills 215ft into the steep gorge below; Taughannock Falls State Park (📞607-387-6739; www.nysparks. com; 2221 Taughannock Rd, Trumansburg) has two major hiking trails, craggy gorges, tent-trailer sites and cabins.

A little further along on Rte 89 near the village of Interlaken is the Creamery (☉11am-8pm), a roadside eatery that in addition to conventional ice cream sundaes serves buzz-inducing wine-infused sorbets. Just past here is Lucas Vineyards (📞607-532-4825; www.lucasvineyards.com; 3862 Cty Rd 150, Interlaken; ☉10:30am-5:30pm Mon-Sat, from 11am Sun Mar-Oct; 10:30am-6pm Mon-Sun Memorial Day-Labor Day), one of the pioneers of Cayuga wineries, and a little further north down by the lake shore is Sheldrake Point (📞607-532-9401; www.sheldrakepoint.com; 7448 County Rd; ☉11am-5pm Fri-Mon Jan-Mar, 10am-5:30pm daily Apr-Dec), which has lake views and award-winning whites.

The small, sleepy town of Seneca Falls is where the country's organized women's rights movement was born. After being excluded from an anti-slavery meeting, Elizabeth Cady Stanton and her friends drafted an 1848 declaration asserting that 'all men and women are created equal.' The inspirational Women's Rights National Historical Park (📞315-568-2991; www.nps.gov/wori;

136 Fall St; ☉9am-5pm) **FREE** has a small but impressive museum with an informative film, plus a visitor center offering tours of Cady Stanton's house.

Seneca & Keuka Lakes

Geneva, at the northern tip of Seneca Lake, has an architecturally historic exterior and a lively vibe with both Hobart and William Smith colleges calling it home. South Main St is lined with an impressive number of immaculate turn-of-the-century homes. The restored 1894 Smith Opera House (📞315-781-5483; www.thesmith.org; 82 Seneca St, Geneva) is the place to go for performing arts. Stop by Microclimate (38 Linden St, Geneva; ☉6pm-midnight Mon, 4:30pm-1am Thu-Sun), a cool little wine bar with wine flights where you can compare locally produced varietals with their international counterparts.

Y-shaped Keuka Lake is surrounded by two small state parks that keep it relatively pristine. One of its old canals has been converted into a rustic bike path and it's a favorite lake for trout fishing. Just south of Penn Yan, the largest village on the lake's shores, you come to Keuka Spring Vineyards (📞315-536-3147; www.keukaspringwinery. com; 54 E Lake Rd, Penn Yan; ☉10am-5pm Mon-Sat, from 11am Sun summer, mostly weekends other months) and then Rooster Hill Vineyards (📞315-536-4773; www.roosterhill.com; 489 Rte 54, Penn Yan; ☉10am-5pm Mon-Sat, from 11am Sun) – two local favorites that offer tastings and tours in pastoral settings.

🛏 Sleeping

⭐ **William Henry Miller Inn**   B&B $$
(📞607-256-4553; www.millerinn.com; 303 N Aurora St, Ithaca; r incl breakfast $115-215; ❋🅿🛜) Gracious and grand, and only a few steps from the commons, this is a completely restored historic home with luxuriously designed rooms – three have Jacuzzis – and a gourmet breakfast.

Inn on Columbia   INN $$
(📞607-272-0204; www.columbiabb.com; 228 Columbia St, Ithaca; r incl breakfast $175-225; ❋🛜🅿) Also recommended; a modern, contemporary home on a quiet residential street.

Gone with the Wind B&B   B&B $$
(📞607-868-4603; www.gonewiththewindonkeukalake.com; 14905 West Lake Rd, Branchport; r incl breakfast $110-200; ❋) This lakeside B&B has

WORTH A TRIP

CORNING

Around 44 miles to the southwest is the charming town of Corning, home to Corning Glass Works and the hugely popular **Corning Museum of Glass** (☑800-732-6845; www.cmog.org; One Museum Way; adult/child $15/free; ⊙9am-5pm, to 8pm Memorial Day–Labor Day; ♿). The massive complex is home to fascinating exhibits on glassmaking arts, complete with demonstrations and interactive items for kids. After visiting the museum, stop by **Vitrix Hot Glass Studio** (www.vitrixhotglass.com; 77 W Market St; ⊙9am-8pm Mon-Fri, from 10am Sat, noon-5pm Sun) in the charming Market Street district to take a gander at museum-quality glass pieces.

The **Rockwell Museum of Western Art** (☑607-937-5386; www.rockwellmuseum. org; 111 Cedar St; adult/child $8/free; ⊙9am-5pm, to 8pm summer; ♿), housed in the former City Hall, has a large collection of art of the American West, including great works by Bierstadt, Russell and Remington.

---

two accommodation choices: the original stone mansion and a log lodge annex – both have generally homey furnishings.

Hotel Clarence　　　BOUTIQUE HOTEL $$
(☑315-712-4000; www.hotelclarence.com; 108 Fall St, Seneca Falls; r $140; ❈ ☎ ☀) Originally a 1920s-era hotel, the downtown building housing the Clarence has undergone a stylish renovation with a nod to the past. The standard rooms are small and the upscale restaurant called the Kitchen is the best in town.

Buttonwood Grove Winery　　CABIN $$
(☑607-869-9760; www.buttonwoodgrove.com; 5986 Rte 89; r $135; ☀) Has four fully furnished log cabins nestled in the hills above Lake Cayuga (open April to December); free wine tasting included.

Belhurst Castle　　　INN $$$
(☑315-781-0201; www.belhurst.com; 4069 Rte 14 S, Geneva; r from $160-415; ❈ ☎) Even if you're not planning a wedding, this fairybook castle overlooking Lake Seneca might inspire you to take the plunge. Check out the three separate properties with a variety of room types. Two restaurants, the more casual Stone Cutters with live music on weekends and the more formal Edgar's.

✖ Eating

A half-dozen restaurants with outdoor seating, including Japanese, Middle Eastern, Mexican and Spanish tapas, line North Aurora St between East State and East Seneca Sts at the east end of the Ithaca Commons. Upscale **Mercato** (www.mercatobarandkitchen. com; 108 N Aurora St, Ithaca; mains $25; ⊙5:30-10pm Mon-Sat) is one of the best. **Ithaca's Farmers Market** (www.ithacamarket.com; Third St; ⊙Apr-Dec) is considered one of the region's standouts; local wines and cheeses are highlights; check the website for operating hours.

Glenwood Pines　　　BURGERS $
(1213 Taughannock Blvd; burgers $6; ⊙11am-10pm) According to locals in the know, this modest roadside restaurant, overlooking Lake Cayuga on Rte 89 and 4 miles north of Ithaca, serves the best burgers.

Yerba Maté Factor Café
& Juice Bar　　　SANDWICHES $
(143 The Commons, Ithaca; mains $8; ⊙9am-9pm Mon-Thu, to 3pm Fri, from noon Sun) Run by members of a fairly obscure religious organization, this large restaurant, housed in a converted historic building on the Ithaca Commons, is good for Belgian waffles, sandwiches and coffee.

★**Hazelnut Kitchen**　　MODERN AMERICAN $$
(☑607-387-4433; 53 East Main St, Trumansburg; mains $14-23; ⊙5-9pm Thu-Mon) ✔ The new owners, a young couple from Chicago interested in collaborating with area farmers, have maintained Hazlenut's status as arguably the finest restaurant in the region. Local ingredients, of course, seasonally inspired menu and au courant meat dishes such as pig face torchon.

Moosewood Restaurant　　VEGETARIAN $$
(www.moosewoodcooks.com; 215 N Cayuga St, Ithaca; mains $8-18; ⊙11:30am-8:30pm, 5:30-9pm Sun; ✔) Famous for its creative and constantly changing vegetarian menu and recipe books by founder Mollie Katzen.

❶ Getting There & Away

Shortline Bus (www.coachusa.com) has frequent departures to New York City ($53, four hours). Delta Airlines has direct flights from the **Ithaca Tompkins Regional Airport** (ITH; www.flyithaca. com) to Detroit, Newark and Philadelphia.

The Adirondacks

Majestic and wild, the Adirondacks, a mountain range with 42 peaks over 4000ft high, rival any of the nation's wilderness areas for sheer awe-inspiring beauty. The 9375 sq miles of park and forest preserve that climb from central New York State to the Canadian border include towns, mountains, lakes, rivers and more than 2000 miles of hiking trails. There's good trout, salmon and pike fishing, along with excellent camping spots. The Adirondack Forest Preserve covers 40% of the park, preserving the area's pristine integrity. In colonial times settlers exploited the forests for beaver fur, timber and hemlock bark, but by the 19th century 'log cabin' wilderness retreats, both in the form of hotels and grand estates, became fashionable.

Lake George

Maybe it's a blessing that the primary gateway to the Adirondacks, the village of Lake George, is a kitsch tourist town full of cotton candy, arcades and cheap souvenirs. The real reason for coming is the 32-mile-long lake itself, with its crystalline waters and forested shoreline, and once you leave the town behind the contrast is only more striking. Paddlewheel boat cruises, parasailing, kayaking and fishing trips are popular.

The state maintains wonderfully remote **campgrounds** (☑800-456-2267; www.dec. ny.gov/outdoor; tent sites $25) on Lake George's islands, and small motels line the main street of Lake George toward the northern end of town with dozens more on Rte 9 all the way to the village of Bolton Landing. Two with lake views that can be recommended are **Georgian Lakeside Resort** (☑518-668-5401; www.georgianresort.com; r incl breakfast from $99; ❄☞☀) and renovated **Surfside on the Lake** (☑800-342-9795; www.surfsideonthelake. com; 400 Canada St; r from $60; ❄☞☀).

Lake Placid & Saranac Lake

It's something of a stretch to imagine that this small mountain resort was once the center of the world's attention – well, twice.

In 1932 and 1980, Lake Placid hosted the Winter Olympics, and the facilities and infrastructure remain; elite athletes still train here. Hockey fans will recognize the **Olympic Center** (☑518-302-5326; www.whiteface. com; 2634 Main St; adult/child $7/5; ⊙10am-5pm; ⊞) on Main St as the location of the 1980 'Miracle on Ice' when the upstart US hockey team managed to defeat the seemingly unstoppable Soviets. Not far from town on Rte 73 is the **Olympic Jumping Complex** (☑518-523-2202; www.whiteface.com; 5486 Cascade Rd ; adult/child $11/8; ⊙hours vary seasonally) where you can take the elevator 20 stories up for impressive views. Seven miles to the south is **Mt Van Hoevenberg** (☑518-523-4436; 8 John Brown Rd, Rte 73, Lake Placid; adult/child $10/8, bobsled rides $30; ⊙hr vary seasonally; ⊞), home to Olympic 'sliding sports' where you can sign up for a bone-rattling, adrenalin-pumping ride on a bobsled, skeleton or luge during certain times of the year. Skiers should head to nearby **Whiteface Mountain** (www.whiteface.com), with 80 trails and a serious 3400ft vertical drop. Hotels, restaurants, bookstores and shops line the frontier-like main street in town, which actually fronts Mirror Lake. **Golden Arrow Lakeside Resort** (☑800-582-5540; www.golden-arrow.com; 2559 Main St, Lake Placid; r from $130; ❄⊖❄☞☀⊞) ☞, the only accommodation directly on the lake, has a variety of room types for families and couples alike.

South of Lake Placid town, **Adirondack Loj** (☑518-523-3441; www.adk.org; dm/r incl breakfast $50/155), run by the Adirondack Mountain Club (ADK), is a rustic retreat surrounded by mountains on the shore of peaceful Heart Lake. Wilderness campsites, lean-tos and cabins are also available.

Further north is the Saranac Lake region, where you'll find even more secluded wilderness areas – small lakes and ponds, ancient forests and wetlands. The town of Saranac Lake itself, once a center for tuberculosis treatments, feels a little down on its luck. Fourteen miles to the north is **White Pine Camp** (☑518-327-3030; www. whitepinecamp.com; 432 White Pine Rd, Paul Smiths; 2-person cottage from $105 late Oct-late Jun; weekly from $1085 mid-May–late Oct), one of the few remaining Adirondack 'great camps' where you can spend a night. Far from ostentatious or grand, White Pine is a collection of rustically cozy cabins set on scenic Osgood Pond.

THE THOUSAND ISLANDS

Virtually unknown to downstate New Yorkers, in part because of its relative inaccessibility, this region of over 1800 islands – from tiny outcroppings just large enough to lie down on to larger islands with roads and towns – is a scenic wonderland separating the US from Canada. From its source in the Atlantic Ocean far to the north, the wide and deceptively fast-moving St Lawrence River East empties into Lake Ontario at Cape Vincent. This portion of the river was once a summer playground for the very rich, who built large, stately homes here. It is still a popular vacation area known for its boating, camping and even shipwreck scuba diving.

The site of a major battle during the War of 1812, Sackets Harbor is on Lake Ontario but isn't technically part of the Thousand Islands. Still, it is a convenient starting point for touring the region. Several inviting restaurants with waterside patio seating line the street that runs down to the harbor front.

The relaxing, French-heritage village of Cape Vincent is at the western end of the river where it meets the lake. Drive out to the Tibbetts Point Lighthouse for stunning lake views; an attractive hostel (315-654-3450; www.hihostels.com; 33439 Co Rte 6; dm $25; Jul 1-Sep 15) shares the property. Nearby Burnham Point State Park (315-654-2522; Rte 12E; campsites $25) has wooded, lakeside campsites.

Fifteen miles to the east along the Seaway Trail (Rte 12), Clayton has more than a dozen marinas and a few good eating choices in an area generally bereft of them. The Antique Boat Museum (315-686-4104; www.abm.org; 750 Mary St, Clayton; adult/child $13/free; 9am-5pm mid-May–mid-Oct;) actually lets you sail or row the old vessels as you learn about them. TI Adventures (315-686-2500; www.tiadventures.com; 1011 State St; half-day kayak rental $30) rents kayaks and runs white-water-rafting trips down the Black River. Similar activities are also organized by several companies in Watertown, a sizable city half an hour's drive to the south.

Lyric Coffee House (315-686-4700; 246 James St, Clayton; mains $7-24; 8am-8pm;), surprisingly contemporary for Clayton, serves specialty coffee drinks, gelato and pastries. as well as meat, fish and pasta mains.

Further east, Alexandria Bay (Alex Bay), an early-20th-century resort town, is still the center of tourism on the American side – its sister city is Gananoque in Canada. While it is run-down and tacky, there's enough around to keep you occupied: go-karts, mini-golf and a drive-in movie theater (www.baydrivein.com; adult/child $5/2;) are only minutes away. It's also the departure point for ferries to Heart Island, where Boldt Castle (315-482-9724; www.boldtcastle.com; adult/child $8/5.50; 10am-6:30pm mid-May–mid-Oct) marks the love story of a rags-to-riches New York hotelier who built the castle for his beloved wife, who died before its completion. The same hotelier once asked his chef to create a new salad dressing, which was popularized as 'Thousand Island' – an unfortunate blend of ketchup, mayonnaise and relish. Uncle Sam's Boat Tours (315-482-2611; www.usboattours.com; 45 James St; 2-nation tour adult/child $20/10) has several departures daily for its recommended two-nation cruise (visiting both the US and Canadian sides of the river), which allows you to stop at Boldt Castle and ride back on one of its half-hourly ferries for free.

Wellesley Island State Park (518-482-2722; www.nysparks.com; campsites from $15) offers camping, which is probably the best accommodations option even for the raccoon-averse. Many sites are almost directly on the riverfront and some have their own 'private' beaches. The island is only accessible by crossing a toll portion ($2.50) of the Thousand Islands Bridge.

There are several supposedly upscale resorts around Alex Bay, though none is especially good value. Probably the best midrange choice is Capt Thomson's Resort (315-482-9961; www.captthomsons.com; 45 James St; r $130-200;) on the waterfront next to the office for Uncle Sam's Boat Tours.

JetBlue (p653) has regular daily flights to Hancock International Airport (SYR) in Syracuse, 90 minutes south. Several major car-rental agencies have offices in the airport. Cyclists will enjoy the mostly flat Scenic Byway Trail.

Around Lake Champlain

Since it was taken from the British in 1775 by the 'Green Mountain Boys,' **Fort Ticonderoga** (☑518-585-2821; www.fortticonderoga.org; 100 Fort Ti Rd; adult/child $17.50/8; ◷9:30am-5pm May 17-Oct 20) has been synonymous with the American Revolution. Nowadays its buckling stone walls afford stellar views of Lake Champlain, and every summer the carefully preserved fort opens its museum and grounds for tours and reenactments.

Further north is **Crown Point State Historic Site** (☑518-597-4666; www.nysparks.com; 21 Grandview Dr, Crown Point; ◷grounds 9am-6pm), the remains of two major 18th-century forts on a strategic promontory where Lake Champlain narrows between New York and Vermont.

Ausable Chasm (☑518-834-9990; www.ausablechasm.com; 2144 Rte 9; adult/child $17/10; ◷9am-5pm summer, to 4pm rest of yr; ♿) is a dramatically beautiful 2-mile long fissure carved from the sandstone by a gushing river over thousands of years. There are trails and walkways and rafting in summertime. **Essex Inn** (☑518-963-4400; www.essexinnessex.com; 2297 Main St, Essex; r from $225; ❋🖧) in the town of Essex has beautifully renovated rooms in a 200-year old landmark building.

❶ Getting There & Around

Both **Greyhound** (www.greyhound.com) and **Adirondack Trailways** (www.trailwaysny.com) serve various towns in the region. A car is essential for exploring the area.

Western New York

Still trying to find their feet after hemorrhaging industries and population for over a decade, most of the cities in this region live in the shadow of Niagara Falls, a natural wonder that attracts upward of 12 million visitors from around the world per year. Buffalo was once a booming industrial center and the terminus of the Erie Canal, which used to serve as the transportation lifeline connecting the Great Lakes and the Atlantic Ocean; it now boasts an indigenous culinary scene and Bohemian enclaves. Syracuse and Rochester are both home to big universities.

Buffalo

This often maligned working-class city does have long, cold winters and its fair share of abandoned industrial buildings, but Buffalo also has a vibrant community of college students and thirty-somethings living well in cheap real estate and gorging on the city's affordable and tasty cuisine. Settled by the French in 1758 – its name is believed to derive from *beau fleuve* (beautiful river) – the city's illustrious past as a former trading post and later a booming manufacturing center and terminus of the Erie Canal means there's a certain nostalgia and hopefulness to ambitious revitalization plans (one calls for a massive expansion and relocation of the University of Buffalo medical school to downtown). Buffalo is about an eight-hour trip from New York City through the Finger

DON'T MISS

TUPPER & BLUE MOUNTAIN LAKES

Only a few miles east of Tupper Lake, an otherwise nondescript town, is the **Wild Center** (☑518-359-7800; www.wildcenter.org; 45 Museum Dr, Tupper Lake; adult/child $17/10, under 3 free; ◷10am-6pm daily late May-early Sep, 10am-5pm Fri-Sun Sep-Mar, closed Apr; ♿) ✐, a jewel of a museum dedicated to the ecology and conservation of the Adirondacks. Interactive exhibits make it great for kids, and walking trails lead to an oxbow overlook and the Raquette River. Don't miss the back-of-the-house tour, where you see the nuts and bolts of the operation such as freezers full of dead mice to feed the center's snakes, owls, skunks and other animals.

A wonderful more-than-a-full-day pairing with the Wild Center is the **Adirondack Museum** (☑518-352-7311; www.adkmuseum.org; 9097 Rte 30; adult/child $18/6; ◷10am-5pm May 24-Oct 14; ♿), which occupies a 30-acre compound overlooking Blue Mountain Lake. Lots of hands-on exhibits explore the human-centered story of the mountains, from the history of mining, logging and boat building to the role of tourism in the region's development.

Lakes region and only a half hour or so south of Niagara Falls.

The very helpful **Buffalo Niagara Convention & Visitors Bureau** (☑800-283-3256; www.visitbuffaloniagara.org; 617 Main St; ☺10am-4pm Mon-Fri, 10am-2pm Sat) located in a light-filled beaux arts–style shopping arcade (c 1892) has good walking-tour pamphlets and a small gift shop.

◉ Sights & Activities

Architecture buffs will enjoy a stroll around downtown – you can't miss City Hall – and the 'theater district,' which has several late-19th-century buildings with baroque, Italianate and art nouveau facades (for details check out www.walkbuffalo.com).

Once derelict, the city's redeveloped waterfront, now called **Canalside** (www.canalsidebuffalo.com), includes an attractive park space where you can board boat cruises and rent kayaks. Also check out the **Naval & Military Park** (www.buffalonavalpark.org; 1 Naval Park Cove; adult/child $10/6; ☺10am-5pm Apr-Oct, Sat & Sun Nov, closed Dec-Mar), a small museum with maritime war-related exhibits but more impressive are the two huge WWII-era ships and submarine (museum admission includes access to the ships). North of downtown, sprawling **Delaware Park** was designed by Frederick Law Olmsted. The **Elmwood** neighborhood is dotted with hip cafes, restaurants, boutiques and bookstores.

This is a hard-core sports town and locals live and die with the **NFL Buffalo Bills** (www.buffalobills.com) football team who play in Ralph Wilson Stadium in the suburb of Orchard Park and the **Buffalo Sabres** (www.sabres.com), the city's NHL ice-hockey team. In 2014 the Sabres are moving from the waterfront First Niagara Center to the **HARBORcenter**, a new development next door. A no less recommended option is to catch the **Buffalo Bisons** (www.bisons.com), the AAA affiliate of the major-league baseball team, the New York Mets, in their trendy-traditional downtown ballpark.

★**Albright-Knox Art Gallery**   MUSEUM
(☑716-882-8700; www.albrightknox.org; 1285 Elmwood Ave; adult/child $12/5; ☺10am-5pm, closed Mon; car 198 West to Elmwood Ave S/Art Gallery) This low slung and sizable museum with a neoclassical facade includes some of the best of French Impressionists and American masters.

Darwin Martin House   ARCHITECTURAL TOUR
(☑716-856-3858; www.darwinmartinhouse.org; 125 Jewett Pkwy; basic tour $15; in-depth tour incl Barton House $30; ☺guided tours by reservation only, closed Tue) One of Frank Lloyd Wright's most elaborate or fully realized Prairie-style homes, with especially remarkable designed glass, can be toured by appointment. The modernist visitor center next door provides historical context for Wright and the home.

Theodore Roosevelt Inaugural National Historic Site   MUSEUM
(☑716-884-0095; www.nps.gov/thri; 641 Delaware Ave; adult/child $10/5; ☺tours hourly 9:30am-3:30pm Mon-Fri, from 12:30pm Sat & Sun) Guided tours of the Ansley-Wilcox house examine the tale of Teddy's emergency swearing-in here following the assassination of William McKinley in 1901 at the Pan American Exposition in Buffalo.

Burchfield Penney Art Center   MUSEUM
(☑716-878-6011; www.burchfieldpenney.org; 1300 Elmwood Ave; adult/child $10/free; ☺10am-5pm Tue, Wed, Fri & Sat, to 9pm Thu, 1-5pm Sun) This modern museum exhibits mostly American art, from the late 19th century to contemporary.

🛏 Sleeping

Standard chains line the highways around the city and downtown has several large ones that cater mainly to business travelers like the Hyatt Regency and the affordable and recommended Hampton Inn & Suites Buffalo Downtown (rooms from $159).

Hostelling International – Buffalo Niagara   HOSTEL $
(☑716-852-5222; www.hostelbuffalo.com; 667 Main St; dm/r $25/65; ❋@☎) Budget travelers should head to this hostel conveniently located in Buffalo's downtown 'theater district' on the street where the light rail train runs. Though the furnishings could use an update – the basement and 2nd-floor lounges resemble suburban rec rooms c 1970 – it's a homey and secure place to bed down. Free coffee, tea, oatmeal and even complimentary bicycles available.

★**Hotel @ the Lafayette**   BOUTIQUE HOTEL $$
(☑716-853-1505; www.thehotellafayette.com; 391 Washington St; r $169, ste from $200; P❋☎) This grand seven-story French Renaissance building of the early 1900s, now restored and open for business in 2012, stands

impressively intact. The cool and stylish furnishings in the rooms and suites can't compete with the art-deco lobby and marble hallway; several recommended restaurants and a bar on the premises.

★ **Mansion on Delaware Avenue** HOTEL $$$
(☑716-886-3300; www.mansionondelaware.com; 414 Delaware Ave; r/ste incl breakfast from $190/390; P✳@☜) For truly special and classy accommodations and flawless service, head to this hotel housed in a grand and regal house c 1862. Ask for room 200 – it has a fireplace and floor-to-ceiling windows. Noteworthy complimentary perks are two daily self-serve drinks from the light-filled lounge area and car service within a range of 3 miles of the hotel.

✗ Eating

Buffalo has an abundance of eateries serving unique, tasty and cheap dishes. Stylish and quality restaurants are scattered around downtown, Allentown, Elmwood and the suburbs. Chef-cum-restaurateur Mike Andrzejewski has a burgeoning mini-empire that includes Seabar (Japanese), Tappo (Italian), Mike A's (steakhouse) and Cantina Loco (Mexican); all are recommended for both their food and ambience.

★ **Anchor Bar** AMERICAN $
(☑716-886-8920; 1047 Main St; 10/20 wings $13/20; ☉10am-11pm Mon-Thu, 10am-1am Fri & Sat) For the famous deep-fried chicken wings covered in a spicy sauce (as well as pizza, pasta, sandwiches, burgers, etc), head to this landmark, which claims credit for inventing the delicacy. Walls are covered with license plates and other roadside memorabilia, and the whole place, including the central bar, has a honky-tonk vibe.

Cantina Loco MEXICAN $
(www.cantinaloco.com; 191 Allen St; mains $7; ☉4-10pm Mon-Thu, to 11pm Fri & Sat, 4-8pm Sun) Hip and lively, even on summertime Monday nights when the backyard patio also fills up, this Allentown restaurant serves up tacos, burritos and quesadillas. Some come with a twist like the Koreatown (Kalbi short ribs, kimchee and soy sauce). The desserts are excellent and super-efficient bartenders really know their mescals.

Ted's FAST FOOD $
(www.tedsonline.com; 7018 Transit Rd; hot dog $2; ☉10:30am-11pm Mon-Sun) Ted's fast-food specialty is hot dogs, foot-longs, any way you like 'em.

Ulrich's Tavern GERMAN $$
(☑716-855-8409; 674 Ellicott St; mains $15; ☉11am-3pm Mon-Wed, 11am-10pm Thu & Fri, 3-9pm Sat) One of Buffalo's oldest taverns has warped floors, dark-wood walls and gut-busting German specialties like liverwurst and red onions on rye, and a fish fry that comes with red cabbage, sauerkraut, potatoes and vegetables.

Betty's MODERN AMERICAN $$
(☑716-362-0633; 370 Virginia St; mains $9-22; ☉8am-9pm Tue, 8am-10pm Wed-Fri, 9am-10pm Sat, 9am-3pm Sun) On a quiet Allentown corner, slightly funky and bohemian Betty's does healthy and flavorful interpretations of American comfort food like meatloaf. Brunch is deservedly popular.

🍷 Drinking & Entertainment

A handful of bars along Chippewa St (aka Chip Strip) are open until 4am and cater primarily to the frat-boy crowd. More eclectic neighborhoods such as Elmwood, Linwood and Allentown have more than their fair share of late-night options. Allen St has a few dive bars with live music clustered near one another, including Nietzches and Duke's Bohemian Grove Bar. Several gay bars are around the south end of Elmwood. From June through August a summer concert series (☑716-856-3150; www.buffaloplace.com) draws an eclectic mix of new and established artists to outdoor spaces in downtown.

Pan American Grill & Brewery BREWERY
(☑716-856-0062; 391 Washington St, Hotel Lafayette; mains $9-18; ☉11am-10pm Mon-Thu, to midnight Fri & Sat, noon-10pm Sun) Several rooms, including two massive old-school mahogany bars, a lounge themed on a Teddy Roosevelt hunting lodge, and a mural room with vaulted ceilings, make up this space, which occupies a good chunk of Hotel Lafayette's ground floor. Their own beer is brewed in the basement and an excellent kitchen does standards such as burgers ($13) and chops ($14), but also dishes like a flatbread duck confit and goat cheese ($8).

Founding Fathers BAR
(75 Edward St; ☉11:30am-1am Mon-Thu, to 2am Fri, to 4am Sat, 5-11pm Sun) The theme of this small, laid-back neighborhood bar just north of downtown is American presidents, and this, ironically or not, attracts a coterie of local po-

liticos. A small menu with good sandwiches ($9) and free popcorn and nachos.

Allen Street Hardware Cafe   BAR
(☑716-882-8843; 245 Allen St) Amid a block of dive bars, this more sophisticated bar and restaurant (mains $14 to $25) hosts performances by the best local musicians.

❶ Getting There & Around

Buffalo Niagara International Airport (BUF; ☑716-630-6000; www.buffaloairport.com), about 10 miles east of downtown, is a regional hub. Jet Blue Airways offers affordable round-trip fares from New York City. Buses arrive and depart from the **Greyhound terminal** (181 Ellicott St) (aka Buffalo Transportation Center). **NFTA** (www.nfta.com) local bus 40 and express bus 60 go to the transit center on the American side of Niagara Falls ($2, one hour). From the downtown **Amtrak train station** (☑716-856-2075; 75 Exchange St), you can catch trains to major cities to NYC ($88, eight hours) and Albany ($48, six hours). The Exchange Street station can feel dodgy, especially at night; locals recommend the **Buffalo-Depew station** (55 Dick Rd), 6 miles east.

Niagara Falls & Around

It's a tale of two cities and two falls, though either side of this international border affords views of an undeniably dramatic natural wonder. There are honeymooners and heart-shaped Jacuzzis, arcades, tacky shops and kitsch boardwalk-style sights, but as long as your attention is focused nothing can detract from the majestic sight. The closer to the falls you get the more impressive they seem and the wetter you become. For good reason, the Canadian side is where almost everyone visits, though it's easy to stroll back and forth between the two (bring your passport). The New York side is dominated by the purple, glass-covered Seneca Niagara Casino & Hotel, which towers over the surrounding derelict blocks.

◎ Sights & Activities

The falls are in two separate towns: Niagara Falls, New York (USA) and Niagara Falls, Ontario (Canada). The towns face each other across the Niagara River, spanned by the Rainbow Bridge, which is accessible for cars and pedestrians. Famous landscape architect Frederick Law Olmstead helped rescue and preserve the New York side, which by the 1870s was dominated by industry and gaudy signs. You can see views of the American Falls and their western portion, the Bridal Veil Falls, which drop 180ft from the Prospect Point Observation Tower (☑716-278-1796; admission $1, free from 5pm; ⊙9:30am-7pm). Cross the small bridge to Goat Island for close-up viewpoints, including Terrapin Point, which has a fine view of Horseshoe Falls and pedestrian bridges to the Three Sisters Islands in the upper rapids. From the north corner of Goat Island, an elevator descends to the Cave of the Winds (☑716-278-1730; adult/child $11/8), where walkways go within 25ft of the cataracts (raincoats provided).

The Maid of the Mist (☑716-284-8897; www.maidofthemist.com; 151 Buffalo Ave; adult/child $15.50/9; ⊙9am-7pm summer, times vary so check website) boat trip around the bottom of the falls has been a major attraction since 1846 and is highly recommended. Boats leave from the base of the Prospect Park Observation Tower on the US side and from the bottom of Clifton Hill on the Canadian side.

For those seeking more of an adrenaline rush, check out Whirlpool Jet Boat Tours

---

BORDER CROSSING: CANADIAN NIAGARA FALLS

When people say they are visiting the falls they usually mean the Canadian side, which is naturally blessed with superior views. Canada's Horseshoe Falls are wider and especially photogenic from Queen Victoria Park; at night they're illuminated with a colored light show. The Journey Behind the Falls (☑905-354-1551; 6650 Niagara Pkwy; adult/child Apr-Dec $15.95/10.95, Dec-Apr $11.25/6.95; ⊙9am-6pm, opens later in summer) gives access to a spray-soaked viewing area beneath the falls. Niagara on the Lake, 15km to the north, is a small town full of elegant B&Bs and a famous summertime theater festival.

Virtually every major hotel chain has at least several locations on the Canadian side of the falls. Obvious tourist-trap restaurants are a dime a dozen in and around Clifton Hill. American fare and chains dominate the culinary scene. The Lundy's Lane area has tons of cheap eats.

(☑ 888-438-4444; www.whirlpooljet.com; 1hr adult/child $50/42), which leave from Lewiston, a charming town with several good eateries 8 miles north of Niagara Falls. Shoppers can head to the Fashion Outlets of Niagara Falls, a few miles west of town, for designer-wear discounts.

Northeast of Niagara Falls is the town of Lockport, the western terminus of the Erie Canal. There's an excellent visitors center and museum and boat tours during the summer months.

🛏 Sleeping & Eating

Most all of the national hotel chains are represented – Ramada Inn, Howard Johnson, Holiday Inn. However, the quality of the pickings are poor compared to the Canadian side. There are a few restaurants near the bridge area, including several Indian takeaway places.

★ **Giacomo**   BOUTIQUE HOTEL **$$**
(☑ 716-299-0200; www.thegiacomo.com; 220 First St; r from $150; ☐ ❊ 🕾) The equal of any Canadian-side lodging in terms of stylish comfort, the Giacomo occupies a renovated 1929 art-deco office tower. While the majority of floors are taken up by high-end condos, the three-dozen spacious rooms are luxuriously appointed and the 19th-floor lounge offers spectacular falls views.

Buzzy's   PIZZA **$**
(☑ 716-283-5333; 7617 Niagara Falls Blvd; mains $6-15; ☺ 11am-11pm Sun-Thu, to midnight Fri & Sat) New York–style pizza, spicy buffalo wings, calzones, subs and hoagies for hungry crowds who like to drink beer and watch sports.

❶ Information

On the US side, the **Niagara Tourism & Convention Corporation** (☑ 716-282-8992; www.niagara-usa.com; 10 Rainbow Blvd; ☺ 9am-7pm Jun-Sep 15, to 5pm Sep 16-May 31) has all sorts of guides; its Canadian counterpart is located near the base of the **Skylon Tower** (☑ 905-356-6061; www.niagarafallstourism.com; 5400 Robinson St, Skylon Tower; ☺ 9am-5pm).

❶ Getting There & Around

NFTA (Niagara Frontier Transportation Authority; www.nfta.com) bus 40 and express bus 60 connect downtown Buffalo and Niagara Falls ($2, one hour). The stop in Niagara Falls is at First and Rainbow Blvd (there's no reason to go to the terminal at Main and Pine Sts). Taxis run

around $75. The **Amtrak train station** (27th St, at Lockport Rd) is about 2 miles northeast of downtown. From Niagara Falls, daily trains go to Buffalo (35 minutes), Toronto (three hours) and New York City (nine hours); fares vary depending on time and day. **Greyhound** (www.greyhound.com; 303 Rainbow Blvd) buses are run out of the Daredevil Museum.

Parking costs $8 to $10 a day on either side of the falls. Most of the midrange hotels offer complimentary parking to guests, while upscale hotels (on the Canadian side) tend to charge $15 to $20 a day for the privilege.

Crossing the Rainbow Bridge to Canada and returning costs US$3.25/1 per car/pedestrian. There are customs and immigration stations at each end – US citizens and overseas visitors are required to have their passport or an enhanced driver's license. Driving a rental car from the US over the border should not be a problem, but check with your rental company before you depart.

NEW JERSEY

There are McMansions, à la the *Real Housewives of New Jersey*, guys who speak with thick Jersey accents like characters from a TV crime drama, and guidos and guidettes who spend their days GTL'ing (gym, tan and laundry) on the Shore. However, the state is at least as well defined by high-tech and banking headquarters and sophisticated, progressive people living in charming towns. Get off the exits, flee the malls and you are privy to a beautiful side of the state: a quarter is farmland and it has 127 miles of beautiful beaches and charming and fun beachside towns, as well as two of New York City's greatest icons: the Statue of Liberty and Ellis Island.

❶ Information

NJ.com (www.nj.com) Statewide news from all the major dailies including the *Newark Star-Leger* and Hudson County's *Jersey Journal*.

New Jersey Monthly (www.njmonthly.com) Monthly glossy with features on attractions and other stories relevant to visitors.

New Jersey Department of Environmental Protection (www.state.nj.us/dep/parksandforests) Comprehensive information on all state parks, including camping and historic sites.

❶ Getting There & Away

Though NJ is made up of folks who love their cars, there are other transportation options:

New Jersey PATH Train (www.panynj.gov/path) Connects lower Manhattan to Hoboken, Jersey City and Newark.

New Jersey Transit (www.njtransit.com) Operates buses out of NYC's Port Authority and trains out of Penn Station, NYC.

New York Waterway (☑800-533-3779; www.nywaterway.com) Its ferries make runs up the Hudson River Valley and from Midtown to Yankee Stadium in the Bronx. A popular commuter route goes from the New Jersey Transit train station in Hoboken to the World Financial Center in Lower Manhattan.

Northern New Jersey

Stay east and you'll experience the Jersey urban jungle. Go west to find its opposite: the peaceful, refreshing landscape of the Delaware Water Gap and rolling Kittatinny Mountains.

Hoboken & Jersey City

A sort of TV-land version of a cityscape, Hoboken is a cute little urban pocket just across the Hudson River from NYC – and, because of cheaper rents that lured pioneers almost 15 years ago, a sort of sixth city borough, too. On weekends the bars and live-music venues come alive, but the town also has loads of restaurants lining commercial Washington St, some lovely residential lanes and a leafy, revitalized waterfront – a far cry from when the gritty *On the Waterfront* was filmed here.

High-rise buildings housing condominiums and the offices of financial firms seeking lower rents have transformed Jersey City for better or worse from a primarily blue-collar and immigrant neighborhood into a 'restored' area for the upwardly mobile. Its biggest draw is the 1200-acre Liberty State Park (☑201-915-3440; www.libertystatepark.org; ⊙6am-10pm), which hosts outdoor concerts with the Manhattan skyline as a backdrop and has a great bike trail, and also operates ferries (☑201-604-2800, 877-523-9849; www.statuecruises.com; adult/child $17/9; ⊙every 30min 9am-5pm, extended summer hr) to Ellis Island and the Statue of Liberty. Also in the park and great for kids – virtually every exhibit is interactive – is the expansive and modern Liberty Science Center (☑201-200-1000; www.lsc.org; adult/child $19.75/14.75, extra for IMAX & special exhibits; ⊙9am-4pm Mon-Fri, to 5:30pm Sat & Sun;).

Delaware Water Gap

The Delaware River meanders in a tight S-curve through the ridge of NJ's Kittatinny Mountains, and its beauteous image turned this region into a resort area, beginning in the 19th century. The Delaware Water Gap National Recreation Area (☑570-426-2452; www.nps.gov), which comprises land in both New Jersey and Pennsylvania, was established as a protected area in 1965, and today it's still an unspoiled place to swim, boat, fish, camp, hike and see wildlife – just 70 miles east of New York City. The 30 mile stretch of good paved road on the Pennsylvania side has many worthwhile stops including Raymondskill Falls and the Pocono Environmental Education Center (☑570-828-2319; www.peec.org; 538 Emery Rd,

---

NEW JERSEY FACTS

Nickname Garden State

Population 8.8 million

Area 8722 sq miles

Capital city Trenton (population 85,000)

Other cities Newark (population 277,000)

Sales tax 7%

Birthplace of Musician Count Basie (1904–84), singer Frank Sinatra (1915–98), actor Meryl Streep (b 1949), musician Bruce Springsteen (b 1949), actor John Travolta (b 1954), musician Jon Bon Jovi (b 1962), rapper Queen Latifah (b 1970), pop band Jonas Brothers: Kevin (b 1987), Joseph (b 1989), Nicolas (b 1992)

Home of The first movie (1889), first professional baseball game (1896), first drive-in theater (1933), the Statue of Liberty

Politics Republican governor Chris Christie, though strong traditionally Democratic legislature

Famous for *The Jersey Shore* (the real thing and the MTV reality show), the setting for *The Sopranos*, Bruce Springsteen's musical beginnings

Number of wineries Thirty six

Driving distances Princeton to NYC 55 miles, Atlantic City to NYC 135 miles

Dingman's Ferry; ⊞) 𝄞; the very developed but stunning Bushkill Falls (☑ 570-588-6682; Rte 209, Bushkill; adult/child $12.50/7; ⊙ opens 9am, closing times vary, closed Dec-Mar) is several miles to the north. On the New Jersey side, take Old Mine Rd, one of the oldest continually operating commercial roads in the US, to trailheads for day hikes such as the one to the top of the 1574ft Mt Tammany in Worthington State Forest (☑ 908-841-9575; www.njparksandforests.org).

For river fun, contact Adventure Sports (☑ 570-223-0505, 800-487-2628; www.adventuresport.com; Rte 209; per day canoe/kayak $40/44; ⊙ 9am-6pm Mon-Fri, from 8am Sat & Sun May-Oct) in Marshalls Creek, Pennsylvania. There are several different put-in and take-out points that allow a variety of itineraries. Camping is allowed at many points along the way and is a great way to experience the beauty of the area.

Northeast of here, High Point State Park (☑ 973-875-4800; www.njparksandforests. org; 1480 Rte 23, Sussex; ⊙ 8am-8pm Apr-Oct, to 4:30pm other months), which is also great for camping and hiking, has a monument that, at 1803ft above sea level, affords wonderful views of surrounding lakes, hills and farmland.

The nearby town of Milford across the border in Pennsylvania is a charming place with several good restaurants and Grey Towers (☑ 570-296-9630; www.greytowers. org; Old Owego Turnpike; tours adult/child $8/ free; ⊙ grounds dawn-dusk), once the gorgeous French chateau-style home of Gifford Pinchot, the first director of the US Forest Service and a two-term governor of Pennsylvania.

Princeton & Around

Settled by an English Quaker missionary, the tiny town of Princeton is filled with lovely architecture and several noteworthy sites, number one of which is its Ivy League Princeton University (www.princeton.edu), which was built in the mid-1700s and soon became one of the largest structures in the early colonies. The town's Palmer Square, built in 1936, is a lovely place to shop and stroll. The Historical Society of Princeton (☑ 609-921-6748; www.princetonhistory.org; 158 Nassau St; tours adult/child $7/4) leads historical walking tours of the town on Sundays at 2pm, and the Orange Key Guide Service & Campus Information Office (☑ 609-258-3060; www.princeton.edu/orangekey) offers free university tours. The Princeton University Art Museum (☑ 609-258-3788; www.princetonart-museum.org; McCormack Hall, Princeton University Campus; ⊙ 10am-5pm, to 10pm Thu) FREE is akin to a mini-Metropolitan Museum of Art in terms of its variety and quality of works, which range from ancient Greek pottery to Andy Warhol.

Accommodations are expensive and hard to find during graduation time in May and June, but beyond that it should be easy to arrange for a stay at one of several atmospheric inns, including the traditionally furnished Nassau Inn (☑ 609-921-7500; www. nassauinn.com; 10 Palmer Sq; r incl breakfast from $169; ▒ 🛜 🞅). For reasonably priced healthy Mediterranean-style food with a Greek emphasis stop by Olives (22 Witherspoon St, Princeton; sandwiches $7; ⊙ 7am-8pm) for lunchtime takeout.

It may not be the most beautiful place, but New Jersey's capital, Trenton, has several historic sites, a museum and a farmers market worth visiting – especially if you can pair it up with a trip to Philly or Atlantic City.

Jersey Shore

Perhaps the most famous and revered feature of New Jersey is its sparkling shore (www.visitthejerseyshore.com), stretching from Sandy Hook to Cape May and studded with resort towns ranging from tacky to classy. You'll find as many mothers pushing strollers as throngs proudly clutching souvenir beer bongs. Though it's mobbed during summer weekends, you could find yourself wonderfully alone on the sand come early fall. Beach access varies across communities, though the majority charge reasonably priced fees for the day. Putting up a tent in a state park or private campground is a low cost alternative during the summer months when finding good-value accommodations is nearly as difficult as locating un-tattooed skin.

Sandy Hook & Around

At the northernmost tip of the Jersey Shore is the Sandy Hook Gateway National Recreation Area (☑ 718-354-4606), a 7-mile sandy barrier beach at the entrance to New York Harbor. You can see the city skyline from your beach blanket on clear days, which only heightens the sense of pleasure and feeling of dislocation. The ocean side of the peninsula has wide, sandy beaches (including a nude beach, the only legal one in NJ, at Gunnison Beach) edged by an extensive system of bike trails, while the bay side is great for fishing or wading. The brick buildings of the abandoned coast-guard station, Fort Hancock (⊙1-5pm Sat & Sun) FREE, house a small museum. The Sandy Hook Lighthouse, which offers guided tours, is the oldest in the country. Bug spray is recommended as biting flies can be a nuisance at dusk.

A fast ferry service, Seastreak (☑800-262-8743; www.seastreak.com; 2 First Ave, Atlantic Highlands; return $45), runs between Sandy Hook (and the Highlands) and Pier 11 in downtown Manhattan or East 35th St, NYC.

Long Branch, Asbury Park & Ocean Grove

Sanitized and slightly generic compared to other shore locations, Long Branch is the first major beach town south of the Highlands. Just a bit inland from here is the famed Monmouth Park Race Track (☑732-222-5100; www.monmouthpark.com; grandstand/clubhouse $3/5; ⊙11:30am-6pm May-Aug), where you can see thoroughbred racing in a gracious, historic setting.

Just south of Long Branch, massive homes the size of museums in the community of Deal are worth gawking at. However, once you cross over Deal Lake into Asbury Park, luxury gives way to abandoned row houses and potholed streets. But the town, which experienced passing prominence in the 1970s when Bruce Springsteen 'arrived' at the Stone Pony (☑732-502-0600; 913 Ocean Ave) nightclub and then a major decline, has been revitalized. Led by wealthy gay men from NYC who snapped up blocks of forgotten Victorian homes and storefronts to refurbish, the downtown (the liveliest on the shore), which includes several blocks of Cookman and Bangs Aves, is lined with charming shops, restaurants, bars and a restored art-house cinema. The sprawling Antique Emporium of Asbury Park (☑732-774-8230; 646 Cookman Ave; ⊙11am-5pm Mon-Sat & noon-5pm Sun) has two levels of amazing finds.

The town immediately to the south, Ocean Grove, is a fascinating place to wander. Founded by Methodists in the 19th century, the place retains what's left of a post–Civil War revival camp called Tent City – now a historic site with 114 cottage-like canvas tents clustered together, which are used as summer homes. The town has dazzling well-preserved Victorian architecture and a 6500-seat wooden auditorium, and there are many beautiful, big-porched Victorian inns to choose from for a stay; visit www.oceangrovenj.com for guidance. A few miles inland just off the Garden State Pkwy is a very utilitarian-looking Premium outlet mall.

Bradley Beach to Spring Lake

Bradley Beach has row after row of adorable summer cottages and a beautiful stretch of shore. Belmar Beach is equally inviting and has a boardwalk with a few food shacks and a handful of restaurants and busy bars on the oceanfront road. The New Jersey Sandcastle Contest (www.njsandcastle.com) is held here in mid-July.

South of here is Spring Lake, a wealthy community once known as the 'Irish Riviera,' with manicured lawns, grand oceanfront Victorian houses, a gorgeous beach and elegant accommodations. This quiet low-key base is about as far from the typical shore boardwalk experience as you can get. Try the bright and airy Grand Victorian at Spring Lake (☑732-449-5237; www.grandvictorianspringlake.com; 1505 Ocean Ave; r with shared/private bath with breakfast from $100/150; ❀ 🛜).

HURRICANE SANDY

In late October 2012 Hurricane Sandy devastated much of the New York and New Jersey coastline, destroying homes, breaching barrier islands, ripping away boardwalks and washing away entire waterfront communities. In New York the hardest hit were Staten Island, the Rockaways and Red Hook, while the Jersey Shore from Sandy Hook to Atlantic City suffered the brunt of the hurricane's impact. The dimensions and profiles of many beaches were diminished and it remains to be seen whether rebuilding efforts will add dunes and other storm surge impediments where none existed before. More than six months later, there are still significant pockets of desolation: piles of debris, houses with their sides ripped away and others that teeter at gravity-defying angles.

Only 5 miles inland from Spring Lake is quirky Historic Village at Allaire (☑732-919-3500; www.allairevillage.org; adult/child $3/2; ☺noon-4pm Wed-Sun late May-early Sep, noon-4pm Sat & Sun Nov-May), the remains of what was a thriving 19th-century village called Howell Works. You can still visit various 'shops,' all run by folks in period costume.

Ocean County Beaches

Just south of the Manasquan River is Point Pleasant. The northern end of the town boardwalk is backed by small, idiosyncratic vacation homes only feet from the beach-going hordes; the southern half, called Jenkinson's Boardwalk, has the usual salt-water taffy shops, eateries and amusement rides, as well as an aquarium good for kids and an enormous bar and restaurant for adults jutting out over the beach. A few sea-food restaurants with outdoor patios built over the water can be found on a marina and inlet of the river – try the Shrimp Box (75 Inlet Dr; sandwiches $10, mains $17; ☺noon-10:30pm). Just north of here in Manasquan, Inlet Beach has the Shore's most reliable year-round waves for surfers.

Just below there, the narrow Barnegat Peninsula barrier island extends some 22 miles south from Point Pleasant. In its center, Seaside Heights of MTV reality-show Jersey Shore fame sucks in the raucous twenty-something summer crowds with two amusement piers (one of these was torn apart by Hurricane Sandy, leaving the Star Jet roller coaster stranded in the ocean until June 2013) and an above-average number of boardwalk bars. Because the beach is relatively narrow, this is not the place to go for privacy or quiet. Better yet, ride the chair lift running from the Casino Pier to the northern end of the boardwalk. If the ocean is not to your taste, beat the heat on the lazy river at the Breakwater Beach Waterpark (www.casinopiernj.com/breakwaterbeach; admission $25; ☺10am-7pm May-Aug; 🌴). There isn't much to recommend about a stay at one of the crash pads on the neglected sun-baked streets inland from the boardwalk. Camping at Surf & Stream Campground (☑732-349-8919; www.surfnstream.com; 1801 Ridgeway Rd/Rte 571, Toms River; campsites $45) in Tom's River about 6 miles to the west is a convenient option. Tucked away in the K-Mart shopping plaza in Tom's River is the silly and sarcastically named Shut Up and Eat! (☑732-349-4544; 213 Rte 37 East; mains $9), where waitresses in pajamas adept at snappy repartee serve up stuffed French toast, pancakes and more. Just to the north of Seaside Heights in Lavallette is Music Man (☑732-854-2779; www.njmusicman.com; 2305 Grand Central Ave/Rte 35, Lavallette; ice cream $3-8; ☺takeout 6am-

---

OFF THE BEATEN TRACK

PINE BARRENS

Locals call this region the Pinelands – and like to carry on the lore about the one million acres of pine forest being home to a mythical beast known as the 'Jersey Devil.' Containing several state parks and forests, the area is a haven for bird-watchers, hikers, campers, canoeists and all-round nature enthusiasts. Inland is the Wharton State Forest (☑609-561-0024), one of the good places to canoe – as well as hike and picnic. To understand the region's early history, begin at the well-preserved village of Batsto founded in 1766 to forge 'bog iron' for the Revolutionary War. The best-known trail is the epic 50-mile Batona Trail, which cuts through several state parks and forests and passes by the Apple Pie Hill Fire Tower, from which there are magnificent 360-degree views of hundreds of square miles of forest. A good outfitter is Micks Pine Barrens Canoe and Kayak Rental (☑609-726-1515; www.pinebarrenscanoe.com; 3107 Rte 563; per day kayak/canoe $37/48), which has maps and other details about boating trips in the area. Further south along the coast is the Edwin B Forsythe National Wildlife Refuge (☑609-652-1665), 40,000 acres of bays, coves, forests, marshes, swamps, and barrier beaches and a paradise for bird-watchers. A recommended camping spot is the lakeside Atsion Family Campground (☑609-268-0444; www.state.nj.us; 31 Batsto Rd; tent sites $20; ☺Apr 31-Oct 1) in Wharton State Forest; nearby, between Atsion and the town of Hammonton is Penza's (☑609-567-3412; 51 Myrtle St, Hammonton; mains 5-$10; ☺8am-5pm), an old-fashioned cafe in a red barn serving great omelets and homemade fruit pies.

midnight, shows 6pm-midnight; 🍴), an ice-cream shop where servers belt out Broadway show tunes tableside.

Occupying the southern third of Barnegat Peninsula is Island Beach State Park (☑ 732-793-0506; www.islandbeachnj.org; per car weekday/weekend $6/10), a 10-mile barrier island that's pure, untouched dunes and wetlands. Although the very southern tip of the park is within throwing distance of Long Beach Island, just across a narrow inlet to the bay south of here, to reach this long sliver of an island with beautiful beaches and impressive summer homes you have to backtrack all the way to Seaside Heights and travel along Rte 9 or the Garden State Pkwy. The landmark Barnegat Lighthouse State Park (☑ 609-494-2016; www.njparksandforests.org; off Long Beach Blvd; ⊙ 8am-4pm), at the very northern tip of the island, offers panoramic views at the top while fishermen cast off from a jetty extending 2000ft along the Atlantic Ocean. Tucked down a residential street in North Beach Haven is Hudson House (13th St, Beach Haven; ⊙ 5pm-1am), a nearly locals-only dive bar about as worn and comfortable as an old pair of flip-flops. A few miles south of Rte 72, which bisects Long Beach Island, is Daddy O (☑ 609-361-5100; www.daddyohotel.com; 4401 Long Beach Blvd; r $195-375), a sleek boutique hotel and restaurant near the ocean.

Atlantic City

It's not exactly Vegas, but for many a trip to AC conjures up *Hangover*-like scenes of debauchery. And inside the casinos, which never see the light of day, it's easy to forget there's a sandy beach just outside and boarded-up shop windows a few blocks in the other direction. The 'AC' that was known throughout the late 19th and early 20th century for its grand boardwalk and Oceanside amusement pier, and for the glamorous corruption depicted in the HBO series *Boardwalk Empire* set in 1920 Prohibition-era AC, has been thoroughly overturned. Gray-haired retirees and vacationing families are at least as common as bachelors and bachelorettes.

It's worth nothing that AC's famous boardwalk, 8 miles long and still the lifeline of the city, was the first in the world. Built in 1870 by local business owners who wanted to cut down on sand being tracked into hotel lobbies, it was named in honor of Alexander Boardman who came up with the idea – Boardman's Walk later became 'Boardwalk'.

The Steel Pier, directly in front of the Taj Mahal casino, was the site of the famous high-diving horse that plunged into the Atlantic before crowds of spectators. Today it's a collection of amusement rides, games of chance, candy stands and a go-kart track.

The small Atlantic City Historical Museum (☑ 609-347-5839; www.acmuseum.org; Garden Pier; ⊙ 10am-5pm) FREE provides a quirky look at AC's past. At the time of research it was closed due to damage from Hurricane Sandy, but was expected to reopen.

🛏 Sleeping & Eating

A handful of motor inns and cheap motels line Pacific Ave, a block inland from the boardwalk. Most of the big boardwalk hotel casinos offer extremely reduced rates midweek out of season (September to May). Some of the best in-casino dining is to be had at the Borgata. Good (and more affordable) food can be found in the 'real' part of downtown and in nearby Ventnor and Margate.

Chelsea   BOUTIQUE HOTEL **$**
(☑ 800-548-3030; www.thechelsea-ac.com; 111 S Chelsea Ave; r from $80; ⓟ❄@📶🏊) Non-casino, trendy with art-deco-style furnishings. Rooms in the attached annex are less expensive. Also houses a retro diner, steakhouse and cabana club.

Revel AC   RESORT **$$**
(☑ 609-572-6488; www.revelresorts.com; 500 Boardwalk; r from $160; ⓟ❄@📶🏊🏊) This 47-story $2.4 billion newcomer occupies a relatively isolated spot at the far northern end of the AC boardwalk; with a big beach in front – all rooms have ocean views. The Revel has all the bells and whistles you'd expect plus a concert hall and 12 restaurants, including a Mexican food truck parked indoors.

Kelsey & Kim's Café   BARBECUE **$**
(201 Melrose Ave; mains $9; ⊙ 7am-10pm) Excellent Southern comfort food like fried whiting, pulled BBQ beef brisket sandwich and fried chicken.

Angelo's Fairmount Tavern   ITALIAN **$**
(2300 Fairmount Ave; mains $7; ⊙ 11:30am-3pm & 5-10pm) Angelo's Fairmount Tavern is a beloved family-owned Italian restaurant. The outdoor patio makes a nice spot to take in the sunset and have a pint and a burger.

❶ Information

The **Atlantic City Convention & Visitors Bureau** (☑ 609-348-7100; www.atlanticcitynj. com; 2314 Pacific Ave; ☺ 9am-5pm) has a location in the middle of the Atlantic City Expwy and another right on the boardwalk at Mississippi Ave. **Atlantic City Weekly** (www.acweekly.com) has useful info on events, clubs and eateries.

❶ Getting There & Away

Air Tran and Spirit Airlines fly into the small **Atlantic City International Airport** (ACY; ☑ 609-645-7895; www.acairport.com), a 20-minute drive from the center of Atlantic City and a great option for reaching any part of South Jersey or Philadelphia.

There are many bus options to AC, including NJ Transit (one way $36, 2½ hours) and Greyhound (one way $25, 2½ hours), both leaving from New York's Port Authority (p110). A casino will often refund much of the fare (in chips, coins or coupons) if you get a bus directly to its door. Take note that when leaving AC, buses first stop at various casinos and only stop at the bus station when not full.

New Jersey Transit (☑ 800-772-2287; www. njtransit.com) trains only go to Atlantic City from Philadelphia (one way $10, 1½ hours).

Ocean City & The Wildwoods

South of Atlantic City, Ocean City is an old-fashioned family-holiday spot, home to dune-swept beaches and a number of child-centric arcades, a small waterpark, mini-golf courses and themed playlands along its lively boardwalk. Motels are plentiful, relatively cheap and old-fashioned, as are the myriad crab shacks and seafood joints.

Further south on the way to Cape May, the three towns of North Wildwood, Wildwood and Wildwood Crest are an archaeological find – whitewashed motels with flashing neon signs, turquoise curtains and pink doors, especially in Wildwood Crest, a kitsch slice of 1950s Americana. Check out eye-catching motel signs like the Lollipop at 23rd and Atlantic Aves. Wildwood, a party town popular with teens, twenty-somethings and the young people who staff the restaurants and shops, is the main social focus. The width of the beach, more than 1000ft in parts, makes it the widest in NJ and means there's always space. Several massive piers are host to water parks and amusement parks – easily the rival of any Six Flags Great Adventure – with roller coasters and rides best suited to aspir-ing astronauts anchoring the 2-mile-long Grand Daddy of Jersey Shore boardwalks. Glow-in-the-dark 3D mini-golf is a good example of the Wildwood boardwalk ethos – take it to the limit, then one step further. Maybe the best ride of all, and one that doesn't induce nausea, is the tram (one-way $2.50; ☺ 9am-1am) running the length of the boardwalk from Wildwood Crest to North Wildwood. There's always a line for a table at Jersey Shore staple pizzeria Mack & Manco's on the boardwalk (it has other shore boardwalk locations).

About 250 small motels – no corporate chains here – offer rooms for $50 to $250; however, it makes sense to narrow your search to the more salubrious area of Wildwood Crest. The sea-green and white Starlux (☑ 609-522-7412; www.thestarlux.com; Rio Grande & Atlantic Aves, Wildwood; r $130-310; ⊛) has a soaring profile, lava lamps, boomerang-decorated bedspreads and even two chrome-sided Airstream trailers. If you're here for waterslides and roller coasters, book a room at the Heart of Wildwood (☑ 609-522-4090; www.heartofwildwood.com; Ocean & Spencer Aves, Wildwood; r $125-245; ⊛), facing the amusement piers. It's not fancy but it gets high marks for cleanliness.

Cape May

Founded in 1620, Cape May – the only place in the state where the sun rises and sets over the water – is on the state's southern tip and is the country's oldest seashore resort. Its sweeping beaches get crowded in summer, but the stunning Victorian architecture is attractive year-round.

In addition to 600 gingerbread-style houses, the city boasts antique shops and the opportunity to watch dolphins, whales (May to December) and birds. It's just outside the Cape May Point State Park and its 157ft Cape May Lighthouse (adult/child $7/3); there's an excellent visitors center and museum with exhibits on wildlife in the area. A mile-long loop of the nearby Cape May Bird Observatory (☑ 609-861-0700, 609-898-2473; www.birdcapemay.org; 701 East Lake Dr; ☺ 9am-4:30pm) is a pleasant stroll through preserved wetlands. The wide sandy beaches at the park (free) and in the town are the main attraction in summer months. Aqua Trails (☑ 609-884-5600; www. aquatrails.com; single/double from $40/70) offers kayak tours of the coastal wetlands.

Cape May's B&B options are endless, though the majority lean toward overstuffed and chintzy; check out www.capemaytimes.com for up-to-date listings. The classic, sprawling Congress Hall (☑888-944-1816; www.caperesorts.com; 251 Beach Ave; r $100-465) has a range of beautiful quarters overlooking the ocean, plus it has a cool on-site restaurant and bar; the affiliated Beach Shack (☑877-7422-507; www.caperesorts.com; 205 Beach Ave; r from $120; ☎) and Star Inn (☑800-297-3779; www.caperesorts.com; 29 Perry St; r from $150; ☎) offer a variety of accommodations for various budgets (look for deep discounts out of summer season).

The flapjacks at Uncle Bill's Pancake House (Beach Ave at Perry St; mains $7; ☺6:30am-2pm), which resembles a 1950s high-school cafeteria in its size and decor, have been drawing in crowds for 50 years. For unarguably fresh seafood – the restaurant's own boats haul in the day's catch – try the Lobster House (906 Schellengers Landing Rd, Fisherman's Wharf; mains $12-27; ☺11:30am-3pm & 4:30-10pm Apr-Dec, to 9pm other times). No reservations mean long waits are the norm; in that case grab a seat at the dockside raw bar. Otherwise, head to the Washington Street Mall, a cobblestone street lined with shops and more than a half-dozen restaurants.

To continue your journey further south without having to backtrack north and far inland, the Cape May-Lewes Ferry (www.cmlf.com; car/passenger $44/8; ☺hourly in summer 6am–9:30pm; check website out of season) crosses the bay to Lewes, Delaware, near Rehoboth Beach. The journey takes 1½ hours.

PENNSYLVANIA

In a state so large it's unsurprising that geography helps determine identity. The further west you go the closer you are to the rest of America. Philadelphia, once the heart of the British colonial empire and the intellectual and spiritual motor of its demise, is firmly ensconced culturally in the East Coast. Residents of Pittsburgh and western Pennsylvania (PA), on the other hand, are proud to identify themselves as part of the city or immediate region, relishing their blue-collar reputation and their distinctiveness from East Coasters. Moving east to west, the terrain becomes more rugged and you begin to appreciate

the sheer size and diversity of the state. Philly's Independence Park and historic district offer an ideal opportunity to come to some understanding of this nation's origins. Nearby, the battle sites of Gettysburg and Valley Forge provide another chance to travel back in time. But the city and state offer more than the clichés associated with school field trips. Stunning natural forests and mountain areas such as the Poconos and Allegheny National Forest provide endless outdoor adventures. Both Philly and Pittsburgh are vibrant university cities with thriving music, performance and art scenes. Frank Lloyd Wright's architectural masterpiece, Fallingwater, and Amish country, not to mention the region's small, artsy towns, are perfect for weekend getaways.

PENNSYLVANIA FACTS

Nicknames Keystone State, Quaker State

Population 12.7 million

Area 46,058 sq miles

Capital city Harrisburg (population 53,000)

Other cities Philadelphia (population 1.45 million), Pittsburgh (population 313,000), Erie (population 102,000)

Sales tax 6%

Birthplace of Writer Louisa May Alcott (1832–88), dancer Martha Graham (1878–1948), artist Andy Warhol (1928–87), movie star Grace Kelly (1929–82), comic Bill Cosby (b 1937)

Home of US Constitution, the Liberty Bell, first daily newspaper (1784), first auto service station (1913), first computer (1946)

Politics 'Swing state,' Republican governor, progressive Philly and blue-collar Democrats elsewhere

Famous for Soft pretzels, Amish people, Philadelphia cheesesteak, Pittsburgh steel mills

Wildlife Home of the largest herd of wild elk east of the Mississippi

Driving distances Philadelphia to NYC 100 miles, Philadelphia to Pittsburgh 306 miles

Philadelphia

Although it may seem like a little sibling to NYC, which is less than 90 miles away, Philadelphia is more representative of what East Coast city living is like. And in the minds of many, it offers every upside of urban life: burgeoning food, music and art scenes, neighborhoods with distinct personalities, copious parkland and, just as importantly, relatively affordable real estate. The older, preserved buildings in historic Philadelphia provide a picture of what colonial

Philadelphia

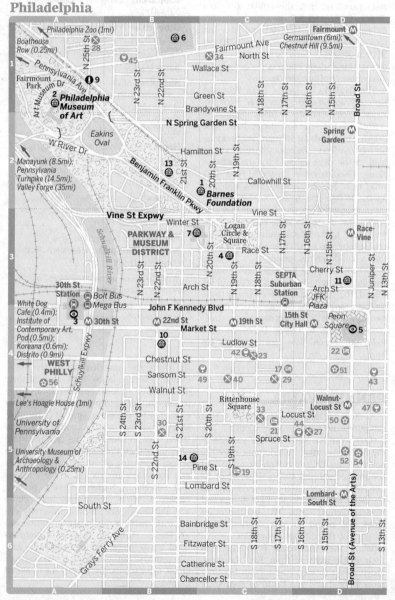

American cities once looked like – based on a grid with wide streets and public squares.

For a time the second-largest city in the British Empire (after London), Philadelphia became a center for opposition to British colonial policy. It was the new nation's capital at the start of the Revolutionary War and again after the war until 1790, when Washington, DC, took over. By the 19th century, NYC had superseded Philadelphia as the nation's cultural, commercial and industrial center. Though urban renewal has been going on for decades, parts of the city formerly populated by industrial workers are blighted

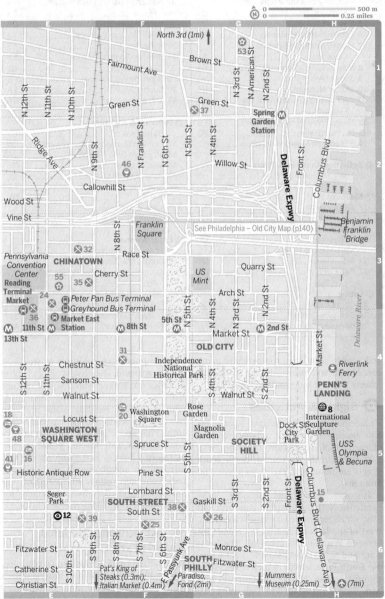

Philadelphia

and worlds away from the carefully manicured lawns and historic district around the Liberty Bell and Independence Hall.

⊙ Sights & Activities

Philadelphia is easy to navigate. Most sights and hotels are within walking distance of each other, or a short bus ride away. East–west streets are named; north–south streets are numbered, except for Broad and Front Sts.

Historic Philadelphia includes Independence National Historic Park and Old City, which extends east to the waterfront. West of the historic district is Center City, home to Penn Sq and City Hall. The Delaware and Schuylkill (*skoo*-kill) Rivers border South Philadelphia, which features the colorful Italian Market, restaurants and bars. West of the Schuylkill, University City

has two important campuses as well as a major museum. Northwest Philadelphia includes the genteel suburbs of Chestnut Hill and Germantown, plus Manayunk, with plenty of bustling pubs and hip eateries. The South St area, between S 2nd, 10th, Pine and Fitzwater Sts, has grungy youthful bars, eateries and music venues. Northern Liberties and Fishtown are two burgeoning neighborhoods with eclectic bars, cafes and restaurants, a sort of Williamsburg and Greenpoint tandem for those who know Brooklyn.

⊙ Independence National Historic Park

This L-shaped park, along with Old City, has been dubbed 'America's most historic square mile.' Once the backbone of the United States government, it has become the backbone of Philadelphia's tourist trade. Stroll around and you'll see storied buildings in which the seeds for the Revolutionary War were planted and the US government came into bloom. You'll also find beautiful, shaded urban lawns dotted with plenty of benches and costumed actors wandering about. Look for any of the 10 'Once Upon a Nation' signs for free dramatic historic storytelling sessions (11am to 4pm). Only the National Constitution Center charges admission; all other sites are free, though they may require reservations.

Liberty Bell Center HISTORIC SITE
(Map p140; ☑215-597-8974; www.nps.gove/inde; 6th & Market Sts; ☺9am-5pm) Philadelphia's top tourist attraction, the Liberty Bell was commissioned to commemorate the 50th anniversary of the Charter of Privileges (Pennsylvania's constitution, enacted in 1701 by William Penn). The 2080lb bronze bell was made in London's East End by the Whitechapel Bell Foundry in 1751. The bell's inscription, from Leviticus 25:10, reads: 'Proclaim liberty through all the land, to all the inhabitants thereof.' The bell was secured in the belfry of the Pennsylvania State House (now Independence Hall) and tolled on important occasions, most notably the first public reading of the Declaration of Independence in Independence Sq. The bell became badly cracked during the 19th century; despite initial repairs, it became unusable in 1846 after tolling for George Washington's birthday.

★National Constitution Center MUSEUM
(Map p140; ☑215-409-6700; www.constitutioncenter.org; 525 Arch St; adult/child $14.50/8; ☺9:30am-5pm Mon-Fri, to 6pm Sat, noon-5pm Sun; ☑) This highly recommended museum makes the United States Constitution sexy and interesting for a general audience through theater-in-the-round reenactments. There are exhibits such as interactive voting booths and Signer's Hall, which contains lifelike bronze statues of the signers in action.

Independence Hall HISTORIC BUILDING
(Map p140; ☑215-597-8974; Chestnut St, btwn 5th & 6th Sts) Independence Hall is the 'birthplace of American government,' where delegates from the 13 colonies met to approve the Declaration of Independence on July 4, 1776. An excellent example of Georgian architecture, it sports understated lines that reveal Philadelphia's Quaker heritage.

Other Attractions HISTORIC BUILDINGS
Other attractions in this historic park include Carpenters' Hall, owned by the Carpenter Company, the USA's oldest trade guild (1724), which is the site of the First Continental Congress in 1774; Library Hall (Map p140), where you'll find a copy of the Declaration of Independence, handwritten in a letter by Thomas Jefferson, plus first editions of Darwin's *On the Origin of the Species* and Lewis and Clark's field notes; Congress Hall (Map p140; S 6th & Chestnut Sts), the meeting place for US Congress when Philly was the nation's capital; and Old City Hall (Map p140), finished in 1791, which was home to the US Supreme Court until 1800. The Franklin Court (Map p140) complex, a row of restored tenements, pays tribute to Benjamin Franklin with a clever underground museum displaying his inventions, and details his many other contributions (as statesman, author and journalist) to society. Christ Church (Map p140; ☑215-627-2750; N 2nd St), completed in 1744, is where George Washington and Franklin worshipped.

Philosophical Hall (Map p140; ☑215-440-3400; 104 S 5th St; admission $1; ☺10am-4pm Thu-Sun Mar–Labor Day & Fri-Sun Labor Day–Feb), south of Old City Hall, is the headquarters of the American Philosophical Society, founded in 1743 by Benjamin Franklin. Past members have included Thomas Jefferson, Marie Curie, Thomas Edison, Charles Darwin and Albert Einstein.

Second Bank of the US (Map p140; Chestnut St, btwn 4th & 5th Sts), modeled after the Greek Parthenon, is an 1824 marble-faced Greek Revival masterpiece that was home to the world's most powerful financial institution until President Andrew Jackson dissolved its charter in 1836. The building then became the Philadelphia Customs House until 1935, when it became a museum. Today it's home to the National Portrait Gallery (Map p140; Chestnut St; ☺11am-4pm Wed-Sun), housing many paintings by Charles Willson Peale, America's top portrait artist at the time of the American Revolution.

⊙ Old City

Old City – the area bounded by Walnut, Vine, Front and 6th Sts – picks up where Independence National Historical Park leaves off. Along with Society Hill, Old City was early Philadelphia. The 1970s

Philadelphia – Old City

saw revitalization, with many warehouses converted into apartments, galleries and small businesses. Today it's a quaint and fascinating place for a stroll. Check out the 9ft-tall Ben Franklin sculpture at Fourth and Arch Sts.

Elfreth's Alley
HISTORIC SITE

(Map p140; www.elfrethsalley.org; off 2nd St, btwn Arch & Race Sts; ⏲ museum 10am-5pm Wed-Sat, from noon Sun) The tiny, cobblestone alleyway – a little slice of colonial America in miniature – is believed to be the oldest continuously occupied street in the USA. One

of the homes has been converted into a museum (tours $5, noon & 3pm). Its 32 well-preserved brick row houses are inhabited by real-live Philadelphians, so be considerate as you walk down the narrow space.

National Museum of American Jewish History
MUSEUM

(Map p140; ☑ 215-923-3811; www.nmajh.org; 101 South Independence Mall E; adult/child $12/free; ⏲ 10am-5pm Tue-Fri, to 5:30pm Sat & Sun) The distinct translucent facade of this museum houses state-of-the-art exhibits that examine the historical role of Jews in the USA.

Philadelphia – Old City

Betsy Ross House   HISTORIC SITE
(Map p140; ☑ 215-686-1252; www.betsyross-house.org; 239 Arch St; suggested donation adult/child $3/2; ⊙ 10am-5pm daily Apr-Sep, closed Mon Oct-Mar) It's believed that Betsy Griscom Ross (1752–1836), upholsterer and seamstress, may have sewn the first US flag here.

United States Mint   TOUR
(Map p140; ☑ 215-408-0110; www.usmint.gov; 151 N Independence Mall E; ⊙ tours 9am-4:30pm Mon-Fri, incl Sat in summer) FREE Line up for same-day, self-guided tours that last about 45 minutes.

⊙ Society Hill

Architecture from the 18th and 19th centuries dominates the lovely residential neighborhood of Society Hill, bounded by Front and 8th Sts from east to west, and Walnut and Lombard Sts north and south. Along the cobblestoned streets you'll see mainly 18th- and 19th-century brick row houses, mixed in with the occasional modern high-rise, such as the Society Hill Towers designed by IM Pei. Washington Square was conceived as part of William Penn's original city plan, and offers a peaceful respite from sightseeing. Two 18th-century brownstones, the Physick House and Powel House are open to the public for tours through the Philadelphia Society for the Preservation of Landmarks (☑ 215-925-2251; www.philalandmarks.org; 321 S 4th St; adult/child $5/free; ⊙ noon-4pm Thu-Sat, from 1pm Sun, by appt Jan & Feb).

⊙ Center City, Rittenhouse Square & Around

Philadelphia's center of creativity, commerce, culture and just about everything else, this region is the engine that drives the city. It contains the city's tallest buildings, the financial district, big hotels, museums, concert halls, shops and restaurants.

The leafy Rittenhouse Square, with its wading pool and fine statues, is the best known of William Penn's city squares. Surrounded by upscale cafes, restaurants, condominiums and hotels, it feels like a little slice of European elegance.

City Hall   BUILDING
(Map p136; ☑ 215-686-2840; www.phila.gov; cnr Broad & Market Sts; ⊙ 9:30am-4:30pm Tue-Fri) FREE The majestic City Hall, completed in 1901, stands 548ft tall in Penn Sq. It's the world's tallest masonry construction (and larger than the US Capitol) without a steel frame, and it's topped by a 27-ton bronze statue of William Penn. A gentleman's agreement to keep City Hall the tallest building in the city lasted until 1987. Access to the tower observation deck and guided tours available.

Rosenbach Museum & Library   MUSEUM
(Map p136; ☑ 215-732-1600; www.rosenbach.org; 2008 Delancey Pl; adult/child $10/5; ⊙ noon-5pm Tue & Fri, Wed & Thu to 8pm, to 6pm Sat & Sun) This place is for bibliophiles, as it features rare books and manuscripts, including James Joyce's *Ulysses,* and incunabula, basically the earliest printed books from 1450

to 1500. Docent-led tours of the elegant home highlight period-furnished rooms, Thomas Sully portraits and the Marianne Moore room – essentially the modernist poet's Greenwich Village apartment lock, stock and barrel.

Mutter Museum   MUSEUM
(Map p136; ☑ 215-563-3737; www.collphyphil.org; 19 S 22nd St; adult/child $14/10; ☺ 10am-5pm) Skip med school and visit this seriously twisted museum to learn all about the history of medicine in the US.

⊙ Fairmount

Modeled after the Champs Elysées in Paris, the Benjamin Franklin Parkway is a center of museums and other landmarks.

★ Philadelphia Museum of Art   MUSEUM
(Map p136; ☑ 215-763-8100; www.philamuseum. org; 2600 Benjamin Franklin Pkwy; adult/child $20/free; ☺ 10am-5pm Tue, Thu, Sat & Sun, to 8:45pm Wed & Fri) It's one of the nation's largest and most important museums, featuring excellent collections of Asian art, Renaissance masterpieces, post-impressionist works and modern pieces by Picasso, Duchamp and Matisse. The grand stairway at its entrance was immortalized when Sylvester Stallone ran up the steps in the 1976 flick *Rocky*. Music, food and wine Friday nights.

★ Barnes Foundation   MUSEUM
(Map p136; ☑ 866-849-7056; www.barnesfoundation.org; 2025 Benjamin Franklin Pkwy; adult/child $18/10; ☺ 9:30am-6pm Wed-Mon, to 10pm Fri) The Barnes Foundation moved from it's original location in Merion, PA (the arboretum and archives are still there) to a strikingly contemporary building in May, 2012. An exceptionally fine collection of impressionist, post-impressionist and early French modern paintings, including works by Cézanne, Degas, Matisse, Monet, Picasso, Renoir and Van Gogh are displayed in the same idiosyncratic and unconventional arrangement as before; walls are cluttered in the 'gallery style' in accordance with Albert C Barnes' own particular 'objective method' to art education and appreciation.

Rodin Museum   MUSEUM
(Map p136; ☑ 215-763-8100; www.rodinmuseum. org; 2154 Benjamin Franklin Pkwy; suggested admission $8; ☺ 10am-5pm Wed-Mon) The newly renovated museum has Rodin's great works *The Thinker* and *Burghers of Calais*.

Pennsylvania Academy of the Fine Arts   MUSEUM
(Map p136; ☑ 215-972-7600; www.pafa.org; 118 N Broad St; adult/child $15/free; ☺ 10am-5pm Tue-Sat, from 11am Sun) A prestigious academy that has a museum with works by American painters, including Charles Willson Peale and Thomas Eakins.

Franklin Institute Science Museum   MUSEUM
(Map p136; ☑ 215-448-1200; www.fi.edu; 222 N 20th St; adult/child $16.50/12.50; ☺ 9:30am-5pm; ⬤) This is where hands-on science displays were pioneered; a highlight is the Ben Franklin exhibit.

Academy of Natural Sciences Museum   MUSEUM
(Map p136; ☑ 215-299-1000; www.ansp.org; 1900 Benjamin Franklin Pkwy; adult/child $15/13; ☺ 10am-4:30pm Mon-Fri, to 5pm Sat & Sun) The museum features a terrific dinosaur exhibition where you can dig for fossils on weekends.

Eastern State Penitentiary   MUSEUM
(Map p136; www.easternstate.org; 2027 Fairmount Ave; adult/child $14/10; ☺ 10am-5pm) Take an audio or guided tour of this decomissioned medieval fortress-like prison where Al Capone once did time.

⊙ Fairmount Park

The snaking Schuylkill River bisects this 9200-acre green space that's bigger than New York's Central Park and, in fact, the largest city park in the country. Scattered all throughout the park are some notable monuments, including one, at the far east end, of Joan of Arc (Map p136). From the earliest days of spring every corner is thrumming with activity – ball games, runners, picnickers, you name it. Runners will love the tree-lined, riverside trails, which range from 2 miles to 10 miles in length. Park trails are also great for cycling. Stop by Fairmount Bicycles (☑ 267-507-9370; www.fairmountbicycles. com; 2015 Fairmount Ave; full/half-day $18/30) for rentals and information.

Boathouse Row   HOUSE
(www.boathouserow.org; 1 Boathouse Row; early American houses adult/child $5/2) On the east bank, Boathouse Row has Victorian-era rowing-club buildings that lend a lovely old-fashioned flavor to this stretch. Across the park are a number of early American houses that are open to the public.

Shofuso Japanese
House and Garden   GARDEN
(☑ 215-878-5097; www.shofuso.com; Landsdowne & Horticultural Dr; adult/child $6/4; ⊙ 11am-5pm, check website) Check out the picturesque home and teahouse constructed in the traditional 16th-century style.

Philadelphia Zoo   ZOO
(☑ 215-243-1100; www.philadelphiazoo.org; 3400 W Girard Ave; adult/child $20/18; ⊙ 9:30am-5pm Mar-Oct, to 4pm Nov-Feb; ⛵) The country's oldest zoo has tigers, pumas, polar bears – you name it – in naturalistic habitats.

◉ South Street
Sort of an East Village or Williamsburg of Philly, slightly grungy South Street is lined with tattoo parlors, art-supply stores, tiny cheapskate eateries and bars, and the teenage and college-age goth chicks and dudes who populate them.

Philadelphia's Magic Garden   GARDEN
(Map p136; ☑ 215-733-0390; www.phillymagicgardens.org; 1020 South St; adult/child $7/3; ⊙ 11am-6pm Sun-Thu, to 8pm Fri & Sat Apr-Oct, to 5pm Nov-Mar; ⛵) A hidden gem worth seeking out, the garden is a mystical, art-filled pocket of land that's the passion of mosaic muralist Isaiah Zager.

◉ South Philadelphia
★ Italian Market   MARKET
(S 9th St, btwn Wharton & Fitzwater Sts; ⊙ 9am-5pm Tue-Sat, 9am-2pm Sun) These days, the country's oldest outdoor market is as much Mexican as Italian and you'll probably find more taquiles than prosciutto; however, it's still a highlight of South Philadelphia. Butchers and artisans still hawk produce and cheese and a handful of authentic old-school Italian shops sell homemade pastas, pastries and freshly slaughtered fish and meats. Anthony's (915 S 9th St; gelato $3.50; ⊙ 7am-7pm), a small cafe, is a good place to take a break with an espresso or gelato.

Mummers Museum   MUSEUM
(☑ 215-336-3050; www.mummersmuseum.com; 1100 S 2nd St; adult/child $3.50/2.50; ⊙ 9:30am-4:30pm Wed-Sat) Amid all the foodie frenzy is the Mummers Museum, celebrating the tradition of disguise and masquerade. It has an integral role in the famed Mummers Parade, which takes place here every New Year's Day.

◉ Chinatown & Around
The fourth-largest Chinatown in the USA, Philly's version has existed since the 1860s. Chinese immigrants who built America's transcontinental railroads started out west and worked their way here. Now many of the neighborhood's residents come from Malaysia, Thailand and Vietnam, in addition to every province in China. The multicolored, four-story Chinese Friendship Gate is Chinatown's most conspicuous landmark.

African American
Museum in Philadelphia   MUSEUM
(Map p140; ☑ 215-574-0380; www.aampmuseum.org; 701 Arch St; adult/child $14/10; ⊙ 10am-5pm Thu-Sat, from noon Sun) Housed in a foreboding concrete building, it contains excellent collections on African American history and culture.

◉ Penn's Landing
Back in its heyday Penn's Landing – the waterfront area along the Delaware River between Market and Lombard Sts – was a very active port area. Eventually those transactions moved further south down the Delaware, and today most of the excitement is about boarding boats, such as the Spirit of Philadelphia (Map p136; ☑ 866-455-3866; www.spiritofphiladelphia.com; tours from $40), for booze cruises, or simply strolling along the water's edge. The 1.8-mile Benjamin Franklin Bridge, the world's largest suspension bridge when completed in 1926, spans the Delaware River and dominates the view.

Independence Seaport Museum   MUSEUM
(Map p136; ☑ 215-413-8655; www.phillyseaport.org; 211 S Columbus Blvd; adult/child $13.50/10; ⊙ 10am-5pm, to 7pm Thu-Sat summer; ⛵) This interactive riverside museum highlights Philadelphia's maritime history (its shipyard closed in 1995 after 200 years). You can hop aboard two ships, an 1892 Cruiser and a WWII submarine.

◉ University City
This neighborhood, separated from downtown Philly by the Schuylkill River, feels like one big college town. That's because it's home to both Drexel University and the Ivy League University of Pennsylvania (commonly called 'U Penn'), founded in 1740. The

leafy, bustling campus makes for a pleasant afternoon stroll, and it's got two museums definitely worth a visit.

University Museum of Archaeology & Anthropology
MUSEUM

(☑215-898-4000; www.penn.museum; 3260 South St; adult/child $15/10; ☺10am-5pm Tue & Thu-Sun, to 8pm Wed; ☐No 21, 30, 40) The University Museum of Archaeology & Anthropology is Penn's magical museum, containing archaeological treasures from ancient Egypt, Mesopotamia, the Mayan peninsula, Greece, Rome and North America.

Institute of Contemporary Art
GALLERY

(☑215-898-7108; www.icaphila.org; 118 S 36th St; ☺11am-8pm Wed, to 6pm Thu & Fri, to 5pm Sat & Sun) FREE An excellent place to catch shows by folks making a big splash at the cutting edge of the art world.

30th Street Station
LANDMARK

(Map p136; ☑215-349-2153; 30th St, at Market St) Whether you're catching a train or not, be sure to pop your head into this romantic, neoclassical station while you're in the 'hood.

☞ Tours

Ed Mauger's Philadelphia on Foot
TOUR

(☑215-627-8680; www.ushistory.org/more/mauger; tours per person $20) Historian and author Ed Mauger offers walking tours with a variety of themes, including Exercise Your Rights (Conservatives Tour), Exercise Your Lefts (Liberals Tour) and Women in the Colony.

Mural Tours
TOUR

(☑215-389-8687; www.muralarts.org/tours; tours free to $30) Guided trolley tour of the city's diverse and colorful outdoor murals, the largest collection in the country.

Philadelphia Trolley Works & 76 Carriage Company
TOUR

(☑215-389-8687; www.phillytour.com; adult/child from $25/10) Tour part of the city or just about every last corner, either on a narrated trolley ride or a quieter horse-drawn carriage.

Taste of Philly Food Tour
TOUR

(☑215-545-8007; www.tasteofphillyfoodtour.com; adult/chid $16/9; ☺10am Wed & Sat) Explore the Reading Terminal Market with a knowledgeable food-obsessed expert.

☆ Festivals & Events

Mummers' Parade
PARADE

(www.mummers.com; ☺Jan 1) A very Philly parade, this is an elaborate celebration of costumes every New Year's Day.

Manayunk Arts Festival
CULTURE

(www.manayunk.com; ☺Jun) It's the largest outdoor arts and crafts show in the Delaware Valley, with more than 250 artists from across the country.

Philadelphia Live Arts Festival & Philly Fringe
PERFORMING ARTS

(www.livearts-fringe.org; ☺Sep) Catch the latest in cutting-edge performance.

🛏 Sleeping

Though the majority of places are found in and around Center City, alternatives are sprinkled throughout other neighborhoods. There's certainly no shortage of places to stay, but it's primarily national chains. The Lowes, Sofitel and Westin can all be recommended. Note that most hotels offer some kind of parking service, usually costing about $20 to $45 per day, or in the very least have discounted arrangements with nearby garages.

Apple Hostels
HOSTEL $

(Map p140; ☑215-922-0222; www.applehostels.com; 32 S Bank St; dm $38, r from $84; 🌡@🛜) This sparkling clean gem of a hostel is hidden down an alleyway, just a short walk from major sights. Everything, from the bunk beds to dishes in the spacious kitchen, looks like it's straight out of an Ikea catalogue – not a bad thing. And every need and desire has been accounted for: ear plugs, breath-rite strips for snorers, power outlets in lockers, USB ports at every bed, Nintendo Wii, free coffee and of course old-school amenities like laundry machines, Foosball, darts and even a guitar. Very friendly and helpful staff and nightly 'events' like walking tours, pasta nights (Wednesday) and free whiskey and bar crawl (Thursday).

Chamounix Mansion Hostel
HOSTEL $

(☑215-878-3676; www.philahostel.org; 3250 Chamounix Dr, West Fairmount Park; dm $23; ☺8am-11am, 4:30-midnight, closed 15 Dec-15 Jan; 🅿@) Looking more like a B&B than a hostel, Chamounix is in a lovely wooded area in Fairmount Park, north of the city, on the way to Manayunk; should only be considered by those with a car. Despite the 19th-century-style parlor and large communal rooms, the dorms themselves are basic but clean.

Morris House Hotel   BOUTIQUE HOTEL $$
(Map p136; ☑ 215-922-2446; www.morrishousehotel.com; 225 S 8th St; r incl breakfast from $179; ❄️🐾) If Benjamin Franklin were a hotelier, he would have designed a place like the Morris House Hotel. Upscale colonial-era boutique, this Federal-era building has the friendly charm and intimacy of an elegant B&B and the professionalism and good taste of a designer-run 21st-century establishment.

Penn's View Hotel   BOUTIQUE HOTEL $$
(Map p140; ☑ 215-922-7600; www.pennsviewhotel.com; cnr Front & Market Sts; r from $149-329; ❄️🐾) Housed in three early-19th-century buildings overlooking the Delaware waterfront, Penn's View is ideal for exploring the Old City. Quaint and full of character but not overly nostalgic or a prisoner to history, the rooms have marble bathrooms and modern conveniences. An authentic Italian trattoria and charming wine bar are part of the hotel.

Hotel Palomar   BOUTIQUE HOTEL $$
(Map p136; ☑ 888-725-1778; www.hotelpalomar-philadelphia.com; 117 S 17th St; r from $149; 🅿️❄️🐾) Part of the Kimpton chain, the Palomar occupies a former office building a few blocks from Rittenhouse Sq. Marble and dark wood accents add warmth to the hip and stylish room furnishings. On offer are wine and snacks, hot chocolate (in winter), a gym and an attached restaurant. Valet parking $42 per night.

Independent Philadelphia   BOUTIQUE HOTEL $$
(Map p136; ☑ 215-772-1440; www.theindependenthotel.com; 1234 Locust St; r incl breakfast from $150; ❄️🐾) A good Center City option housed in a handsome brick Georgian-Revival building with a four-story atrium. The wood-floored rooms are cozy and bright and the complimentary off-site gym-pass and wine and cheese every evening sweeten the deal.

Alexander Inn   BOUTIQUE HOTEL $$
(Map p136; ☑ 215-923-3535; www.alexanderinn.com; 12th & Spruce Sts; s/d incl breakfast from $120/130; ❄️@🐾; 🚇12, 23) Though the outside is a weird combination of brick walls accented with vinyl-sided bay windows, the small rooms at this inn look and feel pretty good and the lobby boasts dark wood, a fireplace and some stained-glass windows. The hotel, because of its helpful, accepting staff and great location near Philly's gay neighbourhood, attracts lots of same-sex couples.

La Reserve   B&B $$
(Map p136; ☑ 215-735 1137; www.lareservebandb.com; 1804 Pine St; r with shared/private bath incl breakfast from $80/125; ❄️🐾) This lovely 1850s row house sits on a quiet stretch of

---

WORTH A TRIP

PHILLY'S OUTLYING 'HOODS

Manayunk
A compact residential neighborhood northwest of the city, with steep hills and Victorian row houses, Manayunk, from a Native American expression meaning 'where we go to drink,' is a lovely place for an afternoon and evening. Just be aware that thousands of others have the same idea on weekend nights, when this otherwise peaceful area overlooking the Schuylkill River has the feel of a raucous frat party. As well as drinking, visitors are also permitted to eat and shop (check out **Dalessandro's** and **Chubby's** for classic Philly sandwiches and cheesesteaks). Parking is near impossible to come by here on weekends, so cycling is a good option – there's a towpath that runs alongside the neighborhood.

Germantown & Chestnut Hill
An odd mix of blight and preserved grandeur, the Germantown historic district – a good 20-minute drive or ride north on the Septa 23 from central downtown Philly – has a handful of tiny museums and notable homes worth checking out. And just to the north is Chestnut Hill with its quaint, small-town-like main strip of shops and eateries and huge historic residential homes and mansions.

Pine Street a few blocks south of Rittenhouse Sq. The B&B's seven rooms come stocked with well-worn charm – often in the form of faded oriental rugs, plush draperies, tall ceilings, inoperative fireplaces and (it seems) the fragile furniture of a minor 19th-century French aristocrat.

Ritz-Carlton
HOTEL $$$

(Map p136; ☎ 215-523-8000; www.ritzcarlton.com/hotels/philadelphia; 10 Ave of the Arts; r from $300; P ✲ @ ☎ ☎) This Ritz possesses one of the most lavish lobbies in North America, modelled after the Pantheon. In the afternoon, a formal tea is held in the rotunda. The 331 rooms are contained in a pre–WWII adjoining tower. Spacious, marble-clad bathrooms feel about as clean as an operating room.

Rittenhouse 1715
HOTEL $$$

(Map p136; ☎ 215-546-6500; www.rittenhouse1715.com; 1715 Rittenhouse Square St; r $249-305, ste $309-699; ✲ ☎) Just steps from Rittenhouse Sq, this is an elegant, top-notch choice. Housed in a 1911 mansion and infused with old-world sophistication, it's brimming with modern amenities: iPod docking stations, plasma TVs and rain showerheads. The friendly and efficient staff is also worth noting.

✕ Eating

Philly is deservedly known for its cheesesteaks – local aficionados debate the relative merits of various shops as if they are biblical scholars parsing the meaning of Deuteronomy. The city's dining scene has grown exponentially, in part due to the contributions of the Starr and Garces groups, which have added a range of quality international eateries. Starr in particular has seemingly targeted every cuisine and theme known to humanity.

The locavore, farm-to-table modern American trend is going strong (even a single block, 20th St and Rittenhouse Sq has three) as are gastropubs, which obsess equally about the provenance of their brews and burgers (Fairmount neighborhood has a handful). Up-and-coming culinary hotspots inlcude Northern Liberties (Modomio for Northern Italian and Fette Sau for barbecue), Fishtown (Pickled Heron for creative French bistro) and East Passyunk in South Philadelphia (Le Virtu for locavore Italian). And food trucks, from gourmet, ethnic and everything in between, can be found in the City Hall area. Because of Pennsylvania's arcane liquor laws, many restaurants are Bring Your Own Bottle (BYOB).

✕ Old City

★ Franklin Fountain
ICE CREAM $

(Map p140; ☎ 215-627-1899; 116 Market St; sundaes $10; ☺ noon-11pm Sun-Thu, to midnight Fri & Sat; ☝) One of the more romantic date spots in the city, especially on weekend nights, this old-timey ice-cream parlor features locally grown fruit and huge sundaes.

Amada
SPANISH $$

(Map p140; ☎ 215-625-2450; 217 Chestnut St; tapas $6-20; ☺ 11:30am-10pm Mon-Thu, to midnight Fri, 5pm-midnight Sat, 4-10pm Sun) Run by renowned restaurateur Jose Garces. The long communal tables foster a bustling, happening and loud atmosphere. The combination of bold and traditional dishes (try the crab-stuffed peppers) is phenomenal.

Cuba Libre
CARIBBEAN $$

(Map p140; ☎ 215-627-0666; www.cubalibrerestaurant.com; 10 S 2nd St; dinner $15-24; ☺ 11:30am-11pm Mon-Fri, from 10:30am Sat & Sun) Colonial America couldn't feel further away at this festive, multistoried Cuban eatery and rum bar. The creative and inspired menu includes Cuban sandwiches, guava-spiced BBQ, and savory black beans and salads tossed with smoked fish.

La Locanda del Ghiottone
ITALIAN $$

(Map p140; ☎ 215-829-1465; 130 N 3rd St; mains $16; ☺ 5-11pm Tue-Sun) The name means 'the Place of the Glutton,' and chef Giussepe and Joe the head waiter encourage overeating. Small and modestly designed, unlike other nearby trendy spots. Try the gnocchi, mushroom crepes and mussels. BYOB.

Silk City Diner
DINER $$

(Map p136; 435 Spring Garden St; mains $13; ☺ 4pm-1am, from 10am Sat & Sun) Cocktails have replaced milkshakes at this classic-looking diner on the edge of the Old City and Northern Liberties. It's worth noting Silk City is as much a late-night dance spot – Jerseyites come in for Saturday DJ nights. Outdoor beer garden in summer.

Zahav
MIDDLE EASTERN $$

(Map p140; ☎ 215-625-8800; 237 St James Pl, off Dock St; mains $11; ☺ 5-10pm Sun-Thu, to 11pm Fri & Sat) Small plates of sophisticated and modern Israeli and North African cuisine on Society Hill Towers' grounds.

✗ Center City & Around

★ Reading Terminal Market   MARKET $
(Map p136; ☑ 215-922-2317; www.readingterminalmarket.org; 51 N 12th St; ⊙ 8am-5:30pm Mon-Sat, 9am-4pm Sun) A wonderful one-stop shop for every appetite. Wander down the aisles past lines for famous Philly cheesesteaks, Amish food, lobster rolls, sushi, barbecue, and every cuisine and delicacy you can imagine.

Mama Palmas   PIZZERIA $
(Map p136; ☑ 215-735-7357; 2229 Spruce St; pizzas $10; ⊙ 4-10pm Mon-Thu, 11am-11pm Fri & Sat, 2-10pm Sun) This small BYOB place serves up some of the best thin-slice brick-oven pizza in the city. It does have a reputation for not tolerating little tykes – if they're rowdy.

Philly Flavors   ICE CREAM $
(Map p136; ☑ 215-232-7748; 2004 Fairmount Ave, at 20th St; ⊙ 11am-11pm Sun-Thu, to midnight Fri & Sat) The best place for Italian ices in the city; even the small kiddie size is large enough for most.

Lemon Hill Food & Drink   MODERN AMERICAN $$
(Map p136; www.lemonphilly.com; 747 N 25th St; mains $14; ⊙ 5-10pm, closed Sat & Sun) If you're in a hurry, do not ask for information about how the duck confit *poutine* is prepared or the type of rum in a cocktail. This Fairmount neighborhood gastropub takes the provenance of its ingredients seriously. Spiel or no spiel, food and drinks are worth the wait. Bar stays open till 1am.

La Viola   ITALIAN $$
(Map p136; ☑ 215-735-8630; 253 S 16th St, at Spruce St; mains $13; ⊙ 11am-10pm Mon-Thu, to 11pm Fri & Sat, 4-10pm Sun) Facing off across the street from one another are two La Violas – both BYOB. The former is a cramped and unpretentious dining room, while the latter is larger and more modern; the cuisine at both, however, is fresh and reasonably priced.

Continental   DINER $$
(Map p136; www.continentalmidtown.com; 1801 Chestnut St; mains $10-20) A fashionably mod update on a diner, Continental boasts hip crowds, eclectic, fusiony tapas and specialty cocktails. Dishes are hit or miss, from a satisfying quinoa salad to a mediocre lunchtime Asian bento box. Another location on Market St.

Luke's Lobster   SEAFOOD $$
(Map p136; 130 S 17th St; sandwiches $10-17; ⊙ 11am-9pm Sun-Thu, to 10pm Fri & Sat) For an authentic taste of a Maine lobster, crab or shrimp roll, head to this casual 'shack' in the Rittenhouse Sq area.

★ Morimoto   JAPANESE $$$
(Map p136; ☑ 215-413-9070; 723 Chestnut St; mains $25; ⊙ 11:30am-10pm Mon-Fri, to midnight Fri & Sat) Morimoto is high concept and heavily stylized, from a dining room that looks like a futuristic aquarium to a menu of globe-spanning influence and eclectic combinations. A meal at this *Iron Chef* regular's restaurant is a theatrical experience.

Parc Brasserie   FRENCH $$$
(Map p136; ☑ 215-545-2262; 227 S 18th St; mains from $23; ⊙ 7:30am-11pm, to midnight Fri & Sat) This enormous polished bistro is in a prime people-watching spot on Rittenhouse Sq. Brunch and lunch menus hit the right notes and are good value.

Zama   JAPANESE $$$
(Map p136; www.zamaphilly.com; 128 S 19th St; mains $20; ⊙ 11:30am-10pm Mon-Fri, to 11pm Fri, 5-11pm Sat, 5-9pm Sun) This upscale place around the corner from Rittenhouse Sq is for sushi and sake connoissieurs. The 'sake sommelier' can guide you to interesting choices.

✗ South Street

Jim's Steaks   STEAKHOUSE $
(Map p136; ☑ 877-313-5467; 400 South St, at 4th St; steak sandwiches $6-8; ⊙ 10am-1am Mon-Thu, to 3am Fri & Sat, noon-10pm Sun) If you can brave the long lines – which bust out of the front door and snake around the side of the building – you'll be in for a treat at this Philly institution, which serves mouthwatering cheesesteaks and hoagies (plus soups, salads and breakfasts).

South Street Souvlaki   GREEK $$
(Map p136; ☑ 215-925-3026; 507 South St; mains $13-18; ⊙ noon-9:30pm Tue-Thu, to 10pm Fri & Sat, to 9pm Sun) A long-running and modest place that is still one of the best places for Greek food in the city. The very large Tom's special salad (Tom is the owner) is recommended.

Horizons   VEGAN $$
(Map p136; ☑ 215-923-6117; www.horizonsphiladelphia.com; 611 S 7th St; mains $15-20; ⊙ 6-10pm Tue-Thu, 6-11pm Fri & Sat; ☑) Satisfying, healthy

and guilt-free dishes made of soy and veg-gies for the vegan gourmand.

Supper

MODERN AMERICAN $$$

(Map p136; ☑ 215-592-8180; 926 South St; mains $24; ☺ 6-11:30pm) Truly farm-to-table, sup-plied with fresh seasonal produce by its very own farm, Supper epitomizes the current culinary spirit, which weds the rural with the urban. Entrees are inventive and tasty creations like crispy confit duck leg with pecan waffles.

Chinatown

Nan Zhou Hand Drawn Noodle House

CHINESE $

(Map p136; ☑ 215-923-1550; 1022 Race St; mains $6-10; ☺ 11am-10pm) Now in a relatively sleek and larger space a block away from the old hole-in-the-wall but still serving delicious and inexpensive meat noodle soups.

Rangoon

BURMESE $

(Map p136; ☑ 215-829-8939; 112 N 9th St; mains $6-15; ☺ 11:30am-9pm Sun-Thu, to 10pm Fri & Sat) This Burmese spot offers a huge array of tantalizing specialties from spicy red-bean shrimp and curried chicken with egg noo-dles to coconut tofu.

Dim Sum Garden

CHINESE $

(Map p136; 59 N 11th St; mains $6; ☺ 10:30am-10:30pm) Overall, not the most salubrious looking hole-in-the-wall near the bus station but some of the tastiest steamed buns in the city.

★ Han Dynasty

CHINESE $$

(Map p140; 108 Chestnut St; mains $15; ☺ 11:30am-11:30pm) Innovative and burn-your-tongue spicy soups and noodle dishes in a more up-scale dining room.

South Philadelphia

The area around the corner of Washing-ton and 11th Sts is chockablock with tasty family-owned Vietnamese restaurants, not to mention the Italian Market (p143).

Pat's King of Steaks

FAST FOOD $

(☑ 215-468-1546; www.patskingofsteaks.com; cnr S 9th St & Passyunk Ave; sandwiches $7; ☺ 24hr) An iconic Philly institution, Pat's is fre-quented by tourists and diehard locals, often inebriated patrons, possibly unaware of the level of grease they're ingesting. It's competitor Geno's is diagonally across the street.

Tony Luke's

SANDWICHES $

(☑ 215-551-5725; www.tonylukes.com; 39 E Oregon Ave; sandwiches $7; ☺ 6am-midnight Mon-Thu, to 2am Fri & Sat) A typical spot out by the sports stadiums with picnic tables and an ordering window, this place is famous for its roast pork and roast beef with hot peppers.

Paradiso

ITALIAN $$

(☑ 215-271-2066; www.paradisophilly.com; 1627 E Passyunk Ave; mains $10-28; ☺ 11:30am-3pm & 5-10pm Mon-Thu, to 11pm Fri & Sat, 4-9pm Sun) Elegantly airy, Paradiso turns out upscale Italian feasts such as pistachio-crusted lamb chops, homemade gnocchi and New York strip steak glazed with anchovy butter.

Fond

AMERICAN $$$

(☑ 212-551-5000; 1617 E Passyunk Ave; mains $25; ☺ 5:30-10pm) Tired of the neighbor-hood sandwich shops? Head to this upscale fine-dining restaurant whose young chefs turn out creatively conceived fish, meat and chicken dishes with French accents and sea-sonal ingredients.

University City

Abyssinia Ethiopian Restaurant

ETHIOPIAN $

(229 S 45th St; mains $9; ☺ 10am-midnight) Ex-cellent *foul madamas* (bean dip) and good brunch with a recommended bar upstairs.

Lee's Hoagie House

SANDWICHES $

(☑ 215-387-0905; 4034 Walnut St; sandwiches $7; ☺ 10am-10pm Mon-Sat, 11am-9pm Sun) For meat and chicken sandwiches, definitely the best in area.

Koreana

KOREAN $

(☑ 215-222-2240; 3801 Chestnut St; mains $7; ☺ noon-10pm) Satisfying students and others interested in good, inexpensive Korean fare; enter from the parking lot in the back of the shopping plaza.

Distrito

MEXICAN $$

(☑ 215-222-1657; 3945 Chestnut St; mains $9-30; ☺ 11:30am-11pm Mon-Fri, 5-11pm Sat, to 10pm Sun) The vibrant pink and lime decor doesn't drown out the taste of the contemporary Mexican fare.

White Dog Cafe

ORGANIC $$

(☑ 215-386-9224; 3420 Sansom St; dinner mains $12-29; ☺ 11:30am-2:30pm Mon-Sat, 5-10pm Mon-Thu, to 11pm Fri & Sat, 10:30am-2:30pm & 5-10pm Sun) This neighborhood institution is the kind of funky-yet-upscale place that college students get their visiting parents to take them to for special dinners or brunch. The local, largely organic menu offers creative interpretations of meat and fish dishes.

Pod ASIAN $$
(☎ 215-387-1803; 3636 Sansom St; dinner mains $14-29; ⊙ 11:30am-11pm Mon-Thu, to midnight Fri, 5pm-midnight Sat, to 10pm Sun) Part of the restaurateur Stephen Starr's empire, this space-age-looking theme restaurant has pan-Asian treats including dumplings and some of the best sushi in Philly, plus plenty of quirky cocktails and original desserts.

🍷 Drinking & Entertainment

Judging Philly's bar scene by the over-the-top, raunchy TV series *It's Always Sunny in Philadelphia* is of course a mistake. Old-school dive bars are well represented but there's at least as many sophisticated cocktail lounges, wine bars and gastropubs intensely focused on local brews.

Apart from New Orleans, Old City boasts the highest concentration of liquor licenses in the US; to find a spot that appeals to your sensibilities, just stroll along S 2nd and S 3rd Sts. There are a fair number of spots where recently legal drinkers go for volume such as Lucy's Hat Shop, Drinker's Tavern and Buffalo Billiard's; South St can feel like an alternative fraternity row on weekend nights. Meanwhile, Center City hotels like the Le Meridien and the Bellevue have classy lounges and bars with popular happy hours. The area between Broad and 12th Sts and Walnut and Pine Sts has been dubbed Midtown Village and unofficially called 'gay'borhood and is permanently decked out with rainbow-flag-festooned street signs. Because nights and venues change frequently, check out www.phillygaycalendar.com. And finally, in the Fairmount neighborhood around the Eastern State Penitentiary there's a handful of recommended gastropubs.

Bars & Nightlife

⭐ **Paris Wine Bar** WINE BAR
(Map p136; 2301 Fairmount Ave; ⊙ 5pm-midnight Thu-Sat) Run by the duo behind the London Grill (an equally recommended gastropub next door to this bar and one of the first in the city), the owners have come up with another novel approach to satisfying sophisticated Philadelphians: Pennsylvania wines on tap! Kegs behind the bar are filled with two whites, three reds and a rose. There's

excellent French-bistro-style food on the menu.

North 3rd GASTROPUB
(www.norththird.com; 801 N 3rd St; ⊙ 4pm-2am) A Northern Liberties gem equally recommended for drinks like huge mojito martinis as for its tremendous food like steamed clams and pork chorizo in a tomato and cilantro broth. Expect extensively tattooed waitstaff and struggling conversations because of the noise level. Dinner served from 5pm to midnight and brunch on weekends, and every Tuesday night films are screened.

Mcgillin's Olde Ale House BAR
(Map p136; ☎ 215-735-5562; www.mcgillins.com; 1310 Drury St; ⊙ 11am-2am Mon-Sat, to midnight Sun) Philadelphia's oldest continually operated tavern (since 1860) – it remained open as a speakeasy in the Prohibition years. Great buffalo wings (Tuesday is special wing night) and karaoke on Wednesdays and Fridays.

Dirty Frank's BAR
(Map p136; 347 S 13th St; ⊙ 11am-2am) Recently discovered by hipsters, this has been a classic neighborhood dive bar since the 1970s. Expect sawdust on the floor and cheap shots and beer.

Shampoo CLUB
(Map p136; ☎ 215-922-7500; www.shampoooonline. com; on Willow St btwn N 7th & 8th Sts; cover $7-12; ⊙ 9pm-2am) Home to foam parties, hot tubs and velvet seating, this giant nightclub's weekly repertoire includes an immensely popular gay night on Fridays, a long-standing Wednesday Goth night, and a conventional free-for-all on Saturdays.

Monk's Cafe BAR
(Map p136; www.monkscafe.com; 264 S 16th St; ⊙ 11:30am-2am) A Belgian beer bar with a big bottle selection as well as a good selection of – what else? – Belgian and Belgian-style beers on tap as well as a bistro menu; the mussels and fries are recommended.

Brasil's CLUB
(Map p140; www.brasilsnightclub-philly.com; 112 Chestnut St; cover $10) The place to bump and grind to Latin, Brazilian and Caribbean sounds, with DJ John Rockwell.

Village Whiskey BAR
(Map p136; 118 S 20th St; ⊙ 11:30am-midnight, to 1am Fri & Sat) Cool vibe, long whiskey menu and creative cuisine.

Franklin Mortgage & Investment Co
COCKTAIL BAR

(Map p136; 112 S 18th St; ☺5pm-2am) Expertly made rye, whiskey and gin drinks in a classy setting.

Tavern on Camac
BAR, CLUB

(Map p136; ☑215-545-0900; www.tavernoncamac. com; 243 S Camac St; ☺6pm-3am) One of the older gay bars in Philly, while a small upstairs dance floor gets packed with dance-happy folks.

Sisters
LESBIAN

(Map p136; ☑215-735-0735; www.sistersnightclub. com; 1320 Chancellor St; ☺5pm-2am, closed Mon) A huge nightclub and restaurant for the ladies.

Dock Street Brewery & Restaurant
BREWERY

(701 S 50th St; ☺3-11pm, to 1am Fri & Sat) Artisan beer and brick-oven pizza in West Philly.

Live Music

Chris' Jazz Club
BLUES, JAZZ

(Map p136; ☑215-568-3131; www.chrisjazzcafe. com; 1421 Sansom St; cover $10-20) Showcasing local talent along with national greats, this intimate space features a 4pm piano happy hour Tuesday through Friday and good bands Monday through Saturday nights.

Ortlieb's Jazzhaus
JAZZ

(Map p136; ☑267-324-3348; www.ortliebsphilly. com; 847 N 3rd St; cover Tue-Thu $3-10, Fri $10, Sat $15, Sun $3) A respectable jazz lineup with a house band jamming every Tuesday night and Cajun cuisine on the menu (mains $20).

World Cafe Live
LIVE MUSIC

(Map p136; ☑215-222-1400; www.worldcafelive. com; 3025 Walnut St; cover $10-40) Located on the eastern edge of University City, World Cafe Live has upstairs and downstairs performance spaces featuring a restaurant and bar and is home to the radio station WXPN. It hosts an eclectic variety of live acts.

Theater & Culture

Kimmel Center for the Performing Arts
PERFORMING ARTS

(Map p136; ☑215-790-5800; www.kimmelcenter. org; cnr Broad & Spruce Sts) Philadelphia's most active center for fine music, the Kimmel Center organizes a vast array of performances, including the Philadelphia Dance Company and the Philadelphia Orchestra.

Tours available at 1pm Tuesday through Saturday.

Philadelphia Theatre Company
THEATER

(Map p136; ☑215-985-0420; www.philadelphia theatrecompany.org; 480 S Broad St, at Lombard St, Suzanne Roberts Theatre; tickets $35-70) This company, which produces quality contemporary plays with regional actors, has a high-end home in the heart of the arts district.

Pennsylvania Ballet
DANCE

(☑215-551-7000; www.paballet.org; tickets $25-130) An excellent dance company that performs in the beautiful Academy of Music (Map p136; 240 S Broad St) and the next-door Merriam Theater, part of the Kimmel Center.

Trocadero Theater
PERFORMING ARTS

(Map p136; ☑215-922-6888; www.thetroc.com; 1003 Arch St; cover $10-40) A rock-and-roll showcase in Chinatown housed in a 19th-century Victorian theater. The calendar encompasses a hodgepodge of musicians, spoken-word artists and comedians; Monday night is movie night.

Sports

Football is all about the Philadelphia Eagles (www.philadelphiaeagles.com), who play at state-of-the-art Lincoln Financial Field from August through January, usually twice a month, on Sunday. The baseball team is the National League Philadelphia Phillies (www.phillies.mlb.com), who play 81 home games at Citizen's Bank Park from April to October. Finally, basketball comes courtesy of the Philadelphia 76ers (www.nba.com/sixers) at Wells Fargo Center.

❶ Information

MEDIA

Philadelphia Daily News (www.phillydailynews.com) A tabloid-style daily.

Philadelphia Magazine (www.phillymag.com) A monthly glossy.

Philadelphia Weekly (www.philadelphiaweekly. com) Free alternative newspaper available at street boxes around town.

Philly.com (www.philly.com) News, listings and more, courtesy of the Philadelphia Inquirer.

WHYY 91-FM (www.whyy.org) Local National Public Radio affiliate.

MEDICAL SERVICES

Pennsylvania Hospital (☑800-789-7366; www.pennmedicine.org; 800 Spruce St; ☺24hr)

TOURIST INFORMATION

Greater Philadelphia Tourism Marketing Corp (Map p140; www.gophila.com; 6th St, at Market St) The highly developed, nonprofit visitors bureau has comprehensive visitor information. Its welcome center shares space with the Independence Visitor Center.

Independence Visitor Center (Map p140; ☑ 215-965-7676; www.independencevisitor-center.com; 6th St btwn Market & Arch Sts; ⊙ 8:30am-5pm) Run by the National Park Service, the center has maps and brochures for all of the sights in the city and around.

🛈 Getting There & Away

AIR

Philadelphia International Airport (PHL; ☑ 215-937-6937; www.phl.org; 8000 Essington Ave), 7 miles south of Center City, is served by direct international flights; domestically, it has flights to over 100 destinations in the USA.

BUS

Greyhound (Map p136; ☑ 215-931-4075; www.greyhound.com; 1001 Filbert St) and **Peter Pan Bus Lines** (Map p136; www.peterpanbus.com; 1001 Filbert St) are the major bus carriers; **Bolt Bus** (Map p136; www.boltbus.com) and **Megabus** (Map p136; www.us.megabus.com) are popular and comfortable competitors. Greyhound connects Philadelphia with hundreds of cities nationwide, while Peter Pan and the others concentrate on the northeast. When booked online a round-trip fare to NYC can be as low as $18 (2½ hours one way), to Atlantic City it's $20 (1½ hours) and to Washington, DC, it's $28 (4½ hours). **NJ Transit** (www.njtransit.state.nj.us), based at the Greyhound terminal, carries you from Philly to various points in New Jersey.

CAR

From the north and south, the I-95 (Delaware Expwy) follows the eastern edge of the city beside the Delaware River, with several exits for Center City. The I-276 (Pennsylvania Turnpike) runs east across the northern part of the city and over the river to connect with the New Jersey Turnpike.

TRAIN

Beautiful **30th St Station** (☑ 215-349-2153; www.30thstreetstation.com; 30th St, at Market St) is one of the biggest train hubs in the country. **Amtrak** (www.amtrak.com) provides services from here to Boston (regional and Acela express service one way $87 to $206, five to 5¾ hours) and Pittsburgh (regional service from $55, seven to eight hours). A cheaper but longer and more complicated way to get to NYC is to take the Septa R7 suburban train to Trenton in New Jersey. From there you can con-nect with NJ Transit to Newark's Penn Station, then continue on NJ Transit to New York City's Penn Station.

🛈 Getting Around

Downtown distances are short enough to let you see most places on foot, and a train, bus or taxi can get you to places further out with relative ease.

Septa (www.septa.org) operates Philadelphia's municipal buses, plus two subway lines and a trolley service. Though extensive and reliable, the web of bus lines (120 routes servicing 159 sq miles) is difficult to make sense of. The one-way fare on most routes is $2.25, for which you'll need exact change or a token. Many subway stations and transit stores sell discounted packages of two tokens for $3.60.

The fare for a taxi to Center City from the airport is a flat fee of $28.50. Septa's airport line ($6.50) will drop you off in University City or at numerous stops in Center City.

Cabs, especially around City Center, are easy to hail. The flag drop or fare upon entry is $2.70, then $2.30 per mile or portion thereof. All licensed taxis have GPS and most accept credit cards.

The **Phlash** (www.ridephillyphlash.com; ⊙ 10am-6pm daily summer, 10am-6pm Fri-Sun May, Sep & Oct) shuttle bus looks like an old-school trolley and loops between Penn's Landing and the Philadelphia Museum of Art (one way/all day $2/12). It runs approximately every 15 minutes.

Around Philadelphia

Valley Forge

After the defeat at the Battle of Brandywine Creek and the British occupation of Philadelphia in 1777, General Washington and 12,000 Continental troops withdrew to Valley Forge. Today, Valley Forge symbolizes Washington's endurance and leadership. The **Valley Forge National Historic Park** (☑ 610-783-1099; www.nps.gov/vafo; cnr N Gulph Rd & Rte 23, park grounds; ⊙ 6am-10pm, welcome center & Washington's Headquarters 9am-5pm) **FREE** contains 5½ sq miles of scenic beauty and open space 20 miles northwest of downtown Philadelphia – a remembrance of where 2000 of George Washington's 12,000 troops perished from freezing temperatures, hunger and disease, while many others returned home. A 22-mile cycling path along the Schuylkill River connects Valley Forge to Philadelphia.

New Hope & Lambertville

About 40 miles north of Philadelphia, New Hope and its sister town, Lambertville, across the Delaware River in NJ, sit equidistant from Philadelphia and NYC, and are a pair of quaint, artsy little towns. Both are edged with long and peaceful towpaths, perfect for runners, cyclists and strollers, and a bridge with a walking lane lets you crisscross between the two with ease. The towns draw a large number of gay folk; rainbow flags hanging outside various businesses demonstrate the town's gay-friendliness.

The Golden Nugget Antique Market (☑609-397-0811; www.gnmarket.com; 1850 River Rd; ⊙6am-4pm), 1 mile south of Lambertville, has all sorts of finds, from furniture to clothing, from a variety of dealers. Or spend a few picturesque hours gliding downstream in a canoe, kayak, raft or tube, courtesy of Bucks County River Country (☑215-297-5000; www.rivercountry.net; 2 Walters Lane; tube $18-22, canoe $62; ⊙rental 9am-2:30pm, return by 5pm), about 8 miles north of New Hope, just off Rte 32.

Both towns have a plethora of cute B&Bs if you decide to make a weekend out of it. Try Porches on the Towpath (☑215-862-3277; www.porchesnewhope.com; 20 Fisher's Alley; r from $115 Mon-Fri, from $155 Sat & Sun), a quirky Victorian with porches and canal views.

For a meal in a divinely renovated former church try the Marsha Brown Creole Kitchen and Lounge (☑215-862-7044; 15 S Main St; mains $15-30; ⊙11:30am-10pm Mon-Thu, to 11pm Fri & Sat, to 9pm Sun) in New Hope for catfish, steaks and lobster. Or head to DeAnna's (☑609-397-8957; 54 N Franklin St; mains $18-25; ⊙5-9:30pm Tue-Thu, to 10pm Fri & Sat) in Lambertville for homemade pastas and delicious meat and fish dishes prepared by the owner/chef.

Pennsylvania Dutch Country

The core of Pennsylvania Dutch Country lies in the southeast region of Pennsylvania, in an area about 20 miles by 15 miles, east of Lancaster. The Amish (*ah*-mish), Mennonite and Brethren religious communities are collectively known as the 'Plain People.' All are Anabaptist sects (only those who choose the faith are baptized), who were persecuted in their native Switzerland, and from the early 1700s settled in tolerant Pennsylvania. Speaking German dialects, they became known as 'Dutch' (from 'Deutsch'). Most Pennsylvania Dutch live on farms and their beliefs vary from sect to sect. Many do not use electricity, and most opt for horse-drawn buggies – a delightful sight, and sound, in the area. The strictest believers, the Old Order Amish, wear dark, plain clothing, and live a simple, Bible-centered life – but have, ironically, become a major tourist attraction, thus bringing busloads of gawkers and the requisite strip malls, chain restaurants and hotels that lend this entire area an oxymoronic quality, to say the least. Because there is so much commercial development continually encroaching on multigenerational family farms, it takes some doing to appreciate the unique nature of the area. Try to find your way through a series of back roads snaking their way through rural countryside between Intercourse and Strasburg.

◉ Sights & Activities

On the western edge of Amish country, the city of Lancaster – a mix of art galleries, well-preserved brick row houses and somewhat derelict blocks – was briefly the US capital in September 1777, when Congress stopped here overnight. The monthly First Friday (www.lancasterarts.com) celebration brings out a friendly local crowd for gallery hops along artsy Prince St.

Probably named for its crossroads location, Intercourse includes Kitchen Kettle Village, which has touristy shops selling clothing, quilts, candles, furniture, fudge and, of course, souvenirs with off-color jokes. The Tanger Outlet stores on Rte 30 draw tourists with their 21st-century designer clothes.

★ Strasburg Railroad   TRAIN
(☑717-687-7522; www.strasburgrailroad.com; Rte 741, Strasburg; coach class adult/child $14/8; ⊙multiple trips daily, times vary by season; 🎫) Since 1832 the Strasburg Railroad has run steam-driven trains along the same route to Paradise and back (at the same speed as well). The wooden train carriages are gorgeously restored with stained glass, shiny brass lamps and plush burgundy seats. The Railroad Museum of Pennsylvania (☑717-687-8628; www.rrmuseumpa.org; Rte 741, Strasburg; adult/child $10/8; ⊙9am-5pm Mon-Sat, noon-5pm Sun, closed Sun Nov-Mar; 🎫) across the street has 100 gigantic mechanical marvels to climb aboard and admire.

Landis Valley Museum MUSEUM
(☑ 717-569-0401; www.landisvalleymuseum.org;
2451 Kissel Hill Rd, Lancaster; adult/child $12/8;
☺ 9am-5pm, from noon Sun) In the 18th century,
German immigrants flooded southeastern
Pennsylvania and only some were Amish.
Most lived like the costumed docents at this
museum, a re-creation of village life that
includes a working smithy, weavers, stables
and more.

Ephrata Cloister MUSEUM
(☑ 717-733-6600; www.ephratacloister.org; 632 W
Main St, Ephrata; adult/child $10/6; ☺ 9am-5pm
Mon-Sat, from noon Sun) One of the country's
earliest religious communities was founded
here in 1732 by Conrad Beissel, a German
emigre escaping persecution in his native
land and dissatisfied with wordly ways and
distractions. There's a small museum in the
visitor center and you can walk or take a
guided tour of its collection of medieval-style
buildings.

Sturgis Pretzel House FACTORY TOUR
(☑ 717-626-4354; www.juliussturgis.com; 219 E
Main St, Lititz; admission $3; ☺ 9am-5pm Mon-Sat;
🖼) Try your hand at twisting and rolling
dough at the USA's first pretzel factory.

Aaron & Jessica's Buggy Rides TOUR
(☑ 717-768-8828; 3121 Old Philadelphia Pike, Bird-
in-Hand; adult/child $10/6; ☺ 9am-5pm Mon-Sat;
🖼) A fun 2-mile tour narrated by an Amish
driver.

🛏 Sleeping

There's a slew of inns and B&Bs in Amish
country and virtually every national motel
chain is represented along a strip-mall-filled
stretch of Rte 30/Lincoln Hwy just east of
Lancaster.

★ **General Sutter Inn** INN $
(☑ 717-626-2115; www.generalsutterinn.com; 14
East Main St, Lititz; r from $70; 🖼🖼) The bones
of this atmospheric and charming inn anchoring one end of Lititz's main street date to
1764. Ten wood-floored and cheerful rooms
are tastefully furnished with antiques. A
new top-floor annex called the Rock Lititz
Penthouse has six, decidedly modern suites
with a playful rock-and-roll theme. Attached
is the extremely popular craft-beer-centric
Bull's Head Pub.

A Farm Stay ACCOMMODATION SERVICE $
(www.afarmstay.com; r from $60-180; 🖼) If you
like your vacations to be working ones,
check out this website which represents
several dozen farm stays that range from
stereotypical B&Bs to Amish farms. Most
include breakfast, private bathrooms and
some activity like milking cows or gathering
eggs or simply petting a goat.

Fulton Steamboat Inn HOTEL $$
(☑ 717-299-9999; 1 Hartman Bridge Rd, Lancaster; r
from $100; 🖼🖼🖼) A nautically themed hotel
in landlocked Amish country seems like a
gimmick even if the inventor of the steam-
boat was born nearby. The slight kitsch
works, however. From shiny brass old-timey
light fixtures to painterly wallpaper, the
hotel's interior is rather elegant and its
rooms are spacious and comfy.

Red Caboose Motel & Restaurant MOTEL $$
(☑ 888-687-5005; www.redcaboosemotel.com;
312 Paradise Lane, Ronks; r from $120; 🖼🖼🖼)
There's nothing very hobo-esque about
a night's sleep in one of these 25-ton ca-
booses – TVs and mini-fridges included –
though the basic furnishings aren't the
draw. Even if spaces are narrow – the
width of a train car – the novelty appeals
to adults as well as kids. Set on a beautiful rural lane surrounded by picturesque
countryside.

Cork Factory BOUTIQUE HOTEL $$
(☑ 717-735-2075; www.corkfactoryhotel.com; 480
New Holland Ave, Lancaster; r incl breakfast from
$125; 🖼🖼) An abandoned brick behemoth
now houses a stylishly up-to-date hotel
only a few miles northeast of the Lan-
caster city center. Sunday brunch at the
hotel's restaurant is a fusion of seasonal
new American and down-home comfort
cooking.

🍴 Eating

To sample one of the famous family-style
restaurants and hearty dishes of Amish
country, get prepared to rub elbows with
lots of tourists.

★ **Bird-in-Hand Farmers Market** MARKET
(☑ 717-393-9674; 2710 Old Philadelphia Pike,
Bird-in-Hand; ☺ 8:30am-5:30pm Wed-Sat Jul-Oct,
call for other times of year) A one-stop shop
of Dutch Country highlights. It has fudge,
quilts and crafts but primarily great deals
on tasty locally made jams, cheeses, pretzels,
beef jerky and more specialties like scrap-
ple (pork scraps mixed with cornmeal and
wheat flour, shaped into a loaf and fried);
two lunch counters serve meals.

Central Market
MARKET $

(www.centralmarketlancaster.com; 23 N Market St, Lancaster; ☺6am-4pm Tue & Fri, to 2pm Sat) The bustling market offers local produce, cheese, meats, Amish baked goods and crafts and all the regional gastronomic delicacies – fresh horseradish, whoopie pies, soft pretzels, sub sandwiches stuffed with cured meats and dripping with oil – as well as ethnic eateries.

Tomato Pie Cafe
SANDWICHES $

(23 N Broad St, Lititz; mains $6; ☺7am-9pm Mon-Sat; ☎) Housed in a charming yellow and green home just around the corner from Main St, this cafe gets crowded especially at lunchtime on weekends. Besides the signature tomato pie, the menu has salads and sandwiches like a peanut butter, nutella and banana panini, excellent breakfasts and baristas who take their coffee seriously.

Dutch Haven
DESSERT $

(2857 Lincoln Hwy/Rte 30, Ronks; 6-inch pies $7) Stop by for a sticky-sweet shoofly pie.

Good 'N Plenty Restaurant
AMERICAN $$

(Rte 896, Smoketown; mains $11; ☺11:30am-8pm Mon-Sat, closed Jan; ☎) Sure, you'll be dining with busloads of tourists and your cardiologist might not approve, but hunkering down at one of the picnic tables for a family-style meal ($21) is a lot of fun. Besides the main dining room, which is the size of a football field, there are a couple of other mini-areas where you can order from an à la carte menu.

Bube's Brewery
EUROPEAN, BREWERY $$

(www.bubesbrewery.com; 102 North Market St, Mt Joy) This well-preserved 19th-century German brewery cum restaurant complex contains several atmospheric bars and four separate dining rooms (one underground), hosts costumed 'feasts' and, naturally, brews its own beer.

Lancaster Brewing Co
AMERICAN, BREWERY $$

(302 N Plum St, Lancaster; mains $9-22; ☺11:30am-10pm) Just down the street from the Cork Factory Hotel in Lancaster, the bar here draws young neighborhood regulars. The menu is a big step up from standard pub fare – rack of wild boar and cranberry sausage is an example – but you can't beat specials like 35¢-wing night.

❶ Information

Use a map to navigate the back roads, avoiding main Rtes 30 and 340, or visit in winter when tourism is down. Even better, rent a bicycle from **Rails to Trail Bicycle Shop** (☎717-367-7000;

GETTYSBURG

This tranquil, compact and history-laden town, 145 miles west of Philadelphia, saw one of the Civil War's most decisive and bloody battles. It's also where Lincoln delivered his Gettysburg Address. Much of the ground where Robert E Lee's Army of Northern Virginia and Maj Gen Joseph Hooker's Union Army of the Potomac skirmished and fought can be explored either in your own car with a map and guide, on an audio CD tour, a bus tour or a two-hour guided ranger tour ($65 per vehicle) – the latter is most recommended, but if short on time, it's still worth driving the narrow lanes past fields with dozens of monuments marking significant sites and moments in the battle. The centerpiece of any visit (and where tours are booked) is the massive new **Gettysburg National Military Park Museum & Visitor Center** (☎717-334-1124; www.gettysburgfoundation.org; 1195 Baltimore Pike; adult/child $12.50/8.50; ☺8am-5pm Nov-Mar, to 6pm Apr-Oct) several miles south of town. It houses an incredible museum filled with artifacts and displays exploring every nuance of the battle, a film explaining Gettysburg's context, and Paul Philippoteaux's 377ft cyclorama painting of Pickett's Charge.

The annual **Civil War Heritage Days**, a festival held in the first weekend of July, features living-history encampments and battle reenactments drawing aficionados from near and far.

For accommodations, try the stately three-story Victorian **Brickhouse Inn** (☎717-338-9337; www.brickhouseinn.com; 452 Baltimore St; r with breakfast $119-189; ❗✷☎), built c 1898, a wonderful B&B with charming rooms and an outdoor patio. For a meal in Gettysburg's oldest home, built in 1776, head to **Dobbin House Tavern** (☎717-334-2100; 89 Steinwehr Ave; mains $8-30; ☺11:30am-9pm), which serves heaping sandwiches and more elaborate meat and fish meals in kitschy themed dining rooms.

www.railstotrail.com; 1010 Hershey Rd; rental per day $25; ⊙10am-6pm) between Hershey and Lancaster, pack some food and hit the road. The **Dutch Country Visitors Center** (☑800-723-8824; www.padutchcountry.com; 501 Greenfield Rd; ⊙9am-5pm Mon-Sat, 10am-4pm Sun), off Rte 30 in Lancaster, offers comprehensive information.

ⓘ Getting There & Around

RRTA (www.redrosetransit.com) local buses link the main towns, but a car is much more convenient for sightseeing. The **Amtrak train station** (53 McGovern Ave) has trains to and from Philadelphia ($16, 70 minutes) and Pittsburgh ($51, six hours).

Pennsylvania Wilds

Interspersed throughout this rural region are regal buildings and grand mansions, remnants of a time when lumber, coal and oil brought great wealth and the world's attention to this corner of Pennsylvania. Several museums (oil ones in Titusville and Bradford and one on lumber in Galeton) tell the boom and bust industrial story. But natural resources of another kind remain – known as 'the Wilds' – roads (especially scenic Rte 6) and hundreds of miles of trails snake through vast national forests and state parks.

The Kinzua railroad viaduct, once the highest and one of the longest railroad suspension bridges in the world and partly destroyed by a tornado in 2011, has been converted into the Kizua Bridge Skywalk (www.visitanf.com). The walkway dead ends 600ft out in an overlook over the gorge; a small section has a glass floor so you can see directly to the valley floor 225ft below. The Lodge at Glendorn (☑800-843-8568; www.glendorn.com; 1000 Glendorn Dr, Bradford; r from $450) in Bradford to the north is a luxurious retreat with outdoor activities galore.

Ponder the immensity of the universe at Cherry Springs State Park (www.dcnr.state. pa.us/state parks/parks/cherrysprings), considered one of the best places for stargazing east of the Mississippi. Crowds of several hundred people are common on clear nights in July and August when the Milky Way is almost directly overhead. Camping is available here or nearby.

Often referred to as the 'Pennsylvania Grand Canyon,' Pine Creek Gorge in the Tioga State Forest has two access points

and parks on either ... and developed Le... Park (☑570-724-... on the east rim ... ton Point State ... have trails to ... floor.

Pittsburgh

Famous as an industrial cent... 19th century, to many Americ... burgh still conjures stark images of bil... ing clouds emanating from steel and coal factories. Today's city, however, has a well-earned reputation for being one of the more livable metropolitan areas in the country. The city sits at the point where the Monongahela (oft referred to as 'the Mon') and Allegheny Rivers join the Ohio River, spreads out over the waterways and has hilly neighborhoods connected by picturesque bridges all with footpaths (more than any other city in the US). Teeming with students from the many universities in town, it's a surprisingly hip and cultured city with top-notch museums, abundant greenery and several bustling neighborhoods with lively restaurant and bar scenes.

Scottish-born immigrant Andrew Carnegie made his fortune here by modernizing steel production, and his legacy is still synonymous with the city and its many cultural and educational institutions. Production dipped during the Great Depression but rose again because of mass-produced automobiles in the 1930s. When the economy and local steel industry took another major hit in the 1970s, the city's pride was buoyed by its local NFL football team: the Steelers achieved a remarkable run of four Super Bowl championships, a feat whose importance to the continuing psyche of some Pittsburghers can't be underestimated. After the steel industry's demise, Pittsburgh's economy refocused on health care, technology and education, and the city is home to several notable Fortune 500 companies, including Alcoa and Heinz.

⊙ Sights & Activities

Points of interest in Pittsburgh are scattered everywhere, and the city's spread-out nature makes it a difficult place to cover thoroughly on foot. The Great Allegheny Passage, a 141-mile hiking and biking path between Cumberland, MD, and Pittsburgh was completed

...r of 2013; from Cumberland, ...nal Towpath carries on all the ...hington, DC.

...gh Parks Conservancy   PARKS
...82-7275; www.pittsburghparks.org) For
... much any outdoor pursuit, the best
...on is the elaborate 1700-acre system of
...e Pittsburgh Parks Conservancy, which
comprises Schenley Park (with a public
swimming pool and golf course), Highland
Park (with swimming pool, tennis courts
and bicycling track), Riverview Park (sporting
ball fields and horseback riding trails)
and Frick Park (with hiking trails, clay
courts and a bowling green), all with beautiful
running, cycling and in-line skating trails.

Downtown

The mystical-sounding Golden Triangle
(mostly only tourist brochures use this
term), between the converging Monongahela
and Allegheny Rivers, is Pittsburgh's
renovated downtown containing the financial
and business districts, as well as 14 or
so blocks filled with theaters, performance
spaces and art galleries referred to as the
'Cultural District'. Every Thursday from
May to November there's a farmers market
in Market Square, a public piazza surrounded
by restaurants – some fast-food
chains – and tall office buildings (a large
complex including a hotel, offices and
parking garage was going up at the time
of research). CONSOL Energy Center
(www.consolenergycenter.com; 1001 Fifth Ave),
just east of downtown, is where the NHL
Pittsburgh Penguins drop the puck (major
concerts held here as well). Just northeast
of here, the Strip offers warehouses, ethnic
food stores, cafes and nightclubs.

Point State Park   PARK
At the tip of the triangle formed by the
meeting of the Monongahela and Allegheny
Rivers is this park containing the Fort Pitt
Museum (☑412-281-9284; www.heinzhistorycenter.org;
601 Commonwealth Pl; adult/child $6/3;
☉10am-5pm), which commemorates the historic
heritage of the French and Indian War.
The renovated and beautified waterfront is
popular during summer with strollers, cyclists,
loungers and runners. For a longer
run, head to the 11-mile gravel-paved Montour
Trail (www.montourtrail.org), accessible by
crossing the 6th St Bridge and catching the
paved path at the Carnegie Science Center.

Senator John Heinz Pittsburgh
Regional History Center   MUSEUM
(☑412-454-6000;   www.heinzhistorycenter.org;
1212 Smallman St; adult/child incl Sports Museum
$15/6; ☉10am-5pm) This remodeled brick
warehouse offers a good take on the region's
past, with exhibits on the French and Indian
War, early settlers, immigrants, steel and the
glass industry. It's also home to the Western
Pennsylvania Sports Museum, focusing
on champs from Pittsburgh; fun interactive
exhibits for kids and for adults who refuse
to admit their shot at professional sports has
passed them by.

August Wilson Center for
African American Culture   ARTS CENTER
(☑412-258-2700;   www.augustwilsoncenter.org;
980 Liberty Ave; special exhibitions adult/child
$8/3; ☉11am-6pm) Named for Pittsburgh native
and award-winning playwright August
Wilson, the strikingly contemporary building
houses a museum, classrooms and performance
spaces.

North Side

This part of town across the Allegheny
River feels lively when Heinz Field (☑412-
323-1200; www.steelers.com; 100 Art Rooney Ave)
or PNC Park (☑412-323-5000; www.pirateball.
com; 115 Federal St) are filled with fans for
a Steelers or Pirates game; bridges from
downtown are closed to vehicular traffic at
this time. One-hour tours of Heinz Field (a
pivotal scene in the latest Batman, *The Dark
Knight Rises,* film was shot here) are open
to the public every Friday from April to the
end of October (adult/child $7/3). Nearby in
the northwest is the Mexican War Streets
neighborhood, named after battles and soldiers
of the 1846 Mexican War. The carefully
restored row houses, with Greek Revival
doorways and Gothic turrets lining the quiet
streets, make for a peaceful, post-museum
stroll. Keep in mind, non-fast-food restaurants
are scarce around here.

★ Andy Warhol Museum   MUSEUM
(☑412-237-8300; www.warhol.org; 117 Sandusky
St; adult/child $20/10; ☉10am-5pm Tue-Thu, Sat &
Sun, to 10pm Fri) This six-story musuem celebrates
Pittsburgh's coolest native son, who
became famous for his pop art, avant-garde
movies, celebrity connections and Velvet
Underground spectaculars. Exhibits include
celebrity portraits, while the museum's
theater hosts frequent film screenings and

quirky performers. Friday-night cocktails at the museum are popular with Pittsburgh's gay community.

Carnegie Science Center
MUSEUM
(☑ 412-237-3400; www.carnegiesciencecenter.org; 1 Allegheny Ave; adult/child $18/12, IMAX & special exhibits extra; ☺ 10am-5pm Sun-Fri, to 7pm Sat; ⊛) Great for kids and a cut above the average hands-on science museum, with innovative exhibits on subjects ranging from outer space to candy.

Children's Museum of Pittsburgh
MUSEUM
(☑ 412-322-5058; www.pittsburghkids.org; 10 Children's Way, Allegheny Sq; adult/child $13/12; ☺ 10am-5pm; ⊛) Features loads of interactive exhibits, including a chance for kids to get under the hood of real cars and some child-friendly Warhol works.

National Aviary
WILDLIFE RESERVE
(☑ 412-323-7235; www.aviary.org; 700 Arch St; adult/child $13/11; ☺ 10am-5pm; ⊛) More than 600 exotic and endangered birds.

Mattress Factory
ARTS CENTER
(☑ 412-231-3169; www.mattress.org; 500 Sampsonia Way; adult $15; ☺ 10am-5pm Tue-Sat, 1-5pm Sun) Hosts avant-garde contemporary installation art and performances.

◎ South Side & Mt Washington

Across the Monongahela River is the South Side, whose Slopes rise up to Mt Washington; at the Flats, youthful and funky E Carson St bustles with clubs and restaurants. In the 10 blocks between the 10th St Bridge and Birmingham Bridge there are dozens of bars, including a bunch of hole-in-the-wall joints. Rising up from the bustling South Side valley is the neighborhood called the South Side Slopes, a fascinating community of houses that seem perilously perched on the edge of cliffs, accessible via steep, winding roads and hundreds of stairs.

★ Monongahela & Duquesne Incline
CABLE CAR
(One-way adult/child $2.50/1.25; ☺ 5:30am-12:45am Mon-Sat, from 7am Sun) The historic funicular railroads (c 1877) that run up and down Mt Washington's steep slopes afford great city views, especially at night. At the start of the Monongahela Incline, which is just over the Smithfield St bridge, is Station Square (☑ 800-859-8959; www.stationsquare.com; Station Square Dr), a group of beautiful, renovated railway buildings that now houses a few restaurants, nightclubs and bars. About halfway between the two inclines along the Monongahela River is Highmark Stadium, a new 3500 seat soccer stadium. Grandview Ave, at the top of the Duquesne Incline, has several excellent restaurants with romantic views including the five-star Le Mont.

◎ Oakland & Around

The University of Pittsburgh and Carnegie Mellon University are here, and the surrounding streets are packed with cheap eateries, cafes, shops and student homes.

Carnegie Museums
MUSEUM
(☑ 412-622-3131; www.carnegiemuseums.org; 4400 Forbes Ave; adult/child $18/12; ☺ 10am-5pm Tue-Sat, from noon Sun; ⊛) The Carnegie Museum of Art, has terrific exhibits of architecture, impressionist, postimpressionist and modern American paintings; and the Carnegie Museum of Natural History features a complete Tyrannosaurus skeleton and exhibits on Pennsylvania geology and Inuit prehistory.

Frick Art & Historical Center
MUSEUM
(☑ 412-371-0600; www.thefrickpittsburgh.org; 7227 Reynolds St; museum & grounds free, Clayton tours $12; ☺ 10am-5pm Tue-Sun) **FREE** East of Oakland, in Point Breeze, this museum displays some of Henry Clay Frick's Flemish, French and Italian paintings; assorted Frickmobiles like a 1914 Rolls Royce in the Car & Carriage Museum; more than 5 acres of grounds and gardens; and Clayton, the restored 1872 Frick mansion. Bus 71 C from downtown heads out this way.

Phipps Conservatory
GARDENS
(☑ 412-622-6914; www.phipps.conservatory.org; One Schenley Park; adult/child $15/11; ☺ 9:30am-5pm, to 10pm Fri; ⊛) 🌿 An impressive steel-and-glass greenhouse with beautifully designed and curated gardens.

Cathedral of Learning
TOWER
(☑ 412-624-6000; 4200 Fifth Ave; tours $3; ☺ 9am-3pm Mon-Sat, from 11am Sun) **FREE** Rising up from the center of the University of Pittsburgh campus is this soaring grand, 42-story Gothic tower, which at 535ft is the second-tallest education building in the world. It houses the elegant Nationality Classrooms, each representing a different style and period; most are accessible only with a guided tour.

Squirrel Hill & Shadyside

These upscale neighborhoods feature wide streets, excellent restaurants, chain stores and independent boutiques and bakeries (try the burnt-almond tortes, a classic Pittsburgh dessert). Squirrel Hill is home to Pittsburgh's large Jewish community, the city's best kosher eateries, butchers and Judaica shops. Apartment buildings, duplexes and more modest housing are almost as common as the grand mansions the neighborhood is known for.

In Shadyside, Walnut St is the bustling main strip. The leafy campus of Chatham University, located between the two neighborhoods, is a nice place to stroll.

Greater Pittsburgh

Formerly gritty Lawrenceville has become the city's Interior Design District, comprising the stretch on and around Butler St from 16th to 62nd Sts. It's a long and spotty strip of shops, galleries, studios, bars and eateries that's on every hipster's radar, and runs into the gentrifying Garfield neighborhood, a good place for cheap ethnic eats.

Bloomfield, a really little Little Italy, is a strip of groceries, Italian eateries and, of all things, a landmark Polish restaurant, the Bloomfield Bridge Tavern. The Pittsburgh zoo and aquarium and a water park are nearby.

Kennywood Amusement Park
AMUSEMENT PARK

(✐ 412-461-0500; www.kennywood.com; 4800 Kennywood Blvd, West Mifflin; adult/child $40/27; ⊙ 10:30am-10pm Jun-Aug; ⊕) A nationally historic landmarked amusement park 12 miles southeast of downtown with four old wooden roller coasters.

🕝 Tours

Rivers of Steel
TOUR

(✐ 412-464-4020; www.riversofsteel.com) This organization is dedicated to preserving the physical heritage as well as the memories and stories of the region's industrial past. It's worth touring Carrie Furnace (Fridays & Saturdays April to end-October), the long ago decommissioned US Steel blast furnace that now stands like a decaying post-apocalyptic memento mori. At its height in the late 1800s it produced 9000 tons of molten iron every day. Several films and music videos have been shot here.

Tour-Ed Mine
TOUR

(✐ 724-224-4720; www.tour-edmine.com; 748 Bull Creek Rd, Tarentum; adult/child $10/9; ⊙ 10am-4pm, closed Tue, Jun-Sep; ⊕) To experience something of the claustrophobia and learn about the working lives of coal miners, take this tour 160ft below the earth's surface.

Alan Irvine Storyteller Tours
CULTURAL TOUR

(✐ 412-508-2077; www.alanirvine.com/walking_tour; tours $15) This historian brings the city's past to life in a journey through several neighborhoods.

'Burgh Bits & Bites Food Tour
CULTURAL TOUR

(✐ 412-901-7150; www.burghfoodtour.com; tours $37) Wonderful way to discover the city's unique ethnic eats.

Pittsburgh History & Landmarks Foundation
CULTURAL TOUR

(✐ 412-471-5808; www.phlf.org; Station Sq; some tours free, others from $5) Specialized historic, architectural or cultural tours by foot or motor coach.

🛏 Sleeping

Straight-up chain hotels, especially around Oakland, dominate the city's lodging options.

Inn on Negley
INN $$

(✐ 412-661-0631; www.innonnegley.com; 703 Negley Ave; r $180-280; P ❋ 🛜) Formerly a pair of Shadyside inns, these two Victorian houses have been combined into one refurbished gem with a clean-line aesthetic that still bursts with romance. It features four-poster beds, handsome furniture and fireplaces, large windows and, in some rooms, hot tubs.

Priory
INN $$

(✐ 412-231-3338; www.thepriory.com; 614 Pressley St; s/d/ste incl breakfast from $99/150/180; P ❋ 🛜) Housed in a former Catholic monastery on the North Side just over the Veterans Bridge, the Priory is a mix of old-fashioned furnishings with contemporary design touches. It has a parlor with a fireplace and an interior courtyard good for drinks in warm months. A wing with an additional 17 rooms was added in 2011. Attached is the magnificent Grand Hall, a former church, now host to weddings and events.

Inn on the Mexican
War Streets
BOUTIQUE HOTEL **$$**

(☑412-231-6544; www.innonthemexicanwarstreets
.com; 604 W North Ave; r incl breakfast $139-199;
P❋🐾) This historic, gay-owned mansion on
the North Side is near the museums and right
on the bus line that takes you downtown. Ex-
pect hearty homemade breakfasts, charming
hosts, stunning antique furnishings and an
elegant porch, plus a martini lounge and the
four-star restaurant Acanthus.

Morning Glory Inn
B&B **$$**

(☑412-431-1707; www.gloryinn.com; 2119 Sarah St;
r incl breakfast $155-195, ste $190-450; P❋🐾)
An Italianate-style Victorian brick town
house popular for weddings, the Morning
Glory is in the heart of the busy South Side.
The overall decor is slightly chintzy – think
floral patterns, wicker furniture, four-poster
beds – but you can relax in the charming
backyard patio, and delicious breakfasts are
a major plus.

Parador Inn
B&B **$$**

(☑412-231-4800; www.theparadorinn.com; 939
Western Ave; r incl breakfast $150; P❋🐾) This
lovingly restored mansion on the North Side
not far from the National Aviary and Heinz
Field is a charming hodgepodge of aesthetic
influence – from Victorian to Caribbean
and everything in between. The owner is on
hand to answer any questions and there are
public rooms and a garden to relax in.

Sunnyledge
HOTEL **$$**

(☑412-683-5014; www.sunnyledge.com; 5124 Fifth
Ave; r/ste $189/275; P❋🐾) Though it refers
to itself as a 'boutique hotel,' it would be
more accurate to describe the Sunnyledge
as a 'historic' one. Housed in an 1886 mansion in Shadyside, the atmosphere is one of
traditional elegance, overwrought at times.
The restaurant on the premises gets mixed
reviews.

★ Omni William Penn Hotel
HOTEL **$$$**

(☑412-281-7100; www.omnihotels.com; 530 Wil-
liam Penn Place; r from $200; P❋🐾) Though
originally built by Henry Clay Frick nearly
100 years ago, his European inspiration is
alive and well in this elegant and stately
downtown behemoth. High tea is served
in the grand lobby, which is (surprisingly)
otherwise a welcoming meeting place for
nonguests. Above-average service, contem-
porary room furnishings, a spa, several din-
ing options and a newly opened basement
speakeasy bar round out the offerings.

✖ Eating

⊗ Downtown & the Strip

For a taste of the city's ethnic texture, head
to the Strip district just east of downtown,
stretching from 14th St to 30th St between the
Allegheny River and Liberty Ave. A stroll along
Penn Ave from 17th to 23rd is the bustling
heart where local chefs go to shop at one-of-a-
kind food markets like **Stamoolis Brothers**,
Pennsylvania Macaroni and **Wholey**. The
best time to visit is between 10am and 3pm;
during the holiday season (parking close to
impossible), it's especially celebratory and in-
toxicating, literally, as homemade wine is typi-
cally passed out for free.

★ Original Oyster House
SEAFOOD **$**

(20 Market Sq; sandwich $6; ⊙10am-10pm Mon-
Sat) Operating in one form or another since
1870 and still drawing crowds of devotees
for its deep-fried fish sandwiches. Locals of
all stripes form a line out the door at lunch-
time but it's a strictly lowdown pretension-
free place with paper plates and plastic
silverware.

Primanti Bros
FAST FOOD **$**

(☑412-263-2142; www.primantibros.com; 18th
St, near Smallman St; sandwiches $6; ⊙24hr) A
Pittsburgh institution on the Strip, this al-
ways-packed place specializes in greasy and
delicious hot sandwiches, from knockwurst
and cheese to the 'Pitts-burger cheesesteak.'
Other outlets are in Oakland, Market Sq
downtown and South Side.

Pamela's
DINER **$**

(www.pamelasdiner.com; 60 21st St; mains $7;
⊙7am-3pm Mon-Sat, 8am-3pm Sun) Even Presi-
dent Obama liked this breakfast and sand-
wich joint in the Strip district. Several other
Pamela's throughout the city, all with a clas-
sic chrome diner look, are renowned for their
crepe-like crispy-around-the-edges pancakes.

★ Enrico Biscotti Company
ITALIAN **$$**

(www.enricobiscotti.com; 2022 Penn Ave; mains $10;
⊙11am-3pm Mon-Fri, from 8am Sat) The owner
Enrico, a charming raconteur, is as adept
at regaling customers with colorful neighborhood tales as he is at churning out delicious homemade bread and wood-burning-
oven pizzas. Housed in a former auto me-
chanic's garage in the Strip with high ceilings, brick walls and reclaimed furniture.
Check out the romantic comedy *The Bread,
My Sweet* for a version of Enrico's life. Bread,

wine and cheese-making classes ($65) are offered Sunday mornings.

Southside

Cafe du Jour
MEDITERRANEAN $$
(☑412-488-9695; 1107 E Carson St; mains $15-35; ⊙11:30am-10pm Mon-Sat) A constantly changing menu of Mediterranean dishes includes especially good soups and salads for lunch; try to get a seat in the small outside courtyard. It's BYOB.

Dish Osteria Bar
MEDITERRANEAN $$
(☑412-390-2012; www.dishosteria.com; 128 S 17th St; mains $14-25; ⊙5pm-2am Mon-Sat) A tucked-away, intimate locals' fave. The simple wood tables and floors belie the at times extravagant Mediterranean creations, which range from fresh sardines with caramelized onions to fettuccine with lamb ragout.

Gypsy Café
MEDITERRANEAN $$
(☑412-381-4977; www.gypsycafe.net; 1330 Bingham St; mains $14-19; ⊙11:30am-midnight) The purple floors and walls and brightly colored rugs make patrons here as happy as the fresh, seasonal fare. Menu items include a smoked trout plate and a stew of shrimp, scallop and feta. Hours are changeable so call ahead

Café Zenith
VEGETARIAN $$
(86 S 26th St; mains $10; ⊙11am-9pm Thu-Sat, 11am-3pm Sun; ☑) A meal here is like eating in an antique shop, and everything from the formica tables and up is for sale. Regardless, the Sunday brunch ($10) and lengthy tea menu are up to date.

Other Neighborhoods

Original Hot Dog Shop
FAST FOOD $
(☑412-621-7388; 3901 Forbes Ave; sandwiches $3-7; ⊙10am-3:30am) Affectionately nicknamed 'dirty Os' or 'the O' by locals, this is an Oakland favorite for its cheap dogs, subs, pizza, chicken wings, milk shakes and mounds of crispy fries – especially after a night at the bars. Inebriation isn't necessary for enjoyment, just very common.

Emil's Lounge
AMERICAN $
(414 Hawkins Ave, Braddock; mains $6; ⊙10am-7pm Tue-Thu, to 8pm Fri, to 4pm Sat) Venture around 8.5 miles east of downtown to Braddock to experience a family-run survivor from the steel-mill era. Old, old, old school Emil's has been serving up artery-clogging portions of

chicken parm, catfish, burgers and other sandwiches for 60 years. Expect wood paneling, carpeting and a friendly welcome from the daughter of the original owners.

Ritter's Diner
DINER $
(5221 Baum Blvd; mains $7; ⊙24hr) A classic greasy spoon where locals of the Bloomfield neighborhood head for a pierogi after a long night out. Each table has its own jukebox.

Quiet Storm Coffeehouse & Restaurant
CAFE $
(☑412-661-9355; www.qspgh.com; 5430 Penn Ave; mains $6-11; ⊙8am-5pm Mon-Thu, to 10pm Fri, 9am-4pm Sat & Sun; ☑) This hipster-filled, multiuse cafe in Garfield specializes in veggie and vegan cuisine and hosts frequent readings and musical performances.

Dinette
PIZZERIA $$
(☑412-362-0202; www.dinette-pgh.com; 5996 Penn Circle South; pizzas $15; ⊙5-10pm Tue-Thu, to 11pm Fri & Sat) Two time James Beard award semifinalist Sonja Finn has elevated this casual Shadyside eatery into a destination for local foodies. The individual gourmet thin-crust pizzas are topped with locally sourced meat and produce. Excellent wine selection.

Industry Public House
MODERN AMERICAN $$
(www.industrypgh.com; 4305 Butler St; mains $10; ⊙11am-2am) Comfort food with a twist – eg lobster mac 'n' cheese, wild boar bacon burgers, artisanal cocktails and locally brewed beers – means this gastropub is prototypical Lawrenceville.

★ Isabela on Grandview
MODERN AMERICAN $$$
(☑412-431-5882; www.isabelaongrandview.com; 1318 Grandview Ave; meals $70; ⊙5-10pm Mon-Sat) Perched atop Mt Washington with gorgeous nighttime city views, this small romantic restaurant is worthy of anniversary or proposal dinners. The seven-course prixe-fixe meal might include lobster and duck and always fresh, seasonal ingredients.

♥ Drinking & Entertainment

Bars & Nightclubs
Most nightlife is centered on the South Side and the Strip. Carson St is ground zero for bar-hopping. You'll find several big, frenzied dance clubs, known as 'meatmarkets,' clustered at the edge of the Strip district. Most gay bars are in a concentrated stretch of Liberty Ave downtown.

Wigle Whiskey
DISTILLERY
(www.wiglewhiskey.com; 2401 Smallman St; ☺10am-6pm Tue-Sun) Pittsburgh's one and only distillery is family owned (almost every member has made a dramatic career change) and uses organic and local ingredients to produce artisan batches of rye and wheat whiskey. Head to this renovated brick warehouse in the Strip for tours ($20) and $5 sample flights.

Bar Marco
COCKTAIL BAR
(2216 Penn Ave; ☺5-11pm Mon, to 2am Tue-Fri, 10am-2am Sat, to 10am-3pm Sun) Sample the top-flight wine menu and cocktails, expertly prepared by bartending pros, at this sophisticated space in a renovated fire house in the Strip. Excllent brunch on weekends.

Bloomfield Bridge Tavern
PUB, LIVE MUSIC
(☑412-682-8611; 4412 Liberty Ave; ☺5pm-2am Mon-Sat) 'The only Polish restaurant in Lil' Italy' is a gritty pub serving beers with excellent sides of pierogi, and indie-rock bands on the weekends.

Church Brew Works
BREWERY
(☑412-688-8200; 3525 Liberty Ave) Serves handcrafted beers in a massive former church space. A standout in Lawrenceville.

Hofbräuhaus
BEER HALL
(☑412-235-7065; 2705 S Water St) An imitation of the famous Munich beer hall and only a block off Carson.

Gooski
BAR
(3117 Brereton St; ☺3pm-2am) Hipster-cum-dive bar in Polish Hill neighborhood with cheap drinks and jukebox.

Brillo Box Bar
BAR, LIVE MUSIC
(www.brillobox.net; 4104 Penn Ave; ☺5pm-2am Tue-Sun) Live music, excellent menu and a good Sunday brunch at this popular spot in Lawrenceville.

Dee's Cafe
BAR
(☑412-431-1314; www.deescafe.com; 1314 E Carson St; ☺11am-2am) A notable punk bar with Pabst on tap and dirt-cheap bottles.

Live Music

AVA Bar & Lounge
CLUB
(www.avapgh.net; 126 S Highland Ave; ☺7pm-2am Mon-Sat, to midnight Sun) One of the coolest and most cutting-edge clubs in the city is ironically located in a generic strip in the East Liberty neighborhood (near Shadyside). The same owner and vibe from the recently closed Shadow Lounge, AVA has DJs and live hip-hop, jazz and other music.

Rex Theater
LIVE MUSIC
(☑412-381-6811; www.rextheatre.com; 1602 E Carson St) A favorite South Side venue, a converted movie theater, for touring jazz, rock and indie bands, as well as a venue for the Moth Storyslam.

MCG Jazz
LIVE MUSIC
(☑412-323-4000; www.mcgjazz.org; 1815 Metropolitan St) Live concerts/recordings of top jazz musicians are held at this venue on the north side of the city.

Club Café
LIVE MUSIC
(☑412-431-4950; www.clubcafelive.com; 56-58 S 12th St) Live music nightly, mostly of the singer-songwriter type.

Theater & Culture

Pittsburgh Cultural Trust
PERFORMING ARTS
(☑412-471-6070; www.pgharts.org; 803 Liberty Ave) Promotes all downtown arts, from the Pittsburgh Dance Council and PNC Broadway in Pittsburgh to visual art and opera. Go to the website for tickets to the Benedum Center, Byham Theater, Theater Square, Heinz Hall and other venues.

Gist Street Readings
PERFORMING ARTS
(www.giststreet.org; 305 Gist St, 3rd fl; readings $10) Holds monthly readings from local and well-known national literary figures. Best to get there when doors open at 7:15pm, since turnout is typically large. Bring your own refreshments.

ⓘ Information

MEDIA
Pittsburgh City Paper (www.pghcitypaper.com) Free alternative weekly with extensive arts listings.
Pittsburgh Post-Gazette (www.post-gazette.com) A major daily.
Pittsburgh Tribune-Review (www.triblive.com) Another major daily.
Pittsburgh's Out (www.outonline.com) Free monthly gay newspaper.

MEDICAL SERVICES
Allegheny County Health Department (☑412-687-2243; 3333 Forbes Ave) Has a walk-in medical center.
University of Pittsburgh Medical Center (☑412-647-8762; 200 Lothrop St; ☺24hr) Emergency, high-ranking medical care.

THE LAUREL HIGHLANDS

A Frank Lloyd Wright masterpiece, Fallingwater (☎724-329-8501; www.fallingwater.org; 1491 Mill Run Rd; adult/child $23/17; ⊙ hours vary, closed Jan & Feb) is south of Pittsburgh on Rte 381. Completed in 1939 as a weekend retreat for the Kaufmanns, owners of the Pittsburgh department store, the building blends seamlessly with its natural setting. To see inside you must take one of the hourly guided tours, and reservations are recommended. A more intensive two-hour tour, with photography permitted, is offered ($55; times vary depending on day and month, reservations required). The rather attractive forested grounds open at 8:30am.

Much less visited is Kentuck Knob (☎724-329-1901; www.kentuckknob.com; 723 Kentuck Rd; adult/child $20/14; ⊙ hours vary, closed Jan 2-Mar 2), another Frank Lloyd Wright house (designed in 1953), built into the side of a rolling hill. It's noted for its natural materials, hexagonal design and honeycomb skylights. House tours last about an hour and include a jaunt through the onsite sculpture garden, with works by Andy Goldsworthy, Ray Smith and others.

From the end of May to the beginning of September the postage-stamp-sized town of Ohiopyle swells with visitors looking to ride the rapids of the Youghiogheny River (locals simply say 'the Yough' pronounced 'yawk') and explore Ohiopyle State Park. Laurel Highlands River Tours (☎800-472-3846; www.laurelhighlands.com) is a highly recommended operator and offers rock climbing and kayaking clinics if rafting is too tame. Laurel Guesthouse (☎724-329-8531; www.laurelhighlands.com/lodging; Grant St, Ohiopyle; s/d $80/90; ❋) has three bedrooms furnished like a comfortable suburban home.

Fort Ligonier (☎724-238-9701; www.fortligonier.org; 200 South Market St, Ligonier; adult/child $10/6; ⊙10am-4:30pm Mon-Sat, noon-4:30pm Sun mid-Apr–mid-Nov), both a museum and a reconstructed fort with enthusiastic historical interpreters, does a great job of explaining the area's importance in the French and Indian War, as does the visitor center at the nearby Fort Necessity (www.nps.gov/fone; 1 Washington Pkwy/Rte 40 , Farmington; ⊙9am-5pm).

You can even spend a night in a Frank Lloyd Wright design at the Duncan House (☎877-833-7829; www.polymathpark.com; 187 Evergreen Ln, Acme; up to 3 people $400, per additional person $50, up to 6; ❋☎), part of Polymath Park, a wooded property with three other homes designed by Wright apprentices. Don't expect Wright pyrotechnics – the house is a modest Eusonia-style and none of the furniture or interior pieces are Wright's but rather standard mid-century modern. Or try the swank Nemacolin Woodlands Resort & Spa (☎724-329-8555; www.nemacolin.com; 1001 Lafayette Dr, Farmington; r from $200; ❋@☎≈❋❋) in Farmington with a spa, golf course and several restaurants.

TOURIST INFORMATION

Greater Pittsburgh Convention & Visitors Bureau Main Branch (☎412-281-7711; www. visitpittsburgh.com; Suite 2800, 120 Fifth Ave; ⊙10am-6pm Mon-Fri, to 4pm Sat, to 3pm Sun) Publishes the *Official Visitors Guide* and provides maps and tourist advice.

WEBSITES

Citysearch (pittsburgh.citysearch.com) Nightlife, restaurant and shopping listings.

Pittsburgh.net (www.pittsburgh.net) Listings, neighborhoods and events.

Pop City (www.popcitymedia.com) Weekly e-magazine highlighting arts and cultural events.

ⓘ Getting There & Away

AIR

Pittsburgh International Airport (☎412-472-3525; www.pitairport.com), 18 miles west of downtown, has direct connections to Europe, Canada and major US cities via a slew of airlines.

BUS

From its station near the Strip, **Greyhound** (☎412-392-6500; www.greyhound.com; 55 11th St) has frequent buses to Philadelphia (from $30, six to seven hours), New York ($56, 8½ to 14 hours) and Chicago, IL ($68, 10 to 14 hours).

CAR

Pittsburgh is easily accessible via major highways, from the north or south on the I-76 or I-79, from the west on Rte 22 and from the east on the I-70. It's about an eight-hour drive from NYC and about three hours from Buffalo.

TRAIN

Amtrak (☎ 800-872-7245; www.amtrak.com; 1100 Liberty Ave) is behind the magnificent original train station, with trains heading to cities including Philadelphia (from $55, seven to eight hours) and NYC (from $73, nine to 11 hours).

❶ Getting Around

The excellent **28X Airport Flyer** (www.portauthority.org; One-way $3.75) public bus makes runs from the airport to Oakland and downtown every 20 minutes. Taxis are readily available and cost about $40 (not including tip) to downtown. Various shuttles also make downtown runs and cost $15 to $20 per person one way.

Driving around Pittsburgh can be extremely frustrating – roads end with no warning, one-way streets can take you in circles and there are various bridges to contend with.

Port Authority Transit (www.portauthority.org) operates an extensive bus system and a limited light-rail system, the 'T,' which is useful for going from downtown to the South Side. Bus and T fares range from free to $2.50, depending on the zones (traveling between the four downtown T stops is free).

For taxis, call **Yellow Cab Co of Pittsburgh** (☎ 412-321-8100), which charges by zone.

New England

Why Go?

Sure, you could drive from one end of New England to the other in a day, but why would you want to? Let the region's many diversions slow you down. The cities offer a vibrant mix of historical sites, chef-driven restaurants and Ivy League campuses. On the coast you'll find age-old fishing villages and sandy beaches begging a dip. Heading inland, the northern states are as rural and rugged as the mountains that run up their spines.

So take it easy. Crack open a lobster and let the sweet juices run down your fingers. Hike quiet trails. Or just get lost on a scenic back road and count the covered bridges. And if you're lucky enough to be here in autumn, you'll be rewarded with the most brilliant fall foliage you'll ever see.

Best Places to Eat

→ Giacomo's Ristorante (p182)

→ Chatham Fish Pier Market (p192)

→ Nudel (p203)

→ Haven Brothers Diner (p206)

→ Hen of the Wood (p223)

Best Places to Stay

→ Harborside Inn (p180)

→ Carpe Diem (p195)

→ Hopkins Inn (p215)

→ Sea Breeze Inn (p209)

→ Inn at Shelburne Farms (p225)

When to Go
Boston

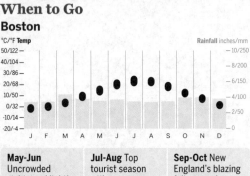

May-Jun Uncrowded sights and lightly trodden trails. Whale-watching begins.

Jul-Aug Top tourist season with summer festivals, warm ocean water and beach parties.

Sep-Oct New England's blazing foliage peaks from mid-September to mid-October.

Getting There & Around

Getting to New England is easy, but once you arrive you'll need a car if you want to explore the region thoroughly. The coastal I-95 and the inland I-91, the main north–south highways, transverse New England from Connecticut to Canada. Public transportation is fine between major cities but scarce in the countryside. Greyhound (www.greyhound.com) operates the most extensive bus service.

Amtrak (800-872-7245; www.amtrak.com) has a Northeast Corridor service that connects Boston, Providence, Hartford and New Haven with New York City; smaller regional services operate elsewhere in New England.

Boston's Logan International Airport (BOS) is New England's main hub. TF Green Airport (PVD) in Providence, RI, and Manchester Airport (MHT) in New Hampshire – both about an hour's drive from Boston – are growing 'minihubs' with less congestion and cheaper fares.

NEW ENGLAND PARKS

Acadia National Park (p243), on the rugged, northeastern coast of Maine, is the region's only national park but numerous other large tracts of New England's forest, mountains and shoreline are set aside for preservation and recreation.

The White Mountain National Forest (p229) is a vast 800,000-acre expanse of New Hampshire and Maine, offering a wonderland of scenic drives, hiking trails, campgrounds and ski slopes. Vermont's Green Mountain National Forest (p219) covers 400,000 acres of unspoiled forest. Both are crossed by the Appalachian Trail.

Another gem of federally protected land is the Cape Cod National Seashore (p193), a 44,600-acre stretch of rolling dunes and stunning beaches that's perfect for swimming, cycling and seaside hikes.

State parks are plentiful throughout New England, ranging from green niches in urban locations to the remote, untamed wilderness of Baxter State Park (p247) in northern Maine.

Seafood Specialties

→ **Clam chowder** Or, as Bostonians say, *chow-dah;* combines chopped clams, potatoes and clam juice in a milk base

→ **Oysters** Served raw on the half-shell or, for the less intrepid, broiled; sweetest are Wellfleet oysters from Cape Cod

→ **Steamers** Soft-shelled clams steamed and served in a bucket of briny broth

→ **Clambake** A meal of steamed lobster, clams and corn on the cob

DON'T MISS

Don't leave New England without cracking open a steamed lobster at a beachside seafood shack, such as the Lobster Dock (p241) in Boothbay Harbor.

NEW ENGLAND

Fast Facts

→ **Hub cities** Boston (population 636,000), Providence (population 178,000)

→ **Time zone** Eastern

→ **Highest point** Mt Washington (6288ft)

→ **Miles of coastline** 4965

Faux Pas

Don't mock, mimic or otherwise imitate a local's accent. New Englanders know they talk differently from other Americans, but they don't care.

Resources

→ **Yankee Magazine** (www.yankeemagazine.com) Great destination profiles, recipes and events.

→ **Mountain Summits** (www.mountainsummits.com) Everything you need to plan a hike in the New England hills.

→ **Maine Lobster Council** (www.lobsterfrommaine.com) How to catch, order, buy, prepare and eat lobster.

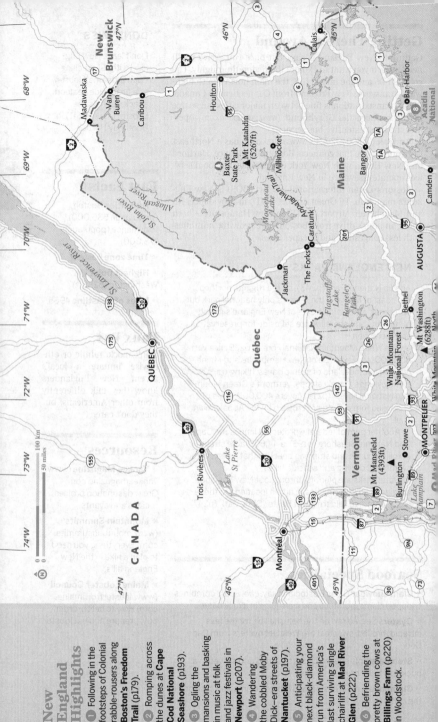

New England Highlights

1 Following in the footsteps of Colonial rabble-rousers along **Boston's Freedom Trail** (p179).

2 Romping across the dunes at **Cape Cod National Seashore** (p193).

3 Ogling the mansions and basking in music at folk and jazz festivals in **Newport** (p207).

4 Wandering the cobbled Moby Dick–era streets of **Nantucket** (p197).

5 Anticipating your next black-diamond run from America's last surviving single chairlift at **Mad River Glen** (p222).

6 Befriending the pretty brown cows at **Billings Farm** (p220) in Woodstock.

7 Driving the **Kancamagus Highway** (p230) across the craggy White Mountains.

8 Hiking and cycling the carriage roads of **Acadia National Park** (p243).

9 Gawking at fall foliage in the **Berkshires** (p202) and **Litchfield Hills** (p215).

43°N

42°N

41°N

68°W

69°W

70°W

71°W

72°W

73°W

74°W

ATLANTIC OCEAN

Monhegan Island

Boothbay Harbor

Portland

Cape Cod National Seashore **2**

Stellwagen Bank National Marine Sanctuary

Provincetown

Rockport
Gloucester
Portsmouth
Salem
Lexington
BOSTON 1
Plymouth
Hyannis
Nantucket **4**
New Bedford
Newport **3**
Fall River
Martha's Vineyard

6
6
3
24
128
95
93
495
90
44
95
395
1
95

Lake Winnipesaukee
Lake Winnipesaukee
Sebago Lake

New Hampshire
CONCORD
Manchester
Hanover
Woodstock
Brattleboro
Connecticut River
Green Mountain National Forest
Bennington
Williamstown
North Adams
Pittsfield
Lenox
Stockbridge
Great Barrington

National Forest
Appalachian Trail
Rutland
16
93
25
11
16
125
101
4
3
9
93
91
107
4

New York
Glens Falls
Buffalo (220mi)
ALBANY
30
87
88
90
4
7

Massachusetts
Amherst
Northampton
Springfield
Worcester
Sturbridge
Concord
Massachusetts Turnpike
Becket
The Berkshires **9**
2
9
202
90

Connecticut
HARTFORD
Bradley International Airport
East Haddam
Deep River
Essex
Old Lyme
Mystic
New Haven
Ledyard
Narragansett
Watch Hill
Block Island
Litchfield
Litchfield Hills **9**
Lake Waramaug State Park
84
91
9
44
395
95
1
84

Rhode Island
PROVIDENCE

Long Island Sound
Long Island
NY
NJ
New York
278
495
95
87

NEW ENGLAND IN...

One Week

Start in **Boston**, cruising the **Freedom Trail**, dining at a cozy **North End bistro** and exploring the city's highlights. Next, tramp through the mansions in **Newport**, then hit the beaches on **Cape Cod** and hop a ferry for a day trip to **Nantucket** or **Martha's Vineyard**. End the week with a jaunt north to New Hampshire's **White Mountains**, circling back down the **Maine coast**.

Two Weeks

Now you've got time for serious exploring. Use your second week to to take a leisurely drive through the **Litchfield Hills** and the **Berkshires**. Bookend the week with visits to the lively burgs of **Providence** and **Burlington**.

Alternatively, extend your stay on the Maine coast, with time to explore **Bar Harbor** and kayak along the shores of **Acadia National Park**. Wrap it up in Maine's vast wilderness, where you can work up a sweat on a hike up the northernmost peak of the **Appalachian Trail** or take an adrenaline-pumping ride down the **Kennebec River**.

History

When the first European settlers arrived, New England was inhabited by native Algonquians who lived in small tribes, raising corn and beans, hunting game and harvesting the rich coastal waters.

English captain Bartholomew Gosnold landed at Cape Cod and sailed north to Maine in 1602 but it wasn't until 1614 that Captain John Smith, who charted the region's coastline for King James I, christened the land 'New England.' With the arrival of the Pilgrims at Plymouth in 1620, European settlement began in earnest. Over the next century the colonies expanded, often at the expense of the indigenous people.

Although subjects of the British crown, New Englanders governed themselves with their own legislative councils and they came to view their affairs as separate from those of England. In the 1770s King George III imposed a series of costly taxes to pay for England's involvement in costly wars. The colonists, unrepresented in the English parliament, protested under the slogan 'no taxation without representation.' Attempts to squash the protests eventually led to battles at Lexington and Concord, setting off the War of Independence. The historic result was the birth of the USA in 1776.

Following independence, New England became an economic powerhouse, its harbors booming centers for shipbuilding, fishing and trade. New England's famed Yankee Clippers plied ports from China to South America. A thriving whaling industry brought unprecedented wealth to Nantucket and New Bedford. The USA's first water-powered cotton-spinning mill was established in Rhode Island in 1793. In the years that followed, New England's swift rivers became the engines of vast mills turning out clothing, shoes and machinery.

But no boom lasts forever. By the early 20th century many of the mills had moved south. Today education, finance, biotechnology and tourism are linchpins of the regional economy.

Local Culture

New Englanders tend to be reserved by nature, with the Yankee brusqueness standing in marked contrast to the casual outgoing nature of some other American regions. This taciturn quality shouldn't be confused with unfriendliness, as it's simply a more formal regional style.

Particularly in rural areas, folks take pride in their ingenuity and self-sufficient character. These New Englanders remain fiercely independent, from the fishing-boat crews who brave Atlantic storms to the Vermont small farmers who fight to keep operating independently within America's agribusiness economy.

Fortunately for the farmers and fishers, buy-local and go-organic movements have grown by leaps and bounds throughout New England. From bistros in Boston to small towns in the far north the menus are greening.

One place you won't find that ol' Yankee reserve is at the ball field. New Englanders are fanatical about sports. Attending a Red

Sox game is as close as you'll come to a modern-day gladiators-at-the-coliseum scene – wild cheers and nasty jeers galore.

Generally regarded as a liberal enclave, New England is in the forefront on progressive political issues from gay rights to health-care reform. Indeed, the universal health-insurance program in Massachusetts became the model for President Obama's national plan.

MASSACHUSETTS

From the woodsy hills of the Berkshires to the sandy beaches of Cape Cod, Massachusetts is filled with opportunities to explore the great outdoors. From Plymouth Rock to the Revolutionary War, the Commonwealth is rich with history. And from Boston's universities and museums to the Berkshires' summer theaters and Tanglewood, the cultural offerings are world-class. Your challenge lies in deciding: which Massachusetts will you discover?

ℹ Information

Massachusetts Department of Conservation and Recreation (☑617-626-1250; www.mass.gov/eea) Offers camping in 29 state parks.
Massachusetts Office of Travel & Tourism (☑617-973-8500; www.massvacation.com) Provides information on the entire state.

Boston

The winding streets and stately architecture recall a history of revolution and renewal; and still, today, Boston is among the country's most forward-looking and barrier-breaking cities.

For all intents and purposes, Boston is the oldest city in America. And you can hardly walk a step over its cobblestone streets without running into some historic site. But Boston has not been relegated to the past. The city's art and music scenes continue to charm and challenge contemporary audiences; cutting-edge urban planning projects are reshaping the city; and scores of universities guarantee an infusion of cultural energy every September.

History

When the Massachusetts Bay Colony was established by England in 1630, Boston became its capital. It's a city of firsts: Boston

Latin School, the first public school in the USA, was founded in 1635, followed a year later by Harvard, the nation's first university. The first newspaper in the colonies was printed here in 1704, America's first labor union organized here in 1795 and the country's first subway system opened in Boston in 1897.

Not only were the first battles of the American Revolution fought nearby, but Boston was also home to the first African American regiment to fight in the US Civil War. Waves of immigrants, especially Irish in the mid-18th century and Italians in the early 20th, have infused the city with European influences.

Today Boston remains at the forefront of higher learning and its universities have spawned world-renowned industries in biotechnology, medicine and finance.

◉ Sights & Activities

Boston's small size means that it's easy to walk and difficult to drive. Most of Boston's

---

MASSACHUSETTS FACTS

Nickname Bay State

Population 6.5 million

Area 7840 sq miles

Capital city Boston (population 625,100)

Other cities Worcester (population 181,600), Springfield (population 153,200)

Sales tax 6.25%

Birthplace of Inventor Benjamin Franklin (1706–90), five presidents including John F Kennedy (1917–63), authors Jack Kerouac (1922–69) and Henry David Thoreau (1817–62)

Home of Harvard University, Boston Marathon, Plymouth Rock

Politics Lefty

Famous for Boston Tea Party, first state to legalize gay marriage

State Sweets Boston Cream Pie, Dunkin' Donuts, Fig Newtons

Driving distances Boston to Provincetown 145 miles, Boston to Northampton 98 miles, Boston to Acadia National Park 310 miles

Boston

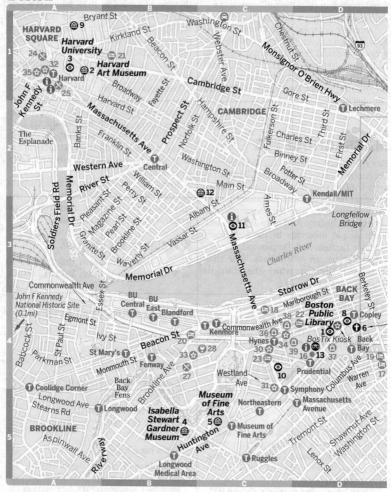

main attractions are found in or near the city center. Begin at Boston Common, where you'll find the tourist office and the start of the Freedom Trail.

◉ Boston Common & Public Garden

★ **Boston Common**   PARK
(Map p174; btwn Tremont, Charles, Beacon & Park Sts; ⏰ 6am-midnight; ♿; Ⓣ Park St) The Boston Common has served many purposes over the years, including as a campground

for British troops during the Revolutionary War and as green grass for cattle grazing until 1830. Although there is still a grazing ordinance on the books, the common today serves picnickers, sunbathers and people-watchers.

★ **Public Garden**   GARDENS
(Map p174; www.friendsofthepublicgarden.org; btwn Charles, Beacon, Boylston & Arlington Sts; ⏰ 6am-midnight; ♿; Ⓣ Arlington) Adjoining Boston Common, the 24-acre Public Garden provides an inviting oasis of bountiful flowers and shady trees. Its centerpiece, a tranquil

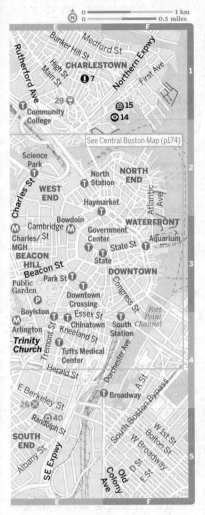

★**Massachusetts State House**   NOTABLE BUILDING

(Map p174; www.sec.state.ma.us; cnr Beacon & Bowdoin Sts; ⊘9am-5pm, tours 10am-4pm Mon-Fri; ⊤Park St) **FREE** High atop Beacon Hill, Massachusetts' leaders and legislators attempt to turn their ideas into concrete policies and practices within the State House. Charles Bulfinch designed the commanding state capitol, but it was Oliver Wendell Holmes who called it 'the hub of the solar system' (thus earning Boston the nickname 'the Hub'). Knowledgeable 'Doric Docents' give free tours showcasing the building's history, artwork, architecture and political personalities.

Granary Burying Ground   CEMETERY

(Map p174; Tremont St; ⊘9am-5pm; ⊤Park St) Dating to 1660, this atmospheric atoll is crammed with historic headstones, many with evocative (and creepy) carvings. This is the final resting place of all your favorite revolutionary heroes including Paul Revere, Samuel Adams, John Hancock and James Otis. Benjamin Franklin is buried in Philadelphia, but the Franklin family plot contains his parents.

Old South Meeting House   HISTORIC BUILDING

(Map p174; www.osmh.org; 310 Washington St; adult/child/senior & student $6/1/5; ⊘9:30am-5pm Apr-Oct, 10am-4pm Nov-Mar; ♿; ⊤Downtown Crossing) 'No tax on tea!' That was the decision on December 16, 1773, when 5000 angry colonists gathered here to protest British taxes, leading to the Boston Tea Party. Check out an exhibit about the history of the building and listen to an audio of the historic pre–Tea Party meeting.

Old State House   HISTORIC BUILDING

(Map p174; www.bostonhistory.org; 206 Washington St; adult/child $8.50/free; ⊘9am-5pm; ♿; ⊤State) Dating to 1713, the Old State House is Boston's oldest surviving public building, where the Massachusetts Assembly used to debate the issues of the day before the revolution. The building is best known for its balcony, where the Declaration of Independence was first read to Bostonians in 1776.

Faneuil Hall   HISTORIC BUILDING

(Map p174; www.faneuilhall.com; Congress St; ⊘9am-5pm; ⊤Haymarket, Aquarium) **FREE** 'Those who cannot bear free speech had best go home,' said Wendell Phillips. 'Faneuil Hall

---

lagoon with old-fashioned pedal-powered **Swan Boats** (Map p174; www.swanboats.com; adult/child/senior $2.75/1.50/2; ⊘10am-4pm, to 5pm mid-Jun–Aug), has been delighting children for generations.

◉ **Beacon Hill & Downtown**

Rising above Boston Common is Beacon Hill, one of the city's most historic and affluent neighborhoods. To the east is Downtown Boston, with a curious mix of Colonial sights and modern office buildings.

Boston

is no place for slavish hearts.' Indeed, this public meeting place was the site of so much rabble-rousing that it earned the nickname the 'Cradle of Liberty.' The 1st floor houses the National Park Service (NPS) Visitors Center, while the 2nd-floor meeting space is also open to the public.

★ **New England Aquarium**   AQUARIUM
(Map p174; www.neaq.org; Central Wharf; adult/child/senior $23/16/21; ⊙9am-5pm Mon-Fri, to 6pm Sat & Sun, 1hr later Jul & Aug; P ⊞; T Aquarium) ✐ The aquarium's main attraction is the newly renovated, three-story, cylindrical saltwater tank, which swirls with more than 600 creatures great and small, including turtles, sharks and eels. At the base of the tank the penguin pool is home to three species of fun-loving penguins. Other special features include the marine mammal exhibit and the shark-and-ray touch tank. The aquarium also organizes whale-watching cruises (Map p174; www.neaq. org; Central Wharf; adult/child/child under 3yr $40/32/15; ⊙10am Apr-Oct, additional cruises May-Sep; ⊞; T Aquarium).

◎ North End & Charlestown

An old-world warren of narrow streets, the Italian North End offers visitors an irresistible mix of colorful period buildings and mouthwatering eateries. Colonial sights spill across the river into Charlestown, home to America's oldest battleship.

Paul Revere House   HISTORIC HOUSE
(Map p174; ☎617-523-2338; www.paulreverehouse. org; 19 North Sq; adult/child/senior & student $3.50/1/3; ⊙9:30am-5:15pm, shorter hours Nov-Apr; ⊞; T Haymarket) When silversmith Paul Revere rode to warn patriots of the British march to Lexington and Concord, he set out from his home on North Sq. This small clapboard house was built in 1680, making it the oldest house in Boston. A self-guided tour through the house and courtyard gives a glimpse of what life was like for the Revere family (which included 16 children!).

Old North Church   CHURCH
(Map p174; www.oldnorth.com; 193 Salem St; donation $1, tour adult/child $5/4; ⊙9am-5pm Mar-Oct, 10am-4pm Tue-Sun Nov-Feb; T Haymarket or North

Station) Every American knows the line from Longfellow's poem 'Paul Revere's Ride': 'One if by land, Two if by sea...' It was here, on the night of April 18, 1775, that the sexton hung two lanterns from the steeple, as a signal that the British would march on Lexington and Concord via the sea route. Also called Christ Church, this 1723 place of worship is Boston's oldest church.

USS Constitution

HISTORIC SITE

(Map p170; www.oldironsides.com; Charlestown Navy Yard; ☺10am-6pm Tue-Sun Apr-Oct, to 4pm Thu-Sun Nov-Mar; ♿; ☐93 from Haymarket, ⛴F4 from Long Wharf) FREE 'Her sides are made of iron!' So cried a crewman as he watched a shot bounce off the thick hull of the USS *Constitution* during the War of 1812. This bit of irony earned the legendary ship her nickname, Old Ironsides. The USS *Constitution* is still the oldest commissioned US Navy ship. Free 30-minute guided tours show off the top deck, gun deck and cramped quarters. The museum (Map p170; www.ussconstitutionmuseum.org; First Ave, Charlestown Navy Yard; adult/senior/child $5/3/2; ☺9am-6pm Apr-Oct, 10am-5pm Nov-Mar; ♿; ☐93 from Haymarket, ⛴F4 from Long Wharf) is great for history and activities for kids.

Bunker Hill Monument

MONUMENT

(Map p170; www.nps.gov/bost; Monument Sq; ☺9am-5pm Sep-Jun, to 6pm Jul & Aug; ☐93 from Haymarket, ⓣCommunity College) FREE Remembering the eponymous battle of June 17, 1775, the 220ft granite obelisk monument is visible from across the harbor in the North End, from the expanse of the Zakim Bridge and from almost anywhere in Charlestown. Climb the 294 steps to the top of the monument and enjoy the 360° panorama.

⊙ Seaport District

Following the HarborWalk, it's a pleasant stroll across the Northern Ave Bridge and into the up-and-coming Seaport District.

Institute of Contemporary Art

MUSEUM

(ICA; www.icaboston.org; 100 Northern Ave; adult/child/student/senior $15/free/10/13; ☺10am-5pm Tue, Wed, Sat & Sun, to 9pm Thu & Fri; ℗♿; ☐SL1 or SL2, ⓣSouth Station) The dramatic building of the ICA is a work of art in itself: a glass structure cantilevered over a waterside plaza. The light-filled interior allows for unique exhibitions and programs, including multimedia presentations and performance art. Most importantly, it allows for the development of the ICA's permanent collection, which has focused on artists featured in past exhibits.

★ Boston Tea Party Ships & Museum

MUSEUM

(Map p174; www.bostonteapartyship.com; Congress St Bridge; ♿; ⓣSouth Station) After years of anticipation and restoration, the Tea Party Ships are now moored at the reconstructed Griffin's Wharf, alongside a shiny new museum dedicated to the revolution's most catalytic event. Interactive exhibits allow visitors to meet reenactors in period costume, explore the ships, learn about contemporary popular perceptions through multimedia presentations and even participate in the protest.

⊙ Chinatown, Theater District & South End

Compact Chinatown offers enticing Asian eateries placed cheek by jowl, while the overlapping Theater District is clustered

---

BOSTON IN...

Two Days

Spend one day reliving revolutionary history by following the **Freedom Trail**. Take time to lounge on **Boston Common**, peek in the **Old State House** and imbibe a little history at the **Union Oyster House**. Afterwards, stroll into the **North End** for an Italian dinner.

On your second day, rent a bicycle and ride along the Charles River. Go as far as **Harvard Square** to cruise the campus and browse the bookstores.

Four Days

On your third day, peruse the impressive American collection at the **Museum of Fine Arts**. In the evening, catch a performance of the world-famous **Boston Symphony Orchestra** or watch the Red Sox play at **Fenway Park**.

Spend your last day discovering Back Bay. Window-shop and gallery-hop on **Newbury St**, go to the top of the **Prudential Center** and browse the **Boston Public Library**.

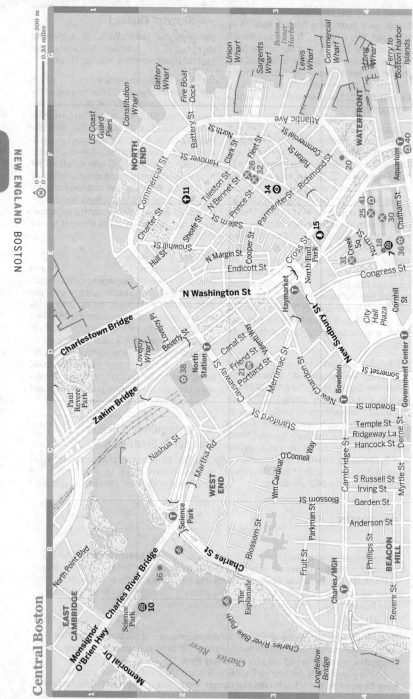

NEW ENGLAND BOSTON

Central Boston

500 m
0.25 miles

Boston Inner Harbor

Ferry to Boston Harbor Islands

Long Wharf

Commercial Wharf

Lewis Wharf

Sargents Wharf

Union Wharf

WATERFRONT

Atlantic Ave

Aquarium

40

Commercial St

Fulton St

Richmond St

North St

Fire Boat Dock

Battery Wharf

Constitution Wharf

US Coast Guard Piers

Battery St

Clark St

Fleet St

Hanover St

NORTH END

Commercial St

Charter St

Tileston St

N Bennet St

Prince St

Salem St

Parmenter St

Cross St

Cooper St

Endicott St

N Margin St

Snowhill St

Hull St

Sheafe St

11

26

32

14

15

25 41

30

Chatham St

18

7

36

31

North End Park

North St

Creek Sq

Congress St

Cornhill St

City Hall Plaza

Haymarket

N Washington St

New Sudbury St

Government Center

Somerset St

Bowdoin

Bowdoin St

Charlestown Bridge

Lovejoy Pl

Lovejoy Wharf

Beverly St

North Station

Canal St

Valenti Way

Friend St

Portland St

Causeway St

Merrimac St

New Chardon St

Temple St

Ridgeway La

Hancock St

Derne St

Paul Revere Park

Zakim Bridge

Nashua St

Martha Rd

O'Connell Way

Stanford St

WEST END

Cambridge St

S Russell St

Irving St

Garden St

Anderson St

Myrtle St

BEACON HILL

Phillips St

Revere St

Wm Cardinal

Blossom St

Parkman St

Fruit St

Charles/MGH

Science Park

38

North Point Blvd

EAST CAMBRIDGE

Monsignor O'Brien Hwy

Charles River Bridge

Memorial Dr

Science Park

10

16

Charles St

The Esplanade

Charles River Bike Path

Charles River

Longfellow Bridge

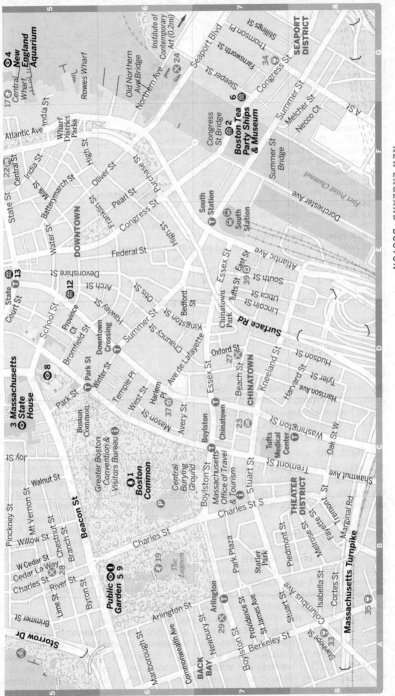

Central Boston

with performing-arts venues. To the west, the sprawling South End boasts one of America's largest concentrations of Victorian row houses, a burgeoning art community and a terrific restaurant scene.

◎ Back Bay

Extending west from Boston Common, this well-groomed neighborhood boasts graceful brownstone residences, grand edifices and the tony shopping mecca of Newbury St.

Copley Square   PLAZA
(Map p170; T Copley) Here you'll find a cluster of handsome historic buildings, including the masterwork of architect HH Richardson, the ornate neo-Romanesque **Trinity Church** (Map p170; www.trinitychurchboston.org; 206 Clarendon St; adult/child/senior & student $7/ free/5; ◎10am-3:30pm Mon-Fri, 9am-4pm Sat, 1-5pm Sun). Across the street, the Renaissance Revival **Boston Public Library** (Map p170; www.bpl.org; 700 Boylston St; ◎9am-9pm Mon-Thu, 9am-5pm Fri & Sat year-round, 1-5pm Sun Oct-May) FREE is America's first municipal library, lending credence to this city's reputation as the 'Athens of America.' Pick

up a self-guided tour brochure and wander around, noting gems such as the murals by John Singer Sargent and sculpture by Augustus Saint-Gaudens.

Prudential Center
Skywalk Observatory   LOOKOUT
(Map p170; www.prudentialcenter.com; 800 Boylston St; adult/child/senior & student $15/10/13; ◎10am-10pm Mar-Oct, to 8pm Nov-Feb; P ; T Prudential) Technically called the Shops at Prudential Center, this landmark city building is not much more than a fancy shopping mall. But it does provide a bird's-eye view of Boston from its 50th-floor Skywalk. Completely enclosed by glass, the Skywalk offers spectacular 360° views of Boston and Cambridge, accompanied by an entertaining audio tour (with a special version catering to kids).

Mary Baker Eddy
Library & Mapparium   LIBRARY
(Map p170; www.marybakereddylibrary.org; 200 Massachusetts Ave; adult/child/senior & student $6/ free/4; ◎10am-4pm Tue-Sun; ; T Symphony) Ever had a hankering to walk across the entire planet? The Mary Baker Eddy Library contains a room-size stained-glass globe,

known as the Mapparium. Walk across the glass bridge and feel you're at the center of the world.

Fenway & Kenmore Square

Kenmore Sq is best for baseball and beer, while the southern part of the Fenway is dedicated to higher-minded cultural pursuits.

★**Museum of Fine Arts** MUSEUM
(MFA; Map p170; www.mfa.org; 465 Huntington Ave; adult/child/senior & student $22/10/20; ⊙10am-5pm Sat-Tue, to 10pm Wed-Fri; ⓘ; Ⓣ Museum of Fine Arts or Ruggles) The Museum of Fine Arts collection encompasses all eras, from the ancient world to contemporary times, and all areas of the globe, making it truly encyclopedic in scope. The museum's latest addition is its new wings dedicated to the Art of the Americas and to Contemporary Art, which has significantly increased its exhibition space and broadened its focus, contributing to Boston's emergence as an art center in the 21st century.

★**Isabella Stewart Gardner Museum** MUSEUM
(Map p170; www.gardnermuseum.org; 280 The Fenway; adult/child/student/senior $15/free/5/12; ⊙11am-5pm Wed-Mon, to 9pm Thu; ⓘ; Ⓣ Museum of Fine Arts) The Gardner is filled with almost 2000 priceless objects, primarily European, including outstanding tapestries and exquisit paintings from the Italian Renaissance and the Dutch Golden Age. The four-story greenhouse courtyard is a tranquil oasis that alone is worth the price of admission.

Cambridge

On the north side of the Charles River lies politically progressive Cambridge, home to academic heavyweights Harvard University and the Massachusetts Institute of Technology (MIT). Thousands of resident students guarantee a diverse, lively atmosphere. At its hub, Harvard Square overflows with cafes, bookstores and street performers.

BOSTON FOR CHILDREN

Boston is one giant history museum, the setting for many educational and lively field trips. Cobblestone streets and costume-clad tour guides can bring to life events from American history. Hands-on experimentation and interactive exhibits fuse education and entertainment.

Changing stations are ubiquitous in public restrooms and many restaurants offer children's menus and highchairs. You'll have no trouble taking your kid's stroller on the T.

Boston's small scale makes it easy for families to explore. A good place to start is the Public Garden (p170), where Swan Boats ply the lagoon and tiny tots climb on the bronze statues (Map p174) from Robert McCloskey's classic Boston tale *Make Way for Ducklings*. Across the street on Boston Common (p170), kids can cool their toes in the Frog Pond, ride the carousel and romp in the playground. At the New England Aquarium (p172), kids of all ages will enjoy face-to-face encounters with underwater creatures.

OTHER GREAT MUSEUMS FOR KIDS:

Boston Children's Museum (Map p174; www.bostonchildrensmuseum.org; 300 Congress St; admission $14, Fri evening $1; ⊙10am-5pm Sat-Thu, 10am-9pm Fri; ⓘ; Ⓣ South Station) ✈ Oodles of fun for the youngest set.

Museum of Science (Map p174; www.mos.org; Charles River Dam; adult/child/senior $22/19/20, theater & planetarium $10/8/9; ⊙9am-5pm Sat-Thu Sep-Jun, to 7pm Jul & Aug, to 9pm Fri year-round; Ⓟ ⓘ; Ⓣ Science Park) ✈ Hours of educational entertainment for all ages.

GREAT TOURS FOR KIDS:

Boston for Little Feet (p178) The only Freedom Trail walking tour designed especially for children aged six to 12.

Urban AdvenTours (p178) Rents kids' bicycles and helmets, as well as cycle trailers for toddlers.

Boston Duck Tours (p178) Quirky, quackiness is always a hit.

★**Harvard University**   UNIVERSITY
(Map p170; www.harvard.edu; Massachusetts Ave; tours free; ⊙ tours 10am, noon & 2pm Mon-Fri, 2pm Sat; Ⓣ Harvard) Founded in 1636 to educate men for the ministry, Harvard is America's oldest college. (No other college came along until 1693.) The original Ivy League school has eight graduates who went on to be US presidents, not to mention dozens of Nobel laureates and Pulitzer Prize winners. The university's historic heart is Harvard Yard, its ancient oaks and redbrick buildings exuding an air of academia.

There are also several excellent museums on campus, including the Harvard Art Museum (Map p170; www.harvardartmuseum.org; 32 Quincy St), which is due to have completed a multiyear renovation and expansion by 2014, and the longstanding Harvard Museum of Natural History (Map p170; www.hmnh.harvard.edu; 26 Oxford St; adult/child/senior & student $12/8/10; ⊙ 9am-5pm; 🖌). Tours are more frequent in summer.

☞ Tours

Boston Duck Tours   BOAT TOUR
(Map p170; ☑ 617-267-3825; www.bostonducktours.com; adult/child/senior $34/23/28; 🖌; Ⓣ Aquarium, Science Park or Prudential) These wildly popular tours use WWII amphibious vehicles that cruise the downtown streets before splashing into the Charles River. Tours depart from the Museum of Science (Map p174; www.bostonducktours.com; Museum of Science, 1 Science Park; Ⓣ Science Park) or from behind the Prudential Center, with more

---

WORTH A TRIP

MASSACHUSETTS INSTITUTE OF TECHNOLOGY

The Massachusetts Institute of Technology (MIT; Map p170; www.mit.edu; 77 Massachusetts Ave; Ⓣ Kendall/MIT) offers a completely novel perspective on Cambridge academia: proudly nerdy, but not quite as tweedy as Harvard. The campus has an impressive collection of public art; and a recent frenzy of building has resulted in some of the most architecturally intriguing structures you'll find on either side of the river. The on-campus MIT Museum (Map p170; museum.mit.edu; 265 Massachusetts Ave; adult/child $8.50/4; ⊙ 10am-5pm; Ⓟ 🖌; Ⓣ Central) might be the city's quirkiest.

---

limited departures from the New England Aquarium. Reserve in advance.

Boston by Foot   WALKING TOUR
(www.bostonbyfoot.com; adult/child $12/8; 🖌) This fantastic nonprofit offers 90-minute walking tours, with specialty themes such as Literary Landmarks, Boston Underfoot (with highlights from the Big Dig and the T) and Boston for Little Feet – a kid-friendly version of the Freedom Trail.

★**Urban AdvenTours**   BICYCLE TOUR
(Map p174; ☑ 617-670-0637; www.urbanadventours.com; 103 Atlantic Ave; tours $50; 🖌; Ⓣ Aquarium) 🖋 Founded by avid cyclists who believe the best views of Boston are from a bicycle. The City View Ride provides a great overview of how to get around by bike, but there are other specialty tours such as Bikes at Night and Bike & Brew Tour.

NPS Freedom Trail Tour   WALKING TOUR
(Map p174; www.nps.gov/bost; Faneuil Hall; ⊙ 10am & 2pm Apr-Nov; 🖌; Ⓣ State) FREE Show up at least 30 minutes early to snag a spot on one of the free, ranger-led Freedom Trail tours provided by the National Park Service. Tours depart from the visitor center in Faneuil Hall and follow a portion of the Freedom Trail (not including Charlestown), for 90 minutes. Each tour is limited to 30 people.

⭐ Festivals & Events

★**Boston Marathon**   SPORTING EVENT
(www.baa.org; ⊙ 3rd Mon Apr) One of the country's most prestigious marathons takes runners on a 26.2-mile course ending at Copley Sq on Patriots' Day, a Massachusetts holiday.

Fourth of July   HOLIDAY
(www.july4th.org) Boston hosts one of the biggest Independence Day bashes in the USA, with a free Boston Pops concert on the Esplanade and a nationally televised fireworks display.

🛌 Sleeping

Boston has a reputation for high hotel prices, but online discounts can lessen the sting at even high-end places. You'll typically find the best deals on weekends. The majority of hotels are in the downtown area and the Back Bay, both convenient to public transportation and sightseeing.

Try also Bed & Breakfast Associates Bay Colony (☑ 781-449-5302, 888-486-6018,

City Walk
Freedom Trail

START BOSTON COMMON
FINISH BUNKER HILL MONUMENT
LENGTH 2.5 MILES; THREE HOURS

Trace America's earliest history along the Freedom Trail, which covers Boston's key revolutionary sites. The well-trodden route is marked by a double row of red bricks, starting at the 1 **Boston Common** (p170), America's oldest public park. Follow the trail north to the gold-domed 2 **State House** (p171), designed by Charles Bulfinch, America's first homegrown architect. Rounding Park St onto Tremont St takes you past the Colonial-era 3 **Park Street Church**; the 4 **Granary Burying Ground** (p171), where victims of the Boston Massacre lie buried; and 5 **King's Chapel**, topped with one of Paul Revere's bells. Continue down School St, past the site of 6 **Boston's first public school** and the 7 **Old Corner Bookstore**, a haunt of 19th-century literati.

Nearby, the 8 **Old South Meeting House** (p171) tells the back story of the Boston Tea Party. There are more Revolutionary exhibits at the 9 **Old State House** (p171). Outside, a ring of cobblestones at the intersection marks the 10 **Boston Massacre Site**, the first violent conflict of the American Revolution. Next up is 11 **Faneuil Hall** (p171), a public market since Colonial times.

Cross the Greenway to Hanover St, the main artery of Boston's Italian enclave. Treat yourself to lunch before continuing to North Sq, where you can tour the 12 **Paul Revere House** (p172), the Revolutionary hero's former home. Follow the trail to the 13 **Old North Church** (p172), where a lookout in the steeple signaled to Revere that the British were coming, setting off his famous midnight gallop.

Continue northwest on Hull St, where you'll find more Colonial graves at 14 **Copp's Hill Burying Ground**. Then cross the Charlestown Bridge to reach the 15 **USS Constitution** (p173), the world's oldest commissioned warship. To the north lies 16 **Bunker Hill Monument** (p173), the site of the first battle fought in the American Revolution.

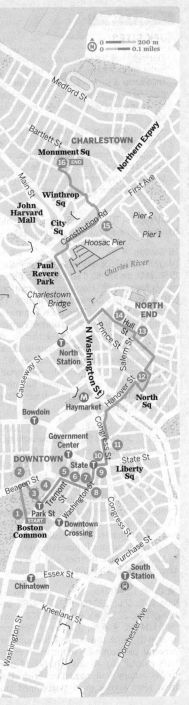

WORTH A TRIP

JFK SITES

The legacy of JFK is ubiquitous in Boston, but the official memorial to the 35th president is the John F Kennedy Library & Museum (www.jfklibrary.org; Columbia Point; adult/child/senior & student $12/9/10; ⊙9am-5pm; Ⓟ; Ⓣ JFK/UMass), a striking, modern, marble building designed by IM Pei. The museum is a fitting tribute to JFK's life and legacy. The effective use of video recreates history for visitors who may or may not remember the early 1960s.

In the streetcar suburb of Brookline, the John F Kennedy National Historic Site (www.nps.gov/jofi; 83 Beals St; ⊙9:30am-5pm Wed-Sun May-Oct; Ⓣ Coolidge Corner) FREE occupies the modest three-story house that was JFK's birthplace and boyhood home. Guided tours allow visitors to see furnishings, photographs and mementos that have been preserved from the time the family lived here. Take the Green Line (C branch) to Coolidge Corner and walk north on Harvard St.

from UK 08-234-7113; www.bnbboston.com), which handles B&Bs, rooms and apartments.

HI Boston HOSTEL $
(Map p174; ☎617-536-9455; www.bostonhostel.org; 19 Stuart St; dm $50-60, d $179; ❋@☎; Ⓣ China-town or Boylston) 🏊 Hostelling International (HI) Boston has a brand-new facility. The historic Dill Building has been completely revamped to allow for expanded capacity and community space, wheelchair access and – most impressively – state-of-the-art green amenities and energy efficiency. What stays the same? The reliably comfortable accommodations and excellent line-up of cultural activities that HI Boston has offered for the past three decades.

Friend Street Hostel HOSTEL $
(Map p174; ☎617-934-2413; www.friendstreethostel.com; 234 Friend St; dm $48-54; @☎; Ⓣ North Station) We believe them when they say it's the friendliest hostel in Boston. But there are other reasons to love this affable hostelry, such as the spic-and-span kitchen and the comfy common area with the huge flatscreen TV. Sleeping six to 10 people each, dorm rooms have painted brick walls, wide-plank wood floors and sturdy pine bunk beds.

Also: breakfast, bicycles and lots of free activities. What's not to love? Street noise.

★Oasis Guest House GUESTHOUSE $$
(Map p170; ☎617-230-0105, 617-267-2262; www.oasisgh.com; 22 Edgerly Rd; r $136-228, without bath $114-148; Ⓟ❋☎; Ⓣ Hynes or Symphony) True to its name, this homey guesthouse is a peaceful, pleasant oasis in the midst of Boston's chaotic city streets. Thirty-odd guest rooms occupy four attractive, brick, bow-front town houses on this tree-lined lane.

The modest, light-filled rooms are tastefully and traditionally decorated, most with queen beds, floral quilts and nondescript prints.

★Harborside Inn BOUTIQUE HOTEL $$
(Map p174; ☎617-723-7500; www.harborsideinnboston.com; 185 State St; r from $169; Ⓟ❋@☎; Ⓣ Aquarium) Housed in a respectfully renovated 19th-century warehouse, this waterfront hostelry strikes just the right balance between historic digs and modern conveniences. Apparently, the architects who did the renovation cared about preserving historic details, as guest rooms have original exposed brick-and-granite walls and hardwood floors. They're offset perfectly by Oriental carpets, sleigh beds and reproduction Federal-era furnishings. Add $20 for a city view.

Irving House GUESTHOUSE $$
(Map p170; ☎617-547-4600; www.irvinghouse.com; 24 Irving St; r $165-270, s without bath $135-160, d without bath $165-205; Ⓟ❋@☎; Ⓣ Harvard) 🏊 Call it a big inn or a homey hotel, this property welcomes the world-weariest travelers. The 44 rooms range in size, but every bed is covered with a quilt, and big windows let in plenty of light. Free continental breakfast.

Chandler Inn HOTEL $$
(Map p170; ☎617-482-3450, 800-842-3450; www.chandlerinn.com; 26 Chandler St; r from $170; ❋☎; Ⓣ Back Bay) The Chandler Inn is looking fine, after a complete overhaul. Small but sleek rooms have benefited from a designer's touch, giving them a sophisticated, urban glow. Modern travelers will appreciate the plasma TVs and iPod docks, all of which come at surprisingly affordable pric-

es. As a bonus, congenial staff provide super service. On site is the South End drinking institution, Fritz.

Hotel Buckminster · HOTEL $$
(Map p170; ✆617-727-2825; www.bostonhotelbuckminster.com; 645 Beacon St; r $149-209, ste from $219; P❋❀☻; T Kenmore) Designed by the architect of the Boston Public Library, the Buckminster is a convergence of Old Boston charm and affordable elegance. It offers nearly 100 rooms of varying shapes and sizes: economy rooms are small and stuffy, with slightly worn furniture (but still a great bargain); by contrast, the European-style suites are quite roomy, with all the tools and toys of comfort and convenience.

463 Beacon Street Guest House · GUESTHOUSE $$
(Map p170; ✆617-536-1302; www.463beacon.com; 463 Beacon St; d with/without bath from $149/99; P❋☻; T Hynes) What's more 'Boston' than a handsome, historic brownstone in Back Bay? This guesthouse lets you live the blue-blood fantasy – and save your cash for the boutiques and bars on Newbury St. Rooms vary in size and decor, but they all have the basics (except daily maid service, which is not offered). Bathrooms are cramped, but hopefully you won't be spending too much time in there.

40 Berkeley · HOSTEL $$
(Map p170; ✆617-375-2524; www.40berkeley.com; 40 Berkeley St; s/d/tr/q from $108/130/144/169; ☻; T Back Bay) Straddling the South End and Back Bay, this safe, friendly Y rents over 200 small rooms (some overlooking the garden) to guests on a nightly and long-term basis. Bathrooms are shared, as are other useful facilities such as the telephone, library, TV room and laundry. All rates include a generous and delicious breakfast.

★ Newbury Guest House · GUESTHOUSE $$$
(Map p170; ✆617-437-7666, 617-437-7668; www.newburyguesthouse.com; 261 Newbury St; r $219-249; P❋☻; T Hynes or Copley) Dating to 1882, these three interconnected brick and brownstone buildings offer a prime location in the heart of Newbury St. A recent renovation has preserved charming features such as ceiling medallions and in-room fireplaces, but now the rooms feature clean lines, luxurious linens and modern amenities. Each morning, a complimentary continental breakfast is laid out next to the marble fireplace in the salon.

✖ Eating

New England cuisine is known for summertime clambakes and Thanksgiving turkey. But the Boston dining scene changes it up with wide-ranging international influences and contemporary interpretations. Indulge in affordable Asian fare in Chinatown and Italian feasts in the North End; or head to the South End for the city's trendiest foodie scene.

✖ Beacon Hill & Downtown

Quincy Market · FOOD COURT $
(Map p174; Congress St; ⏰10am-9pm Mon-Sat, noon-6pm Sun; ✎♿; T Haymarket) Northeast of the intersection of Congress and State Sts, this food hall offers a variety of places under one roof: the place is packed with about 20 restaurants and 40 food stalls. Choose from chowder, bagels, Indian, Greek, baked goods and ice cream, and take a seat at one of the tables in the central rotunda.

★ Paramount · CAFETERIA $$
(Map p174; www.paramountboston.com; 44 Charles St; breakfast & lunch $8-12, dinner $15-30; ⏰7am-10pm Mon-Thu, from 8am Sat-Sun, to 11pm Fri-Sat; ✎♿; T Charles/MGH) This old-fashioned cafeteria is a neighborhood favorite. Basic diner fare includes pancakes, steak and eggs, burgers and sandwiches, and big, hearty salads. For dinner, add table service and candlelight, and the place goes upscale without losing its down-home charm. The menu is enhanced by homemade pastas, a selection of meat and fish dishes and an impressive roster of daily specials.

BOSTON BOMBING

On Patriots' Day 2013, the nation (and the world) turned their eyes to Boston when two bombs exploded near the finish line of the Boston Marathon, killing three and injuring hundreds. Several days later, an MIT police officer was shot dead and the entire city was locked down, as Boston became a battleground for the War on Terror. The tragedy was devastating, but Boston can claim countless heroes, especially the many victims that have inspired others with their courage and fortitude throughout their recoveries.

BOSTON GOES GREEN

Once there was a hulking highway that bisected the city center; now there is a ribbon of green parkland, reconnecting neighborhoods from the North End to Chinatown. Named for JFK's mother, the **Rose Kennedy Greenway** (Map p174; www.rosekennedygreenway.org; ⊞; Ⓣ Aquarium or Haymarket) reclaims the land that was once obscured by the elevated section of I-93. The interconnecting parks offer shady respite from the city bustle, replete with water fountains, blooming gardens and – new in 2013 – a custom-designed Boston-themed carousel. If you're wondering what happened to the highway, it now runs through tunnels beneath the city, thanks to the 'Big Dig,' the costliest highway project in US history.

Durgin Park   AMERICAN **$$**
(Map p174; www.durgin-park.com; North Market, Faneuil Hall; lunch mains $9-15, dinner $15-30; ⊙11:30am-9pm; ⊞; Ⓣ Haymarket) Known for no-nonsense service and sawdust on the floorboards, Durgin Park hasn't changed much since the restaurant opened in 1827. Nor has the menu, which features New England standards such as prime rib, fish chowder, chicken pot pie and Boston baked beans, with strawberry shortcake and Indian pudding for dessert. Be prepared to make friends with the other parties seated at your table.

Union Oyster House   SEAFOOD **$$**
(Map p174; www.unionoysterhouse.com; 41 Union St; mains $15-25; ⊙11am-9:30pm; Ⓣ Haymarket) The oldest restaurant in Boston, ye olde Union Oyster House has been serving seafood in this historic redbrick building since 1826. Countless history-makers have propped themselves up at this bar, including Daniel Webster and John F Kennedy. Apparently JFK used to order the lobster bisque, but the raw bar is the real draw here. Order a dozen on the half-shell and watch the shucker work his magic.

✕ North End

Volle Nolle   SANDWICHES **$**
(Map p174; 351 Hanover St; sandwiches $8-12; ⊙11am-11pm; ⊞ ⊞; Ⓣ Haymarket) Apparently,

volle nolle is Latin for 'willy-nilly,' but there is nothing haphazard about this much-beloved North End sandwich shop. Black-slate tables and pressed-tin walls adorn the simple, small space. The chalkboard menu features fresh salads, delicious flatbread sandwiches and dark rich coffee. A perfect lunchtime stop along the Freedom Trail.

★**Giacomo's Ristorante**   ITALIAN **$$**
(Map p174; www.giacomosblog-boston.blogspot. com; 355 Hanover St; mains $14-19; ⊙4:30-10pm Mon-Sat, 4-9:30pm Sun; ⊠; Ⓣ Haymarket) Customers line up before the doors open so they can guarantee themselves a spot in the first round of seating at this North End favorite. Enthusiastic and entertaining waiters, plus cramped quarters, ensure that you get to know your neighbors. The cuisine is no-frills southern Italian fare, served in unbelievable portions. Cash only.

✕ Seaport District

Barking Crab   SEAFOOD **$$**
(Map p174; www.barkingcrab.com; 88 Sleeper St; mains $12-30; ⊙11:30am-10pm Sun-Wed, to 11pm Thu-Sat; ⊠ SL1 or SL2, Ⓣ South Station) Big buckets of crabs (Jonah, blue, snow, Alaskan etc), steamers dripping in lemon and butter, paper plates piled high with all things fried... The food is plentiful and cheap, and you eat it at communal picnic tables overlooking the water. Beer flows freely. Service is slack, but the atmosphere is jovial. Be prepared to wait for a table if the weather is warm.

✕ Chinatown, Theater District & South End

★**Gourmet Dumpling House**   CHINESE, TAIWANESE **$**
(Map p174; www.gourmetdumpling.com; 52 Beach St; lunch $8, dinner mains $10-15; ⊙11am-1am; ⊠; Ⓣ Chinatown) *Xiao long bao*. That's all the Chinese you need to know to take advantage of the specialty at the Gourmet Dumpling House (or GDH, as it is fondly called). They are Shanghai soup dumplings, of course, and they are fresh, doughy and delicious. The menu offers plenty of other options, including scrumptious crispy scallion pancakes. Come early or be prepared to wait.

Myers & Chang   ASIAN **$$$**
(Map p170; ☏617-542-5200; www.myersand-chang.com; 1145 Washington St; small plates $10-18; ⊙11:30am-11pm Fri & Sat, to 10pm Sun-Thu;

; SL4 or SL5, T Tufts Medical Center) This super-hip Asian spot blends Thai, Chinese and Vietnamese cuisines, which means delicious dumplings, spicy stir-fries and oodles of noodles. The kitchen staff does amazing things with a wok and the menu of small plates allows you to sample a wide selection of dishes. The vibe is casual but cool, international and independent.

Back Bay & Fenway

Tasty Burger   BURGERS $
(Map p170; www.tastyburger.com; 1301 Boylston St; burgers $4-6; ⊙11am-2am; ; T Fenway) Once a Mobile station, it's now a retro burger joint, with picnic tables outside and a pool table inside. The name of the place is a nod to *Pulp Fiction*, as is the poster of Samuel L Jackson on the wall. You won't find a half-pound of Kobe beef on your bun, but you will have to agree 'That's a tasty burger.'

Aside from the burgers, this is a fun place to drink cheap beer and watch sports on TV.

Parish Café   SANDWICHES $$
(Map p174; www.parishcafe.com; 361 Boylston St; sandwiches $12-15; ⊙noon-2am; ; T Arlington) Sample the creations of Boston's most famous chefs without exhausting your expense account. The menu at Parish features a rotating roster of salads and sandwiches, each designed by a local celebrity chef, including Lydia Shire, Ken Oringer and Barbara Lynch.

Cambridge

★ Clover Food Lab   VEGETARIAN $
(Map p170; www.cloverfoodlab.com; 7 Holyoke St; mains $6-7; ⊙7am-midnight; ; T Harvard) Clover is on the cutting edge. It's all high-tech with its 'live' menu updates and electronic ordering system. But it's really about the food – local, seasonal, vegetarian food – which is cheap, delicious and fast. How fast? Check the menu. Interesting tidbit: Clover started as a food truck (and still has a few trucks making the rounds).

Cambridge, 1   PIZZERIA $$
(Map p170; www.cambridge1.us; 27 Church St; pizzas $17-22; ⊙11:30am-midnight; ; T Harvard) Set in the old fire station, this pizzeria's name comes from the sign chiseled into the stonework out front. The interior is sleek, sparse and industrial, with big windows overlooking the Old Burying Ground in the back. The menu is equally simple: pizza, soup, salad, dessert. These oddly-shaped pizzas are delectable, with crispy crusts and creative topping combos.

Drinking & Nightlife

★ Bleacher Bar   SPORTS BAR
(Map p170; www.bleacherbarboston.com; 82a Lansdowne St; T Kenmore) Tucked under the bleachers at Fenway Park, this classy bar offers a view onto center field (go Jacoby baby!). It's not the best place to watch the game, as the place gets packed, but it's an

GAY & LESBIAN BOSTON

Out and active gay communities are visible all around Boston and Cambridge, especially in the South End. **Calamus Bookstore** (Map p174; www.calamusbooks.com; 92 South St; ⊙9am-7pm Mon-Sat, noon-6pm Sun; T South Station) is an excellent source of information about community events and organizations. Pick up a copy of the free weekly *Bay Windows* (www.baywindows.com).

There is no shortage of entertainment options catering to GLBT travelers. From drag shows to dyke nights, this sexually diverse community has something for everybody.

Club Cafe (Map p174; www.clubcafe.com; 209 Columbus Ave; ⊙11am-2am; T Back Bay) Always hopping, it's a cool cafe by day and a crazy club by night. Aimed at men, open to all.

Diesel Cafe (www.diesel-cafe.com; 257 Elm St; ⊙6am-11pm Mon-Sat, 7am-11am Sun; T Davis Sq) Shoot stick, drink coffee and swill beer in this industrial cafe popular with students and queers.

Fritz (Map p174; www.fritzboston.com; 26 Chandler St; ⊙noon-2am; T Back Bay) Watch the boys playing sports on TV or watch the boys watching the boys playing sports on TV.

awesome way to experience America's oldest ballpark, even when the Sox are not playing.

If you want a seat in front of the window, get your name on the waiting list an hour or two before game time; once seated, diners have 45 minutes in the hot seat.

★ **Drink** COCKTAIL BAR
(Map p174; www.drinkfortpoint.com; 348 Congress St S; ⊙4pm-1am; ☐SL1 or SL2, T South Station) There is no cocktail menu at Drink. Instead you have a little chat with the bartender, and he or she will whip something up according to your specifications. The bar takes seriously the art of drink mixology – and you will too, after you sample one of its concoctions. The subterranean space creates a dark, sexy atmosphere, which makes for a great date destination.

Warren Tavern HISTORIC PUB
(Map p170; www.warrentavern.com; 2 Pleasant St; ⊙11am-1am; T Community College) One of the oldest pubs in Boston, the Warren Tavern has been pouring pints for its customers since George Washington and Paul Revere drank here. It is named for General Joseph Warren, a fallen hero of the Battle of Bunker Hill (shortly after which – in 1780 – this pub was opened).

☆ Entertainment

Boston's entertainment scene offers something for everyone.

Live Music

★ **Club Passim** FOLK MUSIC
(Map p170; ☑617-492-7679; www.clubpassim.org; 47 Palmer St; tickets $15-30; T Harvard) Folk music in Boston seems to be endangered outside of Irish bars, but the legendary Club Passim does such a great job booking top-notch acts that it practically fills in the vacuum by itself. The colorful, intimate room is hidden off a side street in Harvard Sq, and those attending shows are welcome to order filling dinners from Veggie

---

> **ⓘ CHEAP SEATS**
>
> Half-price tickets to same-day theater and concerts in Boston are sold at by BosTix (www.bostix.org; ⊙10am-6pm Tue-Sat, 11am-4pm Sun) at Faneuil Hall and Copley Sq. No plastic – these deals are cash only.

Planet, an incredibly good restaurant that shares the space.

★ **Red Room @ Café 939** LIVE MUSIC
(Map p170; www.cafe939.com; 939 Boylston St; T Hynes) Run by Berklee students, the Red Room @ 939 is emerging as one of Boston's best music venues. The place has an excellent sound system and a baby grand piano; most importantly, it books interesting, eclectic up-and-coming musicians. This is where you'll see that band that's about to make it big. Buy tickets in advance at the Berklee Performance Center (Map p170; www.berklee-bpc.com; 136 Massachusetts Ave; T Hynes).

Sinclair LIVE MUSIC
(Map p170; www.sinclaircambridge.com; 52 Church St; tickets $15-18; ⊙11am-1am Tue-Sun, 5pm-1am Mon; T Harvard) Great new small venue to see and hear live music. The acoustics are excellent and the mezzanine level allows you to escape the crowds on the floor. The club attracts a good range of local and regional bands and DJs. Bonus: under the direction of Michael Schlow, the attached kitchen puts out some delicious and downright classy food (though service seems to be a little spotty).

Classical Music & Theater

The big venues in the Theater District are lavish affairs, all restored to their early-20th-century glory.

★ **Boston Symphony Orchestra** CLASSICAL MUSIC
(BSO; Map p170; ☑617-266-1200; www.bso.org; Symphony Hall, 301 Massachusetts Ave; tickets $30-115; T Symphony) Near-perfect acoustics match the ambitious programs of the world-renowned Boston Symphony Orchestra. From September to April, the BSO performs in the beauteous Symphony Hall, featuring an ornamental high-relief ceiling and attracting a fancy-dress crowd. The building was designed in 1861 with the help of a Harvard physicist who pledged to make the building acoustically perfect (he succeeded).

Boston Ballet DANCE
(☑617-695-6950; www.bostonballet.org; tickets $15-100) Boston's skillful ballet troupe performs both modern and classic works at the Opera House (Map p174; www.bostonoperahouse.com; 539 Washington St; T Downtown Crossing). During the Christmas season, it puts on a wildly popular performance of the *Nutcracker*. Student and child 'rush'

tickets are available for $20 two hours before the performance.

Sports

Boston loves its sports teams. And why not, with its professional teams bringing home the 'Grand Slam of American Sports' by winning the four major championships in recent years.

★ **Fenway Park**   SPORT

(Map p170; www.redsox.com; 4 Yawkey Way; tickets $25-125; ⊤ Kenmore) From April to September you can watch the Red Sox play at Fenway Park, the nation's oldest and most storied ballpark. Unfortunately, it is also the most expensive – not that this stops the Fenway faithful from scooping up the tickets. There are sometimes game-day tickets on sale starting two hours before the opening pitch.

TD Garden   BASKETBALL, HOCKEY

(Map p174; ☑ information 617-523-3030, tickets 617-931-2000; www.tdgarden.com; 150 Causeway St; ⊤ North Station) This reincarnation of the Boston Garden is still home to the Bruins, who play hockey here from September to June, and the Celtics, who play basketball from October to April.

🔒 Shopping

Newbury St in the Back Bay and Charles St on Beacon Hill are Boston's best shopping destinations for the biggest selection of shops, both traditional and trendy. Harvard Sq is famous for bookstores and the South End is the city's up-and-coming art district. **Copley Place** (Map p170; www.simon.com; 100 Huntington Ave; ⊘ 10am-8pm Mon-Sat, noon-6pm Sun; ⊤ Back Bay) and the **Prudential Center** (Map p170; www.prudentialcenter.com; 800 Boylston St; ⊘ 10am-9pm; 🛜; ⊤ Prudential), both in Back Bay, are big indoor malls.

Lucy's League   CLOTHING

(Map p174; www.thecolorstores.com; North Bldg, Faneuil Hall; ⊤ Government Center) We're not advocating those pink Red Sox caps. But sometimes a girl wants to look good while she's supporting the team. At Lucy's League, fashionable sports fans will find shirts, jackets and other gear sporting the local teams' logos – but in super-cute styles designed to flatter the female figure.

Life is Good   CLOTHING, GIFTS

(Map p170; www.lifeisgood.com; 285 Newbury St; ⊤ Hynes) Life *is* good for this locally designed brand of T-shirts, backpacks and other gear.

Styles depict the fun-loving stick figure Jake engaged in guitar playing, dog walking, coffee drinking, mountain climbing and just about every other good-vibe diversion you might enjoy. Jake's activity may vary, but his 'life is good' theme is constant.

Converse   SHOES, CLOTHING

(Map p170; www.converse.com; 348 Newbury St; ⊤ Hynes) Converse started making shoes right up the road in Malden, MA, way back in 1908. Chuck Taylor joined the 'team' in the 1920s and the rest is history. This retail store (one of three in the country) has an incredible selection of sneakers, denim and other gear.

The iconic shoes come in all colors and patterns; you can make them uniquely your own in the in-store customization area.

ℹ️ Information

INTERNET ACCESS

Aside from hotels, wireless access is common at cafes, on buses and even in public spaces such as Faneuil Hall and the Greenway. Many cafes charge a fee, though they may offer the first hour free.

Boston Public Library (www.bpl.org; 700 Boylston St; ⏰9am-9pm Mon-Thu, to 5pm Fri & Sat year-round, 1-5pm Sun Oct-May; 🖥; Ⓣ Copley) Internet access free for 15-minute intervals. Or get a visitor courtesy card at the circulation desk and sign up for one hour of free terminal time. Arrive first thing in the morning to avoid long waits.

Wired Puppy (www.wiredpuppy.com; 250 Newbury St; ⏰6:30am-7:30pm; 🖥; Ⓣ Hynes) Free wireless access and free computer use in case you don't have your own. This is also a comfortable, cozy place to just come and drink coffee.

MEDIA

Boston Globe (www.boston.com) One of two major daily newspapers, the *Globe* publishes an extensive Calendar section every Thursday and the daily Sidekick, both of which include entertainment options.

Improper Bostonian (www.improper.com) A sassy biweekly distributed free from sidewalk dispenser boxes.

MEDICAL SERVICES

CVS Pharmacy (www.cvs.com) Cambridge (www.cvs.com; 1426 Massachusetts Ave, Cambridge; ⏰24hr; Ⓣ Harvard); Back Bay (📞617-437-8414; 587 Boylston St; ⏰24hr; Ⓣ Copley)

Massachusetts General Hospital (📞617-726-2000; www.massgeneral.org; 55 Fruit St; ⏰24hr; Ⓣ Charles/MGH) Arguably the city's biggest and best. It can often refer you to smaller clinics and crisis hotlines.

POST

Main post office (www.usps.com; 25 Dorchester Ave; ⏰6am-midnight; Ⓣ South Station) One block southeast of South Station.

TOURIST INFORMATION

Cambridge Visitor Information Kiosk (Map p170; www.cambridge-usa.org; Harvard Sq; ⏰9am-5pm Mon-Fri, 1-5pm Sat & Sun; Ⓣ Harvard) Detailed information on current Cambridge happenings and self-guided walking tours.

Greater Boston Convention & Visitors Bureau (GBCVB; www.bostonusa.com) Boston

Common (Map p174; 📞617-426-3115; 148 Tremont St, Boston Common; ⏰8:30am-5pm Mon-Fri, 9am-5pm Sat & Sun; Ⓣ Park St); Prudential Center (Map p170; www.bostonusa.com; 800 Boylston St, Prudential Center; ⏰9am-6pm; Ⓣ Prudential)

WEBSITES

Boston Central (www.bostoncentral.com) A solid resource for families, with listings for activities good for kids.

City of Boston (www.cityofboston.gov) Official website of Boston city government with links to visitor services.

ⓘ Getting There & Away

Getting in and out of Boston is easy. The train and bus stations are conveniently side by side, and the airport is a short subway ride away.

AIR

Logan International Airport (📞800-235-6426; www.massport.com/logan), just across Boston Harbor from the city center, is served by major US and foreign airlines and has full services.

BUS

South Station (Map p174; 700 Atlantic Ave) is the terminal for an extensive network of long-distance buses operated by Greyhound and regional bus companies.

TRAIN

MBTA Commuter Rail (📞800-392-6100, 617-222-3200; www.mbta.com) trains connect Boston's North Station with Concord and Salem and Boston's South Station with Plymouth and Providence.

The **Amtrak** (📞800-872-7245; www.amtrak.com; South Station) terminal is at South Station; trains to New York cost $73 to $126 (4¼ hours) or $147 on the speedier *Acela Express* (3½ hours).

ⓘ Getting Around

TO/FROM THE AIRPORT

Logan International Airport is just a few miles from downtown Boston: take the blue-line subway or the silver-line bus.

CAR

Driving in Boston is not for the faint of heart. It's best to stick to public transportation within the city. If you're traveling onward by rental car, pick up your car at the end of your Boston visit.

SUBWAY

The **MBTA** (📞800-392-6100, 617-222-3200; www.mbta.com; per ride $2-2.50; ⏰5:30am-

---

ⓘ GETTING TO NYC

The cheapest travel between Boston and NYC is by bus. **Yo! Bus** (www.yobus.com; one-way $12-28; 🖥; Ⓣ South Station) runs six buses a day from South Station, while **Go Buses** (www.gobuses.com; one-way from $15; 🖥; Ⓣ Alewife) depart from Cambridge.

12:30am) operates the USA's oldest subway (known as the 'T'), built in 1897. Five color-coded lines – red, blue, green, orange and silver – radiate from the downtown stations of Park St, Downtown Crossing and Government Center. 'Inbound' trains are headed for one of these stations, 'outbound' trains away from them. Note that the silver line is actually a 'bus rapid transit service' that is useful for Logan airport and some other destinations.

TAXI

Taxis are plentiful; expect to pay between $15 and $25 between two points within the city limits. Flag taxis on the street, find them at major hotels or call **Metro Cab** (☑617-242-8000) or **Independent** (Map p170; ☑617-426-8700).

Around Boston

Up and down the coast, destinations with rich histories, vibrant cultural scenes and unique events merit a venture outside the city. Easily accessible from Boston by car or train, most of these are excellent day-trip destinations.

Lexington & Concord

In Lexington, 15 miles northwest of Boston, the historic Battle Green (Massachusetts Ave) is where a skirmish between patriots and British troops jump-started the War of Independence in 1775. Following the battle, the British Redcoats marched west to Concord, following a route now known as Battle Road. The Minutemen and the Redcoats faced off again at the Old North Bridge – the first American victory. This whole area is preserved as Minute Man National Historic Park (www.nps.gov/mima; 250 North Great Rd, Lincoln; ☉9am-5pm Apr-Oct, 9am-4pm Nov; ☑) FREE, with visitor centers at the east end of Battle Rd and near the bridge.

Aside from its revolutionary history, Concord also harbored a vibrant literary community in the 19th century. Next to the Old North Bridge is the Old Manse (www.thetrustees.org; 269 Monument St; adult/child/senior & student $8/5/7; ☉noon-5pm Tue-Sun May-Oct, Sat & Sun only Mar-Apr & Nov-Dec), former home of author Nathaniel Hawthorne. Within a mile of the town center are the Ralph Waldo Emerson house (www.rwe.org; 28 Cambridge Turnpike; adult/child/senior & student $7/free/5; ☉10am-4:30pm Thu-Sat, 1-4:30pm Sun mid-Apr–Oct) and Louisa May Alcott's Orchard House (www.louisamayalcott.org; 399 Lexington Rd; adult/child/senior & student

GRAB A BICYCLE

Boston's brand new cycle-share program (sponsored by New Balance, as you will be repeatedly reminded) is the Hubway (www.thehubway.com; 30min free, 60/90/120min $2/6/14; ☉24hr). There are now 60 Hubway stations around town, stocked with 600 bikes that are available for short-term loan. Purchase a temporary membership at any bicycle kiosk, then pay by the half-hour for the use of the bikes (free under 30 minutes). Return the bike to any station in the vicinity of your destination.

The Hubway pricing is designed so that cycling can substitute a cab ride (eg to make a one-way trip or run an errand). For leisurely riding or long trips, rent a bike from Urban Adventours (p178).

$10/5/8; ☉10am-4:30pm Mon-Sat, 1-4:30pm Sun Apr-Oct, 11am-3pm Mon-Fri, 10am-4:30pm Sat, 1-4:30pm Sun Nov-Mar).

Henry David Thoreau lived and wrote his most famous treatise at Walden Pond (www.mass.gov/dcr/parks/walden; 915 Walden St; ☉dawn-dusk) FREE, 3 miles south of the town center. Visit his cabin site and take an inspiring hike around the pond. All these authors are laid to rest in Sleepy Hollow Cemetery (www.friendsofsleepyhollow.org; Bedford St; ☉dawn-dusk) in the town center. The Concord Chamber of Commerce (www.concordchamberofcommerce.org; 58 Main St; ☉9:30am-4:30pm Apr-Oct) has full details on sites, including opening hours for the homes, which vary with the season.

Salem

Salem is renowned for the witch hysteria in 1692, when innocent folks were put to death for practicing witchcraft. Nowadays, the town embraces its role as 'Witch City' with witchy museums, spooky tours and Halloween madness.

These incidents obscure the city's true claim to fame: its glory days as a center for clipper-ship trade with the Far East. The Salem Maritime National Historic Site (www.nps.gov/sama; 193 Derby St; ☉9am-5pm) FREE comprises the custom house, the wharves and the other buildings along Derby St that are remnants of the shipping industry that

WITCH CITY

The city of Salem embraces its witchy past with a healthy dose of whimsy. But the history offers a valuable lesson about what can happen when fear and frenzy are allowed to trump common sense and compassion.

By the time the witch hysteria of 1692 had finally died down, a total of 156 people had been accused, 55 people had pleaded guilty and implicated others to save their own lives, and 14 women and five men had been hanged. Stop by at the Witch Trials Memorial (Charter St), a simple but dramatic monument that honors the innocent victims.

The most authentic of more than a score of witchy museums, the Witch House (Jonathan Corwin House; www.salemweb.com/witchhouse; 310 Essex St; adult/child/senior $8.25/4.25/6.25, tour add $2; ⊘10am-5pm May-Nov) was once the home of Jonathan Corwin, a local magistrate who investigated witchcraft claims.

For an informative, accurate overview of Salem's sordid past, sign up with Hocus Pocus Tours (www.hocuspocustours.com; adult/child $16/8), which is neither hokey nor pokey.

once thrived in Salem. Stroll out to the end of Derby Wharf and peek inside the 1871 lighthouse or climb aboard the tall ship Friendship. Get complete information from the NPS Regional Visitor Center (www.nps.gov/sama; 2 New Liberty St; ⊘9am-5pm).

This overview of Salem's maritime exploits is the perfect introduction to the exceptional Peabody Essex Museum (www.pem.org; 161 Essex St; adult/child $15/free; ⊘10am-5pm Tue-Sun; ⊞). The museum was founded upon the art, artifacts and curios collected by Salem traders during their early expeditions to the Far East. As the exhibits attest, they had deep pockets and refined taste. In addition to world-class Chinese and Pacific Island displays, the museum boasts an excellent Native American collection.

Plymouth

Plymouth calls itself 'America's Home Town.' It was here that the Pilgrims first settled in the winter of 1620, seeking a place where they could practice their religion without interference from government. An innocuous, weathered ball of granite – the famous Plymouth Rock – marks the spot where where they supposedly first stepped ashore in this foreign land. Nearby, Mayflower II (www.plimoth.org; State Pier, Water St; adult/child $10/7; ⊘9am-5pm Apr-Nov; ⊞) is a replica of the small ship in which they made the fateful voyage across the ocean.

Three miles south of Plymouth center, Plimoth Plantation (www.plimoth.org; MA 3A; adult/child $26/15; ⊘9am-5pm Apr-Nov; ⊞) authentically recreates the Pilgrims' settlement, in its primary exhibit entitled '1627

English Village.' Everything in the village – costumes, implements, vocabulary, artistry, recipes and crops – has been painstakingly researched and remade. The Wampanoag Homesite replicates the life of a Native American community in the same area during that time.

Cape Cod

Clambering across the National Seashore dunes, cycling the Cape Cod Rail Trail, eating oysters at Wellfleet Harbor – this sandy peninsula serves up a bounty of local flavor. Fringed with 400 miles of sparkling shoreline, 'the Cape,' as it's called by Cape Codders, rates as New England's top beach destination. But there's a lot more than just beaches here. When you've had your fill of sun and sand, get out and explore artist enclaves, take a cruise, or join the free-spirited street scene in Provincetown.

Cape Cod Chamber of Commerce (☑508-362-3225; www.capecodchamber.org; MA 132 at US 6, Hyannis; ⊘9am-5pm Mon-Sat, 10am-2pm Sun) has info.

Sandwich

The Cape's oldest village wraps its historic center around a picturesque swan pond with a gristmill (c 1654) and several small museums.

◉ Sights

If you're ready for salt spray, head to Sandy Neck Beach (Sandy Neck Rd, West Barnstable), off MA 6A, a 6-mile dune-backed strand (parking $15–20) ideal for beachcombing and a bracing swim.

Sandwich Glass Museum · MUSEUM
(📞508-888-0251; www.sandwichglassmuseum. org; 129 Main St; adult/child $6/1.25; ⏱9:30am-5pm) Artfully displayed here is the town's 19th-century glass-making heritage. Glass-blowing demonstrations are given hourly throughout the day.

Heritage Museums & Gardens · MUSEUM
(📞508-888-3300; www.heritagemuseumsandgardens.org; 67 Grove St; adult/child $15/7; ⏱10am-5pm; 🚗) Fun for kids and adults alike, this 76-acre site sports a superb vintage automobile collection in a Shaker-style round barn, a working 1912 carousel, folk-art collections and one of the finest rhododendron gardens in America.

Cape Cod Canal · CANAL
(www.capecodcanal.us; 🚗🚲) FREE Cape Cod isn't connected by land to the mainland, but it's not exactly an island, or at least wasn't until the Cape Cod Canal was dug in 1914 to save ships from having to sail an extra 135 miles around the treacherous tip of the Cape. A 6-mile path ideal for walking, cycling and in-line skating runs along the south side of the canal from Sandwich Harbor.

🛏 Sleeping & Eating

Shawme-Crowell
State Forest · CAMPGROUND $
(📞508-888-0351; www.reserveamerica.com; MA 130; tent sites $14) You'll find 285 shady campsites in this 760-acre woodland near MA 6A.

Belfry Inne & Bistro · B&B $$$
(📞508-888-8550; www.belfryinn.com; 8 Jarves St; r incl breakfast $149-299; 🚗🛜) Ever fall asleep in church? Then you'll love the rooms, some with stained-glass windows, in this creatively restored former church, now an upmarket B&B. If, however, you're uneasy about the angel Gabriel watching over you in bed, Belfry has two other nearby inns with conventional rooms.

Seafood Sam's · SEAFOOD $$
(www.seafoodsams.com; 6 Coast Guard Rd; mains $8-20; ⏱11am-9pm; 🚗) Sam's is a good family choice for fish and chips, fried clams and lobster rolls. Dine at outdoor picnic tables overlooking Cape Cod Canal and watch the fishing boats sail by.

Falmouth

Fantastic beaches and a scenic seaside bike trail highlight the Cape's second-largest town.

⊙ Sights & Activities

Old Silver Beach · BEACH
(off MA 28A; 🚗) Deeply indented Falmouth has 70 miles of coastline, but none of it is finer than this long, sandy stretch of beach. A rock jetty, sandbars and tidal pools provide fun diversions for kids. Parking costs $20.

★Shining Sea Bikeway · CYCLING
(🚲) A bright star among the Cape's stellar bike trails, this 10.7-mile beaut runs along the entire west coast of Falmouth, offering unspoiled views of salt ponds, marsh and seascapes. Bike rentals are available at the north end of the trail.

🛏 Sleeping & Eating

Falmouth Heights Motor Lodge · MOTEL $$
(📞508-548-3623; www.falmouthheightsresort. com; 146 Falmouth Heights Rd; r incl breakfast $129-259; ❄🛜🚗) Don't be fooled by the name. This tidy operation is no drive-up motor lodge – it's not even on the highway. All 28 rooms are a cut above the competition. The beach and Vineyard ferry are minutes away.

Clam Shack · SEAFOOD $
(📞508-540-7758; 227 Clinton Ave; light meals $6-15; ⏱11:30am-7:30pm) A classic of the genre, right on Falmouth Harbor. It's tiny, with picnic tables on the back deck and lots of fried seafood. The clams, huge juicy bellies cooked to a perfect crisp, are the place to start.

DON'T MISS

LOBSTER ICE CREAM, ANYONE?

Lobster mania takes a new twist at Ben & Bill's Chocolate Emporium (209 Main St, Falmouth; cones $5; ⏱9am-11pm) where the crustacean has crawled onto the ice-cream menu. Forget plain vanilla. Step up to the counter and order a scoop of lobster ice cream. Now there's one you won't find with the old 31-flavors folks.

Maison Villatte CAFE $

(☏ 774-255-1855; 267 Main St; snacks $3-10; ☼ 7am-7pm Wed-Sat, to 5pm Sun) A pair of French bakers work the ovens, creating crusty artisan breads, flaky croissants and sinful pastries at this bakery-cafe. Hearty sandwiches and robust coffee make it an ideal lunch spot.

Hyannis

Cape Cod's commercial hub, Hyannis is best known to visitors as the summer home of the Kennedy clan and a jumping-off point for ferries to Nantucket and Martha's Vineyard.

Cape Cod, Martha's Vineyard & Nantucket

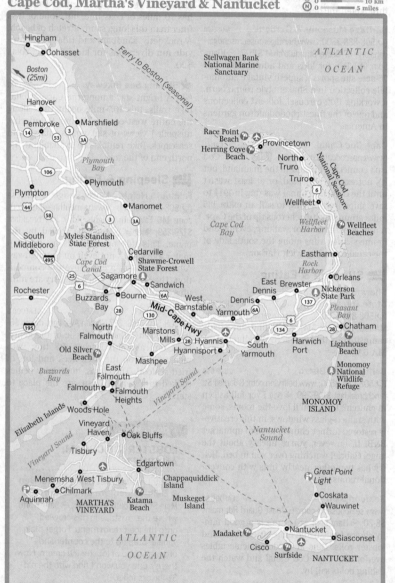

WORTH A TRIP

WOODS HOLE

The tiny village of Woods Hole is home to the largest oceanographic institution in the US. Research at the Woods Hole Oceanographic Institution (WHOI, pronounced 'hooey') has covered the gamut from exploring the sunken *Titanic* to global warming studies.

You can join one of the free tours departing from the WHOI information office (93 Water St). You'll also gain insights into scientists' work at the WHOI Ocean Science Exhibit Center (15 School St; ⊗10am-4:30pm Mon-Sat) FREE.

Woods Hole Science Aquarium (http://aquarium.nefsc.noaa.gov; 166 Water St; ⊗11am-4pm Tue-Sat; ⊕) FREE has little flash and dazzle, but you'll find unusual sea-life specimens, local fish and the *Homarus americanus* (aka lobster). Kids will enjoy the touch-tank creatures. Coolest time to come is at 11am or 4pm when the seals are fed.

Keeping with the nautical theme, head over to the drawbridge where you'll find Fishmonger Café (www.fishmongercafe.com; 56 Water St; mains $10-25; ⊗7am-9:30pm), with water views in every direction and an eclectic menu emphasizing fresh seafood.

To get to Woods Hole from Falmouth center take Woods Hole Rd south from MA28.

⊙ Sights

The town's mile-long Main St is fun to stroll and the place for dining, drinking and shopping. Kalmus Beach (Ocean St, Hyannis) is popular for windsurfing, while Craigville Beach (Craigville Beach Rd, Centerville) is where the college set goes; parking at either costs $15 to $20.

John F Kennedy Hyannis Museum   MUSEUM
(☑508-790-3077; http://jfkhyannismuseum.org; 397 Main St, Hyannis; adult/child $8/3; ⊗9am-5pm Mon-Sat, noon-5pm Sun) This museum celebrates America's 35th president with photographs, videos and mementos. It also houses the Cape Cod Baseball League Hall of Fame.

🛏 Sleeping

HI-Hyannis   HOSTEL $
(☑508-775-7990; http://capecod.hiusa.org; 111 Ocean St, Hyannis; dm incl breakfast $32; @🛜) 🚲 For a million-dollar view on a backpacker's budget, book yourself a bed at this hostel overlooking the harbor and within walking distance of Main St, beaches and ferries. Just 37 beds, so book early.

SeaCoast Inn   MOTEL $$
(☑508-775-3828; www.seacoastcapecod.com; 33 Ocean St, Hyannis; r incl breakfast $128-168; ❄@🛜) This family-run motel is just a two-minute walk from the harbor in one direction and Main St restaurants in the other. There's no view or pool, but the rooms are thoroughly comfy, most have kitchenettes and the price is a deal for Hyannis.

🍴 Eating

★Bistrot de Soleil   MEDITERRANEAN $$
(www.bistrotdesoleil.com; 350 Stevens St, at Main St, Hyannis; mains $10-25; ⊗11:30am-9pm) Mediterranean influences meet fresh local ingredients in a menu that ranges from gourmet wood-fired pizzas to filet mignon. A smart setting, organic wine list and $20 prix fixe dinner specials round out the appeal.

Raw Bar   SEAFOOD $$
(www.therawbar.com; 230 Ocean St, Hyannis; lobster rolls $26; ⊗11am-7pm) Come here for the mother of all lobster rolls – it's like eating an entire lobster in a bun. The view overlooking Hyannis Harbor isn't hard to swallow either.

Brewster

Woodsy Brewster, on the Cape's bay side, makes a good base for outdoorsy types. The Cape Cod Rail Trail cuts clear across town and there are excellent options for camping, hiking and water activities.

⊙ Sights & Activities

Nickerson State Park   PARK
(☑508-896-3491; 3488 MA 6A; per car $5; ⊗dawn-dusk; ⊕) Miles of cycling and walking trails and eight ponds with sandy beaches highlight this 2000-acre oasis.

Jack's Boat Rental   BOATING
(☑508-349-9808; www.jacksboatrental.com; rentals per hr $25-45; ⊗10am-6pm) This operation, within Nickerson State Park, rents canoes, kayaks and sailboats.

DON'T MISS

CYCLING THE RAIL TRAIL

A poster child for the rails-to-trail movement, the **Cape Cod Rail Trail** follows a former railroad track for 22 glorious miles past cranberry bogs and along sandy ponds ideal for a dip. It's one of the finest cycling trails in all New England. There's a hefty dose of Olde Cape Cod scenery en route and you can detour into quiet villages for lunch or sightseeing. The path begins in Dennis on MA 134 and continues all the way to Wellfleet. If you have time to do only part of the trail, begin at Nickerson State Park in Brewster and head for the Cape Cod National Seashore in Eastham. Bicycle rentals are available at the trailhead in Dennis, at Nickerson State Park and opposite the National Seashore's Salt Pond Visitor Center (p193).

Barb's Bike Rental　　　　CYCLING
(☑508-896-7231; www.barbsbikeshop.com; bicycles per half/full day $18/24; ☺9am-6pm) Rents bicycles by the park entrance.

🛏 Sleeping

★**Nickerson State Park**　　CAMPGROUND $
(☑877-422-6762; www.reserveamerica.com; campsites $17; yurts $30-40) Head here for Cape Cod's best camping with 418 wooded campsites. It often fills, so reserve early.

★**Old Sea Pines Inn**　　　　B&B $$
(☑508-896-6114; www.oldseapinesinn.com; 2553 MA 6A; r incl breakfast $85-195; @🛜) A former girls' boarding school dating to 1840, this inn retains an engaging yesteryear look. It's a bit like staying at grandma's house: antique fittings, sepia photographs, claw-foot bathtubs. No TV to spoil the mood, but rocking chairs await on the porch.

🍴 Eating

★**Brewster Fish House**　　SEAFOOD $$
(www.brewsterfish.com; 2208 MA 6A; mains $14-32; ☺11:30am-3pm & 5-9:30pm) A favorite of seafood lovers. Start with the lobster bisque, naturally sweet with chunks of fresh lobster. From there it's safe to cast your net in any direction. Just 11 tables, and no reservations, so think lunch or early dinner to avoid long waits.

Cobie's　　　　　　　　SEAFOOD $$
(www.cobies.com; 3256 MA 6A; mains $9-23; ☺11am-9pm) Conveniently located near Nickerson State Park, this roadside clam shack dishes out fried seafood that you can crunch and munch at outdoor picnic tables.

Chatham

Upscale inns and tony shops are a hallmark of the Cape's most genteel town, but some of Chatham's finest pleasures come free for the taking. Start your exploring on Main St, with its old sea captains' houses and cool art galleries.

At **Chatham Fish Pier** (Shore Rd) watch fishermen unload their catch and spot seals basking on nearby shoals. A mile south on Shore Rd is **Lighthouse Beach**, an endless expanse of sea and sandbars that offers some of the finest beach strolling on Cape Cod. The 7600-acre **Monomoy National Wildlife Refuge** (www.fws.gov/northeast/monomoy) 🦅 covers two uninhabited islands thick with shorebirds; to see it up close take the 1½-hour boat tour with **Monomoy Island Excursions** (☑508-430-7772; www.monomoysealcruise.com; 702 MA 28, Harwich Port; 1½hr tours adult/child $35/30).

🛏 Sleeping & Eating

Bow Roof House　　　　　B&B $$
(☑508-945-1346; 59 Queen Anne Rd; r incl breakfast $115) This homey, six-room, c 1780 house is delightfully old-fashioned in price and offerings, and within easy walking distance of the town center and beach.

Chatham Cookware Café　　　CAFE $
(☑508-945-1250; 524 Main St; sandwiches $8; ☺6:30am-4pm) No, it's not a place to buy pots and pans, but rather *the* downtown spot for a coffee fix, homemade muffins and sandwiches.

★**Chatham Fish Pier Market**　SEAFOOD $$
(www.chathamfishpiermarket.com; 45 Barcliff Ave; mains $12-25; ☺10am-7pm Mon-Thu, to 8pm Fri-Sun) If you like it fresh and local to the core, this salt-sprayed fish shack, with its own sushi chef and day boats, is for you. The chowder's incredible and the fish so fresh it was swimming earlier in the day. It's all takeout, but there are shady picnic tables nearby as well as a harbor full of sights.

Cape Cod National Seashore

Extending some 40 miles around the curve of the Outer Cape, Cape Cod National Seashore (www.nps.gov/caco) encompasses most of the shoreline from Eastham to Provincetown. It's a treasure-trove of unspoiled beaches, dunes, salt marshes and forests. Thanks to President John F Kennedy, this vast area was set aside for preservation in the 1960s, just before a building boom hit the rest of his native Cape Cod. The Salt Pond Visitor Center (☎508-255-3421; 50 Doane Rd, cnr US 6 & Nauset Rd, Eastham; ⏰9am-5pm) FREE is the place to start and has a great view to boot. Here you will find exhibits and films about the area's ecology and the scoop on the park's numerous cycling and hiking trails, some of which begin right at the center.

You brought your board, didn't you? Coast Guard Beach, just down the road from the visitor center, is a stunner that attracts everyone from surfers to beachcombers. And the view of untouched Nauset Marsh from the dunes above the beach is nothing short of spectacular. Nauset Light Beach, running north from Coast Guard Beach, takes its name from the lighthouse perched above it; three other classic lighthouses are nearby. Summertime beach parking passes cost $15/45 per day/season and are valid at all Cape Cod National Seashore beaches including Provincetown.

Wellfleet

Art galleries, primo beaches and those famous Wellfleet oysters lure visitors to this little seaside town.

◉ Sights

Wellfleet Beaches BEACHES
backed by undulating dunes, Marconi Beach has a monument to Guglielmo Marconi, who sent the first wireless transmission across the Atlantic from this site. The adjacent White Crest Beach and Cahoon Hollow Beach offer high-octane surfing. SickDay Surf Shop (☎508-214-4158; www.sickdaysurf.com; 361 Main St; surfboards per day $25-30; ⏰9am-9pm Mon-Sat) rents surfboards.

Wellfleet Bay Wildlife Sanctuary NATURE RESERVE
(☎508-349-2615; www.massaudubon.org; West Rd, off US 6; adult/child $5/3; ⏰8:30am-dusk; ▥) ◈ Birders flock to Mass Audubon's 1100-acre sanctuary, where trails cross tidal creeks, salt marshes and beaches.

☆ Festivals & Events

Wellfleet OysterFest FOOD
(www.wellfleetoysterfest.org; ⏰mid-Oct) The town becomes a food fair for a weekend, with a beer garden, an oyster-shucking contest and, of course, belly-busters of the blessed bivalves.

▦ Sleeping & Eating

Even'Tide Motel MOTEL $$
(☎508-349-3410; www.eventidemotel.com; 650 US 6; r from $135, cottages per week $1100-2800; ▧ ▨) This 31-room motel, set back from the highway in a grove of pine trees, also has nine cottages. Pluses include a large indoor pool, picnic facilities and a playground.

PB Boulangerie & Bistro BAKERY $
(www.pbboulangeriebistro.com; 15 Lecount Hollow Rd; pastries from $3; ⏰7am-7pm Tue-Sun) Incredible pastries, artisan breads and delicious sandwiches.

Mac's Seafood Market SEAFOOD $$
(www.macsseafood.com; 265 Commercial St, Wellfleet Town Pier; mains $7-20; ⏰11am-3pm Mon-Fri, to 8pm Sat & Sun; ▨) Head here for market-fresh seafood at bargain prices. Fried fish standards are paired with snappy-fresh oysters harvested from nearby flats. Order at a window and chow down at picnic tables overlooking Wellfleet Harbor.

☆ Entertainment

★Beachcomber LIVE MUSIC
(☎508-349-6055; www.thebeachcomber.com; 1120 Cahoon Hollow Rd; ⏰5pm-1am) 'Da Coma' is *the* place to rock the night away. It's a bar. It's a restaurant. It's a dance club. It's the

---

LOCAL KNOWLEDGE

SCENIC DRIVE: CAPE COD BAY

When exploring the Cape, eschew the speedy Mid-Cape Hwy (US 6) and follow instead the Old King's Hwy (MA 6A), which snakes along Cape Cod Bay. The longest continuous stretch of historic district in the USA, it's lined with gracious period homes, antique shops and art galleries, all of which make for good browsing en route.

coolest summertime hangout on the entire Cape, set in a former lifesaving station right on Cahoon Hollow Beach. You can watch the surf action till the sun goes down, and after dark some really hot bands take the stage.

Wellfleet Harbor Actors Theater　THEATER
(WHAT; ☎ 508-349-9428; www.what.org; 2357 US 6) This acclaimed theater produces edgy, contemporary plays.

Wellfleet Drive-In　CINEMA
(☎ 508-349-7176; www.wellfleetcinemas.com; US 6; adult/child $9/6; ⌘) Enjoy an evening of nostalgia at this old-fashioned drive-in theater.

Truro

Squeezed between Cape Cod Bay on the west coast and the open Atlantic on the east, narrow Truro abounds with water views and beaches.

◉ Sights

Cape Cod Highland Light　LIGHTHOUSE
(www.capecodlight.org; Light House Rd; admission $4; ⊘10am-5:30pm) Sitting on the Cape's highest elevation (a mere 120ft!), Cape Cod Highland Light casts the brightest beam on the New England coast and offers a sweeping view.

🛏 Sleeping

Hostelling International Truro　HOSTEL **$**
(☎ 508-349-3889; http://capecod.hiusa.org; N Pamet Rd; dm incl breakfast $39; @) Budget digs don't get more atmospheric than at this former coast-guard station perched amid undulating dunes. Book early.

Provincetown

This is it: as far as you can go on the Cape, and more than just geographically. The draw is irresistible. Fringe writers and artists began making a summer haven in Provincetown a century ago. Today this sandy outpost has morphed into the hottest gay

and lesbian destination in the Northeast. Flamboyant street scenes, brilliant art galleries and unbridled nightlife paint the town center. But that's only half the show. Provincetown's untamed coastline and vast beaches beg to be explored. Sail off on a whale watch, cruise the night away, get lost in the dunes – but whatever you do, don't miss this unique corner of New England.

◉ Sights & Activities

Province Lands Visitor Center　BEACH
(☎ 508-487-1256; www.nps.gov/caco; Race Point Rd; ⊘9am-5pm; ℗) 🏷 **FREE** Overlooking Race Point Beach, this Cape Cod National Seashore visitor center has displays on dune ecology and a rooftop observation deck with an eye-popping 360° view of the outermost reaches of Cape Cod.

Race Point Beach　BEACH
(Race Point Rd) On the wild tip of the Cape, Race Point is a breathtaking stretch of sand, with crashing surf and undulating dunes as far as the eye can see.

Herring Cove Beach　BEACH
(Province Lands Rd) This popular swimming beach faces west, making it a spectacular place to be at sunset.

★**Pilgrim Monument & Provincetown Museum**　MUSEUM
(www.pilgrim-monument.org; High Pole Rd; adult/child $12/4; ⊘9am-7pm Jul & Aug, to 5pm Sep-Jun) Climb to the top of the USA's tallest all-granite structure (253ft) for a sweeping view of town and coast. At the base of the c 1910 tower an evocative museum depicts the landing of the *Mayflower* Pilgrims and other Provincetown history.

★**Provincetown Art Association & Museum**　MUSEUM
(PAAM; www.paam.org; 460 Commercial St; adult/child $7/free; ⊘11am-8pm Mon-Thu, to 10pm Fri, to 5pm Sat & Sun) Founded in 1914 to celebrate the town's thriving art community, this vibrant museum showcases the works of artists who have found their inspiration in Provincetown. Chief among them is Edward Hopper, who had a home and gallery in the Truro dunes.

Whydah Pirate Museum　MUSEUM
(www.whydah.com; MacMillan Wharf; adult/child $10/8; ⊘10am-5pm) See the salvaged booty from a pirate ship that sank off Cape Cod in 1717.

GALLERY BROWSING

Provincetown hosts scores of art galleries. For the best browsing begin at PAAM and walk southwest along waterfront Commercial St. Over the next few blocks every second storefront harbors a gallery worth a peek.

★ **Dolphin Fleet**
Whale Watch WHALE-WATCHING
(☎508-240-3636; www.whalewatch.com; MacMillan Wharf; adult/child $44/29; ⊘Apr-Oct; ⊕) ✐
Provincetown is the perfect launch point for whale-watching, since it's the closest port to Stellwagen Bank National Marine Sanctuary, a summer feeding ground for humpback whales. Dolphin offers as many as 12 whale-watch tours daily. Expect splashy fun. Humpback whales have a flair for acrobatic breaching and come surprisingly close to the boats, offering great photo ops.

Cape Cod National
Seashore Bike Trails CYCLING
(www.nps.gov/caco) Eight exhilarating miles of paved bike trails crisscross the forest and undulating dunes of the Cape Cod National Seashore and lead to Herring Cove and Race Point beaches. There are several bike rental shops around town.

⚔ Festivals & Events

Provincetown Carnival CARNIVAL
(www.ptown.org/carnival.asp; ⊘3rd week of August) Mardi Gras, drag queens, flowery floats – this is the ultimate gay party event in this gay party town, attracting tens of thousands of revelers.

🛌 Sleeping

Provincetown offers nearly 100 guesthouses, without a single chain hotel to mar the view. In summer it's wise to book ahead, doubly so on weekends. If you do arrive without a booking, the chamber of commerce keeps tabs on available rooms.

Dunes' Edge Campground CAMPGROUND $
(☎508-487-9815; www.dunesedge.com; 386 US 6; tent/RV sites $42/54) Camp amid the dunes at this family-friendly campground.

Moffett House GUESTHOUSE $$
(☎508-487-6615; www.moffetthouse.com; 296a Commercial St; r without bath $90-159; ❋🕾🐾) Set back in a quiet alleyway, this guesthouse has a bonus: free bicycles. Rooms are basic – it's more like crashing with a friend than doing the B&B thing – but you get kitchen privileges and lots of ops to meet fellow travelers.

Race Point Lighthouse INN $$
(☎508-487-9930; www.racepointlighthouse.net; Race Point; r $155-185) ✐ Want to *really* get away? If unspoiled sand dunes and a 19th-

DON'T MISS

PROVINCETOWN'S FIRST PORT OF CALL

In a town of quirky attractions the **Provincetown Public Library** (www.provincetownlibrary.org; 356 Commercial St; ⊘10am-5pm Mon & Fri, to 8pm Tue-Thu, 1-5pm Sat & Sun) might be the last place you'd expect to find a hidden treasure. Erected in 1860 as a church, it was turned into a museum a century later, complete with a replica of Provincetown's race-winning schooner *Rose Dorothea*. When the museum went bust, the town converted the building to a library. One catch: the boat, which occupies the building's upper deck, was too big to remove. So it's still there, with bookshelves built around it. Pop upstairs and take a look.

century lighthouse sound like good company, book one of the three bedrooms in the old lighthouse-keeper's house. Cool place – powered by solar panels and a wind turbine, and literally on the outer tip of the Cape, miles from the nearest neighbor.

Ampersand Guesthouse B&B $$
(☎508-487-0959; www.ampersandguesthouse.com; 6 Cottage St; r incl breakfast $130-200; ❋🕾) It's not the fanciest place in town but it's friendly and cozy and its summer rates are good value.

Revere Guesthouse B&B $$
(☎508-487-2292; www.reverehouse.com; 14 Court St; r incl breakfast $155-345; ❋🕾) Tasteful rooms and a peaceful setting, yet just minutes from all the action.

★ **Carpe Diem** BOUTIQUE HOTEL $$$
(☎508-487-4242; www.carpediemguesthouse.com; 12 Johnson St; r incl breakfast $229-419; ❋@🕾) Sophisticated and relaxed, with smiling Buddhas, orchid sprays and a European-style spa. Each guest room is inspired by a different gay literary genius; the room themed on poet Raj Rao, for example, has sumptuous embroidered fabrics and hand-carved Indian furniture.

🍴 Eating

Every third building on Commercial St houses some sort of eatery, so that's the place to start.

Cafe Heaven
CAFE $

(📞508-487-9639; 199 Commercial St; mains $7-12; ⊙8am-3pm) Light and airy but small and crowded, this art-filled storefront is an easy-on-the-wallet lunch and breakfast place. The menu ranges from sinful croissant French toast to healthy salads. Don't be deterred by the wait – the tables turn over quickly.

Spiritus Pizza
PIZZERIA $

(www.spirituspizza.com; 190 Commercial St; slices/pizzas $3/20; ⊙11:30am-2am) A favorite place for a late-night bite and cruising after the clubs close.

Purple Feather Cafe & Treatery
CAFE $

(www.thepurplefeather.com; 334 Commercial St; snacks $3-10; ⊙11am-midnight; 🛜🍴) Head to this stylish cafe for killer panini sandwiches, a rainbow of gelati and decadent desserts made from scratch. Lemon cupcakes never looked so lusty.

Fanizzi's by the Sea
SEAFOOD $$

(📞508-487-1964; www.fanizzisrestaurant.com; 539 Commercial St; mains $10-25; ⊙11:30am-9:30pm; 🍴) An amazing water view and reasonable prices make Fanizzi's a local favorite. You'll find something for everyone, from fresh seafood and salads to comfort food and a kids' menu.

★ Mews Restaurant & Cafe
MODERN AMERICAN $$$

(📞508-487-1500; www.mews.com; 429 Commercial St; mains $14-35; ⊙5:30-10pm) Want affordable gourmet? Skip the excellent but pricey restaurant and go upstairs to the bar for a fab view, great martinis and scrumptious bistro fare.

Lobster Pot
SEAFOOD $$$

(📞508-487-0842; www.ptownlobsterpot.com; 321 Commercial St; mains $22-37; ⊙11:30am-9pm) True to its name, this bustling fish house is *the* place for lobster. Service can be s-l-o-w. Best way to beat the crowd is to come mid-afternoon.

🍷 Drinking & Nightlife

Provincetown is awash with gay clubs, drag shows and cabarets. And don't be shy if you're straight – everyone's welcome.

Patio
CAFE

(www.ptownpatio.com; 328 Commercial St; ⊙11am-11pm) Grab yourself a sidewalk table and order up a ginger *mojito* at this umbrella-shaded cafe hugging the pulsating center of Commercial St.

Ross' Grill
BAR

(www.rossgrille.com; 237 Commercial St; ⊙11:30am-10pm) For an romantic place to have a drink with a water view, head to the bar at this smart bistro.

Pied Bar
GAY & LESBIAN

(www.piedbar.com; 193 Commercial St) A popular waterfront lounge that attracts both lesbians and gay men. Particularly hot place to be around sunset.

A-House
CLUB

(Atlantic House; www.ahouse.com; 4 Masonic Pl) A hot dance spot for the gay community.

☆ Entertainment

Provincetown boasts a rich theater history. Eugene O'Neill began his writing career here and several stars including Marlon Brando and Richard Gere performed on Provincetown stages before they hit the big screen.

Provincetown Theater
THEATER

(📞508-487-7487; www.provincetowntheater.org; 238 Bradford St) There's almost always something of interest on here – anything from splashy Broadway musicals to offbeat local themes.

Crown & Anchor
GAY & LESBIAN

(www.onlyatthecrown.com; 247 Commercial St) The queen of the gay scene, this multiwing complex has a nightclub, a leather bar and a steamy cabaret.

🛍 Shopping

Shops lining Commercial St sell everything from kitsch and tourist T-shirts to quality crafts and edgy clothing.

Shop Therapy
ADULT

(www.shoptherapy.com; 346 Commercial St; ⊙10am-10pm) Downstairs, it's patchouli and tie-dye clothing. But everyone gravitates upstairs, where the sex toys are wild enough to make an Amsterdam madam blush. Parents, you'll need to use discretion: your teenagers *will* want to go inside.

Womencrafts
CRAFT

(www.womencrafts.com; 376 Commercial St; ⊙11am-6pm) The name says it all: jewelry, pottery, books and music by female artists from across America.

ℹ Information

Post office (www.usps.com; 219 Commercial St)

Provincetown Business Guild (www.ptown.org) Oriented to the gay community.

Provincetown Chamber of Commerce (www.ptownchamber.com; 307 Commercial St; ⊘9am-6pm) The town's helpful tourist office is at MacMillan Wharf, where the ferries dock.

Provincetown on the Web (www.provincetown.com) Online guide with the entertainment scoop.

Seamen's Bank (221 Commercial St) Has a 24-hour ATM.

Wired Puppy (www.wiredpuppy.com; 379 Commercial St; ⊘6:30am-10pm; 🛜) Free online computers for the price of an espresso.

ℹ Getting There & Away

Plymouth & Brockton buses (www.p-b.com) connect Boston and Provincetown ($35, 3½ hours). From mid-May to mid-October, **Bay State Cruise Company** (📞877-783-3779; www.boston-ptown.com; 200 Seaport Blvd, Boston; round-trip adult/child fast ferry $85/62, slow ferry $46/free; ⊘mid-May–mid-Oct) runs a ferry between Boston's World Trade Center Pier and MacMillan Wharf.

Nantucket

Once home port to the world's largest whaling fleet, Nantucket's storied past is reflected in its period homes and cobbled streets. When whaling went bust in the mid-19th century the town plunged from riches to rags. The population dwindled and grand old houses sat idle until wealthy urbanites discovered Nantucket made a fine place to spend summer. High-end tourism has been Nantucket's mainstay ever since.

⊙ Sights & Activities

Step off the boat and you're in the only place in the USA where the entire town is a National Historic Landmark. It's a bit like stepping into a museum – wander around, soak up the atmosphere. Start your explorations by strolling up Main St, where you'll find the grandest whaling-era mansions lined up in a row.

⭐**Nantucket Whaling Museum**　MUSEUM
(13 Broad St; adult/child $20/5; ⊘10am-5pm mid-May–Oct, 11am-4pm Nov–mid-May) A top sight is this evocative museum in a former spermaceti (whale-oil) candle factory.

Nantucket Beaches　BEACHES

If you have young 'uns head to **Children's Beach**, right in Nantucket town, where the water's calm and there's a playground. **Surfside Beach**, 2 miles to the south, is where the college crowd heads for an active scene and bodysurfing waves. The best place to catch the sunset is **Madaket Beach**, 5.5 miles west of town.

Cycling　CYCLING

No destination on the island is more than 8 miles from town and thanks to Nantucket's relatively flat terrain and dedicated bike trails, cycling is an easy way to explore. For a fun outing, cycle to the picturesque village of **Siasconset** ('Sconset), known for its rose-covered cottages. A couple of companies rent bikes ($30 a day) right at the ferry docks.

🛌 Sleeping

HI Nantucket　HOSTEL $
(📞508-228-0433; http://capecod.hiusa.org; 31 Western Ave; dm incl breakfast $35; ⊘mid-May–mid-Sep; @) Known locally as Star of the Sea, this atmospheric hostel in an 1873 lifesaving station has a million-dollar setting near Surfside Beach. As Nantucket's sole nod to the budget traveler, it's booked well in advance.

⭐**Centerboard Inn**　B&B $$$
(📞508-228-2811; www.centerboardinn.com; 8 Chestnut St; r incl breakfast $249-419; ⊛@🛜) A welcoming innkeeper who pampers guests with extras, and loans iPads, gives this chic B&B a leg up on the competition. Rooms sport an upscale island decor, breakfast includes savory treats and the location is perfect for sightseeing. After a day on the town slip back to relax over cheese and wine at afternoon tea.

Barnacle Inn　B&B $$$
(📞508-228-0332; www.thebarnacleinn.com; 11 Fair St; r with/without bath incl breakfast from $200/140) Folksy owners and simple, quaint accommodations that hearken to earlier times are in store at this turn-of-the-19th-century inn.

🍴 Eating

Centre Street Bistro　CAFE $$
(www.nantucketbistro.com; 29 Centre St; mains $8-30; ⊘11:30am-9:30pm Wed-Sat; 🛜🍴) Settle in at a parasol-shaded sidewalk table and watch the traffic trickle by at this relaxed cafe. The chef-owners make everything from scratch, including delicious warm goat's-cheese tarts.

Club Car
PUB **$$**

(www.theclubcar.com; 1 Main St; mains $12-30; ⊙11:30am-1am) This converted railroad car, a vestige of the actual railroad that sank in the sands of Nantucket, dishes up consistently good food, including the best lobster roll in town.

Black-Eyed Susan's
CAFE **$$**

(www.black-eyedsusans.com; 10 India St; mains $9-30; ⊙7am-1pm daily & 6-10pm Mon-Sat) Snag a seat on the back patio and try the sourdough French toast topped with caramelized pecans and Jack Daniel's butter. At dinner the fish of the day with black-eyed peas takes top honors. BYOB.

❶ Information

Visitor Services & Information Bureau
(☑508-228-0925; www.nantucket-ma.gov; 25 Federal St; ⊙9am-5pm) Maintains a summer-season kiosk at the ferry dock.

❶ Getting There & Around

AIR

Cape Air (www.flycapeair.com) flies from Boston, Hyannis and Martha's Vineyard to Nantucket Memorial Airport (ACK).

BOAT

The **Steamship Authority** (☑508-477-8600; www.steamshipauthority.com) runs ferries throughout the day between Hyannis and Nantucket. The fast ferry (round-trip adult/child $69/35) takes an hour; the slow ferry (round-trip adult/child $35/18) takes 2¼ hours.

BUS

Getting around Nantucket is a snap. The **NRTA Shuttle** (www.shuttlenantucket.com; rides $1-2, day pass $7; ⊙late May-Sep) operates buses around town and to 'Sconset, Madaket and the beaches. Buses have bike racks, so cyclists can bus one way and pedal back.

Martha's Vineyard

New England's largest island is a world unto itself. Home to 15,500 year-round residents, its population swells to 100,000 in summer. The towns are charming, the beaches good, the restaurants chef-driven. And there's something for every mood here – fine-dine in gentrified Edgartown one day and hit the cotton-candy and carousel scene in Oak Bluffs the next.

Martha's Vineyard Chamber of Commerce (☑508-693-0085; www.mvy.com; 24 Beach Rd, Vineyard Haven; ⊙9am-5pm Mon-Fri) has visitor information. There are also summertime visitor kiosks at the ferry terminals.

Oak Bluffs

Odds are this ferry-port town, where the lion's share of boats arrive, will be your introduction to the island. Welcome to the Vineyard's summer fun mecca – a place to wander with an ice-cream cone in hand, poke around honky-tonk sights and go clubbing into the night.

◉ Sights & Activities

Campgrounds & Tabernacle
HISTORIC SITE

Oak Bluffs started out in the mid-19th century as a summer retreat for a revivalist church, whose members enjoyed a day at the beach as much as a gospel service. They built some 300 cottages, each adorned with whimsical gingerbread trim. These brightly painted cottages – known today as the Campgrounds – surround Trinity Park and its open-air Tabernacle (1879), a venue for festivals and concerts.

Flying Horses Carousel
HISTORIC SITE

(www.mvpreservation.org; 15 Lake Ave, at Circuit Ave; rides $2.50; ⊙10am-10pm; ⊞) Take a nostalgic ride on the USA's oldest merry-go-round, which has been captivating kids of all ages since 1876. The antique horses have manes of real horse hair and, if you stare into their glass eyes, you'll see neat little silver animals inside.

Bike Trail
CYCLING

A scenic bike trail runs along the coast connecting Oak Bluffs, Vineyard Haven and Edgartown – it's largely flat so makes a good pedal for families. Rent bicycles at **Anderson's Bike Rental** (☑508-693-9346; www.andersonsbikerentals.com; 1 Circuit Ave Extension; bicycles per day adult/child $18/10; ⊙9am-6pm) near the ferry terminal.

🛏 Sleeping

Nashua House
INN **$$**

(☑508-693-0043; www.nashuahouse.com; 30 Kennebec Ave; r without bath $99-219; ⊛🔊) The Vineyard the way it used to be: no phones, no TV, no in-room bath. Instead you'll find suitably simple and spotlessly clean accommodations at this small inn right in the center of town.

IF YOU HAVE A FEW MORE DAYS

Known as **Up-Island**, the rural western half of Martha's Vineyard is a patchwork of rolling hills, small farms and open fields frequented by wild turkeys and deer. Feast your eyes and your belly at the picturesque fishing village of **Menemsha**, where you'll find seafood shacks with food so fresh the boats unload their catch at the back door. They'll shuck you an oyster and steam you a lobster while you watch and you can eat alfresco on a harborside bench.

The coastal **Aquinnah Cliffs**, also known as the Gay Head Cliffs, are so special they're a National Natural Landmark. These 150ft-high cliffs glow with an amazing array of colors that can be best appreciated in the late-afternoon light. You can hang out at **Aquinnah Public Beach** (parking $15), just below the multihued cliffs, or walk a mile north along the shore to an area that's popular with nude sunbathers.

Cedar Tree Neck Sanctuary (www.sheriffsmeadow.org; Indian Hill Rd; ⊘8:30am-5:30pm) FREE, off State Rd, has an inviting 2.5-mile hike across native bogs and forest to a coastal bluff with views of Cape Cod. The Massachusetts Audubon Society's **Felix Neck Wildlife Sanctuary** (www.massaudubon.org; Edgartown–Vineyard Haven Rd; adult/child $4/3; ⊘dawn-dusk; 🚻) is a birder's paradise with 4 miles of trails skirting marshes and ponds.

Narragansett House   B&B $$

(📞508-693-3627; www.narragansetthouse.com; 46 Narragansett Ave; r incl breakfast $150-300; 🅿🛜) On a quiet residential street, this B&B occupies two adjacent Victorian gingerbread-trimmed houses just a stroll from the town center. It's old-fashioned without being cloying and, unlike other places in this price range, all rooms have private baths.

✖ Eating

Linda Jean's   DINER $

(www.lindajeansrestaurant.com; 25 Circuit Ave; mains $5-15; ⊘6am-10:30pm) The town's best all-around inexpensive eatery rakes in the locals with unbeatable blueberry pancakes, juicy burgers and simple but filling dinners.

MV Bakery   BAKERY $

(www.mvbakery.com; 5 Post Office Sq; baked goods $1-3; ⊘7am-5pm) Inexpensive coffee, apple fritters and cannoli are served all day, but the best time to swing by is from 9pm to midnight, when folks line up at the back door to buy hot doughnuts straight from the baker.

Slice of Life   CAFE $$

(www.sliceoflifemv.com; 50 Circuit Ave; mains $8-24; ⊘8am-9pm; 🚭) The look is casual; the fare is gourmet. At breakfast, there's kick-ass coffee, portobello omelets and fab potato pancakes. At dinner the roasted cod with sun-dried tomatoes is a savory favorite. And the desserts – decadent crème brûlée and luscious lemon tarts – are as good as you'll find anywhere.

🍷 Drinking & Nightlife

Offshore Ale Co   BREWERY

(www.offshoreale.com; 30 Kennebec Ave) This popular microbrewery is the place to enjoy a pint of Vineyard ale.

Lampost   CLUB

(www.lampostmv.com; 6 Circuit Ave) Head to this combo bar and nightclub for the island's hottest dance scene. In the unlikely event you don't find what you're looking for here, keep cruising Circuit Ave where you'll stumble across several dive bars (one actually named the **Dive Bar**, another the **Ritz**), both dirty and nice.

Vineyard Haven

A harbor full of classic wooden sailboats and streets lined with eye-catching restaurants and shops, lure visitors to this appealing town.

🛏 Sleeping & Eating

HI Martha's Vineyard   HOSTEL $

(📞508-693-2665; http://capecod.hiusa.org; 525 Edgartown–West Tisbury Rd; dm $35; ⊘mid-May–mid-Oct; @🛜) Reserve early for a bed at this popular purpose-built hostel in the center of the island. It has everything you'd expect of a top-notch hostel: a solid kitchen, bike delivery and no curfew. The public bus stops out front and it's right on the bike path.

★ Art Cliff Diner   CAFE $$

(📞508-693-1224; 39 Beach Rd; mains $10-16; ⊘7am-2pm Thu-Tue) 🚭 *The* place for breakfast and lunch. Chef-owner Gina Stanley adds flair to everything she touches, from the almond-encrusted French toast to the fresh-fish tacos. The eclectic menu utilizes farm-fresh island ingredients. Expect a line – it's worth the wait.

Edgartown

Perched on a fine natural harbor, Edgartown has a rich maritime history and a patrician air. At the height of the whaling era it was home to more than 100 sea captains whose fortunes built the grand old homes that line the streets today.

Stroll along Main St where you'll find several historic buildings, some of which open to visitors during the summer.

⊙ Sights

Katama Beach   BEACH
(Katama Rd) The Vineyard's best beach lies 4 miles south of Edgartown center. Also called South Beach, Katama stretches for three magnificent miles. Rugged surf will please surfers on the ocean side. Some swimmers prefer the protected salt ponds on the inland side.

🛏 Sleeping & Eating

Edgartown Inn   GUESTHOUSE **$$**
(☎508-627-4794; www.edgartowninn.com; 56 N Water St; r with /without bath from $175/125; ❄) The best bargain in town, with 20 straightforward rooms spread across three adjacent buildings. The oldest dates to 1798 and claims Nathaniel Hawthorne and Daniel Webster among its earliest guests! Ask about last-minute specials; you might score a discount if things are slow.

Among the Flowers Café   CAFE **$$**
(☎508-627-3233; 17 Mayhew Lane; mains $8-20; ⊙8am-3:30pm; ✑) Join the in-the-know crowd on the garden patio for homemade soups, waffles, sandwiches, crepes and even lobster rolls. Although everything's served on paper or plastic, it's still kinda chichi. In July and August, they cafe adds on dinner as well and kicks it up a notch.

☆ Entertainment

★**Flatbread Company**   LIVE MUSIC
(www.flatbreadcompany.com; 17 Airport Rd; ⊙3pm-late) Formerly the home of Carly Simon's legendary Hot Tin Roof, Flatbread continues the tradition, staging the best bands on the island. And it makes damn good organic pizzas too. It's adjacent to Martha's Vineyard Airport.

❶ Getting There & Around

BOAT

Frequent ferries operated by the **Steamship Authority** (☎508-477-8600; www.steamshipauthority.com) link Woods Hole to both Vineyard Haven and Oak Bluffs, a 45-minute voyage. If you're bringing a car, book well in advance.

From Falmouth Harbor, the passenger-only ferry **Island Queen** (☎508-548-4800; www.islandqueen.com; 75 Falmouth Heights Rd) sails to Oak Bluffs several times daily in summer.

From Hyannis, **Hy-Line Cruises** (☎508-778-2600; www.hylinecruises.com; Ocean St Dock; round-trip adult/child slow ferry $45/free, fast ferry $72/48) operates a slow ferry (1½ hours) once daily to Oak Bluffs and a high-speed ferry (55 minutes) five times daily.

BUS

Martha's Vineyard Regional Transit Authority (www.vineyardtransit.com; 1-/3-day pass $7/15) operates a bus network with frequent service between towns. It's a practical way to get around and you can even reach out-of-the-way destinations including the Aquinnah Cliffs.

Central Massachusetts

Poking around this central swath of Massachusetts, between big-city Boston and the fashionable Berkshires, provides a taste of the less-touristed stretch of the state. But it's no sleeper, thanks largely to a score of colleges that infuse a youthful spirit into the region.

The **Central Massachusetts Convention & Visitors Bureau** (☎508-755-7400; www.centralmass.org; 91 Prescott St, Worcester; ⊙9am-5pm Mon-Fri) and the **Greater Springfield Convention & Visitors Bureau** (☎413-787-1548; www.valleyvisitor.com; 1441 Main St, Springfield; ⊙8:30am-5pm Mon-Fri) provide regional visitor information.

Worcester

The state's second-largest city had its glory days in the 19th century. The industries that made the town rich went bust but the old barons left a legacy at the first-rate **Worcester Art Museum** (☎508-799-4406; www.worcesterart.org; 55 Salisbury St; adult/child $14/free; ⊙11am-5pm Wed-Fri & Sun, 10am-5pm Sat; ❸), which showcases works by luminary French Impressionists and American masters such as Whistler.

Springfield

Workaday Springfield's top claim to fame is as the birthplace of the all-American game of basketball. The **Naismith Memorial Basketball Hall of Fame** (www.hoophall.com; 1000 W Columbus Ave; adult/child $19/14; ⏰10am-5pm; P ♿) celebrates the sport with exhibits and memorabilia from all the big hoop stars.

It's also the hometown of Theodor Seuss Geisel, aka children's author Dr Seuss. You'll find life-size bronze sculptures of the Cat in the Hat and other wonky characters at the **Dr Seuss National Memorial Sculpture Garden** (www.catinthehat.org; cnr State & Chestnut Sts; ♿) FREE.

Northampton

The region's best dining, hottest nightlife and most interesting street scenes all await in this uber-hip burg known for its liberal politics and outspoken lesbian community. Easy to explore on foot, the eclectic town center is chockablock with cafes, funky shops and art galleries. **Greater Northampton Chamber of Commerce** (☑413-584-1900; www.explorenorthampton.com; 99 Pleasant St; ⏰9am-5pm Mon-Fri; 10am-2pm Sat & Sun) is information central.

◎ Sights

Smith College　　　　COLLEGE CAMPUS
(www.smith.edu; Elm St; P) The Smith College campus, covering 127 acres with lovely gardens, is well worth a stroll.

Smith College Museum of Art　　MUSEUM
(☑413-585-2760; www.smith.edu/artmuseum; Elm St, at Bedford Tce; adult/child $5/2; ⏰10am-4pm Tue-Sat, noon-4pm Sun; P) Don't miss the Smith College Museum of Art, which boasts an impressive collection of 19th- and 20th-century European and North American paintings, including works by John Singleton Copley, Picasso and Monet.

⌊ Sleeping

Autumn Inn　　　　　　MOTEL $$
(☑413-584-7660; www.hampshirehospitality.com; 259 Elm St/MA 9; r incl breakfast $115-169; P@♠🐾) Despite its motel-like layout, this two-story place near Smith campus sports an agreeable inn-style ambience and large, comfy rooms.

WORCESTER DINERS

Worcester nurtured a great American icon: the diner. Here, in this rust-belt city, you'll find a dozen of them tucked behind warehouses, underneath old train trestles, or steps from dicey bars. **Miss Worcester Diner** (☑508-753-5600; 300 Southbridge St; meals $5-9; ⏰6am-2pm Mon-Sat, 7am-2pm Sun) is a classic of the genre. Built in 1948, it was a showroom diner of the Worcester Lunch Car Company, which produced 650 diners at its factory right across the street. Harleys parked on the sidewalk and Red Sox paraphernalia on the walls set the tone. Enticing selections such as banana-bread French toast compete with the usual greasy-spoon menu of chili dogs and biscuits with gravy. It's one tasty slice of Americana.

Hotel Northampton　　HISTORIC HOTEL $$$
(☑413-584-3100; www.hotelnorthampton.com; 36 King St; r $185-275; P🛜) Northampton's finest sleep since 1927, this 100-room hotel in the town center features period decor and well-appointed rooms.

✗ Eating

Woodstar Cafe　　　　CAFE $
(www.woodstarcafe.com; 60 Masonic St; mains $5-8; ⏰8am-8pm; 🛜♿) Students flock to this family-run bakery-cafe, just a stone's throw from Smith campus, for tasty sandwiches and luscious pastries at bargain prices. Perhaps the smoked salmon and chevre on an organic baguette?

Green Bean　　　　　　CAFE $
(www.greenbeannorthampton.com; 241 Main St; mains $6-9; ⏰7am-3pm; 🛜) 🍃 Pioneer Valley farmers stock the kitchen at this cute eatery that dishes up organic eggs at breakfast and juicy hormone-free beef burgers at lunch.

Haymarket Café　　　　CAFE $
(www.haymarketcafe.com; 185 Main St; items $4-10; ⏰7am-10pm; 🛜♿) Northampton's coolest hangout for bohemians and caffeine addicts, the Haymarket serves up heady espresso, fresh juices and an extensive vegetarian menu.

♀ Drinking & Entertainment

Northampton Brewery BREWERY
(www.northamptonbrewery.com; 11 Brewster Ct; ⊙ 11:30am-2am Mon-Sat, noon-1am Sun) The oldest operating brewpub in New England enjoys a loyal summertime following thanks to its generously sized outdoor deck.

Calvin Theatre CONCERT VENUE
(☑ 413-584-0610; www.iheg.com; 19 King St) This gorgeously restored theater hosts big-name performances with everything from hot rock and indie bands to comedy shows.

Diva's LESBIAN
(www.divasofnoho.com; 492 Pleasant St; ⊙ Wed-Sat) The city's main gay-centric dance club keeps its patrons sweaty thanks to a steady diet of thumping house music.

Iron Horse Music Hall CONCERT VENUE
(☑ 413-584-0610; www.iheg.com; 20 Center St) Nationally acclaimed folk and jazz artists line up to play in this intimate setting.

Amherst

This college town, a short drive from Northampton, is built around the mega **University of Massachusetts** (UMass; www.umass.edu) and two small colleges, the liberal **Hampshire College** (www.hampshire.edu) and the prestigious **Amherst College** (www.amherst.edu). Contact them for campus tours and event information; there's always something happening. If hunger strikes, you'll find the usual bevy of college-town eateries radiating out from Main St in the town center.

The lifelong home of poet Emily Dickinson (1830–86), the 'belle of Amherst,' is open to the public as the **Emily Dickinson Museum** (☑ 413-542-8161; www.emilydickinsonmuseum.org; 280 Main St; adult/child $10/5; ⊙ 10am-5pm Wed-Mon). Admission includes a 40-minute tour.

The Berkshires

Tranquil towns and a wealth of cultural attractions are nestled in these cool green hills. For more than a century the Berkshires have been a favored retreat for wealthy Bostonians and New Yorkers. And we're not just talking Rockefellers – the entire Boston symphony summers here as well. The **Berkshire Visitors Bureau** (☑ 413-743-4500; www.berkshires.org; 3 Hoosac St; ⊙ 10am-5pm) can provide information on the entire region.

Great Barrington

Hands-down the best place in the Berkshires to be at mealtime. Head straight to the intersection of Main (US 7) and Railroad Sts in the town center where you'll find an artful mix of galleries and eateries serving mouthwatering food – everything from bakeries to ethnic cuisines.

For wholesome Berkshire-grown meals on a budget, go to the **Berkshire Co-op Market Cafe** (www.berkshire.coop; 42 Bridge St; meals $6-10; ⊙ 8am-8pm Mon-Sat, 10am-8pm Sun; ☑) ✿ inside the local co-op. For fine dining, **Castle Street Cafe** (☑ 413-528-5244; www.castlestreetcafe.com; 10 Castle St; mains $21-29; ⊙ 5-9pm Wed-Mon; ☑) ✿ serves up an innovative menu that reads like a who's who of local farms: Ioka Valley Farm grass-fed natural beef, Rawson Brook chevre and more. For a little green with your suds, head to **Barrington Brewery** (www.barringtonbrewery.net; 420 Stockbridge Rd; mains $8-20; ⊙ 11:30am-9:30pm; ☎) ✿, where the hoppy brews are created using solar power.

Stockbridge

This timeless New England town, sans even a single traffic light, looks like something straight out of a Norman Rockwell drawing. Oh wait...it is! Rockwell (1894–1978), the most popular illustrator in US history, lived on Main St and used the town and its residents as subjects. At the evocative **Norman Rockwell Museum** (☑ 413-298-4100; www.nrm.org; 9 Glendale Rd/MA 183; adult/child $16/5; ⊙ 10am-5pm), Rockwell's slice-of-Americana paintings come to life when examined up close.

Lenox

The cultural heart of the Berkshires, the refined village of Lenox hosts one of the country's premier musical events, the open-air **Tanglewood Music Festival** (☑ 888-266-1200; www.tanglewood.org; 297 West St/MA 183, Lenox; ⊙ late Jun-early Sep), featuring the Boston Symphony Orchestra and guest artists such as James Taylor and Yo-Yo Ma. Buy a lawn ticket, spread a blanket, uncork a bottle of wine and enjoy the quintessential Berkshires experience.

Shakespeare & Company (☑ 413-637-1199; www.shakespeare.org; 70 Kemble St; ⊙ Tue-Sun) gives performances of the Bard's work in evocative settings throughout the summer. The renowned Jacob's Pillow Dance Festival (☎413-243-0745; www.jacobspillow.org; 358 George Carter Rd, Becket; ☺mid-Jun–Aug), 10 miles east of Lenox in Becket, stages contemporary dance performances.

The Mount (www.edithwharton.org; 2 Plunkett St; adult/child $18/free; ☺10am-5pm May-Oct), the former estate of novelist Edith Wharton (1862–1937), offers tours of her mansion and inspirational gardens.

🛏 Sleeping & Eating

Birchwood Inn INN $$$
(☎413-637-2600; www.birchwood-inn.com; 7 Hubbard St; r incl breakfast $200-375; ✳🛜🅿) Charming period inns abound in Lenox. The senior of them, Birchwood Inn, registered its first guest in 1767 and continues to offer warm hospitality today.

Cornell in Lenox B&B $$$
(☎413-637-4800; www.cornellbb.com; 203 Main St; r incl breakfast $145-265; @🛜) Spread across three historic houses, this B&B provides good value in a high-priced town.

★Nudel AMERICAN $$$
(☎413-551-7183; www.nudelrestaurant.com; 37 Church St; mains $22-25; ☺5:30-9:30pm Tue-Sat) Get a delicious taste of the area's sustainable food movement at Nudel, whose seasonally inspired menu takes a back-to-basics approach with the likes of heritage-bred pork chops and spaetzle pasta with rabbit.

Bistro Zinc FRENCH $$$
(☎413-637-8800; www.bistrozinc.com; 56 Church St; mains $15-30; ☺11:30am-3pm & 5:30-10pm) You'll find stylish bistros along Church St in the town center, including Bistro Zinc with hot postmodern decor and French-inspired New American fare.

🍷 Drinking & Nightlife

Olde Heritage Tavern PUB
(www.theheritagetavern.com; 12 Housatonic St; mains $7-15; ☺11:30am-12:30am Mon-Fri, 8am-12:30am Sat & Sun; 👶) For family fare at honest prices visit Olde Heritage Tavern, an upbeat pub whose menu ranges from waffles to steaks.

Pittsfield

Just west of the town of Pittsfield is Hancock Shaker Village (☎413-443-0188; www.hancockshakervillage.org; US 20; adult/child $18/free; ☺10am-5pm mid-Apr–Oct; 👶), a fascinating museum illustrating the lives of the Shakers, the religious sect that founded the village in 1783. The Shakers believed in communal ownership, the sanctity of work and celibacy, the latter of which proved to be their demise. Their handiwork – graceful in its simplicity – includes wooden furnishings and 20 buildings, the most famous of which is the round stone barn.

Williamstown & North Adams

Cradled by the Berkshire's rolling hills, Williamstown is a picture-perfect New England college town revolving around the leafy campus of Williams College. Williamstown and neighboring North Adams boast three outstanding art museums, each a worthy destination in itself.

◉ Sights & Activities

★Clark Art Institute MUSEUM
(☎413-458-2303; www.clarkart.edu; 225 South St, Williamstown; adult/child Jun-Oct $15/free, Nov-May all free; ☺10am-5pm, closed Mon Sep-Jun) The Sterling & Francine Clark Art Institute is a gem among US art museums. Even if you're not an avid art lover, don't miss it. The collections are particularly strong in the impressionists, with significant works by Monet, Pissarro and Renoir. Mary Cassatt, Winslow Homer and John Singer Sargent represent contemporary American painting.

Williams College Museum of Art MUSEUM
(☎413-597-2429; www.wcma.org; 15 Lawrence Hall Dr, Williamstown; ☺10am-5pm Tue-Sat, 1-5pm Sun) FREE This sister museum of the Clark Art Institute graces the center of town and has an incredible collection of its own. Around half of its 13,000 pieces comprise the American Collection, with substantial works by

---

WORTH A TRIP

SCENIC FOLIAGE DRIVE

For the finest fall foliage drive in Massachusetts, head west on MA 2 from Greenfield to Williamstown on the 63-mile route known as the Mohawk Trail. The lively Deerfield River slides alongside, with roaring, bucking stretches of whitewater that turn leaf-peeping into an adrenaline sport for kayakers.

notables such as Edward Hopper (*Morning in a City*), Winslow Homer and Grant Wood, to name only a few.

MASS MoCA MUSEUM
(☑413-662-2111; www.massmoca.org; 1040 Mass Moca Way, North Adams; adult/child $15/5; ☺10am-6pm Jul & Aug, 11am-5pm Wed-Mon Sep-Jun; ⊕) The USA's largest contemporary art museum, MASS MoCA sprawls across an amazing 222,000 sq ft and includes art construction areas, performance centers and 19 galleries. One gallery is the size of a football field, giving installation artists the opportunity to take things into a whole new dimension. Bring your walking shoes!

Mt Greylock State Reservation PARK
(☑413-499-4262; www.mass.gov/dcr/parks/mt-Greylock; ☺visitor center 9am-5pm) FREE Just south of North Adams, this park has both a road and trails up to Massachusetts' highest peak (3491ft), where there's a panoramic view of several mountain ranges and, on a clear day, five different states. Among the park's 45 miles of hiking trails is a portion of the Appalachian Trail. In addition, you'll find a rustic summit lodge.

✥ Festivals & Events

Williamstown Theatre Festival THEATER
(☑413-597-3400; www.wtfestival.org; 1000 Main St, Williamstown; ☺late Jun–late Aug) Stars of the theater world descend upon Williamstown every year. The festival mounts a mix of classics and contemporary works by up-and-coming playwrights. Bradley Cooper and Gwyneth Paltrow are just two of the well-known thespians who have performed here.

🛏 Sleeping & Eating

River Bend Farm B&B B&B $$
(☑413-458-3121; www.riverbendfarmbb.com; 643 Simonds Rd/US 7, Williamstown; r without bath incl breakfast $120; ❄🛜) Step back to the 18th century in this Georgian Colonial B&B furnished with real-deal antiques and boasting five fireplaces. Four doubles share two bathrooms here. Despite the name it's not on a farm but along US 7 in Williamstown.

Maple Terrace Motel MOTEL $$
(☑413-458-9677; www.mapleterrace.com; 555 Main St, Williamstown; r incl breakfast $121-157; 🛜🏊) On the eastern outskirts of Williamstown, the Swedish innkeepers here offer 15 simple, yet cozy rooms.

Porches BOUTIQUE HOTEL $$$
(☑413-664-0400; www.porches.com; 231 River St, North Adams; r incl breakfast $189-285; ❄🛜🏊🐾) Across the street from MASS MoCA in North Adams, the artsy rooms here combine well-considered color palettes, ample lighting and French doors into a pleasant sleeping experience.

Moonlight Diner & Grille DINER $
(☑413-458-3305; 408 Main St, Williamstown; mains $6-10; ☺7am-8:30pm Mon-Thu, to 9:30pm Fri & Sat) This old-school diner on the east side of Williamstown dishes up all the classics at honest prices. Think retro '50s decor, huge burgers and cheesy omelets.

Public Eat & Drink PUB $$
(www.publiceatanddrink.com; 34 Holden St, North Adams; mains $10-22; ☺5-9pm; 🐾) Come to this cozy North Adams pub for an excellent selection of craft beers and gourmet pub fare, including brie burgers, flatbread pizzas and bistro steak. Some decent vegetarian options as well.

★**Mezze Bistro & Bar** FUSION $$$
(☑413-458-0123; www.mezzerestaurant.com; 777 Cold Spring Rd/US 7, Williamstown; mains $20-30; ☺5-9pm) East meets West at this chic restaurant that blends contemporary American cuisine with classic French and Japanese influences. Mezze's farm-to-table approach begins with an edible garden right on site. Much of the rest of the seasonal menu, from small-batch microbrews to organic meats, is locally sourced as well.

RHODE ISLAND

America's smallest state packs a lot into a compact package, more than making up for its lack of land with 400 miles of craggy coastline, deeply indented bays and lovely beaches. The state's engaging capital, Providence, is small enough to be friendly but big enough to offer top-notch dining and attractions. Newport, a summer haunt of the well-heeled, brims with opulent mansions, pretty yachts and world-class music festivals. Should you want to take it further afield, hopping on a ferry to Block Island makes a perfect day trip.

History

Ever since it was founded in 1636 by Roger Williams, a religious outcast from Boston,

Rhode Island's capital, Providence has enjoyed an independent frame of mind. Williams' guiding principle, the one that got him ostracized from Massachusetts, was that all people should have freedom of conscience. He put his liberal beliefs into practice when settling Providence, remaining on friendly terms with the local Narragansett Native Americans after purchasing from them the land for a bold experiment in tolerance and peaceful coexistence.

Williams' principles would not last long. As Providence and Newport grew and merged into a single colony, competition and conflict with area tribes sparked several wars, leading to the decimation of the Wampanoag, Pequot, Narragansett and Nipmuck peoples. Rhode Island was also a prolific slave trader and its merchants would control much of that industry in the years after the Revolutionary War.

The city of Pawtucket gave birth to the American industrial revolution with the establishment of the water-powered Slater Mill in 1790. Industrialism impacted the character of Providence and surrounds, particularly along the Blackstone River, creating urban density. As with many small east-coast cities, these urban areas went into a precipitous decline in the 1940s and '50s as manufacturing industries (textiles and costume jewelry) faltered. In the 1960s preservation efforts salvaged the historic architectural framework of Providence and Newport. The former has emerged as a lively place with a dynamic economy and the latter, equally lively, survives as a museum city.

RHODE ISLAND FACTS

Nicknames Ocean State, Little Rhody

Population 1,050,300

Area 1034 sq miles

Capital city Providence (population 178,400)

Other city Newport (population 24,000)

Sales tax 7%

Birthplace of Broadway composer George M Cohan (1878–1942) and toy icon Mr Potato Head (b 1952)

Home of The first US tennis championships

Politics Majority vote Democrat

Famous for Being the smallest state

Official state bird A chicken? Why not? The Rhode Island Red revolutionized the poultry industry

Driving distances Providence to Newport 37 miles, Providence to Boston 50 miles

downtown. Along the way you'll have opportunities to lounge in the sidewalk cafe of an art-house theater, dine in a stellar restaurant and knock back a few pints in a cool bar. At night, take in a play at the Trinity Repertory, squeeze into a club or eat some 3am burgers aboard the mobile Haven Brothers Diner.

ℹ️ Information

Providence Journal (www.providencejournal.com) The state's largest daily newspaper.

Rhode Island Parks (www.riparks.com) Offers camping in five state parks.

Rhode Island Tourism Division (☑800-250-7384; www.visitrhodeisland.com) Distributes visitor information on the whole state.

Providence

Rhode Island's capital city, Providence presents its visitors with some of the finest urban strolling this side of the Connecticut River. In the crisp air and falling leaves of autumn, wander through Brown University's green campus on 18th-century College Hill and follow the Riverwalk into

◉ Sights

Exit 22 off I-95 deposits you downtown. The university area is a short walk to the east. The colorful Italian enclave of Federal Hill centers on Atwells Ave, a mile west of the city center.

College Hill   NEIGHBORHOOD
East of the Providence River, College Hill, headquarters of **Brown University** (www.brown.edu), contains over 100 Colonial, Federal and Revival houses dating from the 18th century. Stroll down **Benefit Street's** 'Mile of History' for the best of them. Amidst them you'll find the clean lines of William Strickland's 1838 **Providence Athenaeum** (☑401-421-6970; www.providenceathenaeum.org; 251 Benefit St; ⊙9am-7pm Mon-Thu, 9am-5pm Fri & Sat, 1-5pm Sun) **FREE**,

NEW ENGLAND PROVIDENCE

DON'T MISS

BONFIRES AFTER DARK

Move over, Christo. Providence has blazed onto the public-art installation scene with WaterFire (www.waterfire. org), set on the river that meanders through the city center. Nearly 100 braziers poke above the water, each supporting a bonfire that roars after dark. Flames dance off the water, music plays, black-clad gondoliers glide by, and party-goers pack the riverbanks. A captivating blend of art and entertainment, WaterFire takes place about a dozen times between May and September, mostly on a Saturday, from sunset to 1am.

inside which plaster busts of Greek gods and philosophers preside over a collection that dates from 1753.

Free tours of the campus begin from the Brown University Admissions Office (☑401-863-2378; Corliss Brackett House, 45 Prospect St). Call or drop by for times.

Museum of Art   MUSEUM
(☑401-454-6500; www.risdmuseum.org; 224 Benefit St; adult/child $12/3; ☺10am-5pm Tue-Sun, to 9pm Thu; ♿) Wonderfully eclectic, the Rhode Island School of Design's art museum showcases everything from ancient Greek art to 20th-century American paintings and decorative arts. Pop in before 1pm Sunday and admission is free.

State House   HISTORIC BUILDING
(☑401-222-3983; 82 Smith St; ☺8:30am-4:30pm Mon-Fri, free tours 9am, 10am & 11am) FREE Providence's focal point is crowned with one of the world's largest self-supporting marble domes. Check out the Gilbert Stuart portrait of George Washington, then compare it to the $1 bill in your wallet.

Roger Williams Park   PARK
(1000 Elmwood Ave) FREE In 1871 Betsey Williams, great-great-great-granddaughter of the founder of Providence, donated her farm to the city as a public park. Today this 430-acre expanse of greenery, only a short drive south of Providence, includes lakes and ponds, forest copses, broad lawns, picnic grounds and a Planetarium and Museum of Natural History (☑401-785-9457; museum $2, planetarium $4; ☺10am-4pm, planetarium shows 2pm Sat & Sun; ♿).

🛏 Sleeping

Christopher Dodge House   B&B $$
(☑401-351-6111; www.providence-hotel.com; 11 W Park St; r incl breakfast $120-180; P) This 1858 Federal-style house is furnished with early American reproduction furniture and marble fireplaces. Austere on the outside, it has elegant proportions, large, shuttered windows and wooden floors.

Providence Biltmore   HISTORIC HOTEL $$$
(☑401-421-0700; www.providencebiltmore.com; 11 Dorrance St; r/ste $146/279; P✺) The granddaddy of Providence's hotels, the Biltmore dates from the 1920s. The lobby, both intimate and regal, nicely combines dark wood, twisting staircases and chandeliers, while well-appointed rooms stretch many stories above the old city. Ask for one of the 292 rooms that are on a high floor.

🍴 Eating

Both the Rhode Island School of Design and Johnson & Wales University have top-notch culinary programs that annually turn out creative new chefs. The large student population on the East Side ensures that there are plenty of good places around College Hill and Fox Point. To experience old Providence, head over to Atwells Ave in Federal Hill.

East Side Pockets   MEDITERRANEAN $
(www.eastsidepocket.com; 278 Thayer St; mains $4-7; ☺10am-1am Mon-Sat, 10am-10pm Sun; ☑) Fabulous falafels and baklava at student-friendly prices.

★Haven Brothers Diner   DINER $
(Washington St; meals $5-10; ☺5pm-3am) As legend has it, the Haven Brothers started as a horse-drawn lunch wagon in 1893. Climb up a rickety ladder to get basic diner fare alongside everyone from prominent politicians, to college kids pulling an all-nighter, to drunks.

Flan y Ajo   SPANISH $
(☑401-432-6656; 225a Westminster St; tapas $3-7; ☺6-11pm) This BYOB tapas bar serves lip-smacking *pintxos* (bites) such as single shell-on prawn with *salsa verde*, mussels in white wine and succulent *lomito* (pork tenderloin). Buy a bottle of wine from Eno Fine Wines next door.

Abyssinia   ETHIOPIAN $$
(☑401-454-1412; www.abyssinia-restaurant.com; 333 Wickenden St; meals $20; ☺11am-10pm; ☑) From the plum-colored banquettes to the

roaring (or is that smiling?) Lion of Judah on the wall, get ready to experience the heady flavors of Ethiopian cooking. Vegetarian lentils and split-pea curries tempt the taste buds before the spicy onslaught of *doro wat* (chicken stew) and beef *key wot*.

★ **birch** MODERN AMERICAN $$$
(☑ 401-272-3105; www.birchrestaurant.com; 200 Washington St; meals $25-35; ⊙ 5pm-midnight Thu-Tue) With a background at the fabulous Dorrance at the Biltmore, chef Benjamin Sukle and his wife, Heidi, now have their own place. Its intimate size and its style means attention to detail is exacting in both the decor and the food, which focuses on small-batch and hyper-seasonal produce.

⬤ Drinking & Entertainment

Trinity Brewhouse BREWERY
(☑ 401-453-2337; www.trinitybrewhouse.com; 186 Fountain St; ⊙ 11:30am-1am Sun-Thu, noon-2am Fri & Sat) This microbrewery in the entertainment district creates terrific British-style beers. Don't miss the stouts.

The Salon BAR, CLUB
(www.thesalonpvd.com; 57 Eddy St; ⊙ 5pm-1am Mon-Fri, 7pm-2am Sat) The Salon mixes ping-pong tables and pinball machines with '80s pop and pickleback shots (whiskey with a pickle juice chaser) upstairs, and live shows, open mic, DJs and dance parties downstairs.

**Providence Performing
Arts Center** PERFORMING ARTS
(☑ 401-421-2787; www.ppacri.org; 220 Weybosset St) This popular venue for touring Broadway musicals and other big-name performances is in a former Loew's Theater dating from 1928. It has a lavish art-deco interior.

AS220 CLUB
(☑ 401-831-9327; www.as220.org; 115 Empire St; ⊙ 5pm-1am) A longstanding outlet for all forms of Rhode Island art, AS220 (say 'A-S-two-twenty') books experimental bands (Lightning Bolt, tuba and banjo duos), hosts readings and provides gallery space for a very active community. Hours given here are for the bar, but the gallery opens midday Wednesday through Saturday, and the cafe closes at 10pm.

🛍 Shopping

Providence Place (www.providenceplace.com; 1 Providence Place) in the city center is Rhode Island's largest mall. For more individual, quirky shops head to Westminster St, Thayer St and Wickenden St.

ⓘ Information

Providence Visitor Information Center
(☑ 401-751-1177; www.goprovidence.com; Rhode Island Convention Center, 1 Sabin St; ⊙ 9am-5pm Mon-Sat)

ⓘ Getting There & Away

TF Green Airport (PVD; www.pvdairport.com; I-95, exit 13, Warwick), 20 minutes south of downtown Providence, is served by major US airlines and car-rental companies.

Peter Pan Bus Lines (www.peterpanbus.com) connects Providence with Boston ($8, one hour) and New York ($35, 3¾ hours). **Amtrak** (www.amtrak.com; 100 Gaspee St) trains also link cities in the Northeast with Providence.

Rhode Island Public Transit Authority (RIPTA; www.ripta.com; one way $2, day pass $6) runs city-wide bus services from downtown Kennedy Plaza; other RIPTA buses link Providence with Newport.

Newport

Established by religious moderates fleeing persecution from Massachusetts Puritans, 'new port' flourished to become the fourth richest city in the newly independent colony and the harbor remains one of the most active and important yachting centres in the country. Downtown the Colonial-era architecture is beautifully preserved, although it struggles to compete with the opulent 'summer cottages' built by latter-day industrialists on the back of shipping, railroad and mining fortunes. Modeled on Italianate *palazzi*, French *chateaux* and Elizabethan manor houses, these buildings remain the town's premier attraction alongside a series of summer music festivals, which are among the most important in the US.

◉ Sights & Activities

★ **Preservation Society
of Newport County** HISTORIC BUILDINGS
(☑ 401-847-1000; www.newportmansions.org; 424 Bellevue Ave; 5-site ticket adult/child $49/19) Five of Newport's grandest mansions are managed by this society. Each mansion takes about 90 minutes to tour.

➡ **Breakers**
(44 Ochre Point Ave; adult/child $19.50/5.50; ⊙ 9am-5pm Apr-mid-Oct, hours vary mid-Oct–Mar;

P) If you have time for only one Newport mansion, make it this extravagant 70-room, 1895 Italian Renaissance mega-palace built for Cornelius Vanderbilt II, patriarch of America's then-richest family.

➡ **Rosecliff**

(548 Bellevue Ave; adult/child $14.50/5.50; ☺10am-5pm Apr-mid-Oct, hrs vary mid-Oct–Mar; P) A 1902 masterpiece of architect Stanford White, Rosecliff resembles the Grand Trianon at Versailles. Its immense ballroom had a starring role in Robert Redford's *The Great Gatsby*.

➡ **The Elms**

(www.newportmansions.org; 367 Bellevue Ave; adult/child $14.50/5.50, servant-life tour adult/child $15/5; ☺10am-5pm Apr-mid-Oct, hours vary mid-Oct–Mar; P ⓗ) Built in 1901, the Elms is a replica of Château d'Asnières, built near Paris in 1750. You can take a 'behind-the-scenes' tour which will have you snaking through the servants' quarters and up onto the roof.

★ **Rough Point**   HISTORIC BUILDING

(www.newportrestoration.com; 680 Bellevue Ave; adult/child $25/free; ☺10am-2pm Thu-Sat mid-Apr–mid-May, 10am-3.45pm Tue-Sat mid-May–mid-Nov; P) Once called the 'richest little girl in the world,' Doris Duke (1912–93) was just 13 years old when she inherited this English manor estate from her father. Duke had a passion for travel and art collecting; Rough Point houses many of her holdings, from Ming dynasty ceramics to Renoir paintings.

International Tennis Hall of Fame   MUSEUM

(☑401-849-3990; www.tennisfame.com; 194 Bellevue Ave; adult/child $12/free; ☺9:30am-5pm) To experience something of the American aristocracy's approach to 19th-century leisure, visit this museum. It lies inside the historic Newport Casino building (1880), which served as a summer club for Newport's wealthiest residents. For $110 you can jump into your whites and play a game on the classic grass courts.

Touro Synagogue National Historic Site   SYNAGOGUE

(☑401-847-4794; www.tourosynagogue.org; 85 Touro St; adult/child $12/free; ☺10am-4pm Sun-Fri Jul-Sep, 10am-2pm Sun-Fri Sep-Oct, noon-1.30pm Sun-Fri May-Jun, noon-1.30pm Sun Nov-Apr) Tour the oldest synagogue (c 1763) in the USA, an architectural gem that treads the line between austere and lavish.

Cliff Walk   WALKING TRAIL

(www.cliffwalk.com) For a glorious hike take the 3.5-mile Cliff Walk, which hugs the coast behind the mansions. You will not only enjoy the same dramatic ocean views, but you will get to gawk at mansions along the way. The Cliff Walk stretches from Memorial Blvd to Bailey's Beach; a scenic place to start is at Ruggles Ave near the Breakers.

★ **Fort Adams State Park**   PARK

(www.fortadams.org; Harrison Ave; fort tours adult guided/self-guided $12/6, child $6/3; ☺sunrise-sunset) Fort Adams is America's largest coastal fortification and is the centerpiece of this gorgeous state park, which juts out into Narragansett Bay. It's the venue for the Newport Jazz and Folk Festivals. Swimming is OK at Fort Adams, but **Easton's Beach** (First Beach; Memorial Blvd) and **Sachuest (Second) Beach** (Purgatory Rd) are better.

★ **Sail Newport**   SAILING

(☑401-846-1983; www.sailnewport.org; 60 Fort Adams Dr; 1-/2-week sessions $365/475, sailboat rental per 3hr $73-138; ☺9am-7pm; ⓗ) As you'd expect in the hometown of the prestigious America's Cup, the sailing in breezy Newport is phenomenal.

Adirondack II   CRUISE

(☑401-847-0000; www.sail-newport.com; Bowen's Wharf; 1½hr cruise $30-39; ☺11am-7pm) This schooner sails from Bowen's Wharf five times a day.

⚜ Festivals & Events

For a full schedule of events, see www.gonewport.com.

Newport Folk Festival   MUSIC

(www.newportfolkfest.net; Fort Adams State Park; 1-/3-day pass $49/120, parking $12; ☺late Jul) Big-name stars and up-and-coming groups perform at Fort Adams State Park. Bring sunscreen.

Newport Jazz Festival   MUSIC

(www.newportjazzfest.net; Fort Adams State Park; tickets $47.50-100; ☺early Aug) The roster reads like a who's who of jazz, with the likes of Dave Brubeck and Wynton Marsalis.

Newport Music Festival   MUSIC

(www.newportmusic.org; tickets $20-42; ☺mid-Jul) This internationally regarded festival offers classical music concerts in many of the great mansions.

🛏 Sleeping

★ Newport International Hostel   HOSTEL $

(William Gyles Guesthouse; ☎ 401-369-0243; www.newporthostel.com; 16 Howard St; dm without bath incl breakfast $35-119; ☉ Apr-Dec; ☎) Welcome to Rhode Island's only hostel, run by an informal and knowledgeable host. Book as early as you can. The tiny guesthouse contains fixings for a simple breakfast, a laundry machine and spare, clean digs in a dormitory room. Private rooms are available but you need to enquire by email.

Stella Maris Inn   INN $$

(☎ 401-849-2862; www.stellamarisinn.com; 91 Washington St; r incl breakfast $125-225; ℗) This quiet, stone-and-frame inn has numerous fireplaces, heaps of black-walnut furnishings, Victorian bric-a-brac and some floral upholstery. Rooms with garden views rent for less than those overlooking the water. The owner can be a bit gruff, but the prices are good (for Newport, that is). Oddly, it doesn't accept credit cards.

★ The Attwater   BOUTIQUE HOTEL $$$

(☎ 401-846-7444; www.theattwater.com; 22 Liberty St; r $180-309; ℗✳☎) Newport's newest hotel has the bold attire of a midsummer beach party with turquoise, lime-green and coral prints, ikat headboards and snazzily patterned geometric rugs. Picture windows and porches capture the summer light and rooms come furnished with thoughtful luxuries such as iPads, Apple TV and beach bags.

🍴 Eating

★ Rosemary & Thyme Cafe   BAKERY, CAFE $

(☎ 401-619-3338; www.rosemaryandthymecafe.com; 382 Spring St; baked goods $2-5, sandwiches & pizza $5.95-7.95; ☉ 7.30am-3pm Tue-Sat, to 11.30am Sun; ☎) With a German baker in the kitchen, it is hardly surprising that the counter here is piled high with buttery croissants, apple and cherry tarts and plump muffins. At lunchtime gourmet sandwiches feature herbed goat's cheese and Tuscan dried tomatoes and an Alsatian cheese mix.

Franklin Spa   DINER $

(☎ 401-847-3540; 229 Spring St; meals $3-10; ☉ 6am-2pm; ☎) This old-school joint slings hash, eggs and grease for cheap. It's locally loved and opens early. Enjoy freshly squeezed orange juice, homemade turkey noodle soup or coffee cabinet (milkshake with ice cream) at a Formica-topped table on a worn white-and-red-tiled floor.

Mamma Luisa   ITALIAN $$

(☎ 401-848-5257; www.mammaluisa.com; 673 Thames St; mains $14-25; ☉ 5-10pm Thu-Tue) This cozy restaurant serves authentic Italian fare to its enthusiastic customers, who recommend this low-key pasta house as a place to escape the Newport crowds. There are classic pasta dishes (cheese ravioli with fava beans, spaghetti *alle vongole*), as well as meat and fish entrees.

OFF THE BEATEN TRACK

IF YOU HAVE A FEW MORE DAYS

Unspoiled Block Island, separated from the rest of Rhode Island by 12 miles of open ocean, offers simple pleasures: rolling farms, uncrowded beaches and miles of quiet hiking and cycling trails.

Ferries dock at Old Harbor, the main town, which has changed little since its gingerbread houses were built in the late 19th century. The beaches begin right at the north side of town. If you continue north 2 miles you'll come to the Clay Head Nature Trail, which follows high clay bluffs above the beach offering good bird-watching along the way. Rodman Hollow, a 100-acre wildlife refuge at the island's south end, is also laced with interesting trails.

A mere 7 miles long, Block Island begs to be explored by bicycle; several places near the ferry dock rent them for $25 a day. The Block Island Chamber of Commerce (☎ 800-383-2474; www.blockislandchamber.com), at the ferry dock, can help with accommodations, but be aware the island's four-dozen inns typically book out in summer and many require minimum stays. The Sea Breeze Inn (☎ 401-466-2275; www.seabreeze-blockisland.com; Spring St, Old Harbor; r $230-310, with shared bath $150-180; ℗) offers the cutest digs in seafront cottages sat above a wild meadow.

The Block Island Ferry (☎ 401-783-4613; www.blockislandferry.com; adult/child round-trip ferry $25.55/12.50, high-speed $35.85/19.50) operates high-speed (30 minutes) and traditional (55 minutes) ferries from Galilee State Pier in Point Judith.

The Mooring

SEAFOOD $$$

(☑401-846-2260; www.mooringrestaurant.com; Sayer's Wharf; meals $15-40; ⊗11:30am-10pm) A harbor-front setting and a menu brimming with fresh seafood make this an unbeatable combination for seaside dining. Tip: if it's packed, take the side entrance to the bar, grab a stool and order the meaty clam chowder and a 'bag of doughnuts' (tangy lobster fritters).

🍷 Drinking & Entertainment

Fastnet

BAR

(www.thefastnetpub.com; 1 Broadway; ⊗11am-1am) Named for a lighthouse off the coast of Cork, this pub serves classics such as bangers and mash and fish and chips, beside an ever-flowing river of Guinness. There's live Irish music every Sunday night.

Newport Blues Café

CLUB

(☑401-841-5510; www.newportblues.com; 286 Thames St) This popular rhythm-and-blues bar and restaurant draws top acts to an old brownstone that was once a bank. It's an intimate space with many enjoying quahogs, house-smoked ribs or pork loins at tables adjoining the small stage. Dinner is offered 6pm to 10pm; the music starts at 9:30pm.

ℹ Information

Newport Visitor Center (☑401-845-9123; www.gonewport.com; 23 America's Cup Ave; ⊗9am-5pm) Offers maps, brochures, local bus information, tickets to major attractions, public restrooms and an ATM. There's free parking for 30 minutes adjacent to the center.

ℹ Getting There & Away

Peter Pan Bus Lines (www.peterpanbus.com) Has several buses daily to Boston ($27, 1¾ hours).

RIPTA (www.ripta.com) State-run RIPTA operates frequent buses (one way $2, day pass $6) from the visitor center to the mansions, beaches and Providence.

Scooter World (☑401-619-1349; www.scooterworldri.com; 11 Christie's Landing; bicycles per day $30; ⊗9am-7pm) Rents bicycles

Rhode Island Beaches

If you're up for a day at the beach, Rhode Island's southwestern coastal towns fit the bill. It is the Ocean State, after all.

The mile-long Narragansett Town Beach in Narragansett is the place to go for surfing. Nearby Scarborough State Beach is among Rhode Island's finest, with a wide sandy shore, a classic pavilion and inviting boardwalks. Watch Hill at the state's southwestern tip is a wonderful place to turn back the clock, with its Flying Horse Carousel and Victorian mansions. The South County Tourism Council (☑800-548-4662; www.southcountyri.com) has details on the entire area.

CONNECTICUT

Sandwiched between sexy New York City and northerly New England's quainter quarters, Connecticut typically gets short shrift from travelers. Sure, the brawny I-95 coastal corridor is largely industrial, but take a closer look and you're in for pleasant surprises. Seaside Mystic, with its nautical attractions, and the time-honored towns bordering the Connecticut River are a whole other world, and the Litchfield Hills, in the state's northwestern corner, are as charmingly rural as any place in New England.

History

A number of Native American tribes (notably the Pequot and the Mohegan, whose name for the river became the name of the state) were here when the first European explorers, primarily Dutch, appeared in the early 17th century. The first English settlement was at Old Saybrook in 1635, followed a year later by the Connecticut Colony, built by Massachusetts Puritans under Thomas Hooker. A third colony was founded in 1638 in New Haven. After the Pequot War (1637), the Native Americans were no longer a check to colonial expansion in New England, and Connecticut's English population grew. In 1686, Connecticut was brought into the Dominion of New England.

The American Revolution swept through Connecticut, leaving scars with major battles at Stonington (1775), Danbury (1777), New Haven (1779) and Groton (1781). Connecticut became the fifth state in 1788. It embarked on a period of prosperity, propelled by its whaling, shipbuilding, farming and manufacturing industries (from firearms to bicycles to household tools), which lasted well into the 19th century.

The 20th century brought world wars and the depression but, thanks in no small part to Connecticut's munitions industries, the state was able to fight back. Everything from planes to submarines was made in the state, and when the defense industry began to decline in the 1990s the growth of other businesses (such as insurance) helped pick up the slack.

ℹ️ Information

There are welcome centers at the Hartford airport and on I-95 and I-84 when entering the state by car.

Connecticut Tourism Division (www.ctvisit. com) Distributes visitor information for the entire state.

Hartford Courant (www.courant.com) The state's largest newspaper.

Connecticut Coast

The Connecticut Coast is not all of a piece. The western end is largely a bedroom community connected by commuter rail to New York City. By the time you get to New Haven, Connecticut's artsier side shines through. Mystic, at the eastern end of the state, is the location of the state's biggest attraction, Mystic Seaport, a recreated 19th-century whaling town spread across 17 acres.

New Haven

For visitors, New Haven is all about Yale. Head straight to New Haven Green, graced by old Colonial churches and Yale's hallowed ivy-covered walls. The oldest planned city in America (1638), New Haven is laid out in orderly blocks spreading out from the Green, making it a cinch to get around. INFO New Haven (203-773-9494; www.infonewhaven. com; 1000 Chapel St; 10am-9pm Mon-Sat, noon-5pm Sun) is the city's helpful tourist office.

◉ Sights

★Yale University UNIVERSITY
(www.yale.edu) Each year, thousands of high-school students make pilgrimages to Yale, nursing dreams of attending the country's third-oldest university, which boasts such notable alumni as Noah Webster, Eli Whitney, Samuel Morse, and Presidents William H Taft, George HW Bush, Bill Clinton and George W Bush. You don't need to share the students' ambitions in order to take a stroll around the campus, just pick up a map at the visitors center (www.yale.edu/visitor; cnr Elm & Temple Sts; 9am-4:30pm Mon-Fri,

11am-4pm Sat & Sun) or join a free, one-hour guided tour.

★Yale University Art Gallery MUSEUM
(203-432-0600; artgallery.yale.edu; 1111 Chapel St; 10am-5pm Tue-Fri, 11am-5pm Sat & Sun) FREE America's oldest university art museum boasts American masterworks by Edward Hopper and Jackson Pollock, as well as a superb European collection that includes Vincent van Gogh's *The Night Café*.

Peabody Museum of Natural History MUSEUM
(203-432-5050; www.yale.edu/peabody; 170 Whitney Ave; adult/child $9/5; 10am-5pm Mon-Sat, noon-5pm Sun; P 🚼) Wannabe paleontologists will be thrilled by the dinosaurs here.

Yale Center for British Art MUSEUM
(203-432-2800; ycba.yale.edu; 1080 Chapel St; 10am-5pm Tue-Sat, noon-5pm Sun) FREE The most comprehensive British art collection outside the UK.

CONNECTICUT FACTS

Nicknames Constitution State, Nutmeg State

Population 3.6 million

Area 4845 sq miles

Capital city Hartford (population 124,890)

Other cities New Haven (population 129,585)

Sales tax 6.35%

Birthplace of Abolitionist John Brown (1800–59), circus man PT Barnum (1810–91), actress Katharine Hepburn (1909–2003)

Home of The first written constitution in the US; the first lollipop, Frisbee and helicopter

Politics Democrat-leaning

Famous for Starting the US insurance biz and building the first nuclear submarine

Quirkiest state song lyrics 'Yankee Doodle', which entwines patriotism with doodles, feathers and macaroni

Driving distances Hartford to New Haven 40 miles, Hartford to Providence 75 miles

🛏 Sleeping

Hotel Duncan
HISTORIC HOTEL $

(☎ 203-787-1273; www.hotelduncan.net; 1151 Chapel St; s/d $60/80; ❉) Though the shine has rubbed off this New Haven gem it's the enduring features that still make it worth a stay, including the handsome lobby and the hand-operated elevator. Check out the wall in the manager's office, filled with autographed pictures of celebrity guests such as Jodie Foster and Christopher Walken.

Study at Yale
HOTEL $$$

(☎ 203-503-3900; www.studyhotels.com; 1157 Chapel St; r $219-359; P 🛜) The Study at Yale manages to evoke 'Mad Men chic' without being over the top. Ultra-contemporary touches include in-room iPod docking stations and cardio machines with built-in televisions. There's also an in-house restaurant and cafe, into which you can stumble for morning snacks.

🍴 Eating

⭐ Frank Pepe
PIZZERIA $$

(☎ 203-865-5762; www.pepespizzeria.com; 157 Wooster St; pizza $7-20; ⏲ 11:30am-10pm) Pepe's serves immaculate pizza fired in a coal oven, just as it has since 1925, in frenetic white-walled surroundings. Prices vary depending on size and toppings; the large mozzarella pizza runs at $12. Try the white-clam pizza. No credit cards.

Caseus Fromagerie Bistro
CHEESE SHOP $$$

(☎ 203-624-3373; www.caseusnewhaven.com; 93 Whitney Ave; meals $10-30; ⏲ 11:30am-2:30pm Mon-Tue, 11:30am-2:30pm & 5:30-9pm Wed-Sat) With a boutique cheese counter piled with locally sourced labels and a concept menu devoted to *le grand fromage*, Caseus has hit upon a winning combination. After all, what's not to like about a perfectly executed mac 'n' cheese or the dangerously delicious poutine (pommes frites, cheese curds and velouté)? There's also pavement seating.

Soul de Cuba
CUBAN $$$

(☎ 203-498-2822; www.souldecuba.com; 283 Crown St; meals $15-25; ⏲ 11:30am-10pm) With its peach-colored walls, Afro-Caribbean soundtrack and spirit-rousing cocktails, Soul de Cuba is warm and inviting. Aside from the enormous and excellent-value Cuban sandwiches the menu is packed with sunshine flavors from fried chicken with Spanish olives, to oxtail cooked in red wine.

⭐ Entertainment

New Haven has a first-rate theatre scene. The free weekly *New Haven Advocate* (www.newhavenadvocate.com) has current entertainment listings.

Toad's Place
MUSIC

(☎ 203-624-8623; www.toadsplace.com; 300 York St) Toad's is arguably New England's premier music hall, having earned its rep hosting the likes of the Rolling Stones, U2 and Bob Dylan.

Shubert Theater
THEATER

(☎ 203-562-5666; www.shubert.com; 247 College St) Dubbed 'Birthplace of the Nation's Greatest Hits,' since 1914 the Shubert has been hosting ballet and Broadway musicals on their trial runs before heading off to New York City.

Yale Repertory Theatre
THEATER

(☎ 203-432-1234; www.yale.edu/yalerep; 1120 Chapel St) Performing classics and new works in a converted church.

ℹ Getting There & Away

By train from New York City skip Amtrak and take **Metro North** (www.mta.info; one way $14-19), which has near-hourly services and the lowest fares. **Greyhound Bus Lines** (www.greyhound.com) connects New Haven to scores of cities including Hartford ($12.75, one hour) and Boston ($33, four hours).

Mystic

A centuries-old seaport, Mystic boasts a top-notch nautical museum, a stellar aquarium and attractive period accommodations. Yes, it gets inundated with summer tourists, but there's a good reason why everyone stops here (including fans of the 1988 film *Mystic Pizza*), so get off the highway and check it out. The **Greater Mystic Chamber of Commerce** (☎ 860-572-1102; www.mysticchamber.org; 2 Roosevelt Ave; ⏲ 9am-4:30pm), at the old train station, has visitor information.

👁 Sights

⭐ Mystic Seaport Museum
MUSEUM

(☎ 860-572-5315; www.mysticseaport.org; 75 Greenmanville Ave/CT 27; adult/child $24/15; ⏲ 9am-5pm mid-Feb-Oct, to 4pm Nov-Dec; P) America's maritime history springs to life as costumed interpreters ply their trades at this sprawling re-created 19th-century seaport village. You can scurry aboard several historic sailing vessels, including the *Charles W Morgan* (built in 1841), the last surviving wooden whaling ship in the world. If you want to experience a little voyage yourself, the Sabino, a 1908 steamboat, departs hourly (adult/child $5.50/4.50) on jaunts up the Mystic River.

★ **Mystic Aquarium & Institute for Exploration** AQUARIUM
(☑ 860-572-5955; www.mysticaquarium.org; 55 Coogan Blvd; adult/child 3-17 yr $29.95/21.95; ☺ 9am-5pm Apr-Oct, to 4pm Nov & Mar, 10am-4pm Dec-Feb; 🅰) This state-of-the-art aquarium boasts more than 6000 species of sea creatures (including three beluga whales), an outdoor viewing area for watching seals and sea lions below the waterline, a penguin pavilion and the 1400-seat Marine Theater for dolphin shows.

🛏 Sleeping

★ **Mermaid Inn** B&B $$
(☑ 860-536-6223; www.mermaidinnofmystic.com; 2 Broadway Ave; d incl breakfast $175-225; 🅿) This quirky Italianate B&B sits on a quiet street within walking distance of the town center. Its three rooms each have special touches such as fresh flowers and Italian chocolates. In warm weather, guests enjoy breakfast on the porch.

★ **Steamboat Inn** INN $$$
(☑ 860-536-8300; www.steamboatinnmystic.com; 73 Steamboat Wharf; d incl breakfast $160-295; 🅿❄🛜) Located right in the heart of downtown Mystic, the 11 rooms of this historic inn have wraparound water views and luxurious amenities, including two-person whirlpool tubs. Antiques lend the interior a romantic atmosphere and service is top-notch with baked goods for breakfast, complimentary bikes, boat docks and gym facilities.

🍴 Eating

Mystic Drawbridge Ice Cream ICE CREAM $
(www.mysticdrawbridgeicecream.com; 2 W Main St; cones $4, panini $7.50; ☺ 9am-11pm; 🅰) Strolling through town is best done with an ice-cream cone in hand. Some of the more quirky flavors, such as pumpkin pie and southern peach, are seasonal, but on any given day there will be something innovative to try.

★ **Captain Daniel Packer Inne** AMERICAN $$
(☑ 860-536-3555; www.danielpacker.com; 32 Water St; meals $14-24; ☺ 11am-10pm) This 1754 historic house has a low-beam ceiling,

creaky floorboards and a casual (and loud) pub downstairs. Upstairs, the dining room has river views and an imaginative American menu.

Oyster Club SEAFOOD $$$
(☑ 860-415-9266; www.oysterclubct.com; 13 Water St; Noank oysters $2, meals $12-35; ☺ 4-9pm Mon-Thu, 11am-2pm & 4-9pm Fri-Sun; 🅿) A little off the main drag, this is the place locals come for oysters served grilled or raw on the deck out back. Classics such as chowder and cherrystone clams satisfy traditionalists, while mussels steamed in lemongrass and coconut milk tempt more adventurous palates.

Lower Connecticut River Valley

Several Colonial-era towns grace the banks of the Connecticut River, offering up their rural charm at an unhurried pace. The **River Valley Tourism District** (☑ 860-787-9640; www.visitctriver.com) provides information on the region.

Old Lyme

Set near the mouth of the Connecticut River, Old Lyme was home to some 60 sea captains in the 19th century. Today its claim to fame is its art community. In the early 1900s art patron Florence Griswold opened her estate to visiting artists, many of whom offered paintings in lieu of rent. Her Georgian mansion, now the **Florence Griswold Museum** (☑ 860-434-5542; www.flogris.org; 96 Lyme St; adult/child $10/free; ☺ 10am-5pm Tue-Sat, 1-5pm Sun; 🅿) contains a fine selection of both impressionist and Barbizon paintings.

Nearby, the classy **Bee & Thistle Inn & Spa** (☑ 860-434-1667; www.beeandthistleinn. com; 100 Lyme St; r $180-280; 🅿🛜), a 1756 Dutch Colonial farmhouse, has antique-filled rooms and a romantic dining room serving New American cuisine (meals $30 to $60).

Essex

Tree-lined Essex, established in 1635, stands as the chief town of the region and features well-preserved Federal-period houses, legacies of rum and tobacco fortunes made in the 19th century.

The **Connecticut River Museum** (☑ 860-767-8269; www.ctrivermuseum.org; 67 Main St; adult/child $8/5; ☺ 10am-5pm Tue-Sun; 🅿), next to **Steamboat Dock**, recounts the region's history and includes a replica of the world's first submarine, built by Yale student David Bushnell in 1776. The museum runs summer river **cruises** (adult/child $26/16; ⏱ Jun-Oct) and weekend **eagle-watch tours** Friday to Sunday between February and mid-March ($40 per person).

Alternatively, take the **Essex Steam Train & Riverboat Ride** (📞860-767-0103; www.essexsteamtrain.com; 1 Railroad Ave; adult/child $17/9, with cruise $26/17; ♿), an antique steam locomotive that runs 6 scenic miles to Deep River, where you can cruise on a Mississippi-style riverboat up to East Haddam before returning by train.

The landmark **Griswold Inn** (📞860-767-1776; www.griswoldinn.com; 36 Main St; r incl breakfast $110-190, ste $190-305; 🅿🛜) has been Essex's physical and social centerpiece since 1776.

East Haddam

Two intriguing attractions mark this small town on the east bank of the Connecticut River. The medieval-style **Gillette Castle** (📞860-526-2336; www.ct.gov/dep/gillettecastle; 67 River Rd; adult/child $6/2; ⏱10am-4:30pm late May–mid-Oct; 🅿) is a wildly eccentric stone-turreted mansion built in 1919 by actor William Gillette, who made his fortune playing Sherlock Holmes.

With residents such as Gillette and banker William Goodspeed, East Haddam became a regular stopover on the summer circuit for New Yorkers, who travelled up on Goodspeed's steam ship to visit the **Goodspeed Opera House** (📞860-873-8668; www.goodspeed.org; 6 Main St; tickets $45-70; ⏱performances Wed-Sun Apr-Dec), an elegant 1876 Victorian music hall known as 'the birthplace of the American musical.'

Hartford

Despite its depressing reputation as the 'filing cabinet of America,' Connecticut's capital city, Hartford, is full of surprises. Settled in the 17th century by Dutch traders and, later, Puritans fleeing persecution in Massachusetts, it is one of New England's oldest cities and as such harbors a collection of impressive sights and museums. The **Greater Hartford Welcome Center** (📞860-244-0253; www.letsgoarts.org/welcomecenter; 100 Pearl St; ⏱9am-5pm Mon-Fri) distributes tourist information.

◉ Sights

★ Mark Twain House & Museum MUSEUM
(📞860-247-0998; www.marktwainhouse.org; 351 Farmington Ave; adult/child $16/10; ⏱9:30am-5:30pm Mon-Sat, noon-5:30pm Sun) It was at this former home of Samuel Langhorne Clemens, aka Mark Twain, that the legendary author penned many of his greatest works, including *The Adventures of Huckleberry Finn* and *Tom Sawyer*. The house itself, a Victorian Gothic with fanciful turrets and gables, reflects Twain's quirky character.

Harriet Beecher Stowe House MUSEUM
(📞860-522-9258; www.harrietbeecherstowe.org; 77 Forest St; adult/child $9/6; ⏱9:30am-4:30pm Tue-Sat, noon-4:30pm Sun) Next door is the house of the woman who wrote the antislavery book *Uncle Tom's Cabin*. The book so rallied Americans against slavery that Abraham Lincoln once credited Stowe with starting the Civil War.

★ Wadsworth Atheneum MUSEUM
(📞860-278-2670; www.thewadsworth.org; 600 Main St; adult/child $10/free; ⏱11am-5pm Wed-Fri, 10am-5pm Sat & Sun) The nation's oldest public-art museum, the Wadsworth Atheneum houses nearly 50,000 pieces. On display are paintings by members of the Hudson River School, European old masters, 19th-century Impressionist works, sculptures by Connecticut artist Alexander Calder and a small yet outstanding array of surrealist works.

Old State House HISTORIC BUILDING
(📞860-522-6766; www.ctoldstatehouse.org; 800 Main St; adult/child $6/3; ⏱10am-5pm Tue-Sat Jul 4-Columbus Day, Mon-Fri Columbus Day-Jul 4; ♿) Connecticut's original capitol building (from 1797 to 1873) was designed by Charles Bulfinch, who also designed the Massachusetts State House in Boston, and was the site of the trial of the *Amistad* prisoners. Gilbert Stuart's famous 1801 portrait of George Washington hangs in the senate chamber.

🛏 Sleeping & Eating

Hartford Marriott Downtown BUSINESS HOTEL $$
(📞866-373-9806, 860-249-8000; www.marriott.com; 200 Columbus Blvd; d/ste $159/299; 🅿@🛜🏊) This colossal Marriott hotel is located in the Adriaen's Landing District overlooking the Connecticut River. There are 401 stylish rooms spread over 22-stories alongside an indoor rooftop pool and fitness

center. There's also an affiliated spa and an upscale Mediterranean restaurant.

Bin 228 ITALIAN **$$**
(☑860-244-9463; www.bin228winebar.com; 228 Pearl St; paninis & small plates $8-12; ☺11:30am-10pm Mon-Thu, to midnight Fri, 4pm-midnight Sat) This wine bar serves Italian fare – paninis, cheese platters, salads – alongside its expansive all-Italian wine list. For those eager to avoid the louder late-night eateries, this is a good option on weekends, when the kitchen stays open to midnight (later for drinks).

🍸 Drinking & Nightlife

Vaughan's Public House PUB
(☑860-882-1560; www.irishpublichouse.com; 59 Pratt St; pub fare $9-16; ☺11:30am-1am) This popular Irish pub serves a full pub menu – including beer-battered cod and chips, Guinness lamb stew and farmhouse pie – at a long wooden bar. There are also two taps of Guinness, an excellent happy hour (3pm to 7pm, $3 for 16oz pints) and an amusing mural celebrating famous Irish.

ℹ️ Getting There & Away

Central **Union Station** (☑860-247-5329; www.amtrak.com; 1 Union Pl) links Hartford to cities throughout the Northeast, including New Haven ($13, one hour) and New York City ($40 to $57, three hours).

Litchfield Hills

The rolling hills in the northwestern corner of Connecticut are sprinkled with lakes and carpeted with forests. Historic Litchfield is the hub of the region, but lesser-known villages like Bethlehem, Washington, Preston, Warren and Kent boast similarly illustrious lineages and are just as photogenic. The **Western Connecticut Convention & Visitors Bureau** (☑800-663-1273; www.litchfieldhills.com) has information on the region.

Litchfield

Founded in 1719, Litchfield prospered from the commerce brought by stagecoaches en route between Hartford and Albany, and its many handsome period buildings are a testimony to that era. Stroll along North and South Sts to see the finest homes, including the 1773 **Tapping Reeve House & Law School** (☑860-567-4501; www.litchfieldhistoricalsociety.org; 82 South St; adult/child $5/free;

☺11am-5pm Tue-Sat, 1-5pm Sun mid-Apr–Nov), the country's first law school, which trained 129 members of Congress.

Connecticut's largest wildlife preserve, the **White Memorial Conservation Center** (☑860-567-0857; www.whitememorialcc.org; US 202; park free, museum adult/child $6/3; ☺park sunrise-sunset, museum 9am-5pm Mon-Sat, noon-5pm Sun) is 2.5 miles west of town and has 35 miles of walking trails and good bird-watching.

Lake Waramaug

The most beautiful of the dozens of lakes and ponds in the Litchfield Hills is Lake Waramaug. As you make your way around North Shore Rd, stop at **Hopkins Vineyard** (☑860-868-7954; www.hopkinsvineyard.com; 25 Hopkins Rd; ☺10am-5pm Mon-Sat, 11am-5pm Sun May-Dec) for wine tastings. It's next to the 19th-century **Hopkins Inn** (☑860-868-7295; www.thehopkinsinn.com; 22 Hopkins Rd, Warren; r $120-135, apt $150; 🅿🌀🐾), which has lake-view accommodations and a restaurant with Austrian-influenced country fare. **Lake Waramaug State Park** (☑860-868-0220; www.ct.gov/deep; 30 Lake Waramaug Rd; tent sites $17-$27) has lakeside campsites, but book well in advance.

VERMONT

Artisanal cheeses, buckets of maple syrup, Ben & Jerry's ice cream…just try to get out of this state without gaining 10lb. Fortunately, there are plenty of ways to work it off: hike the trails of the Green Mountains, paddle a kayak on Lake Champlain or hit Vermont's snowy slopes.

Vermont gives true meaning to the word rural. Its capital would barely rate as a small town in other states and even its largest city, Burlington, has just 42,500 content souls. The countryside is a blanket of rolling green, with 80% of the state forested and most of the rest given over to some of the prettiest farms you'll ever see. So take your time, meander down quiet side roads, stop in those picturesque villages, and sample a taste of the good life.

History

Frenchman Samuel de Champlain explored Vermont in 1609, becoming the first European to visit these lands long inhabited by the native Abenaki.

Vermont & New Hampshire

Vermont played a key role in the American Revolution in 1775 when Ethan Allen led a local militia, the Green Mountain Boys, to Fort Ticonderoga, capturing it from the British. In 1777 Vermont declared independence as the Vermont Republic, adopting the first New World constitution to abolish slavery and establish a public school system. In 1791 Vermont was admitted to the USA as the 14th state.

The state's independent streak is as long and deep as a vein of Vermont marble. Historically a land of dairy farmers, Vermont is still largely agricultural and has the lowest population of any New England state.

ℹ Information

Vermont Dept of Tourism (www.vermont vacation.com) Online information by region, season and other user-friendly categories.

Vermont Public Radio (VPR; www.vpr.net) Vermont's excellent statewide public radio station. The radio frequency varies depending on where you are in the state, but the following selection covers most areas: Burlington (northwestern Vermont) 107.9; Brattleboro (southeastern Vermont) 94.5; Manchester (southwestern Vermont) 92.5; and St Johnsbury (northeastern Vermont) 88.5.

Vermont State Parks (☑ 888-409-7579; www.vtstateparks.com) Complete camping and parks information.

Southern Vermont

The southern swath of Vermont holds the state's oldest towns and plenty of scenic back roads.

Brattleboro

Ever wondered where the 1960s counterculture went? It's alive and well in this riverside burg overflowing with artsy types and more tie-dye per capita than any other place in New England.

◉ Sights

Paralleling the Connecticut River, Main St is lined with period buildings, including the handsome art-deco Latchis Building. The surrounding area boasts several covered bridges; pick up a driving guide at the Chamber of Commerce (p218).

Brattleboro Museum & Art Center MUSEUM (www.brattleboromuseum.org; 10 Vernon St; adult/child $8/4; ⊙ 11am-5pm Sun-Mon & Wed-Thu, 11am-7pm Fri, 10am-5pm Sat) Located in a 1915 railway station, this museum hosts rotating exhibitions of contemporary art, including multimedia works by local artists.

🛏 Sleeping

If all you're after is a cheap sleep, there are plenty of motels on Putney Rd north of town; take Exit 3 off I-91.

Latchis Hotel HOTEL $$ (☑ 800-798-6301, 802-254-6300; http://hotel.latchis.com; 50 Main St; tw $80-100, d $105-180, ste $160-210; 🖥) You can't beat the prime downtown location of this art-deco hotel with a historic theater right next door.

★ Forty Putney Road B&B B&B $$$ (☑ 800-941-2413, 802-254-6268; www.fortyputneyroad.com; 192 Putney Rd; r incl breakfast $159-329; @ 🖥) In a sweet riverside location just north of town, this 1930 B&B has a cheery pub, a glorious backyard, four rooms and a separate, self-contained cottage. On-site boat and bike rentals allow guests to explore the adjacent West River estuary.

🍴 Eating

Amy's Bakery Arts Cafe BAKERY, CAFE $ (113 Main St; sandwiches & salads $7-12; ⊙ 8am-6pm Mon-Sat, 9am-5pm Sun) Enjoy pastries and coffee, local artwork and Connecticut River views at this popular bakery. Lunchtime offerings include salads, soups and sandwiches.

Brattleboro Food Co-op DELI $ (www.brattleborofoodcoop.com; 2 Main St; ⊙ 7am-9pm Mon-Sat, 9am-9pm Sun) 🍴 Load up your basket with wholefood groceries, organic produce and local cheeses at this thriving community co-op, or visit the juice bar and deli for healthy takeaway treats.

Whetstone Station PUB $$ (www.whetstonestation.com; 36 Bridge St; mains $10-20; ⊙ 11:30am-10pm Sun-Thu, 11:30am-11pm Fri & Sat) Brattleboro's newest eatery has a dozen-plus craft brews on tap and excellent pub fare, but the real show-stopper is its outstanding roof deck with a bird's eye view of the Connecticut River. It's the ideal spot for a beer and a bite at sundown.

TJ Buckley's AMERICAN $$$ (☑ 802-257-4922; www.tjbuckleys.com; 132 Elliot St; mains $40; ⊙ 5:30-9pm Thu-Sun) 🍴 Chef-owner Michael Fuller founded this exceptional, upscale 18-seat eatery in an authentic 1927

VERMONT FACTS

Nickname Green Mountain State

Population 626,000

Area 9217 sq miles

Capital city Montpelier (population 7860)

Other city Burlington (population 42,500)

Sales tax 6%

Birthplace of Mormon leader Brigham Young (1801–77), President Calvin Coolidge (1872–1933)

Home of More than 100 covered bridges

Politics Independent streak, leaning Democrat

Famous for Ben & Jerry's ice cream

Sudsiest state Most microbreweries per capita in the USA

Driving distances Burlington to Brattleboro 151 miles, Burlington to Boston 216 miles

diner over 30 years ago. The oral menu of four nightly changing items is sourced largely from local organic farms. Reserve ahead.

❶ Information

Brattleboro Chamber of Commerce (☑877-254-4565, 802-254-4565; www.brattleborochamber.org; 180 Main St; ☉9am-5pm Mon-Fri)

Mt Snow

Family-oriented **Mt Snow** (☑800-245-7669; www.mountsnow.com; VT 100, West Dover; adult lift ticket midweek/weekend $75/85) is the southernmost of Vermont's big ski resorts. When the snow melts, its lifts and trail system draw hikers and mountain bikers. The **Mt Snow Valley Chamber of Commerce** (☑877-887-6884, 802-464-8092; www.visitvermont.com; 21 W Main St; ☉8:30am-4:30pm Mon-Wed, to 6pm Thu & Fri, 10am-4pm Sat & Sun) has information on accommodations and activities. Mt Snow is reached via Wilmington, midway between Brattleboro and Bennington.

Bennington

A measure of how rural southern Vermont really is, cozy Bennington, with just 15,000 inhabitants, ranks as the region's largest town. You'll find an interesting mix of cafes and shops downtown along Main St, while the adjacent Old Bennington historic district boasts age-old Colonial homes and a trio of covered bridges. A hilltop granite obelisk commemorating the 1777 Battle of Bennington towers above it all.

❍ Sights

Old First Church   HISTORIC SITE
(cnr Monument Ave & VT 9) Gracing the center of Old Bennington, this early 19th-century church is best known for its churchyard, which holds the remains of five Vermont

---

VERMONT FRESH NETWORK

Finding locavore food in Vermont is a piece of cake. The farm-and-chef partnership **Vermont Fresh Network** (www.vermontfresh.net) ✐ identifies restaurants that focus on sustainable, locally sourced produce, cheese and meats. Just look for the green-and-white square sticker with a plate and silverware, proudly displayed at farms and eateries throughout the state.

---

governors, numerous American Revolutionary soldiers and Vermont's beloved 20th-century poet Robert Frost (1874–1963).

Bennington Battle Monument   HISTORIC SITE
(www.benningtonbattlemonument.com; 15 Monument Circle; adult/child $3/1; ☉9am-5pm mid-Apr–Oct) Vermont's loftiest structure offers an unbeatable 360-degree view of the surrounding countryside. An elevator whisks you painlessly to the top.

Bennington Museum   MUSEUM
(☑802-447-1571; www.benningtonmuseum.org; 75 Main St; adult/child $10/free; ☉10am-5pm daily, closed Jan, closed Wed Nov-Jun) Between downtown and Old Bennington, this museum's outstanding early Americana collection includes furniture, glassware, Bennington pottery, the world's oldest surviving American Revolutionary flag and works by American folk artist 'Grandma Moses.'

🛏 Sleeping & Eating

Greenwood Lodge
& Campsites   HOSTEL, CAMPGROUND $
(☑802-442-2547; www.campvermont.com/greenwood; VT 9, Prospect Mountain; 2-person tent/RV site $27/35, dm/d from $29/70; ☉mid-May–late Oct) Nestled in the Green Mountains 8 miles east of town, this 120-acre space with three ponds holds one of Vermont's best-sited hostels and campgrounds.

Henry House   B&B $$
(☑802-442-7045; www.thehenryhouseinn.com; 1338 Murphy Rd, North Bennington; r incl breakfast $100-155; ☎) Sit on the rocking chair and watch the traffic trickle across a covered bridge at this Colonial home on 25 peaceful acres, built in 1769 by American Revolution hero William Henry.

Blue Benn Diner   DINER $
(☑802-442-5140; 314 North St; mains $5-12; ☉6am-4:45pm Mon-Fri, 7am-3:45pm Sat & Sun) This classic 1950s-era diner serves breakfast all day and a healthy mix of American and international fare. Enhancing the retro experience are little tabletop jukeboxes on which you can play Willie Nelson's 'Moonlight in Vermont' till your neighbors scream for mercy.

★Pangaea   INTERNATIONAL $$$
(☑802-442-7171; www.vermontfinedining.com; 1 Prospect St, North Bennington; lounge mains $11-23, restaurant mains $30-39; ☉lounge 5-9pm daily, restaurant 5-9pm Tue-Sat) Offering fine dining for every budget, this top-end North Ben-

nington restaurant sits side-by-side with a more casual, intimate lounge. Opt for gourmet burgers served on the riverside terrace out back, or head to the tastefully decorated dining room next door for international specialties such as Provence-herbed Delmonico steak topped with gorgonzola.

❶ Information

Bennington Area Chamber of Commerce
(☑ 800-229-0252, 802-447-3311; www. bennington.com; 100 Veterans Memorial Dr; ◷ 9am-5pm) One mile north of downtown.

Manchester

Sitting in the shadow of Mt Equinox, Manchester's been a fashionable summer retreat since the 19th century. The mountain scenery, the agreeable climate and the Batten Kill River – Vermont's best trout stream – continue to draw vacationers today.

Manchester Center, at the town's north end, sports cafes and upscale outlet stores. Further south lies dignified Manchester Village, lined with marble sidewalks, stately homes and the posh Equinox hotel.

◉ Sights & Activities

The **Appalachian Trail**, which overlaps the Long Trail (p222) in southern Vermont, passes just east of Manchester. For trail maps and details on shorter day hikes, stop by the **Green Mountain National Forest office** (☑ 802-362-2307; 2538 Depot St, Manchester Center; ◷ 8am-4:30pm Mon-Fri).

★**Hildene**   HISTORIC SITE
(☑ 800-578-1788, 802-362-1788; www.hildene.org; 1005 Hildene Rd/VT 7A; adult/child $16/5, tours $5/2; ◷ 9:30am-4:30pm) This stately 24-room Georgian Revival mansion was home to members of Abraham Lincoln's family from the 1800s until 1975, when it was converted into a museum. The collection of family heirlooms includes the hat Lincoln probably wore while delivering the Gettysburg Address. The gorgeous grounds offer 8 miles of walking and cross-country ski trails.

American Museum of Fly Fishing & Orvis   MUSEUM
(www.amff.com; 4070 Main St; adult/child $5/3; ◷ 10am-4pm Tue-Sun Jun-Oct, Tue-Sat Nov-May) This museum has perhaps the world's best display of fly-fishing equipment, including flies and rods used by Ernest Hemingway,

SCENIC DRIVE: COVERED BRIDGES

A 30-minute detour takes you across three picture-perfect covered bridges spanning the Wallomsac River at Bennington's rural north end. To get started turn west onto VT 67A just north of Bennington's tourist office and continue 3.5 miles, bearing left on Murphy Rd at the 117ft-long **Burt Henry Covered Bridge** (1840). Exhale, slow down: you're back in horse-and-buggy days. After curving to the left, Murphy Rd next loops through the **Paper Mill Bridge**, which takes its name from the 1790 mill whose gear works are still visible along the river below. Next turn right onto VT 67A, go half a mile and turn right onto Silk Rd where you'll soon cross the **Silk Road Bridge** (c 1840). Continue southeast for two more miles, bearing left at two T-intersections, to reach the Bennington Battle Monument (p218).

Bing Crosby and US president Herbert Hoover.

BattenKill Canoe   BOATING
(☑ 802-362-2800; www.battenkill.com; 6328 VT 7A, Arlington; ◷ 9am-5:30pm daily May-Oct, Wed-Fri Nov-Apr) These outfitters 6 miles south of Manchester rent paddling equipment and organize trips on the lovely Battenkill River.

Skyline Drive   SCENIC DRIVE
(☑ 802-362-1114; car & driver $15, extra passenger $5; ◷ 9am-sunset May-Oct) For spectacular views, drive to the summit of **Mt Equinox** (3816ft) via Skyline Drive, a private 5-mile toll road off VT 7A.

🛏 Sleeping & Eating

Aspen Motel   MOTEL $
(☑ 802-362-2450; www.theaspenatmanchester. com; 5669 Main St/VT 7A; r $85-150; ✳ 🕲 🗵) This family-run motel set back serenely from the road has 25 comfortable rooms and a convenient location within walking distance of Manchester Center.

Inn at Manchester   INN $$
(☑ 800-273-1793, 802-362-1793; www.innatmanchester.com; 3967 Main St/VT 7A; r/ste incl breakfast from $155/205; ✳ @ 🕲 🗵) In the heart of

town, this delightful inn and carriage house offers comfy rooms with quilts and country furnishings, along with a big front porch, afternoon teas, an expansive backyard and a wee pub.

Spiral Press Café　　　　　CAFE $
(cnr VT 11 & VT 7A; mains $6-10; ⊙7:30am-7pm; 🙴) Attached to the fabulous Northshire Bookstore, Manchester Center's favorite cafe draws locals and tourists alike with good coffee, flaky croissants and delicious panini sandwiches.

Ye Olde Tavern　　　　　AMERICAN $$$
(✆802-362-0611; www.yeoldetavern.net; 5183 Main St; mains $17-34; ⊙5-9pm) At this gracious roadside 1790s inn, hearthside dining at candlelit tables complementary the wide-ranging menu of 'Yankee favorites' that feature traditional pot roast (cooked in the tavern's own ale) or local venison (a regular Friday special).

ℹ Information

Manchester and the Mountains Regional Chamber of Commerce (✆802-362-6313, 800-362-4144; www.visitmanchestervt.com; 39 Bonnet St, Manchester Center; ⊙9am-5pm Mon-Fri, 10am-4pm Sat, 11am-3pm Sun; 🙴) Spiffy new office with free wi-fi.

Central Vermont

Nestled in the Green Mountains, central Vermont is classic small-town, big-countryside New England. Its picturesque villages and venerable ski resorts have been luring travelers for generations.

Woodstock & Quechee

The archetypal Vermont town, Woodstock has streets lined with graceful Federal- and Georgian-style houses. The Ottauquechee River, spanned by a covered bridge, meanders right through the heart of town. Quechee (*kwee*-chee), 7 miles to the northeast, is famous for its dramatic gorge, dubbed 'Vermont's Little Grand Canyon.'

⊙ Sights

★**Quechee Gorge**　　　　　CANYON
Quechee Gorge, an impressive 170ft-deep, 3000ft-long chasm cut by the Ottauquechee River, can be viewed from above or explored via nearby walking trails.

Marsh-Billings-Rockefeller National Historical Park　　　PARK
(✆802-457-3368; www.nps.gov/mabi; Woodstock; mansion tours adult/child $8/free, trails free; ⊙10am-5pm late May–Oct) Encompassing the historic home and estate of early American conservationist George Perkins Marsh, Vermont's only national park offers mansion tours every 30 minutes, plus 20 miles of trails and carriage roads for walkers, cross-country skiers and snowshoers.

Billings Farm & Museum　　　FARM
(✆802-457-2355; www.billingsfarm.org; 69 Old River Rd, Woodstock; adult/child $12/6; ⊙10am-5pm daily May-Oct, to 3:30pm Sat & Sun Nov-Feb; 🙴) 🞢 A mile north of the village green, this historic farm delights children with pretty Jersey cows and hands-on demonstrations of traditional farm life. The family-friendly seasonal events include wagon and sleigh rides, pumpkin and apple festivals and old-fashioned Halloween, Thanksgiving and Christmas celebrations.

VINS Nature Center　　WILDLIFE CENTER
(✆802-359-5000; www.vinsweb.org; US 4; adult/child $13/11; ⊙10am-5:30pm; 🙴) 🞢 Visit this nature center, a mile west of Quechee Gorge, for close-up looks at the magnificent bald eagles and other raptors that are rehabilitated here.

🛌 Sleeping

Quechee State Park　　CAMPGROUND $
(✆802-295-2990; www.vtstateparks.com/htm/quechee.htm; 5800 US 4, Quechee; tent & RV sites/lean-tos $20/27; ⊙mid-May–mid-Oct) Perched on the edge of Quechee Gorge, this 611-acre spot has 45 pine-shaded campsites and seven lean-tos.

Ardmore Inn　　　　　　B&B $$
(✆802-457-3887; www.ardmoreinn.com; 23 Pleasant St, Woodstock; r incl breakfast $155-230; 🙴) Congenial owners and lavish breakfasts enhance the considerable appeal of this stately, centrally located 1867 Victorian–Greek Revival inn with five antique-laden rooms.

Shire Riverview Motel　　　MOTEL $$
(✆802-457-2211; www.shiremotel.com; 46 Pleasant St/US 4, Woodstock; r $128-228; ❄🙴) Within walking distance of the town center, this 42-room motel features a wraparound porch overlooking the Ottauquechee River. Some rooms have fireplaces and most have river views.

✕ Eating

★ **Skunk Hollow Tavern** AMERICAN **$$**
(☑802-436-2139; www.skunkhollowtavern.com;
12 Brownsville Rd, Hartland Four Corners; mains
$13-25; ☺5pm-late Wed-Sun) Exuding rustic
historic charm, this 200-year-old crossroads
tavern 8 miles south of Woodstock serves
burgers, fish and chips or rack of lamb
downstairs at the bar, or in the more inti-
mate space upstairs. There's live music on
Friday evenings.

Osteria Pane e Salute ITALIAN **$$**
(☑802-457-4882; www.osteriapaneesalute.com;
61 Central St, Woodstock; mains $16-23; ☺6-10pm
Thu-Sun, closed Apr & Nov) This popular downtown bistro specializes in northern Italian
classics, plus thin-crust Tuscan pizza in
winter, complemented by an extensive list
of Italian wines from small boutique vineyards. Book ahead.

★ **Simon Pearce**
Restaurant NEW AMERICAN **$$$**
(☑802-295-1470; www.simonpearce.com; 1760
Main St, Quechee; lunch mains $13-18, dinner mains
$23-35; ☺11:30am-2:45pm & 5:30-9pm) Reserve
ahead for a window table suspended over
the river in this converted brick mill, where
fresh-from-the-farm local ingredients are
used to inventive effect. The restaurant's
beautiful stemware is blown by hand in the
Simon Pearce Glass workshops next door.

ℹ Information

Woodstock Area Chamber of Commerce
Welcome Center (☑802-432-1100; www.
woodstockvt.com; Mechanic St, Woodstock;
☺10am-4pm Mon-Fri, 9am-5pm Sat & Sun)
On a riverside backstreet, two blocks from the
village green.

Killington

A half-hour's drive west of Woodstock, Kil-
lington Resort (☑802-422-6200; www.kil-
lington.com; adult/senior/youth lift ticket weekend
$88/75/68, midweek $80/68/62) is New Eng-
land's answer to Vail, boasting 200 runs on
seven mountains, a vertical drop of 3150ft
and more than 30 lifts. Thanks to the world's
most extensive snowmaking system, Killing-
ton has one of the East's longest ski seasons.
Come summer, mountain bikers and hikers
claim the slopes.

Killington is jam-packed with accom-
modations, from cozy ski lodges to chain
hotels. Most are along Killington Rd, the
6-mile road that heads up the mountain
from US 4. The Killington Chamber of
Commerce (☑800-337-1928, 802-773-4181;
www.killingtonchamber.com; 2046 US 4, Killington;
☺10am-4:30pm Mon-Fri, 9am-1pm Sat) has all
the nitty-gritty.

Middlebury

Straddling the pretty falls of Otter Creek,
this former mill town nowadays revolves
around Middlebury College, whose Bread-
loaf School of English and summer language
programs lure writers and linguists from
around the world. The Addison County
Chamber of Commerce (☑802-388-7951;
www.addisoncounty.com; 93 Court St; ☺9am-5pm
Mon-Fri) has area information.

There's excellent lakeside camping, just
10 miles south of town at Branbury State
Park (☑802-247-5925; www.vtstateparks.com/
htm/branbury.htm; VT 53; campsite/lean-to
$20/27; ☺late May–mid-Oct). Back in Middle-
bury itself, the gracious 1803 Federal-style
Inn on the Green (☑888-244-7512, 802-388-
7512; www.innonthegreen.com; 71 S Pleasant St; r
incl breakfast $159-299; ☒@☎) has 11 attrac-
tive rooms that overlook the town green.

Go retro at A&W Drive-In (middaw.com;
1557 US 7; mains $3-10; ☺11:30am-8:30pm),
where carhops deliver root-beer floats,
cheeseburgers and onion rings directly
to your car window. For dining with river
views, try the high-ceilinged, student-driven
51 Main (☑802-388-8209; www.go51main.com;

NEW ENGLAND CENTRAL VERMONT

WORTH A TRIP

SCENIC DRIVE: VERMONT'S GREEN MOUNTAINS

Following Vermont's Green Mountain
spine through the rural heart of the
state, the VT 100 rambles past roll-
ing pastures speckled with cows,
tiny villages with country stores and
white-steepled churches, and verdant
mountains crisscrossed with hiking
trails and ski slopes. It's the quintes-
sential side trip for those who want to
slow down and experience Vermont's
bucolic essence. The road runs north to
south all the way from Massachusetts
to Canada. Even if your time is limited,
don't miss the scenic 45-mile stretch
between Waterbury and Stockbridge,
an easy detour off I-89.

51 Main St; mains $9-24; ⊙5pm-late Tue-Sat; 🛜), a restaurant-bar, or the outdoor terrace at Storm Cafe (✅802-388-1063; www.thestormcafe.com; 3 Mill St; mains $6-25; ⊙11:30am-2:30pm & 5-10pm Tue & Wed, 7:30am-2:30pm & 5-10pm Thu-Sat, 7:30am-2:30pm Sun), just below the waterfall.

Mad River Valley

The Mad River Valley, centered around the towns of Warren and Waitsfield, boasts two significant ski areas: Sugarbush (✅800-537-8427, 802-583-6300; www.sugarbush.com; 1840 Sugarbush Access Rd, Warren; adult lift ticket weekend/midweek $89/84; 10% discount if purchased online) and Mad River Glen (✅802-496-3551; www.madriverglen.com; VT 17; adult lift ticket weekend/midweek $71/55), in the mountains west of VT 100. Opportunities abound for cycling, canoeing, horseback riding, kayaking, gliding and other activities. Stop at the Mad River Valley Chamber of Commerce (✅800-828-4748, 802-496-3409; www.madrivervalley.com; 4061 Main St, Waitsfield; ⊙8am-5pm Mon-Fri) for a mountain of information.

Northern Vermont

Boasting some of New England's lushest and prettiest landscapes, northern Vermont cradles the fetching state capital of Montpelier, the ski mecca of Stowe, the vibrant college town of Burlington and the state's highest mountains.

Montpelier

America's smallest capital, Montpelier is a thoroughly likable town of period buildings backed by verdant hills and crowned by the gold-domed 19th-century State House (www.vtstatehouse.org; 115 State St; ⊙tours 10am-3:30pm Mon-Fri, 11am-2:30pm Sat Jul-Oct) FREE. Tours of the capitol building run on the half hour. Right across the street, the Capitol Region Visitors Center (✅802-828-5981; cri.center@state.vt.us; 134 State St; ⊙6am-5pm Mon-Fri, 9am-5pm Sat & Sun) has tourist information.

Bookstores, boutiques and restaurants throng the town's twin thoroughfares, State and Main Sts. Forget about junk food – Montpelier prides itself on being the only state capital in the USA without a McDonald's! The bakery-cafe La Brioche (www.neci.edu/labrioche; 89 Main St; pastries & sandwiches $2-8; ⊙7am-5pm Mon-Fri, to 3pm Sat), run by students from Montpelier's New England

Culinary Institute, gets an A-plus for its innovative sandwiches and flaky French pastries. Other terrific options include Hunger Mountain Co-op (✅802-223-8000; hungermountain.coop; 623 Stone Cutters Way; deli items $5-10; ⊙8am-8pm), a health-food store and deli with cafe tables perched above a river, and Threepenny Taproom (www.threepennytaproom.com; 108 Main St; mains $9-18; ⊙11am-late Mon-Fri, noon-late Sat, noon-5pm Sun), with 25 microbrews on tap and locally sourced bistro fare.

Stowe & Around

With Vermont's highest peak, Mt Mansfield (4393ft), as its backdrop, Stowe ranks as Vermont's classiest ski destination. It packs all the Alpine thrills you could ask for – both cross-country and downhill skiing, with gentle runs for novices and challenging drops for pros. Cycling, hiking and kayaking take center stage in the summer. Lodgings and eateries are thick along VT 108 (Mountain Rd), which continues northwest from Stowe village to the ski resorts.

❍ Sights & Activities

In warm weather, don't miss the drive through dramatic Smugglers Notch, northwest of Stowe on VT 108 (closed by heavy snows in winter). This narrow pass slices through mountains with 1000ft cliffs on either side. Roadside trails lead into the surrounding high country.

★ Ben & Jerry's
Ice Cream Factory   FACTORY
(✅802-882-1240; www.benjerrys.com; 1281 VT 100, Waterbury; adult/child $4/free; ⊙9am-9pm Jul–mid-Aug, 9am-7pm mid-Aug–Oct, 10am-6pm Nov-Jun; ♿) A far cry from the abandoned Burlington gas station where ice-cream pioneers Ben Cohen and Jerry Greenfield first set up shop in 1978, this legendary factory, just north of I-89 in Waterbury, still draws crowds for tours that include a campy moovie and a taste tease of the latest flavor. Behind the factory, a mock cemetery holds 'graves' of Holy Cannoli and other longforgotten flavors.

Long Trail   HIKING
Vermont's 300-mile Long Trail, which passes west of Stowe, follows the crest of the Green Mountains and runs the entire length of Vermont with rustic cabins, lean-tos and campsites along the way. Its caretaker, the Green Mountain Club (✅802-244-7037; www.

greenmountainclub.org; 4711 Waterbury-Stowe Rd/ VT 100) 🖉, has full details on the Long Trail and shorter day hikes around Stowe.

★ **Stowe Recreation Path** OUTDOORS
(www.stowe-village.com/BikePath; 🖉) This flat to gently rolling 5.5-mile path offers a fabulous four-season escape for all ages, as it rambles through woods, meadows and outdoor sculpture gardens along the West Branch of the Little River, with sweeping views of Mt Mansfield unfolding in the distance. Bike, walk, skate, ski and/or swim in one of the swimming holes along the way.

Stowe Mountain Resort SKIING
(☑888-253-4849, 802-253-3000; www.stowe. com; 5781 Mountain Rd) This venerable resort encompasses two major mountains, Mt Mansfield (vertical drop 2360ft) and Spruce Peak (1550ft). It offers 48 beautiful trails – 16% beginner, 59% intermediate and 25% for hard-core backcountry skiers.

Umiak Outdoor Outfitters OUTDOORS
(☑802-253-2317; www.umiak.com; 849 S Main St; ⊙9am-6pm) Rents kayaks, snowshoes and telemark skis, offers boating lessons and leads boating and moonlight snowshoe tours.

AJ's Ski & Sports EQUIPMENT RENTAL
(☑800-226-6257, 802-253-4593; www.stowe-sports.com; 350 Mountain Rd; ⊙10am-6pm) Rents bikes, kayaks, skiing and snowboarding equipment in the village center.

🛏 Sleeping

Smugglers Notch State Park CAMPGROUND $
(☑802-253-4014; www.vtstateparks.com/htm/ smugglers.htm; 6443 Mountain Rd; tent & RV sites $20, lean-tos $27; ⊙mid-May–mid-Oct) This 35-acre park, 8 miles northwest of Stowe, is perched on the mountainside, with 20 tent and trailer sites and 14 lean-tos.

Fiddler's Green Inn INN $
(☑800-882-5346, 802-253-8124; www.fiddlers-greeninn.com; 4859 Mountain Rd; r incl breakfast midweek/weekend $90/125; ❄) A throwback to simpler times, this unembellished 1820s farmhouse a mile below the ski lifts has rustic pine walls, a fieldstone fireplace and seven humble guest rooms, the best of which overlook the river out back.

Stowe Motel & Snowdrift MOTEL, APARTMENT $$
(☑800-829-7629, 802-253-7629; www.stowemo-tel.com; 2043 Mountain Rd; r $85-200, ste $182-240, apt $162-250; @ 🛜 🏊) With units ranging from simple to deluxe, this motel set on 16 acres comes complete with a tennis court, hot tubs, lawn games and free bicycles or snowshoes for use on the adjacent Stowe Recreation Path.

Trapp Family Lodge LODGE $$$
(☑800-826-7000, 802-253-8511; www.trappfamily. com; 700 Trapp Hill Rd; r from $275; @ 🛜 🏊) Surrounded by wide-open fields and mountain vistas, this Austrian-style chalet, built by Maria von Trapp of *Sound of Music* fame, boasts Stowe's best setting. Traditional lodge rooms are complemented by guesthouses scattered across the 2700-acre property. A network of trails offers stupendous hiking, snowshoeing and cross-country skiing.

🍴 Eating

Harvest Market MARKET $
(www.harvestatstowe.com; 1031 Mountain Rd; ⊙7am-7pm) Before heading for the hills, stop here for coffee, pastries, Vermont cheeses, sandwiches, gourmet deli items, wines and local microbrews.

Pie-casso PIZZERIA $$
(☑802-253-4411; www.piecasso.com; 1899 Mountain Rd; mains $9-22; ⊙11am-9pm) Portobello panini and organic arugula chicken salad supplement the menu of excellent hand-tossed pizzas. There's a bar and live music too.

Gracie's Restaurant BURGERS $$
(☑802-253-8741; www.gracies.com; 18 Edson Hill Rd; mains $11-35; ⊙5-9:30pm) Halfway between the village and the mountain, this animated, dog-themed eatery serves big burgers, hand-cut steaks, Waldorf salad and garlic-laden shrimp scampi.

★ **Hen of the Wood** AMERICAN $$$
(☑802-244-7300; www.henofthewood.com; 92 Stowe St, Waterbury; mains $18-32; ⊙5-10pm Mon-Sat) 🖉 Arguably the finest dining in northern Vermont, this chef-driven restaurant in Waterbury gets rave reviews for its innovative farm-to-table cuisine. The setting in a historic grist mill rivals the extraordinary food, which features densely flavored dishes such as smoked duck breast and sheep's-milk gnocchi.

ℹ Information

Stowe Area Association (☑802-253-7321; www.gostowe.com; 51 Main St; ⊙9am-5pm Mon-Sat, to 8pm Jun-Oct & Jan-Mar) In the heart of the village.

Burlington

This hip college town on the shores of scenic Lake Champlain is one of those places that makes you think, wouldn't it be great to live here? The cafe and club scene is on par with a much bigger city, while the slow, friendly pace is pure small town. And where else can you walk to the end of Main St and paddle off in a kayak?

○ Sights

Burlington's shops, cafes and pubs are concentrated around Church St Marketplace, a bustling brick-lined pedestrian mall midway between the University of Vermont and Lake Champlain.

★ Shelburne Museum   MUSEUM

(☑802-985-3346; www.shelburnemuseum.org; US 7, Shelburne; adult/child $22/11, after 3pm $15/7; ☉10am-5pm mid-May–Oct; ⊞) This extraordinary 45-acre museum, 9 miles south of Burlington, showcases a Smithsonian-caliber collection of Americana – 150,000 objects in all. The mix of folk art, decorative arts and more is housed in 39 historic buildings, most of them relocated here from other parts of New England to ensure their preservation.

Shelburne Farms   FARM

(☑802-985-8686; www.shelburnefarms.org; 1611 Harbor Rd, Shelburne; adult/child $8/5; ☉9am-5:30pm mid-May–mid-Oct, 10am-5pm mid-Oct–mid-May; ⊞) ✐ This 1400-acre estate, designed by landscape architect Frederick Law Olmsted (who also designed New York's Central Park), was both a country house for the aristocratic Webb family and a working farm, with stunning lakefront perspectives.

LOCAL KNOWLEDGE

BURLINGTON'S SECRET GARDEN

Hidden away less than 2 miles from Burlington's city center is one of Vermont's most idyllic green spaces. Tucked among the lazy curves of the Winooski River, the **Intervale Center** (www.intervale.org; 180 Intervale Rd) FREE encompasses a dozen organic farms and a delightful trail network, open to the public 365 days a year for hiking, cycling, skiing, berry picking and more; check its website for details.

Sample the farm's superb Cheddar cheese, tour the magnificent barns, walk the network of trails, and enjoy afternoon tea or dinner at its award-winning inn (p225).

Echo Lake Aquarium & Science Center   SCIENCE CENTER

(☑802-864-1848; www.echovermont.org; 1 College St; adult/child $13.50/10.50; ☉10am-5pm; ⊞) Examining the colorful past, present and future of Lake Champlain, this lakeside museum features a multitude of small aquariums and rotating science exhibits with plenty of hands-on, kid-friendly activities.

Magic Hat Brewery   BREWERY

(☑802-658-2739; www.magichat.net; 5 Bartlett Bay Rd, South Burlington; ☉10am-6pm Mon-Sat, noon-5pm Sun) Drink in the history of one of Vermont's most dynamic microbreweries on the fun, free, self-guided tour. Afterwards, sample a few experimental brews from the four dozen taps in the on-site Growler Bar.

🏃 Activities

Ready for outdoor adventures? Head to the waterfront, where options include boating on **Lake Champlain** and cycling, in-line skating and walking on the 7.5-mile shorefront **Burlington Bike Path**. Jump-off points and equipment rentals for all these activities are within a block of each other near the waterfront end of Main St.

Local Motion   BICYCLE RENTAL

(☑802-652-2453; www.localmotion.org; 1 Steele St; bicycles per day $30; ☉10am-6pm; ⊞) ✐ Rents quality bikes.

Whistling Man Schooner Company   SAILING

(☑802-598-6504; www.whistlingman.com; Boathouse, College St, at Lake Champlain; 2hr cruises adult/child $40/25; ☉3 trips daily, late May–early Oct) Explore Lake Champlain on the *Friend Ship*, a 17-passenger, 43-ft sailboat.

🛏 Sleeping

Burlington's budget and midrange motels are on the outskirts of town, clustered along Shelburne Rd (US 7) in South Burlington, Williston Rd (US 2) east of I-89 exit 14, and US 7 north of Burlington in Colchester (I-89 exit 16).

North Beach Campground   CAMPGROUND $

(☑802-862-0942; www.enjoyburlington.com; 60 Institute Rd; tent/RV site $26/36; ☉May–mid-Oct; ☎) Two miles north of downtown, this wonderful spot on Lake Champlain offers 69 tent sites on 45 wooded acres, with picnic tables, fire rings, hot showers, a playground, beach and bike path.

Burlington Hostel
HOSTEL $

(802-540-3043; www.theburlingtonhostel.com; 53 Main St; dm incl breakfast midweek/weekend $35/40; ❊@🛜) Just minutes from Church St and Lake Champlain, Burlington's hostel accommodates up to 48 guests and offers both mixed and women-only dorms.

Lang House
B&B $$

(802-652-2500; www.langhouse.com; 360 Main St; r incl breakfast $145-245; ❊🛜) Burlington's most elegant B&B occupies a centrally located, tastefully restored 19th-century Victorian home and carriage house. Reserve ahead for one of the 3rd-floor rooms with lake views.

Willard Street Inn
INN $$

(802-651-8710; www.willardstreetinn.com; 349 S Willard St; r incl breakfast $150-265; 🛜) Perched on a hill within easy walking distance of the University of Vermont and the Church St Marketplace, this late-19th-century Queen Anne–Georgian Revival mansion has a fine-wood and cut-glass elegance, with several guest rooms overlooking Lake Champlain.

★ Inn at Shelburne Farms
INN $$$

(802-985-8498; www.shelburnefarms.org/stay dine; 1611 Harbor Rd, Shelburne; r with private/without bath from $289/169, cottage $289-430, guesthouse $436-926; 🛜) At this historic 1400-acre lakefront estate (p224), 7 miles south of Burlington, guests stay in a gracious, welcoming country manor house, or in four independent, kitchen-equipped cottages and guesthouses scattered across the property. The attached farm-to-table restaurant is superb.

✖ Eating

On Saturday mornings, don't miss Burlington's thriving farmers market in City Hall Park.

★ Penny Cluse Cafe
CAFE $

(www.pennycluse.com; 169 Cherry St; mains $7-11; ⏱6:45am-3pm Mon-Fri, 8am-3pm Sat & Sun) One of Burlington's most popular downtown eateries whips up pancakes, biscuits and gravy, omelets and tofu scrambles, along with sandwiches, fish tacos, salads and the best *chile relleno* you'll find east of the Mississippi. Expect long lines on weekends.

City Market
MARKET $

(www.citymarket.coop; 82 S Winooski Ave; ⏱7am-11pm) If there's a natural-foods heaven, it must look something like this: chock-full of local produce and products (with over 1600 Vermont-based producers represented) and a huge takeout deli.

Stone Soup
VEGETARIAN $

(www.stonesoupvt.com; 211 College St; buffet per lb $9.75, light meals $5-10; ⏱7am-9pm Mon-Fri, 9am-9pm Sat; 🛜🖋) Best known for its excellent vegetarian- and vegan-friendly buffet, this longtime local favorite also features homemade soups, sandwiches on home-baked bread, a salad bar and pastries.

★ American Flatbread
PIZZERIA $$

(www.americanflatbread.com/restaurants/burlington-vt; 115 St Paul St; flatbreads $14-23; ⏱restaurant 11:30am-2:30pm & 5-10pm, taproom 11:30am-late) Its central downtown location, great microbrews on tap, a back-alley outdoor terrace and scrumptious wood-fired flatbread (thin-crust pizza) topped with organic local ingredients make this a perennial local favorite.

Daily Planet
INTERNATIONAL $$

(802-862-9647; www.dailyplanet15.com; 15 Center St; mains $11-20; ⏱4-11pm Mon-Sat, 10am-2pm & 4-11pm Sun; 🛜🖋) This stylish downtown haunt serves everything from burgers with exotic trimmings to barbecued duck confit to Prince Edward Island mussels to pecan-crusted rainbow trout. The bar stays open late nightly, and there's a good Sunday brunch.

Leunig's Bistro
FRENCH $$$

(802-863-3759; www.leunigsbistro.com; 115 Church St; lunch mains $10-17, dinner mains $21-32; ⏱11am-10pm Mon-Fri, 9am-10pm Sat & Sun) With sidewalk seating and an elegant, tin-ceilinged dining room, this convivial Parisian-style brasserie is a longstanding Burlington staple. It's as much fun for the people-watching (windows face busy Church St Marketplace) as for the excellent wine list and food.

🍸 Drinking & Entertainment

The free weekly *Seven Days* (www.7dvt.com) has event and entertainment listings.

Radio Bean
BAR, CAFE

(www.radiobean.com; 8 N Winooski Ave; ⏱8am-2am; 🛜) This funky cafe-bar features its own low-power FM radio station, a trendy attached eatery serving international street food and live performances nightly that include jazz, acoustic music and poetry readings.

Vermont Pub & Brewery MICROBREWERY
(www.vermontbrewery.com; 144 College St; ⊙ 11:30am-1am Sun-Wed, to 2am Thu-Sat) Specialty and seasonal brews, including weekly limited releases, are made on the premises, accompanied by British-style pub fare (mains $6 to $16).

Splash at the Boathouse BAR
(☑ 802-658-2244; www.splashattheboathouse.com; 0 College St; ⊙ 11:30am-2am) Perched atop Burlington's floating boathouse, this restaurant-bar with stellar views over Lake Champlain is perfect for kicking back with an evening cocktail or microbrew at sunset.

Nectar's LIVE MUSIC
(www.liveatnectars.com; 188 Main St; ⊙ 7pm-2am Sun-Tue, 5pm-2am Wed-Sat) Indie darlings Phish got their start here, and the joint still rocks out with a mix of theme nights and live acts.

Red Square LIVE MUSIC
(www.redsquarevt.com; 136 Church St; ⊙ 4pm-late Sun-Thu, 2pm-late Fri & Sat) With a stylish Soho-like ambience, this Church St institution is best in summertime when live bands play on its outdoor stage.

🛍 Shopping

You'll find boutiques and smart craft shops along Church St Marketplace. Don't miss the **Frog Hollow Craft Center** (www.froghollow.org; 85 Church St), a collective featuring some of the finest work in Burlington.

ℹ Information

Fletcher Allen Health Care (☑ 802-847-0000; www.fletcherallen.org; 111 Colchester Ave; ⊙ 24hr) Vermont's largest hospital.
Lake Champlain Regional Chamber of Commerce (☑ 877-686-5253, 802-863-3489; www.vermont.org; 60 Main St; ⊙ 8am-5pm Mon-Fri, 9am-5pm Sat & Sun) Downtown tourist office.

ℹ Getting There & Away

Greyhound (☑ 800-231-2222; www.greyhound.com; 219 S Winooski St) offers bus service to Boston and Montreal. **Amtrak's Vermonter train** (☑ 800-872-7245; www.amtrak.com/vermonter-train) runs south to Brattleboro, New York City and Washington DC. **Lake Champlain Ferries** (☑ 802-864-9804; www.ferries.com; King St Dock; adult/child/car $8/3.10/30) runs summer-only ferries across the lake to Port Kent, NY (one hour).

NEW HAMPSHIRE

You're gonna like the scale of things in the Granite State: the towns are small and personable, the mountains majestic and rugged. The heart of New Hampshire is unquestionably the granite peaks of the White Mountain National Forest. Outdoor enthusiasts of all stripes flock to New England's highest range (6288ft at Mt Washington) for cold-weather skiing, summer hiking and the brilliant fall foliage scenery. Oh, and don't be fooled by that politically conservative label that people stick on the state. The state mantra, 'Live Free or Die,' indeed rings from every automobile license plate but, truth be told, residents here pride themselves on their independent spirit more than right-wing politics.

History

Named in 1629 after the English county of Hampshire, New Hampshire was one of the first American colonies to declare its independence from England in 1776. In the 19th century industrialization boom, the state's leading city, Manchester, became such a powerhouse that its textile mills were the world's largest.

New Hampshire played a high-profile role in 1944 when president Franklin D Roosevelt gathered leaders from 44 Allied nations at remote Bretton Woods for a conference to rebuild global capitalism. It was at the Bretton Woods Conference that the World Bank and the International Monetary Fund emerged.

In 1963 New Hampshire, long famed for its anti-tax sentiments, found another way to raise revenue – by becoming the first state in the USA to have a legal lottery.

ℹ Information

Welcome centers are situated at major state border crossings, including one at the south end of I-93 that's open 24/7.
New Hampshire Division of Parks & Recreation (☑ 603-271-3556; www.nhstateparks.org) Offers information on a statewide bicycle route system and a very comprehensive camping guide.
New Hampshire Division of Travel & Tourism Development (☑ 603-271-2665; www.visitnh.gov) Information including ski conditions and fall foliage reports.
Union Leader (www.unionleader.com) The state's largest newspaper.

Portsmouth

America's third-oldest city (1623), Portsmouth wears its history on its sleeve. Its roots are in shipbuilding, but New Hampshire's sole coastal city also has a hip, youthful energy. The old maritime warehouses along the harbor now house cafes and boutiques. Elegant period homes built by shipbuilding tycoons have been converted into B&Bs.

◉ Sights & Activities

Strawbery Banke Museum   MUSEUM
(☏ 603-433-1100; www.strawberybanke.org; cnr Hancock & Marcy Sts; adult/child $17.50/10; ⊙ 10am-5pm May-Oct) Spread across a 10-acre site, the Strawbery Banke Museum is an eclectic blend of period homes that date back to the 1690s. Costumed guides recount tales of events that took place among the 40 buildings (10 furnished). Strawbery Banke includes **Pitt Tavern** (1766), a hotbed of American revolutionary sentiment, **Goodwin Mansion** (a grand 19th-century house from Portsmouth's most prosperous time) and **Abbott's Little Corner Store** (1943). The admission ticket is good for two consecutive days.

USS Albacore   MUSEUM
(☏ 603-436-3680; http://ussalbacore.org; 600 Market St; adult/child $6/3; ⊙ 9:30am-5pm Jun–mid-Oct, to 4pm Thu-Mon mid-Oct–May) Like a fish out of water, this 205ft-long submarine is now a beached museum on a grassy lawn. Launched from Portsmouth Naval Shipyard in 1953, the *Albacore* was once the world's fastest submarine.

Isles of Shoals Steamship Co   CRUISE
(☏ 603-431-5500; www.islesofshoals.com; 315 Market St; adult/child $28/18; ⊛) From mid-June to October the company runs an excellent tour of the harbor and the historic Isles of Shoals aboard a replica 1900s ferry. Look into the all-day whale-watching and shorter sunset, hip-hop and dinner cruises.

⛱ Sleeping

Ale House Inn   INN $$
(☏ 603-431-7760; www.alehouseinn.com; 121 Bow St; r $150-280; ℗✨) This brick warehouse for the Portsmouth Brewing Company is now Portsmouth's snazziest boutique, fusing contemporary design with comfort. Rooms are modern with clean lines of white and flatscreen TVs, plush tan sofas fill the suites, and deluxe rooms feature an in-room iPad. Rates include use of vintage cruising bikes.

Inn at Strawbery Banke   B&B $$
(☏ 603-436-7242; www.innatstrawberybanke.com; 314 Court St; r incl breakfast $170-190; ℗✨) Set amid the historic buildings of Strawbery Banke, this colonial charmer has seven small but attractive rooms, each uniquely set with quilted bedspreads and brass or canopy beds.

✗ Eating & Drinking

Head to the intersection of Market and Congress Sts, where restaurants and cafes are thick on the ground.

Friendly Toast   DINER $
(113 Congress St; mains $7-12; ⊙ 7am-10pm Sun-Thu, to 2am Fri & Sat; ✨✎) Fun, whimsical furnishings set the scene for filling sandwiches, omelets, Tex-Mex and vegetarian fare at this retro diner. The breakfast menu is huge and is served around the clock – a good thing since weekend morning waits can be long.

NEW HAMPSHIRE FACTS

Nicknames Granite State, White Mountain State

Population 1.3 million

Area 8968 sq miles

Capital city Concord (population 42,800)

Other cities Manchester (population 109,800), Portsmouth (1.3 million)

Sales tax None

Birthplace of America's first astronaut Alan Shepard (1923–98), *The Da Vinci Code* author Dan Brown (b 1964)

Home of The highest mountains in northeastern USA

Politics New England's most Republican state

Famous for Being the first to vote in US presidential primaries, which gives the state enormous political influence for its size

Most extreme state motto Live Free or Die

Driving distances Boston to Portsmouth 60 miles, Portsmouth to Hanover 118 miles

★ **Black Trumpet Bistro**   INTERNATIONAL **$$$**
(☑ 603-431-0887; www.blacktrumpetbistro.com; 29 Ceres St; mains $17-38; ⊘5:30-9pm) With brick walls and oozing sophisticated ambience, this bistro serves unique combinations (anything from housemade sausages infused with cocoa beans to seared haddock with yuzu and miso). The full menu is also available at its wine bar upstairs, which whips up equally inventive cocktails.

Jumpin' Jays Fish Cafe   SEAFOOD **$$$**
(☑ 603-766-3474; www.jumpinjays.com; 150 Congress St; mains $20-28; ⊘5:30-10pm) This exceptional seafood cafe offers fresh catches of the day simply grilled or seared (with a choice of six sauces, such as 'tamarind and guava' or 'citrus and Dijon'), plus unconventional twists: bouillabaisse with lemongrass and coconut, or haddock Piccata. Add a raw bar and a huge warm and cold appetizer menu plus a buzzing modern space and Jumpin' Jays wins on all counts.

Portsmouth Brewery   MICROBREWERY
(www.portsmouthbrewery.com; 56 Market St; ⊘11:30am-12:30am; 🐾) Classically set with tin ceilings and exposed brick walls, this airy brewpub serves excellent homegrown pilsners, porters and ales. Come for the beer, not for the pub fare.

Thirsty Moose Taphouse   PUB
(www.thirstymoosetaphouse.com; 21 Congress St; bar snacks $3-11, brunch $10-17; ⊘11:30-1am Mon-Sat, 10:30am-1pm Sun) More of a bar than a restaurant, this convivial spot pours more than 100 beers on tap, leaning heavily on New England brews (and a staff that can walk you through most – it's impressive). A fine spot to kick back and relax, bites include poutine (a Montreal fave: fries drenched in cheese and gravy), corn dogs and a handful of salads.

❶ Information

Greater Portsmouth Chamber of Commerce
(☑ 603-436-3988; www.portsmouthchamber. org; 500 Market St; ⊘8:30am-5pm Mon-Fri) Also operates an information kiosk in the city center at Market Sq.

Monadnock State Park

The 3165ft Mt Monadnock (www.nh-stateparks.org; NH 124; adult/child $4/2), in the southwestern corner of the state, is the most hiked summit in New England.

'Mountain That Stands Alone' in Algonquian, Monadnock is relatively isolated from other peaks, which means hikers who make the 5-mile round-trip to the summit are rewarded with unspoiled views of three states.

Lake Winnipesaukee

A popular summer retreat for families looking for a break from the city, New Hampshire's largest lake stretches 28 miles in length, contains 274 islands and offers abundant opportunities for swimming, boating and fishing.

Weirs Beach

This lakeside town dishes up a curious slice of honky-tonk Americana with its celebrated video arcades, mini-golf courses and go-cart tracks. The Lakes Region Chamber of Commerce (☑ 603-524-5531; www.lakesregion-chamber.org; 383 S Main St, Laconia ; ⊘8:30am-4:30pm Mon-Fri) supplies information on the area.

Mount Washington Cruises (☑ 603-366-5531; www.cruisenh.com; cruises $27-43) operates scenic lake cruises, the pricier ones with champagne brunch, from Weirs Beach aboard the old-fashioned MS *Mount Washington*.

Winnipesaukee Scenic Railroad (☑ 603-279-5253; www.hoborr.com; adult/child $15/12) offers train rides along the shore of Lake Winnipesaukee.

Wolfeboro

On the opposite side of Lake Winnipesaukee, and a world away from the ticky-tacky commercialism of Weirs Beach, sits genteel Wolfeboro. Anointing itself 'the oldest summer resort in America,' the town is awash with graceful period buildings, including several that are open to the public. The Wolfeboro Chamber of Commerce (☑ 603-569-2200; www.wolfeborochamber.com; 32 Central Ave; ⊘10am-3pm Mon-Fri, to noon Sat), in the old train station, has the scoop on everything from boat rentals to lakeside beaches.

Wolfeboro is home to the Great Waters Music Festival (☑ 603-569-7710; www.greatwaters.org; ⊘Jul & Aug), featuring folk, jazz and blues artists at venues throughout town.

Off NH 28, about 4 miles north of town, is lakeside **Wolfeboro Campground** (603-569-9881; www.wolfeborocampground.com; 61 Haines Hill Rd; tent & RV sites $32; mid-May–mid-Oct) with 50 wooded campsites.

The classic stay is the **Wolfeboro Inn** (603-569-3016; www.wolfeboroinn.com; 90 N Main St; r incl breakfast $189-290;), the town's principal lodging since 1812. Some of the rooms have balconies overlooking the lake. The inn's cozy pub, **Wolfe's Tavern** (mains $10-26; 8am-10pm), offers a varied menu ranging from pizza to seafood. The old-school **Wolfeboro Diner** (5 N Main St; mains $5-12; 7am-2pm) hits the mark with juicy cheeseburgers and straightforward breakfast fare at honest prices.

White Mountains

What the Rockies are to Colorado the White Mountains are to New Hampshire. New England's loftiest mountain range is a magnet for adventurers, with boundless opportunities for everything from hiking and kayaking to skiing. Those who prefer to take it in from the comfort of a car seat won't be disappointed either, as scenic drives wind over rugged mountains rippling with waterfalls, sheer rock faces and sharply cut gorges.

You'll find information on the White Mountains at ranger stations throughout the **White Mountain National Forest** (www.fs.fed.us/r9/white) and chambers of commerce in the towns along the way.

Waterville Valley

In the shadow of Mt Tecumseh, Waterville Valley was developed as a resort community during the latter half of the 20th century, when hotels, condos, golf courses and ski trails were all laid out. It's very much a planned community and arguably a bit too groomed but there's plenty to do, including tennis, indoor ice skating, cycling and other family fun. The **Waterville Valley Region Chamber of Commerce** (603-726-3804; www.watervillevalleyregion.com; 12 Vintinner Rd, Campton; 9am-5pm), off I-93 exit 28, has all the details.

Like many New England ski mountains, the **Waterville Valley Ski Area** (www.waterville.com; lift ticket adult/student $63/53) is open in the summer for mountain biking and hiking.

Mt Washington Valley

Stretching north from the eastern terminus of the Kancamagus Hwy (p230), Mt Washington Valley includes the towns of Conway, North Conway, Intervale, Glen, Jackson and Bartlett. Every conceivable outdoor activity is available. The area's hub and biggest town, North Conway, is also a center for outlet shopping, including some earthy stores including LL Bean.

🏃 Activities

★ **Conway Scenic Railroad**   TRAIN
(603-356-5251; www.conwayscenic.com; NH 16, North Conway; Notch Train adult/child from $27/16, Valley Train from $14/10; daily May-Oct, Sat & Sun Apr & Nov;) The **Notch Train**, built in 1874 and restored in 1974, offers New England's most scenic journey. The spectacular five- to 5½-hour trip passes through Crawford Notch. Accompanying live commentary recounts the railroad's history and folklore. Reservations required.

Alternatively, the same company operates the antique steam **Valley Train**, which makes a shorter journey south through the Mt Washington Valley, stopping in Conway and Bartlett. Sunset trains, dining trains and other special events are all available.

Echo Lake State Park   PARK
(www.nhstateparks.org; River Rd; adult/child $4/2) Two miles west of North Conway via River Rd, this placid mountain lake lies at the foot of **White Horse Ledge**, a sheer rock wall. A scenic trail circles the lake. There is also a mile-long auto road and hiking trail leading to the 700ft-high

---

WORTH A TRIP

NEW HAMPSHIRE WINE & CHEESE TRAILS

Watch out, Vermont. New Hampshire's small cheese producers are multiplying and small wineries are popping up left and right. The tourism board has put together an excellent leaflet, *New Hampshire Wine & Cheese Trails*, detailing three itineraries across 21 farms and wineries, including a few cider producers. Pick it up from any tourist office or download it from the web (http://agriculture.nh.gov/publications/documents/winecheesepdf.pdf).

DON'T MISS

SCENIC DRIVE: WHITE MOUNTAIN NATIONAL FOREST

One of New England's finest, the 35-mile Kancamagus Highway (NH 112) is a beauty of a road cutting through the White Mountain National Forest (p229) between Conway and Lincoln. Laced with excellent hiking trails, scenic lookouts and swimmable streams, this is as natural as it gets. There's absolutely no development along the entire highway, which reaches its highest point at Kancamagus Pass (2868ft).

You can pick up brochures and hiking maps at the Saco Ranger District Office (☑603-447-5448; 33 Kancamagus Hwy; ◷8am-4:30pm) at the eastern end of the highway near Conway.

Coming from Conway, 6.5 miles west of the Saco ranger station, you'll see Lower Falls on the north side of the road – stop here for the view and a swim. No trip along this highway is complete without taking the 20-minute hike to the breathtaking cascade of Sabbaday Falls; the trail begins at Mile 15 on the south side of the road. The best place to spot moose is along the shores of Lily Pond; stop at the roadside overview at Mile 18. At the Lincoln Woods ranger station, which is near the Mile 29 marker, cross the suspension footbridge over the river and hike 3 miles to Franconia Falls, the finest swimming hole in the entire national forest, complete with a natural rock slide. Parking anywhere along the highway costs $3 per day (honor system) or $5 per week; just fill out an envelope at any of the parking areas.

The White Mountain National Forest is ideal for campers, and you'll find several campgrounds run by the forest service, accessible from the Kancamagus Hwy. Most are on a first-come, first-served basis; pick up a list at the Saco ranger station.

Cathedral Ledge, with panoramic White Mountains views. Both Cathedral Ledge and White Horse Ledge are excellent for rock climbing. This is also a fine spot for swimming and picnicking.

Saco Bound   CANOEING
(☑603-447-2177; www.sacobound.com; 2561 E Main/US 302, Conway; rentals per day $28) Saco Bound Inc rents out canoes and kayaks and organizes guided canoe trips, including the introductory trip to Weston's Bridge ($22) and overnight camping trips.

Attitash   SKIING
(☑603-374-2368; www.attitash.com; US 302, Bartlett; weekends & holidays lift ticket adult/child 13-18 yr/child 6-12 yr & seniors $70/55/50, weekdays $63/48/39) West of Glen, you can play and stay at Attitash. The resort includes two mountains, Attitash and Bear Peak, which offer a vertical drop of 1750ft, 12 lifts and 70 ski trails. Half the trails are intermediate level, while the other half are equally divided between expert and beginner level. From mid-June to mid-October the resort offers a slew of activities, including an alpine slide, horseback riding, mountain biking, bungy trampolines, a chair-lift ride, a water slide, a climbing wall and a mountain coaster (a roller coaster that barrels down the mountain).

Black Mountain Ski Area   SKIING
(☑603-383-4490; www.blackmt.com; NH 16B; weekends & holidays lift ticket adult/child $49/32, weekdays $35/25; ⛷) This smaller ski area has a vertical drop of 1100ft. Forty trails – about equally divided between beginner, intermediate and expert slopes – are served by four lifts. This is a good place for beginners and families with small children.

🛏 Sleeping

North Conway in particular is thick with sleeping options from resort hotels to cozy inns.

White Mountains Hostel   HOSTEL $
(☑603-447-1001; www.whitemountainshostel.com; 36 Washington St, Conway; dm/r $24/60; ◉) 🌱 Set in an early-1900s farmhouse, New Hampshire's only youth hostel is this cheery place off Main St (NH 16) in Conway. The environmentally conscientious hostel has five bedrooms with bunk beds, four family-size rooms and a communal lounge and kitchen. Excellent hiking and cycling opportunities are just outside the door, and canoeists can easily portage to two nearby rivers. Our only gripe is the location, which puts you 5 miles south of the action in North Conway. This place is smoke- and alcohol-free.

Saco River Camping Area CAMPGROUND $
(✆603-356-3360; www.sacorivercampingarea.
com; 1550 NH 16; tent/RV sites $33/39; ☺May–
mid-Oct; 🛜 🔲) A riverside campground, away
from the highway, with 140 wooded and
open sites as well as rustic huts (literally
walls and a roof; no electricity or kitchen).
Canoe and kayak rental available.

Cranmore Inn B&B $$
(✆603-356-5502; www.cranmoreinn.com; 80 Kear-
sarge St; r incl breakfast $99-169; 🛜 🔲) The Cran-
more has been operating as a country inn
since 1863, and it has been known as reliably
good value for much of that time. Traditional
country decor predominates, meaning lots
of floral and frills. In addition to standard
rooms, there is one two-room suite and one
apartment with a kitchen, and there's a hot
tub on site, perfect for post-hike sore muscles.

🍴 Eating

Peach's CAFE $
(www.peachesnorthconway.com; 2506 White Moun-
tain Hwy; mains $6-11; ☺7am-2:30pm) Away
from the in-town bustle, this perennially
popular little house is an excellent option for
soups, sandwiches and breakfast. Who can
resist fruit-smothered waffles and pancakes
and fresh-brewed coffee, served in some-
body's cozy living room?

**★Moat Mountain Smoke
House & Brewing Co** PUB $$
(✆603-356-6381; www.moatmountain.com; 3378
White Mountain Hwy; mains $10-24; ☺11:30am-
11pm) Come here for a variety of American
with a nod to southern fare: BBQ Reuben
sandwiches, bowls of beefy chili, juicy burgers, luscious salads, wood-grilled pizzas and
cornmeal-crusted catfish. Wash it down with
one of the eight brews made on-site. The
friendly bar is also a popular local hangout.

ℹ Information

Mt Washington Valley Chamber of Commerce
(✆603-356-5701; www.mtwashingtonvalley.
org; 2617 White Mountain Hwy; ☺9am-5pm)
Tourist information just south of the town
center. Hours are notoriously unreliable.

North Woodstock & Lincoln

You'll pass right through the twin towns of
Lincoln and North Woodstock on your way
between the Kancamagus Hwy (p230) and
Franconia Notch State Park, so it's a handy
place to break for a bite or a bed. The towns

straddle the Pemigewasset River at the intersection of NH 112 and US 3. If you're ready
for some action, **Loon Mountain** (✆603-
745-8111; www.loonmtn.com; Kancamagus Hwy, Lincoln; tubing walk-up/lift $10/16, gondola adult/child
$17/11, lift ticket adult/child 13-18/child 6-12 & seniors
$79/69/59; ☺tubing 6-9:40pm Wed-Sun, gondola
9:30am-5:30pm late Jun–mid-Oct) offers winter
skiing and snowboarding, and in summer
has mountain-bike trails, climbing walls and
New Hampshire's longest gondola ride. Or
ratchet the adrenaline up a notch by zipping
2000ft down a hillside while strapped to just
a cable with the treetop zip line at **Alpine Adventure** (✆603-745-9911; www.alpinezipline.com;
41 Main St, Lincoln; zips $92; ☺9am-4pm).

🛏 Sleeping & Eating

Woodstock Inn INN $$
(✆603-745-3951; www.woodstockinnnh.com; US 3;
r incl breakfast with/without bath from $120/78; 🛜)
This Victorian country inn is North Wood-
stock's centerpiece. It features 33 individu-
ally appointed rooms across five separate
buildings (three in a cluster, two across the
street), each with modern amenities but old-
fashioned style. For dinner, you have your
choice of the on-site upscale restaurant and
microbrewery (Woodstock Station & Micro-
brewery), with outdoor seating on the lovely
flower-filled patio.

Woodstock Inn Station & Brewery PUB $$
(✆603-745-3951; US 3; mains $12-28; ☺11:30am-
10pm) Formerly a railroad station, this eatery tries to be everything to everyone. In the
end, with more than 150 items, it can probably satisfy just about any food craving, but
pasta, sandwiches and burgers are the most
interesting. The beer-sodden rear tavern
here is one of the most happening places in
this neck of the woods.

ℹ Information

Lincoln/Woodstock Chamber of Commerce
(✆603-745-6621; www.lincolnwoodstock.com;
Main St/NH 112, Lincoln; ☺9am-5pm Mon-Fri)
Offers area information.

Franconia Notch State Park

Franconia Notch is the most celebrated
mountain pass in New England, a narrow
gorge shaped over the eons by a rushing
stream slicing through the craggy granite.
I-93, in places feeling more like a country
road than a highway, runs straight through
the state park. The Franconia Notch State

Park visitor center (☎603-745-8391; www.franconianotchstatepark.com; I-93, exit 34A), which is 4 miles north of North Woodstock, can give you details on hikes in the park, ranging from short nature walks to day-long treks.

◉ Sights & Activities

★ Frost Place   HISTORIC SITE

(☎603-823-5510; www.frostplace.org; 158 Ridge Rd, Franconia; adult/child $5/3; ⊙1-5pm Sat & Sun late May-Jun, 1-5pm Wed-Mon Jul–mid-Oct) Robert Frost (1874–1963) was America's most renowned and best-loved poet in the mid-20th century. For several years he lived with his wife and children on a farm near Franconia, now known as the Frost Place. Many of his best and most famous poems describe life on this farm and the scenery surrounding it, including 'The Road Not Taken' and 'Stopping by Woods on a Snowy Evening.' The farmhouse has been kept as faithful to the period as possible, with numerous exhibits of Frost memorabilia.

Cannon Mountain
Aerial Tramway   CABLE CAR

(☎603-823-8800; www.cannonmt.com; I-93, exit 34B; round-trip adult/child $15/12; ⊙9am-5pm late May–mid-Oct; ⛷) This tramway shoots up the side of Cannon Mountain, offering a breathtaking view of Franconia Notch. In 1938 the first passenger aerial tramway in North America was installed on this slope. It was replaced in 1980 by the current, larger cable car, capable of carrying 80 passengers up to the summit of Cannon Mountain in five minutes – a 2022ft, 1-mile ride. Or, visitors can hike up the mountain and take the tramway down.

Flume Gorge   HIKING

(www.flumegorge.com; adult/child $14/11; ⊙9am-5pm May-Oct) To see this natural wonder, take the 2-mile self-guided nature walk that includes the 800ft boardwalk through the Flume, a natural cleft (12ft to 20ft wide) in the granite bedrock. The granite walls tower 70ft to 90ft above you, with moss and plants growing from precarious niches and crevices. Signs along the way explain how nature formed this natural phenomenon. A nearby covered bridge is thought to be one of the oldest in the state, perhaps erected as early as the 1820s.

Echo Lake   BEACH

(☎603-823-8800; I-93, exit 34C; adult/child $4/2; ⊙10am-5:30pm) Despite its proximity to the highway, this little lake at the foot of Can-non Mountain is a pleasant place to pass an afternoon swimming, kayaking or canoeing (rentals from $11 per hour) in the crystal-clear waters. And many people do. The small beach gets packed, especially on weekends.

🛏 Sleeping

Lafayette Place Campground   CAMPGROUND $

(☎603-271-3628; www.reserveamerica.com; campsites $21; ⊙mid-May–early Oct) This popular campground has 97 wooded tent sites that are in heavy demand in summer. Reservations are accepted for 88 of the sites. For the others, arrive early in the day and hope for the best. Many of the state park's hiking trails start here.

Bretton Woods & Crawford Notch

Before 1944, Bretton Woods was known primarily as a low-key retreat for wealthy visitors who patronized the majestic Mt Washington Hotel. After President Roosevelt chose the hotel for the historic conference that established a new post-WWII economic order, the town's name gained worldwide recognition. The countryside, with Mt Washington looming above it, is as magnificent today as it was back then. The Twin Mountain–Bretton Woods Chamber of Commerce (☎800-245-8946; www.twinmountain.org; cnr US 302 & US 3) has details on the area.

The region's largest ski area, Bretton Woods Ski Station (☎603-278-3320; www.brettonwoods.com; US 302; weekends & holidays lift ticket adult/child 13-17/child 6-12 & seniors $79/64/49, weekdays $54/43/33) offers downhill and cross-country skiing as well as a zip line.

US 302 heads south from Bretton Woods to Crawford Notch (1773ft) through stunning mountain scenery ripe with towering cascades. Crawford Notch State Park (☎603-374-2272; www.nhstateparks.org; adult/child $4/2) maintains an extensive system of hiking trails, including short hikes around a pond and to a waterfall, and a longer trek up Mt Washington.

🛏 Sleeping

Dry River Campground   CAMPGROUND $

(☎603-271-3628; www.reserveamerica.org; US 302; campsites $25; ⊙late May-early Oct) Near the southern end of Crawford Notch State Park, this quiet state-run campground has 36 tent sites with a nicely kept bathhouse, showers and laundry facilities. Thirty of the sites can be reserved in advance.

★**Omni Mt Washington**
Hotel & Resort   HOTEL **$$$**
(✆603-278-1000; www.brettonwoods.com; 310 Mt Washington Hotel Rd, Bretton Woods; r $299-480, ste $560; ✳@🛜❄) Open since 1902, this grand hotel maintains a sense of fun – note the moose's head overlooking the lobby and the framed local wildflowers in many of the guest rooms. Also offers 27 holes of golf, red-clay tennis courts, an equestrian center and a spa. There's a $25 daily resort fee.

Mt Washington

From Pinkham Notch (2032ft), on NH 16 about 11 miles north of North Conway, a system of hiking trails provides access to the natural beauties of the Presidential Range, including lofty Mt Washington (6288ft), the highest mountain east of the Mississippi and north of the Smoky Mountains.

Hikers need to be prepared: Mt Washington's weather is notoriously severe and can turn on a dime. Dress warmly – not only does the mountain register New England's coldest temperatures (in summer, the average at the summit is 45°F/7°C) but unrelenting winds make it feel colder than the thermometer reading. In fact, Mt Washington holds the record for the USA's strongest wind gust – 231mph!

The **Pinkham Notch Visitor Center** (✆603-466-2727; www.outdoors.org; NH 16; ◷6:30am-10pm), run by the Appalachian Mountain Club (AMC), is the area's informational nexus for like-minded adventurers and a good place to buy hiking necessities, including topographic trail maps and the handy *AMC White Mountain Guide*.

One of the most popular trails up Mt Washington begins at the visitor center and runs 4.2 strenuous miles to the summit, taking four to five hours to reach the top and a bit less on the way down.

If your quads aren't up for a workout, the **Mt Washington Auto Road** (✆603-466-3988; www.mountwashingtonautoroad.com; off NH 16; car & driver $26, extra adult/child $8/6; ◷mid-May–mid-Oct), 2.5 miles north of Pinkham Notch Camp, offers easier summit access, weather permitting.

While purists walk and the out-of-shape drive, the quaintest way to reach the summit is to take the **Mt Washington Cog Railway** (✆603-278-5404; www.thecog.com; adult/child $62/39; ◷May-Oct). Since 1869, coal-fired steam-powered locomotives have followed a

3.5-mile track up a steep mountainside trestle for a jaw-dropping excursion.

Dolly Copp Campground (✆603-466-2713; www.campsnh.com; NH 16; tent/RV sites $22/26; ◷mid-May–mid-Oct), a USFS campground 6 miles north of the AMC's Pinkham Notch facilities, has 176 simple campsites.

Hanover

The archetypal New England college town, Hanover has a town green that is bordered on all four sides by the handsome brick edifices of Dartmouth College. Virtually the whole town is given over to this Ivy League school; chartered in 1769, Dartmouth is the nation's ninth-oldest college.

Main St, rolling down from the green, is surrounded by perky pubs, shops and cafes that cater to the collegian crowd.

◉ Sights

Dartmouth College   COLLEGE
(www.dartmouth.edu) Hanover is all about Dartmouth College, so hit the campus. Join a free student-guided **campus walking tour** (✆603-646-2875) or just pick up a map at the admissions office and head off on your own. Don't miss the **Baker-Berry Library**, splashed with the grand *Epic of American Civilization*, painted by the outspoken Mexican muralist José Clemente Orozco (1883–1949), who taught at Dartmouth in the 1930s.

Hood Museum of Art   MUSEUM
(✆603-646-2808; E Wheelock St; ◷10am-5pm Tue-Sat, to 9pm Wed, noon-5pm Sun) **FREE** Shortly after the university's founding in 1769 Dartmouth began to acquire artifacts of artistic or historical interest. Since then the collection has expanded to include nearly 70,000 items, which are housed at the Hood Museum of Art. The collection is particularly strong in American pieces, including Native American art. One of the highlights is a set of Assyrian reliefs from the Palace of Ashurnasirpal that date to the 9th century BC. Special exhibits often feature contemporary artists.

🍴 Sleeping & Eating

Storrs Pond Recreation Area   CAMPGROUND **$**
(✆603-643-2134; www.storrspond.com; NH 10; tent/RV sites $28/36; ◷late May–early Sep; 🛜) In addition to 37 woodsy sites next to a 15-acre pond, this private campground has tennis courts and two sandy beaches for

swimming. From I-89 exit 13, take NH 10 north and look for signs.

Hanover Inn
INN $$$

(☑800-443-7024, 603-643-4300; www.hanoverinn.com; cnr W Wheelock & S Main Sts; r from $280; 🐾) Owned by Dartmouth College, Hanover's loveliest guesthouse has nicely appointed rooms with elegant wood furnishings. It has a wine bar and an award-winning restaurant on site.

Lou's
DINER $

(www.lousrestaurant.net; 30 S Main St; mains $6-12; ☺6am-3pm Mon-Fri, 7am-3pm Sat & Sun) A Dartmouth institution since 1947, this is Hanover's oldest establishment, always packed with students meeting for a coffee or perusing their books. From the retro tables or the Formica-topped counter, order typical diner food: eggs, sandwiches and burgers. The bakery items are also highly recommended.

Canoe Club Bistro
CAFE $$

(☑603-643-9660; www.canoeclub.us; 27 S Main St; mains $10-23; ☺11:30am-11:30pm) 🍴 This smart cafe does a fine job with grilled food – not just burgers and steaks, but also tasty treats such as duck breast with fig port glaze. There's also live entertainment nightly – anything from acoustic to jazz.

🍸 Drinking & Entertainment

Murphy's on the Green
PUB

(☑603-643-4075; 11 S Main St; mains $8-18; ☺11am-12:30am) This classic collegiate tavern is where students and faculty meet over pints (it carries over 10 beers on tap, including local microbrews like Long Trail Ale) and satisfying pub fare (mains $8 to $18). Stained-glass windows and church-pew seating enhance the cozy atmosphere.

Hopkins Center for the Arts
PERFORMING ARTS

(☑603-646-2422; www.hop.dartmouth.edu; 2 E Wheelock St) A long way from the big-city lights of New York and Boston, Dartmouth hosts its own entertainment at this outstanding performing arts venue. The season brings everything from movies to live performances by international companies.

❶ Information

Hanover Area Chamber of Commerce (☑603-643-3115; www.hanoverchamber.org; 53 S Main St, Suite 216; ☺9am-4pm Mon-Fri) For tourist information. It's inside the Nugget Building and also maintains an information booth on the village green, staffed July to mid-September.

MAINE

Maine is New England's frontier – a land so vast it could swallow the region's five other states with scarcely a gulp. The sea looms large with mile after mile of sandy beaches, craggy sea cliffs and quiet harbors. While time-honored fishing villages and seaside lobster joints are the fame of Maine, inland travel also offers ample reward. Maine's rugged interior is given over to rushing rivers, dense forests and lofty mountains just aching to be explored.

As a traveler in Maine, your choices are as spectacularly varied as the landscape. You can opt to sail serenely along the coast on a graceful schooner or rip through white-water rapids on a river raft, spend the night in an old sea captain's home-turned-B&B, or camp among the moose on a backwoods lake.

History

It's estimated that 20,000 Native Americans from tribes known collectively as Wabanaki ('People of the Dawn') inhabited Maine when the first Europeans arrived. The French and English vied to establish colonies in Maine during the 1600s but, deterred by the harsh winters, these settlements failed.

In 1652 Massachusetts annexed the territory of Maine to provide a front line of defense against potential attacks during the French and Indian War. And Maine at times did indeed become a battlefield between English colonists in New England and French forces in Canada. In the early 19th century, in an attempt to settle sparsely populated Maine, 100-acre homesteads were offered free to settlers willing to farm the land. In 1820 Maine broke from Massachusetts and entered the Union as a state.

In 1851 Maine became the first state to ban the sale of alcoholic beverages, the start of a temperance movement that eventually took hold throughout the United States. It wasn't until 1934 that Prohibition was finally lifted.

❶ Information

If you're entering the state on I-95 heading north, stop at the well-stocked visitor information center on the highway.

Maine Bureau of Parks and Land (☑800-332-1501; www.campwithme.com) Offers camping in 12 state parks.

Maine Office of Tourism (☑888-624-6345; www.visitmaine.com; 59 State House Station,

Augusta) These folks maintain information centers on the principal routes into the state: Calais, Fryeburg, Hampden, Houlton, Kittery and Yarmouth. Each facility is open 9am to 5pm, with extended hours in summer.

Southern Maine Coast

Maine's most touristed quarter, this seaside region lures visitors with its sandy beaches, resort towns and outlet shopping. The best place to stop for the latter is the southernmost town of Kittery, which is chockablock with outlet stores.

Ogunquit

Aptly named, Ogunquit means 'Beautiful Place by the Sea' in the native Abenaki tongue, and its 3-mile beach has long been a magnet for summer visitors. Ogunquit Beach, a sandy barrier beach, separates the Ogunquit River from the Atlantic Ocean, offering beachgoers the appealing option to swim in cool ocean surf or in the warmer, calmer cove.

As a New England beach destination, Ogunquit is second only to Provincetown for the number of gay travelers who vacation here. Most of the town lies along Main St (US 1), lined with restaurants, shops and motels. For waterfront dining and boating activities head to Perkins Cove at the south end of town.

◉ Sights & Activities

A highlight is walking the scenic 1.5-mile Marginal Way, the coastal footpath that skirts the 'margin' of the sea from Shore Rd, near the center of town, to Perkins Cove. A sublime stretch of family-friendly coastline, Ogunquit Beach, also called Main Beach by locals, begins right in the town center at the end of Beach St.

Finestkind Scenic Cruises   CRUISES
(☑207-646-5227; www.finestkindcruises.com; Perkins Cove; adult/child from $17/9) Offers many popular trips, including a 50-minute lobstering trip, a sunset cocktail cruise and a two-hour cruise aboard the twin-sailed *Cricket*.

⌂ Sleeping

Pinederosa Camping   CAMPGROUND $
(☑207-646-2492; www.pinederosa.com; 128 North Village Rd, Wells; campsites $30; ☎) This wholesome, wooded campground has 162 well-

tended sites, some of which overlook the Ogunquit River. Amenities include a lovely in-ground pool, camp store and summer shuttle to Ogunquit Beach, about 3 miles away.

Gazebo Inn   B&B $$
(☑207-646-3733; www.gazeboinnogt.com; 572 Main St; r incl breakfast $109-245; ☎☒) This stately 1847 farmhouse features 14 rooms that feel more like a private boutique hotel. Rustic-chic touches include heated wood floors, stone fireplaces in the bathrooms, and a media room with beamed ceilings and a wall-sized TV.

Ogunquit Beach Inn   B&B $$
(☑207-646-1112; www.ogunquitbeachinn.com; 67 School St; r incl breakfast $139-179; @☎) In a tidy little arts-and-crafts-style bungalow, this gay-and-lesbian-friendly B&B has colorful, homey rooms and chatty owners who know all about the best new bistros and bars in town. The central location makes walking to dinner a breeze.

✖ Eating

You'll find Ogunquit's restaurants on the south side of town at Perkins Cove and in the town center along Main St.

MAINE FACTS

Nickname Pine Tree State

Population 1.3 million

Area 35,387 sq miles

Capital city Augusta (population 18,700)

Other cities Portland (population 66,400)

Sales tax 5%

Birthplace of Poet Henry Wadsworth Longfellow (1807–82)

Home of Horror novelist Stephen King

Politics Split between Democrats and Republicans

Famous for Lobster, moose, blueberries, LL Bean

State drink Maine gave the world Moxie, America's first (1884) and spunkiest soft drink

Driving distances Portland to Acadia National Park 160 miles, Portland to Boston 150 miles

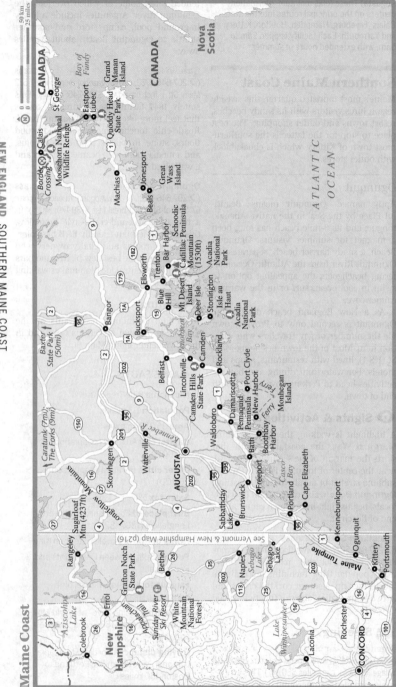

Maine Coast

50 km
25 miles

New Hampshire

Aziscohos Lake

Colebrook

Errol

Rangeley

Grafton Notch State Park

Bethel

Sunday River Ski Resort

Appalachian Trail

White Mountain National Forest

Naples

Sebago Lake

Rochester

Laconia

Lake Winnipesaukee

CONCORD

Portsmouth

Kittery

Ogunquit

Kennebunkport

Maine Turnpike

Cape Elizabeth

Portland

Casco Bay

Freeport

Brunswick

Sabbathday Lake

Bath

Boothbay Harbor

Damariscotta

Pemaquid Peninsula

New Harbor

Monhegan Island

Port Clyde

Rockland

Camden

Lincolnville

Camden Hills State Park

Belfast

Bucksport

Bangor

Baxter State Park (50mi)

Waterville

AUGUSTA

Skowhegan

Longfellow Mountains

Sugarloaf Mtn (4237ft)

Caratunk (7mi)
The Forks (9mi)

Kennebec R

Penobscot Bay

Blue Hill

Ellsworth

Trenton

Bar Harbor

Mt Desert Island

Acadia National Park

Cadillac Mountain (1530ft)

Deer Isle

Stonington

Isle au Haut

Acadia National Park

Schoodic Peninsula

Beals

Great Wass Island

Jonesport

Machias

Calais

Border Crossing

Moosehorn National Wildlife Refuge

Eastport

Lubec

St George

Quoddy Head State Park

Grand Manan Island

Bay of Fundy

CANADA

Nova Scotia

ATLANTIC OCEAN

See Vermont & New Hampshire Map (p216)

Bread & Roses
BAKERY $

(www.breadandrosesbakery.com; 246 Main St; snacks $3-9; ⊘7am-7pm; 🖉) 🍴 Get your coffee and blueberry-scone fix at this teeny slip of a bakery, in the heart of downtown Ogunquit. The cafe fare, such as veggie burritos and organic egg-salad sandwiches, is good for a quick lunch. No seating.

Lobster Shack
SEAFOOD $$

(110 Perkins Cove Rd; mains $10-25; ⊘11am-8pm) If you want good seafood and aren't particular about the view, this reliable joint serves lobster in all its various incarnations, from lobster rolls to lobster in the shell.

Barnacle Billy's
SEAFOOD $$$

(☎207-646-5575; www.barnbilly.com; 183 Shore Rd; mains $12-35; ⊘11am-9pm) This big, noisy barn of a restaurant overlooking Perkins Cove is a longtime favorite for casual seafood: steamers, crab rolls, clam chowder, and, of course, whole lobsters.

☆ Entertainment

Ogunquit Playhouse
THEATER

(☎207-646-5511; www.ogunquitplayhouse.org; 10 Main St; 🖮) First opened in 1933, presents both showy Broadway musicals and children's theater each summer.

❶ Information

Ogunquit Chamber of Commerce (☎207-646-2939; www.ogunquit.org; 36 Main St; ⊘9am-5pm Mon-Fri, 10am-3pm Sat & Sun) Located on US 1, near the Ogunquit Playhouse and just south of the town's center.

Kennebunkport

On the Kennebunk River, Kennebunkport fills with tourists in summer who come to stroll the streets, admire the century-old mansions and get their fill of sea views. Be sure to take a drive along Ocean Ave, which runs along the east side of the Kennebunk River and then follows a scenic stretch of the Atlantic that holds some of Kennebunkport's finest estates, including the summer home of former president George Bush Snr.

Three public beaches extend along the west side of the Kennebunk River and are known collectively as Kennebunk Beach. The center of town spreads out from Dock Sq, which is along ME 9 (Western Ave) at the east side of the Kennebunk River bridge.

The **Kennebunk/Kennebunkport Chamber of Commerce** (☎207-967-0857; www.visitthekennebunks.com; 17 Western Ave; ⊘10am-5pm Mon-Fri year-round, to 3pm Sat Jun-Sep) has tourist information.

🛏 Sleeping

Franciscan Guest House
GUESTHOUSE $$

(☎207-967-4865; www.franciscanguesthouse.com; 26 Beach Ave; r incl breakfast $89-159; 🛜🞕) You can almost smell the blackboard chalk inside this high-school-turned-guesthouse, on the peaceful grounds of the St Anthony Monastery. Guest rooms, once classrooms, are basic and unstylish – acoustic tile, fauxwood paneling, motel beds. If you don't mind getting your own sheets out of the supply closet (there's no daily maid service), staying here's great value and a unique experience.

Colony Hotel
HOTEL $$

(☎207-967-3331; www.thecolonyhotel.com; 140 Ocean Ave; r incl breakfast $129-299; 🛜🞕) Built in 1914, this grand dame of a summer resort evokes the splendor of bygone days. Inside, the 124 old-fashioned rooms have vintage cabbage-rose wallpaper and authentically creaky floors. Outside, ladies recline on Adirondack chairs on the manicured lawn, while young men in polo shirts play badminton nearby and children splash around at the private beach across the street.

Green Heron Inn
INN $$$

(☎207-967-3315; www.greenheroninn.com; 126 Ocean Ave; r incl breakfast $190-225; 🞕@🛜) In a fine neighborhood, overlooking a picturesque cove, this engaging inn has 10 cozy rooms and is within walking distance of a sandy beach and several restaurants. Breakfast is a multicourse event.

✗ Eating

Clam Shack
SEAFOOD $$

(2 Western Ave; mains $7-22; ⊘11am-9:30pm) Standing in line at this teeny gray hut that's perched on stilts above the river is a time-honored Kennebunkport summer tradition. Order a box of fat, succulent fried whole-belly clams or a 1lb lobster roll, which is served with your choice of mayo or melted butter. Outdoor seating only.

Bandaloop
BISTRO $$$

(☎207-967-4994; www.bandaloop.biz; 2 Dock Sq; mains $17-27; ⊘5-9:30pm; 🖉) 🍴 Local, organic and deliciously innovative, running the gamut from grilled rib-eye steak to baked tofu with hemp-seed crust. For the perfect starter, order the skillet-steamed Casco Bay mussels and a Peak's organic ale.

Hurricane
AMERICAN **$$$**

(☑207-967-9111; www.hurricanerestaurant.com; 29 Dock Sq; mains $12-45; ⊙11:30am-9:30pm) On Dock Sq, this popular fine-dining bistro specializes in the classics: crab-stuffed baked lobster, rack of lamb in a red wine reduction, bread pudding. Small plates are more modern and creative: tempura-fried spicy tuna rolls, duck-liver mousse with fig jam. Crowds tend to be middle-aged, well-heeled and high on wine.

Portland

The 18th-century poet Henry Wadsworth Longfellow referred to his childhood city as the 'jewel by the sea' and, thanks to a hefty revitalization effort, Portland once again sparkles. Its lively waterfront, burgeoning gallery scene and manageable size add up to great exploring. Foodies, rev up your taste buds: cutting-edge cafes and chef-driven restaurants have turned Portland into the hottest dining scene north of Boston.

Portland sits on a hilly peninsula surrounded on three sides by water: Back Cove, Casco Bay and the Fore River. It's easy to find your way around. Commercial St (US 1A) runs along the waterfront through the Old Port, while the parallel Congress St is the main thoroughfare through downtown.

⊙ Sights

Old Port
NEIGHBORHOOD

Handsome 19th-century brick buildings line the streets of the Old Port. Portland's most enticing shops, pubs and restaurants are located within this five-square-block district. By night, flickering gas lanterns add to the atmosphere. What to do here? Eat some wicked fresh seafood, down a local microbrew, buy a nautical-themed T-shirt from an up-and-coming designer, peruse the many tiny local art galleries. Don't forget to wander the authentically stinky wharfs, ducking into a fishmongers to order some lobsters.

Portland Museum of Art
MUSEUM

(☑207-775-6148; www.portlandmuseum.org; 7 Congress Sq; adult/child $12/6, 5-9pm Fri free; ⊙10am-5pm Sat-Thu, to 9pm Fri, closed Mon mid-Oct–May) Founded in 1882, this well-respected museum houses an outstanding collection of American artists. Maine artists, including Winslow Homer, Edward Hopper, Louise Nevelson and Andrew Wyeth, are particularly well represented. You'll also find a few works by European masters, including Degas, Picasso and Renoir. The collections are spread across three separate buildings. The majority of works are found in the postmodern Charles Shipman Payson building, designed by the firm of famed architect IM Pei. The 1911 beaux-arts-style LDM Sweat Memorial Gallery and the 1801 Federal-style McLellan House hold the 19th-century American art collection.

Fort Williams Park
LIGHTHOUSE

(⊙sunrise-sunset) 🅵 **FREE** Four miles southeast of Portland on Cape Elizabeth, 90-acre Fort Williams Park is worth visiting simply for the panoramas and picnic possibilities. Stroll around the ruins of the fort, a late-19th-century artillery base, checking out the WWII bunkers and gun emplacements (a German U-boat was spotted in Casco Bay in 1942) that still dot the rolling lawns. Strange as it may seem, the fort actively guarded the entrance to Casco Bay until 1964.

Adjacent to the fort stands the **Portland Head Light**, the oldest of Maine's 52 functioning lighthouses. It was commissioned by George Washington in 1791 and staffed until 1989, when machines took over. The keeper's house has been passed into service as the **Museum at Portland Head Light** (☑207-799-2661; www.portlandheadlight.com; 1000 Shore Rd; adult/child $2/1; ⊙10am-4pm Jun-Oct), which traces the maritime and military history of the region.

Portland Observatory Museum
HISTORIC SITE

(☑207-774-5561; www.portlandlandmarks.org; 138 Congress St; adult/child $8/5; ⊙10am-5pm late May-early Oct) History buffs won't want to miss this hilltop museum, built in 1807 as a maritime signal station to direct ships entering the bustling harbor. Its function was roughly on a par with that of an airport traffic-control tower today. From the top of this observatory, the last of its kind remaining in the USA, you'll be rewarded with a sweeping view of Casco Bay.

Longfellow House
HISTORIC BUILDING

(☑207-879-0427; www.mainehistory.org; 489 Congress St; adult/child $12/3; ⊙10am-5pm Mon-Sat, noon-5pm Sun May-Oct) The revered American poet Henry Wadsworth Longfellow grew up in this Federal-style house, built in 1788 by his Revolutionary War hero grandfather. The house has been impeccably restored to look like it did in the 1800s, complete with original furniture and artifacts.

Children's Museum of Maine MUSEUM
(📌207-828-1234; www.childrensmuseumofme.org; 142 Free St; admission $9; ⊙10am-5pm Mon-Sat, noon-5pm Sun, closed Mon Sep-May; 🚼) Kids aged zero to 10 shriek and squeal as they haul traps aboard a replica lobster boat, milk a fake cow on a model farm, or monkey around on an indoor rock-climbing wall. The highlight of this ultra-interactive museum might be the 3rd-floor camera obscura, where a single pinhole projects a panoramic view of downtown Portland.

🏃 Activities

For a whole different angle on Portland and Casco Bay, hop on one of the boats offering narrated scenic cruises out of Portland Harbor.

Casco Bay Lines CRUISE
(📌207-774-7871; www.cascobaylines.com; 56 Commercial St; adult $13-24, child $7-11) This outfit cruises the Casco Bay islands delivering mail, freight and visitors. It also offers cruises to Bailey Island (adult/child $25/12).

Maine Island Kayak Company KAYAKING
(📌207-766-2373; www.maineislandkayak.com; 70 Luther St, Peaks Island; tour $70; ⊙May-Nov) On Peak Island, a 15-minute cruise from downtown on the Casco Bay Lines, this well-run outfitter offers fun day and overnight trips exploring the islands of Casco Bay.

Portland Schooner Company CRUISE
(📌207-776-2500; www.portlandschooner.com; 56 Commercial St; adult/child $35/10; ⊙May-Oct) Offers tours aboard an elegant, early-20th-century schooner. In addition to two-hour sails, you can book overnight tours ($240 per person, including dinner and breakfast).

**Maine Narrow Gauge
Railroad Co & Museum** RAILROAD
(📌207-828-0814; www.mngrr.org; 58 Fore St; adult/child $10/6; ⊙10am-4pm mid-May–Oct, shorter hours off-season; 🚼) Ride antique steam trains along Casco Bay; journeys depart on the hour.

🛏 Sleeping

Portland has a healthy selection of midrange and upscale B&Bs, though very little at the budget end. The most idyllic accommodations are in the old town houses and grand Victorians in the West End.

Inn at St John INN $
(📌207-773-6481; www.innatstjohn.com; 939 Congress St; r incl breakfast $79-169; P🏠) This turn-of-the-century hotel has a stuck-in-time feel, from the old-fashioned pigeonhole mailboxes behind the lobby desk to the narrow, sweetly floral rooms. Ask for a room away from noisy Congress St.

Morrill Mansion B&B $$
(📌207-774-6900; www.morrillmansion.com; 249 Vaughan St; r incl breakfast $149-239; 🏠) Charles Morrill, the original owner of this 19th-century West End town house, made his fortune by founding B&M baked beans, still a staple of Maine pantries. His home has been transformed into a handsome B&B, with seven guest rooms furnished in a trim, classic style. Think hardwood floors, lots of tasteful khaki and taupe shades. Some rooms are a bit cramped; if you need lots of space, try the two-room Morrill Suite.

La Quinta Inn HOTEL $$
(📌207-871-0611; www.laquinta.com; 340 Park St; r incl breakfast $75-149; ❄@🏠🏊) Best value among the chains, La Quinta has well-maintained rooms and a convenient location opposite the ballpark of the Portland Sea Dogs, a Boston Red Sox–affiliate team.

Portland Harbor Hotel HOTEL $$$
(📌207-775-9090; www.portlandharborhotel.com; 468 Fore St; r from $269; P🏠) This independent hotel has a classically coiffed lobby, where guests relax on upholstered leather chairs surrounding the glowing fireplace. The rooms carry on the classicism, with sunny gold walls and pert blue toile bedspreads. The windows face Casco Bay, the interior garden or the street; garden rooms are quieter. Parking is $16.

🍴 Eating

Two Fat Cats Bakery BAKERY $
(📌207-347-5144; www.twofatcatsbakery.com; 47 India St; treats $3-7; ⊙8am-6pm Mon-Fri, to 5pm Sat, 10am-4pm Sun) Tiny bakery serving pastries, pies, melt-in-your-mouth chocolate-chip cookies and fabulous whoopie pies.

WHOOPIE!

Looking like steroid-pumped Oreos, these marshmallow-cream-filled chocolate snack cakes are a staple of bakeries and seafood-shack dessert menus across the state. Popular both in Maine and in Pennsylvania's Amish country, whoopie pies are said to be so named because Amish farmers would shout 'whoopie!' when they discovered one in their lunch pail. Don't leave the state without trying at least one. For our money, Portland's Two Fat Cats Bakery (p239) has the best.

★ **Green Elephant** VEGETARIAN **$$**
(☑ 207-347-3111; www.greenelephantmaine.com; 608 Congress St; mains $9-13; ⊙ 11:30am-2:30pm Tue-Sat & 5-9:30pm Tue-Sun; 🖐) Even carnivores shouldn't miss the brilliant vegetarian fare at this Zen-chic, Thai-inspired cafe. Start with the crispy spinach wontons, then move on to one of the exotic soy creations, perhaps gingered 'duck' with shiitake mushrooms. Save room for the incredible chocolate-orange mousse pie.

Susan's Fish & Chips SEAFOOD **$$**
(www.susansfishnchips.com; 1135 Forest Ave/US 302; mains $7-19; ⊙ 11am-8pm) Pop in for fish and chips at this no-fuss eatery on US 302, where the tartar sauce comes in mason jars. Located in a former garage.

J's Oyster SEAFOOD **$$**
(www.jsoyster.com; 5 Portland Pier; mains $6-24; ⊙ 11:30am-11:30pm Mon-Sat, noon-10:30pm Sun) This well-loved dive has the cheapest raw oysters in town. Eat 'em on the deck overlooking the pier. The oyster-averse have plenty of sandwiches and seafood mains to choose from.

★ **Fore Street** MODERN AMERICAN **$$$**
(☑ 207-775-2717; www.forestreet.biz; 288 Fore St; mains $20-31; ⊙ 5:30-11pm) Chef-owner Sam Hayward has turned roasting into a high art at Fore Street, one of Maine's most lauded restaurants. Chickens turn on spits in the open kitchen as chefs slide iron kettles of mussels into the wood-burning oven. Local, seasonal eating is taken very seriously here and the menu changes daily to offer what's freshest. A recent dinner included a fresh pea salad, periwinkles (a local shell-fish) in herbed cream, and roast bluefish with pancetta. The large, noisy dining room nods towards its warehouse past with exposed brick and pine paneling. It's also ecofriendly.

Hugo's FUSION **$$$**
(☑ 207-774-8538; www.hugos.net; 88 Middle St; mains $24-30; ⊙ 5:30-9pm Tue-Sat) James Beard Award–winning chef Rob Evans presides over this temple of molecular gastronomy. The menu, which changes regularly, might include such palate-challenging dishes as oxtail and monkfish dumplings, crispy fried pig ears, and bacon crème brûlée. The 'blind' tasting menu – diners only find out what they've eaten after they've eaten it – is the culinary equivalent of an avant-garde opera.

🍷 Drinking & Entertainment

Gritty McDuff's Brew Pub BREWPUB
(www.grittys.com; 396 Fore St; ⊙ 11am-1am) Gritty is an apt description for this party-happy Old Port pub. You'll find a generally raucous crowd here drinking excellent beers – Gritty brews its own award-winning ales downstairs.

Big Easy Blues Club CLUB
(www.bigeasyportland.com; 55 Market St; ⊙ 9pm-1am Tue-Sat, 4-9pm Sun, 6-10pm Mon) This small music club features a mostly local lineup of rock, jazz and blues bands, as well as open-mic hip-hop nights.

🛍 Shopping

Go to Exchange and Fore Sts for gallery row.

Portland Farmers Market FARMERS MARKET
(http://portlandmainefarmersmarket.org; ⊙ 7am-noon Sat, to 2pm Mon & Wed) On Saturdays in Deering Oak Park, vendors hawk everything from Maine blueberries to homemade pickles. On Monday and Wednesday the market is in Monument Sq.

Harbor Fish Market FOOD
(www.harborfish.com; 9 Custom House Wharf; ⊙ 7am-noon Mon-Sat) On Custom House Wharf, this iconic fishmonger packs lobsters to ship anywhere in the US.

Maine Potters Market CERAMICS
(www.mainepottersmarket.com; 376 Fore St; ⊙ 10am-8pm Mon-Fri, to 6pm Sat & Sun) A cooperatively owned gallery featuring the work of a dozen or so different Maine ceramists.

❶ Information

Greater Portland Convention & Visitors Bureau (www.visitportland.com; Ocean Gateway Bldg, 239 Park Ave; ⊙ 8am-5pm Mon-Fri, 10am-5pm Sat)

❶ Getting There & Around

Portland International Jetport (PWM; ☑ 207-874-8877; www.portlandjetport.org) has nonstop flights to cities in the eastern US.

Greyhound (www.greyhound.com) buses and **Amtrak** (☑ 800-872-7245; www.amtrak.com) trains connect Portland and Boston; both take about 2½ hours and charge $20 to $24 one way.

The local bus **Metro** (www.gpmetrobus.com; fares $1.50), which runs throughout the city, has its main terminus at Monument Sq, the intersection of Elm and Congress Sts.

Central Maine Coast

Midcoast Maine is where the mountains meet the sea. You'll find craggy peninsulas jutting deep into the Atlantic, alluring seaside villages and endless opportunities for hiking, sailing and kayaking.

Freeport

The fame and fortune of Freeport, 16 miles northeast of Portland, began a century ago when Leon Leonwood Bean opened a shop to sell equipment to hunters and fishers heading north into the Maine wilderness. Bean's good value earned him loyal customers. Over the years the **LL Bean store** (www.llbean.com; Main St; ⊙ 24hr) has expanded to add sportswear to its outdoor gear. Though a hundred other stores have joined the pack, the wildly popular LL Bean is still the epicenter of town.

The Victorian-era **White Cedar Inn** (☑ 207-865-9099; www.whitecedarinn.com; 178 Main St; r incl breakfast $150-185; ☏) is conveniently located within walking distance of the shops. The former home of Arctic explorer Donald MacMillan, it has seven atmospheric rooms, with brass beds and working fireplaces.

For the best atmosphere, head to the casual, harborside **Harraseeket Lunch & Lobster Co** (☑ 207-865-4888; www.harraseeketlunchandlobster.com; 36 Main St, South Freeport; mains $10-26; ⊙ 11am-7:45pm, to 8:45pm Jul & Aug; ♿), 3 miles south of Freeport center, for its popular lobster dinners, steamers and fried seafood. Feast at picnic tables within spitting distance of the bay.

Bath

Bath has been renowned for shipbuilding since Colonial times and that remains the raison d'être for the town today. **Bath Iron Works**, one of the largest shipyards in the USA, builds steel frigates and other ships for the US Navy. The substantial **Maine Maritime Museum** (☑ 207-443-1316; www.mainemaritimemuseum.org; 243 Washington St; adult/child $15/10; ⊙ 9:30am-5pm), south of the ironworks on the Kennebec River, showcases the town's centuries-old maritime history, which included construction of the six-mast schooner *Wyoming*, the largest wooden vessel ever built in the USA.

Boothbay Harbor

On a fjordlike harbor, this achingly picturesque fishing village with narrow, winding streets is thick with tourists in the summer. Other than eating lobster, the main activity here is hopping on boats. **Balmy Days Cruises** (☑ 207-633-2284; www.balmydayscruises.com; Pier 8; harbor tour adult/child $15/8, day trip cruise to Monhegan adult/child $32/18, sailing tour $24/18) runs one-hour harbor tour cruises, day trips to Monhegan Island and 1½-hour sailing trips around the scenic islands near Boothbay. The **Boothbay Harbor Region Chamber of Commerce** (☑ 207-633-2353; www.boothbayharbor.com; 192 Townsend Ave; ⊙ 8am-5pm Mon-Fri) provides visitor information.

🛏 Sleeping & Eating

Topside Inn   B&B $$
(☑ 207-633-5404; www.topsideinn.com; 60 McKown St; r incl breakfast $165-275; ☏) Atop McKown Hill, this grand gray mansion has Boothbay's best harbor views. Rooms are elegantly turned out in crisp nautical prints and beachy shades of sage, sea glass and khaki. Main-house rooms have more historic charm, but rooms in the two adjacent modern guesthouses are sunny and lovely, too. Enjoy the sunset from an Adirondack chair on the inn's sloping manicured lawn.

Lobster Dock   SEAFOOD $$
(www.thelobsterdock.com; 49 Atlantic Ave; mains $10-26; ⊙ 11:30am-8:30pm) Of all the many lobster joints in Boothbay Harbor, this sprawling wooden waterfront shack is one of the best and cheapest. It serves traditional

fried seafood platters, sandwiches and steamers, but whole, butter-dripping lobster is definitely the main event.

Monhegan Island

This small granite island with high cliffs and crashing surf, 9 miles off the Maine coast, attracts summer day-trippers, artists and nature-lovers who find inspiration in the dramatic views and agreeable isolation. Tidy and manageable, Monhegan is just 1.5 miles long and a half-mile wide. The online Monhegan Island Visitor's Guide (www.monheganwelcome.com) has information and accommodation links. Rooms typically book out in summer, so plan ahead if you're not just visiting on a day trip.

In addition to its 17 miles of walking trails, there's an 1824 lighthouse with a small museum in the former keeper's house and several artists studios that you can poke your head into.

Departing from Port Clyde, the Monhegan Boat Line (207-372-8848; www.monheganboat.com; round-trip adult/child $32/18) runs

OFF THE BEATEN TRACK

PEMAQUID PENINSULA

Adorning the southernmost tip of the Pemaquid Peninsula, Pemaquid Point is one of the most wildly beautiful places in Maine, with its tortured igneous rock formations pounded by treacherous seas. Perched atop the rocks in the 7-acre Lighthouse Park (207-677-2494; www.bristolparks.org; Pemaquid Point; adult/child $2/free; sunrise-sunset) is the 11,000-candle-power Pemaquid Light, built in 1827, and a star of the 61 surviving lighthouses along the Maine coast. A climb to the top will reward you with a fine coastal view. You may well be carrying an image of Pemaquid Light in your pocket without knowing it – it's the beauty featured on the back of the Maine state quarter. The keeper's house now serves as the Fishermen's Museum (9am-5:15pm mid-May–mid-Oct) displaying period photos, old fishing gear and lighthouse paraphernalia. Admission is included in the park fee. Pemaquid Peninsula is 15 miles south of US 1 via ME 130.

three trips daily to Monhegan from late May to mid-October, once a day for the rest of the year. The MV Hardy III (800-278-3346; www.hardyboat.com; round-trip adult/child $32/18; mid-Jun–Sep) departs for Monhegan twice daily from New Harbor, on the east side of the Pemaquid Peninsula. Both boats take approximately one hour and both have early-morning departures and late-afternoon returns, perfect for day-tripping.

Camden & Around

With rolling hills as a backdrop and a harbor full of sailboats, Camden is a gem. Home to Maine's justly famed fleet of windjammers, it attracts nautical-minded souls. You can get a superb view of pretty Camden and its surroundings by taking the 45-minute climb up Mt Battie in Camden Hills State Park (207-236-3109; 280 Belfast Rd/US 1; adult/child $4.50/1; 7am-sunset) at the north side of Camden.

Lobster fanatics (and who isn't!) won't want to miss the Maine Lobster Festival (www.mainelobsterfestival.com; early Aug), New England's ultimate homage to the crusty crustacean, held in nearby Rockland.

The Camden-Rockport-Lincolnville Chamber of Commerce (207-236-4404; www.camdenme.org; 2 Public Landing; 9am-5pm), near the harbor, provides visitor information on the region.

Two miles south of Camden, the sleepy harborside town of Rockport is a much smaller and more peaceful settlement that's known for the world-renowned Maine Media Workshops (www.mainemedia.edu; 70 Camden St, Rockport).

Sleeping & Eating

Whitehall Inn   INN $$
(207-236-3391; www.whitehall-inn.com; 52 High St, Camden; r incl breakfast $119-230; May-Oct;) Camden-raised poet Edna St Vincent Millay got her start reciting poetry to guests at this old-fashioned summer hotel. Read about her wild, often tragic life in the inn's Millay Room parlor, which still has the Steinway piano she once played. The 45 rooms have a vintage boarding-house character, some with Victorian striped wallpaper, in-room pedestal sinks and claw-foot tubs. Rocking chairs on the wide front porch are a nice place for evening socializing.

HOIST THE SAILS

Feel the wind in your hair and history at your side aboard the gracious, multimasted sailing ships known as windjammers. The sailing ships, both historic and replicas, gather in the harbors at Camden and neighboring Rockland to take passengers out on day trips and overnight sails.

Day sails cruise for two hours in Penobscot Bay from June to October for around $35 and you can usually book your place on the day. On the Camden waterfront, look for the 86ft wooden tall ship **Appledore** (☑207-236-8353; www.appledore2.com) and the two-masted schooner **Olad** (☑207-236-2323; www.maineschooners.com).

Other schooners make two- to six-day cruises, offer memorable wildlife viewing (seals, whales and puffins) and typically include stops at Acadia National Park, small coastal towns and offshore islands for a lobster picnic.

You can get full details on several glorious options in one fell swoop through the **Maine Windjammer Association** (☑800-807-9463; www.sailmainecoast.com), which represents 13 traditional tall ships, several of which have been designated National Historic Landmarks. Among them is the granddaddy of the schooner trade, the *Lewis R French*, America's oldest (1871) windjammer. Rates range from $400 for a two-day cruise to $1000 for a six-day voyage and are a bargain when you consider they include meals and accommodations. Reservations for the overnight sails are a must. Prices are highest in midsummer. June offers long days, uncrowded harbors and lower rates, though the weather can be cool. Late September, when the foliage takes on autumn colors, captures the scenery at its finest.

★ **Shepherd's Pie**   AMERICAN **$$**
(www.shepherdspierockport.com; 18 Central St, Rockport; mains $12-22; ⊙5pm-late) Brian Hill, who runs successful restaurant Francine in neighbouring Camden, opened the more laid-back temple of food in a dark-wood pubby space with a tin ceiling. With a menu boasting four main sections – Bar Snacks, From the Grill, Plates and Sides –you can swing by for a bite or a full meal. Choose from usual suspects with a twist: seasonal pickles, smoked alewife (a fish) Caesar, grilled pork chop with apples sauce and salted caramel or buttermilk potatoes.

Cappy's   SEAFOOD **$$**
(www.cappyschowder.com; 1 Main St, Camden; mains $8-17; ⊙11am-11pm; 🐾) This friendly longtime favorite is better known for its bar and convivial atmosphere than for its food, though it does serve a decent bowl of chowder and other casual New England fare.

Acadia National Park

The only national park in New England, **Acadia** (www.nps.gov/acad) encompasses an unspoiled wilderness of undulating coastal mountains, towering cliffs, surf-pounded beaches and quiet ponds. The dramatic landscape offers a plethora of activities for both leisurely hikers and adrenaline junkies.

The park was established in 1919 on land that John D Rockefeller donated to the national parks system to save it from encroaching lumber interests. Today you can hike and cycle along the same carriage roads on which Rockefeller once rode his horse and buggy. The park covers over 62 sq miles, including most of mountainous Mt Desert Island and tracts of land on the Schoodic Peninsula and Isle au Haut, and has a wide diversity of wildlife including moose, puffins and bald eagles.

⊙ Sights & Activities

Park Loop Road

Park Loop Rd, the main sightseeing jaunt through the park, takes you to several of Acadia's highlights. If you're up for a bracing swim or just want to stroll Acadia's longest beach, stop at **Sand Beach**. About a mile beyond Sand Beach you'll come to **Thunder Hole**, where wild Atlantic waves crash into a deep, narrow chasm with such force that it creates a thundering boom, loudest during incoming tides. Look to the south to see Otter Cliffs, a favorite rock-climbing spot that rises vertically from the sea. At Jordan Pond choose from a 1-mile nature trail loop around the south side of the pond or a 3.5-mile trail that skirts the entire pond perimeter. After you've worked up an appetite, reward yourself with a relaxing afternoon tea on the lawn of Jordan Pond House (p244). Near the end of Park Loop Rd a side road leads up to Cadillac Mountain.

Cadillac Mountain

The majestic centerpiece of Acadia National Park is Cadillac Mountain (1530ft), the highest coastal peak in the eastern US, reached by a 3.5-mile spur road off Park Loop Rd. Four trails lead to the summit from four directions should you prefer hiking boots to rubber tires. The panoramic 360-degree view of ocean, islands and mountains is a winner any time of the day, but it's truly magical at dawn when hardy souls flock to the top to watch the sun rise over Frenchman Bay.

Other Activities

Some 125 miles of hiking trails crisscross Acadia National Park, from easy half-mile nature walks and level rambles to mountain treks up steep and rocky terrain. A standout is the 3-mile round-trip Ocean Trail, which runs between Sand Beach and Otter Cliffs and takes in the most interesting coastal scenery in the park. Pick up a guide describing all the trails at the visitor center.

The park's 45 miles of carriage roads are the prime attraction for cycling. You can rent quality mountain bikes, replaced new at the start of each season, at Acadia Bike (207-288-9605; www.acadiabike.com; 48 Cottage St; per day $22; 8am-8pm).

Rock climbing on the park's sea cliffs and mountains is breathtaking. Gear up with Acadia Mountain Guides (207-288-8186; www.acadiamountainguides.com; 228 Main St, Bar Harbor; half-day outing $75-140; May-Oct); rates include a guide, instruction and equipment.

Scores of ranger-led programs, including nature walks, birding talks and kids' field trips, are available in the park. Check the schedule at the visitor center (p244).

For information on kayaking and other activities see Bar Harbor (p245).

Sleeping & Eating

The park has two campgrounds, both wooded and with running water, showers and barbecue pits.

There are scores of restaurants, inns and hotels in Bar Harbor, just a mile beyond the park.

Acadia National Park Campgrounds CAMPGROUND $
(877-444-6777; www.nps.gov/acad; tent sites $14-24) Four miles south of Southwest Harbor, Seawall has both by-reservation and walk-up sites. Five miles south of Bar Harbor on ME 3, year-round Blackwoods requires reservations in summer. Both sites have restrooms and pay showers. Both are densely wooded but only a few minutes' walk to the ocean.

Jordan Pond House AMERICAN $$
(207-276-3316; www.thejordanpondhouse.com; afternoon tea $9.50, mains $10-28; 11:30am-9pm mid-May–Oct) Afternoon tea at this lodge-like teahouse has been an Acadia tradition since the late 1800s. Steaming pots of Earl Grey come with hot popovers (hollow rolls made with egg batter) and strawberry jam. Eat outside on the broad lawn overlooking the lake. The park's only restaurant, Jordan Pond also does fancy but often mediocre lunches and dinners.

Information

Granite mountains and coastal vistas greet you upon entering Acadia National Park. The park is open year-round, though Park Loop Rd and most facilities are closed in winter. An admission fee is charged from May 1 to October 31. The fee, which is valid for seven consecutive days, is $22 per vehicle between mid-June and early October ($10 at other times) and $12 for cyclists or pedestrians.

Start your exploration at **Hulls Cove Visitor Center** (207-288-3338; ME 3; 7-day park admission per vehicle $22, walkers & cyclists $12; 8am-4:30pm mid-Apr–mid-Jun & Oct, to 6pm mid-Jun–Aug, to 5pm Sep), from where the 20-mile Park Loop Rd circumnavigates the eastern portion of the park.

Getting There & Around

The convenient **Island Explorer** (www.exploreacadia.com; late Jun-early Oct) runs eight shuttle bus routes throughout Acadia National Park and to adjacent Bar Harbor, linking trailheads, campgrounds and accommodations.

Bar Harbor

Set on the doorstep of Acadia National Park, this alluring coastal town once rivaled Newport, RI, as a trendy summer destination for wealthy Americans. Today many of the old mansions have been turned into inviting inns and the town has become a magnet for outdoor enthusiasts. The Bar Harbor Chamber of Commerce (☑207-288-5103; www.barharbormaine.com; 1201 Bar Harbor Rd/ME 3, Trenton; ☺8am-6pm late May–mid-Oct, to 5pm Mon-Fri mid-Oct–late May) has a convenient welcome center just before the bridge onto Mt Desert Island.

🏃 Activities

Bar Harbor Whale Watch Co   CRUISE
(☑207-288-2386; www.barharborwhales.com; 1 West St; adult $34-64, child $22-34; ☺mid-May–Oct) Operates four-hour whale-watching and puffin-watching cruises, among other options.

Downeast Windjammer Cruises   CRUISE
(☑207-288-4585; www.downeastwindjammer.com; 27 Main St; adult/child $40/30) Offers two-hour cruises on the majestic 151ft, four-masted schooner *Margaret Todd*.

Acadian Nature Cruises   CRUISE
(☑207-288-2386; www.acadiannaturecruises.com; 1 West St; adult/child $28/17; ☺mid-May–Oct) See whales, porpoises, bald eagles, seals and more on these narrated two-hour nature cruises.

🛌 Sleeping

There's no shortage of sleeping options in Bar Harbor, ranging from period B&Bs to the usual chain hotels.

Bar Harbor Youth Hostel   HOSTEL $
(☑207-288-5587; www.barharborhostel.com; 321 Main St; dm/r $27/82; 🛜) In a converted home a few blocks south of the village green, this pleasant, friendly and very clean hostel has simple male and female dorm rooms, each sleeping 10, and a private room that sleeps four.

Holland Inn   B&B $$
(☑207-288-4804; www.hollandinn.com; 35 Holland Ave; r incl breakfast $95-185; 🛜) In a quiet residential neighborhood, walking distance from downtown, this restored 1895 house and adjacent cottage has nine homey, unfrilly rooms. Ambience is so low-key you'll feel like you're staying in a friend's private home.

Aysgarth Station Inn   B&B $$
(☑207-288-9655; www.aysgarth.com; 20 Roberts Ave; r incl breakfast $115-165; ❄) On a quiet side street, this 1895 B&B has six cozy rooms with homey touches. Request the Tan Hill room, which is on the 3rd floor, for a view of Cadillac Mountain.

🍴 Eating

Cafe This Way   AMERICAN $$
(☑207-288-4483; www.cafethisway.com; 14½ Mount Desert St; mains breakfast $6-9, dinner $15-25; ☺7-11:30am Mon-Sat, 8am-1pm Sun, 5:30-9pm nightly; 🖉) In a sprawling white cottage, this quirky eatery is *the* place for breakfast, with plump Maine blueberry pancakes and eggs Benedict with smoked salmon. It also serves eclectic, sophisticated dinners, such as roasted duck with blueberries, Moroccan-style squash and tuna tempura. Sit in the garden.

2 Cats   CAFE $$
(☑207-288-2808; www.2catsbarharbor.com; 130 Cottage St; mains $8-19; ☺7am-1pm; 🖉) On weekends crowds line up for smoked-trout omelets and homemade muffins at this sunny, arty little cafe. Lunch offerings include slightly heartier fare, like burritos and seafood dishes. Pick up a kitty-themed gift in the gift shop.

Mâche Bistro   FRENCH $$$
(☑207-288-0447; www.machebistro.com; 135 Cottage St; mains $18-28; ☺5-10:30pm Mon-Sat) Almost certainly Bar Harbor's best restaurant, Mâche serves contemporary French-inflected fare in a stylishly renovated cottage. The changing menu highlights the local riches: think pumpkin-seed-dusted scallops, lobster-and-brie flatbread, and wild-blueberry trifle. Specialty cocktails add to the appeal. Reservations are crucial.

Downeast Maine

The 900-plus miles of coastline running northeast from Bar Harbor are sparsely populated, slower-paced and foggier than southern and western Maine. Highlights include the Schoodic Peninsula, whose tip is a noncontiguous part of Acadia National Park; the lobster fishing villages of

Jonesport and Beals; and Great Wass Island, a nature preserve with walking paths and good bird-watching, including the chance to see puffins.

Machias, with a branch of the University of Maine, is the center of commerce along this stretch of coast. Lubec is about as far east as you can go and still be in the USA; folks like to watch the sun rise at nearby Quoddy Head State Park so they can say they were the first in the country to catch the sun's rays.

Interior Maine

Sparsely populated northern and western Maine is rugged outdoor country. River rafting, hiking trails up Maine's highest mountain and the ski town of Bethel make this region a magnet for adventurers.

Sabbathday Lake

The nation's only active Shaker community is at Sabbathday Lake, 25 miles north of Portland. It was founded in the early 18th century and a handful of devotees keep the Shaker tradition of simple living, hard work and fine artistry alive. You can tour several of their buildings on a visit to the Shaker Museum ([☑207-926-4597; www.shaker.lib. me.us; adult/child $6.50/2; ☺10am-4:30pm Mon-Sat late May–mid-Oct). To get there, take exit 63 off the Maine Turnpike and continue north for 8 miles on ME 26.

Bethel

The rural community of Bethel, nestled in the rolling Maine woods 12 miles east of New Hampshire on ME 26, offers an engaging combination of mountain scenery, outdoor escapades and good-value accommodations. Bethel Area Chamber of Commerce ([☑207-824-2282; www.bethelmaine.com; 8 Station Pl; ☺9am-5pm Mon-Fri) provides information for visitors.

🏃 Activities

Bethel Outdoor Adventure KAYAKING
([☑207-824-4224; www.betheloutdooradventure. com; 121 Mayville Rd/US 2; per day kayak/canoe $46/67; ☺8am-6pm) This downtown outfitter rents canoes, kayaks and bicycles, and it arranges lessons, guided trips and shuttles to and from the Androscoggin River.

Grafton Notch State Park HIKING
([☑207-824-2912; ME 26) If you're ready for a hike, head to this park north of Bethel for pretty mountain scenery, waterfalls and lots of trails of varying lengths.

Sunday River Ski Resort SKIING
([☑800-543-2754; www.sundayriver.com; ME 26; full-day lift ticket adult/child 13-18 yr/child under 12 yr& seniors $87/69/56, half-day $63/55/45; ✚]) Six miles north of Bethel along ME 5/26, Sunday River has eight mountain peaks and 132 trails, with 16 lifts. It's regarded as one of the region's best family ski destinations. It also offers summer activities, including chairlift rides, canoeing, ATV tours and a mountain-bike park. Two huge lodges have more than 400 rooms.

🛏 Sleeping

⭐**Chapman Inn** B&B $
([☑207-824-2657; www.chapmaninn.com; 2 Church St; dm incl breakfast $35, r $89-129; ☎]) Run by a friendly globe-trotting retiree, this roomy downtown guesthouse has character in spades. The nine private rooms are done up in florals and antiques, with slightly sloping floors attesting to the home's age. The cozy common space is stocked with Monopoly and other rainy-day games. In winter, skiers bunk down in the snug dorm, complete with a wood-paneled game room presided over by a massive mounted moose head. Breakfast, a lavish spread of homemade pastries and made-to-order omelets, will keep you full for a day on the slopes. And, oh, if you feel a cold draft, it's probably just the ghost of little Abigail Chapman, the daughter of the home's 19th-century owner.

Sudbury Inn & Suds Pub INN $$
([☑207-824-2174; www.sudburyinn.com; 151 Main St; r incl breakfast $99-159; ✷]) The choice place to stay in downtown Bethel, this historic inn has 17 rooms, a pub with 29 beers on tap, pizza and live weekend entertainment. It also has an excellent dinner restaurant serving Maine-centric fare (mains $18 to $26).

Caratunk & The Forks

For white-water rafting at its best, head to the Kennebec River, below the Harris Dam, where the water shoots through a dramatic 12-mile gorge. With rapids with names like Whitewasher and Magic Falls, you know you're in for an adrenaline rush.

The adjoining villages of Caratunk and The Forks, on US 201 south of Jackman, are at the center of the Kennebec River rafting operations. The options range from rolling rapids and heart-stopping drops to calmer waters where children as young as seven can join in. Rates range from $75 to $130 per person for a day-long outing. Multiday packages, with camping or cabin accommodations, can also be arranged.

Reliable operators include **Crab Apple Whitewater** (☏ 800-553-7238; www.crabapplewhitewater.com) and **Three Rivers Whitewater** (☏ 877-846-7238; www.threeriverswhitewater.com).

Baxter State Park

Set in the remote forests of northern Maine, **Baxter State Park** (☏ 207-723-5140; www.baxterstateparkauthority.com; per car $14) cent-

ers on Mt Katahdin (5267ft), Maine's tallest mountain and the northern terminus of the 2175-mile **Appalachian Trail** (www.nps.gov/appa). This vast 209,500-acre park is maintained in a wilderness state – no electricity and no running water (bring your own or plan on purifying stream water) – and there's a good chance you'll see moose, deer and black bear. Baxter has extensive hiking trails, several leading to the top of Mt Katahdin, which can be hiked round-trip in a day as long as you're in good shape and get an early start.

At **Millinocket**, south of Baxter State Park, there are motels, campgrounds, restaurants and outfitters that specialize in white-water rafting and kayaking on the Penobscot River. Get information from the **Katahdin Area Chamber of Commerce** (☏ 207-723-4443; www.katahdinmaine.com; 1029 Central St, Millinocket).

NEW ENGLAND INTERIOR MAINE

Washington, DC & the Capital Region

Best Places to Eat

➡ Woodberry Kitchen (p287)

➡ Central Michel Richard (p274)

➡ Rasika (p273)

➡ Inn at Little Washington (p317)

➡ Julep's (p306)

Best Places to Stay

➡ Hay-Adams Hotel (p270)

➡ Jefferson Hotel (p306)

➡ Colonial Williamsburg Historic Lodging (p308)

➡ Cottages at Indian River Marina (p296)

➡ Inn at 2920 (p287)

Why Go?

No matter your politics, it's hard not to fall for the nation's capital. Iconic monuments, vast (and free) museums and venerable restaurants serving cuisine from around the globe are just the beginning of the great DC experience. There's much to discover: leafy, cobblestoned neighborhoods, sprawling markets and verdant parks – not to mention the corridors of power where visionaries and demagogues still roam.

Beyond the Beltway, the diverse landscapes of Maryland, Virginia, West Virginia and Delaware offer potent enticement to travel beyond the marble city. Craggy mountains, rushing rivers, vast nature reserves (including islands where wild horses run), sparkling beaches, historic villages and the magnificent Chesapeake Bay form the backdrop to memorable adventures: sail, hike, raft, camp or simply sit on a pretty stretch of shoreline, planning the next seafood feast. It's a region where traditions run deep, from the nation's birthplace to Virginia's still-thriving bluegrass scene.

When to Go
Washington DC

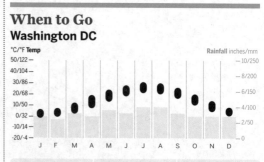

°C/°F **Temp**

Rainfall inches/mm

50/122 —	— 10/250
40/104 —	— 8/200
30/86 —	— 6/150
20/68 —	
10/50 —	— 4/100
0/32 —	— 2/50
-10/14 —	
-20/-4 —	— 0

J F M A M J J A S O N D

Mar-Apr Cherry blossoms bring crowds to the city during DC's most popular festival.

Jun-Aug Beaches and resorts heave; prices are high and accommodations scarce.

Sep-Oct Fewer crowds and lower prices, but pleasant temperatures and fiery fall scenery.

Transportation

The region is served by three major airports: Washington Dulles International Airport (IAD), Ronald Reagan Washington National Airport (DCA) and Baltimore/Washington International Thurgood Marshall Airport (BWI). Norfolk International Airport (ORF) and Richmond International Airport (RIC) are smaller regional hubs.

Train travel is possible in some areas, with service provided by Amtrak (www.amtrak.com). Key towns connected by rail to DC include Baltimore, MD; Wilmington, DE; Harpers Ferry, WV; and, in Virginia: Manassas, Fredericksburg, Richmond, Williamsburg, Newport News and Charlottesville.

TIPS ON VISITING WASHINGTON, DC

DC has a lot of great museums, but you'll be hard pressed to see them all – even if you spend two weeks in the capital. Some sights – including the Washington Monument, US Holocaust Memorial Museum and Ford's Theatre – have limited admittance; if they're high on your list, go early to ensure you get a spot.

Aside from the Museum of the American Indian, which has a great restaurant, dining is limited along the Mall. One strategy: hit Eastern Market first to assemble a picnic for later in the day (on the Mall or around the Tidal Basin).

If possible, leave the car at home. The Metro is excellent and driving in the city can get pricey, with overnight lots charging upward of $25 a night.

Best National Parks

⟶ The New River Gorge National River is utterly Edenlike and home to white-tailed deer and black bears. It also has world-class white-water rafting.

⟶ Shenandoah National Park provides spectacular scenery along the Blue Ridge Mountains, and great hiking and camping, including along the Appalachian Trail.

⟶ Assateague Island National Seashore and Chincoteague are beautiful coastal environments with great blue herons, ospreys, blue crabs and wild horses.

⟶ George Washington and Jefferson National Forests protect more than 1500 sq miles of forests and alpine scenery bordering the Shenandoah Valley.

⟶ Virginia's famous battlefields are also part of the park system. Good places to reconnect with America's darkest hours are Antietam and Manassas.

DON'T MISS

With Chesapeake Bay at its doorstep, this region is pure heaven for seafood-lovers. The Maine Avenue Fish Market (p272) in DC is legendary. In Baltimore, Annapolis and all along Maryland's Eastern Shore, you'll also find top-notch seafood.

Fast Facts

⟶ **Hub cities** Washington, DC (population 632,000), Baltimore (population 620,000), Virginia Beach (population 442,700)

⟶ **Distances from DC** Baltimore (40 miles), Williamsburg (152 miles), Abingdon (362 miles)

⟶ **Time zone** Eastern

Did You Know?

⟶ Thomas Jefferson was one of many Virginians to make wine in the state in the past 400 years. Now Virginia has more than 192 wineries and earns high marks at international awards shows.

Resources

⟶ **Washington** (www.washington.org) Lists upcoming events and loads of DC details.

⟶ **The Crooked Road** (www.thecrookedroad.org) Gateway to Virginia's heritage music trail.

⟶ **Virginia Wine** (www.virginiawine.org) Essential for planning a route through wine country.

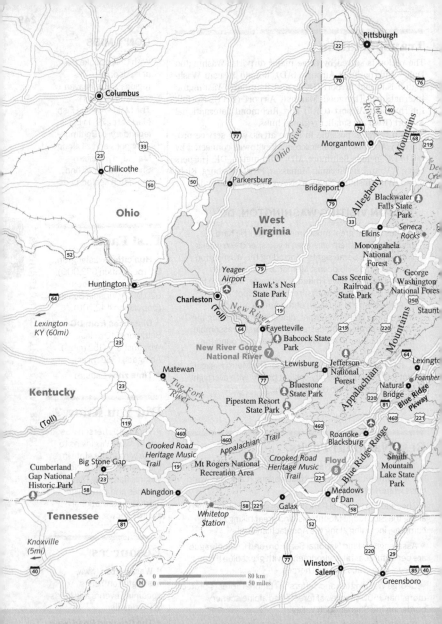

Washington, DC & the Capital Region Highlights

① Visiting Washington's **Smithsonian Institution museums** (p263), then watching the sunset over **Lincoln Memorial** (p261).

② Tracing America's roots at the living-history museum of **Colonial Williamsburg** (p308).

③ Exploring the region's nautical past with a pub crawl

through the cobblestoned port-town neighborhood of **Fells Point** (p286), Baltimore.

④ Taking a Sunday drive along **Skyline Drive** (p316), followed by hiking and

camping under the stars in **Shenandoah National Park** (p315).

5 Marveling at Thomas Jefferson's masterpieces of **Monticello** (p314) and the **University of Virginia** (p313) in historic Charlottesville.

6 Strolling the boardwalk in the family- and gay-friendly resort of **Rehoboth Beach** (p296).

7 Tackling the rapids of **New River Gorge National River** (p325) in Fayetteville.

8 Feeling the beat of the clog dancers at a jamboree in **Floyd, VA** (p321).

History

Native Americans populated this region long before European settlers arrived. Many of the area's geographic landmarks are still known by their Native American names, such as Chesapeake, Shenandoah, Appalachian and Potomac. In 1607 a group of 108 English colonists established the first permanent European settlement in the New World: Jamestown. During the early years, colonists battled harsh winters, starvation, disease and occasionally hostile Native Americans.

Jamestown survived, and the Royal Colony of Virginia came into being in 1624. Ten years later, fleeing the English Civil War, Lord Baltimore established the Catholic colony of Maryland at St Mary's City, where a Spanish Jewish doctor treated a town council that included a black Portuguese sailor and Margaret Brent, the first woman to vote in North American politics. Delaware was settled as a Dutch whaling colony in 1631, was practically wiped out by Native Americans, then later resettled by the British. Celts displaced from Britain filtered into the Appalachians, where they created a fiercely independent culture that persists today. Border disputes between Maryland, Delaware and Pennsylvania led to the creation of the Mason– Dixon line, which eventually separated the industrial North from the agrarian, slave-holding South.

The fighting part of the Revolutionary War finished here with the British surrender at Yorktown in 1781. Then, to diffuse regional tension, central, swampy Washington, District of Columbia (DC), was made the new nation's capital. But divisions of class, race and economy were strong, and this area in particular split along its seams during the Civil War (1861–65): Virginia seceded from the Union while its impoverished western farmers, long resentful of genteel plantation owners, seceded from Virginia. Maryland stayed in the Union but its white slave-owners rioted against Northern troops, while thousands of black Marylanders joined the Union Army.

Local Culture

The North–South tension long defined this area, but the region has also jerked between the aristocratic pretensions of upper-class Virginia, miners, watermen, immigrant boroughs and the ever-changing rulers of Washington, DC. Since the Civil War, local economies have made the shift from agriculture and manufacturing to high technology and the servicing and staffing of the federal government.

Many African Americans settled this border region, either as slaves or escapees running to Northern freedom. Today African Americans still form the visible underclass of major cities, but in the rough arena of the disadvantaged they compete with Latino immigrants, mainly from Central America. At the other end of the spectrum, ivory towers – in the form of world-class universities and research centers such as the National Institute of Health – attract intelligentsia from around the world. The local high schools are often packed with the children of scientists and consultants staffing some of the world's most prestigious think tanks.

All of this has spawned a culture that is, in turns, as sophisticated as a journalists' book club, as linked to the land as bluegrass festivals in Virginia and as hooked into the main vein of urban America as Tupac Shakur, go-go, Baltimore Club and DC Hardcore. And, of course, there's always politics, a subject continually simmering under the surface here.

WASHINGTON, DC FACTS

Nickname DC, the District, Chocolate City

Population 632,300

Area 68.3 sq miles

Capital city Exactly!

Sales tax 5.75%

Birthplace of Duke Ellington (1899–1974), Marvin Gaye (1939–84), Dave Chappelle (b 1973)

Home of The Redskins, cherry blossoms, all three branches of American government

Politics Overwhelmingly Democrat

Famous for National symbols, crime, partying interns, struggle for Congressional recognition

Unofficial motto and license-plate slogan Taxation Without Representation

Driving distances Washington, DC, to Baltimore 40 miles, Washington, DC, to Virginia Beach 210 miles

THE CAPITAL REGION IN...

One Week

Follow a version of the two-day DC itinerary and spend a day exploring underrated **Baltimore** before heading to Maryland's gorgeous **Eastern Shore** and the **Delaware beaches**. Head south to cross over the Chesapeake Bay bridge-tunnel and time-warp through Virginia's history: visit the nation's birthplace at **Jamestown** and take a wander through the 18th century in **Williamsburg**, followed by the nation's post–Civil War reconciliation at **Appomattox Court House**. Swing north through **Richmond**, where students, Dixie aristocracy and African American neighborhoods combine to form a fascinating whole, before rolling back into DC.

Two Weeks

Head to **Charlottesville** to experience Virginia's aristocratic soul (and good dining and B&B scene), then drive down the mountainous backbone through **Staunton**, **Lexington** and **Roanoke**. Follow the **Crooked Road** on a weekend to hear some of the nation's best bluegrass. Truck through West Virginia, stopping to hike, mountain bike or ski in the **Monongahela National Forest**, then go rafting in **New River Gorge** before returning to Washington via the hallowed battlefields of **Antietam**.

WASHINGTON, DC

This is a terrifically exciting city. Whatever you think it may be, Washington, DC is more. A workaholic capital? Absolutely; look at the interns scrabbling across Capitol Hill, the think-tank staff angling for a fellowship and the lobbyist on their smartphone. A study in monumental dignity? Yes; see the wide boulevards, iconic memorials, countless museums and idyllic vistas over the Potomac.

And then, DC is much more than a mere museum piece or marble backdrop to nightly news reports. It's home to tree-lined neighborhoods and a vibrant theater scene, with ethnically diverse restaurants, large numbers of immigrants and a dynamism percolating just beneath the surface. The city has a growing number of markets, historic cobblestoned streets and more over-achieving and talented types than any city of this size deserves.

It also has an underclass, which lives in poverty and high crime (although these metrics have improved), and it has a high price tag. DC has undergone extensive gentrification since the late 1990s. With the exception of a few outlier years, crime has dropped as the cost of living has increased, although this has been accompanied by displacement of many area African Americans to the Maryland and Virginia suburbs. The cost of living in DC is among the highest in the nation, and coupled with waves of politically motivated transplants, the city has a reputation as a place more geared towards transients than families. But it is nevertheless family-friendly if you're visiting with children, and DC's residential outer areas and Beltway suburbs provide a home base for those who want to live amid the capital's undeniable intellectual and cultural energy.

History

Like a lot of American history, the District of Columbia (DC) story is one of compromise. In this case, the balance was struck between Northern and Southern politicians who wanted to plant a federal city between their power bases. As potential capitals such as Boston, Philadelphia and Baltimore were rejected as too urban-industrial by Southern plantation owners, it was decided that a new city would be carved at the 13 colonies' midway point, along the banks of the Potomac River. Maryland and Virginia donated the land (which Virginia took back in the 19th century).

DC was originally run by Congress, was torched by the British during the War of 1812, and lost the south-bank slave port of Alexandria to Virginia in 1846 (when abolition talk was buzzing in the capital). Over the years, DC evolved along diverging tracks; as a marbled temple to federal government and residential city for federal employees on the one hand, and an urban ghetto for northbound African Americans and overseas immigrants on the other.

The city finally got its own mayor in 1973 (Walter Washington, among the first African

Washington, DC

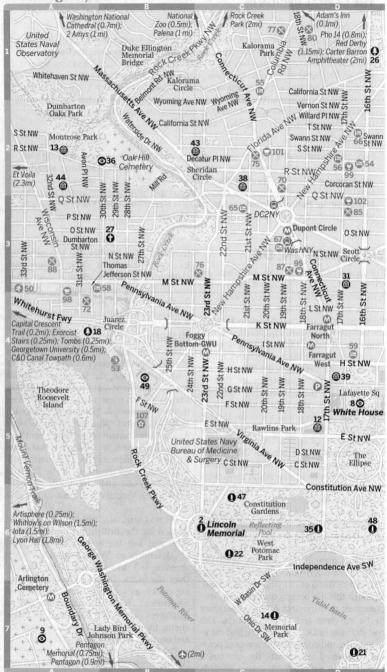

United States Naval Observatory

Washington National Cathedral (0.7mi); 2 Amys (1 mi)

Duke Ellington Memorial Bridge

National Zoo (0.5mi); Palena (1 mi)

Rock Creek Park (2mi)

Adam's Inn (0.1mi)

Pho 14 (1.15mi); Red Derby (1.15mi); Carter Barron Amphitheater (2mi) ❶ 26

77

80

Kalorama Park

Columbia Rd NW

Whitehaven St NW

Massachusetts Ave NW

Belmont Rd NW

Kalorama Circle

Wyoming Ave NW

California St NW

Sheridan Circle

Connecticut Ave NW

California St NW

Vernon St NW

Willard Pl NW

T St NW

Swann St NW

S St NW

R St NW

Swann St NW 66

16th St NW

17th St NW

Dumbarton Oaks Park

Wisconsin Ave NW

S St NW

R St NW

Montrose Park 13 🏛

Et Voila (2.3mi) ←

32nd St NW

44 🏛

Avon Pl NW

Oak Hill Cemetery

🌀 36

Mill Rd

Waterside Dr NW

43 🏛

Decatur Pl NW

38 🏛

New Hampshire Ave NW

Florida Ave NW

101

75

56

99

54

Corcoran St NW

Q St NW

30th St NW

29th St NW

28th St NW

Q St NW

P St NW

O St NW

Dumbarton St NW 27 ❶

N St NW

Thomas Jefferson St NW

27th St NW

Rock Creek

22nd St NW

21st St NW

65 🏛 DC2NY

Dupont Circle Ⓜ

67

WashNY 🏛

95 87

N St NW

O St NW

Scott Circle

31 🏛

102

85

70

R St NW

33rd St NW

31st St NW

88

🏛 50

98

72

58

Pennsylvania Ave NW

23rd St NW

76

M St NW

New Hampshire Ave NW

21st St NW

20th St NW

19th St NW

18th St NW

M St NW

Connecticut Ave NW

L St NW

17th St NW

16th St NW

Whitehurst Fwy

Capital Crescent Trail (0.2mi); Exorcist Stairs (0.25mi); Tombs (0.25mi); Georgetown University (0.5mi); C&O Canal Towpath (0.6mi)

Juarez Circle

❶ 18

K St NW

Farragut North Ⓜ

Farragut West Ⓜ

59

H St NW

53

Foggy Bottom-GWU Ⓜ

25th St NW

24th St NW

23rd St NW

22nd St NW

H St NW

G St NW

F St NW

20th St NW

19th St NW

18th St NW

🏛 39

17th St NW

Theodore Roosevelt Island

49 🎯

F St NW

107 ✪

E St NW

Rawlins Park

Ⓟ

8 🎯 White House

12 🏛

Lafayette Sq

Mount Vernon Trail

United States Navy Bureau of Medicine & Surgery

Virginia Ave NW

D St NW

C St NW

D St NW

C St NW

E St NW

The Ellipse

Artisphere (0.25mi); Whitlow's on Wilson (1.5mi); Iota (1.5mi); Lyon Hall (1.8mi)

Constitution Ave NW

❶ 47

Constitution Gardens

48 ❶

2 ❶ Lincoln Memorial

Reflecting Pool

35 ❶

West Potomac Park

❶ 22

Rock Creek Pkwy

George Washington Memorial Pkwy

Independence Ave SW

Arlington Cemetery

Ⓜ

Boundary Dr

9 🎯

Lady Bird Johnson Park

Pentagon Memorial (0.75mi); Pentagon (0.9mi)

Potomac River

W Basin Dr SW

14 ❶

Ohio Dr SW

Memorial Park

Tidal Basin

❶ 21

✈ (2mi)

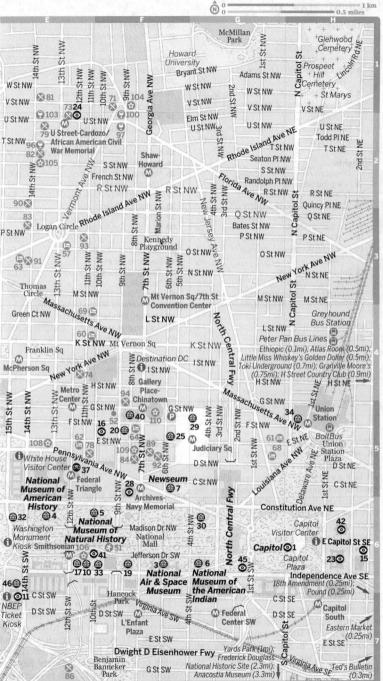

Washington, DC

American mayors of a major American city). DC was ever underfunded and today residents are taxed like other American citizens yet lack a voting seat in Congress. The educated upper class is leagues away from the neglected destitute; almost half the population has a university degree, yet a third is functionally illiterate.

With the election of Barack Obama in 2008, Washington, DC, gained a bit of cool cachet – New Yorkers are coming here now, instead of the other way around. Unfortunately, they've brought with them an NYC cost of living. DC remains quite divided between upwardly mobile transplants and long-term residents. The former possess wealth, while the latter are influential within local politics. In some places these two sectors coexist, but in other neighborhoods tensions can be palpable.

◉ Sights

The capital was designed by its two planners to be perfectly navigable. Unfortunately, their urban visions have mashed up against each other. Pierre L'Enfant's diagonal state-named streets share space with Andrew Ellicott's grid (remember: letters go east–west, numbers north–south). On top of that the city is divided into four quadrants with identical addresses in different divisions – F and 14th NW puts you near the White House, while F and 14th NE puts you near Rosedale Playground.

The majority of sights lie in the Northwest (NW) quadrant, while the most run-down neighborhoods tend to be in the Southeast (SE). Keep your urban wits about you at night, and be prepared for crowds during events such as the Cherry Blossom Festival. The Potomac River is to your south and west; Maryland lies to the north and east; and the Beltway, the capital ring road, encircles the entire package.

○ National Mall

When you imagine Washington, DC, you likely imagine this 1.9-mile-long lawn. Anchored at one end by the Lincoln Memorial and at the other by Capitol Hill, intersected by the Reflecting Pool and WWII Memorial, and centered on the Washington Monument, this is the heart of the city and, in some ways, the American experiment.

Perhaps no other symbol has housed the national ideal of massed voice affecting radical change – from Martin Luther King's 1963 'I Have a Dream' speech to marches for gay marriage in the 2000s. Hundreds of rallies occur here every year; the Mall, framed by great monuments and museums, and shot through with tourists, dog-walkers and idealists, acts as loudspeaker for any cause.

★ **National Air & Space Museum** MUSEUM
(http://airandspace.si.edu/; cnr 6th St & Independence Ave SW; ⊙10am-5:30pm daily, to 7:30pm Jun-Aug; Ⓜ Smithsonian, L'Enfant Plaza, Federal Center) **FREE** The Air & Space Museum is the most popular Smithsonian museum; everyone flocks to see the Wright brothers' flyer, Chuck Yeager's *Bell X-1*, Charles Lindbergh's *Spirit of St Louis* and the *Apollo 11* command module. There's also an IMAX theater, planetarium and simulator (adult/child $9/7.50 each).

★ **National Museum of Natural History** MUSEUM
(www.mnh.si.edu; cnr 10th St & Constitution Ave NW; ⊙10am-5:30pm, to 7:30pm Jun-Aug; 🚸; Ⓜ Smithsonian, Federal Triangle) **FREE** A favorite with the kids, the Museum of Natural History showcases dinosaur skeletons, an archaeology/anthropology collection, wonders from the ocean, and unusual gems and minerals, including the 45-carat Hope Diamond.

National Mall

Folks often call the Mall 'America's Front Yard,' and that's a pretty good analogy. It is indeed a lawn, unfurling scrubby green grass from the Capitol west to the Lincoln Memorial. It's also America's great public space, where citizens come to protest their government, go for scenic runs and connect with the nation's most cherished ideals writ large in stone, landscaping, monuments and memorials.

You can sample quite bit in a day, though it'll be a full one that requires roughly 4 miles of walking. Start at the **Vietnam Veterans Memorial** 1, then head counterclockwise around the Mall, swooping in on the **Lincoln Memorial** 2, **Martin Luther King Jr Memorial** 3 and **Washington Monument** 4. You can also pause for the cause of the Korean War and WWII, among other monuments that dot the Mall's western portion.

Martin Luther King Jr Memorial

Walk all the way around the towering statue of Dr King by Lei Yixin and read the quotes. His likeness, incidentally, is 11ft taller than Lincoln and Jefferson in their memorials.

Tidal Basin

Smithsonian Castle

Seek out the tomb of James Smithson, the eccentric Englishman whose 1826 financial gift launched the Smithsonian Institution. His crypt is in a room by the Mall entrance.

Department of Agriculture

National Air & Space Museum

Simply step inside and look up, and you'll be impressed. Lindbergh's *Spirit of St Louis* and Chuck Yeager's sound barrier–breaking Bell X-1 are among the machines hanging from the ceiling.

West Building

East Building

National Museum of the American Indian

US Capitol

Then it's onward to the museums, all fabulous and all free. Begin at the **Smithsonian Castle** 5 to get your bearings – and to say thanks to the guy making all this awesomeness possible – and commence browsing through the **National Air & Space Museum** 6, **National Gallery of Art & National Sculpture Garden** 7 and **National Museum of Natural History** 8.

TOP TIPS

Start early, especially in summer. You'll avoid the crowds, but more importantly you'll avoid the blazing heat. Try to finish with the monuments and be in the air-conditioned museums by 10:30am. Also, consider bringing snacks, since the only food available is from scattered cart vendors and museum cafes.

Lincoln Memorial

Commune with Abe in his chair, then head down the steps to the marker where Martin Luther King Jr gave his 'Dream' speech. The view of the Reflecting Pool and Washington Monument is one of DC's best.

STEVEN GREAVES / GETTY IMAGES ©

Korean War Veterans Memorial

National WWII Memorial

National Museum of American History

National Sculpture Garden

Vietnam Veterans Memorial

Check the symbol that's beside each name. A diamond indicates 'killed, body recovered.' A plus sign indicates 'missing and unaccounted for.' There are approximately 1200 of the latter.

Washington Monument

As you approach the obelisk, look a third of the way up. See how it's slightly lighter in color at the bottom? Builders had to use different marble after the first source dried up.

National Museum of Natural History

Wave to Henry, the elephant who guards the rotunda, then zip to the 2nd floor's Hope Diamond. The 45.52-carat bauble has cursed its owners, including Marie Antoinette, or so the story goes.

National Gallery of Art & National Sculpture Garden

Beeline to Gallery 6 (West Building) and ogle the Western Hemisphere's only Leonardo da Vinci painting. Outdoors, amble amid whimsical sculptures by Miró, Calder and Lichtenstein. Also check out IM Pei's design of the East Building.

EDDIE BRADY / GETTY IMAGES ©

★ **National Museum of American History** MUSEUM
(www.americanhistory.si.edu; cnr 14th St & Constitution Ave NW; ⊙10am-5:30pm, to 7:30pm Jun-Aug; ⊕; Ⓜ Smithsonian, Federal Triangle) **FREE** The Museum of American History is accented with the daily bric-a-brac of the American experience – synagogue shawls, protest signs and cotton gins – plus an enormous display of the original Star-Spangled Banner and icons such as Dorothy's slippers and Kermit the Frog.

★ **National Museum of the American Indian** MUSEUM
(www.americanindian.si.edu; cnr 4th St & Independence Ave SW; ⊙10am-5:30pm; ⊕; Ⓜ L'Enfant Plaza) **FREE** The Museum of the American Indian, ensconced in honey-colored sandstone, provides a good introduction to the indigenous people of the Americas, with an array of costumes, video and audio recordings, and cultural artifacts. Exhibits are largely organized and presented by individual tribes, which provides an extremely intimate, if sometimes disjointed, overall narrative. Don't miss the regionally specialized menu of Native-inspired dishes at **Mitsitam Native Foods Cafe** (www.mitsitamcafe.com; cnr 4th St & Independence Ave SW, National Museum of the American Indian; mains $8-18; ⊙11am-5pm; Ⓜ L'Enfant Plaza) on the ground floor.

Hirshhorn Museum & Sculpture Garden MUSEUM
(www.hirshhorn.si.edu; cnr 7th St & Independence Ave SW; ⊙10am-5:30pm, sculpture garden 7:30am-dusk; ⊕; Ⓜ Smithsonian) **FREE** The doughnut-shaped Hirshhorn Museum & Sculpture Garden houses a huge collection of modern sculpture, which is rotated regularly. It includes works by Rodin, Henry Moore and Ron Mueck, as well as paintings by O'Keeffe, Warhol, Man Ray and de Kooning.

National Museum of African Art MUSEUM
(www.nmafa.si.edu; 950 Independence Ave SW; ⊙10am-5:30pm; ⊕; Ⓜ Smithsonian) **FREE** The National Museum of African Art showcases masks, textiles and ceramics from the sub-Sahara, as well as ancient and contemporary art from all over the continent.

Arthur M Sackler Gallery GALLERY
(www.asia.si.edu/; 1050 Independence Ave SW; ⊙10am-5:30pm; Ⓜ Smithsonian, L'Enfant Plaza) **FREE** Poring over ancient manuscripts and Japanese silk screens is a peaceful way to spend an afternoon at this quiet gallery and the adjoining Freer Gallery of Art (http://www.asia.si.edu/; cnr 12 St & Jefferson Dr SW). Together they comprise the National Museum of Asian Art. The Freer, rather incongruously, also houses more than 1300 works by the American painter James Whistler.

WASHINGTON, DC, IN...

Two Days

Start your DC adventure at the Mall's much-loved **National Air & Space Museum** and **National Museum of Natural History**. Around lunchtime visit the **National Museum of the American Indian**, for aboriginal lore and a great meal. Wander down the **Mall** to the **Lincoln Memorial** and **Vietnam Veterans Memorial**. Before exhaustion creeps in, go to **U Street** for dining and drinks.

Next day, head to the **US Holocaust Memorial Museum**, **Arthur M Sackler Gallery** and **Freer Gallery of Art**. Catch the illuminated **White House** and the new **Martin Luther King Jr Memorial** at night. For dinner, browse the restaurant-lined **Penn Quarter**.

Four Days

On day three, go to **Georgetown** for a morning stroll along the Potomac, followed by window-shopping and lunch at **Martin's Tavern**. Afterwards, visit the lovely **Dumbarton Oaks** gardens, then take a hike in **Rock Creek Park**. Head to **Columbia Heights** for dinner, followed by drinks at **Meridian Pint**.

On the fourth day, visit the **Newseum**, **Capitol** and **Library of Congress**, then walk to **Eastern Market** for a meal. In the evening, try to catch a show a the **Kennedy Center**.

National Gallery of Art MUSEUM
(www.nga.gov; Constitution Ave NE, btwn 3rd & 4th
Sts NW; ⊙10am-5pm Mon-Sat, 11am-6pm Sun)
FREE Set in two massive buildings, the National Gallery of Art houses a staggering
art collection (more than 100,000 objects),
spanning the Middle Ages to the present.
The neoclassical west building houses European art through the 1800s, with an excellent range of Italian Renaissance works
(including the continent's only da Vinci);
the geometric east building, designed by
IM Pei, showcases modern art, with works
by Picasso, Matisse, Pollock and a massive
Calder mobile over the entrance lobby. An
underground passage with a wonderful indoor waterfall ('Cascade') and cafe connects
the two buildings.

Smithsonian Castle VISITOR CENTER
(☑202-633-1000; www.si.edu; 1000 Jefferson
Dr SW; ⊙8:30am-5:30pm; Ⓜ Smithsonian) The
red-turreted Smithsonian Castle is the visitor center for all museums, but is not that
interesting in and of itself.

◉ Other Museums & Monuments

★Lincoln Memorial MONUMENT
(2 Lincoln Memorial Cir NW) FREE Anchoring
the Mall's west end is the hallowed shrine
to Abraham Lincoln, who gazes peacefully
across the Reflecting Pool beneath his neoclassical Doric-columned abode. To the left
of Lincoln you can read the words of the
Gettysburg Address, and the hall below
highlights other great Lincoln-isms; on the
steps, Martin Luther King Jr delivered his
famed 'I Have a Dream' speech.

★Newseum MUSEUM
(www.newseum.org; 555 Pennsylvania Ave NW;
adult/child $22/13; ⊙9am-5pm; ▣; Ⓜ Archives-
Navy Memorial, Judiciary Sq) Although you'll
have to pay up, this massive, highly interactive news museum is well worth the admission price. You can delve inside the major
events of recent years (the fall of the Berlin
Wall, September 11, Hurricane Katrina), and
spend hours watching moving film footage, perusing Pulitzer Prize–winning photographs and reading works by journalists
killed in the line of duty.

US Holocaust Memorial Museum MUSEUM
(www.ushmm.org; 100 Raoul Wallenberg Pl;
⊙10am-5:20pm) FREE For a deep under-

standing of the Holocaust – its victims, per-
petrators and bystanders – this harrowing
museum is a must-see. The main exhibit
(not recommended for under-11s, who can
go to a separate on-site exhibit that's also
free) gives visitors the identity card of a
single Holocaust victim, whom visitors can
ponder while taking a winding route into a
hellish past amid footage of ghettos, rail cars
and death camps where so many were murdered. Only a limited number of visitors are
admitted each day, so go early.

Washington Monument MONUMENT
(☑202-426-6841; 2 15th St NW; ⊙9am-10pm Jun-
Aug, to 5pm Sep-May) FREE Peaking at 555ft
(and 5in), the Washington Monument is the
tallest building in the district. It took two
phases of construction to complete; note
the different hues of the stone. Tickets are
free but must be reserved from the kiosk
(15th St, btwn Madison Dr NW & Jefferson Dr SW;
⊙8:30am-4:30pm), or you can order them in
advance by calling the National Park Service (☑877-444-6777; www.recreation.gov; tickets
$1.50).

Bureau of Engraving & Printing LANDMARK
(www.moneyfactory.gov; cnr 14th & C Sts SW;
⊙9am-3pm Mon-Fri, to 7:30pm summer; ▣;
Ⓜ Smithsonian) FREE The Bureau of Engraving & Printing, aka the most glorified print
shop in the world, is where all the US paper
currency is designed. Some $32 million of it
rolls off the presses daily. Get in line early at
the ticket kiosk (Raoul Wallenberg Pl, aka 15th
St) on Raoul Wallenberg Pl.

Vietnam Veterans Memorial MONUMENT
(Constitution Gardens) FREE The opposite of
DC's white, gleaming marble is this black,
low-lying 'V', an expression of the psychic
scar wrought by the Vietnam War. The
monument follows a descent deeper into the
earth, with the names of the 58,267 dead soldiers, listed in the order in which they died,
chiseled into the dark wall. It's a subtle, but
profound monument – and all the more surprising as it was designed by 21-year-old undergraduate student Maya Lin in 1981.

Korean War Veterans Memorial MONUMENT
(www.nps.gov/kwvm; 10 Daniel French Drive SW;
Ⓜ Foggy Bottom-GWU) FREE The elaborate
memorial depicts a patrol of ghostly steel
soldiers marching by a wall of etched faces
from that conflict; seen from a distance, the

images on the wall form the outline of the Korean mountains.

National WWII Memorial   MONUMENT

(www.wwiimemorial.com; 17th St; M Smithsonian) FREE Occupying one end of the Reflecting Pool (and, controversially, the center of the Mall – the only war memorial to have that distinction), the National WWII Memorial honors the 400,000 Americans who died in the war, along with the 16 million US soldiers who served during the conflict. Stirring quotes are sprinkled about the monument.

Corcoran Gallery   MUSEUM

(☏ 202-639-1704; www.corcoran.org; cnr 17th St & New York Ave NW; adult/child $10/free; ⊙ 10am-5pm Wed-Sun, to 9pm Thu; M Farragut West) DC's oldest art museum, the Corcoran Gallery has had a tough time standing up to the free, federal competition around the block, but this hasn't stopped it from maintaining one of the most eclectic exhibitions in the country.

⊙ Capitol Hill

The Capitol, appropriately, sits atop Capitol Hill (what Pierre L'Enfant called 'a pedestal waiting for a monument'; we'd say it's more of a stump, but hey), across a plaza from the dignified Supreme Court and Library of Congress. Congressional office buildings surround the plaza. A pleasant brownstone residential district stretches from E Capitol St to Lincoln Park. Union Station, Capitol South and Eastern Market Metro stations serve this area.

★ Capitol   LANDMARK

(East Capitol St NE & First St) Since 1800, this is where the legislative branch of American government – ie Congress – has met to write the country's laws. The lower House of Representatives (435 members) and upper Senate (100) meet respectively in the south and north wings of the building.

A visitor center (www.visitthecapitol.gov; 1st St NE & E Capitol St; ⊙ 8:30am-4:30pm Mon-Sat) showcases the exhaustive background of a building that fairly sweats history. If you book in advance (http://tours.visitthecapitol.gov), you can go on a free tour of the interior, which is as daunting as the exterior, cluttered with the busts, statues and personal mementos of generations of Congress members and a museum-worthy collection

of art. Note that it is also possible to queue for same-day tour passes at a walk-up line near an information desk of the visitor center; arrive early if you want a pass.

To watch Congress in action, US citizens can request visitor passes from their representatives or senators (☏ 202-224-3121); foreign visitors must show their passports at the House gallery. Congressional committee hearings are actually more interesting (and substantive) if you care about what's being debated; check for a schedule, locations and to see if they're open to the public (they often are) at www.house.gov and www.senate.gov.

Library of Congress   LANDMARK

(www.loc.gov; 1st St SE; ⊙ 8:30am-4:30pm Mon-Sat) FREE To prove to Europeans that America is cultured, John Adams plunked the world's largest library on Capitol Hill. The LOC's motivation is simple: 'universality' – the idea that all knowledge is useful. Stunning in scope and design, the building's baroque interior and neoclassical flourishes are set off by a main reading room that looks like an ant colony constantly harvesting 29 million books. The visitor center (p262) and tours of the reading rooms are both located in the Jefferson Building, just behind the Capitol building.

Supreme Court   LANDMARK

(☏ 202-479-3030; www.supremecourt.gov; 1 1st St NE; ⊙ 9am-4:30pm Mon-Fri; M Capitol South) FREE Even non-law students are impressed by the highest court in America. Arrive early to watch arguments (periodic Mondays through Wednesdays October to April). You can visit the permanent exhibits and the building's seven-spiral staircase year-round.

Folger Shakespeare
Library & Theatre   LIBRARY

(www.folger.edu; 201 E Capitol St SE; ⊙ 10am-5pm Mon-Sat, noon-5pm Sun; M Capitol South) FREE The Folger houses the world's largest collection of Shakespeare materials, and is open for both general visitation as well as ticketed performances and lectures.

National Postal Museum   MUSEUM

(www.postalmuseum.si.edu; 2 Massachusetts Ave NE; ⊙ 10am-5:30pm; ♿; M Union Station) FREE This museum has the planet's largest stamp collection, plus an antique mail plane and some moving war letters. A decent microbrewery sits above the museum.

SMITHSONIAN INSTITUTION MUSEUMS

Massive in size and ambition, the 19 Smithsonian museums (☎202-633-1000; www. si.edu; ☉10am to 5:30pm) FREE, galleries and zoo – all admission free – comprise the world's largest museum and research complex. You could spend weeks wandering endless corridors taking in the great treasures, artifacts and ephemera from America and beyond. Massive dinosaur skeletons, lunar modules and artworks from every corner of the globe are all part of the Smithsonian largesse. Thanks go to the curious Englishman James Smithson, who never visited the USA but willed the fledgling nation $500,000 to found an 'establishment for the increase and diffusion of knowledge' in 1826.

The Smithsonian's latest work-in-progress is the $500-million National Museum of African American History and Culture (www.nmaahc.si.edu; cnr Constitution Ave & 14th St NW), scheduled to open in 2015. Until then, you can peruse its temporary galleries on the 2nd floor of the National Museum of American History (p260).

Most museums are open daily (except Christmas Day). Some have extended hours in summer. Be prepared for lines and bag checks.

United States
Botanic Garden   GARDENS
(www.usbg.gov; 100 Maryland Ave SW; ☉10am-5pm; ♿; Ⓜ Federal Center SW) FREE This incongruous addition to the Hill is hot, sticky and green, with more than 4000 different plant species on display.

◉ Tidal Basin

It's magnificent to stroll around this constructed inlet and watch the monument lights wink across the Potomac. The blooms here are loveliest during the Cherry Blossom Festival, the city's annual spring rejuvenation, when the basin bursts into a pink-and-white floral collage. The original trees were a gift from the city of Tokyo, and planted in 1912.

Jefferson Memorial   MONUMENT
(900 Ohio Dr SW) FREE The domed memorial is etched with the Founding Father's most famous writings – although historians criticize some of the textual alterations (edited, allegedly, for space considerations). Regardless, there are wonderful views across the waterfront onto the Mall.

FDR Memorial   MONUMENT
(Memorial Park) FREE This 7.5-acre monument stands as tribute to the longest-serving president in US history and the era he governed. In a thoughtful, well-laid-out path, visitors are taken through the Depression, the New Deal era and WWII. It's best visited at night, when the interplay of rock, fountains and the lights of the Mall are enchanting.

Martin Luther King Jr
Memorial   MONUMENT
(www.mlkmemorial.org) FREE The Martin Luther King Jr Memorial, which overlooks the banks of the Tidal Basin, is the Mall's first memorial dedicated to both a nonpresident and an African American, and pays moving tribute (through quotes taken from a dozen speeches) to one of the world's great peace advocates.

◉ Downtown

Downtown Washington began in what is now called Federal Triangle, but has since spread north and east, encompassing the area east of the White House to Judiciary Sq at 4th St, and from the Mall north to roughly M St.

Reynolds Center for American Art MUSEUM
(cnr F & 8th Sts NW; ☉11:30am-7pm) FREE Don't miss the Reynolds Center for American Art, which combines the National Portrait Gallery (www.npg.si.edu) with the American Art Museum (http://americanart.si.edu) to create perhaps the most immersive, impressive collection of American art anywhere. From haunting depictions of both the inner city and rural heartland to the self-taught visions of itinerant wanderers, the center has dedicated itself to capturing the optimism and critical self-appraisal of American art, and it succeeds. The inner courtyard, roofed with slanting glass that filters the sunlight, is a lovely spot to relax in, while the impressive 3rd floor, once the model building of the national patent office, now serves as a stunning baroque great hall.

National Archives
LANDMARK

(www.archives.gov; 700 Constitution Ave NW; ⊙10am-7pm mid-Mar–early Sep, to 5:30pm early Sep–mid-Mar) **FREE** It's hard not to feel a little in awe of the big three documents in the National Archives: the Declaration of Independence, the Constitution and the Bill of Rights, plus one of four copies of the Magna Carta. Taken together, it becomes clear just how radical the American experiment was for its time. The Public Vaults, a bare scratching of archival bric-a-brac, make a flashy rejoinder to the main exhibit.

International Spy Museum
MUSEUM

(☑202-393-7798; www.spymuseum.org; 800 F St NW; adult/child $20/15; ⊙9am-7pm; ◉; ⓂGallery Place-Chinatown) You like those bits in the Bond movies with Q? Then you'll like the immensely popular International Spy Museum. All the undercover tools of the trade on display make this place great for (secret) history buffs. Get there early.

National Building Museum
MUSEUM

(www.nbm.org; 401 F St NW; adult/child $8/5; ⊙10am-5pm Mon-Sat, from 11am Sun, tours daily 11:30am, 12:30pm & 1:30pm; ◉; ⓂJudiciary Sq) Devoted to architecture and urban design, this underappreciated museum is appropriately housed in a magnificent 19th-century edifice modeled after the Renaissance-era Palazzo Farnese in Rome. Four stories of ornamented balconies flank the dramatic 316ft-wide atrium, and the gold Corinthian columns rise 75ft high. Rotating exhibits on different aspects of the built environment are hidden in rooms off the atrium.

Renwick Gallery
MUSEUM

(www.americanart.si.edu/renwick; 1661 Pennsylvania Ave NW; ⊙10am-5:30pm; ◉; ⓂFarragut West) **FREE** Near the White House, the Renwick Gallery is set in a stately 1859 mansion and exhibits a superb collection of American crafts and decorative-art pieces. Highlights include some over-the-top works such as Larry Fuente's extravagantly kitsch *Game Fish* and Beth Lipman's ethereal *Bancketje (Banquet)*.

Old Post Office Pavilion
LOOKOUT

(www.oldpostofficedc.com; 1100 Pennsylvania Ave NW; ⊙10am-8pm Mon-Sat, to 7pm Sun; ⓂFederal Triangle) **FREE** If you don't want the hassle of the lines at the Washington Monument, head to this little-visited 1899 Romanesque Revival building, whose 315ft observation tower gives great downtown panoramas.

Down below, there's a floodlit atrium and international food court.

Ford's Theatre
HISTORIC SITE

(☑202-426-6924; www.fords.org; 511 10th St NW; tours $2.50; ⊙9am-4:30pm; ⓂMetro Center, Gallery Place-Chinatown) **FREE** On April 14, 1865, John Wilkes Booth assassinated Abraham Lincoln in his box seat here. The theater still operates today; you can also take a tour of the theater and learn about the events that transpired on that fateful April night. There's a restored Lincoln Museum devoted to Lincoln's presidency that you can see as part of the tour. Arrive early to get a ticket, as limited numbers are admitted each day. You can also use your ticket to explore the nearby Petersen House (516 10th St), where Lincoln eventually gave up the ghost.

Marian Koshland Science Museum of the National Academy of Sciences
MUSEUM

(www.koshland-science-museum.org; cnr 6th & E Sts NW; adult/child $7/4; ⊙10am-6pm Wed-Mon; ◉; ⓂJudiciary Sq, Gallery Place-Chinatown) A big, kid-friendly complex of hands-on, educational fun with (as you would expect) a science-oriented focus.

◎ White House & Foggy Bottom

An expansive park called the Ellipse borders the Mall; on the east side is the powerbroker block of Pennsylvania Ave. Foggy Bottom was named for the mists that belched out of a local gasworks; now, as the home of the State Department and George Washington University, it's an upscale (if not terribly lively) neighborhood crawling with students and professionals.

★ White House
LANDMARK

(☑tours 202-456-7041; www.whitehouse.gov; ⊙tours 7:30am-11am Tue-Sat; ⓂFarragut West, Farragut North, McPherson Sq, Metro Center) The White House has survived both fire (the Brits torched it in 1814 – only a thunderstorm saved its complete destruction) and insults (Jefferson groused that it was 'big enough for two emperors, one Pope and the grand Lama'). Although its facade has changed little since 1924, its interior has seen frequent renovations. Franklin Roosevelt added a pool; Truman gutted the whole place (and simply discarded many of its historical features – today's rooms are replicas); Jacqueline Kennedy brought back antique furnishings and historic details; Nixon added a bowling alley; Carter installed solar roof panels, which Reagan then removed; Clinton added a jogging track; and George W Bush included a T-ball field. Cars can no longer pass the White House on Pennsylvania Ave, clearing the area for posing school groups and round-the-clock peace activists.

➜ **Tours**

A self-guided tour will lead you through the ground and 1st floors, but the 2nd and 3rd floors are off-limits, and we have to warn you: due to staffing reductions brought about by the government's inability to settle on a working budget, tours had been canceled until further notice at the time of writing. That said, the tours are so popular, we are confident (fingers crossed) they will resume.

If so, tours must be arranged (up to six months) in advance. Americans must apply via one of their state's members of Congress, and non-Americans must apply through either the US consulate in their home country or their country's consulate in DC. If that sounds like too much work, pop into the White House Visitor Center (www.whitehouse.gov; cnr 15th & E Sts NW; ⊘7:30am-4pm); it's not the real deal, but hey, there's executive paraphernalia scattered about.

➜ **Watergate**

The riverfront Watergate complex (www.watergatehotel.com; 2650 Virginia Ave NW; Ⓜ Foggy Bottom-GWU) encompasses apartments, boutiques and the office towers that made 'Watergate' a byword for political scandal after it broke that President Nixon's 'plumbers' had bugged the headquarters of the 1972 Democratic National Committee.

⊙ U Street, Logan Circle & Shaw

If you need proof that the District is a living, breathing, changing city as opposed to a calcified capital, look no further than U St. Through the 20th century, this road went from a center of African American commerce to a blighted drug-dealing corridor to possibly the most gentrified street in the city. Today the U St area (especially 14th St NW) is a center for dining, nightlife and shopping. The area's African American history is acknowledged by the presence of the African American Civil War Memorial, inscribed with the name of African American Civil War dead, at the U Street metro station. Nearby Shaw and Logan Circle are

> ### STEVEN F UDVAR-HAZY CENTER
>
> The Smithsonian National Air & Space Museum's **Steven F Udvar-Hazy Center** (www.nasm.si.edu/udvarhazy; 14390 Air & Space Museum Parkway; ⊘10am-5:30pm, to 6:30pm late May-early Sep; Ⓟ) FREE, located in Chantilly near Dulles airport, is a huge hangar filled with surplus planes and spacecraft that wouldn't fit at the museum's DC location. Highlights include the space shuttle *Enterprise*, the B-29 *Enola Gay*, SR-71 *Blackbird* and a Concorde supersonic airliner. While the museum is free, parking costs $15.

some of the city's most pleasant residential neighborhoods.

Meridian Hill Park   PARK
(www.nps.gov/mehi; btwn 15th, 16th, Euclid & W Sts NW; ⊘sunrise-sunset; Ⓜ U Street-Cardozo) This is an incredible bit of green space that gets short shrift in the list of America's great urban parks. What makes the park special is the way it emphasizes its distinctive geography. Lying on the fall line between the upland Piedmont Plateau and flat Atlantic Coastal Plain, the grounds are terraced like a hanging garden, replete with waterfalls, sandstone terraces and assorted embellishments that feel almost Tuscan. Many locals still call this Malcolm X Park.

Lincoln Theatre   LANDMARK
(☑202-328-6000; www.thelincolntheatre.org; 1215 U St NW) The historic Lincoln Theatre was an early cornerstone of the nation's African American renaissance when it was founded in 1922. Luminaries such as DC-native Duke Ellington as well as Louis Armstrong, Ella Fitzgerald, Billie Holiday, Sarah Vaughan and many others have lit up the stage here.

⊙ Dupont Circle

A well-heeled splice of gay community and DC diplomatic scene, this is city life at its best. Great restaurants, bars, bookstores and cafes, captivating architecture and the electric energy of a lived-in, happening neighborhood make Dupont worth a linger. The historic mansions have largely been converted into embassies, and Embassy Row (on Massachusetts Ave) runs through DC's thumping gay heart.

Phillips Collection MUSEUM
(www.phillipscollection.org; 1600 21st St NW; admission Mon-Fri free, Sat & Sun $10, ticketed exhibitions $12, chamber-music series per ticket $20; ⊙10am-5pm Tue & Wed, Fri & Sat, to 8:30pm Thu, 11am-6pm Sun, chamber-music series 4pm Sun Oct-May; ⓂDupont Circle) The first modern-art museum in the country (opened in 1921) houses a small but exquisite collection of European and American works – including pieces by Gauguin, van Gogh, Matisse, Picasso, O'Keeffe, Hopper and many other greats. It's partially set in a beautifully restored Georgian Revival mansion.

Textile Museum MUSEUM
(www.textilemuseum.org; 2320 S St NW; suggested donation $8; ⊙10am-5pm Tue-Sat, from 1pm Sun; ⓂDupont Circle) Set in two historic mansions in the Kalorama neighborhood, the oft-overlooked Textile Museum showcases beautifully wrought creations from across the globe, including pre-Columbian weavings, American quilts and Ottoman embroidery.

National Geographic Society Museum GALLERY
(☑202-857-7700; 1145 17 St NW; adult/child $11/7; ⊙10am-6pm; ⓂFarragut North) Rotating exhibits and lectures on the Society's worldwide expeditions are found here. Call ahead for details on what's offered.

⊙ Georgetown

Thousands of the bright and beautiful, from students to ivory-tower academics and diplomats, call this leafy, aristocratic neighborhood home. At night, shop-a-block M St becomes congested with traffic, turning into a weird mix of high-school cruising and high-street boutique.

The best way to explore the neighborhood is a stroll on the C&O Canal Towpath (☑20 2-653-5190; 1057 Thomas Jefferson St NW; ⊙9am-4:30pm Wed-Sun), which runs along a shaded path by a constructed waterway that once transported goods all the way to West Virginia. Also watch out for the Exorcist Stairs (3600 Prospect St NW), where Father Karras tumbled to his death in the eponymous 1973 horror movie.

Dumbarton Oaks MUSEUM, GARDENS
(www.doaks.org; 1703 32nd St NW; museum free, gardens adult/child $8/5; ⊙museum 2-5pm Tue-Sun, gardens 2-6pm Tue-Sun) A museum featuring exquisite Byzantine and pre-Columbian art is housed within this historic mansion. More impressive are the 10 acres of beautifully designed formal gardens, which are simply stunning during the springtime blooms. Visit on weekdays to beat the crowds.

Mt Zion United Methodist Church CHURCH
(www.mtzionumcdc.org; 1334 29th St NW) This church sits on one of the sites that recall the history of Georgetown's 19th-century free black community, who lived in an area known as Herring Hill. Founded in 1816, it claims DC's oldest black congregation. Its original site, on 27th St NW, was once a stop on the Underground Railroad.

Georgetown University UNIVERSITY
(www.georgetown.edu; cnr 37th & O Sts NW) Bill Clinton went to school here, which should give you an idea of the student body: smart, hard-working party people.

Georgetown Waterfront Park PARK
(www.georgetownwaterfrontpark.org; K St NW & Potomac River; ⊛) The Waterfront is a favorite with couples on first dates, singles hoping to hook up, families on an evening stroll and yuppies showing off their big yachts. The park begins at Washington Harbour (look for it east of 31st St NW), a modern complex of towers set around a circular terraced plaza filled with fountains (which light up like rainbows at night). Trees shade the pedestrian-friendly lanes, and benches dot the way, where you can sit and watch the rowing teams out on the water. Kids splash in the fountains at Wisconsin Ave's foot. At 33rd St there's a labyrinth in the grass; walk the circles and see if you feel more connected to the universe.

Oak Hill Cemetery CEMETERY
(www.oakhillcemeterydc.org; cnr 30th & R Sts NW; ⊙9am-4:30pm Mon-Fri, 1-4pm Sun) This 24-acre, obelisk-studded cemetery contains winding walks and 19th-century gravestones set into the hillsides of Rock Creek. It's a fantastic spot for a quiet walk, especially in spring, when it seems as if every wildflower in existence blooms on the grounds. James Renwick designed the lovely gatehouse and charming gneiss-stone chapel.

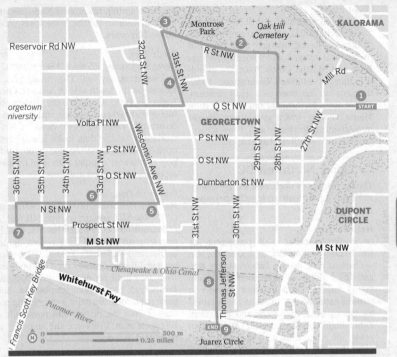

City Walk
Genteel Georgetown

START MT ZION CEMETERY
END GEORGETOWN WATERFRONT PARK
LENGTH 3 MILES; THREE HOURS

If ever a neighborhood was prime for ambling, it's Georgetown, in all its leafy, filigreed-manor glory.

African American **1 Mt Zion Cemetery**, near the intersection of 27th and Q Sts, dates from the early 1800s. The nearby Mt Zion church was a stop on the Underground Railroad; escaping slaves hid in a vault in the cemetery. The entrance to **2 Oak Hill Cemetery** (p266) is a few blocks away at 30th and R Sts NW. Stroll the obelisk-studded grounds and look for gravesites of prominent Washingtonians such as Edwin Stanton (Lincoln's war secretary). Up the road **3 Dumbarton Oaks** (p266) offers exquisite Byzantine art inside and sprawling, fountain-dotted gardens outside. The blooms in springtime are stunning.

George Washington's step-granddaughter Martha Custis Peter owned **4 Tudor Place** (p268), the neoclassical mansion at 1644 31st St. It has some of George's furnishings from Mount Vernon on show.

Head over to Wisconsin Ave NW, and stop in at **5 Martin's Tavern** (p276), where John F Kennedy proposed to Jackie. Walk along N St and you'll pass several Federal-style townhouses in the 3300 block. JFK and Jackie lived at **6 3307 N St**, between 1958 and 1961.

At the corner of 36th St and Prospect Ave, stare down the **7 Exorcist Stairs** (p266). This is where demonically possessed Reagan of the *Exorcist* sent victims to their screaming deaths. Joggers use the stairs by day; at night the steps are legitimately creepy as hell.

Head to M St NW and pop in to whichever boutiques your wallet permits. At Jefferson St turn right and sniff your way to **8 Baked & Wired** (p273) to replenish with a monster cupcake and cappuccino. From there you can stroll down to **9 Georgetown Waterfront Park** (p266) to watch the boats along the Potomac River.

Tudor Place
MUSEUM

(www.tudorplace.org; 1644 31st St NW; 1hr house tour adult/child $10/3, self-guided garden tour $3; ⊙10am-3pm Tue-Sat, from noon Sun) This 1816 neoclassical mansion was owned by Thomas Peter and Martha Custis Peter, the granddaughter of Martha Washington. Today the mansion functions as a small museum, and features furnishings and artwork from Mount Vernon, which give a nice insight into American decorative arts. The 5 acres of grounds are beautifully landscaped.

Upper Northwest DC

The far reaches of northwest DC are primarily made up of leafy residential neighborhoods.

National Zoo
ZOO

(www.nationalzoo.si.edu; 3001 Connecticut Ave NW; ⊙10am-6pm Apr-Oct, to 4:30pm Nov-Mar; Ⓜ Cleveland Park, Woodley Park-Zoo/Adams Morgan) FREE Home to more than 2000 individual animals (400 different species) in natural habitats, this 163-acre zoo is famed for giant pandas Mei Xiang and Tian Tian. Other highlights include: the African lion pride; the Asian trail, with red pandas and giant Japanese salamander; and dangling orangutans swinging 50ft overhead from steel cables and interconnected towers (the 'O Line').

Washington National Cathedral
CHURCH

(☑ 202-537-6200; www.nationalcathedral.org; 3101 Wisconsin Ave NW; suggested donation $5; ⊙10am-5:30pm Mon-Fri, to 4:30pm Sat, 8am-5pm Sun; ☐32, 37) This Gothic cathedral, as dramatic as its European counterparts, blends both the spiritual and the profane in its architectural treasures. The stained-glass windows are stunning (check out the Space Window with its imbedded lunar rock), and you'll need binoculars to spy the Darth Vader gargoyle on the exterior. Specialized tours delve deeper into the esoteric; call or go online for the schedule.

Anacostia

The drive from Georgetown eastbound to Anacostia takes about 30 minutes – and the patience to endure a world of income disparity. The neighborhood's poverty in contrast to the Mall, sitting mere miles away, forms one of DC's (and America's) great contradictory panoramas. Some high end con-

dos have sprung up around Nationals, the baseball stadium for the home team Washington Nationals.

Yards Park
PARK

(www.yardspark.org; 355 Water St SE; ⊙7am to 2hr past sunset; Ⓜ Navy Yard) This lovely park is located on the north side of Anacostia near Nationals Park. It's one of the city's newer bits of sculpted public space, with a wooden boardwalk, excellent river views, a funky modernist bridge that looks like a giant, open-faced plastic straw, and a mini-tidal pool that is very popular with local families, especially on summer evenings.

Frederick Douglass National Historic Site
HISTORIC SITE

(☑ 877-444-6777; www.nps.gov/frdo; 1411 W St SE; ⊙9am-5pm Apr-Oct, to 4:30pm Nov-Mar; ☐B2, B4 from Anacostia Metro) FREE Freedom fighter, author and statesman Frederick Douglass occupied this beautifully sited hilltop house from 1878 until his death in 1895. Original furnishings, books, photographs and other personal belongings paint a compelling portrait of both the private and public life of this great man. Visits into the home are by organized tour only.

Anacostia Museum
MUSEUM

(☑ 202-633-4820; www.anacostia.si.edu; 1901 Fort Pl SE; ⊙10am-5pm; ☐W2, W3 from Anacostia Metro) FREE This Smithsonian museum is surrounded by the community that is the subject of its educational mission, and houses good rotating exhibits on the African American experience in the USA. Call ahead, as the museum closes for about a month between installations.

🏃 Activities

Under the auspices of the National Park Service (NPS), the 1754 acres of Rock Creek Park (www.nps.gov/rocr; ⊙sunrise-sunset; Ⓜ Cleveland Park, Woodley Park-Zoo/Adams Morga) follow Rock Creek as it winds through the northwest of the city. There are miles of bicycling, hiking and horseback-riding trails, and even a few coyotes. The C&O Canal offers cycling and hiking trails in canalside parks, and the lovely 11-mile Capital Crescent Trail (www.cctrail.org; Water St) connects Georgetown north to Silver Spring, MD, via splendid Potomac River views. Fifteen miles north of DC, Great Falls National Park (p300) is an outstanding slice of wilderness, great for rafting or rock climbing on the beautiful cliffs that hang over the Potomac.

The **Potomac Heritage National Scenic Trail** (www.nps.gov/pohe) connects Chesapeake Bay to the Allegheny Highlands along an 830-mile network that includes DC's **C&O Canal Towpath** (adult/child $8/5; ⊙ Apr–mid-Aug), the 17-mile Mt Vernon Trail (Virginia) and the 75-mile Laurel Highlands Trail (Pennsylvania).

Paddleboat rentals (☑ 202-479-2426; www.tidalbasinpaddleboats.com/; 1501 Maine Ave SW; 2-person boat per hr $12) are available at the boathouse at Tidal Basin. At the Potomac River end of Rock Creek Park, **Thompson Boat Center** (www.thompsonboatcenter.com; 2900 Virginia Ave NW; per hr/day water craft from $10/24, bikes from $7/28; ⊙ 8am-5pm Mar-Oct) rents canoes, kayaks and bikes.

Big Wheel Bikes (www.bigwheelbikes.com; 1034 33rd St NW; per 3hr/day $21/35; ⊙ 11am-7pm Tue-Fri, 10am-6pm Sat & Sun) is a good bike-rental outfitter, or try **Capital Bikeshare** (☑ 877-430-2453; www.capitalbikeshare.com; membership 24hr/3 days $7/15), a scheme modeled on bike-sharing schemes in Europe. It has a network of 1000-plus bicycles scattered at 100-odd stations around DC. To check out a bike, select the membership, insert credit card and off you go. The first 30 minutes are free; after that, rates rise exponentially ($1.50/3/6 per extra 30/60/90 minutes). Call or go online for complete details.

☞ Tours

DC Metro Food Tours WALKING TOUR
(☑ 800-979-3370; www.dcmetrofoodtours.com; per person $30-65) These walking tours take in the culinary riches of DC, exploring various neighborhoods and stopping for bites along the way. Offerings include Eastern Market, U St, Little Ethiopia, Georgetown and Alexandria, VA.

DC by Foot WALKING TOUR
(www.dcbyfoot.com) Guides for this free, tip-based walking tour dispense intriguing stories and historical details on different walks covering the National Mall, Arlington Cemetery and Lincoln's assassination.

Bike & Roll CYCLE TOUR
(www.bikethesites.com; adult/child from $40/30; ⊙ mid-Mar–Nov) Offers a handful of day and evening bike tours around the city (plus combo boat–bike trips to Mt Vernon).

WASHINGTON, DC, FOR CHILDREN

The top destination for families is undoubtedly the (free!) National Zoo, and museums around the city will entertain and educate children of all ages. But if you – or they – tire of indoor attractions, there are plenty of enticing green spaces, such as the excellent Yards Park.

The DC-area **Our Kids** (www.our-kids.com) website has listings for kid-centric shows and events, family-friendly restaurants and loads of activity ideas.

Many hotels offer babysitting services, but you can also book through the reputable organization **Mothers' Aides** (☑ 703-250-0700; www.mystaffingsolutions.com/).

The wide-open spaces of the Mall are perfect for outdoor family fun, whether you want to throw a Frisbee, have a picnic, ride the old-fashioned **carousel** (tickets $2.50) or stroll through museums.

Kids like things that go squish and/or make other things go squish; they can find both in the dinosaurs and insects of the National Museum of Natural History (p257). The Kennedy Center (p281) puts on entertaining shows for tots, and the National Air & Space Museum (p257) has moon rocks, IMAX films and a wild simulation ride.

The National Theatre (p281) offers free Saturday-morning performances, from puppet shows to tap dancers (reservations required); the **Discovery Theater** (www.discoverytheater.org; 1100 Jefferson Dr SW; ⊞; Ⓜ Smithsonian) stages entertaining shows for young audiences; and the **Imagination Stage** (☑ 301-961-6060; www.imaginationstage.org; 4908 Auburn Ave, Bethesda, MD; ⊙ 301-961-6060; Ⓜ Bethedsda) is a wonderful children's theater in Bethesda, a Metro-accessible suburb just north of DC.

Located about 15 miles east of downtown in Largo, MD, **Six Flags America** (☑ 301-249-1500; www.sixflags.com/america; 13710 Central Avenue Upper Marlboro, MD ; adult/child $60/38; ⊙ May-Oct, hours vary) offers a full array of roller coasters and tamer kiddie rides. Take the Metro blue line to Largo, then take the C22 bus to the park.

WASHINGTON, DC & THE CAPITAL REGION WASHINGTON, DC

City Segway Tours TOUR
(☎ 202-626-0017; http://citysegwaytours.com/washington-dc; $70) Extremely popular and relaxing way of seeing the major sights along the Mall and in Penn Quarter.

✿✿ Festivals & Events

National Cherry Blossom Festival CULTURE
(www.nationalcherryblossomfestival.org; ⊙ late Mar-early Apr) This festival marks DC at her prettiest.

Smithsonian Folklife Festival CULTURE
(www.festival.si.edu; ⊙ Jun & Jul) This fun family event, held over two weekends in June and July, features distinctive regional folk art, crafts, food and music.

Independence Day CULTURE
(⊙ Jul 4) Not surprisingly, Independence Day is a big deal here, celebrated with a parade, an open-air concert and fireworks over the Mall.

🛏 Sleeping

For B&Bs and private apartments citywide, contact Bed & Breakfast Accommodations (☎ 877-893-3233; www.bedandbreakfast-dc.com).

If you bring a car to DC, plan on $20 upwards per day for in-and-out privileges (or stay in Arlington or Alexandria, where some hotels have free parking). Keep in mind that accommodations prices in DC get hit with a hefty 14.5% hotel tax on top of room rates.

🛏 Capitol Hill

Liaison HOTEL $$
(☎ 202-638-1616; www.affinia.com; 415 New Jersey Ave NW; r from $200; P ⊛ @ 🛜 ≋; Ⓜ Union Station) The Liason has jazzed up the accommodation options in Capitol Hill. Modernist rooms come in a stately slate-and-earth-tones color palette, which creates a feeling that's the right mix of corporate business and playful fun times. That said, the rooftop is all about the latter; there's trippy house music and a rooftop pool that seems perpetually occupied by attractive folks. It's within spitting distance of the Capitol.

Hotel George BOUTIQUE HOTEL $$$
(☎ 202-347-4200; www.hotelgeorge.com; 15 E St NW; r from $290; P ⊛ @ 🛜; Ⓜ Union Station) George was the first DC hotel to take the term 'boutique' to a daring, ultramodern level. The stylish interior is framed by clean

lines, chrome-and-glass furniture and modern art. Rooms exude a cool creamy-white Zen. The pop-art presidential accents (paintings of American currency, artfully rearranged and diced up) are a little overdone, but that's a minor complaint about what is otherwise the hippest lodging on the Hill.

🛏 Downtown & White House Area

Hostelling International – Washington DC HOSTEL $
(☎ 202-737-2333; www.hiwashingtondc.org; 1009 11th St NW; dm incl breakfast $30-55, r $120-150; ⊛ @ 🛜; Ⓜ Metro Center) Top of the budget picks, this large, friendly hostel attracts a laid-back international crowd and has loads of amenities: loungerooms, a pool table, free tours and movie nights, a kitchen and a laundry.

Hotel Monaco HOTEL $$
(☎ 202-628-7177; www.monaco-dc.com; 700 F St NW; r from $410, ste from $670; P ⊖ ⊛ @ 🛜; Ⓜ Gallery Place-Chinatown) The neoclassical facade has aged with considerable grace at this marble temple to stylish glamour. Free goldfish on request and a geometric, deco-inspired interior help polish the 1930s cool-daddy-o vibe. All this is in the historic, grand Corinthian-columned 1839 Tariff Building. The location works well for families: it's across the street from the Spy Museum, Smithsonian American Art Museum and Metro, and just four blocks from the Mall.

Hotel Harrington HOTEL $$
(☎ 800-424-8532, 202-628-8140; www.hotel-harrington.com; 436 11th St NW; r $130-200; P ⊛ 🛜; Ⓜ Federal Triangle) One of the most affordable options near the Mall, this aging, family-run hotel has small, basic rooms that are clean but in definite need of an update. Helpful service and a great location make the Harrington great value for travelers who don't mind a little lack of amenities.

★ Hay-Adams Hotel LUXURY HOTEL $$$
(☎ 202-638-6600; www.hayadams.com; 800 16th St NW; r from $450; P ⊛ @ 🛜 ≋; Ⓜ McPherson Sq) One of the city's great heritage hotels, the Hay is a beautiful old building, where 'nothing is overlooked but the White House.' It's named for two mansions that once stood on the site (owned by secretary of state John Hay and historian Henry Adams) that were the nexus of Washington's political and intellectual elite. Today the hotel has a palaz-

zo-style lobby and probably the best rooms of the old-school luxury genre in the city: puffy mattresses like clouds, four-poster canopies and gold-braid tassels.

Morrison-Clark Inn   HISTORIC HOTEL $$
(☑202-898-1200; www.morrisonclark.com; 1015 L St NW; r $200-350; P🅿❄@🛜; MMt Vernon Sq/7th St Convention Center) Listed on the Register of Historic Places, this elegant inn comprises two 1864 residences filled with fine antiques, chandeliers, richly hued drapes and other features evocative of the antebellum South. Some rooms come with private balconies or decorative marble fireplaces.

U Street, Shaw & Logan Circle

Chester Arthur House   B&B $$
(☑877-893-3233; www.chesterarthurhouse.com; 13th & P Sts NW; r incl breakfast $175-275; ❄🛜; MU Street-Cardozo) Run by a delightful couple with serious travel experience under their belts – they both have National Geographic credentials – this is a good option for those wanting to explore beneath Washington's surface. Accommodations are in one of three rooms in a beautiful Logan Circle row house which is filled with antiques and collected ephemera from the hosts' global expeditions.

Hotel Helix   BOUTIQUE HOTEL $$$
(☑866-508-0658, 202-462-9001; www.hotelhelix.com; 1430 Rhode Island Ave NW; r from $220; P🅿❄@🛜; MDupont Circle, U Street-Cardozo) Modish and highlighter bright, the Helix is playfully hip – the perfect hotel for the bouncy international set that makes up the surrounding neighborhood. Little touches suggest a youthful energy (Pez dispensers in the minibar) balanced with worldly cool, such as the pop-punk decor – just camp enough to be endearing. Specialty rooms include Bunk (that's right, bunk beds) and studios with kitchenettes; all rooms have comfy, crisp-sheet beds and flat-screen TVs.

Adams Morgan

American Guest House   B&B $$
(☑202-588-1180; www.americanguesthouse.com; 2005 Columbia Rd NW; r incl breakfast $160-220; ❄@🛜; MDupont Circle) This 12-room bed-and-breakfast earns high marks for its warm, friendly service, good breakfasts and elegantly furnished rooms. Decor runs the gamut from Victorian vibe (room 203) to New England cottage (room 304) to colonial love nest (room 303). Some quarters are rather small.

Adam's Inn   B&B $$
(☑202-745-3600; www.adamsinn.com; 1746 Lanier Pl NW; r incl breakfast with bath $129-99, without bath $99-159; P🅿❄🛜; MWoodley Park-Zoo/Adams Morgan) On a pretty tree-lined street near Adams Morgan, this townhouse has small but nicely decorated rooms; thin walls mean you might hear your neighbor.

Dupont Circle

Hotel Palomar   HOTEL $$
(☑877-866-3070, 202-448-1800; www.hotelpalomar-dc.com; 2121 P St NW; r $260-380; P🅿❄@🛜✖🛜; MDupont Circle) The Palomar brings in a stylish business clientele, plus a whole lot of pooches. Room decor is bright, colorful and lashed with pop-art accents. The outdoor pool and deck go beyond the norm. Then there's the pet-friendly vibe, which the hotel does up big time. Not only does your dog get pampered each night with gourmet treats at turndown, it can also get a massage. Or drop your pooch off at the Dish, the hotel's pet lounging area.

Dupont Collection   B&B $$
(☑202-467-6777; http://thedupontcollection.com; r $120-260; P🅿❄🛜) If you're craving a good range of B&B coziness in the heart of the capital, check out these three excellent heritage properties. Most-centrally located are the inns at Dupont North (☑202-467-6777; www.thedupontcollection.com; 1620 T St NW; r incl breakfast $115-270; ❄🛜; MDupont Circle) and Dupont South (☑202-467-6777; www.thedupontcollection.com; 1312 19th St NW; r incl breakfast $115-230; ❄🛜; MDupont Circle); the former feels like the modern home of a wealthy friend, while the latter evokes much more of a chintz-and-lacy-linen sensibility. The Brookland (http://thedupontcollection.com; 3742 12th St NE, Brookland Inn) is in the far northeast (but Metro accessible).

Akwaaba   B&B $$$
(☑866-466-3855; www.akwaaba.com; 1708 16th St NW; r $200-265; P🅿❄🛜; MDupont Circle) Part of a small chain of B&Bs that emphasize African American heritage in its properties, the well-located Dupont branch has uniquely furnished rooms set in a late-19th-century mansion. Expect a friendly welcome and excellent cooked breakfasts.

Carlyle Suites APARTMENT **$$$**
(📞 202-234-3200; www.carlylesuites.com; 1731 New Hampshire Ave NW; apt $180-320; 🅿️❄️@📶; Ⓜ️ Dupont Circle) Inside this all-suites art-deco gem, you'll find sizeable, handsomely furnished rooms with crisp white linens, luxury mattresses, 37in flat-screen TVs and full kitchens. The friendly staff is first rate, and the added extras include free use of laptops and complimentary access to the Washington Sports Club. Plus the on-site bar pours a mean martini. Parking is limited to 20 spaces (out of about 170 rooms), and it's first-come, first-served.

🛏️ Georgetown

Graham Georgetown HOTEL **$$$**
(📞 202-337-0900; http://thegrahamgeorgetown. com/; 1075 Thomas Jefferson St NW; r from $330; 🅿️❄️@📶; Ⓜ️ Foggy Bottom-GWU to DC Circulator) Set smack in the heart of Georgetown, the Graham occupies the intersection between stately tradition and modernist hip. Rooms have tasteful floral prints and duochrome furnishings with geometric accents. Even the most basic rooms have linens by Liddell Ireland and Bvlgari White Tea bath amenities, which means you'll be as fresh, clean and beautiful as the surrounding Georgetown glitterati.

🍴 Eating

As you might expect of one of the world's most international cities, DC has an eclectic palate, with a superb array of restaurants serving Ethiopian, Indian, Southeast Asian, French, Italian and more, plus good old-fashioned Southern fare. Annoyingly, this is an expensive town to eat out in; cheap options are rare and midrange dining options can be poor value for money. Well, unless you follow our recommendations, that is.

🍴 Capitol Hill

H St NE forms a continuous stretch of restaurants and bars, and becomes a nightlife miracle mile come weekends. To get to H St, you can either walk from Union Station (H & 14th, which is the far end of the strip, is 1.3 miles away), or take a free H St shuttle from Gallery Place-Chinatown and Minnesota Ave Metro stops. The shuttle runs from 5pm until Metro rail closes (midnight on weekdays, 3am on weekends). And 8th St SE near Eastern Market – also known as Bar-racks Row – is also packed with restaurants and bars.

Eastern Market MARKET **$**
(225 7th St SE; ⏱️ 7am-7pm Tue-Fri, to 6pm Sat, 9am-5pm Sun) One of the icons of Capitol Hill, this covered arcade sprawls with delectable produce and good cheer on the weekends. The crab cakes at the Market Lunch stall are divine.

Toki Underground ASIAN **$**
(📞 202-388-3086; www.tokiunderground.com; 1234 H St NE; mains $10; ⏱️ 5-10pm Mon-Wed, to 11pm Thu, to midnight Fri & Sat, closed Sun; 🚍 H Street shuttle) Spicy, belly-warming ramen noodles and dumplings sum up the menu in wee Toki. Steaming pots and pans obscure the busy chefs, while diners slurp and sigh contentedly. No reservations are taken and there's typically a long wait. Take the opportunity to explore surrounding bars; Toki will text when your table's ready. Despite the name, Toki Underground is on the 2nd floor. It's not marked; look for the Pug bar sign – the restaurant is above it.

Maine Avenue Fish Market SEAFOOD **$**
(1100 Maine Ave SW; meals from $7; ⏱️ 8am-9pm; Ⓜ️ L'Enfant Plaza) In case you didn't know, Washington, DC, is basically in Maryland, and Maryland does the best seafood in America. You get it fresh here – still flopping, in fact – where locals will kill, strip, shell, gut, fry, broil or whatever your fish, crabs, oysters etc in front of your eyes.

Atlas Room AMERICAN **$$**
(📞 202-388-4020; 1015 H St NE; mains $11-25; ⏱️ 5:30-9:30pm Mon, to 10pm Tue-Thu, to 10:30pm Fri & Sat, 5-9:30pm Sun; 🚍 H Street shuttle) The Atlas Room takes some cues from classical French and Italian gastronomy, but blends them in uniquely American ways, while drawing from an entirely seasonal roster of ingredients; in summer you might enjoy crab fritters, while in winter a braised daube of beef will melt your tongue (in a good way!).

Granville Moore's BELGIAN **$$**
(📞 202-399-2546; www.granvillemoores.com; 1238 H St NE; mains $11-16; ⏱️ 5pm-midnight Sun-Thu, to 3am Fri & Sat; 🚍 H Street shuttle) One of the anchors of the bohemian Atlas District (which runs along H St NE), Granville Moore's bills itself as a gastropub with a Belgian fetish. Indeed you'll find more

TOP CAFES

★ **Baked & Wired** (☎ 202-333-2500; www.bakedandwired.com; 1052 Thomas Jefferson St NW; snacks $3-6; ⊙ 7am-8pm Mon-Thu, to 9pm Fri, 8am-9pm Sat, 9am-8pm Sun; 🛜) Baked & Wired is a cheery little Georgetown cafe that whips up beautifully made coffees and delectable desserts; it's a fine spot to join students in both real and virtual chatter (free wi-fi, of course).

Ching Ching Cha (1063 Wisconsin Ave NW; teas $6-12; ⊙ 11am-9pm) This airy, Zenlike tea-house feels a world away from the shopping mayhem of Georgetown's M St. Stop in for a pot of rare tea (more than 70 varieties). CCC also serves steamed dumplings, sweets and simple but flavorful three-course lunches ($30).

Pound (www.poundcoffee.com; 621 Pennsylvania Ave SE; mains $5-8; ⊙ 7am-9:30pm Mon-Sat, 8am-8pm Sun; 🛜; Ⓜ Eastern Market) In Capitol Hill, Pound serves high-quality coffees in an elegant rustic interior (exposed brick and timber, original plaster ceilings, wood floors and nicely lit artwork). Breakfast quesadillas, panini and daily lunch specials are tops – as is the Nutella latte.

Filter (www.filtercoffeehouse.com; 1726 20th St NW; ⊙ 7am-7pm Mon-Fri, 8am-7pm Sat & Sun; 🛜; Ⓜ Dupont Circle) On a quiet street in Dupont, Filter is a jewel-box-sized cafe with a tiny front patio, a hipsterish laptop-toting crowd and, most importantly, great coffee. Those who seek caffeinated perfection can get a decent flat white here.

than 70 Belgian beers, good pub fare and fun crowds most nights.

Ethiopic
ETHIOPIAN $$

(☎ 202-675-2066; 401 H St NE ; mains $12-17; ⊙ 5-10pm Tue-Thu, from noon Fri & Sun; 🚇 H Street shuttle) In a city with no shortage of Ethiopian joints, Ethiopic stands above the rest. We're big fans of the signature ho*t wat* (stews) and *tibs* (sauteed meat and veg), derived from tender lamb that's sat in a bath of herbs and satisfyingly hot spices. Pair with good spongy *injera* bread and simmered *gomen* (collard greens). Plenty of options for vegetarians and vegans.

Ted's Bulletin
AMERICAN $$

(☎ 202-544-8337; www.tedsbulletin.com; 505 8th St SE; mains $10-18; ⊙ 7am-10:30pm, to 11:30pm Fri & Sat; 👶; Ⓜ Eastern Market) Plop into a booth in the art-deco-meets-diner ambience, and loosen the belt. Beer biscuits and sausage gravy for breakfast, meatloaf with ketchup glaze for dinner and other hipster spins on comfort foods hit the table. You've got to admire a place that lets you substitute pop tarts for toast. Breakfast is available all day.

🍴 Downtown & White House Area

Merzi
INDIAN $

(☎ 202-656-3794; 415 7th St NW; meals under $10; ⊙ 11am-10pm Mon-Sat, to 9pm Sun; 🅿; Ⓜ Gallery Place-Chinatown, Archives-Navy Memorial) 🍴 If you need cheap Indian – especially cheap vegetarian Indian – in downtown DC, this is where to be. Merzi's setup is simple: choose a base (roti, rice, salad etc), a protein (chicken, lamb etc) or veg, then add sauces, chutney and such. Your wallet will barely feel lighter for the visit.

★ Rasika
INDIAN $$

(☎ 202-637-1222; www.rasikarestaurant.com; 633 D St NW; mains $16-26; ⊙ 11:30am-2:30pm Mon-Fri, 5:30-10:30pm Mon-Thu, to 11pm Fri, 5-11pm Sun; 🅿; Ⓜ Archives-Navy Memorial) Rasika is as cutting edge as Indian food gets, both in terms of menu and presentation. The latter resembles a Jaipur palace decorated by a flock of modernist art-gallery curators; the former... well, it's *good*. Narangi duck is juicy, almost unctuous, and pleasantly nutty thanks to the addition of cashews; the deceptively simple *dal* (lentils) have the right kiss of sharp fenugreek. Vegans and vegetarians will feel a lot of love here.

Hill Country Barbecue
BARBECUE $$

(☎ 202-556-2050; 410 7th St NW; mains $13-22; ⊙ 11:30am-2am; Ⓜ Archives-Navy Memorial, Gallery Place-Chinatown) Penn Quarter is frankly overflowing with overpriced, overrated eating establishments. Hill Country is none of those things. It's a total anomaly for DC – a Texas-themed joint filled with cowboy hats and boots that doesn't feel corny; a barbecue spot that serves excellent smoked meat;

a live-music venue that hosts great Texas honky-tonk shows.

Zaytinya
MEDITERRANEAN $$

(☑ 202-638-0800; 701 9th St NW; mezze $7-13; ⊙ 11:30am-11:30pm Tue-Sat, to 10pm Sun & Mon) One of the culinary crown jewels of chef José Andrés, ever-popular Zaytinya serves superb Greek, Turkish and Lebanese mezze (small plates) in a long, narrow dining room with soaring ceilings and all-glass walls. Stop in for $4 happy-hour specials from 4:30pm to 6:30pm.

★ Central Michel Richard
FUSION $$$

(☑ 202-626-0015; 1001 Pennsylvania Ave NW; mains $19-34; ⊙ 11:30am-2:30pm Mon-Fri, 5-10:30pm Mon-Thu, to 11pm Fri & Sat; ✐; Ⓜ Federal Triangle, Archives-Navy Memorial) Michel Richard is known for high-end eating establishments in the District, but Central stands out. It's aimed at hitting a comfort-food sweet spot; you're dining in a four-star bistro where the food is old-school favorites with a twist: lobster burgers, a sinfully complex meatloaf and fried chicken that redefines what fried chicken can be. It's an awesome dining experience, well worth a splurge.

Bibiana
ITALIAN $$$

(☑ 202-216-9550; 1100 New York Ave NW; mains $18-34; ⊙ 11:30am-2:30pm Mon-Fri, 5:30-10:30pm Mon-Wed, to 11pm Thu-Sat; ✐) Owned by Ashok Bajaj of Rasika, Bibiana pushes contemporary Italian just as its sister establishment does with Indian cuisine. Chiluluy-esque chandeliers and light fixtures hang over an ultramodern dining room, where diners enjoy tortellini with guinea fowl and foie gras, or poached halibut over green-tomato polenta. A meat-free tasting menu is a standout in DC's vegetarian repertoire.

✕ U Street, Shaw & Logan Circle

American Ice Company
BARBECUE $

(☑ 202-758-3562; 917 V St NW; mains under $10; ⊙ 5pm-2am Mon-Thu, to 3am Fri, 1pm-3am Sat, 1pm-2am Sun; Ⓜ U Street-Cardozo) The usual U St/Columbia Heights crew of hipsters, policy wonks (people who aren't politicians who work in politics as researchers, lobbyists, legislative aides etc) and policy wonks who kind of look like hipsters packs the cluttered interior and much nicer outdoor patio of this casual eatery. The focus is on barbecue and canned beer, pretty much in that order.

Try the gooey pork-and-cheese sandwich or the delicious pork nachos (yes, pork nachos).

Desperados
BURGERS $

(☑ 202-299-0433; 1342 U St NW; mains under $10; ⊙ 11am-1:30am Mon-Thu & Sun, to 2:30am Fri & Sat; Ⓜ U-St/Cardozo) This little cowboy-themed spot is a U St standby when you're out and need a cheap, filling burger. These beef patties don't play; they're the size of your face and come in several variations, including a pleasingly spicy Cajun version. The bar churns out cocktails that will lay you on your back.

El Centro
MEXICAN $$

(☑ 202-328-3131; 1819 14th St NW; mains $9-20; ⊙ 11am-11pm daily, brunch 10:30am-3pm Sat & Sun; ✐; Ⓜ U Street-Cardozo) El Centro is our favorite of Richard Sandoval's many outposts in DC. With sleek furniture, chic clientele and a sexy rooftop deck, it's often known as more nightlife spot than restaurant (the bar is open till 2am). For shame – this is excellent noveau-Mexican cuisine. The guacamole is the best in town, duck tacos are delicious and the slow-roasted carnitas (pork) met in your mouth.

Estadio
SPANISH $$

(☑ 202-319-1404; 1520 14th St NW; tapas $5-15; ⊙ Mon-Thu 5-10pm, to 11pm Fri & Sat, to 9pm Sun, 11:30am-2pm Fri-Sun; ✐; Ⓜ U Street-Cardozo) Estadio stands tall amid the Spanish cuisine purveyors of the capital. The tapas menu (which is the focus) is as deep as an ocean trench; there's three variations of *Iberico* ham and a delicious foie gras, scrambled egg and truffle open-faced sandwich. Wash it down with some traditional *calimocho* (red wine and coke).

Veranda on P
MEDITERRANEAN $$

(☑ 202-234-6870; 1100 P St NW; mains $12-25; ⊙ 5pm-12:30am Mon-Thu, later Sat & Sun; ✐; Ⓜ U Street-Cardozo) The interior of this cozy little nook vaguely brings a Greek Island to mind, but we prefer the outdoor eponymous veranda, which sits amid the handsome red-brick townhouses of Logan Circle. The food is Mediterranean and quite good value; melted Kefalograviera cheese is an excellent appetizer to set up for a main event of silky moussaka.

Pig
AMERICAN $$

(☑ 202-290-2821; 1320 14th St NW; mains $12-21; ⊙ noon-10:30pm Mon & Tue, to 11pm Wed & Thu, to 11:30pm Fri, 11am-11:30pm Sat, to 10pm Sun; Ⓜ U

THE BEAUTY OF BEN'S CHILI BOWL

Ben's Chili Bowl (www.benschilibowl.com; 1213 U St; mains $5-9; ⊙11am-2am Mon-Thu, to 4am Fri & Sat, to midnight Sun; MU Street-Cardozo) is to DC dining what the White House and Capitol are to sightseeing: a must-visit. To take that analogy further, while the White House and Capitol are the most recognizably important symbols of DC as a capital, Ben's holds the same status as regards DC as a place where people live. Opened and operated by Ben and Virginia Ali and family (Ben died in 2009; the alley adjacent is named in his honor), the diner-style Bowl has been around since 1958. It's one of the few businesses on U St to have survived the 1968 riots and the disruption that accompanied construction of the U St Metro stop. The main stock in trade are half-smokes, DC's meatier, smokier version of the hot dog, usually slathered in mustard and the namesake chili. Until recently, Bill Cosby was the only person who ate here for free, but Michelle Obama and daughters Sasha and Malia get the nod, too – though, apparently, not their presidential dad. That's a short list, as a lot of famous faces have passed through these doors, from Bono to both Bushes. Cash only.

Street-Cardozo) The Pig lives up to its name, offering plenty of porcine-inspired treats from crispy shank to a decadent cutlet-and-gruyere sandwich that will leave you lost for words. There's nonporky goodness as well, including some wonderful cornmeal-dusted oysters and a surprisingly vegetarian-friendly chickpea hash (that said, this isn't the best spot for herbivores).

Eatonville SOUTHERN $$
(☏202-332-9672; www.eatonvillerestaurant.com; 2121 U St NW; mains $9-21; ⊙11am-11pm Mon-Thu, to midnight Fri, 3pm-midnight Sat, 3-11pm Sun; MU Street-Cardozo) Novelist Zora Neal Hurston is the unconventional theme at this restaurant. The atmosphere is superb, a sort of bayou dripped through impressionist-style murals of the South, then resurrected upon a modernist, cavernous dining hall that looks like nothing less than a cathedral to black intelligentsia. Catfish come correct with cheese grits, and the andouille-and-sweet-potato hash...don't get us started. Wash it down with lavender lemonade, which, on hot summer days, is sort of like drinking sex.

Pearl Dive Oyster Palace SEAFOOD $$
(www.pearldivedc.com; 1612 14th St NW; mains $19-25; ⊙noon-3pm Fri & Sat, 11am-3pm Sun, 5-10pm daily; MU Street-Cardozo) 🌱 Flashy Pearl Dive serves exceptional sustainable oysters from both coasts, along with braised duck and oyster gumbo, crab cakes and insanely rich peanut-butter chocolate pie. Fresh air from the front windows wafts through the open industrial space, done up in a nautical, weathered-wood motif. No reservations; you'll need to take a number (like a deli).

🍴 Adams Morgan

Adams Morgan, particularly the area around 18th St and Columbia Rd NW, is lined with ethnic eateries and funky diners.

Diner AMERICAN $$
(www.dinerdc.com; 2453 18th St NW; mains $8-16; ⊙24hr; 👶; M Woodley Park-Zoo/Adams Morgan) This is the ideal spot for late-night breakfast, (crowded) weekend bloody Mary brunches or anytime you want unfussy, well-prepared American fare (omelets, stuffed pancakes, mac 'n' cheese, grilled Portobello sandwiches, burgers and the like). It's a good spot for kids, too (staff will even hang their Diner-made colorings on the wall).

Cashion's Eat Place AMERICAN $$$
(☏202-797-1819; www.cashionseatplace.com; 1819 Columbia Rd NW; mains $17-34; ⊙5:30-11pm Tue-Sun; M Woodley Park-Zoo/Adams Morgan) With an original menu and inviting decor, this little bistro is lauded as one of the city's very best. The mismatched furniture and flower boxes create an unpretentious setting for enjoying rich dishes such as scallion-cream sauced crab and bison rib eye with wild mushroom *bordelaise* sauce. The bar serves fancy late-night fare, such as pork cheek and goat's cheese quesadillas, till 2am on Friday and Saturday.

🍴 Dupont Circle

★**Afterwords Cafe** AMERICAN $$
(☏202-387-3825; www.kramers.com; 1517 Connecticut Ave; mains $15-24; ⊙7:30am-1:30am Sun-Thu, 24hr Fri & Sat; M Dupont Circle) Not your average bookstore cafe, this buzzing spot

overflows with good cheer at its packed cafe tables and outdoor patio. The menu features tasty bistro fare and an ample beer selection, making it a prime spot for happy hour or brunch and all hours on weekends.

Bistrot du Coin
FRENCH $$

(☎202-234-6969; www.bistrotducoin.com; 1738 Connecticut Ave; mains $14-24; ☺11:30am-11pm, to 1am Thu-Sat; ⛎Dupont Circle) For a quick culinary journey across the Atlantic, the lively and much-loved Bistro du Coin delivers the goods. You'll find consistently good onion soup, classic *steak-frites* (grilled steak and french fries), cassoulet, open-faced sandwiches and nine varieties of its famous *moules* (mussels).

Blue Duck Tavern
AMERICAN $$

(☎202-419-6755; www.blueducktavern.com; 1201 24th St NW; mains $16-34; ☺6:30am-2:30pm & 5:30-10:30pm Sun-Thu, till 11.30pm Fri & Sat; ⛍; ⛎Dupont Circle) The Blue Duck tries to create a rustic kitchen ambience in the midst of one of M St's uber-urbanized concrete corridors. The menu draws from farms across the country, mixing mains such as a pork terrine and trotter croquette made from pigs in Virginia, and crab cakes sourced from Louisiana.

Malaysia Kopitiam
MALAYSIAN $$

(☎202-833-6232; www.malaysiakopitiam.com; 1827 M St NW; mains $9-15; ☺11:30am-10pm Mon-Thu, to 11pm Fri & Sat, noon-10pm Sun; ⛎Dupont Circle) This hole-in-the-wall restaurant is a good spot to get your Malaysian fix. Standouts include the *laksas* (curry noodle soups), *roti canai* (flatbread served with chicken curry) and crispy squid salad.

★Little Serrow
THAI $$$

(1511 17th St NW; fixed menu per person $45; ☺5:30-10pm Tue-Thu, to 10:30 Fri & Sat) There' are a lot of annoying rules at Little Serrow. There's no phone, and no reservations. It only allows groups of four or less, and you'll be lining up around the block. And what for? Superlative Northern Thai cuisine. The single-option menu changes by the week; you might get chicken livers and long peppers, or shrimp paste, eggplant and chilies, or pig ears garnished with mint. Every dish comes with mountains of heaping fresh herbs.

Komi
FUSION $$$

(☎202-332-9200; www.komirestaurant.com; 1509 17th St NW; set menu $135; ☺5-11pm Tue-Sat; ⛎Dupont Circle) There's an admirable simplicity to Komi's changing menu, which is rooted in Greece and influenced by everything – primarily genius. Suckling pig for two; scallops and truffles; a roasted baby goat. Komi's fairytale of a dining space doesn't take groups larger than four, and you need to reserve way in advance – like, now.

✗ Georgetown

Et Voila
BELGIAN $$

(☎202-237-2300; 5120 MacArthur Blvd NW; mains $16-29; ☺11:30am-2:30pm & 5:30-10pm Tue-Fri & Sat, 11:30am-2:30pm Sat & Sun, 5-9:30pm Mon) A definite local gem, Et Voila sits in a beautiful corner of the Palisades, northwest of Georgetown. While the name suggests French, this spot leans a little north to Belgium. Dishes such as rib eye with *frites*, lobster risotto and roasted chicken have a hearty, rustic heft coupled with a refined execution. The atmosphere is supremely intimate.

Martin's Tavern
AMERICAN $$

(☎202-333-7370; www.martins-tavern.com; 1264 Wisconsin Ave NW; mains $12-25; ☺11am-1:30am Mon-Thu, to 2:30am Fri, 9am-2:30am Sat, 8am-1:30am Sun) Martin's is a favorite with Georgetown students and US presidents, who all enjoy the tavern's old-fashioned dining room and unfussy classics such as thick burgers, crab cakes and prime rib.

✗ Upper Northwest DC

2 Amys
PIZZA $$

(☎202-885-5700; www.2amyspizza.com; 3715 Macomb St NW; mains $9-14; ☺11am-10pm Tue-Thu, to 11pm Fri & Sat, noon-10pm Sun, 5-10pm Mon; ⛍; ⛎Tenleytown-AU then southbound ⛐31, 32, 36, 37) A bit out of the way (but a stone's throw from Washington National Cathedral), 2 Amys serves some of DC's best thin-crust pizzas. Pies are sprinkled with market-fresh ingredients and baked to perfection in a wood-burning oven. Avoid the weekend crowds.

Palena
AMERICAN $$$

(☎202-537-9250; www.palenarestaurant.com; 3529 Connecticut Ave NW; 3-/5-course menu $80/100; ☺5:30-10:30pm Tue-Sat; ⛎Cleveland Park) Tucked away in Cleveland Park, northwest on the Red Line, Palena is one of DC's food-loving heavyweights. Red snapper with ramps (wild leeks) and oyster mushrooms; artichoke risotto; and celery root soup with shrimp and almonds are recent favorites. Reserve ahead or eat in the more casual cafe (mains from $17 to $30).

Columbia Heights & Around

Pho 14   VIETNAMESE $
(202-986-2326; www.dcpho14.com; 1436 Park Rd NW; mains $8-13; 11:30am-9pm Sun-Wed, to 10pm Thu-Sat; Columbia Heights) Smart, solid Pho 14 ladles out steaming bowls of the namesake noodle soup, as well as stir-fry dishes and *banh mi* sandwiches (baguettes filled with meat and/or spicy veggies) to brisk lunchtime and dinner crowds.

Kangaroo Boxing Club   AMERICAN $
(KBC; 202-505-4522; 3410 11th St NW; mains $10-17; 5pm-2am Mon-Thu, to 3am Fri, 10am-3am Sat, to 2am Sun) The gastropub concept – but a hip, laid-back, Brooklyn-esque gastropub – is all the rage among DC's hip young things. Enter the KBC: it has a quirky theme (vintage boxing), delicious food (burgers, BBQ, sweet spoon bread, mac 'n' cheese and the like) and a deep beer menu.

El Chucho   MEXICAN $
(202-290-3313; 3313 11th St NW; tacos $6-12; 4pm-2am, to 3am Fri & Sat) There's a *Day of the Dead*-inspired interior, margaritas on tap, excellent *elote (corn)* smothered in white cheese and spices, and fresh guacamole. The tiny tacos leave us wanting more. Lots of cool tattooed staff members, and customers who love them.

Drinking & Nightlife

See the weekly *Washington City Paper* (p282) or *Washington Post* (p282) weekend section for comprehensive listings. Same-day concert and show tickets at half-price (no phone sales).

Capitol Hill & Downtown

Little Miss Whiskey's Golden Dollar   BAR
(www.littlemisswhiskeys.com; 1104 H St NE; from 5pm; H Street shuttle) If Alice had got back from Wonderland so traumatized by a near-beheading that she needed to start engaging in heavy drinking, we imagine she'd often pop down to Little Miss Whiskey's. She'd love the decor: somewhere between whimsical and the dark nightmares of a lost drug addict. And she'd probably have fun with the club kids partying on the upstairs dance floor on weekends.

H Street Country Club   BAR
(www.thehstreetcountryclub.com; 1335 H St NE; from 5pm Mon-Thu, from 4pm Fri-Sun; H Street shuttle) The Country Club is two levels of great. The bottom floor is packed with pool tables, skeeball and shuffleboard, while the top contains (seriously) its own mini-golf course ($7 to play) done up to resemble a tour of the city on a small scale.

18th Amendment   BAR
(www.18thdc.com; 613 Pennsylvania Ave SE; Eastern Market, Capitol South) The Amendment embraces a speakeasy theme – hence the name. Gangsters and bootleggers should head directly to the basement, where the furniture is made from beer barrels and whiskey crates, and there are pool tables on which to fight your duel.

U Street, Shaw & Logan Circle

Marvin   BAR
(www.marvindc.com; 2007 14th St NW; U Street-Cardozo) Stylish Marvin has a low-lit lounge with vaulted ceilings where DJs spin soul and rare grooves to a mixed 14th St crowd. The upstairs roof deck is a draw both on summer nights and in winter, when folks huddle under roaring heat lamps sipping cocktails and Belgian beers. Good bistro fare, too.

Patty Boom Boom   CLUB
(202-629-1712; 1359 U St NW; 8pm-midnight, to 3am Sat & Sun) A mixed crowd of policy wonks and Howard University undergrads pack this spot, either chilling to soft reggae during cool-down sets or getting freaky when the dancehall DJs get going. Either way the theme is Caribbean, as evinced by the eponymous beef and veg patties on sale for when you need something to soak up a rum punch.

Brixton   BAR
(202-560-5045; 901 U St NW; 5pm-2am, to 3am Sat, from 11am Sun) As the name implies, this is a slice of England in DC, although it's not corny Olde England. Rather, its hip young folk in tight jeans and ethnic scarves, stiff drinks, London slang and East End pop art on the walls. Has a decent pub-grubby menu if such is your fancy, and a rooftop patio with great views over U St.

Eastern & Southern USA Cuisine

Look at the photos of these dishes and tell us your mouth didn't just water. Eating is serious business in the region, and locals' time-honed, fiercely guarded recipes for barbecue sauce, fried chicken, apple pie and more are yours to seek out and yield to.

1. New York hot dog
The garlicky, all-beef frank is griddled to a crackling snap and dressed with spicy brown mustard, sauerkraut and onions.

2. Chicago deep-dish pizza
A hulking mass of crust rises three inches above the plate and cradles a molten pile of cheese and chunky tomato sauce.

3. Gumbo
The spicy soup/stew teems with oysters, shrimp and crab (or smoked meats if you're inland).

4. Pie
The South prefers pecan, Florida likes key lime, the Midwest bakes sugar cream and the Northeast enjoys fruit between its crusts.

5. Southern-style barbecue
The variations are mind-blowing, but expect some version of slow-cooked, wood-smoked pork, with sauces sweet or vinegary.

6. Wisconsin cheese
The chunks go way beyond cheddar, from cave-aged Gouda to cocoa-rubbed goat's-milk cheese and stinky Limburger.

7. Seafood
The region's bounty makes a heckuva chowder (rich, creamy soup), including oysters, clams and Maine's mighty lobsters.

8. Kentucky bourbon
The silky, caramel-colored whiskey gets its unique taste from corn and barrel aging. Drink it straight or with water.

9. Microbrews
It's a golden age for hopheads: you'll find small-batch brewers pouring delicious suds regionwide.

10. Corn bread
Mix cornmeal and buttermilk, bake in a cast-iron skillet, and voila: the bread of the South, best consumed butter-smothered.

11. Southern-fried chicken
All chefs have a secret recipe for the batter, but the constant is that the bird will pop out of the pan crisp outside and moist inside.

12. Cajun food
The bayou country's rustic fare marries native spices like sassafras and chili peppers to provincial French cooking. Try the jambalaya.

3

6

9

12

Bar Pilar
BAR

(www.barpilar.com; 1833 14th St NW; ⓜU Street-Cardozo) Friendly neighborhood favorite Bar Pilar serves seasonal organic tapas dishes and excellent cocktails in a small, nicely designed space. The mustard-colored walls and curious collections (hats, Hemingway regalia) give it an old-fashioned feel.

Dickson Wine Bar
WINE BAR

(www.dicksonwinebar.com; 903 U St NW; ⊘from 6pm Mon-Sat; ⓜU Street-Cardozo) Cozy and candlelit, with walls covered in wine bottles, Dickson pours romantic, first-date ambience throughout a three-story row house. The entrance is not marked by name; look for 'Dickson Building 903' above the door. It's a cool spot to swing into before a show at the 9:30 Club.

Dupont Circle

18th Street Lounge
LOUNGE

(www.eighteenthstreetlounge.com; 1212 18th St NW; ⊘from 5:30pm Tue-Fri, from 9:30pm Sat & Sun; ⓜDupont Circle) Chandeliers, velvet sofas, antique wallpaper and an attractive dance-loving crowd adorn this multifloored mansion. The DJs here – spinning funk, soul and Brazilian beats – are phenomenal, which is not surprising given Eric Hilton (of Thievery Corporation) is co-owner.

Georgetown

Tombs
BAR

(www.tombs.com; 1226 36th St NW; ⊘from 11:30am Mon-Sat, from 9:30am Sun) If it looks familiar, think back to the '80s; this was the setting for *St Elmo's Fire*. Today this cozy windowless bar is a favorite with Georgetown students and teaching assistants boozing under crew regalia.

Columbia Heights & Around

Red Derby
BAR

(www.redderby.com; 3718 14th St NW; ⓜColumbia Heights) The unsigned Derby packs 'em in with an open-air deck up top (with heat lamps), films screening on the wall and riotous crowds. Order the $5 shot-and-Schlitz combo to start the night with a bang.

Wonderland
BAR

(www.thewonderlandballroom.com; 1101 Kenyon St NW; ⓜColumbia Heights) Wonderland is friendly but divey, with a spacious patio in front with outsized wooden benches that are just right on warm evenings. The upstairs dance floor sees a mix of DJs and bands, and gets packed on weekends.

Looking Glass Lounge
BAR

(www.thelookingglasslounge.com; 3634 Georgia Ave NW; ⓜGeorgia Ave-Petworth) Petworth's neighborhood nightspot is an artfully designed dive with a great jukebox, DJs on weekends and a fine outdoor patio.

Meridian Pint
BAR

(www.meridianpint.com; 3400 11th St NW; ⓜColumbia Heights) Staffed by locals from the neighborhood, Meridian Pint is the quintessential corner tavern for Columbia Heights. Sports flicker on TV, folks play pool and shuffleboard, and impressive American craft beers flow from the taps.

DC Reynolds
BAR

(☑202-506-7178; 3628 Georgia Ave NW; ⊘11am-2am, to 3am Fri & Sat; ⓜGeorgia Ave-Petworth) Petworth is one of the edges of DC's gentrification, and some interesting bars are opening here. DC Reynolds is one of our favorites of the bunch, although you need to visit outside the winter months, as the main draw is an enormous outdoor patio that's perfect for a cool beer and a pickle back (whiskey followed by pickle juice).

☆ Entertainment

Live Music

Black Cat
LIVE MUSIC

(www.blackcatdc.com; 1811 14th St NW, U St; admission $5-15; ⓜU Street-Cardozo) A pillar of DC's music scene since the 1990s, the battered Black Cat has hosted all the greats of years past (White Stripes, the Strokes, Arcade Fire among others). If you don't want to pony up for $20-a-ticket bands on the upstairs main stage (or the smaller Backstage below), head to the Red Room for jukebox, pool and strong cocktails.

9:30 Club
LIVE MUSIC

(www.930.com; 815 V St NW, U St; admission from $10; ⓜU Street-Cardozo) The 9:30, which can pack 1200 people into a surprisingly intimate venue, is the granddaddy of the live-music scene in DC. Pretty much every big name that comes through town ends up on this stage, and a concert here is the first-gig memory of many a DC-area teenager. Headliners usually take the stage between 10:30pm and 11:30pm.

GAY & LESBIAN WASHINGTON, DC

One of Washington's gay-bar scenes is concentrated around Dupont Circle.

Cobalt (www.cobaltdc.com; 1639 R St NW; ⊘5pm-2am; Ⓜ Dupont Circle) Featuring lots of hair product and faux-tanned gym bodies, Cobalt tends to gather a better-dressed late-20s to 30-something crowd who come for fun (but loud!) dance parties throughout the week.

Nellie's (www.nelliessportsbar.com; 900 U St NW; Ⓜ U Street-Cardozo) The vibe here is low key, and Nellie's is a good place to hunker down among a friendly crowd for tasty bar bites, events nights (including drag bingo Tuesdays) or early drink specials.

JR's (www.jrsbardc.com; 1519 17th St NW; ⊘from 4pm Mon-Fri, from 1pm Sat & Sun; Ⓜ Dupont Circle) This popular gay hangout is a great spot for happy hour, and is packed more often than not. Embarrassing show tunes karaoke is great fun on Monday nights.

Verizon Center   CONCERT VENUE
(☑202-628-3200; www.verizoncenter.com; 601 F St NW, Gallery Place-Chinatown) DC's great big sports-arena-cum-big-name-band venue.

Performing Arts

Kennedy Center   PERFORMING ARTS
(☑202-467-4600; www.kennedy-center.org; 2700 F St NW, Georgetown; Ⓜ Foggy Bottom-GWU) Perched on 17 acres along the Potomac, the magnificent Kennedy Center hosts a staggering array of performances – more than 2000 each year among its multiple venues including the Concert Hall (home to the National Symphony), the Opera House and Eisenhower Theater. The Millennium Stage puts on free performances at 6pm daily.

**Wolf Trap Farm Park
for the Performing Arts**   PERFORMING ARTS
(☑703-255-1900; www.wolftrap.org; 1645 Trap Rd, Northern Virginia) This outdoor park some 40 minutes from downtown DC hosts summer performances by the National Symphony and other highly regarded musical and theatrical troupes.

National Theatre   THEATER
(☑202-628-6161; www.nationaltheatre.org; 1321 Pennsylvania Ave NW; ⊘box office 10am-9pm Mon-Sat, noon-8pm Sun; Ⓜ Federal Triangle) Washington's oldest continuously operating theater shows big Broadway musicals and similar big-name productions.

Shakespeare Theatre   THEATER
(☑202-547-1122; www.shakespearetheatre.org; 450 7th St NW; tickets from $30; ⊘box office 10am-6pm Mon-Sat, noon-6pm Sun; Ⓜ Archives-Navy Memorial) The nation's foremost Shakespeare company presents masterfully staged pieces by the Bard as well as works by George Bernard Shaw, Oscar Wilde, Ibsen, Eugene O'Neill and other greats.

Carter Barron Amphitheater   THEATER
(☑202-895-6000; www.nps.gov/rocr; 4850 Colorado Ave NW, near 16th St NW, Rock Creek Park; ⊘box office noon-8pm show days; Ⓜ McPherson Sq, then ◻S2, S4) In a lovely wooded setting inside Rock Creek Park, you can catch a mix of theater, dance and music (jazz, salsa, classical and reggae). Some events are free.

Sports

Washington Redskins   FOOTBALL
(☑301-276-6800; www.redskins.com; 1600 Fedex Way, Landover, MD; tickets from $65) The city's football team plays at FedEx Field, east of DC in Maryland. The season runs from September to February.

Washington Nationals   BASEBALL
(www.nationals.com; 1500 S Capitol St SE; Ⓜ Navy Yard) DC's baseball team plays at Nationals Park, along the Anacostia riverfront in southeast DC. The season runs from April through October.

DC United   SOCCER
(www.dcunited.com; 2400 East Capitol St; Ⓜ Stadium-Armory) DC United play at Robert F Kennedy (RFK) Memorial Stadium. The season runs from March through October.

Washington Capitals   HOCKEY
(☑202-397-7328; http://capitals.nhl.com; 601 F St NW; Ⓜ Gallery Place-Chinatown) DC's rough-and-tumble hockey team plays from October through April at the Verizon Center.

Washington Wizards   BASKETBALL
(www.nba.com/wizards; 601 F St NW; ⊘box office 10am-5:30pm Mon-Sat; Ⓜ Gallery Place-Chinatown) NBA season runs from October

WASHINGTON, DC & THE CAPITAL REGION WASHINGTON, DC

through April, with home games played at the Verizon Center. DC's WNBA team, the Washington Mystics (www.wnba.com/mystics), also plays here May to September.

ℹ Information

Destination DC (☎202-789-7000; www.washington.org; 901 7th St NW, 4th fl) Doles out loads of information online, over the phone or in person at a handy downtown location.

George Washington University Hospital (☎202-715-4000; 900 23rd St NW; Ⓜ Foggy Bottom-GWU)

International Visitors Information Desk (⊙9am-5pm Mon-Fri) You'll find helpful multilingual staff at this information desk run by the Meridian International Center. At the arrivals terminal at Washington Dulles Airport.

Kramerbooks (1517 Connecticut Ave NW; ⊙7:30am-1am Sun-Thu, 24hr Fri & Sat) One computer with free access in the bar.

Online Visitor Information (www.washington.org)

Washington City Paper (www.washingtoncitypaper.com) Free edgy weekly with entertainment and dining listings.

Washington Post (www.washingtonpost.com) Respected daily city (and national) paper. Its tabloid-format daily *Express* is free. Check online for events listings.

ℹ Getting There & Away

AIR

Washington Dulles International Airport (IAD; www.metwashairports.com), 26 miles west of the city center, and **Ronald Reagan Washington National Airport** (DCA; ☎703-417-8000), 4.5 miles south, are the main airports serving DC, although **Baltimore/Washington International Thurgood Marshall Airport** (BWI; ☎410-859-7111; www.bwiairport.com), 30 miles to the northeast, is also an option. All three airports, particularly Dulles and National, are major hubs for flights from around the world.

BUS

In addition to Greyhound, there are numerous cheap bus services to New York, Philadelphia and Richmond. Most charge around $20 for a one-way trip to NYC (it takes four to five hours). Pick-up locations are scattered around town, but are always Metro-accessible. Tickets usually need to be bought online, but can also be purchased on the bus itself if there are still seats available.

BoltBus (☎877-265-8287; www.boltbus.com; ☎) The best of the budget options, BoltBus leaves from the upper level of Union Station.

DC2NY (☎202-332-2691; www.dc2ny.com; 20th St & Massachusetts Ave NW; ☎) Leaves from near Dupont Circle.

Greyhound (☎202-589-5141; www.greyhound.com; 1005 1st St NE) Provides nationwide service. The terminal is a few blocks north of Union Station; take a cab after dark.

Megabus (☎877-462-6342; us.megabus.com; ☎) Leaves from Union Station.

Peter Pan Bus Lines (☎800-343-9999; www.peterpanbus.com) Travels to northeastern US; uses a terminal just opposite Greyhound's.

WashNY (☎866-287-6932; www.washny.com; 1320 19th St NW, Union Station; ☎) Has two stops in the city.

TRAIN

Amtrak (☎800-872-7245; www.amtrak.com) Set inside the magnificent beaux-arts Union Station. Trains depart for nationwide destinations, including New York City (3½ hours), Chicago (18 hours), Miami (24 hours) and Richmond, VA (three hours).

MARC (Maryland Rail Commuter; mta.maryland.gov) This regional rail service for the Washington, DC–Baltimore metro area runs trains frequently to Baltimore ($7, 71 minutes) and other Maryland towns (from $4 to $12); and to Harpers Ferry, WV ($15, 80 minutes).

ℹ Getting Around

TO/FROM THE AIRPORT

If you're using Baltimore/Washington International Airport, you can travel between Union Station and the BWI terminal stop on either **MARC** ($7, 40 minutes) or **Amtrak** ($16, 40 minutes). Or consider the **B30 bus**, which runs to Greenbelt Metro ($6.30, 40 minutes)

Metrobus 5A (www.wmata.com) Runs from Dulles to Rosslyn Metro station (35 minutes) and central DC (L'Enfant Plaza, 48 minutes); it departs every 30 to 40 minutes. The combo bus/Metro fare is about $8.

Metrorail (www.wmata.com) National airport has its own Metro rail station, which is fast and cheap.

Supershuttle (☎800-258-3826; www.supershuttle.com; ⊙5:30am-12:30am) A door-to-door shuttle that connects downtown DC with Dulles ($29), National ($14) and BWI ($37).

Washington Flyer (www.washfly.com) Runs every 30 minutes from Dulles to West Falls Church Metro ($10).

PUBLIC TRANSPORTATION

Circulator (www.dccirculator.com) Buses run along handy routes – including Union Station to/from Georgetown. One-way fare costs $1.

Metrobus (www.wmata.com) Operates buses throughout the city and suburbs; have exact change handy ($1.80).

Metrorail (☏202-637-7000; www.wmata. com) One of the best transportation systems in the country will get you to most sights, hotels and business districts, and the Maryland and Virginia suburbs. Trains start running at 5am Monday through Friday (from 7am on weekends); the last service is around midnight Sunday through Thursday and 3am on Fridays and Saturdays. Machines inside stations sell computerized fare cards; fares cost from $1.60 (children under five ride free). Unlimited travel passes are also available (one day/seven days from $14/57.50).

TAXI

For a cab, try **Capitol Cab** (☏202-636-1600), **Diamond** (☏202-387-6200) or **Yellow Cab** (☏202-544-1212).

MARYLAND

Maryland is often described as 'America in Miniature', and for good reason. This small state possesses all of the best bits of the country, from the Appalachian Mountains in the west to sandy white beaches in the east. A blend of Northern streetwise and Southern down-home gives this most osmotic of border states an appealing identity crisis. Its main city, Baltimore, is a sharp, demanding port town; the Eastern Shore jumbles art-and-antique-minded city refugees and working fishermen; while the DC suburbs are packed with government and office workers seeking green space, and the poor seeking lower rents. Yet it all somehow works – scrumptious blue crabs, Natty Boh beer and lovely Chesapeake country being the glue that binds all. This is also an extremely diverse and progressive state, and was one of the first in the country to legalize gay marriage.

History

George Calvert established Maryland as a refuge for persecuted English Catholics in 1634 when he purchased St Mary's City from the local Piscataway, with whom he initially tried to coexist. Puritan refugees drove both Piscataway and Catholics from control and shifted power to Annapolis; their harassment of Catholics produced the Tolerance Act, a flawed but progressive law that allowed freedom of any (Christian) worship in Maryland – a North American first.

MARYLAND FACTS

Nickname The Old Line State, the Free State

Population 5.8 million

Area 12,407 sq miles

Capital city Annapolis (population 39,000)

Other cities Baltimore (population 621,000), Frederick (population 66,000), Hagerstown (population 40,000), Salisbury (population 30,500)

Sales tax 6%

Birthplace of Abolitionist Frederick Douglass (1818–95), baseball great Babe Ruth (1895–1948), actor David Hasselhoff (b 1952), author Tom Clancy (b 1947), swimmer Michael Phelps (b 1985)

Home of 'The Star-Spangled Banner,' Baltimore Orioles, TV crime shows *The Wire* and *Homicide: Life on the Street*

Politics Staunch Democrats

Famous for Blue crabs, lacrosse, Chesapeake Bay

State sport Jousting

Driving distances Baltimore to Annapolis 29 miles, Baltimore to Ocean City 147 miles

That commitment to diversity has always characterized this state, despite a mixed record on slavery. Although state loyalties were split during the Civil War, a Confederate invasion was halted here in 1862 at Antietam. Following the war, Maryland harnessed its black, white and immigrant work force, splitting the economy between Baltimore's industry and shipping, and the later need for services in Washington, DC. Today the answer to 'What makes a Marylander?' is 'all of the above': the state mixes rich, poor, the foreign-born, urban sophisticates and rural villages like few other states do.

Baltimore

Once one of the most important port towns in America, Baltimore – or 'Bawlmer' to locals – is a city of contradictions. On one hand it remains something of an ugly duckling – a defiant, working-class, gritty city still tied to its nautical past. But in recent years Baltimore has begun to grow into a swan or, more accurately, gotten better at showing the world the swan that was always there, in the form of world-class museums, trendy shops, ethnic restaurants, boutique hotels, culture and sports. 'B'more' (another nickname) does this all with a twinkle in the eye and a wisecrack on the lips; this quirky city spawned Billie Holiday and John Waters. Yet it remains intrinsically tied to the water, from the Disney-fied Inner Harbor and cobblestoned streets of portside Fells Point to the shores of Fort McHenry, birthplace of America's national anthem, 'The Star-Spangled Banner.' There's an intense, sincere friendliness to this 'burg, which is why Baltimore lives up to its final, most accurate nickname: 'Charm City.'

◉ Sights & Activities

◉ Harborplace & Inner Harbor

This is where most tourists start and, unfortunately, end their Baltimore sightseeing. The Inner Harbor is a big, gleaming waterfront renewal project of shiny glass, air-conditioned malls and flashy bars that manages to capture the maritime heart of this city, albeit in a safe-for-the-family kinda way. But it's also just the tip of Baltimore's iceberg.

★ **National Aquarium**   AQUARIUM
(☑410-576-3800; www.aqua.org; 501 E Pratt St, Piers 3 & 4; adult/child $35/22; ⊙9am-5pm Mon-Thu, to 8pm Fri, 8:30am-8pm Sat, to 6pm Sun) ✦ Standing seven stories high and capped by a glass pyramid, this is widely considered to be the best aquarium in America. It houses 16,500 specimens of 660 species, a rooftop rainforest, a central ray pool and a multistory shark tank. There's also a reconstruction of the Umbrawarra Gorge in Australia's Northern Territory, complete with a 35ft waterfall, rocky cliffs and free-roaming birds and lizards. Kids will love the dolphin show and 4-D Immersion Theater (together an additional $5). Go on weekdays to beat the crowds.

Baltimore Maritime Museum   MUSEUM
(☑410-396-3453; www.historicships.org; 301 E Pratt St, Piers 3 & 5; 1/2/4 ships adult $11/14/18, child $5/6/7; ⊙10am-4:30pm) Ship-lovers can take a tour through four historic ships: a Coast Guard cutter, lightship, submarine and the USS Constellation, one of the last

sail-powered warships built (in 1797) by the US Navy. Admission to the 1856 Seven Foot Knoll Lighthouse on Pier 5 is free.

◉ Downtown & Little Italy

You can easily walk from downtown to Little Italy, but follow the delineated path as there's a rough housing project along the way.

National Great Blacks in Wax Museum   MUSEUM
(☑410-563-3404; www.greatblacksinwax.org; 1601 E North Ave; adult/child $13/11; ⊙9am-6pm Tue-Sat, noon-6pm Sun, to 5pm Oct-Jan) This excellent African American history museum has exhibits on Frederick Douglass, Jackie Robinson, Martin Luther King Jr and Barack Obama, as well as lesser-known figures such as explorer Matthew Henson. The museum also covers slavery, the Jim Crow era and African leaders – all told in surreal fashion through Madame Tussaud-style figures.

Star-Spangled Banner Flag House & 1812 Museum   MUSEUM
(☑410-837-1793; www.flaghouse.org; 844 E Pratt St; adult/child $8/6; ⊙10am-4pm Tue-Sat; ♿) This historic home, built in 1793, is where Mary Pickersgill sewed the gigantic flag that inspired America's national anthem. Costumed interpreters and 19th-century artifacts transport visitors back in time to dark days during the War of 1812; there's also a hands-on discovery gallery for kids.

Jewish Museum of Maryland   MUSEUM
(☑410-732-6400; www.jewishmuseummd.org; 15 Lloyd St; adult/student/child $8/4/3; ⊙10am-5pm Tue-Thu & Sun) Maryland has traditionally been home to one of the largest, most active Jewish communities in the country, and this is a fine place to explore their experience in America. It also houses two wonderfully preserved historical synagogues.

Babe Ruth Museum   MUSEUM
(☑410-727-1539; www.baberuthmuseum.com; 216 Emory St; adult/child $6/3; ⊙10am-5pm) Celebrates the Baltimore native son who happens to be the greatest baseball player in history. Four blocks east, Sports Legends at Camden Yards (cnr Camden & Sharp Sts, Camden Station; adult/child $8/4) honors more Maryland athletes. The museums share hours; combo tickets cost $12/5.

SCENIC DRIVE: MARITIME MARYLAND

Maryland and Chesapeake Bay have always been inextricable, but there are some places where the old-fashioned way of life on the bay seems to have changed little over the passing centuries.

About 150 miles south of Baltimore, at the edge of the Eastern Shore, is Crisfield, the top working water town in Maryland. Get visiting details at the J Millard Tawes Historical Museum (☎410-968-2501; www.crisfieldheritagefoundation.org/museum; 3 Ninth St; adult/child $3/1; ⊙10am-4pm Mon-Sat), which doubles as a visitor center. Any seafood you eat will be first-rate, but for a true Shore experience, Watermen's Inn (☎410-968-2119; 901 W Main St; mains $12-25; ⊙11am-8pm Thu & Sun, to 9pm Fri & Sat, closed Mon-Wed) is legendary. In a simple, unpretentious setting, you can feast on local catch from an ever-changing menu. You can find local waterfolk at their favorite hangout, having 4am coffee at Gordon's Confectionery (831 W Main St) before shipping off to check and set traps.

From here you can leave your car and take a boat to Smith Island (www.visitsmithsland.com), the only offshore settlement in the state. Settled by fisherfolk from the English West Country some 400 years ago, the island's tiny population still speaks with what linguists reckon is the closest thing to a 17th-century Cornish accent.

We'll be frank: this is more of a dying fishing town than charming tourist attraction, although there are B&Bs and restaurants (check the website for details). But it is also a last link to the state's past, and if you approach Smith Island as such, you may appreciate the limited amenities on offer. These notably include paddling through miles of some of the most pristine marshland on the eastern seaboard. Ferries will take you back to the mainland and the present day at 3:45pm.

Edgar Allan Poe House & Museum   MUSEUM
(☎410-396-7932; 203 N Amity St; adult/child $4/ free; ⊙noon-3:30pm Wed-Sat Apr-Nov) Home to Baltimore's most famous adopted son from 1832 to 1835, it was here that the macabre poet and writer first found fame after winning a $50 short-story contest. After moving around, Poe later returned to Baltimore in 1849, where he died in mysterious circumstances. His grave can be found in nearby Westminster Cemetery.

◎ Mt Vernon

For the best views of Baltimore, climb the 228 steps of Baltimore's Washington Monument (699 Washington Pl; suggested donation $5; ⊙10am-5pm Wed-Sun), a 178ft-tall Doric column that's only slightly less phallic than its DC counterpart.

★Walters Art Museum   MUSEUM
(☎410-547-9000; www.thewalters.org; 600 N Charles St; ⊙10am-5pm Wed-Sun, to 9pm Thu) FREE Don't pass up this excellent, eclectic gallery, which spans more than 55 centuries, from ancient to contemporary, with excellent displays of Asian treasures, rare and ornate manuscripts and books, and a comprehensive French paintings collection.

Maryland Historical Society   MUSEUM
(www.mdhs.org; 201 W Monument St; adult/child $9/6; ⊙10am-5pm Wed-Sat, noon-5pm Sun) With more than 5.4 million artifacts, this is one of the largest collections of Americana in the world, and it includes Francis Scott Key's original manuscript of the 'Star-Spangled Banner.' There are often excellent temporary exhibits, as well as a fascinating permanent one tracing Maryland's maritime history.

◎ Federal Hill & Around

On a bluff overlooking the harbor, Federal Hill Park lends its name to the comfortable neighborhood that's set around Cross St Market and comes alive after sundown.

★American Visionary Art Museum   MUSEUM
(☎410-244-1900; www.avam.org; 800 Key Hwy; adult/child $16/10; ⊙10am-6pm Tue-Sun) AVAM is a showcase for self-taught (or 'outsider' art,) a celebration of unbridled creativity utterly free of arts-scene pretension. Some of the work comes from asylums, other pieces are created by self-inspired visionaries, but it's all fantastically captivating and well worth a long afternoon.

Fort McHenry National Monument & Historic Shrine HISTORIC SITE

(☑410-962-4290; 2400 E Fort Ave; adult/child $7/free; ☺8am-5pm) On September 13 and 14, 1814, the star-shaped fort successfully repelled a British navy attack during the Battle of Baltimore. After a long night of bombs bursting in the air, prisoner Francis Scott Key saw, 'by dawn's early light,' the tattered flag still waving, inspiring him to pen 'The Star-Spangled Banner' (set to the tune of a popular drinking song).

◉ Fell's Point & Canton

Once the center of Baltimore's shipbuilding industry, the historic cobblestoned neighborhood of Fell's Point is now a gentrified mix of 18th-century homes and restaurants, bars and shops. The neighborhood has been the setting for several films and TV series, most notably *Homicide: Life on the Street.* Further east, the slightly more sophisticated streets of Canton fan out, with its grassy square surrounded by great restaurants and bars.

◉ North Baltimore

The 'Hon' expression of affection, an oft-imitated but never quite duplicated 'Bawlmerese' peculiarity, was born in Hampden, an area straddling the line between working class and hipster-creative class. Spend a lazy afternoon browsing kitsch, antiques and vintage clothing along the Avenue (aka W 36th St). To get to Hampden, take the I-83 N, merge onto Falls Rd (northbound) and take a right onto the Avenue. The prestigious Johns Hopkins University (3400 N Charles St) is nearby.

⌖ Tours

Baltimore Ghost Tours WALKING TOUR

(☑410-357-1186; www.baltimoreghosttours.com; adult/child $13/10; ☺7pm Fri & Sat Mar-Nov) Offers several walking tours exploring the spooky and bizarre side of Baltimore. The popular Fells Point ghost walk departs from Max's on Broadway, 731 S Broadway.

★ Festivals & Events

Preakness SPORTS

(www.preakness.com; ☺May) Held on the third Sunday of every May, the 'Freakness' is the second leg of the Triple Crown horse race.

Honfest CULTURE

(www.honfest.net; ☺Jun) Put on your best 'Bawlmerese' accent and head to Hampden for this celebration of kitsch, beehive hair-dos, rhinestone glasses and other Baltimore eccentricities.

Artscape CULTURE

(www.artscape.org; ☺mid-July) America's largest free arts festival features art displays, live music, theater and dance performances.

◉ Sleeping

Stylish and affordable B&Bs are mostly found in the downtown 'burbs of Canton, Fell's Point and Federal Hill.

Mount Vernon Hotel HOTEL $

(☑410-727-2000; www.mountvernonbaltimore.com; 24 W Franklin St, Mt Vernon; d from $90, ste from $120; 🅿❋🐾) The historic 1907 Mount Vernon Hotel is good value for its comfortable, heritage-style rooms in a nice location near the restaurant scene along Charles St. Hearty cooked breakfasts sweeten the deal.

BALTIMORE FOR CHILDREN

Most attractions are centered on the Inner Harbor, including the National Aquarium (p284), perfect for pint-sized visitors. Kids can run wild o'er the ramparts of historic Fort McHenry National Monument & Historic Shrine, too.

Maryland Science Center (☑410-685-5225; www.mdsci.org; 601 Light St; adult/child $17/14; ☺10am-5pm Mon-Fri, to 6pm Sat, 11am-5pm Sun, longer hours in summer) is an awesome center featuring a three-story atrium, tons of interactive exhibits on dinosaurs, outer space and the human body, and the requisite IMAX theater ($4 extra).

Two blocks north, Port Discovery (☑410-727-8120; www.portdiscovery.org; 35 Market Pl; admission $14; ☺10am-5pm Mon-Sat, noon-5pm Sun, reduced hours in winter) is a converted fish market, which has a playhouse, a laboratory, a TV studio and even Pharaoh's tomb. Wear your kids out here.

At Maryland Zoo in Baltimore (www.marylandzoo.org; Druid Hill Park; adult/child $16/11; ☺10am-4pm), lily-pad hopping, adventures with Billy the Bog Turtle and grooming live animals are all in a day's play here. Prices are slightly cheaper on weekdays.

HI-Baltimore Hostel
HOSTEL **$**

(☑ 410-576-8880; www.hiusa.org/baltimore; 17 W Mulberry St, Mt Vernon; dm/d incl breakfast $25/65; ✴ @ ☎) Located in a beautifully restored 1857 mansion, the HI-Baltimore has four dorms with eight and 12-beds, plus a private double room. Helpful management, nice location and a filigreed classical chic look make this one of the region's best hostels.

★ Inn at 2920
B&B **$$**

(☑ 410-342-4450; www.theinnat2920.com; 2920 Elliott St, Canton; r incl breakfast $175-235; ✴ @ ☎) ⚑ Housed in a former bordello, this boutique B&B offers five individual rooms: high-thread-count sheets, sleek avant-garde decor and the nightlife-charged neighborhood of Canton right outside your door. The Jacuzzi bathtubs and green sensibility of the owners add a nice touch.

Inn at Henderson's Wharf
HOTEL **$$**

(☑ 800-584-7065, 410-522-7777; www.hendersonswharf.com; 1000 Fell St; r from $175; P ✴ ☎) A complimentary bottle of wine upon arrival sets the tone at this marvelously situated Fell's Point hotel, which began life as an 18th-century tobacco warehouse. Consistently rated one of the city's best lodges.

Blue Door on Baltimore
B&B **$$**

(☑ 410-732-0191; www.bluedoorbaltimore.com; 2023 E Baltimore St, Fell's Point; r $140-180; ✴ @ ☎) In an early 1900s row house, this spotless inn has three elegantly furnished rooms, each with a king-sized bed, clawfoot bathtub (and separate shower), and thoughtful extras such as an in-room fountain and fresh flowers. It lies just north of Fells Point.

Peabody Court
HOTEL **$$**

(☑ 410-727-7101; www.peabodycourthotel.com; 612 Cathedral St, Mt Vernon; r from $120; P ✴ ☎) Right in the middle of Mt Vernon, this upscale 104-room hotel has large, handsomely appointed guest rooms with all-marble bathrooms and top-notch service. Often has great deals online.

✗ Eating

Baltimore is an ethnically rich town that sits on top of the greatest seafood repository in the world, not to mention the fault line between the down-home South and cutting-edge innovation of the Northeast.

Lexington Market
FAST FOOD **$**

(www.lexingtonmarket.com; 400 W Lexington St, Mt Vernon; ◷ 9am-5pm Mon-Sat) Around since 1782, Mt Vernon's Lexington Market is one of Baltimore's true old-school food markets. It's a bit shabby on the outside, but the food is great. Don't miss the crab cakes at **Faidley's** (☑ 410-727-4898; www.faidleyscrabcakes.com; mains $8-14; ◷ Mon-Sat 9am-5pm) seafood stall, because my goodness, they are truly amazing.

Vaccaro's Pastry
ITALIAN **$**

(www.vaccarospastry.com; 222 Albemarle St, Little Italy; desserts $7; ◷ 9am-10pm Sun-Thu, to midnight Fri & Sat) Vaccaro's serves some of the best desserts and coffee in town. The cannolis are legendary.

LP Steamers
SEAFOOD **$$**

(☑ 410-576-9294; 1100 E Fort Ave, South Baltimore; mains $8-28; ◷ 11:30am-10pm) LP is the best in Baltimore's seafood stakes: working class, teasing smiles and the freshest crabs on the southside.

PaperMoon Diner
DINER **$$**

(227 W 29th St; mains $7-16; ◷ 7am-midnight Sun-Thu, to 2am Fri & Sat) This brightly colored, quintessential Baltimore diner is decorated with thousands of old toys, creepy mannequins and other quirky knickknacks. The real draw here is the anytime breakfast – fluffy French toast, crispy bacon and bagels with lox.

City Cafe
CAFE **$$**

(☑ 410-539-4252; www.citycafebaltimore.com; 1001 Cathedral St, Mt Vernon; mains lunch $10-14, dinner $15-29; ◷ 7:30am-10pm Mon-Fri, 10am-10:30pm Sat, to 8pm Sun; ☎) A bright, inviting Mt Vernon cafe with floor-to-ceiling windows, desserts and gourmet sandwiches; the dining room in back serves high-end bistro fare.

Dukem
ETHIOPIAN **$$**

(☑ 410-385-0318; 1100 Maryland Ave, Mt Vernon; mains $13-22; ◷ 11am-10:30pm) Baltimore hosts one of the largest Ethiopian expat populations in the world, and they've brought their home cuisine to 'Charm City.' Dukem in Mt Vernon is a standout. Delicious mains, including spicy chicken, lamb and vegetarian dishes, all sopped up with spongy flatbread.

★ **Woodberry Kitchen** AMERICAN $$$
(☎410-464-8000; www.woodberrykitchen.com;
2010 Clipper Park Rd, Woodberry; mains $24-45;
☺5-10pm Mon-Thu to 11pm Fri & Sat, to 9pm Sun)
The Woodberry takes everything the Chesapeake region has to offer, plops it into an industrial barn and creates culinary magic. The entire menu is like a playful romp through the best of local produce, seafood and meats, from a 'nose-to-tail' approach to rockfish (Maryland's state fish) to local turkey sausage with pork-fat potatoes, and wood-roasted tomatoes and garlic plucked from nearby farms. The food is just stupidly delicious, the service is warm and the experience is top-notch.

Charleston SOUTHERN $$$
(☎410-332-7373; www.charlestonrestaurant.com; 1000 Lancaster St, Harbor East; 3-/6-courses $79/114; ☺5:30-10pm Mon-Sat) One of Baltimore's most celebrated restaurants, Charleston serves beautifully prepared Southern-accented fare in a plush setting. Extensive wine list and superb desserts (always included).

Salt AMERICAN $$$
(☎410-276-5480; www.salttavern.com; 2127 E Pratt St, Fells Point; mains $18-27; ☺5pm-midnight Tue-Sat, from 4:30pm Sun; ☑) Salt is heavy on the lips of Baltimore foodies (the restaurant, not crystallized sodium). The food is nouveau American, but there's a lot of international influence bordering on the cutting edge; start the meal with some sea-urchin custard, then move on to duck breast served over date puree with Moroccan spices.

BALTIMORE BEEF

Everyone knows Baltimore does crab cakes, but barely anyone outside the city knows about pit beef – thinly sliced top round grilled over charcoal – Baltimore's take on barbecue. The place to grab the stuff is Chaps (☎410-483-2379; 5801 Pulaski Hwy; mains under $10; ☺10:30am-10pm Sun-Thu), out on Pulaski Hwy, about 4 miles east of downtown Baltimore. Park (next to a strip club) and follow your nose to smoky mouthwatering goodness, and get that beef like a local: shaved onto a kaiser roll with a raw onion slice on top, smothered in Tiger Sauce (a creamy blend of horseradish and mayonnaise).

🍷 **Drinking & Nightlife**

On weekends, Fell's Point and Canton turn into temples of alcoholic excess that would make a Roman emperor blush. Mt Vernon and North Baltimore are a little more civilized, but any one of Baltimore's neighborhoods houses a cozy local pub. Closing time is generally 2am.

Brewer's Art PUB
(☎410-547-6925; 1106 N Charles St, Mt Vernon; ☺4pm-2am Mon-Sat, 5pm-2am Sun) This subterranean cave mesmerizes the senses with an overwhelming selection of beers. Its upstairs embodiment serves respectable dinners (sandwiches $9 to $12, mains $19 to $26) in its classy dining room.

Club Charles BAR
(☎410-727-8815; 1724 N Charles St, Mt Vernon; ☺from 6pm) Hipsters adorned in the usual skinny jeans/vintage T-shirt uniform, as well as characters from other walks of life, flock to this 1940s art-deco cocktail lounge to enjoy good tunes and cheap drinks.

Idle Hour BAR
(☎410-276-5480; 201 E Fort Ave, Federal Hill; ☺5pm-2am) Slip past the door that's papered with bumper stickers into a dark bar lit by sexy red Christmas lights and a bartenders' smile. Or, as the case may be, a bartender's surliness (good-hearted surliness, though). A watercolor of Elvis looks down upon you customers, blessing your cheap beers.

Ale Mary's BAR
(☎410-276-2044; 1939 Fleet St, Fell's Point; ☺from 4pm Mon-Thu, from 11:30am Fri-Sun) Its name and decor pay homage to Maryland's Catholic roots, with crosses and rosaries scattered about.

One-Eyed Mike's PUB
(☎410-327-0445; 708 S Bond St, Fell's Point; ☺11am-2am) Handshakes and a hearty welcome will make you feel right at home at this popular pirate-themed spot. With tin ceilings and old-world details, it's one of Baltimore's oldest taverns.

Little Havana BAR
(☎410-837-9903; 1325 Key Hwy, Federal Hill; ☺from 11:30am) A good after-work spot and a great place to sip *mojitos* on the waterfront deck, this converted brick warehouse is a major draw on warm, sunny days (especially around weekend brunch time).

MARYLAND BLUE CRABS

Eating at a crab shack, where the dress code stops at shorts and flip-flops, is the quintessential Chesapeake Bay experience. Folks in these parts take their crabs seriously and can spend hours debating the intricacies of how to crack a crab, the proper way to prepare crabs and where to find the best ones. There is one thing Marylanders can agree on: they must be blue crabs (scientific name: *Callinectes sapidus*, or 'beautiful swimmers'). With all this said, blue crab numbers have suffered with the contuining pollution of the Chesapeake Bay. Sadly, many crabs you eat here are imported from elsewhere. Steamed crabs are prepared very simply, using beer and Old Bay seasoning. One of the best crab shacks in the state is Jimmy Cantler's Riverside Inn (458 Forest Beach Rd; ⊙11am-11pm Sun-Thu, to midnight Fri & Sat), where eating a steamed crab has been elevated to an art form – a hands-on, messy endeavor, normally accompanied by corn on the cob and ice-cold beer. Another fine spot is across the bay at the Crab Claw (p292).

Hippo GAY
(www.clubhippo.com; 1 W Eager St; ⊙from 4pm) The Hippo has been around forever and is still one of the city's largest gay clubs (though some nights the dance floor is dead), with themed nights (gay bingo, karaoke and hip-hop).

Grand Central GAY & LESBIAN
(www.centralstationpub.com; 1001 N Charles St, Mt Vernon; ⊙9pm-2am Wed-Sun) More of a complex than a club, Central spreads a fancy to suit all moods – dance floor, pub and Sappho's (free admission for the ladies). Probably boasts B's best dance floors.

☆ Entertainment

Baltimoreans *love* sports. The town plays hard and parties even harder, with tailgating parties in parking lots and games showing on numerous televisions.

Baltimore Orioles BASEBALL
(☑888-848-2473; www.orioles.com) The Orioles play at Oriole Park at Camden Yards (333 W Camden St, Downtown), arguably the best ballpark in America. Daily tours (adult/child $9/6) of the stadium are offered during regular season (April to October).

Baltimore Ravens FOOTBALL
(☑410-261-7283; www.baltimoreravens.com) The Ravens play at M&T Bank Stadium (1101 Russell St, Downtown) from September to January.

Homewood Field STADIUM
(☑410-516-8000; www.hopkinssports.com; Homewood Field on University Pkwy) Maryland is lacrosse heartland, and is home to arguably the sport's most fanatic followers. The best

place to watch 'lax' is at Johns Hopkins University's Homewood Field.

Pimlico HORSE RACING
(☑410-542-9400; www.pimlico.com; 5201 Park Heights Ave) Horse racing is huge from April to late May, especially at Pimlico, which hosts the Preakness (p286). The track is roughly 7 miles north of downtown.

❶ Information

Baltimore Area Visitor Center (☑877-225-8466; http://baltimore.org; 401 Light St; ⊙9am-6pm Mon-Fri) Located on the Inner Harbor. Sells the Harbor Pass (adult/child $50/40), which gives admission to five major area attractions.

Baltimore Sun (www.baltimoresun.com) Daily city newspaper.

City Paper (www.citypaper.com) Free altweekly.

Enoch Pratt Free Library (400 Cathedral St; ⊙10am-8pm Mon-Wed, to 5pm Thu-Sat, 1-5pm Sun; ☎) Has free wi-fi and some public access computers (also free).

University of Maryland Medical Center (☑410-328-8667; 22 S Greene St) Has a 24-hour emergency room.

❶ Getting There & Away

The Baltimore/Washington International Thurgood Marshall Airport (p282) is 10 miles south of downtown via I-295.

Greyhound (www.greyhound.com) and **Peter Pan Bus Lines** (☑410-752-7682; 2110 Haines St) have numerous buses from Washington, DC, (roughly every 45 minutes, one hour); and from New York (12 to 15 per day, 4½ hours). The **BoltBus** (☑877-265-8287; www.boltbus.com; 1610 St Paul St; ☎) has seven buses a day to/from NYC.

Penn Station (1500 N Charles St) is in north Baltimore. MARC operates weekday commuter trains to/from Washington, DC ($7, 71 minutes). **Amtrak** (☑ 800-872-7245; www.amtrak.com) trains serve the East Coast and beyond.

❶ Getting Around

Light Rail (☑ 866-743-3682; mta.maryland. gov/light-rail; tickets $1.60; ☺ 6am-11pm) runs from BWI airport to Lexington Market and Penn Station. Train frequency is every five to 10 minutes. MARC trains run hourly between Penn Station and BWI airport on weekdays for $5. Supershuttle (p282) provides a BWI-van service to the Inner Harbor for $14. Check **Maryland Transit Administration** (MTA; www.mtamaryland.com) for all local transportation schedules and fares.

Baltimore Water Taxi (☑ 410-563-3900; www.baltimorewatertaxi.com; Inner Harbor; daily pass adult/child $12/6; ☺ 10am-11pm, to 9pm Sun) docks at all harborside attractions and neighborhoods.

Annapolis

Annapolis is as charming as state capitals get. The Colonial architecture, cobblestones, flickering lamps and brick row houses are worthy of Dickens, but the effect isn't artificial; this city has preserved, rather than created, its heritage.

Perched on Chesapeake Bay, Annapolis revolves around the city's rich maritime traditions. It's home to the US Naval Academy, whose 'middies' (midshipmen students) stroll through town in their starched white uniforms. Sailing is not just a hobby, it's a way of life, and the city docks are crammed with vessels of all shapes and sizes.

◉ Sights & Activities

Annapolis has more 18th-century buildings than any other city in America, and they include the homes of all four Marylanders who signed the Declaration of Independence.

Think of the State House as a wheel hub from which most attractions fan out, leading to the City Dock and historic waterfront.

US Naval Academy   UNIVERSITY
(www.usnabsd.com/for-visitors) The undergraduate college of the US Navy is one of the most selective universities in America. The **Armel-Leftwich visitor center** (☑ 410-293-8687; tourinfo@usna.edu; Gate 1, City Dock entrance; tours adult/child $9.50/7.50; ☺ 9am-5pm) is the place to book tours and immerse yourself in all things Academy. Come for the formation weekdays at 12:05pm sharp, when the 4000 midshipmen and midshipwomen conduct a 20-minute military marching display in the yard. Photo ID is required for entry. If you've got a thing for American naval history, go revel in the **Naval Academy Museum** (☑ 410-293-2108; www.usna.edu/museum; 118 Maryland Ave; ☺ 9am-5pm Mon-Sat, 11am-5pm Sun) **FREE**.

Maryland State House   HISTORIC BUILDING
(☑ 410-974-3400; 91 State Circle; ☺ 9am-5pm Mon-Fri, 10am-4pm Sat & Sun, tours 11am & 3pm) **FREE** The country's oldest state capitol in continuous legislative use, the stately (haha) 1772 State House also served as national capital from 1733 to 1734. The Maryland Senate is in action here from January to April. The upside-down giant acorn atop the dome stands for wisdom. Photo ID is required for entry.

Hammond Harwood House   MUSEUM
(☑ 410-263-4683; www.hammondharwoodhouse. org; 19 Maryland Ave; adult/child $7/6; ☺ noon-5pm Tue-Sun Apr-Oct, to 4pm Nov-Dec) Of the many historical homes in town, the 1774 HHH is the one to visit. It has a superb collection of decorative arts, including furniture, paintings and ephemera dating to the 18th century, and is one of the finest existing British Colonial homes in America.

Kunta Kinte–Alex Haley Memorial   MONUMENT
At the City Dock, the Kunta Kinte–Alex Haley Memorial marks the spot where Kunta Kinte – ancestor of *Roots* author Alex Haley – was brought in chains from Africa.

☞ Tours

Four Centuries Walking Tour   WALKING TOUR
(http://annapolistours.com; adult/child $16/10) A costumed docent will lead you on this great introduction to all things Annapolis. The 10:30am tour leaves from the visitor center and the 1:30pm tour leaves from the information booth at the City Dock; there's a slight variation in sights visited by each, but both cover the country's largest concentration of 18th-century buildings, influential African Americans and colonial spirits who don't want to leave. The associated one-hour **Pirates of the Chesapeake Cruise** (☑ 410-263-0002; www.chesapeakepirates.com; adult/child $20/12; ☺ late May-early Sep; ⊞) is good 'yar'-worthy fun, especially for the kids.

Woodwind
CRUISE

(☑410-263-7837; www.schoonerwoodwind. com; 80 Compromise St; sunset cruise adult/ child $42/27; ☺May-Oct) This beautiful 74ft schooner offers two-hour day and sunset cruises. Or splurge for the Woodwind 'boat & breakfast' package (rooms $300, including breakfast), one of the more unique lodging options in town.

🛏 Sleeping

ScotLaur Inn
GUESTHOUSE $

(☑410-268-5665; www.scotlaurinn.com; 165 Main St; r $95-140; P✳☎) The folks from Chick & Ruth's Delly offer 10 simple pink-and-blue rooms with private bath at their B&B (bed and bagel) above the deli.

Historic Inns of Annapolis
HOTEL $$

(☑410-263-2641; www.historicinnsofannapolis. com; 58 State Circle; r $130-205; ✳☎) The Historic Inns comprise three different boutique guesthouses, each set in a heritage building in the heart of old Annapolis: the Maryland Inn, the Governor Calvert House and the Robert Johnson House. Common areas are packed with period details, and the best rooms boast antiques, a fireplace and attractive views (the cheapest are small and could use an update).

🍴 Eating & Drinking

With the Chesapeake at its doorstep, Annapolis has superb seafood.

Chick & Ruth's Delly
DINER $

(☑410-269-6737; www.chickandruths.com; 165 Main St; mains $6-12; ☺6:30am-10pm Sun-Thu, to 11:30pm Fri & Sat;) A cornerstone of Annapolis, the Delly is bursting with affable quirkiness and a big menu, heavy on sandwiches and breakfast fare. Patriots can relive grade-school days reciting the Pledge of Allegiance, weekdays at 8:30am (9:30am on weekends).

★ Vin 909
AMERICAN $$

(☑410-990-1846; 909 Bay Ridge Ave; mains $12-18; ☺5:30-10:30pm Tue, noon-10:30pm Wed-Fri, 5-11pm Sat, to 9pm Sun) Perched on a little wooded hill and exuding intimate but enjoyably casual ambience, Vin is the best thing happening in Annapolis for food. Farm-sourced goodness comes at you in the form of tasty sliders and homemade pizzas (try the Rock Star, with foie gras, truffles and peaches), and there's a wine cellar as deep as a trench.

Galway Bay
PUB $$

(☑410-263-8333; 63 Maryland Ave; mains $8-15; ☺11am-midnight Mon-Sat, from 10:30am Sun) The epitome of a power-broker bar, this Irish-owned and -operated pub is the dark sort of hideaway where political deals go down over Jameson, stouts and mouthwatering seafood specials.

Rams Head Tavern
PUB $$$

(☑410-268-4545; www.ramsheadtavern.com; 33 West St; mains $10-30; ☺from 11am) Serves pub fare and refreshing microbrews in an attractive oak-paneled setting, with live bands (tickets $15 to $55) on stage.

ℹ Information

There's a **visitor center** (www.visitannapolis. org; 26 West St; ☺9am-5pm) and a seasonal information booth at City Dock. A **Maryland Welcome Center** (☑410-974-3400; 350 Rowe Blvd; ☺9am-5pm) is inside the State House, and runs free tours of the building.

ℹ Getting There & Around

Greyhound (www.greyhound.com) runs buses to Washington, DC (once daily). **Dillon's Bus** (www.dillonbus.com; tickets $5) has 26 weekday-only commuter buses between Annapolis and Washington, DC, connecting with various DC Metro lines.

Inexpensive **bicycles** (per day $5; ☺9am-8pm) are available for hire from the Harbormaster's office at the City Dock.

Eastern Shore

Just across the Chesapeake Bay Bridge, a short drive from the urban sprawl of the Baltimore–Washington corridor, Maryland's landscape makes a dramatic about-face. Nondescript suburbs give way to unbroken miles of bird-dotted wetlands, serene waterscapes, endless cornfields, sandy beaches and friendly little villages. The Eastern Shore retains its charm despite the growing influx of city-dwelling yuppies and day-trippers. This area revolves around the water: working waterfront communities still survive off Chesapeake Bay and its tributaries, and boating, fishing, crabbing and hunting are integral to local life.

St Michaels & Tilghman Island

The prettiest little village on the Eastern Shore, St Michaels lives up to its motto as the 'Heart and Soul of Chesapeake Bay.' It's a mix of old Victorian homes, quaint B&Bs, boutique shops and working docks, where escape artists from Washington mix with salty-dog watermen. During the War of 1812, inhabitants rigged up lanterns in a nearby forest and blacked out the town. British naval gunners shelled the trees, allowing St Michaels to escape destruction. The building now known as the Cannonball House (Mulberry St) was the only structure to have been hit. At the lighthouse, the Chesapeake Bay Maritime Museum (☑410-745-2916; www.cbmm.org; 213 N Talbot St; adult/child $13/6; ☉9am-6pm summer; ♿) delves into the deep ties between Shore folk and America's largest estuary.

The Victorian red-brick Parsonage Inn (☑410-745-8383; www.parsonage-inn.com; 210 N Talbot St; r incl breakfast $150-210; P✷) offers floral decadence (curtains, duvets) and brass beds, plus a friendly welcome from its hospitable innkeepers.

Next door to the Maritime Museum, the Crab Claw (☑410-745-2900; 304 Burns St; mains $15-30; ☉11am-10pm) has a splendid open-air setting at the water's edge. Get messy eating delicious steamed crabs ($36 to $60 per dozen) at picnic tables.

At the end of the road over the Hwy 33 drawbridge, tiny Tilghman Island still runs a working waterfront where local captains take visitors out on graceful oyster skipjacks; the historic Rebecca T Ruark (☑410-829-3976; www.skipjack.org; 2hr cruise adult/child $30/15), built in 1886, is the oldest certified vessel of its kind.

Berlin & Snow Hill

Imagine 'small-town, main street Americana,' cute that vision up by a few points, and you've come close to these Eastern Shore villages. Most of the buildings here are preserved or renovated to look preserved. Antiquity hunters will have to budget extra time to browse the antique shops littering this area.

In Berlin, the Globe Theater (☑410-641-0784; www.globetheater.com; 12 Broad St; lunch mains $6-12, dinner $11-25; ☉11am-10pm; ☎) is a lovingly restored main stage that serves as a restaurant, bar, art gallery and theater for nightly live music; the kitchen serves eclectic American fare with global accents (seafood burritos, jerk chicken wraps).

There are B&Bs galore, but we prefer the Atlantic Hotel (☑410-641-3589; www.atlantichotel.com; 2 N Main St; r $115-245; P✷),

a handsome, Gilded-era lodger that gives guests the time-warp experience with all the modern amenities.

A few miles from Berlin, Snow Hill has a splendid location along the idyllic Pocomoke River. Get on the water with the Pocomoke River Canoe Company (☑410-632-3971; www.pocomokerivercanoe.com; 312 N Washington St; canoe per hr/day $15/40). They'll even take you upriver so you can have a leisurely paddle downstream. Nearby Furnace Town (☑410-632-2032; www.furnacetown.com; Old Furnace Rd; adult/child $6/3; ☉10am-5pm Mon-Sat Apr-Oct, from noon Sun; P♿), off Rte 12, is a living-history museum that marks the old location of a 19th-century iron-smelting town. In Snow Hill itself, while away an odd, rewarding half-hour in the Julia A Purnell Museum (☑410-632-0515; 208 W Market St; adult/child $2/0.50; ☉10am-4pm Tue-Sat, from 1pm Sun Apr-Oct), a tiny structure that feels like an attic for the entire Eastern Shore.

Staying in town? Check out Snow Hill's River House Inn (☑410-632-2722; www.riverhouseinn.com; 201 E Market St; r $160-190, cottage $250-300; P✷☎✷), with a lush backyard that overlooks a scenic bend of the river. Palette (☑410-632-0055; 104 W Market St; mains $14-22; ☉11am-3pm Tue-Wed, to 9pm Thu-Sat, 10am-2pm Sun; ☑) ✐ serves a changing menu of contemporary American fare, using organic locally sourced ingredients.

Ocean City

'The OC' is where you'll experience the American seaside resort at its tackiest. Here you can take a spin on nausea-inducing thrill rides, buy a T-shirt with obscene slogans and drink to excess at cheesy theme bars. The center of action is the 2.5-mile-long boardwalk, which stretches from the inlet to 27th St. The beach is attractive, but you'll have to contend with horny teenagers and noisy crowds; the beaches north of the boardwalk are much quieter.

In summer, the town's tiny year-round population of 7100 swells to more than 150,000; traffic is jammed and parking scarce.

🛏 Sleeping

The visitor center (☑800-626-2326; www.ococean.com; Coastal Hwy at 40th St; ☉9am-5pm), in the convention center on Coastal Hwy, can help you find lodging.

ASSATEAGUE ISLAND

Just 8 miles south but a world away from Ocean City is Assateague Island seashore, a perfectly barren landscape of sand dunes and beautiful, secluded beaches. This undeveloped barrier island is populated by the only herd of wild horses on the East Coast, made famous in the book *Misty of Chincoteague*.

The island is divided into three sections. In Maryland there's **Assateague State Park** (☎410-641-2918; Rte 611; admission/campsites $4/31; ☺campground late Apr-Oct) and federally administered **Assateague Island National Seashore** (☎410-641-1441; www. nps.gov/asis; Rte 611; admission/vehicles/campsites per week $3/15/20; ☺visitor center 9am-5pm). **Chincoteague National Wildlife Refuge** (www.fws.gov/northeast/chinco; 8231 Beach Road, Chincoteague Island; daily/weekly pass $8/15 ; ☺5am-10pm Mon-Sat May-Sep, 6am-6pm Nov-Feb, to 8pm Mar, Apr & Oct; P) is in Virginia.

As well as swimming and sunbathing, recreational activities include birding, kayaking, canoeing, crabbing and fishing. There are no services on the Maryland side of the island, so you must bring all your own food and drink. Don't forget insect repellent; the mosquitoes and biting horseflies can be ferocious!

King Charles Hotel GUESTHOUSE $$
(☎410-289-6141; www.kingcharleshotel.com; cnr N Baltimore Ave & 12th St; r $115-190; P) This place could be a quaint summer cottage, except it happens to be a short stroll to the heart of the boardwalk action. It has aging but clean rooms with small porches attached, and it's quiet (owners discourage young partiers).

Inn on the Ocean B&B $$$
(☎410-289-8894; www.innontheocean.com; 1001 Atlantic Ave, at the Boardwalk; r incl breakfast $275-395) This six-roomed B&B is an elegant escape from the usual OC big-box lodging.

✗ Eating & Drinking

Surf 'n' turf and all-you-can-eat deals are the order of the day. Dance clubs cluster around the boardwalk's southern tip.

Liquid Assets MODERN AMERICAN $$
(☎410-524-7037; cnr 94th St & Coastal Hwy; mains $10-28; ☺11:30am-11pm Sun-Thu, to midnight Fri & Sat) Like a diamond in the rough, this bistro and wine shop is hidden in a strip mall in north OC. The menu is a refreshing mix of innovative seafood, grilled meats and regional classics (such as Carolina pork BBQ and 'ahi tuna burger').

Fager's Island MODERN AMERICAN $$$
(☎410-524-5500; www.fagers.com; 60th St; mains $19-36; ☺from 11am) The food can be hit-and-miss, but it's a great place for a drink, with enviable views over Isle of Wight Bay. Live bands and DJs keep the bachelorettes rolling on weekends.

Seacrets BAR
(www.seacrets.com; cnr W 49th St & the Bay; ☺8am-2am) A water-laced, Jamaican-themed, rum-soaked bar straight out of MTV's *Spring Break*. You can drift around in an inner tube while sipping a drink and people-watching at OC's most famous meat market.

❶ Getting There & Around

Greyhound (☎410-289-9307; www.greyhound. com; 12848 Ocean Gateway) buses run daily to and from Washington, DC (four hours), and Baltimore (3½ hours).

Ocean City Coastal Highway Bus (day pass $3) runs up and down the length of the beach, from 6am to 3am. There's also a tram ($3 or $6 all-day pass) that runs 11am to midnight from memorial day to late September.

Western Maryland

The western spine of Maryland is mountain country. The Appalachian peaks soar to 3000ft above sea level, and the surrounding valleys are packed with rugged scenery and Civil War battlefields. This is Maryland's outdoor playground, where hiking, skiing, rock climbing and white-water rafting are just a short drive from Baltimore.

Frederick

Halfway between the battlefields of Gettysburg, PA, and Antietam, Frederick, with its handsome 50-square-block historic district, resembles an almost perfect cliche of a mid-sized city.

The National Museum of Civil War Medicine (www.civilwarmed.org; 48 E Patrick St; adult/child $6.50/4.50; ☉10am-5pm Mon-Sat, from 11am Sun) gives a fascinating, sometimes gruesome look at the health conditions soldiers and doctors faced during the war, as well as important medical advances that resulted from the conflict.

Hollerstown Hill B&B (☑301-228-3630; www.hollerstownhill.com; 4 Clarke Pl; r $135-145; P✳☎) has four pattern-heavy rooms, an elegant billiard room and friendly, knowledgeable hosts.

The bouncy Brewer's Alley (☑301-631-0089; 124 N Market St; burgers $9-13, mains $18-29; ☉11:30am-11:30pm Mon & Tue, to midnight Wed & Thu, to 12:30am Fri & Sat, noon-11:30pm Sun; ☎) is one of our favorite places in town, for several reasons. First, the beer: homemade, plenty of variety, delicious. Second, the burgers: enormous, half-pound monstrosities. Third, the rest of the menu: excellent Chesapeake seafood and Frederick county farm produce. Finally: the beer. Again

Frederick is accessible via Greyhound (☑301-663-3311; www.greyhound.com) and MARC trains (☑301-682-9716) located across from the visitor center at 100 S East St.

Antietam National Battlefield

The site of the bloodiest day in American history is, ironically, supremely peaceful, quiet and haunting, uncluttered save for plaques and statues. On September 17, 1862, General Robert E Lee's first invasion of the North was stalled here in a tactical stalemate that left more than 23,000 dead, wounded or missing – more casualties than America had suffered in all her previous wars combined. Poignantly, many of the battlefield graves are inscribed with German and Irish names, a roll call of immigrants who died fighting for their new homeland. The visitor center (☑301-432-5124; State Rd 65; 3-day pass per person/family $4/6; ☉8:30am-6pm, to 5pm off-season) sells a range of books and materials, including self-guided driving and walking tours of the battlefield.

Cumberland

At the Potomac River, the frontier outpost of Fort Cumberland (not to be confused with the Cumberland Gap between Virginia and Kentucky) was the pioneer gateway across the Alleghenies to Pittsburgh and the Ohio River. Today Cumberland has expanded into the outdoor recreation trade to guide visitors to the region's rivers, forests and mountains. Sights are a short stroll from the pedestrian-friendly streets of downtown Cumberland.

◉ Sights & Activities

C&O Canal National
Historic Park   HIKING, CYCLING
A marvel of engineering, the C&O Canal was designed to stretch alongside the Potomac River from Chesapeake Bay to the Ohio River. Construction on the canal began in 1828 but was halted here in 1850 by the Appalachian Mountains. The park's protected 185-mile corridor includes a 12ft-wide towpath, hiking and cycling trail, which goes all the way from here to Georgetown in DC. The C&O Canal Museum (☑301-722-8226; http://www.nps.gov/choh; 13 Canal Pl; ☉9am-5pm Mon-Fri; P) ✐ has displays chronicling the importance of river trade in eastern seaboard history.

Western Maryland Scenic Railroad   TOUR
(☑800-872-4650; www.wmsr.com; 13 Canal St; adult/child $33/16; ☉11:30am Fri-Sun May-Oct, Sat & Sun Nov-Dec) Outside the Allegheny County visitor center, near the start of the C&O Canal, passengers can catch steam-locomotive rides, traversing forests and steep ravines to Frostburg, a 3½-hour round-trip.

Cumberland Trail Connection   CYCLING
(☑301-777-8724; www.ctcbikes.com; 14 Howard St, Canal Pl; half-day/day/week from $15/25/120; ☉10am-6pm) Conveniently located near the start of the C&O Canal, this outfit rents out bicycles (cruisers, touring bikes and mountain bikes), and also arranges shuttle service anywhere from Pittsburgh to DC. Canoe rentals are in the works.

Allegany Expeditions   ADVENTURE TOUR
(☑301-777-9313; www.alleganyexpeditions.com; 10310 Columbus Ave/Rte 2) Leads adventure tours, including rock-climbing, canoeing, cross-country skiing and fly-fishing.

✖ Eating

Queen City Creamery & Deli   DINER $
(☑301-777-0011; 108 Harrison St; mains $6-8; ☉7am-9pm) This retro soda fountain is like a 1940s time warp, with creamy shakes and homemade frozen custard, thick sandwiches and belly-filling breakfasts.

Deep Creek Lake

In the extreme west of the panhandle, Maryland's largest freshwater lake is an all-seasons playground. The crimson and copper glow of the Alleghenies attracts thousands during the annual Autumn Glory Festival (www.autumngloryfestival. com; ⊘Oct), rivaling New England's leaf-turning backdrops.

DELAWARE

Wee Delaware, the nation's second-smallest state (96 miles long and less than 35 miles across at its widest point) is overshadowed by its neighbors and overlooked by visitors to the Capital Region. And that's too bad, because Delaware has a lot more on offer than just tax-free shopping and chicken farms.

Long white sandy beaches, cute colonial villages, a cozy countryside and small-town charm characterize the 'Small Wonder'. Ignore those tolls: there's a whole state just waiting to be explored, and (forgive us one more joke about Delaware's size), it doesn't take long to get around.

History

In colonial days Delaware was the subject of an aggressive land feud between Dutch, Swedish and British settlers. The former imported classically northern European middle-class concepts, the latter a plantation-based aristocracy, which is partly why Delaware remains a typically mid-Atlantic cultural hybrid today.

The little state's big moment came on December 7, 1787, when Delaware became the first state to ratify the US Constitution and thus the first state in the Union. It remained in that union throughout the Civil War, despite supporting slavery. During this period, as throughout much of the state's history, the economy drew on its chemical industry. DuPont, the world's second-largest chemical company, was founded here in 1802 as a gunpowder factory by French Immigrant Eleuthère Irénée du Pont. Low taxes drew other firms (particularly credit-card companies) in the 20th century, boosting the state's prosperity.

Delaware Beaches

Delaware's 28 miles of sandy Atlantic beaches are the best reason to linger. Most businesses and services are open year-round. Off-season (outside June to August) price bargains abound.

Lewes

In 1631 the Dutch gave this whaling settlement the pretty name of Zwaanendael, or valley of the swans, before promptly getting massacred by local Nanticokes. The name was changed to Lewes (pronounced Loo-iss) when William Penn gained control of the area. Today it's an attractive seaside gem with a mix of English and Dutch architecture.

The visitor center (www.leweschamber. com; 120 Kings Hwy; ⊘9am-5pm Mon-Fri) directs you to sights such as the Zwaanendael Museum (102 Kings Hwy; ⊘10am-4:30pm Tue-Sat, 1:30-4:30pm Sun) FREE, where the friendly staff explains the Dutch roots of this first-state settlement.

For aquatic action, Quest Fitness Kayak (☑302-644-7020; www.questfitnesskayak.com; Savannah Rd; kayak per 2/8hr $25/50) operates a kayak rental stand next to the Beacon Motel. It also runs scenic paddle tours around the Cape (adult/child $65/35).

DELAWARE FACTS

Nickname The First State

Population 917,000

Area 1982 sq miles

Capital city Dover (population 36,000)

Sales tax None

Birthplace of Rock musician George Thorogood (b 1952), actress Valerie Bertinelli (b 1960), actor Ryan Phillippe (b 1974)

Home of Vice President Joe Biden, the Du Pont family, DuPont chemicals, credit-card companies, lots of chickens

Politics Democrat

Famous for Tax-free shopping, beautiful beaches

State bird Blue hen chicken

Driving distances Wilmington to Dover 52 miles, Dover to Rehoboth Beach 43 miles

Restaurant and hotel options in the small historic downtown include Hotel Rodney (302-645-6466; www.hotelrodneydelaware.com; 142 2nd St; r $160-260; P✳︎🐾🛜≋), a charming boutique hotel with exquisite bedding and antique furniture. On the other side of the canal, the Beacon Motel (302-645-4888; www.beaconmotel.com; 514 Savannah Rd; r $95-190; P✳︎🐾🛜) has large, quiet (if a little boring) rooms within 10-minutes' walk to the beach.

There are charming restaurants and cafes sprinkled along 2nd St. Located by the drawbridge over the canal, the clapboard Striper Bites Bistro (302-645-4657; 107 Savannah Rd; lunch mains $10-12, dinner $16-24; ⏲11:30am-late Mon-Sat) specializes in innovative seafood dishes such as Lewes rockfish and fish tacos. Across the drawbridge, the Wharf (302-645-7846; 7 Anglers Rd; mains $15-29; ⏲7am-1am; P🐾) has a relaxing waterfront location (facing the canal), and serves a big selection of seafood and pub grub. Live music throughout the week.

The Cape May–Lewes Ferry (800-643-3779; www.capemaylewesferry.com; 43 Cape Henlopen Dr; per motorcycle/car $36/44, per adult/child $10/5) runs daily 90-minute ferries across Delaware Bay to New Jersey from the terminal, 1 mile from downtown Lewes. For foot passengers, a seasonal shuttle bus ($4) operates between the ferry terminal and Lewes and Rehoboth Beach. Fares are lower Sunday through Thursday and during winter. Reservations recommended.

Cape Henlopen State Park

One mile east of Lewes, more than 4000 acres of dune bluffs, pine forests and wetlands are preserved at this lovely state park (302-645-8983; http://www.destateparks.com/park/cape-henlopen/; 15099 Cape Henlopen Dr; admission $4; ⏲8am-sunset) that's popular with bird-watchers and beachgoers ($6 per out-of-state car). You can see clear to Cape May from the observation tower. North Shores beach draws many gay and lesbian couples. Camping (877-987-2757; campsites $33; ⏲Mar-Nov) includes oceanfront or wooded sites.

Rehoboth Beach & Dewey Beach

As the closest beach to Washington, DC (121 miles), Rehoboth is often dubbed 'the Nation's Summer Capital.' Founded in 1873 as a Christian seaside resort camp, Rehoboth is today a shining example of tolerance. It is both a family-friendly and gay-friendly destination, and has a particularly large lesbian community. There's even a gay beach – aka Poodle Beach – located, appropriately, at the end of Queen St.

Downtown Rehoboth is a mixture of grand Victorian and gingerbread houses, tree-lined streets, boutique B&Bs and shops, posh restaurants, kiddie amusements and wide beaches fronted by a mile-long boardwalk. Rehoboth Ave, the main drag, is lined with restaurants and the usual tacky souvenir shops; it stretches from the visitor center (302-227-2233; www.beach-fun.com; 501 Rehoboth Ave; ⏲9am-5pm Mon-Fri, to 1pm Sat & Sun) at the traffic circle to the boardwalk. Outside of town, Rte 1 is a busy highway crammed with chain restaurants, hotels and outlet malls, where bargain-hunters take advantage of Delaware's tax-free shopping.

Less than 2 miles south on Hwy 1 is the tiny hamlet of Dewey Beach. Unapologetically known as 'Do Me' beach for its hook-up scene (straight) and hedonistic nightlife, it's is a major party beach. Another 3 miles past Dewey is Delaware Seashore State Park (302-227-2800; http://www.destateparks.com/park/delaware-seashore/; 39415 Inlet Rd; admission $4; ⏲8am-sunset), a windswept slice of preserved dunes and salty breezes possessed of a wild, lonely beauty.

🛏 Sleeping

As elsewhere on the coast, prices sky rocket in high season (June to August). Cheaper lodging options are located on Rte 1.

⭐Cottages at Indian River Marina   COTTAGES $$$
(302-227-3071; http://www.destateparks.com/camping/cottages/rates.asp; Inlet 838, Rehoboth Beach; weekly peak/shoulder/off-season $1800/1350/835, 2 days off-season $280 ; P✳︎) These cottages, located in Delaware Seashore State Park five miles south of town, are some of our favorite local vacation rentals. Not for the decor per se, but the patios and unadulterated views across the pristine beach to the ocean. Each cottage has two bedrooms and a loft. They must be rented out by the week during the summer, but they're available in two-day increments off-season.

Bellmoor Inn & Spa   BOUTIQUE HOTEL $$$
(866-899-2779, 302-227-5800; www.thebellmoor.com; 6 Christian St; r $190-260; P✳︎@🛜) If money were no object, we'd splurge for

a room at Rehoboth's most luxurious inn. With its English country decor, fireplaces, quiet garden and secluded setting, this is not your usual seaside resort. A full-service day spa caps the amenities.

Hotel Rehoboth BOUTIQUE HOTEL **$$$**
(☑ 302-227-4300; www.hotelrehoboth.com; 247 Rehoboth Ave; r $230-320; P ✴ @ 🛜 🌊) This boutique hotel has a reputation for great service and luxurious amenities. It offers a free shuttle to the beach.

Crosswinds Motel MOTEL **$$$**
(☑ 302-227-7997; www.crosswindsmotel.com; 312 Rehoboth Ave; r $130-275; P ✴ 🛜) Located in the heart of Rehoboth Ave, this simple motel offers great value for your dollar, with its welcome amenities (minifridge, coffeemaker, flat-screen TV). Walk to the beach in 12 minutes.

🍴 Eating & Drinking

Cheap eats are available on the boardwalk, with favorites such as Thrasher's fries, Grotto's pizza and Dolle's saltwater taffy. For classier dining, browse the inviting restaurants sprinkled along Wilmington Ave.

Ed's Chicken & Crabs AMERICAN **$**
(☑ 302- 227-9484; 2200 Coastal Highway, Dewey Beach; mains $7-18; ⊙ 11am-10pm) It's fried. What's fried? Just about everything at this outdoor dining shack: shrimp, jalapenos, crabs. But not the corn – the corn is boiled and sweet and delicious. Ed's ain't fine dining, but it's tasty and old-school and unhealthy and, in its way, perfect.

★ Planet X FUSION **$$$**
(☑ 302-226-1928; 35 Wilmington Ave; mains $16-33; ⊙ from 5pm; 🖉) This stylish spot shows its Asian influence in menu and decor – red paper lanterns and Buddhas adorn the walls, while diners feast on red Thai curry with jumbo shrimp and crab cakes with spicy Asian sesame noodles. There's alfresco dining on the open-sided front porch.

Henlopen City Oyster House SEAFOOD **$$$**
(50 Wilmington Ave; mains $21-26; ⊙ from 3pm) Oyster- and seafood-lovers won't want to miss this elegant spot, where an enticing raw bar and beautifully prepared plates (soft-shell crabs, bouillabaisse and lobster mac 'n' cheese) draw crowds (arrive early; no reservations). Good microbrews, cocktails

DON'T MISS

CYCLING THE JUNCTION & BREAKWATER TRAIL

For a fantastic ride between Rehoboth and Lewes, rent a bicycle and hit the 6-mile Junction and Breakwater Trail. Named after the former rail line, which operated here in the 1800s, this smooth, graded greenway travels through wooded and open terrain, over coastal marshes and past farmland. Pick up a map from the Rehoboth visitor center or from Atlantic Cycles (☑ 302-226-2543; www.atlanticcycles. net; 18 Wilmington Ave; half-day/day from $16/24), also in Rehoboth, which offers inexpensive rentals. In Lewes, try Ocean Cycles (☑ 302-537-1522; www. oceancycles.com; 526 E Savannah Rd) at the Beacon Motel.

and wine selections make it an ideal early-evening drink-and-eat spot.

Cultured Pearl JAPANESE **$$$**
(☑ 302-227-8493; 301 Rehoboth Ave; mains $16-33; ⊙ 4:30pm-late) A longtime locals' favorite, this Asian restaurant has a Zen feel, with a koi pond at the entrance and a pleasant rooftop deck. The sushi and appetizers are first-rate. Live music most nights.

Dogfish Head MICROBREWERY
(www.dogfish.com; 320 Rehoboth Ave; mains $9-25; ⊙ noon-late) When a place mixes its own brewery with some of the best live music on the Eastern Shore, you know you've got a winning combination.

ℹ Getting There & Around

The **Jolly Trolley** (one way/round-trip $3/5; ⊙ 8am-2am summer) connects Rehoboth and Dewey, and makes frequent stops along the way. Unfortunately, long-distance buses no longer serve Rehoboth.

Bethany Beach & Fenwick Island

Want to get away from it all? The seaside towns of Bethany and Fenwick, about halfway between Rehoboth and Ocean City, are known as 'the Quiet Resorts.' They share a tranquil, almost boring, family-friendly scene.

There are only a few restaurants and even fewer hotels here; most visitors stay in

WASHINGTON, DC & THE CAPITAL REGION DELAWARE BEACHES

rented apartments and beach houses. For a nice change of pace from the usual seafood fare, Bethany Blues BBQ (302-537-1500; www.bethanyblues.com; 6 N Pennsylvania Ave; mains $14-24; 4:30-9pm, to 10pm Fri & Sat) has falling-off-the-bone ribs and pulled-pork sandwiches.

Northern & Central Delaware

The grit of Wilmington is balanced by the rolling hills and palatial residences of the Brandywine Valley, particularly the soaring estate of Winterthur. Dover is cute, friendly and gets a little lively after hours.

Wilmington

A unique cultural milieu (African Americans, Jews and Caribbeans) and an energetic arts scene make this town worth a visit.

The Delaware Art Museum (302-571-9590; www.delart.org; 800 S Madison St; adult/child $12/6, Sun free; 10am-4pm Wed-Sat, from noon Sun) exhibits work of the local Brandywine School, including Edward Hopper, John Sloan and three generations of Wyeths.

The Wilmington Riverfront (www.riverfrontwilm.com) consists of several blocks of redeveloped waterfront shops, restaurants and cafes; the most striking building is the Delaware Center for the Contemporary Arts (302-656-6466; www.thedcca.org; 200 S Madison St; 10am-5pm Tue & Thu-Sat, from noon Wed & Sun) FREE, which consistently displays innovative exhibitions. In the art-deco Woolworth's building, the Delaware History Museum (302-656-0637; www.hsd.org/dhm; 200 S Madison St; adult/child $6/4; 11am-4pm Wed-Fri, 10am-4pm Sat) proves the First State's past includes loads more than being head of the line to sign the Constitution.

The premier hotel in the state, the Hotel du Pont (302-594-3100; www.hoteldupont.com; cnr Market & 11th Sts; r $230-480; P✳︎☏) is luxurious enough to satisfy its namesake (one of America's most successful industrialist families). On the riverfront, Iron Hill Brewery (302-472-2739; 710 South Madison St; mains $10-24; 11am-11pm) is a spacious and airy multilevel space set in a converted brick warehouse. Satisfying microbrews (try the seasonal Belgian ale) match nicely with hearty pub grub.

The visitor center (800-489-6664; www.visitwilmingtonde.com; 100 W 10th St; 9am-5pm Mon-Thu, 8:30am-4:30pm Fri) is downtown. Wilmington is accessible by Greyhound or Peter Pan Bus Lines, which run to major East Coast cities. Both bus lines serve the Wilmington Transportation Center (101 N French St). Amtrak (www.amtrak.com; 100 S French St) trains connect Wilmington with DC (1½ hours), Baltimore (45 minutes) and New York (1¾ hours).

Brandywine Valley

After making their fortune, the French-descended Du Ponts turned the Brandywine Valley into a sort of American Loire Valley, and it remains a nesting ground for the wealthy and ostentatious to this day.

Six miles northwest of Wilmington is Winterthur (302-888-4600; www.winterthur.org; 5105 Kennett Pike (Rte 52) ; adult/child $18/5; 10am-5pm Tue-Sun), the 175-room country estate of industrialist Henry Francis du Pont, housing his collection of antiques and American arts, one of the world's largest.

Brandywine Creek State Park (302-577-3534; http://www.destateparks.com/park/brandywine-creek/; 41 Adams Dam Road, Wilmington; admission $3; 8am-sunset) is the gem of the area. This green space would be impressive anywhere, but is doubly so considering how close it is to prodigious urban development. Nature trails and shallow streams wend through the park; contact Wilderness Canoe Trips (302-654-2227; www.wilderness-canoetrips.com; 2111 Concord Pike; kayak/canoe trip from $46/56, per tube $18) for information on paddling or tubing down the dark-green Brandywine creek.

New Castle

As cute as a colonial kitten, New Castle is a web of cobblestoned streets and beautifully preserved 18th-century buildings lying near a riverfront (that said, the surrounding area, however, is a bit of an urban wasteland). Sights include the Old Court House (302-323-4453; 211 Delaware St, New Castle; 10am-3:30pm Wed-Sat, 1:30-4:30pm Sun) FREE, the arsenal on the Green, churches and cemeteries dating back to the 17th century, and historic houses.

The five-room Terry House B&B (302-322-2505; www.terryhouse.com; 130 Delaware St; r $90-110; P☏) is idyllically set in the historic district. The owner will play the piano for you while you enjoy a full breakfast.

A few doors down, Jessop's Tavern (302-322-6111; 114 Delaware St; mains $12-24; 11:30am-10pm Sun-Thu, to midnight Fri & Sat) serves up Dutch pot roast, Pilgrim's feast (oven-roasted turkey with all the fixings) plus fish and chips and other pub grub in a colonial atmosphere. Half the fun is watching the bored teenage staff chafe in their Colonial-era garb.

Outside of town, check out the Dog House (302-328-5380; 1200 Dupont Hwy, New Castle; mains under $10; 10:30am-midnight). Don't be fooled by the name; while this unassuming diner does hot dogs and does them well (the chili dogs are a treat), it also whips out mean subs and cheese-steaks that could pass muster in Philly.

Dover

Dover's city center is quite attractive; the row-house-lined streets are peppered with restaurants and shops and, on prettier lanes, broadleaf trees spread their branches.

Learn about the first official state at First State Heritage Park (302-744-5055; 121 Martin Luther King Blvd North, Dover; 8am-4:30pm Mon-Fri, from 9am Sat, 1:30-4:30pm Sun) FREE. Located in the local archives, the park serves as a welcome center for the city of Dover, the state of Delaware and the adjacent state house. Access the latter via the Georgian Old State House (302-744-5055; http://history.delaware.gov/museums/; 25 The Green; 9am-4:30pm Mon-Sat, from 1:30pm Sun) FREE, built in 1791 and since restored, which contains art galleries and in-depth exhibits on the First State's history and politics.

The State Street Inn (302-734-2294; www.statestreetinn.com; 228 N State St; r $125-135) is well located near the State House, and has four bright rooms with wood floors and period furnishings.

A short stroll from the State House, Golden Fleece (302-674-1776; 132 W Lockerman St; mains under $10; 4pm-midnight, to late on Sat & Sun, from noon Sun) is our favorite bar in Dover. There's decent food and the atmosphere of an old English pub, which meshes well with the surrounding red-brick historical center.

Bombay Hook National Wildlife Refuge

You're not the only person making a trip to Bombay Hook National Wildlife Refuge (302-653-9345; http://www.fws.gov/refuge/Bombay_Hook; 2591 Whitehall Neck Rd, Smyrna; sunrise-sunset). Hundreds of thousands of waterfowl use this protected wetland as a stopping point along their migration routes.

A 12-mile wildlife driving trail through 16,251 acres of sweet-smelling saltwater marsh, cordgrass and tidal mud flats, which manages to encapsulate all of the soft beauty of the DelMarVa peninsula in one perfectly preserved ecosystem, is the highlight of the sanctuary.

There are also five walking trails, two of which are accessible to travelers with disabilities, as well as observation towers overlooking the entire affair. Across the water you may see the lights and factories of New Jersey, an industrial yin to this area's wilderness yang.

VIRGINIA

Beautiful Virginia is a state steeped in history. It's the birthplace of America, where English settlers established the first permanent colony in the New World in 1607. From there, the Commonwealth of Virginia has played a lead role in nearly every major American drama, from the Revolutionary and Civil Wars to the Civil Rights movement and September 11, 2001.

Virginia's natural beauty is as diverse as its history and people. Chesapeake Bay and the wide sandy beaches kiss the Atlantic Ocean. Pine forests, marshes and rolling green hills form the soft curves of the central Piedmont region, while the rugged Appalachian Mountains and stunning Shenandoah Valley line its back.

The nation's invisible line between North and South is drawn here, somewhere around Richmond; you'll know it as soon as you hear the sweet southern drawl offering plates of biscuits and Virginia ham. With something for everyone, it's easy to appreciate the state's motto: 'Virginia is for Lovers.'

History

Humans have occupied Virginia for at least 5000 years. Several thousand Native Americans were already here in May 1607 when Captain James Smith and his crew sailed up Chesapeake Bay and founded Jamestown, the first permanent English colony in the New World. Named for the 'Virgin Queen' Elizabeth I, the territory originally occupied most of America's eastern seaboard. By 1610 most of the colonists had died from starvation in their quest for gold, until colonist John Rolfe (husband

WASHINGTON, DC & THE CAPITAL REGION VIRGINIA

of Pocahontas) discovered Virginia's real riches: tobacco.

A feudal aristocracy grew out of tobacco farming, and many gentry scions became Founding Fathers, including native son George Washington. In the 19th century the slave-based plantation system grew in size and incompatibility with the industrializing North; Virginia seceded in 1861 and became the epicenter of the Civil War. Following its defeat the state walked a tense cultural tightrope, accruing a layered identity that included older aristocrats, a rural and urban working class, waves of immigrants, to-day, the burgeoning tech-heavy suburbs of DC. The state revels in its history, yet still wants to pioneer the American experiment; thus, while Virginia only reluctantly deseg-regated in the 1960s, today it houses one of the most ethnically diverse populations of the New South.

VIRGINIA FACTS

Nickname Old Dominion

Population 8.2 million

Area 42,774 sq miles

Capital city Richmond (population 205,000)

Other cities Virginia Beach (population 447,000), Norfolk (population 245,800), Chesapeake (population 228,400), Richmond (population 210,300), Newport News (population) 180,700

Sales tax 5.3%

Birthplace of Eight US presidents including George Washington (1732–99), Confederate General Robert E Lee (1807–70), tennis ace Arthur Ashe (1943–93), author Tom Wolfe (b 1931), actress Sandra Bullock (b 1964)

Home of The Pentagon, the CIA, more technology workers than any other state

Politics Republican

Famous for American history, tobacco, apples, Shenandoah National Park

State beverage Milk

Driving distances Arlington to Shenandoah 113 miles, Richmond to Virginia Beach 108 miles

Northern Virginia

Hidden within its suburban sprawl exterior, Northern Virginia (NOVA) mixes small-town charm with metropolitan chic. Colonial villages and battlefields bump up against skyscrapers, shopping malls and world-class arts venues.

You'll discover unexpected green spaces such as **Great Falls National Park** (703-285-2965; www.nps.gov/grfa; 7am-sunset) . It's a well-maintained forest cut through by the Potomac River, which surges over a series of white-water rapids.

Arlington

Just across the Potomac River from DC, Arlington County was once part of Washington until it was returned to Virginia in 1847. In recent years the gentrified neighborhoods of Arlington have spawned some tempting dining and nightlife options.

Sights

Arlington National Cemetery   HISTORIC SITE
(877-907-8585; www.arlingtoncemetery.mil; tour bus adult/child $8.75/4.50; 8am-7pm Apr-Sep, to 5pm Oct-Mar) **FREE** This immensely powerful destination is the somber final resting place for more than 300,000 military personnel and their dependents, with veterans of every US war from the Revolution to Iraq. The cemetery is spread over 612 hilly acres. You can travel around via a **tour bus**, which departs continuously from the visitor center from 8:30am to 4:30pm.

➜ **The Grounds**

Much of the cemetery was built on the grounds of **Arlington House**, the former home of Robert E Lee and his wife Mary Anna Custis Lee, a descendant of Martha Washington. When Lee left to lead Virginia's army in the Civil War, Union troops confiscated the property to bury their dead. The **Tomb of the Unknowns** contains the remains of unidentified American servicemen from both World Wars and the Korean War; military guards retain a round-the-clock vigil and the changing of the guard (every half-hour March to September, every hour October to February) is one of Arlington's most moving sights. An eternal flame marks the **grave of John F Kennedy**, next to those of Jacqueline Kennedy Onassis and two of her infant children.

➡ **Marine Corps Memorial**

Just north of the cemetery, the Marine Corps Memorial (N Meade & 14th Sts) depicts six soldiers raising the American flag on Iwo Jima. The Felix de Weldon–designed sculpture is based on an iconic photo by Associated Press photographer Joe Rosenthal.

Artisphere   ARTS CENTER

(🖉703-875-1100; www.artisphere.com; 1101 Wilson Blvd; ⌨; Ⓜ Rosslyn) For something completely different than memorials and museums, check out the excellent exhibits at this sleek, modern, multistory arts complex. Its several theaters host live performances (many free), including world music, film and experimental theater. Nearby Freedom Park, an elevated greenway that rests in an old road overpass running by Artisphere, is a nice spot to sit for a while and contemplate.

Pentagon   BUILDING

South of Arlington Cemetery is the Pentagon, the largest office building in the world. It's not open to the public, but outside you may visit the Pentagon Memorial (www.whs.mil/memorial; 1 N Rotary Rd, Arlington; ⊙24hr) FREE; 184 illuminated benches honor each person killed in the September 11, 2001, terrorist attack on the Pentagon. Nearby, the three soaring arcs of the Air Force Memorial (🖉703-247-5805; www.airforcememorial.org; 1 Air Force Memorial Dr, Arlington) evoke the contrails of jets.

🛏 **Sleeping & Eating**

In addition to hotels, there are dozens of chic restaurants and bars located along Clarendon and Wilson Blvds, clustered near Rosslyn and Clarendon Metro stations.

⭐**Myanmar**   BURMESE $

(🖉703-289-0013; 7810 Lee Hwy, Falls Church; mains under $10; ⊙11am-10pm) Myanmar's decor is bare bones; the service is slow; the portions are small; and the food is delicious. This is homemade Burmese: curries cooked with lots of garlic, turmeric and oil, plus chili fish, mango salads and chicken swimming in rich gravies.

Lyon Hall   FRENCH $$

(🖉703-741-7636; http://lyonhallarlington.com; 3100 N Washington Blvd; mains $14-25; ⊙11.30am-3pm Mon-Fri, from 10am Sat & Sun, 5pm-10:30pm Sun-Thu, to 11:30pm Fri & Sat; Ⓜ Clarendon) Enter this French-Alsatian bistro under a deco-style sign. Cassoulet is wonderfully rich thanks to its base of duck fat; a trout served

over summer beans is enlivened by vanilla butter. Wash it down with a local cocktail from the popular bar.

Eden Center   VIETNAMESE $$

(www.edencenter.com; 6571 Wilson Blvd, Falls Church; mains $9-15; ⊙9am-11pm; 🖉) One of Washington's most fascinating ethnic enclaves isn't technically in Washington but west of Arlington in Falls Church, VA. The Eden Center is, basically, a bit of Saigon that got lost in America. And we mean 'Saigon' – this is a shopping center/strip mall entirely occupied and operated by South Vietnamese refugees and their descendants. You can buy Vietnamese DVDs, shop for odd fruits and unusual medicines and, of course, eat – anywhere.

Whitlow's on Wilson   AMERICAN $$

(🖉703-276-9693; 2854 Clarendon Blvd; mains $8-21; ⊙11am-2am Mon-Fri, from 9am Sat & Sun) Arlington's best Sunday-brunch menu, plus weekday happy-hour specials and live bands on weekends.

☆ **Entertainment**

⭐**Iota**   LIVE MUSIC

(www.iotaclubandcafe.com; 2832 Wilson Blvd; tickets from $10; ⊙from 8am; 🛜; Ⓜ Clarendon) Iota is the best venue for live music in the area. Bands span genres; folk, reggae, traditional Irish and Southern rock are all possibilities. Tickets are available at the door only (no advance sales). The free open-mic Wednesdays can be lots of fun or painfully self-important, as these things are wont to be.

Alexandria

The charming colonial village of Alexandria is just 5 miles and 250 years away from Washington. Once a salty port town, Alexandria – known as 'Old Town' to locals – is today a posh collection of red-brick colonial homes, cobblestone streets, flickering gas lamps and a waterfront promenade. King St is packed with boutiques, outdoor cafes, and neighborhood bars and restaurants.

⊙ **Sights**

George Washington Masonic National Memorial   MONUMENT, LOOKOUT

(www.gwmemorial.org; 101 Callahan Dr at King St; adult/child $8/free; ⊙9am-4pm Mon-Sat, noon-4pm Sun; Ⓜ King St) Alexandria's most prominent landmark features a fine view from its 333ft tower, where you can see the Capitol,

Mount Vernon and the Potomac River. It is modeled after Egypt's Lighthouse of Alexandria and honors the first president (who was initiated into the shadowy Masons in Fredericksburg in 1752 and later became Worshipful Master of Alexandria Lodge No 22). The only way up is via a guided tour; they depart at 10am, 11:30am, 1:30pm and 3pm (on Sunday the first one is at 12:30pm).

Gadsby's Tavern Museum MUSEUM
(www.gadsbystavern.org; 134 N Royal St; adult/child $5/2; ☉10am-5pm Tue-Sat, 1-5pm Sun & Mon; Ⓜ King St then trolley) Once a real tavern (operated by John Gadsby from 1796 to 1808), this building now houses a museum demonstrating the prominent role of the tavern in Alexandria during the 18th century. As the center of local political, business and social life, the tavern was frequented by anybody who was anybody, including George Washington, Thomas Jefferson and the Marquis de Lafayette. The rooms are restored to their 18th-century appearance, and the tavern occasionally still hosts pricey balls. Guided tours take place at quarter to and quarter past the hour.

Torpedo Factory Art Center ARTS CENTER
(www.torpedofactory.org; 105 N Union St; ☉10am-6pm, to 7pm Thu; Ⓜ King St then trolley) FREE
What do you do with a former munitions dump and arms factory? How about turning it into one of the best art spaces in the region? Three floors of artists studios and free creativity are on offer in Old Town Alexandria, as well as the opportunity to buy paintings, sculptures, glassworks, textiles and jewelry direct from their creators. The Torpedo Factory anchors Alexandria's revamped waterfront with a marina, parks, walkways, residences and restaurants.

✖ Eating & Drinking

Misha's Coffee Roaster CAFE $
(www.mishascoffee.com; 102 S Patrick St; pastries $3-4; ☉6am-8pm; 🛜) Sip a lovely latte next to jars of strong-smelling beans imported from Indonesia and Ethiopia, bang out your play on your laptop (or procrastinate with the free wi-fi), check out the cute nerds at the other tables and reach caffeinated nirvana at this very hip indie cafe. Croissants and cookies add to the buzz.

Hank's Oyster Bar SEAFOOD $$
(1026 King St; mains $6-28; ☉5:30-9:30pm Tue-Thu, 11:30am-midnight Fri & Sat, 11am-9:30pm Sun)

There are a fair few oyster bars in Washington (slurping raw boys is good for political puffery, apparently) and Hank's is our favorite of the bunch. It's got the right testosterone combination, a bit of power-player muscle mixed with good-old-boy ambiance, which isn't to say women won't love it here; just that guys really do. Needless to say, the oyster menu is extensive and excellent; there are always at least four varieties on hand. Quarters are cramped, and you often have to wait for a table – nothing a saki oyster bomb won't fix.

Restaurant Eve AMERICAN $$$
(☎703-706-0450; www.restauranteve.com; 110 S Pitt St; 5-/7-course tasting menus $120/135; ☉lunch Mon-Fri, dinner Mon-Sat; 🖊) While 'fusion' may be an overused adjective when it comes to describing restaurants, the best kitchens always fuse. Innovation and tradition, regional and international influences, comfort and class. Eve contains everything we have described, a combination of great American ingredients, precise French technique and some of the highest levels of service we've encountered in the area. Splurge here on the tasting menus, which are simply on another level of gastronomic experience. This is one of the few vegan-friendly high-end restaurants in the DC metro area; just be sure to call a day ahead and chef-owner Cathal Armstrong's team will be happy to accommodate you.

☆ Entertainment

Birchmere LIVE MUSIC
(www.birchmere.com; 3701 Mount Vernon Ave; tickets $15-35; ☉box office 5-9pm, shows 7:30pm; Ⓜ Pentagon City then 🚌 10A) Known as 'America's Legendary Music Hall,' this is the DC area's premier venue for folk, country, Celtic and bluegrass music. The talent that graces the stage is reason enough to come, but the venue is pretty great too: it sort of looks like a warehouse that collided with an army of LSD-savvy muralists. Located north of Old Town Alexandria off Glebe Rd.

Tiffany Tavern LIVE MUSIC
(www.tiffanytavern.com; 1116 King St; Ⓜ King St) FREE The food is kind of lame and the beer selection weak, but the live bluegrass (from 8:30pm Friday and Saturday) hits the spot at the well-worn Tiffany Tavern. It gets a little rough and a lot raucous on the best nights, when Yuengling on tap, mandolin and fiddle equal hours of roots-music magic.

VIRGINIA VINEYARDS

Now the fifth-biggest wine producer in the USA, Virginia has 192 vineyards around the state, many located in the pretty hills around Charlottesville. Particularly notable is the Virginia Viognier. For more information on Virginia wine, visit www.virginiawine.org.

Jefferson Vineyards (434-977-3042; www.jeffersonvineyards.com; 1353 Thomas Jefferson Pkwy) Known for consistent quality vintage, this winery harvests from its namesake's original 1774 vineyard site.

Keswick Vineyards (434-244-3341; www.keswickvineyards.com; 1575 Keswick Winery Dr) Keswick won a wave of awards for its first vintage and has since been distilling a big range of grapes. It's off Rte 231.

Kluge Estate (434-977-3895; www.klugeestateonline.com; 100 Grand Cru Dr) Oenophiles regularly rate Kluge wine as the best in the state.

ℹ Information

The **visitor center** (703-838-5005; www.visitalexandriava.com; 221 King St; ☉9am-5pm) issues parking permits and discount tickets for historic sites.

ℹ Getting There & Away

To get to Alexandria from downtown DC, get off at the King St Metro station. A free trolley makes the 1-mile journey between the Metro station and the waterfront (every 20 minutes, from 11:30am to 10pm).

Mount Vernon

One of the most visited historic shrines in the nation, Mount Vernon (703-780-2000, 800-429-1520; www.mountvernon.org; 3200 Mount Vernon Memorial Hwy, Mt Vernon; adult/child $17/8; ☉8am-5pm Apr-Aug, 9am-4pm Nov-Feb, to 5pm Mar, Sep & Oct) was the beloved home of George and Martha Washington, who lived here from the time of their marriage in 1759 until Washington's death in 1799. Now owned and operated by the Mount Vernon Ladies Association, the estate offers glimpses of 18th-century farm life and the first president's life as a country planter. Mount Vernon does not gloss over the Founding Father's slave ownership; visitors can tour the slave quarters and burial ground. Other sights include Washington's distillery and grist mill (www.tourmobile.com; adult/child $4/2, incl Mount Vernon adult/child $30/15), 3 miles south of the estate.

Mount Vernon is 16 miles south of DC off the Mount Vernon Memorial Hwy. By public transportation, take the Metro to Huntington, then switch to Fairfax Connector bus 101. Grayline (202-289-1995; www.grayline.

com; adult/child incl Mt Vernon admission from $55/20) tours depart daily from DC's Union Station year-round.

Several companies offer seasonal boat trips from DC and Alexandria; the cheapest is Potomac Riverboat Company (703-684-0580; www.potomacriverboatco.com; adult/child incl Mt Vernon admission $40/20). A healthy alternative is to take a lovely bike ride along the Potomac River from DC (18 miles from Roosevelt Island).

Manassas

On July 21, 1861, Union and Confederate soldiers clashed in the first major land battle of the Civil War. Expecting a quick victory, DC residents flocked here to picnic and watch the First Battle of Bull Run (known in the South as First Manassas). The surprise Southern victory erased any hopes of a quick end to the war. Union and Confederate soldiers again met on the same ground for the larger Second Battle of Manassas in August 1862; again the South was victorious. Today, Manassas National Battlefield Park is a curving green hillscape, sectioned into fuzzy fields of tall grass and wildflowers by split-rail wood fences. Start your tour at the Henry Hill Visitor Center (703-361-1339; www.nps.gov/mana; adult/child $3/free; ☉8:30am-5pm) to watch the orientation film and pick up park and trail maps.

Daily Amtrak (www.amtrak.com; one way $16-28) and Virginia Railway Express (VRE; www.vre.org; one way $9.10; ☉Mon-Fri) trains make the 50-minute journey between DC's Union Station and the historic Old Town Manassas Railroad Station on 9451 West St; from there it's a 6-mile taxi ride to the park. There are several restaurants and bars around the Manassas train station, but the rest of the city is a mess of strip malls and suburban sprawl.

Fredericksburg

Fredericksburg is a pretty town with a historical district that is almost a cliché of small-town Americana. George Washington grew up here, and the Civil War exploded in the streets and surrounding fields. Today the main street is a pleasant amble of bookstores, gastropubs and cafes.

◎ Sights

The **visitor center** (☑540-373-1776; www.visitfred.com; 706 Caroline St; ⊙9am-5pm, from 11am Sun) offers a Timeless Fredericksburg pass ($32), which includes admission to nine local sights.

Fredericksburg & Spotsylvania National Military Park HISTORIC SITE
(adult/child $32/10) More than 13,000 Americans were killed during the Civil War in four battles fought in a 17-mile radius covered by this park that's maintained by the NPS. Don't miss the burial site of Stonewall Jackson's amputated arm near the **Fredericksburg Battlefield visitor center** (☑540-654-5535; www.nps.gov/frsp; 1013 Lafayette Blvd; film $2; ⊙9am-5pm) FREE

James Monroe Museum & Memorial Library HISTORIC SITE
(☑540-654-1043; http://jamesmonroemuseum.umw.edu; 908 Charles St; adult/child $5/1; ⊙10am-5pm Mon-Sat, from 1pm Sun) The museum's namesake was the nation's fifth president.

Mary Washington House HISTORIC SITE
(☑540-373-1569; www.apva.org; 1200 Charles St; adult/child $5/2; ⊙11am-5pm Mon-Sat, noon-4pm Sun) The 18th-century home of George Washington's mother.

⊨ Sleeping & Eating

You'll find dozens of restaurants and cafes along historic Caroline and William Sts.

Richard Johnston Inn B&B $$
(☑540-899-7606; www.therichardjohnstoninn.com; 711 Caroline St; r $125-200; P❋🗢) In an 18th-century brick mansion, this cozy B&B scores points for location, comfort and friendliness (especially from the two resident Scottie dogs). Guests get full breakfast on weekends.

Sammy T's AMERICAN $
(☑540-371-2008; 801 Caroline St; mains $6-14; ⊙11:30am-9:30pm; 🗢🎤) Located in a circa 1805 building in the heart of historic Fredericksburg, Sammy T's serves soups and sandwiches and pub-y fare, with an admirable mix of vegetarian options including a local take on lasagna and black-bean quesadillas.

Foode AMERICAN $$
(☑540-479-1370; 1006 C Caroline St; mains $13-24; ⊙11am-3pm & 4:30pm-8pm Tue-Thu, to 9pm Fri, 10am-2:30pm & 4:30-9pm Sat, 10am-2pm Sun; 🎤) 🍃 Foode takes all the feel-good restaurant trends of the late naughties/early teens — fresh, local, free range, organic and a casual-artsy-rustic-chic decor over white tablecloths and dark lighting — and runs with the above all the way to pretty delicious results.

❶ Getting There & Away

VRE ($11.10, 1½ hours) and **Amtrak** ($25 to $43, 1¼ hours) trains depart from the **Fredericksburg train station** (200 Lafayette Blvd) with service to DC. **Greyhound** has buses to/from DC (five per day, 1½ hours) and Richmond (three per day, one hour). The **Greyhound station** (☑540-373-2103; 1400 Jefferson Davis Hwy) is roughly 1.5 miles west of the historic district.

Richmond

Richmond has been the capital of the Commonwealth of Virginia since 1780. That's the stable part of its identity. What this town is constantly trying to define is its culture: a welcoming, warm Southern city on the one hand, and part of the international milieu of the Northeast Corridor on the other. Maybe it's better to throw away that dichotomy and say Richmond is the northernmost city of the New South: grounded in tradition yet international and well-educated on the one hand, but full of income disparities and social tensions on the other.

This is a handsome town, full of red-brick and brownstone row-houses that leave a softer impression than their sometimes-staid Northeastern counterparts. History is ubiquitous and, sometimes, uncomfortable; this was where patriot Patrick Henry gave his famous 'Give me Liberty, or give me Death!' speech, and where the slave-holding Southern Confederate States placed their capital. Today a population of students and young professionals makes the 'River City' a lot more fun than you might expect.

◉ Sights

The James River bisects Richmond, with most attractions lying to its north. Uptown residential neighborhoods include the Fan district, south of Monument Ave, and Carytown, in the west end. Downtown, Court End holds the capitol and several museums.

On E Cary St between 12th and 15th Sts, converted warehouses in Shockoe Slip are home to shops and restaurants. Once you pass under the trestle-like freeway overpass, you're in Shockoe Bottom. Just north of Court End is the historic African American neighborhood of Jackson Ward. Keep in mind that Cary St is more than 5 miles long; E Cary St is downtown, while W Cary St is in Carytown.

Monument Avenue, a tree-lined boulevard in northeast Richmond, holds statues of such revered Southern heroes as JEB Stuart, Robert E Lee, Matthew Fontaine Maury, Jefferson Davis, Stonewall Jackson and, in a nod to diversity, African American tennis champion Arthur Ashe.

Jackson Ward, an African American neighborhood that was known as Little Africa in the late 19th century, is now a National Historic Landmark district. It comes off as a tough neighborhood (which it is), but there's a deep cultural legacy here as well.

The 1.25-mile waterfront Canal Walk between the James River and the Kanawha (ka-naw) and Haxall Canals is a lovely way of seeing a dozen highlights of Richmond history.

American Civil War Center at Historic Tredegar   MUSEUM
(www.tredegar.org; 500 Tredegar St; adult/child $8/2; ⊙9am-5pm) Located in an 1861 gun foundry, this fascinating site explores the causes and course of the Civil War from the perspectives of Union, Confederate and African American experiences. The center is one of 13 protected area sites that make up Richmond National Battlefield Park (www.nps.gov/rich).

Museum & White House of the Confederacy   HISTORIC SITE
(www.moc.org; cnr 12th & Clay Sts; adult/child $12/7; ⊙10am-5pm Mon-Sat, from noon Sun) While this was once a shrine to the Southern 'Lost Cause,' the Museum of the Confederacy has graduated into an educational institution, and its collection of Confederate artifacts is probably the best in the country. The optional tour of the Confederate White House is recommended for its quirky insights (did you know the second-most powerful man in the Confederacy may have been a gay Jew?).

Virginia State Capitol   BUILDING
(www.virginiacapitol.gov; cnr 9th & Grace Sts, Capitol Sq; ⊙9am-5pm Mon-Sat, 1-4pm Sun) FREE Designed by Thomas Jefferson, the capitol building was completed in 1788 and houses the oldest legislative body in the Western Hemisphere, the Virginia General Assembly, established in 1619. Free tours.

Virginia Historical Society   MUSEUM
(www.vahistorical.org; 428 N Blvd; adult/student $6/4; ⊙10am-5pm Mon-Sat, from 1pm Sun) Changing and permanent exhibits trace the history of the Commonwealth from prehistoric to present times.

St John's Episcopal Church   CHURCH
(www.historicstjohnschurch.org; 2401 E Broad St; tours adult/child $7/5; ⊙10am-4pm Mon-Sat, from 1pm Sun) It was here that firebrand Patrick Henry uttered his famous battle cry, 'Give me Liberty, or give me Death!' during the rebellious 1775 Second Virginia Convention. His speech is reenacted at 2pm on Sundays in summer.

Virginia Museum of Fine Arts   MUSEUM
(VMFA; ☑804-340-1400; www.vmfa.state.va.us; 2800 Grove Ave; ⊙10am-5pm Sat-Wed, to 9pm Thu & Fri) FREE Has a remarkable collection of European works, sacred Himalayan art and one of the largest Fabergé egg collections on display outside Russia. Also hosts excellent temporary exhibitions (admission from free of charge to $20).

Poe Museum   MUSEUM
(☑804-648-5523; www.poemuseum.org; 1914-16 E Main St; adult/student $6/5; ⊙10am-5pm Tue-Sat, from 11am Sun) Contains the world's largest collection of manuscripts and memorabilia of poet Edgar Allan Poe, who lived and worked in Richmond.

Hollywood Cemetery   CEMETERY
(hollywoodcemetery.org; entrance cnr Albemarle & Cherry Sts; ⊙8am-5pm, to 6pm summer) FREE This tranquil cemetery, perched above the James River rapids, contains the gravesites of two US presidents (James Monroe and John Tyler), the only Confederate president (Jefferson Davis) and 18,000 Confederate soldiers. Free walking tours are given at 10am, Monday through Saturday.

WASHINGTON, DC & THE CAPITAL REGION RICHMOND

🛏 Sleeping

Massad House Hotel MOTEL $

(☎804-648-2893; www.massadhousehotel.com; 11 N 4th St; r $75-110) This is the cheapest in-city option and its location for exploring can't be beat. That said, you get what you pay for. The rooms are tiny but clean, but the hotel is in serious need of renovation.

Linden Row Inn BOUTIQUE HOTEL $$

(☎804-783-7000; www.lindenrowinn.com; 100 E Franklin St; r incl breakfast $120-170, ste $250; P✳@🛜) This antebellum gem has 70 attractive rooms (with period Victorian furnishings) spread among neighboring Greek Revival town houses in an excellent downtown location. Friendly southern hospitality and thoughtful extras (free passes to the YMCA, free around-town shuttle service) sweeten the deal.

Museum District B&B B&B $$

(☎804-359-2332; www.museumdistrictbb.com; 2811 Grove Ave; r $100-195; P✳🛜) In a fine location near the dining and drinking of Carytown, this stately 1920s brick B&B has earned many admirers for its warm welcome. Rooms are comfortably set and guests can enjoy the wide front porch, cozy parlor with fireplace, and excellent cooked breakfasts – plus wine and cheese in the evenings.

★ Jefferson Hotel LUXURY HOTEL $$$

(☎804-788-8000; www.jeffersonhotel.com; 101 W Franklin St; r from $250; P✳🛜🏊) The Jefferson is Richmond's grandest hotel and one of the finest in America. The vision of tobacco tycoon and Confederate major Lewis Ginter, the beaux-arts-style hotel was completed in 1895. Today it offers luxurious rooms, topnotch service and one of Richmond's finest restaurants. According to rumor, the magnificent grand staircase in the lobby served as the model for the famed stairs in *Gone with the Wind*.

🍴 Eating

You'll find dozens of restaurants along the cobbled streets of Shockoe Slip and Shockoe Bottom. Further west in Carytown (W Cary St between S Blvd and N Thompson St), you'll find even more dining options.

17th Street Farmers Market MARKET $

(cnr 17th & E Main Sts; ⊙8:30am-4pm Sat & Sun) For cheap eats and fresh produce, check out this bustling market, which runs from early May through October. On Sundays, the market sells antiques.

Burger Bach GASTROPUB $

(☎804-359-1305; 10 S Thompson St; mains $7-12; ⊙11am-10pm Sun-Mon, to 11pm Fri & Sat; ✳🍴🖶) 🍴 We give Burger Bach credit for being the only restaurant in the area that classifies itself as a New Zealand–inspired burger joint. And that said, why yes, they do serve excellent lamb burgers here, although the locally sourced beef (and vegetarian) options are awesome as well. Go crazy with the 14 different sauces available for the thick-cut fries.

Ipanema Café AMERICAN $$

(☎804-213-0190; 917 W Grace St; mains $8-13; ⊙11am-11pm Mon-Fri, from 5:30pm Sat & Sun; 🍴) This underground den is much loved by the bohemian and art-student crowd. It has a tempting selection of vegan and vegetarian fare (tempeh 'bacon' sandwich, curried vegetables, changing specials), plus *moules-frites,* tuna melts and a few other nonveg options. Vegan desserts are outstanding.

★ Julep's MODERN AMERICAN $$$

(☎804-377-3968; 1719 E Franklin St; mains $18-32; ⊙5:30-10pm Mon-Sat; P✳) One of Richmond's finest restaurants serves decadent New Southern cuisine in a classy old-fashioned dining room that's cinematically set inside a restored 1817 building. Start with a mint julep, fried green tomatoes or jumbo lump-crab soup, followed by Julep's signature shrimp and grits with grilled andouille sausage.

Edo's Squid ITALIAN $$$

(☎804-864-5488; 411 N Harrison St; mains $12-30) This is easily the best Italian restaurant in Richmond. Edo's serves up mouthwatering, authentic cuisine such as eggplant parmesan, spicy shrimp *diavolo* pasta, daily specials and, of course, squid. This place can get very crowded and noisy.

Millie's Diner MODERN AMERICAN $$$

(☎804-643-5512; 2603 E Main St; breakfast & lunch $7-12, dinner $20-32; ⊙11am-2:30pm & 5:30-10:30pm Tue-Fri, 10am-3pm & 5:30-10:30pm Sat & Sun) Breakfast, lunch or dinner, Millie's does it all, and does it well. But where this Richmond icon really shines is Sunday brunch: the Devil's Mess – an open-faced omelet with spicy sausage, curry, veg, cheese and avocado – is quite legendary.

🍷 Drinking & Entertainment

Lift CAFE
(218 W Broad St; ⊙7am-7pm Mon-Fri, 8am-8pm Sat, 9am-7pm Sun; 🛜) Part coffeehouse, part art gallery, Lift serves stiff lattes and tasty sandwiches and salads. Sidewalk seating.

Capital Ale House BAR
(623 E Main St; ⊙11am-1:30am) Popular with political wonks from the nearby state capitol, this downtown pub has a superb beer selection (more than 50 on tap and 250 bottled) and decent pub grub. The frozen trough on the bar keeps your drinks ice-cold.

Cary Street Cafe LIVE MUSIC
(☑804-353-7445; www.carystreetcafe.com; 2631 W Cary St; ⊙11am-2pm) Live music (or at least, karaoke) emanates from this excellent bar just about every night of the week. This spot is proudly pro-hippie, but doesn't just bust hippie tunes; the gigs juke from reggae to folk to alt-country.

Byrd Theater CINEMA
(☑804-353-9911; www.byrdtheatre.com; 2908 W Cary St; tickets $5) You can't beat the price at this classic 1928 cinema, which shows second-run films. Wurlitzer-organ concerts precede the Saturday-night shows.

ℹ️ Information

Johnston-Willis Hospital (☑804-330-2000; 1401 Johnston-Willis Dr)
Post office (700 E Main St; ⊙7:30am-5pm Mon-Fri)
Richmond-Times Dispatch (www2.timesdispatch.com) Daily newspaper.
Richmond Visitor Center (☑804-783-7450; www.visitrichmondva.com; 405 N 3rd St; ⊙9am-5pm)

ℹ️ Getting There & Around

The cab fare from **Richmond International Airport** (RIC; ☑804-226-3000), 10 miles east of town, costs about $30.

Amtrak (☑800-872-7245; www.amtrak.com) trains stop at the **main station** (7519 Staples Mill Rd), 7 miles north of town (connected to downtown by bus 27). More convenient but less frequent trains stop downtown at the **Main St Station** (1500 E Main St).
Greater Richmond Transit Company (GRTC; ☑804-358-4782; www.ridegrtc.com) Runs local buses (base fare $1.50; exact change only).
Greyhound/Trailways Bus Station (☑804-254-5910; www.greyhound.com; 2910 N Blvd)

Petersburg

About 25 miles south of Richmond, the little town of Petersburg played a big role in the Civil War; as a major railway junction, it provided Confederate troops and supplies. Union troops laid a 10-month siege of Petersburg in 1864–65, the longest on American soil. The **Siege Museum** (☑804-733-2404; 15 W Bank St; adult/child $5/4, incl Old Blandford Church $11/9; ⊙10am-5pm) relates the plight of civilians during the siege. Several miles east of town, the **Petersburg National Battlefield** (US 36; per vehicle/pedestrian $5/3; ⊙9am-5pm) is where Union soldiers planted explosives underneath a Confederate breastwork, leading to the Battle of the Crater (novelized and cinematized in *Cold Mountain*). West of downtown in Pamplin Historical Park, the excellent **National Museum of the Civil War Soldier** (☑804-861-2408; adult/child 6-12yr $10/5; ⊙9am-5pm) illustrates the hardships faced by soldiers on both sides of the conflict.

Historic Triangle

This is America's birthplace. Nowhere else in the country has such a small area played such a pivotal role in the course of the nation's history. The nation's roots were planted in Jamestown, the first permanent English settlement in the New World. The flames of the American Revolution were fanned at the colonial capital of Williamsburg, and America finally won its independence from Britain at Yorktown.

You'll need at least two days to do the Triangle any justice. A daily free shuttle travels between the Williamsburg visitor center, Yorktown and Jamestown.

Williamsburg

If you visit only one historical town in Virginia, make it Williamsburg, home to Colonial Williamsburg, one of the largest, most comprehensive living-history museums in the world. If any place is going to get kids into history, this is it, but it's plenty of fun for adults too.

The actual town of Williamsburg, Virginia's capital from 1699 to 1780, is a stately place. The prestigious campus of the College of William & Mary adds a decent dash of youth culture, with coffee shops, cheap pubs and fashion boutiques.

◉ Sights

Colonial Williamsburg　　　HISTORIC SITE
(www.colonialwilliamsburg.org; adult/child $42/21;
⊙9am-5pm) The restored capital of England's largest colony in the New World is a must-see attraction for visitors of all ages. This is not some cheesy, fenced-in theme park; Colonial Williamsburg is a living, breathing, working history museum that transports visitors to the 1700s.

➡ **The Site**

The 301-acre historic area contains 88 original 18th-century buildings and several hundred faithful reproductions. Costumed townsfolk and 'interpreters' in period dress go about their Colonial jobs as blacksmiths, apothecaries, printers, bartenders, soldiers and patriots, breaking character only long enough to pose for a snapshot.

Costumed patriots such as Patrick Henry and Thomas Jefferson still deliver impassioned speeches for freedom but, to its credit, Colonial Williamsburg has grown up a little. Where once it was all about projecting a rah-rah version of American-heck-yeah in a powdered wig, today re-enactors debate and question slavery, women's suffrage, the rights of indigenous Americans and the very moral right of revolution.

➡ **Entrance**

Walking around the historic district and patronizing the shops and taverns is free, but entry to building tours and most exhibits is restricted to ticket holders. Expect crowds, lines and petulant children, especially in summer.

To park and to purchase tickets, follow the signs to the **visitor center** (⊘757-220-7645; 101 Visitor Center Drive; ⊙8:45am-5pm), north of the historic district between Hwy 132 and Colonial Pkwy, where kids can hire out period costumes for $25 per day. Start off with a 30-minute film about Williamsburg, and peruse a copy of *Williamsburg This Week,* listing the day's programs and events.

Parking is free; shuttle buses run frequently to and from the historic district, or you can walk along the tree-lined footpath. You can also buy tickets at the **Merchants Square information booth** (west end of Duke of Gloucester St; ⊙9am-5pm).

College of William & Mary　HISTORIC BUILDING
(www.wm.edu; 200 Stadium Dr) Chartered in 1693, the **College of William & Mary** is the second-oldest college in the country and retains the oldest academic building in continued use in the USA, the Sir Christopher Wren Building. The school's alumni include Thomas Jefferson, James Monroe and comedian Jon Stewart.

🛏 Sleeping

The **Williamsburg Hotel & Motel Association** (⊘800-446-9244; www.gowilliamsburg.com) at the visitor center will help find and book accommodations at no cost. If you stay in Colonial Williamsburg, guesthouses can provide discount admission tickets (adult/child $30/15).

Governor's Inn　　　HOTEL $
(⊘757-253-2277; www.colonialwilliamsburgresorts.com; 506 N Henry St; r $70-120; P⃝⛱⃝) Williamsburg's official 'economy' choice is a big box by any other name, but rooms are clean, and guests can use the pool and facilities of the Woodlands Hotel. It's in a great location three blocks from the historic district.

Williamsburg White House　　　B&B $$
(⊘757-229-8580; www.awilliamsburgwhitehouse.com; 718 Jamestown Rd; r $160-200, ste $375; P⃝) This romantic, beautifully furnished B&B decorated with red, white and blue bunting is located across the campus of William & Mary, just a few blocks' walk from Colonial Williamsburg. It's a favorite spot of visiting politicos and bigwigs, but the atmosphere and amicable management exudes more stateliness than stuffiness. The two-room FDR suite can accommodate up to four guests.

Colonial Williamsburg
Historic Lodging　　　GUESTHOUSE $$$
(⊘757-253-2277; www.history.org; r $150-270) For true 18th-century immersion, guests can stay in one of 26 original Colonial houses inside the historic district. Accommodations range in size and style, though the best have period furnishings, canopy beds and wood-burning fireplaces.

Williamsburg Inn　　　INN $$$
(⊘757-253-2277; www.colonialwilliamsburg.com; 136 E Francis St; r from $320; P⃝⛱⃝) Queen Elizabeth II has stayed here twice, so you know this place is palatial. Williamsburg's premier property has a not-so-colonial price tag, but the pampering is nonstop at this prestigious resort.

✕ Eating

You will find many restaurants, cafes and pubs in Merchants Sq, adjacent to Colonial Williamsburg.

Cheese Shop   DELI **$**
(410 Duke of Gloucester St, Merchants Sq; mains $6-7; ⊙10am-8pm Mon-Sat, 11am-6pm Sun) Adjoining Fat Canary, this gourmet deli showcases some flavorful sandwiches and antipasti, plus baguettes, pastries, wine, beer and wonderful cheeses.

King's Arms Tavern   MODERN AMERICAN **$$**
(☑757-229-2141; 416 E Duke of Gloucester St; lunch mains $13-15, dinner $31-37; ⊙11:30am-2:30pm & 5-9pm) Of the four restaurants located within Colonial Williamsburg, this is the most elegant, serving early-American cuisine such as game pie – venison, rabbit and duck braised in port-wine sauce.

Fat Canary   AMERICAN **$$$**
(☑757-229-3333; 410 Duke of Gloucester St, Merchants Sq; mains $28-39; ⊙5-10pm) For a splurge, there's no better place in the historic triangle. Top-notch service, excellent wines and heavenly desserts are only slightly upstaged by the magnificent seasonal cuisine (recent favorites: pan-seared sea scallops with oyster pork belly; wild rice stuffed quail; and seared foie gras and hazelnut toast).

ⓘ Getting There & Around

Williamsburg Transportation Center (☑757-229-8750; cnr Boundary & Lafayette Sts)
Amtrak (www.amtrak.com) trains run from here twice a day to Washington, DC ($43, four hours), Richmond ($33, 50 minutes) and New York ($84 to $152, eight hours). Greyhound buses run to Richmond ($18, one hour) five times daily. Buses to other destinations require a transfer in Richmond.

Triangle Theme Parks

Three miles east of Williamsburg on Hwy 60, Busch Gardens (☑800-343-7946; www.buschgardens.com; adult/child $70/60; ⊙Apr-Oct; ⊛) is a European-themed park with some of the best roller coasters on the East Coast. Just down the road, off Hwy 199 east of Williamsburg, Water Country USA (☑800-343-7946; www.watercountryusa.com; adult/child $49/42; ⊙May-Sep; ⊛) is a kids' paradise, with twisty slides, raging rapids and wave pools. A three-day combo ticket

for both parks costs $75. Parking costs $13 at both places.

Jamestown

On May 14, 1607, a group of 104 English men and boys settled on this swampy island with a charter from the Virginia Company of London to search for gold and other riches. Instead, they found starvation and disease. By January of 1608, only about 40 colonists were still alive, and these had resorted to cannibalism to survive. The colony survived the 'Starving Time' with the leadership of Captain James Smith and help from Powhatan, a local king. In 1619 the elected House of Burgesses convened, forming the first democratic government in the Americas.

Historic Jamestowne (☑757-856-1200; www.historicjamestowne.org; 1368 Colonial Pkwy; adult/child $14/free; ⊙8:30am-4:30pm), run by the NPS, is the original Jamestown site. Start your visit at the on-site museum and check out the statues of John Smith and Pocahontas. The original Jamestown ruins were rediscovered in 1994; visitors can watch the ongoing archaeological work at the site.

More child-friendly, the state-run Jamestown Settlement (☑757-253-4838; www.historyisfun.org; 2110 Jamestown Rd; adult/child $16/7.50, incl Yorktown Victory Center $20.50/10.25; ⊙9am-5pm; P⊛) reconstructs the 1607 James Fort, a Native American village and full-scale replicas of the first ships that brought the settlers to Jamestown, along with multimedia exhibits and costumed interpreters portraying life in the 17th century.

Yorktown

On October 19, 1781, British General Cornwallis surrendered to George Washington here, effectively ending the American Revolution. Overpowered by massive American guns on land and cut off from the sea by the French, the British were in a hopeless position. Although Washington anticipated a much longer siege, the devastating barrage quickly overwhelmed Cornwallis, who surrendered within days.

Yorktown Battlefield (☑757-898-3400; 1000 Colonial Pkwy; incl Historic Jamestowne adult/child $10/free; ⊙9am-5pm; P⊛) 🄿, run by the NPS, is the site of the last major battle of the American Revolution. Start your tour at the visitor center and check out the orientation film and the display of Washington's original tent. The 7-mile Battlefield Rd Tour takes you past the major highlights. Don't miss a walk through the last British defensive sites, Redoubts 9 and 10.

The state-run Yorktown Victory Center (☑757-887-1776; www.historyisfun.org; 200 Water St; adult/child $9.75/5.50; ☺9am-5pm; P☷) ❦ is an interactive, living-history museum that focuses on reconstruction, reenactment and the Revolution's impact on the people who lived through it. At the re-created encampment, costumed Continental soldiers fire cannons and discuss food preparation and field medicine of the day.

The actual town of Yorktown is a pleasant waterfront village overlooking the York River with a nice range of shops, restaurants and pubs. Set in an atmospheric 1720 house, the Carrot Tree (☑757-988-1999; 411 Main St; mains $10-16; ☺11am-3:30pm daily, 5-8:30pm Thu-Sat) is a good, affordable spot serving playfully named dishes such as Lord Nelson's BBQ and Battlefield beef stroganoff.

James River Plantations

The grand homes of Virginia's slave-holding aristocracy were a clear sign of the era's class divisions. A string of them line scenic Hwy 5 on the north side of the river, though only a few are open to the public.

Sherwood Forest (☑804-829-5377; sherwoodforest.org; 14501 John Tyler Memorial Hwy), the longest frame house in the country, was the home of 10th US president John Tyler. Tours are available by appointment for $35 per person. The grounds (and a touching pet cemetery) are open to self-guided tours (adult/child $10/free; ☺9am-5pm).

Berkeley (☑804-829-6018; www.berkeleyplantation.com; 12602 Harrison Landing Rd; adult/child $11/7.50; ☺9:30am-4:30pm) was the site of the first official Thanksgiving in 1619. It was the birthplace and home of Benjamin Harrison V, a signatory to of the Declaration of Independence, and his son William Henry Harrison, the ninth US president.

Shirley (☑800-232-1613; www.shirleyplantation.com; 501 Shirley Plantation Rd; adult/child $11/7.50; ☺9am-5pm), situated picturesquely on the river, is Virginia's oldest plantation (1613) and perhaps the best example of how a British-model plantation actually appeared, with its tidy row of brick service and trade houses – tool barn, ice house, laundry etc – leading up to the big house.

Hampton Roads

The Hampton Roads (named not for asphalt, but the confluence of the James, Nansemond and Elizabeth Rivers and Chesapeake Bay) have always been prime real estate. The Powhatan Confederacy fished these waters and hunted the fingerlike protrusions of the Virginia coast for thousands of years before John Smith arrived in 1607. Today Hampton Roads is known for congestion and a cultural mishmash of history, the military and the arts.

Norfolk

Home to the world's largest naval base, it's not surprising that Norfolk had a reputation as a rowdy port town filled with drunken sailors. In recent years, the city has worked hard to clean up its image through development, gentrification and focusing on its burgeoning arts scene.

◉ Sights

Naval Station Norfolk   NAVY BASE
(☑757-444-7955; www.cnic.navy.mil/norfolksta; 9079 Hampton Blvd; adult/child $10/5) The world's largest navy base, and one of the busiest airfields in the country, this is a must-see. The 45-minute bus tours are conducted by naval personnel and must be booked in advance (hours vary). Photo ID is required for adults.

Nauticus   MUSEUM
(☑757-664-1000; www.nauticus.org; 1 Waterside Dr; adult/child $16/11.50; ☺10am-5pm Tue-Sun) This massive interactive maritime-themed museum has exhibits on undersea exploration, aquatic life of the Chesapeake Bay and US Naval lore. The museum's highlight is clambering around the decks and inner corridors of the USS Wisconsin. Built in 1943, it was the largest (887ft long) and last battleship built by the US Navy.

Chrysler Museum of Art   MUSEUM
(☑757-664-6200; www.chrysler.org; 245 W Olney Rd; ☺10am-9pm Wed, to 5pm Thu-Sat, noon-5pm Sun) FREE A glorious setting for a spectacular and eclectic collection of artifacts from ancient Egypt to the present day, including works by Monet, Matisse, Renoir, Warhol and a world-class collection of Tiffany blown glass. Set to re-open with a brand new facade and interior in April 2014.

🛏 Sleeping

For waterfront digs, there are tons of budget to midrange options lining Ocean View Ave (which actually borders the bay).

Residence Inn   HOTEL **$$**
(📞757-842-6216; www.marriott.com; 227 W Brambleton Ave; r $140, ste $210; 🅿🛜🐾) A short stroll to the Granby St eating strip, this friendly chain hotel has a boutique feel, with stylish, spacious rooms featuring small kitchenettes and excellent amenities.

Page House Inn   B&B **$$$**
(📞757-625-5033; www.pagehouseinn.com; 323 Fairfax Ave; r $155-230; 🅿❄🛜) Opposite the Chrysler Museum of Art, this luxurious B&B is a cornerstone of Norfolk elegance.

✖ Eating

Two of the best dining strips are downtown's Granby St and Ghent's Colley Ave.

Doumar's   DINER **$**
(1919 Monticello Ave, at E 20th St; mains $2-4; 🕙8am-11pm Mon-Sat) Since 1904 this slice of Americana has been the drive-up home of the world's original ice-cream-cone machine, plus great BBQ.

Luna Maya   LATIN AMERICAN **$$**
(📞757-622-6986; 2010 Colley Ave, Ghent; mains $13-19; 🕙4:30-10pm Tue-Sat; 🍴) On Ghent's restaurant-lined Colley Ave, Luna Maya serves up delectable pan-Latin fare and ever-flowing *mojitos* in a stylish, rustic open dining room. It's run by two Bolivian sisters, and standouts include the *pastel de choclo con chorizo,* a Bolivian corn casserole with spicy chicken sausage.

Press 626 Cafe &
Wine Bar   MODERN AMERICAN **$$$**
(📞757-282-6234; 150 W Main St; mains $19-35; 🕙11am-11pm Mon-Fri, from 5pm Sat, 10:30am-2:30pm Sun; 🍴) Embracing the Slow Food movement, Press 626 has a small high-end menu (pan-seared swordfish with sun-dried tomato polenta, for example), plus delectable cheeses and sharing plates.

🍷 Drinking & Entertainment

Elliot's Fair Grounds   CAFE
(806 Baldwin Ave; 🕙7am-10pm Mon-Sat, from 8am Sun; 🛜) This tiny, funky coffeehouse attracts everyone from students to sailors. The menu also includes vegan and kosher items such as Boca burgers.

Taphouse Grill at Ghent   PUB
(931 W 21st St) Good microbrews are served and good local bands jam at this warm little pub.

ℹ Getting There & Around

The region is served by **Norfolk International Airport** (NIA; 📞757-857-3351), 7 miles northeast of downtown Norfolk. **Greyhound** (📞757-625-7500; www.greyhound.com; 701 Monticello Ave) runs buses to Virginia Beach ($16, 35 minutes), Richmond ($32, 2¾ hours) and Washington, DC ($50, 6½ hours).

Hampton Roads Transit (📞757-222-6100; www.hrtransit.org) serves the entire Hampton Roads region. Buses ($1.50) run from downtown throughout the city and to Newport News and Virginia Beach. **Norfolk Electronic Transit** (NET; 🕙6:30am-11pm Mon-Fri, noon-midnight Sat, to 8pm Sun) is a free bus service that connects Norfolk's major downtown sites, including Nauticus and the Chrysler Museum.

Newport News

The city of Newport News comes off as a giant example of suburban sprawl, but there are several attractions here, notably the amazing Mariners' Museum (📞757-596-2222; www.marinersmuseum.org; 100 Museum Dr; adult/child $12/7; 🕙9am-5pm Wed-Sat, from 11am Sun), one of the biggest, most-comprehensive maritime museums in the world. The on-site USS Monitor Center houses the dredged carcass of the Civil War–era *Monitor,* one of the world's first ironclad warships, as well as a life-sized replica of the real deal.

The Virginia Living Museum (📞757-595-1900; thevlm.org; 524 J Clyde Morris Blvd; adult/child $17/13; 🕙9am-5pm, from noon Sun; 🅿♿) 🍃 is a fine introduction to Virginia's terrestrial and aquatic life set in naturalistic ecosystems. The complex comprises open-air animal enclosures, an aviary, gardens and a planetarium.

Virginia Beach

With 35 miles of sandy beaches, a 3-mile concrete oceanfront boardwalk and nearby outdoor activities, it's no surprise that Virginia Beach is a prime tourist destination. The city has worked hard to shed its reputation as a rowdy 'Redneck Riviera,' and, hey, the beach is wider and cleaner and there are fewer louts. But the town's appeal is limited: uninspiring high-rise hotels dominate the horizon, and the crowded beachfront and traffic-choked streets leave much to be desired.

Surfing is permitted at the beach's southern end near Rudee Inlet and alongside the 14th St pier.

◎ Sights

Virginia Aquarium & Marine Science Center
AQUARIUM

(☎757-385-3474; www.virginiaaquarium.com; 717 General Booth Blvd; adult/child $22/15; ⊙9am-5pm) If you want to see an aquarium done right, come here. You can get up close in a tidal pool with playful seals ($175) or observe the feeding and interact with the local sea turtles ($20).

Mt Trashmore
PARK

(310 Edwin Dr; ⊙7:30am-dusk) **FREE** Off I-64 exit 17B, Virginia Beach's only verticality was the creative solution to a landfill problem. Today the 165-acre park serves as a prime picnicking and kite-flying venue, with two lakes, playgrounds, a skate park and other recreational areas.

First Landing State Park
NATURE RESERVE

(☎800-933-7275; 2500 Shore Dr; per vehicle $4-5) Virginia's most-visited state park is a vast 2888-acre woodland with 20 miles of hiking trails, plus opportunities for camping, cycling, fishing, kayaking and swimming.

Contemporary Arts Center of Virginia
MUSEUM

(www.virginiamoca.org; 2200 Parks Ave; adult/child $7.70/5.50; ⊙10am-9pm Tue, to 5pm Wed-Fri, to 4pm Sat & Sun) Has excellent rotating exhibitions housed in a fresh, ultramodern building that lovingly focuses natural light onto an outstanding collection of local and international artwork.

Back Bay National Wildlife Refuge
NATURE RESERVE

(www.fws.gov/backbay; per vehicle/pedestrian $5/2 Apr-Oct, free Nov-Mar; ⊙sunrise-sunset) This 9250-acre wildlife and migratory bird marshland habitat is most stunning during the December migration season.

Great Dismal Swamp National Wildlife Refuge
NATURE RESERVE

(☎757-986-3705; www.fws.gov/refuge/great_dismal_swamp; 3100 Desert Rd, Suffolk, GPS 36.631509,-76.559715; ⊙sunrise-sunset; 🐾) **FREE** Some 30 miles southwest of Virginia Beach, this 112,000-acre refuge, which straddles the North Carolina border, is rich in flora and fauna, including black bears, bobcats and more than 200 species of bird.

⎝ Sleeping

Angie's Guest Cottage & Hostel
GUESTHOUSE $

(☎757-491-1830; www.angiescottage.com; 302 24th St; dm $23-31, s/d $55/70; P❄) Located just one block from the beach, Angie's HI-USA-affiliated hostel offers dormitories, two private rooms and a communal kitchen. It's as good value as you'll find in the area and, besides that, it has a communal, hostel-y feel that encourages hanging out with other budget travelers.

First Landing State Park
CAMPGROUND $

(☎800-933-7275; http://dcr.virginia.gov; Cape Henry; campsites $24-30, cabins from $75; P) 🐾 You couldn't ask for a prettier campground than the one at this bayfront state park, though cabins have no water view.

Cutty Sark Motel
MOTEL $$

(☎757-428-2116; www.cuttysarkvb.com; 3614 Atlantic Ave; r $140-160, apt per week from $1000; P❄) Rooms at Cutty Sark have private balconies and kitchenettes, but check that the view you're promised doesn't look out onto a parking lot. Rates drop like a rock off-season.

Hilton Virginia Beach Oceanfront
HOTEL $$$

(☎757-213-3000; www.hiltonvb.com; 3001 Atlantic Ave; r $180-250, ste from $290; P🛜❄) The premier place to stay on the beach, this 21-story hotel is superluxurious. The oceanfront rooms are spacious, comfortable and packed with amenities including huge flat-screen TVs, dreamy bedding and large balconies that open out to the beach and Neptune Park below.

✖ Eating

There is no shortage of restaurants along the boardwalk and Atlantic Ave, most geared toward local seafood. A bevy of interchangeable clubs and bars sits between 17th and 23rd Sts around Pacific and Atlantic Aves.

Jewish Mother
DELI $

(☎757-428-1515; 600 Nevan Rd; mains $5-14; ⊙10am-9pm Mon-Thu, 8am-2am Fri & Sat, to 9pm Sun) Get your nosh on here with packed deli sandwiches, 'penicillin soup' (chicken and matzo ball) and monster-sized pie. Excellent live music staged nightly.

Mary's Restaurant
DINER $

(☎ 757-428-1355; 616 Virginia Beach Blvd; mains $4-9; ⊙ 6am-3pm) A local institution for more than 40 years, Mary's is a great place to start the day with a tasty, filling, cheap breakfast. Fluffy, gooey, chocolate-chip waffles have earned many fans.

Catch 31
SEAFOOD $$$

(☎ 757-213-3474; 3001 Atlantic Ave; mains $18-35; ⊙ 7am-11pm) One of the top seafood restaurants on the boardwalk has a sleek interior and a popular deck that's great for people-watching and catching a bit of an ocean breeze. Find it in the Hilton.

❶ Information

The I-264 runs straight to the **visitor center** (☎ 800-822-3224; www.visitvirginiabeach.com; 2100 Parks Ave; ⊙ 9am-5pm) and the beach.

❶ Getting There & Around

Greyhound (☎ 757-422-2998; www.greyhound. com; 971 Virginia Beach Blvd) has several buses a day to Richmond (3½ hours), which also stop in Norfolk and Newport News; transfer in Richmond for services to Washington, DC, Wilmington, NYC and beyond. Buses depart from Circle D Food Mart, 1 mile west of the boardwalk. **Hampton Roads Transit** runs the Virginia Beach Wave trolley (tickets $1), which plies Atlantic Ave in summer.

The Piedmont

Central Virginia's rolling central hills and plateaus separate the coastal lowlands from the mountainous frontier. The fertile valley gives way to dozens of wineries, country villages and grand Colonial estates.

Charlottesville

Set in the shadow of the Blue Ridge Mountains, Charlottesville is regularly ranked as one of the country's best places to live. This culturally rich town of 45,000 is home to the University of Virginia (UVA), which attracts Southern aristocracy and artsy lefties in equal proportion. With the UVA grounds and pedestrian downtown area overflowing with students, couples, professors and the occasional celebrity under a blanket of blue skies, 'C-ville' is practically perfect.

Charlottesville Visitor Center (☎ 877-386-1103; www.visitcharlottesville.org; 610 E Main St; ⊙ 9am-5pm) is a helpful office in the heart of downtown.

◉ Sights

Blenheim Vineyards
WINERY

(☎ 434-293-5366; http://blenheimvineyards.com; 31 Blenheim Farm, Charlottesville; tastings $5; ⊙ 11am-5:30pm) Blenheim is owned by Dave Matthews, who in some ways – what with his folkie-preppie vibe and eternal gap-year sunniness, and the fact that he owns a vineyard – is the Platonic ideal of a UVA student. The wines are great and the setting is sheer bucolic joy.

University of Virginia
UNIVERSITY

(☎ 434-924-0311; www.virginia.edu; 400 Ray C Hunt Dr, Charlottesville) Thomas Jefferson founded the University of Virginia, where the classically designed buildings and grounds embody the spirit of communal living and learning that Jefferson envisioned. The centerpiece is the Jefferson-designed **Rotunda** (☎ 434-924-7969; 1826 University Ave; ⊙ tours daily 10am, 11am, 2pm, 3pm & 4pm), a scale replica of Rome's Pantheon. Free, student-led tours of the Rotunda meet inside the main entrance. UVA's **Fralin Art Museum** (☎ 434-924-3592; 155 Rugby Rd; ⊙ noon-5pm Tue-Sun) FREE has an eclectic and interesting collection of American, European and Asian arts.

⌷ Sleeping

There's a good selection of budget and mid-range chain motels lining Emmet St/US 29 north of town. If you're after a reservation service, try **Guesthouses** (☎ 434-979-7264; www.va-guesthouses.com; r from $150), which provides cottages and B&B rooms in private homes. Two-night minimum stays are common on weekends.

White Pig
B&B $$

(☎ 434-831-1416; www.thewhitepig.com; 5120 Irish Rd; r $180-190; P ✳) ✎ It's worth the pilgrimage to the White Pig, about 22 miles southwest of Monticello. Rooms have pleasant meadow and garden views, and there's a hot tub for guests. Located on the 170-acre Briar Creek Farm, this B&B-cum–animal sanctuary has one of the most innovative vegan menus in the state.

English Inn
HOTEL $$

(☎ 434-971-9900; www.englishinncharlottesville. com; 2000 Morton Dr; r incl breakfast $100-160; P ⊛ ✳) British hospitality and furnishings and a Tudor facade accent this unique hotel. It's 1.5 miles north of UVA. Cheaper rates on weekdays.

DON'T MISS

MONTICELLO & AROUND

Monticello (☎434-984-9800; www.monticello.org; 931 Thomas Jefferson Pkwy; adult/child $24/16; ⊙9am-6pm Mar-Oct, 10am-5pm Nov-Feb) is an architectural masterpiece designed and inhabited by Thomas Jefferson, Founding Father and third US president. 'I am as happy nowhere else and in no other society, and all my wishes end, where I hope my days will end, at Monticello,' wrote Jefferson, who spent 40 years building his dream home, finally completed in 1809. Today it is the only home in America designated a UN World Heritage site. Built in Roman neoclassical style, the house was the centerpiece of a 5000-acre plantation tended by 150 slaves. Monticello today does not gloss over the complicated past of the man who declared that 'all men are created equal' in the Declaration of Independence, while owning slaves and likely fathering children with slave Sally Hemings. Jefferson and his family are buried in a small wooded plot near the home.

Visits to the house are by guided tours only; you can take self-guided tours of the plantation grounds, gardens and cemetery. A high-tech exhibition center delves deeper into Jefferson's world – including exhibits on architecture, enlightenment through education, and the complicated idea of liberty. Frequent shuttles run from the visitor center to the hilltop house, or you can take the wooded footpath.

Tours are also offered of the nearby 1784 Michie Tavern (☎434-977-1234; www.michietavern.com; 683 Thomas Jefferson Pkwy; adult/child $5/2; ⊙9am-4:20pm) and James Monroe's estate Ash Lawn-Highland (☎434-293-8000; www.ashlawnhighland.org; adult/child $14/8; ⊙9am-6pm Apr-Oct, 11am-5pm Nov-Mar), 2.5 miles east of Monticello. A combo ticket for all three sites costs $36. Visit the Michie Tavern during lunchtime, when its dining room, the Ordinary (buffet $17; ⊙11:15am-3:30pm), serves lunch buffets of Southern delights such as fried chicken with biscuits.

Monticello is about 4.5 miles northwest of downtown Charlottesville.

South Street Inn
B&B $$$
(☎434-979-0200; www.southstreetinn.com; 200 South St; r incl breakfast $150-255; [P][❀]) In the heart of downtown Charlottesville, this elegant 1856 building went through previous incarnations as a girl's finishing school, boarding house and brothel. Now it houses heritage-style rooms – a total of two dozen, which gives this place more depth and diversity than your average B&B.

✖ Eating

The Downtown Mall, a pedestrian zone lined with dozens of shops and restaurants, is great for people-watching and outdoor dining on warm days. At night the bars along University Ave attract students and 20-somethings.

Whiskey Jar
SOUTHERN $
(☎434-202-1549; 227 West Main St; mains $9-16; [♪]) The Whiskey Jar does neo-Southern comfort food in an affected rustic setting of wooden furniture where wait staff wear plaid and drinks are served out of Mason jars. We're tempted to say it's all a little too cute, but honestly, the Jar nails it – simple, fresh food, such as mustard-braised rabbit, is delicious and exceedingly good value.

Local
MODERN AMERICAN $$
(☎434-984-9749; 824 Hinton Ave; mains $11-25; ⊙5:30-10pm Sun-Thu, to 11pm Fri & Sat) The Local has earned many fans for its locavore-loving menu (try black truffle mac 'n' cheese or roast duck with blood orange gastrique) and the elegant, warmly lit interior (exposed brick adorned with colorful oil paintings). There's sidewalk and rooftop dining in warmer months, plus great cocktails.

Blue Moon Diner
AMERICAN $$
(512 W Main St; mains $10-20; ⊙8am-10pm Mon-Fri, from 9am Sat, 9am-3pm Sun) One of Charlottesville's best breakfast and weekend brunch spots is a festive retro-style diner that serves up delicious fare using locally sourced ingredients. You'll also find Virginia beers on tap, old-school rock on the radio and the occasional live band.

Continental Divide
MEXICAN $$
(☎434-984-0143; 811 W Main St; mains $10-15; ⊙5-10:15pm, to 10:45pm Fri & Sat, to 9:45pm Sun) This fun, easy-going spot has no sign (look for the neon 'Get in Here' in the window) but is well worth seeking out for its Mexican fusion fare – tacos with slow-cooked pork, tuna tostadas, nachos with bison chili – and C-ville's best margaritas. Equally popular

with students on a budget and professors looking for a bargain night out.

South Street Brewery
SOUTHERN $$

(106 W South St; mains $9-18; ⊗ from 5pm Mon-Sat) In a restored 1800s brick warehouse, you'll find tasty craft brews, good Southern bistro fare (barbecue pulled pork, crawfish-and-mushroom-stuffed trout) and occasional live bands (currently Wednesday nights from 10pm). It's a short stroll from the Downtown Mall.

Zocalo
FUSION $$$

(☑434-977-4944; 201 E Main St; mains $19-26; ⊗5:30pm-2am Tue-Sun) This sleek and stylish restaurant-bar serves nicely turned out Latin-inspired dishes (spicy tuna tartar, chili-dusted sea scallops and achiote-rubbed grilled pork). There's an outdoor patio for warm nights and a crackling fireplace in winter.

❶ Getting There & Around

Amtrak (www.amtrak.com; 810 W Main St) Two daily trains to Washington, DC ($33, three hours).

Charlottesville Albemarle Airport (CHO; ☑434-973-8342; www.gocho.com) Ten miles north of downtown; offers regional flights.

Greyhound/Trailways Terminal (☑434-295-5131; 310 W Main St) Runs three daily buses to both Richmond ($20, 1¼ hours) and Washington, DC ($26, three hours).

Trolley (⊗6:40am-11:30pm Mon-Sat, 8am-5pm Sun) A free trolley connects W Main St with UVA.

Appomattox Court House & Around

At the McLean House in the town of Appomattox Court House, General Robert E Lee surrendered the Army of Northern Virginia to General Ulysses S Grant, in effect ending the Civil War. Instead of coming straight here, follow Lee's retreat (☑800-673-8732; www.varetreat.com) on a winding 25-stop tour that starts in Petersburg at Southside Railroad Station (River St and Cockade Alley) and cuts through some of the most attractive countryside in Virginia. Best take a detailed road map, as the trail is not always clearly marked. You'll finish at the 1700-acre Appomattox Court House National Historic Park (☑434-352-8987; www.nps.gov/apco; Jun-Aug $4, Sep-May $3; ⊗8:30am-5pm).

Most of the 27 restored buildings are open to visitors.

If you need a place to stay, consider Longacre (☑800-758-7730; www.longacreva.com; 1670 Church St; r from $105, ste $275; P❋), which looks as if it got lost somewhere in the English countryside and decided to set up shop in Virginia. Seriously, amid the six elegantly furnished rooms there could be children lost in magical kingdoms after slipping through wardrobes.

Shenandoah Valley

Local lore says Shenandoah was named for a Native American word meaning 'Daughter of the Stars.' True or not, there's no question this is God's country, one of the most beautiful places in America. The 200-mile-long valley and its Blue Ridge Mountains are packed with picturesque small towns, wineries, preserved battlefields and caverns. This was once the western border of colonial America, settled by Scotch-Irish frontiersmen who were Highland Clearance refugees. Outdoor activities – hiking, camping, fishing, horseback riding and canoeing – abound.

Shenandoah National Park

One of the most spectacular national parks in the country, Shenandoah (☑540-999-3500; www.nps.gov/shen; week pass per car Mar-Nov $15) is like a new smile from nature: in spring and summer the wildflowers explode, in fall the leaves burn bright red and orange, and in winter a cold, starkly beautiful hibernation period sets in. White-tailed deer are a common sight and, if you're lucky, you might spot a black bear, bobcat or wild turkey. The park lies just 75 miles west of Washington, DC.

🏃 Activities

There are two visitor centers in the park, Dickey Ridge (☑540-635-3566; Skyline Dr, Mile 4.6; ⊗9am-5pm Apr-Nov) in the north and Harry F Byrd (Mile 51; ⊗8:30am-5pm Mar 31-Oct 27) in the south. Both have maps, backcountry permits and information on horseback riding, hang gliding, cycling (only on public roads) and other wholesome goodness. Shenandoah has more than 500 miles of hiking trails, including 101 miles of the Appalachian Trail. The trails described in this section are listed from north to south.

DON'T MISS

SCENIC ROUTE: SKYLINE DRIVE

A 105-mile-long road running down the spine of the Blue Ridge Mountains, Shenandoah National Park's Skyline Drive redefines the definition of 'Scenic Route.' You're constantly treated to an impressive view, but keep in mind the road is bendy, slow-going (35mph limit) and (in peak season) congested. It's best to start this drive just south of Front Royal, VA; from here you'll snake over Virginia wine and hill country. Numbered mile posts mark the way and there's lots of pull-offs. Our favorite is around Mile 51.2, where you can take a moderately difficult 3.6 mile-loop hike to Lewis Spring Falls.

Old Rag Mountain
HIKING

This is a tough, 8-mile circuit trail that culminates in a rocky scramble only suitable for the physically fit. Your reward is the summit of Old Rag Mountain and, along the way, some of the best views in Virginia.

Big Meadows
HIKING

A very popular area with four easy to medium difficulty hikes. The Lewis Falls and Rose River trails run by the park's most spectacular waterfalls, and the former accesses the Appalachian Trail.

Bearfence Mountain
HIKING

A short trail leads to a spectacular 360-degree viewpoint. The circuit hike is only 1.2 miles, but it involves a strenuous scramble over rocks.

Riprap
HIKING

Three trails of varying difficulty. Blackrock Trail is an easy 1-mile loop that yields fantastic views. You can either hike the moderate 3.4-mile Riprap Trail to Chimney Rock, or detour and make a fairly strenuous 9.8-mile circuit that connects with the Appalachian Trail.

Sleeping & Eating

Camping is at four NPS campgrounds (877-444-6777; www.recreation.gov; $15-25): Mathews Arm (Mile 22.1; campsites $15), Big Meadows (Mile 51.3; campsites $20), Lewis Mountain (Mile 57.5; campsites $15, no reservations) and Loft Mountain (Mile 79.5; campsites $15). Most are open from mid-May to Oc-

tober. Camping elsewhere requires a free backcountry permit, available from any visitor center.

For not-so-rough lodging, stay at Skyland Resort (877-247-9261; www.goshenandoah.com/Skyland-Resort.aspx; Skyline Dr, Mile 41.7; r from $140, incl breakfast $150; Apr-Oct; P), Big Meadows Lodge (540-999-2255; www.goshenandoah.com/Big-Meadows-Lodge.aspx; Skyline Dr, Mile 51.2; r $130-210; late May-Oct;) or Lewis Mountain Cabins (877-247-9261; www.goshenandoah.com/Lewis-Mountain-Cabins.aspx; Skyline Dr, Mile 57.6; cabins $90-100, campsites $16; Apr-Oct; P).

Skyland and Big Meadows both have restaurants and taverns with occasional live music. Big Meadows offers the most services, including gas, laundry and camp store. It's best to bring your own food into the park if you're going camping or on extended hikes.

Getting There & Around

Amtrak (www.amtrak.com) trains run to Staunton, in the Shenandoah Valley, once a day from Washington, DC ($65, four hours). You'll really need your own wheels to explore the length and breadth of the park, which can be easily accessed from several exits off I-81.

Front Royal & Around

The northernmost tip of Skyline Dr looks like a drab strip of gas stations, but there's a friendly main street and some cool caverns nearby. Stop at the visitor center (800-338-2576; 414 E Main St; 9am-5pm) and the Shenandoah Valley Travel Association (800-847-4878; www.visitshenandoah.org; US 211 W, I-81 exit 264; 9am-5pm) before heading 'up' the valley.

Front Royal's claim to fame is Skyline Caverns (800-296-4545; www.skylinecaverns.com; entrance to Skyline Dr; adult/child $16/8; 9am-5pm), which boast rare white-spiked anthodites – delicate mineral formations that resemble sea urchins. Kids may enjoy mini-train rides ($3) and the mirror maze ($5).

Woodward House on Manor Grade (800-635-7011, 540-635-7010; www.acountry-home.com; 413 S Royal Ave/US 320; r $110-155, cottage $225; P) has seven cheerful rooms and two separate cottages (with wood-burning fireplaces). Sip your coffee from the deck and don't let the busy street below distract from the Blue Ridge Mountain vista.

Element (☑540-636-9293; jsgourmet.com; 206 S Royal Ave; mains $12-22; ⊙11am-3pm & 5-10pm Tue-Sat; 🅿) 🍴 is a foodie favorite for quality bistro fare. The small dinner menu features changing specials such as horse-radish-crusted red snapper; for lunch, come for gourmet sandwiches, soups and salads. Upstairs, Apartment 2G (☑540-636-9293; 206 S Royal Ave; 5 courses $50, tapas $6-14; ⊙from 6:30pm Sat & 3rd Thur) 🍴 serves decadent five-course dinners on Saturday evening in a cozy space (like dining at a friend's place). Reservations essential. Check the website for other culinary happenings. Jalisco's (☑540-635-7348; 1303 N Royal Ave; mains $8-15; ⊙11am-10pm Mon-Thu, to 11pm Fri & Sat, to 9:30pm Sun) has surprisingly good Mexican; the chili *relleños* (stuffed peppers) go down a treat.

Some 25 miles north, in the town of Winchester, the Museum of the Shenandoah Valley (☑540-662-1473, 888-556-5799; www.shenandoahmuseum.org; 901 Amherst St; adult/student $10/8; ⊙10am-4pm Tue-Sun) comprises an 18th-century period-filled house museum, 6-acre garden and a multimedia museum that delves into the valley's history. There's also a cafe.

If you can only fit one cavern into your itinerary, head 25 miles south from Front Royal to the world-class Luray Caverns (☑540-743-6551; www.luraycaverns.com; Rte 211; adult/child $21/10; ⊙9am-7pm Jun-Aug, to 6pm Sep-Nov, Apr & May, to 4pm Mon-Fri Dec-Mar) and hear the 'Stalacpipe Organ,' hyped as the largest musical instrument on earth.

Staunton & Around

You may want to end your trip and look into local real estate when you get here. There are some towns in the USA that just, for lack of a better term, nail it, and Staunton is one of those towns.

⦿ Sights

The pedestrian-friendly, handsome center boasts more than 200 buildings designed by noted Victorian architect TJ Collins. There's an artsy yet unpretentious bohemian vibe thanks to the presence of Mary Baldwin, a small women's liberal-arts college, and the gem of the Shenandoah mountains: Blackfriars Playhouse (☑540-851-1733; www.americanshakespearecenter.com; 10 S Market St; tickets $20-42). This is the world's only re-creation of Shakespeare's original indoor theater. The facility hosts the immensely talented American Shakespeare Center company, which puts on performances throughout the year. See a show here. It will do you good.

SCENIC DRIVE: VIRGINIA'S HORSE COUNTRY

About 40 miles west of Washington, DC, suburban sprawl gives way to endless green farms, vineyards, quaint villages and palatial estates and ponies. This is 'Horse Country,' where wealthy Washingtonians pursue their equestrian pastimes.

The following route is the most scenic drive to Shenandoah National Park. From DC, take Rte 50 West to Middleburg, a too-cute-for-words town of B&Bs, taverns, wine shops and boutiques. The National Sporting Library (☑540-687-6542; www.nsl.org; 102 The Plains Rd; ⊙10am-4pm Wed-Sat, from noon Sun) FREE is a museum and research center devoted to horse and field sports such as foxhunting, dressage, steeplechase and polo.

Griffin Tavern (☑540-675-3227; 659 Zachary Taylor Hwy; mains $9-18; ⊙11:30am-9pm Mon-Fri, to 10pm Sat, 10:30am-9pm Sun) is a quintessential British pub with English and Irish food and beer. Head southwest on Rte 522 and 211 to Flint Hill.

Six miles down Rte 211 is Little Washington, another cute town that's home to one of the finest B&B restaurants in America, the Inn at Little Washington (☑540-675-3800; www.theinnatlittlewashington.com; cnr Middle & Main Sts, Washington, VA; dinner prix fixe $148-165; ⊙5:30-11pm). The Inn at Little Washington has been perfecting locally sourced, seasonally selected menus since well before that practice became a culinary trend. The result is New American cuisine inspired by the best of the Piedmont and the Chesapeake, served in an atmosphere that puts one in mind of a romantic French country inn. Book early and eat well. Further down the road at the foothills of the Blue Ridge Mountains is Sperryville. Its many galleries and shops are a must-stop for antique-lovers. Continue 9 miles west to reach the Thornton Gap entrance of Skyline Dr in Shenandoah National Park.

History buffs should check out the **Woodrow Wilson Presidential Library** (www.woodrowwilson.org; 18-24 N Coalter St; adult/student/child $14/7/5; ⊙ 9am-5pm Mon-Sat, from noon Sun) across town. Stop by and tour the hilltop Greek Revival house where Wilson grew up, which has been faithfully restored to its original 1856 appearance.

The excellent **Frontier Culture Museum** (☎ 540-332-7850; overlooking I-81 exit 222; adult/student/child $10/9/6; ⊙ 9am-5pm mid-Mar–Nov, 10am-4pm Dec–mid-Mar) has authentic historic buildings from Germany, Ireland and England, plus re-created West African dwellings and a separate area of American frontier dwellings on the site's 100-plus acres. Costumed interpreters (aided by bleating livestock) do an excellent job showing what life was like for the disparate ancestors of today's Virginians.

🛏 Sleeping

Frederick House B&B $$
(☎ 540-885-4220; www.frederickhouse.com; 28 N New St; r incl breakfast $130-240; 🅿✳🛜) To stay right downtown, the thoroughly mauve and immensely welcoming Frederick House consists of five historical residences with 25 varied rooms and suites, all with private bathrooms and some with antique furnishings and decks.

Anne Hathaway's Cottage B&B $$
(☎ 540-885-8885; www.anne-hathaways-cottage.com; 950 West Beverley St; r $150-170; 🅿✳🛜) Head out of town to Anne Hathaway's Cottage, named for Shakespeare's wife, who would have thoroughly enjoyed a night in one of the three rooms in this ridiculously romantic Tudor-style, thatched-roof cottage.

🍴 Eating

West Beverley St is sprinkled with restaurants and cafes.

Pompeii Lounge ITALIAN $
(☎ 540-885-5553; 23 East Beverley St; snacks $4-9; ⊙ 5pm-1am Tue-Thu, to 2am Fri & Sat; 🍴) The Pompeii is a three-story Italian restaurant that doubles as the nicest spot in Staunton to grab a drink. The jewel in the crown is the top-floor deck, from where you can stare out over the Staunton skyline and enjoy live music, antipasto-style small plates and some fine locally crafted cocktails.

Mugshots CAFE $
(☎ 540-887-0005; 32 S New St, Staunton; pastries under $5; ⊙ 7am-5:30pm Mon-Fri, 8am-5pm Sat, 8am-4pm Sun; 🛜) This simple cafe is a prime spot to sit down, catch up on your email, sip a coffee and enjoy a bagel or a muffin.

AVA Restaurant & Wine Bar AMERICAN $$
(☎ 540-886-2851; 103 W Beverley St, Staunton; mains $10-30; ⊙ 4-9:30pm Wed-Thu, noon-10pm Fri & Sat, 10:30am-2:30pm Sun; 🍴) 🍴 AVA offers fine dining with Creole-style catfish and roasted duck breast, plus the best vegetarian food in town – the vegetarian Beef Wellington uses beets in place of beef.

Lexington & Around

This is the place to see Southern gentry at their stately best, as cadets from the Virginia Military Institute jog past the prestigious academics of Washington & Lee University. The **visitor center** (☎ 540-463-3777; 106 E Washington St; ⊙ 9am-5pm) has free parking.

◉ Sights & Activities

Founded in 1749, colonnaded Washington & Lee University is one of the top small colleges in America. The **Lee Chapel & Museum** (☎ 540-458-8768; ⊙ 9am-4pm, from 1pm Sun) inters Robert E Lee, while his horse Traveller is buried outside. One of the four Confederate banners surrounding Lee's tomb is set in an original flagpole, a branch of a rebel soldier turned into a makeshift standard.

Virginia Military Institute UNIVERSITY
(VMI; Letcher Ave; ⊙ 9am-5pm when campus & museums open) You'll either be impressed or put off by the extreme discipline of the cadets at Virginia Military Institute, the only university to have sent its entire graduating class into combat (plaques to student war dead are touching and ubiquitous). A full-dress parade takes place most Fridays at 4:30pm during the school year. The school's **George C Marshall Museum** (☎ 540-463-7103; http://www.marshallfoundation.org/museum/; adult/student $5/2; ⊙ 9am-5pm Tue-Sat, from 1pm Sun) honors the creator of the Marshall Plan for post-WWII European reconstruction. The **VMI Cadet Museum** (☎ 540-464-7334; ⊙ 9am-5pm) **FREE** houses the stuffed carcass of Stonewall Jackson's horse, a homemade American flag made by an alumnus prisoner of war in Vietnam, and a tribute to VMI students killed in the War on Terror. Contact

the museum for a free guided tour of the campus offered at noon.

Natural Bridge & Foamhenge   LANDMARK
Yes, it's a kitschy tourist trap, and yes, vocal creationists who insist it was made by the hand of God are dominating the site, but the 215ft-high Natural Bridge (www.naturalbridgeva.com; bridge adult/child $21/12, bridge & caverns $29/17; ⊙9am-dusk), 15 miles from Lexington, is still pretty cool. It was surveyed by 16-year-old George Washington, who supposedly carved his initials into the wall, and was once owned by Thomas Jefferson. You can also take a tour of some exceptionally deep caverns here. Just up the road, check out Foamhenge (Hwy 11) FREE, a marvelous full-sized replica of Stonehenge made entirely of Styrofoam. There are fine views – and even an on-site wizard. It's a mile north of Natural Bridge.

🛏 Sleeping

Historic Country Inns   INN $$
(☎877-283-9680; 11 N Main St; r $110-145, ste $170-190; P ❀) Historic Country Inns operates two inns in downtown Lexington and one outside town. All of the buildings have some historical significance to Lexington, and most of the rooms are individually decorated with period antiques.

Applewood Inn & Llama Trekking   INN $$
(☎800-463-1902; www.applewoodbb.com; 242 Tarn Beck Lane; r $155-165; P ❀) The charming, ecominded Applewood Inn & Llama Trekking offers accommdations and a slew of outdoorsy activities (including, yes, Llama trekking) on a farm a 10-minute drive away from downtown Lexington in a positively bucolic valley.

🍴 Eating

Red Hen   SOUTHERN $$
(☎540-464-4401; 11 E Washington St; mains $17-26; ⊙5:30-9pm Tue-Sat; 🖋) 🍷 Reserve well ahead for a memorable meal at Red Hen, which features a creative menu showcasing the fine local produce. Try the roasted pork loin with savory beer bread pudding and oyster mushrooms.

Bistro On Main   BISTRO $$
(8 N Main St; mains $9-24; ⊙11:30am-2:30pm & 5-9pm Tue-Sat) This is a bright, welcoming spot with big windows onto Lexington's main street, tasty bistro fare and a bar.

☆ Entertainment

Hull's Drive-in   CINEMA
(☎540-463-2621; http://hullsdrivein.com; 2367 N Lee Hwy/US 11; per person $6; ⊙7pm Thu-Sun May-Oct) For old-fashioned amusement, catch a movie at Hull's Drive-in, 5.5 miles north of Lexington.

Blue Ridge Highlands & Southwest Virginia

The southwestern tip of Virginia is the most rugged part of the state. Turn onto the Blue Ridge Pkwy or any side road and you'll immediately plunge into dark strands of dogwood and fir, fast streams and white waterfalls. You're bound to see Confederate flags in the small towns, but will find there's a proud hospitality behind the fierce veneer of independence.

Blue Ridge Parkway

Where Skyline Dr ends, the Blue Ridge Pkwy (www.blueridgeparkway.org) picks up. The road is just as pretty and runs from the southern Appalachian ridge in Shenandoah National Park at Mile 0 to North Carolina's Great Smoky Mountains National Park at Mile 469. Wildflowers bloom in spring, and fall colors are spectacular, but watch out for foggy days; the lack of guardrails can make for hairy driving. There are a dozen visitor centers scattered over the Pkwy, and any of them make a good kick-off point to start your trip.

◉ Sights & Activities

There are all kinds of sights running along the Pkwy.

Mabry Mill   HISTORIC SITE
(Mile 176) One of the most-photographed buildings in the state, the mill nests in such a fuzzy green vale you'll think you've entered the opening chapter of a Tolkien novel.

Humpback Rocks   HIKING
(Mile 5.8) Tour 19th-century farm buildings or take the steep trail to Humpback Rocks, offering spectacular 360-degree views.

Sherando Lake Recreation Area   SWIMMING
(☎540-291-2188; off Mile 16) In George Washington National Forest, you'll find two pretty lakes (one for swimming, one for fishing), with hiking trails and campsites. To get there, take Rte 664 W.

Peaks of Otter HIKING

(Mile 86) There are trails to the tops of these mountains: Sharp Top, Flat Top and Harkening Hill. Shuttles run to the top of Sharp Top or you can try a fairly challenging hike (3 miles return) to the summit.

🛏 Sleeping

There are nine local campgrounds (☑877-444-6777; www.recreation.gov; campsites $19; ☺May-Oct), four in Virginia. Every year the staggered opening date of facilities changes, but sites are generally accessible from April to November. Two NPS-approved indoor facilities are on the Pkwy in Virginia.

Rocky Knob Cabins CABIN $

(☑540-593-3503; www.rockyknobcabins.com; 266 Mabry Mill Rd; cabin without bath $75; ☺May-Oct; ☀ ℗) Rustic cabins set in a secluded stretch of forest. Bring food, as eating options are limited along the Pkwy.

Peaks of Otter LODGE $$

(☑540-586-1081; www.peaksofotter.com; Mile 86, 85554 Blue Ridge Pkwy; r from $130; ☀) A pretty, split-rail-surrounded lodge on a small lake that's nestled between two of its namesake mountains. There's a restaurant, but no public phones and no cellphone reception.

Roanoke & Around

Illuminated by the giant star atop Mill Mountain, Roanoke is the largest city in the valley and is the self-proclaimed 'Capital of the Blue Ridge.'

The striking Taubman Museum of Art (www.taubmanmuseum.org; 110 Salem Ave SE; ☺10am-5pm Tue-Sat, to 9pm Thu & 1st Fri of month; ℗) FREE, opened in 2008, is set in a sculptural steel-and-glass edifice that's reminiscent of the Guggenheim Bilbao (it's no coincidence, as architect Randall Stout was a one-time associate of Frank Gehry). Inside, you'll find a superb collection of artworks spanning 3500 years (it's particularly strong in 19th- and 20th-century American works).

About 30 miles east of Roanoke, the tiny town of Bedford suffered the most casualties per capita during WWII, and hence was chosen to host the moving National D-Day Memorial (☑540-586-3329; US 460 & Hwy 122; adult/child $7/5; ☺10am-5pm). Among its towering arch and flower garden is a cast of bronze figures re-enacting the storming of the beach, complete with bursts of water symbolizing the hail of bullets the soldiers

faced. Walking tours ($3) leave hourly between 10:30am and 3:30pm.

Rose Hill (☑540-400-7785; www.bandbrosehill.com; 521 Washington Ave; r $100-125) is a charming and welcoming three-room B&B in Roanoke's historic district.

For eats, head to Wildflour (☑540-343-4543; 1212 4th St SW; sandwiches under $10, dinner mains $15-24; ☺11am-9pm Mon-Sat; ℗) 🍴, which serves wonderful homemade sandwiches and a rustic fusion-meets-New-American menu, with entrees such as maple-soy-glazed salmon and a hearty meatloaf.

Mt Rogers National Recreation Area

This seriously beautiful district is well worth a visit for outdoor enthusiasts. Hike, fish or cross-country ski among ancient hardwood trees and the state's tallest peak. The park headquarters (☑800-628-7202, 276-783-5196; www.fs.usda.gov/gwj; 3714 Hwy 16, Marion) offers maps and recreation directories. The NPS operates five campgrounds in the area; contact park headquarters for details.

Abingdon

One of the most photogenic towns in Virginia, Abingdon retains fine Federal and Victorian architecture in its historic district, and hosts the bluegrass Virginia Highlands Festival over the first half of August. The visitor center (☑800-435-3440; 335 Cummings St; ☺9am-5pm) has exhibits on local history.

Fields-Penn 1860 House Museum (208 W Main St; adult/child $3/2; ☺11am-4pm Wed, from 1pm Thu-Sat) has exhibits on 19th-century life in southwest Virginia. Founded during the Depression, Barter Theatre (☑276-628-3991; www.bartertheatre.com; 133 W Main St; performances from $20) earned its name from audiences trading food for performances. Actors Gregory Peck and Ernest Borgnine (and uh, Wayne Knight, *Seinfeld*'s 'Newman') cut their teeth on Barter's stage.

The Virginia Creeper Trail (www.vacreepertrail.org), named for the railroad that once ran this route, travels 33 miles between Whitetop Station near the North Carolina border and downtown Abingdon. Several outfitters rent bicycles, organize outings and run shuttles, including Virginia

CARTER FAMILY FOLD

In a tiny hamlet of SW Virginia, formerly known as Maces Spring (today part of Hiltons), you'll find one of the hallowed birthplaces of mountain music. The Carter Family Fold (☑276-386-6054; www.carterfamilyfold.org; 3449 AP Carter Hwy, Hiltons; adult/child $8/1; ⊙7:30pm Sat) continues the musical legacy begun by the talented Carter family back in 1927. Every Saturday night, the 900-person arena hosts first-rate bluegrass and gospel bands; there's also a museum with family memorabilia and the original mid-1800s log cabin where AP Carter was born. With no nearby lodging, your best bet is to stay in Abingdon (30 miles east), Kingsport, TN (12 miles southwest) or Bristol (25 miles southeast).

Creeper Trail Bike Shop (☑276-676-2552; www.vacreepertrailbikeshop.com; 201 Pecan St; bike hire 2hr/day $10/20; ⊙9am-6pm Sun-Fri, from 8am Sat) near the trailhead.

Martha Washington Inn (☑276-628-3161; www.marthawashingtoninn.com; 150 W Main St; r from $173; P❈@🐾🛜), opposite the Barter, is the region's premier historic hotel, a Victorian sprawl of elegant rooms and excellent amenities (wood-paneled library, outdoor Jacuzzi, saltwater pool and tennis courts).

Step back in time at Pop Ellis Soda Shoppe (217 W Main St; mains $8-11; ⊙11am-4pm Mon, to 9pm Tue-Sat) with a beautifully restored interior reminiscent of 1920s-era soda fountains. Thick burgers, wraps and nachos are a fine accompaniment to hand-jerked sodas and milkshakes.

Equal parts cafe and bookstore, Zazzy'z (380 E Main St; mains around $5; ⊙8am-6pm Mon-Sat, 9am-3pm Sun) serves inexpensive quiches, lasagnas and paninis, plus decent coffee.

The Crooked Road

When Scotch–Irish fiddle-and-reel married African American banjo-and-percussion, American mountain or 'old-time' music was born, with such genres as country and bluegrass. The latter genre still dominates the Blue Ridge, and Virginia's Heritage Music Trail, the 250-mile-long Crooked Road (www.thecrookedroad.org), takes you through nine sites associated with that history, along with some eye-stretching mountain scenery. It's well worth taking a detour and joining the music-loving fans of all ages who kick up their heels (many arrive with tap shoes) at these festive jamborees. During a live show you'll witness elders connecting to deep cultural roots and a new generation of musicians keeping that heritage alive and evolving.

FLOYD

Tiny, cute-as-a-postcard Floyd is nothing more than an intersection between Hwys 8 and 221, but life explodes on Friday nights at the Floyd Country Store (☑540-745-4563; www.floydcountrystore.com; 206 S Locust St; ⊙11am-5pm Tue-Thu, to 11pm Fri, to 5pm Sat, noon-5pm Sun). Every Friday starting at 6:30pm, $5 gets you four bluegrass bands in four hours and the chance to watch happy crowds jam along to regional heritage. No smokin', no drinkin', but there's plenty of dancin' (of the jig-and-tap style) and good cheer. On weekends, there's lots of live music happening nearby.

Built in 2007 with ecofriendly materials and furnishings, Hotel Floyd (☑540-745-6080; www.hotelfloyd.com; 120 Wilson St; r $85-145; P❈🛜🐾) 🍃 is one of the most 'green' hotels in Virginia, and is a model of sustainability. Each of the 14 unique rooms were decorated by local artisans. Eight miles west of Floyd, Miracle Farm B&B (☑540-789-2214; www.miraclefarmbnb.com; 179 Ida Rose Lane; r $125-155; P❈🛜) has lovely ecofriendly cabins amid lush scenery.

When you're all jigged out, head for Oddfella's (☑540-745-3463; 110 N Locust St; lunch mains $7-14, dinner $8-21; ⊙11am-2:30pm Wed-Sat, 5-9pm Thu-Sun, 10am-3pm Sun; P🐾) 🍃, which has a woodsy, organic mostly Tex-Mex menu, and satisfying locally produced microbrews from the Shooting Creek Brewery.

Above the Harvest Moon health-food store, Natasha's Market Cafe (☑540-745-2450; 227 N Locust St; lunch/dinner mains from $8/16; ⊙11am-3pm Tue-Sat, 5:30-9pm Thu-Sat) is a bright and cheery spot serving organic local produce.

GALAX

Galax claims to be the world capital of mountain music, although it feels like anywhere-else-ville outside of the immediate

WASHINGTON, DC & THE CAPITAL REGION BLUE RIDGE HIGHLANDS

downtown area, which is on the National Register of Historic Places. The main attraction is the Rex Theater (☑276-236-0329; www.rextheatergalax.com; 113 E Grayson St), a musty, red-curtained belle of yore. Frequent bluegrass acts cross its stage, but the easiest one to catch is the free Friday-night live WBRF 98.1 show, which pulls in crowds from across the mountains.

Tom Barr of Barr's Fiddle Shop (☑276-236-2411; http://barrsfiddleshop.com/; 105 S Main St; ☺9am-5pm Mon-Sat) is the Stradivarius of the mountains, a master craftsman sought out by fiddle and mandolin aficionados from across the world. The Old Fiddler's Convention (www.oldfiddlersconvention.com) is held on the second weekend in August in Galax; it's one of the premier mountain-music festivals in the world.

Doctor's Inn (☑276-238-9998; thedoctorsinnvirginia.com; 406 W Stuart Dr; r $140-150; P✳🗗) is a welcoming guesthouse with antique-filled chambers and excellent breakfasts.

The Galax Smokehouse (☑276-236-1000; 101 N Main St; mains $7-18; ☺11am-9pm Mon-Sat, to 3pm Sun) serves platters of sweetly sauced Memphis-style BBQ.

WEST VIRGINIA

Wild and wonderful West Virginia is often overlooked by American and foreign travelers. It doesn't help that the state can't seem to shake its negative stereotypes. That's too bad, because West Virginia is one of the prettiest states in the Union. With its line of unbroken green mountains, raging white-water rivers and snowcapped ski resorts, this is an outdoors-lovers' paradise.

Created by secessionists from secession, the people here still think of themselves as hardscrabble sons of miners, and that perception isn't entirely off. But the Mountain State is also gentrifying and, occasionally, that's a good thing: the arts are flourishing in the valleys, where some towns offer a welcome break from the state's constantly evolving outdoor activities.

History

Virginia was once the biggest state in America, divided between the plantation aristocracy of the Tidewater and the mountains of what is now West Virginia. The latter were settled by tough farmers who staked out independent freeholds across the Appalachians. Always resentful of their Eastern brethren and their reliance on cheap (ie slave) labor, the mountaineers of West Virginia declared their independence from Virginia when the latter tried to break off from America during the Civil War.

Yet the scrappy, independent-at-all-costs stereotype was challenged in the late 19th and early 20th centuries, when miners here formed into cooperative unions and fought employers in some of the bloodiest battles in American labor history. That mix of chip-on-the-shoulder resentment toward authority and look-out-for-your-neighbor community values continues to characterize West Virginia today.

ℹ️ Information

West Virginia Division of Tourism (☑800-225-5982; www.wvtourism.com) operates welcome centers at interstate borders and in Harpers Ferry (☑304-535-2482). Check www.adventuresinwv.com for info on the state's myriad adventure-tourism opportunities.

Many hotels and motels tack on a $1 'safe' fee, refundable upon request at checkout. So if you didn't use that room safe, get your dollar back.

Eastern Panhandle

The most accessible part of the state has always been a mountain getaway for DC types.

Harpers Ferry

History lives on in this attractive town, set with steep cobblestoned streets, framed by the Shenandoah Mountains and the confluence of the rushing Potomac and Shenandoah Rivers. The lower town functions as an open-air museum, with more than a dozen buildings that you can wander through to get a taste of 19th-century life in the small town. Exhibits narrate the town's role at the forefront of westward expansion, American industry and, most famously, the slavery debate. In 1859 old John Brown tried to spark a slave uprising here and was hanged for his efforts; the incident rubbed friction between North and South into the fires of Civil War.

Pick up a pass to visit the historic buildings at the Harpers Ferry National Historic Park Visitor Center (☑304-535-6029; www.nps.gov/hafe; 171 Shoreline Dr; per person/

vehicle $5/10; ☉8am-5pm; ⓘ) 🗲 off Hwy 340. You can also park and take a free shuttle from here. Parking is extremely limited in Harpers Ferry proper.

◎ Sights & Activities

There are great hikes in the area, from three-hour scrambles to the scenic overlook from the Maryland Heights Trail, past Civil War fortifications on the Loudoun Heights Trail or along the Appalachian Trail. You can also cycle or walk along the C&O Canal towpath.

Master Armorer's House   HISTORIC SITE
(☑304-535-6029; www.nps.gov/hafe; 171 Shoreline Dr, Harpers Ferry) **FREE** Among the free sites in the historic district, this 1858 house explains how rifle technology developed here revolutionized the firearms industry.

Storer College Building   MUSEUM
(☑304-535-6029; www.nps.gov/hafe; 171 Shoreline Dr, Harpers Ferry) **FREE** Long ago a teachers' college for freed slaves, it now traces the town's African American history.

John Brown Wax Museum   MUSEUM
(☑304-535-6342; www.johnbrownwaxmuseum. com; 168 High St, Harpers Ferry; adult/child $7/5; ☉9am-4:30pm winter, 10am-5:30pm summer) For those of you who appreciate kitsch, the ultimate, if overpriced, attraction to seek out in these parts is the John Brown Wax Museum. A somewhat imbalanced albeit brave zealot, Brown led an ill-conceived slave rebellion here that helped spark the Civil War. The museum dedicated to his life and the event is laughably old-school, and worth a visit for all that; nothing says historical accuracy like scratchy vocals, jerky animatronics and a light-and-sound show that sounds as if it was recorded some time around the late Cretaceous.

Appalachian Trail Conservancy   HIKING
(☑304-535-6331; www.appalachiantrail.org; 799 Washington Trail, cnr Washington & Jackson Sts; ☉9am-5pm Mon-Fri Apr-Oct) The 2160-mile Appalachian Trail is headquartered here at this tremendous resource for hikers.

River Riders   ADVENTURE SPORTS
(☑800-326-7238; www.riverriders.com; 408 Alstadts Hill Rd) The go-to place for rafting, canoeing, tubing, kayaking and multiday cycling trips, plus cycle rental.

WEST VIRGINIA FACTS

Nickname Mountain State

Population 1.85 million

Area 24,230 sq miles

Capital city Charleston (population 52,000)

Other cities Huntington (population 49,000), Parkersburg (population 31,500), 4 Morgantown (population 29,500), Wheeling (population 28,500)

Sales tax 6%

Birthplace of Olympic gymnast Mary Lou Retton (b 1968), writer Pearl S Buck (1892–1973), pioneer aviator Chuck Yeager (b 1923), actor Don Knotts (1924–2006)

Home of The National Radio Astronomy Observatory, much of the American coal industry

Politics Republican

Famous for Mountains, John Denver's 'Take Me Home, Country Roads,' the Hatfield–McCoy feud

State slogan 'Wild and Wonderful'

Driving distances Harpers Ferry to Fayetteville 280 miles, Fayetteville to Morgantown 148 miles

🛏 Sleeping & Eating

HI-Harpers Ferry Hostel   HOSTEL $
(☑301-834-7652; www.hiusa.org; 19123 Sandy Hook Rd, Knoxville, MD; dm $20; ☉mid-Apr–mid-Oct; Ⓟ▣@⃝) Located 2 miles from downtown on the Maryland side of the Potomac River, this friendly hostel has plenty of amenities including a kitchen, laundry and lounge area with games and books.

Jackson Rose   B&B $$
(☑304-535-1528; www.thejacksonrose.com; 1167 W Washington St; r weekday/weekend $135/150; ▣⃝) This marvelous brick 18th-century residence with stately gardens has three attractive guestrooms, including a room where Stonewall Jackson briefly lodged during the Civil War. Antique furnishings and vintage curios are sprinkled about the house, and the cooked breakfast is excellent. It's a 600m walk downhill to the historic district. No children under 12.

ROADSIDE MYSTERIES

See gravity and the known limits of tackiness defied at the **Mystery Hole** ([📞]304-658-9101; www.mysteryhole.com/; 16724 Midland Trail, Ansted; adult/child $6/5; [⊘]10:30am-6pm), one of the great attractions of roadside America. Everything inside this madhouse *tilts at an angle!* It's located 1 mile west of Hawks Nest State Park. Call ahead to check open days.

Town's Inn INN $$

([📞]877-489-2447, 304-702-1872; www.thetownsinn. com; 175 & 179 High St; r $70-140; [❄]) Spread between two neighboring pre–Civil War residences, the Town's Inn has rooms ranging from small and minimalist to charming heritage-style quarters. It's set in the middle of the historic district and has an indoor-outdoor restaurant as well.

Canal House AMERICAN $$

(1226 Washington St; mains $7-14; [⊘]11am-3pm Wed-Sat, 5:30-8:30pm Thu-Sat, noon-6pm Sun; [🖬]) Roughly 1 mile west (and uphill) from the historic district, Canal House is a perennial favorite for delicious sandwiches and friendly service in a flower-trimmed stone house. Outdoor seating.

Anvil AMERICAN $$

([📞]304-535-2582; 1270 Washington St; lunch mains $8-12, dinner mains $15-24; [⊘]11am-9pm Wed-Sun) Local trout melting in honey-pecan butter and an elegant Federal dining room equals excellence at Anvil, in next-door Bolivar.

Beans in the Belfry AMERICAN $$

([📞]301-834-7178; 122 W Potomac St, Brunswick, MD; mains under $10; [⊘]9am-9pm Mon-Sat, to 7pm Sun; [🛜🖬]) Across the river in Brunswick, MD (roughly 10 miles east), you'll find this converted red-brick church, sheltering mismatched couches and kitsch-laden walls, light fare (chili, sandwiches, quiche) and a tiny stage where live folk, blues and bluegrass bands strike up most nights. Sunday jazz brunch ($18) is a hit.

❶ Getting There & Around

Amtrak (www.amtrak.com) trains run to Washington's Union Station ($14, one daily, 71 minutes). **MARC trains** (mta.maryland.gov) run three times daily Monday to Friday.

Berkeley Springs

America's first spa town (George Washington relaxed here) is an odd jumble of spiritualism, artistic expression and pampering spa centers. Farmers in pickups, sporting Confederate flags, and acupuncturists in tie-dye smocks regard each other with bemusement on the roads of Bath (still the official name).

The Berkeley Springs State Park's **Roman Baths** ([📞]304-258-2711; www.berkeleyspringssp.com/spa.html; 2 S Washington St; bath $22; [⊘]10am-6pm) are uninspiring soaks in dimly lit individual tile-lined rooms, but it's the cheapest spa deal in town. (Fill your water bottle with some of the magic stuff at the fountain outside the door.) For a more indulgent experience, book a treatment (massage, facial, aromatherapy) across the green at the **Bath House** ([📞]800-431-4698; www.bathhouse. com; 21 Fairfax St; 1hr massage $75; [⊘]10am-5pm).

Cacapon State Park ([📞]304-258-1022; 818 Cacapon Lodge Dr; lodge/cabins from $85/91) has simple lodge accommodations plus modern and rustic cabins (with fireplaces) in a peaceful wooded setting, 9 miles south of Berkeley Springs (off US 522). There's hiking, lake swimming and a golf course.

Tari's ([📞]304-258-1196; 33 N Washington St; lunch $8-12, dinner $19-27; [⊘]11am-9pm; [🖊]) [🍴] is a very Berkeley Springs sort of spot, with fresh local food and good vegetarian options served in a laid-back atmosphere, where all the right hints of good karma abound.

Monongahela National Forest

Almost the entire eastern half of West Virginia is marked green parkland on the map, and all that goodness falls under the auspices of this stunning national forest. Within its 1400 sq miles are wild rivers, caves and the highest peak in the state (Spruce Knob). More than 850 miles of trails include the 124-mile **Allegheny Trail**, for hiking and backpacking, and the 75-mile rails-to-trails **Greenbrier River Trail**, popular with cyclists.

Elkins, at the forest's western boundary, is a good base of operations. The **National Forest Service Headquarters** ([📞]304-636-1800; 200 Sycamore St; campsites $5-30, primitive camping free) distributes recreation directories for hiking, cycling and camping. Stock up on trail mix, energy bars and hippie auras at Good Energy Foods (214 3rd St; ☺9am-5:30pm Mon-Sat).

In the southern end of the forest, Cranberry Mountain Nature Center (☎304-653-4826; cnr Hwys 150 & 39/55; ☺9am-4:30pm Thu-Mon May-Oct) has scientific information on the forest and the surrounding 750-acre bog ecosystem, the largest of its kind in the state.

The surreal landscapes at Seneca Rocks, 35 miles southeast of Elkins, attract rock climbers up the 900ft-tall sandstone strata. Seneca Shadows Campground (☎877-444-6777; campsites $11-30; ☺Apr-Oct) lies 1 mile east.

Southern West Virginia

This part of the state has carved out a viable stake as adventure-sports capital of the eastern seaboard.

New River Gorge National River

The New River is actually one of the oldest in the world, and the primeval forest gorge it runs through is one of the most breathtaking in the Appalachians. The NPS protects a stretch of the New River that falls 750ft over 50 miles, with a compact set of rapids up to Class V concentrated at the northernmost end.

Canyon Rim visitor center (☎304-574-2115; www.nps.gov/neri; 162 Visitor Center Road Lansing, WV , GPS 38.07003 N, 81.07583 W; ☺9am-5pm; 📶) 📶, just north of the impressive gorge bridge, is only one of five NPS visitor centers along the river. It has information on scenic drives, river outfitters, gorge climbing, hiking and mountain biking, as well as white-water rafting to the north on the Gauley River. Rim and gorge trails offer beautiful views. There are several free basic camping areas.

Nearby Hawks Nest State Park offers views from its rim-top lodge (☎304-658-5212; www.hawksnestsp.com; r $86-128; ❄📶); from June through October it operates an aerial tram (closed Wednesdays) to the river, where you can catch a cruising boat ride.

Babcock State Park (☎304-438-3004; www.babcocksp.com; cabins $77-88, campsites $20-23) has hiking, canoeing, horseback riding, camping and cabin accommodations. The park's highlight is its photogenic Glade Creek Grist Mill.

Fayetteville & Around

Pint-sized Fayetteville acts as jumping-off point for New River thrill-seekers and is an artsy mountain enclave besides. On the third Saturday in October, hundreds of base jumpers parachute from the 876ft-high New River Gorge Bridge for the Bridge Day Festival.

Among the many state-licensed rafting outfitters in the area, Cantrell Ultimate Rafting (☎304-574-2500, 304-663-2762; www.cantrellultimaterafting.com/; 49 Cantrell Dr; packages from $60) stands out for its white-water rafting trips. Hard Rock (☎304-574-0735; www.hardrockclimbing.com; 131 South Court St; half-/full day from $75/140) offers trips and training courses for rock climbers

The Beckley Exhibition Coal Mine (☎304-256-1747; www.beckleymine.org; adult/child $20/12; ☺10am-6pm Apr-Oct) in nearby Beckley is a museum for the region's coal heritage. Visitors can descend 1500ft to a former coal mine. Bring a jacket, as it's cold underground!

River Rock Retreat Hostel (☎304-574-0394; www.riverrockretreatandhostel.com; Lansing-Edmond Rd; dm $23; 📶❄), located less than 1 mile north of the New River Gorge Bridge, has basic, clean rooms and plenty of common space. Owner Joy Marr is a wealth of local information. Two miles south of the bridge, Rifrafters Campground (☎304-574-1065; www.rifrafters.com; Laurel Creek Rd; campsites per person $12, cabins d/q $40/80) has primitive campsites, comfy cabins and hot-shower and bathroom facilities.

Start the day with breakfast and coffee under stained-glass windows at Cathedral Café & Bookstore (☎304-574-0202; 134 S Court St; mains $5-8; ☺7:30am-4pm; 📶📶) 📶.

WASHINGTON, DC & THE CAPITAL REGION SOUTHERN WEST VIRGINIA

The South

Best Places to Stay

➡ 21c Museum Hotel (p383)

➡ Nashville Downtown Hostel (p372)

➡ Lodge on Little St Simons (p407)

➡ Shack Up Inn (p417)

➡ Mansion on Forsyth Park (p403)

Best Places to Eat

➡ Proof (p384)

➡ Prince's Hot Chicken (p373)

➡ Boucherie (p441)

➡ Octopus Bar (p397)

➡ Restaurant August (p440)

Why Go?

More than any other part of the country, the South has an identity all its own – a lyrical dialect, a complicated political history and a pride in a shared culture that cuts across state lines. Nurtured by deep roots yet shaped by hardship, the South has a rich legacy in politics and culture. Icons and leaders like Martin Luther King Jr, Rosa Parks, and Bill Clinton, novelists like William Faulkner, Eudora Welty and Flannery O'Connor are all Southern-born. So is barbecue, bourbon and Coca-Cola, and the blues. Which, of course, gave birth to rock and roll, soul and American popular music as a whole. The cities of the South are some of the country's most fascinating, from antebellum beauties like New Orleans and Savannah to New South powerhouses like Atlanta and Nashville.

But it's the legendary Southern hospitality that makes travel in the region such a pleasure. People round here love to talk. Stay long enough and you'll no doubt be invited for dinner.

When to Go
New Orleans

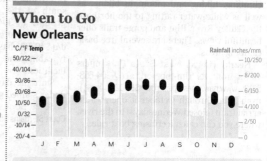

Nov–Feb Winter is generally mild here, and Christmas is a capital-E Event.	Apr–Jun Springs are lush and warm, abloom with fragrant jasmine, gardenia and tuberose.	Jul–Sep Summer is steamy, often unpleasantly so, and locals hit the beaches.

Understanding Southern Culture

Southerners have long been the butt of their fellow countrymen's jokes. They're slow-moving, hard-drinking, funny-talking and spend all their time fixing their pickup trucks and marrying their cousins. Or so the line goes. Well, while Southerners do tend to be relatively friendly and laid-back, the drawling country bumpkin is more the exception than the norm. Today's Southerner is just as likely to be a Mumbai-born motel owner in rural Arkansas, a fast-talking Atlanta investment banker with a glitzy high-rise condo, or a 20-something gay hipster in trendy Midtown Memphis.

Southerners do love sports, especially football, college basketball and Nascar, while fine arts thrive in historic cities like Charleston and Savannah, and college towns like Chapel Hill, Knoxville and Athens are famed for their indie-music scenes. Religion is hugely important here – the so-called Bible belt runs smack through the South, with about half of all Southerners identifying as Evangelical Christians.

THE SOUTH FOR MUSIC LOVERS

The history of American music is the history of Southern music: the blues, bluegrass, jazz, gospel, country and rock 'n' roll were all born here. Music hot spots include: Nashville, the birthplace of country music and home to more boot-stompin' honky-tonks than anywhere in the world; Memphis, where bluesmen still groove in the clubs of Beale St; and New Orleans, where you can hear world-class jazz, blues and zydeco every night of the week. Asheville, NC, is an emerging center of Appalachian revival music, while Kentucky claims bluegrass as its own.

Must-Eat Southern Foods

⇒ **Barbecue** (region-wide, especially in North Carolina and Tennessee)

⇒ **Fried chicken** (region-wide)

⇒ **Cornbread** (region-wide)

⇒ **Shrimp and grits** (South Carolina and Georgia coasts)

⇒ **Boudin** (Cajun pork and rice sausage; Southern Louisiana)

⇒ **Gumbo/jambalaya/étouffée** (rice and seafood or meat stew or a mixture; Southern Louisiana)

⇒ **Po'boy** (sandwich, traditionally with fried seafood or meat; Southern Louisiana)

⇒ **Hot tamales** (cornmeal stuffed with spiced beef or pork; Mississippi Delta)

⇒ **Collards** (a leafy green, often cooked with ham; region-wide)

⇒ **Pecan pie, coconut cake, red velvet cake, sweet-potato pie** (region-wide)

⇒ **Bourbon** (Kentucky)

DID YOU KNOW?

The South is America's fastest-growing region, with 14.3% of the country's population.

Fast Facts

⇒ **Nickname** Dixie

⇒ **Biggest cities** Atlanta, Charlotte, Memphis

⇒ **Time zones** Eastern, Central

Scenic Drives

⇒ **Blue Ridge Parkway** North Carolina to Virginia (www.blueridgeparkway.org)

⇒ **Natchez Trace** Tennessee to Mississippi (www.nps.gov/natr)

⇒ **Hwy 12** North Carolina's Outer Banks

⇒ **Kentucky Bourbon Trail** (p387) Sniff, taste and enjoy the locals' favorite liquor

⇒ **Blues Highway** (p417) Take the mythic Hwy 61 from Memphis to the Crossroads

Resources

⇒ **Visit South** (www. visitsouth.com) Sights and activities across the region

⇒ **South Carolina** (www. discoversouthcarolina.com) This state's official tourism site; better than most

⇒ **North Carolina** (www. visitnc.com) Roadtrips, Asheville and the coast

⇒ **Tennessee** (www. tnvacation.com) Events, activities and sights

⇒ **Louisiana** (www. louisianatravel.com) Info on the Cajun countryside

THE SOUTH

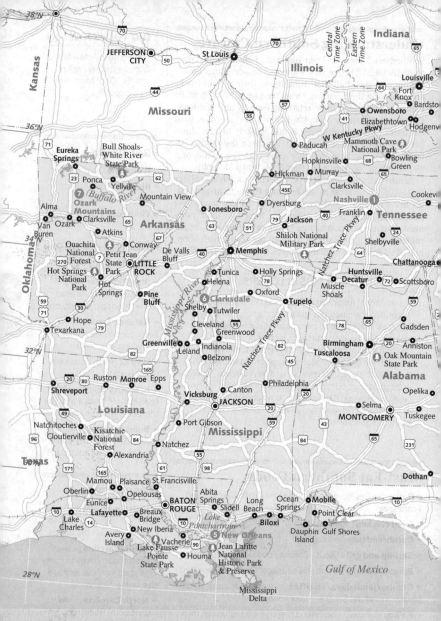

The South Highlights

1 Stomping your boots at **Tootsie's Orchid Lounge** (p376) on Nashville's honky-tonk-lined Lower Broadway.

2 Hiking and camping in the magnificent **Great Smoky**

Mountains National Park (p345 and p380).

3 Driving windswept Hwy 12 the length of North Carolina's **Outer Banks** (p331) and riding the ferry to Ocracoke Island.

4 Touring the grand antebellum homes and cotton plantations of **Charleston** (p348).

5 Putting yourself into a Cajun-Creole food-induced

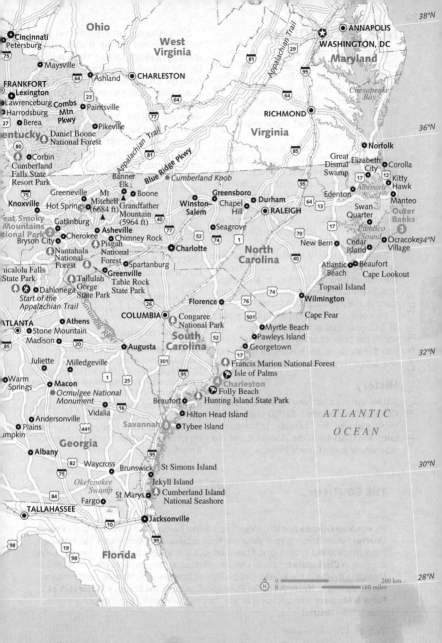

coma in **New Orleans** (p428), one of America's most treasured foodie havens.

⑥ Immersing yourself in the soul, rhythm, history and perseverance of the **Delta Blues Museum** (p416) in Clarksdale, MS.

⑦ Exploring the caverns, mountains, rivers and forests of Arkansas' **Ozark Mountains** (p425), where folk music reigns.

⑧ Falling for the hauntings, murderous tales and Southern hospitality in Georgia's living romance novel, the architecturally pristine **Savannah** (p402).

NORTH CAROLINA

Hipsters, hog farmers and hi-tech wunder-kinds – all cross paths in fast-growing North Carolina, where the Old South and the New South stand shoulder to shoulder. From the ancient mountains in the west to the sandy barrier islands of the Atlantic you'll find a variety of cultures and communities not easy to stereotype.

Agriculture is North Carolina's leading moneymaker, with 50,400 farms, and the state is the second-largest producer of hogs and pigs in the nation. But new technologies are also an economic force, with more than with 170 global companies operating in Research Triangle Park alone. Other important industries include finance, nanotechnology, tobacco and Christmas trees.

Though the bulk of North Carolinians live in the business-oriented urban centers of the central Piedmont region, most travelers stick to the scenic routes along the coast and through the Appalachian Mountains.

So come on down, ya'll, grab a platter of barbecue and a hoppy microbrew, and watch the Duke Blue Devils battle the Carolina Tar Heels on the basketball court. College hoops rival Jesus for Carolinians' souls.

History

Native Americans have inhabited North Carolina for more than 10,000 years. Major tribes included the Cherokee, in the mountains, the Catawba in the Piedmont and the Waccamaw in the Coastal Plain.

North Carolina was the second territory to be colonized by the British, named in memory of King Charles I (Carolus in Latin), but the first colony to vote for independence from the Crown. Several important Revolutionary War battles were fought here.

The state was a sleepy agricultural backwater through the 1800s, earning it the nickname the 'Rip Van Winkle State.' Divided on slavery (most residents were too poor to own slaves), North Carolina was the last state to secede during the Civil War, but went on to provide more Confederate soldiers than any other state.

North Carolina was a civil rights hotbed in the mid-20th century, with highly publicized lunch-counter sit-ins in Greensboro and the formation of the influential Student Nonviolent Coordinating Committee (SNCC) in Raleigh. The later part of the century brought finance to Charlotte, and technology and medicine to the Raleigh-Durham area, driving a huge population boom and widening cultural diversity.

ℹ Information

North Carolina Division of Tourism (☎919-733-8372; www.visitnc.com; 301 N Wilmington St, Raleigh; ⊗8am-5pm Mon-Fri) Sends out good maps and information, including its annual *Official Travel Guide*.

North Carolina State Parks (www.ncparks. gov) Offers info on North Carolina's 38 state parks and recreation areas, some have camping (prices range from free to more than $20 a night).

THE SOUTH IN...

One Week

Fly into **New Orleans** and stretch your legs with a walking tour in the legendary **French Quarter** before devoting your remaining time to celebrating jazz history and partying the night away in a zydeco joint. Then wind your way upward through the languid Delta, stopping in **Clarksdale** for a sultry evening of blues at the juke joints before alighting in **Memphis** to walk in the footsteps of the King at **Graceland**. From here, head on down the Music Hwy to **Nashville** to see Elvis' gold Cadillac at the **Country Music Hall of Fame & Museum** and practice your line dancing at the honky-tonks (country-music clubs) of the **District**.

Two to Three Weeks

From Nashville, head east to hike amid the craggy peaks and waterfalls of **Great Smoky Mountains National Park** before a revitalizing overnight in the arty mountain town of **Asheville** and a tour of the scandalously opulent **Biltmore Estate**, America's largest private home. Plow straight through to the coast to loll on the sandy barrier islands of the isolated **Outer Banks**, then head down the coast to finish up in **Charleston**, with decadent food and postcard-pretty architecture.

North Carolina Coast

The coast of North Carolina remains remarkably under-developed. Yes, the wall of cottages stretching south from Corolla can seem endless, but for the most part the state's shores remain free of flashy, highly commercialized resort areas. Instead you'll find rugged, windswept barrier islands, Colonial villages once frequented by pirates, and laid-back beach towns full of locally owned ice-cream shops and mom 'n' pop motels. Even the most touristy beaches have a small-town vibe.

If it's solitude you seek, head to the isolated Outer Banks (OBX), where fishermen still make their living hauling in shrimp and the older locals speak in an archaic British-tinged brogue. The Hwy 158 bypass from Kitty Hawk to Nags Head gets congested in summer, but the beaches themselves still feel uncrowded. Further south, Wilmington is known as a center of film and TV production, and its surrounding beaches are popular with local spring breakers and tourists.

Outer Banks

These fragile ribbons of sand trace the coastline for 100 miles, cut off from the mainland by various sounds and waterways. From north to south, the barrier islands of Bodie (pronounced 'Body'), Roanoke, Hatteras and Ocracoke, essentially large sandbars, are linked by bridges and ferries. The far-northern communities of Corolla (pronounced kur-*all*-ah, not like the car), Duck and Southern Shores are former duck-hunting grounds for the northeastern rich, and are quiet and upscale. The nearly contiguous Bodie Island towns of Kitty Hawk, Kill Devil Hills and Nags Head are heavily developed and more populist in nature, with fried-fish joints, drive-thru beer shops, motels and dozens of sandals 'n' sunblock shops. Roanoke Island, west of Bodie Island, offers Colonial history and the quaint waterfront town of Manteo. Further south, Hatteras Island is a protected national seashore with a few teeny villages and a wild, windswept beauty. At the southern end of OBX, wild ponies run free and old salts shuck oysters and weave hammocks on Ocracoke Island, accessible only by ferry.

A meandering drive down Hwy 12, which connects much of the Outer Banks, is one of the truly great American road trips, whether

NORTH CAROLINA FACTS

Nickname Tar Heel State

Population 9.7 million

Area 48,711 sq miles

Capital city Raleigh (population 416,000)

Other city Charlotte (population 751,000)

Sales tax 6.75%, plus an additional hotel-occupancy tax of up to 6%

Birthplace of President James K Polk (1795–1849), jazzman John Coltrane (1926–67), Nascar driver Richard Petty (b 1937), singer-songwriter Tori Amos (b 1963)

Home of America's first state university, the Biltmore House, Krispy Kreme doughnuts

Politics Conservative in rural areas, increasingly liberal in urban ones

Famous for The Andy Griffith Show, first airplane flight, college basketball

Pet name Natives are called 'tar heels,' a nickname of uncertain origin but said to be related to their pine tar production and their legendary stubbornness

Driving distances Asheville to Raleigh 247 miles, Raleigh to Wilmington 131 miles

you come during the stunningly desolate winter months or the sunny summer.

◉ Sights

Corolla, the northernmost town on US 158, is famed for its wild horses. Descendants of Colonial Spanish mustangs, the horses roam the northern dunes, and numerous commercial outfitters go in search of them. The non-profit Corolla Wild Horse Fund (www.corollawildhorses.com; 1129 Corolla Village Rd; ◎9:30am-5pm Mon-Fri, 10am-4pm Sat Jun-Aug, 10am-4pm Mon-Fri Sep-May) FREE runs a small museum and leads tours.

The following places are listed from north to south.

Currituck Heritage Park HISTORIC BUILDINGS (Corolla; ◎dawn-dusk) The sunflower-yellow, art-nouveau-style Whalehead Club (www.whaleheadclub.org; tours $10; ◎tours 10am-5pm Mon-Sat mid-Mar–Dec, 11am-4pm Dec–mid-Mar), built in the 1920s as a hunting 'cottage' for a Philadelphia industrialist, is the centerpiece of this manicured park in the village of Corolla. You can also climb the Currituck Beach Lighthouse (www.currituckbeachlight.com; adult/child $7/free; ⊙9am-5pm Mar 23-Nov 23), or check out the modern Outer Banks Center for Wildlife Education (www.ncwildlife.org/obx; 1160 Village Ln; ⊙9am-4:30pm Mon-Sat) FREE for an interesting film about area history, info on local hiking trails and a life-size marsh diorama.

Wright Brothers National Memorial
PARK, MUSEUM

(www.nps.gov/wrbr; Mile 7.5, US 158 Bypass; adult/child $4/free; ⊙9am-5pm, to 6pm summer) Self-taught engineers Wilbur and Orville Wright launched the world's first successful airplane flight on December 17, 1903 (it lasted 12 seconds). A boulder now marks the take-off spot. Climb a nearby hill, where the brothers conducted earlier glider experiments, for fantastic views of sea and sound. The on-site Wright Brothers Visitor Center has a reproduction of the 1903 flyer and exhibits.

The 30-minute 'Flight Room Talk,' a lecture about the brother's dedication and ingenuity, is excellent. For an up-close look at the plane's intricacies, check out the bronze-and-steel replica behind the hill; it's okay to scramble aboard.

Fort Raleigh National Historic Site
HISTORIC BUILDINGS

In the late 1580s, three decades before the Pilgrims landed at Plymouth Rock, a group of 116 British colonists disappeared without a trace from their Roanoke Island settlement. Were they killed off by drought? Did they run away with a Native American tribe? Did they try to sail home and capsize? The fate of the 'Lost Colony' remains one of America's greatest mysteries, and one of the site's star attractions is the beloved musical the Lost Colony Outdoor Drama (www.thelostcolony.org; 1409 National Park Dr; adult/child $26.50/9.50; ⊙8pm Mon-Sat Jun-late Aug).

The play, from Pulitzer Prize–winning North Carolina playwright Paul Green, dramatizes the fate of the colonists and celebrated its 75th anniversary in 2012. It plays at the Waterside Theater throughout summer.

Other attractions include exhibits, artifacts, maps and a free film to fuel the imagination, hosted at the visitor center (www.nps.gov/fora; 1401 National Park Dr, Manteo; ⊙grounds dawn-dusk, visitor center 9am-5pm) FREE. The 16th-century-style Elizabethan Gardens (www.elizabethangardens.org; 1411 National Park Dr; adult/child $9/6; ⊙9am-7pm Jun-Aug, shorter hours Sep-May) include a Shakespearian herb garden and rows of beautifully manicured flower beds.

Cape Hatteras National Seashore
ISLANDS

(www.nps.gov/caha) Extending some 70 miles from south of Nags Head to the south end of Ocracoke Island, this fragile necklace of islands remains blissfully free of overdevelopment. Natural attractions include local and migratory water birds, marshes, woodlands, dunes and miles of empty beaches.

Bodie Island Lighthouse
LIGHTHOUSE

(☎252-441-5711, ticket reservations 255-475-9417; Bodie Island Lighthouse Rd, Bodie Island; museum free, tours adult/child $8/4; ⊙museum 9am-6pm Jun-Aug, to 5pm Sep-May, tours 9am-5:45pm late Apr-early Oct; ⚐) This photogenic lighthouse opened its doors to visitors in 2013. The 156ft-high structure still has its original Fresnel lens, a rarity. Entry is by guided tour. Tickets can be purchased by advance reservation by phone (☎255-475-9417), but not on the day of the tour. Tickets are also available on a first-come, first-served basis.

Pea Island National Wildlife Refuge
PRESERVE

(☎252-987-2394; www.fws.gov/peaisland; Hwy 12; ⊙visitor center 9am-4pm, trails dawn-dusk) At the northern end of Hatteras Island, this 5834-acre preserve is a birdwatcher's heaven, with two nature trails (one fully disabled-accessible) and 13 miles of unspoiled beach.

Chicamacomico Lifesaving Station
MUSEUM

(www.chicamacomico.net; adult/child $6/4; ⊙10am-5pm Mon-Fri Apr-Nov) Built in 1874, this was the first lifesaving station in the state. It's now a museum filled with pre–Coast Guard artifacts.

Cape Hatteras Lighthouse
LIGHTHOUSE

(www.nps.gov/caha; climbing tours adult/child $8/4; ⊙visitor center 9am-5pm Sep-May, to 6pm Jun-Aug, lighthouse late Apr-early Oct) At 208ft, this striking black-and-white-striped edifice is the tallest brick lighthouse in the US and is one of North Carolina's most iconic images. Climb the 248 steps and check out the visitor center.

OCRACOKE ISLAND

Crowded in summer and desolate in the winter, Ocracoke Village (www.ocracokevillage.com) is a funky little community that moves at a slower pace. The village is at the southern end of 14-mile-long Ocracoke Island and is accessed from Hatteras via the free Hatteras–Ocracoke ferry (p335). The ferry lands at the northeastern end of the island. With the exception of the village, the National Park Service owns the island.

The older residents still speak in the 17th-century British dialect known as 'Hoi Toide' (their pronunciation of 'high tide') and refer to non-islanders as 'dingbatters.' Edward Teach, aka Blackbeard the pirate, used to hide out in the area and was killed here in 1718. You can camp by the beach where wild ponies run, have a fish sandwich in a local pub, bike around the village's narrow streets or visit the 1823 Ocracoke Lighthouse, the oldest one still operating in North Carolina.

The island makes a terrific day trip from Hatteras Island, or you can stay the night. There are a handful of B&Bs, a park service campground and rental cottages.

For good eats, try the shrimp basket special on the patio of Dajio (dajiorestaurant.com; 305 Irvin Garrish Hwy) from 3pm to 5pm, followed by the to-die-for lemon berry marscapone. For drinks, savor a Grasshopper latte with chocolate mint and toffee at Ocracoke Coffee (www.ocracokecoffee.com; 226 Back Rd) or quaff a beer at Howard's Pub (mains $8-23; ⊙ 11am-10pm early Mar-late Nov, may stay open later on Fri & Sat), a big old wooden pub that's been an island tradition for beer and fried seafood since the 1850s.

Want to get on the water? Take a a kayaking tour with Ride the Wind (☑252-928-6311; www.surfocracoke.com; 2-2½ hr tours adult/child $35/15). The sunset tours are easy on the arms, and the guides are easy on the eyes.

Graveyard of the Atlantic Museum MUSEUM
(☑252-986-2995; www.graveyardoftheatlantic.com; 59200 Museum Dr; donations appreciated; ⊙10am-4pm Mon-Sat Apr-Oct, Mon-Fri Nov-Mar) FREE Exhibits about shipwrecks, piracy and salvaged cargo are highlights at this maritime museum at the end of the road. According to one exhibit, in 2006 a container washed ashore near Frisco, releasing thousands of Doritos bags.

🏃 Activities

The same strong wind that helped the Wright brothers launch their biplane today propels windsurfers, sailors and hang gliders. Other popular activities include kayaking, fishing, cycling, horse tours, stand-up paddleboarding and scuba diving. The coastal waters kick up between August and October, creating perfect conditions for bodysurfing.

Kitty Hawk Kites ADVENTURE SPORTS
(☑877-359-2447, 252-441-2426; www.kittyhawk.com; 3933 S Croatan Hwy; hang gliding $99, bike rental per day $25, kayaks $39-49, stand-up paddleboards $59) Has locations all over OBX offering beginners' kiteboarding lessons (two hours $300) and hang-gliding lessons at Jockey's Ridge State Park (from $99). It also rents kayaks, sailboats, stand-up paddleboards, bikes and inline skates and offers a variety of tours and courses.

Corolla Outback Adventures DRIVING TOURS
(☑252-453-4484; www.corollaoutback.com; 1150 Ocean Trail, Corolla; 2hr tour adult/child $50/25) Owner Jay Bender, whose family started Corolla's first guide service, knows his local history and his local horses. Tours bounce you down the beach and through the dunes to see the wild mustangs that roam the northern Outer Banks.

Outer Banks Dive Center DIVING
(☑252-449-8349; www.obxdive.com; 3917 S Croatan Hwy; wreck dives $120) Has NAUI-certified instructors who run everything from basic classes to guided dives of the shipwrecks of the Graveyard of the Atlantic.

🛏 Sleeping

Crowds swarm the Outer Banks in summer, so reserve in advance. The area has few massive chain hotels, but hundreds of small motels, rental cottages and B&Bs; the visitor centers offer referrals. Also check www.outer-banks.com. For cottage rentals, try www.sunrealtync.com or www.southern shores.com.

DON'T MISS

SCENIC DRIVE: BLUE RIDGE PARKWAY

Commissioned by President Franklin D Roosevelt as a Depression-era public-works project, the Blue Ridge Parkway traverses the southern Appalachians from Virginia's Shenandoah National Park at Mile 0 to the Great Smoky Mountains National Park at Mile 469.

North Carolina's piece of the parkway twists and turns for 262 miles of killer alpine vistas. The **National Park Service** (NPS; www.nps.gov/blri; ⊘ May-Oct) runs campgrounds and visitor centers. Note that restrooms and gas stations are few and far between. For details about the Parkway in Virginia, see p319.

Parkway highlights and campgrounds include the following, from the Virginia border south:

Cumberland Knob (Mile 217.5) NPS visitor center, easy walk to the knob.

Doughton Park (Mile 241.1) Trails and camping.

Blowing Rock (Mile 291.8) Small town named for a craggy, commercialized cliff that offers great views, occasional updrafts and a Native American love story.

Moses H Cone Memorial Park (Mile 294.1) A lovely old estate with carriage trails and a craft shop.

Julian Price Memorial Park (Mile 296.9) Camping.

Grandfather Mountain (Mile 305.1) Hugely popular for its mile-high pedestrian 'swinging bridge.' Also has a nature center and small animal reserve.

Linville Falls (Mile 316.4) Short hiking trails to the falls, campsites.

Little Switzerland (Mile 334) Old-style mountain resort.

Mt Mitchell State Park (Mile 355.5) Highest peak east of the Mississippi (6684ft); hiking and camping.

Craggy Gardens (Mile 364) Hiking trails explode with rhododendron blossoms in summer.

Folk Art Center (Mile 382) High-end Appalachian crafts for sale.

Blue Ridge Parkway Visitor Center (Mile 384) Inspiring film, interactive map, trail information.

Mt Pisgah (Mile 408.8) Hiking, camping, restaurant, inn.

Graveyard Fields (Mile 418) Short hiking trails to waterfalls.

Campgrounds   CAMPGROUND **$**
(☑ 252-473-2111; www.nps.gov/caha; tent sites $20-23; ⊘ late spring-early fall) The National Park Service runs four campgrounds on the islands which feature cold-water showers and flush toilets. They are located at Oregon Inlet (near Bodie Island Lighthouse), Cape Point and Frisco (near Cape Hatteras Lighthouse) and **Ocracoke** (☑ 800-365-2267; www.recreation.gov). Sites at Ocracoke can be reserved; the others are first-come, first-served.

Breakwater Inn   MOTEL **$$**
(☑ 252-986-2565; www.breakwaterhatteras.com; 57896 Hwy 12; r/ste inn $159/189, motel $104/134; P ❋ 🛜 🌊) The end of the road doesn't look so bad at this three-story inn. Rooms come with kitchenettes and private decks that have views of the sound. On a budget? Try one of the older 'Fisherman's Quarters' rooms, with microwave and refrigerator. The inn is near the Hatteras–Ocracoke ferry landing.

Shutters on the Banks   HOTEL **$$**
(☑ 800-848-3728; www.shuttersonthebanks.com; 405 S Virginia Dare Trail; r $149-289; P ❋ 🛜 🌊) Formerly Colony IV by the Sea, this welcoming beachfront hotel exudes a sassy, colorful style. The inviting rooms come with plantation windows and colorful bedspreads, as well as a flatscreen TV, refrigerator and microwave.

Sanderling Resort & Spa   RESORT **$$$**
(☑ 252-261-4111; www.sanderling-resort.com; 1461 Duck Rd; r/ste from $299/539; P ❋ 🛜 🌊) These

posh digs have impeccably tasteful neutral-toned rooms with decks and flatscreen TVs, several restaurants and bars, and a spa offering luxe massage.

✖ Eating

The main tourist strip on Bodie Island has the most restaurants and nightlife, but many are only open Memorial Day (last Monday in May) through early fall.

John's Drive-In   SEAFOOD, ICE CREAM **$**
(www.johnsdrivein.com; 3716 N Virginia Dare Trail; mains $2-13; ⊘11am-5pm Mon, Tue & Thu, to 6pm Fri-Sun May-Sep) A Kitty Hawk institution for perfectly fried baskets of 'dolphin' (mahi-mahi) and rockfish, to be eaten at outdoor picnic tables and washed down with one of hundreds of possible milkshake varieties. Some folks just come for the ice cream.

★**Kill Devil Grill**   SEAFOOD, AMERICAN **$$**
(☑252-449-8181; www.thekilldevilgrill.com; Beach Rd, Mile 9¾; lunch $7-11, dinner $9-20; ⊘11:30am-10pm Tue-Sat) Yowza, this place is good. It's also a bit historic – the entrance is a 1939 diner that's listed in the National Registry of Historic Places. Pub grub and seafood arrive with tasty flair, and portions are generous. Check out the specials, where the kitchen can really shine.

Tortugas' Lie   SEAFOOD **$$**
(www.tortugaslie.com; 3014 S Virginia Dare Trail/Mile 11; lunch $9-18, dinner $12-24; ⊘11:30am-9:30pm Sun-Thu, to 10pm Fri & Sat) With its surfboards and license plates, the interior of this divey stand-by isn't dressed to impressed, but who cares? The reliably good seafood, burritos and burgers go down well with the beer. Guy Fieri stopped by in 2012 and scrawled his signature on the wall. Fills up by 6:30pm. Kids are okay.

Mama Quan's OBX
Grill & Tiki Bar   CALIFORNIAN, SEAFOOD **$$**
(www.mamakwans.com; 1701 S Virginia Dare Trail; lunch $9-15, dinner $10-25; ⊘11:30am-2am Mon-Sat, to midnight Sat) Five words: Mama's World Famous Fish Tacos. Upon your first bite of these mahimahi-filled wonders, a baby angel earns it wings.

❶ Orientation

Hwy 12, also called Virginia Dare Trail or 'the coast road,' runs close to the Atlantic for the length of the Outer Banks. US 158, usually called 'the Bypass,' begins just north of Kitty Hawk and merges with US 64 as it crosses onto Roanoke Island. Locations are usually given in terms of 'mile posts' (Mile or MP), beginning with Mile 0 at the foot of the Wright Memorial Bridge at Kitty Hawk.

❶ Information

The best sources of information are at the main visitor centers. Many smaller centers are open seasonally. Also useful is www.outerbanks.org. The entire Manteo waterfront has free wi-fi.

Aycock Brown Visitor Center (☑252-261-4644; www.outerbanks.org; Mile 1, US 158, Kitty Hawk; ⊘9am-5pm)

Corolla Public Library (1123 Ocean Trail/Hwy 12; ☏) Free wi-fi and internet access.

Hatteras Island Visitor Center (☑252-441-5711; www.nps.gov/caha; ⊘9am-6pm Jun-Aug, to 5pm Sep-May) Beside Cape Hatteras Lighthouse.

Ocracoke Island Visitor Center (☑252-928-4531; www.nps.gov/caha; ⊘9am-5pm)

Outer Banks Welcome Center on Roanoke Island (☑877-629-4386, 252-473-2138; www.outerbanks.org; 1 Visitors Center Cir, Manteo; ⊘9am-5pm)

❶ Getting There & Away

No public transportation exists to or on the Outer Banks. However, the **North Carolina Ferry System** (☑800-293-3779; www.ncdot.gov/ferry) operates several routes, including the free 40-minute Hatteras–Ocracoke car ferry, which runs at least hourly from 5:15am to 11:45pm from Hatteras in high season; reservations aren't accepted. North Carolina ferries also run between Ocracoke and Cedar Island (one-way $15, 2¼ hours) and Ocracoke and Swan Quarter on the mainland ($15, 2½ hours) every two hours or so; reservations are recommended in summer for these two routes.

Crystal Coast

The southern Outer Banks are collectively called the 'Crystal Coast,' at least for tourist offices' promotional purposes. Less rugged than the northern beaches, they include several historic coastal towns, a number of sparsely populated islands, and some vacation-friendly beaches.

An industrial and commercial stretch of US 70 goes through Morehead City, with plenty of chain hotels and restaurants. Stop here for shrimp burgers at El's Drive-In (3706 Arendell St; mains $2-13; ⊘10:30am-10pm Sun-Thu, to 10:30pm Fri & Sat), a legendary seafood spot where your food is brought to you by carhop.

Down the road, postcard-pretty Beaufort (*bow*-fort), the third-oldest town in the state, has a charming boardwalk and lots of B&Bs. Nibble chili-lime shrimp tacos beside Taylor's Creek at stylish Front Street Grill at Stillwater (www.frontstreetgrillatstillwater.com; 300 Front St; brunch & lunch $11-17, dinner $19- 24; ⊘11:30am-9pm Tue-Thu, to 10:30pm Sat & Sun), then rest your head at the homey Beaufort Inn (☑252-728-2600; www.beaufort-inn.com; 101 Ann St; r/ ste incl breakfast from $139/189). The pirate Blackbeard was a frequent visitor to the area in the early 1700s – in 1996 the wreckage of his flagship, the *Queen Anne's Revenge*, was discovered at the bottom of Beaufort Inlet. See artifacts from the ship at the North Carolina Maritime Museum (www.ncmaritimemuseum.org; 315 Front St; ⊘9am-5pm Mon-Fri, 10am-5pm Sat, 1-5pm Sun) FREE. Blackbeard himself is said to have lived in the Hammock House off Front St. You can't go inside, but some claim you can still hear the screams of the pirate's murdered wife at night.

Currently, small commercial ferries leave regularly from the Beaufort boardwalk for the isolated islands of the Cape Lookout National Seashore (www.nps.gov/calo; ferries $10-16). Highlights include Shackleford Banks, an uninhabited sandbar with spectacular seashells and herds of wild ponies, and the diamond-patterned Cape Lookout Lighthouse (adult/child $8/4; ⊘mid-May–mid-Sep). Primitive camping is allowed in some areas – the coolest place to sleep is on Portsmouth Island, where you can wander an abandoned 18th-century settlement and sleep on the beach. Bring plenty of bug spray – the mosquitoes are notorious. There are also rustic multiroom cabins (☑877-444-6777; www.nps.gov/calo; www.reserve.com; from $76 Jun-Aug, from $101 fall & spring) popular with fishermen. At press time the park service was moving forward with plans to work with one ferry operator; check the park website for the latest details.

The Bogue Banks, across the Sound from Morehead City via the Atlantic Beach Causeway, have several well-trafficked beach communities – try Atlantic Beach if you like the smell of coconut suntan oil and doughnuts. Pine Knoll Shores is home to the North Carolina Aquarium (www.ncaquariums.com; 1 Roosevelt Blvd; adult/child $8/6; ⊘9am-5pm; 🖈), with fast-moving river otters and a cool exhibit re-creating the local shipwreck of a U-352 German submarine. In Atlantic Beach, Fort Macon State Park (www.ncparks.gov; ⊘8am-9pm Jun-Aug, shorter hours Sep-May) FREE draws crowds to its reconstructed Civil War fort.

Wilmington

If you're driving down the coast, carve out a day or two for Wilmington. This seaside charmer may not have the name recognition of Charleston and Savannah, but eastern North Carolina's largest city has historic neighborhoods, azalea-choked gardens and cute cafes aplenty. All that plus reasonable hotel prices and a lack of crowds. At night the historic riverfront downtown becomes the playground for local college students, tourists and the occasional Hollywood type – there are so many movie studios here the town has earned the nickname 'Wilmywood.'

HOLLYWOOD EAST

North Carolina is one of the top states for TV and film production, and its scenery is known to millions.

Wilmington *Dawson's Creek* and *One Tree Hill* were both shot on sets at EUE/Screen Gem Studios. In 2012, stunts for *Iron Man III* were filmed over the Cape Fear River. Check www.visitnc.com for a list of *Iron Man III*–related sites or take a delightfully campy movie tour with Hollywood Location Walk (www.hollywoodnc.com; adult/child $13/11).

Asheville Pay homage to Katniss Everdeen with a stop by the visitor center (p345) where you can pick-up a list of *Hunger Games* film sites in the area. Henry River Mill Village, about an hour east of Asheville, doubled as District 12.

Blue Ridge Mountains and around The final 17 minutes of *The Last of the Mohicans* was filmed in Chimney Rock State Park, and Grandfather Mountain was a backdrop for *Forrest Gump*. The Cheoah Dam near the Nantahala Outdoor Center (p347) appears in *The Fugitive*.

WILMINGTON-AREA BEACHES

While riverfront Wilmington doesn't have its own beach, there are plenty of sandy stretches just a few minutes away. These are listed from north to south.

Topsail Beach A clean, white-sand beach, home to a sea-turtle rehab center.

Wrightsville Beach The closest to Wilmington, with plenty of fried-fish joints, sunglasses shops and summer crowds.

Carolina Beach Warm water and a boardwalk equal row upon row of beach umbrellas.

Kure Beach A popular fishing beach and home to the North Carolina Aquarium at Fort Fisher.

Southport Not a swimming beach, but a quaint town with antique stores and the famed **Provision Company** (www.provisioncompany.com) seafood shack.

Sights

Wilmington sits at the mouth of the Cape Fear River, about 8 miles from the beach. The historic **riverfront** is perhaps the city's most important sight, abounding with boutiques and boardwalks.

A **free trolley** (www.wavetransit.com) runs through the historic district from morning through evening.

★**Cape Fear Serpentarium** SNAKE ZOO
(☎910-762-1669; www.capefearserpentarium.com; 20 Orange St; admission $8; ⏰11am-5pm Mon-Fri, to 6pm Sat & Sun) Herpetologist Dean Ripa's museum is fun and informative – if you don't mind standing in a building slithering with venomous snakes, giant constrictors and big-teethed crocodiles. They're all behind glass but…sssssss. Just hope there's not an earthquake. One sign explains the effects of a bite from a bushmaster: 'It is better to just lie down under a tree and rest, for you will soon be dead.' Enjoy!

The Serpentarium may close on Monday and Tuesday in the off-season. Live feedings are held at 3pm on Saturdays and Sundays, but call ahead to confirm.

Battleship North Carolina HISTORIC SHIP
(www.battleshipnc.com; 1 Battleship Rd; adult/child $12/6; ⏰8am-5pm Sep-May, to 8pm Jun-Aug) Take a river taxi ($5 round-trip) or cross the Cape Fear Bridge to get here. Self-guided tours take you through the decks of this 45,000-ton megaship, which earned 15 battle stars in the Pacific theater in WWII before being decommissioned in 1947.

Airlie Gardens GARDEN
(www.airliegardens.org; 300 Airlie Rd; adult/child $8/3; ⏰9am-5pm, closed Mon winter) Wander beneath the wisteria, with 67 acres of bewitching formal flower beds, pine trees, lakes and trails. The Airlie Oak dates back to 1545.

Sleeping & Eating

There are numerous budget hotels on Market St, just north of downtown. Restaurants directly on the waterfront can be crowded and mediocre; head a block or two inland for the best eats and nightlife.

CW Worth House B&B $$
(☎910-762-8562; www.worthhouse.com; 412 S 3rd St; r $154-194; ❄@📶) Within a few blocks of downtown, this turreted 1893 home is dotted with antiques and Victorian touches, but still manages to feel kick-back and cozy. Breakfasts are top-notch.

Blockade Runner Beach Resort HOTEL $$$
(☎910-256-2251; www.blockade-runner.com; 275 Waynick Blvd, Wrightsville Beach; r from $204) It's not as glossy as most boutique hotels, with a little wear around the edges, but rooms have a spare, smart style, and the beach is just steps away. For the best sunset views, stay on the sound side.

Flaming Amy's Burrito Barn MEXICAN $
(☎910-799-2919; www.flamingamys.com; 4002 Oleander Dr; mains $5-9; ⏰11am-10pm) The burritos are big and tasty at Flaming Amy's, a scrappy barn filled with kitschy decor from Elvis to Route 66. Burritos include the Philly Phatboy, the Thai Mee Up and the jalapeno-and-pepper-loaded Flaming Amy itself. Everyone is here or on the way.

Manna NEW AMERICAN $$$
(☎910-763-5252; www.mannaavenue.com; 123 Princess St; ⏰5-10pm Tue-Thu, to 11pm Fri & Sat, to 9pm Sun) The menu changes daily at this stylish downtown dinner spot, where fresh and farm-to-table form the credo. Look for

intriguing, savory dishes like vanilla-seared tuna and sherry-brined duck breast. The carefully crafted cocktails are also a highlight.

Drinking & Nightlife

Front Street Brewery
PUB
(www.frontstreetbrewery.com; 9 N Front St; mains $7-15; ⊙11am-midnight) This two-story downtown pub is madly popular for its simple grub, like drippy burgers and crab cakes, and its microbrews. There are free beer tastings and brewery tours daily from 3pm to 5pm.

Information

Visitor Center (📞877-406-2356, 910-341-4030; www.wilmingtonandbeaches.com; 505 Nutt St; ⊙8:30am-5pm Mon-Fri, 9am-4pm Sat, 1-4pm Sun) The visitor center, an 1800s freight warehouse, has a walking-tour map.

The Triangle

The central Piedmont region is home to the cities of Raleigh, Durham and Chapel Hill, which form a rough triangle. Three top research universities – Duke, University of North Carolina and North Carolina State – are located here, as is the 7000-acre computer and biotech-office campus known as Research Triangle Park. Swarming with egghead computer programmers, bearded peace activists and hip young families, each town has its own unique personality, despite being only a few miles apart. In March, everyone – we mean *everyone* – goes crazy for college basketball.

Getting There & Around

Raleigh-Durham International Airport (RDU; 📞919-840-2123; www.rdu.com), a significant hub, is a 25-minute (15 mile) drive northwest of downtown Raleigh. **Greyhound** (📞919-834-8275; 314 W Jones St) serves Raleigh and Durham. The **Triangle Transit Authority** (📞919-549-9999; www.triangletransit.org; adult $2) operates buses linking Raleigh, Durham and Chapel Hill to each other and the airport. Rte 100 runs from downtown Raleigh to the airport and the Regional Transit Center in Durham.

Raleigh

Founded in 1792 specifically to serve as the state capital, Raleigh remains a rather staid government town with major sprawl issues. Still, the handsome downtown has some neat (and free!) museums and galleries, and the food and music scene is on the upswing.

Sights

★ North Carolina Museum of Art
MUSEUM
(www.ncartmuseum.org; 2110 Blue Ridge Rd; ⊙10am-5pm Tue-Thu, Sat & Sun, 10am-9pm Fri) FREE The light-filled glass-and-anodized-steel West Building won praise from architecture critics nationwide when it opened in 2010. The fine and wide-ranging collection, with everything from ancient Roman sculpture to Raphael to graffiti artists, is worthy as well, as is the winding outdoor sculpture trail. A few miles west of downtown.

North Carolina Museum of Natural Sciences
MUSEUM
(www.naturalsciences.org; 11 W Jones St; ⊙9am-5pm Mon-Wed, Fri & Sat, to 9pm Thu & 1st Fri of every month, noon-5pm Sun) FREE The museum was the state's most visited attraction in 2012, surpassing even the Biltmore. Thanks goes to the glossy **Nature Research Center**, a new wing that's fronted by a three-story multimedia globe. The research center spotlights scientists and their projects, and visitors can watch them at work. Skywalks lead to the main museum building, which holds habitat dioramas, taxidermy and the world's only dinosaur with a heart (it's fossilized).

There's also a scary exhibit about the Acrocanthosaurus dinosaur, a three-ton carnivore known as the Terror of the South. Its toothy skull is the stuff of nightmares.

North Carolina Museum of History
MUSEUM
(www.ncmuseumofhistory.org; 5 E Edenton St; ⊙9am-5pm Mon-Sat, noon-5pm Sun) FREE This engaging museum is low on tech but high on straightforward information. Artifacts include a 3000-year-old canoe, Civil War photos, and a 1960s sit-in lunch counter. There's a special exhibit about stock-car racing.

Raleigh State Capitol
HISTORIC BUILDING
(Edenton St) Check out the handsome 1840 state capitol, one of the best examples of Greek Revival architecture. It's open for visitors.

Sleeping & Eating

Downtown is pretty quiet on nights and weekends, except for the City Market area at E Martin and S Person Sts. Just to the northwest, the Glenwood South neighborhood hops with cafes, bars and clubs. You'll find plenty of moderately priced chain hotels around exit 10 off I-440 and off I-40 near the airport.

Umstead Hotel & Spa HOTEL $$$
(☑919-447-4000; www.theumstead.com; 100 Woodland Pond Dr; r/ste from $279/369; P❉☎⊜) Computer chips embedded in the silver room-service trays alert bellhops to whisk away leftovers post haste at this lavish boutique hotel. How's that for taking care of details? In a wooded suburban office park, the Umstead caters to visiting biotech CEOs with simple, sumptuous rooms and a Zen-like spa.

Raleigh Times PUB $
(14 E Hargett St; mains $10-12; ⊙11:30am-2am) Chase plates of BBQ nachos with pints of North Carolina craft brews at this popular downtown pub.

Poole's Downtown Diner MODERN AMERICAN $$
(www.ac-restaurants.com; 426 S McDowell St; mains $18-22; ⊙5:30pm-midnight) Chef Ashley Christensen sautés burgers in duck fat and bakes the world's most exquisitely creamy mac 'n' cheese at this Southern diner–meets–Parisian bistro, the toast of the local food scene. Don't miss the haute takes on classic American pies like banana cream. No reservations.

ℹ Information

Raleigh Visitor Information Center (☑919-834-5900; www.visitraleigh.com; 500 Fayetteville St; ⊙9am-5pm Mon-Sat) Hands out maps and other info.

Durham & Chapel Hill

Ten miles apart, these two university towns are twinned by their rival basketball teams and left-leaning attitudes. Chapel Hill is a pretty Southern college town whose culture revolves around the nearly 30,000 students at the prestigious University of North Carolina, founded in 1789 as the nation's first state university. A funky, forward-thinking place, Chapel Hill is renowned for its indie rock scene and loud 'n' proud hippie culture. Down the road, Durham is a once-gritty tobacco-and-railroad town whose fortunes collapsed in the 1960s and have only recently begun to revive. Though still fundamentally a working-class Southern city, the presence of top-ranking Duke University has long drawn progressive types to the area and Durham is now making its name as a hot spot for gourmands, artists and gays and lesbians.

The hip former mill town of Carrboro is just west of downtown Chapel Hill. Here,

the big lawn at Weaver Street Market (www.weaverstreetmarket.com) grocery co-op serves as an informal town square, with live music and free wi-fi.

In Durham, activity revolves around the renovated brick tobacco warehouses of the handsome downtown: check out Brightleaf Sq and the American Tobacco Campus for shopping and outdoor dining.

◉ Sights

★**Duke Lemur Center** ZOO
(☑919-489-3364; www.lemur.duke.edu; 3705 Erwin Rd, Durham; adult/child $10/7; 🐾) Perhaps the coolest, least-known sight in Durham, the Lemur Center has the largest collection of endangered prosimian primates outside their native Madagascar. Only a robot could fail to melt at the sight of these big-eyed fuzzy-wuzzies. Call well in advance for tours, held Monday to Saturday by appointment only.

Duke University UNIVERSITY, GALLERY
(www.duke.edu; Campus Dr, Durham) Endowed by the Duke family's cigarette fortune, the university has a Georgian-style East Campus and a neo-Gothic West Campus notable for its towering 1930s chapel. The Nasher Museum of Art (2001 Campus Dr; admission $5; ⊙10am-5pm Tue, Wed, Fri & Sat, to 9pm Thu, noon-5pm Sun) is also worth a gander, as is the heavenly 55-acre Sarah P Duke Gardens (420 Anderson St; ⊙8am to dusk) FREE. Metered parking at both sites is $2 per hour.

University of North Carolina UNIVERSITY
(www.unc.edu; Chapel Hill) America's oldest public university has a classic quad lined with flowering pear trees and gracious antebellum buildings. Don't miss the Old Well, said to give good luck to students who drink from it. Pick up a map of the site at the visitor center (☑919-962-1630; 250 E Franklin St; ⊙9am-5pm Mon-Fri) inside the Morehead Planetarium and Science Center.

Durham Bulls Athletic Park SPECTATOR SPORT
(www.dbulls.com; 409 Blackwell St, Durham; tickets $7-9; 🐾) Have a quintessentially American afternoon of beer and baseball watching the minor-league Durham Bulls (of 1988 Kevin Costner film *Bull Durham* fame), who play from April to September.

🛏 Sleeping

There are plenty of cheap chain motels off I-85 in north Durham.

Duke Tower HOTEL $

(☎866-385-3869, 919-687-4444; www.duke-tower.com; 807 W Trinity Ave, Durham; ste $88-98; P✻🛜🏊) For less than most local hotel rooms you can enjoy a condo with hardwood floors, full kitchen, and a tempur-pedic mattress. Premium suites have flatscreen TVs. Located in Durham's historic downtown tobacco-mill district.

Inn at Celebrity Dairy B&B $$

(☎919-742-5176; www.celebritydairy.com; 144 Celebrity Dairy Way, Siler City; r incl breakfast $100-165, ste $165; P✻🛜) Thirty miles west of Chapel Hill in rural Chatham County, this working goat dairy offers B&B accommodations in a Greek Revival farmhouse. Savor goat's-cheese omelets for breakfast then head out to the barn to pet the goat who provided the milk.

Carolina Inn HOTEL $$

(☎919-933-2001; www.carolinainn.com; 211 Pittsboro St, Chapel Hill; r from $179; P✻🛜) Even if you're not a Tar Heel, this lovely on-campus inn will win you over with hospitality and historic touches. The charm starts in the bright lobby then continues through the hallways, lined with photos of alums and championship teams. At press time the inn had finished renovating some of the guestrooms, adding eco-friendly features.

🍴 Eating

Durham was named 'The South's Tastiest Town' by *Southern Living* in 2013, and for good reason. The area abounds with top-notch restaurants. Downtown Durham has scads of great eateries, coffee shops and bars. Most of Chapel Hill's better restaurants are found along Franklin St.

Neal's Deli BREAKFAST, DELI $

(www.nealsdeli.com; 100 E Main St, Carrboro; breakfast $3-6, lunch $5-9; ⊙7:30am-7pm Tue-Fri, 8am-4pm Sat & Sun) Before starting your day, chow down on a delicious buttermilk breakfast biscuit at this tiny deli in downtown Carrboro. The egg, cheese and bacon is some kind of good. For lunch, Neal's serves sandwiches and subs, from chicken salad to pastrami to a three-cheese pimiento with a splash of bourbon.

Toast SANDWICHES $

(www.toast-fivepoints.com; 345 W Main St, Durham; sandwiches $7; ⊙11am-8pm Mon-Fri, to 3pm Sat) Families, couples, solos and the downtown lunch crowd – everybody loves this tiny Italian sandwich shop, one of the eateries at the forefront of downtown Durham's revitalization. Order your panini at the counter then grab a table by the window – if you can – for people watching.

Guglhupf Bakery & Cafe BAKERY, CAFE $$

(www.guglhupf.com; 2706 Durham-Chapel Hill Blvd, Durham; lunch $8-11, dinner $15-24; ⊙bakery 7am-5pm Tue-Sat, 8:30am-2pm Sun, cafe 8am-4:30pm Tue-Sat, 9am-3pm Sun) Mornings, a tart cherry Danish and a cappuccino are the way to go at this superior German-style bakery and cafe. In the afternoon, try a Westphalian ham sandwich and a pilsner on the sunny patio.

★ Lantern ASIAN $$$

(☎919-969-8846; www.lanternrestaurant.com; 423 W Franklin St, Chapel Hill; mains $23-32; ⊙5:30-10pm Mon-Sat) If you only have time for one dinner in the Triangle, dine here. Tea-smoked chicken and roll-your-own bento boxes have earned this modern Asian spot a shower of James Beard Awards. For special occasions, the stylish front rooms are just right, but for a casual more convivial atmosphere try the bar and lounge in back. And the eat-the-shell salt and pepper shrimp? Excellent.

Watts Grocery NEW SOUTHERN $$$

(☎919-416-5040; www.wattsgrocery.com; 1116 Broad St, Durham; lunch $8-13, dinner $18-23, brunch $7-13; ⊙11am-2:30pm Wed-Sun, 5:30-10pm Tue-Sun) Durham's hippest 'farm-to-table' joint serves upscale takes on local bounty in an airy renovated storefront. Sausage- and avocado-laden bowls of grits might be the best weekend brunch in town.

🍷 Drinking & Entertainment

Chapel Hill has an excellent music scene, with shows nearly every night of the week. For entertainment listings, pick up the free weekly *Independent* (www.indyweek.com).

★ Cocoa Cinnamon COFFEE SHOP

(www.cocoacinnamon.com; 420 W Geer St, Durham; ⊙7:30am-10pm Mon-Thu, 7:30am-midnight Fri & Sat, 9am-9pm Sun) If someone tells you that you *must* order a hot chocolate at Cocoa Cinnamon, ask them to be more specific. This new, talk-of-the town coffee shop offers several cocoas, and newbies may be paralyzed by the plethora of chocolatey awesomeness. Come here to enjoy cocoa, teas, single-source coffee and the energetic vibe.

Fullsteam Brewery   BREWPUB
(www.fullsteam.ag; 726 Rigsbee Ave, Durham; ☺4pm-midnight Mon-Thu, to 2am Fri, noon-2am Sat, to midnight Sun) Calling itself a 'plow-to-pint' brewery, Fullsteam has gained national attention for pushing the boundaries of beer with wild, super-Southern concoctions like sweet-potato lager and persimmon ale. Mixed-age crowds.

Top of the Hill   PUB
(www.thetopofthehill.com; 100 E Franklin St, Chapel Hill; ☺11am-2am) The 3rd-story patio of this downtown restaurant and microbrewery is *the* place for the Chapel Hill preppy set to see and be seen after football games.

Cat's Cradle   MUSIC
(☎919-967-9053; www.catscradle.com; 300 E Main St, Carrboro) Everyone from Nirvana to Arcade Fire has played the Cradle, hosting the cream of the indie-music world for three decades. Most shows are all-ages.

ℹ Information

Chapel Hill Visitor Center (☎919-968-2060; www.visitchapelhill.org; 501 W Franklin St, Chapel Hill; ☺8:30am-5pm Mon-Fri, 10am-2pm Sat)

Durham Visitor Center (☎800-446-8604, 919-687-0288; www.durham-nc.com; 101 E Morgan St, Durham; ☺8:30am-5pm Mon-Fri, 10am-2pm Sat) The visitor center has information and maps.

Charlotte

The largest city in North Carolina and the biggest US banking center after New York, Charlotte has the sprawling, sometimes faceless look of many New South suburban megalopolises. But although the Queen City, as it's known, is primarily a business town, it's got a few good museums, stately old neighborhoods and lots of fine food.

Busy Tryon St cuts through skyscraper-filled 'uptown' Charlotte, home to banks, hotels, museums and restaurants. The renovated textile mills of the NoDa neighborhood (named for its location on N Davidson St) and the funky mix of boutiques and restaurants in the Plaza–Midwood area, just northeast of uptown, have a hipper vibe.

THE BARBECUE TRAIL

North Carolina pulled-pork BBQ is practically a religion in these parts, and the rivalry between Eastern Style (with a thin vinegar sauce) and Western Style (with a sweeter, tomato-based sauce) occasionally comes to blows. The North Carolina Barbecue Society has an interactive Barbecue Trail Map (www.ncbbqsociety.com), directing pilgrims to the best spots. So try both styles, then take sides (hint: Eastern style is better. Just kidding! Sort of.).

◉ Sights & Activities

Billy Graham Library   RELIGIOUS
(www.billygrahamlibrary.org; 4330 Westmont Dr; ☺9:30am-5pm Mon-Sat) **FREE** This multimedia 'library' is a tribute to the life of superstar evangelist and 'pastor to the presidents' Billy Graham, a Charlotte native. The 90-minute tour starts with a gospel-preaching animatronic cow and ends with a paper questionnaire asking whether or not you've been moved to accept Christ today.

Levine Museum of the New South   MUSEUM
(www.museumofthenewsouth.org; 200 E 7th St; adult/child $8/5; ☺10am-5pm Mon-Sat, noon-5pm Sun) This slick museum has an informative permanent exhibit on post–Civil War Southern history and culture, from sharecropping to sit-ins.

★**US National Whitewater Center**   ADVENTURE SPORTS
(www.usnwc.org; 5000 Whitewater Center Pkwy; all-sport day pass adult/child $54/44, individual activities $20-25, 3hr canopy tour $89; ☺dawn-dusk) A beyond-awesome hybrid of nature center and waterpark, this 400-acre facility is home to the largest artificial white-water river in the world, whose rapids serve as training grounds for Olympic canoe and kayak teams. Paddle it as part of a guided rafting trip, or try one of the center's other adventurous activities: ziplines, an outdoor rock-climbing wall, ropes courses, paddleboarding, aerial canopy tours of the surrounding forest, miles of hiking and mountain-biking trails. Parking is $5.

Charlotte Motor Speedway   SPEEDWAY
(www.charlottemotorspeedway.com; tours $12; ☺tours 9:30am-3:30pm Mon-Sat, 1:30-3:30pm Sun) Nascar races, a homegrown Southeastern

obsession, are held at the visible-from-outer-space speedway, 12 miles northeast of town. For the ultimate thrill/near-death experience, ride shotgun at up to 160 miles per hour in a real stock car with the Richard Petty Driving Experience (☑800-237-3889; www.drivepetty.com; rides from $59).

🛏 Sleeping & Eating

Many uptown hotels cater to business travelers, so rates are often lower on weekends. Cheaper chains cluster off I-85 and I-77. Uptown eating and drinking options cater to the preppy banker set; you'll see more tattoos at the laid-back pubs and bistros of NoDa.

Duke Mansion   B&B $$
(☑704-714-4400; www.dukemansion.com; 400 Hermitage Rd; r $99-219, ste $279; P☀@☎) Tucked away in an oak-shaded residential neighborhood, this stately white-columned inn was the residence of 19th-century tobacco millionaire James B Duke and still retains the quiet, discreet feel of a posh private home. Most rooms have high ceilings and their own screened-in sleeping porches.

Hyatt House   HOTEL $$
(☑704-373-9700; www.charlottecentercity.house. hyatt.com; 435 E Trade St; r from $239; P☀@☎) Formerly the Hotel Sierra, this chic hotel has a space-agey lime-and-charcoal color scheme and a gleaming lobby. Parking is $22 per night.

★ Price's Chicken Coop   SOUTHERN $
(www.priceschickencoop.com; 1614 Camden Rd; mains $2-11; ⊙10am-6pm Tue-Sat) A Charlotte institution, scruffy Price's regularly makes 'Best Fried Chicken in America' lists. Line up to order your 'dark quarter' or 'white half' from the army of white-jacketed cooks, then take your bounty outside – there's no seating. Cash only.

Mac's Speed Shop   SOUTHERN $$
(☑704-522-6227; www.macspeedshop.com; 2511 South Blvd; mains $8-16; ⊙11am-midnight Sun-Tue, 11am-2am Wed-Sat) Rev it up for Mac's Speed Shop, a BBQ joint in an old service station that also dishes out local brews and live music. Sit inside or outside on the patio, where you might see a fine array of motorcycles.

Soul Gastrolounge Tapas   SUSHI $$
(☑704-348-1848; www.soulgastrolounge.com; 1500 Central Ave; mains $5-18; ⊙5pm-2am Mon-Sat, 11am-3pm & 5pm-2am Sun) In Plaza Midtown, this sultry speakeasy serves a glo-bally inspired selection of small plates, from spanakopita to Korean BBQ, a Cuban panini and sushi rolls.

❶ Information

Check out the alt-weekly *Creative Loafing* (charlotte.creativeloafing.com) for entertainment listings.

Public Library (College St) The public library has 90 terminals with free internet.

Visitor Center (☑800-231-4636, 704-331-2700; www.charlottesgotalot.com; 330 S Tryon St; ⊙8:30am-5pm Mon-Fri, 9am-3pm Sat) The downtown visitor center publishes maps and a visitors' guide.

❶ Getting There & Around

Charlotte Douglas International Airport (CLT; ☑704-359-4027; www.charmeck.org/departments/airport; 5501 Josh Birmingham Pkwy) is a US Airways hub with direct flights from Europe and the UK. Both the **Greyhound station** (601 W Trade St) and **Amtrak** (1914 N Tryon St) are handy to Uptown. **Charlotte Area Transit** (www.charmeck.org; 310 E Trade St) runs local bus and light-rail services.

North Carolina Mountains

These ancient mountains have drawn seekers for generations. Cherokee came here to hunt, followed by 18th-century Scots-Irish immigrants looking for a better life. Lofty towns like Blowing Rock drew the sickly, who came for the fresh air. Today, scenic drives, leafy trails and roaring rivers draw outdoor adventurers.

The Appalachians in the western part of the state include the Great Smoky, Blue Ridge, Pisgah and Black Mountain subranges. Carpeted in blue-green hemlock, pine and oak trees, these cool hills are home to cougars, deer, black bears, wild turkeys and great horned owls. Hiking, camping, climbing and rafting adventures abound, and there's another jaw-dropping photo opportunity around every bend.

High Country

The northwestern corner of the state is known as 'High Country.' Its main towns are Boone, Blowing Rock and Banner Elk, all short drives from the Blue Ridge Pkwy. Boone is a lively college town, home to Appalachian State University (ASU). Blowing Rock and Banner Elk are quaint tourist centers near the winter ski areas.

⊙ Sights & Activities

Hwy 321 from Blowing Rock to Boone is studded with gem-panning mines and other tourist traps. In Boone, check out the shops on King St and keep an eye out for the bronze statue of local bluegrass legend Doc Watson. He's strumming his guitar on the corner of King and Depot Sts.

Tweetsie Railroad AMUSEMENT PARK
(☑877-893-3874; www.tweetsie.com; 300 Tweetsie Railroad Ln; adult/child $37/23; ⊙9am-6pm daily Jun-Aug, Fri-Sun mid-Apr–May, Sep & Oct; ➍) A much-loved Wild West–themed amusement park. The highlight is a 1917 coal-fired steam train that chugs past marauding Indians and heroic cowboys.

Grandfather Mountain HIKING
(☑828-733-4337; www.grandfather.com; Blue Ridge Pkwy Mile 305; adult/child 4-12yr $18/8; ⊙8am-7pm Jun-Aug) Tiptoe across a vertigo-inducing mile-high suspension bridge then lose the crowds on one of 11 hiking trails, the most difficult of which include steep hands-and-knees scrambles. In 2008 the family that owns the mountain sold the backcountry to the state park system, which opened Grandfather Mountain State Park (www.ncparks.gov) the following year.

River and Earth Adventures OUTDOORS
(☑828-963-5491; www.raftcavehike.com; 1655 Hwy 105; half-/full-day rafting from $60/100; ➍) Offers everything from family-friendly caving trips to rafting Class V rapids at Watauga Gorge. Eco-conscious guides even pack organic lunches. Canoe and kayak rentals.

🛏 Sleeping & Eating

Chain motels abound in Boone. You'll find private campgrounds and B&Bs scattered throughout the hills.

Mast Farm Inn B&B $$
(☑828-963-5857; www.themastfarminn.com; 2543 Broadstone Rd, Vale Crucis; r/cottages incl breakfast from $209/349; ♇❋❀) In the beautiful hamlet of Valle Crucis, this restored farmhouse defines rustic chic with worn hardwood floors, claw-foot tubs and handmade toffees on your bedside table. The upscale mountain cuisine at the inn's restaurant, Simplicity, is worth a trip in itself.

Six Pence Pub PUB $$
(www.sixpencepub.com; 1121 Main St, Blowing Rock; mains $9-18; ⊙restaurant 11:30am-10:30pm Sun-Thu, to midnight Fri & Sat, bar to 2am) The bartenders keep a sharp but friendly eye on things at this lively British pub, where the shepherd's pie comes neat, not messy.

Hob Nob Farm Cafe CAFE $$
(www.hobnobfarmcafe.com; 506 West King St, Boone; breakfast & lunch $3-12, dinner $8-15; ⊙10am-10pm Wed-Sun; ➋) Gobble up avocado-tempeh melts, Thai curry bowls and sloppy burgers made from local beef at a wildly painted cottage near ASU. Brunch is served until 5pm.

ℹ Information

Visitor Center (☑800-438-7500, 828-264-1299; www.highcountryhost.com; 1700 Blowing Rock Rd; ⊙9am-5pm Mon-Sat, to 3pm Sun) The High Country visitor center has info on accommodations and outdoors outfitters.

Asheville

With its homegrown microbreweries, decadent chocolate shops and stylish New Southern eateries, Asheville is one of the trendiest small cities in the East. Glossy magazines swoon for the place. But don't be put off by the hipsters and the flash. At heart, Asheville is still an overgrown mountain town, and it holds tight to its traditional roots. Just look around. There's a busker fiddling a high lonesome tune on Biltmore Ave and hikers chowing down after climbing Mt Pisgah. Cars swoop on and off the Blue Ridge Parkway, which swings around the city. A huge artist population and a visible contingent of hardcore hippies also keep things real.

⊙ Sights

Downtown is compact and easy to negotiate on foot. The art-deco buildings remain much as they were in 1930. The shopping's fantastic, with everything from hippie-dippy candle shops to vintage shops to high-end local art. West Asheville is an up-and-coming area, still gritty but very cool.

★ Biltmore Estate HOUSE, GARDENS
(☑800-543-2961; www.biltmore.com; 1 Approach Rd; adult/child under 16yr from $59/30; ⊙house 9am-4:30pm) The country's largest private home, and Asheville's number-one tourist attraction, the Biltmore was built in 1895 for shipping and railroad heir George Washington Vanderbilt II. He modeled it after the grand chateaux he'd seen on his various European jaunts. Viewing the estate and its 250 acres of gorgeously manicured grounds and gardens takes several hours.

THE SOUTH NORTH CAROLINA MOUNTAINS

Tours of the house are self-guided. To get the most out of your visit, pay an extra $10 for the audio tour. Also available are behind-the-scenes guided tours ($17) covering the architecture, the family or the servants.

Beyond the house, there are numerous cafes, a gift shop the size of a small supermarket, a hoity-toity hotel, and an award-winning winery that offers free tastings. In Antler Village, the new Biltmore Legacy exhibit, 'The Vanderbilts at Home and Abroad,' provides a more personal look at the family.

Chimney Rock Park   PARK

(www.chimneyrockpark.com; Hwy 64/74A; adult/child $15/7; ⊙ 8:30am-5:30pm late Mar-Oct, hours vary Nov-Feb) The American flag flaps in the breeze atop this popular park's namesake 315ft granite monolith. An elevator takes visitors up to the chimney, but the real draw is the exciting hike around the cliffs to a 404ft waterfall. The park, once privately owned, is now part of the state park system; access to the rock is still managed commercially. The park is a 20-mile drive southeast of Asheville.

Thomas Wolfe Memorial   HOUSE

(www.wolfememorial.com; 52 N Market St; museum free, house tour $5; ⊙ 9am-5pm Tue-Sat) **FREE** This downtown memorial, with a small museum and a separate house tour, honors *Look Homeward Angel* author Thomas Wolfe. The author grew up in Asheville, which was the inspiration for the novel's setting.

☞ Tours

Brews Cruise   MICROBREWERIES

(☎ 828-545-5181; www.ashevillebrewscruise.com; per person $50-55) Tour several of Asheville's microbreweries on the Brews Cruise.

Lazoom Comedy Tour   COMEDY

(☎ 828-225-6932; www.lazoomtours.com; per person $21-24) For a hysterically historical tour of the city, hop on the purple bus – and bring your own booze.

🛏 Sleeping

The **Asheville Bed & Breakfast Association** (☎ 877-262-6867; www.ashevillebba.com) handles bookings for numerous area B&Bs, from gingerbread cottages to alpine cabins.

Sweet Peas   HOSTEL $

(☎ 828-285-8488; www.sweetpeashostel.com; 23 Rankin Ave; dm/pod/r $28/35/60; P ❋ @ 🛜) This spic-and-span hostel gleams with IKEA-like style, with shipshape steel bunk beds and blond wood sleeping 'pods.' The loftlike space is very open and can be noisy (a downstairs pub adds to the ruckus) – what you lose in privacy and quiet, you gain in style, cleanliness, sociability and an unbeatable downtown location.

Campfire Lodgings   CAMPGROUND $$

(☎ 828-658-8012; www.campfirelodgings.com; 116 Appalachian Village Rd; tent/RV sites $38/45, yurts from $115, cabins $160; P ❋ 🛜) All yurts should have flatscreen TVs, don't you think? Sleep like the world's most stylish Mongolian nomad in one of these furnished multiroom tents, on the side of a wooded hill. Cabins and tent sites are also available. Wi-fi access at RV sites, which have stunning valley views.

Grove Park Inn Resort & Spa   RESORT $$$

(☎ 828-252-2711; www.groveparkinn.com; 290 Macon Ave; r from $269; P ❋ @ 🛜 ⊛ 🏊) This titanic arts-and-crafts-style stone lodge, which celebrates its centennial in 2013, has a hale-and-hearty look that sets the mood for adventure. But no worries all you modern mavens, the well-appointed rooms come with 21st-century amenities. The spa is an underground grotto with stone pools and an indoor waterfall. The Nantahala Outdoor Center (p347) just opened a 'basecamp' here, certified by Leadership in Energy and Environmental Design (LEED).

Aloft Asheville   HOTEL $$$

(☎ 828-232-2838; www.aloftasheville.com; 51 Biltmore Ave; r from $242; P ❋ @ 🛜 ⊛ 🏊) At first glance this new downtown hotel looks like the 7th ring of hipster: giant chalkboard in the lobby, groovy young staff, a neon lounge with bright retro chairs. The only thing missing is a wool-cap-wearing bearded guy drinking a hoppy microwbr– oh, wait, over there. We jest. Once settled, you'll find the staff knowledgeable, the rooms spacious, and the vibe convivial. The hotel is close to downtown hotspots, including the Orange Peel (p345).

✗ Eating

Asheville is a great foodie town – many visitors come here just to eat!

★ 12 Bones   BARBECUE $

(www.12bones.com; 5 Riverside Dr; dishes $4-20; ⊙ 11am-4pm Mon-Fri) Sooooiiieeee, this place is good. The slow-cooked meats are smoky tender, and the sides, from the jalapeño cheese grits to the buttery green beans, will have you kissing your mama and blessing the day you were born. Order at the counter, grab a picnic table, die happy.

Sunny Point Cafe
CAFE $

(www.sunnypointcafe.com; 626 Haywood Rd; breakfast & lunch $8-12, dinner $8-17; ☻8:30am-2:30pm Sun & Mon, to 9pm Tue-Sat) This bright West Asheville spot is beloved for its hearty, homemade fare. The huevos rancheros, with feta cheese and chorizo sausage, is deservedly popular. The cafe embraces the organic and fresh, and even has its own garden. The biscuits are divine.

French Broad Chocolate Lounge
BAKERY, DESSERTS $

(www.frenchbroadchocolates.com; 10 S Lexington; snacks $2-6; ☻11am-11pm Sun-Thu, to midnight Fri & Sat) Small-batch organic chocolates, a sippable 'liquid truffle,' pints of local stout served á la mode with vanilla ice cream... hey, where'd you go?

★ Admiral
MODERN AMERICAN $$

(☑828-252-2541; www.theadmiralnc.com; 400 Haywood Rd; small plates $10-14, large plates $22-30; ☻5-10pm) This concrete bunker next to a car junkyard looks divey on the outside, but inside? That's where the magic happens. This low-key West Asheville spot is one of the state's finest New American restaurants serving wildly creative dishes – flat-iron steak with soy-sauce mashed potatoes and Vietnamese slaw – that taste divine. No reservation? Grab a seat at the bar.

Tupelo Honey
NEW SOUTHERN $$

(☑828-255-4863; www.tupelohoneycafe.com; 12 College St; breakfast $7-15, lunch & dinner $10-28; ☻9am-10pm) A longtime favorite for New Southern fare like shrimp and grits with goat cheese. Breakfasts are superb but no matter the meal, say yes to the biscuit. And add a drop of honey.

🍷 Drinking & Entertainment

Downtown Asheville has a range of bars and cafes, from frat-boy beer halls to hookah-n-sprout hippie holes-in-the-wall. West Asheville has a more laid-back townie vibe. For more about the region's 20-plus microbreweries and beer pubs, visit www.asheville-aletrail.com.

Wicked Weed
MICROBREWERY

(www.wickedweedbrewing.com; 91 Biltmore Ave) Henry VIII called hops 'a wicked and pernicious weed' that ruined the taste of beer. His subjects kept quaffing it anyway – just like the hordes at this new microbrewery, which overflows with hoppy brews. In a former gas station with a wide front patio, it's a big and breezy spot to chill.

Thirsty Monk
BREW PUB

(www.monkpub.com; 95 Patton Ave; ☻4pm-midnight Mon-Thu, noon-2am Fri & Sat, noon-10pm Sun) Try a variety of North Carolina craft beers and plenty of Belgian ales at this scruffy but lovable beer bar.

Jack of the Wood
PUB

(www.jackofthewood.com; 95 Patton Ave) This Celtic pub is a good place to bond with local 20- and 30-somethings over a bottle of organic ale.

Asheville Pizza & Brewing Company
BREWERY, CINEMA

(www.ashevillebrewing.com; 675 Merrimon Ave; movies $3; ☻movies 1pm, 4pm, 7pm & 10pm) Catch a flick at the small theater inside this one-of-a-kind spot.

Orange Peel
LIVE MUSIC

(www.theorangepeel.net; 101 Biltmore Ave; tickets $15-33) For live music, try this warehouse-sized place for big-name indie and punk.

Grey Eagle
LIVE MUSIC

(www.thegreyeagle.com; 185 Clingman Ave; tickets $5-20) For bluegrass and jazz.

ℹ️ Information

Public Library (67 Haywood Ave) Has computers with free internet.

Visitor Center (☑828-258-6129; www.exploreasheville.com; 36 Montford Ave; ☻9am-5:30pm Mon-Fri, 9am-5pm Sat & Sun) The shiny new visitor center is at I-240 exit 4C.

ℹ️ Getting There & Around

Asheville Transit (www.ashevilletransit.com; tickets $1) has 16 local bus routes, with most running from 6:30am to about 8pm Monday to Saturday. Twenty minutes south of town, **Asheville Regional Airport** (AVL; ☑828-684-2226; www.flyavl.com) has a handful of non-stop flights, including to/from Atlanta, Charlotte, Chicago and New York. **Greyhound** (2 Tunnel Rd) is just northeast of downtown.

Great Smoky Mountains National Park

The Great Smoky Mountains National Park is a moody, magical place. Covering 521,000-acres, it is one of the world's most diverse areas. Landscapes range from deep,

SMOKY MOUNTAINS DAY HIKES

These are a few of our favorite short hikes in the North Carolina side of the park.

Big Creek Trail Hike an easy 2 miles to Mouse Creek Falls or go another 3 miles to a backcountry campground; the trailhead's near I-40 on the park's northeastern edge.

Boogerman Trail Moderate 7-mile loop passing old farmsteads; accessible via Cove Creek Rd.

Chasteen Creek Falls From Smokemont campground, this 4-mile round-trip passes a small waterfall.

Shuckstack Tower Starting at massive Fontana Dam, climb 3.5 miles for killer views from an old fire tower.

dim spruce forest to sunny meadows carpeted with daisies and Queen Anne's lace to wide, coffee-brown rivers. There's ample hiking and camping, and opportunities for horseback riding, bike rental and fly-fishing. Unfortunately, with more than 9.6 million annual visitors – which is the highest of any national park in the US – the place can get annoyingly crowded. The North Carolina side has less traffic than the Tennessee side, however, so even at the height of summer tourist season you'll still have room to roam (p380).

Newfound Gap Rd/Hwy 441 is the only thoroughfare that crosses Great Smoky Mountains National Park, winding through the mountains from Gatlinburg, TN, to the town of Cherokee and the busy Oconaluftee Visitor Center (☑ general information 865-436-1200, visitor center 865-436-1200; www.nps.gov/grsm; Hwy 441; ◷ 8am-7pm Jun-Aug, hours vary Sep-May) FREE, in the southeast. Pick up your backcountry camping permits here. The Oconaluftee River Trail, one of only two in the park that allows leashed pets, leaves from the visitor center and follows the river for 1.5 miles.

The on-site Mountain Farm Museum (☑ 423-436-1200; www.nps.gov/grsm; ◷ dawn-dusk) is a restored 19th-century farmstead, complete with barn, blacksmith shop and smokehouse (with real pig heads!), assembled from original buildings from different parts of the park. Just north is the 1886 Min-

gus Mill (self-guided tours free; ◷ 9am-5pm daily mid-Mar–mid-Nov, plus Thanksgiving weekend 9am-5pm), a turbine-powered mill that still grinds wheat and corn much as it always has. A few miles away the Smokemont Campground (www.nps.gov/grsm; tent & RV sites $20) is the only North Carolina campground open year-round.

To the east, remote Cataloochee Valley has several historic buildings to wander through and is a prime location for elk and black bears.

Around Great Smoky Mountains National Park

The state's westernmost tip is blanketed in parkland and sprinkled with tiny mountain towns. The area has a rich but sad Native American history – many of the original Cherokee inhabitants were forced off their lands during the 1830s and marched to Oklahoma on the Trail of Tears. Descendants of those who escaped are known as the Eastern Band of the Cherokee, about 12,000 of whom still live on the 56,000-acre Qualla Boundary territory at the edge of Great Smoky Mountains National Park.

The town of Cherokee anchors the Qualla Boundary with ersatz Native American souvenir shops, fast-food joints and Harrah's Cherokee Casino (www.harrahs cherokee.com; 777 Casino Dr), which has an impressive water and video display, the Rotunda, in the lobby. The best sight is the modern and engaging Museum of the Cherokee Indian (☑ 828-497-3481; www.cherokeemuseum. org; 589 Tsali Blvd/Hwy 441, at Drama Rd; adult/child 6-12yr $10/6; ◷ 9am-5pm daily, to 7pm Mon-Sat Jun-Aug), with an informative exhibit about the Trail of Tears.

South of Cherokee, the contiguous Pisgah and Nantahala National Forests have more than a million acres of dense hardwood trees, windswept mountain balds and some of the country's best white water. Both contain portions of the Appalachian Trail. Pisgah National Forest highlights include the bubbling baths in the village of Hot Springs (www.hotspringsnc.org), the natural waterslide at Sliding Rock, and the 3.2-mile round-trip hike to the summit of 5721ft Mt Pisgah, which has a view of Cold Mountain of book and movie fame. Nantahala National Forest has several recreational lakes and dozens of roaring waterfalls.

Just north of Nantahala is quaint Bryson City, an ideal jumping-off point for outdoor adventures. It's home to the huge and highly recommended Nantahala Outdoor Center (NOC; ☑828-488-2176, 888-905-7238; www.noc.com; 13077 Hwy 19/74; kayak/canoe rental per day $30/50, guided trips $30-189), which specializes in wet and wild rafting trips down the Nantahala, French Broad, Pigeon and Ocoee Rivers. There's also a zipline and an alpine tower. It even has its own lodge and restaurant. The Appalachian Trail rolls across the property too. From the Bryson City depot, the Great Smoky Mountains Railroad (☑800-872-4681; www.gsmr.com; 226 Everett St, Bryson City; Nantahala Gorge trip adult/child 2-12yr from $55/31; ⊗Mar-Dec) runs scenic train excursions through the dramatic river valley. For lodging and dining try the lofty Fryemont Inn (☑828-488-2159; www.fryemontinn.com; 245 Fryemont St; lodge/ste/cabins from $110/$180/245; nonguests breakfast $6-9, dinner $20-29 ; ⊗restaurant 8am-10am & 6-8pm Sun-Tue, 6-9pm Fri & Sat mid-Apr–late Nov; P✷), a family-owned lodge and restaurant. The bark-covered inn has a front-porch view of the Smokies and downtown Bryson City.

SOUTH CAROLINA

The air is hotter, the accents thicker and the traditions more dear in South Carolina, where the Deep South begins. From its Revolutionary War patriots to its 1860s secessionist government to its current crop of feisty legislators, the Palmetto State has never shied away from a fight.

From the silvery sands of the Atlantic Coast, the state climbs westward from the Coastal Plain across the Piedmont and up into the Blue Ridge Mountains. Most travelers stick to the coast, with its splendid antebellum cities and palm-tree-studded beaches. But the interior has a wealth of sleepy old towns, wild and undeveloped state parks and spooky black-water swamps. Along the sea islands you hear the sweet songs of the Gullah, a culture and language created by former slaves who held onto many West African traditions through the ravages of time.

From genteel, gardenia-scented Charleston to bright, tacky Myrtle Beach, South Carolina is always an engaging destination.

History

More than 28 separate tribes of Native Americans have lived in what is now South Carolina, many of them Cherokee who were later forcibly removed during the Trail of Tears era.

The English founded the Carolina colony in 1670, with settlers pouring in from the royal outpost of Barbados, giving the port city known as Charles Towne a Caribbean flavor. West African slaves were brought over to turn the thick coastal swamps into rice paddies and by the mid-1700s the area was deeply divided between the slave-owning aristocrats of the Lowcountry and the poor Scots-Irish and German farmers of the rural backcountry.

South Carolina was the first state to secede from the Union, and the first battle of the Civil War occurred at Fort Sumter in Charleston Harbor. The end of the war left much of the state in ruins.

South Carolina traded in cotton and textiles for most of the 20th century. It remains a relatively poor agricultural state, though with a thriving coastal tourism business.

In recent years the Palmetto State has garnered headlines because of its politicians, from Nikki Haley, the state's first woman and first Indian American governor, to disgraced ex-governor and now Congressman, Mark Sanford. While governor, Sanford famously claimed that he was hiking the

THE SOUTH SOUTH CAROLINA

GULLAH CULTURE

African slaves were transported from the region known as the Rice Coast (Sierra Leone, Senegal, the Gambia and Angola) to a landscape of remote islands that was shockingly similar – swampy coastlines, tropical vegetation and hot, humid summers.

These new African Americans were able to retain many of their homeland traditions, even after the fall of slavery and well into the 20th century. The resulting Gullah (also known as Geechee) culture has its own language, an English-based Creole with many African words and sentence structures, and many traditions, including fantastic storytelling, art, music and crafts. The Gullah culture is celebrated annually with the energetic Gullah Festival (www.gullahfestival.org; ⊗late May) in Beaufort. For a Gullah-style meal, stop in Mt Pleasant for the lunch buffet at Gullah Cuisine (www.gullahcuisine.net; 1717 Hwy 17 N; buffet adult/child $8.25/4.50).

SOUTH CAROLINA FACTS

Nickname Palmetto State

Population 4.7 million

Area 30,109 sq miles

Capital city Columbia (population 130,500)

Other city Charleston (122,700)

Sales tax 6%, plus up to 10% extra tax on accommodations

Birthplace of Jazzman Dizzy Gillespie (1917–93), political activist Jesse Jackson (b 1941), boxer Joe Frazier (b 1944), *Wheel of Fortune* hostess Vanna White (b 1957)

Home of The first US public library (1698), museum (1773) and steam railroad (1833)

Politics Leans Republican

Famous for Firing the first shot of the Civil War, from Charleston's Fort Sumter

State dance The shag

Driving distances Columbia to Charleston 115 miles, Charleston to Myrtle Beach 97 miles

Appalachian Trail when he was in fact visiting his Argentinian honey.

ℹ Information

South Carolina Department of Parks, Recreation & Tourism (☏803-734-1700; www.discoversouthcarolina.com; 1205 Pendleton St, room 505; ☎) Sends out the state's official vacation guide. The state's nine highway welcome centers offer wi-fi. Ask inside for password.

South Carolina State Parks (☏camping reservations 866-345-7275, 803-734-0156; www.southcarolinaparks.com) The helpful website lists activities, hiking trails and allows online reservations for campsites (prices vary).

Charleston

This lovely city will embrace you with the warmth and hospitality of an old and dear friend – who died in the 1700s. We jest, but the cannons, cemeteries and carriage rides do conjure an earlier era. And that historic romanticism, along with the food and Southern graciousness, is what makes Charleston one of the world's favorite cities and

one of the most popular tourist destinations in the South. In fact, Charleston was named the Best City to Visit in The World by readers of *Condé Nast Traveler* in 2012.

How best to enjoy its charms? Charleston is a city for savoring – stroll past the historic buildings, admire the antebellum architecture, stop to smell the blooming jasmine and enjoy long dinners on the verandah. It's also a place for romance, everywhere you turn another blushing bride is standing on the steps of yet another charming church.

In the high season the scent of gardenia and honeysuckle mixes with the tang of horse from the aforementioned carriage tours that clip-clop down the cobblestones. In winter the weather is milder and the crowds thinner, making Charleston a great bet for off-season travel.

History

Well before the Revolutionary War, Charles Towne (named for Charles II) was one of the busiest ports on the eastern seaboard, the center of a prosperous rice-growing and trading colony. With influences from the West Indies and Africa, France and other European countries, it became a cosmopolitan city, often compared to New Orleans.

The first shots of the Civil War rang out at Fort Sumter, in Charleston's harbor. After the war, as the labor-intensive rice plantations became uneconomical without slave labor, the city's importance declined. But much of the town's historic fabric remains, to the delight of more than four million tourists every year.

◉ Sights

◉ Historic District

The quarter south of Beaufain and Hasell Sts has the bulk of the antebellum mansions, shops, bars and cafes. At the southernmost tip of the peninsula are the antebellum mansions of the Battery.

Gateway Walk   CHURCHES
Long a culturally diverse city, Charleston gave refuge to persecuted French Protestants, Baptists and Jews over the years and earned the nickname the 'Holy City' for its abundance of houses of worship. The Gateway Walk, a little-known garden path between Archdale St and Philadelphia Alley,

connects four of the city's most beautiful historic churches: the white-columned St John's Lutheran Church (5 Clifford St), the Gothic Revival Unitarian Church (4 Archdale St), the striking Romanesque Circular Congregational Church (150 Meeting St) originally founded in 1681; and St Philip's Church (146 Church St), with its picturesque steeple and 17th-century graveyard, parts of which were once reserved for 'strangers and transient white persons.'

Gibbes Museum of Art · GALLERY
(www.gibbesmuseum.org; 135 Meeting St; adult/child $9/7; ⊘10am-5pm Tue-Sat, 1-5pm Sun) Houses a decent collection of American and Southern works. The contemporary collection includes works by local artists, with Lowcountry life as a highlight.

Old Slave Mart Museum · MUSEUM
(www.nps.gov/nr/travel/charleston/osm.htm; 6 Chalmers St; adult/child $7/5; ⊘9am-5pm Mon-Sat) African men, women and children were once auctioned off here, it's now a museum of South Carolina's shameful past. Text-heavy exhibits illuminate the slave experience; the few artifacts, such as leg shackles, are especially chilling. For first-hand stories, listen to the oral recollections of former slave Elijah Green.

Old Exchange & Provost Dungeon · HISTORIC BUILDING
(www.oldexchange.org; 122 E Bay St; adult/child $8/4; ⊘9am-5pm; ⊙) Kids love the dungeon, used as a prison for pirates and for American patriots held by the British during the Revolutionary War. The cramped space sits beneath a stately Georgian Palladian customs house completed in 1771. Costumed guides lead the dungeon tours.

Kahal Kadosh Beth Elohim · SYNAGOGUE
(www.kkbe.org; 90 Hasell St; ⊘tours 10am-noon & 1:30-3:30pm Mon-Thu, 10am-noon & 1-3pm Fri, 1-4pm Sun) The oldest continuously used synagogue in the country. There are free docent-led tours.

The Battery & White Point Gardens · GARDEN
The Battery is the southern tip of the Charleston Peninsula, buffered by a seawall. Stroll past cannons and statues of military heroes in the gardens then walk the promenade and look for Fort Sumter.

Rainbow Row · NEIGHBORHOOD
Around the corner from White Point Gardens, this stretch of lower E Bay St is one of the most photographed areas of town for its candy-colored houses.

Historic Homes
About half a dozen majestic historic homes are open to visitors. Discounted combination tickets may tempt you to see more, but one or two will be enough for most people. Guided tours run every half-hour.

Aiken-Rhett House · HISTORIC BUILDING
(www.historiccharleston.org; 48 Elizabeth St; admission $10; ⊘10am-5pm Mon-Sat, 2-5pm Sun) The only surviving urban plantation, this house gives a fascinating glimpse into antebellum life. The role of slaves is also presented, and you can wander into the dorm-style quarters behind the main house. The Historic Charleston Foundation manages the house with a goal of preserving and conserving, but not restoring, the property, meaning there have been few alterations.

Joseph Manigault House · HISTORIC BUILDING
(www.charlestonmuseum.org; 350 Meeting St; admission $10; ⊘10am-5pm Mon-Sat, 1-5pm Sun) The three-story Federal-style house was once the showpiece of a French Huguenot rice planter. Don't miss the tiny neoclassical temple in the garden.

Nathaniel Russell House · HISTORIC BUILDING
(www.historiccharleston.org; 51 Meeting St; adult/child $10/5; ⊘10am-5pm Mon-Sat, 2-5pm Sun, last tour 4:15pm) Built by a Rhode Islander, known in Charleston as 'the king of the Yankees,' the 1808 Federal-style house is noted especially for its spectacular, self-supporting spiral staircase and lush English garden.

◉ Marion Square
Formerly home to the state weapons arsenal, this 10-acre park is Charleston's living room, with various monuments and an excellent Saturday farmers market.

Charleston Museum · MUSEUM
(www.charlestonmuseum.org; 360 Meeting St; adult/child $10/5; ⊘9am-5pm Mon-Sat, 1-5pm Sun) Founded in 1773, this claims to be the country's oldest museum. It's informative if you're looking for more historic background after strolling through the Historic District. Exhibits

spotlight various periods of Charleston's long and storied history, and artifacts range from prehistoric whale skeletons to slave tags and Civil War weapons.

◉ Aquarium Wharf

Aquarium Wharf surrounds pretty Liberty Sq and is a great place to stroll and watch the tugboats guiding ships into the fourth-largest container port in the US. The wharf is one of two embarkation points for tours to Fort Sumter, the other is at Patriot's Point (p353).

Fort Sumter   HISTORIC SITE

The first shots of the Civil War rang out at Fort Sumter, on a pentagon-shaped island in the harbor. A Confederate stronghold, the fort was shelled to bits by Union forces from 1863 to 1865. A few original guns and fortifications give a feel for the momentous history. The only way to get here is by boat tours (boat tour 843-722-2628, park 843-883-3123; www.nps.gov/fosu; adult/child $18/11), which depart from 340 Concord St at 9:30am, noon and 2:30pm in summer (less often in winter) and from Patriot's Point in Mt Pleasant, across the river, at 10:45am, 1:30pm and 4pm from mid-March to late August (less in winter).

South Carolina Aquarium   AQUARIUM

(www.scaquarium.org; 100 Aquarium Wharf; adult/child $25/15; 9am-5pm Mar-Aug, to 4pm Sep-Feb;) Ticket prices are steep, so this riverside aquarium is best for a rainy day. Exhibits showcase the state's diverse aquatic life. The highlight is the 42ft Great Ocean Tank, which teems with sharks and alien-looking puffer fish.

Arthur Ravenel Jr Bridge   BRIDGE

Stretching across the Cooper River like some massive stringed instrument, the 3-mile-long Arthur Ravenel Jr Bridge is a triumph of contemporary engineering. Cycling or jogging across the protected no-car lane is one of active Charlestonians' go-to weekend activities. There are parking lots on either side of the bridge. Rent a cruiser at Affordabike (843-789-3281; www.affordabike.com; 534 King St; bikes per day from $20).

☞ Tours

Listing all of Charleston's walking, horse-carriage, bus and boat tours could take up this entire book. Ask at the visitor center for the gamut.

Culinary Tours of Charleston   CULINARY

(843-722-8687; www.culinarytoursofcharleston.com; 2½hr tour $42) You'll likely sample grits, pralines, BBQ and more on this walking tour of Charleston's restaurants and markets.

Adventure Harbor Tours   BOAT

(843-442-9455; www.adventureharbortours.com; adult/child $55/30.) Runs fun trips to uninhabited Morris Island, great for shelling.

Charleston Footprints   WALKING

(843-478-4718; www.charlestonfootprints.com; 2hr tour $20) A highly rated walking tour of historical Charleston sights.

Olde Towne Carriage Company   CARRIAGE

(843-722-1315; www.oldetownecarriage.com; 20 Anson St; 1hr tour adult/child $22/12) Guides on this popular horse-drawn-carriage tour offer colorful commentary as you clip-clop around town.

✹✹ Festivals & Events

Lowcountry Oyster Festival   OYSTER

(www.charlestonrestaurantassociation.com/lowcountry-oyster-festival; Jan) In January oyster-lovers in Mt Pleasant feast on 65,000lb of the salty bivalves.

Spoleto USA   PERFORMING ARTS

(www.spoletousa.org; May) This 17-day performing-arts festival is Charleston's biggest event, with operas, dramas and musicals staged across the city, and artisans and food vendors lining the streets.

MOJA Arts Festival   ARTS

(www.mojafestival.com; Sep) Spirited poetry jams and gospel concerts mark this two-week celebration of African American and Caribbean culture.

🛏 Sleeping

Staying in the historic downtown is the most attractive option, but it's also the most expensive, especially on weekends and in high season. The rates below are for high season (spring and early summer). The chain hotels on the highways and near the airport offer significantly lower rates. Hotel parking in central downtown is usually between $12 and $20 a night; accommodations on the fringes of downtown often have free parking.

The city is bursting with charming B&Bs serving Southern breakfasts and Southern hospitality. They fill up fast, so try using an agency such as Historic Charleston B&B

(☎843-722-6606; www.historiccharlestonbedand-breakfast.com; 57 Broad St).

NotSo Hostel   HOSTEL $

(☎843-722-8383; www.notsohostel.com; 156 Spring St; dm/r $26/62; P✳@⛱) On the north edge of downtown, three tottering old houses have been carved into dorms and private rooms. Get local tips from friendly staff members during the shared morning breakfast. A new nearby annex at 33 Cannon St offers private rooms with queen beds ($70) and a quieter vibe, good for couples.

James Island County Park   CAMPGROUND $

(☎843-795-4386; www.ccprc.com; 871 Riverland Dr; tent sites from $25, 8-person cottages $169) Southwest of town, this 643-acre park has meadows, a marsh and a dog park. Rent bikes and kayaks or play the disc golf course. The park offers shuttle services downtown ($10). Reservations are highly recommended. Cottages require one-week rental June to August.

Indigo Inn   BOUTIQUE $$

(☎843-577-5900; www.indigoinn.com; 1 Maiden Ln; r $171) Our favorite part? The tasty ham biscuits at breakfast. Other perks include a prime location in the middle of the historic district and an oasis-like private courtyard, where guests can enjoy free wine and cheese by the fountain. Decor gives a nod to the 18th century, and the beds are quite comfy. A good value.

1837 Bed & Breakfast   B&B $$

(☎877-723-1837, 843-723-7166; www.1837bb.com; 126 Wentworth St; r incl breakfast $129-169; P✳⛱) Close to the College of Charleston, this B&B may bring to mind the home of your eccentric, antique-loving aunt. The 1837 has nine charmingly overdecorated rooms, including three in the old brick carriage house.

Anchorage Inn   INN $$

(☎843-723-8300; www.anchoragecharleston.com; 26 Vendue Range; r from $159; ✳⛱) One of the best values of Charleston's intimate Historic District inns, its rooms have the dark and small feel of ship's quarters but they're plenty plush.

★Ansonborough Inn   HOTEL $$$

(☎800-522-2073; www.ansonboroughinn.com; 21 Hasell St; r incl breakfast $209-259; P✳@⛱) A central atrium done up with burnished pine, exposed beams and nautical-themed oil paintings makes this intimate Historic District hotel feel like an antique sailing ship. Droll neo-Victorian touches like the Persian-carpeted glass elevator, the closet-sized British pub and the formal portraits of dogs add a sense of fun. Huge guest rooms mix old and new, with worn leather couches, high ceilings and flatscreen TVs. Complimentary wine and cheese social from 5pm to 6pm.

Vendue Inn   INN $$$

(☎843-577-7970; www.vendueinn.com; 19 Vendue Range; r incl breakfast $205-425, ste $395-465; P✳⛱) This boutique hotel, in the part of downtown known as the French Quarter, is decked out in a trendy mix of exposed brick and eccentric antiques. Rooms have cool amenities like deep soaking tubs and gas fireplaces. Even cooler is the aptly named Rooftop bar. Parking is $14 per night.

✕ Eating

Charleston is one of America's finest eating cities, and there are enough fabulous restaurants here for a town three times its size. The 'classic' Charleston establishments stick to fancy seafood with a French flair, while many of the trendy up-and-comers are reinventing Southern cuisine with a focus on the area's copious local bounty, from oysters to heirloom rice to heritage pork. On Saturday, stop by the terrific **farmers market** (Marion Sq; ⊙8am-1pm Sat Apr-Oct).

Sugar Bakeshop   BAKERY $

(www.sugarbake.com; 59 Cannon St; pastries $1-4; ⊙10am-6pm Mon-Fri, 11am-5pm Sat) The staff is as sweet as the cupcakes at Sugar, a teensy space north of downtown. Pop in on Thursdays for the Lady Baltimore cupcake, a retro Southern specialty with dried fruit and white frosting.

The Ordinary   SEAFOOD $$

(☎843-414-7060; www.eattheordinary.com; 544 King St; small plates $5-25, large $24-28; ⊙from 3pm Tue-Sun) Stepping through the door you feel like you've arrived at the best party in town at the Ordinary, a buzzy seafood hall and oyster bar inside a cavernous 1927 bank building. The menu is short, but the savory dishes are prepared with finesse – from the oyster sliders to the lobster rolls to the nightly fish dishes. Efficient but welcoming bar works well for solos.

This is the latest venue from Chef Mike Lata, a James Beard winner and owner of beloved FIG.

Poe's Tavern
PUB $$

(www.poestavern.com; 2210 Middle St, Sullivan's Island; meals $9-13; ⊙11am-10pm, bar to midnight) On a sunny day the front porch of Poe's on Sullivan's Island is the place to be. The tavern's namesake, master of the macabre Edgar Allen Poe, was once stationed at nearby Fort Moultrie. The burgers, are superb, and the Amontillado comes with guacamole, jalapeño jack, pico de gallo and chipotle sour cream. Quoth the raven: 'Gimme more.'

Gaulart & Maliclet
FRENCH $$

(www.fastandfrenchcharleston.com; 98 Broad St; mains $5-16; ⊙8am-11pm Mon-Sat) Locals crowd around the shared tables at this tiny spot, known as 'Fast & French,' to nibble on Gallic cheeses and sausages or nightly specials ($16) that include bread, soup, a main dish and wine.

Monza
PIZZA $$

(www.monzapizza.com; 451 King St; mains $12-14; ⊙11am-10pm Sun-Thu, to 11pm Fri & Sat) Burnt out on shrimp and grits? We know, it happens. After shopping on King St, pop into this exposed-brick spot. Monza is an Italian raceway, and the names of the wood-fired pizzas are inspired by racing legends. The Volpini is topped with prosciutto and argula. Salads and pastas are also on the menu.

Hominy Grill
NEW SOUTHERN $$

(www.hominygrill.com; 207 Rutledge Ave; mains $8-18; ⊙7:30am-9pm Mon-Fri, 9am-9pm Sat, to 3pm Sun; ✍) Slightly off the beaten path, this neighborhood cafe serves modern, vegetarian-friendly Lowcountry cuisine in an old barbershop. The shady patio is tops for brunch.

Husk
NEW SOUTHERN $$$

(☎843-577-2500; www.huskrestaurant.com; 76 Queen St; brunch & lunch $10-16, dinner $27-30; ⊙11:30am-2:30pm Mon-Sat, 10am-2:30pm Sun , 5:30-10pm Sun-Thu, 5:30-11pm Fri & Sat) Everything – *everything* – on the menu at this buzzed-about restaurant is grown or raised in the South, from the jalapeño marmalade-topped Georgia corn soup to the yuzu-scented Cooper River oysters, to the local lard featured in the 'pork butter' brought out with the restaurant's addictive sesame-seed rolls.

The setting, in a two-story mansion, is elegant but unfussy, and the adjacent speakeasy-style bar is near-close to perfect – if only they would expand the bar food menu.

FIG
NEW SOUTHERN $$$

(☎843-805-5900; www.eatatfig.com; 232 Meeting St; mains $28-31; ⊙5:30-10:30pm Mon-Thu, to 11pm Fri & Sat) Foodies swoon over inspired nouvelle-Southern fare like crispy pig's trotters (that means 'feet' – local and hormone-free, of course) with celery-root remoulade in this rustic-chic dining room. FIG stands for Food is Good. And the gourmands agree.

S.N.O.B.
NEW SOUTHERN $$$

(☎843-723-3424; www.mavericksouthernkitchens.com; 192 E Bay St; lunch $10-14, dinner $18-34; ⊙11:30am-3pm Mon-Fri, 5:30pm-late nightly) The cheeky name (it stands for 'slightly north of Broad,' as in Broad St) reflects the anything-goes spirit of this upscale-casual spot, which draws raves for its eclectic menu, filled with treats such as BBQ tuna with fried oysters and sautéed squab breast over South Carolina rice.

🍸 Drinking & Nightlife

Balmy Charleston evenings are perfect for lifting a cool cocktail or dancing to live blues. Check out the weekly *Charleston City Paper* and the 'Preview' section of Friday's *Post & Courier*.

Husk Bar
BAR

(www.huskrestaurant.com; 76 Queen St; ⊙from 4pm) Adjacent to Husk restaurant, this intimate brick-and-worn-wood spot recalls a speakeasy, with historic cocktails such as the Monkey Gland (gin, OJ, raspberry syrup).

Rooftop at Vendue Inn
BAR

(www.vendueinn.com; 23 Vendue Range; ⊙11:30am-midnight) This rooftop bar has the best views of downtown, and the crowds to prove it. Enjoy afternoon nachos or late-night live blues.

Blind Tiger
PUB

(www.blindtigercharleston.com; 36-38 Broad St; ⊙11:30am-2am Mon-Sat, 11am-2am Sun) A cozy and atmospheric dive, with stamped-tin ceilings, a worn wood bar and good pub grub.

Closed for Business
PUB

(www.closed5business.com; 535 King St; ⊙11am-2am Mon-Sat, 10am-2pm Sun) Charleston's best beer selection and a raucous neighborhood pub vibe.

🛍 Shopping

The historic district is clogged with over-priced souvenir shops and junk markets. Head instead to King St: hit lower King for antiques, middle King for cool boutiques, and upper King for trendy design and gift shops. The main stretch of Broad St is known as 'Gallery Row' for its many art galleries.

**Shops of Historic
Charleston Foundation** GIFTS
(www.historiccharleston.org; 108 Meeting St; ⊙9am-6pm Mon-Sat, noon-5pm Sun) This place showcases jewelry, home furnishings and furniture inspired by the city's historic homes, like earrings based on the cast-iron railings at the Aiken-Rhett House. Pick up a 'Charleston' candle, scented with hyacinth, white jasmine and tuberose.

Charleston Crafts Cooperative CRAFT
(www.charlestoncrafts.org; 161 Church St; ⊙10am-6pm) A pricey, well-edited selection of contemporary South Carolina–made crafts such as sweetgrass baskets, hand-dyed silks and wood carvings.

Blue Bicycle Books BOOKS
(www.bluebicyclebooks.com; 420 King St; ⊙10am-7:30pm Mon-Sat, 1-6pm Sun) Excellent new-and-used bookshop with a great selection of Southern history and culture.

ⓘ Information

The City of Charleston maintains free public internet (wi-fi) access throughout the downtown area.
Charleston City Paper (www.charlestoncitypaper.com) Published each Wednesday, this alt-weekly has good entertainment and restaurant listings.
Main Police Station (🗷non-emergencies 843-577-7434; 180 Lockwood Blvd)
Post & Courier (www.postandcourier.com) Charleston's daily newspaper.
Post Office (www.usps.com; 83 Broad St; ⊙11:30am-3:30pm)
Public Library (68 Calhoun St; ⊙9am-8pm Mon-Thu, to 6pm Fri & Sat, 2-5pm Sun) Free internet access.
University Hospital (Medical University of South Carolina; 🗷843-792-1414; 171 Ashley Ave; ⊙24hr) Emergency room.
Visitor Center (🗷843-853-8000; www.charlestoncvb.com; 375 Meeting St; ⊙8:30am-5pm) Find help with accommodations and tours or watch a half-hour video on Charleston history in this spacious renovated warehouse.

ⓘ Getting There & Around

Charleston International Airport (CHS; 🗷843-767-7000; www.chs-airport.com; 5500

International Blvd) is 12 miles outside of town in North Charleston, with 124 daily flights to 17 destinations.

The **Greyhound station** (3610 Dorchester Rd) and the **Amtrak train station** (4565 Gaynor Ave) are both in North Charleston.

CARTA (www.ridecarta.com; fare $1.75) runs city-wide buses; the free DASH streetcars do three loop routes from the visitor center.

Mt Pleasant

Across the Cooper River from Charleston is the residential and vacation community of Mt Pleasant, originally a summer retreat for early Charlestonians, along with the slim barrier resort islands of Isle of Palms and Sullivan's Island. Though increasingly glutted with traffic and strip malls, the area still has some charm, especially in the historic downtown, called the Old Village. Some good seafood restaurants sit overlooking the water at Shem Creek, where it's fun to dine creekside at sunset and watch the incoming fishing-boat crews unload their catch. This is also a good place to rent kayaks to tour the estuary.

⊙ Sights

**Patriot's Point Naval
& Maritime Museum** MUSEUM
(www.patriotspoint.org; 40 Patriots Point Rd; adult/child $18/11; ⊙9am-6:30pm) Patriot's Point Naval & Maritime Museum is home to the USS *Yorktown*, a giant aircraft carrier used extensively in WWII. You can tour the ship's

flight deck, bridge and ready rooms and get a glimpse of what life was like for its sailors. Also on site are a small museum, submarine, naval destroyer, Coast Guard cutter and a re-created 'fire base' from Vietnam. You can also catch the Fort Sumter boat tour from here.

Boone Hall Plantation HISTORIC BUILDING
(☑843-884-4371; www.boonehallplantation.com; 1235 Long Point Rd; adult/child $20/10; ⊙8:30am-6:30pm Mon-Sat, noon-5pm Sun early Mar-Aug, shorter hours Sep-Feb, closed Jan) Just 11 miles from downtown Charleston on Hwy 17N, Boone Hall Plantation is famous for its magical Avenue of Oaks, planted by Thomas Boone in 1743. Boone Hall is still a working plantation, though strawberries, tomatoes and Christmas trees long ago replaced cotton as the primary crop. The main house, built in 1936, is the fourth house on the site. The most compelling buildings are the Slave Street cabins, built between 1790 and 1810 and now lined with exhibits.

Ashley River Plantations

Only a 20-minute drive northwest from Charleston, there are three spectacular plantations. You'll be hard-pressed for time to visit all three in one outing, but you could squeeze in two (allow at least a couple of hours for each). Ashley River Rd is also known as SC 61, which can be reached from downtown Charleston via Hwy 17.

◉ Sights

★**Middleton Place** HISTORIC BUILDING, GARDENS
(☑843-556-6020; www.middletonplace.org; 4300 Ashley River Rd; gardens adult/child $28/10, house museum tour adult & child extra $15; ⊙9am-5pm) Designed in 1741, this plantation's vast gardens are the oldest in the US. One hundred slaves spent a decade terracing the land and digging the precise geometric canals for the owner, wealthy South Carolina politician Henry Middleton. The bewitching grounds are a mix of classic formal French gardens and romantic woodland, bounded by flooded rice paddies and rare-breed farm animals. Union soldiers burned the main house in 1865; a 1755 guest wing, now housing the house museum, still stands.

The on-site inn is a series of ecofriendly modernist glass boxes overlooking the Ashley River. Enjoy a traditional Lowcountry plantation lunch of she-crab soup and pole beans at the highly regarded cafe.

Magnolia Plantation HOUSE, GARDENS
(www.magnoliaplantation.com; 3550 Ashley River Rd; adult/child $15/10, tours $8; ⊙8am-5:30pm) On 500 acres owned by the Drayton family since 1676, Magnolia Plantation is a veritable plantation theme park, complete with a tram tour, a swamp walk, a petting zoo, and a guided house tour. At the reconstructed slave cabins, the Slavery to Freedom Tour traces the African American experience at the plantation.

Drayton Hall PLANTATION
(☑843-769-2600; www.draytonhall.org; 3380 Ashley River Rd; adult/child $18/8; ⊙9am-5pm Mon-Sat, 11am-5pm Sun, last tour 3:30pm) This 1738 Palladian brick mansion was the only plantation house on the Ashley River to survive the Revolutionary and Civil Wars and the great earthquake of 1886. Guided tours explore the unfurnished house, which has been preserved, but not restored. Walking trails wander along the river and a marsh.

Lowcountry

From just north of Charleston, the southern half of the South Carolina coast is a tangle of islands cut off from the mainland by inlets and tidal marshes. Here, descendants of West African slaves known as the Gullah maintain small communities in the face of resort and golf-course development. The landscape ranges from tidy stretches of shimmery, oyster-gray sand, to wild, moss-shrouded maritime forests.

Charleston County Sea Islands

The following islands are all within an hour's drive from Charleston.

About 8 miles south of Charleston, Folly Beach is good for a day of sun and sand. Folly Beach County Park (☑843-588-2426; www.ccprc.com; 1100 W Ashley Ave, Folly Beach; admission per vehicle $8, walk-in/bicycle free; ⊙10am-6pm), on the west side, has public changing areas and beach-chair rentals. The other end of the island is popular with surfers.

Upscale rental homes and golf courses abound on Kiawah Island, just southeast of Charleston, while nearby Edisto Island (ed-is-tow) is a homespun family vacation spot without a single traffic light. At its southern tip, Edisto Beach State Park (☑843-869-2156; www.southcarolinaparks.com; adult/child $5/3, tent sites from $21, furnished cabins from $80) has a gorgeous, uncrowded beach and oak-shaded hiking trails and campgrounds.

Beaufort & Hilton Head

The southernmost stretch of South Carolina's coast is popular with a mostly up-scale set of golfers and B&B aficionados, but the area's got quirky charms aplenty for everyone.

On Port Royal Island, the darling colonial town of Beaufort (byoo-furt) is often used as a set for Hollywood films about the South. The streets of the historic district are lined with antebellum homes and magnolias dripping with Spanish moss, and the riverfront downtown has gobs of linger-worthy cafes and galleries. The most romantic of the city's handful of B&Bs is Cuthbert House (☑843-521-1315; www.cuthberthouseinn.com; 1203 Bay St; r incl breakfast $179-245; P ✿ ☎), a sumptuously grand white-columned mansion straight out of *Gone With the Wind II*. Bay St has the bulk of the cute bistros, but for hardcore local flavor head inland to Sgt White's (1908 Boundary St; mains $7-12; ☺11am-3pm Mon-Fri), where a retired Marine sergeant serves up juicy BBQ ribs, collards and cornbread.

South of Beaufort, some 20,000 young men and women go through boot camp each year at the Marine Corps Recruit Depot on Parris Island, made notorious by Stanley Kubrick's *Full Metal Jacket*. The fascinating Parris Island Museum (☑843-228-2951; www.mcrdpi.usmc.mil; 111 Panama St; ☺10am-4:40pm) **FREE** has antique uniforms and weaponry, and covers marine corps history. Come for Friday graduations to see newly minted marines parade proudly for family and friends. You may be asked to show ID and car registration before driving onto the base.

East of Beaufort, the Sea Island Pkwy/ Hwy 21 connects a series of marshy, rural islands, including St Helena Island, considered the heart of Gullah country. Once one of the nation's first schools for freed slaves, the Penn Center (☑843-838-2432; www.discoversouthcarolina.com; 16 Penn Center Circle W; adult/child $5/3; ☺11am-4pm Mon-Sat) has a small museum that covers Gullah culture and traces the history of Penn School, which was one of the nation's first schools for freed slaves. Further down the road, Hunting Island State Park (☑843-838-2011; www.southcarolinaparks.com; 2555 Sea Island Pkwy; adult/child $5/3, tent sites $17-38, cabins $210; ☺visitor center 9am-5pm Mon-Fri, 11am-5pm Sat & Sun) has acres of spooky maritime forest, tidal lagoons, and empty, bone-white beach. The Vietnam War scenes from *Forrest Gump* were filmed in the marsh, a nature-lover's dream. Campgrounds fill up quickly in summer.

Across Port Royal Sound, tony Hilton Head Island is South Carolina's largest barrier island and one of America's top golf spots. There are dozens of courses, many enclosed in posh private residential communities called 'plantations.' Though summer traffic and miles of stoplights make it hard to see the forest (or a tree) along Hwy 278,

THE SOUTH LOWCOUNTRY

LOWCOUNTRY CUISINE

The traditional cooking style of the South Carolina and Georgia coasts, Lowcountry cuisine is seafood-centric Southern fare with a heavy dash of West African influence. Dishes to look for:

Benne wafers Sesame-seed cookies.

Country Captain Curried chicken stew, brought to the city via India by British sea captains.

Hoppin' John A rice-and-bean dish, sometimes spicy.

Lowcountry boil/Frogmore stew Crabs, shrimp, oysters and other local seafood boiled in a pot with corn and potatoes, generally eaten at picnics.

Perlau A rice-and-meat dish, cousin to rice pilaf.

She-crab soup Cream-based crab soup fortified with sherry.

Shrimp and grits A classic Charleston fisherman's breakfast of shrimp and ground corn, now a ubiquitous main course.

DON'T MISS

BOWEN'S ISLAND RESTAURANT

Down a long dirt road through Low-country marshland near Folly Beach, this unpainted wooden shack (1870 Bowen's Island Rd; ⊙ 5-10pm Tue-Sat) is one of the South's most venerable seafood dives – grab an oyster knife and start shucking! Cool beer and friendly locals give the place its soul.

there are some lush nature preserves and wide, white beaches hard enough to ride a bike on. Stop by the visitor center (☎ 800-523-3373; wwwhiltonheadisland.org; 1 Chamber of Commerce Dr; ⊙ 8:30am-5pm), on the island, for information and brochures.

North Coast

The coastline from the North Carolina border to the city of Georgetown is known as the Grand Strand, with some 60 miles of fast-food joints, beach resorts and three-story souvenir shops. What was once a laid-back summer destination for working-class people from across the Southeast has become some of the most overdeveloped real estate in the country. Whether you're ensconced in a behemoth resort or sleeping in a tent at a state park, all you need to enjoy your stay is a pair of flip-flops, a margarita and some quarters for the pinball machine.

Myrtle Beach

Love it or hate it, Myrtle Beach means summer vacation, American-style.

Bikers take advantage of the lack of helmet laws to let their graying ponytails fly in the wind, bikini-clad teenagers play Pac-Man and eat hot dogs in smoky arcades, and whole families roast like chickens on the white sand.

North Myrtle Beach, actually a separate town, is slightly lower-key, with a thriving culture based on the 'shag' (no, not that kind of shag) – a jitterbug-like dance invented here in the 1940s.

It ain't for nature-lovers, but with enormous outlet malls and innumerable mini-golf courses, water parks, daiquiri bars and t-shirt shops, it's a rowdy good time.

◉ Sights & Activities

The beach itself is pleasant enough – wide, hot and crowded with umbrellas. Beach-front Ocean Blvd has the bulk of the hamburger stands and seedy gift shops. Hwy 17 is choked with mini-golf courses, boasting everything from animatronic dinosaurs to faux volcanoes spewing lurid-pink water.

Several amusement park–shopping mall hybrids teem with people at all hours.

Brookgreen Gardens   GARDENS
(www.brookgreen.org;   adult/child $14/7;
⊙ 9:30am-5pm) These magical gardens, 16 miles south of town on Hwy 17S, are home to the largest collection of American sculpture in the country, set amid 9000 acres of rice plantation turned subtropical garden paradise. Seasonal blooms are listed on the website.

Wonderworks   MUSEUM
(www.wonderworksonline.com; 1313 Celebrity Circle; adult/child from $23/15; ⊙ 9am-9pm Sun-Thu, to 10pm Fri & Sat, hours vary; ⊕) The Inversion Tunnel, which 'flips' visitors as they enter, is pretty darn freaky. It's also just the start of the fun at this interactive museum/amusement zone, with ropes courses, laser tag, beeping and flashing 'science' exhibits and more. We dare you to lie on the bed of nails.

Broadway at the Beach   MALL
(www.broadwayatthebeach.com;   1325 Celebrity Circle) With shops, restaurants, nightclubs, rides and an IMAX theater, this is Myrtle Beach's nerve center.

Family Kingdom   AMUSEMENT PARK
(www.family-kingdom.com; combo pass $36; ⊕) An old-fashioned amusement-and-water-park combo overlooking the ocean. Hours vary by season. Closed in winter.

🛏 Sleeping

Hundreds of hotels, ranging from retro family-run motor inns to vast resort complexes, have prices that vary widely by season; a room might cost $30 in January and more than $150 in July. The following are high-season rates.

Myrtle Beach State Park   CAMPGROUND $
(☎ 843-238-5325;   www.southcarolinaparks.com; 4401 S Kings Hwy; tent & RV sites $21-52, cabins & apts $65-210; ℗ 🐾 ✉) Sleep beneath the pines or rent a cabin, all just steps from the shore. The park is 3 miles south of central Myrtle Beach. Wi-fi available at the ranger station.

Serendipity Inn   INN **$$**
(☎800-762-3229; www.serendipityinn.com; 407
71st Ave N; r incl breakfast $99, ste $109-149;
P❄🐾🛜🏊) This intimate Spanish-style inn
hides from the city's buzz on a quiet side
street. Rooms, done up with florals and
knickknacks, are comfy but not fancy.

Compass Cove   RESORT **$$**
(☎855-330-6258; www.compasscove.com; 2311 S
Ocean Blvd; r from $172; P❄🐾@🛜🏊) Got the
kids? Go full Myrtle Beach at this three-tow-
ered resort with 23 water attractions, including eight pools and two waterslides.

✕ Eating

The hundreds of restaurants are mostly
high-volume and middlebrow – think buffets longer than bowling alleys and 24-hour
doughnut shops. Ironically, good seafood is
hard to come by; locals go to the nearby fishing village of Murrells Inlet.

Prosser's BBQ   SOUTHERN **$$**
(3750 Business Hwy 17, Murrells Inlet; buffet break-
fast/lunch $6/8.30, dinner $9.30-13; ☺6am-2pm
Mon-Sat, plus 4-8pm Wed-Sat; 👶) The gut-bust-
ing lunch buffet is downhome delicious. It
includes fried fish and chicken, sweet pota-
toes, mac 'n' cheese, green beans, and vine-
gary pulled pork. Hours vary by season. Your
best bet on Murrells Inlet's 'restaurant row.'
Worth the drive.

Duffy Street Seafood Shack   SEAFOOD **$$**
(www.duffyst.com; 202 Main St; mains $10-23;
☺noon-10pm) This place has a divey, peanut-
shells-on-the-floor ambience and a raw bar
'happy hour' with 35¢ shrimp.

☆ Entertainment

★Fat Harold's Beach Club   DANCE
(www.fatharolds.com; 212 Main St; ☺from 4pm
Mon & Tue, from 11am Wed-Sun) Folks groove
to doo-wop and old-time rock and roll at
this North Myrtle institution, which calls
itself 'Home of the Shag.' The dance, that is.
Free shag lessons are offered at 7pm every
Tuesday.

❶ Information

Chapin Memorial Library (www.chapinlibrary.
org; 400 14th Ave N; 🛜) Internet access.
Visitor Center (☎800-356-3016, 843-626-
7444; www.myrtlebeachinfo.com; 1200 N Oak
St; ☺8:30am-5pm Mon-Fri, 10am-2pm Sat)
Has loads of maps and brochures.

❶ Getting There & Around

The traffic coming and going on Hwy 17 Busi-
ness/Kings Hwy can be infuriating. To avoid 'the
Strand' altogether, stay on the Hwy 17 bypass, or
take Hwy 31/Carolina Bays Pkwy, which parallels
Hwy 17 between Hwy 501 and Hwy 9.

Myrtle Beach International Airport (MYR;
☎843-448-1589; www.flymyrtlebeach.com;
1100 Jetport Rd) is located within the city limits,
as is the **Greyhound** (☎843-448-2472; 511 7th
Ave N) station.

Around Myrtle Beach

Fifteen minutes down I-17 is Pawleys Island, a narrow strip of pastel sea cottages
that's worlds away from the neon of Myrtle
Beach. There's not much to do here but kayak and fish, but that's just fine. Another 15
minutes will bring you to mellow Georgetown, South Carolina's third-oldest city.
Have lunch on Front St, with photogenic
19th-century storefronts overlooking the
water, or use it as a quiet jumping-off point
for exploring the Francis Marion National
Forest.

Greenville &
The Upcountry

Cherokee Indians once roamed the state's
mountain foothills, which they called 'The
Great Blue Hills of God.' The region today
is known as the Upcountry. Geographically,
it's the spot where the Blue Ridge mountains
drop dramatically to meet the Piedmont.

The region is anchored by Greenville,
home to one of the most inviting downtowns
in the South. The Reedy River twists through
the city center, and its dramatic falls tumble
beneath Main St at Falls Park (www.fallspark.
com). Main St itself rolls past a lively array of
indie shops, good restaurants and craft-beer
pubs. Whimsical quotes, called 'Thoughts
on a Walk' dot the sidewalk. Kids will get a
kick out of Mice on Main, a find-the-bronze-
mouse scavenger hunt inspired by the book
Goodnight Moon. Nibble porchetta and sip
wine beside the river at much-lauded Lazy
Goat (☎864-679-5299; www.thelazygoat.com;
170 River Pl; lunch $5-15, dinner small plates $5-10,
dinner mains $12-25; ☺11:30am-9pm Mon-Wed,
to 10pm Thu-Sat), a stylish spot known for its
Mediterranean small plates. For a welcoming B&B that's close to downtown, try Petti-
gru Place (☎864-242-4529; www.pettigruplace.

EXPLORING SOUTH CAROLINA SWAMPS

Inky-black water, dyed with tannic acid leached from decaying plant matter. Bone-white cypress stumps like the femurs of long-dead giants. Spanish moss as dry and gray as witches' hair. There's nothing like hiking or canoeing through one of South Carolina's unearthly swamps to make you feel like a character in a Southern Gothic novel.

Near Columbia, the 22,000-acre Congaree National Park (☑803-776-4396; www. nps.gov/cong; 100 National Park Rd, Hopkins; ☉visitor center 9am-5pm), America's largest contiguous, old-growth floodplain forest, has camping and free ranger-led canoe trips (reserve in advance). Casual day-trippers can wander the 2.4-mile elevated boardwalk. Look carefully at the cool Blue Sky mural in the visitor center – the scene seems to change as you move.

Between Charleston and Myrtle Beach, Francis Marion National Forest (☑843-928-3368; www.fs.usda.gov/scnfs; 5821 Hwy 17 N, Awendaw; ☉visitor center 9am-5pm Tue-Sat) has 259,000 acres of black-water creeks, camping, and hiking trails, including the 42-mile Palmetto Trail, which runs along old logging routes. Charleston-based Nature Adventures Outfitters (☑843-568-3222; www.kayakcharleston.com; adult/child half-day $55/39) leads kayak and canoe trips.

com; 302 Pettrigru St; r incl breakfast $145-225; P❋☞).

The region's marquee natural attraction is Table Rock Mountain, a 3124ft-high mountain with a striking granite face. The 7.2-mile round trip hike to its summit at Table Rock State Park (☑864-878-9813; www.southcarolinaparks.com; 158 Ellison Ln, Pickens; adult/child $2/free; ☉7am-7pm Sun-Thu, to 9pm Fri & Sat, extended hours mid-May–early Nov) is a popular local challenge. For overnight stays, camping is available (campsites $16 to $21), as are cabins built by the Civilian Conservation Corps ($52 to $181).

TENNESSEE

Most states have one official state song. Tennessee has seven. And that's not just a random fact – Tennessee has music deep within its soul. Here, the folk music of the Scots-Irish in the eastern mountains combined with the bluesy rhythms of the African Americans in the western Delta to give birth to the modern country music that makes Nashville famous.

These three geographic regions, represented by the three stars on the Tennessee flag, have their own unique beauty: the heather-colored peaks of the Great Smoky Mountains descend into lush green valleys in the central plateau around Nashville and then onto the hot, sultry lowlands near Memphis.

In Tennessee you can hike shady mountain trails in the morning, and by evening whoop it up in a Nashville honky-tonk or walk the streets of Memphis with Elvis' ghost.

From country churches where snake handlers still speak in tongues, to modern cities where record execs wear their sunglasses at night, Tennesseans are a passionate, diverse lot.

ℹ Information

Department of Environment & Conservation (☑888-867-2757; www.state.tn.us/environment/parks) Check out the well-organized website for camping (prices range from free to $27 or more), hiking and fishing info for Tennessee's more than 50 state parks.

Department of Tourist Development (☑800-462-8366, 615-741-2159; www.tnvacation.com; 312 8th Ave N, Nashville) Has welcome centers at the state borders.

Memphis

Memphis doesn't just attract tourists. It draws pilgrims. Music-lovers lose themselves to the throb of blues guitar on Beale St. Barbecue connoisseurs descend to stuff themselves psychotic on smoky pulled pork and dry-rubbed ribs. Elvis fanatics fly in to worship at the altar of the King at Graceland. You could spend days hopping from one museum or historic site to another, stopping only for barbecue, and leave happy.

But once you get away from the lights and the tourist buses, Memphis is a different place entirely. Named after the capital of ancient Egypt, it has a certain baroque ruined quality that's both sad and beguiling. Poverty is rampant – Victorian mansions sit beside tumbledown shotgun shacks (a narrow style of house popular in the South), college campuses lie in the shadow of eerie abandoned factories, and whole neighborhoods seem to have been almost reclaimed by kudzu and honeysuckle vines. Memphis' wild river-town spirit reveals itself to visitors willing to look, and wherever you wander, you'll quickly feel the open-hearted warmth of the people.

◉ Sights

◉ Downtown

The pedestrian-only stretch of Beale St is a 24-hour carnival zone, where you'll find deep-fried funnel cakes, to-go beer counters, and music, music, music. Although locals don't hang out here much, visitors tend to get a kick out of it.

★ **National Civil Rights Museum** MUSEUM
(Map p362; www.civilrightsmuseum.org; 450 Mulberry St; adult/student & senior/child $10/9/8; ⊙9am-5pm Mon & Wed-Sat, 1-5pm Sun Sep-May, to 6pm Jun-Aug) Housed across the street from the Lorraine Motel, where the Reverend Dr Martin Luther King Jr was fatally shot on April 4, 1968, is the gut-wrenching National Civil Rights Museum. Five blocks south of Beale St, this museum's extensive exhibits and detailed timeline chronicle the struggle for African American freedom and equality. Both Dr King's cultural contribution and his assassination serve as prisms for looking at the Civil Rights movement, its precursors and its continuing impact on American life. The turquoise exterior of the 1950s motel and two preserved interior rooms remain much as they were at the time of King's death, and serve as pilgrimage points in their own right.

Memphis Rock 'n' Soul Museum MUSEUM
(Map p362; ☑901-205-2533; www.memphisrocknsoul.org; cnr Lt George W Lee Ave & 3rd St; adult/child $11/8; ⊙10am-7pm) The Smithsonian's museum, next to FedEx Forum, examines how African American and white music mingled in the Mississippi Delta to create the modern rock and soul sound. The audio tour has more than 100 songs.

Gibson Beale Street Showcase FACTORY TOUR
(Map p362; www.gibson.com; 145 Lt George W Lee Ave; admission $10, no children under 5 yr; ⊙tours 11am-4pm Mon-Sat, noon-4pm Sun) Take the fas-

cinating 45-minute tour of this enormous place to see master craftspeople transform solid blocks of wood into Stratocasters. Tours leave on the hour.

WC Handy House Museum MUSEUM
(Map p362; ☑901-522-1556; www.wchandymemphis.org; 352 Beale St; adult/child $6/4; ⊙11am-4pm Tue-Sat winter, 10am-5pm Tue-Sat summer) On the corner of 4th St, this shotgun shack once belonging to the composer called the 'father of the blues.' He was the first to transpose the 12 bars and later wrote 'Beale Street Blues' in 1916.

Peabody Ducks MARCHING DUCKS
(Map p362; www.peabodymemphis.com; 149 Union Ave; ⊙11am & 5pm; ♠) FREE Every day at 11am sharp, five ducks file from the Peabody Hotel's gilded elevator, waddle across the red-carpeted lobby, and decamp in the marble lobby fountain for a day of happy splashing. The ducks make the reverse march at 5pm, when they retire to their penthouse

THE SOUTH MEMPHIS

TENNESSEE FACTS

Nickname Volunteer State

Population 6.35 million

Area 41,217 sq miles

Capital city Nashville (population 641,000)

Other city Memphis (population 634,000)

Sales tax 7%, plus local taxes of up to about 15%

Birthplace of Frontiersman Davy Crockett (1786–1836), soul diva Aretha Franklin (b 1942), singer Dolly Parton (b 1946)

Home of Graceland, Grand Ole Opry, Jack Daniel's distillery

Politics Pretty darn conservative, with liberal hot spots in urban areas

Famous for 'Tennessee Waltz,' country music, Tennessee walking horses, soul music

Odd law In Tennessee, it's illegal to fire a gun at any wild game, other than whales, from a moving vehicle

Driving distances Memphis to Nashville 213 miles, Nashville to Great Smoky Mountains National Park 223 miles

accompanied by their red-coated Duckmaster. The march of the ducks dates back to the 1930s and always draws major crowds – get here early to secure your spot (the mezzanine has the best views).

North of Downtown

Mud Island   PARK
(www.mudisland.com; 125 N Front St; ☉10am-5pm Tue-Sun Apr-Oct, later Jun-Aug; ⊞) **FREE** A small peninsula jutting into the Mississippi, Mud Island is downtown Memphis' best-loved green space. Hop the monorail ($4, or free with Mississippi River Museum admission) or walk across the bridge to the park, where you can jog and rent bikes.

Mississippi River Museum   MUSEUM
(Map p362; www.mudisland.com/c-3-mississippi-river-museum.aspx; 350 East 3rd St; adult/child $15/10; ☉10am-5pm Apr-Oct) Located on Mud Island, this place is part Aquarium, part geological and historical examination of America's greatest river. You'll find a full-size replica of a packet boat and a scale model of the lower Mississippi, which includes a Gulf of Mexico aquarium schooling with sharks and rays, where visitors tool around in pedal boats.

Slave Haven Underground
Railroad Museum/Burkle Estate   MUSEUM
(Map p361; ☎901-527-3427; www.slavehaven-undergroundrailroadmuseum.org; 826 N 2nd St; adult/child $10/8; ☉10am-1pm Mon-Sat) An unimposing clapboard house, it's thought to have been a way station for runaway slaves on the Underground Railroad, complete with trapdoors and tunnels.

East of Downtown

★ Sun Studio   STUDIO TOUR
(Map p361; ☎800-441-6249; www.sunstudio.com; 706 Union Ave; adult/child $12/free; ☉10:30am-5:30pm) It doesn't look like much from outside, but this dusty storefront is ground zero for American rock and roll music. Starting in the early 1950s, Sun's Sam Phillips recorded blues artists such as Howlin' Wolf, BB King and Ike Turner, followed by the rockabilly dynasty of Jerry Lee Lewis, Johnny Cash, Roy Orbison and, of course, the King himself (who started here in 1953).

Packed 40-minute guided tours through the tiny studio offer a chance to hear original tapes of historic recording sessions. Guides are full of anecdotes; you can pose for photos on the 'X' where Elvis once stood,

or buy a CD of the 'Million Dollar Quartet,' Sun's spontaneous 1956 jam session between Elvis, Johnny Cash, Carl Perkins and Jerry Lee Lewis. From here, hop on the studio's free shuttle (hourly, starting at 11:15am), which does a loop between Sun Studio, Beale St and Graceland.

Children's Museum of Memphis   MUSEUM
(Map p361; www.cmom.com; 2525 Central Ave; admission $12; ☉9am-5pm; ⊞) Gives the kids a chance to let loose and play in, on and with exhibits such as an airplane cockpit, tornado generator and waterwheel. For $5 extra you can maraud through the fun **Splash Park**, a plaza with over 40 spouts and sprayers that will keep the kids cool and smiling.

Overton Park

Off Poplar Ave in Midtown, stately homes surround this 342-acre rolling green oasis in the middle of this often gritty city. If Beale St is Memphis' heart, then Overton Park is its lungs.

Memphis Zoo   ZOO
(Map p361; www.memphiszoo.org; 2000 Prentiss Pl; adult/child $15/10; ☉9am-5pm Mar-Oct, to 4pm Nov-Feb; ⊞) At the park's northwestern corner, this world-class zoo hosts two giant panda stars in a $16-million exhibit on native Chinese habitat. Other residents include the full gamut of monkeys, polar bears, penguins, eagles and sea lions.

Brooks Museum of Art   GALLERY
(Map p361; www.brooksmuseum.org; 1934 Poplar Ave; adult/child $7/3; ☉10am-4pm Wed & Fri, to 8pm Thu, to 5pm Sat, from 11am Sun) A well-regarded art museum on the park's western fringe, the excellent permanent collection encompasses everything from Renaissance sculpture to Impressionists to abstract expressionists.

Levitt Shell   ARCHITECTURE
(Map p361; www.levittshell.org) A historic band shell and the site of Elvis' first concert, in 1954. Today the mod-looking white shell hosts free concerts all summer.

South of Downtown

★ Graceland   HISTORIC BUILDING
(Map p361; ☎901-332-3322; www.elvis.com; Elvis Presley Blvd/US 51; tours house only adult/child $33/30, full tour $37/33; ☉9am-5pm Mon-Sat, to 4pm Sun, shorter hour & closed Tue winter; ℙ)

N
0 —————— 5 km
0 —————— 3 miles

See Memphis Map (p362)

THE SOUTH MEMPHIS

If you only make one stop in Memphis, it ought to be here: the sublimely kitschy, gloriously bizarre home of the King of Rock and Roll. Though born in Mississippi, Elvis Presley was a true son of Memphis, raised in the Lauderdale Courts public housing projects, inspired by blues clubs on Beale St, and discovered at Sun Studio. In the spring of 1957, the already-famous 22-year-old spent $100,000 on a Colonial-style mansion, named Graceland by its previous owners.

The King himself had the place, ahem, redecorated in 1974. With a 15ft couch, fake waterfall, yellow vinyl walls and green shag-carpet ceiling – it's a virtual textbook of ostentatious '70s style. You'll begin your tour at the visitor plaza on the other side of Elvis Presley Blvd. Book ahead in the busy season to ensure a prompt tour time. The basic self-guided mansion tour comes with an engaging headset audio narration. Pay just $4 extra to see the car museum, and two custom planes (check out the blue-and-gold private bathroom on the *Lisa Marie*, a Convair 880 Jet).

Priscilla Presley (who divorced Elvis in 1973) opened Graceland to tours in 1982, and now millions come here to pay homage to the King who died here (in the upstairs bathroom) from heart failure in 1977. Throngs of fans still weep at his grave, next to the swimming pool out back. Graceland is 9 miles south of Downtown on US 51, also called 'Elvis Presley Blvd.' You can also hop on the free shuttle from Sun Studio. Parking costs $10.

★ **Stax Museum of American Soul Music**　　　　MUSEUM
(Map p361; ☎ 901-942-7685; www.staxmuseum. com; 926 E McLemore Ave; adult/child $12/9; ⊗ 10am-5pm Tue-Sat, 1-5pm Sun Mar-Oct, closed Mon Nov-Mar) Wanna get funky? Head directly to Soulsville USA, where this 17,000-sq-ft museum sits on the site of the old Stax

Memphis

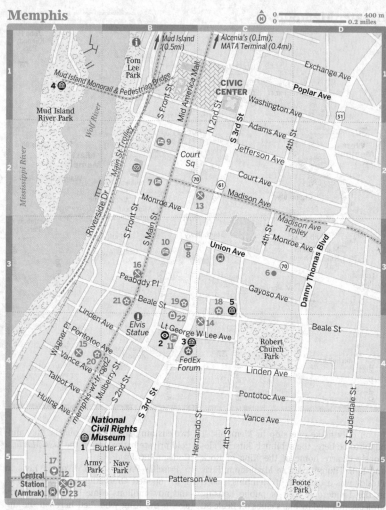

recording studio. This venerable spot was soul music's epicenter in the 1960s, when Otis Redding, Booker T and the MGs and Wilson Pickett recorded here. Dive into soul music history with photos, displays of '60s and '70s peacock clothing and, above all, Isaac Hayes' 1972 Superfly Cadillac outfitted with shag-fur and 24-carat-gold exterior trim.

Full Gospel Tabernacle Church CHURCH
(www.algreenmusic.com; 787 Hale Rd; ☉ services 11:30am & 4pm Sun) If you're in town on a Sunday, put on your smell goods and head to services in South Memphis, where soul

music legend turned reverend Al Green presides over a powerful choir. Visitors are welcome, and usually take up about half the pews. Join in the whooping 'hallelujahs,' but don't forget the tithe (a few bucks is fine). Green is not around every weekend, but services are a fascinating cultural experience nonetheless.

⛵ Tours

★ **American Dream Safari** CULTURE
(☎901-527-8870; www.americandreamsafari.com; walking tour per person $15, driving tours per vehicle from $200) Southern culture junkie

Tad Pierson shows you the quirky, personal side of Memphis – juke joints, gospel churches, decaying buildings – on foot or in his pink Cadillac. Ask about day trips to the Delta and special photography tours.

Blues City Tours BUS TOUR
(Map p362; ☎901-522-9229; www.bluescitytours. com; adult/child from $24/19) A variety of themed bus tours, including an Elvis tour and a Memphis Music Tour.

✪ Festivals & Events

Trolley Night ART WALK
(www.southmainmemphis.net; S Main St; per person $10; ☉6-9pm last Fri of month) On Trolley Night galleries on South Main stay open late, and pour wine for the people.

★ Beale Street Music Festival MUSIC
(www.memphisinmay.org; Tom Lee Park; 3-day pass $85; ☉1st weekend in May) You've heard of Coachella, New Orleans Jazz Fest and Bonnaroo, but Memphis' Beale Street Music Festival gets very little attention, though it offers one of the country's best line-ups of old school blues masters, up-and-coming rockers and gloriously past their prime pop and hip-hop artists.

It runs over three days and attracts 100,000 people.

International Blues Challenge MUSIC
(www.blues.org; ☉Jan/Feb) Sponsored by the Blues Foundation, blues acts do battle in front of a panel of judges.

Memphis in May CULTURAL
(www.memphisinmay.org; ☉May) Every Friday, Saturday and Sunday in May, something's cookin', whether it's the Beale Street Music Festival (p363), the barbecue contest or the grand-finale sunset symphony.

🛏 Sleeping

Chain motels lie off I-40, exit 279, across the river in West Memphis, AR. Prices jump during the Memphis in May festival.

🛏 Downtown

★ Talbot Heirs GUESTHOUSE **$$**
(Map p362; ☎901-527-9772, 800-955-3956; www. talbothouse.com; 99 S 2nd St; ste from $130; ❄ 🐾) Inconspicuously located on the 2nd floor of a busy Downtown street, this cheerful guesthouse is one of Memphis' best kept and most unique secrets. Spacious suites are more like hip studio apartments than hotel rooms, with Asian rugs and funky local artwork, and kitchens stocked with snacks.

When big stars, like Harvey Keitel, Kathy Bates or Eric Clapton are in town, they nest here. Parking costs $10.

JACK DANIEL'S DISTILLERY

The irony of the Jack Daniel's Distillery (www.jackdaniels.com; Rte 1; ⊙9am-4:30pm) **FREE** being in a 'dry county' is lost on no one – local liquor laws dictate that no hard stuff can be sold within county lines, but they do give out small samples on their free hour-long tours. For $10 you can take a two-hour Distillery Tour (book in advance), where you'll get a more generous sample. The oldest registered distillery in the US, the folks at Jack Daniels have been dripping whiskey through layers of charcoal then aging it in oak barrels since 1866. It's located off Hwy 55 in tiny Lynchburg.

Sleep Inn at Court Square   HOTEL $$
(Map p362; ☎901-522-9700; www.sleepinn.com; 400 N Front St; r from $114; P❄🖥) Our pick of the cheaper Downtown digs, this stubby stucco box, part of a jumble of corporate sleeps, has pleasant, airy rooms with flat-screen TVs. Parking is $12.

Madison Hotel   BOUTIQUE $$$
(Map p362; ☎901-333-1200; www.madison-hotelmemphis.com; 79 Madison Ave; r from $264; P❄@🖥) If you're looking for a sleek treat, check in to this swanky, boutique sleep. The rooftop garden is one of the best places in town to watch a sunset, and rooms have nice touches, like high ceilings, Italian linens and whirlpool tubs.

Peabody Hotel   HOTEL $$$
(Map p362; ☎901-529-4000; www.peabodymemphis.com; 149 Union Ave; r from $229; ❄🖥) The city's most storied hotel has been catering to a who's who of Southern gentry since the 1860s. The current incarnation, a 13-story Italian Renaissance Revival–style building, dates to the 1920s, and it remains a social center, with a spa, shops, various restaurants and an atmospheric marble-and-gold lobby bar. The daily march of the lobby fountain's resident ducks (p359) is a Memphis tradition.

**Westin Memphis
Beale Street Hotel**   HOTEL $$$
(Map p362; ☎901-334-5900; www.westinmemphisbealestreet.com; 170 Lt George W Lee Ave; r from $189) Directly across from the FedEx Forum and the gateway to Beale St, this is Memphis' newest and flashiest hotel. Spacious rooms have all the four-star trimmings and excellent service.

East of Downtown

Pilgrim House Hostel   HOSTEL $
(☎901-273-8341; www.pilgrimhouse.org; 1000 S Cooper St; dm $20, r $30-50; P❄@🖥) Yes, it's in a church. No, no one will try to convert you. Dorms and private rooms are clean and spare. An international crowd plays cards and chats (no alcohol) in a sunny, open common area resembling an IKEA catalog, and all guests must do a brief daily chore, like taking out the trash.

South of Downtown

**Memphis Graceland
RV Park & Campground**   CAMPGROUND $
(☎901-396-7125; www.elvis.com; 3691 Elvis Presley Blvd; tent sites/cabins from $27/51; P🖥) Keep Lisa Marie in business when you camp out or sleep in the no-frills log cabins (with shared bathrooms) next to Graceland.

Heartbreak Hotel   HOTEL $$
(☎877-777-0606, 901-332-1000; www.elvis.com/epheartbreakhotel/; 3677 Elvis Presley Blvd; d from $120; ❄@🖥) At the end of Lonely St (seriously) across from Graceland, this basic hotel is tarted up with all things Elvis. Ramp up the already-palpable kitsch with one of the themed suites, such as the red-velvet Burnin' Love room.

Days Inn Graceland   MOTEL $$
(☎901-346-5500; www.daysinn.com; 3839 Elvis Presley Blvd; r from $104; P❄🖥) With a guitar-shaped pool, gold records and Elvis memorabilia in the lobby and neon Cadillacs on the roof, the Days Inn manages to out-Elvis the neighboring Heartbreak Hotel. Guest rooms themselves are clean but nothing special. You'll need wheels or to depend upon the shuttle to get Downtown.

✖ Eating

Locals come to blows over which of the city's chopped-pork sandwiches or dry-rubbed ribs are the best. Barbecue joints are scattered across the city; the ugliest exteriors often yield the tastiest goods. Hip young locals head to the South Main Arts District or Midtown's Cooper-Young neighborhood, a hip bloom of tasty restaurants and bars.

Downtown

Gus's World Famous
Fried Chicken
CHICKEN $

(Map p362; ☑ 901-527-4877; 310 S Front St; mains $6-9; ⊙ 11am-9pm Sun-Thu, to 10pm Fri & Sat) Fried-chicken connoisseurs across the globe twitch in their sleep at night, dreaming about the gossamer-light fried chicken at this Downtown concrete bunker with the fun, neon-lit interior and vintage juke box. On busy nights, waits can top an hour.

Alcenia's
SOUTHERN $

(www.alcenias.com; 317 N Main St; mains $6-9; ⊙ 11am-5pm Tue-Fri, 9am-3pm Sat) The only thing sweeter than Alcenia's famous 'ghetto juice' (a diabetes-inducing fruit drink) is owner Betty-Joyce 'BJ' Chester-Tamayo – don't be surprised to receive a kiss on the top of the head as soon as you sit down. The lunch menu at this funky little gold- and purple-painted cafe rotates daily – look for killer fried chicken and catfish, melt-in-your-mouth spiced cabbage and an exquisite eggy custard pie.

Arcade
DINER $

(Map p362; www.arcaderestaurant.com; 540 S Main St; mains $8-10; ⊙ 7am-3pm, plus dinner Fri) Elvis used to eat at this ultra-retro diner, Memphis' oldest. Crowds still pack in for sublime sweet-potato pancakes – as fluffy, buttery and addictive as advertised. The rest of the dishes are standard greasy-spoon fare.

Dyer's
FAST FOOD $

(Map p362; www.dyersonbeale.com; 205 Beale St; burgers $4-7; ⊙ 11am-midnight Sun-Thu, to late Fri & Sat) Purportedly one of America's best burgers – annointed so by both *Esquire* and *Playboy* – the meat is smacked flat with a spatula at least 4in wide then submerged in bubbling grease, which is continuously filtered like it is a life-giving elixir when, well, it's probably the opposite.

Charlie Vergos' Rendezvous
BARBECUE $$

(Map p362; ☑ 901-523-2746; www.hogsfly.com; 52 S 2nd St; mains $10-20; ⊙ 4:30-10:30pm Tue-Thu, 11am-11pm Fri, from 11:30am Sat) Tucked in an alleyway off Union Ave, this subterranean institution sells an astonishing 5 tons of its exquisite dry-rubbed ribs weekly. The ribs don't come with any sauce, but the pork shoulder does, so try a combo and you'll have plenty of sauce to enjoy. The beef brisket is also tremendous. With a superb, no-nonsense wait staff, and walls plastered with historic memorabilia, eating here is an event. Expect a wait.

Majestic Grille
CONTINENTAL $$$

(Map p362; ☑ 901-522-8555; www.majesticgrille.com; 145 S Main St; mains $17-36; ⊙ 11am-10pm Mon-Thu, to 11pm Fri & Sat, to 9pm Sun) Set in an old silent-movie theater, with pre-talkie black and whites strobing in the handsome dark-wood dining room, here is classic continental fare, from roasted half chickens, to seared tuna and grilled pork tenderloin, and four varieties of hand-cut filet mignon. Just a stone's throw from Beale St.

East of Downtown

Bar DKDC
GASTROPUB $

(www.facebook.com/BARDKDC; 964 S Cooper St; dishes $3-8; ⊙ 5pm-3am Wed-Sun) It's all tapas here, and the food is cheap and flavorful. Per the menu's suggestions, 'begin' with sugar-cane shrimp, 'continue' with an island jerk fish club sandwich, 'keep going' with jerk chicken or lamb chops or a guava-glazed pork chop. The space sports an eclectic decor, chalkboard wine list, and friendly bartenders.

Payne's Bar-B-Q
BARBECUE $

(1762 Lamar Ave; sandwihes $4-7, plates $7-9; ⊙ 11am-6:30pm Tue-Sat) We'd say this converted gas station has the best chopped-pork sandwich in town, but we don't want to have to fight anyone. Decide for yourself.

Neely's Interstate Bar-B-Q
BARBECUE $

(☑ 901-775-1045; www.interstatebarbecue.com; 2265 S 3rd St; mains $8-20; ⊙ 11am-11pm Sun-Thu, to midnight Fri & Sat; ▣) Two words: barbecued spaghetti. It's just as weird as it sounds, but not half bad. Jim Neely's ribs and chopped-shoulder sandwiches are superb, so is the smoked turkey, and the atmosphere is homey and family-friendly.

★ Cozy Corner
BARBECUE $$

(www.cozycornerbbq.com; 745 N Pkwy; mains $7-12; ⊙ 11am-9pm Tue-Sat) Slouch in a torn vinyl booth and devour an entire barbecued Cornish game hen, the house specialty at this pug-ugly cult favorite. Ribs and wings are spectacular too, and the fluffy, silken sweet-potato pie is an A-plus specimen of the classic Southern dessert.

Alchemy
SOUTHERN TAPAS $$

(☑ 901-726-4444; www.alchemymemphis.com; 940 S Cooper St; tapas $10-13, mains $23-28;

⊙4pm-1am Mon-Sat, to 10pm Sun) A flash spot in the Cooper-Young district, serving tasty southern tapas like diver scallops with truffled cauliflower purée, roasted asparagus with Benton's bacon, and cornmeal dusted and flash-fried calamari. The kitchen stays open until 1am.

Soul Fish Cafe SEAFOOD $$
(☑901-755-6988; www.soulfishcafe.com; 862 S Cooper St; mains $10-13; ⊙11am-10pm Mon-Sat, to 9pm Sun) A cute cinderblock cafe in the Cooper-Young neighborhood, known for delectable po'boys, fried fish plates and, in a departure, some rather indulgent cakes.

Restaurant Iris NEW SOUTHERN $$$
(☑901-590-2828; www.restaurantiris.com; 2146 Monroe Ave; mains $25-37; ⊙5-10pm Mon-Sat) Chef Kelly English crafts special, avant-garde Southern fusion dishes that delight foodies, hence the James Beard noms. He's got a fried-oyster-stuffed steak, a sublime shrimp 'n' grits and an American Kobe beef garnished with aloo gobi and mint chutney. There's brunch on the third Sunday of each month.

Sweet Grass SOUTHERN $$$
(☑901-278-0278; www.sweetgrassmemphis.com; 937 S Cooper St; mains $21-27; ⊙5:30pm-late Tue-Sun, 11am-2pm Sun) Contemporary Low Country cuisine (the seafood-heavy cooking of the South Carolina and Georgia coasts) wins raves at this sleek new Midtown bistro. Shrimp and grits, a classic fisherman's breakfast, is a crowd-pleaser. However, the vibe can be a bit stuffy.

🍸 Drinking & Nightlife

Last call for alcohol is 3am, but bars do close early on quiet nights.

★Earnestine & Hazel's BAR
(Map p362; 531 S Main St) One of the great dive bars in Memphis has a 2nd floor full of rusty bedsprings and claw-foot tubs, remnants of its brothel past. The Soul Burger, the bar's only food, is the stuff of legend. Things heat up after midnight.

Cove BAR
(www.thecovememphis.com; 2559 Broad Ave) This hipsterish new dive rocks a nautical theme while serving retro cocktails and upscale bar snacks (oysters on the half shell, chips with fresh anchovies). A good place to meet locals.

☆ Entertainment

Beale St is the obvious spot for live blues, rock and jazz. There's no cover for most clubs, or it's only a few bucks, and the bars are open all day, while neighborhood clubs tend to start filling up around 10pm. To find out the latest, check the Memphis Flyer (p367) online calendar.

★FedEx Forum SPORTS ARENA
(Map p362; ☑box office 901-205-2640; www.fedexforum.com; 191 Beale St, Beale Street Entertainment District) A Downtown arena home to the Memphis Grizzlies, the city's only major professional sports team. Memphis does love their basketball squad, and this place gets electric loud when the team is rolling. It hosts big-name concerts too.

Wild Bill's BLUES
(1580 Vollentine Ave; ⊙10pm-late Fri & Sat) Don't even think of showing up at this gritty, hole-in-the-wall before midnight. Order a 40oz beer and a basket of wings then sit back to watch some of the greatest blues acts in Memphis. Expect some stares from the locals; it's worth it for the kick-ass, ultra-authentic jams.

Hi-Tone Cafe LIVE MUSIC
(www.hitonememphis.com; 1913 Poplar Ave) Near Overton Park, this unassuming little dive is one of the city's best places to hear live local bands and touring indie acts.

Young Avenue Deli LIVE MUSIC
(www.youngavenuedeli.com; 2119 Young Ave; ⊙11am-3pm Mon-Sat, from 11:30am Sun) This Midtown favorite has food, pool, occasional live music and a laid-back young crowd.

New Daisy Theater LIVE MUSIC
(Map p362; ☑901-525-8971; events hotline 901-525-8979; www.newdaisy.com; 330 Beale St; ⊙varies) Where popular indie acts like Minus the Bear, Gorilla, and Napalm Death (their band, their name) perform on Beale St.

Rum Boogie BLUES
(Map p362; ☑912-528-0150; www.rumboogie.com; 182 Beale St) Huge, popular and loud, this Cajun-themed Beale club hops every night to the tunes of a tight house blues band.

Rumba Room DANCE
(Map p362; www.memphisrumbaroom.com; 303 S Main St; ⊙7:30-11:30pm Mon, 6pm-2am Thu, 6:30pm-3am Fri, 8pm-3am Sat, to 1am Sun) Crave something other than the blues? This arts district ballroom hosts DJs, swing and salsa

nights that will get you spinning and twirling like a pro after a few drinks.

The Orpheum VENUE
(Map p362; ☑ 901-525-7800; www.orpheum-memphis.com; 203 S Main St; ☺ times vary) Broadway shows and big-name concerts in historic, 1928 environs. Its walk of fame glitters out front, and beware the ghost of a pigtailed little girl named Mary, said to giggle eerily between acts.

🛍 Shopping

Beale St abounds with cheesy souvenir shops, while Cooper-Young is the place for boutiques and bookshops. The streets around South Main have been branded an arts district. That's where some of the most interesting shopping happens these days, and it has a monthly Trolley Night (p363) too.

★ Hoot & Louise VINTAGE
(Map p362; www.facebook.com/hootandlouise; 109 GE Patterson Ave; ☺ 10:30am-6:30pm Mon-Sat, noon-5pm Sun) This store combines new vintage-inspired design with affordable and classic vintage pieces, along with quirky jewelry. Brand new, the space is special in its own right.

A Schwab's GIFTS
(Map p362; ☑ 901-523-9782; www.a-schwab.com; 163 Beale St; ☺ noon-7pm Mon-Wed, to 9pm Thu, to 10pm Fri & Sat) It has everything from denim shirts to flasks to rubber duckies to fine hats to overalls. But the real attractions are the antiques upstairs. Think: vintage scales and irons, hat stretchers and a cast-iron anchor of a cash register.

D'Edge GALLERY
(Map p362; www.dedgeart.com; 550 S Main St; ☺ 11am-5pm) A colorful art gallery with a whimsical, musical soul, combining classic Mississippi Delta–inspired, African American art with creative landscapes. Here is fun, exuberant art of the people for the people.

Lanksy Brothers CLOTHING
(Map p362; ☑ 901-529-9070; www.lanskybros.com; 149 Union Ave; ☺ 9am-6pm Sun-Wed, to 9pm Thu-Sat) The 'Clothier to the King,' this mid-century men's shop once outfitted Elvis with his two-tone shirts. Today it has a retro line of menswear, plus gifts and women's clothes. It's located in the Peabody Hotel.

ℹ Information

Almost all hotels, and many restaurants, have free wi-fi.

Commercial Appeal (www.commercialappeal.com) Daily newspaper with local entertainment listings.

Main Post Office (Map p362; 555 S 3rd St)

Memphis Flyer (www.memphisflyer.com) Free weekly distributed on Thursday; has entertainment listings.

Police Station (☑ 901-545-2677; 545 S Main St)

Public Library (www.memphislibrary.org; 33 S Front St; ☺ 10am-5pm Mon-Fri) Computers with free internet access.

Regional Medical Center at Memphis (☑ 901-545-7100; www.the-med.org; 877 Jefferson Ave) Has the only level-one trauma center in the region.

Tennessee State Visitor Center (Map p362; ☑ 888-633-9099, 901-543-5333; www.memphistravel.com; 119 N Riverside Dr; ☺ 9am-5pm Nov-Mar, to 6pm Apr-Oct) Brochures for the whole state.

ℹ Getting There & Around

Memphis International Airport (MEM; ☑ 901-922-8000; www.memphisairport.org; 2491 Winchester Rd) is 12 miles southeast of Downtown via I-55; taxis to Downtown cost about $30.

Memphis Area Transit Authority (MATA; www.matatransit.com; 444 N Main St; fares $1.75) operates local buses; buses 2 and 32 go to the airport.

MATA's vintage **trolleys** ($1, every 12 minutes) ply Main St and Front St downtown. **Greyhound** (Map p362; www.greyhound.com; 203 Union Ave) is right downtown, as is **Central Station** (www.amtrak.com; 545 S Main St), the Amtrak terminal.

Shiloh National Military Park

'No soldier who took part in the two day Battle at Shiloh ever spoiled for a fight again,' said one veteran of the bloody 1862 clash, which took place among these lovely fields and forests. Ulysses S Grant, then a major general, led the Army of Tennessee. After a vicious Confederate assault on the first day that took Grant by surprise, his creative maneuver on the second day held Pittsburgh Landing, and turned the Confederates back. During the fight over 3500 soldiers died and nearly 24,000 were wounded. A relative unknown at the beginning of the war, Grant went on to lead the Union to victory and eventually became the 18th president of the United States.

The vast Shiloh National Military Park (www.nps.gov/shil; 1055 Pittsburg Landing Rd; ☺ park dawn-dusk, visitor center 8am-5pm) FREE is located just north of the Mississippi border near the town of Crump, TN, and can only be seen by car. Sights include the Shiloh National Cemetery, and an overlook of the Cumberland River where Union reinforcement troops arrived by ship. The visitor center gives out maps, shows a video about the battle, and sells an audio driving tour.

Nashville

Imagine you're an aspiring country singer arriving in downtown Nashville after days of hitchhiking, with nothing but your battered guitar on your back. Gaze up at the neon lights of Lower Broadway, take a deep breath of smoky, beer-perfumed air, feel the boot-stompin' rumble from deep inside the crowded honky-tonks, and say to yourself 'I've made it.'

For country-music fans and wannabe songwriters all over the world, a trip to Nashville is the ultimate pilgrimage. Since the 1920s the city has been attracting musicians who have taken the country genre from the 'hillbilly music' of the early 20th century to the slick 'Nashville sound' of the 1960s to the punk-tinged alt-country of the 1990s.

Its many musical attractions range from the Country Music Hall of Fame to the revered Grand Ole Opry to Jack White's niche of a record label. It also has a lively university community, some excellent down-home grub, and some seriously kitschy souvenirs.

◉ Sights

◎ Downtown

The historic 2nd Ave N business area was the center of the cotton trade in the 1870s and 1880s, when most of the Victorian warehouses were built; note the cast-iron and masonry facades. Today it's the heart of the District, with shops, restaurants, underground saloons and nightclubs. It's a bit like the French Quarter meets Hollywood Boulevard drenched in bourbon and country twang. Two blocks west, Printers Alley is a narrow cobblestoned lane known for its nightlife since the 1940s. Along the Cumber-land River, Riverfront Park is a landscaped promenade, featuring Fort Nashborough, a replica of the city's original outpost. The brand-new Music City Center (www.nashvillemusiccitycenter.com; Broadway St btwn 5th & 8th Aves) convention and events complex looks up-to-the-nanosecond modern.

★ Country Music
Hall of Fame & Museum   MUSEUM
(www.countrymusichalloffame.com; 222 5th Ave S; adult/child $22/14, audio tour additional $2, Studio B 1hr tour adult/child $13/11; ☺ 9am-5pm) 'Honor Thy Music' is the catchphrase of this monumental museum, reflecting the near-biblical importance of country music to Nashville's soul. Gaze at Patsy Cline's cocktail gown, Hank Williams' guitar, Elvis' gold Cadillac and Conway Twitty's yearbook picture (back when he was Harold Jenkins).

Written exhibits trace country's roots, computer touch screens access recordings and photos from the enormous archives, and the fact- and music-filled audio tour is narrated by contemporary stars. From here you can also take the Studio B Tour, which shuttles you to Radio Corporation of America's (RCA's) famed Music Row studio, where Elvis recorded 'Are You Lonesome Tonight?' and Dolly Parton cut 'I Will Always Love You.'

Ryman Auditorium   HISTORIC BUILDING
(www.ryman.com; 116 5th Ave N; self-guided tour adult/child $13/6.50, backstage tour $17/10.50; ☺ 9am-4pm) The so-called 'Mother Church of Country Music' has hosted a laundry list of 20th-century performers, from Martha Graham to Elvis to Katherine Hepburn to Bob Dylan. The soaring brick tabernacle was built in 1890 by wealthy riverboat captain Thomas Ryman to house religious revivals, and watching a show from one of its 2000 seats can still be described as a spiritual experience.

The Grand Ole Opry took place here for 31 years, until it moved out to the Opryland complex in Music Valley in 1974. Today the Opry returns to the Ryman during winter.

Tennessee State Capitol   HISTORIC BUILDING
(www.tnmuseum.org; Charlotte Ave; ☺ tours 9am-4pm Mon-Fri) FREE At the northeast edge of downtown, this 1845 Greek Revival building was built from local limestone and marble by slaves and prison inmates working alongside European artisans. Around back, steep stairs lead down to the Tennessee Bicen-

tennial Mall, whose outdoor walls are covered with historical facts about Tennessee's history, and the wonderful daily Farmers Market.

Tennessee State Museum MUSEUM
(www.tnmuseum.org; 5th Ave, btwn Union & Deaderick Sts; ☉10am-5pm Tue-Sat, 1-5pm Sun) FREE For history buffs, this engaging but not flashy museum on the ground floor of a massive office tower, offers a worthy look at the state's past, with Native American handicrafts, a life-size log cabin and quirky historical artifacts such as President Andrew Jackson's inaugural hat. Rotating exhibits pass through, as well.

Frist Center for the Visual Arts GALLERY
(www.fristcenter.org; 919 Broadway; adult/senior/child $10/7/free; ☉10am-5:30pm Mon-Wed & Sat, to 9pm Thu & Fri, 1-5pm Sun) A top-notch art museum and complex hosting traveling exhibitions of everything from American folk art to Picasso in the grand, refurbished post-office building. There was a Rembrandt show on when we passed through.

Fort Nashborough FORT
(1st Ave) Down along the banks of the Cumberland River is a reconstruction of a late-18th-century wooden fort, the first flagpost of a pioneer settlement that later became Nashville.

☉ West End

Along West End Ave, starting at 21st Ave, sits prestigious Vanderbilt University, founded in 1883 by railway magnate Cornelius Vanderbilt. The 330-acre campus buzzes with some 12,000 students, and student culture influences much of Midtown's vibe.

Parthenon PARK, GALLERY
(www.parthenon.org; 2600 West End Ave; adult/child $6/4; ☉9am-4:30pm Tue-Sat, plus Sun summer) Yes, that is indeed a reproduction Athenian Parthenon sitting in Centennial Park. Originally built in 1897 for Tennessee's Centennial Exposition and rebuilt in 1930 due to popular demand, the full-scale plaster copy of the 438 BC original now houses an art museum with a collection of American paintings and a 42ft statue of the Greek goddess Athena.

Music Row NEIGHBORHOOD
(Music Sq West & Music Sq East) Just west of downtown, sections of 16th and 17th Aves, called Music Sq West and Music Sq East,

FIVE POINTS

Five Points in East Nashville is the epicenter of a new hipster scene, and despite all appearances, this is actually the old part of town. Yes, Nashville originally developed east of the Cumberland River but after a great fire the folks moved across the river where downtown presently stands. These days, Five Points is sprinkled with cafes and restaurants, with most of the action focused on Woodlawn Ave between 10th and 11th.

are home to the production companies, agents, managers and promoters who run Nashville's country-music industry. There's not much to see, but you can pay to cut your own record at some of the smaller studios, and the famed RCA Studio B is here too.

RCA Studio B LANDMARK
(www.countrymusichalloffame.org; 1611 Roy Acuff Pl; tours adult/child $35/26) One of Music Row's most historic studios, this is where Elvis, the Everly Brothers and Dolly Parton all recorded numerous hits. It's marked by the Heartbreak Hotel guitar sculpture emblazoned with a pelvis jutting image of the King. You can tour the studio via the Country Music Hall of Fame's (p368) Studio B Tour, included with the Platinum Package.

☉ Music Valley

This suburban tourist zone is about 10 miles northeast of downtown at Hwy 155/Briley Pkwy, exits 11 and 12B, and reachable by bus.

Grand Ole Opry House MUSEUM
(☑615-871-6779; www.opry.com; 2802 Opryland Dr; tours adult/child $18.50/13.50; ☉museum 10:30am-6pm Mar-Dec) This unassuming modern brick building seats 4400 for the Grand Ole Opry (p376) on Friday and Saturday from March to November. Guided backstage tours are offered daily by reservation – book online up to two weeks ahead. Across the plaza, a small, free museum tells the story of the Opry with wax characters, colorful costumes and dioramas.

THE SOUTH NASHVILLE

Nashville

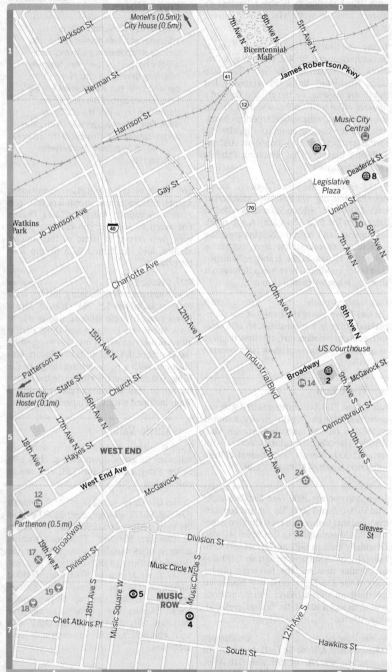

Monell's (0.5mi);
City House (0.6mi)

Bicentennial
Mall

James Robertson Pkwy

Music City
Central

Deaderick St

Legislative
Plaza

Union St

Watkins
Park

Jo Johnson Ave

Charlotte Ave

12th Ave N

10th Ave N

8th Ave N

7th Ave N

6th Ave N

5th Ave N

7th Ave N

Jackson St

Herman St

Harrison St

Gay St

US Courthouse

Patterson St

State St

Church St

Music City
Hostel (0.1mi)

15th Ave N

16th Ave N

17th Ave N

Hayes St

18th Ave N

Industrial Blvd

Broadway

McGavock St

9th Ave S

Demonbreun St

10th Ave S

WEST END

West End Ave

McGavock

Parthenon (0.5mi)

Broadway

12th Ave S

Division St

Division St

Music Circle N

Music Circle S

Gleaves
St

12th Ave S

Hawkins St

South St

Chet Atkins Pl

Music Square W

19th Ave N

18th Ave S

MUSIC
ROW

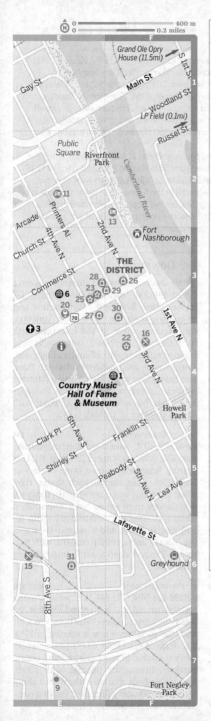

Nashville

◎ Top Sights
1 Country Music Hall of Fame & Museum F4

◎ Sights
2 Frist Center for the Visual Arts D4
3 Music City Center E4
4 Music Row.. B7
5 RCA Studio B...................................... B7
6 Ryman Auditorium E3
7 Tennessee State Capitol..................... D2
8 Tennessee State Museum.................. D2

◎ Activities, Courses & Tours
9 NashTrash E7

⊟ Sleeping
10 Hermitage Hotel................................. D3
11 Hotel Indigo E2
12 Hutton Hotel....................................... A6
13 Nashville Downtown Hostel............... F2
14 Union Station Hotel D4

⊗ Eating
15 Arnold's.. E6
16 Southern F4
17 Tavern A6

◎ Drinking & Nightlife
18 Rebar A7
19 Soulshine A7
20 Tootsie's Orchid Lounge.................... E3
21 Whiskey Kitchen C5

◎ Entertainment
22 Nashville Symphony............................ F4
23 Robert's Western World E3
Ryman Auditorium .... (see 6)
24 Station Inn... D5
25 Tootsie's Orchid Lounge.................... E3

⊡ Shopping
26 Boot Country...................................... F3
27 Ernest Tubb E3
28 Gruhn Guitars..................................... E3
29 Hatch Show Print............................... F3
30 Johnny Cash Museum Store.............. F3
31 Third Man Records E6
32 Two Old Hippies................................. D6

PLANTATIONS NEAR NASHVILLE

The former home of seventh president Andrew Jackson, **Hermitage** (615-889-2941; www.thehermitage.com; 4580 Rachel's Lane; adult/child $19/14; 8:30am-5pm Apr-Oct, 9am-4:30pm Oct-Mar), lies 15 miles east of downtown. The 1000-acre plantation is a peek into what life was like for a Mid-South gentleman farmer in the 19th century. Tour the Federal-style brick mansion, now a furnished house museum with costumed interpreters, and see Jackson's original 1804 log cabin and the old slave quarters (Jackson was a lifelong supporter of slavery, at times owning up to 150 slaves; a special exhibit tells their stories).

The Harding-Jackson family began raising thoroughbreds at **Belle Meade Plantation** (615-356-0501; www.bellemeadeplantation.com; 5025 Harding Pike; adult/student 13-18 yr/child under 13 yr $16/10/8; 9am-5pm Mon-Sat, 11am-5pm Sun), 6 miles west of Nashville, in the early 1800s. Nearly every horse entered in the Kentucky Derby in the past six years is a descendant of Belle Meade's studly sire, Bonnie Scotland, who died in 1880. Yes, Bonnie can be a boy's name! The 1853 mansion is open to visitors, as are various interesting outbuildings, including a model slave cabin.

Tours

★ **NashTrash** BUS TOUR
(615-226-7300; www.nashtrash.com; 900 8th Ave N; 1½hr tours $35) The big-haired 'Jugg Sisters' lead a campy frolic through the risqué side of Nashville history while guests sip BYO booze on the big pink bus. Buy in advance: tours can sell out *months* in advance.

Tommy's Tours BUS TOUR
(615-335-2863; www.tommystours.com; tours from $35) Wisecracking local Tommy Garmon leads highly entertaining three-hour tours of country-music sights.

General Jackson Showboat BOAT TOUR
(615-458-3900; www.generaljackson.com; tours from $45) Paddleboat sightseeing cruises of varying length on the Cumberland River, some with music and food.

Festivals & Events

CMA Music Festival MUSIC
(www.cmafest.com; Jun) Draws tens of thousands of country-music fans to town.

Tennessee State Fair FAIR
(www.tennesseestatefair.org; Sep) Nine days of racing pigs, mule-pulls and cake bake-offs.

Sleeping

Bargain-bin chain motels cluster on all sides of downtown, along I-40 and I-65. Music Valley has a glut of family-friendly midprice chains.

Downtown

★ **Nashville Downtown Hostel** HOSTEL $
(615-497-1208; www.nashvillehostel.com; 177 1st Ave N; dm/r $28/85; P) Well located and up-to-the-minute in style and function, the common space in the basement with its rather regal exposed stone walls and beamed rafters is your all-hours mingle den. Dorm rooms are upstairs on the 4th floor, and have lovely wood floors, exposed timber columns, silver beamed ceilings and four brand new bunks to a room. All come with shared bathrooms. Parking is $12.

Union Station Hotel HOTEL $$$
(615-726-1001; www.unionstationhotelnashville. com; 1001 Broadway; r from $359; P✳🛜) This soaring Romanesque grey stone castle was Nashville's train station back in the days when rail travel was a grand affair; today it's downtown's most iconic hotel. The vaulted lobby is dressed in peach and gold with inlaid marble floors and a stained-glass ceiling. Rooms are tastefully modern, with flatscreen TVs and deep soaking tubs. Parking costs $20.

Hermitage Hotel HOTEL $$$
(888-888-9414, 615-244-3121; www.thehermitagehotel.com; 231 6th Ave N; r from $399; P✳🛜) Nashville's first million-dollar hotel was a hit with the socialites when it opened in 1910. The lobby feels like a Czar's palace, every surface covered in rich tapestries and ornate carvings. Rooms are upscale, with plush, four-poster beds, marble baths with soaking tubs, and mahogany furniture. Parking costs $20. Service is a cut above here too.

Hotel Indigo
BOUTIQUE **$$$**

(☑615-891-6000; www.ihg.com; 301 Union St; r from $299; ℗) Part of a smallish international-al chain, the Indigo has a fun, pop-art look, with 130 rooms, 24 of which were recently remodeled at research time. Those King Rooms are spacious, with brand new wood floors, high ceilings, flatscreens, leather headboards and office chairs, and the loca-tion, on Capitol Hill, walking distance to the honky tonks, is ideal. Parking is $20.

🛏 West End

Music City Hostel
HOSTEL **$**

(☑615-692-1277; www.musiccityhostel.com; 1809 Patterson St; dm/r $28/85; ℗✳@✶) These squat brick bungalows are less than scenic, but Nashville's West End hostel is lively and welcoming, with bike rental, and a common kitchen. The crowd is young, international and fun, and many hoppin' West End bars are within walking distance. Private rooms share showers but have their own toilet.

★ Hutton Hotel
HOTEL **$$$**

(☑615-340-9333; www.huttonhotel.com; 1808 West End Ave; r from $289; ℗✳@✶) 🍴 Our favorite Nashville boutique hotel riffs on mid-century-modern design with bamboo-paneled walls and grown-up beanbags in the lobby. Rust- and chocolate-colored rooms are sizable and well appointed with marble rain showers, glass wash basins, king beds, ample desk space, fat flatscreens, high-end carpet and linens, and top-level service.

🛏 Music Valley

Gaylord Opryland Hotel
RESORT **$$**

(☑866-972-6779, 615-889-1000; www.gaylordhotels. com; 2800 Opryland Dr; r from $149; ℗✳@✶☀) This whopping 2881-room hotel is a universe unto itself. Why set foot outdoors when you could ride a paddleboat along an artificial river, eat sushi beneath a faux waterfall in an indoor garden, shop for bolo ties in a model 19th-century town, or sip scotch in an ante-bellum-style mansion, all *inside* the hotel's three massive glass atriums.

🍴 Eating

The classic Nashville meal is the 'meat-and-three' – a heaping portion of meat, served with your choice of three home-style sides. Gentrifying Germantown offers a hand-ful of cafes and restaurants, including two standouts. Five Points is worth exploring, and do not miss the best fried chicken of your life!

🍴 Five Points

★ Prince's Hot Chicken
FRIED CHICKEN **$**

(123 Ewing Dr; quarter/half/whole chicken $5/9/18; ☺noon-10pm Tue-Thu, to 4am Fri, 2pm-4am Sat; ℗) Cayenne-rubbed 'hot chicken,' fried to succulent perfection and served on a piece of white bread with a side of pickles, is Nash-ville's unique contribution to the culinary universe.

Tiny, faded, family-owned Prince's, set in a gritty, northside strip mall, is a local legend that's gotten shout-outs everywhere from the *New York Times* to *Bon Appétit* and at-tracts everyone from hipsters to frat boys to entire immigrant families to local heads to hillbillies. Fried up mild (a total lie), medium (what a joke), hot (verging on insanity) and extra hot (extreme masochism), its chicken will burn a hole in your stomach, and take root in your soul. You may wait an hour for yours – time well spent. It's cash only.

VIVA NASHVEGAS!

Brash, glittery Nashville is proud to have earned the nickname NashVegas. So put on your rhinestone cowboy boots and explore its weird and wild side.

'Outlaw Country' star Willie Nelson sold all his worldly goods to pay off $16.7 million in unpaid taxes in the early 1990s. You can see them at the **Willie Nelson Museum** (www. willienelsongeneralstore.com; 2613 McGavock Pike; admission $8; ☺8:30am-9pm).

The **Doyle and Debbie** show at **Zanies Comedy Club** (www.nashville.zanies.com; 2025 8th Ave S) is a cult-hit parody of a washed-up country-music duo.

The **Johnny Cash Museum Store** (www.facebook.com/johnnycashmuseum; 119 3rd Ave; ☺11am-7pm) is less a museum and more a gift shop where fans of the Man In Black descend for all things Cash, from leather to books to CDs to vintage vinyl.

In the quirky 12th Ave S neighborhood, a former stylist to New York City's drag queens stocks bouffant wigs, vintage cowboy boots and handmade bolo ties at **Katy K's Ranch Dressing** (www.katyk.com; 2407 12th Ave S).

Pied Piper Creamery
ICE CREAM $

(www.thepiedpipercreamery.com; 114 S 11th St; scoops under $3; ⊙ noon-9pm Sun-Thu, to 10pm Fri & Sat) Thicker, smoother and more packed with goodness than any other ice-cream shop in town, we love the toffee lovers coffee flavor, but it does have two dozen varieties available to explore at any one time. It's in Five Points.

I Dream of Weenie
HOT DOGS $

(www.facebook.com/IDreamofWeenie; 113 S 11th St; hot dogs $3-5; ⊙ 11am-4pm Mon-Thu, to 6pm Fri, 10:30am-7pm Sat, to 4pm Sun) If you want something quick and easy hit this VW bus turned hot dog stand in Five Points, pick a tubular product made from beef, turkey or tofu and get yours creatively topped. Picnic In A Bun includes baked beans, bacon, coleslaw and BBQ sauce, or just go simple with a Kraut Weenie (sauerkraut and spicy mustard).

King Market Cafe
LAOTIAN, THAI $

(300 Church St, Antioch Pike; dishes $6-10; ⊙ 8:30am-7pm) An authentic Southeast Asian cafe set inside an Asian Grocer in the Antioch Pike area – an east Nashville suburb where this city suddenly seems much less homogenous. It does noodle dishes, soups, curries and stirfrys, a Thai-style country pork sausage, deep-fried mackerel, and adventurous eats like fried pork intestine. Food comes rapidly and in heaping portions.

Marché Artisan Foods
BISTRO $$

(www.marcheartisanfoods.com; 1000 Main St; mains $9-16; ⊙ 8am-9pm Tue-Sat, to 4pm Sun) In rapidly gentrifying Five Points, this lovely and bright glass box of a farm-to-table cafe offers a corned-beef Ruben on marble rye, a popular lamb burger and a delicious warm broccoli salad with brown rice at lunch. It hosts special beer and wine dinners too.

Downtown

Arnold's
SOUTHERN $

(www.facebook.com/Arnoldsmeatand3; 605 8th Ave S; mains $5-8; ⊙ 10:30am-2:30pm Mon-Fri) Grab a tray and line up with college students, garbage collectors and country-music stars at Arnold's, king of the meat-and-three. Slabs of drippy roast beef are the house specialty, along with fried green tomatoes, cornbread two ways, and big gooey wedges of chocolate cream pie.

Monell's
SOUTHERN $$

(☎ 615-248-4747; www.monellstn.com; 1235 6th Ave N; all-you-can-eat $13-19; ⊙ 10:30am-2pm Mon, 10:30am-2pm & 5-8:30pm Tue-Fri, 8:30am-3pm & 5-8:30pm Sat, 8:30am-4pm Sun) In an old brick house just north of the District, Monell's is beloved for down-home Southern food served family style. This is not just a meal, it's an experience. Especially at breakfast when platter after platter of sausage, bacon, bone in ham, skillet-fried chicken, hominy, corn pudding, baked apples and potatoes are served along with baskets of biscuits and bowls of sugary cinnamon rolls.

City House
NEW SOUTHERN $$$

(☎ 615-736-5838; www.cityhousenashville.com; 1222 4th Ave N; mains $15-24; ⊙ 5-10pm Mon & Wed-Sat, to 9pm Sun) This signless brick building in Nashville's gentrifying Germantown hides one of the city's best restaurants. The food, cooked in an open kitchen in the warehouse-like space, is a crackling bang-up of Italy meets New South.

It does tangy kale salads, a tasty chickpea and octopus dish flavored with fennel, onion, lemon and garlic, and pastas featuring twists like rigatoni rabbit, or gnocchi in cauliflower ragu. It cures its own sausage and salamis, and takes pride in the cocktail and wine list. Save room for dessert. Sunday supper features a stripped-down menu.

Southern
BAR & GRILL $$$

(www.thesouthernnashville.com; 150 3rd Ave; lunch mains $11-15, dinner mains $14-48; ⊙ 7:30am-10pm Mon-Thu, to midnight Fri, 10am-midnight Sat, 10am-10pm Sun) A brand-new eatery in the heart of downtown with a nice oyster menu sourced from Cape Cod, the Pacific Northwest, and Gulf Coast. Craftsman draft beers are poured at the marble bar and an open kitchen serves up everything from gourmet burgers to fish tacos to double-smoked pork chops and a plethora of steaks.

It's part of the new, ahem, SoBro area. Their terminology. Not ours, bro.

West End

Fido
CAFE $

(www.fidocafe.com; 1812 21st S; mains $6-12; ⊙ 7am-11pm; 🖭) A Hillsboro institution, known for excellent coffees and breakfasts, as well as an affordable menu of salads and sandwiches, some creative entrees like green chile mac and cheese, a nice crispy tofu stirfry, and a kale and collard green salad.

FRANKLIN

About 20 miles south of Nashville off I-65, the historic town of Franklin (www.historic-franklin.com) has a charming downtown and beautiful B&Bs. It was also the site of one of the Civil War's bloodiest battlefields. On November 30, 1864, 37,000 men (20,000 Confederates and 17,000 Union soldiers) fought over a 2-mile stretch of Franklin's outskirts. Nashville's sprawl has turned much of that battlefield into suburbs, but the Carter House (📞 615-791-1861; www.carter-house.org; 1140 Columbia Ave, Franklin; adult/senior/child $8/7/4; ⊘ 9am-5pm Mon-Sat, 1-5pm Sun; 🚻 👹) property is a preserved 8-acre chunk of the Battle of Franklin. The house is still riddled with 1000-some bullet holes. Before leaving town stop off at Puckett's Grocery (www.puckettsgrocery.com; 120 4th Ave S, Franklin; mains $10-20; ⊘ 7am-3pm Mon, to 9pm Tue-Sat, to 7pm Sun) for a fried catfish sandwich and some bluegrass.

It's generally packed, yet spacious enough to accomodate the rather appealing crowd.

Pancake Pantry　　　BREAKFAST $
(www.pancakepantry.com; 1796 21st Ave S; mains $7-11; ⊘ 6am-3pm) For 50-plus years, crowds have been lining up around the block for tall stacks of pancakes done up every-which-way at this iconic breakfast joint. Try the sweet-potato kind.

Provence　　　BAKERY, CAFE $
(www.provencebreads.com; 1705 21st Ave S; mains $7-11; ⊘ 7am-8pm Mon-Fri, to 8pm Sat, to 6pm Sun) A popular spot in the Hillsboro District, lovers of breads will want to stop here for a loaf or a ready-made turkey, chicken salad or tuna sandwich. It also does frittatas, salads, tasty pastries, and a French toast made with a peach compote. Order your flavor and grab a table in the bright dining area that's popular at lunch.

Tin Angel　　　NEW AMERICAN $$
(📞 615-298-3444; www.tinangel.net; 3201 West End Ave; mains $14-22; ⊘ 11am-10pm Mon-Fri, 5-10pm Sat, 11am-3pm Sun) This low-key West End bistro serves a business crowd some good New American grub. With a house-smoked pork loin, vegetarian moussaka, maple bourbon duck breast and tasty entree salads, there really is something for everyone in this darkwood, intimately lit dining room. The only issue we had was that 1980s smooth jazz soundtrack. Ain't this Nashville?!

Tavern　　　GASTROPUB $$
(www.mstreetnashville.com; 1904 Broadway; mains $9-22; ⊘ 11am-1am Mon-Thu, to 3am Fri, 10am-3am Sat, to 1am Sun) This Music Row gatsropub does everything from a Thai Cobb salad to wood-grilled artichokes to Ozzie-style meat pies to steak and seafood. All afford-ably priced. It has a nice whiskey list, and a handsome minimalist interior of moulded concrete booths, brick walls and built-in book cases.

🍸 Drinking & Nightlife

Nashville has the nightlife of a city three times its size, and you'll be hard-pressed to find a place that *doesn't* have live music. College students, bachelor-party-goers, Danish backpackers and conventioneers all rock out downtown, where neon-lit Broadway looks like a country-fried Las Vegas. Bars and venues west and south of downtown tend to attract more locals, with many places clustered near Vanderbilt University. Last call is at 3am.

3 Crow Bar　　　BAR
(www.3crowbar.com; 1024 Woodland St; ⊘ 11am-3am; 🛜) Garage-door windows roll open onto this truly divey cinderblock cavern with ample table and bar space in Five Points. This is the kinda joint you can lay back and enjoy not for a few minutes, but a few hours. The crowd is young and local, and there isa great back patio, as well.

Whiskey Kitchen　　　PUB
(www.whiskeykitchen.com; 118 12th Ave S) In the Gulch, an up-and-coming patch of rehabbed warehouses adjacent to downtown, this neo-Southern gastropub with a mile-long whiskey menu attracts an upmarket crowd.

Bongo Java　　　COFFEE HOUSE
(www.bongojava.com; 107 S 11th St; ⊘ 6:30am-6pm Mon-Fri, from 7:30am Sat & Sun) A low-key hipster habitat, pretty goth girls expose fishnets and melancholy on the shady porch, and more serious thinker/writers/(web)surfers hunch over laptops in the cavernous interior where the coffee is

house-roasted and sacked, and where Robert Plant has been known to grab a cup when he's in town.

Rebar
BAR

(www.rebarnashville.com; 1919 Division St; ⊙2pm-3am Mon-Fri, from 11am Sat & Sun) Set in an old brick-and-stone house with an attractive tiled bar and low ceilings, wide concrete patio and flatscreens strobing the ball game – any ball game – this is a popular day-drinking spot among locals in Midtown, thanks to its two-for-one drinks from 2pm to 7pm daily.

Soulshine
PUB

(www.soulshinepizza.com; 1907 Division St; ⊙11am-1am Sun-Thu, to 2am Fri & Sat) A two-story, concrete-floor, brickhouse pub and pizzeria in Midtown. Bands rock the wide rooftop patio on weekend nights.

☆ Entertainment

Nashville's opportunities for hearing live music are unparalleled. As well as the big venues, many talented country, folk, bluegrass, Southern-rock and blues performers play smoky honky-tonks, college bars, coffee shops and organic cafes for tips. Most places are free Monday to Friday.

★ Station Inn
BLUEGRASS

(☎615-255-3307; www.stationinn.com; 402 12th Ave S; ⊙open mic 7pm, live bands 9pm) Sit at one of the small cocktail tables, squeezed together on the worn-wood floor in this beer-only dive, illuminated with stage lights, and neon signs, and behold the lightning fingers of bluegrass savants. We are talking stand-up bass, banjo, mandolin, fiddle and a modicum of yodelling.

Bluebird Cafe
CLUB

(☎615-383-1461; www.bluebirdcafe.com; 4104 Hillsboro Rd; cover free-$15; ⊙shows 6:30pm & 9:30pm) It's in a strip mall in suburban South Nashville, but don't let that fool you: some of the best original singer-songwriters in country music have graced this tiny stage. Steve Earle, Emmylou Harris and the Cowboy Junkies have all played the Bluebird, which is the setting for the popular television series, *Nashville.* Try your luck at Monday open mic nights.

It's first-come, first-serve seating, and it's best to show up at least an hour before the show begins. No talking during the show or you will get bounced.

Tootsie's Orchid Lounge
HONKY-TONK

(☎615-726-7937; www.tootsies.net; 422 Broadway; ⊙10am-late) **FREE** The most venerated of the downtown honky-tonks, Tootsie's is a blessed dive oozing boot-stomping, hillbilly, beer-soaked grace. In the 1960s club owner and den mother 'Tootsie' Bess nurtured Willie Nelson, Kris Kristofferson and Waylon Jennings on the come up.

No-name country musicians still play her two tiny stages, but it's not unusual for big stars to stop by for an impromptu jam.

Grand Ole Opry
MUSICAL THEATER

(☎615-871-6779; www.opry.com; 2802 Opryland Dr; adult $28-88, child $18-53) Though you'll find a variety of country shows throughout the week, the performance to see is the *Grand Ole Opry,* a lavish tribute to classic Nashville country music, every Tuesday, Friday and Saturday night. Shows return to the Ryman from November to February.

Robert's Western World
HONKY-TONK

(www.robertswesternworld.com; 416 Broadway; ⊙11am-2am) **FREE** Buy a pair of boots, a beer or a burger at Robert's, a longtime favorite on the strip. Music starts at 11am and goes all night; Brazilbilly, the house band, rocks it after 10pm on weekends. All ages are welcome before 10pm, afterward it's strictly 21 and up.

Ryman Auditorium
CONCERT VENUE

(☎info 615-889-3060, tickets 615-458-8700; www.ryman.com; 116 5th Ave) The Ryman's excellent acoustics, historic charm and large seating capacity have kept it the premier venue in town, with big names frequently passing through. The *Opry* returns for winter runs.

Belcourt
CINEMA

(www.belcourt.org; 2012 Belcourt Ave; child/adult $7.25/9.25; ⊙hour vary) A sweet art-house cinema playing new indie releases and a lot of old classics in a historic cinema space. Occasional live concerts too.

Nashville Symphony
SYMPHONY

(☎615-687-6500; www.nashvillesymphony.org; 1 Symphony Pl) Hosts maestros, the local symphony and major pop stars from Randy Travis to Smokey Robinson, in the shiny new, yet beautifully antiquated, Schemerhorn Symphony Hall.

LP Field
FOOTBALL

(☎615-565-4200; www.titansonline.com; 1 Titans Way; ticket prices vary; ⊙games Sep-Dec) Home of Nashville's own Tennessee Titans, part of

SCENIC DRIVE: NASHVILLE'S COUNTRY TRACKS

About 25 miles southwest of Nashville off Hwy 100, drivers pick up the Natchez Trace Pkwy, which leads 444 miles southwest to Natchez, MS. This northern section is one of its most attractive stretches, with broad-leafed trees leaning together to form an arch over the winding road. There are three primitive campsites along the way, free and available on a first-come, first-served basis. Near the parkway entrance, stop at the landmark Loveless Cafe (☑ 615-646-9700; www.lovelesscafe.com; 8400 Hwy 100, Nashville, TN 37221), a 1950s roadhouse famous for its biscuits with homemade preserves, country ham and ample portions of Southern fried chicken.

the National Football League. It's linked to downtown by a pedestrian bridge that spans the Cumberland River.

🛍 Shopping

Lower Broadway has tons of record shops, boot stores and souvenir stalls. The 12th Ave South neighborhood is the spot for ultra-trendy boutiques and vintage stores.

★ Hatch Show Print   ART, SOUVENIRS

(www.hatchshowprint.com; 316 Broadway; ⊙9am-5pm Mon-Fri, from 10am Sat) One of the oldest letterpress print shops in the US, Hatch has been using old-school, hand-cut blocks to print its bright, iconic posters since the early days of Vaudeville. The company has produced graphic ads and posters for almost every country star since, and they're still in business.

If you don't have a special order in mind, you can buy reproductions of original Louis Armstrong, Patsy Cline, Hank Williams and Bill Monroe publicity posters.

Third Man Records   MUSIC

(www.thirdmanrecords.com; 623 7th Ave S; ⊙10am-6pm Mon-Sat, 1-4pm Sun) In a still-industrial slice of downtown, you'll find Jack White's boutique record label and shop complete with its own vinyl press. It sells only Third Man recordings on vinyl and CD, collectible t-shirts, stickers, and headphones, and its own Spinerette record players. You'll also find old White Stripes records and White's more recent Raconteurs recordings.

Live shows go off in the studio's Blue Room once a month. They're typically open to the public, cost about $10, but are only announced a couple weeks in advance. Often those shows become limited-edition vinyl – such as Jerry Lee Lewis' performance – sold in store.

Boot Country   BOOTS

(www.facebook.com/bootcountrynashville; 304 Broadway; ⊙10am-10:30pm Mon-Thu, to 11pm Fri & Sat, 11am-7:30pm Sun) If you're into leather, or worn rawhide, or anything close, they do all manner of boot here. From sexy to staid, flamboyant to stern, worn and frayed to polished and glossy. Buy one, get two free. No joke!

Two Old Hippies   CLOTHING, MUSIC

(www.twooldhippies.com; 401 12th Ave S) Only in Nashville would an upscale retro-inspired clothing shop have a bandstand with regular live shows of high quality. And, yes, just like the threads, countrified hippie rock is the rule. The shop itself has special jewelry, fitted tees, excellent belts, and an unfortunate collection of man purses.

As well, it has, ahem, $2000 leather jackets (including a beaded rpelica of the one Jimmie wore at Woodstock), and superb guitars! It's part of the Gulch shopping center.

A Thousand Faces   GIFTS

(www.athousandfaces.com; 1720 21st Ave S; ⊙10am-6pm Mon-Thu, to 7pm Fri & Sat, to 5pm Sun) A lovely gift boutique specializing in handmade ceramics, exquisite silver jewelry and interesting art. We loved the intriguing guitar sculpture that you simply have to see.

Ernest Tubb   RECORDS

(www.etrecordshop.com; 417 Broadway) Marked by a giant neon guitar sign, this is the best place to shop for country and bluegrass records. Open late.

Parnassus Books   BOOKS

(www.parnassusbooks.net; 3900 Hillsboro Pike; ⊙10am-8pm Mon-Sat, noon-5pm Sun) Anne Patchett's Parnassus Books is arguably one of America's most famous indie booksellers. The bright space hosts special events, readings, and signings, promotes local authors and even sells e-books.

Gruhn Guitars   MUSIC
(www.gruhn.com; 400 Broadway; ⊙9:30am-
5:30pm Mon-Fri, to 2:30pm Sat) This renowned
vintage instrument store has expert staff,
and at any minute some unassuming virtuo-
so may just walk in, grab a guitar, mandolin
or banjo off the wall and jam.

Pangaea   GIFTS
(www.pangaeanashville.com; 1721 21st Ave S;
⊙10am-6pm Mon-Thu, to 9pm Fri & Sat, noon-
5pm Sun) There are no groovier shops in
town. What with the beaded belts and silly
scarves, funky hats and summery dresses,
Not to mention the triple milled soap, Frida
Kahlo match holders, stunning mirrors and
light fixtures all of which scream vintage, as
do the worn wood floors. Welcome to your
sweet-smelling, good-vibing blast of Nashville bohemia.

❶ Information

Downtown Nashville and Centennial Park have
free wi-fi, as do nearly all hotels and many restaurants and coffee shops.

InsideOut (www.insideoutnashville.com) A
weekly covering the local gay and lesbian
scene.

Main Police Station (☑615-862-8600; 310
1st Ave S)

Nashville Scene (www.nashvillescene.com)
Free alternative weekly with entertainment
listings.

Nashville Visitors Information Center
(☑800-657-6910, 615-259-4747; www.visit-
musiccity.com; 501 Broadway, Sommet Center;
⊙8:30am-5:30pm) Pick up free city maps here
at the glass tower. Great online resource.

Post Office (1718 Church St)

Public Library (www.library.nashville.org; 615
Church St; ☎) Free internet access.

Tennessean (www.tennessean.com) Nashville's
daily newspaper.

Vanderbilt University Medical Center (☑615-
322-5000; 1211 22nd Ave S)

❶ Getting There & Around

Nashville International Airport (BNS; ☑615-
275-1675; www.nashintl.com), 8 miles east
of town, is not a major air hub. **Metropolitan
Transit Authority** (MTA; www.nashvillemta.
org; fares $1.70-2.25) bus 18 links the airport
and downtown; the **Gray Line Airport Express**
(www.graylinenashville.com; one-way/return
$14/25; ⊙5am-11pm) serves major downtown
and West End hotels. Taxis charge a flat rate of
$25 to $27 to downtown or Opryland.

Greyhound (www.greyhound.com; 709 5th
Ave S) is downtown. The MTA operates city bus
services, based downtown at **Music City Central** (400 Charlotte Ave). Express buses go to
Music Valley.

Eastern Tennessee

Dolly Parton, Eastern Tennessee's most famous native, loves her home region so much
she has made a successful career out of singing about girls who leave the honeysuckle-
scented embrace of the Smoky Mountains
for the false glitter of the city. They're always
sorry. Largely a rural region of small towns,
rolling hills and river valleys, the eastern
third of the state has friendly folks, hearty
country food and pastoral charm. The lush,
heather-tinted Great Smoky Mountains are
great for hiking, camping and rafting, while
the region's two main urban areas, Knoxville
and Chattanooga, are easygoing riverside
cities with lively student populations.

Chattanooga

Named 'the dirtiest city in America' in the
1960s, today the city is recognized as being
one of the country's greenest, with miles of
well-used waterfront trails, electric buses
and pedestrian bridges crossing the Tennessee River. With world-class rock-climbing,
hiking, biking and water-sports opportunities, it's one of the South's best cities for outdoorsy types.

The city was once a major railway hub
throughout the 19th and 20th centuries,
hence the 'Chattanooga Choo-Choo,' which
was originally a reference to the Cincinnati
Southern Railroad's passenger service from
Cincinnati to Chattanooga and later the title
of a 1941 Glen Miller tune. The eminently
walkable downtown is an increasingly
gentrified maze of historic stone and brick
buildings and some tasty gourmet kitchens.
There's a lot to love about Chattanooga.

❍ Sights & Activities

Coolidge Park is a good place to start a riverfront stroll. There's a carousel, well-used
playing fields and a 50ft climbing wall attached to one of the columns supporting the
Walnut Street Bridge. Abutting that park,
the city has installed gabions to restore the
wetlands and attract more bird life. Check
them out by strolling to the edge of the cool,
floating decks that jut over the marsh. The

much larger Tennessee River Park is an 8-mile, multi-use greenway that runs from downtown through Amincola Marsh and along South Chickamauga Creek. Plans are to expand its reach to a full 22 miles.

Tennessee Aquarium   AQUARIUM
(www.tnaqua.org; 1 Broad St; adult/child $25/15; ⊘10am-8pm, last entry 6pm; 🚼) That glass pyramid looming over the riverside bluffs is the world's largest freshwater aquarium. Climb aboard the aquarium's high-speed catamaran for two-hour excursions through the Tennessee River Gorge (adult/child $29/22).

Hunter Museum of American Art   GALLERY
(www.huntermuseum.org; 10 Bluff View; adult/child $10/5, 1st Sun of month free; ⊘10am-5pm Mon, Tue, Fri & Sat, to 8pm Thu, noon-5pm Wed & Sun) Set high on the river bluffs, east of the aquarium, is this equally striking melted-steel and glass edifice, easily the most singular architectural achivement in Tennessee. Oh, and the 19th- and 20th-century art collection is fantastic.

Lookout Mountain   OUTDOORS
(www.lookoutmountain.com; 827 East Brow Rd; adult/child $48/25; ⊘varies; 🚼) Some of Chattanooga's oldest and best-loved attractions are 6 miles outside the city. Admission price includes: the Incline Railway, which chugs up a steep incline to the top of the mountain; the world's longest underground waterfall, Ruby Falls; and Rock City, a garden with a dramatic clifftop overlook.

The mountain is also a popular hang-gliding location. The folks at Lookout Mountain Flight Park (☏800-688-5637; www.hanglide.com; 7201 Scenic Hwy; intro tandem flight $149) offer tandem flights.

Outdoor Chattanooga   OUTDOORS
(☏423-643-6888; www.outdoorchattanooga.com; 200 River St) A city-run agency promoting active recreation, the website is a good resource for outdoor information, river and trail suggestions, though walk-in visitors may be disappointed in the lack of spur-of-the-moment guidance. It occasionally runs guided trips.

🛏 Sleeping & Eating

You can find plenty of budget motels around I-24 and I-75.

★Stone Fort Inn   BOUTIQUE HOTEL $$
(☏423-267-7866; www.stonefortinn.com; 120 E 10th St; r from $135-155; P🌸🛜) In the midst of a

---

refurbish at research time, rooms at this historic hotel have flatscreens and soaker Jacuzzi tubs and new fixtures in the bathrooms. Ceilings are high, the furnishings are vintage and service is phenomenal. The Appalachia-style, farm-to-table restaurant is the newest winner in town. Some beds do sag.

Sheraton Read House   HOTEL $$
(☏423-266-4121; www.sheratonreadhouse.com; 827 Broad St; r from $149; P🌸🛜) Set in a historic building dating to 1926, this is the nicest of Chattanooga's chain hotels, and the only one in the downtown center (most are on the northern edge near the river). Rooms are clean and good sized with high ceilings, crown mouldings, wood desks and flatscreens. It's within walking distance of the best restaurants and the riverside. Parking is $15

Chattanooga Choo-Choo   HOTEL $$
(☏423-308-2440; www.choochoo.com; 1400 Market St; r/railcars from $133; P🌸@🛜🏊) One hundred years old at research time, the city's grand old railway terminal has been transformed into a bustling hotel, complete with 48 authentic Victorian railcar rooms, a retro Gilded Age bar, and stunning grand portico in the lobby. Standard rooms and suites, in separate buildings, are ordinary.

★Public House   NEW AMERICAN $$
(☏423-266-3366; www.publichousechattanooga.com; 1110 Market St; mains $9-22; ⊘5-9pm Mon-Thu, to 10pm Fri & Sat) A rather chic pub and restaurant in the refurbished warehouse district, the in-house bar, Social, is a dark

welcoming brick house, the dining room is draped, bright and homey, and both rooms serve a tasty upscale menu.

Think: duck confit with red cabbage, grilled pork tenderloin with green-apple chutney, or sautéed trout with cauliflower and tomato preserve.

St John's Meeting Place NEW AMERICAN $$$ (☑ 423-266-4400; www.stjohnsrestaurant.com; 1278 Market St; mains $28-36; ⊙ 5-9:30pm Mon-Thu, to 10pm Fri & Sat) Set on the south end of downtown is another of Chattanooga's creative new culinary habitats, and it's widely considered the best. A black granite floor, black-glass chandeliers and drapes lend a mod elegance, and the menu is fine farm-to-table cuisine featuring roast pork, antelope, lamb, shortrib and duck mains.

❶ Getting There & Around

Chattanooga's modest **airport** (CHA; ☑ 423-855-2202; www.chattairport.com; 1001 Airport Rd) is just east of the city. The **Greyhound station** (960 Airport Rd) is just down the road. For access to most downtown sites, ride the free electric **shuttle buses** that ply the center. The **visitor center** (☑ 800-322-3344, 423-756-8687; www.chattanoogafun.com; 215 Broad St; ⊙ 8:30am-5:30pm) has a route map. If you'd rather pedal, fill out an online application and take part in **Bike Chattanooga** (www.bikechattanooga.com), a city sponsored, bicycle-sharing program. Bikes are lined and locked up at 31 stations throughout the city. Rides under 60 minutes are free.

Knoxville

Once known as the 'underwear capital of the world' for its numerous textile mills, Knoxville is home to the University of Tennessee. Downtown's Market Square is full of ornate, 19th-century buildings and lovely outdoor cafes shaded by pear trees, while Old Town, an arty, renovated warehouse district centered on Gay St, is where the best nightlife blooms.

The city's visual centerpiece is the Sunsphere (☑ 865-251-6860; World's Fair Park, 810 Clinch Ave; ⊙ 9am-10pm Apr-Oct, 11am-6pm Nov-Mar), a gold orb atop a tower that's the main remnant of the 1982 World Fair. You can take the elevator up to the (usually deserted) viewing deck to see the skyline and a dated exhibit on Knoxville's civic virtues. You can't miss the massive orange basketball that marks the Women's Basketball Hall of Fame (www.wbhof.com; 700 Hall of Fame Dr; adult/child $8/6; ⊙ 10am-5pm Mon-Sat summer, 11am-5pm Tue-Sat winter), a nifty look at the sport from the time when women competed in full-length dresses.

For dinner, find Tupelo Honey Cafe (www.tupelohoneycafe.com; 1 Market Sq; mains $9-19; ⊙ 9am-10pm Mon-Thu, to 11pm Fri, 8am-11pm Sat, to 9pm Sun) a bustling, eclectic dining room on Market Sq serving chorizo-crusted sea scallops, pulled pork with jalapeño BBQ sauce, and shrimp and goat cheese grits. It does a handful of vegetarian dishes too. The Oliver Hotel (☑ 865-521-0050; www.theoliver-hotel.com; 407 Union Ave; r from $145) is the most stylish nest.

Great Smoky Mountains National Park

The Cherokee called this territory Shaconage (shah-*cone*-ah-jey), meaning roughly 'land of the blue smoke,' for the heather-colored mist that hangs over the ancient peaks. The Southern Appalachians are the world's oldest mountain range, with mile upon mile of cool, humid deciduous forest.

The 815-sq-mile park (www.nps.gov/grsm) FREE is the country's most visited and, while the main arteries and attractions can get crowded, 95% of visitors never venture further than 100 yards from their cars, so it's easy to leave the teeming masses behind. There are sections of the park in Tennessee and North Carolina.

Unlike most national parks, Great Smoky charges no admission fee. Stop by a visitor center to pick up a park map and the free *Smokies Guide*. The remains of the 19th-century settlement at Cades Cove are some of the park's most popular sights, as evidenced by the teeth-grinding summer traffic jams on the loop road.

Mt LeConte offers terrific hiking, as well as the only non-camping accommodations, LeConte Lodge (☑ 865-429-5704; www.lecontelodge.com; cabins per person adult/child 4-12yr $126/85). Though the only way to get to the lodge's rustic, electricity-free cabins is via an 8-mile uphill slog. It's so popular you need to reserve up to a year in advance. You can drive right up to the dizzying heights of Clingmans Dome, the third-highest mountain east of the Mississippi, with a futuristic observation tower.

With 10 developed campgrounds offering about 1000 campsites, you'd think finding a place to pitch would be easy. Not so in the busy summer season, so plan ahead. You can

make reservations (☎800-365-2267; www.
nps.gov/grsm; tent site per night $14-23) for some
sites; others are first-come, first-served.
Cades Cove and Smokemont campgrounds
are open year-round; others are open March
to October.

Backcountry camping (☎reservations
865-436-1231; www.nps.gov/grsm/planyourvisit/
backcountry-camping.htm; per night $4) is an ex-
cellent option. A permit is required; you can
make reservations and get permits at the
ranger stations or visitor centers.

❶ Information

The park's three interior visitor centers are
Sugarlands Visitor Center (☎865-436-1291;
www.nps.gov/grsm; ☺8am-7pm Jun-Aug, hours
vary Sep-May), at the park's northern entrance
near Gatlinburg; **Cades Cove Visitor Center**
(☎877-444-6777; ☺9am-7pm Apr-Aug, earlier
Sep-Mar), halfway up Cades Cove Loop Rd,
off Hwy 441 near the Gatlinburg entrance; and
Oconaluftee Visitor Center (p346), at the park's
southern entrance near Cherokee in North
Carolina.

Gatlinburg

Wildly kitschy Gatlinburg hunkers at the
entrance of the Great Smoky Mountains
National Park, waiting to stun hikers with
the scent of fudge and cotton candy. Amuse
yourself Gatlinburg-style at the city's various
Ripley's franchise attractions (a 'Believe it
or Not!' museum of oddities, a mirror maze,
a haunted house, a massive aquarium),
or by riding the scenic 2-mile aerial **tram-
way** (www.obergatlinburg.com; 1001 Parkway;
adult/child $11/8.50; ☺7:30am-6:20pm Sun, to
10:40pm Mon, Fri & Sat, 9:30am-9:49pm Tue-Thu)
to the Bavarian-themed Ober Gatlinburg
Ski Resort (www.obergatlinburg.com; lift ticket
adult $35-54, child $25-44, equipment rental packages ski/snowboard $25/30). Afterwards, suck
down free samples of white lightnin' at the
Ole Smoky Moonshine Distillery (☎865-
436-6995; www.olesmokymoonshine.com; 903
Parkway; ☺10am-10pm), the country's first
licensed moonshine maker (sounds like an
oxymoron to us!). If you plan on sleeping
it off in Gatlinburg, find homey and inviting Bearskin Lodge (☎877-795-7546; www.
thebearskinlodge.com; 840 River Rd; r from $110)
on the river. Wild Boar Saloon & Howard's
Steakhouse (☎865-436-3600; www.wildboar-
saloon.com; 976 Parkway; mains $9-30; ☺10am-
10pm Sun-Thu, to 1:30am Fri & Sat) will make you
feel right at home, come dinner time.

DOLLYWOOD

Dollywood (☎865-428-9488; www.
dollywood.com; 2700 Dollywood Parks
Blvd; adult/child $57/45; ☺Apr-Dec) is a
self-created ode to the patron saint of
East Tennessee, the big-haired, bigger-
bosomed country singer Dolly Parton.
The park features Appalachian-themed
rides and attractions, from the Mystery
Mine roller coaster to the faux one-
room chapel named after the doctor
who delivered Dolly. Find it looming
above the outlet mall mosh pit of
Pigeon Forge (www.mypigeonforge.
com), 9 miles north of Gatlinburg.

KENTUCKY

With an economy based on bourbon, horse
racing and tobacco, you might think Kentucky would rival Las Vegas as Sin Central.
Well, yes and no. For every whiskey-soaked
Louisville bar there's a dry county where
you can't get anything stronger than ginger
ale. For every racetrack there's a church.
Kentucky is made of such strange juxtaposi-
tions. A geographic and cultural crossroads,
the state combines the friendliness of the
South, the rural frontier history of the West,
the industry of the North and the aristocratic charm of the East. Every corner is easy
on the eye, but there are few sights more
heartbreakingly beautiful than the rolling
limestone hills of horse country, where thoroughbred breeding is a multimillion-dollar
industry. In spring the pastures bloom with
tiny azure buds, earning it the moniker
'Bluegrass State.'

❶ Information

The boundary between Eastern and Central time
goes through the middle of Kentucky.
Kentucky State Parks (☎800-255-7275; www.
parks.ky.gov) Offers info on hiking, caving, fishing, camping and more in Kentucky's 52 state
parks. So-called 'Resort Parks' have lodges.
'Recreation Parks' are for roughin' it.
Kentucky Travel (☎800-225-8747, 502-564-
4930; www.kentuckytourism.com) Sends out a
detailed booklet on the state's attractions.

Louisville

Best known as the home of the Kentucky
Derby, Louisville (or Louahvul, as the locals
say) is handsome and underrated. A major

KENTUCKY FACTS

Nickname Bluegrass State

Population 4.4 million

Area 39,728 sq miles

Capital city Frankfort (pop 28,000)

Other cities Louisville (pop 600,000), Lexington (pop 300,000)

Sales tax 6%

Birthplace of 16th US president Abraham Lincoln (1809–65), 'gonzo' journalist Hunter S Thompson (1937–2005), boxer Muhammad Ali (b 1942), actresses Ashley Judd (b 1968) and Jennifer Lawrence (b 1990)

Home of Kentucky Derby, Louisville Slugger, bourbon

Politics Generally to extremely conservative in rural areas

Famous for Horses, bluegrass music, basketball, bourbon, caves

Ongoing internal conflict North vs South allegiance during the Civil War

Driving distances Louisville to Lexington 77 miles, Lexington to Mammoth Cave National Park 135 miles

Ohio River shipping center during the days of westward expansion, Kentucky's largest city is on the come up, with hip bars, superb farm-to-table restaurants, and an engaging, young and increasingly progressive population. It's a fun place to spend a few days, checking out the museums, wandering the old neighborhoods, and sipping some bourbon.

Sights & Activities

The Victorian-era Old Louisville neighborhood, just south of downtown, is worth a stroll. Don't miss St James Court, just off Magnolia Ave, with its utterly charming gas lamp–lit park. There are several wonderful historic homes (www.historichomes.org) in the area open for tours, including Thomas Edison's old shotgun cottage.

⭐ **Churchill Downs**   RACETRACK
(www.churchilldowns.com; 700 Central Ave) On the first Saturday in May, a who's who of uppercrust America puts on their searsucker suits and most flamboyant hats and descends for the 'greatest two minutes in sports,' the Ken-

tucky Derby. After the race, the crowd sings 'My Old Kentucky Home' and watches as the winning horse is covered in a blanket of roses. Then they party.

Actually, they've been partying for a while. The Kentucky Derby Festival (www.kdf.org), which includes a balloon race, a marathon, and the largest fireworks display in North America, starts two weeks before the big event. Most seats at the derby are by invitation only or have been reserved years in advance. On Derby Day, $50 gets you into the infield, which is a debaucherous rave with no seats. It's so crowded you won't see much of the race. Not that you'll mind. If you are a conniseur of the thoroughbreds, from April through to November, you can get a $3 seat at the Downs for exciting warm-up races leading up to the big event.

Kentucky Derby Museum   MUSEUM
(www.derbymuseum.org; Gate 1, Central Ave; adult/child $14/6; ⊙8am-5pm Mon-Sat, 11am-5pm Sun) On the racetrack grounds, the museum has exhibits on derby history, including a peek into the life of jockeys and a roundup of the most illustrious horses. There is a 360-degree audiovisual about the race, and admission includes a 30-minute walking tour of the horse staging area and the track, which includes some engaging yarns.

The 90-minute Inside the Gates Tour ($11) leads you through the jockey's quarters and posh VIP seating areas known as Millionaire's Row.

Muhammad Ali Center   MUSEUM
(www.alicenter.org; 144 N 6th St; adult/senior & student/child 4-12 yr $9/8/5; ⊙9:30am-5pm Tue-Sat, noon-5pm Sun) A love offering to the city from its most famous native, and an absolute must-see. Start on the 5th level where there is a wonderful orientation film. The video archives on the 4th floor enable you to watch every Ali fight!

'Confidence' is a wonderful exhibit about how Ali's supposed swaggering braggadocio more accurately signified rare self love and confidence. For a black man from the South during his era, to rejoice in his own greatness and beauty, was revolutionary and inspiring to behold.

Louisville Slugger Museum   MUSEUM
(www.sluggermuseum.org; 800 W Main St; adult/senior/child $11/10/6; ⊙9am-5pm Mon-Sat, 11am-5pm Sun; 👪) Look for the 120ft baseball bat leaning against the museum. Hillerich & Bradsby Co have been making the famous

Louisville Slugger here since 1884. Admission includes a plant tour, a hall of baseball memorabilia including Babe Ruth's bat, a batting cage and a free mini slugger.

Frazier International History Museum
MUSEUM

(www.fraziermuseum.org; 829 W Main St; adult/student/child $10.50/7.50/6; ⊙9am-5pm Mon-Sat, noon-5pm Sun) Surprisingly ambitious for a midsized city, this state-of-the-art museum covers 1000 years of history with grisly battle dioramas and costumed interpreters demonstrating swordplay and staging mock debates.

State Science Center of Kentucky
MUSEUM

(☑502-561-6100; www.kysciencecenter.org; 727 W Main St; adult/child $13/11; ⊙9:30am-5:30pm Sun-Thu, to 9pm Fri & Sat; ⊛) Set in a historic building on Main St there are three floors of exhibits that illuminate biology, physiology, physics, computing and more for families (kids love it). For an extra $7 you can catch a film in the IMAX theatre.

Big Four Bridge
WALKING, CYCLING

(East River Rd) Town's latest attraction, is an old bridge fixed up new. Built between 1888 and 1895, the Big Four Bridge, which spans the Ohio River and reaches the Indiana shores, had been closed to vehicular traffic since 1969 and was reopened in 2013 as a pedestrian and cycling path, with excellent city and river views throughout.

Dogs are allowed. Skates and skateboards are not. Ample parking.

🛏 Sleeping

Chain hotels cluster near the airport off I-264.

Rocking Horse B&B
B&B $$

(☑888-467-7322, 502-583-0408; www.rockinghorse-bb.com; 1022 S 3rd St; r incl breakfast $125-215) On a stretch of 3rd St once known as Millionaire's Row, this 1888 Romanesque mansion has six guest rooms decorated with Victorian antiques and splendid stained glass. Guests can eat their two-course breakfast in the English country garden or sip complimentary port in the parlor.

★ 21c Museum Hotel
HOTEL $$$

(☑502-217-6300; www.21chotel.com; 700 W Main St; r from $269; P⊛🛜) This contemporary art museum–hotel would be edgy anywhere; in laid-back Louisville, it's mind expanding.

Video screens project your distorted image and falling language on the wall as you wait for the elevator. Chandeliers made from scissors dangle in the hallways. Urban loft-like rooms have iPod docks and mint julep kits in the mini-fridge.

The hotel restaurant, Proof (p384), is one of the city's hippest New Southern bistros, and service could not be finer. Parking is $18.

Brown Hotel
HOTEL $$$

(☑502-583-1234; www.brownhotel.com; 335 West Broadway; r from $250; P⊖⊛🛜) Opera stars, queens and prime ministers have trod the marble floors of this storied downtown hotel, now restored to all its 1920s gilded glamour with 293 comfy rooms and a swank bar. Parking is $18.

🍴 Eating

The number of incredible kitchens multiplies every year, especially in the engaging NuLu area, where there are numerous galleries and boutiques to explore. The Highlands area around Bardstown and Baxter Rds is another popular nightlife and dining spot.

★ Hillbilly Tea
APPALACHIAN $$

(☑502-587-7350; 120 S First St; dishes $10-17; ⊙10am-9pm Tue-Sat, to 4pm Sun) An excellent value cafe off Main St specializing in Appalachian food with a modern twist. You may find smoked catfish served over smashed potatoes or a smoked cornish hen over brussels and parsnips, and the grilled moonshine pork loin looks fantastic.

THE HAUNTED HOSPITAL

Towering over Louisville like a mad king's castle, the abandoned Waverly Hills Sanatorium once housed victims of an early 20th-century tuberculosis epidemic. When patients died, workers dumped their bodies down a chute into the basement. No wonder the place is said to be one of America's most haunted buildings. Search for spooks with a nighttime ghost-hunting tour (☑502-933-2142; www.therealwaverlyhills.com; 4400 Paralee Ln; 2hr tours/2hr ghost hunt/overnight $22/50/100; ⊙Mar-Aug); the genuinely fearless can even spend the night! Many claim it's the scariest place they've ever been.

Garage Bar
GASTROPUB $$

(www.garageonmarket.com; 700 E Market St; dishes $7-16) The best thing to do on a warm afternoon in Louisville is to make your way to this über-hip converted NuLu service station (accented by two kissing Camaros) and order a round of basil gimlets and the ham platter: a tasting of four regionally cured hams, served with fresh bread and preserves.

Then move onto the menu which ranges from the best brick-oven pizza in town, to pork meatballs and turkey wings, to rolled oysters that are divine.

Wiltshire on Market
NEW AMERICAN $$

(502-589-5224; www.wiltshirepantry.com; 636 Market St; mains $14-23; 5-10pm Thu & Sun, to 11pm Fri & Sat) The live music on Sunday nights and community-activist chef are appealing, sure, but the reasonably priced gourmet eats are why you're here. Choose from a half dozen oyster platters paired with a weekly charcuterie board, or go with the country sausage flatbread, the lamb bolognese, or the seriously good veggie burger.

Eiderdown
GASTROPUB $$

(502-290-2390; www.eiderdowngernantown. com; 983 Goss Ave; dishes $4-17; 4-10pm Tue-Thu, 11:30am-11pm Fri & Sat, noon-10pm Sun) When this Kentucky-born, 30-something, French-trained chef fled the corporate confines of a local Outback kitchen, he envisioned this exposed-brick, dark-wood destination pub suffused with the aroma of duck fat popcorn, cabbage, bacon, and *spaetzle* – a melange of root vegetables and sausage dripping with sage butter.

It's in the still-gritty, mostly residential corner of Louisville known as Germantown.

Ghyslain
MARKET CAFE $$

(502-690-8645; www.Ghyslain.com; 721 E Market St; dishes $10-13; 7am-9pm) An inviting market cafe with a menu of delectable baguettes stuffed with roast pork and broccoli, or pesto meatballs, and it does a nice chicken curry wrapped in naan. It also simmers some tasty gumbo (a roux-based stew) and chili. Grab a marble-table top, and finish with fine chocolates or gelato.

★ Proof
NEW SOUTHERN $$$

(502-217-6360; www.proofonmain.com; 702 W Main St; mains $17-36; 7-10am, 11am-2pm & 5:30-10pm Mon-Thu, to 11pm Fri & 7am-3pm, 5:30-11pm Sat, to 10pm Sun) Arguably Louisville's best, and certainly its most lauded restaurant. The cocktails are incredible, the wine and bourbon list (they're known to pour from exclusive and rare barrels of Woodford Reserve and Van Winkle) is long and satsifying, and mains range from a bone-in pork chop, to a succulent bison burger to a high-minded take on chicken and dumplings.

Did we mention they grow and raise some of the ingredients on their own farm? The art is loud and inspired, the servers hip and deadly serious, and the bar crowd is well dressed and festive.

Drinking & Entertainment

The free *Weekly Leo* (www.leoweekly.com) lists local gigs. You'll have no problem finding a watering hole in the Highlands area. Check out the many galleries, restaurants and cafes in NuLu and downtown on the **First Friday Trolley Hop** (www.ldmd.org/First-Friday-Trolley-Hop.html; Main & Market St; 5-11pm, 1st Fri of month) FREE.

Holy Grale
PUB

(www.holygralelouisville.com; 1034 Bardstown Rd; 4pm-late) One of Bardstown's best bars is housed in an old church, with a menu of funked-up pub grub (Scotch quail eggs, kimchee hot dogs) and a dozen rare German, Belgian and Japanese brews on tap. The most intense beers (up to 13% alcohol) can be found in the choir loft.

Please & Thank You
CAFE

(www.pleaseandthankyoulouisville.com/welcome; 800 E Market St; drinks $2-5; 7am-6pm Mon-Fri, 10am-2pm Sat & Sun) The kind of indie cafe that makes a neighborhood. It does tasty coffee drinks and home-baked bread pudding, creative scones and coffee cakes, zucchini bread and gooey chocolate-chip cookies. Oh, and it also sells vinyl, which only adds to the anti-Starbucks mystique.

Rudyard Kipling
BAR, MUSIC

(www.therudyardkipling.com; 422 W Oak St) In Old Louisville, this place is loved by arty locals for its intimate indie-bluegrass shows, way-off-broadway plays and Kentucky bar food (try the 'snappy cheese').

KFC Yum! Center
BASKETBALL

(502-690-9000; www.gocards.com; 1 Arena Plaza) A flood of Cardinal red floods into this downtown arena on game day. The University of Louisville Cardinals, National Collegiate Athletic Association national basketball champs at research time, are led by famed coach Rick Pitino, and the games are almost always sold out. If you love basketball, you should definitely see a game here. The arena also lures the odd pop star.

🛍 Shopping

★ **Joe Ley Antiques**   ANTIQUES
(www.joeley.com; 615 E Market St; ⊙10am-5pm Tue-Sat) A massive, four-story brick-and-stained glass antique emporium crammed with collectibles from eight decades. Think homely dolls, freaky furniture and chunky jewelry.

Butchertown Market   BOUTIQUES
(www.thebutchertownmarket.com; 1201 Story Ave; ⊙10am-6pm Mon-Fri, to 5pm Sat) It's new and ambitious, and you simply have to see this converted slaughterhouse complex that's been turned into a grab bag of quirky, cute and artsy boutiques. Whether it's funky jewelry, kooky gifts, exquisite chocolates, craftsman metal fixtures, bath and body products or baby clothes, someone is selling it here.

Cellar Door Chocolates   CHOCOLATIER
(www.thebutchertownmarket.com; 1201 Story Ave, Butchertown Market; ⊙10am-6pm Mon-Fri, to 5pm Sat) The choclates are as creative as they are delectable, and it has the awards to prove it. Green chili? Check. Coconut milk chocolate? Indeed. Wasabi truffles, white-chocolate bark, sea-salt caramel? Yes please. It haseaspresso too.

Flea Off Market   FLEA MARKET
(www.facebook.com/thefleaoffmarket; 1007 E Jefferson St; ⊙2nd weekend of month) A monthly, weekend-long bazaar of 1980s-era Adidas, rockabilly vinyl, artful terrariums, local craftsman preserves and jerky, and jewelry. Not to mention plenty of vintage threads. The whole thing is catered by food trucks. Somewhere in Portlandia, Fred Armisted is smiling.

Taste   WINE
(☑502-409-4646;   www.tastefinewinesandbourbons.com; 634 E Market Street; tastings $4-8; ⊙11am-8pm Tue-Wed, noon-late Thu & Fri, 10:30am-late Sat) A high-end wine shop that sells small-batch wines and bourbons, and offers sips of either (or both) to help you decide (or perhaps it muddles the whole process). The point is, come, sip, buy.

ℹ Information

Public Library (301 York St) Surf the web free, downtown.

Visitor Center (☑888-568-4784, 502-582-3732; www.gotolouisville.com; 301 S 4th St; ⊙10am-6pm Mon-Sat, noon-5pm Sun)

WORTH A TRIP

INTERNATIONAL BLUEGRASS MUSIC MUSEUM

Kentuckian Bill Monroe is considered the founding father of bluegrass music; his band, the Blue Grass Boys, gave the genre its name. Bluegrass has its roots in the old-time mountain music, mixed with the fast tempo of African songs and spiced with lashings of jazz. Any banjo picker or fiddle fan will appreciate the historic exhibits at the **International Bluegrass Music Museum** (www.bluegrassmuseum.org; 107 Daviess St; adult/student $5/2; ⊙10am-5pm Tue-Sat, 1-4pm Sun) in Owensboro, where you can stumble into a jam session on the first Thursday of the month. The pretty Ohio River town, about 100 miles west of Louisville, also hosts the **ROMP Bluegrass Festival** (www.rompfest.com; ⊙late Jun).

ℹ Getting There & Around

Louisville's International Airport (SDF; ☑502-367-4636; www.flylouisville.com) is 5 miles south of town on I-65. Get there by cab for a flat rate of $20 or by local bus 2. The **Greyhound station** (www.greyhound.com; 720 W Muhammad Ali Blvd) is just west of downtown. **TARC** (www.ridetarc.org; 1000 W Broadway) runs local buses ($1.75) from the Union Station depot.

Bluegrass Country

Drive through northeast Kentucky's Bluegrass Country on a sunny day and glimpse horses grazing in the brilliant-green hills dotted with ponds, poplar trees and handsome estate houses. These once-wild woodlands and meadows have been a center of horse breeding for almost 250 years – the region's natural limestone deposits, and you'll see limestone bluffs rise majestic from out of nowhere, are said to produce especially nutritious grass. The area's principal city, Lexington, is called the 'Horse Capital of the World.'

Lexington

Even the prison looks like a country club in Lexington, home of million-dollar houses and multimillion-dollar horses. Once the wealthiest and most cultured city west of the Allegheny Mountains, it was called 'the Athens of the West.' It's home to the University of

Kentucky and is the heart of the thoroughbred industry. The small downtown has some pretty Victorian neighborhoods, but most of the attractions are in the countryside.

◉ Sights

Kentucky Horse Park   MUSEUM, PARK
(www.kyhorsepark.com; 4089 Iron Works Pkwy; adult/child $16/8, horseback riding $25; ⊘ 9am-5pm daily mid-Mar–Oct, Wed-Sun Nov–mid-Mar; ⊞) An educational theme park and equestrian sports center sits on 1200 acres just north of Lexington. Horses representing 50 different breeds live in the park and participate in special live shows. Also included, the international Museum of the Horse has neat dioramas of the horse through history, from the tiny prehistoric 'eohippus' to Pony Express mail carriers. Guided 35 minute horseback rides are offered seasonally.

Thoroughbred Center   FARM
(www.thethoroughbredcenter.com; 3380 Paris Pike; adult/child $15/8; ⊘ tours 9am Mon-Sat Apr-Oct, Mon-Fri Nov-Mar) Most farms are closed to the public, but you can see working racehorses up close here, with tours of the stables, practice tracks and paddocks.

Ashland   LANDMARK
(www.henryclay.org; 120 Sycamore Rd; adult/child $10/5; ⊘ 10am-4pm Tue-Sat, 1-4pm Sun) Just 1.5 miles east of downtown, part historic home of one of Kentucky's favorite sons, part public park, this was the Italianate estate of statesman Henry Clay (1777–1852) famed for his contribution to Abraham Lincoln's cabinet.

A gorgeous property set in the midst of a tony historic neighborhood, you'll need to pay to enter the home, but you can walk the property for free, peer into the carriage house where his coach is on display, and you can see the, ahem, privy too.

Mary Todd-Lincoln House   HISTORIC BUILDING
(www.mtlhouse.org; 578 W Main St; adult/child $10/5; ⊘ 10am-4pm Mon-Sat) Just behind Rupp Arena, this modest (compared to Ashland) 1806 house has articles from the first lady's childhood and her years as Abe's wife.

⊫ Sleeping

Kentucky Horse Park   CAMPGROUND $
(☑ 800-370-6416, 859-259-4257; www.kyhorsepark.com; 4089 Iron Works Pkwy; sites $20, powered sites $28-35; ⊘ year-round; ⊛) There are 260 paved sites and showers, laundry, a grocery, playgrounds and more. Primitive camping is also available.

Gratz Park Inn   HOTEL $$
(☑ 800-752-4166; www.gratzparkinn.com; 120 W 2nd St; r from $179; ℗ ❄ 🛜) On a quiet downtown street, this 41-room hotel feels like a genteel hunt club, with mahogany furnishings and Old World oil paintings in heavy frames, and a baby grand in the lobby. It's the only boutique choice downtown.

✖ Eating

There are several downtown cafes and bars with outdoor seating around Main and Limestone Sts.

Magee's   BAKERY $
(www.mageesbakery.com; 726 E Main St; donuts & pastries $1-3, mains $6-8; ⊘ 6:30am-2pm Mon & Sat, to 4pm Tue-Fri, 8am-2pm Sun; ℗) Lexington's guiltiest pleasure is this adorable brickhouse bakery with high-arced ceilings, and happy-making cinnamon and pecan rolls, hulking doughnuts and frosted cupcakes. It's especially popular on Sunday morns.

Village Idiot   GASTROPUB $$
(☑ 859-252-0099; www.lexingtonvillageidiot.com; 307 West Short St; dishes $7-17; ⊘ 5pm-midnight Sun-Wed, to 1am Thu-Sat) Hip young foodies descend for dishes comfy and familiar, but with a twist. Think: duck confit and waffles, or scallop and foie gras benedict. The baked brie is wrapped in phyllo dough, drizzled in fig vinegar, and is transcendent. There is a decent bourbon selection too.

★ Table Three Ten   NEW AMERICAN $$$
(☑ 859-309-3901; www.table-three-ten.com; 310 West Short St; dishes $8-32; ⊘ 4:30-11pm Mon-Fri, 11am-3pm Sat, 11am-9pm Sun) Everyday farmers pull up in old pick-ups hauling baskets of rabbits, hens, pork shoulder and veggies, the raw material from which Lexington's best chefs work. Mains are listed on the blackboard, and all the dishes are imganitive (think: lobster mac and cheese) and flavorful. Cocktails are tasty too.

A la Lucie   BISTRO $$$
(☑ 859-252-5277; www.alalucie.com; 159 N Limestone St; mains $19-30; ⊘ 11am-2pm Tue-Fri, 5-10pm Mon-Thu, to 11pm Fri & Sat) An intimate and whimsically decorated bistro serving the classics: a lamb shank here, steak frites there. Don't overlook the white-wine-and-herb-braised Kentucky rabbit. The local choice on date night.

⭐ Entertainment

Keeneland Association   RACETRACK
(☎859-254-3412; www.keeneland.com; 4201 Versailles Rd; general admission $5; ☺races Aug & Oct) Second only to Churchill Downs in terms of quality of competition, races run in April and October, when you can also glimpse champions training from sunrise to 10am. Frequent horse auctions lure sheiks, sultans, hedge fund princes and those who love (or serve) them.

Red Mile   RACETRACK
(www.theredmile.com; 1200 Red Mile Rd; ☺races Aug-Oct) Head here to see harness racing, where jockeys are pulled behind horses in special two-wheeled carts. Live races are in the fall, but you can watch and wager on simulcasts year-round.

Rupp Arena   ARENA
(www.rupparena.com; 430 W Vine St) The home court of perennial national title contender, University of Kentucky basketball. Set in the middle of downtown, it also hosts conventions, concerts and other happenings.

THE BOURBON TRAIL

Silky, caramel-colored bourbon whiskey was likely first distilled in Bourbon County, north of Lexington, around 1789. Today 90% of all bourbon that comes out of the US is produced here in Kentucky, thanks to its pure, limestone-filtered water. Bourbon must contain at least 51% corn, and is stored in charred oak barrels for a minimum of two years. While connoisseurs drink it straight or with water, you must try a mint julep, the archetypal Southern drink made with bourbon, simple syrup and crushed mint.

The Oscar Getz Museum of Whiskey History (www.whiskeymuseum.com; 114 N 5th St; donations appreciated; ☺10am-4pm Tue-Sat, noon-4pm Sun), in Bardstown, tells the bourbon story with old moonshine stills and other artifacts.

Most of Kentucky's distilleries, which are centered on Bardstown and Frankfort, offer free tours. Check out Kentucky's official Bourbon Trail website (www.kybourbontrail. com). Note that it doesn't include every distillery.

Distilleries near Bardstown include:

Heaven Hill (www.bourbonheritagecenter.com; 1311 Gilkey Run Rd; tours $3-5) Distillery tours are offered, but you may also opt to explore the interactive Bourbon Heritage Center.

Jim Beam (www.jimbeam.com; 149 Happy Hollow Rd; tours per person $8; ☺9am-5:30pm Mon-Sat, noon-4:30pm Sun) Watch a film about the Beam family and sample small-batch bourbons at the country's largest bourbon distillery. Beam makes Knob Creek (good), Knob Creek Single Barrel (better), Basil Hayden's (velvety) and the fabulous Booker's (high-proof enlightenment).

Maker's Mark (www.makersmark.com; 3350 Burks Spring Rd; tours $7; ☺10am-4:30pm Mon-Sat, 1-4:30pm Sun) This restored Victorian distillery is like a bourbon theme park, with an old gristmill and a gift shop where you can seal your own bottle in red wax.

Willet (☎502-348-0899; www.kentuckybourbonwhiskey.com; Loretto Rd, Bardstown; tours $7) A craftsman, family-owned distillery making small-batch bourbon in its own patented style. It's a gorgeous 120-acre property and one of our favorites. Tours run throughout the day.

Distilleries near Frankfort/Lawrenceburg:

Buffalo Trace (www.buffalotrace.com; 1001 Wilkinson Blvd) The nation's oldest continuously operating distillery has highly regarded tours and free tastings.

Four Roses (☎502-839-2655; www.fourrosesbourbon.com; 1224 Bonds Mills Rd; ☺9am-4pm Mon-Sat, noon-4pm Sun, closed summer) FREE One of the most scenic distilleries, in a riverside Spanish Mission–style building. Free tastings.

Woodford Reserve (www.woodfordreserve.com; 7855 McCracken Pike; tour per person $7; ☺10am-5pm) The historic site along a creek is restored to its 1800s glory; the distillery still uses old-fashioned copper pots. By far the most scenic of the lot.

❶ Information

Pick up maps and area information from the **visitor center** (☑ 800-845-3959, 859-233-7299; www.visitlex.com; 301 E Vine St; ⊘ 8:30am-5pm Mon-Fri, 10am-4pm Sat). The **public library** (140 E Main St; ⊘ 10am-5pm Tue-Fri, noon-5pm Sat & Sun; 🛜) has free internet access and free wi-fi for laptop luggers.

❶ Getting There & Around

Blue Grass Airport (LEX; ☑ 859-425-3114; www.bluegrassairport.com; 4000 Terminal Dr) is west of town, with about a baker's dozen domestic nonstops. **Greyhound** (www.greyhound.com; 477 W New Circle Rd) is 2 miles from downtown. **Lex-Tran** (www.lextran.com) runs local buses (bus 6 goes to the Greyhound station).

Central Kentucky

The Bluegrass Pkwy runs from I-65 in the west to Rte 60 in the east, passing through some of the most luscious pasturelands in Kentucky.

About 40 miles south of Louisville is Bardstown, the 'Bourbon Capital of the World'. The historic downtown comes alive for the Kentucky Bourbon Festival (www.kybourbonfestival.com; Bardstown; ⊘ Sep). Have a meal, some bourbon and a good night's sleep in the dim limestone environs of Old Talbott Tavern (☑ 502-348-3494; www.talbotts.com; 107 W Stephen Foster Ave; r from $69-109, mains $8-11; 🅿 ✳), which has been welcoming the likes of Abraham Lincoln and Daniel Boone since the late 1700s.

Follow Hwy 31 southwest to Hodgenville and the Abraham Lincoln Birthplace (www.nps.gov/abli; 2995 Lincoln Farm Road, Hodgenville; ⊘ 8am-4:45pm, to 6:45pm summer) **FREE**, a faux-Greek temple constructed around an old log cabin. Ten minutes away is Honest Abe's boyhood home at Knob Creek, with access to hiking trails.

About 25 miles (30 minutes) southwest of Lexington is Shaker Village at Pleasant Hill (www.shakervillageky.org; 3501 Lexington Rd; adult/child $15/5, riverboat rides $10/5; ⊘ 10am-5pm), home to a community of the Shaker religious sect until the early 1900s. Tour impeccably restored buildings, set amid buttercup meadows and winding stone paths. There's a charming inn (☑ 859-734-5611; www.shakervillageky.org; 3501 Lexington Rd; r from $100; 🅿🛜) and restaurant, a paddle-boat ride beneath the limestone bluffs along the Kentucky River, and a gift shop.

Daniel Boone National Forest

Over 700,000 acres of rugged ravines and gravity-defying sandstone arches cover much of the Appalachian foothills of eastern Kentucky. The main ranger station (☑ 859-745-3100; www.fs.fed.us/r8/boone; 1700 Bypass Rd) is in Winchester.

An hour southeast of Lexington is the Red River Gorge, whose cliffs and natural arches make for some of the best rock climbing in the country. Red River Outdoors (☑ 859-230-3567; www.redriveroutdoors.com; 415 Natural Bridge Rd; full-day guided climb from $115) offers guided climbing trips. Red River Climbing (www.redriverclimbing.com) offers detailed route information on its website. Climbers (only) can also pay $2 to camp out behind Miguel's Pizza (www.miguelspizza.com; 1890 Natural Bridge Rd; mains $10-14; ⊘ 7am-10pm Mon-Thu, to 11pm Fri & Sat) in the hamlet of Slade. Bordering Red River Gorge is the Natural Bridge State Resort Park (☑ 606-663-2214; www.parks.ky.gov; 2135 Natural Bridge Rd; r $70-150, cottages $100-170), notable for its sandstone arch. It's a family-friendly park, with camping, and some short hiking trails.

Mammoth Cave National Park

With the longest cave system on earth, Mammoth Cave National Park (www.nps.gov/maca; 1 Mammoth Cave Pkwy, exit 53, off I-65; tours adult $5-48, child $3.50-18; ⊘ 8:45am-5:15pm fall-spring, 8:15am-6:30pm summer) has some 400 miles of surveyed passageways. Mammoth is at least three times bigger than any other known cave, with vast interior cathedrals, bottomless pits and strange, undulating rock formations. The caves have been used for prehistoric mineral-gathering, as a source of saltpeter for gunpowder and as a tuberculosis hospital. Tourists started visiting around 1810 and guided tours have been offered since the 1830s. The area became a national park in 1926 and now brings nearly two million visitors each year.

The only way to see the caves is on the excellent ranger-guided tours (☑ 800-967-2283; adult $5-48, child $3-18) and it's wise to book ahead, especially in summer. Tours range from subterranean strolls to strenuous, daylong spelunking adventures (adults only). The history tour is especially interesting.

In addition to the caves, the park contains 70 miles of trails for hiking, horseback riding and mountain biking. There are also three campsites with restrooms, but no electricity or water hookups ($12 to $30), and 13 free backcountry campsites. Get your backcountry permit at the visitor center at the caves.

GEORGIA

The largest state east of the Mississippi River is a labyrinth of geographic and cultural extremes: right-leaning Republican politics rub against liberal idealism; small, conservative towns merge with sprawling, progressive, financially flush cities; northern mountains rise to the clouds and produce roaring rivers, while coastal marshlands teem with fiddler crabs and swaying cordgrass. Georgia's southern beaches and islands are a treat. And so are its kitchens.

ℹ Information

For statewide tourism information, contact **Discover Georgia** (☑ 800-847-4842; www.exploregeorgia.org). For information on camping and activities in state parks, contact the **Georgia Department of Natural Resources** (☑ 800-864-7275; www.gastateparks.org). Cars are the most convenient way to move around Georgia. I-75 bisects the state running north–south; I-20 runs east–west.

Atlanta

With five million residents in the metro and outlying areas, the so-called capital of the South continues to experience explosive growth thanks to southbound Yankees and international immigrants alike. It's also booming as a tourist destination. Beyond the big-ticket downtown attractions you'll find a constellation of superlative restaurants, a palpable Hollywood influence as Atlanta has become something of a production center, and iconic African American history.

Without natural boundaries to control development, Atlanta keeps growing, yet for all this suburbanization, Atlanta is a pretty city covered with trees and elegant homes. Distinct neighborhoods are like friendly small towns sticthed together. The economy is robust, the population is young and creative, and racial tensions are minimal in 'the city too busy to hate.'

THE SOUTH ATLANTA

◉ Sights & Activities

◉ Downtown

In recent years developers and politicians have been focusing on making the urban core more vibrant and livable. Big attractions in the city have contributed to the success.

World of Coca-Cola   MUSEUM
(www.woccatlanta.com; 121 Baker St; adult/senior/child $16/14/12; ⊙ 9am-7:30pm Mon-Fri, to 8:30pm Sat, 10am-7:30pm Sun) Next door to the Georgia Aquarium, this self-congratulatory museum might prove entertaining to fizzy beverage and rash commercialization fans. The climactic moment comes when guests sample Coke products from around the world – a taste-bud-twisting good time! But there are also Andy Warhol pieces on view, a 4D film to catch, company history to learn, and promotional materials aplenty.

Atlanta

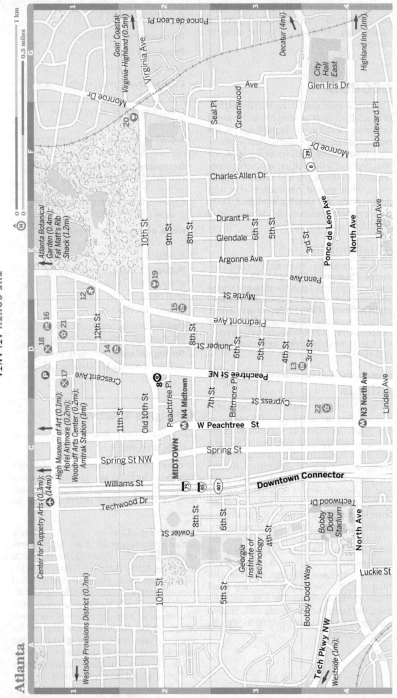

THE SOUTH ATLANTA

1 km
0.5 miles

Westside Provisions District (0.7mi);

Center for Puppetry Arts (0.3mi);
(14mi)

High Museum of Art (0.1mi);
Hotel Artmore (0.2mi);
Woodruff Arts Center (0.2mi);
Amtrak Station (1mi)

Atlanta Botanical
Garden (0.4mi);
Fat Matt's Rib
Shack (1.2mi)

Goin' Coastal;
Virginia-Highland (0.5mi)

Ponce de Leon Pl

Virginia Ave

Monroe Dr

Decatur (4mi)

Highland Inn (1mi)

City
Hall
East

Glen Iris Dr

Ave

Seal Pl

Greenwood

Boulevard Pl

Monroe Dr

Charles Allen Dr

Ponce de Leon Ave

North Ave

Linden Ave

Durant Pl
Glendale
Argonne Ave

10th St
9th St
8th St
6th St
5th St
3rd St

Penn Ave
Myrtle St
Piedmont Ave

8th St
Juniper St
6th St
5th St
4th St
3rd St

Peachtree St NE

Old 10th St
Peachtree Pl
Crescent Ave
11th St
12th St

Spring St NW
Williams St
Techwood Dr

Spring St

W Peachtree St

MIDTOWN

Downtown Connector

7th St
Cypress St
Biltmore Pl

10th St
Fowler St
8th St
6th St
4th St
5th St

Georgia
Institute of
Technology

Bobby
Dodd
Stadium

Techwood Dr

North Ave

Luckie St

Bobby Dodd Way

Tech Pkwy NW

Westside (1mi)

Linden Ave

20
29
8
19
12
16
21
18
14
15
13
22
17
8
75
85
401

N4 Midtown
N3 North Ave

THE SOUTH ATLANTA

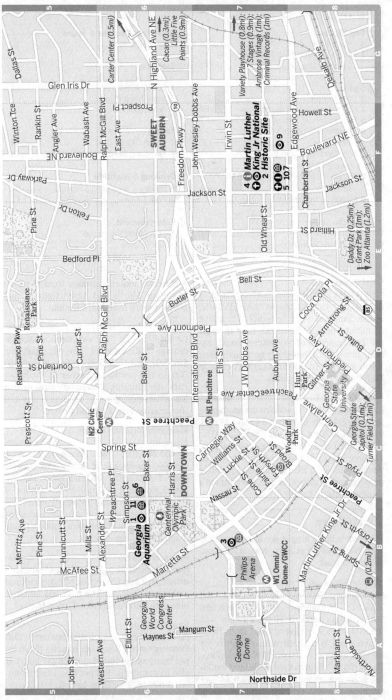

Dallas St

Winton Tce

Glen Iris Dr

Rankin St

N Angier Ave

Wabash Ave

Ralph McGill Blvd

Prospect Pl

East Ave

Carter Center (0.5mi)

N Highland Ave NE

Cacao (0.3mi);
Little Five
Points (0.9mi)

Boulevard NE

SWEET
AUBURN

Freedom Pkwy

John Wesley Dobbs Ave

Jackson St

Irwin St

Variety Playhouse (0.8mi);
7 Stages (0.9mi);
Ambrose Vintage (1mi);
Criminal Records (1mi)

Martin Luther
King Jr National
Historic Site

Edgewood Ave

Howell St

4 1
2
1
5 10 7

9

Chamberlain St

Jackson St

DeKalb Ave

Parkway Dr

Pine St

Felton Dr

Bedford Pl

Old Wheat St

Hilliard St

Bell St

Daddy Dz (0.25mi);
Grant Park (1mi);
Zoo Atlanta (12mi)

Renaissance
Park

Renaissance Pkwy

S Pine St

Currier St

Ralph McGill Blvd

Baker St

Butler St

Piedmont Ave

International Blvd

Ellis St

J W Dobbs Ave

Auburn Ave

Coca Cola Pl

Armstrong St

Butler St

85

Prescott St

Courtland St

Renaissance St

N2 Civic
Center

Prescott St

Spring St

W Peachtree Pl

Simpson St

Baker St

Peachtree St

N1 Peachtree

Peachtree Center Ave

Central Ave

Piedmont Ave

Gilmer St

Hurt
Park

Woodruff
Park

Georgia
State
University

Armstrong Ave

Merritts Ave

Pine St

Hunnicutt St

Mills St

Alexander St

Georgia
Aquarium

1 11
6

Centennial
Olympic
Park

Harris St

Carnegie Way

Williams St

Luckie St

Cone St

Fairlie St

Forsyth St

Broad St

Nassau St

DOWNTOWN

Peachtree St

Pryor St

Georgia-State
Capitol (0.1mi);
Turner Field (1.1mi)

McAfee St

Marietta St

3

Philips
Arena

W1 Omni/
Dome/GWCC

Martin Luther King Jr Dr

Forsyth St

Spring St

(0.2mi)

John St

Western Ave

Elliott St

Haynes St

Mangum St

Georgia
World Congress
Center

Georgia
Dome

Markham St

Northside Dr

Markham St

Northside Dr

Atlanta

CNN Center
TV STUDIO

(☑ 404-827-2300; www.cnn.com/tour/atlanta; 1 CNN Center; tour adult/senior/child $15/14/12; ☺ 9am-5pm) You might be tempted to take a 55-minute behind-the-scenes tour through the headquarters of the international, 24-hour news giant, but don't be heartbroken if you miss it. Visitors don't get very close to Wolf Blitzer (or his cronies).

Georgia State Capitol
LANDMARK

(☑ 404-463-4536; www.libs.uga.edu/capitol-museum; 214 State Capitol; ☺ 8am-5pm Mon-Fri, tours 10am, 10:30am, 11am & 11:30am) **FREE** The gold-domed capitol is Atlanta's political hub. The free tours (choose to be guided or self-guided) include a film about the legislative process and a glance at the government's communications facility.

◎ Midtown

Midtown is like a hipper, second downtown, with plenty of great bars, restaurants and cultural venues.

★ High Museum of Art
GALLERY

(www.high.org; 1280 Peachtree St NE; adult/child $19.50/12; ☺ 10am-5pm Mon-Sat, noon-5pm Sun) Atlanta's modern High Museum was the first to ever exhibit art lent from Paris' Louvre, and is a destination as much for its architecture as its world-class exhibits. The striking whitewashed multilevel building houses a permanent collection of eye-catching late-19th-century furniture, early American modern canvases from the likes of George Morris and Albert Gallatin, and postwar work from Mark Rothko.

Atlanta Botanical Garden
GARDENS

(☑ 404-876-5859; www.atlantabotanicalgarden.org; 1345 Piedmont Ave NE; adult/child $18.95/12.95; ☺ 9am-5pm Tue-Sun, to 7pm Apr-Oct) In the northwest corner of Piedmont Park, the stunning 30-acre botanical garden has a Japanese garden, winding paths and the amazing Fuqua Orchid Center.

Margaret Mitchell House & Museum
LANDMARK

(☑ 404-249-7015; www.margaretmitchellhouse.com; 990 Peachtree St, at 10th St; adult/student/child $13/10/8.50; ☺ 10am-5:30pm Mon-Sat, noon-5:30pm Sun) A shrine to the author of *Gone With the Wind*. Mitchell wrote her epic in a small apartment in the basement of this historic house, though nothing inside it actually belonged to her.

Piedmont Park
PARK

(www.piedmontpark.org) A glorious, rambling urban park and the setting of many cultural and music festivals. The park has fantastic bike paths, and a Saturday Green Market.

Skate Escape
CYCLING

(☑ 404-892-1292; www.skateescape.com; 1086 Piedmont Ave NE) Rents out bicycles (from $6 per hour) and in-line skates ($6 per hour). It also has tandems ($12 per hour) and mountain bikes ($25 for three hours).

◉ Sweet Auburn

Auburn Ave was the thumping commercial and cultural heart of African American culture in the 1900s. Today a collection of sights is associated with its most famous son, Martin Luther King Jr, who was born and preached here and whose grave now looks onto the street. All of the King sites are a few blocks' walk from the MARTA (p400) King Memorial station.

★Martin Luther King Jr
National Historic Site   HISTORIC SITE
(☑ 404-331-5190, 404-331-6922; www.nps.gov/malu/index.htm; 450 Auburn Ave; ☉ 9am-5pm)
FREE The historic site commemorates the life, work and legacy of a civil rights leader and one of the great Americans. The center takes up several blocks. A stop by the excellent bustling visitor center (☉ 9am-5pm, to 6pm summer) will help you get oriented with a map and brochure of area sites, and exhibits that elucidate the context – ie the segregation, systematic oppression and racial violence that inspired and fueled King's work. A 1.5-mile long, landscaped trail leads from here to the Carter Center (p394).

Martin Luther King Jr Birthplace   LANDMARK
(www.nps.gov/malu; 501 Auburn Ave; ☉ tours 10am, 11am, 2pm, 3pm, 4pm & 4:30pm) FREE Free guided tours of King's childhood home take about 30 minutes to complete and require reservations, which can be made at the National Historic Site visitor center.

King Center for Non-Violent
Social Change   MUSEUM
(www.thekingcenter.org; 449 Auburn Ave NE; ☉ 9am-5pm, to 6pm summer) Across from the National Historic Site visitor center, this place has more information on King's life and work and a few of his personal effects, including his Nobel Peace Prize. His gravesite is surrounded by a long reflecting pool and can be viewed any time.

First Ebenezer Baptist Church   CHURCH
(www.historicebenezer.org; 407 Auburn Ave NE; ☉ tours 9am-6pm Mon-Sat, 1:30-6pm Sun) FREE
Martin Luther King Jr, his father and grandfather were all pastors here, and King Jr's mother was the choir director. Sadly she was murdered here by a deranged gunwan while she sat at the organ in 1974. A multimillion-dollar restoration, completed in 2011, brought the church back to the 1960–68 period when King Jr served as co-pastor with his father.

THE SOUTH ATLANTA

ATLANTA FOR CHILDREN

Atlanta has plenty of activities to keep children entertained, delighted and educated.

Georgia Aquarium (www.georgiaaquarium.com; 225 Baker St; adult/child $35/29; ☉ 10am-5pm Sun-Fri, 9am-6pm Sat; P ⛲) The world's largest aquarium is Atlanta's showstopper. Here are whale sharks (certified divers can swim with them), beluga whales and a, gulp, dolphin show, where human actors/trainers and majestic bottlenose dolphins perform together in a Vegas-meets-Broadway production of spectacle and cheese (think more Pirates of the Caribbean than underwater Cirque du Soleil).

Imagine It! Children's Museum of Atlanta (☑ 404-659-5437; www.childrensmuseumatlanta.org; 275 Centennial Olympic Park Dr NW; admission $12.75; ☉ 10am-4pm Mon-Fri, to 5pm Sat & Sun; ⛲) A hands-on museum geared toward kids aged eight and under. Adults aren't allowed in without a youngster in tow.

Center for Puppetry Arts (☑ tickets 404-873-3391; www.puppet.org; 1404 Spring St NW; museum $8.25, performances $16.50-25; ☉ 9am-3pm Tue-Fri, 10am-5pm Sat, noon-5pm Sun; ⛲) A wonderland for visitors of all ages and, hands-down, one of Atlanta's most unique attractions, the museum houses a treasury of puppets, some of which you get to operate yourself. Separate tickets are required for performances, which delight children and often sell out.

Grant Park (www.grantpark.org) A verdant oasis on the southeast edge of the city center, the park is home to Zoo Atlanta (www.zooatlanta.org; Grant Park; adult/child $22/17; ☉ 9:30am-5:30pm Mon-Fri, to 6:30pm Sat & Sun; ⛲), which features flamingos, elephants, kangaroos and the odd tiger. But the zoo's pride and joy are the giant pandas. Their cubs will slaughter you with cuteness.

LITTLE FIVE POINTS & EAST ATLANTA

While much of Atlanta keeps getting ever more hipster and hipsterer, Little Five Points (L5P) has always been Atlanta's bohemian home, though it is becoming more gentrified and touristy by the year. The epicenter is a three-way intersection with a mini plaza where drifters and hippies congregate and strum broke-down guitars and panhandle for smokes. As L5P becomes increasingly yuppified, East Atlanta has emerged as the new hot spot where the hip, gay and ghetto chic converge, conflict and party.

Both are dominated by a main drag – Euclid Ave in L5P and Flat Shoals Ave in East Atlanta – and anchored by popular music venues, Variety Playhouse (p399) and the EARL (p399), respectively.

You can sit in this time capsule, as his voice booms beautifully through the sanctuary. Sunday services are now held at a new Ebenezer across the street.

Virginia-Highland

Leafy and bucolic, families enjoy the historic homes and quiet streets off North Highland Ave. The main focal point of the area is the triangular Virginia-Highland intersection-turned-commercial district, chockablock with restaurants cafes and boutiques – corporate and indie.

Carter Center　　　　　　LIBRARY, MUSEUM
(☑ 404-865-7100; www.jimmycarterlibrary.org; 441 Freedom Pkwy; adult/senior/child $8/6/free; ☺ 9am-4:45pm Mon-Sat, noon-4:45pm Sun) Located on a hilltop overlooking downtown, it features exhibits highlighting Jimmy Carter's 1977–81 presidency, including a replica of the Oval Office. Carter's Nobel Prize is also on display. Don't miss the tranquil Japanese garden out back. The 1.5-mile long, landscaped, Freedom Park Trail leads from here to the Martin Luther King Jr National Historic Site (p393) through Freedom Park.

Festivals & Events

Atlanta Jazz Festival　　　　　　MUSIC
(www.atlantafestivals.com; Piedmont Park; ☺ May) The month-long event culminates in live concerts in Piedmont Park on Memorial Day weekend.

Atlanta Pride Festival　　　　GAY & LESBIAN
(www.atlantapride.org; ☺ Oct) Atlanta's annual GLBT festival.

National Black Arts Festival　　　　CULTURAL
(☑ 404-730-7315; www.nbaf.org; ☺ Jul) Artists from across the country converge to celebrate African American music, theater, literature and film.

Sleeping

Rates at downtown hotels tend to fluctuate wildly depending on whether there is a large convention in town. The least expensive option is to stay in one of the many chain hotels along the MARTA line outside downtown and take the train into the city for sightseeing.

Hotel Artmore　　　　BOUTIQUE HOTEL $$
(☑ 404-876-6100; www.artmorehotel.com; 1302 W Peachtree St; r $134-274; P ❄ @ ☞) This funky art-deco gem wins all sorts of accolades: excellent service, a wonderful, wine-inviting courtyard with fire pit and a superb location across the street from Arts Center MARTA station. The 1924 Spanish-Mediterranean architectural landmark was completely revamped in 2009 resulting in an artistic boutique hotel that's become an urban sanctuary for those who appreciate their trendiness with a dollop of discretion. Parking is $18.

Hotel Indigo　　　　　　BOUTIQUE $$
(☑ 404-874-9200; www.hotelindigo.com; 683 Peachtree St; r $129-179; P) A boutique-style hotel that's actually part of a chain, the Indigo has a boisterous blue color scheme and a sunny personality. More important is the outstanding Midtown location, across the street from restaurants and entertainment and within walking distance of MARTA. Parking costs $18.

Highland Inn　　　　　　INN $$
(☑ 404-874-5756; www.thehighlandinn.com; 644 N Highland Ave; r from $81; P ❄ ☞) This European-style inn, built in 1927, has appealed to touring musicians over the years. Rooms aren't huge, and that carpet is a bit threadbare, but it's as affordably comfy as Atlanta gets and is well located in the Virginia-Highland area. Paying $10 more gets you a much bigger room and a queen bed.

W Midtown   HOTEL $$

(☎ 404-892-6000; www.watlantamidtown.com; 188 14th St NE; r from $190; P ✳ @ 🛜 🏊) A short stroll from Piedmont Park this iteration of the W offers the typical mod style you've come to expect. Rooms aren't huge but are plenty spacious with flatscreens, love seats and excellent views from top floors. The in-house Whiskey Park club attracts scenesters on the weekends.

This place caters mostly to a corporate crowd which means rates soar midweek but you can score great deals on the weekends.

★ Stonehurst Place   B&B $$$

(☎ 404-881-0722; www.stonehurstplace.com; 923 Piedmont Ave NE; r $159-399; P ✳ @ 🛜) Built in 1896 by the Hinman family, this elegant B&B has all the modern amenities one could ask for, is fully updated with eco-friendly water treatment and heating systems, and has original Warhol illustrations on the wall. Well located, it's an exceptional choice if you have the budget.

Loews Atlanta   HOTEL $$$

(☎ 404-745-5000; www.loewshotels.com; 1065 Peachtree St; r from $269; ✳ @ 🛜) Smart and modern, arguably Atlanta's finest luxury hotel is part of the Loews chain and offers all the over-the-top comforts in the heart of Midtown. The attached Exhale Spa will soothe your weary heart after board meetings and its art collection adds some flair.

✕ Eating

After New Orleans, Atlanta is the best city in the South to eat and food culture here is nothing short of obsessive.

✕ Downtown & Midtown

Fat Matt's Rib Shack   BARBECUE $$
(www.fatmattsribshack.com; 1811 Piedmont Ave NE; mains $6-21; ⊙ 11:30am-11:30pm Mon-Fri, to 12:30am Sat, 1-11:30pm Sun) A classic shrine to two great Southern traditions: barbecue and the blues. Take special note of the Brunswick stew, a delicious side dish best described as barbecue soup.

Daddy Dz   BARBECUE $$
(☎ 404-222-0206; www.daddydz.com; 264 Memorial Dr; sandwiches $6-12, plates $13-20; P) This juke joint of a BBQ shack, consistently voted tops in town, has soul to spare. From the graffiti murals on the red, white and blue exterior to the all-powerful smoky essence to the reclaimed booths on the covered patio. Order the succulent ribs or a pulled-pork plate. You'll leave smiling.

Tamarind Seed   THAI $$
(www.tamarindseed.com; 1197 Peach Tree St NE; mains $14-28; ⊙ 11am-10pm Mon-Thu, to 11pm Fri, 4-11pm Sat, noon-10pm Sun; P) A bustling and sleek Thai eatery amidst the Midtown towers, serving the upwardly mobile business crowd. It does all the Thai staples and some intriguing departures like spicy lamb with

THE SOUTH ATLANTA

MARTIN LUTHER KING JR: A CIVIL RIGHTS GIANT

Martin Luther King Jr, the quintessential figure of the American Civil Rights movement and arguably America's greatest leader, was born in 1929, the son of an Atlanta preacher and choir leader. His lineage was significant not only because he followed his father to the pulpit of Ebenezer Baptist Church, but also because his political speeches rang out with a preacher's inflections.

In 1955 King led the year-long 'bus boycott' in Montgomery, AL, which resulted in the US Supreme Court removing laws that enforced segregated buses. From this successful beginning King emerged as an inspiring moral voice.

His nonviolent approach to racial equality and peace, which he borrowed from Gandhi and used as a potent weapon against hate, segregation and racially motivated violence – a Southern epidemic at the time – makes his death all the more tragic. He was assassinated on a Memphis hotel balcony in 1968, four years after receiving the Nobel Peace Prize and five years after giving his legendary 'I Have a Dream' speech in Washington, DC.

King remains one of the most recognized and respected figures of the 20th century. Over 10 years he led a movement that essentially ended a system of statutory discrimination in existence since the country's founding. The Martin Luther King Jr National Historic Site (p393) and the King Center for Non-Violent Social Change (p393) in Atlanta are testaments to his moral vision, his ability to inspire others and his lasting impact on the fundamental fabric of American society.

basil and baked scallops with Penang curry. It validates parking.

South City Kitchen SOUTHERN $$$
(📞404-873-7358; www.southcitykitchen.com; 1144 Crescent Ave; mains $17-36; ⊙11am-3:30pm, 5-10pm Sun-Thu, to 10:30pm Fri & Sat) An upscale Southern kitchen featuring tasty updated staples like buttermilk fried chicken served with sautéed collards and mash, and a Georgia trout, pan fried with lemon mascarpone. Start with flash fried oysters dipped in cornmeal, served with shellfish etoufee, grilled andouille and fried capers.

🍴 Westside

The **Westside Provisions District** (www. westsidepd.com; 100-1210 Howell Mill Rd; P) is an inviting new complex of hip, farm-to-table-inspired restaurants sprinkled among upscale shops and lofts on Atlanta's Westside. There is a lot to choose from here.

★West Egg Cafe DINER $
(www.westeggcafe.com; 1100 Howell Mill Rd; mains $6-12; ⊙9am-9pm Mon & Tue, to 10pm Wed-Fri, 8am-10pm Sat, to 9pm Sun; P🍴) Belly up to the marble breakfast counter or grab a table and dive into a salmon cake Benedict, eggs and grits, banana-bread french toast, a fried green tomato BLT, sugar bacon pancakes, or short rib hash. All the dishes are reimagined versions of old school classics, served in a stylish and spare dining room.

The tasty Irish coffees and cute wait staff don't hurt.

Star Provisions SELF-CATERING $
(📞404-365-0410; www.starprovisions.com; 1198 Howell Mill Rd; ⊙10am-midnight Mon-Sat) DIY gourmands will feel at home among the cheese shops and butcher cases, bakeries and kitchen hardware depots. The meat department has an exceptional array of house-cured meats, including pepperoni, bresaola, lonzino and prosciutto, if you have picnic on the brain.

Yeah! Burger BURGERS $
(www.yeahburger.com; 1168 Howell Mill Rd; burgers $6-11; ⊙11:30am-10pm Sun-Thu, to 11pm Fri & Sat; P🍴) A creative, cheap-and-cheerful burger joint where you pick the patty: grass-fed beef, bison, turkey, veggie or chicken breast, tap a bun (including a gluten-free option), select one of nine cheeses and 22 toppings among rarities like jalapeños, ni-

trate-free bacon or fig jam, and add one of 18 sauces.

Kids love it, there's a full bar, and the plastic cups are compostable.

JCT Kitchen & Bar NEW AMERICAN $$
(📞404-355-2252; www.jctkitchen.com; 1198 Howell Mill Rd; mains $9-24; ⊙11am-2:30pm Mon-Sat, 5-10pm Mon-Thu, to 11pm Fri & Sat, 5-9pm Sun) Think: stylish wood floors and glass walls with bird-cage lighting, a knotty-wood bar and a tasty array of plates from chicken liver mousse on toast to shrimp and grits to slow-cooked rabbit to a tasty lump crab roll. It does a damn fine hanger steak too.

Abattoir CHOPHOUSE $$$
(📞404-892-3335; www.starprovisions.com/abattoir; 1170 Howell Mill Rd; mains $15-35; ⊙6-11pm Tue-Sat; P) An aptly named, upscale, carnivorous kitchen with a gorgeous bar area. The burger is top shelf, the fried quail comes with braised greens and a cornbread waffle, the shrimp and grits is curry spiced, and the hanger steak is a classic. This is a chophouse, pure and simple, complete with laid-back swank.

Bacchanalia FINE DINING $$$
(📞404-365-0410; www.starprovisions.com/bacchanalia; 1198 Howell Mill Rd; prix-fixe per person $85; ⊙from 6pm) Widely considered the top restaurant in the city at research time, the menu rotates daily and you may choose from six dishes for each of the five courses. Start with a Hawaiian hamachi with preserved lemon shoyu and raddish or perhaps a foie gras confit. Move into a Gulf crab fritter, a sweet-potato angilotti or poached halibut.

Then comes the lamb strip steak or quail or local Berkshire pork and winter kale, before the decadent cheese course and dessert. The atmosphere verges on chilly. Reserve ahead.

🍴 Virginia-Highland & Around

Little Five has a fun vibe on weekends. Inman Park is a transitional neighborhood, set just east of downtown. And amidst the mayhem of East Atlanta, there is a lobster roll that will make you quiver.

Sevananda SELF-CATERING $
(www.sevananda.coop; 467 Moreland Ave NE, Little Five Points; ⊙8am-10pm) Voted Atlanta's best health-food store and a gold mine for self caterers, this co-op has a decent deli, hot soups, organic produce, natural health rem-

edies, and that unmistakable sniff of left-leaning food politics.

Cacao
CHOCOLATIER $

(www.cacaoatlanta.com; 312 N Highland Ave NE; sweets $4-6; ☉11am-9pm Mon-Thu, 10am-10pm Fri & Sat, 11am-6pm Sun) Chocolate lovers should duck into this sleek boutique for sinful truffles and gelato (the dark choclate is absurdly good), an outrageous-looking, four-layer chocolate cake, and soul-warming mocha.

★ Fox Brothers
BARBECUE $$

(☑404-577-4030; www.foxbrosbbq.com; 1238 DeKalb Ave NE; dishes $8-25; ☉11am-10pm Sun-Thu, to 11pm Fri & Sat) Another longtime Atlanta classic, set in Inman Park, ribs are scorched and smoked perfectly with a hint of charcoaled crust on the outside and tender on the inside. They're also known for their exceptional Texas-style brisket, and they bottle their own sauce.

Octopus Bar
ASIAN FUSION $$

(www.octopusbaratl.com; 560 Gresham Ave SE, East Atlanta; dishes $3-14; ☉10:30pm-2:30am Mon-Sat) Do they keep odd hours? Is seating difficult to come by? Does it take so long to get your fusion grub because the chefs are maybe, sorta, getting high in the back alley? And, finally, is that bartender the handsomest man in Georgia? The answer, of course, is yes, to all of the above. So leave your hang-ups at the hotel and get to know what good is at this indoor-outdoor patio dive nuanced with graffed-up walls and ethereal electronica. Offerings include the best dish in the city: the lobster roll of enlightenment. No reservations, so line up early.

★ Goin' Coastal
SEAFOOD $$$

(www.goincoastalseafood.com; 1021 Virginia Ave NE; mains $18-26; ☉5-10pm Sun-Thu, to 11pm Fri & Sat) A casual neighborhood seafood kitchen in the heart of the Highlands lists fresh catch on the blackboard, supplemented by stunning staples such as lobster tacos ($18), coastal trout ($24) and a heap of delicious sides (creamy grits, jalapeño cornbread pudding). Whole Maine lobsters are just $20 on Monday nights.

🍴 Decatur

Independent Decatur, 6 miles east of downtown, has grown into a countercultural enclave and a bonafide foodie destination. Like most traditional Southern towns, the gazebo-crowned Courthouse Square is the center of the action, with a number of restaurants, cafes and shops surrounding it.

Victory
SANDWICHES $

(www.vicsandwich.com; 340 Church St, Decatur; sandwiches $4; ☉11am-2am) One of two area locations, the other is in Inman Park, this spare, converted Decatur brick house is a wonderful bargain gourmet sandwich counter where baguettes are stuffed with white anchovies and lemon mayo, or prosciutto, arugula and apples, among other intriguing options.

★ Leon's Full Service
FUSION $$

(☑404-687-0500; www.leonsfullservice.com; 131 E Ponce de Leon Ave; mains $11-24; ☉5pm-1am Mon, 11:30am-1am Tue-Thu & Sun, to 2am Fri & Sat) No pretense, just a gorgeous concrete bar and an open floorplan that spills out of a former service station and onto a groovy heated deck with floating beams. Everything, from the beer, wine and cocktails (their spirits are all craftsman, small-batch creations) to the menu (think pan-roasted trout served with roasted cauliflower and an apple-curry broth or house-made chicken sausage in green curry with baby bok choi) show love and attention to detail. No wonder this place is packed. No reservations.

No. 246
ITALIAN $$

(☑678-399-8246; www.no246.com; 129 E Ponce de Leon Ave; mains $12-25; ☉11am-3pm & 5-10pm Mon-Sat, to 9pm Sun) An upscale woodfired pizza and house-made pasta joint with gourmet gravitas. It does charcuterie and cheese to start, and the wonderful agnolotti is stuffed with goat cheese, roasted beets, radish and tarragon. The gnocchi with fennel sausage meatballs is worthy too. So are the pizzas. Service is superb.

Cake's & Ale
NEW AMERICAN $$$

(☑404-377-7994; www.cakesandalerestaurant.com; 155 Sycamore St; mains $24-36; ☉6-11pm Tue-Thu, 5:30pm-midnight Fri & Sat) A recent Top Chef alum and pastry mastermind opened this hip and new eatery on the square. The bakery next door has life-affirming hot chocolate along with a case of delecatable pastries, but it closes early. Fear not, have a port at the molded-concrete bar and pair it with a ricotta cheesecake and blood-orange sorbet, or make that the pineapple fritters folded in brioche dough and topped with rum ice cream.

The dinner menu is spare, and rotates almost weekly, but usually offers oysters, a rib eye, and intriguing options like pork belly and shrimp served over fennel purée. That crispy rabbit leg looks good too.

🍷 Drinking & Nightlife

Brick Store Pub   BAR
(www.brickstorepub.com; 125 E Court Sq) Beer hounds geek out on Atlanta's best beer selection at this pub in Decatur, with some 17 meticulously chosen draughts, and a separate, and more intimate Belgian beer bar upstairs. In total, it serves nearly 200 beers by the bottle and draw a fun, young crowd every night.

Ormsby's   BAR
(www.ormsbysatlanta.com; 1170 Howell Mill Rd, Westside; ⊙11am-3am Mon-Fri, from noon Sat, noon-midnight Sun) Submerged beneath the Westside Provisions District (p396), this sprawling, well populated, underground pub not only has over a dozen craftsman beers on tap, and dozens more from Germany, Belgium, Sri Lanka and other exotic ports, it has games! Bocce ball, shuffleboard, billiards, ski ball and board games like Connect Four are yours to play until the wee smalls.

Rumor has it, this joint was originally a prohibition-era burlesque haunt with S&M proclivities.

Graveyard Tavern   BAR
(www.graveyardtavern.com; 1245 Glenwood Ave SE; ⊙5pm-2am Mon-Sat, 7pm-midnight Sun) Here the rafters are exposed along with the building's age, not out of high design impulse, but because this dive in East Atlanta is deliciously decrepit. The octagonal wood bar and vinyl booths host all kinds: hipsters, queers, hip-hoppers, gangsters and retirees.

Park Tavern   BAR
(www.parktavern.com; 500 10th Street NE; ⊙4:30pm-midnight Mon-Fri, from 11:30am Sat & Sun) This microbrewery-restaurant may not be all that hip, but its outdoor patio on the edge of Piedmont Park is one of the most beautiful spots in Atlanta to sit back and drink away a weekend afternoon. It pours $1 drafts on rainy days.

Blake's   GAY & LESBIAN
(www.blakesontheparkatlanta.com; 227 10th St NE) On Piedmont Park, Blake's bills itself as 'Atlanta's favorite gay bar since 1987.'

☆ Entertainment

Atlanta has big-city nightlife with lots of live music and cultural events. For listings, check out **Atlanta Coalition of Performing Arts** (www.atlantaperforms.com). The **Atlanta Music Guide** (www.atlantamusicguide.com) maintains a live-music schedule, plus a directory of local venues and links to online ticketing. Smartphone addicts should check into the **Bandsintown** app. It's especially useful in big-city America.

Theater

Woodruff Arts Center   ARTS CENTER
(www.woodruffcenter.org; 1280 Peachtree St NE, at 15th St) An arts campus hosting the High Museum, the Atlanta Symphony Orchestra and the Alliance Theatre.

Fox Theatre   THEATER
(☑855-285-8499; www.foxtheatre.org; 660 Peachtree St NE; ⊙box office 10am-6pm Mon-Fri, to 3pm Sat) A spectacular 1929 movie palace with fanciful Moorish and Egyptian designs. It hosts Broadway shows and concerts in an auditorium holding more than 4500 people.

14th Street Playhouse   THEATRE
(☑404-733-5000; www.14thstplayhouse.org; 173 14th St NE; admission from $25) If you crave a night at the Theatre, head here for professional productions of mainstream, and some avant-garde, plays and musical theatre.

7 Stages   THEATRE
(☑404-523-7647; www.7stages.org; 1105 Euclid Ave) An independently operated, nonprofit

---

GAY & LESBIAN ATLANTA

Atlanta – or 'Hotlanta' as some might call it – is one of the few places in Georgia with a noticeable and active gay and lesbian population. Midtown is the center of gay life; the epicenter is around Piedmont Park and the intersection of 10th St and Piedmont Ave, try Blake's (p398). The town of Decatur, east of downtown Atlanta, has a significant lesbian community. For news and information, grab a copy of *David Atlanta* (www.david-atlanta.com); also check out www.gayatlanta.com.

Atlanta Pride Festival (p394) is a massive annual celebration of the city's gay and lesbian community. Held in October in and around Piedmont Park.

theatre complex specializing in productions featuring local playwrights.

Live Music & Nightclubs

Cover charges at the following vary nightly. Check their respective websites for music calendars and ticket prices.

EARL LIVE MUSIC
(www.badearl.com; 488 Flat Shoals Ave, East Atlanta) The indie rocker's pub of choice – with a busy live-music calendar and surprisingly good food.

Eddie's Attic LIVE MUSIC
(☑404-377-4976; www.eddiesattic.com; 515b N McDonough St) One of the city's best venues to hear live folk and acoustic music, renowned for breaking local artists, in a nonsmoking atmosphere seven nights a week. In East Atlanta.

Variety Playhouse LIVE MUSIC
(www.variety-playhouse.com; 1099 Euclid Ave NE) A smartly booked and well-run concert venue for a variety of touring artists. It's the anchor that keeps Little Five Points relevant.

Sports

Order tickets to sporting events through **Ticketmaster** (☑404-249-6400; www.ticketmaster.com).

Atlanta Braves BASEBALL
(☑404-522-7630; www.atlantabraves.com; 755 Hank Aaron Dr SE; tickets $8-90) The Major League Baseball (MLB) team plays at **Turner Field**. The MARTA/Braves shuttles to the games leave from **Underground Atlanta** (www.underground-atlanta.com; cnr Peachtree & Alabama Sts; ⊘10am-9pm Mon-Sat, 11am-6pm Sun) at Steve Polk Plaza beginning 90 minutes before first pitch.

🛍 Shopping

Ambrose Vintage VINTAGE
(www.facebook.com/AmbroseVintage; 1160 Euclid Ave; ⊘11am-7pm) By far the finest of Little Five's vintage boutiques. You'll find a nice selection of blazers and leathers for men, tweed jackets and slacks, ties and denim jackets, skirts, sweaters, blouses and hats for the ladies – all of it spanning four decades. It has tasty rock on the sound system too.

Criminal Records MUSIC
(www.criminalatl.com; 1154 Euclid Ave; ⊘11am-9pm Mon-Sat, noon-7pm Sun) A throwback record store with used and new pop, soul, jazz, and

metal, on CD or vinyl, here for your perusal. It has a fun music-related book section, and some decent comic books.

ℹ Information

EMERGENCY & MEDICAL SERVICES

Atlanta Medical Center (www.atlantamedcenter.com; 303 Pkwy Dr NE) A 460-bed tertiary care hospital operating since 1901.
Atlanta Police Department (☑404-614-6544; www.atlantapd.org)
Emory University Hospital (www.emoryhealthcare.org; 1364 Clifton Rd NE)
Piedmont Hospital (www.piedmonthospital.org; 1968 Peachtree Rd NW)

INTERNET ACCESS

Central Library (www.afpls.org; 1 Margaret Mitchell Sq; ⊘9am-9pm Mon-Sat, 2-6pm Sun; 🛜) Many branches of the public library offer two free 15-minute internet sessions daily, including this main branch.

MEDIA

Atlanta (www.atlantamagazine.com) A monthly general-interest magazine covering local issues, arts and dining.
Atlanta Daily World (www.atlantadailyworld.com) The nation's oldest continuously running African American newspaper (since 1928).
Atlanta Journal-Constitution (www.ajc.com) Atlanta's major daily newspaper, with a good travel section on Sunday.
Creative Loafing (www.clatl.com) For hip tips on music, arts and theater, this free alternative weekly comes out every Wednesday.

POST

For general postal information call 800-275-8777. There are post office branches at **CNN Center** (190 Marietta St NW, CNN Center); **Little Five Points** (455 Moreland Ave NE); **North Highland** (1190 N Highland Ave NE) and **Phoenix Station** (41 Marietta St NW).

Useful Websites

Scout Mob (www.scoutmob.com) Tips on what's new and hot in Atlanta.
Dixie Caviar (www.dixiecaviar.com) Recipes and restaurant recommendations from a young, brainy Atlanta-area foodie in the know.
Atlanta Travel Guide (www.atlanta.net) Official site of the Atlanta Convention & Visitors Bureau with excellent links to shops, restaurants, hotels and upcoming events. Its website also lets you buy a CityPass, a tremendous money saver that bundles admission to five of the city's attractions for a discounted price (see www.citypass.com/atlanta for more).

ⓘ Getting There & Away

Atlanta's huge **Hartsfield-Jackson International Airport** (ATL; Atlanta; www.atlanta-airport.com), 12 miles north of downtown, is a major regional hub and an international gateway.

The **Greyhound terminal** (232 Forsyth St) is next to the MARTA Garnett station. Some destinations include Nashville, TN (five hours), New Orleans, LA (10½ hours), New York (20 hours), Miami, FL (16 hours) and Savannah, GA (4¾ hours).

The **Amtrak station** (1688 Peachtree St NW, at Deering Rd) is just north of downtown.

ⓘ Getting Around

The **Metropolitan Atlanta Rapid Transit Authority** (MARTA; ☑ 404-848-5000; www.its-marta.com; fares $2.50) rail line travels to/from the airport to downtown, along with less useful commuter routes. Each customer must purchase a Breeze card ($1), which can be loaded and reloaded as necessary.

The shuttle and car-rental agencies have desks in the airport, situated at baggage claim.

Driving in Atlanta can be infuriating. You'll often find yourself sitting in traffic jams, and it's easy to get disoriented – Google Maps is invaluable. Some cyclists brave the city streets.

North Georgia

The southern end of the great Appalachian Range extends some 40 miles into Georgia's far north, providing superb mountain scenery, some damn decent wines, and frothing rivers. Fall colors emerge late here, peaking in October. A few days are warranted to see sites like the 1200ft-deep Tallulah Gorge (www.gastateparks.org/tallulahgorge), and the mountain scenery and hiking trails at Vogel State Park (www.gastateparks.org/vogel) and Unicoi State Park (www.gastateparks.org/unicoi).

Dahlonega

In 1828 Dahlonega was the site of the first gold rush in the USA. The boom these days, though, is in tourism, as it's an easy day excursion from Atlanta and is a fantastic mountain destination. The visitor center (☑ 706-864-3513; www.dahlonega.org; 13 S Park St; ⊙ 9am-5:30pm Mon-Fri, 10am-5pm Sat), on Courthouse Sq has plenty of information on area sights and activities (including hiking, canoeing, kayaking, rafting and mountain biking). Amicalola Falls State Park (☑ 706-265-4703; www.amicalolafalls.com; entry per vehi-

cle $5), 18 miles west of Dahlonega on Hwy 52, features the 729ft Amicalola Falls, the highest waterfall in Georgia.

A dozen or so wineries on the town's outskirts produce tasty products. You can sip on the square at the Naturally Georgia (www.naturallygeorgia.com; 90 Public Sq N; ⊙ noon-5pm Mon-Thu, to 8pm Fri-Sun) tasting room, but it's well worth seeking out Frogtown Cellars (☑ 706-878-5000; www.frogtownwine.com; 700 Ridge Point Dr; tastings $15; ⊙ noon-5pm Mon-Fri, to 6pm Sat, 12:30-5pm Sun), a beautiful winery with a killer deck on which to sip libations, and behind it, Three Sisters (☑ 706-865-9463; www.threesistersvineyards.com; tastings $15; ⊙ 1-5pm Thu-Sun). They pair their fine wine with bluegrass and Cheetos.

Crimson Moon Café (www.thecrimsonmoon.com; 24 N Park St; mains $8-15; ⊙ 11am-3pm Mon, to 9pm Wed, to 9:30pm Thu-Sun) is an organic coffeehouse offering Southern comfort food and an intimate live-music venue. The seafood at Back Porch Oyster Bar (☑ 706-864-8623; www.facebook.com/backporchoysterbar; 19 North Chestatee St; mains $9-30; ⊙ 11:30am-8pm) is delivered fresh daily.

★ Hiker Hostel (☑ 770-312-7342; www.hikerhostel.com; 7693 Hwy 19N; dm/r $18/42; P ✳ @ ⟩), on Hwy 19N near the Three Gap Loop, is owned by avid outdoors enthusiasts and caters to those looking to explore the Appalachian Trail, which begins nearby. Each bunk room has its own bathroom and it is wonderfully neat and clean.

Central Georgia

Central Georgia is a mostly rural catch-all for everything that's not metro Atlanta, mountainous north Georgia or swampy Savannah. It feels rustic, real and definitively Southern.

Athens

A beery, artsy and laid-back college town roughly 70 miles east of Atlanta, Athens has an extremely popular football team (the University of Georgia Bulldogs), a world-famous music scene (which has launched artists including the B-52s, R.E.M. and Widespread Panic) and a burgeoning restaurant culture. The university drives the culture of Athens and ensures an ever-replenishing supply of young bar-hoppers and concert goers, some of whom stick around long after graduation and become 'townies.' The pleasant, walkable downtown offers a plethora of funky choices for eating, drinking and shopping.

◎ Sights

★ Georgia Museum of Art   MUSEUM

(www.georgiamuseum.org; 90 Carlton St; suggested donation $3; ⊘10am-5pm Tue-Wed, Fri & Sat, to 9pm Thu, 1-5pm Sun) A smart, modern gallery open to the public where brainy, arty types set up in the wired lobby for personal study and art hounds gawk at modern sculpture in the courtyard garden and a tremendous collection from American realists of the 1930s. Rotating exhibitions always inspire.

State Botanical Garden
of Georgia   GARDENS

(☑706-369-5884;   www.uga.edu/~botgarden; 2450 S Milledge Ave; ⊘8am-8pm) **FREE** Truly gorgeous, with winding outdoor paths and a socio-historical edge to boot, Athens' gardens rivals Atlanta's. Signs provide smart context for its amazing collection of plants, which runs the gamut from rare and threatened species to nearly 5 miles of top-notch woodland walking trails.

🛏 Sleeping & Eating

Athens does not have a great selection of lodging. There are standard chains just out of town on W Broad St.

★ Hotel Indigo   BOUTIQUE HOTEL $$

(☑706-546-0430; www.indigoathens.com; 500 College Ave; r weekend/weekday from $159/139; P❋@🛜🛝) 🍃 Rooms are spacious, loft-like pods of cool at this eco-chic boutique hotel. Part of the Indigo chain, it's a Leadership in Energy and Environmental Design gold-certified sustainable standout. Green elements include regenerative elevators and priority parking for hybrid vehicles, and 30% of the building was constructed from recycled content.

Foundry Park Inn & Spa   INN $$

(☑706-549-7020; www.foundryparkinn.com; 295 E Dougherty St; r from $110; P❋@🛜🛝) A cute, indie choice on pleasant grounds that include a restored Confederate iron foundry. In addition to its on-site spa, the hotel campus includes a restaurant and a cozy music venue.

Ike & Jane   CAFE $

(www.ikeandjane.com; 1307 Prince Ave; mains $3.50-7; ⊘6:30am-5pm Mon-Fri) If your idea of a balanced breakfast is doughnuts and cof-fee, you might be a police officer, an 85-year-old man or a fan of this sunny little shingle in Normal Town, where the doughnuts involve creative ingredients like red velvet, caramel, peanut butter, banana and bacon.

The coffee is gourmet, and it does quiche, bagels, and gourmet soups, salads and sandwiches too.

Heirloom Cafe   CAFE $$

(☑706-354-7901; www.heirloomathens.com; 815 N Chase St; mains $10-15; ⊘11am-3pm & 5:30-9pm Mon-Thu, to 10pm Fri, 9:30am-2:30pm & 5:30-10pm Sat, 9:30am-2:30pm Sun; 🅿) A new spot specializing in locally sourced ingredients folded into tasty dishes like shrimp and grits, a prosciutto, cheese and apple baguette, and a mean pulled-pork sandwich. Weekend brunch features a popular gruyere-and-fig omelet.

★ Five & Ten   AMERICAN $$$

(☑706-546-7300; www.fiveandten.com; 1653 S Lumpkin St; mains $18-29; ⊘10:30am-2:30pm Sun, 5:30-10pm Sun-Thu, to 11pm Fri & Sat) 🍃 Driven by sustainable ingredients, Five & Ten ranks among the South's best restaurants. Its menu is earthy and slightly gamey: sweatbreads, hand-cut pasta and Frogmore stew (stewed corn, sausage and potato). Reservations mandatory.

National   NEW SOUTHERN $$$

(☑706-549-3450; www.thenationalrestaurant.com; 232 W Hancock Ave; mains $20-28; ⊘11:30am-10pm Mon-Thu, to late Fri & Sat, 5-10pm Sun) An effortlessly cool bistro on the downtown outskirts, favored for the kale Caesar, the peppery crawfish bisque, a nice pan-roasted trout, and mussels steamed in an orange-saffron-chili vinaigrette. The bar is one where you may want to sit and sip a while.

🍷 Drinking & Entertainment

Nearly 100 bars and restaurants dot Athens' compact downtown area, so it's not hard to find a good time. Pick up a free *Flagpole* (www.flagpole.com) to find out what's on.

Normal Bar   BAR

(www.facebook.com/normal.bar.7; 1365 Prince Ave; ⊘4pm-2am Mon-Thu, from 3pm Fri & Sat) This lovable dark storefront bar, a bit out of the way in Normal Town, is very un-student but still very much Athens. The beer goes from PBR cheap to local craftsman IPA-sophiticati. It has a terrific wine list and the crowd is young, cute and doesn't care either way.

Grab a candlelit booth inside, belly up to the bar or hang on the back patio.

Flicker
BAR

(www.flickertheatreandbar.com; 263 W Washington St; ⊙4pm-2am Mon-Fri, from 1pm Sat) A happening hipster scene simmers. It hosts live bands and has a slender smoking patio populated with intellectual, self-confident hairdos and the occasional vaguely sexy fire twirler. It's always busy. Even on Monday nights.

Cutter's
SPORTS BAR

(www.facebook.com/cutterspub; 120 E Clayton St; ⊙2:30pm-2am Mon-Fri, from noon Sat) A popular sports bar with gargantuan flatscreens. If victory is grasped by the UGA Bulldogs, the interior becomes a sloshed dance hall of depravity. But in a good way.

Walker's Coffee & Pub
PUB

(www.walkerscoffee.com; 128 College Ave; ⊙7am-2am) Where grad students and a few sophisticated under grads stretch out in the built-in wooden booths that wrap around the room. It specializes in an array of liquored-up coffee drinks. But you can get a sensible coffee here too.

40 Watt Club
LIVE MUSIC

(☑706-549-7871; www.40watt.com; 285 W Washington St; admission $5-30) This legendary joint has lounges, a tiki bar, $2 PBRs, and has welcomed indie rock to its stage since R.E.M., the B-52s and Widespread Panic owned this town. It's still where the big hitters play when they visit.

Georgia Theatre
VENUE

(☑706-850-7670; www.georgiatheatre.com; 215 N Lumpkin St; ⊙11:30am-midnight Mon-Sat) When this historic movie theater burnt down it was rebuilt as a hip music venue. Only the facade and marquee remain from the original, and there is a brand-new bar on the rooftop with stunning views of uplit downtown.

Sanford Stadium
STADIUM

(☑706-542-9036; www.georgiadogs.com; 100 Sanford Dr) Home of the beloved University of Georgia Bulldogs football team.

ⓘ Information

The **Athens Welcome Center** (☑706-353-1820; www.athenswelcomecenter.com; 280 E Dougherty St; ⊙10am-5pm Mon-Sat, noon-5pm Sun), in a historic antebellum house at the corner of Thomas St, provides maps and information on local tours – these include a Civil War tour and the 'Walking Tour of Athens Music History.'

Savannah

Like a proper Southern belle with a an electric-blue streak in her hair, this grand historic town revolves around formal antebellum architecture and the revelry of local students from Savannah College of Art & Design (SCAD). It sits alongside the Savannah River, about 18 miles from the coast, amid Lowcountry swamps and mammoth live oak trees dripping with Spanish moss. With its colonial mansions, and beautiful squares, Savannah preserves its past with pride and grace. However, unlike its sister city of Charleston, SC, which retains its reputation as a dignified and refined cultural center, Savannah is a little gritty, lived in, and real.

◎ Sights & Activities

The Central Park of Savannah is a sprawling rectangular green space called **Forsyth Park**. The park's beautiful fountain is a quintessential photo op. Savannah's **riverfront** is mostly populated with forgettable shops and cafes. But it's worth a short stroll. As is **Jones Street**, among Savannah's prettiest thanks to the mossy oaks that hold hands from either side.

A $20 multi-venue ticket gets you into the Jepson Center for the Arts, Telfair Academy and the Owen-Thomas House.

★Wormsloe Plantation
Historic Site
PLANTATION

(www.gastateparks.org; 7601 Skidaway Rd; adult/senior/youth 6-17yr/child 1-5yr $10/9/4.50/1; ⊙9am-5pm Tue-Sun) A short drive from downtown, on the beautiful **Isle of Hope**, this is one of the most photographed sites in town. The real draw is the dreamy entrance through a corridor of mossy, ancient oaks that runs for 1.5 miles, known as the **Avenue of the Oaks**.

But there are other draws, including an existing antebellum mansion still lived in by the descendants of the original owner, Noble Jones, some old colonial ruins, and a touristy site where you can see folks demonstrate blacksmithing and other bygone trades. There are two flat, wooded walking trails here too. The one-miler takes in the main sights. A 3-mile trail extends to the plantation boundary.

Owens-Thomas House
HISTORIC BUILDING

(www.telfair.org; 124 Abercorn St; adult/child $15/5; ☺noon-5pm Mon, 10am-5pm Tue-Sat, 1-5pm Sun) Completed in 1819 by British architect William Jay, this gorgeous villa exemplifies English Regency-style architecture, which is known for its symmetry. The guided tour is fussy, but it delivers interesting trivia about the spooky 'haint blue' ceiling paint in the slaves' quarters (made from crushed indigo, buttermilk and crushed oyster shells) and the number of years by which this mansion preceded the White House in getting running water (nearly 20).

Jepson Center for the Arts
GALLERY

(JCA; www.telfair.org; 207 W York St; adult/child $12/5; ☺10am-5pm Mon, Wed, Fri & Sat, to 8pm Thu, noon-5pm Sun; 🖼) Looking pretty darn space-age by Savannah's standards, the JCA focuses on 20th- and 21st-century art. Its contents are modest in size but intriguing. There's also a neat interactive area for kids.

Mercer-Williams House
HISTORIC BUILDING

(www.mercerhouse.com; 429 Bull St; adult/child $12.50/8) Although Jim Williams, the Savannah art dealer portrayed by Kevin Spacey in the film version of *Midnight in the Garden of Good and Evil*, died back in 1990, his infamous mansion didn't become a museum until 2004. You're not allowed to see the upstairs, where Williams' family still lives, but the downstairs is an interior decorator's fantasy.

Telfair Academy of Arts & Sciences
MUSEUM

(www.telfair.org; 121 Barnard St; adult/child $12/5; ☺noon-5pm Mon, 10am-5pm Tue-Sat, 1-5pm Sun) Considered Savannah's top art museum, the historic Telfair family mansion is filled with 19th-century American art, silver from that century, and a smattering of European pieces.

SCAD Museum of Art
ART MUSEUM

(www.scadmoa.org; 601 Turner Blvd; adult/child under 14 yr $10/free; ☺10am-5pm Tue, Wed & Fri, to 8pm Thu, noon-5pm Sat & Sun) Brand new and architecturally striking, this brick, steel, concrete and glass longhouse delivers your modern fix. With groovy, creative sitting areas inside and out, and fun rotating exhibitions.

Cathedral of St John the Baptist
CHURCH

(222 E Harris St) If you like old churches, you will love it here. Completed in 1896 but destroyed by fire two years later, this impressive cathedral, reopened in 1912, features stunning stained-glass transept windows from Austria depicting Christ's ascension into heaven, as well as ornate Station of the Cross woodcarvings from Bavaria. The pipe organ is equally spectacular.

Ralph Mark Gilbert Civil Rights Museum
MUSEUM

(460 Martin Luther King Jr Blvd; adult/senior/child $8/6/4; ☺9am-5pm Tue-Sat) Set in what was once the most successful black-owned bank in America, this private museum focuses on the local history of segregated schools, hotels, hospitals, jobs and lunch counters. Push the buttons at Levy's lunch counter for a stinging dramatization.

Savannah Bike Tours
CYCLING

(☎912-704-4043; www.savannahbiketours.com; 41 Habersham St) Operating out of a cute little storefront on Habersham St, this outfit offers two-hour bike tours on its fleet of cruisers (with baskets of course).

🛏 Sleeping

Luckily for travelers, it's become stylish for Savannah hotels and B&Bs to serve hors d'oeuvres and wine to guests in the evening. Cheap sleeps are difficult to find and all accommodations should be booked in advance.

Azalea Inn
INN $$

(☎912-236-2707; www.azaleainn.com; 217 E Huntingdon St; r from $199; P❄🛜🏊) A humble stunner on a quiet street, we love this sweet canary-yellow historic inn near Forsyth Park. The 10 rooms aren't huge, but are well done with varnished dark-wood floors, crown mouldings, four-post beds and a small dipping pool out back.

Bed & Breakfast Inn
B&B $$

(☎912-238-0518; www.savannahbnb.com; 117 W Gordon St; r $179-229; P❄🛜) Spittin' distance from Savannah's most architecturally diverse square (Monterrey), this is a well-loved, well-worn establishment. Meaning it does show its age. Easy to walk right by on a uniform street of 1850 row houses, the location is ideal.

Mansion on Forsyth Park
HOTEL $$$

(☎912-238-5158; www.mansiononforsythpark.com; 700 Drayton St; r weekend/weekday $249/199; P❄@🛜🏊) A choice location and chic design highlight the luxe accommodations on offer at the 18,000-sq-ft Mansion – the sexy bathrooms alone are practically

Savannah

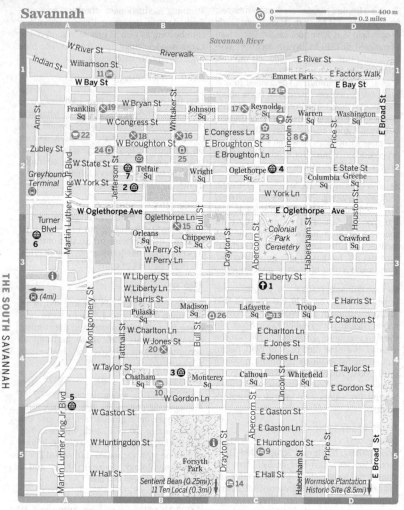

worth the money. The best part of the hotel-spa is the amazing local and international art that crowds its walls and hallways, over 400 pieces in all. Parking costs $20 per day.

Bohemian Hotel BOUTIQUE HOTEL $$$
(☏ 912-721-3800; www.bohemianhotelsavannah.com; 102 West Bay St; r from $299; P❋@🛜) Enjoy sleek, dark, Gothic hallways, a riverside perch and small touches like driftwood and oyster chandeliers. Rooms are stunning, though too low-lit for some. Personalized service makes it feel far more intimate than its 75 rooms indicate. Parking is $25

East Bay Inn INN $$$
(☏ 912-238-1225; www.eastbayinn.com; 225 E Bay St; r from $235) Wedged between corporate rivals, this brick behemoth offers just 28 huge rooms all with original wood floors, exposed brick walls, soaring ceilings, slender support columns and fat flatscreens, along with much charm and warmth.

Hamilton Turner Inn INN $$$
(☏ 912-233-1833; www.hamilton-turnerinn.com; 330 Abercorn St; d from $189; ❋🛜) Set on picturesque Lafayette Sq and built in classic French style in 1873, all 17 rooms offer

Savannah

elegant antique decor that may make you swoon, though service is not one of the inn keepers' strong points.

✕ Eating

Angel's BBQ
BARBECUE $

(www.angels-bbq.com; 21 West Oglethorpe Lane; sandwiches/plates $6/8; ⊘11:30am-3pm Tue, to 6pm Wed-Sat) Utterly low-brow and hidden down an uneventful lane, Angel's pulled-pork sandwich and sea-salted fries will leave you humbled and thoroughly satisfied – and that's before you tear through the impressive list of housemade sauces.

Vinnie Van GoGo's
PIZZERIA $

(www.vinnievangogo.com; 317 W Bryan St; pizza slices from $2.50; ⊘4-11pm Mon-Thu, noon-midnight Fri & Sat, noon-11:30pm Sun) This locally owned pizzeria draws legions of locals for its Neapolitan brick-oven pies.

Wilkes' House
SOUTHERN $$

(www.mrswilkes.com; 107 W Jones St; lunch $16; ⊘11am-2pm Mon-Fri) The line outside can begin as early as 8am at this first-come, first served, Southern comfort food institution. Once the lunch bell rings and you are seated family-style, the kitchen unloads on you: fried chicken, beef stew, meatloaf, cheese potatoes, collard greens, black-eyed peas, mac 'n' cheese, rutabaga, candied yams, squash casserole, creamed corn *and* biscuits.

It's like Thanksgiving and the Last Supper rolled into one massive feast chased with sweet tea.

Papillote
CAFE $$

(www.papillote-savannah.com; 218 W Broughton St; mains $9-14; ⊘10:30am-7pm Wed-Fri, 9:30am-5pm Sat & Sun) One of our favorite new spots in town serves creative yet simple delights, like a chicken curry pot pie, and a baguette stuffed with braised pork, roasted red peppers and melted Swiss. The omelets and brioche French toast for brunch are popular too.

Circa 1875
BISTRO $$

(☏912-443-1875; www.circa1875.com; 48 Whitaker St; mains $12-28; ⊘bar 5pm-2am, dinner 6-11pm) A gorgeous little bistro downtown with high tin ceilings, turn-of-the-century tiled floors, and a dynamite burger drenched in peppercorn sauce and served with truffle fries. It also does frog legs, escargot, pâté, steak tartare and steak frites, of course.

★11 Ten Local
NEW AMERICAN $$$

(☏912-790-9000; www.local11ten.com; 1110 Bull St; mains $24-32; ⊘6-10pm Mon-Sat) Upscale, sustainable, local, fresh: these elements help create an elegant, well-run restaurant, that's, hands down, the best in Savannah. Start with a spring roll salad, an unfurled spring roll speckled with ginger dressing, then move on to the fabulous big eye tuna,

THE SOUTH SAVANNAH

seared perfectly fresh and plated with kim chi and green-pea purée.

Or just pick a grilled protein – fillet, fresh catch, scallops, or chicken breast – and one or three of their awesome sauces and sides like brussels with walnuts and sausage or a historically good mac and cheese.

Olde Pink House   NEW SOUTHERN $$$

(☑912-232-4286; www.plantersinnsavannah.com/ savannah-dining.htm; 23 Abercorn St; mains $25-31; ⊙11am-10:30pm) Classic Southern food done upscale, our favorite appetizer is southern sushi – shrimp and grits rolled in a coconut-crusted nori roll. Dine in the slender digs upstairs, or go underground to the fabulous tavern where the piano player rumbles and the room is cozy, funky and perfect. The buidling is a 1771 landmark.

🍷 Drinking & Nightlife

Rocks on the Roof   BAR

(www.bohemianhotelsavannah.com/dining/lounge; 102 West Bay St; ⊙from 11am; 🐾) The expansive rooftop bar at the Bohemian Hotel is breezy, fun and best when the weather is nice and the firepit is glowing. The views are sensational.

Lulu's Chocolate Bar   CAFE

(www.luluschocolatebar.net; 42 Martin Luther King Jr Blvd) More a place to sink yourself into a sugar coma than catch a buzz, Lulu's is an adorable yet chic neighborhood martini and dessert bar. The heavenly signature Lulutini is pure chocolate decadence.

Sentient Bean   CAFE

(www.sentientbean.com; 13 E Park Ave; ⊙7am-10pm; 🐾) 🍴 Everything you want from an indie coffee house: terrific brew, gourmet scones, spacious boho interior and hipster clientele and baristas. It's Savannah's favorite and just across from Forsyth Park.

Abe's on Lincoln   BAR

(17 Lincoln St) Ditch the tourists – drink with the locals in dark, dank, all-wood environs. It hosts open-mic nights and occasional live performances.

☆ Entertainment

Lucas Theatre for the Arts   THEATER

(☑912-525-5040; www.lucastheatre.com; 32 Abercorn St) Hosting concerts (guitarist Jonny Lang), plays (*Guys and Dolls*) and films (*The Day the Earth Stood Still*) in a historic building dating from 1921.

🔒 Shopping

West Broughton St is Savannah's preeminent shopping district – with both corporate and indie entities shoulder to shoulder, and all of it punctuated with a distinctly SCAD flavor.

★Satchel   HANDBAGS

(☑912-233-1008; www.shopsatchel.com; 311 W Broughton St) After graduating from SCAD, 29-year-old designer and owner, Elizabeth Seeger, didn't want to get a real job (or move away from Savannah), so she opened a store. She makes her all-leather goods in-house, and we're talking about an amazing collection of high-end bespoke hand bags that belong on a runway. Her men's wallets are terrific too.

Savannah Bee Company   FOOD

(www.savannahbee.com; 104 W Broughton St; ⊙10am-8pm Mon-Sat, 11am-5pm Sun) This internationally renowned honey dreamland is one of Savannah's must-stops. Expect artisanal honey of infinite variety and limitless free tastings.

ShopSCAD   ARTS & CRAFTS

(www.shopscadonline.com; 340 Bull St; ⊙9am-5:30pm Mon-Wed, to 8pm Thu & Fri, 10am-8pm Sat, noon-5pm Sun) All the wares at this funky, kitschy boutique were designed by students, faculty and alumni of Savannah's prestigious art college.

ℹ Information

Candler Hospital (www.sjchs.org; 5353 Reynolds St)

CVS Pharmacy (cnr Bull & W Broughton Sts)

Live Oak Public Library (www.liveoakpl.org; 2002 Bull St; ⊙9am-8pm Mon-Tue, to 6pm Wed-Fri, 2-6pm Sun; 🐾) Offers free internet and wi-fi access.

Post Office Historic District (118 Barnard Street; ⊙8am-5pm Mon-Fri); Main (1 E Bay St; ⊙8am-5:30pm Mon-Fri, 9am-1pm Sat)

Savannah Chatham Metropolitan Police (☑912 651-6675; www.scmpd.org; cnr E Oglethorpe Ave & Habersham St)

Visitor Center (☑912-944-0455; www.savannahvisit.com; 301 Martin Luther King Jr Blvd; ⊙8:30am-5pm Mon-Fri, 9am-5pm Sat & Sun) Excellent resources and services are available in this center, based in a restored 1860s train station. Many privately operated city tours start here. There is also a small interactive tourist-info kiosk in the new Visitor Center at Forsyth Park.

ℹ Getting There & Around

The **Savannah/Hilton Head International Airport** (SAV; www.savannahairport.com) is about 5 miles west of downtown off I-16. Taxis from the airport to the Historic District cost a standard $28. **Greyhound** (www.greyhound.com; 610 W Oglethorpe Ave) has connections to Atlanta (about five hours), Charleston, SC (about two hours) and Jacksonville, FL (2½ hours). The **Amtrak station** (www.amtrak.com; 2611 Seaboard Coastline Dr) is just a few miles west of the Historic District.

You won't need a car. It's best to park and walk. **Chatham Area Transit** (CAT; www.catchacat.org; per ride $1.50) operates local buses that run on bio-diesel, including a free shuttle (the Dot) that makes its way around the Historic District and stops within a couple of blocks of nearly every major site.

Brunswick & the Golden Isles

Georgia has a coast? Oh yes, a righteously beautiful one, blessed with a string of picturesque islands ranging from rustic to kitschy to indulgent. With its large shrimp-boat fleet and downtown historic district shaded beneath lush live oaks, Brunswick dates from 1733 and has charms you might miss when sailing by on I-95 or the Golden Isle Pkwy (US Hwy 17). During WWII Brunswick shipyards constructed 99 Liberty transport ships for the navy. Today a 23ft scale model at Mary Ross Waterfront Park (Bay St) stands as a memorial to those ships and their builders. On the first Friday of the month quirky Brunswick opens up its fun antique and art galleries and pours wine for all comers.

St Simons Island

Famous for its golf courses, resorts and majestic live oaks, St Simons Island is the largest and most developed of the Golden Isles. It lies 75 miles south of Savannah and just 5 miles from Brunswick. The southern half of the island is a thickly settled residential and resort area. However the northern half and adjacent Sea Island (www.explorestsimonsisland.com) offer tracts of coastal wilderness amid a tide-water estuary. East Beach, the island's best, is accessible from Massengale Park (1350 Ocean Blvd). Munch tasty seafood at Crab Trap (☑912-638-3552; www.thecrabtrapssi.com; 1209 Ocean Blvd; dishes $11-25). Bed down near the main downtown drag at St Simons Inn by the Lighthouse (☑912-

638-1101; www.saintsimonsinn.com; 609 Beachview Dr; r from $179; P❋✿🛜≋).

Little St Simons is an all-natural jewel, accessible by boat only to guests at the exclusive Lodge on Little St Simons (☑912-638-7472; www.littlessi.com; 1000 Hampton Pt, Little St Simons Island; all-inclusive d from $475; ☺May-Sep) or to their day trippers (☑912-638-7472; www.littlestsimonsisland.com; Hampton Point Dr; ☺trips 10:30am).

Jekyll Island

An exclusive refuge for millionaires in the late 19th and early 20th centuries, Jekyll is a 4000-year-old barrier island with 10 miles of beaches. Today it's an unusual clash of wilderness, historically preserved buildings, modern hotels and a massive campground. It's an easily navigable place – you can get around by car, horse or bicycle, but there's a $5 parking fee per day.

An endearing attraction is the Georgia Sea Turtle Center (☑912-635-4444; www.georgiaseaturtlecenter.org; 214 Stable Rd; adult/child $7/5; ☺9am-5pm Sun-Tue, 10am-2pm Mon, tours 8:30pm & 9:30pm from Jun 1; ♿), a conservation center and turtle hospital where patients are on view for the public. Come sunrise, you must find Driftwood Beach.

The posh yet antiquated Jekyll Island Club Hotel (☑800-535-9547; www.jekyllclub.com; 371 Riverview Dr; d/ste from $179/279; P❋@✿≋) is a great place for a drink after a sunset seafood dinner at its waterfront Latitude 31 Restaurant & Rah Bar (www.latitude31andrahbar.com; mains $14-23; ☺from 11:30am Tue-Sun), located right on the wharf. For something closer to the best beaches, find Villas By The Sea (☑912-635-2521, 800-841-6262; www.villasbythesearesort.com; 1175 N Beachview Dr; condos from $149).

Cumberland Island & St Marys

An unspoiled paradise, a backpacker's fantasy, a site for day trips or extended stays – it's clear why the family of 19th-century industrialist and philanthropist Andrew Carnegie used Cumberland as a retreat long ago. Most of this southernmost barrier island is now occupied by the Cumberland Island National Seashore (www.nps.gov/cuis; admission $4). Almost half of its 36,415 acres consists of marsh, mudflats and tidal creeks. On the ocean side are 16 miles of wide, sandy beach that you might have all to yourself. The island's interior is characterized by maritime forest. Ruins from the Carnegie estate Dungeness are astounding, as are the wild turkeys, tiny fiddler crabs and beautiful butterflies. Feral horses roam the island and are a common sight.

The only public access to the island is via boat to/from the quirky, lazy town of St Marys (www.stmaryswelcome.com). Convenient and pleasant ferries (☑912-882-4335; www.nps.gov/cuis; round-trip adult/senior/child $20/18/14) leave from the mainland at the St Marys dock at 9am and 11:45am and return at 10:15am and 4:45pm. Reservations are staunchly recommended well before you arrive, and visitors are required to check in at the visitor's center (☑912-882-4336; www.nps.gov/cuis; ⊘8am-4:30pm) at the dock at least 30 minutes prior to departure. December through February, the ferry does not operate on Tuesday or Wednesday.

St Marys caters to tourists visiting Cumberland. This tiny, lush one-horse town has a number of comfortable B&Bs, including the lovely Spencer House Inn (☑912-882-1872; www.spencerhouseinn.com; 200 Osborne St; r $135-245), circa 1872. It's brushed-up pink, with 14 spacious rooms on three floors. The staff book ferry reservations, pack lunches for day trippers and serve a full gourmet breakfast each morning. When you're hungry, find Riverside Cafe (www.riversidecafesaintmarys.com; 106 St Marys Rd; mains $8-18; ⊘11am-9pm Mon-Fri, from 8:30am Sat & Sun), a wonderful Greek diner with sea views.

On Cumberland Island, the only private accommodations are at the Greyfield Inn (☑904-261-6408; www.greyfieldinn.com; r incl meals $425-635), a mansion built in 1900, with a two-night minimum stay. Camping is available at Sea Camp Beach (☑912-882-4335; www.nps.gov/cuis; tent sites per person $4), a campground set among magnificent verdant oaks.

Note: there are no stores or waste bins on the island. Eat before arriving or bring lunch, and take your trash with you.

ALABAMA

Football and history are two things Southerners never stop discussing, and Alabama is the perfect prism for both. It was home to one of gridiron's most legendary coaches, Paul 'Bear' Bryant, and to Jefferson Davis, the first president of the Confederacy in 1861 (the year the Civil War began).

More significantly, in the 1950s and '60s, Alabama became a civil rights battleground pitting racial segregationists against nonviolent activists who demanded freedom. The ripple effects were felt in legislation that affected the entire country, and exploring this state provides powerful insight into uniquely American racial dynamics, and the United States' checkered history as a whole.

Geographically, Alabama has a surprising diversity of landscapes, from leafy foothills in the north to the subtropical Gulf Coast down south. And let's not forget endearing Birmingham, a shining light of progress in a state that all too often seems to be shadow boxing with its own demons.

❶ Information

Alabama Bureau of Tourism & Travel (www.alabama.travel) Sends out a vacation guide and has a website with extensive tourism options.
Alabama State Parks (☑800-252-7575; www.alapark.com) There are 23 parks statewide with camping facilities ranging from primitive ($12) to RV hookups ($26). Advanced reservations are suggested for weekends and holidays.

Birmingham

No one can ignore Birmingham's checkered past – civil rights violence earned it the nickname 'Bombingham.' Yet this midsize, blue-collar city will show you a good time, has a surprising amount of culture, and has integrated its civil rights struggle into the tourist experience. Such perspective, and a bustling economy – Mercedes Benz manufactures here – has allowed the city to look forward, and become modern, open and new.

◎ Sights & Activities

Art-deco buildings in trendy Five Points South house shops, restaurants and nightspots. Equally noteworthy is the newer and more upscale Homewood community's quaint commercial drag on 18th St S, close to the Vulcan who looms illuminated above the city and is visible from nearly all angles, day and night.

★**Birmingham Civil Rights Institute** — MUSEUM
(www.bcri.org; 520 16th St N; adult/senior/child $12/5/3, Sun free; ⊘10am-5pm Tue-Sat, 1-5pm Sun) A maze of moving audio, video and photography exhibits tell the story of racial segregation in America, and the Civil Rights

movement – with a focus on activities in and around Birmingham. There's an extensive exhibit on the 16th Street Baptist Church bombing in 1963, and it's the beginning of the city's new Civil Rights Memorial Trail.

16th Street Baptist Church
CHURCH
(www.16thstreetbaptist.org; cnr 16th St & 6th Ave N; donation $5; ⊙ministry tours 10am-4pm Tue-Fri, to 1pm Sat) This church became a gathering place for organizational meetings and a launch pad for protests in the 1950s and '60s. During a massive desegregation campaign directed at downtown merchants in 1963, Ku Klux Klan members bombed the church during Sunday school, killing four little girls. Today the rebuilt church is a memorial and a house of worship (services 10:45am Sunday).

Vulcan Park
PARK
(www.visitvulcan.com; 1701 Valley View Dr; observation tower adult/child $6/4; ⊙7am-10pm, observation tower 10am-6pm Mon-Sat, from 1pm Sun) Visible from all over the city thanks to the world's largest cast-iron statue, the park offers fantastic views for free, and an observation tower.

Birmingham Museum of Art
GALLERY
(www.artsbma.org; 2000 Rev Abraham Woods Jr Blvd; ⊙10am-5pm Tue-Sat, noon-5pm Sun) FREE Collects work from Asia, Africa, Europe and the Americas. Don't miss the work of Rodin, Botero and Dalí in the sculpture garden.

Birmingham Civil Rights Memorial Trail
WALKING TOUR
(www.bcri.org; 520 16th St N;) Seven blocks long, a poignant walk perfect for the whole family, and installed in 2013 for the 50th anniversary of the Civil Rights campaign, the walk depicts 22 moving scenes with statues and photography, and peels back yet another layer of the sweat and blood behind a campaign that changed America.

For instance, you'll learn that Martin Luther King Jr's strategy was to flood the city jails, but to spare families from losing their bread winners, they recruited high-school students who became known as 'foot soldiers' within the movement.

🛏 Sleeping

★ Aloft
HOTEL $$
(205-874-8055; www.aloftbirminghamsohosquare.com; 1903 29th Ave S; r from $129; P❄🛜) Yes, it's a chain, but this W-conceived kid sister in the Homewood area is a steal with

---

ALABAMA FACTS

Nickname the Heart of Dixie

Population 4.8 million

Area 52,419 sq miles

Capital city Montgomery (population 205,600)

Other city Birmingham (population 212,038)

Sales tax 4%, but up to 11% with local taxes

Birthplace of Author Helen Keller (1880–1968), civil rights activist Rosa Parks (1913–2005), musician Hank Williams (1923–53)

Home of US Space & Rocket Center

Politics Republican stronghold – Alabama hasn't voted Democratic since 1976

Famous for Rosa Parks and the Civil Rights movement

Bitter rivalry South vs North (yes, still!), University of Alabama vs Auburn University

Driving distances Montgomery to Birmingham 91 miles, Mobile to Dauphin Island 38 miles, Mobile to Tuscaloosa 196 miles

---

new, modern interiors, king beds and high ceilings, up-to-the-minute electronics, ample light, and luscious bathrooms and linens. There's a fun bar with a pool table and a news ticker in the groovy lobby.

Redmont Hotel
HISTORIC HOTEL $$
(205-324-2101; 2101 5th Ave N; r/ste from $89/129; ❄@🛜) A historic hotel built in 1925, the piano and chandelier in the lobby lend a certain historical, old-world feel and all deluxe rooms are just renovated giving it modern edge. The spacious rooftop bar doesn't hurt, either. It's walking distance to the civil rights sights.

Hotel Highland
HOTEL $$
(205-271-5800; www.thehotelhighland.com; 1023 20th St S; r from $129; P❄@🛜) Nuzzled right up next to the lively Five Points district, this colorful, slightly trippy, modern hotel manages to be very comfortable and a good deal. The rooms are thankfully a bit less bright and funky than the lobby.

✗ Eating & Drinking

For such a small Southern city, student-tilted Birmingham has a wide variety of eateries and cafes, and plenty of free live music on weekends.

Garage Café   CAFE $
(www.garagecafe.us; 2304 10th Ter S; sandwiches $7; ☺3pm-midnight Sun-Mon, 11am-2am Tue-Sat) By day it's a great soup and create-your-own-sandwich spot; by night eclectic crowds knock back myriad beer choices while tapping their toes to live music in a courtyard full of junk, antiques, ceramic statues *and* the kitchen sink.

★ Hot & Hot Fish Club   SEAFOOD $$$
(☑205-933-5474; www.hotandhotfishclub.com; 2180 11th Court South; mains $29-36; ☺5:30-10:30pm Tue-Sat) This crazy-awesome Southside Birmingham restaurant – one of the South's best – will bring you to your knees hollerin' gastro-hallelujah's! Chef Chris Hastings was a James Beard Best Chef in the South finalist three years in a row – his daily-changing seasonal menu (including cocktails) is a knockout.

Bottega   ITALIAN $$$
(☑205-939-1000; www.bottegarestaurant.com; 2240 Highland Ave S; lunch mains $13-19, dinner $25-42; ℗) Enjoy a spot of Birmingham posh at this fine Italian bistro in the Highlands. It impresses with creative pizzas like fried oyster and pancetta or the Persian piadine with watercress, mint, dill, walnuts and raddish. It also does a nice pasta with pork meatballs and a popular hanger steak. Not to mention a pan-roasted venison.

Bottletree Cafe   BAR
(☑205-533-6288; www.thebottletree.com; 3719 3rd Ave S; ☺5pm-2am Mon, 11am-2am Tue-Sat, 11am-3pm Sun) A bit out if the way, in an industrial area north of downtown, this funky dive with Delta-blues art and vintage decor is best for late-night mingling and indie bands. The food gets good reviews too.

Pale Eddie's   PUB
(☑205-297-0052; www.paleeddiespourhouse.com; 2308 2nd Ave N; ☺from 4pm Mon-Thu, from 2pm Fri, from 6pm Sat) On the groovy northern edge of downtown this pub wins for its brick house environs, the array of craftsman brews, including a gluten-free cider (et tu beer man?), and free live music every weekend.

➊ Getting There & Around

The **Birmingham International Airport** (BHM; www.flybirmingham.com) is about 5 miles northeast of downtown.

Greyhound (☑205-253-7190; www.greyhound.com; 618 19th St N), north of downtown, serves cities including Huntsville, Montgomery, Atlanta, GA, Jackson, MS, and New Orleans, LA (10 hours). **Amtrak** (☑205-324-3033; www.amtrak.com; 1819 Morris Ave), downtown, has trains daily to New York and New Orleans.

Birmingham Transit Authority (www.bjcta.org; adult $1.25) runs local buses.

Around Birmingham

North of Birmingham, the aerospace community of Huntsville hosts the US space program that took off and attracted international aerospace-related companies. **US Space & Rocket Center** (www.spacecamp.com/museum; 1 Tranquility Base, I-565, exit 15; museum adult/child $25/20; ☺9am-5pm; 👶) is a competition science museum and theme park. A great place to take a kid, or to become one again. Admission includes an IMAX film, exhibits, rides and video presentations.

East of Huntsville, in Scottsboro, you'll find the infamous **Unclaimed Baggage Center** (☑256-259-1525; www.unclaimedbaggage.com; 509 W Willow St; ☺9am-6pm Mon-Thu, to 7pm Fri, 8am-7pm Sat), which draws pilgrims from far and wide who peruse the now-for-sale belongings of unfortunate air travelers who have lost their baggage irrevocably down the dark annals of fate. Finders keepers.

Fans of Ricky Bobby, or, you know, Nascar racing, should find **Talladega Superspeedway** (☑877-462-3342; ww.talladegasuperspeedway.com; 3366 Speedway Blvd; tickets $45-200), 48 miles east of Birmingham on the I-20. Pitched to absurd angles, it's the biggest and fastest oval in the circuit and an absolute adrenaline rush on race day.

Montgomery

In 1955 Rosa Parks refused to give up her seat to a white man on a city bus, launching a bus boycott and galvanizing the Civil Rights movement nationwide. The city has commemorated that incident with a museum, which along with a few other civil rights sights, is the main reason to visit. Alabama's capital, Montgomery is an otherwise pleasant but sleepy city.

⊙ Sights

Montgomery's pleasant Riverwalk is accessed via a tunnel from downtown and is an extended plaza along a bend in the river with a natural amphitheater and a riverboat dock.

★ Rosa Parks Museum   MUSEUM
(www.trojan.troy.edu/community/rosa-parks-museum; 251 Montgomery St; adult/child 4-12yr $7.50/5.50; ⊙9am-5pm Mon-Fri, 9am-3pm Sat; 🅿) A tribute to Mrs Parks (who died in October 2005), the museum, set in front of the bus stop where she took her stand, features a sophisticated video re-creation of that pivotal moment that launched the 1955 boycott. While it is true that she worked as a tailor, do not believe the myth that Parks was simply an ordinary woman pushed too far.

She was an activist with a sharp, strategic intellect who volunteered for the local National Association for the Advancement of Colored People chapter and was trained in the principles of nonviolent civil disobedience before her moment arrived.

Civil Rights Memorial Center   MEMORIAL
(www.civilrightsmemorialcenter.org; 400 Washington Ave; adult/child $2/free; ⊙9am-4:30pm Mon-Fri, 10am-4pm Sat) With its circular design crafted by Maya Lin, this haunting memorial focuses on 40 martyrs of the Civil Rights movement, all murdered senselessly. Some cases remain unsolved. Martin Luther King Jr was the most famous, but there were many 'faceless' deaths along the way, white and African American alike.

The memorial is part of the Southern Poverty Law Center, a legal foundation committed to racial equality and equal opportunity for justice under the law. They are best known for their landmark victory in 1987 that found the Ku Klux Klan responsible for the death of a young black man, Michael Donald, in 1981. The judgment bankrupted the Klan nationwide.

Dexter Avenue King Memorial Church   CHURCH
(☏334-263-3970; www.dexterkingmemorial.org; 454 Dexter Ave; adult/child 3-12yr $10/6; ⊙10am-4pm Tue-Fri, to 2pm Sat) Formerly known as Dexter Avenue Baptist Church, here a 26-year-old Atlanta minister began his long march toward freedom. Built in 1885, Martin Luther King was the minister here (he planned the Montgomery bus boycott from his office) from 1954 to 1960. The nearby Dexter Parsonage Museum, is the humble house where King lived with his family. It was bombed in 1956.

One-hour tours must be booked in advance.

Scott & Zelda Fitzgerald Museum   MUSEUM
(www.fitzgeraldmuseum.net; 919 Felder Ave; donation adult/child $5/2; ⊙10am-2pm Wed-Fri, 1-5pm Sat & Sun) The writers' home from 1931 to 1932 now houses first editions, translations and original artwork including a mysterious self-portrait of Zelda. We loved the handwritten letters from Zelda to Scott, and the typed letters from Scott to his great foil and friend, Ernest Hemingway.

Hank Williams Museum   MUSEUM
(www.thehankwilliamsmuseum.com; 118 Commerce St; admission $10; ⊙9am-4:30pm Mon-Fri, 10am-4pm Sat, 1-4pm Sun) Pays homage to the

---

ROLL TIDE!

Roll Tide! It's the call you'll hear, well pretty much everywhere in the town of Tuscaloosa, 60 miles southwest of Birmingham, but especially on Saturday afternoons in the fall. During football season, students and alumni gather in the University of Alabama (www.ua.edu) quad, hours before kickoff, for a pre-game party like none other. White tents, wired with satellite TV, fill the expansive lawn. Barbecue is smoked and devoured, cornhole (drunken bean-bag toss) is played. At game time all migrate to Bryant-Denny Stadium (☏205-348-3600; www.rolltide.com; 920 Paul W Bryant Dr), a 102,000 capacity football stadium that looks out onto the rolling hills and is always packed with rabid fans, and with good reason. The Alabama Crimson Tide have won 19 national championships, including the last two, and three of the last four. Get a full dose of Crimson Tide football history, at the Paul W Bryant Museum (☏205-348-4668; www.bryantmuseum.com; 300 Paul W Bryant Dr; adult/senior & child $2/1; ⊙9am-4pm), named for the greatest coach of them all. Or so the legend goes...

ECHOES OF A KING

After the long march from Selma to Montgomery on March 25, 1965, Dr Martin Luther King Jr gave his speech 'Our God is Marching On!' on the steps of the state capitol. Here are some highlights:

There never was a moment in American history more honorable and more inspiring than the pilgrimage of clergymen and laymen of every race and faith pouring into Selma to face danger at the side of its embattled Negroes.

...Our aim must never be to defeat or humiliate the white man but to win his friendship and understanding. We must come to see that the end we seek is a society at peace with itself, a society that can live with its conscience. That will be a day not of the white man, not of the black man. That will be the day of man as man. I know you are asking today, 'How long will it take?' I come to say to you this afternoon however difficult the moment, however frustrating the hour, it will not be long, because truth pressed to earth will rise again.

How long? Not long, because no lie can live forever.

How long? Not long, because you still reap what you sow.

How long? Not long. Because the arm of the moral universe is long but it bends toward justice.

country-music giant and Alabama native, a pioneer who effortlessly fused hillbilly music with the blues.

🛏 Sleeping & Eating

Montgomery isn't known for its restaurants and accommodations, and can be done on a day trip, but there are a couple of finds. **The Alley**, a dining and entertainment district, has helped perk up a dormant downtown.

Renaissance Hotel HOTEL $
(☑ 334-481-5000; www.marriott.com; 201 Tallapoosa St; r from $189; [P][✳][@][🤖][🏊]) Yes, it's a corporate monstrosity, but it is also well located and is easily Montgomery's nicest address.

Dreamland BBQ BARBECUE $
(www.dreamlandbbq.com; 101 Tallapoosa St; mains $8-11; ⊙ 11am-9pm Sun-Thu, to 10pm Sat) It's an Alabama chain and the ribs, chopped-pork sandwich and traditional banana pudding are all solid. It's the culinary cradle of the Alley, the focal point of Montgomery's downtown makeover.

★ Central CHOPHOUSE $$$
(www.central129coosa.com; 129 Coosa St; mains $18-33; ⊙ 11am-2pm Mon-Fri, 5:30pm-late Mon-Sat) The gourmand's choice, this stunner has a creative interior with a reclaimed-wood bar. The booths are sumptuous and it specializes in wood-fired fish, chicken, steaks and chops.

ℹ Information

Montgomery Area Visitor Center (☑ 334-262-0013; www.visitingmontgomery.com; 300 Water St; ⊙ 8:30am-5pm Mon-Sat) Has tourist information and a helpful website.

ℹ Getting There & Around

Montgomery Regional Airport (MGM; www.montgomeryairport.org; 4445 Selma Hwy) is about 15 miles from downtown and is served by daily flights from Atlanta, Charlotte and Dallas.
Greyhound (☑ 334-286-0658; www.greyhound.com; 950 W South Blvd) also serves the city.
The **Montgomery Area Transit System** (www.montgomerytransit.com; tickets $1) operates the infamous city buses.

Selma

On Bloody Sunday, March 7, 1965, the media captured state troopers and deputies beating and gassing African Americans and white sympathizers near the **Edmund Pettus Bridge** (Broad St & Walter Ave). The crowd was marching to the state capital (Montgomery) to demonstrate against the murder of a local black activist by police, during a demonstration for voting rights. When the scene was broadcast on every network later that night, it marked one of the first times Americans outside the South had witnessed the horrifying images of the struggle. Shock and outrage was widespread, and support for the movement grew. Martin

Luther King arrived swiftly to Selma and after another aborted attempt due to the threat of violence, helped lead what became 8000 people on a four-day, 54 mile march to Montgomery, culminating with a classic King speech on the capitol steps. Soon after, President Johnson signed the Voting Rights Act of 1965.

Selma's story is told at the National Voting Rights Museum ([☏]334-327-8218; www. nvrm.org; 1012 Water Ave; adult/senior & student $6/4; ⊘10am-4pm Mon-Thu), near the Edmund Pettus Bridge, and in more detail at the Lowndes County Interpretive Center (www.nps.gov/semo; 7002 US Hwy 80; ⊘9am-4:30pm) halfway between Selma and Montgomery. Oddly, as we are writing this, the US Supreme Court has ruled that the Voting Rights Act is unconstitutional – a controversial decision that has cut down party lines. The passage of that federal law was the key to victory during this phase of the Civil Rights movement. The ramifications of the decision are still unclear, though many observers fear it could potentially make access to the polls more difficult. Some states, like Florida, have been plagued by accusations of racial discrimination when it comes to voting rights.

Mobile

Wedged between Mississippi and Florida, the only real Alabama coastal city is Mobile (mo-*beel*), a busy industrial seaport with green spaces, shady boulevards and four historic districts. It's ablaze with azaleas in early spring, and festivities are held throughout February for Mardi Gras (www.mobilemardigras.com), which has been celebrated here for nearly 200 years. The Dauphin St historic district is where you'll find most bars and restaurants, and it's where much of the Mardi Gras action blooms.

USS Alabama (www.ussalabama.com; 2703 Battleship Pkwy; adult/child $15/6; ⊘8am-6pm Apr-Sep, to 5pm Oct-Mar), a 690ft behemoth famous for escaping nine major WWII battles unscathed, is a worthwhile self-guided tour. Parking's $2.

Battle House ([☏]251-338-2000; www.marriott.com; 26 N Royal St; r from $159; [P][✳][@][🛜][🏊]) is the best address in downtown Mobile. You'll want to stay in the original historic wing with its ornate domed marble lobby, though the striking new tower is on the waterfront. Home to Mobile's best burg-

ers and consistently voted one of America's best bars, the ramshackle Callaghan's Irish Social Club (www.callaghansirishsocialclub.com; 916 Charleston St; burgers $7-9; ⊘11am-9pm Mon, 11am-10pm Tue & Wed, 11am-11pm Thu-Sat) in a 1920s-era building that used to house a meat market in the Oakleigh District, is unmissable. Closer to the town center, Wintzell's ([☏]251-432-4605; www.wintzellsoysterhouse.com; 605 Dauphin St; mains $11-23; ⊘11am-10pm Sun-Thu, to 11pm Fri & Sat), open since 1938, serves oysters raw, chargrilled or fried in brewhouse environs.

MISSISSIPPI

One of the USA's most misunderstood (and yet most mythologized) states, Mississippi is home to gorgeous country roads, shabby juke joints, crispy catfish, hallowed authors and acres of cotton. Most people feel content to malign Mississippi, long scorned for its lamentable civil rights history and low-ranking on the list of nearly every national marker of economy and education, without ever experiencing it. But unpack your bags for a moment and you'll feel its bottomless soul.

❶ Getting There & Away

There are three routes most folks take when traveling through Mississippi. I-55 and US-61 both run north–south from the state's northern to southern borders. US-61 goes through the delta, and I-55 flows in and out of Jackson. The gorgeous Natchez Trace Parkway, runs diagonally across the state from Tupelo to Natchez.

❶ Information

Mississippi Division of Tourism Development ([☏]601-359-3297; www.visitmississippi.org) Has a directory of visitor bureaus and thematic travel itineraries to choose from. Most are well thought out and run quite deep.

Mississippi Wildlife, Fisheries, & Parks ([☏]1-800-467-2757; www.mississippistateparks.reserveamerica.com) Camping costs $12 to $28, depending on the facilities, and some parks have cabins for rent.

Tupelo

Unless you want to pick up the Natchez Trace Pkwy, you probably won't plan to spend a long time here. But an afternoon pop-in is rewarding indeed for devotees of the King.

MISSISSIPPI FACTS

Nickname the Magnolia State

Population 3 million

Area 48,430 sq miles

Capital city Jackson (population 175,437)

Sales tax 7%

Birthplace of Author Eudora Welty (1909–2001), musicians Robert Johnson (1911–38), Muddy Waters (1913–83), BB King (b 1925) and Elvis Presley (1935–77), activist James Meredith (b 1933) and puppeteer Jim Henson (1936–90)

Home of The blues

Politics Traditionally conservative, but has voted for third-party candidates more than any other state since WWII

Famous for Cotton fields

Kitschiest souvenir Elvis lunchbox in Tupelo

Driving distances Jackson to Clarksdale 187 miles, Jackson to Ocean Springs 176 miles

Elvis Presley's Birthplace (☑ 662-841-1245; www.elvispresleybirthplace.com; 306 Elvis Presley Blvd; adult/senior/child $15/12/6; ⊗ 9am-5:30pm Mon-Sat, 1-5pm Sun) is east of downtown off Hwy 78. The 15-acre complex contains the two-room shack Elvis lived in as a boy, a museum displaying personal items, the modest chapel where a very young Elvis attended church with his mother, got bit by the music bug and danced in the aisles, and a massive gift shop.

Oxford

Oxford is one of those rare towns that seeps into your bones and never leaves. Local culture revolves around the quaint-yet-hip Square, where you'll find inviting bars, wonderful food and decent shopping, and the regal University of Mississippi (www.olemiss.edu), aka Ole Miss. All around and in between are quiet residential streets, sprinkled with antebellum homes, shaded by majestic oaks, including William Faulkner's old lair. Oxford has just 10,000 year-round residents, but the 18,000 students infuse the town with youth and life.

Oxford is best reached via Hwy 6, which runs between Clarksdale and Tupelo in Northern Mississippi.

◎ Sights & Activities

The gorgeous, 0.6-miles long and rather painless Bailee's Woods Trail connects two of the town's most popular sights, Rowan Oak and the University of Mississippi Museum.

Rowan Oak　　　　　HISTORIC BUILDING
(www.rowanoak.com; Old Taylor Rd; adult/child $5/free; ⊗ 10am-4pm Tue-Sat, 1-4pm Sun) Literary pilgrims head directly here, to the graceful 1840s home of William Faulkner, who authored so many brilliant and dense novels set in Mississippi, and whose work is celebrated in Oxford with an annual conference in July. Tours of Rowan Oak – where Faulkner lived from 1930 until he died in 1962 – are self-guided. The staff can also provide directions to Faulkner's grave, which is located in St Peter's Cemetery, northeast of the Square.

University of Mississippi Museum　MUSEUM
(www.museum.olemiss.edu; University Ave at 5th St; admission $5; ⊗ 10am-6pm Tue-Sat) This museum has fine and folk arts, a Confederate uniform and a plethora of science-related marvels, including a microscope and electromagnet from the 19th century.

⊨ Sleeping & Eating

The cheapest accommodations are chains on the outskirts of town. A number of high-quality restaurants dot the Square.

★ **(5) Twelve**　　　　　B&B $$
(☑ 662-234-8043; www.the5twelve.com; 512 Van Buren Ave; r from $115; P ❋ 🎧) This six-room B&B has an antebellum-style exterior and modern interior (think: tempurpedic beds and flatscreens). Room rates include full Southern breakfasts to order. It's an easy walk from shops and restaurants, and the inn keepers will make you feel like family.

Inn at Ole Miss　　　　　HOTEL $$
(☑ 662-234-2331; www.theinnatolemiss.com; 120 Alumni Dr; r from $129; P ❋ @ 🎧 ▥) Unless it's a football weekend, in which case, you'd be wise to book well ahead, you can usually find a nice room at this 180-room hotel and conference center right on the Ole Miss

Grove. Although less personal than the local inns, it's comfortable, well-located and walkable to downtown.

Bottletree Bakery
BAKERY $
(www.bottletreebakery.net; 923 Van Buren; pastries $3-4, mains $6-9; ☺7am-4pm Tue-Fri, 9am-4pm Sat, to 2pm Sun; 🛜) This place trades in exquisite pastries including saucer-sized cinnamon rolls, a brioche of the day, shortbread streusel, mammoth chocolate croissants, and a nice collection of sandwiches and salads.

⭐ Snackbar
NEW AMERICAN $$
(🗷662-236-6363; www.cityceryonline.com; 721 N Lamar Blvd; small plates $6-12, mains $11-26; ☺4pm-midnight Mon-Sat) A fabulous find in an otherwise nondescript mini-mall. It specializes in craftsman cocktails, and are also known for its exquisite raw bar (oysters, blue crab, Gulf shrimp) and small plates that wander from oysters and grits to a kale Caesar. The burger is legendary. All served in rather dark and groovy hardwood environs.

Taylor Grocery
SEAFOOD $$
(www.taylorgrocery.com; 4 County Rd 338A; dishes $9-15; ☺5-10pm Thu-Sat, to 9pm Sun) Be prepared to wait – and to tailgate in the parking lot – at this splendidly rusticated catfish haunt. Get yours fried or grilled, and bring a marker to sign your name on the wall. The joint is about 7 miles from downtown Oxford, south on Old Taylor Rd.

☆ Entertainment

On the last Tuesday of the month, an increasingly popular Art Crawl, connects galleries across town with free buses carrying well-lubricated art lovers. Nibbles and wine aplenty.

Proud Larry's
LIVE MUSIC
(🗷662-236-0050; www.proudlarrys.com; 211 S Lamar Blvd; ☺shows 9:30pm) On the Square, this iconic music venue hosts consistently good bands, and it does a nice pub grub business at lunch and dinner before stage lights dim.

Rooster's Blues House
BLUES
(www.roostersblueshouse.com; 114 Courthouse Sq) Enjoy soulful crooning on the weekends.

The Lyric
VENUE
(🗷662-234-5333; www.thelyricoxford.com; 1006 Van Buren St) This old brickhouse, and rather intimate theater with concrete floors, exposed rafters and a mezzanine, is where you come to see indie acts like Beach House or Band of Horses.

🔒 Shopping

Square Books
BOOKSTORE
(🗷662-236-2262; www.squarebooks.com; 160 Courthouse Sq; ☺9am-9pm Mon-Thu, to 10pm Fri & Sat, to 6pm Sun) Square Books, one of America's great independent bookstores, is the epicenter of Oxford's lively literary scene and a frequent stop for traveling authors. There's a cafe and balcony upstairs, along with an immense section devoted to Faulkner. Nearby Square Books Jr is where you can find children's and young adult lit. Off Square trades in used fare.

JAMES MEREDITH'S MARCH

The Grove, the shady heart center of Ole Miss (the University of Mississippi), is generally peaceful, except on football Saturdays, when it buzzes with brass-band, pre-game anticipation.

Yet it was also the setting of one of the Civil Rights movement's most harrowing scenes. Here, on October 1, 1962, James Meredith, a young student,, accompanied by his advisor, National Association for the Advancement of Colored People state chair Medgar Evers, marched through a violent mob of segregationists to become the first African American student to register for classes at Ole Miss. He was supposed to have registered 10 days before, but riots ensued and the Kennedy administration had to call in 500 federal marshalls and the National Guard to ensure his safety.

Evers was eventually assasinated, and Meredith later walked across the state to raise awareness about racial violence in Mississippi. Some of Meredith's correspondence is on display at the Center for Southern Culture (🗷662-915-5855; 1 Library Loop, University of Mississippi; ☺8am-9pm Mon-Thu, to 4pm Fri, to 5pm Sat, 1-5pm Sun; 🚹) FREE, at the campus library.

Southside Gallery   ART
(www.southsideartgallery.com; 150 Courthouse
Sq; ⊙10am-6pm Tue-Sat) The best of Oxford's
downtown art galleries puts an emphasis
on local, young, up-and-coming artists who
create modern works from abstract to real-
ist; from big format to smaller than seems
reasonable.

Mississippi Delta

In the cultivated flood plain, along Hwy 61,
American music took root. It arrived from
Africa in the souls of slaves, morphed into
field songs, and wormed into the brain of
a sharecropping troubadour waiting for a
train. In Tutweiler, WC Handy eavesdropped
and wrote the rhythm down. In Clarksdale,
at the crossroads, Robert Johnson made a
deal with the devil and became America's
first guitar hero. Yes, the Delta has soul food
and a blood-soaked history, but its chief
export, its white-hot legacy will always be
the blues. There is no Beatles, no Stones,
no Hendrix, Zeppelin, or even hip-hop
without the music of the Mississippi Delta,
which runs from Memphis all the way to
Vicksburg.

Clarksdale

Clarksdale is the Delta's most useful
base – with more comfortable hotel rooms
and modern, tasteful kitchens here than the
rest of the Delta combined. It's within a couple of hours from all the blues sights, and
big-name blues acts honor Clarksdale on the
weekends.

⊙ Sights

The Crossroads of Hwys 61 and 49, is the
intersection where the great Robert Johnson made his mythical deal with the devil,
immortalized in his tune 'Cross Road Blues.'

Delta Blues Museum   MUSEUM
(www.deltabluesmuseum.org; 1 Blues Alley; adult/
senior & student $7/5; ⊙9am-5pm Mon-Sat) A
small but well-presented collection of memorabilia is on display. The shrine to Delta
legend Muddy Waters includes the actual
cabin where he grew up; local art exhibits
and a gift shop round out the revelry.

**Rock N' Roll & Blues
Heritage Museum**   MUSEUM
(✆901-605-8662; www.blues2rock.com; 113 E
Second St; admission $5; ⊙11am-5pm Tue-Sat) A
jovial Dutch transplant and blues fanatic
displays an impressive personal collection
of records, memorabilia and artifacts that
trace the roots of rock and roll from blues
through the '70s.

✯ Festivals & Events

Clarksdale has two blues parties.

Juke Joint Festival   MUSIC
(www.jukejointfestival.com; tickets $15; ⊙Apr)
There are more than 100 daytime and over
20 night venues at this three-day festival held in joints sprinkled in and around
Clarksdale.

**Sunflower River
Blues & Gospel Festival**   MUSIC
(www.sunflowerfest.org; ⊙Aug) Draws bigger
names than the Juke Joint Festival.

A WHOLE LOTTA JUKIN' GOING ON

It's believed that 'juke' is a West African word that survived in the Gullah language, the
Creole–English hybrid spoken by isolated African Americans in the US. The Gullah 'juke'
means 'wicked and disorderly.' Little wonder, then, that the term was applied to the
roadside sweatboxes of the Mississippi Delta, where secular music, suggestive dancing,
drinking and, in some cases, prostitution were the norm. The term 'jukebox' came into
vogue when recorded music, spun on automated record-changing machines, began to
supplant live musicians in such places, as well as in cafes and bars.

Most bona-fide juke joints are African American neighborhood clubs, and outside visitors can be a rarity. Many are mostly male hangouts. There are very few places that local
women, even in groups, would turn up without a male chaperone. Otherwise, women
can expect a lot of persistent, suggestive attention.

For a taste of the juke-joint scene, we recommend Red's, which is usually open on
Friday and Saturday nights. It can be intimidating to first-timers, but it is one of Clarksdale's best jukes. If the pit's smoking, order whatever's cooking.

🛏 Sleeping & Eating

★ Shack Up Inn
INN **$**
(☑ 662-624-8329; www.shackupinn.com; Hwy 49; d $75-165; P❄🛜) At the cheeky Hopson Plantation, this self-titled 'bed and beer' 2 miles south on the west side of Hwy 49 evokes the blues like no other. Guests stay in refurbished sharecropper cabins or the creatively renovated cotton gin. The cabins have covered porches and are filled with old furniture and musical instruments.

The old commissary, the Juke Joint Chapel (equipped with pews), is an atmospheric venue inside the cotton gin for live-music performances. The whole place reeks of down-home dirty blues and Deep South character – possibly the coolest place you'll ever stay.

Lofts at the Five & Dime
LOFTS **$$**
(☑ 888-510-9604; www.fiveanddimelofts.com; 211 Yazoo St; lofts $150-175) Set in a 1954 building are six plush, loft-style apartments with molded-concrete counters in the full kitchen, massive flatscreens in the living room and bedroom, terrazzo showers and free sodas and water throughout your stay. They sleep up to four comfortably.

Abe's
BBQ **$**
(☑ 662-624-9947; 616 State St; sandwiches $4-6, plates $6-14; ⊙ 10am-9pm Mon-Thu, to 10pm Fri & Sat, 11am-2pm Sun; 🅿) Abe's has served zesty pork sandwiches, vinegary slaw and slow-burning tamales at the Crossroads since 1924.

★ Yazoo Pass
CAFE **$$**
(www.yazoopass.com; 207 Yazoo Ave; lunch mains $6-10, dinner $13-26; ⊙ 7am-9pm Mon-Sat; 🛜) A contemporary space where you can enjoy fresh scones and croissants in the mornings, salad bar, sandwiches and soups at lunch, and pan-seared ahi, filet mignon, burgers and pastas at dinner.

Rust
SOUTHERN **$$**
(www.rustclarksdale.com; 218 Delta Ave; mains $12-36; ⊙ 6-9pm Tue-Thu, to 10pm Fri & Sat) The souped-up Southern comfort food served here (blackened rib eye with red chili mustard, crawfish cakes with grilled asparagus) amid junkyard-chic decor makes it a nice place for a bite before a show.

☆ Entertainment

Red's
BLUES CLUB
(☑ 662-627-3166; 395 Sunflower Ave; cover $10; ⊙ live music 9pm Fri & Sat) Clarksdale's best juke joint, with its neon-red mood lighting, plastic-bag ceiling and general soulful disintegration is the best place to see blues men howl. Red runs the bar, and may have some moonshine hidden back there?

Ground Zero
BLUES CLUB
(www.groundzerobluesclub.com; 0 Blues Alley; ⊙ 11am-2pm Mon-Tue, to 11pm Wed & Thu, to 1am Fri & Sat) For blues in more polished environs, we recommend Morgan Freeman's Ground Zero, a huge and friendly hall with a dancefloor surrounded by tables. Bands take the stage Wednesday to Saturday.

🛍 Shopping

Cat Head Delta Blues & Folk Art
ARTS & CRAFTS
(www.cathead.biz; 252 Delta Ave; ⊙ 10am-5pm Mon-Sat) Friendly St Louis carpetbagger and author, Roger Stolle runs a colorful, all-purpose, blues emporium. The shelves are jammed with books, face jugs, local art and blues records. Stolle seems to be connected to everyone in the Delta, and knows when and where the bands will play.

Around Clarksdale

For such a poor, flat part of the country, the Delta has a surprisingly deep list of funky little towns to explore.

Down Hwy 49, Tutwiler is where the blues began its migration from oral tradition to popular art form. Here, WC Handy, known as the Father of the Blues, first heard a share cropper moan his 12-bar prayer while the two waited for a train in 1903. He transcribed it in 1912, but wasn't recognized as a blues pioneer until his 'Beale Street Blues' became a hit in 1916. That meeting is immortalized by a mural at the Tutwiler Tracks (off Hwy 49, Tutwiler; 🅿).

East of Greenville, Hwy 82 heads out of the Delta. The Highway 61 Blues Museum (www.highway61blues.com; 307 N Broad St; ⊙ 10am-4pm Tue-Sat Nov-Feb, 10am-5pm Mon-Sat Mar-Oct), at the start of the route known as the Blues Highway' packs a mighty wallop in a condensed, six-room space venerating local bluesman from the Delta. Leland (www.lelandms.org) hosts the Highway 61 Blues Festival in June.

Stopping in the tiny Delta town of Indianola is well worthwhile, to visit the incredible, modern BB King Museum and Delta Interpretive Center (www.bbkingmuseum.org; 400 Second St; adult/student/child $10/5/free;

⌚10am-5pm Tue-Sat, noon-5pm Sun-Mon, closed Mon Nov-Mar). The best blues museum in the Delta is filled with interactive displays, video exhibits and an amazing array of BB King artifacts, effectively communicating the history and legacy of the blues while shedding light on the soul of the Delta.

Greenwood is a once-poor Delta town infused with a dose of opulence thanks to Viking Range Corporation's investment (its headquarters are here). Visitors are usually wealthy patrons or splurging travelers who want to take advantage of the Delta's most refined sleep, the **Alluvian** (☎662-453-2114; www.thealluvian.com; 318 Howard St; r $200-215; P❄@ᯤ), owned by Viking. The nearby **Delta Bistro** (☎662-455-9575; www.deltabistro.com; 117 Main St, Greenwood; mains $9-24; ⌚11am-9pm Mon-Sat) is the best restaurant in the region.

Vicksburg

Vicksburg is famous for its strategic location in the Civil War, on a high bluff overlooking the Mississippi River. General Ulysses S Grant besieged the city for 47 days, until its surrender on July 4, 1863, at which point the North gained dominance over North America's greatest river, and the war was all but over.

Sights & Activities

The major sights are readily accessible from I-20 exit 4B (Clay St).

National Military Park (www.nps.gov/vick; Clay St; per car/individual $8/4; ⌚8am-5pm Oct-Mar, to 7pm Apr-Sep), north of I-20 is Vicksburg's main attraction. A 16-mile driving tour passes historic markers explaining battle scenarios and key events. You can buy an audio tour in the visitor center gift shop, or drive through on your own using the free map distributed on-site. Plan for at least two hours to do it justice. If you have your bike, cycling is a fantastic way to take it in. The cemetery contains some 17,000 Union graves. **Civil War re-enactments** are held in May and July.

Historic downtown stretches along several cobblestoned blocks of Washington St. Down by the water is a block of murals depicting the history of the area, and a **Children's Art Park**. The surprsingly interesting **Lower Mississippi River Museum** (☎601-638-9900; www.lmrm.org; 910 Washington St; ⌚9am-5pm Tue-Sat year-round, 1-5pm Sun Apr-Oct) FREE delves into such topics as the famed 1927 flood. Kids will dig the aquarium and clambering around the dry-docked research vessel, the **M/V Mississippi IV**. Don't leave town without stopping by the **Attic Gallery** (☎601-638-9221; www.atticgallery.net; 1101 Washington St; ⌚10am-5pm Mon-Sat), a treasure trove of fine and folk art from across the Delta.

Sleeping & Eating

Corners Mansion B&B $$
(☎601-636-7421; www.thecorners.com; 601 Klein St; r incl breakfast from $125; P❄ᯤ) The best part of this 1873 B&B is looking over the Yazoo and Mississippi Rivers from your porch-swing. The gardens and Southern breakfast don't hurt either.

Rusty's Riverfront Grill SOUTHERN $$
(www.rustysriverfront.com; 901 Washington St; mains $17-29; ⌚11am-2pm & 5-9:30pm Tue-Fri, 11am-9:30pm Sat) Set at the north end of downtown, this down-home grill is known for the terriffic rib eye, but it has a nice selection of Southern-style seafood too, including crab cakes, blackened redfish, and a nice New Orleans–style gumbo.

Jackson

Mississippi's capital and largest city is victim to the common car-culture phenomenon of a latent (though stately and gentrifying) downtown surrounded by plush suburbs. However, interesting areas like the funky Fondren District, along with a cluster of well-done museums, historic sites and bars and restaurants, give insight into the culture of Mississippi and are elevating Jackson to a good time.

Sights

★**Mississippi Museum of Art** GALLERY
(www.msmuseumart.org; 380 South Lamar St; permenant collections free, special exhibitions $5-12; ⌚10am-5pm Tue-Sat, noon-5pm Sun) FREE This is the one fantastic attraction in Jackson. The collection of Mississippi art – a permanent exhibit dubbed 'The Mississippi Story' – is superb.

Old Capitol Museum MUSEUM
(www.mdah.state.ms.us/museum; 100 State St; ⌚9am-5pm Tue-Sat, 1-5pm Sun) FREE The state's Greek Revival capitol building from 1839 to 1903 now houses a Mississippi

history museum filled with films and exhibits. You'll learn that secession was far from unanimous, and how reconstruction brought some of the harshest, pre-segregation 'black codes' in the South.

Eudora Welty House   LANDMARK
([J]601-353-7762; www.mdah.state.ms.us/welty; 1119 Pinehurst St; ⊘tours 9am, 11am, 1pm & 3pm Tue-Fri) Literature buffs should make a reservation to tour the Pulitzer Prize–winning author's Tudor Revival house, where she lived for more than 75 years. It's now a true historical preservation down to the most minute details.

Smith Robertson Museum   MUSEUM
(www.jacksonms.gov/visitors/museums/smith-robertson; 528 Bloom St; adult/child $4.50/1.50; ⊘9am-5pm Mon-Fri, 10am-2pm Sat, 2-5pm Sun) Housed in Mississippi's first public school for African American kids is the alma mater of author Richard Wright. It offers insight and explanation into the pain and perseverance of the African American legacy in Mississippi.

🛏 Sleeping & Eating

Fondren District is the budding artsy, boho area of town, with fun restaurants, art galleries and cafes dotting the happening commercial strip.

Old Capitol Inn   BOUTIQUE HOTEL $$
([J]601-359-9000; www.oldcapitolinn.com; 226 N State St; r incl breakfast from $135; [P][✻][@][🛜][⌨]) This 24-room, all-suite, boutique hotel, near museums and restaurants, is terrific. The rooftop garden includes a hot tub. A full Southern breakfast (and early-evening wine and cheese) are included and the rooms are all comfortable and uniquely furnished.

Fairview Inn   INN $$
([J]601-948-3429; www.fairviewinn.com; 734 Fairview St; r incl breakfast $129-329; [P][✻][@][🛜]) For a colonial estate experience, the 18-room Fairview Inn, set in a converted historic mansion, will not let you down. The antique decor is stunning. It also has a full spa.

High Noon Cafe   VEGETARIAN $
(www.rainbowcoop.org; 2807 Old Canton Rd; mains $7-10; ⊘11:30am-2pm Mon-Fri; [P][🛜][J]) 🖉 Tired of fried, green, pulled-pork-covered catfish? This organic vegetarian grill, inside the Rainbow Co-op grocery store in the Fondren District does beet burgers, portabello Reubens and other healthy delights. Stock up on organic groceries too.

★Walker's Drive-In   SOUTHERN $$$
([J]601-982-2633; www.walkersdrivein.com; 3016 N State St; lunch mains $10-17, dinner $25-35; ⊘11am-2pm Mon-Fri & from 5:30pm Tue-Sat) This retro diner has been restored with love and infused with new Southern foodie ethos. Lunch is diner 2.0 fare with grilled redfish sandwiches, tender burgers and grilled oyster po'boys, as well as an exceptional seared, chili-crusted tuna salad, which comes with spiced calamari and seaweed.

Things get even more gourmet at dinner. Think lamb porterhouse, wood-grilled octopus and miso-marinated seabass. There's an excellent wine list and service is impeccable.

Mayflower   SEAFOOD $$$
([J]601-355-4122; 123 W Capitol St; mains $21-29; ⊘11am-2:30pm & 4:30-9:15pm Mon-Fri, 4:30-9:30pm Sat) It looks like just another downtown dive, but it's a damn fine seafood house. Locals swear by the broiled redfish, and the Greek salad, which becomes a meal when you add pan-seared scallops (sensational!). Everything is obscenely fresh.

☆ Entertainment

★F Jones Corner   BLUES
(www.fjonescorner.com; 303 N Farish St; ⊘11am-2pm Tue-Fri, 10am-late Thu-Sat) All shapes and sizes, colors and creeds descend on this down-home Farish St club when everywhere else closes. It hosts authentic Delta musicians who have been known to play until sunrise. Don't show up before 1am.

119 Underground   BLUES
(www.underground119.com; 119 S President St; ⊘5-11pm Tue, 4pm-midnight Wed-Thu, 4pm-2am Fri & Sat, 6pm-2am Sat) A funky, supremely cool supper club serving up blues, jazz and bluegrass alongside excellent eats (the chef's Southern fusion comes from his extended travels and backyard urban garden).

🛈 Information

Convention & Visitors Bureau ([J]601-960-1891; www.visitjackson.com; 111 E Capitol St, suite 102; ⊘8am-5pm Mon-Fri) Free information.

❶ Getting There & Away

At the junction of I-20 and I-55, it's easy to get in and out of Jackson. Its international **airport** (JAN; www.jmaa.com) is 10 miles east of downtown. **Greyhound** (☏ 601-353-6342; www.greyhound.com; 300 W Capitol St) buses serve Birmingham, AL, Memphis, TN, and New Orleans, LA. Amtrak's *City of New Orleans* stops at the station.

Natchez

A tiny dollop of cosmopolitan in Mississippi, adorable Natchez is home to gay log-cabin Republicans, intellectual liberals, and down-home folks, who've never left. Perched on a bluff overlooking the Mississippi, it's the oldest town on the river and attracts tourists in search of antebellum history and architecture – 668 antebellum homes pepper the oldest civilized settlement on the Mississippi River (beating New Orleans by two years). It's also the end (or the beginning!) of the scenic 444-mile Natchez Trace Pkwy, the state's cycling and recreational jewel.

The **visitor and welcome center** (☏ 601-446-6345; www.visitnatchez.org; 640 S Canal St; tours adult/child $12/8; ☉ 8:30am-5pm Mon-Sat, 9am-4pm Sun) is a large, well-organized tourist resource. Tours of the historic downtown and antebellum mansions leave from here. During the 'pilgrimage' seasons in spring and fall, local mansions are opened to visitors.

Ever wish you could sleep in one of those historic homes? At the **Historic Oak Hill Inn** (☏ 601-446-2500; www.historicoakhill.com; 409 S Rankin St; r incl breakfast from $125; P ✲ 🛜), you can sleep in an original 1835 bed and dine on pre–Civil War porcelain under 1850 Waterford crystal gasoliers – it's all about purist antebellum aristocratic living at this classic Natchez B&B. You can skip rocks into the Mississippi from the **Mark Twain Guesthouse** (☏ 601-446-8023; www.underthehillsaloon.com; 33 Silver St; r without bathroom $65-85; ✲ 🛜) where three rooms (two with views) sit on top of a classic local watering hole, **Under the Hill Saloon** (☏ 601-446-8023; 25 Silver St; ☉ 9am-late). (Check-in for the guesthouse is at the saloon).

To get your fill of Southern fusion eats, follow your nose to the **Magnolia Grill** (☏ 601-446-7670; www.magnoliagrill.com; 49 Silver St; mains $13-20; ☉ 11am-9pm, to 10pm Fri & Sat; 🍴). **Cotton Alley** (www.cottonalleycafe.com; 208 Main St; mains $10-15; ☉ 11am-10pm Mon-Sat) is a good place for lighter fare.

Gulf Coast

In the backyard of New Orleans, the Gulf Coast's economy, traditionally based on the seafood industry, got a shot of adrenaline in the 1990s when Vegas-style casinos muscled in alongside sleepy fishing villages. And then a double whammy of disasters: just when the casinos in Biloxi had been rebuilt following Hurricane Katrina in 2005, the Gulf's Deepwater Horizon oil spill in 2010 dealt the coast another unexpected blow. However, Mississippi's barrier islands helped divert much of the oil problems toward New Orleans and Alabama.

Through it all, **Ocean Springs** remains charming with a romantic line up of shrimp boats in the harbor alongside recreational sailing yachts, a historic downtown core, and a powdery fringe of white sand on the Gulf. The highlight is the **Walter Anderson Museum** (www.walterandersonmuseum.org; 510 Washington St; adult/child $10/5; ☉ 9:30am-4:30pm Mon-Sat, 12:30-4:30pm Sun). A consummate artist and lover of Gulf Coast nature, Anderson suffered from mental illness, which spurred his monastic existence and fuelled his life's work. After he died, the beachside shack where he lived on **Horn Island** was discovered to be painted in mind-blowing murals, which you'll see here.

Hotels line the highway as you approach downtown. Nice camping (and a visitor center) can be found at **Gulf Islands National Seashore Park** (www.nps.gov/guis; camping $16-20), just out of town.

PADDLING THE MISSISSIPPI

According to Keith Benoist, a photographer, landscaper and co-founder of the **Phatwater Challenge** (www.kayakmississippi.com) marathon kayak race, the Mississippi has more navigable river miles than any other state in the union. Natchez-born Benoist trains for his 42-mile race by paddling 10 miles of the Old River, an abandoned section of the Mississippi fringed with cypress and teeming with gators. If you're lucky enough to meet him at Under the Hill, he may just take you with him.

ARKANSAS

Hiding out between the Midwest and the Deep South, Arkansas (*ar*-kan-saw) is America's overlooked treasure. This is a nature lover's Shangri La, with the worn slopes of the Ozarks and the Ouachita (wash-*ee*-tah) mountains; clean, gushing rivers; and lakes bridged by crenelated granite and limestone outcrops. The entire state is dotted with exceptionally well-presented state parks and tiny, empty roads crisscrossing dense forests that let out onto breathtaking vistas and gentle pastures dotted with grazing horses. The rural towns of Mountain View and Eureka Springs hold quirky charm, and don't be fooled by talk of Wal-Mart or backwoods culture. As one local put it, 'Say what you want about Arkansas, but it's an outdoor paradise.'

ⓘ Information

Arkansas State Parks (☑888-287-2757; www.arkansasstateparks.com) Arkansas' well-reputed park system has 52 state parks, 30 offering camping (tent and RV sites are $12 to $55, depending on amenities). A number of the parks offer lodge and cabin accommodations. Due to popularity, reservations on weekends and holidays often require multiday stays.

Little Rock

It's tempting for those who zip in and out of this leafy, attractive state capital on the Arkansas River to dismiss it as quiet, maybe a little dull, certainly conservative. They're wrong. Little Rock is young, up-and-coming, gay- and immigrant-friendly, and just friendly in general. Downtown has perked up thanks to the burgeoning River Market district, and the Hillcrest neighborhood is a tiny epicenter of cafes and funky shops. If you know where to look, you'll enjoy this town.

◎ Sights

The best stroll is in the River Market district (www.rivermarket.info; W Markham St & President Clinton Ave), an area of shops, galleries, restaurants and pubs along the riverbank.

★ Little Rock Central
High School HISTORIC SITE
(www.nps.gov/chsc; 2125 Daisy Bates Dr; ⊙9:30am-4:30pm, tours 9am & 1:15pm Mon-Fri mid-Aug–early Jun) Little Rock's most riveting attraction is the site of the 1957 desegrega-

tion crisis that changed the country forever. It was here that a group of African American students known as the Little Rock Nine were first denied entry inside the then all-white high school (despite a unanimous 1954 Supreme Court ruling forcing the integration of public schools).

Eventually, President Eisenhower commanded the 1200-man 101st Airborne Battle Group to keep the crowds at bay and escort the students inside, a pivotal moment in the American Civil Rights movement. Today it's both a National Historic Site and a working high school. There's a spiffy new visitor center airing all the dirty laundry and putting the crisis into perspective alongside the greater Civil Rights movement.

William J Clinton
Presidential Center LIBRARY
(☑501-748-0419; www.clintonlibrary.gov; 1200 President Clinton Ave; adult/student & senior/child $7/5/3, with audio $10/8/6; ⊙9am-5pm Mon-Sat, 1-5pm Sun) ✎ This library houses the largest

ARKANSAS DELTA

Roughly 120 miles east of Little Rock, and just 20 from Clarksdale, Hwy 49 crosses the Mississippi River into the Arkansas Delta. Helena, a formerly prosperous, currently depressed mill town with a blues tradition (Sonny Boy Williamson made his name here), awakens for its annual Arkansas Blues & Heritage Festival (www.kingbiscuitfestival.com; tickets $45; ☺Oct) when blues musicians and their fans take over downtown for three days in early October. Year-round, blues fans and history buffs should visit the Delta Cultural Center (☑870-338-4350; www.deltaculturalcenter.com; 141 Cherry St; ☺9am-5pm Tue-Sat) FREE. The museum displays all manner of memorabilia such as Albert King's and Sister Rosetta Tharpe's guitars, and John Lee Hooker's signed handkerchief.

The world's longest-running blues radio program, *King Biscuit Time*, is broadcast here (12:15pm Monday to Friday), and *Delta Sounds* (1pm Monday to Friday) often hosts live musicians; both air on KFFA AM-1360. Before leaving town, make like Robert Plant and stop by the wonderfully cluttered, Bubba's Blues Corner (☑870-995-1326; 105 Cherry St, Helena; ☺9am-5pm Tue-Sat; ⏩) FREE, to pick up a blues record. Bubba puts on the Arkansas Delta Rockabilly Festival (www.deltarockabillyfest.com; tickets $30; ☺May).

archival collection in presidential history, including 80 million pages of documents and two million photographs. Peruse the full-scale replica of the Oval Office, the exhibits on all stages of Clinton's life or the gifts from visiting dignitaries. The entire complex is built to environmentally friendly 'green' standards.

Old State House Museum MUSEUM
(www.oldstatehouse.com; 300 W Markham St; ☺9am-5pm Mon-Sat, 1-5pm Sun) FREE The state capitol from 1836 to 1911 now holds restored legislative chambers and displays on Arkansas history and culture.

Riverfront Park PARK
Just northwest of downtown, Riverfront Park rolls pleasantly along the Arkansas River and both pedestrians and cyclists take advantage of this fantastic city park daily. You can't miss the Big Dam Bridge (www.bigdambridge.com; ⏩), which connects 17 miles of multiuse trails that form a complete loop thanks to the renovation of the recently renamed, Clinton Presidential Park Bridge.

For a proper perusal of Riverfront Park, rent a bike (or tandem) from Fike's Bike (☑501-374-5505; www.fikesbikes.com; 200 S Olive St; 4hr/day from $12/20; ☺3-8pm Tue-Fri, 7-11am & 3-8pm Sat & Sun) – outside opening hours you can call for a reservation. In the River Market area, saddle up at Bobby's Bike Hike (☑501-613-7001; www.bobbysbikehike.com/

littlerock; 400 President Clinton Ave; 4hr $17-30, day $28-55).

🛏 Sleeping & Eating

Because of government and convention-center traffic, it's difficult to find inexpensive hotels downtown, and rates fluctuate wildly. Budget motels lie off the interstates. The fun-loving pubs in the River Market district buzz at night. Ottenheimer Market Hall (btwn S Commerce & S Rock Sts; ☺7am-6pm Mon-Sat) houses an eclectic collection of inexpensive food stalls.

Capital Hotel BOUTIQUE HOTEL $$
(☑888-293-4121, 501-374-7474; www.capitalhotel.com; 111 W Markham St; r from $160; P❀@⏩) This 1872 former bank building with a cast-iron facade – a near-extinct architectural feature – is the top digs in Little Rock. There is a wonderful outdoor mezzanine for cocktails (and, unfortunately, smokers).

Rooms are plush, and the chef at Ashley's, one of two restaurants on the premises, won the *Food & Wine* People's Choice Best New Chef for the Midwest in 2011 (except this ain't the Midwest, though it's no fault of the food).

Rosemont HISTORIC B&B $$
(☑501-374-7456; www.rosemontoflittlerock.com; 515 W 15th St; r incl breakfast from $99; P❀⏩) An 1880s restored farmhouse near the Governor's mansion that oozes cozy Southern charm. The proprietors have also opened a few historic cottages nearby (from $125).

River City CAFE $
(www.rivercityteacoffeeandcream.com; 2715 Ka-
vanaugh Blvd; ⊙ 6am-9pm Mon-Fri, from 7am Sat
& Sun; 🐟) A killer Hillcrest tea and coffeehouse, cozy and homey with cushy sofas and
an excellent selection of loose leaf tea. It has
good ice cream too.

House PUB $
(www.facebook.com/thehouseinhillcrest; 722 N
Palm St; mains $8-11; ⊙ 11am-2pm, 5pm-late Mon-
Sat; 🐟) Arkansas' first gastropub is really all
about the excellent burgers. The jerk burger
comes smothered in warm mango chutney
and jerk spices, the mac and cheese burger
comes with, well, mac and cheese and the
black-apple bourbon burger is drizzled with
bourbon glaze and topped with a slice of
crisp Arkansas black apple and bacon.

Get yours with a turkey or veggie patty if
you must.

Acadia SOUTHERN $$$
(www.acadiahillcrest.com; 3000 Kavanaugh Blvd;
dinner mains $18-23; ⊙ 5:30-10pm Mon-Sat; 🐟)
Another Hillcrest standout, Acadia's multi-
level patio with twinkling lights is a fabu-
lous place to enjoy fancy-shmancy Southern
dishes like oven-roasted duck breast glazed
with Guinness-honey mustard paired with
white truffled portobello-mushroom jack-
cheese grits.

🛈 Getting There & Around

Bill & Hillary Clinton National Airport (LIT;
☑ 501-372-3439; www.lrn-airport.com) lies
just east of downtown. The **Greyhound station**
(☑ 501-372-3007; www.greyhound.com; 118 E
Washington St), in North Little Rock, serves Hot
Springs (one to two hours), Memphis, TN (2½
hours), and New Orleans (18 hours). Amtrak
occupies **Union Station** (☑ 501-372-6841; 1400
W Markham St). **Central Arkansas Transit** (CAT;
☑ 501-375-6717; www.cat.org) runs local buses
and the **River Rail Streetcar**, a trolley which
makes a loop on W Markham and President
Clinton Ave (adult/child $1/50¢).

Hot Springs

The little city of Hot Springs once hosted
the vacationing organized-crime elite. At
full throttle in the 1930s, the city was a hot-
bed of gambling, bootlegging, prostitution,
opulence and dangerous thugs. Yet it was
also a spot of truce between warring gangs,
a place where it was decreed that all crimi-
nals could be gluttonous hedonists in peace.

When gambling was squelched, so was the
city's economy.

Though it still hasn't recovered from that
blow, the healing waters have always drawn
people, everyone from Native Americans
to present-day pilgrims. Elaborate restored
bathhouses, where you can still get old-
school spa treatments, line Bathhouse Row
behind shady magnolias on the east side of
Central Ave.

◉ Sights & Activities

A promenade runs through the park around
the hillside behind Bathhouse Row, where
some springs survive intact, and a network
of trails covers Hot Springs' mountains.
Only two of the historic bathhouses are in
operation.

Gangster Museum of America MUSEUM
(www.tgmoa.com; 510 Central Ave; adult/child
$12/free; ⊙ 10am-5pm Sun-Thu, to 6pm Fri & Sat)
Learn about the sinful glory days of prohi-
bition when this small town in the middle
of nowhere turned into a pinpoint of lav-
ish wealth thanks to Chicago bootleggers
like Capone, and his NYC counterparts.
Highlights include original slots and a
tommy gun.

**Hot Springs Museum
of Contemporary Art** ART
(☑ 501-608-9966; www.museumofcontempo-
raryart.org; 425 Central Ave; adult/child $5/free;
⊙ 9am-4pm Tue-Sat, noon-3pm Sun) The historic
Ozark bathhouse is now home to 11,000 sq ft
of gallery space housing rotating exhibits.
Given Hot Springs' arts reputation, it is
worth a look.

NPS Visitor Center MUSEUM
(☑ 501-620-6715; www.nps.gov/hosp; 369 Central
Ave; ⊙ 9am-5pm) On Bathhouse Row, tra-
ditionally set up in the 1915 Fordyce bath-
house, the NPS visitor center and museum
have exhibits about the park's history first as
a Native American free-trade zone, and later
as a turn-of-the-19th-century European spa.
At research time, however, the Fordyce was
under renovation and a temporary center
was set up in the Lamar bathhouse down
the street.

Hot Springs Mountain Tower OUTDOORS
(401 Hot Springs Mountain Rd; adult/child $7/4;
⊙ 9am-5pm Nov-Feb, to 6pm Mar-May 15 & Labor
Day-Oct, to 9pm May 16-Labor Day) On top of
Hot Springs Mountain, the 216ft tower has

spectacular views of the surrounding mountains covered with dogwood, hickory, oak and pine – lovely in the spring and fall.

★ **Buckstaff Bathhouse**   SPA
(☑ 501-623-2308; www.buckstaffbaths.com; 509 Central Ave; thermal bath $30, with 20min massage $60; ⊘ 7-11:45am & 1:30-3pm Mon-Sat) Spa service Hot Springs style was never a 'foofy' experience. Buckstaff's no-nonsense staff whip you through the baths, treatments and massages, just as in the 1930s. And it is wonderful.

Quapaw Baths   SPA
(www.quapawbaths.com; 413 Central Ave; thermal bath $18, massage $50-80; ⊘ 10am-6pm Mon & Wed-Sat, 10am-3pm Sun) 🕿 If the traditional 'wham, bam, thank you, ma'am' approach isn't your thing, the newly remodeled Quapaw offers a more 21st-century vibe, with lovely restored thermal baths and gentle treatments.

🛏 Sleeping & Eating

Restaurants congregate along the Central Ave tourist strip and offer ho-hum food.

★ **Alpine Inn**   INN $
(☑ 501-624-9164; www.alpine-inn-hot-springs.com; 741 Park Ave/Hwy 7 N; r $55-90; P ❄ 🛜 ☎) The friendly Scottish owners of this inn, less than a mile from Bathhouse Row, have spent a few years upgrading an old motel to remarkable ends. The rooms are impeccable, comfortable and include new flatscreen TVs and sumptuous beds.

Arlington Resort Hotel & Spa   HISTORIC HOTEL $
(☑ 501-623-7771; www.arlingtonhotel.com; 239 Central Ave; s/d from $88/98, with mineral bath $145; P ❄ 🛜 ☎) This imposing historic hotel tops Bathhouse Row and constantly references its glory days. The grand lobby buzzes at night when there might be a live band. There's an in-house spa, and rooms are well-maintained, if aging. There's even a half-hearted Starbucks! Corner rooms with a view are a steal.

Colonial Pancake House   DINER $
(111 Central Ave; mains $6-10; ⊘ 7am-3pm) A Hot Springs classic, with turquoise booths and homey touches like quilts and doilies on the walls, it's almost like your grandma's kitchen. Except the pancakes, French toast (made with Texas toast) and malted or buckwheat

waffles are better'n grandma's. Get yours with pecans inside. It does burgers and other diner grub at lunch.

McClard's   BARBECUE $$
(www.mcclards.com; 505 Albert Pike; mains $4-15; ⊘ 11am-8pm Tue-Sat) Southwest of the center, Bill Clinton's favorite boyhood BBQ is still popular for ribs, slow-cooked beans, chili and tamales. It's on the outskirts of downtown.

Central Park Fusion   ASIAN FUSION $$$
(☑ 501-623-0202; www.centralparkfusion.com; 200 Park Ave; mains $19-33) The town favorite at research time, this east-meets-west kitchen grills steaks Hawaiian style, steams mussels in Thai curry, does an Asian duck salad, and glazes salmon in Thai chili. All served in a contemporary dining space accented with local art.

☆ Entertainment

Maxine's   BAR
(☑ 501-321-0909; www.maxineslive.com; 700 Central Ave) If you're looking for some (loud) night music, head to this infamous cathouse turned live music venue. It hosts bands out of Austin regularly, and cater to a younger crowd.

ⓘ Getting There & Away

Greyhound (☑ 501-623-5574; www.greyhound.com; 1001 Central Ave) has buses heading to Little Rock (1½ hours, three daily).

Around Hot Springs

The wild, pretty Ouachita National Forest (☑ 501-321-5202; www.fs.usda.gov/ouachita; welcome center 100 Reserve St; ⊘ 8am-4:30pm) is studded with lakes and draws hunters, fisherfolk, mountain-bike riders and boaters. The small roads through the mountains unfailingly bring hidden nooks and wonderful views. The Ouachita boasts two designated National Forest Scenic Byways: Arkansas Scenic Hwy 7 and Talimena Scenic Byway, navigating mountain ranges from Arkansas into Oklahoma.

Clinton buffs might stop at Hope, where the ex-pres spent his first seven years, but there's not much to see other than the spiffy Hope Visitor Center & Museum (www.hopearkansas.net; 100 E Division St; ⊘ 8:30am-5pm Mon-Fri, from 9am Sat, 1-4pm Sun), in the old depot, and the President Bill Clinton

First Home Museum (www.clintonchildhood-homemuseum.com; 117 S Hervey St; ⊙8:30am-4:30pm) FREE.

Arkansas River Valley

The Arkansas River cuts a swath across the state from Oklahoma to Mississippi. Folks come to fish, canoe and camp along its banks and tributaries. The excellently maintained trails of Petit Jean State Park (☑501-727-5441; www.petitjeanstatepark.com; 愛), west of Morrilton, wind past a lush 95ft waterfall, romantic grottoes, expansive vistas and dense forests. There's a rustic stone lodge, reasonable cabins (per night $105-180) and campgrounds. Another stellar state park is Mount Magazine (☑479-963-8502; www.mountmagazinestatepark.com; 16878 Hwy 309 S), which maintains 14 miles of trails around Arkansas' highest point. Outdoor enthusiasts enjoy great hang gliding and rock climbing here as well as hiking.

The spectacular Highway 23/Pig Trail Byway, lined with wild echinacea and lilies, climbs through Ozark National Forest and into the mountains; an excellent way to reach Eureka Springs.

Ozark Mountains

Stretching from northwest and central Arkansas into Missouri, the Ozark Mountains (☑870-404-2741; www.ozarkmountainregion.com) are an ancient range, once surrounded by sea and now well worn by time. Verdant rolling mountains give way to misty fields, and dramatic karst formations line sparkling lakes, meandering rivers and scenic back roads. Though some of the towns bank on kitschy hillbilly culture, scratch below the surface to find unique cultural traditions, such as acoustic folk music and home-cooked hush puppies and catfish.

Mountain View

Detour east of US 65 or along Hwy 5 to this wacky Ozark town, known for its tradition of informal music-making at Courtsquare. Creeping commercialism is taking its toll, as the Visitor Information Center (☑870-269-8068; www.yourplaceinthemountains.com; 107 N Peabody Ave; ⊙9am-4:30pm Mon-Sat) promotes the place as the 'Folk Music Capital of the World,' but cutesy sandstone architecture downtown, and impromptu folk, gospel and bluegrass hootenannies (jam sessions) by the Stone County Courthouse (especially on Saturday night) – and on porches all around town anytime – make a visit here rather harmonious.

Ozark Folk Center State Park (☑800-264-3655; www.ozarkfolkcenter.com; 1032 Park Ave; auditorium adult/child $12/7; ⊙10am-5pm Tue-Sat Apr-Nov), just north of town, hosts ongoing craft demonstrations and a traditional herb garden, as well as frequent live music from 7pm that attracts an avid, older crowd. The zip and slack lines, free-fall and climbing wall at LocoRopes (☑870-269-6566; www.locoropes.com; 1025 Park Ave; per zip line $7.50; ⊙10am-5pm Mar 1-Nov 30) is strictly for the young and wild at heart.

The spectacular Blanchard Springs Caverns (☑870-757-2211; www.blanchardsprings.org; NF 54, Forest Rd, off Hwy 14; adult/child Drip Stone Tour $10.50/5.50, Wild Cave Tour $75; ⊙10:30am-4:30pm; 愛), located 15 miles northwest of Mountain View, were carved by an underground river and rival those at Carlsbad Caverns National Park. Three Forest Service guided tours range from disabled-accessible to adventurous three- to four-hour spelunking sessions. The welcoming and historic 1918 Wildflower B&B (☑870-269-4383; www.wildflowerbb.com; 100 Washington; r incl breakfast from $89; ℙ❀🛜) is right on the Courtsquare with a rocking chair–equipped, wrap-around porch, and cozy down-home trappings. Tommy's Famous Pizza and BBQ (cnr Carpenter & W Main Sts; pizza $7-26, mains $7-13; ⊙from 3pm) is run by the friendliest bunch of backwoods hippies you could ask for. The pulled-pork BBQ pizza marries Tommy's specialties perfectly.

Eureka Springs

Artsy, quirky and drop-dead gorgeous, Eureka Springs, near Arkansas' northwestern corner, perches in a steep valley and is one of the coolest towns in the South. Victorian buildings line crooked streets and a crunchy local population welcomes all – it's one of the most explicitly gay-friendly towns in the Ozarks and an island of Democratic blue in a sea of Republican red. On the surface, art galleries and kitschy shops compete with commercialized country music and the 70ft Christ of the Ozarks statue for your attention. But bend a local's ear and find out who's playing at the nearest pub, or the location of their favorite swimming hole, and this idiosyncratic village will take on new

DON'T MISS

A LOVELY LOOP

Downtown Eureka Springs is beautiful in and of itself, but the town's real coup is its easily overlooked Historic Loop, a 3.5-mile ring of history through downtown and neighboring residential neighborhoods. The route is dotted with over 300 Victorian homes, all built before 1910, each and every one of them a jaw-dropper and on par with any preserved historic district in the USA.

Pick up a *Six Scenic Walking Tours* brochure from the visitor center in Eureka Springs, rent a bike from Adventure Mountain Outfitters (☑479-253-0900; www. adventuremountainoutfitters.com; 151 Spring St, Eureka Springs; half day from $50; ⏰9am-5pm Wed-Sat); or catch the Red Line of the Eureka Trolley (www.eurekatrolley.org; day pass adult/child $6/2; ⏰9am-5pm Jan-Apr & Nov-Dec, to 8pm Sun May-Oct).

dimensions. Hiking, cycling, and horseback-riding opportunities abound. There are no red lights or perpendicular cross streets, so zipping around its historical beauty is a breeze. Well, except for those steep hills.

The visitor center (☑479-253-8737; www. eurekaspringschamber.com; 516 Village Circle, Hwy 62 E; ⏰9am-5pm) has information about lodging, activities, tours and local attractions, such as the rockin' Blues Festival (www.eurekaspringsblues.com; ⏰Jun). The old ES & NA Railway (☑479-253-9623; www. esnarailway.com; 299 N Main St; adult/child $14/7; ⏰Tue-Sat Apr-Oct) puffs through the Ozark hills on an hour-long tour three times a day (four times on Saturday).

Thorncrown Chapel (☑479-253-7401; www.thorncrown.com; 12968 Hwy 62 W; donation suggested; ⏰9am-5pm Apr-Nov, 11am-4pm Mar & Dec) is a magnificent sanctuary made of glass, with its 48ft-tall wooden skeleton holding 425 windows. There's not much between your prayers and God's green earth here. It's just outside of town in the woods.

You can nest downtown at the historic New Orleans Hotel and Suchness Spa (☑479-253-8630; www.neworleanshotelandspa.com; 63 Spring St; r from $89; P☀☎), which would send you reeling back in time, except for the New Age, chakra balancing spa in the lobby. Treehouse Cottages (☑479-253-8667; www. treehousecottages.com; 165 W Van Buren St; cottages $149-169; P☀☎) offers gorgeous sunlit, Jacuzzi-equipped tree houses (that are more like cottages on stilts) in the woods on the canyon rim.

At Mud Street Café (www.mudstreetcafe. com; 22G S Main St; mains $9-13; ⏰8am-3pm Thu-Tue), downtown, the coffee drinks and breakfasts are renowned. After dark, find Chelsea's Pizzeria (☑479-253-8231; www. chelseascornercafe.com; 10 Mountain St; mains $10-20; ⏰noon-10pm Sun-Thu, to midnight Fri &

Sat), for good pies and Mediterranean fare, and an excellent live music scene in the cavernous bar downstairs.

Buffalo National River

Yet another under-acknowledged Arkansas gem, and perhaps the best of them all, this 135-mile river flows beneath dramatic bluffs through unspoiled Ozark forest. The upriver section tends to have most of the white water, while the lower reaches ease lazily along – perfect for an easy paddle. The Buffalo National River (☑870-741-5443; www.nps.gov/ buff) has 10 campgrounds and three designated wilderness areas; the most accessible is through the Tyler Bend visitor center (☑870-439-2502; ⏰8:30am-4:30pm), 11 miles north of Marshall on Hwy 65, where you can also pick up a list of approved outfitters for self-guided rafting or canoe trips, the best way to tour the park and see the gargantuan limestone bluffs. Or simply seek out Buffalo Outdoor Center (BOC; ☑800-221-5514; www. buffaloriver.com; cnr Hwys 43 & 74; kayak/canoe per day $58/60, car shuttle from $18, zipline tour $89; ⏰8am-5pm; ☀☎) in Ponca. They will point you in the right direction and rent out attractive cabins in the woods too. Thanks to its National River designation in 1972, the Buffalo is one of the few remaining unpolluted, free-flowing rivers in America.

LOUISIANA

Southerners will often tell you they're different from other Americans. They say it's their intensely felt local traditions and connection to the land, though they might say this sitting on the porch of a cookie-cutter subdivision that could be Anywhere, America. But in Louisiana, that regional pride becomes actual regionalism, a palpable sense that you are somewhere different.

A French colony turned Spanish protectorate turned reluctant American purchase; a southern fringe of swampland, bayou and alligators dissolving into the Gulf of Mexico; a northern patchwork prairie of heartland farm country, and everywhere, a population tied together by a deep, unshakeable appreciation for the good things: food and music.

Louisiana's first city, New Orleans, lives and dies by these qualities, and her restaurants and music halls are second to none, but everywhere, the state shares a love for this joie de vivre. We're not dropping French for fun, by the way; while the language is not a cultural component of North Louisiana, near I-10 and below it is a generation removed from the household – if it has been removed at all.

History

The lower Mississippi River area was dominated by the Mississippian mound-building culture until around 1592 when Europeans arrived and decimated the Native Americans with the usual combination of disease, unfavorable treaties and outright hostility.

The land was then passed back and forth between France, Spain and England. Under the French 'Code Noir,' slaves were kept, but retained a somewhat greater degree of freedom, and thus native culture, than their counterparts in British North America.

After the American Revolution the whole area passed to the USA in the 1803 Louisiana Purchase, and Louisiana became a state in 1812. The resulting blend of American and Franco-Spanish traditions, plus the influence of Afro-Caribbean communities, gave Louisiana a unique culture she retains to this day.

Steamboats opened a vital trade network across the continent. New Orleans was a major port, and Louisiana's slave-based plantation economy kept up a flowing export of rice, tobacco, indigo, sugarcane and especially cotton. After the Civil War, Louisiana was readmitted to the Union in 1868, and the next 30 years saw political wrangling, economic stagnation and renewed discrimination against African Americans.

In the 1920s, industry and tourism developed, but so did a tradition of unorthodox and sometimes ruthless politics; in 1991, former Ku Klux Klan leader David Duke ran for Governor against Edwin Edwards; Edwards, a famously colorful and corrupt politician. Edwards won the race and was eventually convicted on racketeering charges.

Hurricane Katrina (2005) and the BP Gulf Coast Oil Spill (2010) significantly damaged the local economy and infrastructure. Louisiana remains a bottom-rung state in terms of per capita income and education levels, yet on the flip side, ranks high in national happiness scales.

ℹ Information

Sixteen welcome centers dot freeways throughout the state, or contact the **Louisiana Office of Tourism** (☑ 800-993-7515, 225-342-8100; www.louisianatravel.com).

Louisiana State Parks (☑ 877-226-7652; www.crt.state.la.us/parks; primitive/premium sites $1/18) Louisiana has 22 state parks that offer camping. Some parks offer lodge accommodations and cabins. Reservations (☑ 877-226-7652; http://reservations2. usedirect.com/LAStateParksHome/) can be made online, by phone, or on a drop-in basis if there's availability.

LOUISIANA FACTS

Nicknames Bayou State, Pelican State, Sportsman's Paradise

Population 4.6 million

Area 51,843 sq miles

Capital city Baton Rouge (population 229,553)

Other cities New Orleans (population 360,740)

Sales tax 4%, plus local city and county taxes

Birthplace of Jazz, naturalist John James Audubon (1785–1851), trumpeter Louis 'Satchmo' Armstrong (1901–71), author Truman Capote (1924–84), musician Antoine 'Fats' Domino (b 1928), pop star Britney Spears (b 1981)

Home of Tabasco sauce, chef Emeril Lagasse

Politics Republican stronghold with a very liberal large city (New Orleans)

Famous for Drive-thru margaritas

Official state reptile Alligator

Driving distances New Orleans to Lafayette 137 miles, New Orleans to St Francisville 112 miles

New Orleans

New Orleans is very much of America, and extraordinarily removed from it as well. 'Nola' is something, and somewhere, else. Founded by the French and administered by the Spanish (and then the French again), she is, with her sidewalk cafes and iron balconies, the most European city in America, yes. But she is also, with her *vodoun* (voodoo), weekly second-line parades (essentially, neigborhood parades), Mardi Gras Indians, jazz and brass and gumbo, the most African and Caribbean city in the country as well. New Orleans celebrates; while America is on deadline, this city is getting a cocktail after a long lunch. But if you saw how people here rebuilt their homes after floods and storms, you'd be foolish to call the locals lazy.

Tolerating everything and learning from it is the soul of this city. When her citizens aspire to that great Creole ideal – a mix of all influences into something better – we get: jazz; Nouveau Louisiana cuisine; storytellers from African *griots* (West African bards) to Seventh Ward rappers to Tennessee Williams; French townhouses a few blocks from Foghorn Leghorn mansions groaning under sweet myrtle and bougainvillea; Mardi Gras celebrations that mix pagan mysticism with Catholic pageantry. Just don't forget the indulgence and immersion, because that Creole-ization gets watered down when folks don't live life to its intellectual and epicurean hilt.

New Orleans may take it easy, but it takes it. The whole hog. Stuffed with crawfish.

History

The town of Nouvelle Orléans was founded as a French outpost in 1718 by Jean-Baptiste Le Moyne de Bienville. Early settlers arrived from France, Canada and Germany, and the French imported thousands of African slaves. The city became a central port in the slave trade; due to local laws some slaves were allowed to earn their freedom and assume an established place in the Creole community as *les gens de couleur libres* (free people of color).

The Spanish were largely responsible for building the French Quarter as it still looks today because fires in 1788 and 1794 decimated the earlier French architecture. The influx of Anglo Americans after the Louisiana Purchase led to an expansion of the city into the Central Business District (CBD), Garden District and Uptown.

New Orleans survived the Civil War intact after an early surrender to Union forces, but the economy languished with the end of the slavery-based plantations. In the early 1900s, New Orleans was the birthplace of jazz music. Many of the speakeasies and homes of the jazz originators have been destroyed through neglect, but the cultural claim was canonized in 1994 when the National Park Service established the New Orleans Jazz National Historical Park to celebrate the origins and evolution of America's most widely recognized indigenous musical art form. Oil and petrochemical industries developed in the 1950s, and today tourism is the other lifeblood of the local economy.

In 2005 Katrina, a relatively weak Category 3 hurricane, overwhelmed New Orleans' federal flood protection system in over 50 places. Some 80% of the city was flooded, over 1800 people lost their lives and the entire city was evacuated. Today the population has largely returned (80% of pre-Katrina population levels), and cheap housing and the vibrant culture has attracted a whole generation of entrepreneurs.

⊙ Sights

◉ French Quarter

Elegant, Caribbean-colonial architecture, lush gardens and wrought-iron accents are the visual norm in the French Quarter. But this is also the heart of New Orleans' tourism scene. Bourbon St generates a loutish membrane that sometimes makes the rest of the Quarter difficult to appreciate. Look past this. The Vieux Carré (Old Quarter; first laid out in 1722) is the focal point of much of this city's culture and in the quieter back lanes and alleyways there's a sense of faded time shaken and stirred with joie de vivre.

Jackson Square   SQUARE, PLAZA
(☑ 504-568-6968; www.jackson-square.com; Decatur & St Peter Sts) Jackson Sq is the heart of the Quarter. Sprinkled with lazing loungers, surrounded by fortune-tellers, sketch artists and traveling showmen, and overlooked by cathedrals, offices and shops plucked from a fairy tale, this is one of America's great green spaces.

St Louis Cathedral
CATHEDRAL

(📋 504 525-9585; Jackson Sq; donations accepted; ⏰ 9am-5pm Mon-Sat, 1-5pm Sun) St Louis Cathedral is Jackson Sq's masterpiece. Designed by Gilberto Guillemard, this is one of the finest examples of French ecumenical (church) architecture in America.

Louisiana State Museum
MUSEUM

(http://lsm.crt.state.la.us; per bldg adult/child $6/free; ⏰ 10am-4:30pm Tue-Sun) This institution operates several buildings across the state. The standouts here include the 1911 Cabildo (701 Chartres St), on the left of the cathedral, a Louisiana history museum located in the old city hall where Plessy vs Ferguson (which legalized segregation) was argued. The huge number of exhibits inside can easily eat up half a day (don't miss the 1875 Upright Piano on the 3rd floor), the remainder of which can be spent in the Cabildo's sister building, on the right of the church, the 1813 Presbytère (751 Chartres St; 📷). Inside is an excellent Mardi Gras museum, with displays of costumes, parade floats and royal jewelry; and a poignant Katrina & Beyond exhibit, chronicling the before and after of this devastating storm – a surefire don't-miss for understanding the effects of this disaster on the city.

Historic New Orleans Collection
MUSEUM

(www.hnoc.org; 533 Royal St; tours $5; ⏰ 9:30am-4:30pm Tue-Sat, 10:30am-4:30pm Sun) FREE In several exquisitely restored buildings are thoughtfully curated exhibits with an emphasis on archival materials, such as the original transfer documents of the Louisiana Purchase. Separate home, architecture/courtyard and history tours also run at 10am, 11am, 2pm and 3pm.

Old Ursuline Convent
HISTORIC BUILDING

(1112 Chartres St; adult/child $5/3; ⏰ tours 10am-4pm Mon-Sat) In 1727, 12 Ursuline nuns arrived in New Orleans to care for the French garrison's 'miserable little hospital' and to educate the young girls of the colony. Between 1745 and 1752 the French colonial army built what is now the oldest structure in the Mississippi River Valley and the only remaining French building in the Quarter.

NEW ORLEANS IN...

Two Days

On the first day, wander Jackson Sq and the French Quarter's museums. The **Cabildo** and **Presbytere** are adjacent to each other and give a good grounding in Louisiana culture, as does the nearby **Historic New Orleans Collection**. Afterwards, stroll along the mighty Mississippi.

Grab dinner at **Bayona**, localvore base of hometown legend Susan Spicer. Enjoy drinks at **Tonique** and go see some live music at **Preservation Hall**.

Next morning, stroll along Magazine St in a state of shopping nirvana. Then walk north, pop into **Lafayette Cemetery No 1**, consider having a drink at **Commander's Palace** – it helps to be well-dressed – and hop onto the St Charles Avenue Streetcar. Have a haute Southern dinner at **Boucherie**.

Four Days

On day three, join the morning Creole Neighborhoods bike tour with **Confederacy of Cruisers**. This is exceptionally easy riding, and takes in all elements of the funky Marigny and Bywater, but if you don't fancy bikes, walk past Washington Sq Park and soak up the Marigny's vibe.

Have dinner at **Bacchanal** and enjoy great wine and cheese in this musical garden.

If you're feeling edgy, head to St Claude Avenue where the offerings range from punk to hip-hop to bounce to '60s mod. For more traditional Nola jazz and blues, head down Frenchmen St.

The next day drive, or consider renting a bicycle, and explore around the Tremé – don't miss the **Backstreet Cultural Museum** or **Willie Mae's** fried chicken.

Head up Esplanade Ave and gawk at all the gorgeous Creole mansions sitting pretty under the big live oaks. Take Esplanade all the way to **City Park** and wander around the **New Orleans Museum of Art**.

New Orleans

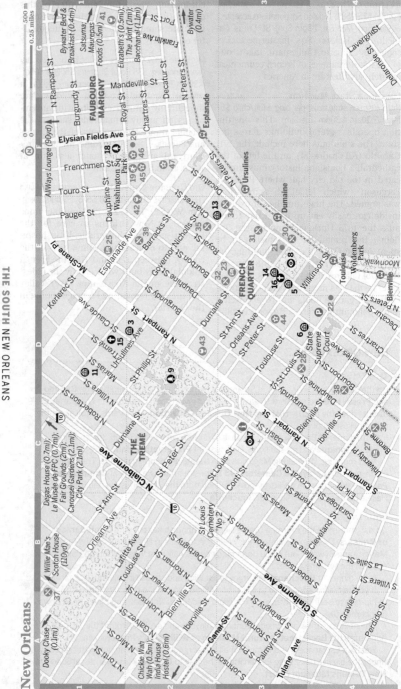

0   500 m
0   0.25 miles

FAUBOURG MARIGNY

Bywater Bed & Breakfast (0.4mi);
Satsuma; Maurepas Foods (0.5mi) 41
Elizabeth's (0.5mi); The Joint (1mi); Bacchanal (1.1mi)
Franklin Ave
Port St
Bywater (0.4mi)

N Rampart St
Burgundy St
Royal St
Chartres St
Decatur St
N Peters St

Mandeville St
Elysian Fields Ave
18
Frenchmen St
Touro St
Pauger St
Dauphine St
Washington Sq Park
19 45 46 20
42 47
25
39

AllWays Lounge (90yd)

Esplanade
Ursulines
Dumaine
Toulouse

Esplanade Ave
McShane Pl
Kerlerec St
St Claude Ave

Barracks St
Governor Nicholls St
Bourbon St
Dauphine St
Burgundy St
Dumaine St
St Ann St
Orleans Ave
St Peter St
Toulouse St
St Louis St
Bienville St
Iberville St

Royal St
Chartres St
Decatur St
N Peters St

13
34
35
31
30
21 8
14
16 1
5
32 23
FRENCH QUARTER

Degas House (0.7mi);
Le Musée de FPC (0.7mi);
Fair Grounds (2mi);
Carousel Gardens (2.1mi);
City Park (2.1mi)

N Claiborne Ave
N Robertson St
N Villere St
N Prieur St
N Roman St
N Johnson St
N Galvez St
N Miro St
N Tonti St

THE TREMÉ
15
3
11
9
43

Ursulines St
St Philip St
Dumaine St
St Peter St
St Louis St
Conti St

10
1
10

St Louis Cemetery No 2

Willie Mae's Scotch House (110yd)
Dooky Chase (0.1mi)
37

Chickie Wah Wah (0.5mi);
India House Hostel (0.6mi)

N Rampart St
Basin St
Burgundy St
Dauphine St
Bourbon St
St Charles Ave
N Peters St
Decatur St
Chartres St
Wilkinson St
N Peters St
Bienville St

44
6
28
38
22
State
Supreme Court
P

Woldenberg Park
Moonwalk
Toulouse
Bienville

S Rampart St
Elk Pl
Saratoga St
Treme St
Marais St
N Villere St
N Robertson St
N Derbigny St
Cleveland St
University Pl
Basin St

36
27

S Claiborne Ave
S Villere St
La Salle St
S Robertson St
S Derbigny St

Orleans Ave
Toulouse St
Bienville St
Iberville St
Canal St
Tulane Ave
Gravier St
Perdido St

S Roman St
S Prieur St
S Johnson St
Palmyra St

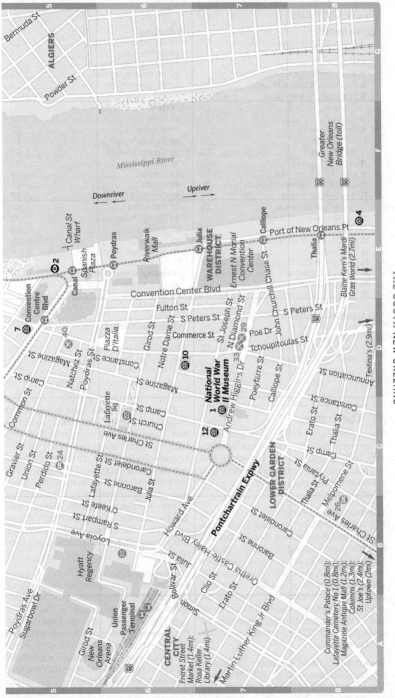

THE SOUTH NEW ORLEANS

New Orleans

◎ The Tremé

The oldest African American neighborhood in the city is obviously steeped in a lot of history. Leafy **Esplanade Avenue**, which borders the neighborhood, is full of old-school Creole mansions, and is one of the prettiest streets in the city.

Louis Armstrong Park   PARK
(701 N Rampart St; ☺9am-10pm) Louis Armstrong Park encompasses **Congo Square**, an American cultural landmark. Now a lovely landscaped park, it was the one place where enslaved people were allowed to congregate and play the music they had carried over the seas – a practice outlawed in most other slave-holding societies. The preservation of this musical heritage helped lay the groundwork for rhythms that would eventually become jazz.

Backstreet Cultural Museum   MUSEUM
(www.backstreetmuseum.org; 1116 St Claude Ave; admission $8; ☺10am-5pm Tue-Sat) This is the place to see one facet of this town's distinctive customs – its African American side – and how they're expressed in daily life. The term 'backstreet' refers to New Orleans' 'back o' town,' or the poor African American neighborhoods. If you have any interest in Mardi Gras Indian suits (African Americans who dress up in Carnival-esque Native American costume), second lines and the activities of social aid and pleasure clubs (the local African American community version of civic associations), you need to stop by.

Le Musée de FPC   MUSEUM
(Free People of Color Museum; www.lemuseed-efpc.com; 2336 Esplanade Ave; adult/child $10/5; ☺11am-4pm Wed-Sat) Inside a lovely 1859 Greek Revival mansion in the Upper Tremé, this museum showcases a 30-year collection of artifacts, documents, furniture and art, telling the story of a forgotten subculture: the 'free people of color' before the Civil War. Also opens by appointment.

St Louis Cemetery No 1 CEMETERY
(Basin St; ⊙ 9am-3pm Mon-Sat, to noon Sun; 🚹)
This cemetery received the remains of most
early Creoles. The shallow water table ne-
cessitated above ground burials, with bodies
placed in the family tombs you see to this
day. The supposed grave of voodoo queen
Marie Laveau is here, scratched with XXXs
from spellbound devotees – this is graffiti
you shouldn't add to, per the request of the
family that owns the tomb. Do not come
here at night; the area can be dangerous.

New Orleans African
American Museum MUSEUM
(www.thenoaam.org; 1418 Governor Nicholls St;
adult/student/child $7/5/3; ⊙ 11am-4pm Wed-Sat)
This small museum features rotating displays of local artists and semi-permanent installations on slavery and African American
history in a series of tidy Creole homes.

St Augustine's Church CHURCH
(☑ 504-525-5934; www.staugustinecatholic-
church-neworleans.org; 1210 Governor Nicholls St)
The 1824 church is the second-oldest African American Catholic church in the US;
many jazz funeral processions originate
here. It has Sunday services but you'll need
to call ahead for a tour. Note the haunting
cross fashioned from chains on the side of
the building marking the Tomb of the Unknown Slave.

◉ Faubourg Marigny, the
Bywater & the Ninth Ward

North of the French Quarter are the Creole
suburbs (*faubourgs*, which more accurately
means 'neighborhoods') of the Marigny
and the Bywater. The Marigny is the heart
of the local gay scene. Frenchmen Street,
which runs through the center of the 'hood,
is a fantastic strip of live-music goodness. It
used to be known as a locals' Bourbon, but
recently it's been inundated with tourists,
although it's still nowhere near as tacky as
Bourbon. Nearby St Claude Avenue now
boasts a collection of good live music venues that are fairly undiscovered by outsiders,
but don't expect Dixie-style jazz joints; folks
here rock out to punk and bounce (a local
style of frenetic dance music).

The Bywater is a collection of candy-
colored shotgun houses (local houses that
are laid out one room after another with
no hallway) and Creole cottages. It has the
heaviest concentration of transplants in

the city and an ever-expanding number of
sometimes awesome, sometimes cloyingly
hip new restaurant and bars.

Old New Orleans Rum Distillery FACTORY
(☑ 504-945-9400; www.oldneworleansrum.com;
2815 Frenchmen St; admission $10; ⊙ tours noon,
2pm & 4pm Mon-Fri, 2pm & 4pm Sat) A short
drive north of the Marigny is the Old New
Orleans Rum distillery. Founded by local
artists James Michalopoulos and his artist-
musician friends, the distillery makes great
spirits you'll find in most local bars. You can
sample all of them, including a rare vintage
unavailable outside the factory, on an entertaining 45-minute distillery tour. The rum
distillery is in an industrial area 2 miles
north of Faubourg Marigny.

Washington Square Park PARK
(cnr Frenchmen & Royal St) Also known as
'Marigny Green,' this park is a popular
spot for locals to play with their dogs, toss
Frisbees and, based on the frequent smell,
smoke things that aren't cigarettes. There's a
touching HIV/AIDS memorial on the north
side of the park.

◉ CBD & Warehouse District

★ National World War II Museum MUSEUM
(☑ 504-528-1944; www.ddaymuseum.org; 945
Magazine St; adult/child $22/13, with 1/2 films
add $5/10; ⊙ 9am-5pm) The extensive, heart-
wrenching museum should satisfy the historical curiosity of anyone with even a passing interest in WWII. The museum presents
an admirably nuanced and thorough analy-
sis of the biggest war of the 20th century.
Of particular note is the D-Day exhibition,
arguably the most in-depth of its type in the
country. *Beyond All Boundaries*, a film narrated by Tom Hanks and shown on a 120ft-
wide immersive screen in the new Solomon
Victory Theater, is a loud, proud and awesome extravaganza. *Final Mission* places
27 audience members on the submarine
USS *Tang* during her final mission; you will
become a crew member with naval respon-
sibilities and learn the ultimate fate of the
ship's complement.

Ogden Museum of Southern Art MUSEUM
(☑ 504-539-9600; www.ogdenmuseum.org; 925
Camp St; adult/student/child $10/8/5; ⊙ 10am-
5pm Wed-Mon, 10am-5pm & 6-8pm Thu) New Orleans entrepreneur Roger Houston Ogden
has assembled one of the finest collections
of Southern art anywhere – far too large

LOCAL KNOWLEDGE

ART FOR EVERY WEEKEND

Lindsay Glatz from the Arts Council of New Orleans fills us in on the places where you can discover local art and meet local artists every weekend in New Orleans.

New Orleans Arts District Art Walk (www.neworleansartsdistrict.com; Julia St; ☺6-9pm 1st Sat of month) The fine-art galleries in New Orleans Art District celebrate the opening night of month-long feature artist exhibitions. In the Warehouse District/CBD.

Freret Street Market (www.freretmarket.org; cnr Freret St & Napoleon Ave; ☺noon-5pm 1st Sat of month Sep-Jun) A combination farmers market, flea market and art show in Uptown, this offers a great mix of local culture.

Saint Claude Arts District Gallery Openings (www.scadnola.com; ☺2nd Sat of month) New Orleans' newest arts district, this growing collective of art-exhibition spaces spans Faubourg Marigny and the Bywater, home to some of New Orleans' more eclectic artists. Ask locals for weekend recommendations and you may be rewarded with a fire-eating display or impromptu collective installations at a secret, hidden art space.

Art Market of New Orleans (www.artscouncilofneworleans.org; Palmer Park, cnr Carrolton & Claiborne Aves; ☺last Sat of month) Featuring hundreds of the area's most creative local artists, this monthly Uptown market is juried for quality and always features local food, music and kids' activities. Perfect on warm-weather days.

to keep to himself – which includes huge galleries ranging from Impressionist landscapes to outsider folk-art quirkiness, to contemporary installation work. There's live music from 6pm to 8pm Thursday with normal museum admission.

Blaine Kern's Mardi Gras World MUSEUM
(☑504-655-9586; www.mardigrasworld.com; 1380 Port of New Orleans Pl; adult/child $19.95/12.95; ☺tours 9:30am-4:30pm; 🚹) This garish and good-fun spot houses (and constructs) many of the greatest floats used in Mardi Gras parades. The tour takes you through the giant workshops where artists create elaborate floats for New Orleans *krewes* (marching clubs), Universal Studios and Disney World.

Aquarium of the Americas AQUARIUM
(☑504-581-4629; www.auduboninstitute.org; 1 Canal St; adult/child $22.50/16, with IMAX $29/23, with Audubon Zoo $36/25; ☺10am-5pm; 🚹) Simulates an eclectic selection of watery habitats – look for the rare white alligator. You can buy combination tickets to the IMAX theater next door, the nearby Insectarium, the Audubon Zoo in Uptown or all of the above (adult/child $44.50/27.50).

Insectarium MUSEUM, GARDEN
(☑504-581-4629; www.auduboninstitute.org; 423 Canal St; adult/child $16.50/12; ☺10am-5pm; 🚹) A supremely kid-friendly learning center that's a joy for budding entomologists. The Japanese garden dotted with whispering butterflies is particularly beautiful. Has

a nice exhibit on New Orleans' notorious cockroaches.

☺ Garden District & Uptown

The main architectural division in New Orleans is between the elegant townhouses of the Creole and French northeast and the magnificent mansions of the American district, settled after the Louisiana Purchase. These huge structures, plantationesque in their appearance, are most commonly found in the Garden District and Uptown. Magnificent oak trees arch over St Charles Ave, which cuts through the heart of this sector and where the supremely picturesque **St Charles Avenue streetcar** (per ride $1.25; 🚹) runs. The boutiques and galleries of **Magazine Street** form the best shopping strip in the city.

Lafayette Cemetery No 1 CEMETERY
(Washington Ave at Prytania St; ☺9am-2:30pm) This necropolis was established in 1833 by the former City of Lafayette. Sitting as it does just across from **Commander's Palace** and shaded by magnificent groves of lush greenery, the cemetery has a strong sense of Southern subtropical gothic about it. Some of the wealthier family tombs were built of marble, with elaborate detail rivaling the finest architecture in the district. You'll notice many German and Irish names on the above ground graves, testifying that immigrants were devastated by 19th-century yellow-fever epidemics. Take bus 11 or 12.

Audubon Zoological Gardens　　ZOO
(www.auduboninstitute.org; 6500 Magazine St; adult/child $17.50/12; ⊙10am-5pm Mon-Fri, to 6pm Sat & Sun; 🖝) This wonderful zoo is great for kids and adults. It contains the ultracool Louisiana Swamp exhibit, full of alligators, bobcats, foxes, bears and snapping turtles.

◉ City Park & Mid-City

City Park　　PARK
(www.neworleanscitypark.com; City Park Ave) The Canal streetcar (p444) makes the run from the CBD to City Park. Three miles long, 1 mile wide, stroked by weeping willows and Spanish moss and dotted with museums, gardens, waterways, bridges, birds and the occasional alligator, City Park is the nation's fifth-largest urban park (bigger than Central Park in NYC) and New Orleans' prettiest green lung.

New Orleans Museum of Art　　MUSEUM
(www.noma.org; 1 Collins Diboll Circle; adult/child $10/6; ⊙10am-6pm Tue-Thu, to 9pm Fri, 11am-5pm Sat & Sun) Inside City Park, this elegant museum was opened in 1911 and is well worth a visit both for its special exhibitions and top-floor galleries of African, Native American, Oceanic and Asian art (don't miss the outstanding Qing-dynasty snuff-bottle collection). Its sculpture garden (⊙10am-4:30pm Sat-Thu, to 8:45pm Fri) FREE contains a cutting-edge collection in lush, meticulously planned grounds.

Fair Grounds　　PARK
(1751 Gentilly Blvd, btwn Gentilly Blvd & Fortin St; ⊙late April-early May) Besides hosting the reg-

ular horse-racing season, the fair grounds are also home to the huge springtime New Orleans Jazz & Heritage Festival.

🥢 Courses

New Orleans School of Cooking　　COOKING
(☑800-237-4841; www.neworleansschoolofcooking.com; 524 St Louis St; courses $24-29) Most open courses are food demonstrations. Menus rotate daily, but rest assured you'll be snacking on creations such as gumbo, jambalaya and pralines at the end of class, all the while learning about the history of the city as told by the charismatic chefs. A hands-on class in cooking Creole cuisine is offered as well ($125).

⟅ゔ Tours

The Jean Lafitte National Historic Park and Preserve (p443) visitor center leads free walking tours of the French Quarter at 9:30am (get tickets at 9am).

Confederacy of Cruisers　　CYCLING
(☑504-400-5468; www.confederacyofcruisers.com; tours from $49) Get yourself out of the Quarter and on two wheels – this superinformative, laid-back bike tour takes you through Nola's non-Disneyland neighborhoods – Faubourg Marigny, Esplanade Ridge, the Tremé – often with a bar stop and the occasional jazz funeral pop-in along the way. Offers cocktail ($85) and culinary ($89) tours as well.

Friends of the Cabildo　　WALKING
(☑504-523-3939; 1850 House Museum Store, 523 St Ann St; adult/student $15/10; ⊙tours 10am

THE SOUTH NEW ORLEANS

SWAMP TOURS

Arrange swamp tours in New Orleans or go on your own and contract directly with a bayou-side company.

Louisiana Lost Land Tours (☑504-400-5920; http://lostlandstours.org) Wonderful tours that include kayak paddles into the wetlands and a motorboat tour of Barataria Bay. Excursions focus on land loss and wildlife threats, and are led by folks who genuinely love this land. Check out their blog on environemtnal issues in South Louisiana, http://lostlandstours.org/category/blog, maintained by Pulitzer Prize–winning journalist Bob Marshall.

Annie Miller's Son's Swamp & Marsh Tours (☑985-868-4758; www.annie-miller.com; 3718 Southdown Mandalay Rd, Houma; adult/child $15/10; 🖝) The son of legendary swamp guide Annie Miller has taken up his mom's tracks. The tours run about 50 miles outside New Orleans; call to arrange transportation.

Cajun Encounters (☑504-834-1770; www.cajunencounters.com; without/with pick-up from $25/50, night tours $40/70) Popular, well-run and offering a wide variety of tour options, including night tours.

& 1:30pm Tue-Sun) Volunteers lead the best available walking tours of the Quarter.

City Segway Tours SEGWAY
(☎504-619-4162; neworleans.citysegwaytours.com; 3-/2-/1-hr tours $75/65/45) Get on a Segway and glide around the French Quarter, the Tremé and the river front.

✯✯ Festivals & Events

New Orleans never needs an excuse to party. Just a few listings are included below; check www.neworleansonline.com for a good events calendar.

Mardi Gras CULTURAL
(www.mardigrasneworleans.com; ☺Feb or early Mar) Fat Tuesday marks the orgasmic finale of the Carnival season.

St Patrick's Day CULTURAL
(www.stpatricksdayneworleans.com; ☺Mar) March 17 and its closest weekend see parades of cabbage-wielding partiers all dressed in green.

St Joseph's Day – Super Sunday CULTURAL
(☺Mar) March 19 and its nearest Sunday bring the tribes of Mardi Gras Indians out into the streets in all their feathered, drumming glory. The Super Sunday parade usually begins around noon at Bayou St John and Orleans Ave, but follows no fixed route.

Tennessee Williams Literary Festival LITERARY
(www.tennesseewilliams.net; ☺Mar) Five days of literary panels, plays and parties celebrate the author's work.

French Quarter Festival MUSIC
(www.fqfi.org; ☺2nd weekend Apr) Free music on multiple stages.

Jazz Fest MUSIC
(www.nojazzfest; ☺Apr-May) The last weekend of April and the first weekend of May; a world-renowned extravaganza of music, food, crafts and good living.

🛏 Sleeping

Rates peak during Mardi Gras and Jazz Fest, and fall in the hot summer months. Book early and call or check the internet for special deals. Parking in the Quarter costs $15 to $30 per day.

Bywater Bed & Breakfast B&B $
(☎504-944-8438; www.bywaterbnb.com; 1026 Clouet St, Bywater; r without bathroom $100) An artsy B&B, Bywater is particularly popular with the LGBT crowd (particularly lesbians), and is about as homey and laid-back as it gets. It's a restored double-shotgun, very colorful, with a kitchen and parlors in which guests can cook or loiter. The walls double as gallery space, showcasing a collection of vibrant outsider and folk art. The four guest rooms are simple and comfortable with more cheery paint and art.

Prytania Park Hotel HOTEL $
(☎504-524-0427; www.prytaniaparkhotel.com; 1525 Prytania St, Garden District; r from $75, ste from $100; P ❋ ☎) This great-value complex of three separate hotels in the Garden District offers friendly, well-located bang-for-the-buck. The **Prytania Park** offers clean-cut, smallish rooms with flatscreen TVs for budget travelers. The **Prytania Oaks** (rooms from $110) is sleeker and the **Queen Anne** (rooms from $120) is an exquisite boutique hotel, nicely renovated and bedecked with antiques. It's a perfect spot for folks of all budgets bouncing between the Quarter and the Garden District and/or Uptown. Parking is free and so is access to St Charles Ave Athletic Club.

India House Hostel HOSTEL $
(☎504-821-1904; www.indiahousehostel.com; 124 S Lopez St, Mid-City; dm/d $20/55; @ ☎ ☒) In Mid-City, this place has a free-spirited party atmosphere. A large aboveground swimming pool and cabana-like patio add ambience to the three well-used old houses that serve as sparse but nice dorms. Private rooms are so-so.

Columns HISTORIC HOTEL $$
(☎504-899-9308; www.thecolumns.com; 3811 St Charles Ave, Garden District; r incl breakfast weekend/weekday from $170/134; ❋ ☎) A steal in low season (from $99), still a deal in high, this stately 1883 Italianate mansion in the Garden District is both elegant and relaxed, boasting all sorts of extraordinary original features: a stained-glass-topped staircase, elaborate marble fireplaces, richly carved woodwork throughout etc. To top it off, there's a lovely 2nd-floor porch overlooking oak-draped St Charles Ave and a damn inviting bar. It's everything that's wonderful about Nola.

Melrose Mansion B&B $$$
(☎504-944-2255, 800-650-3323; www.melrose-mansion.com; 937 Esplanade Ave, French Quarter; ste weekdays/weekends from $150/330; ☎ ☒)

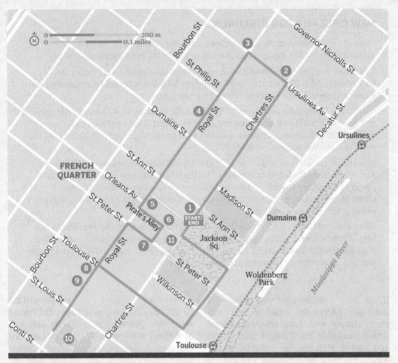

🏃 City Walk
French Quarter

START JACKSON SQ
END JACKSON SQ
LENGTH 1.1 MILE; 1 HOUR 30 MINUTES

Begin your walk at the **1 Presbytère** (p429) on Jackson Sq and head down Chartres St to the corner of Ursulines Ave. Directly across Chartres St, at No 1113, the 1826 **2 Beauregard-Keyes House** combines Creole and American styles of design. Walk along Ursulines Ave to Royal St – the soda fountain at the **3 Royal Pharmacy** is a preserved relic from halcyon malt-shop days.

When it comes to quintessential New Orleans postcard images, Royal St takes the prize. Cast-iron galleries grace the buildings and a profusion of flowers garland the facades.

At No 915 Royal, the **4 Cornstalk Hotel** (p438) stands behind one of the most frequently photographed fences anywhere. At Orleans Ave, stately magnolia trees and lush tropical plants fill **5 St Anthony's Garden**, behind **6 St Louis Cathedral** (p429).

Alongside the garden, take the inviting Pirate's Alley and turn right down Cabildo Alley and then right up St Peter St toward Royal St. Tennessee Williams shacked up at No 632 St Peter, the **7 Avart-Peretti House** in 1946–47, while he wrote *A Streetcar Named Desire*.

Turn left on Royal St. At the corner of Royal and Toulouse Sts stands a pair of houses built by Jean François Merieult in the 1790s. The building known as the **8 Court of Two Lions**, at 541 Royal St, opens onto Toulouse St and next door is the **9 Historic New Orleans Collection** (p429).

On the next block, the massive 1909 **10 State Supreme Court Building** was the setting for many scenes in director Oliver Stone's movie *JFK*.

Turn around and head right on Toulouse St to Decatur St and turn left. Cut across the road and walk the last stretch of this tour along the river. As Jackson Sq comes into view, cross back over to the Presbytère's near-identical twin, the **11 Cabildo** (p429).

NEW ORLEANS FOR CHILDREN

Many of New Orleans' daytime attractions are well suited for kids, including the Audubon Zoo (p435), Aquarium of the Americas (p434) and Insectarium (p434).

Carousel Gardens (☑504-483-9402; www.neworleanscitypark.com; 7 Victory Ave, City Park; admission $3; ⊙10am-3pm Tue-Fri, 11am-6pm Sat & Sun, extended hours summer) The 1906 carousel is a gem of vintage carny-ride happiness.

Louisiana Children's Museum (☑504-523-1357; www.lcm.org; 420 Julia St; admission $8; ⊙9:30am-4:30pm Tue-Sat, from noon Sun, to 5pm summer) Great hands-on exploratory exhibits and toddler area. Children under 16 must be accompanied by an adult. The museum is in the Warehouse District/CBD.

Milton Latter Memorial Library (☑504-596-2625; www.nutrias.org; 5120 St Charles Ave; ⊙9am-8pm Mon & Wed, to 6pm Tue & Thu, 10am-5pm Sat, noon-5pm Sun) Poised elegantly above shady strands of palm on St Charles Ave in New Orleans' Uptown area, the Latter Memorial Library was once a private mansion residence. Now it's a lovely library with a great children's section.

Rosa Keller Library (☑504-596-2660; 4300 S Broad St; ⊙10am-7pm Mon-Thu, to 5pm Sat) This local library, in the neighborhood of Broadmoor, is an architectural gem with huge windows that let in brilliant amounts of natural light. There's a nice children's section and a cafe that doubles as a communtiy center.

If you were a millionaire with a New Orleans pied-à-terre, this could be it. It's austerely elegant with hand-selected antiques sitting alongside the freshest modern art, and during high season you'll be regaled with a home-baked breakfast and evening wine and cheese in the chic parlor. A chic studio option offers sleeker, more modern accommodations.

Roosevelt Hotel   HOTEL $$$
(☑504-648-1200; www.therooseveltneworleans. com; 123 Baronne St, Warehouse District/CBD; r from $200, ste from $290; P@🖂) With its majestic, block-long lobby, this was the city's elite establishment when it opened in 1893. By the 1930s, its swanky bar was frequented by governor Huey Long. After a meticulous $145 million renovation, the Roosevelt reopened its doors in June 2009 as part of the Waldorf-Astoria Collection. Swish rooms have classical details, but the full spa, a John Besh restaurant and the storied Sazerac Bar are at least half the reason to stay.

Cornstalk Hotel   B&B $$$
(☑504-523-1515; www.cornstalkhotel.com; 915 Royal St, French Quarter; r $125-250; 🏵🖂) Pass through the famous cast-iron fence and into a plush, antiqued B&B where the serenity sweeps away the whirl of the busy streets outside. Gemlike rooms are all luxurious and clean – carpets are given the once-over monthly! Limited parking.

Le Pavillon   HISTORIC HOTEL $$$
(☑504-581-3111; www.lepavillon.com; 833 Poydras Ave, French Quarter; r $160-299, ste $199-499; P🏵🖂🖂) Built in 1907, this elegant European-style hotel's opulent marble lobby, plush, classic rooms and rooftop pool are a steal. Decadent suites might prevent you from ever leaving the building. If booking a queen room, request a bay window. Parking costs $25.

Degas House   HISTORIC HOTEL $$$
(☑504-821-5009; www.degashouse.com; 2306 Esplanade Ave; r incl breakfast from $199; P🏵🖂) Edgar Degas, the famed French Impressionist, lived in this 1852 Italianate house in Treme when visiting his mother's family in the early 1870s. Arty rooms recall the painter's stay with reproductions of his work and period furnishings. The suites have balconies and fireplaces, while the less-expensive garret rooms are the cramped top-floor quarters that once offered resident artists some much-need respite.

✖ Eating

Louisiana may have the greatest native culinary tradition in the USA – not necessarily by dint of the quality of food (although quality is very high) but from the long history that lies behind dishes that are older than most American states. While the rest of us eat to live, New Orleanians live to eat.

French Quarter

Croissant D'Or Patisserie CAFE $
(617 Ursulines Ave; items $1.50-5.75; ⊙6:30am-3pm Mon & Wed-Sun) This wonderful pastry shop is where many Quarter locals start their day. Bring a paper, order coffee and a croissant and bliss out. On your way in, check out the tiled sign on the threshold that says 'ladies entrance' – a holdover from pre-feminist days that is no longer enforced.

Clover Grill DINER $
(900 Bourbon St; mains $3-8; ⊙24hr) Gay greasy spoon? Yup. It's all slightly surreal, given this place otherwise totally resembles a '50s diner, but nothing adds to the Americana like a prima-donna-style argument between an out-of-makeup drag queen and a drunk club kid, all likely set to blaring disco music.

Café du Monde CAFE $
(800 Decatur St; beignets $2.14; ⊙24hr; 🖶) Du Monde is overrated, but you're probably gonna go there, so here goes: the coffee is decent and the beignets (square, sugar-coated fritters) are inconsistent. The atmosphere is off-putting: you're a number forced through the wringer, trying to shout over Bob and Fran while they mispronounce 'jambalaya' and a street musician badly mangles John Lennon's 'Imagine.' At least it's open 24 hours.

Coop's CAJUN, CREOLE $$
(1109 Decatur St; mains $8-17.50; ⊙11am-3am) For a cheap but thoroughly satisfying meal in the Quarter, this Cajun country shack disguised as a divey bar is as good as it gets: try the rabbit and sausage jambalaya or the red beans and rice for a taste of Cajun heaven.

Port of Call BAR $$
(☎504 523-0120; 838 Esplanade Ave; mains $7-21; ⊙11am-late) The Port of Call burger is, simply put, one of the best we've had, anywhere. The meat is unadulterated and, well, meaty, and the burger is enormous – a half pound that easily looks the size, and we mean this, of your face. There are a lot of other menu items, but we can't get enough of that burger-y heaven, and neither can the locals, who willingly wait outside in long lines for a seat (no reservations).

Central Grocery ITALIAN $$
(923 Decatur St; half/full muffuletta $7.50/14.50; ⊙9am-5pm Mon-Sat) Here, in 1906, a Sicilian immigrant invented the world-famous *muf-fuletta* sandwich – a round, seeded loaf of bread stuffed with ham, salami, provolone and marinated olive salad that's roughly the size of a manhole cover. This is still the best place in town to get one.

Bayona MODERN AMERICAN $$$
(☎504-525-4455; www.bayona.com; 430 Dauphine St; mains $27-32; ⊙11:30am-2pm Mon-Fri, plus 6-10pm Mon-Thu, to 11pm Fri & Sat) Bayona is a great splurge in the Quarter. It's rich but not overwhelming, classy but unpretentious, innovative without being precocious. Expect fish, fowl and game on the daily-changing menu divided between long-time classics and daily specials (about four of each), all done up in a way that makes you raise an eyebrow, then smile like you've discovered comfort food gone classy.

Galatoire's CREOLE $$$
(☎504 525 2021; 209 Bourbon St; mains $17-38; ⊙11:30am-10pm Tue-Sat, noon-10pm Sun) The century-plus history of this institution, which only accepted cash until quite recently, drips from the unchanged walls. Ask a tuxedo-ed waiter for what's fresh, don a jacket if you're a guy and treat yourself to the old-line masterpieces and mainstays: *pompano meunière,* liver with bacon and onions, and the signature chicken *clemenceau.* Friday lunch (which lasts all day) is a boozy affair that attracts many local aristocrats.

The Tremé

Willie Mae's Scotch House SOUTHERN $$
(2401 St Ann St; fried chicken $10; ⊙11am-7pm Mon-Sat) The fried chicken at Willie Mae's is good. Very good. Some may claim it's the best in the world (we say: it's a contender for sure).

Dooky Chase SOUTHERN $$
(☎504-821-0600; 2301 Orleans Ave; buffet $17.95; ⊙11am-3pm Tue-Fri, plus 5-9pm Fri) Ray Charles wrote 'Early in the Morning' about Dooky's, local civil rights leaders used the spot as an informal headquarters in the 1960s and Bush and Barack have tucked into the refined soul food at this overpriced Tremé backbone.

Bywater

The Joint BARBEQUE $
(☎504-949-3232; 701 Mazant St; mains $7-17; ⊙11:30am-10pm Mon-Sat) The Joint's smoked pork has the olfactory effect of the Sirens'

sweet song, pulling you, the proverbial traveling sailor, off course from your Ithaca into the gnashing rocks of savory meat-induced blissful death (classical Greek analogies ending now). Knock some ribs or pulled pork or brisket back with some sweet tea in the backyard garden and learn to love life.

Satsuma   HEALTH FOOD $
(☑504-304-5962; 3218 Dauphine St; breakfast & lunch under $10, dinner mains $8-16; ⊙7am-7pm) With its chalkboard menu of organic soups and sandwiches, Mediterranean-inspired salads, pasta, seafood and lamb, ginger limeade (seriously, the ginger limeade on a hot day – heaven), graphic/pop art-decorated walls – and lots of MacBooks – it's like the cute hipster girl with a frock, bangs and thick eyeglass frames you've secretly had a crush on, given restaurant form. The fact said girls are largely the clientele of this place confirms: the Bywater is becoming Brooklyn.

Bacchanal   CAFE $$
(www.bacchanalwine.com; 600 Poland Ave; cheese from $5, mains $8-16; ⊙11am-midnight) Grab a bottle of wine, let the folks behind the counter prep some *fromage* into a work of art, then kick back in an overgrown garden green scattered with rusted-out lawn chairs and tatty foldouts set to whoever showed up to play live music that day. Or order from the inventive full menu cooked out of the kitchen in the back (cash only).

Maurepas Foods   AMERICAN $$
(☑504-267-0072; 3200 Burgundy St; mains $7-16; ⊙11am-midnight, closed Wed; ☑) Maurepas isn't your typical Bywater spot. It's got high ceilings, minimalist decor, polished floors and metal fixtures. And holy hell is the food good: the organic chicken, market greens, grits and a poached egg are delicious. Vegetarians should snack on the soba noodles, and everyone should get drunk on the craft cocktails.

Elizabeth's   CAJUN, CREOLE $$$
(www.elizabeths-restaurant.com; 601 Gallier St; mains $16-26; ⊙8am-2:30pm & 6-10pm Tue-Sat, 8am-2:30pm Sun) Elizabeth's is deceptively divey, mixing corner-shack ambiance, folk-art music gallery and damned excellent food. The food can be startlingly out-of-the-box and is rich as all get out. But it tastes as

good as the best haute New Orleans chefs can offer. Be sure to order praline bacon, no matter the time of day: fried up in brown sugar and, as far as we can tell, God's own cooking oil. If you're into steak, the smoked ribeye is heaven.

✕ CBD & Warehouse District

Domenica   ITALIAN $$
(☑504-648-6020; 123 Baronne St; mains $13-30; ⊙11am-11pm; ☑) Domenica's rustic pies are loaded with nontraditional but savory toppings – spicy lamb meatballs, roast pork shoulder – and are big enough that solo diners should have a slice or two leftover. With its wooden refectory tables, white lights and soaring ceiling, Domenica feels like a village trattoria gone posh.

Butcher   CAJUN, SOUTHERN $$
(www.cochonbutcher.com; 930 Tchoupitoulas St; sandwiches $9-12; ⊙10am-10pm Mon-Thu, to 11pm Fri & Sat, to 4pm Sun) Around the corner from Cochon, chef Donald Link makes his in-house cured meat philosophy accessible to all budgets at this don't-miss butcher shop–deli and bar. Sandwich highlights here include milk-fed pork Cubans, Carolina-style pulled pork, the Cochon *muffaletta* and the Buckboard bacon melt.

★Cochon   CONTEMPORARY CAJUN $$$
(☑504-588-2123; www.cochonrestaurant.com; 930 Tchoupitoulas St; mains $19-25; ⊙11am-10pm Mon-Fri, 5:30-10pm Sat) James Beard Award–winning chef Donald Link's fabulous brasserie serves up gourmet Southern comfort food in such curious and intriguing ways, you won't know what to do with yourself. The house-made Louisiana *cochon* – moist, pulled-pork heaven on the inside, crusty, pan-seared perfection on the outside – is probably the best swine you will ever have, unless you eat here twice. Reservations essential.

Restaurant August   CREOLE $$$
(☑504 299-9777; 301 Tchoupitoulas St; mains $24-45; ⊙5-9pm Tue-Thu & Sat, 11am-2pm & 5-9pm Fri; ☑) August's converted 19th-century tobacco warehouse gets the nod for most aristocratic dining room in New Orleans. Candles flicker soft, warm shades over a meal that will, quite likely, blow your mind. If you're ready to splurge and eat like an emperor, consider arranging a private tasting menu dinner.

Garden District & Uptown

Dat Dog
HOT DOGS $

(☑504-899-6883; 5031 Freret St, Uptown; mains under $8; ⊙11am-10pm Mon-Sat, to 9pm Sun; ♠) Every part of your dog, from the steamed link to the toasted sourdough bun to the flavor-packed toppings, is produced with tasty exuberance at this outdoor joint. There's an enormous amount of sausages and toppings, from olive salad to crawfish etuofee, to pick from. If you like your dawgs spicy, try the Louisiana hot sausage from nearby Hanrahan.

★Boucherie
NEW SOUTHERN $$

(☑504-862-5514; www.boucherie-nola.com; 8115 Jeannette St, Uptown; large plates $13-18;

⊙11am-3pm & 5:30-9pm Tue-Sat) Just when you thought a Krispy Kreme doughnut was already perfection personified, Boucherie comes along and turns it into a bread pudding. When married to a honey-glaze, drowning in syrup, that heavy bread pudding becomes airy yet drool-tastically unforgettable! For dinner, blackened shrimp-and-grits cakes are darkly sweet and savory, garlic Parmesan fries are gloriously stinky and gooey and the smoked Wagyu beef brisket melts in your mouth. Just amazing.

Domilise's Po-Boys
CREOLE $$

(5240 Annunciation St, Uptown; po'boys $9-15; ⊙10am-7pm Mon-Wed & Fri, 10:30am-7pm Sat) A dilapidated white shack by the river serving Dixie beer (brewed in Wisconsin!), staffed

---

FROM THE MEKONG TO THE MISSISSIPPI

Following the Vietnam War, thousands of South Vietnamese fled to America, settling in Southern California, Boston, the Washington, DC, area and New Orleans. If the last choice seems odd, remember that many of these refugees were Catholic and the New Orleans Catholic community – one of the largest in the country – was helping to direct refugee resettlement. In addition, the subtropical climate, rice fields and flat wetlands must have been geographically reassuring. For a Southeast Asian far from home, the Mississippi delta may have borne at least a superficial resemblance to the Mekong delta.

Restaurants

Probably the most pleasant way to experience local Vietnamese culture is by eating its delicious food. The following are all in the suburbs of Gretna or New Orleans East.

Pho Tau Bay (☑504 368 9846; 113 Westbank Expwy, Gretna; mains under $10; ⊙9am-8:30pm Mon-Wed, Fri & Sat) Fantastic executions of Vietnamese mains and some of the best *pho* (rice-noodle soup) we've tried in metropolitan New Orleans.

Dong Phuong Oriental Bakery (☑504 254 0214; 14207 Chef Menteur Hwy, New Orleans East; mains under $10) For the best *banh mi* (Vietnamese sandwiches of sliced pork, cucumber, cilantro and other lovelies, locally called a 'Vietnamese po'boy') around and some very fine durian cake.

Tan Dinh (☑504 361 8008; 2005 Belle Chasse Hwy, Gretna; mains $8-15; ⊙9:30am-9pm Mon & Wed-Fri, 9am-9pm Sat, 8am-9pm Sun) We'd happily contend that Tan Dinh is one of the best restaurants in greater New Orleans. The garlic butter chicken wings could be served in heaven's pub, and the Korean short ribs are mouthwatering. Also contends with PhoTau Bay for some of that high quality *pho*.

Markets

Try not to miss the local markets either.

Hong Kong Food Market (☑394-7075; 925 Behrman Highway, Gretna; ⊙8am-9pm) Hong Kong Food Market is a general Asian grocery store that serves plenty of Chinese and Filipinos, but the main customer base is Vietnamese.

Vietnamese Farmers' Market (☑394-7075; 14401 Alcee Fortier Blvd, New Orleans East; ⊙6am-9am) The closest you'll come to witnessing Saigon on a Saturday morning (by the way, lots of local Vietnamese, being southern refugees, still call it 'Saigon') is the Vietnamese Farmers' Market, also known as the 'squat market' thanks to the ladies in *non la* (conical straw hats) squatting over their fresh, wonderful-smelling produce.

by folks who've worked here for decades and dressing one of the most legendary po'boys (traditional Louisiana submarine sandwich) in the city. It's cash-only and prepare to hurry up and wait on weekends.

Mat and Naddie's CONTEMPORARY CREOLE **$$$**
(☑504-861-9600; 937 Leonidas St, Uptown; mains $22-29; ⊙5:30-9:30pm Thu-Sat, Mon & Tue) Set in a beautiful riverfront shotgun house with a Christmas-light-bedecked patio in the back, M&N's is rich, innovative, even outlandish: artichoke, sun-dried tomato and roasted garlic cheesecake (oh yes!), sherry-marinated grilled quail with waffles, pecan sweet-potato pie – all crazy delicious. High quality topped with quirkiness.

Commander's Palace CONTEMPORARY CREOLE **$$$**
(☑504-899-8221; 1403 Washington Ave, Garden District; dinner mains $28-45; ⊙11:30am-2pm & 6:30-10pm Mon-Fri, 11:30am-1pm & 6:30-10pm Sat, 10:30am-1:30pm Sun) It's no small coincidence that some of the most famous Nola chefs – check that, US chefs – got their start in this kitchen (Paul Prudhomme, Emeril Lagasse); this New Orleans grand dame is outstanding across the board. It's an impeccable mainstay of Creole cooking and knowledgeable, friendly service, in the heart of the gorgeous Garden District. Pop in for the lunchtime 25¢ martinis and a cup of the signature turtle soup. No shorts allowed.

🍸 Drinking

New Orleans is a drinking town. Heads up: Bourbon St sucks. Get into the neighborhoods and experience some of the best bars in America.

Most bars open every day, often by noon, get hopping around 10pm, and can stay open all night. There's no cover charge unless there's live music. It's illegal to have open glass liquor containers in the street, so all bars dispense plastic 'go cups' when you're ready to wander.

Tonique BAR
(www.bartonique.com; 820 Rampart St, French Quarter) If you're going to drink in the Quarter (on the edge of it, anyway), this serious cocktail bar is the place, where cool folks who appreciate an excellent concoction gather over the best Sazerac we had in town. And we had many.

Mimi's in the Marigny BAR
(2601 Royal St, Faubourg Marigny; ⊙to 5am) Great bi-level bar (pool downstairs, music upstairs) serving up excellent Spanish tapas ($5 to $8) and a casual neighborhood vibe.

St Joe's BAR
(5535 Magazine St, Uptown) Good-time Uptown pious-themed bar with great blueberry mojitos (praise the Lord!), a cool back courtyard and friendly ambience.

R Bar BAR
(1431 Royal St, Marigny) Somewhere between a dive and a neighborhood joint; a beer and a shot runs you $5.

☆ Entertainment

What's New Orleans without live local music? Almost any weekend night you can find something for every taste: jazz, blues, brass band, country, Dixieland, zydeco (Cajun dance music), rock or Cajun. Free shows in the daytime abound. Check *Gambit* (www.bestofneworleans.com), *Offbeat* (www.offbeat.com) or www.nolafunguide.com for schedules.

★ Spotted Cat LIVE MUSIC
(www.spottedcatmusicclub.com; 623 Frenchmen St, Faubourg Marigny) A throwback retro cool permeates through this excellent Frenchmen staple you might recognize from numerous episodes of *Tremé*. Hipster jazz is on nightly and there's never a cover unless a special event is on.

Three Muses JAZZ
(www.thethreemuses.com; 536 Frenchmen St, Marigny; ⊙4-10pm Wed, Thu, Sun & Mon, to 2am Fri & Sat) Three Muses has managed to happily marry an excellent soundtrack with gourmet cuisine in a more intimate room than most on Frenchmen. There's loads of great local art to peruse between acts and courses. Start here.

AllWays Lounge THEATER
(☑504-218-5778; 2240 St Claude Ave, Marigny) In a city full of funky music venues, the AllWays stands out as one of the funkiest. On any given night of the week you may see experimental guitar, local theater, thrash-y rock or a '60s-inspired shagadelic dance party. Also: the drinks are super cheap.

Chickie Wah Wah LIVE MUSIC
(☑504-304-4714; www.chickiewahwah.com; 2828 Canal St, Mid-City; ⊙shows around 8pm) Despite the fact it lies on one of the most unremarkable stretches of Canal St as you please, Chickie Wah Wah is a great jazz club.

It hosts some good names such as John Mooney, Jolly House and Papa Mali in a cozy little setting where the French Quarter feels several universes away.

Tipitina's   LIVE MUSIC
(www.tipitinas.com; 501 Napoleon Ave, Uptown) Always drawing a lively crowd, this legendary Uptown club rocks out like the musical mecca it is: local jazz, blues, soul and funk acts stop in, as well as national touring bands.

Rock & Bowl   LIVE MUSIC
(☑504-861-1700; www.rockandbowl.com; 3000 S Carrollton Ave, Mid-City; ☺5pm-late, live music Wed-Sat; ☝) A night at the Rock & Bowl is a quintessential New Orleans experience. Come see a strange, wonderful combination of bowling alley, deli, and a huge live music and dance venue, where patrons get down to New Orleans roots music while trying to avoid that 7-10 split. Thursday night zydeco shows will knock your socks off.

Snug Harbor   JAZZ
(www.snugjazz.com; 626 Frenchmen St, Marigny) In the Marigny, the city's best contemporary jazz venue is all about world-class music and a good variety of acts. If you can't spring for the show (cover $15 to $25), sit downstairs at the bar and watch on closed-circuit.

Preservation Hall   JAZZ
(www.preservationhall.com; 726 St Peter St, French Quarter; cover $15; ☺8-11pm) A veritable museum of traditional and Dixieland jazz, Preservation Hall is a pilgrimage. But like many religious obligations, it ain't necessarily easy, with no air-conditioning, limited seating and no refreshments (you can bring your own water, that's it).

🔒 Shopping

Magazine Antique Mall   ANTIQUES
(☑504 896 9994; www.magazineantiquemall.com; 3017 Magazine St; ☺10:30am-5:30pm Mon-Sat, from noon Sun) Hard-core rummagers are likely to score items of interest in the dozen or so stalls here, where independent dealers peddle an intriguing and varied range of antique bric-a-brac.

Maple Street Book Shop   BOOKSHOP
(www.maplestreetbookshop.com; 7523 Maple St, Uptown; ☺9am-7pm Mon-Sat, 11am-5pm Sun) A mainstay independent bookstore in Uptown, with a used bookstore affiliate next door.

❶ Information

DANGERS & ANNOYANCES
New Orleans has a high violent-crime rate, and neighborhoods go from good to ghetto very quickly. Be careful walking too far north of Faubourg Marigny and the Bywater (St Claude Ave is a good place to stop), south of Magazine St (things get dodgier past Laurel St) and too far north of Rampart St (Lakeside) from the French Quarter into Tremé without a specific destination in mind. Stick to places that are well peopled, particularly at night, and spring for a cab to avoid dark walks. In the Quarter, street hustlers frequently approach tourists – just walk away. With all that said, don't be paranoid. Crime here, as in most of America, tends to be between people who already know each other.

INTERNET ACCESS
There's pretty good wi-fi coverage in the CBD, French Quarter, Garden and Lower Garden Districts and Uptown. Almost every coffee shop in the city has wi-fi coverage. Libraries have free internet access for cardholders.

MEDIA
Gambit Weekly (www.bestofneworleans.com) Free weekly hot sheet of music, culture, politics and classifieds.

Offbeat Magazine (www.offbeat.com) Free monthly specializing in music.

WWOZ 90.7 FM (www.wwoz.org) Tune in here for Louisiana music and more.

MEDICAL SERVICES
Tulane University Medical Center (☑504-988-5800; http://tulanehealthcare.com; 1415 Tulane Ave; ☺24hr) Has an emergency room; located in the CBD.

POST
Post Office Lafayette Sq (610 S Maestri Pl, Lafayette Sq; ☺8:30am-4:30pm Mon-Fri); Main branch (701 Loyola Ave; ☺7am-7pm Mon-Fri, 8am-4pm Sat) Mail sent General Delivery, New Orleans, LA 70112, goes to the main branch at 701 Loyola Ave. Postboxes in outlying areas are not necessarily reliable since Katrina.

TOURIST INFORMATION
The city's official visitor website is www.neworleansonline.com.

Jean Lafitte National Historic Park and Preserve Visitor Center (☑504-589-2133, 504-589-3822; www.nps.gov/jela; 419 Decatur St, French Quarter; ☺9am-5pm) Operated by the NPS, with exhibits on local history, guided walks and daily live music.

Basin St Visitor's Center (☑504-293-2600; www.neworleanscvb.com; 501 Basin St, French Quarter; ☺9am-5pm) This interactive tourist info center inside the former freight administration building of the Southern Railway has loads of helpful info and maps, as well as an historical overview film and a small rail museum component.

ℹ Getting There & Away

Louis Armstrong New Orleans International Airport (MSY; www.flymsy.com; 900 Airline Hwy), 11 miles west of the city, handles primarily domestic flights.

The **Union Passenger Terminal** (☑504-299-1880; 1001 Loyola Ave) is home to **Greyhound** (☑504-525-6075; ⊙5:15am-1pm & 2:30-6pm), which has regular buses to Baton Rouge (two hours), Memphis, TN (11 hours) and Atlanta, GA ($84 to $106, 12 hours). **Amtrak** (☑504-528-1610; ⊙ticketing 5:45am-10pm) trains also operate from the Union Passenger Terminal, running to Jackson, MS; Memphis, TN; Chicago, IL. Birmingham, AL; Atlanta, GA; Washington, DC; New York City; Los Angeles, CA; and Miami, FL.

ℹ Getting Around

TO/FROM THE AIRPORT

There's an information booth at the airport's A&B concourse. The **Airport Shuttle** (☑866-596-2699; www.airportshuttleneworleans.com; one way $20) runs to downtown hotels. The **Jefferson Transit** (☑504-364-3450; www.jeffersontransit.org; adult $2) airport route E2 picks up outside entrance 7 on the airport's upper level; it stops along Airline Hwy (Hwy 61) on its way into town (final stop Tulane and Loyola Aves). After 7pm it only goes to Tulane and Carrollton Aves in Mid-City; a solid 5 miles through a dreary neighborhood to get to the CBD, from here you must transfer to a Regional Transit Authority (RTA) bus – a haphazard transfer at best, especially with luggage.

Taxis downtown cost $34 for one or two people, $14 more for each additional passenger.

CAR & MOTORCYCLE

Bringing a car is a useful way of exploring beyond the Quarter; just be aware that parking in the Quarter is a hassle. Garages charge about $13 for the first three hours and $30 to $35 for 24 hours.

PUBLIC TRANSPORTATION

The **Regional Transit Authority** (RTA; www.norta.com) runs the local bus service. Bus and streetcar fares are $1.25, plus 25¢ for transfers; express buses cost $1.50. Exact change is required. RTA Visitor Passes for one/three days cost $5/12.

The RTA also operates three **streetcar** lines (one-way $1.25, day pass $3; have exact change). The historic St Charles streetcar is running only a short loop in the CBD due to hurricane damage to the Uptown tracks. The Canal streetcar makes a long journey up Canal St to City Park, with a spur on Carrollton Ave. The Riverfront line runs 2 miles along the levee from the Old US Mint, past Canal St, to the upriver convention center and back.

For a taxi, call **United Cabs** (☑504-522-9771; www.unitedcabs.com).

Rent bicycles at **Bicycle Michael's** (☑504-945-9505; www.bicyclemichaels.com; 622 Frenchmen St, Faubourg Marigny; per day $35; ⊙10am-7pm Mon, Tue & Thu-Sat, to 5pm Sun).

Around New Orleans

Leaving gritty, colorful New Orleans quickly catapults you into a world of swamps, bayous, antebellum plantation homes, laid-back small communities and miles of bedroom suburbs and strip malls.

Barataria Preserve

This section of the Jean Lafitte National Historical Park & Preserve, south of New Orleans near the town of Marrero, provides the easiest access to the dense swamplands that ring New Orleans. The 8 miles of platform trails are a stunning way to tread lightly through the fecund, thriving swamp where you can check out gators and other fascinating plant life and creatures. The preserve is home to alligators, nutrias (read: big invasive rats), tree frogs and hundreds of species of birds. It is well worth taking a ranger-led walk to learn about the many ecosystems that make up what are often lumped together as 'wetlands.'

Start at the NPS Visitors Center (☑504-589-2330; www.nps.gov/jela; Hwy 3134; ⊙9am-5pm; ♿) FREE, 1 mile west of Hwy 45 off the Barataria Blvd exit, where you can pick up a map or join a guided walk or canoe trip (most Saturday mornings and monthly on full-moon nights; call to reserve a spot). To rent canoes or kayaks for a tour or an independent paddle, go to Bayou Barn (☑504-689-2663; http://bayoubarn.com; 7145 Barataria Blvd; canoes per person $20, 1-person kayak per day $25; ⊙10am-6pm Thu-Sun) about 3 miles from the park entrance.

The North Shore

Bedroom communities sprawl along Lake Pontchartrain's north shore, but head north of Mandeville and you'll reach the bucolic village of Abita Springs, which was popular in the late 1800s for its curative waters. Today the spring water still flows from a fountain in the center of the village, but the primary liquid attraction here is the Abita Brew Pub (☑985-892-5837; www.abitabrewpub. com; 7201 Holly St; ☺11am-9pm Tue-Thu, to 10pm Fri & Sat, closed Mon), where you can choose from the many Abita beers on tap that are made a mile west of town at Abita Brewery (www.abita.com; 166 Barbee Rd; tours free; ☺tours 2pm Wed-Fri, 11am, noon, 1pm & 2pm Sat).

The 31-mile Tammany Trace trail (www. tammanytrace.org) connects north shore towns, beginning in Covington, passing through Abita Springs and Fontainebleau State Park, on the lakeshore near Mandeville, and terminating in Slidell. This converted railroad makes for a lovely bike ride that drops you into each town's center. In Lacombe, about 9 miles east of Mandeville, you can rent bicycles and kayaks at Bayou Adventures (☑985-882-9208; www.bayou-adventure.com; 27725 Main St, Lacombe; bicycles per hr/day $8/25, single/double kayaks per day $35/50; ☺5am-6pm).

River Road

Elaborate plantation homes dot the east and west banks of the Mississippi River between New Orleans and Baton Rouge. First indigo, then cotton and sugarcane, brought great wealth to these plantations, many of which are open to the public. Most tours focus on the lives of the plantation owners, the restored architecture and the ornate gardens of antebellum Louisiana.

◉ Sights

Laura Plantation   PLANTATION
(www.lauraplantation.com; 2247 Hwy 18, Vacherie; adult/child $20/6; ☺10am-4pm) Laura Plantation, in Vacherie on the west bank, offers the most dynamic and informative tour of the River Road plantations. This ever-evolving and popular tour teases out the distinctions between Creole, Anglo, free and enslaved African Americans via meticulous research and the written records of the Creole women who ran the place for generations. Laura is

also fascinating because it was a Creole mansion, founded and maintained by a continental European-descended elite, as opposed to Anglo-Americans; the cultural and architectural distinctions between this and other plantations is obvious and striking.

Oak Alley Plantation   PLANTATION
(www.oakalleyplantation.com; 3645 Hwy 18, Vacherie; adult/child $20/7.50; ☺9am-4:40pm) The most impressive aspect of Oak Alley Plantation is its canopy of 28 majestic live oaks lining the entry to the grandiose Greek Revival–style house – even better with a fresh mint julep. The tour is relatively staid, but there are guest cottages ($145 to $200) and a restaurant on-site.

River Road African American
Museum   MUSEUM
(www.africanamericanmuseum.org; 406 Charles St, Donaldsonville; admission $5; ☺10am-5pm Wed-Sat, 1-5pm Sun) Be sure to flesh out any plantation tour with a visit to the River Road African American Museum, 25 miles beyond Vacherie in Donaldsonville. This excellent museum preserves the important history of African Americans in the rural communities along the Mississippi, and offers insight into the free people of color, a unique sociopolitical demographic within Louisiana that had huge bearing on the state's culture. Tours are by appointment only.

Baton Rouge

In 1699 French explorers named this area *baton rouge* (red stick) when they came upon a reddened cypress pole that Bayagoulas and Houma Native Americans had staked in the ground to mark the boundaries of their respective hunting territories. From one pole grew a lot of sprawl; Baton Rouge stretches out in an unplanned clutter in many directions. Visitors are mostly drawn to Baton Rouge for Louisiana State University (LSU) and Southern University; the latter is one of the largest historically African American universities in the country.

◉ Sights & Activities

Louisiana State Capitol   HISTORIC BUILDING
(☺9am-4pm Tue-Sat) **FREE** The art-deco skyscraper looming over town was built at the height of the Great Depression to the tune of $5 million. It's the most visible leftover legacy of populist governor 'Kingfish' Huey

THE SOUTH AROUND NEW ORLEANS

Long. The 27th-floor observation deck offers stunning views and the ornate lobby is equally impressive. There are hourly free tours.

Louisiana Arts & Science Museum
MUSEUM

(www.lasm.org; 100 S River Rd; adult/child $7.25/6.25, with planetarium show $9/8; ⊙10am-3pm Tue-Fri, to 5pm Sat, 1-4pm Sun; 🖈) Interesting arts and natural-history installations, and planetarium shows. If you just want a good stretch of the legs, there's a pleasant pedestrian/bike path along the Mississippi River, covering 2.5 miles from the downtown promenade to LSU.

Old State Capitol
HISTORIC BUILDING

(☑225-342-0500; www.louisianaoldstatecapitol. org; 100 North Blvd; ⊙9am-4pm Tue-Sat) FREE The Gothic Revival, pink, fairytale castle is... well, look, it's a pink castle. Should tell you something about how eccentric the government of its resident state can be. Today the structure houses exhibits about the colorful political history of the state.

LSU Museum of Art
MUSEUM

(LSUMOA; www.lsumoa.com; 100 Lafayette St; adult/child $5/free; ⊙10am-5pm Tue-Sat, to 8pm Thu, 1-5pm Sun) The physical space this museum is ensconced in, the clean, geometric lines of the Shaw Center, is as impressive as the on-site galleries, which include a permanent collection of over 5000 works and temporary, curated galleries exploring regional artistic heritage and contemporary trends.

Rural Life Museum
MUSEUM

(☑225-765-2437; 4560 Essen Ln; adult/child $7/6; ⊙8am-5pm; 🅿🖈) This outdoor museum promises a trip into the architecture, occupations and folkways of rural Louisiana. Numerous rough-hewn buildings are scattered over the bucolic campus, and exhibits are refreshingly honest and informative, lacking any rose-colored romanticization of the hard country legacy that built Louisiana.

Dixie Landin & Blue Bayou
AMUSEMENT PARK

(☑225-753-3333; www.bluebayou.com; 18142 Perkins Rd; adult/child $37/30; 🖈) Just east of town at I-10 and Highland Rd. Kids will love the respective amusement and water parks; check the online calendar for opening hours.

🛏 Sleeping & Eating

Stockade Bed & Breakfast
B&B $$$

(☑888-900-5430, 225-769-7358; www.thestockade.com; 8860 Highland Rd; r incl breakfast $135-215; 🅿❄🖥) Chain hotels line the sides of I-10, but for a more intimate stay, try this wonderful B&B with five spacious, comfortable and elegant rooms just 3.5 miles southeast of LSU and within earshot of several standout neighborhood restaurants. Book ahead on weekends, especially during football season.

Schlittz & Giggles
BAR, PIZZERIA $$

(www.schlittz.com; 301 3rd St; pizzas $10-22; ⊙11am-midnight Mon-Thu, to 3am Fri-Sun; 🖥) The food stands up to the awesomely named downtown late-night bar and pizzeria. Bubbly coeds serve up thin-as-black-ice pizza slices ($3 to $3.50) and fabulous paninis to a student crowd, while a gaggle of old-timer locals tend to belly up at the bar.

Buzz Café
CAFE $

(www.thebuzzcafe.org; 340 Florida St; meals $7-9; ⊙7:30am-2pm Mon-Fri; 🖥) For an awesome cup of joe and a plethora of creative wraps and sandwiches at a funky coffee shop in a historic building, try the Buzz.

☆ Entertainment

Varsity Theatre
LIVE MUSIC

(☑225-383-7018; www.varsitytheatre.com; 3353 Highland Rd; ⊙8pm-2am) At the gates of LSU, you'll find live music here, often on weeknights. The attached restaurant boasts an extensive beer selection and a raucous college crowd.

Boudreaux and Thiboudeux
LIVE MUSIC

(☑225-636-2442; www.bandtlive.com; 214 3rd St) Try this place downtown for live music Thursday to Saturday and a great upstairs balcony bar. Named for the dumb and dumber duo of classic Cajun comedy.

❶ Information

Visitor Center (☑225-383-1825, 800-527-6843; www.visitbatonrouge.com; 359 3rd St; ⊙8am-5pm) The downtown city branch has maps, brochures of local attractions and festival schedules.

Capital Park (☑225-219-1200; www. louisianatravel.com; 702 River Rd N; ⊙8am-4:30pm) Near the visitor center, it's even more extensive.

ℹ Getting There & Around

Baton Rouge lies 80 miles west of New Orleans on I-10. **Baton Rouge Metropolitan Airport** (BTR; www.flybtr.com) is north of town off I-110; it's about 1½ hours from New Orleans, so it's a viable airport of entry if you're renting a car. **Greyhound** (☎225-383-3811; 1253 Florida Blvd, at N 12th St) has regular buses to New Orleans, Lafayette and Atlanta, GA. **Capitol Area Transit System** (CATS; ☎225-389-8282; www.brcats. com) operates buses around town.

St Francisville

Lush St Francisville is the quintessential Southern artsy small town, a blend of historical homes, bohemian shops and outdoors activities courtesy of the nearby Tunica Hills (you read that right – hills in Louisiana). During the antebellum decade this was home to plantation millionaires, and much of their architecture is still intact.

◉ Sights & Activities

In town, stroll down historic Royal St to catch a glimpse of antebellum homes and buildings-turned-homes. The visitor center has pamphlets that lead you on self-guided tours.

Myrtles Plantation   HISTORIC BUILDING
(☎225-635-6277,   800-809-0565;   www.myrtlesplantation.com; 7747 US Hwy 61 N; ⊙9am-4:30pm, tours 6pm, 7pm & 8pm Fri & Sat) An especially notable B&B because supposedly it's haunted, and it has night mystery tours (by reservation) on the weekend. We heard secondhand corroboration of the supernatural presence, so it might be fun to stay overnight (rooms from $115) to commune with the other world.

Oakley Plantation & Audubon
State Historic Site   HISTORIC SITE
(☎225 342 8111; www.crt.state.la.us; 11788 Hwy 965; admission $2; ⊙9am-5pm) Outside of St Francisville is Oakley Plantation & Audubon State Historic Site, where John James Audubon spent his tenure, arriving in 1821 to tutor the owner's daughter. Though his assignment lasted only four months (and his room was pretty darn spartan), he and his assistant finished 32 paintings of birds found in the plantation's surrounding forest. Furnishing of the small West Indies–influenced house (1806) includes several original Audubon prints.

Mary Ann Brown Preserve   NATURE RESERVE
(☎225-338-1040; 13515 Hwy 965; ⊙sunrise-sunset) Operated by the Nature Conservancy, the Mary Ann Brown Preserve takes in some of the beech woodlands, dark wetlands and low, clay-soil hill country of the Tunica uplands. A 2-mile series of trails and boardwalks crosses the woods, the same trees that John James Audubon tramped around when he began work on *Birds of America*.

🛏 Sleeping & Eating

★ Shadetree Inn
Bed & Breakfast   B&B $$
(☎225-635-6116; www.shadetreeinn.com; cnr Royal & Ferdinand Sts; r from $165; P❋🖤) Sidled up against the historic district and a bird sanctuary, this super-cozy B&B has a gorgeous flower-strewn, hammock-hung courtyard and spacious, upscale rustic rooms. A deluxe continental breakfast can be served in your room and is included along with a bottle of wine or champagne.

3-V Tourist Court   HISTORIC INN $$
(☎225-721-7003; 5689 Commerce St; 1-/2-bed cabins $80/130; P❋🖤) One of the oldest motor inns in the United States (started in the 1930s and on the National Register of Historic Places), these five units bring you back to simpler times. Rooms have period decorations and fixtures, though a recent renovation upgraded the beds, hardwood floors and flatscreen TVs into borderline trendy territory.

Birdman Coffee & Books   CAFE $
(Commerce St; mains $5-6.50; ⊙7-5pm Tue-Fri, 8am-5pm Sat, to 4pm Sun; 🖤) Right in front of the Magnolia Café lies the Birdman, *the* spot for a local breakfast (old-fashioned yellow grits, sweet-potato pancakes etc) and local art.

Magnolia Café   CAFE $$
(☎225-635-2528;   www.themagnoliacafe.com; 5687 Commerce St; mains $7-12; ⊙10am-4pm Sun-Wed, to 9pm Thu & Sat, to 10pm Fri) The nucleus of what's happening in St Francisville, the Magnolia Café used to be a health-food store/VW bus repair shop. Now it's where people go to eat, socialize and dance to live music on Friday night. Try the cheesy shrimp po'boy.

ℹ Information

Tourist Information (☑ 225-635-4224; www.stfrancisville.us; 11757 Ferdinand St) Provides helpful information about the numerous plantations open for viewing in the area, many of which offer B&B services.

Cajun Country

When people think of 'Louisiana,' this (and New Orleans) is the image that comes to mind: miles of bayou, sawdust-strewn shacks, a unique take on French and lots of good food. Welcome to Cajun Country, also called Acadiana for French settlers exiled from L'Acadie (now Nova Scotia, Canada) by the British in 1755.

Cajuns are the largest French-speaking minority in the US – prepare to hear it on radios, in church services and in the sing-song lilt of local English accents. While Lafayette is the nexus of Acadiana, getting out and around the waterways, villages and ramshackle roadside taverns really drops you straight into Cajun living. This is largely a socially conservative region, but the Cajuns also a have well-deserved reputation for hedonism. It's hard to find a bad meal here; jambalaya (a rice-based dish with tomatoes, sausage and shrimp) and crawfish étouffée (a thick Cajun stew) are prepared slowly with pride (and cayenne!), and if folks aren't fishing, then they are probably dancing. Don't expect to sit on the sidelines...*allons danson* (let's dance).

Lafayette

The term 'undiscovered gem' gets thrown around too much in travel writing, but Lafayette really fits the bill. The bad first: this town is deader then a cemetery on Sundays. The rest: there's an entirely fantastic amount of good eating and lots of music venues here, plus one of the best free music festivals in the country. This is a university town; bands are rocking most any night. Heck, even those quiet Sundays have a saving grace: some famously delicious brunch options.

⊙ Sights

Vermilionville CULTURAL BUILDING
(☑ 337-233-4077; www.vermilionville.org; 300 Fisher Rd; adult/student $8/6; ⊙10am-4pm Tue-Sun; ⊞) A tranquil restored/re-created 19th-century Cajun village wends along the bayou near the airport. Friendly, enthusiastic costumed docents explain Cajun, Creole and Native American history, and local bands perform on Sundays. Also offers guided **boat tours** (☑ 337-233-4077; adult/student $12/8; ⊙10:30am Tue-Sat Mar-May & Sep-Nov) of Bayou Vermilion.

Acadiana Center for the Arts GALLERY
(☑ 337-233-7060; www.acadianacenterforthearts.org; 101 W Vermilion St; adult/student/child $5/3/2; ⊙9am-5pm Tue-Fri, to 6pm Sat) This arts center in the heart of downtown maintains three chic galleries and hosts dynamic theater, lectures and special events.

CAJUNS, CREOLES &...CREOLES

A lot of tourists in Louisiana use the terms 'Cajun' and 'Creole' interchangeably, but the two cultures are different and distinct. 'Creole' refers to descendants of the original European settlers of Louisiana, a blended mix of mainly French and Spanish ancestry. The Creoles tend to have urban connections to New Orleans and considered their own culture refined and civilized. Many (but not all) were descended from aristocrats, merchants and skilled tradesmen.

The Cajuns can trace their lineage to the Acadians, colonists from rural France who settled Nova Scotia. After the British conquered Canada, the proud Acadians refused to kneel to the new crown, and were exiled in the mid-18th century – an act known as the Grand Dérangement. Many exiles settled in South Louisiana; they knew the area was French, but the Acadians ('Cajun' is an English bastardization of the word) were often treated as country bumpkins by the Creoles. The Acadians-cum-Cajuns settled in the bayous and prairies, and to this day self-conceptualize as a more rural, frontier-stye culture.

Adding confusion to all of the above is the practice, standard in many post-colonial French societies, of referring to mixed-race individuals as 'Creoles.' This happens in Louisiana, but there is a cultural difference between Franco-Spanish Creoles and mixed-race Creoles, even as these two communities very likely share actual blood ancestry.

Acadian Cultural Center   MUSEUM
(www.nps.gov/jela; 501 Fisher Rd; ⊙8am-5pm)
This National Parks Service museum has extensive exhibits on Cajun culture, next door
to Vermilionville.

⚔ Festivals & Events

Festival International de Louisiane   MUSIC
(www.festivalinternational.com; ⊙last weekend
Apr) At the fabulous Festival International
de Louisiane, hundreds of local and international artists rock out for five days – the
largest free music festival of its caliber in the
US. Although 'Festival' avowedly celebrates
Francophone music and culture, the event's
remit has grown to accommodate other music styles and languages.

🛏 Sleeping & Eating

Chain hotels clump near exits 101 and 103,
off I-10 (doubles from $65). Head to Jeffer-
son St mid-downtown to take your choice of
bars and restaurants, from sushi to Mexican.

★Blue Moon Guest House   GUESTHOUSE $
(☑337-234-2422, 877-766-2583; www.blue-
moonguesthouse.com; 215 E Convent St; dm $18,
r $73-94; P❀@☎) This tidy old home is
one of Louisiana's travel gems, an upscale
hostel-like hangout that's walking distance
from downtown. Snag a bed and you'll be
on the guest list for Lafayette's most popular down-home music venue, located in the
backyard. The friendly owners, full kitchen
and camaraderie among guests create a
unique music-meets-migration environment catering to backpackers, flashpackers
and those in transition (flashbackpackers?).
Prices skyrocket during festival time. Decidedly not a quiet spot.

Buchanan Lofts   BOUTIQUE APARTMENTS $$
(☑337-534-4922; www.buchananlofts.com; 403
S Buchanan; r per night/week from $110/600;
P❀@☎) These über-hip lofts could be in
New York City if they weren't so big. Doused
in contemporary-cool art and design – all
fruits of the friendly owner's globetrotting –
the extra spacious units all come with kitch-
enettes and are awash in exposed brick and
hardwoods.

Johnson's Boucanière   CAJUN $
(1111 St John St; mains under $10; ⊙10am-6pm Tue-
Thu, to 9pm Fri, 7am-9pm Sat) This resurrected
70-year-old family prairie smoker business

turns out detour-worthy *boudin* (Cajun-
style pork and rice sausage) and an unstop-
pable smoked pork-brisket sandwich topped
with smoked sausage.

Artmosphere   AMERICAN $
(☑337-233-3331; 902 Johnston St; mains under
$10; ⊙11am-2am Mon-Sat, to midnight Sun; ☑)
Your place if you're jonesing for vegan/veg-
etarian food, or even just a hookah, plus a
lovely selection of beer on offer. Live music
every night and a crowd that largely consists
of the student and artist set.

★French Press   BREAKFAST $$$
(www.thefrenchpresslafayette.com; 214 E Vermillion;
breakfast $6-$10.50, dinner mains $29-38; ⊙7am-
2pm Tue-Thu, 7am-2pm & 5:30-9pm Fri, 9am-2pm &
5:30-9pm Sat, 9am-2pm Sun; ☎) This French-
Cajun hybrid is the best culinary thing going in Lafayette. Breakfast is mind blowing,
with a sinful Cajun benedict (*boudin* instead of ham), cheddar grits (that will kill
you dead) and organic granola (offset the
grits). Dinner is wonderful as well; that rack
of lamb with the truffled gratin is a special
bit of gastronomic dreaminess.

☆ Entertainment

To find out what's playing around town, pick
up the free weekly *Times* (www.theadvertiser.
com – check under Times of Acadiana) or
Independent (www.theind.com).

Besides the places below, Cajun restaurants like **Randol's** (☑337-981-7080; www.ran-
dols.com; 2320 Kaliste Saloom Rd; ⊙5-10pm Sun-
Thu, to 11pm Fri & Sat) and **Prejean's** (☑337-
896-3247; www.prejeans.com; 3480 NE Evangeline
Thruway/I-49) feature live music on weekends
nights.

Blue Moon Saloon   LIVE MUSIC
(www.bluemoonpresents.com; 215 E Convent St;
cover $5-8) This intimate venue on the back
porch of the accompanying guesthouse is
what Louisiana is all about: good music,
good people and good beer. What's not to
love?

Artmosphere   LIVE MUSIC
(902 Johnston St; ⊙11am-2am Mon-Sat, to midnight Sun) Graffiti, hookahs, hipsters and an
edgy line-up of acts; it's more CBGB's than
Cajun dancehall, but it's a lot of fun, and
there's good Mexican food to boot.

THE TAO OF FRED'S

Deep in the heart of Cajun Country, Mamou is a typical South Louisiana small town six days of the week, worth a peek and a short stop before rolling to Eunice. But on Saturday mornings, Mamou's hometown hangout, little Fred's Lounge (420 6th St; ⊗8am-2pm Sat), becomes the apotheosis of a Cajun dancehall.

OK, to be fair: Fred's is more of a dance shack than hall. It's a little bar and it gets more than a little crowded from 8:30am to2ish in the afternoon, when owner 'Tante' (auntie) Sue and her staff host a Francophone-friendly music morning, with bands, beer, cigarettes and dancing (seriously, it gets smoky in here. Fair warning). Sue herself will often take to the stage to dispense wisdom and songs in Cajun French, all while taking pulls off a bottle of brown liquor she keeps in a pistol holster.

ⓘ Information

Visitor Center (⌨800-346-1958, 337-232-3737; www.lafayettetravel.com; 1400 NW Evangeline Thruway; ⊗8:30am-5pm Mon-Fri, 9am-5pm Sat & Sun)

ⓘ Getting There & Away

From I-10, exit 103A, the Evangeline Thruway (Hwy 167) goes to the center of town. **Greyhound** (⌨337-235-1541; 100 Lee Ave) operates from a hub beside the central commercial district, making several runs daily to New Orleans (3½ hours) and Baton Rouge (one hour). The **Amtrak** (100 Lee Ave) train *Sunset Limited* goes to New Orleans three times a week.

Cajun Wetlands

In 1755, the Grand Dérangement, the British expulsion of rural French settlers from Acadiana (now Nova Scotia, Canada), created a homeless population of Acadians who searched for decades for a place to settle. In 1785, seven boatloads of exiles arrived in New Orleans. By the early 19th century, 3000 to 4000 Acadians occupied the swamplands southwest of New Orleans. Native American tribes such as the Attakapas helped them learn to eke out a living based upon fishing and trapping, and the aquatic way of life is still the backdrop to modern living.

East and south of Lafayette, the Atchafalaya Basin is the preternatural heart of the Cajun wetlands. Stop in to the Atchafalaya Welcome Center (⌨337-228-1094; www.louisianatravel.com/atchafalaya-welcome-center; I-10, exit 121; ⊗8:30am-5pm) to learn how to penetrate the dense jungle protecting these swamps, lakes and bayous from the casual visitor (incidentally, it also screens one of the most gloriously cheesy nature films in existence). They'll fill you in on camping in Indian Bayou and exploring the Sherburne Wildlife Management Area, as well as the exquisitely situated Lake Fausse Pointe State Park.

Eleven miles east of Lafayette in the compact, crawfish-lovin' town of Breaux Bridge, you'll find the utterly unexpected Café des Amis (www.cafedesamis.com; 140 E Bridge St; mains $17-26; ⊗11am-2pm Tue, to 9pm Wed & Thu, 7:30am-9:30pm Fri & Sat, 8am-2pm Sun), where you can relax amid funky local art as waiters trot out sumptuous weekend breakfasts, sometimes set to a zydeco jam. Just 3.5 miles south of Breaux Bridge, Lake Martin (Lake Martin Rd) is a wonderful introduction to bayou landscapes. This bird sanctuary hosts thousands of great and cattle egrets, blue heron and more than a few gators.

Check out the friendly tourist center (⌨337-332-8500; www.breauxbridgelive.com; 318 E Bridge St; ⊗8am-4pm Mon-Fri, to noon Sat), who can hook you up with one of numerous B&Bs in town, or the wonderful Bayou Cabins (⌨337-332-6158; www.bayoucabins.com; 100 W Mills Ave; cabins $60-125): 14 completely individualized cabins situated on Bayou Teche, some with 1950s retro furnishings, others decked out in regional folk art. The included breakfast is delicious, but the smoked meats may shave a few years off your lifespan. If you're in town the first week of May, don't miss the gluttony of music, dancing and Cajun food at the Crawfish Festival (www.bbcrawfest.com; ⊗May)

Cajun Prairie

Think: dancing cowboys! Cajun and African American settlers in the higher, drier terrain north of Lafayette developed a culture based around animal husbandry and farming, and the 10-gallon hat still rules. It's also the hotbed of Cajun and zydeco music (and thus accordions) and crawfish farming.

Opelousas squats sleepily alongside Hwy 49, and its historic downtown is home to the esoteric Museum & Interpretive Center (337-948-2589; 315 N Main St; ⊙8am-4:30pm Mon-Fri, 10am-3pm Sat) FREE; check out the doll collection.

The top zydeco joints in Acadiana, Slim's Y-Ki-Ki (www.slimsykiki.com; cnr Main St & Park St, Opelousas), a few miles north on Main St, across from the Piggly Wiggly, and the Zydeco Hall of Fame (11154 Hwy 190), 4 miles west in Lawtell, strike it up most weekends. Wear your dancing shoes and don't be afraid to sweat!

Plaisance, northwest of Opelousas, hosts the grassroots, fun-for-the-family Southwest Louisiana Zydeco Festival (www.zydeco.org; ⊙late Aug).

In Eunice (www.eunice-la.com) there's the Saturday-night (6pm to 7:30pm) 'Rendez-Vous des Cajuns' at the Liberty Theater (337-457-7389; 200 Park Ave; admission $5), which is broadcast on local radio. In fact, visitors are welcome all day at KBON (www.kbon.com; 109 S 2nd St), 101.1FM. Browse the capacious Wall of Fame, signed by visiting musicians. Two blocks away, the Cajun Music Hall of Fame & Museum (337-457-6534; www.cajunfrenchmusic.org; 230 S CC Duson Dr; ⊙9am-5pm Tue-Sat) FREE is a dusty colletion of instruments and cultural ephemera that caters to the die-hard music buff. The NPS runs the Prairie Acadian Cultural Center (337-457-8499; www.nps.gov/jela; 250 West Park Ave; ⊙8am-5pm Tue-Fri, to 6pm Sat) FREE, which has exhibits on rural life and Cajun culture and shows a variety of documentaries explaining the history of the area.

If all this leaves you in need of a respite, try centrally located Potier's Cajun Inn (337-457-0440; 110 W Park Ave, Eunice; r from $55; P ✳) for spacious, down-home-Cajun-style cozy apartments with kitchenettes. Ruby's Café (337-550-7665; 123 S 2nd St, Eunice; meals under $10; ⊙6am-2pm Mon-Fri, 5-9pm Wed & Thu, to 10pm Fri & Sat) does popular plate lunches in a 1950s diner setting and Café Mosaic (202 S 2nd St, Eunice; meals $3-4.50; ⊙6am-10pm Mon-Fri, from 7am Sat, 7am-7pm Sun; ☎) is a smart coffeehouse with waffles and grilled sandwiches.

Northern Louisiana

Make no mistake: the rural, oil-industry towns along the Baptist Bible belt make northern Louisiana as far removed from New Orleans as Paris, TX, is from Paris, France. There's a lot of optimistic tourism development, but at the end of the day, most folks come here from states like Texas and Arkansas to gamble.

Captain Henry Shreve cleared a 165-mile logjam on the Red River and founded the river-port town of Shreveport, in 1839. The city boomed with oil discoveries in the early 1900s, but declined after WWII. Some revitalization came in the form of huge Vegas-sized casinos and a riverfront entertainment complex. The visitor center (888-458-4748; www.shreveport-bossier.org; 629 Spring St; ⊙8am-5pm Mon-Fri, 10am-2pm Sat) is downtown. If you're a rose-lover, it would be a shame to miss the Gardens of the American Rose Center (318-938-5402, 800-637-6534; www.ars.org; 8877 Jefferson Paige Rd; admission by donation, tours $10; ⊙9am-5pm Mon-Sat, 1-5pm Sun), which contains more than 65 individual gardens designed to show how roses can be grown in a home garden – take exit 5 off the I-20. If you're hungry, stop by Strawn's Eat Shop (318-868-0634; 125 E Kings Hwy; mains under $10; ⊙6am-8pm Mon-Sat, to 3pm Sun). This basic diner serves good, hearty Americana fare with a lot of Southern charm – think chicken-fried steak and mustard greens – but it's most notable for its delicious pies.

About 50 miles northeast of Monroe on Hwy 557 near the town of Epps, the Poverty Point State Historic Site (888-926-5492, 318-926-5492; www.crt.state.la.us; 6859 Highway 577, Pioneer; adult/child $4/free; ⊙9am-5pm) has a remarkable series of earthworks and mounds along what was once the Mississippi River. A two-story observation tower gives a view of the site's six concentric ridges, and a 2.6-mile hiking trail meanders through the grassy countryside. Around 1000 BC this was the hub of a civilization comprising hundreds of communities, with trading links as far north as the Great Lakes.

THE SOUTH NORTHERN LOUISIANA

Florida

Best Places to Eat

- ➡ Blue Heaven (p482)
- ➡ Floridian (p488)
- ➡ Michy's (p466)
- ➡ Broken Egg (p496)
- ➡ Ella's Folk Art Cafe (p493)

Best Places to Stay

- ➡ Pelican Hotel (p465)
- ➡ Biltmore Hotel (p465)
- ➡ Dickens House (p494)
- ➡ Pillars (p469)
- ➡ Everglades International Hostel (p473)

Why Go?

Juan Ponce de León came in search of the fountain of youth. Henry Flagler built a railroad for snowbirds looking for a little sunshine. And Walt Disney put Florida on many a bucket list when he chose it as the location of his legendary theme park.

For centuries, people have flocked to Florida in search of a little magic, and they seldom leave disappointed. The Sunshine State is built on tourism and it insists that everyone have a good time, packing an extraordinary amount into a narrow peninsula.

It's home to glitzy theme parks and campy roadside attractions, white-sand beaches and laid-back islands, and top-notch art museums and fascinating historical sites (including the oldest city in the US). It's nearly impossible to be bored here, and if you are, just hop on a roller coaster, kayak alongside some alligators or swim with a manatee. We're betting it will pass.

When to Go

Miami

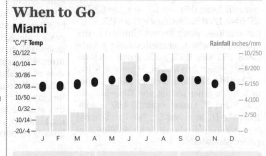

Feb-Apr Winter ends and high season begins, coinciding with spring break.

Jun-Aug The hot, humid wet months are peak season for northern Florida beaches and theme parks.

Sep-Oct The ideal shoulder season with fewer crowds, cooler temperatures and warm waters.

Spring Training

Forget daylight savings – for many Florida residents, the seasons are measured by the beginning and end of baseball spring training. Every March, 15 major league baseball teams hold their spring training in stadiums across central and south Florida, where sunshine is practically guaranteed. The intimate stadiums put you within spitting and signing distance of big leaguers and future hall of famers, making it a pilgrimage for fans of teams like the Boston Red Sox, the New York Yankees and the Philadelphia Phillies (not to mention several Florida-based teams). Around 240 exhibition games are held over 30 days, and fans have been known to camp out for prime seats. For information, visit www.floridagrapefruitleague.com.

AMERICA'S BEST STATE PARKS

Encountering Florida's bizarre, beautiful terrain and its wealth of ancient critters, migratory seabirds and imposing wildlife is unquestionably a highlight. Thankfully, Florida makes it easy for travelers with one of the nation's best state park systems. It is the first and only state to be a two-time recipient of the National Gold Medal Award for Excellence (in 1999 and 2005).

The state's 160 state parks span an overwhelming array of environments, home to epic coral reefs (John Pennekamp), thousands of alligators (Myakka River), otherworldly limestone karst terrain (Paynes Prairie) and crystal springs (Wakulla Springs). Of course, Florida is also legendary for the quality of its beaches, including such top beach parks as Grayton Beach, Fort DeSoto, Honeymoon Island and St Joseph Peninsula.

For the full list, visit Florida State Parks (www.floridastateparks.org). For advice on wildlife watching (what, when and how), visit the Florida Fish & Wildlife Commission (www.myfwc.com), which also facilitates boating, hunting and fishing.

Green Florida

Until recently, Florida wasn't known for conservation and ecotourism, but that's changing fast.

➡ **Department of Environmental Protection** (www.dep.state.fl.us) State-run agency tackles ecological and sustainability issues.

➡ **Green Lodging Program** (www.dep.state.fl.us/greenlodging) DEP-run program recognizes lodgings committed to conservation and sustainability.

➡ **Florida Sierra Club** (http://florida.sierraclub.org) Venerable outdoors and advocacy group.

➡ **Florida Surfrider** (http://florida.surfrider.org) Venerable outdoors and advocacy group.

➡ **Greenopia** (www.greenopia.com) Rates ecofriendly businesses in more than a dozen Florida cities.

HIAASEN'S FLORIDA

Writer Carl Hiaasen's unique, black-comic vision of Florida is a hilarious gumbo of misfits and murderous developers. Try *Skinny Dip* (for adults), *Hoot* (for kids) and *Paradise Screwed* (for his selected columns).

Fast Facts

➡ **Population** Miami (population 413,892), Miami-Dade County (2.5 million)

➡ **Distances from Miami** Key West (160 miles), Orlando (235 miles)

➡ **Time zones** Eastern (eastern Florida), Central Time Zone (western Panhandle)

Best Beaches

You'll never want for shoreline in the Sunshine State. Here are a few of our favorites.

➡ Siesta Key (p495)
➡ South Beach (p457)
➡ Bahia Honda (p479)
➡ Apollo Beach (p484)
➡ St George Island (p507)

Resources

➡ **Visit Florida** (www.visitflorida.com) The official state tourism website.

➡ **My Florida** (www.myflorida.com) The official government portal.

➡ **Florida Smart** (www.floridasmart.com/news) Provides comprehensive Florida links.

FLORIDA

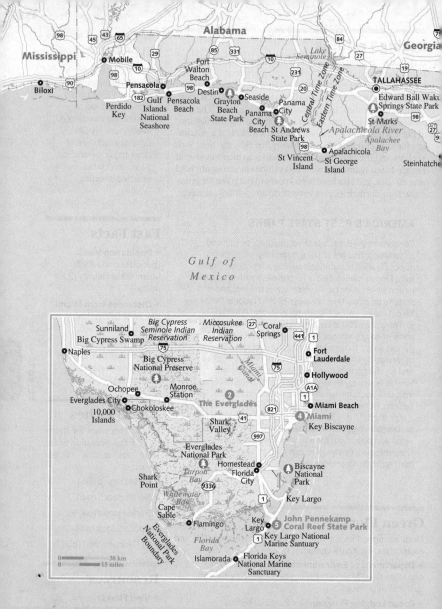

Florida Highlights

1 Join Mallory Square's **sunset bacchanal** (p479) in Key West.

2 Paddle among alligators and sawgrass in the **Everglades** (p472).

3 Be swept up in nostalgia and thrill rides at **Walt Disney World** (p502).

4 Marvel at the **murals** (p461) all around Wynwood in Miami.

5 Snorkel the USA's most extensive coral reef at **John Pennekamp** (p475).

6 Relax on the sugar-sand beaches of Sarasota's **Siesta Key** (p495).

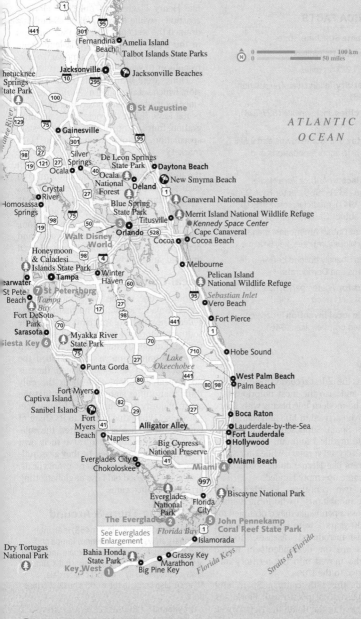

ATLANTIC
OCEAN

See Everglades
Enlargement

7 Ponder the symbolism of
The Hallucinogenic Toreador
at **Dalí Museum** (p495).

8 Growl like a pirate among
the historic Spanish buildings
of **St Augustine** (p487).

FLORIDA HISTORY

FLORIDA FACTS

Nickname Sunshine State

Population 19.3 million

Area 53,927 sq miles

Capital city Tallahassee (population 182,965)

Other cities Jacksonville (827,908), Tampa (346,037)

Sales tax 6% (some towns add 9.5% to 11.5% to accommodations and meals)

Birthplace of Author Zora Neale Hurston (1891–1960), actor Faye Dunaway (b 1941), musician Tom Petty (b 1950), author Carl Hiaasen (b 1953)

Home of Cuban Americans, manatees, Mickey Mouse, retirees, key lime pie

Politics Sharply divided between Republicans and Democrats

Famous for Theme parks, beaches, alligators, art deco

Notable local invention Frozen concentrated orange juice (1946)

History

Florida has the oldest recorded history of any US state, and also the most notorious and bizarre. The modern tale begins with Ponce de León, who arrived in 1513 and claimed La Florida for Spain. Supposedly, he was hunting for the mythical fountain of youth (the peninsula's crystal springs), while later Spanish explorers like Hernando de Soto sought gold. All came up empty handed.

Within two centuries, Florida's original native inhabitants – who formed small tribes across a peninsula they'd occupied for over 11,000 years – were largely decimated by Spanish-introduced diseases. Today's Seminoles are the descendents of native groups who moved into the territory and intermingled in the 1700s.

Through the 18th century, Spain and England played hot potato with Florida as they struggled to dominate the New World, finally tossing the state to America, who admitted it to the Union in 1845. Meanwhile, developers and speculators were working hard to turn the swampy peninsula into a vacation and agricultural paradise. By the turn of the 20th century, railroad tycoons like Henry Flagler had unlocked Florida's coastlines, while a frenzy of canal-building drained the wetlands. The rush was on, and in the 1920s the South Florida land boom transformed Miami from sandbar to metropolis in 10 years.

Things went bust with the Great Depression, which set the pattern: Florida has ever since swung between intoxicating highs and brutal lows, riding the vicissitudes of immigration, tourism, hurricanes and real estate speculation (not to mention a thriving black market).

Following Castro's Cuban revolution in the 1960s, Cuban exiles flooded Miami, and each successive decade has seen the ranks of Latin immigrants grow and diversify. As for tourism, it was never the same after 1971, when Walt Disney built his Magic Kingdom, embodying the vision of eternal youth and perfected fantasy that Florida has packaged and sold since the beginning.

Local Culture

Florida is one of the USA's most diverse states. Broadly speaking, northern Florida reflects the culture of America's South, while southern Florida has welcomed so many Cuban, Caribbean, and Central and South American immigrants, it's been dubbed 'the Capital of Latin America.' As such, there is no 'typical Floridian,' and about the only thing that unifies state residents is that the great majority are transplants from someplace else. While this has led to its share of conflicts, tolerance is more often the rule. Most Floridians are left to carve their own self-defined communities, be they gays, retirees, Cubans, Haitians, bikers, evangelicals, Nascar-loving good old boys or globetrotting art-world sophisticates.

ℹ Getting There & Around

Miami International Airport (p468) is an international gateway, as are Orlando, Tampa and Fort Lauderdale. The Fort Lauderdale and Miami airports are about 30 minutes apart; it's almost always cheaper to fly into Fort Lauderdale. Miami is also home to the world's busiest cruise port.

Greyhound (☑ 800-231-2222; www.greyhound.com) has widespread service throughout the state. **Amtrak** (www.amtrak.com) *Silver Meteor* and *Silver Star* trains run daily between New York and Miami.

Car-rental rates in Florida tend to fluctuate, but expect to pay at least $300 a week for a typical economy car.

SOUTH FLORIDA

Exemplifying the state's diversity, South Florida is a vivid pastiche of all that makes Florida wicked and wild. First is the multicultural entrepôt of Miami, and the sophisticated, rich beach communities stretching north from Fort Lauderdale to Palm Beach. In striking contrast, the beaches are bordered by the subtropical wilderness of the Everglades, while the tip of the state peters out in an ellipsis of fun-loving islands, culminating in anything-goes Key West.

Miami

Miami moves to a different rhythm from anywhere else in the USA. Pastel-hued, subtropical beauty and Latin sexiness are everywhere: from the cigar-filled dance halls where Havana expats dance to *son* and boleros to the exclusive nightclubs where stiletto-heeled Brazilian models shake to Latin hip-hop. Whether you're meeting avant-garde gallery hipsters or passing the buffed, perfect bodies recumbent along South Beach, everyone can seem oh-so-artfully posed. Meanwhile, street vendors and restaurants dish out flavors of the Caribbean, Cuba, Argentina and Haiti. For travelers, the city can be as intoxicating as a sweaty-glassed *mojito*.

Miami is its own world, an international city whose tempos, concerns and inspirations often arrive from distant shores. Over half the population is Latino and over 60% speak predominantly Spanish. In fact, many northern Floridians don't consider immigrant-rich Miami to be part of the state, and many Miamians, particularly Cubans, feel the same way.

◎ Sights

Greater Miami is a sprawling metropolis. Miami is on the mainland, while Miami Beach lies 4 miles east across Biscayne Bay. South Beach refers to the southern part of Miami Beach, extending from 5th St north to 21st St. Washington Ave is the main commercial artery. North of downtown (along NE 2nd Ave from about 17th St to 41st St), Wynwood and the Design District are focal points for art, food and nightlife. Just north again is Little Haiti. To reach Little Havana, head west on SW 8th St, or Calle Ocho, which pierces the heart of the neighborhood (and becomes the Tamiami Trail/Hwy

41). Just south of Little Havana are Coconut Grove and Coral Gables.

For more on South Florida, pick up a copy of Lonely Planet's guide to *Miami & the Keys*.

◎ Miami Beach

Miami Beach has some of the best beaches in the country, with white sand and warm aquamarine water. That movie in your head of art-deco hotels, in-line-skating models, preening young studs and cruising cars? That's Ocean Drive (from 1st to 11th Sts), with the beach merely a backdrop for strutting peacocks. This confluence of waves, sunshine and exhibitionist beauty is what made South Beach (or 'SoBe') world-famous.

Just a few blocks north, Lincoln Road (between Alton Rd and Washington Ave) becomes a pedestrian mall, or outdoor fashion runway, so all may admire SoBe's fabulously gorgeous creatures.

★ Art Deco Historic District   NEIGHBORHOOD
(Map p460) The well-preserved, pastel-hued Art Deco Historic District verily screams 'Miami.' It's the largest concentration of deco anywhere in the world, with approximately 1200 buildings lining the streets around Ocean Dr and Collins Ave. For tours and info, make your

---

FLORIDA IN...

One Week

Start in **Miami** and plan on spending three full days exploring museums and galleries, the art-deco district, Little Havana and the South Beach scene. Take a day to hike and kayak the **Everglades**, and don't miss **Coral Castle**. Then spend three days in the Keys: snorkel at **John Pennekamp Coral Reef State Park**, go tarpon fishing in **Islamorada** and let yourself get loose in **Key West**.

Two Weeks

Spend one or two days at the theme parks of **Orlando**, then scoot over to **Tampa** for fine cuisine and Ybor City nightlife. Get surreal in **St Petersburg** at the **Salvador Dalí Museum**, and visit a few **Tampa Bay Area beaches**. Finally, save a couple of days for **Sarasota**, with its jaw-dropping **Ringling Museum Complex** and the dreamy sands of **Siesta Key**.

Greater Miami

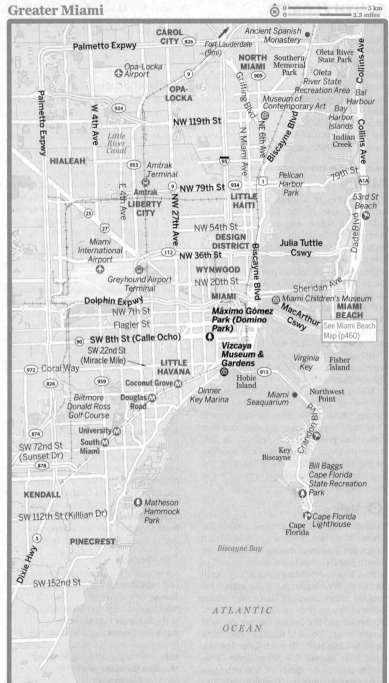

0 — 5 km
0 — 2.5 miles

CAROL CITY 826
Palmetto Expwy
Fort Lauderdale (9mi)
Ancient Spanish Monastery
NORTH MIAMI 909
Southern Memorial Park
Oleta River State Park
Collins Ave
Opa-Locka Airport
Oleta River State Recreation Area
Palmetto Expwy
OPA-LOCKA
NW 119th St
Griffing Blvd
Museum of Contemporary Art
Bal Harbour
Bay Harbor Islands
924
W 4th Ave
N Miami Ave
NE 6th Ave
Biscayne Blvd
Indian Creek
Collins Ave
Little River Canal
HIALEAH
95
Amtrak Terminal
953
NW 79th St
934
Pelican Harbor Park
79th St
A1A
E 4th Ave
Amtrak
LIBERTY CITY
NW 27th Ave
LITTLE HAITI
1
53rd St Beach
25
NW 54th St
27
Miami International Airport
DESIGN DISTRICT
112
NW 36th St
WYNWOOD
Julia Tuttle Cswy
Biscayne Blvd
Greyhound Airport Terminal
NW 20th St
MIAMI
Sheridan Ave
Miami Children's Museum
Dolphin Expwy
NW 7th St
Máximo Gómez Park (Domino Park)
MacArthur Cswy
MIAMI BEACH
See Miami Beach Map (p460)
Flagler St
90
SW 8th St (Calle Ocho)
Vizcaya Museum & Gardens
Virginia Key
Fisher Island
SW 22nd St (Miracle Mile)
972 Coral Way
LITTLE HAVANA
Hobie Island
913
826
959
Coconut Grove
Dinner Key Marina
Miami Seaquarium
Northwest Point
Biltmore Donald Ross Golf Course
Douglas Road
874
University
Crandon Blvd
SW 72nd St (Sunset Dr)
South Miami
Key Biscayne
878
KENDALL
Bill Baggs Cape Florida State Recreation Park
SW 112th St (Killlian Dr)
Matheson Hammock Park
5
Cape Florida Lighthouse
Cape Florida
PINECREST
Dixie Hwy
Biscayne Bay
SW 152nd St

ATLANTIC
OCEAN

first stop the Art Deco Welcome Center (Map p460; ☎305-531-3484; 1001 Ocean Dr, South Beach; guided tour per adult/child/senior $20/free/15; ☺tours 10:30am Fri-Wed, 6:30pm Thu).

★**Wolfsonian-FIU**   MUSEUM
(Map p460; www.wolfsonian.org; 1001 Washington Ave; adult/child 6-12 $7/5; ☺noon-6pm Thu-Tue, to 9pm Fri) A fascinating collection that spans transportation, urbanism, industrial design, advertising and political propaganda from the late 19th to mid-20th century.

Bass Museum of Art   MUSEUM
(www.bassmuseum.org; 2121 Park Ave; adult/child $8/6; ☺noon-5pm Wed-Sun) The best art museum in Miami Beach has a playfully futurist facade, and the collection isn't shabby either, ranging from 16th-century European religious works to Renaissance paintings.

World Erotic Art Museum   MUSEUM
(Map p460; www.weam.com; 1205 Washington Ave; adult over 18yr $15; ☺11am-10pm Mon-Thu, to midnight Fri-Sun) Unfazed by SoBe's bare flesh? Something will get your attention here, with an amazingly extensive collection of naughty and erotic art, and even furniture depicting all sorts of parts and acts.

◉ Downtown Miami

Downtown isn't a tourist magnet, but it is home to a couple of worthwhile museums. Look for the brand new Pérez Art Museum Miami (MAM; www.miamiartmuseum.org), formerly Miami Art Museum, at its new location in Bicentennial Park.

History Miami   MUSEUM
(www.historymiami.org; 101 W Flagler St; adult/child $8/5; ☺10am-5pm Tue-Fri, from noon Sat & Sun) South Florida's complex, excitable history of Seminole warriors, rumrunners, pirates, land grabbers, tourists and Latin American immigrants is succinctly and vividly told. In a plaza just off W Flagler St.

◉ Little Havana

As SW 8th St heads away from downtown, it becomes Calle Ocho (pronounced *kah*-yeh *oh*-cho, Spanish for 'Eighth Street'). That's when you know you've arrived in Little Havana, the most prominent community of Cuban Americans in the US. Despite the cultural monuments, this is no Cuban theme park. The district remains a living, breathing immigrant enclave, though one whose residents have become, admittedly, more broadly Central American. One of the best times to come is the last Friday of the month during Viernes Culturales (www.viernesculturales.org), or 'Cultural Fridays,' a street fair showcasing Latino artists and musicians.

★**Máximo Gómez Park**   PARK
(SW 8th St at SW 15th Ave; ☺9am-6pm) Get a sensory-filled taste of old Cuba. It's also known as 'Domino Park,' and you'll understand why when you see the old-timers throwing bones.

El Crédito Cigars   CIGARS
(☎305-858-4162; 1106 SW 8th St) One of Miami's most popular cigar stores; watch *tabaqueros* hand-roll them.

MIAMI IN...

Two Days

Focus your first day on South Beach. Bookend an afternoon of sunning and swimming with a walking tour through the **Art Deco Historic District** and a visit to **Wolfsonian-FIU**, which explains it all. That evening, sample some Haitian cuisine at **Tap Tap**, while away the evening with swanky cocktails at **Skybar** or, for a low-key brew, head to **Room**. For a late jolt, stop by the **World Erotic Art Museum**, open to midnight on weekends. Next morning, shop for Cuban music along Calle Ocho in **Little Havana**, followed by classic Cuban cuisine at **Versalles**. Go for a stroll at **Vizcaya Museum & Gardens**, cool off with a dip at the **Venetian Pool**, then end the day with dinner and cocktails at **Senora Martinez**.

Four Days

Follow the two-day itinerary, then head to the **Everglades** on day three and jump in a kayak. For your last day, immerse yourself in art and design in **Wynwood** and the **Design District**, followed by a visit to the **Miami Art Museum** or **Museum of Contemporary Art**. In the evening, party with the hipsters at the **Electric Pickle** or check out some live music: enjoy rock at **Tobacco Road** or Latin grooves at **Hoy Como Ayer**.

Miami Beach

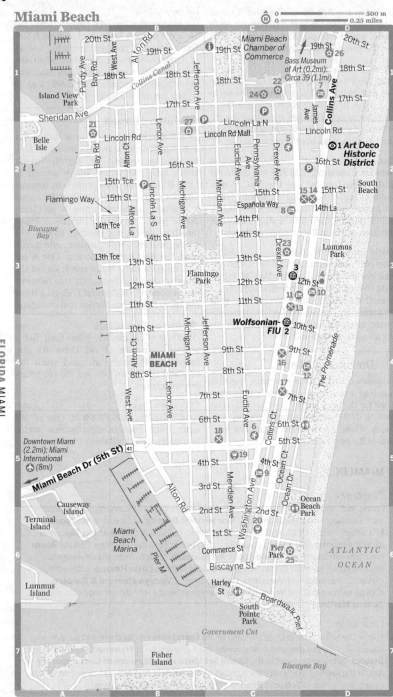

Miami Beach

⊙ Design District, Wynwood & Little Haiti

Proving that SoBe doesn't hold the lease on hip, these two trendy areas north of downtown – all but deserted 25 years ago – have ensconced themselves as bastions of art and design. The Design District is a mecca for interior designers, home to dozens of galleries and contemporary furniture, fixture and design showrooms. Just south of the Design District, Wynwood is a notable arts district, with myriad galleries and art studios housed in abandoned factories and warehouses.

The home of Miami's Haitian refugees, Little Haiti is defined by brightly painted homes, markets and *botanicas* (voodoo shops).

Wynwood Walls   PUBLIC ART
(www.thewynwoodwalls.com; NW 2nd Ave btwn 25th & 26th St; ☺ noon-8pm Wed-Sat) Not a gallery per se, Wynwood Walls is a collection of murals and paintings laid out over an open courtyard in the heart of Wynwood. What's on offer tends to change with the coming and going of major arts events like Art Basel (one of the US's major annual art shows); when we visited the centerpiece was an enormous and fantastic piece by artist Shepard Fairey.

⊙ Coral Gables & Coconut Grove

For a slower pace and a more European feel, head inland. Designed as a 'model suburb' by George Merrick in the early 1920s, Coral Gables is a Mediterranean-style village that's centered around the shops and restaurants of the Miracle Mile, a four-block section of Coral Way between Douglas and LeJeune Rds.

★ Vizcaya Museum & Gardens   HISTORIC BUILDING
(www.vizcayamuseum.org; 3251 S Miami Ave; adult/child 6-12 $15/6; ☺ 9:30am-4:30pm Wed-Mon) In Coconut Grove, this Italian Renaissance–style villa, the housing equivalent of a Fabergé egg, is Miami's most fairy-tale residence. The 70 rooms are stuffed with centuries-old furnishings and art, and the 30-acre grounds contain splendid formal gardens and Florentine gazebos.

Biltmore Hotel   HISTORIC BUILDING
(☏ 855-311-6903; www.biltmorehotel.com; 1200 Anastasia Ave) Architecturally speaking, the crown jewel of Coral Gables is this magnificent edifice that once housed a speakeasy run by Al Capone. Even if you don't stay, drop by for a drink at the bar and gawk at the pool, or catch a free tour on Sunday afternoons.

FLORIDA MIAMI

City Walk
Art-Deco Magic

START ART DECO WELCOME CENTER
END EDISON HOTEL
LENGTH 1-2 MILES; 30 MINUTES

There are excellent walking tours available for the Art Deco Historic District – both guided and self-guided – but if you just want to hit the highlights, follow this quick and easy path.

Start at the ❶ **Art Deco Welcome Center** (p459) at the corner of Ocean Dr and 12th St, and head inside for a taste of deco style. Next, go north on Ocean Dr. Between 12th and 14th Sts, you'll see three classic examples of deco hotels: the ❷ **Leslie**, with classic 'eyebrows' and a typically boxy shape; the ❸ **Carlyle**, which was featured in the film *The Birdcage;* and the graceful ❹ **Cardozo Hotel**, with sleek, rounded edges. At 14th St, peek inside ❺ **Winter Haven** to see its fabulous terrazzo floors.

Turn left and head along 14th St to Washington Ave, and turn left again to find the

❻ **US Post Office** at 13th St. Step inside to admire the domed ceiling and marble stamp tables, and try whispering into the domed ceiling. Two blocks down on your left is the ❼ **11th St Diner** (p466), a gleaming aluminum deco-style Pullman car where you can also stop for lunch. At 10th St, you'll find the ❽ **Wolfsonian-FIU** (p459), an excellent museum with many deco-era treasures, and across the street is the beautifully restored ❾ **Hotel Astor**.

Turn left on 8th St and head east to Collins Ave. On the corner, you'll see ❿ **The Hotel** – originally the Tiffany Hotel and still topped by a deco-style neon spire bearing that name. Continue to Ocean Dr and turn right to see the ⓫ **Colony Hotel** and its famous neon sign, then double back to find the 1935 ⓬ **Edison Hotel**, another creation of deco legend Henry Hohauser, half a block past 9th St.

Venetian Pool SWIMMING

(www.coralgablesvenetianpool.com; 2701 De Soto Blvd; adult/child $11/7.35; ⏰hours vary; 🚻) 'Swimming pool' doesn't even begin to describe it: with waterfalls, grottos and an Italianate feel, this spring-fed pool made by filling in the limestone quarry used to build Coral Gables looks like a vacation home for rich mermaids.

Lowe Art Museum MUSEUM

(www.lowemuseum.org; 1301 Stanford Dr; adult/student $10/5; ⏰10am-4pm Tue-Sat, from noon Sun) The Lowe's tremendous collection satisfies a wide range of tastes, but it's particularly strong in Asian, African and South Pacific art and archaeology, and its pre-Columbian and Mesoamerican collection is stunning.

◉ Greater Miami

Museum of Contemporary Art MUSEUM

(MoCA; www.mocanomi.org; 770 NE 125th St; adult/student & senior $5/3; ⏰11am-5pm Tue & Thu-Sat, 1-9pm Wed, noon-5pm Sun) North of downtown, MoCA has frequently changing exhibitions focusing on international, national and emerging artists.

Ancient Spanish Monastery CHURCH

(☎305-945-1461; www.spanishmonastery.com; 16711 W Dixie Hwy; adult/child $8/4; ⏰10am-4:30pm Mon-Sat, from 11am Sun) Said to be the oldest building in the Western Hemisphere, this monastery was built in Segovia, Spain, in 1141 and shipped here by William Randolph Hearst. Call to confirm hours.

◉ Key Biscayne

Bill Baggs Cape Florida State Park PARK

(www.floridastateparks.org/capeflorida; 1200 S Crandon Blvd; per car $8, pedestrian $2; ⏰8am-sunset) If you don't make it to the Florida Keys, come to this park for a taste of their unique island ecosystems. The 494-acre space is a tangled clot of tropical fauna and dark mangroves, all interconnected by sandy trails and wooden boardwalks and surrounded by miles of pale ocean. A concession shack rents kayaks, bikes, in-line skates, beach chairs and umbrellas. At the southernmost tip, the 1825 brick **Cape Florida Lighthouse** offers free tours at 10am and 1pm Thursday through Monday.

WYNWOOD GALLERIES

In Wynwood, Miami's hip proving ground for avant-garde art, 'Wypsters' (Wynwood hipsters) stock dozens of galleries with 'guerrilla' installations, new murals, graffiti and other inscrutableness. The neighborhood is roughly bound by NW 20th and NW 37th streets on the south and north, and N Miami Ave and NW 3rd Ave east and west. The best way to experience the scene is to attend the **Wynwood and Design District Arts Walks** (www.artcircuits.com; ⏰second Saturday of the month 7-10pm) FREE, with music, food and wine on the second Saturday of the month from 7pm to 10pm.

🏃 Activities

Cycling & In-Line Skating

Skating or cycling the strip along Ocean Dr in South Beach is pure Miami; also try the Rickenbacker Causeway to Key Biscayne.

Fritz's Skate, Bike & Surf SPORTS RENTALS

(Map p460; ☎305-532-1954; www.fritzsmiamibeach.com; 1620 Washington Ave; hour/day/week bike & skate rentals $10/24/69; ⏰10am-9pm Mon-Sat, to 8pm Sun) Sports equipment rentals and free in-line skate lessons (10:30am Sunday).

Miami Beach Bicycle Center CYCLING

(Map p460; www.bikemiamibeach.com; 601 5th St; per hr/day from $5/14; ⏰10am-7pm Mon-Sat, to 5pm Sun) Convenient bike rentals in the heart of SoBe.

Water Sports

Boucher Brothers Watersports WATER SPORTS

(☎305-535-8177; www.boucherbrothers.com; ⏰10:30am-4:30pm) Rentals and lessons for all sorts of water-related activities: kayaking, waterskiing, windsurfing, parasailing, waverunners and boats. You can find locations up and down the beach; your best bet is to call first to find out where to go for whatever it is you want to rent.

Sailboards Miami WATER SPORTS

(☎305-892-8992; www.sailboardsmiami.com; 1 Rickenbacker Causeway; ⏰10am-6pm Fri-Tue) The waters off Key Biscayne are perfect for windsurfing, kayaking and kiteboarding; get your gear and lessons here.

☞ Tours

Miami Design Preservation League WALKING

(Map p460; ☑ 305-531-3484; guided tours adult/child $20/free, audio tours $15; ⊙ 10:30am Fri-Wed, 6:30pm Thu) Learn about art deco and its icons on a 90-minute walking tour departing from the Art Deco Welcome Center at 1200 Ocean Dr, Miami Beach.

History Miami Tours WALKING, CYCLING

(☑ 305-375-1621; www.historymiami.org/tours; tours $20-54) Historian extraordinaire Dr Paul George leads fascinating bike, boat, coach and walking tours, including those that focus on Stiltsville. Get the full menu online.

South Beach Bike Tours CYCLING

(☑ 305-673-2002; www.southbeachbiketours.com; half-day tour per person $59) Three-hour, two-wheel tours of South Beach.

✦ Festivals & Events

Calle Ocho Festival CULTURAL

(www.carnavalmiami.com) This massive street party in March is the culmination of Carnaval Miami, a 10-day celebration of Latin culture.

Winter Music Conference MUSIC

(www.wmcon.com) The SXSW of dance music and electronica takes place every March.

Art Basel Miami Beach ART

(www.artbaselmiamibeach.com) An internationally known art show held each December.

⛏ Sleeping

Miami Beach is the well-hyped mecca for stylish boutique hotels in renovated art-deco buildings. To find them and other chic options, check out www.miamiboutiquehotels.com. Rates vary widely by season and all bets are off during spring break, when rates can quintuple; the summer months are slowest. For hotel parking, expect to pay $20 to $35 a night.

▦ South Beach

Clay Hotel HOTEL **$$**

(Map p460; ☑ 305-534-2988, 800-379-2529; www.clayhotel.com; 1438 Washington Ave; r $88-190; ❋@☎) Located in a 100-year-old Spanish-style villa – legend has it that Al Capone once slept here – the Clay has clean and comfortable rooms and is right on Espanola Way.

MIAMI FOR CHILDREN

The best beaches for kids are in Miami Beach north of 21st St, especially at 53rd St, which has a playground and public toilets, and the dune-packed beach around 73rd St. Also head south to Matheson Hammock Park, which has calm artificial lagoons.

Miami Seaquarium (www.miamiseaquarium.com; 4400 Rickenbacker Causeway; adult/child $40/30; ⊙9:30am-6pm, last entry 4:30pm) On the way to Key Biscayne, this 38-acre marine-life park is more extensive than the usual aquarium; it also rehabilitates dolphins, manatees and sea turtles, and presents great animal shows. You can swim with the dolphins.

Miami Children's Museum (www.miamichildrensmuseum.org; 980 MacArthur Causeway; admission $16; ⊙10am-6pm) On Watson Island, between downtown Miami and Miami Beach, this hands-on museum has fun music and art studios, as well as some branded 'work' experiences that make it feel a tad corporate.

Jungle Island (www.jungleisland.com; 1111 Parrot Jungle Trail, off MacArthur Causeway; adult/child $35/27; ⊙10am-5pm) Jungle Island is packed with tropical birds, alligators, orangutans, chimps and (to the delight of *Napoleon Dynamite* fans) a liger, a cross between a lion and a tiger.

Zoo Miami (Metrozoo; www.miamimetrozoo.com; 12400 SW 152nd St; adult/child $16/12; ⊙9:30am-5:30pm, last admission 4pm) Miami's tropical weather makes strolling around Zoo Miami almost feel like a day in the wild. For a quick overview (and because the zoo is so big), hop on the Safari Monorail; it departs every 20 minutes. There's a glut of grounds tours available, and kids will love feeding the Samburu giraffes ($2).

Monkey Jungle (www.monkeyjungle.com; 14805 SW 216th St; adult/child $30/24; ⊙9:30am-5pm, last entry 4pm) The tagline, 'Where humans are caged and monkeys run wild,' tells you all you need to know – except for the fact that it's in far south Miami.

GUIDE TO MIAMI BEACHES

The beaches around Miami are some of the best in the country. The water is clear and warm. They're also informally zoned into areas with their own unique crowds so that everyone can enjoy them at their own speed.

Scantily-Clad Beaches In South Beach between 5th St and 21st St, modesty is in short supply.

Family-Fun Beaches North of 21st St is where you'll find the more family-friendly beaches, and the beach at 53rd St has a playground and public toilets.

Nude Beaches Nude bathing is legal at Haulover Beach Park in Sunny Isles. North of the lifeguard tower is predominantly gay; south is straight.

Gay Beaches All of South Beach is gay-friendly, but a special concentration seems to hover around 12th St.

Windsurfing Beaches Hobie Beach, along the Rickenbacker Causeway on the way to Key Biscayne, is actually known as 'Windsurfing Beach.'

★**Hotel St Augustine** BOUTIQUE HOTEL **$$**
(Map p460; ☑ 305-532-0570; www.hotelstaugustine.com; 347 Washington Ave; r $126-289; P ❋ ⊛ ☎) Wood that's blonder than Barbie and a crisp-and-clean deco theme combine to create one of South Beach's most elegant yet stunningly modern sleeps. A hip-and-homey standout.

Lords Hotel BOUTIQUE HOTEL **$$**
(Map p460; ☑ 877-448-4754; www.lordssouthbeach.com; 1120 Collins Ave; r $120-240, ste $330-540; P ❋ ⊛ ☎) The epicenter of South Beach's gay scene is this 'appropriately oriented' hotel, with rooms decked out in lemony yellow and offset by pop art. Lords is hip, yet doesn't affect an attitude.

Kent Hotel BOUTIQUE HOTEL **$$**
(Map p460; ☑ 305-604-5068; www.thekenthotel.com; 1131 Collins Ave; r $69-199; P ❋ ⊛ ☎) The lobby is a kick, filled with fuchsia and electric-orange geometric furniture plus bright Lucite toy blocks. Rooms continue the playfulness. One of South Beach's better deals.

★**Pelican Hotel** BOUTIQUE HOTEL **$$$**
(Map p460; ☑ 305-673-3373; www.pelicanhotel.com; 826 Ocean Dr; r $165-425, ste $295-555; ❋ ☎) The name and deco facade don't hint at anything unusual, but the decorators went wild inside with great themes such as 'Best Whorehouse,' 'Executive Zebra' and 'Me Tarzan, You Vain.'

Cadet Hotel BOUTIQUE HOTEL **$$$**
(Map p460; ☑ 305-672-6688; www.cadethotel.com; 1701 James Ave; r $189-280; ❋ ☎ ⊛) This unassuming little boutique hotel has the perfect deco aesthetic, with creative embellishments everywhere and a shaded verandah that's an oasis of calm.

🛏 Northern Miami Beach

★**Circa 39** BOUTIQUE HOTEL **$$**
(☑ 305-538-4900; www.circa39.com; 3900 Collins Ave; r $85-144; P ❋ ⊛ @ ⊛) If you love South Beach style but loathe South Beach attitude, Circa has got your back. Combines one of the funkiest lobbies in Miami, hip icy-blue-and-white rooms and a welcoming attitude. Web rates are phenomenal.

🛏 Coral Gables

Hotel St Michel HOTEL **$$**
(☑ 305-444-1666; www.hotelstmichel.com; 162 Alcazar Ave; r $85-225; P ❋ ☎) You could conceivably think you're in Europe in this vaulted place at Coral Gables, with inlaid floors, old-world charm and just 28 rooms.

★**Biltmore Hotel** HISTORIC HOTEL **$$$**
(☑ 855-311-6903; www.biltmorehotel.com; 1200 Anastasia Ave; r from $209; P ❋ ⊛ ☎ ⊛) This 1926 hotel is a National Historic Landmark and an icon of luxury. Standard rooms may be small, but public spaces are palatial; its fabulous pool is the largest hotel pool in the country.

🍴 Eating

Florida's most international city has an international-level food scene.

🍴 South Beach

Walking up Ocean Ave, you'll find a veritable gauntlet of restaurants taking over the patios and sidewalks of almost every hotel facing the beach, all hawking lunch specials and happy hour deals. Competition is fierce, which means you can eat inexpensively. Stroll till you find something that suits, anywhere between 5th St and 14th Pl.

Puerto Sagua
CUBAN $

(Map p460; ☎305-673-1115; 700 Collins Ave; most mains $6-20; ⊙7:30am-2am) Pull up to the counter for authentic, tasty and inexpensive *ropa vieja* (shredded beef), black beans and *arroz con pollo* (rice with chicken) – plus some of the best Cuban coffee in town – at this beloved Cuban diner.

11th St Diner
DINER $

(Map p460; www.eleventhstreetdiner.com; 1065 Washington Ave; mains $9-18; ⊙24hr except midnight-7am Wed) This deco diner housed inside a gleaming Pullman train car sees round-the-clock activity and is especially popular with people staggering home from clubs.

Pizza Rustica
PIZZERIA $

(Map p460; www.pizza-rustica.com; 863 Washington Ave; slices $5, other mains $8-10; ⊙11am-6pm) Big square slices that are a meal in themselves – when you're wandering around hungry, there's nothing better. Also at 667 Lincoln Rd.

★Tap Tap
HAITIAN $$

(Map p460; ☎305-672-2898; www.taptaprestaurant.com; 819 5th St; mains $9-20; ⊙noon-11:30pm) In this tropi-psychedelic Haitian eatery, you dine under bright murals of Papa Legba, enjoying cuisine that's a happy marriage of West Africa, France and the Caribbean: try spicy pumpkin soup, curried goat and *mayi moulen,* a signature side of cornmeal.

Jerry's Famous Deli
DELI $$

(Map p460; ☎305-532-8030; www.jerrysfamousdeli.com; 1450 Collins Ave; most mains $9-18; ⊙24hr) Jerry's does it all – from pastrami melts to Chinese chicken salad to fettuccine

Alfredo – and does it all day long. It also does it big, with huge portions served in a large, open, deco space or delivered to you.

★Osteria del Teatro
ITALIAN $$$

(Map p460; ☎305-538-7850; http://osteriadelteatromiami.com; 1443 Washington Ave; mains $17-38; ⊙6-11pm Mon-Thu, to 1am Fri-Sun) Stick to the specials of one of Miami's oldest and best Italian restaurants, and you can't go wrong. Better yet, let the gracious Italian waiters coddle and order for you. They never pick wrong.

Downtown Miami

Azul
FUSION $$$

(☎305-913-8288; 500 Brickell Key Dr; mains $35-65; ⊙7-11pm Tue-Sat) Be pampered at this terrific restaurant on Brickell Key with a stellar Asian fusion menu. In addition to a massive wine list and waterfront views of downtown, Azul offers some of the best service in Miami.

Little Havana

Versailles
CUBAN $$

(☎305-444-0240; www.versaillesrestaurant.com; 3555 SW 8th St; mains $5-26; ⊙8am-1am) *The* Cuban restaurant in town is not to be missed. It finds room for everybody in the large, cafeteria-style dining rooms.

Design District & Wynwood

Michy's
FUSION $$$

(☎305-759-2001; http://michysmiami.com; 6927 Biscayne Blvd; meals $29-38; ⊙6-10:30pm Tue-Thu, to 11pm Fri-Sat, to 10pm Sun; ☑) Organic, locally sourced ingredients and a stylish, fantastical decor are what you'll find at Michelle 'Michy' Bernstein's place – one of the brightest stars in Miami's culinary constellation.

LATIN AMERICAN SPICE IN MIAMI

Thanks to its immigrant heritage, Miami is legendary for its authentic Cuban, Haitian, Brazilian and other Latin American cuisines. Cuban food is a mix of Caribbean, African and Latin American influences, and the fertile cross-pollination of these traditions has given rise to endlessly creative, tasty gourmet fusions, sometimes dubbed 'nuevo Latino,' 'nouvelle Floridian' or 'Floribbean' cuisine.

For a good introduction to Cuban food, sidle up to a Cuban *loncheria* (snack bar) and order a *pan cubano*: a buttered, grilled baguette stuffed with ham, roast pork, cheese, mustard and pickles. For dinner, order the classic *ropa vieja*: shredded flank steak cooked in tomatoes and peppers, and accompanied by fried plantains, black beans and yellow rice.

Other treats to look for include Haitian *griots* (marinated fried pork), Jamaican jerk chicken, Brazilian BBQ, Central American *gallo pinto* (red beans and rice) and *batidos*, a milky, refreshing Latin American fruit smoothie.

🍸 Drinking & Entertainment

Miami truly comes alive at night. There is always something going on, and usually till the wee hours, with many bars staying open till 3am or 5am. For events calendars and gallery, bar and club reviews, check out www.cooljunkie.com and www.beachedmiami.com.

Bars

There are tons of bars along Ocean Dr; a meander at happy hour will get you half-price drinks.

★Room
BAR

(Map p460; www.theotheroom.com; 100 Collins Ave; ◎7pm-5am) This dark, atmospheric, boutique beer bar in SoBe is a gem: hip and sexy as hell but with a low-key attitude. Per the name, it's small and gets crowded.

★Abraxas
BAR

(Map p460; 407 Meridian Ave; ◎7pm-3am Sun-Mon, 5pm-5am Tue-Sat) In a classic deco building, Abraxas couldn't be friendlier. Uncrowded and serving fantastic beer from around the world, it's tucked away in a residential part of South Beach.

Electric Pickle
BAR

(www.electricpicklemiami.com; 2826 N Miami Ave; ◎10pm-5am Wed-Sat) In Wynwood, arty hipsters become glamorous club kids in this two-story hepcat hot spot. The Pickle is sexy, gorgeous and literate.

Nightclubs

To increase your chances of getting into the major nightclubs, call ahead to get on the guest list. Having gorgeous, well-dressed females in your group doesn't hurt either (unless you're going to a gay bar). In South Beach clubs and live music venues, cover charges range from $20 to $25; elsewhere you'll get in for around half that.

Skybar
CLUB

(Map p460; ☎305-695-3100; Shore Club, 1901 Collins Ave; 4pm-2am Mon-Wed, to 3am Thu-Sat) Sip chic cocktails on the alfresco terrace – they're too expensive to guzzle. Or, if you're 'somebody,' head for the indoor A-list Red Room. Both have a luxurious Moroccan theme and beautiful-people-watching.

Twist
CLUB

(Map p460; ☎305-538-9478; www.twistsobe.com; 1057 Washington Ave; ◎1pm-5am) This gay hangout has serious staying power and a little bit of something for everyone, including dancing, drag shows and go-go dancers.

Nikki Beach Club
CLUB

(Map p460; ☎305-538-1111; www.nikkibeach.com; 1 Ocean Dr; cover from $25; ◎11am-6pm Mon-Tue, to 11pm Wed-Sat, to 5pm Sun) Lounge on beds or inside your own tipi in this beach-chic outdoor space that's right on the sand.

Mansion
CLUB

(Map p460; ☎305-532-1525; www.mansionmiami.com; 1235 Washington Ave; cover from $20; ◎11pm-5am Wed-Sat) Prepare for some quality time with the velvet rope and wear fly duds to enter this grandiose, exclusive megaclub, which lives up to its name.

Live Music

Hoy Como Ayer
LIVE MUSIC

(☎305-541-2631; www.hoycomoayer.us; 2212 SW 8th St; ◎from 9pm Thu-Sat) Authentic Cuban music.

Tobacco Road
LIVE MUSIC

(☎305-374-1198; www.tobacco-road.com; 626 S Miami Ave; ◎11:30am-5am) Old-school roadhouse around since 1912; blues, jazz and occasional impromptu jams by well-known rockers.

Jazid
LOUNGE

(Map p460; ☎305-673-9372; www.jazid.net; 1342 Washington Ave; ◎10pm-5am) Jazz in a candlelit lounge; upstairs, DJ-fueled soul and hip-hop.

Theater & Culture

Adrienne Arsht Center for the Performing Arts
PERFORMING ARTS

(www.arshtcenter.org; 1300 Biscayne Blvd) Showcases jazz from around the world, as well as theater, dance, music, comedy and more.

New World Center
CLASSICAL MUSIC

(Map p460; www.newworldcenter.com; 500 17th St) The new home of the acclaimed New World Symphony is one of the most beautiful buildings in Miami.

Colony Theater
PERFORMING ARTS

(Map p460; www.mbculture.com; 1040 Lincoln Rd) Everything – from off-Broadway productions to ballet and movies – plays in this renovated 1934 art-deco showpiece.

Fillmore Miami Beach
PERFORMING ARTS

(Map p460; www.fillmoremb.com; 1700 Washington Ave) Miami Beach's premier showcase for Broadway shows and headliners.

Sports

Miami hosts pro teams in all four major US team sports.

Miami Dolphins FOOTBALL
(☑ 305-943-8000; www.miamidolphins.com; Sun Life Stadium, 2269 Dan Marino Blvd; tickets from $35) NFL football season runs from August to December.

Florida Marlins BASEBALL
(http://miami.marlins.mlb.com; Marlins Park, 501 Marlins Way; tickets from $15) MLB baseball season is May to September.

Miami Heat BASKETBALL
(☑ 786-777-1000; www.nba.com/heat; American Airlines Arena, 601 Biscayne Blvd; tickets from $20) NBA basketball season is November to April.

Florida Panthers HOCKEY
(☑ 954-835-7825; http://panthers.nhl.com; BB&T Center, 1 Panther Pkwy, Sunrise; tickets from $15) NHL hockey season runs mid-October to mid-April.

🛍 Shopping

Browse for one-of-a-kind and designer items at the South Beach boutiques around Collins Ave between 6th and 9th Sts and along Lincoln Rd mall. For unique items, try Little Havana and the Design District.

Bal Harbour Shops MALL
(www.balharbourshops.com; 9700 Collins Ave) Miami's most elegant mall.

Bayside Marketplace MALL
(www.baysidemarketplace.com; 401 Biscayne Blvd) Near the marina, a buzzy if touristy shopping and entertainment hub.

Books & Books BOOKS
(Map p460; ☑ 305-532-3222; www.booksand-books.com; 927 Lincoln Rd) Best indie bookstore in South Florida; the original location is in Coral Gables at 265 Aragon Ave and there's another in Bal Harbour Shops.

ℹ Information

DANGERS & ANNOYANCES

Miami has a few areas considered dangerous at night: Little Haiti, stretches of the Miami riverfront and Biscayne Blvd, and areas below 5th St in South Beach. Downtown, use caution near the Greyhound station and shantytowns around causeways, bridges and overpasses.

EMERGENCY

Beach Patrol (☑ 305-673-7714)

INTERNET ACCESS

Most hotels offer wi-fi access (as do Starbucks), and libraries also have free internet terminals.

INTERNET RESOURCES

Art Circuits (www.artcircuits.com) Insider info on art events; neighborhood-by-neighborhood gallery maps.

Mango & Lime (www.mangoandlime.net) The best local food blog.

Miami Beach 411 (www.miamibeach411.com) A great general guide for Miami Beach visitors.

MEDIA

Miami Herald (www.miamiherald.com) The city's major English-language daily.

El Nuevo Herald (www.elnuevoherald.com) Spanish-language daily published by the *Miami Herald*.

Miami New Times (www.miaminewtimes.com) Edgy, alternative weekly.

MEDICAL SERVICES

Mount Sinai Medical Center (☑ 305-674-2121, 24hr visitors medical line 305-674-2222; 4300 Alton Rd) The area's best emergency room.

MONEY

Bank of America has branch offices all over Miami and Miami Beach.

TOURIST INFORMATION

Greater Miami & the Beaches Convention & Visitors Bureau (☑ 305-539-3000; www.miamiandbeaches.com; 701 Brickell Ave, 27th fl; ⊘ 8:30am-5pm Mon-Fri) Located in an oddly intimidating high-rise building.

Miami Beach Chamber of Commerce (Map p460; ☑ 305-674-1300; www.miamibeach-chamber.com; 1920 Meridian Ave; ⊘ 9am-5pm Mon-Fri) You can purchase a Meter Card from the **Miami Beach Chamber of Commerce**. Denominations come in $10, $20 and $25 (and meters cost $1 per hour).

🔶 Getting There & Away

Miami International Airport (MIA; www.miami-airport.com) is about 6 miles west of downtown and is accessible by **SuperShuttle** (☑ 305-871-8210; www.supershuttle.com), which costs about $21 to South Beach.

Greyhound (☑ 800-231-2222; www.grey-hound.com) serves all the major cities in Florida with four stations in Miami; check their website to see which location is best for you.

Amtrak (☑ 800-872-7245, 305-835-1222; www.amtrak.com; 8303 NW 37th Ave) has a main Miami terminal. The **Tri-Rail** (☑ 800-874-7245; www.tri-rail.com) commuter system serves Miami (with a free transfer to Miami's transit system) and MIA, Fort Lauderdale and its airport, and West Palm Beach and its airport ($11.55 round-trip).

❶ Getting Around

Metro-Dade Transit (☎305-891-3131; www.miamidade.gov/transit/routes.asp; tickets $2) runs the local Metrobus and Metrorail ($2), as well as the free Metromover monorail serving downtown.

Fort Lauderdale

Fort Lauderdale was once known as spring-break party central, but like the drunken teens who once littered the beach, the town has grown up and moved on. It's now a stylish, sophisticated city known more for museums, Venice-style waterways, yachting and open-air cafes than wet T-shirt contests and beer bongs. It's also a very popular gay and lesbian destination, along with most of South Florida. And the beach is as lovely as always.

For local information, head to the visitor bureau (☎800-227-8669, 954-765-4466; www.sunny.org; 100 E Broward Blvd, Suite 200; ⊗8:30-5pm Mon-Fri).

◉ Sights & Activities

Fort Lauderdale Beach & Promenade
BEACH

Fort Lauderdale's promenade – a wide, brick, palm-tree-dotted pathway swooping along the beach and A1A – is a magnet for runners, in-line skaters, walkers and cyclists. The white-sand beach is one of the nation's cleanest and best, stretching 7 miles to Lauderdale-by-the-Sea.

Museum of Art
MUSEUM

(www.moafl.org; 1 E Las Olas Blvd; adult/child 6-17 $10/5; ⊗10am-5pm Mon-Sat, noon-5pm Sun) A curvaceous Florida standout known for its William Glackens collection (among Glackens fans) and its exciting exhibitions (among everyone else).

Museum of Discovery & Science
MUSEUM

(www.mods.org; 401 SW 2nd St; adult/child 2-12 $14/12; ⊗10am-5pm Mon-Sat, noon-6pm Sun; ⁂) A 52ft kinetic-energy sculpture greets you, and fun exhibits include Gizmo City and Runways to Rockets – where it actually *is* rocket science. Plus there's an Everglades exhibit and IMAX theater.

Bonnet House
HISTORIC HOME

(www.bonnethouse.org; 900 N Birch Rd; adult/child $20/16, grounds only $10; ⊗9am-4pm Tue-Sat, from 11am Sun) Wandering the 35 acres of lush, subtropical gardens, you might just spot the resident Brazilian squirrel monkeys. The art-filled house is open to guided tours only.

★ Carrie B
BOAT TOURS

(☎954-642-1601, 888-238-9805; www.carriebcruises.com; tours adult/child $23/13) Hop aboard this replica 19th-century riverboat for a narrated 90-minute 'lifestyles of the rich and famous' tour of the ginormous mansions along the Intracoastal and New River.

Water Taxi
BOAT TOURS

(www.watertaxi.com; all-day pass adult/child $20/13) The fun, yellow Water Taxi travels the canals and waterways between 17th St to the south, Atlantic Blvd/Pompano Beach to the north, the Riverfront to the west and the Atlantic Ocean to the east. A daily pass entitles you to unlimited rides.

🛏 Sleeping

The area from Rio Mar St in the south to Vistamar St in the north, and from Hwy A1A in the east to Bayshore Dr in the west, offers the highest concentration of accommodations in all price ranges. Check out the CVB's list of superior small lodgings (www.sunny.org/ssl).

Shell Motel
MOTEL $

(☎954-463-1723; www.sableresorts.com; 3030 Bayshore Dr; r/ste from $90/150; P🛜❄) One of six modest motels owned by the same company, this sweet Old Florida–style spot has bright, clean rooms surrounding a small pool. Splash out for a roomy suite.

Riverside Hotel
HOTEL $$

(☎954-467-0671; www.riversidehotel.com; 620 E Las Olas Blvd; r $129-224; P❄🛜❄⛱) This Fort Lauderdale landmark – fabulously located downtown on Las Olas – has three room types: more modern rooms in the newer tower, restored rooms in the original property and the more old-fashioned 'classic' rooms.

★ Pillars
B&B $$$

(☎954-467-9639; www.pillarshotel.com; 111 N Birch Rd; r $179-520; P❄🛜❄) From the harp in the sitting area to the private balconies and the intimate prearranged dinners for two, this tiny boutique B&B radiates hushed good taste. A block from the beach, facing one of the best sunsets in town.

🍴 Eating

★ Gran Forno
ITALIAN $

(www.gran-forno.com; 1235 E Las Olas Blvd; mains $6-12; ⊗7am-6pm Tue-Sun) The best lunch spot in downtown Fort Lauderdale is this delightfully old-school Milanese-style

FLORIDA FORT LAUDERDALE

GAY & LESBIAN FORT LAUDERDALE

Sure, Miami's South Beach is a mecca for gay travelers, but Fort Lauderdale has long been nipping at the high heels of its southern neighbor. For information on local gay life, visit www.gayftlauderdale.com. Other resources that cover South Florida include the glossy weekly Hot Spots (www.hotspotsmagazine.com), the insanely comprehensive www.jumponmarkslist.com, and www.sunny.org/glbt.

bakery and cafe: warm crusty pastries, bubbling pizzas, and fat golden loaves of ciabatta, sliced and stuffed with ham, roast peppers, pesto and other delicacies.

11th Street Annex AMERICAN $

(http://twouglysisters.com; 14 SW 11th St; lunch $9; ☺ 11:30am-2pm Mon-Fri) In this off-the-beaten-path peach cottage, the owners serve whatever strikes their fancy: perhaps brie mac 'n' cheese, chicken confit, and sour cream chocolate cake. Most of the vegetables are grown from the cottage's garden.

★ **Le Tub** BURGERS, AMERICAN $$

(www.theletub.com; 1100 N Ocean Dr, Hollywood; mains $9-20; ☺ 11am-1am Mon-Fri, noon-2am Sat & Sun; ☀) Decorated exclusively with flotsam collected over four years of daybreak jogs along Hollywood Beach, this quirky intracoastal-side institution features multiple tiers of outdoor seating, plus bathtubs and toilet bowls (!) sprouting lush plants. The thing to order here is the sirloin burger – it's bigger than your head (seriously) and is routinely named 'Best in America' by the likes of *GQ*. Expect a wait, both for seating and for cooking time. It's worth it.

Casablanca Cafe MEDITERRANEAN $$$

(☎954-764-3500; www.casablancacafeonline.com; 3049 Alhambra St; mains $10-38; ☺ 11:30am-2am) Try to score a seat on the upstairs balcony of this Moroccan-style home where Mediterranean-inspired food and Florida-style ocean views are served. Live music Wednesday through Sunday.

Rustic Inn SEAFOOD $$$

(☎954-584-1637; www.rusticinn.com; 4331 Anglers Ave; mains $14-30; ☺ 11:30am-10:30pm Mon-Sat, noon-9:30pm Sun) Hungry locals at this messy, noisy crab-house use wooden mallets at long, newspaper-covered tables to get at the Dungeness crab, blue crab and golden crab drenched in garlic.

🍸 Drinking & Entertainment

Bars generally stay open until 4am on weekends and 2am during the week. Meander the Riverwalk (www.goriverwalk.com) along the New River, where you'll find the alfresco mall Las Olas Riverfront (SW 1st Ave at Las Olas Blvd), with stores, restaurants, a movie theater and entertainment.

Elbo Room BAR

(www.elboroom.com; 241 S Fort Lauderdale Beach Blvd; ☺ 10am-2am) Featured in the movie *Where the Boys Are,* Elbo Room hangs onto its somewhat seedy reputation as one of the oldest and diviest bars around.

Lulu's Bait Shack BAR

(www.lulusbaitshack.com; 17 S Atlantic Blvd; ☺ 11am-1am) Get lured in by the buckets of beer, bowls of mussels and fishbowl drinks at the ocean's edge.

ℹ️ Getting There & Around

The **Fort Lauderdale-Hollywood International Airport** (☎ 866-435-9355, 954-359-6100; www.broward.org/airport; 320 Terminal Dr) is served by more than 35 airlines, some with non-stop flights from Europe. A taxi from the airport to downtown costs around $20.

The **Greyhound station** (www.greyhound.com; 515 NE 3rd St) is four blocks from Broward Central Terminal, with multiple daily services. The **train station** (200 SW 21st Tce) serves **Amtrak** (☎ 800-872-7245; www.amtrak.com; 200 SW 21st Tce), and the **Tri-Rail** (www.tri-rail.com; 6151 N Andrews Ave) has services to Miami and Palm Beach.

Hail a **Sun Trolley** (www.suntrolley.com; fare 50¢) for rides between downtown, the beach, Las Olas and the Riverfront.

Palm Beach & Around

Palm Beach isn't all yachts and mansions – but just about. This is where railroad baron Henry Flagler built his winter retreat, and it's also home to Donald Trump's Mar-a-Lago (1100 S Ocean Blvd). In other words, if you're looking for middle-class tourism or Florida kitsch, keep driving. Contact the Palm Beach County Convention & Visitor Bureau (☎800-554-7256; www.palmbeachfl.com; 1555 Palm Beach Lakes Blvd) in West Palm Beach for area information and maps.

Boca Raton

Halfway between Fort Lauderdale and Palm Beach is this largely residential stretch of picturesque coast that's been preserved from major development. For a great taste, hike the elevated boardwalks of the Gumbo Limbo Nature Center (☑561-544-8605; www.gumbolimbo.org; 1801 N Ocean Blvd; admission by donation; ☺9am-4pm Mon-Sat, noon-4pm Sun; 🚻), a beautiful wetlands preserve; also visit its sea turtle rehabilitation center. Another good reason to stop is the outstanding Boca Raton Museum of Art (☑561-392-2500; www.bocamuseum.org; 501 Plaza Real; adult/student $8/5; ☺10am-5pm Tue-Fri, noon-5pm Sat & Sun), with a permanent collection of contemporary works by Picasso, Matisse, Warhol and more. The museum is in Mizner Park (www.miznerpark.org), a ritzy outdoor mall with stores, restaurants and regular free concerts.

Palm Beach

About 30 miles north of Boca Raton are Palm Beach and West Palm Beach. The two towns have flip-flopped the traditional coastal hierarchy: Palm Beach, the beach town, is more upscale, while West Palm Beach on the mainland is younger and livelier.

Palm Beach is an enclave of the ultra-wealthy, especially during its winter 'social season,' so the main tourist activities involve gawking at oceanfront mansions and window-shopping the boutiques along the aptly named Worth Avenue (www.worth-avenue.com). You can also visit one of the country's most fascinating museums, the resplendent Flagler Museum (www.flaglermuseum.us; 1 Whitehall Way; adult/child $18/10; ☺10am-5pm Tue-Sat, noon-5pm Sun), housed in the railroad magnate's 1902 winter estate, Whitehall Mansion. The elaborate 55-room palace is an evocative immersion in Gilded Age opulence.

Flagler's opulent oceanfront 1896 hotel, the Breakers (☑888-273-2537, 561-655-6611; www.thebreakers.com; 1 S County Rd; r $270-1250, ste $510-5500; 🅿@🛜🏊), is a super-luxurious world unto itself, modeled after Rome's Villa Medici. It encompasses two golf courses, 10 tennis courts, a three-pool Mediterranean beach club and a trove of restaurants.

For a low-end treat, kick it Formica-style with an egg cream and a low-cal platter at the lunch counter in Green's Pharmacy (151 N County Rd; mains $4-11; ☺8am-6pm Mon-Fri, to 4pm Sat).

West Palm Beach

Henry Flagler initially developed West Palm Beach as a working-class community to support Palm Beach. Today West Palm works harder, plays harder and is simply cooler and more relaxed. It's a groovy place to explore.

Florida's largest museum, the Norton Museum of Art (☑561-832-5196; www.norton.org; 1451 S Olive Ave; adult/child $12/5; ☺10am-5pm Tue-Sat, to 9pm Thu, 11am-5pm Sun) houses an enormous collection of American and European modern masters and Impressionists, along with a large Buddha head presiding over an impressive Asian art collection. If you like that, you'll love the outdoor Ann Norton Sculpture Garden (www.ansg.org; 253 Barcelona Rd; admission adult/under 5 $7/free; ☺10am-4pm Wed-Sun). This serene collection of sculptures sprinkled among verdant gardens is a real West Palm gem.

If you have children, take them to Lion Country Safari (www.lioncountrysafari.com; 2003 Lion Country Safari Rd; adult/child $28.50/21; ☺9:30am-5:30pm; 🚻), the country's first cageless drive-through safari, where around 900 creatures roam freely around 500 acres.

The coolest lodging in town is Hotel Biba (☑561-832-0094; www.hotelbiba.com; 320 Belvedere Rd; r $69-129; 🅿🛜🏊) 🅿. The retro-funky exterior looks like a cute 1950s motel, but the rooms have a modern, boutique style that would be right at home in Miami's SoBe.

Much of the action centers around City-Place (www.cityplace.com; 700 S Rosemary Ave; ☺10am-10pm Mon-Sat, noon-6pm Sun), a European village-style outdoor mall with splashing fountains and a slew of dining and entertainment options. Clematis St also has several worthy bars, live-music clubs and restaurants, and every Thursday Clematis by Night (www.clematisbynight.net) hosts friendly outdoor concerts. If you're hungry, try Rocco's Tacos & Tequila Bar (www.roccostacos.com; 224 Clematis St; mains $12-23; ☺11:30am-11pm Sun-Wed, to midnight Thu-Sat), a saucy *nuevo* Mexican restaurant with funky decor, tableside guacamole and 175 different kinds of tequila – no wonder it's so loud in here!

Admirably servicing its migration of snowbirds is Palm Beach International Airport (PBI; ☑561-471-7420; www.pbia.org), 2.5 miles west of downtown West Palm Beach. The downtown Tri-Rail station (☑800-875-7245; www.tri-rail.com; 203 S Tamarind Ave) also serves as the Amtrak station (☑561-832-6169; www.amtrak.com; 209 S Tamarind Ave).

FLORIDA PALM BEACH & AROUND

The Everglades

Contrary to what you may have heard, the Everglades isn't a swamp. Or at least, it's not *only* a swamp. It's most accurately characterized as a wet prairie – grasslands that happen to be flooded most of the year. Nor is it stagnant. In the wet season, a horizon-wide river creeps ever-so-slowly beneath the rustling saw grass and around the subtly raised cypress and hardwood hammocks toward the ocean. The Everglades are indeed filled with alligators – and perhaps a few dead bodies, as *CSI: Miami* would have it. Yet its beauty is not measured in fear or geological drama, but in the timeless, slow Jurassic flap of a great blue heron as it glides over its vast and shockingly gentle domain.

Which is one reason that exploring the Everglades by foot, bicycle, canoe and kayak (or camping) is so much more satisfying than by noisy, vibrating airboat. There is an incredible variety of wonderful creatures to see within this unique, subtropical wilderness, and there are accessible entrances that, at the cost of a few hours, get you easily into the Everglades' soft heart.

The Everglades has two seasons: the summer wet season and the winter dry season. Winter – from December to April – is the prime time to visit: the weather is mild and pleasant, and the wildlife is out in abundance. In summer – May through October – it's stiflingly hot, humid and buggy, with frequent afternoon thunderstorms. In addition, as water sources spread out, so the animals disperse.

Everglades National Park

While the Everglades has a history dating back to prehistoric times, the park wasn't founded until 1947. It's considered the most endangered national park in the USA, but the Comprehensive Everglades Restoration Plan (www.evergladesplan.org) has been enacted to undo some of the damage done by draining and development.

The park has three main entrances and areas: in the south along Rte 9336 through Homestead and Florida City to Ernest Coe Visitor Center and, at road's end, Flamingo; along the Tamiami Trail/Hwy 41 in the north to Shark Valley; and on the Gulf Coast near Everglades City.

The main park entry points have visitor centers where you can get maps, camp-ing permits and ranger information. You only need to pay the entrance fee (per car/pedestrian $10/5 for seven days) once to access all points.

Even in winter it's almost impossible to avoid mosquitoes, but they're ferocious in summer: bring *strong* repellent. Alligators are also prevalent. As obvious as it sounds, never, ever feed them: it's illegal and is a sure way to provoke attacks. Four types of poisonous snakes call the Everglades home; avoid all snakes, just in case, and wear long, thick socks and lace-up boots.

◯ Sights & Activities

Shark Valley   PARK
(☑ 305-221-8776;   www.nps.gov/ever/planyour-visit/svdirections.htm; 36000 SW 8th St; car/cyclist $10/5; ☉ 9:15am-5:15pm) One of the best places to dip your toe into the Everglades (figuratively speaking) is Shark Valley, where you can take an excellent two-hour **tram tour** (☑ 305-221-8455; www.sharkvalleytramtours.com; adult/child $20/12.75) along a 15-mile asphalt trail and see copious amounts of alligators in the winter months. Not only do you get to experience the park from the shady comfort of a breezy tram, but the tours are narrated by knowledgeable park rangers who give a fascinating overview of the Everglades. The pancake-flat trail is perfect for bicycles, which can be rented at the entrance for $7.50 per hour. Bring water with you.

Ernest Coe Visitor Center   PARK
(☑ 305-242-7700; www.nps.gov/ever; Hwy 9336; ☉ 9am-5pm) Those with a day to give the Glades could start with this visitor center in the south. It has excellent, museum-quality exhibits and tons of activity info: the road accesses numerous short trails and lots of top-drawer canoeing opportunities. Call for a schedule of fun ranger-led programs, such as the two-hour 'slough slog.' At the nearby **Royal Palm Area** (☑ 305-242-7700; Hwy 9336), you can catch two short trails: the **Anhinga Trail** is great for wildlife spotting, especially alligators in winter; and the **Gumbo-Limbo Trail** showcases plants and trees.

Flamingo Visitor Center   PARK
(☑ 239-695-2945; ☉ 8am-4:30pm) From Royal Palm, Hwy 9336 cuts through the belly of the park for 38 miles until it reaches the isolated Flamingo Visitor Center, which has maps of canoeing and hiking trails. Call ahead about the status of facilities: the former Flamingo Lodge was wiped out by hurricanes in 2005.

Flamingo Marina (✆239-695-3101; ✪store hours 7am-5:30pm Mon-Fri, from 6am Sat & Sun) has reopened and offers backcountry boat tours and kayak/canoe rentals for self-guided trips along the coast.

Gulf Coast Visitor Center   PARK
(✆239-695-3311; 815 Oyster Bar Lane, off Hwy 29, Everglades City; ✪9am-4:30pm) Those with more time should also consider visiting the northwestern edge of the Everglades, where the mangroves and waterways of the 10,000 Islands offer incredible canoeing and kayaking opportunities, and great boat tours with a chance to spot dolphins. The visitor center is next to the marina, with rentals (from $13 per hour) and various guided boat trips (from $25). Everglades City also has other private tour operators who can get you camping in the 10,000 Islands.

⊨ Sleeping

Everglades National Park has two developed campgrounds, both of which have water, toilets and grills. The best are the first-come, first-served sites at Long Pine Key (✆305-242-7873; campsite/RV site $16/30), just west of Royal Palm Visitor Center; reserve ahead for campsites at Flamingo (✆877-444-6777; www.recreation.gov; campsite/RV site $16/30), which have cold-water showers and electricity. Backcountry camping (permit $10, plus per person per night $2) is throughout the park and includes beach sites, ground sites and chickees (covered wooden platforms above the water). A permit from the visitor center is required.

❶ Getting There & Around

The largest subtropical wilderness in the continental USA is easily accessible from Miami. The Glades, which comprise the 80 southernmost miles of Florida, are bound by the Atlantic Ocean to the east and the Gulf of Mexico to the west. The Tamiami Trail (US Hwy 41) goes east–west, parallel to the more northern (and less interesting) Alligator Alley (I-75).

You need a car to properly enter the Everglades and once you're in, wearing a good pair of walking boots is essential to penetrate the interior. Having a canoe or kayak helps as well; these can be rented from outfits inside and outside of the park, or else you can seek out guided canoe and kayak tours. Bicycles are well suited to the flat roads of Everglades National Park, particularly in the area between Ernest Coe and Flamingo Point, but they're useless off the highway. In addition, the road shoulders in the park tend to be dangerously small.

Around the Everglades

Coming from Miami, the gateway town of Homestead on the east side of the park can make a good base, especially if you're headed for the Keys.

Biscayne National Park

Just south of Miami (and east of Homestead), this national park is only 5% land. The 95% that's water is Biscayne National Underwater Park (✆305-230-1100; www.nps.gov/bisc), containing a portion of the world's third-largest coral reef, where manatees, dolphins and sea turtles highlight a vibrant, diverse ecosystem. Get general park information from Dante Fascell Visitor Center (✆305-230-7275; www.nps.gov/bisc; 9700 SW 328th St; ✪8:30am-5pm). The park offers canoe/kayak rentals, snorkel and dive trips, and popular three-hour glass-bottom boat tours; all require reservations.

Homestead & Florida City

Homestead and Florida City don't look like much, but they have some true Everglades highlights. Don't miss Robert Is Here (www.robertishere.com; 19200 SW 344th St, Homestead; ✪8am-7pm Nov-Aug) – a kitschy Old Florida institution with a petting zoo, live music and crazy-good milk shakes.

The Homestead–Florida City area has no shortage of chain motels along Krome Ave. For a seriously good hostel experience, consider the Everglades International Hostel

CORAL CASTLE

'You will be seeing unusual accomplishment' reads the inscription on the rough-hewn quarried wall. That's an understatement. Exemplifying all that is weird and wacky about South Florida, Coral Castle (✆305-248-6345; www.coralcastle.com; 28655 S Dixie Hwy; adult/child $15/7; ✪8am-6pm Sun-Thu, to 8pm Fri & Sat) is a unique monument to unrequited love. Of course, what's an altar-jilted Latvian to do, except move to Florida and hand carve, unseen, in the dead of night, a rock compound that includes a 'throne room,' a sun dial, a stone stockade and a revolving boulder gate that engineers to this day cannot explain...

(☎ 800-372-3874, 305-248-1122; www.everglade-shostel.com; 20 SW 2nd Ave, Florida City; camping $18, dm $28, d $61-75, ste $125-225; ⓟ❄️🛜🐾). Rooms are good value, the vibe is very friendly, but the back gardens – wow. It's a fantasia of natural delights, and the hostel conducts some of the best Everglades tours around. For a more personal touch than the chain hotels, book a room at the historic **Redland Hotel** (☎ 800-595-1904; www.hotel-redland.com; 5 S Flagler Ave, Homestead; r $100-140; ⓟ🛜). Homestead's modestly quaint main street, along Krome Ave, is the central restaurant and shopping district.

Tamiami Trail

The Tamiami Trail/Hwy 41 starts in Miami and beelines to Naples along the north edge of Everglades National Park. Just past the entrance to the Everglades' Shark Valley is **Miccosukee Village** (www.miccosukee.com; MM 70 Hwy 41; adult/child/5yr and under $10/6/ free; ☺ 9am-5pm), an informative, entertaining open-air museum showcasing Miccosukee culture. Tour traditional homes, attend performances (from dance to gator wrestling), take an airboat ride ($16) and peruse handmade crafts in the gift store.

About 20 miles west of Shark Valley, you reach the **Oasis Visitor Center** (☎ 941-695-1201; ☺ 8am-4:30pm Mon-Fri; 🚻) for 1139-sq-mile **Big Cypress National Preserve** (☎ 239-695-4758; 33000 Tamiami Trail E; ☺ 8:30am-4:30pm). Good exhibits and short trails bring the region's ecology to life, though the adventurous might consider tackling a portion of the **Florida National Scenic Trail** (www.nps.gov/bicy/planyourvisit/florida-trail.htm); 31 miles cut through Big Cypress.

Half a mile east of the visitor center, drop into the **Big Cypress Gallery** (☎ 941-695-2428; www.clydebutcher.com; Tamiami Trail; ☺ 10am-5pm Wed-Mon) 🖌, displaying Clyde Butcher's work; his large-scale B&W landscape photographs spotlight the region's unusual beauty.

The tiny town of **Ochopee** is home to the country's smallest post office. If that's not enough to make you pull over, then stop into the eccentric **Skunk Ape Research Headquarters** (☎ 239-695-2275; www.skunkape.info; 40904 Tamiami Trail E; ☺ 7am-7pm, 'zoo' closes around 4pm), dedicated to tracking Bigfoot's legendary, if stinky, Everglades kin. It's goofy but sincere. Based out of Skunk Ape HQ, **Everglades Adventure Tours** (EAT; ☎ 800-504-6554; www.evergladesadventuretours.com; tours from $69) offers knowledgeable swamp hikes, 'safaris,' airboats and, best of all, trips being poled around in a canoe or skiff.

Finally, just east of Ochopee, is the quintessential 1950s-style swamp shack, **Joanie's Blue Crab Cafe** (joaniesbluecrab-cafe.com; Tamiami Trail; mains $9-17; ☺ 9am-5pm), with open rafters, colorful, shellacked picnic tables and a swamp dinner of gator nuggets and fritters.

A KINDER, GENTLER WILDERNESS ENCOUNTER

As you explore Florida's outdoors and encounter its wildlife, keep in mind the following guidelines.

Airboats and swamp buggies For exploring wetlands, airboats are better than big-wheeled buggies, but nonmotorized (and silent) canoes and kayaks are least-damaging and disruptive.

Wild dolphins Captive dolphins are typically rescued animals already acclimated to humans. However, federal law makes it illegal to feed, pursue or touch wild dolphins in the ocean.

Manatee swims When swimming near manatees, a federally protected endangered species, look but don't touch. 'Passive observation' is the standard.

Feeding wild animals In a word, don't. Acclimating wild animals to humans usually leads to the animal's death, whether because of accidents or aggression.

Sea-turtle nesting sites It's a federal crime to approach nesting sea turtles or hatchling runs. Observe beach warning signs. If you encounter nesting turtles, keep your distance and no flash photos.

Coral-reef etiquette Never touch the coral reef. It's that simple. Coral polyps are living organisms. Touching or breaking coral creates openings for infection and disease.

Everglades City

This small town at the edge of the park makes a good base for exploring the 10,000 Islands region. With large renovated rooms, Everglades City Motel (☑800-695-8353, 239-695-4244; www.evergladescitymotel.com; 310 Collier Ave; r from $80; ❈ 🤶) is exceptionally good value, and the fantastically friendly staff can hook you up with any kind of tour. The same can be said for the Ivey House Bed & Breakfast (☑877-567-0679, 239-695-3299; www.iveyhouse.com; 107 Camellia St; lodge $74-120, inn $99-209; ❈🤶). Choose between basic lodge accommodations or somewhat sprucer inn rooms, then book some of the region's best nature trips with the on-site North American Canoe Tours (NACT; ☑877-567-0679, 239-695-3299; www.ever-gladesadventures.com; 107 Camellia St, Ivey House Bed & Breakfast; tours $124, canoe rentals $25-35; ☺Nov–mid-Apr). Ask about room/tour packages. For dinner, try the Seafood Depot (102 Collier Ave; mains $6-20; ☺10:30am-9pm), a haven of fried seafood and a great place to sample gator and frog's legs; just douse with Tabasco and devour.

Florida Keys

Before Henry Flagler completed his railroad in 1912, which connected the Keys to the mainland, this 126-mile string of islands was just a series of untethered bumps of land accessible only by boat. (Little surprise, then, that their early economies were built on piracy, smuggling, ship salvaging and fishing.) Flagler's railroad was destroyed by a hurricane in 1935, but what remained of its bridges allowed the Overseas Hwy to be completed in 1938. Now, streams of travelers swarm down from the mainland to indulge in the alluring jade-green waters, laid-back island lifestyle, great fishing, and idyllic snorkeling and diving.

The islands are typically divided into the Upper Keys (Key Largo to Islamorada), Middle Keys and Lower Keys (from Little Duck Key). Yet far from petering out, they crescendo at highway's end, reaching their grand finale in Key West – the Keys' gloriously unkempt, bawdy, freak-loving exclamation point.

Many addresses in the Keys are noted by their proximity to mile markers (indicated as MM), which start at MM 126 in Florida City and count down to MM 0 in Key West.

They also might indicate whether they're 'oceanside' (the south side of the highway) or 'bayside' (which is north).

The Florida Keys & Key West Visitors Bureau (☑800-352-5397; www.fla-keys.com) has information; also check www.keysnews.com.

Key Largo

Stretching from Key Largo to Islamorada, the Upper Keys are cluttered with touristy shops and motels. At first you can't even see the water from the highway, then – bam – you're in Islamorada and water is everywhere.

Key Largo has long been romanticized in movies and song, so it can be a shock to arrive and find...no Bogart, no Bacall, no love-sick Sade. Yes, Key Largo is underwhelming, a sleepy island and town with middling views. That is, if all you do is stick to the highway and keep your head above water. On the side roads you can find some of those legendary island idiosyncracies, and dive underwater for the most amazing coral reef in the continental US.

For maps and brochures, visit the chamber of commerce (☑305-451-1414; www.key-largo.org; MM 106 bayside; ☺9am-6pm), located in a yellow building just past Seashell World (not to be confused with the *other* yellow visitor center at 10624 that makes reservations and works on commission).

🏃 Activities

John Pennekamp Coral
Reef State Park   PARK
(www.pennekamppark.com; MM 102.6 oceanside; car/motorcycle/cyclist or pedestrian $8/4/2; ☺8am-sunset, aquarium 8am-5pm; 🖰) The USA's first underwater park, Pennekamp contains the third largest coral barrier reef in the world – the only one in the US – and is home to a panoply of sea life and the oft-photographed statue *Christ of the Deep*. Your options for seeing the reef are many: take a 2½-hour glass-bottom boat tour (☑305-451-6300; adult/child $24/17; ☺9:15am, 12:15pm & 3:15pm) on a thoroughly modern 65ft catamaran. Dive in with a snorkeling trip (☑305-451-6300; adult/child $30/25) or two-tank diving trip (☑305-451-6322; $55); half-day trips leave twice daily, usually around 9am and 1pm. Or go DIY and rent a canoe or kayak (per hour single/double $12/17) and journey through a 3-mile network of water trails. Call the park for boat-rental information.

African Queen
BOAT TOUR

(☑ 305-451-8080; www.africanqueenflkeys.com; MM 100 oceanside at the Holiday Inn Marina; canal cruise $49, dinner cruise $89) For years, the African Queen – the steamboat used in the 1951 movie starring Humphrey Bogart and Katherine Hepburn – has been docked in Key Largo, but the owners have restored her to her former, er, splendor, and now offer canal and dinner cruises. Canal cruises are every two hours from 10am to 6pm; best to call for reservations: the tiny vessel only accommodates six.

Florida Bay Outfitters
KAYAKING

(☑ 305-451-3018; www.kayakfloridakeys.com; MM 104 bayside; kayak rental per half-day $40) See the keys from the water: rent a kayak or canoe or catch a guided trip.

Horizon Divers
DIVING

(☑ 305-453-3535; www.horizondivers.com; 100 Ocean Dr, off MM 100 oceanside; snorkel/scuba trips $50/80) Get beneath the surface on a scuba or snorkel trip with Horizon's friendly crew.

🛏 Sleeping

In addition to luxe resorts, Key Largo has loads of bright, cheery motels and camping.

John Pennekamp Coral Reef State Park
CAMPGROUND $

(☑ 800-326-3521; www.pennekamppark.com; campsite/RV site both $36; P) Sleep with–er, *near* the fishes at one of the 47 coral-reef-adjacent sites here. Camping's popular; reserve well in advance.

Largo Lodge
HOTEL $$

(☑ 305-451-0424; www.largolodge.com; MM 102 bayside; cottages $150-265; P) These six charming, sunny cottages with their own private beach are surrounded by palm trees, tropical flowers and lots of roaming birds, for a taste of Florida in the good old days.

Key Largo House Boatel
HOTEL $$

(☑ 305-766-0871; www.keylargohouseboatel.com; Shoreland Dr, MM 103.5 oceanside; houseboat small/medium/large from $75/100/150) These five houseboats are a steal. The largest is incredibly spacious, sleeping six people comfortably. The boats are right on the docks, so there's no possibility of being isolated from land (or booze). Call for directions.

Kona Kai Resort & Gallery
HOTEL $$$

(☑ 305-852-7200; www.konakairesort.com; MM 97.8 bayside; r $199-439; P ✳ 🗑 ☀) This intimate hideaway features 11 airy rooms and suites (with full kitchens). They're all bright and comfortable, though some feel a little old-fashioned. Tons of activities, plus its own beach.

🍴 Eating & Drinking

Mrs Mac's Kitchen
AMERICAN $

(☑ 305-451-3722; www.mrsmacskitchen.com; MM 99.4 bayside; breakfast & lunch $8-12, dinner $9-22; ⊙ 7am-9:30pm Mon-Sat) This cute roadside diner bedecked with rusty license plates serves classic highway food such as burgers and fish baskets. Look for a second location just half a mile south on the opposite side of the road.

Alabama Jack's
SEAFOOD, BAR $

(http://alabamajacks.com; 58000 Card Sound Rd; mains $7-14; ⊙ 11am-7pm) On the back road between Key Largo and Florida City (about 15 miles north of Key Largo), this funky open-air joint draws an eclectic booze-hungry crowd of genuine Keys characters. Try the rave-worthy conch fritters.

★ Key Largo Conch House
FUSION $$

(☑ 305-453-4844; www.keylargocoffeehouse.com; MM 100.2 oceanside; mains $8-26; ⊙ 8am-10pm) Now *this* feels like the islands: Conch architecture, tropical foliage, and crab and conch dishes that ease you off the mainland.

Fish House
SEAFOOD $$

(☑ 305-451-4665; www.fishhouse.com; MM 102.4 oceanside; mains $9-24; ⊙ 11:30am-10pm; 🖰) Delivers on its name, serving fish, fish and more fish that's as fresh as it gets. Your main decision: fried, broiled, jerked, blackened or grilled?

Islamorada

It sounds like an island, but Islamorada is actually a string of several islands, the epicenter of which is Upper Matecumbe Key. It's right around here that the view starts to open up, allowing you to fully appreciate the fact that you're surrounded by water. Several little nooks of beach are easily accessible, providing scenic rest stops. Housed in an old red caboose, the chamber of commerce (☑ 305-664-4503; www.islamoradachamber.com; MM 83.2 bayside; ⊙ 9am-5pm Mon-Fri, to 4pm Sat, to 3pm Sun) has area information.

👁 Sights & Activities

Billed as 'the Sportfishing Capital of the World,' Islamorada is an angler's paradise.

Indeed, most of its highlights involve getting on or in the sea.

Indian Key Historic State Park   ISLAND

(☑ 305-664-2540; www.floridastateparks.org/indiankey; MM 78.5 oceanside; per person $2.50; ☺ 8am-sunset) A few hundred yards offshore, this peaceful island contains the crumbling foundations of a 19th-century settlement that was wiped out by Native Americans during the Second Seminole War. It's a moody ramble, accessible only by kayak or boat, which you can rent from Robbie's Marina.

Lignumvitae Key
Botanical State Park   ISLAND

(☑ 305-664-2540; www.floridastateparks.org/lignumvitaekey; admission $2.50, tour $2; ☺ tours 10am & 2pm Fri-Sun) It'll feel like just you and about a jillion mosquitoes on this bayside island park, with virgin tropical forests and the 1919 Matheson House. Come for the shipwrecked isolation. Robbie's Marina offers boat rentals and tours.

Florida Keys History
of Diving Museum   MUSEUM

(☑ 305-664-9737; www.divingmuseum.org; MM 83; adult/child $12/6; ☺ 10am-5pm) Don't miss this collection of diving paraphernalia from around the world, including diving 'suits' and technology from the 19th century. This charmingly eccentric museum embodies the quirky Keys.

Windley Key Fossil Reef
Geological State Site   PARK

(☑ 305-664-2540; www.floridastateparks.org/windleykey; MM 85.5 oceanside; admission $2.50, tour $2; ☺ 8am-5pm, closed Tue & Wed) Wander through layer after layer of geological history in the quarry, with 8ft walls of fossilized coral. Tours are offered Friday to Sunday at 10am and 2pm.

Anne's Beach   BEACH

(MM 73.5 oceanside) The area's best public beach; shaded picnic tables and a ribbon of sand.

★ Robbie's Marina   MARINA

(☑ 305-664-8070; www.robbies.com; MM 77.5 bayside; half-day kayak & canoe rentals $40-75; ☺ 9am-8pm) This marina/roadside attraction offers the buffet of boating options: fishing charters, jet skiing, party boats, ecotours, snorkeling trips, kayak rentals and more (come here to visit the area's island parks). At a minimum, stop to feed the freakishly large tarpon from the dock ($3 per bucket, $1 to watch), and sift the flea market/tourist shop for tacky seaside trinkets.

Theater of the Sea   DOLPHIN ENCOUNTER

(☑ 305-664-2431; www.theaterofthesea.com; MM 84.7 bayside; adult/child 3-10 $30/21; ☺ 9:30am-5pm) Dolphins and sea lions perform in an intimate, close-up setting, and for an extra fee you can meet or swim with them.

🛏 Sleeping

Long Key State
Recreation Area   CAMPGROUND $

(☑ 305-664-4815, 305-326-3521; www.floridastateparks.org/longkey; MM 67.5; campsite/RV site both $38.50) Book as far ahead as possible for the 60 coveted oceanfront campsites in this shady 965-acre park.

Lime Tree Bay Resort Motel   MOTEL $$

(☑ 800-723-4519, 305-664-4740; www.limetreebayresort.com; MM 68.5 bayside; r $135-175, ste $185-395) A plethora of hammocks and lawn chairs provide front-row seats for the spectacular sunsets at this 2.5-acre waterfront hideaway.

Ragged Edge Resort   RESORT $$

(☑ 305-852-5389; www.ragged-edge.com; 243 Treasure Harbor Rd; apt $69-259; P ❄ ⊛) Swim off the docks at this happily unpretentious oceanfront complex off MM 86.5. It has 10 spotless and popular studios and apartments, and a happily comatose vibe.

Casa Morada   HOTEL $$$

(☑ 888-881-3030, 305-664-0044; www.casamorada.com; 136 Madeira Rd, off MM 82.2; ste incl breakfast $279-659; P ❄ ⊚ ⊛) Come for a welcome dash of South Beach sophistication mixed with laid-back Keys style. The slick bar is a great oceanside sunset perch.

🍴 Eating

★ Midway Cafe   CAFE $

(☑ 305-664-2622; 80499 Overseas Hwy; menu items $2-11; ☺ 7am-3pm Thu-Tue, to 2pm Sun; ⊛) Celebrate your Keys adventure with a friendly cup of joe, a smoothie or a treat from the overflowing bakery case. The lovely folks who run this art-filled cafe roast their own beans and make destination-worthy baked goods.

Hog Heaven   BAR $$

(☑ 305-664-9669; MM 83 oceanside; mains $10-18; ☺ 11am-4am) From sandwiches and salads to chicken wings and steaks, the diverse menu rocks. Come during happy hour (3pm to 7pm) and bring a designated driver; the drinks are cheap and plentiful.

Morada Bay
AMERICAN $$$

(☎ 305-664-0604; www.moradabay-restaurant. com; MM 81.6 bayside; mains $14-33; ⊙ 11:30am-10pm) Grab a table under a palm tree on the white-sand beach and sip a rum drink with your fresh seafood for a lovely, easy-going Caribbean experience. Don't miss the monthly full-moon party.

Grassy Key

To reach Grassy Key in the Middle Keys, you enjoy a vivid sensation of island-hopping, ending with the biggest hop, the Seven Mile Bridge, one of the world's longest causeways.

◉ Sights

Dolphin Research Center WILDLIFE RESERVE
(☎ 305-289-1121; www.dolphins.org; MM 59 bayside; adult/child under 4yr/child 4-12yr/senior $20/free/15/17.50, swim program $180-650; ⊙ 9am-4pm) By far the most popular activity on Grassy Key is swimming with the descendants of Flipper. Of all the dolphin swimming spots in the Keys, this one stands out; the dolphins are free to leave the grounds and a lot of marine-biology research goes on behind the (still pretty commercial) tourist activities, such as getting a dolphin to paint your T-shirt or playing 'trainer for a day' ($650).

Marathon

Halfway between Key Largo and Key West, Marathon is the most sizable town; it's a good base and a hub for commercial fishing and lobster boats. Get local information at the visitor center (☎ 305-743-5417; www.floridakeys-marathon.com; MM 53.5 bayside; ⊙ 9am-5pm).

◉ Sights & Activities

Crane Point Museum MUSEUM
(www.cranepoint.net; MM 50.5 bayside; adult/child $12.50/8.50; ⊙ 9am-5pm Mon-Sat, from noon Sun; ♿) Escape all the development at this 63-acre reserve, where you'll find a vast system of nature trails and mangroves, a raised boardwalk and a rare early-20th-century Bahamian-style house. Kids will enjoy pirate and wreck exhibits, a walk-through coral reef tunnel and the bird hospital.

Pigeon Key National
Historic District ISLAND
(☎ 305-743-5999; www.pigeonkey.net; tours leave from MM 47 oceanside; adult/child/under 5yr $12/9/free; ⊙ tours 10am, noon & 2pm) On the Marathon side of Seven Mile Bridge, this tiny key served as a camp for the workers who toiled to build the Overseas Hwy in the 1930s. You can tour the historic structures or just sun and snorkel on the beach. Reach it by ferry, included in admission, or walk or bike your way there on the Old Seven Mile Bridge, which is closed to traffic but serves as the 'World's Longest Fishing Bridge.'

Sombrero Beach BEACH
(Sombrero Beach Rd, off MM 50 oceanside) This beautiful little white-sand beach has a playscape, shady picnic spots and big clean bathrooms.

Marathon Kayak KAYAKING
(☎ 305-395-0355; www.marathonkayak.com; 3hr tours $60) Kayak Dave is a reliable source for kayak instruction and excellent guided tours.

🛏️ Sleeping & Eating

Siesta Motel MOTEL $
(☎ 305-743-5671; www.siestamotel.net; MM 51 oceanside; r $75-105; ▣ ❄ 🛜) Head here for one of the cheapest, cleanest flops in the Keys, located in a friendly cluster of cute Marathon homes – with great service, to boot.

Seascape Motel & Marina MOTEL $$
(☎ 305-743-6212; www.seascapemotelandmarina. com; 1275 76th St Ocean E, btwn MM 51 & 52; r from $99; ▣ ❄ 🛜 🏊) Choose one of the nine crisp, clean rooms or an apartment that sleeps six at this oceanfront hideaway with a waterfront pool, boat dock and barbecue area.

★ Keys Fisheries SEAFOOD $
(www.keysfisheries.com; 3502 Gulfview Ave; mains $7-16; ⊙ 11am-9pm) Shoo the seagulls from your picnic table on the deck and dig in to fresh seafood in a down-and-dirty dockside atmosphere. The lobster reuben is the stuff of legend.

Wooden Spoon AMERICAN $
(7007 Overseas Hwy; menu items $2-10; ⊙ 5:30am-1:30pm) It's the best breakfast around, served by sweet Southern women who know their way around a diner. The biscuits are fluffy, the sausage gravy is delicious, and the grits buttery and creamy.

Hurricane AMERICAN $$
(☎ 305-743-2200; MM 49.5 bayside; mains $9-19; ⊙ 11am-midnight) As well as being a favorite Marathon bar, the Hurricane also serves an excellent menu of creative South Florida–inspired goodness, like snapper stuffed with

crabmeat and conch sliders jerked in Caribbean seasoning.

Island Fish Co SEAFOOD **$$**
(☑ 305-743-4191; www.islandfishco.com; MM 54 bayside; mains $8-22; ⊙ 8am-11pm) Grab a spicy bowl of conch chowder and a seat overlooking the water at this huge, open-air tiki hut that has a raw bar and copious fish specialties.

Lower Keys

The Lower Keys (MM 46 to MM 0) are fierce bastions of Conch culture in all its variety. The chamber of commerce (☑ 305-872-2411; www.lowerkeyschamber.com; MM 31 oceanside; ⊙ 9am-5pm Mon-Fri, 9am-3pm Sat) is on Big Pine Key.

One of Florida's most acclaimed beaches – and certainly the best in the Keys for its shallow, warm water – is at Bahia Honda State Park (☑ 305-872-3210; www.bahiahondapark.com; MM 36.8; per car/motorcycle/cyclist $5/4/2; ⊙ 8am-sunset; ⬢), a 524-acre park with nature trails, ranger-led programs, watersports rentals and some of the best coral reefs outside Key Largo.

Offshore from Looe Key is a marine sanctuary teeming with colorful tropical fish and coral; try Looe Key Dive Center (☑ 305-872-2215; www.diveflakeys.com; snorkel/dive $44/84) on Ramrod Key for snorkeling and diving day trips, including wreck drives.

Overnight camping at Bahia Honda State Park (☑ 305-872-2353; www.reserveamerica.com; MM 37, Bahia Honda Key; sites $36, cabins $160; ℗) is sublime; it'd be perfect except for the sandflies. There are also six popular waterfront cabins. Reserve far ahead for all. For a completely different experience, book one of the four cozily scrumptious rooms at Deer Run Bed & Breakfast (☑ 305-872-2015; www.deerrunfloridabb.com; 1997 Long Beach Dr, Big Pine Key, off MM 33 oceanside; r $235-355; ℗ ❄). This state-certified green lodge and vegetarian B&B is a garden of quirky delights, and the owners are extremely helpful.

On Big Pine Key, stop in for a pizza, beer and ambience at No Name Pub (☑ 305-872-9115; N Watson Blvd, Big Pine Key, off MM 30.5 bayside; mains $7-18; ⊙ 11am-11pm) – if you can find it. The quirky hideout is right before the causeway that gets you to No Name Key. While you're there, staple a dollar bill to the wall to contribute to the collection of approximately $60,000 wallpapering the room.

Key West

Key West's funky, laid-back vibe has long attracted artists, renegades and free spirits. In the words of one local: 'It's like they shook the United States and all the nuts fell to the bottom.' Part of that independent streak is rooted in Key West's geography: it's barely connected to the USA, and it's closer to Cuba than to the rest of the States. There's only one road in, and it's not on the way to anywhere. In other words, it's an easy place to do your own thing.

Originally called 'Cayo Hueso' – Spanish for 'Bone Island' – Key West was named for all the skeletons early explorers found littering the beach. Since then, the island has enjoyed a long and colorful history that includes pirates, sunken treasures, literary legends and lots of ghosts.

These days, people flock to Key West to soak up the sun, the mellow atmosphere and more than a little booze. They listen to tales of the past. They snorkel the crystal clear water. And they find their internal clocks set to 'island time.'

⊙ Sights

Key West has more than its fair share of historic homes, buildings and districts (like the colorful Bahama Village); it's a walkable town that rewards exploring. Naturally, you'll snap a pic at the USA's much ballyhooed Southernmost Point Marker, even though it's not technically the southernmost point in the USA. (That distinction goes to a point about half a mile down the beach, but since it's part of a naval air station, it's hardly tourist-friendly.)

★ Mallory Square SQUARE
Sunset at Mallory Sq, at the end of Duval St, is a bizzaro attraction of the highest order. It takes all those energies, subcultures and oddities of Keys life – the hippies, the rednecks, the foreigners and the tourists – and focuses them into one torchlit, playfully edgy (but family-friendly) street party. Come for the jugglers, fire-eaters, sassy acrobats and tightrope-walking dogs, and stay for the after-dark madness.

Duval Street STREET
Key West locals have a love–hate relationship with their island's most famous road. Duval, Old Town Key West's main drag, is a miracle mile of booze, tacky everything and awful behavior that still manages, somehow,

to be fun. At the end of the night, the 'Duval Crawl' is one of the best pub crawls in the country.

Hemingway House
HOUSE

(☑305-294-1136; www.hemingwayhome.com; 907 Whitehead St; adult/child $13/6; ☺9am-5pm) Ernest Hemingway lived in this Spanish-Colonial house from 1931 to 1940 – to write, drink and fish, if not always in that order. Tours run every half-hour, and as you listen to docent-spun yarns of Papa, you'll see his studio, his unusual pool, and the descendents of his six-toed cats languishing in the sun, on furniture and pretty much wherever they feel like.

Florida Keys
Eco-Discovery Center
MUSEUM

(☑305-809-4750; http://eco-discovery.com/ ecokw.html; 35 East Quay Rd; ☺9am-4pm Tue-Sat; P⛵) FREE This excellent nature center pulls together all the plants, animals and habitats that make up the Keys' unique ecosystem and presents them in fresh, accessible ways. A great place for kids and the big picture.

Key West Cemetery
CEMETERY

(cnr Margaret & Angela Sts; ☺7am - 6pm; ⛵) This dark, alluring Gothic labyrinth is in the center of town. Livening up the mausoleums are famous epitaphs like 'I told you I was sick.'

Key West Butterfly &
Nature Conservatory
ANIMAL SANCTUARY

(☑305-296-2988; www.keywestbutterfly.com; 1316 Duval St; adult/child 4-12 $12/8.50; ☺9am-5pm; ⛵) Even if you have only the faintest interest in butterflies, you'll find yourself entranced by the sheer quantity flittering around you here.

Museum of Art & History
at the Custom House
MUSEUM

(☑305-295-6616; www.kwahs.com/customhouse; 281 Front St; adult/child $7/5; ☺9:30am-4:30pm) Offering a more low-key, less swashbuckling version of Key West history, this is an interesting collection of folklore, international art and historical exhibits housed in the impressive former Customs House.

Fort East Martello
Museum & Gardens
MUSEUM

(☑305-296-3913; www.kwahs.com/martello.htm; 3501 S Roosevelt Blvd; adult/child $7/5; ☺9:30am-4:30pm) This fortress preserves interesting historical artifacts and some fabulous folk art by Mario Sanchez and 'junk' sculptures

by Stanley Papio. But Martello's most famous resident is Robert the Doll – a genuinely creepy, supposedly haunted, 19th-century doll that's kept in a glass case to keep him from making mischief.

🏃 Activities

Seeing as how you're out in the middle of the ocean, getting out on or in the water is one of the top activities. Charters abound for everything from fishing to snorkeling to scuba diving, including dive trips to the USS Vandenberg, a 522-foot transport ship sunk off the coast to create the world's second largest artificial reef.

Fort Zachary Taylor
BEACH

(www.floridastateparks.org/forttaylor; 601 Howard England Way; per car/pedestrian $6/2; ☺8am-sunset) Key West has three city beaches, but they aren't special; most people head to Bahia Honda. That said, Fort Zachary Taylor has the best beach on Key West, with white sand, decent swimming and some near-shore snorkeling; it's great for sunsets and picnics.

Dive Key West
DIVING

(☑305-296-3823; www.divekeywest.com) Everything you need for wreck-diving trips, from equipment to charters.

★ Jolly Rover
CRUISE

(☑305-304-2235; www.schoonerjollyrover.com; cnr Greene & Elizabeth Sts, Schooner Wharf; cruise $45) Set sail on a pirate-esque schooner offering daytime and sunset cruises.

Reelax Charters
KAYAKING

(☑305-304-1392; www.keyskayaking.com; MM 17 Sugarloaf Key Marina; kayak trips $240) Take a guided kayak tour from nearby Sugarloaf Key.

Sunny Days Catamaran
SNORKELING

(☑866-878-2223; www.sunnydayskeywest.com; 201 Elizabeth St; adult/child $35/22) Our favorite for snorkel trips, water sports and other aquatic adventures.

Clearly Unique
KAYAKING

(☑877-282-5327; www.clearlyuniquecharters.com) Rents out glass-bottomed kayaks, providing a unique view of the water.

🧭 Tours

Both the Conch Tour Train (☑305-294-5161; www.conchtourtrain.com; adult/child under 13yr/ senior $29/free/26; ☺tours 9am-4:30pm; ⛵)

and Old Town Trolley (☎305-296-6688; www.trolleytours.com/key-west; adult/child under 13yr/senior $29/free/26; ⊙tours 9am-4:30pm; ☑) offer tours leaving from Mallory Sq. The train offers a 90-minute narrated tour in a breezy, open car, while the hop-on, hop-off trolley makes 12 stops around town.

Original Ghost Tours   GHOST
(☎305-294-9255; www.hauntedtours.com; adult/child $15/10; ⊙8pm & 9pm) Is your guesthouse haunted? Probably. Why should you fear Robert the Doll in East Martello? You're about to find out.

✦ Festivals & Events

Key West hosts a party every sunset, but residents don't need an excuse to go crazy.

Conch Republic
Independence Celebration   CULTURE
(www.conchrepublic.com) A 10-day tribute to Conch Independence, held every April; vie for (made-up) public offices and watch a drag queens footrace.

Hemingway Days Festival   CULTURE
(www.hemingwaydays.net) Includes a bull run, marlin tournament and look-alike contest, as well as literary events, in late July.

Fantasy Fest   CULTURE
(www.fantasyfest.net) Room rates get hiked to the hilt for this raucous, 10-day Halloween-meets-Carnivale event in late October.

🛏 Sleeping

Key West lodging is generally pretty expensive – especially in the wintertime and even *more* especially during special events, when room rates can triple. Book ahead, or you may well end up joining the long traffic jam headed back to the mainland.

You can find chain motels in New Town, but you've got to stay in Old Town to truly experience Key West. Visit the Key West Innkeepers Association (www.keywestinns.com) for more guesthouses; pretty much all are gay-friendly.

Caribbean House   GUESTHOUSE $
(☎305-296-0999; www.caribbeanhousekw.com; 226 Petronia St; summer $89, winter $119-139; P❄@) In the heart of Bahama Village, rooms are tiny, but they're clean, cozy and cheery. Add free breakfast and welcoming hosts and you get a rare find in Key West: a bargain.

★ **Key West Bed & Breakfast**   B&B $$
(☎800-438-6155, 305-296-7274; www.keywestbandb.com; 415 William St; r summer $79-155, winter $89-265; ❄⚡) Sunny, airy and full of artistic touches: hand-painted pottery here, a working loom there – is that a ship's masthead in the corner? There are also a range of rooms to fit every budget.

L'Habitation   GUESTHOUSE $$
(☎305-293-9203; www.lhabitation.com; 408 Eaton St; r $119-189; ❄⚡) At this beautiful classic Keys cottage, the friendly, bilingual owners welcome guests in English or French. The cute rooms come kitted out in light tropical shades, with lamps that look like contemporary art pieces and skittles-bright quilts.

Key Lime Inn   HOTEL $$
(☎800-549-4430; www.historickeywestinns.com; 725 Truman Ave; r $99-229; P⚡❄) These cozy cottages are scattered around a tropical hardwood backdrop. Inside, the blissfully cool rooms are greener than a jade mine, with wicker furniture and tiny flat-screens to keep you from ever leaving.

Mermaid & the Alligator   GUESTHOUSE $$$
(☎305-294-1894; www.kwmermaid.com; 729 Truman Ave; r summer $168-228, winter $258-328, P❄@⚡) Book way ahead: with only nine rooms, this place's charm exceeds its capacity. It's chock-a-block with treasures collected from the owners' travels, giving it a worldly flair that's simultaneously European and Zen.

Curry Mansion Inn   HOTEL $$$
(☎305-294-5349; www.currymansion.com; 511 Caroline St; r summer $195-285, winter $240-365; P❄⚡❄) In a city full of stately 19th-century homes, the Curry Mansion is especially handsome. It's a pleasing mix of aristocratic American elements, but especially the bright Floridian rooms with canopied beds. Enjoy bougainvillea and breezes on the verandah.

Big Ruby's Guesthouse   HOTEL $$$
(☎305-296-2323; www.bigrubys.com; 409 Appelrouth Lane; r $179-499; P❄⚡❄) Catering exclusively to a gay clientele, the hotel's exterior is all refined Conch mansion, while inside, the rooms are sleekly contemporary. The capper is the clothing-optional lagoon pool. Breakfast is included.

FLORIDA FLORIDA KEYS

GAY & LESBIAN KEY WEST

Gay and lesbian visitors can get information at the Gay & Lesbian Community Center (☑ 305-292-3223; www.glcckeywest.org; 513 Truman Ave). While you'll find the entire island extraordinarily welcoming, several bars and guesthouses cater specifically to a gay clientele. Toast your arrival in town at one of the following:

801 Bourbon Bar (www.801bourbon.com; 801 Duval St), where boys will be boys.

Aqua (☑ 305-294-0555; www.aquakeywest.com; 711 Duval St) caters to both gays and lesbians.

Pearl's Patio (☑ 305-292-1450; www.pearlsrainbow.com; 525 United St; ☺ noon-10pm Sun-Thu, to midnight Fri & Sat) is a lesbian bar at Pearl's Guesthouse.

✖ Eating

You aren't technically allowed to leave the island without sampling the conch fritters – like hushpuppies, but made with conch – or the key lime pie, made with key limes, sweetened condensed milk, eggs and sugar on a Graham-cracker crust.

Help Yourself Organic Foods   VEGETARIAN $
(☑ 315-296-7766; www.helpyourselfcafe.com; 829 Fleming St; dishes $5-12; ☺ 8am-6pm) Vegetarian, vegan and gluten-free options abound in this cute, colorful cafe that serves wraps, salads, smoothies and other hippified offerings – a nice break from fried fish and key lime pie.

Camille's   FUSION $$
(☑ 305-296-4811; www.camilleskeywest.com; 1202 Simonton St; breakfast & lunch $4-13, dinner $15-25; ☺ 8am-3pm & 6-10pm; ☑) Ditch Duval St and dine with the locals at Camille's; this healthy and tasty neighborhood joint is where local families go for a casual meal. Their inventive menu ranges from French toast with Godiva liqueur to tasty chicken salad.

El Siboney   CUBAN $$
(900 Catherine St; mains $8-16; ☺ 11am-9:30pm) Key West is only 90 miles from Cuba, so this awesome rough-and-ready corner establishment is quite literally the closest you can get to real Cuban food in the US. Cash only.

Mo's Restaurant   CARIBBEAN $$
(☑ 305-296-8955; 1116 White St; mains $6-17; ☺ 11am-10pm Mon-Sat) If the phrase 'Caribbean home cooking' causes drool to form in the corners of your mouth, don't hesitate. The dishes are mainly Haitian, and they're delicious.

BO's Fish Wagon   SEAFOOD $$
(☑ 305-294-9272; 801 Caroline St; mains $8-22; ☺ 11am-9pm) This looks like the backyard shed of a crazy old fisherman (but in a good way). Fried fish, conch fritters and cold beer – not to mention great prices – will win over any scaredy-cats in your group.

★ Blue Heaven   AMERICAN $$$
(☑ 305-296-8666; http://blueheavenkw.homestead.com; 729 Thomas St; dinner $17-35; ☺ 8am-4pm, until 2pm Sun & 5-10:30pm daily) One of the island's quirkiest venues (and it's a high bar), where you dine in an outdoor courtyard with a flock of chickens. Customers gladly wait, bemusedly, for Blue Heaven's well-executed, Southern-fried interpretation of Keys cuisine.

★ Café Solé   FRENCH $$$
(☑ 305-294-0230; www.cafesole.com; 1029 Southard St; dinner $20-34; ☺ 5:30-10pm) Conch carpaccio with capers? Yellowtail fillet and foie gras? Oh yes. This locally and critically acclaimed venue is known for its cozy back-porch ambience and innovative menus, the result of a French-trained chef exploring island ingredients.

🍷 Drinking & Entertainment

Hopping (or staggering) from one bar to the next – also known as the 'Duval Crawl (p479)' – is a favorite pastime here in the Conch Republic, and there are plenty of options for your drinking pleasure.

★ Green Parrot   BAR
(www.greenparrot.com; 601 Whitehead St; ☺ 10am-4am) This rogue's cantina has the longest tenure of any bar on the island (since 1890). It's a fabulous dive drawing a lively mix of locals and out-of-towners, with a century's worth of strange decor. Men, don't miss the urinal.

Captain Tony's Saloon   BAR
(www.capttonyssaloon.com; 428 Greene St) This former icehouse, morgue and Hemingway haunt is built around the town's old hanging tree. The eclectic decor includes emancipated bras and signed dollar bills.

Porch
BAR

(www.theporchkw.com; 429 Caroline St; ⊘10am-2am Mon-Sat, noon-2am Sun) Escape the Duval St frat boy bars at the Porch, where knowledgeable bartenders dispense artisan beers. It sounds civilized, and almost is, by Key West standards.

Garden of Eden
BAR

(224 Duval St) You can make like Adam and Eve at this clothing-optional rooftop bar; the fig leaf is also optional.

Virgilio's
JAZZ

(www.virgilioskeywest.com; 524 Duval St) Thank God for a little variety. This town needs a dark, candlelit martini lounge where you can chill to jazz and salsa. Enter on Appelrouth Lane.

La Te Da
CABARET

(www.lateda.com; 1125 Duval St) While the outside bar is where locals gather for mellow chats over beer, you can catch high-quality drag acts – big names come here from around the country – upstairs at the fabulous Crystal Room on weekends. More low-key cabaret acts grace the downstairs lounge.

❶ Information

A great trip-planning resource is www.fla-keys.com/keywest. In town, get maps and brochures at **Key West Chamber of Commerce** (☑305-294-2587; www.keywestchamber.org; 510 Greene St; ⊘8:30am-6:30pm Mon-Sat, to 6pm Sun).

❶ Getting There & Around

The easiest way to travel around Key West and the Keys is by car, though traffic along the one major route, US 1, can be maddening during the winter high season. **Greyhound** (☑305-296-9072; www.greyhound.com; 3535 S Roosevelt Blvd) serves the Keys along US Hwy 1 from downtown Miami.

You can fly into **Key West International Airport** (EYW; www.keywestinternationalairport.com) with frequent flights from major cities, most going through Miami. Or, take a fast catamaran from Fort Myers or Miami; call the **Key West Express** (☑888-539-2628; www.seakeywestexpress.com; adult/child round-trip $146/81, one-way $86/58) for schedules and fares; discounts apply for advance booking.

Within Key West, bicycles are the preferred mode of travel (rentals along Duval St run $10 to $25 per day). **City Transit** (☑305-600-1455; www.kwtransit.com; tickets $2) runs color-coded buses through downtown and the Lower Keys.

ATLANTIC COAST

Florida's Atlantic Coast isn't all beach volleyball, surfing and lazing in the sun. It offers travelers a remarkably well-rounded experience, with something for everyone from history buffs to thrill seekers to art lovers.

WORTH A TRIP

DRY TORTUGAS

Seventy miles west of the Keys in the middle of the Gulf, **Dry Tortugas National Park** (☑305-242-7700; www.nps.gov/drto; adult/15yr and under $5/free) is America's most inaccessible national park. Reachable only by boat or plane, it rewards your efforts to get there with amazing snorkeling, diving, bird-watching and stargazing.

Ponce de León christened the area Tortugas (tor-too-guzz) after the sea turtles he found here, and the 'Dry' part was added later to warn about the absence of fresh water on the island. But this is more than just a pretty cluster of islands with no drinking water. The never-completed Civil War-era **Fort Jefferson** provides a striking hexagonal centerpiece of red brick rising up from the emerald waters on **Garden Key**, meaning along with your bottled water, you should definitely bring your camera.

So how do you get there? **Yankee Freedom** (☑800-634-0939, 305-294-7009; www.yankeefreedom.com; Historic Seaport) is a fast ferry that leaves from the north end of Grinnell St in Key West; fare includes breakfast, a picnic lunch, snorkeling gear and tour of the fort. Or, you can hop on a **Key West Seaplane** (☑305-293-9300; www.keywestseaplanecharters.com/; half-day trip adult/child 3-12 $280/224) for a half-day or full-day trip. Whichever you choose, reserve at least a week ahead.

If you really want to enjoy the isolation, stay overnight at one of Garden Key's 13 **campsites** (per person $3). Reserve early through the park office, and bring everything you need, because once that boat leaves, you're on your own.

Space Coast

The Space Coast's main claim to fame (other than being the setting for the iconic 1960s TV series *I Dream of Jeannie*) is being the real-life home to the Kennedy Space Center and its massive visitor complex. Cocoa Beach is also a magnet for surfers, with Florida's best waves. Visitor information is available through Florida's Space Coast Office of Tourism (☑321-433-4470; www.visitspacecoast.com; 430 Brevard Ave, Cocoa Village; ◷8am-5pm Mon-Sat).

◉ Sights

Kennedy Space Center
Visitor Complex   MUSEUM
(☑321-449-4444; www.kennedyspacecenter. com; adult/child $50/40, parking $10; ◷9am-5pm) Once a working space-flight facility, Kennedy Space Center is shifting from a living museum to a historical one since the end of NASA's space shuttle program in 2011. Devote most of your day to the new Space Shuttle Atlantis attraction, IMAX theaters and Rocket Garden, featuring replicas of classic rockets towering over the complex. And don't miss the Shuttle Launch Simulator, which reaches a top 'speed' of 17,500mph and feels just like a space-shuttle takeoff (but without the teary goodbyes). But first take the hop-on, hop-off bus tour of working NASA facilities that depart every 15 minutes from 10am to 2:45pm.

Add-on options abound, depending on how serious you are about your astronaut experience (they're popular – book in advance). Hungry space enthusiasts can have Lunch with an Astronaut (☑866-737-5235; adult/child $30/16), and the action-oriented Astronaut Training Experience (ticket $145) prepares you for space flight, should the opportunity arise.

★Merritt Island National
Wildlife Refuge   WILDLIFE RESERVE
(www.fws.gov/merrittisland; I-95 exit 80; ◷park dawn-dusk; visitor center 8am-4:30pm Mon-Fri, 9am-5pm Sat & Sun, closed Sun Apr-Oct) This unspoiled 140,000-acre refuge is one of the country's best birding spots, especially from October to May (early morning and after 4pm). More endangered and threatened species of wildlife inhabit the swamps, marshes and hardwood hammocks here than at any other site in the continental US. The best viewing is on Black Point Wildlife Dr.

Canaveral National Seashore   PARK
(☑321-267-1110; www.nps.gov/cana; car/bike $5/1; ◷dawn-dusk) The 24 miles of pristine, windswept beaches comprise the longest stretch of undeveloped beach on Florida's east coast. On the north end is family-friendly Apollo Beach, which shines in a class of its own with gentle surf and miles of solitude. On the south end, Playalinda Beach is surfer central. And in between the two is untrammeled Klondike Beach, a favorite of campers and nature lovers.

Mosquito Lagoon, with islands and mangroves teeming with wildlife, hugs the west side of the barrier island. Rent kayaks in Cocoa Beach. Rangers offer pontoon boat tours (per person $20) from the visitor information center on most Sundays. From June through August, rangers lead groups on nightly sea turtle nesting tours (adult/child 8-16yr $14/free; 7am-11:30pm); reservations required.

🏃 Activities

Despite all the sunshine and shoreline, Florida is no *Endless Summer*. The water around Miami tends to stay flat, and much of the Gulf Coast is too protected to get much of a swell. But the 70 miles of beaches from New Smyrna to Sebastian Inlet are surfer central. Ten-time world champion surfer Kelly Slater was born in Cocoa Beach, which remains the epicenter of the surf community. For the local scene and surf reports, visit Florida Surfing (www.floridasurfing.com) and Surf Guru (www.surfguru.com).

Ron Jon's Surf Shop   WATER SPORTS
(☑321-799-8888; 4151 N Atlantic Ave; ◷24 hrs) Rents just about anything water-related from fat-tired beach bikes ($15 daily) to surfboards ($30 daily).

Ron Jon Surf School   SURFING
(☑321-868-1980; www.cocoabeachsurfingschool. com; 150 E Columbia Lane, Cocoa Beach; per hr $50-65) The best surf school in Cocoa Beach for all ages and levels is the state's largest, Ron Jon Surf School run by ex-pro surfer and Kelly Slater coach, Craig Carroll.

Cocoa Beach Jetski Rentals   BOATING
(☑321-454-7661; http://cocoabeachjetskirentals. com; 1872 E 520 Causeway, Cocoa Beach; kayaks/ jet skis per hr $20/90; ◷8:45am-5pm) Rent boats, kayaks, surfboards – and of course jetskis. You can even buy live bait.

🛏 Sleeping

Charming Cocoa Beach has the most options, as well as the most chains. For a quieter stay, Vero Beach is also attractive.

Fawlty Towers   MOTEL $
(📞 321-784-3870; www.fawltytowersresort.com; 100 E Cocoa Beach Causeway, Cocoa Beach; r $72-92; 🅿 ❋ 🛜 ☒) Beneath this motel's gloriously garish and extremely pink exterior lie fairly straightforward rooms with an unbeatable beachside location; quiet pool and tiki bar.

South Beach Place   MOTEL $$
(📞 772-231-5366; www.southbeachplacevero.com; 1705 S Ocean Dr, Vero Beach; ste per day $125-175, per week $700-1100; 🛜 ☒) Old Florida with a facelift, this tasteful and bright two-story motel in Vero Beach sits in a particularly quiet stretch across from the beach. One-bedroom suites have a full kitchen.

Beach Place Guesthouses   APARTMENT $$$
(📞 321-783-4045; www.beachplaceguesthouses. com; 1445 S Atlantic Ave, Cocoa Beach; ste $195-395; 🛜) A slice of heavenly relaxation in Cocoa Beach's partying beach scene, this laid-back two-story guesthouse in a residential neighborhood has roomy suites with hammocks and a lovely deck, all just steps from the dunes and beach.

🍴 Eating

Simply Delicious   CAFE $
(125 N Orlando Ave, Cocoa Beach; mains $6-12; ☺ 8am-3pm Tue-Sat, to 2pm Sun) You can't miss this little yellow house on the southbound stretch of A1A. It's a homey Americana place – nothing fancy, nothing trendy, just simply delicious.

Slow and Low Barbecue   BARBECUE $$
(http://slowandlowbarbeque.com; 306 N Orlando Ave, Cocoa Beach; mains $7-15; ☺ 11am-10pm Mon-Sat, from noon Sun) After a day on the beach, nothing satisfies better than a plate overflowing with barbecue ribs, fried okra, turnip greens and sweet fried potatoes. There's a daily happy hour and live music Thursday through Sunday.

Fat Snook   SEAFOOD $$$
(📞 321-784-1190; http://thefatsnook.com; 2464 S Atlantic Ave, Cocoa Beach; mains $22-36; ☺ 5:30-10pm) Hidden inside an uninspired building, yet sporting cool, minimalist decor, tiny Fat Snook stands out as an oasis of fine cooking. Yes, there's a distinct air of food snobbery here, but it's so tasty, no one seems to mind.

3-2-1...BLASTOFF

Along the Space Coast, even phone calls get a countdown, thanks to the local area code: 321. It's no coincidence; in 1999 residents led by Robert Osband petitioned to get the digits in honor of the rocket launches that took place at Cape Canaveral.

Maison Martinique   FRENCH $$$
(📞 772-231-7299; Caribbean Court Hotel, 1603 S Ocean Dr, Vero Beach; mains $24-42; ☺ 5-10pm Tue-Sat) In Vero Beach, outstanding French cuisine with first-rate service and intimate surrounds. On warm evenings, eat by the little pool; for something more casual, head to the piano bar upstairs.

ℹ Getting There & Away

From Orlando take Hwy 528 east, which connects with Hwy A1A. **Greyhound** (www.greyhound.com) has services from West Palm Beach and Orlando to Titusville. **Vero Beach Shuttle** (📞 772-200-7427; www.verobeachshuttle.com) provides shuttle service from area airports.

Daytona Beach

With typical Floridian hype, Daytona Beach bills itself as 'The World's Most Famous Beach.' But its fame is less about quality than the size of the parties this expansive beach has witnessed during spring break, Speed-Weeks, and motorcycle events when half a million bikers roar into town. One Daytona title no one disputes is 'Birthplace of NASCAR,' which started here in 1947. Its origins go back as far as 1902 to drag races held on the beach's hard-packed sands.

The **Daytona Beach Convention & Visitors Bureau** (📞 386-255-0415; www.daytonabeach.com; 126 E Orange Ave; ☺ 9am-5pm Mon-Fri) has great lodging listings. Gay and lesbian travelers can visit www.gaydaytona.com.

◉ Sights & Activities

Museum of Arts & Sciences   MUSEUM
(www.moas.org; 1040 Museum Blvd; adult/student $13/7; ☺ 9am-5pm Tue-Sat, from 11am Sun) A wonderful mishmash of everything from Cuban art to Coca-Cola relics to a 13ft giant sloth skeleton.

Ponce Inlet Lighthouse
& Museum
LIGHTHOUSE

(www.ponceinlet.org; 4931 S Peninsula Dr; adult/child $5/1.50; ⏱10am-6pm winter, to 9pm summer) About 6 miles south of Daytona Beach, it's 203 steps to the top of Florida's tallest lighthouse.

Daytona Beach
BEACH

(per car $5) This stretch of sand was once the city's raceway. You can still drive sections at a strictly enforced top speed of 10mph. Or rent an ATV, fat-tired cruiser or recumbent trike. Water sports rentals are ubiquitous.

Daytona International
Speedway
RACETRACK

(☎800-748-7467; www.daytonaintlspeedway.com; 1801 W International Speedway Blvd; tickets from $20, adult tours $16-23, child 6-12 $10-17) The Holy Grail of raceways has a diverse race schedule. Ticket prices accelerate rapidly for the big races, headlined by the **Daytona 500** in February, but you can wander the massive stands for free on nonrace days. Two first-come, first-served **tram tours** take in the track, pits and behind-the-scenes areas. Real fanatics can indulge in the **Richard Petty Driving Experience** (☎800-237-3889; www.drivepetty.com), where you can either ride shotgun ($84 to $135) around the track or take a day to become the driver ($550 to $3200); check schedule online.

🛏 Sleeping

Daytona lodging is plentiful and spans all budgets and styles. Prices soar during events; book well ahead.

Shores
RESORT $$

(☎386-767-7350; www.shoresresort.com; 2637 N Atlantic Ave; r from $109; P❀🛜🏊) One of Daytona's most elegant offerings, this chic, beachfront boutique has hand-striped walls, a full-service spa and sophisticated color palette.

★ August Seven Inn
B&B $$

(☎386-248-8420; www.jpaugust.net; 1209 S Peninsula Dr; r $140-225; P❀🛜🏊) The friendly innkeepers of this gorgeous B&B have stocked it with period antiques and stylish deco, creating a soothing haven from Daytona's typical Nascar-and-spring-break carnival.

Tropical Manor
RESORT $$

(☎386-252-4920; www.tropicalmanor.com; 2237 S Atlantic Ave; r $80-315; P❀🛜🏊) This beachfront property is vintage Florida, with motel rooms, studios and cottages all blanketed in a frenzy of murals and bright pastels.

Sun Viking Lodge
RESORT $$

(☎800-815-2846; www.sunviking.com; 2411 S Atlantic Ave; r $79-259; P❀🛜🏊) Most rooms have kitchenettes, but they could stand a reno – oh never mind. For families, it's ideal: two pools, a 60ft waterslide, beach access, shuffleboard, endless activities and a Viking theme!

🍴 Eating & Drinking

Dancing Avocado Kitchen
MEXICAN $

(110 S Beach St; mains $6-10; ⏱8am-4pm Tue-Sat; 🍴) Fresh, healthful Mexican dishes like extreme burritos and quesadillas dominate the menu at this vegetarian-oriented cafe, but the signature Dancing Avocado Melt is tops.

Pasha
MIDDLE EASTERN $

(www.pashamideastcafe.com; 919 W International Speedway Blvd; mains $5-14; ⏱11am-7:30pm Mon-Sat) Bread unchanged since it opened in the '70s, this place combines an Aladdin's cave deli of imported Middle Eastern goods and a cafe with authentic dishes like Armenian breaded cheese pie and platters served with the owner's grandma's pita bread.

Aunt Catfish's on the River
SOUTHERN $$

(☎386-767-4768; www.auntcatfishontheriver.com; 4009 Halifax Dr, Port Orange; mains $8-25; ⏱11:30am-9pm Mon-Sat, from 9am Sun) Southern-style seafood lolling in butter and Cajun-spice catfish make this place insanely popular.

The Cellar
ITALIAN $$$

(☎386-258-0011; www.thecellarrestaurant.com; 220 Magnolia Ave; mains $19-37; ⏱5-10pm Tue-Sun) Classic, upscale Italian fare and elegant ambience (located in the summer mansion of 29th US President Warren G Harding) has made this go-to spot for special-occasion dinners. Reservations recommended.

🍸 Drinking & Entertainment

Daytona's entertainment scene skews to rocking biker bars (mostly along Main St) and high-octane dance clubs (on or near Seabreeze Blvd).

Froggy's Saloon
BAR

(www.froggyssaloon.net; 800 Main St) Outside this train wreck of a bar, a bone chopper gleams in the window. Inside, a sign asks, 'Ain't drinking fun?' You better believe they mean it: opening at 7am, this is Party Central for bikers and others who want to go bonkers. Expect to see flashing chicks, smoky beards and more leather than on an African safari.

Razzles CLUB
(www.razzlesnightclub.com; 611 Seabreeze Blvd; ⊛8pm-3am) The reigning dance club, permanently thumping.

ⓘ Getting There & Around

Daytona Beach International Airport (☑386-248-8030; www.flydaytonafirst.com; 700 Catalina Dr) is just east of the Speedway, and the **Greyhound bus station** (www.greyhound.com; 138 S Ridgewood Ave) is the starting point for services around Florida.

Daytona is close to the intersection of two of Florida's major interstates: I-95 is the quickest way to Jacksonville (about 90 miles) and Miami (260 miles), and I-4 leads to Orlando in an hour.

Votran (www.votran.org; fare $1.25) runs buses and trolleys throughout the city.

St Augustine

The first this, the oldest that... St Augustine was founded by the Spanish in 1565, which means it's chock-full of age-related superlatives. Tourists flock here to stroll the ancient streets, and horse-drawn carriages clip-clop past townsfolk dressed in period costume around the National Historic Landmark District, aka the oldest permanent settlement in the US.

At times St Augustine screams, 'Hey, everyone, look how quaint we are!' but it stops just short of feeling like a historic theme park because, well, the buildings and monuments are real, and the narrow, cafe-strewn lanes are genuinely charming. Walk the cobblestoned streets or stand where Juan Ponce de León landed in 1513, and the historical distance occasionally collapses into present-moment chills.

The main **visitor center** (☑904-825-1000; www.ci.st-augustine.fl.us; 10 Castillo Dr; ⊛8:30am-5:30pm) screens a 45-minute film on the town's history.

◉ Sights & Activities

The town's two Henry Flagler buildings shouldn't be missed.

★**Lightner Museum** MUSEUM
(☑904-824-2874; www.lightnermuseum.org; 75 King St; adult/child $10/5; ⊛9am-5pm) Flagler's former Hotel Alcazar is now home to this wonderful museum, with a little bit of everything from ornate Gilded Age furnishings to collections of marbles and cigar-box labels.

Hotel Ponce de León HISTORIC BUILDING
(74 King St; tours adult/child $10/1; ⊛tours hourly in summer 10am-3pm, 10am & 2pm during school year) This gorgeous former hotel was built in the 1880s and is now the world's most gorgeous dormitory, belonging to Flagler College. Take a guided tour – or at least step inside to gawk at the lobby for free.

Colonial Quarter HISTORIC BUILDINGS
(33 St George St; adult/child $13/7; ⊛9am-6pm) See how they did things back in the 18th century at this re-creation of Spanish-Colonial St Augustine, complete with craftspeople demonstrating blacksmithing, leather working and other trades.

Pirate & Treasure Museum MUSEUM
(www.thepiratemuseum.com; 12 S Castillo Dr; adult/child $13/7; ⊛9am-8pm; ⊞) A mash-up of theme park and museum, this celebration of all things pirate has real historical treasures (and genuine gold) as well as animatronic pirates, blasting cannons and a kid-friendly treasure hunt.

Castillo de San Marcos National Monument FORT
(☑904-829-6506; www.nps.gov/casa; 1 S Castillo Dr, St Augustine; adult/child under 16 $7/free; ⊛8:45am-5:15pm; ⊞) This incredibly photogenic fort is another atmospheric monument to longevity: it's the country's oldest masonry fort, completed by the Spanish in 1695. Park rangers lead programs hourly and shoot off cannons most weekends.

Fountain of Youth HISTORIC SITE
(www.fountainofyouthflorida.com; 11 Magnolia Ave; adult/child 6-12 $12/8; ⊛9am-5pm) Step right up for an acrid cup of eternal youth at this 'archaeological park.' As the story goes, Spanish explorer Juan Ponce de León came ashore here in 1513, and he considered this freshwater stream the possible legendary fountain of youth.

Anastasia State Recreation Area PARK
(☑904-461-2033; www.floridastateparks.org; 1340 Hwy A1A; car/bike $8/2; ⊛8am-sundown) Locals escape the tourist hordes here, with a terrific beach, a campground (campsites $28) and rentals for all kinds of water sports.

☞ Tours

St Augustine City Walks WALKING

(☑904-540-3476; www.staugustinecitywalks.com; tours $12-49) Extremely fun walking tours of all kinds, from silly to serious to spooky.

Old Town Trolley Tours TOUR

(☑888-910-8687; www.trolleytours.com; adult/child 6-12 $23/10) Hop-on, hop-off narrated trolley tours.

St Augustine Sightseeing Trains TRAIN

(☑904-829-6545; www.redtrains.com; 170 San Marco Ave; tour adult/child $20/9) Hop-on, hop-off narrated train tours or get creeped out on the Ghost Train.

🛏 Sleeping

St Augustine is a popular weekend escape; expect room rates to rise about 30% on Friday and Saturday. Inexpensive motels and chain hotels line San Marco Ave, near where it meets US Hwy 1. More than two dozen atmospheric B&Bs can be found at www.staugustineinns.com.

Pirate Haus Inn HOSTEL $

(☑904-808-1999; www.piratehaus.com; 32 Treasury St; dm $20, r $65-109; P❋☏) Yar, if ye don't be needing anything fancy, this family-friendly European-style guesthouse/hostel has an unbeatable location and includes a pirate pancake breakfast.

★ At Journey's End B&B $$

(☑904-829-0076; www.atjourneysend.com; 89 Cedar St; r $149-199; P❋☏) Free from the grannyish decor that haunts many St Augustine B&Bs, this pet-friendly, kid-friendly and gay-friendly spot is outfitted in a chic mix of antiques and modern furniture, and run by some affable hosts. Breakfast is included.

Casa de Solana B&B $$

(☑877-824-3555; www.casadesolana.com; 21 Aviles St; r $149-279; P☏) Just off pedestrian-only Aviles St in the oldest part of town, this utterly charming little inn remains faithful to its early-1800s period decor. Rooms are a bit small, but price and location make it a good deal.

Casa Monica HISTORIC HOTEL $$$

(☑904-827-1888; www.casamonica.com; 95 Cordova St; r $179-379; P❋☏☰) ✐ Built in 1888, this is *the* luxe hotel in town, with turrets and fountains adding to the Spanish-Moorish castle atmosphere. Rooms are richly appointed, with wrought-iron beds and every amenity.

✗ Eating & Drinking

St Augustine has a notable dining scene, though it's also rife with overpriced tourist traps.

★ Spanish Bakery BAKERY $

(www.thespanishbakery.com; 42½ St George St; mains $3.50-5.50; ☉9:30am-3pm) Through an arched gate in a table-filled courtyard, this diminutive stucco bakeshop serves empanadas, sausage rolls and other conquistador-era favorites. Don't hesitate; they sell out quick.

★ Floridian MODERN AMERICAN $$

(☑904-829-0655; www.thefloridianstaug.com; 39 Cordova St; mains $12-20; ☉lunch 11am-3pm Wed-Mon, dinner 5-9pm Mon-Thu, 5-10pm Fri & Sat) Though it oozes with hipster-locavore earnestness, this new farm-to-table restaurant is so friggin' fabulous you won't mind. The chef-owners serve whimsical neo-Southern creations in an oh-so-cool dining room.

Collage INTERNATIONAL $$$

(☑904-829-0055; www.collagestaug.com; 60 Hypolita St; mains $28-38; ☉from 5:30pm) This upscale spot feels a world away from the bustling touristy downtown. The seafood-heavy menu wins raves for its subtle touch with global flavors.

Scarlett O'Hara's PUB

(www.scarlettoharas.net; 70 Hypolita St; ☉11am-1am) Good luck grabbing a rocking chair: the porch of this pine building is packed all day, every day. Built in 1879, today Scarlett's serves regulation pub grub, but it's got the magic ingredients – hopping happy hour, live entertainment nightly, hardworking staff, funky bar – that draw folks like spirits to a séance.

★ Taberna del Gallo BAR

(35 St George St; ☉noon-7pm Sun-Thu, to 11pm Fri & Sat) Flickering candles provide the only light at this 1736 stone tavern. Sing sea shanties on weekends.

AIA Ale Works PUB

(www.a1aaleworks.com; 1 King St; ☉11am-11:30pm Sun-Thu, to midnight Fri & Sat) Who needs historical ambience with fine-crafted beer like this?

ℹ Getting There & Around

The **Greyhound bus station** (☑904-829-6401; 52 San Marcos Ave) is just a few blocks north of the visitor's center. Once you're in Old Town, you can get almost everywhere on foot.

Jacksonville

Are we there yet? Have we left yet? It's hard to tell, because Jacksonville sprawls out over a whopping 840 sq miles, making it the largest city by area in the continental US (eclipsed only by Anchorage, AK). Jacksonville Beach, known locally as 'Jax Beach,' is about 17 miles east of the city center and is where you'll find white sand and most of the action. For information, peruse www.visitjacksonville.com.

⦿ Sights & Activities

★ Cummer Museum of Art & Gardens   MUSEUM
(www.cummer.org; 829 Riverside Ave; adult/student $10/6; ⊙10am-9pm Tue, to 4pm Wed-Sat, noon-4pm Sun) This handsome museum, Jacksonville's premier cultural space, has a genuinely excellent collection of American and European paintings, Asian decorative art and antiquities.

Museum of Science & History   MUSEUM
(www.themosh.org; 1025 Museum Circle; adult/child $10/8; ⊙10am-5pm Mon-Thu, to 8pm Fri, to 6pm Sat, noon-5pm Sun; ⓘ) Packing kids? This museum offers dinosaurs, a planetarium and educational exhibits on Jacksonville's cultural and natural history.

Jacksonville Museum of Modern Art   MUSEUM
(www.mocajacksonville.org; 333 N Laura St; adult/child $8/5; ⊙11am-5pm Tue-Sat, to 9pm Thu, noon-5pm Sun) The focus of this ultramodern space extends beyond painting: get lost among contemporary sculpture, prints, photography and film.

Jacksonville Landing   PROMENADE
(www.jacksonvillelanding.com; 2 Independent Dr) At the foot of the high-rise downtown, this prominent shopping and entertainment district has about 40 mostly touristy shops surrounding a tip-top food court with outdoor tables and regular, free live entertainment.

Anheuser-Busch Budweiser Brewery   BREWERY
(www.budweisertours.com; 111 Busch Dr; ⊙10am-4pm Mon-Sat) Enjoy a free tour (and free beer if you're over 21).

🛏 Sleeping & Eating

The cheapest rooms are along I-95 and I-10, where the lower-priced chains congregate. Beach lodging rates often rise in summer.

Riverdale Inn   B&B $$
(☑904-354-5080; www.riverdaleinn.com; 1521 Riverside Ave; r $110-190, ste $200-220; ⓟ❋🎧) In the early 1900s this was one of 50 or so mansions lining Riverside. Now there are only two left, and you're invited to enjoy its lovely rooms with full breakfast.

★ Clark's Fish Camp   SOUTHERN $$
(☑904-268-3474; www.clarksfishcamp.com; 12903 Hood Landing Rd; mains $13-22; ⊙4:30-9:30pm Mon-Thu, 4:30-10pm Fri, 11:30am-10pm Sat, 11:30am-9:30pm Sun) Sample Florida's Southern 'Cracker' cuisine of gator, snake, catfish and frog's legs while surrounded by the animal menagerie of 'America's largest private taxidermy collection.' This swamp shack is unforgettable. It's far south of downtown Jacksonville.

★ Aix   MEDITERRANEAN $$$
(☑904-398-1949; www.bistrox.com; 1440 San Marco Blvd; mains $10-28; ⊙11am-10pm Mon-Thu, to 11pm Fri, 5-11pm Sat, 5-9pm Sun) Dine with the fashionable food mavens on fusion-y Mediterranean dishes at Aix, whose menu bursts with global flavors. Reservations recommended.

River City Brewing Company   SEAFOOD $$$
(☑904-398-2299; www.rivercitybrew.com; 835 Museum Circle; mains $19-32; ⊙11am-4pm & 5-10pm Mon-Sat, 10:30am-2:30pm Sun) The perfect place to quaff a microbrew and enjoy some upscale seafood overlooking the water.

☆ Entertainment

Freebird Live   LIVE MUSIC
(☑904-246-2473; www.freebirdlive.com; 200 N 1st St; ⊙8pm-2am on show nights) At the beach, a rocking music venue and home of the band Lynyrd Skynyrd.

❶ Getting There & Around

North of the city, **Jacksonville International Airport** (JAX; ☑904-741-4902; www.flyjax.com) has rental cars. **Greyhound** (www.greyhound.com; 10 N Pearl St) serves numerous cities, and **Amtrak** (☑904-766-5110; www.amtrak.com; 3570 Clifford Lane) has trains from the north and south. The **Jacksonville Transportation Authority** (www.jtafla.com) runs the free Skyway monorail and city buses (fare $1.50).

Amelia Island & Around

Residents are quick to tell you: Amelia Island is just as old as that braggart St Augustine – they just can't prove it. Unfortunately, no Ponce de León, no plaque, so they have to content themselves with being a pretty little island of moss-draped Southern charm and home to Fernandina Beach, a shrimping village with 40 blocks of historic buildings and romantic B&Bs. Pick up walking-tour maps and information at the visitor center (☑904-277-0717; www.ameliaisland.com/; 102 Centre St; ☉10am-4pm).

Take a half-hour horse-drawn carriage tour with the Old Towne Carriage Co (☑904-277-1555; www.ameliacarriagetours.com; half-hour adult/child $15/7). If you'd rather a carriage didn't come between you and your horse, Kelly's Seahorse Ranch (☑904-491-5166; www.kellyranchinc.com; 1hr rides $60; ☉10am, noon, 2pm & 4pm) offers beachfront trail rides for riders aged 13 and over .

◎ Sights & Activities

Fort Clinch State Park   PARK
(2601 Atlantic Ave; park pedestrian/car $2/6; ☉park 8am-sunset, fort 9am-5pm) Capping the north end of the island, the Spanish moss–draped Fort Clinch State Park has beaches, camping ($26), bike trails and a commanding Civil War–era fort, with re-enactments taking place the first full weekend of every month.

Amelia Island
Museum of History   MUSEUM
(www.ameliamuseum.org; 233 S 3rd St; adult/student $7/4; ☉10am-4pm Mon-Sat, 1-4pm Sun) Learn about Amelia Island's intricate history, which has seen it ruled under eight different flags starting with the French in 1562. Admission includes tours at 11am and 2pm.

Talbot Islands State Parks   PARK
(☑904-251-2320; ☉8am-dusk) Amelia Island is part of the Talbot Islands State Parks, which includes the pristine shoreline at Little Talbot Island and the 'boneyard beach' at Big Talbot Island State Park, where silvered tree skeletons create a dramatic landscape. Both are south of Amelia Island down the First Coast Hwy.

⌸ Sleeping

Florida House Inn   HOTEL $$
(☑904-491-3322; www.floridahouseinn.com; 20 & 22 S 3rd St; r $140-160) Fernandina does beat out St Augustine with Florida's oldest hotel, Florida House Inn, which stays modern with beautifully restored rooms, wi-fi and free use of zippy, red scooters.

Hoyt House   B&B $$$
(☑800-432-2085, 904-277-4300; www.hoythouse.com; 804 Atlantic Ave; r $239-359; ❀ ☎ ☲) This tall Victorian, perched on the edge of downtown, boasts an enchanting gazebo that begs time with a cool drink. Ten rooms each have their own stylish mix of antiques and found treasures. Want a really unique stay? The owners will rent out their luxury yacht for overnights.

★Elizabeth Pointe Lodge   B&B $$$
(☑904-277-4851; www.elizabethpointelodge.com; 98 S Fletcher Ave; r $225-335, ste $385-470; ❀ ☎) Located right on the ocean, this lodge looks like an old Nantucket-style sea captain's house with wraparound porches, gracious service and beautifully appointed rooms.

★Fairbanks House   B&B $$$
(☑904-277-0500; www.fairbankshouse.com; 227 S 7th St; r $185-240, ste $265-450; ❀ ☎) This grand, Gothic Victorian is stuffed to the gills with silk carpets, heavy leather-bound books and global knickknacks. Guest rooms are so large they feel like suites; we especially like the downstairs room carved out of the house's original 1800s kitchen.

✕ Eating & Drinking

Café Karibo & Karibrew   FUSION, PUB $$
(☑904-277-5269; www.cafekaribo.com; 27 N 3rd St; mains $7-22; ☉11am-9pm Tue-Sat, 11am-8pm Sun, 11am-3pm Mon) This funky side-street favorite serves a large and eclectic menu in a sprawling two-story space. The adjacent Karibrew brewpub has its own menu of global pub grub.

★29 South   SOUTHERN $$$
(☑904-277-7919; www.29southrestaurant.com; 29 S 3rd St; mains lunch $8-13, dinner $18-28; ☉lunch 11:30am-2:30pm Wed-Sat, 10am-2pm Sun, dinner 5:30-9:30pm daily) Small plates and mains link arms happily at the tiny, stylish neo-Southern gourmet bistro.

Merge   MODERN AMERICAN $$$
(☑904-277-8797; www.mergerestaurant.com; 510 S 8th St; meals $19-32; ☉from 5-9pm Sun-Thu, to 10pm Fri & Sat) Run by the former chef from the island's Ritz-Carlton resort, this new bistro is a bit off the beaten path on the side of busy 8th St. Local foodies rave about exquisite seafood dishes using local ingredients – think sea scallops over braised rhubarb, and cornmeal-breaded oysters in white cheddar cream.

★**Palace Saloon** BAR
(www.thepalacesaloon.com; 113-117 Centre St; ⊘noon-2am daily) One more superlative for Fernandina: Florida's oldest bar, sporting swinging doors, draped velvet and a deadly Pirate's Punch.

WEST COAST

If Henry Flagler's railroad made the east coast of Florida what it is today, his non-attention to the rest of the state similarly affected the west coast. Things are calmer here, with fewer tourist hordes and more room for nature to amuse with shelling beaches, swamp lands and nature preserves. The west coast has front-row seats to flame-red sunsets emblazoned over the Gulf of Mexico, as well as adrenaline-pumping roller coasters, hand-rolled cigars and lip-synching mermaids.

Tampa

From the outside, Florida's third-largest city seems all business, even generically so. But Tampa surprises: its revitalized riverfront is a sparkling green swathe dotted with intriguing cultural institutions, and its historic Ybor City district preserves the city's Cuban cigar-industry past while, at night, transforming into the Gulf Coast's hottest bar and nightclub scene. South Tampa, meanwhile, has a cutting-edge dining scene that's drawing food mavens from Orlando and Miami.

◉ Sights

◉ Downtown Tampa

Aside from the zoo, downtown's sights are in or along Tampa's attractive green space, Riverwalk (www.thetampariverwalk.com).

★**Florida Aquarium** AQUARIUM
(☑813-273-4000; www.flaquarium.org; 701 Channelside Dr; adult/child $22/17; ⊘9:30am-5pm) Tampa's excellent aquarium is among the state's best. Cleverly designed, the re-created swamp lets you walk among herons and ibis as they prowl the mangroves. Programs let you swim with the fishes (and the sharks) or take a catamaran ecotour in Tampa Bay.

★**Lowry Park Zoo** ZOO
(☑813-935-8552; www.lowryparkzoo.com; 1101 W Sligh Ave; adult/child $25/20; ⊘9:30am-5pm; ℙ⊞) North of downtown, Tampa's zoo gets you as close to the animals as possible, with several free-flight aviaries, a camel ride, giraffe feeding, wallaby enclosure and rhino 'encounter.'

Tampa Museum of Art MUSEUM
(☑813-274-8130; www.tampamuseum.org; 120 W Gasparilla Plaza; adult/child $10/5; ⊘11am-7pm Mon-Thu, to 8pm Fri, to 5pm Sat & Sun) In 2010 the museum christened its dramatically cantilevered new home. Six galleries balance Greek and Roman antiquities, contemporary photography and new media with major traveling exhibitions.

FLORIDA TAMPA

TAMPA BAY AREA BEACHES

The barrier islands of the Tampa Bay Area are graced with some of Florida's best beaches, whether you define 'best' as 'gorgeous untrammeled solitude' or 'family fun and thumping beach parties.' For more information, visit www.tampabaybeaches.com and www.visitstpeteclearwater.com. North to south, some highlights:

Honeymoon & Caladesi Islands Two of Florida's most beautiful beaches; unspoiled, lightly visited Caladesi Island is only reachable by ferry.

Clearwater Beach Idyllic soft white sand hosts raucous spring-break-style parties; huge resorts cater to the masses.

St Pete Beach Double-wide strand is an epicenter of activities and all-ages fun; packed with hotels, bars and restaurants.

Pass-a-Grille Beach Most popular with city-based day-trippers; extremely long and backed by houses (not resorts); cute-as-a-button village for eats.

Fort Desoto Park & Beach North Beach is one of Florida's finest white-sand beaches; ideal for families. Extensive park includes bike and kayak rentals, fishing piers and a cafe.

Tampa Bay History Center
MUSEUM

(☑813-228-0097; www.tampabayhistorycenter.org; 801 Old Water St; adult/child $13/8; ⊘10am-5pm) This first-rate history museum presents the region's Seminole people, Cracker pioneers and Tampa's Cuban community and cigar industry. The cartography collection dazzles.

Henry B Plant Museum
MUSEUM

(☑813-254-1891; www.plantmuseum.com; 401 W Kennedy Blvd; adult/child 4-12yrs $10/5; ⊘10am-5pm Tue-Sat, from noon Sun) The silver minarets of Henry B Plant's 1891 Tampa Bay Hotel glint majestically. Now part of the University of Tampa, one section re-creates the original hotel's luxurious, gilded late-Victorian world.

Glazer Children's Museum
MUSEUM

(☑813-443-3861; www.glazermuseum.org; 110 W Gasparilla Plaza; adult/child under 12 yr $15/9.50; ⊘10am-5pm Mon-Fri, to 6pm Sat, 1-6pm Sun; ▣) Creative play spaces for kids don't get any better than this crayon-bright, inventive museum. Eager staff and tons of coolio fun; adjacent Curtis Hixon Park is picnic-and-playground friendly.

◉ Ybor City

Like the illicit love child of Key West and Miami's Little Havana, Ybor City's cobblestoned 19th-century historic district is a redolent mix of wrought-iron balconies, globe streetlamps, immigrant history, ethnic cuisine, cigars and hip, happening nightlife. Diverse and youthful, Ybor (ee-bore) City oozes rakish, scruffy charm.

Get a great overview plus walking tour maps at the visitor center (☑813-241-8838; www.ybor.org; 1600 E 8th Ave; ⊘10am-5pm Mon-Sat, from noon Sun) – itself an excellent small museum. The main drag – along 7th Ave (La Septima) between 14th and 21st Sts – is packed with eats, drinks, shops and cigar stores.

Ybor City Museum State Park
MUSEUM

(☑813-247-6323; www.ybormuseum.org; 1818 E 9th Ave; adult/child under 5yr $4/free; ⊘9am-5pm) Join a walking tour (☑813-428-0854; tour $18 incl museum admission; ⊘by appt) run by a cigar-maker with a PhD, check out the cool museum store, or delve into the old-school history museum that preserves a bygone era, with cigar-worker houses and wonderful photos.

◉ Busch Gardens & Adventure Island

No, it's not as thematically immersive as Orlando's Disney World or Universal, but Tampa's big theme park, Busch Gardens (☑813-987-5600; www.buschgardens.com; 10165 McKinley Dr; adult/child 3-9yr $85/77, discounts online; ⊘varies by day & season), will satisfy your adrenaline craving with epic roller coasters and flume rides that weave through an African-theme wildlife park. Music, performances and interactive 4D movies round out a full day. Check the website for opening hours, which vary seasonally.

Adjacent Adventure Island (☑813-987-5600; www.adventureisland.com; 10001 McKinley Dr; adult/child 3-9yr $46/42; ⊘hours vary; daily

---

MANATEES & MERMAIDS

Apparently, Florida's Spanish discoverers confused manatees with mermaids, but it's not hard to tell them apart. Mermaids are those beautiful long-haired women with the spangly tails swimming in the underwater theater at Weeki Wachee Springs (☑352-592-5656; www.weekiwachee.com; 6131 Commercial Way, Spring Hill; adult/child 6-12yr $13/8; ⊘9am-5:30pm). Their graceful adagios and The Little Mermaid show (three times daily) are Florida's most delightfully kitschy entertainment (just 45 minutes north of Tampa).

Lovable, ponderous, 1000lb manatees are the ones nibbling lettuce in the crystal bathtub of Homosassa Springs Wildlife State Park (☑352-628-5343; www.floridastateparks.org/homosassasprings; 4150 S Suncoast Blvd; adult/child 6-12yr $13/5; ⊘9am-5:30pm, last entrance 4pm), with its own underwater observatory (20 minutes north of Weeki Wachee).

Sadly, you can't swim with the mermaids, but you can with the manatees. Head a few miles north to King's Bay, within the Crystal River National Wildlife Refuge (☑352-563-2088; www.fws.gov/crystalriver; 1502 SE Kings Bay Dr; ⊘visitor center 8am-4pm Mon-Fri), where the visitor center can guide you to nearly 40 commercial operators that, had they existed, would have spared the Spaniards lots of heartache.

mid-Mar–Aug, weekends Sep-Oct) is a massive water park with slides and rides galore. Discounts and combination tickets are available online.

🛏 Sleeping

Chains abound along Fowler Ave and Busch Blvd (Hwy 580), near Busch Gardens.

Gram's Place   HOSTEL $

(☑813-221-0596; www.grams-inn-tampa.com; 3109 N Ola Ave; dm $23, r $25-70; ❄@) As charismatic as an aging rock star, Gram's is a tiny, welcoming hostel for international travelers who prefer personality over perfect linens. Dig the in-ground hot tub and Saturday night jams.

Tahitian Inn   HOTEL $$

(☑813-877-6721; www.tahitianinn.com; 601 S Dale Mabry Hwy; r $79-139, ste $149-199; P❄@🛜🏊) The name is reminiscent of a tiki-theme motel, but this family-owned, full-service hotel offers fresh, boutique stylings at midrange prices. Nice pool, and airport transportation.

Don Vicente de Ybor
Historic Inn   HISTORIC HOTEL $$

(☑813-241-4545; www.donvicenteinn.com; 1915 Republica de Cuba; r $139-219; P❄🛜) Slightly faded, the 1895 Don Vicente recalls Ybor City's glory days. Unfortunately, rooms are less warmly dramatic than the atmospheric Old World public spaces. Breakfast included.

🍴 Eating

At mealtime, focus on Ybor City, South Tampa's SoHo area (South Howard Ave) and up-and-coming Seminole Heights.

Wright's Gourmet House   SANDWICHES $

(1200 S Dale Mabry Hwy; sandwiches & salads $5-9; ⏱7am-6pm Mon-Fri, 8am-4pm Sat) It doesn't look like much from the outside. Heck, it doesn't look like much from the inside. But they've been slinging sandwiches since 1963, and their unique combinations and hearty portions win them plenty of fans.

★Ella's Americana
Folk Art Cafe   AMERICAN $$

(www.ellasfolkartcafe.com; 5119 N Nebraska Ave; mains $11-22; ⏱5-11pm Tue-Thu, to midnight Fri & Sat, 11am-8pm Sun) Ten minutes from downtown in Seminole Heights, artsy Ella's aims to please with tasty flavor combinations, funky folk art, occasional live music, and pork ribs in their Bloody Marys during Soul Food Sundays.

Datz & Datz Dough   AMERICAN $$

(www.datztampa.com; 2616 S MacDill Ave; mains $10-19; ⏱7am-10pm Mon-Thu, to 11pm Fri, 8:30am-11pm Sat, 8:30am-3pm Sun) Perfect for a casual meal, this big, bustling place dishes out the humor, with menu items like Brie Bardot, Havana Hottie and When Pigs Fly. Next door, Datz Dough takes on the overflow, serving breakfast, lunch, baked goods and gelato.

Refinery   FUSION $$

(www.thetamparefinery.com; 5137 N Florida Ave; mains $12-18; ⏱5-10pm Sun-Thu, to 11pm Fri & Sat, brunch 11am-3pm Sun; 🚗) 🍴 This blue-collar gourmet joint promises chipped plates and no pretensions, just playful, delicious hyper-local cuisine that cleverly mixes a sustainability ethic with a punk attitude.

★Columbia Restaurant   SPANISH $$$

(☑813-248-4961; www.columbiarestaurant.com; 2117 E 7th Ave; mains lunch $9-15, dinner $18-29; ⏱11am-10pm Mon-Thu, to 11pm Fri & Sat, noon-9pm Sun) Definitely reserve ahead for the exuberant, twice-nightly flamenco shows, and enjoy robust, classic Spanish cuisine and heady *mojitos* and sangria. It's an Old World Iberian time warp.

★Bern's Steak House   STEAKHOUSE $$$

(☑813-251-2421; www.bernssteakhouse.com; 1208 S Howard Ave; mains $25-60; ⏱from 5pm) This legendary, nationally renowned steakhouse is an event as much as a meal. Dress up, order caviar and on-premises dry-aged beef, ask to tour the wine cellar and kitchens, and *don't* skip dessert.

🍷 Drinking & Entertainment

For nightlife, Ybor City is party central, though SoHo and Seminole Heights are also hip and happening. Tampa Bay's alternative weekly, Creative Loafing (www.cltampa. com), lists events and bars. Ybor City is also the center of Tampa's GLBT life; check out the GaYBOR District Coalition (www.gaybor.com) and Tampa Bay Gay (www.tampabaygay.com).

★Skipper's Smokehouse   LIVE MUSIC

(☑813-971-0666; www.skipperssmokehouse.com; 910 Skipper Rd; cover $5-25; ⏱11am-midnight Tue-Fri, from noon Sat, from 1pm Sun) Feeling like it blew in from the Keys, Skipper's is a beloved, unpretentious open-air venue for blues, folk, reggae and gator-swamp rockabilly about ten miles north of downtown. Get directions online.

Straz Center for the Performing Arts
PERFORMING ARTS

(☑ 813-229-7827; www.strazcenter.org; 1010 Mac-Innes Pl) This enormous, multivenue complex draws the gamut of fine arts performances: touring Broadway shows, pop concerts, opera, ballet, drama and more.

ℹ Information

MEDIA

The area has two major daily newspapers, the **St Petersburg Times** (www.tampabay.com) and **Tampa Tribune** (www.tampatrib.com).

TOURIST INFORMATION

Tampa Bay Convention & Visitors Bureau
(☑ 813-223-1111; www.visittampabay.com; 615 Channelside Dr; ⊙ 10am-5:30pm Mon-Sat, 11am-5pm Sun) The visitor center has good free maps and lots of information. Book hotels directly through the website.

ℹ Getting There & Around

Tampa International Airport (TPA; www.tampaairport.com) has car-rental agencies. **Greyhound** (www.greyhound.com; 610 E Polk St) has numerous services. Trains run south to Miami and north through Jacksonville from the **Amtrak station** (☑ 813-221-7600; www.amtrak.com; 601 N Nebraska Ave). **Hillsborough Area Regional Transit** (HART; ☑ 813-254-4278; www.gohart.org; 1211 N Marion St; fare $2) connects downtown and Ybor City with buses, trolleys and old-style streetcars.

St Petersburg

In the bay area, St Petersburg is the more arty, youthful sibling. It also has a more compact and walkable tourist district along its attractive harbor. For a cultural city base within easy striking distance of the region's excellent beaches, St Pete is a great choice.

For maps and info, drop by the **chamber of commerce** (☑ 727-821-4069; www.stpete.com; 100 2nd Ave N; ⊙ 9am-5pm Mon-Fri). For planning help, visit www.visitstpeteclearwater.com.

⦿ Sights

Most of the action is around and along Central Ave, from 8th Ave to Bayshore Dr, which fronts the harbor and tourist pier.

St Petersburg Museum of Fine Arts
MUSEUM

(☑ 727-896-2667; www.fine-arts.org; 255 Beach Dr NE; adult/child $17/10; ⊙ 10am-5pm Mon-Sat, to 8pm Thu, from noon Sun) The Museum of Fine Arts collection is as broad as the Dalí's is deep, traversing the world's antiquities and following art's progression through nearly every era.

Florida Holocaust Museum
MUSEUM

(☑ 727-820-0100; www.flholocaustmuseum.org; 55 5th St S; adult/child $16/8; ⊙ 10am-5pm) The understated exhibits of this Holocaust museum, one of the country's largest, present these mid-20th-century events with moving directness.

Chihuly Collection
GALLERY

(☑ 727-896-4527; www.chihulycollectionstpete.com; 400 Beach Dr; adult/child $15/11; ⊙ 10am-5pm Mon-Sat, from noon Sun) A paean to Dale Chihuly's glass artistry, with galleries designed to hold the dramatic installations.

🛏 Sleeping

★ Dickens House
B&B $$

(☑ 727-822-8622; www.dickenshouse.com; 335 8th Ave NE; r $119-245; P ❋ @ ☎) Five lushly designed rooms await in this passionately restored arts-and-crafts-movement home. The gregarious, gay-friendly owner whips up a gourmet breakfast.

Ponce de Leon
BOUTIQUE HOTEL $$

(☑ 727-550-9300; www.poncedeleonhotel.com; 95 Central Ave; r $99-119, ste $169; P ❋ @ ☎) A boutique hotel with Spanish flair in the heart of downtown. Splashy murals, designer-cool decor, and the hot restaurant and bar are highlights; off-site parking is not.

Renaissance Vinoy Resort
LUXURY HOTEL $$$

(☑ 727-894-1000; www.vinoyrenaissanceresort.com; 501 5th Ave NE; r $169-359; P ❋ @ ☎ ☎) St Pete's coral pink grande dame, the newly renovated 1925 Vinoy is a sumptuous concoction with standout off-season and online deals. It's worth it just for the gorgeous pool.

🍴 Eating & Drinking

At night, focus on Central Ave between 2nd and 3rd Sts, and along the harborfront. Many restaurants have lively, late bar scenes.

AnnaStella Cajun Bistro
CAJUN $

(☑ 727-498-8978; www.annastellacajunbistro.com; 300 Beach Dr N; dishes $6-16; ⊙ 8am-10pm Sun-Thu, to 11pm Fri & Sat; ☎) Enjoy a Cajun-spiced breakfast or lunch and harbor views; great gumbo and fresh beignets (French-style doughnuts).

SALVADOR DALÍ MUSEUM

Of course St Petersburg was the logical place to put a museum dedicated to Salvador Dalí, the eccentric Spanish artist who painted melting clocks, grew an exaggerated handlebar mustache to look like King Philip, and once filled a Rolls Royce with cauliflower. Right? In fact, The Dalí Museum (✆727-823-3767; www.thedali.org; 1 Dali Blvd; adult/child 6-12yr $21/7, after 5pm Thu $10; ⊙10am-5:30pm Mon-Sat, to 8pm Thu, noon-5:30pm Sun) is the largest Dalí collection outside of Spain. So how did that happen exactly?

In 1942, A. Reynolds Morse and his wife Eleanor began what would become the largest private Dalí collection in the world. When it came time to find a permanent home for the collection, they had one stipulation: that the collection had to stay together. Only three cities could agree to the terms, and St Petersburg won out for its waterfront location.

The museum now has a brand-new building with a theatrical exterior that, when seen from the bay side, looks like a geodesic atrium oozing out of a shoebox. It doesn't have *the* melting clocks, but it does have *some* melting clocks, as well as an impressive collection of paintings with titles such as *The Ghost of Vermeer of Delft Which Can Be Used as a Table*.

★Ceviche   TAPAS $$
(✆727-209-2299; www.ceviche.com; 10 Beach Dr; tapas $5-13, mains $15-23; ⊙11am-10pm) Panache counts and Ceviche has it in spades, with an upbeat Spanish atmosphere and flavorful, creative, generously portioned tapas. End the evening in the sexy, cavernlike Flamenco Room below, with live flamenco Thursday and Saturday nights.

Bella Brava   ITALIAN $$
(✆727-895-5515; www.bellabrava.com; 204 Beach Dr NE; lunch $7-10, dinner $14-20; ⊙11:30am-10pm, to 11pm Fri & Sat, 3-9pm Sun) Anchoring the prime waterfront intersection, Bella Brava specializes in contemporary northern Italian cooking and breezy, sidewalk dining.

Garden   MEDITERRANEAN $$
(✆727-896-3800; www.thegardendtsp.com; 217 Central Ave; lunch $7-12, dinner $15-24; ⊙11am-10pm Sun-Thu, to 11pm Fri & Sat) In a pretty hidden courtyard, Garden emphasizes Mediterranean-influenced salads and pastas. There's live jazz and DJs on weekends.

☆ Entertainment

★Jannus Live   CONCERT VENUE
(✆727-565-0551; www.jannuslive.com; 16 2nd St N) Well-loved outdoor concert venue inside an intimate courtyard; national and local bands reverberate downtown.

❶ Getting There & Around

St Petersburg-Clearwater International Airport (www.fly2pie.com; Roosevelt Blvd & Hwy 686, Clearwater) is served by several major carriers. Greyhound (✆727-898-1496; www.greyhound.com; 180 Dr Martin Luther King Jr St N) services include Tampa.

Pinellas Suncoast Transit Authority (PSTA; www.psta.net; 340 2nd Ave N; fare $2; ⊙5am-9pm Mon-Sat, 7am-5pm Sun) operates buses citywide and the Suncoast Beach Trolley that links the beaches from Clearwater to Pass-a-Grille.

Sarasota

Artists, writers, musicians, entertainers – artsy types have flocked to Sarasota since the 1920s, with John Ringling leading the way. He set it on this course in 1911, when he made the town the winter home of his famous circus. Today the Ringling Museum Complex is a regional highlight, and Sarasota spills over with opera, theater and art. For arts and performance information, check out the Arts and Cultural Alliance (www.sarasotaarts.org). The all-encompassing Van Wezel Performing Arts Hall (✆800-826-9303, 941-953-3368; www.vanwezel.org; 777 N Tamiami Trail; tickets $25-80) showcases all types of performances, while the Asolo Repertory Theatre (✆941-351-8000; www.asolorep.org; 5555 N Tamiami Trail; tickets $15-50; ⊙Nov-Jul) is a lauded regional theater company.

Another considerable boost to Sarasota's popularity is its luscious white-sand beaches. Lido Beach is closest and has free parking, but 5 miles away Siesta Key has sand like confectioner's sugar and is one of Florida's best and most popular strands; Siesta Village is also a lively, family-friendly beach town.

Want more nature? Mote Aquarium (✆941-388-4441; www.mote.org; 1600 Ken Thompson Pkwy, City Island; adult/child $17/14; ⊙10am-5pm) is a

RINGLING COMPLEX

Who doesn't love the circus? Well, people who are afraid of clowns, perhaps, but a little coulrophobia isn't necessarily a deal breaker at the Ringling Museum Complex (☑ 941-359-5700; www.ringling.org; 5401 Bay Shore Rd; adult/child 6-17yr $25/5; ☺ 10am-5pm daily, to 8pm Thu; ☑). On the grounds of the 66-acre complex are three separate museums, all included in your admission and each one a worthy attraction on its own. Railroad, real-estate and circus baron John Ringling and his wife Mabel put down roots here, building a Venetian Gothic waterfront mansion called Ca d'Zan. You can wander the ground floor at your own pace, or take a guided tour – totally worth it – which grants you access to the upstairs bedrooms.

Also on the grounds, the John & Mabel Museum of Art is an excellent art museum with impressive high ceilings, intimidatingly large paintings and a re-created room from the Astor mansion. But the real standout here is the one-of-a-kind Museum of the Circus, with costumes, props, posters, antique circus wagons and an extensive miniature model that let you relive the excitement of the big-top era.

leading shark research center providing intimate encounters with sharks, manatees, sea turtles, rays and more, plus marine biologist-led sea-life cruises. Boasting the world's largest scientific collection of orchids and bromeliads, Marie Selby Botanical Gardens (☑ 941-366-5731; www.selby.org; 811 S Palm Ave; adult/child 6-11yr $17/6; ☺ 10am-5pm) is a relaxing yet fascinating botanical encounter. And about a half-hour from downtown, visit Myakka River State Park (www.myakkariver.org; 13208 State Road 72, Sarasota; car/bike $6/2; ☺ 8am-sunset) to kayak or airboat among hundreds of alligators, and for the area's best hiking and camping; get directions and tour times online.

Stop by the Visitor Information Center (☑ 941-706-1253; www.sarasotafl.org; 701 N Tamiami Trail; ☺ 10am-5pm Mon-Sat, 11am-2pm Sun; ☎) for info and maps.

🛏 Sleeping & Eating

In addition to downtown Sarasota and Siesta Village, St Armands Circle on Lido Key is an evening social hub, with a proliferation of stylish shops and restaurants.

★ Hotel Ranola   BOUTIQUE HOTEL $$
(☑ 941-951-0111; www.hotelranola.com; 118 Indian Pl; r $109-149, ste $209; P ❄ @) The nine rooms feel like a designer's brownstone apartment: free-spirited and effortlessly artful, but with real working kitchens. It's urban funk, walkable to downtown Sarasota.

Sunsets on the Key   APARTMENT $$$
(☑ 941-312-9797; www.sunsetsonthekey.com; 5203 Avenida Navarre; apt in-season $230-340, off-season $149-209; P ❄ ☎ ⊠) In Siesta

Village, eight well-kept, rigorously clean condo apartments are run like a hotel.

★ Broken Egg   BREAKFAST $
(www.thebrokenegg.com; 140 Avenida Messina; mains $7-14; ☺ 7:30am-2:30pm; ☑) This diner-style breakfast institution on Siesta Key, known for huge pancakes and cheddary home fries, is a social hub each morning.

★ Owen's Fish Camp   SOUTHERN $$
(☑ 941-951-6936; www.owensfishcamp.com; 516 Burns Lane; mains $9-22; ☺ from 4pm) This ironically hip swamp-shack downtown serves upscale versions of Florida-style Southern cuisine with an emphasis on seafood.

Fort Myers

Workaday, sprawling Fort Myers is overshadowed by the region's pretty beaches and upscale, sophisticated towns. However, a recent facelift has spruced up the historic riverfront district (along 1st St between Broadway and Lee St) into an attractive, brick-lined collection of restaurants and bars. Visit www.fortmyers.org for information.

Fort Myers' main claim to fame is the Edison & Ford Winter Estates (☑ 239-334-7419; www.edisonfordwinterestates.org; 2350 McGregor Blvd; adult/child $20/11; ☺ 9am-5:30pm). Famous inventor Thomas Edison built a winter home and lab here in 1885, and automaker Henry Ford became his neighbor in 1916. The excellent museum focuses mainly on the overwhelming scope of Edison's genius, and their homes are genteel, landscaped delights.

From November through March, one of the easiest ways to encounter wintering manatees is at Lee County Manatee Park (☑239-690-5030; www.leeparks.org; 10901 State Rd 80; parking per hr/day $2/5; ⊘8am-sunset daily) **FREE**, a warm-water power-plant discharge canal that's now a protected sanctuary. The park is signed off Hwy 80, about 6.5 miles from downtown.

For an easily accessible taste of South Florida wetlands, meander the 1.2-mile boardwalk trail of the Six Mile Cypress Slough Preserve (☑239-533-7550; www.leeparks.org/sixmile; 7791 Penzance Blvd; parking per hr/day $1/5; ⊘dawn-dusk, nature center 10am-4pm Tue-Sat, to 2pm Sun) **FREE**.

Fort Myers Beach

Fifteen miles south of Fort Myers, Fort Myers Beach is 7 miles of talcum powder-fine sand along Estero Island, presided over by one of Florida's quintessential activity-and-party-fueled beach towns. Families often prefer Fort Myers Beach because it's more affordable than neighboring coastal towns, and coeds like it because its bars are louder and more raucous. For town information, visit www.fortmyersbeachchamber.org.

The only draw, and it's a good one, is the beachy fun, but nearby Lovers Key State Park (☑239-463-4588; www.floridastateparks.org; 8700 Estero Blvd; per car/bike $8/2; ⊘8am-sunset) adds great shelling as well as hiking and kayaking among quiet islands and canals (frequented by manatees).

Impeccably clean and well maintained, Edison Beach House (☑239-463-1530; www.edisonbeachhouse.com; 830 Estero Blvd; r $145-415; ✽🛜🐾) is perfectly situated near action central (the so-called Times Sq area), yet soothingly comfortable, with full kitchens. For funky charm in a more low-key beach section, nab one of the six rooms at Mango Street Inn (☑239-233-8542; www.mangostreetinn.com; 126 Mango St; r $95-150; ✽🛜🐾), an idiosyncratic B&B serving delectable breakfasts by a Cajun-trained chef.

Sanibel & Captiva Islands

Shaped like a fish hook trying to lure Fort Myers, these two slivers of barrier island lie across a 2-mile causeway (toll $6). Upscale but unpretentious, with a carefully managed shoreline that feels remarkably lush and undeveloped, the islands are idyllic, cushy getaways, where bikes are the preferred mode of travel, the shelling is legendary and

romantic meals are a reservation away. The Sanibel & Captiva Islands Chamber of Commerce (☑239-472-1080; www.sanibel-captiva.org; 1159 Causeway Rd, Sanibel; ⊘9am-5pm; 🐾) is one of the most helpful visitors centers around and can help with accommodations.

In addition to its fabulous beaches, Sanibel's 6300-acre JN 'Ding' Darling National Wildlife Refuge (☑239-472-1100; www.fws.gov/dingdarling; 1 Wildlife Drive; per car/cyclist $5/1; ⊘Wildlife Drive from 7am, closed Fri, visitor center 9am-5pm) is a splendid refuge that's home to an abundance of seabirds and wildlife. It has an excellent nature center, a 5-mile Wildlife Drive, narrated tram tours and easy kayaking in Tarpon Bay. For tours and boat rentals, contact Tarpon Bay Explorers (☑239-472-8900; www.tarponbayexplorers.com; 900 Tarpon Bay Rd, Sanibel; ⊘8am-6pm).

Like a mermaid's jewel box, the Bailey-Matthews Shell Museum (☑239-395-2233; www.shellmuseum.org; 3075 Sanibel-Captiva Rd, Sanibel; adult/child 5-16yr $9/5; ⊘10am-5pm) is a natural history of the sea, with covetous displays of shells worldwide. To rent bikes or any other wheeled contrivance, visit Billy's Rentals (☑239-472-5248; www.billysrentals.com; 1470 Periwinkle Way, Sanibel; bikes per 2hr/day from $5/15; ⊘8:30am-5pm).

On Captiva, the 'Tween Waters Inn (☑239-472-5161; www.tween-waters.com; 15951 Captiva Dr, Captiva; r $175-275, ste $265-390, cottages from $245; ✽@🛜🐾) is a full-service yet low-key resort with a variety of good-value lodging choices; ask for a renovated room. In addition to a big pool, tennis courts and spa, its marina offers various kayak rentals, guided trips and boat cruises. Or, for a more personal experience, stay in the five-room Tarpon Tale Inn (☑239-472-0939; www.tarpontale.com; 367 Periwinkle Way, Sanibel; r $80-219; ✽@🛜🐾), which does a nice imitation of a charming, hammock-strung B&B, but without breakfast.

Start your day at the Over Easy Cafe (www.overeasycafesanibel.com; 630 Tarpon Bay Rd at Periwinkle Way, Sanibel; mains $8-14; ⊘7am-3pm daily; 🐾), a social hub where everyone goes for a diner-style breakfast. Island Cow (☑239-472-0606; www.sanibelislandcow.com; 2163 Periwinkle Way; mains $8-19; ⊘7am-10pm) has an extensive menu and a cheery interior, making it an easy choice any time of day. Or, for romantic gourmet, Sweet Melissa's Cafe (☑239-472-1956; www.sweetmelissascafe.net; 1625 Periwinkle Way, Sanibel; tapas $9-16, mains $26-34; ⊘11:30am-2:30pm Mon-Fri, from 5pm Mon-Sat) offers creative, relaxed refinement.

Naples

The Gulf Coast's answer to Palm Beach, Naples is a perfectly manicured, rich town with an adult sense of self and one of the most pristine, relaxed city beaches in the state. While it is certainly family friendly, it appeals most to romance-minded travelers seeking fine art and fine dining, trendy cocktails, fashion-conscious shopping and luscious sunsets. Visit www.napleschamber. org for city information.

For contemporary art, the sophisticated Naples Museum of Art (239-597-1900; www.thephil.org; 5833 Pelican Bay Blvd; adult/child under 17 $10/free; 10am-4pm Tue-Sat, noon-4pm Sun) is a rewarding collection with cleverly designed exhibits. Meanwhile, one of the state's best nature conservancies and rehabilitation centers is Naples Nature Center (239-262-0304; www.conservancy.org; 1450 Merrihue Dr; adult/child 3-12 $13/9; 9:30am-4:30pm Mon-Sat), with a LEED-certified campus and fantastic exhibits.

For well-polished, Mediterranean-style luxury in the heart of downtown's 5th Ave corridor, stay at the historic Inn on 5th (239-403-8777; www.innonfifth.com; 699 5th Ave S; r $180-500;). For a well-located, good-value midrange motel, the Lemon Tree Inn (239-262-1414; www.lemontreeinn.com; 250 9th St S, at 3rd Ave S; r $89-169;) is a pretty, bright choice.

Good eats are abundant. Top choices for a special meal include Cafe Lurcat (239-213-3357; www.cafelurcat.com; 494 5th Ave; dinner $24-39; 5-10pm), a sexy, multi-level restaurant and lively bar (open to 11pm or midnight nightly), and the off-the-beaten-path IM Tapas (239-403-8272; http://imtapas.com; 965 4th Ave N; tapas $9-18; from 5:30pm Mon-Sat), where a mother-and-daughter team serves Madrid-worthy Spanish tapas.

CENTRAL FLORIDA

Before Disney – BD – most tourists came to Florida to see two things: the white-sand beaches and the alligator-infested Everglades. Walt Disney changed all that when he opened the Magic Kingdom in 1971. Today Orlando is the theme park capital of the world, and Walt Disney World is Florida's number one attraction.

Orlando

Like Las Vegas, Orlando is almost entirely given over to fantasy. It's a place to come when you want to imagine you're somewhere else: Hogwarts, perhaps, or Cinderella's Castle, or Dr Seuss' world, or an African safari. And like Vegas' casinos, Orlando's theme parks work hard to be constantly entertaining thrill rides where the only concern is your pleasure. Even outside the theme parks, Orlando can exhibit a hyper atmosphere of fiberglass-modeled, cartoon-costumed pop culture amusement.

Yet there is, in fact, a real city to explore, one with tree-shaded parks of the natural variety, art museums, orchestras, and dinners that don't involve high-fiving Goofy. And just outside the city, Florida's wilderness and wildlife, particularly its crystal springs, can be as memorably bizarre as anything Ripley ever dreamed up.

Sights & Activities

Downtown & Loch Haven Park

Fashionable Thornton Park has several good restaurants and bars, while Loch Haven Park is home to a cluster of cultural institutions.

★ Orlando Museum of Art   MUSEUM
(407-896-4231; www.omart.org; 2416 N Mills Ave; adult/child $8/5; 10am-4pm Tue-Fri, from noon Sat & Sun) Spotlighting American and African art as well as unique traveling exhibits.

Mennello Museum of
American Art   MUSEUM
(407-246-4278; www.mennellomuseum.com; 900 E Princeton St; adult/child 6-18yr $5/1; 10:30am-4:30pm Tue-Sat, from noon Sun) Features the bright folk art of Earl Cunningham, plus traveling exhibitions.

Orlando Science Center   MUSEUM
(407-514-2000; www.osc.org; 777 E Princeton St; adult/child 3-11yr $19/13; 10am-5pm Thu-Tue) Candy-coated hands-on science for the whole family.

Harry P Leu Gardens   PARK
(www.leugardens.org; 1920 N Forest Ave; adult/student $10/3; 9am-5pm) One mile east of Loch Haven Park is this 50-acre tranquil escape from all the gloss.

⊙ International Drive

Like a theme park itself, International Dr (I-Dr) is shoulder to shoulder with high-energy amusements: sprinkled among the major theme, wildlife and water parks, smaller attractions shout for attention: Ripley's Believe It or Not, the upside-down WonderWorks and an indoor skydiving experience. Chain restaurants and hotels also crowd the thoroughfare.

Check online for combo tickets with Discovery Cove and Aquatica.

★**Universal Orlando Resort**   THEME PARK
(☎407-363-8000;   www.universalorlando.com; 1000 Universal Studios Plaza; single/both parks $92/128, discounts on multiday; ☺daily, hours vary) Universal is giving Disney a run for its money with this mega-complex that features two theme parks, a water park, three hotels and Universal CityWalk, an entertainment district that connects the two parks. But where Disney World is all happy and magical, Universal Orlando gets your adrenaline pumping with revved-up rides and entertaining shows. The first of the two parks, Universal Studios, has a Hollywood backlot feel and simulation-heavy rides dedicated to television and the silver screen, from The Simpsons and Shrek to Revenge of the Mummy and Twister. Universal's Islands of Adventure is tops with coaster-lovers but also has plenty for the little ones in Toon Lagoon and Seuss Landing.

But the absolute highlight – and the hottest thing to hit Orlando since Cinderella's Castle – is the Wizarding World of Harry Potter. Located within Islands of Adventure, it's easily the most fantastically realized themed experience in Florida. Muggles are invited to poke along the cobbled streets and impossibly crooked buildings of Hogsmeade, sip frothy Butter Beer and mail a card via Owl Post, all in the shadow of Hogwarts Caste. The detail and authenticity tickle the fancy at every turn, from the screeches of the mandrakes in the shop windows to the groans of Moaning Myrtle in the bathroom; keep your eyes peeled for magical happenings.

Review multiple ticket options online, which can include add-ons like Express Plus line skipping and a dining plan; resort hotel guests also get nice park perks. Parking is $16.

SeaWorld   AMUSEMENT PARK
(☎407-351-3600; www.seaworld.com; 7007 SeaWorld Dr; adult/child 3-9 $92/84; ☺from 9am) A peculiarly Floridian blend of marine animal shows and thrill rides, SeaWorld is home to both Shamu the killer whale and Kraken the floorless roller coaster. While the rides provide jolts of adrenaline, the real draws are the up-close sea life encounters (with manta rays, sharks, penguins, beluga whales) and the excellent dolphin, sea lion and killer whale shows. Look online for admission discounts and package deals. Make sure to check show and feeding times online before visiting, and plan your day accordingly.

Discovery Cove   WATER PARK
(☎877-557-7404; www.discoverycove.com; 6000 Discovery Cove Way; admission $169-269, incl dolphin swim $229-379; ☺8am-5:30pm) Attendance is limited, ensuring Discovery Cove retains the feel of an exclusive tropical resort, complete with beaches, a fish-filled reef and an aviary. No high-speed thrills or frantic screaming, just blessed relaxation and the chance to swim with dolphins. The price is steep, but everything is included: buffet lunch, beer, towels, parking, even a day pass to SeaWorld.

⊙ Winter Park

On the northern edge of Orlando, Winter Park is a friendly college town with some outstanding museums and a relaxing downtown.

**Charles Hosmer Morse
Museum of American Art**   MUSEUM
(www.morsemuseum.org; 445 N Park Ave; adult/child $5/free; ☺9:30am-4pm Tue-Sat, from 1pm Sun) Internationally famous, with the world's most comprehensive collection of Tiffany glass; its stunning centerpiece is a chapel interior.

Scenic Boat Tour   BOAT TOUR
(www.scenicboattours.com; 1 E Morse Blvd; adult/child $12/6; ☺hourly 10am-4pm) This recommended one-hour **boat ride** floats through 12 miles of tropical canals and lakes. The enthusiastic tour guide talks about the mansions, Rollins College and other sites along the way. Boats are small pontoons, holding about 10 people each.

⊙ Greater Orlando

★**Gatorland**   AMUSEMENT PARK
(www.gatorland.com; 14501 S Orange Blossom Trail/ Hwy 17; adult/child $25/17; ☺10am-6pm) This Old Florida throwback is small, silly and kitschy. It's all about alligators, with gator wrestling, gator jumping, feeding gators hot dogs and other great squeal-worthy moments.

Greater Orlando & Theme Parks

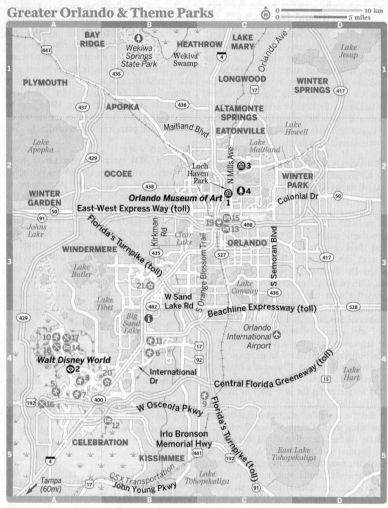

🛏 Sleeping

In addition to the Walt Disney World resorts, Orlando has countless lodging options. Most are clustered around I-Dr, US 192 in Kissimmee and I-4. **Reserve Orlando** (www.reserveorlando.com) is a central booking agency. **Universal Orlando Resort** (☎407-363-8000; www.universalorlando.com; r & ste from $270) also has three recommended hotels.

⭐ **EO Inn & Spa**   BOUTIQUE HOTEL $$
(☎407-481-8485; www.eoinn.com; 227 N Eola Dr; r $129-229; P✳️🛜❄️) Sleek and understated, this downtown boutique inn overlooks Lake Eola near Thornton Park, with neutral-toned rooms that are elegant in their simplicity.

Courtyard at Lake Lucerne   B&B $$
(☎407-648-5188; www.orlandohistoricinn.com; 211 N Lucerne Circle E; r $99-225; P✳️🛜) This lovely historic inn, with enchanting gardens and genteel breakfast, has roomy art-deco suites and handsome antiques throughout. Complimentary cocktails help you forgive its location under two highway overpasses.

Barefoot'n in the Keys   MOTEL $$
(☎877-978-3314; www.barefootn.com; 2754 Florida Plaza Blvd; ste $89-199; @❄️) Clean, bright

Greater Orlando & Theme Parks

and spacious suites in a yellow six-story building. Low-key, friendly and close to Disney, this makes an excellent alternative to generic chains.

✗ Eating

On and around I-Dr you'll find an explosion of chains; a half-mile stretch of Sand Lake Rd has been dubbed 'restaurant row' for its upscale dining.

Dandelion Communitea Café   VEGETARIAN $
(http://dandelioncommunitea.com; 618 N Thornton Ave; mains $6-10; ☉11am-10pm Mon-Sat, to 5pm Sun; 🖉🖪) ✿ Unabashedly crunchy and definitively organic, this pillar of creative, sustainable, locavore vegetarianism is genuinely delicious, with tons of community spirit. Look for events.

Graffiti Junktion
American Burger Bar   BURGERS $
(www.graffitijunktion.com; 900 E Washington St, Thornton Park; mains $6-13; ☉11pm-2am) This neon graffiti-covered happenin' hangout is all about massive burgers with attitude. Top yours with a fried egg, artichoke hearts, chili, avocado and more.

Yellow Dog Eats   BARBECUE $$
(☑407-296-0609; www.yellowdogeats.com; 1236 Hempel Ave, Windermere; mains $7-14; ☉11am-9pm; 🖉) Housed in an old, tin-roof general store, and quirky to the extreme, it's not your typi-

cal barbecue. Try the excellent Cuban-style black beans and the Florida Cracker (pulled pork with gouda, bacon and fried onions). It's a drive; get directions online.

★**Ravenous Pig**   AMERICAN $$$
(☑407-628-2333; www.theravenouspig.com; 1234 Orange Ave, Winter Park; mains $13-33; ☉11:30am-2pm & 5:30-9:30pm Tue-Sat) One of Orlando's most talked-about foodie destinations, this bustling hot spot serves designer cocktails and creative, delicious versions of shrimp and grits, and lobster tacos. Reservations recommended.

🍸 Drinking & Entertainment

Orlando Weekly (www.orlandoweekly.com) is the best source for entertainment listings. There's plenty to do downtown, where there's a happening bar district around Orange Ave between Church St and Jefferson St.

Universal Studio's **CityWalk** (www.citywalkorlando.com) has a concentration of cinemas, restaurants, clubs and big-name shows.

Latitudes   BAR
(www.churchstreetbars.com; 33 W Church St; ☉4:30pm-2am) Island-inspired rooftop bar, with two more bars below.

Wall Street Plaza   BAR
(☑407-849-0471; www.wallstplaza.net; 25 Wall St Plaza) Eight theme bars, with live music, all in one plaza.

FLORIDA ORLANDO

The Social   LIVE MUSIC
(☏ 407-246-1419; www.thesocial.org; 54 N Orange Ave) Check out great live music.

Parliament House   GAY
(www.parliamenthouse.com; 410 N Orange Blossom Trail; ⊙ 10:30am-3am) Legendary gay resort and drag shows; six bars.

ℹ Information

For city information, discount tickets to attractions, and good multilingual guides and maps, visit Orlando's **Official Visitor Center** (☏ 407-363-5872; www.visitorlando.com; 8723 International Dr; ⊙ 8:30am-6pm). Gay travelers can peruse http://orlando.gaycities.com. For theme park advice, visit www.themeparkinsider.com.

ℹ Getting There & Around

Orlando International Airport (MCO; www.orlandoairports.net) has buses and taxis to major tourist areas. **Mears Transportation** (☏ 407-423-5566; www.mearstransportation.com) provides shuttles for $20 to $30 per person. **Greyhound** (www.greyhound.com; 555 N John Young Pkwy) serves numerous cities. **Amtrak** (www.amtrak.com; 1400 Sligh Blvd) has daily trains south to Miami and north to New York City.

Orlando's bus network is operated by **Lynx** (☏ route info 407-841-8240; www.golynx.com; single ride/day/week pass $2/4.50/16, transfers free). **I-Ride Trolley** (www.iridetrolley.com; rides adult/child under 12yr $1.50/free) buses run along I-Dr.

When driving, note that I-4 is the main north–south connector, though it's confusingly labeled east–west. To go north, take I-4 east (toward Daytona); to go south, get on I-4 west (toward Tampa). The main east–west roads are Hwy 50 and Hwy 528 (the Bee Line Expwy), which accesses Orlando International Airport.

Walt Disney World Resort

Covering 40 sq miles, Walt Disney World (WDW; ☏ 407-939-5277; http://disneyworld.disney.go.com) is the largest theme park resort in the world. It includes four separate theme parks, two water parks, a sports complex, five golf courses, two dozen hotels, 100 restaurants and two shopping and nightlife districts – proving that it's not such a small world, after all. At times it feels ridiculously crowded and corporate, but with or without kids, you won't be able to inoculate yourself against Disney's highly infectious enthusiasm and warm-hearted nostalgia. Naturally, expectations run high, and even the self-proclaimed 'happiest place on earth'

doesn't always live up to its billing. Still, it always happens: Cinderella curtsies to your little Belle, your own Jedi knight vanquishes Darth Maul, or you tear up on that corny ride about our tiny planet, and suddenly you're swept up in the magic.

◉ Sights & Activities

Magic Kingdom   THEME PARK
When most people think of WDW – especially kids – it's really the Magic Kingdom they're picturing. This is where you'll find all the classic Disney experiences, such as the iconic Cinderella's Castle, rides like Space Mountain and the nighttime fireworks and light parade illuminating **Main Street, USA**. For Disney mythology, it doesn't get better.

Cinderella's Castle is at the center of the park, and from there paths lead to the different 'lands':

Tomorrowland is where Space Mountain hurtles you through the darkness of outer space. This indoor roller coaster is the most popular ride in the Magic Kingdom, so come first thing and if the line is already excruciating, get a FastPass.

Fantasyland is the highlight of any Disney trip for the eight-and-under crowd. This is the land of Mickey and Minnie, Goofy and Donald Duck, Snow White and the Seven Dwarves, and many more big names.

Adventureland features pirates and jungles, magic carpets and tree houses, whimsical and silly representations of the exotic locales from storybooks and imagination.

Liberty Square is the home of the the Haunted Mansion, a rambling, 19th century mansion that's a Disney favorite, and **Frontierland** is Disney's answer to the Wild West.

Disney Hollywood Studios   THEME PARK
Formerly Disney-MGM Studios, this is the least charming of Disney's parks. However, it does have two of WDW's most exciting rides: the unpredictable elevator in the **Twilight Zone Tower of Terror** and the Aerosmith-themed **Rock 'n' Roller Coaster**. Wannabe singers can audition for the American Idol Experience, kids can join the Jedi Training Academy, and various programs present Walt Disney himself and how Disney's movies are made.

Epcot   THEME PARK
An acronym for 'Experimental Prototype Community of Tomorrow,' Epcot was Disney's vision of a high-tech city when it opened in 1982. It's divided into two halves: **Future**

World, with rides and corporate-sponsored interactive exhibits, and World Showcase, providing an interesting toe-dip into the cultures of 11 countries. Epcot is much more soothingly low-key than other parks, and it has some of the best food and shopping. Plus, a few rides are WDW highlights, like Soarin' and Mission: Space. The interactive Turtle Talk with Crush is delightful.

Animal Kingdom   THEME PARK
This sometimes surreal blend of African safari, zoo, rides, costumed characters, shows and dinosaurs establishes its own distinct tone. It's best at animal encounters and shows, with the 110-acre Kilimanjaro Safaris as its centerpiece. The iconic Tree of Life houses the fun It's Tough to Be a Bug! show, and Expedition Everest and Kali River Rapids are the top thrill rides.

🛏 Sleeping

While it's tempting to save money by staying elsewhere, the value of staying at a Walt Disney World resort lies in the conveniences they offer. WDW has 24 family-friendly sleeping options, from camping to deluxe resorts, and Disney guests receive great perks (extended park hours, discount dining plans, free transportation, airport shuttles). Disney's thorough website outlines rates and amenities for every property. Don't expect the quality of the room and amenities to match the price: you're paying for Walt Disney World convenience, not for Ritz-like luxury.

One of our favorite deluxe resorts is the Yosemite-style Wilderness Lodge (📞407-824-3200; 901 Timberline Dr; r from $319; P❄🛜🏊); the 'rustic opulence' theme includes erupting geysers, a lakelike swimming area and bunk beds for the kids. And for wilderness on a budget, we love the Fort Wilderness Resort & Campground (📞407-824-2900; campsites $54-120, cabins from $325; ❄🛜🏊🐕) with tent sites and cabins that sleep up to six people.

Disney's Value Resorts (https://disneyworld.disney.go.com; r $90-150) are the least-expensive option (besides camping); quality is equivalent to basic chain hotels, and (fair warning) they are favored by school groups.

Disney's Art of Animation Resort   HOTEL
(📞407-938-7000; 1850 Animation Way; ❄🏊) Inspired by animated Disney classics including *The Lion King, Cars, Finding Nemo* and *The Little Mermaid.*

Disney's All-Star Movies Resort   HOTEL
(📞407-939-7000; 1991 Buena Vista Dr; ❄🏊) Icons from Disney movies including *Toy Story* and *101 Dalmatians.*

Disney's All-Star Music Resort   HOTEL
(📞407-939-6000; 1801 W Buena Vista Dr; ❄🏊) Family suites and motel rooms surrounded by giant instruments.

Disney's All-Star Sports Resort   HOTEL
(📞407-939-5000; 1701 Buena Vista Dr; ❄🏊) Five pairs of three-story buildings divided thematically by sport.

Disney's Pop Century Resort   HOTEL
(📞407-938-4000; 1050 Century Dr; ❄🏊) Each section pays homage to a different decade of the late 20th century.

🍴 Eating

Theme park food ranges from OK to awful; the most interesting is served in Epcot's World Showcase. Sit-down meals are best, but *always* make reservations; seats can be impossible to get without one. For any dining, you can call central reservations (📞407-939-3463) up to 180 days in advance.

Disney has three dinner shows (a luau, country-style BBQ and vaudeville show) and about 15 character meals, and these

---

BEST OF MAGIC KINGDOM

With the exception of Space Mountain, Splash Mountain and the scary introduction to the Haunted Mansion, these are all Disney Perfect for children.

Mickey's Philharmagic 3D movie perfection.

Space Mountain Indoor roller coaster in the dark.

Pirates of the Caribbean Cruise through the world of pirates.

Haunted Mansion Slow-moving ride past lighthearted spooks.

Dumbo the Flying Elephant A favorite with toddlers.

Mad Tea Party Quintessential Disney spinning.

It's a Small World Boat ride through the world – you know the song.

Jungle Cruise Disney silliness at its best.

Splash Mountain Classic water ride.

TICKETS & TIPS

Tickets

Consider buying a ticket that covers more days in the parks than you think you'll need. It's less expensive per day, and it gives you the freedom to break up time at the theme parks with downtime in the pool or at low-key attractions beyond theme-park gates.

You can buy tickets for one park per day, or Park Hopper passes that allow entrance to all four parks. Check online for packages, and buy in advance to avoid lines at the gate. For discounts, check out www.mousesavers.com and www.undercovertourist.com.

When to Go

Anytime schools are out – during summer and holidays – WDW will be the most crowded. The least crowded times are January to February, mid-September through October and early December. Late fall tends to have the best weather; frequent downpours accompany the hot, humid summer months.

On the actual day you go, plan on arriving early so you can see as much of the park as possible before the midday peak. Consider going back to your hotel for to recharge around 2:00 or 3:00 pm when it's the hottest and most crowded, then come back a few hours later and stay till close.

Fast Pass

For the most popular attractions, WDW offers FastPass: a free paper ticket that assigns a time for you to return and skip (most of) the mind-numblingly long lines. Just swipe your park ticket at the automated ticket machine next to the ride (the park map will tell you which ones offer that option) and come back when it tells you to. FastPass waits are usually no more than 15 minutes.

The catch? You can only have one (sometimes two, depending on crowd levels) at a time. Check the bottom of your FastPass to find out when you are eligible to swipe your card for another FastPass. FastPasses for the most popular attractions can run out by midday; if you really want to see something, get your FastPass as early as possible.

---

are insanely popular (see website for details). Book them the minute your 180-day window opens. The most sought-after meal is **Cinderella's Royal Table** (adult $43-54, child $28-33) inside the Magic Kingdom's castle, where you dine with Disney princesses.

★**Sci-Fi Dine-In Theater**   AMERICAN $$
(Hollywood Studios; mains $13-30; ☺11am-10:30pm; 🖼) Dine in Cadillacs and watch classic sci-fi flicks.

O'Hana   HAWAIIAN $$$
(Polynesian Resort; adult $36-43, child $18-20; ☺7:30-11am, 5-10pm) Great South Pacific decor and interactive Polynesian-themed luau shenanigans with all-you-care-to-eat meals served family style.

California Grill   AMERICAN $$$
(Disney's Contemporary Resort; mains $32-49; ☺5-10pm; 🖼) Coveted seats with great views of the Magic Kingdom fireworks.

Boma   BUFFET $$$
(Animal Kingdom Lodge; adult/child breakfast $23/13, dinner $40/19; ☺7:30-11am, 4:30-9:30pm; 🖼) African-inspired eatery with pleasant surroundings and a buffet several notches above the rest.

Victoria and Albert   AMERICAN $$$
(Grand Floridian; prix fixe $135) A true jacket-and-tie, crystal goblet romantic gourmet restaurant – no kidding, and no kids under 10.

☆ Entertainment

In addition to theme park events like Magic Kingdom parades and fireworks and Epcot's Illuminations, Disney has two entertainment districts – Downtown Disney and Disney's Boardwalk – with eats, bars, music, movies, shops and shows.

★**Cirque du Soleil**
La Nouba   PERFORMING ARTS
(☎407-939-7600; www.cirquedusoleil.com; Downtown Disney's West Side; adult $61-144, child 3-9yr

$49-117; ⊙6pm & 9pm Tue-Sat) This mind-blowing acrobatic extravaganza is one of the best shows at Disney.

House of Blues　　　　　　LIVE MUSIC
(☑407-934-2583; www.houseofblues.com; 1490 E Buena Vista Dr) Top acts visit this national chain; Sunday's Gospel Brunch truly rocks.

DisneyQuest　　　　　　ARCADE
(Downtown Disney; 1-day adult/child 3-9yr $48/41; ⊙11:30am-10pm Sun-Thu, to 11pm Fri & Sat) Five floors of virtual reality and arcade games.

❶ Getting There & Around

Most hotels in Kissimmee and Orlando – and all Disney properties – offer free transportation to Walt Disney World. Disney-owned resorts also offer free transportation from the airport. Drivers can reach all four parks via I-4 and park for $14. The Magic Kingdom lot is huge; trams get you to the entrance.

Within Walt Disney World, a complex network of monorails, boats and buses get you between the parks, resorts and entertainment districts. Pick up a transportation map at your resort or at Guest Relations near the main entrance of all four parks.

Around Orlando

Just north of Orlando await some of Florida's best outdoor adventures, particularly swimming, snorkeling and kayaking in its crystal-clear, 72°F (22°C) natural springs. Closest is Wekiwa Springs State Park (☑407-884-2008; www.floridastateparks.org; 1800 Wekiwa Circle, Apopka; car $6, campsite $24; ⊙8am-sundown), with 13 miles of hiking trails, a spring-fed swimming hole and nice campground and the tranquil 'Wild and Scenic' Wekiva River; rent kayaks from Nature Adventures (☑407-884-4311; www.canoewekiva.com; 2hr $18; ⊙8am-8pm).

Blue Spring State Park (www.floridastateparks.org; 2100 W French Ave; car/bike $6/2; ⊙8am-sundown) is a favorite of wintering manatees, and two-hour cruises ply the St John's River. Just north of Deland, De Leon Springs State Park (www.floridastateparks.org; 601 Ponce de Leon Blvd, Ponce de Leon; car/bike $6/2; ⊙8am-sunset) has a huge swimming area, more kayaking and tours of Juan Ponce de León's alleged fountain of youth.

To really escape into raw wilderness, head for the Ocala National Forest (www.fs.usda.gov/ocala), which has dozens of campgrounds, hundreds of miles of trails and 600 lakes. The hiking, biking, canoeing and camping are some of the state's best. See the website for visitor centers and descriptions.

FLORIDA PANHANDLE

Take all the things that are great about the Deep South – friendly people, molasses-slow pace, oak-lined country roads, fried food galore – and then add several hundred miles of sugar-white beaches, dozens of gin-clear natural springs and all the fresh oysters you can suck down, and there you have it: the fantastic, highly underrated Florida Panhandle.

Tallahassee

Florida's capital, cradled between gently rising hills and beneath tree-canopied roadways, is a calm and gracious city. It's closer to Atlanta than it is to Miami – both geographically and culturally – and far more Southern than the majority of the state it administrates. Despite the city's two major universities (Florida State and Florida Agricultural and Mechanical University) and its status as a government center, there's not much to detain a visitor for more than a day or two.

Stop by the visitor center (☑800-628-2866, 850-606-2305; www.visittallahassee.com; 106 E Jefferson St; ⊙8am-5pm Mon-Fri) for information.

◉ Sights & Activities

Mission San Luis　　　　　　HISTORIC SITE
(☑850-245-6406; www.missionsanluis.org; 2100 W Tennessee St; adult/child $5/2; ⊙10am-4pm Tue-Sun) The 60-acre site of a 17th-century Spanish and Apalachee mission that's been wonderfully reconstructed, especially the soaring Council House. Good tours included with admission provide a fascinating taste of mission life 300 years ago.

Museum of Florida History　　　　MUSEUM
(www.museumoffloridahistory.com; 500 S Bronough St; ⊙9am-4:30pm Mon-Fri, from 10am Sat, from noon Sun) FREE Here it is, Florida's history splayed out in fun, crisp exhibits: from mastodon skeletons to Florida's Paleo-Indians and Spanish shipwrecks, the Civil War to 'tin-can tourism.'

Florida Capitol Buildings　　HISTORIC BUILDING
FREE Old and new, side by side. The current Florida State Capitol (cnr Pensacola & Duval Sts; ⊙8am-5pm Mon-Fri) is, in a word,

WAKULLA SPRINGS

Just 15 miles south of Tallahassee is the world's deepest freshwater spring at **Edward Ball Wakulla Springs State Park** (850-561-7276; www.floridastateparks.org; 465 Wakulla Park Dr; car/bike $6/2, boat tours adult/child $8/5; 8am-dusk). The springs flow from massive underwater caves that are an archeologist's dream, with fossilized bones including a mastodon that was discovered around 1850. These days you can swim in the icy springs or enjoy them from a glass-bottom boat. You can also take a boat tour of the wildlife-filled Wakulla River, which was used as a movie set for several Tarzan movies, as well as *The Creature from the Black Lagoon*. Overnighters can stay in the park at the **Wakulla Springs Lodge** (850-926-0700; www.wakul-laspringslodge.com; 465 Wakulla Park Dr; r $85-125), a grand Spanish-style lodge built in 1937 where an 11ft stuffed alligator named 'Old Joe' keeps an eye on things.

ugly, but its top-floor observation deck gives you a bird's-eye view of the city. Next door, the **Historic Capitol** (www.flhistoric-capitol.gov; 400 S Monroe St;) **FREE** is the more charming 1902 predecessor. Inside, the **Florida Legislative Research Center and Museum** (www.flrcm.gov; free admission; 9am-4:30pm Mon-Fri, from 10am Sat, from noon Sun) **FREE** has intriguing government and cultural exhibits, including one on the infamous 2000 US presidential election.

Sleeping & Eating

Chains are clumped at exits along I-10 and along Monroe St between I-10 and downtown.

Hotel Duval　　　　　　　　　　HOTEL **$$**
(850-224-6000; www.hotelduval.com; 415 N Monroe St; r $109-179;) Tallahassee's slickest digs. This new 117-room hotel goes in for a neo-mod look. A rooftop bar and lounge is open until 2am most nights, and Shula's, a fancy chain steakhouse, is off the lobby.

Governor's Inn　　　　　　　　　HOTEL **$$**
(850-681-6855; www.thegovinn.com; 209 S Adams St; r $149-209;) In a stellar downtown location, this warm, inviting inn has

everything from single rooms to two-level loft suites, plus a daily cocktail hour.

Catfish Pad　　　　　　　　　　SEAFOOD **$**
(850-575-0053; www.catfishpad.com; 4229 W Pensacola St; mains $8-15; 11am-3pm & 5-9pm Mon-Fri, 11am-9pm Sat) There's no doubt you're in the South at this home-style seafood joint. Go for a plate of cornmeal-battered catfish with a side of grits, chased down with a cup of sweet tea. Yum.

Reangthai　　　　　　　　　　　THAI **$$**
(reangthai.com; 2740 Capital Circle NE; lunch $9-12, mains $13-20; 11am-2pm Tue-Fri, 5-10pm Mon-Sat) The real deal, and elegant despite its strip mall setting, Reangthai serves the kind of spicy, fish sauce-y, explode-in-your-mouth cuisine so many American Thai restaurants shy away from.

Andrew's　　　　　　　　　　AMERICAN **$$**
(850-222-3444; www.andrewsdowntown.com; 228 S Adams St; mains $9-36; 11:30am-10pm) Downtown's see-and-be-seen political hot spot. At this split-level place, the downstairs grill serves casual burgers and beer, while upstairs serves upscale neo-Tuscan dishes.

☆ Entertainment

Bradfordville Blues Club　　　　LIVE MUSIC
(850-906-0766; www.bradfordvilleblues.com; 7152 Moses Lane, off Bradfordville Rd; tickets $5-25; 10pm Fri & Sat, 8:30pm some Thu; check online) Down the end of a dirt road lit by tiki torches, you'll find a bonfire raging under the live oaks at this hidden-away juke joint that hosts excellent national blues acts.

ℹ Getting There & Around

The **Tallahassee Regional Airport** (www.talgov.com/airport) is about 5 miles southwest of downtown, off Hwy 263. The **Greyhound station** (www.greyhound.com; 112 W Tennessee St) is right downtown. **Star Metro** (www.talgov.com/starmetro; single ride $1.25, unlimited 1/7 days $3/10) provides local bus service.

Apalachicola & Around

Slow, mellow and perfectly preserved, Apalachicola is one of the Panhandle's most irresistible, romantic villages. Perched on the edge of a broad bay famous for its oysters, the oak-shaded town is a hugely popular getaway, with a new wave of bistros, art galleries, eclectic boutiques and historic B&Bs.

For town information, visit www.apala-chicolabay.org. For nature, the pristine St Vincent Island (www.fws.gov/saintvincent) holds pearly dunes, pine forests and wetlands teeming with wildlife. Neighboring St George Island State Park (☎850-927-2111; www.floridastateparks.org/stgeorgeisland; vehicle $6, camping $24; ☺8am-dusk) offers 9 miles of glorious, undeveloped beaches. In town, seek out fishing charters and wildlife cruises.

Ensure romance with a night's stay at Coombs House Inn (☎850-653-9199; www.coombshouseinn.com; 80 6th St; r $129-169, ste $149-269; ❈❀), a stunning Victorian home transformed into a luscious, luxury B&B. Sample the town's famous bivalve, freshly shucked, baked or fried, at Papa Joe's Oyster Bar & Grill (www.papajoesoysterbar.com; 301b Market St; mains $8-18; ☺11am-10pm Mon-Tue, 11am-11pm Thu-Sat).

Panama City Beach

There's no mistaking Panama City Beach for anything other than it is: a quintessentially Floridian, carnival-esqe beach town. Spring breakers and summer vacationers flock here for the beautiful white-sand beaches and the hurdy-gurdy of amusements, while mile after mile of high-rise condos insist on disrupting the view. Stop by the visitor bureau (☎800-722-3224, 850-233-5070; www.visitpanamacitybeach.com; 17001 Panama City Beach Parkway; ☺8am-5pm) for information.

A renowned wreck-diving site, the area around Panama City Beach has dozens of natural, historic and artificial reefs. Dive Locker (☎850-230-8006; www.divelocker.net; 106 Thomas Dr; ☺8am-6pm Mon-Sat) has dives from $90, gear included.

St Andrews State Park (www.floridastateparks.org/standrews; car $8) is a peaceful escape with nature trails, swimming beaches and wildlife. Just offshore, Shell Island has fantastic snorkeling, and shuttles (☎850-233-0504; www.shellislandshuttle.com; adult/child $17/9; ☺9am-5pm) depart every 30 minutes in summer.

🛏 Sleeping

Summer is the high season for Panhandle beaches. Panama City doesn't lack for choice; to avoid spring breakers, look for the code phrase 'family-friendly.'

Beachbreak by the Sea   MOTEL $
(☎850-234-6644; www.beachbreakbythesea.com; 15405 Front Beach Rd; d $79-169; ❂❈❊) A refreshing four-story spot in a sea of high-rises, this place offers basic motel-style rooms, a central beachfront location and continental breakfast.

Wisteria Inn   MOTEL $$
(☎850-234-0557; www.wisteria-inn.com; 20404 Front Beach Rd; d $89-149; ❂❈❊) This sweet little 15-room motel has a bright, Caribbean theme, poolside mimosa (champagne and orange juice drink) hours and an 'adults only' policy that discourages spring breakers.

DON'T MISS

SCENIC DRIVE: THE EMERALD COAST

Along the Panhandle coast between Panama City Beach and Destin, skip the main highway (Hwy 98) in favor of one of the most enchanting drives in Florida: Scenic Hwy 30A. This 18-mile stretch of road hugs what's referred to as the Emerald Coast for its almost fluorescent, gem-colored waters lapping brilliant white beaches of ground-quartz crystal.

Leading off Scenic Hwy 30A are pristine, wild parklands like Grayton Beach State Park (www.floridastateparks.org/graytonbeach; 357 Main Park Rd; car $5), considered one of Florida's prettiest, most pristine strands. About 15 quaint communities hug the coast, some arty and funky, and some master-planned resorts with matchy-matchy architectural perfection. Of these, the most intriguing and surreal is the little village of Seaside (www.seasidefl.com), a Necco Wafer–colored town that was hailed as a model of New Urbanism in the 1980s.

Seaside is such an idealized vision that, unaltered, it formed the setting for the 1998 film The Truman Show, about a man whose 'perfect life' is nothing but a TV show. Other variations on this theme are WaterColor, Alys Beach and Rosemary Beach.

Good online resources are www.30a.com and www.visitsouthwalton.com.

✗ Eating & Drinking

Pineapple Willy's   CARIBBEAN $$
(www.pwillys.com; 9875 S Thomas Dr; mains $10-26; ⊘11am-late) Ask for a table on the restaurant pier for breezy beachside dining. Famed for its signature drinks and its house special: Jack Daniels BBQ ribs.

Firefly   MODERN AMERICAN $$$
(☑850-249-3359; www.fireflypcb.com; 535 Richard Jackson Blvd; mains $23-42; ⊘5-10pm) This uber atmospheric, fine dining establishment beckons with clever seafood dishes and its cool Library Lounge. It's good enough for the US president – Obama ate here in 2010.

Tootsie's Orchid Lounge   HONKY TONK
(www.tootsies.net; 700 S Pier Park Dr; ⊘10am-late) Lacks the dusty character of the Nashville original, but the nonstop live country music is still plenty boot stompin'.

ℹ Getting There & Around

The **Panama City International Airport** (PFN; www.iflybeaches.com) is served by a few major airlines. The **Greyhound Station** (www.greyhound.com; 917 Harrison Ave) is in Panama City, and the limited **Bay Town Trolley** (baytowntrolley.org; tickets $1.50) runs only weekdays from 6am to 8pm.

Pensacola & Pensacola Beach

Neighbors with Alabama, Pensacola and its adjacent beach town welcome visitors driving in from the west. Its gorgeous snow-white beaches and tolerance of the annual

---

GOODBYE, MULLET

Every April, locals gather along the Florida–Alabama state line on Perdido Key for a time-honored tradition: the **Interstate Mullet Toss**. The idea – apart from a great excuse for a party – is to see who can throw their (dead) mullet the furthest into Alabama (we're talking fish, not the unfortunate '80s hairstyle). The event is organized by the **Flora-Bama Lounge, Package and Oyster Bar** (www.florabama.com; 17401 Perdido Key Dr; ⊘11am-3am), a legendary roadhouse that's worth visiting even when the fish aren't flying.

---

spring break bacchanal ensure Pensacola's popularity. There is also a thrumming military culture and a sultry, Spanish-style downtown. The **visitor bureau** (☑800-874-1234, 850-434-1234; www.visitpensacola.com; 1401 E Gregory St; ⊘8am-5pm Mon-Fri, 9am-4pm Sat, 10am-4pm Sun) has maps.

The region has taken its licks in recent years. In 2004 Hurricane Ivan did its best to smash the place, and in 2010 the Deepwater Horizon oil spill in the Gulf of Mexico tainted beaches with tar balls. However, today, all Panhandle beaches are clean of oil, Pensacola's buildings and roads are repaired, and the region is eager to welcome travelers back.

◉ Sights & Activities

★ National Museum of Naval Aviation   MUSEUM
(☑850-452-3604; www.navalaviationmuseum.org; 1750 Radford Blvd; admission free; ⊘9am-5pm Mon-Fri, from 10am Sat & Sun; ⊞) **FREE** The Pensacola Naval Air Station (NAS) is home to both the museum – a don't-miss collection of jaw-dropping military aircraft – and the elite **Blue Angels** (www.blueangels.navy.mil) squadron.

Historic Pensacola Village   HISTORIC BUILDINGS
(www.historicpensacola.org; Zaragoza St, btwn Tarragona & Adams Sts; adult/child $6/3; ⊘10am-4pm Tue-Sat, tours 11am, 1pm & 2:30pm) Pensacola says 'take that, St Augustine!' with this village, a self-contained enclave of historic homes and museums. Admission is good for one week and includes a guided tour and entrance to each building.

TT Wentworth Museum   MUSEUM
(330 S Jefferson St; admission free; ⊘10am-4pm) **FREE** The TT Wentworth Museum has two floors of Florida history, including remnants of the Luna expedition and one floor of Wentworth's collection of oddities, including his famous petrified cat.

Pensacola Museum of Art   MUSEUM
(www.pensacolamuseumofart.org; 407 S Jefferson St; adult/student $5/3; ⊘10am-5pm Tue-Fri, from noon Sat) In the city's old jail (1908), this lovely art museum features an impressive, growing collection of major 20th- and 21st-century artists, spanning cubism, realism, pop art and folk art.

Gulf Islands National Seashore PARK

(www.nps.gov/guis; 7-day pedestrian & cyclist/car $3/8; ☺sunrise-sunset) To enjoy the area's lovely white sands, head to the easy-access Pensacola Beach or the neighboring Gulf Islands National Seashore, part of a 150-mile stretch of undeveloped beach. Aim for the Naval Live Oaks section for a calm, family-friendly beach, and drive out to Fort Pickens (✆850-934-2600; www.nps.gov/guis; Fort Pickens Rd, Pensacola; ⛟) to poke around this crumbling wreck of a 19th-century fort.

🛏 Sleeping

Noble Inn B&B $$

(✆850-434-9544; www.noblemanor.com; 110 W Strong St; r $135-145, ste $160; P☻❄) This B&B has the prettiest rooms in town; 'Bacall' would be opulent enough for its namesake.

New World Inn HOTEL $$

(✆850-432-4111; www.newworldlanding.com; 600 S Palafox St; r from $109; P❄🛜) Peek under the lid of this former box factory and you'll find surprisingly lovely rooms with luxe bedding and real carpeting (a beach-town luxury).

Paradise Inn MOTEL $$

(✆850-932-2319; www.paradiseinn-pb.com; 21 Via de Luna Dr; r $80-200; P❄🛜☰) Across from the beach, this sherbet-colored motel is a lively, cheery place thanks to its popular bar and grill (for quiet, ask for rooms on the parking lot's far side). Rooms are small and clean, with tiled floors and brightly painted walls.

🍴 Eating & Drinking

★Joe Patti's SEAFOOD MARKET $

(www.joepattis.com; 534 South B St, at Main St; ☺7:30am-7pm Mon-Sat, to 6pm Sun) At this beloved seafood emporium, get dock-fresh fish and seafood, prepared picnic food and sushi.

Jerry's Drive-In AMERICAN $

(2815 E Cervantes St; mains $7-12; ☺10am-10pm Mon-Fri, from 7am Sat) No longer a drive-in or owned by Jerry, but this greasy spoon is always packed – possibly because you can hardly eat for less. Cash only.

Dharma Blue INTERNATIONAL $$

(✆850-433-1275; www.dharmablue.com; 300 S Alcaniz St; mains $10-30; ☺11am-4pm & 5-9:30pm Mon-Sat; ⛟) Many locals consider this the area's best restaurant. The eclectic menu goes from fried green tomatoes to luscious sushi rolls.

Peg Leg Pete's SEAFOOD $$

(✆850-932-4139; 1010 Fort Pickens Rd; mains $8-20; ☺11am-10pm; ⛟) Raw? Rockefeller? Casino? Get your oysters any way you like 'em at this popular beach hangout with live music and pirate decor.

McGuire's Irish Pub PUB $$

(www.mcguiresirishpub.com; 600 E Gregory St; mains $11-30; ☺11am-late) Promising 'feasting, imbibery and debauchery,' this barnlike spot delivers all three. Stick to steaks and burgers, and don't mind the animal heads or dollar-bill-adorned walls. Stay late, and be prepared to sing along.

★Seville Quarter CLUB

(www.sevillequarter.com; 130 E Government St; ☺7am-2:30am) Taking up an entire city block, this multi-venue complex always has something going on from breakfast through last call in their seven separate eating, drinking and music venues.

ℹ Getting There & Around

Five miles northeast of downtown, **Pensacola Regional Airport** (www.flypensacola.com; 2430 Airport Blvd) is served by major airlines. The **Greyhound station** (505 W Burgess Rd) is 9 miles north of downtown.

Great Lakes

Includes ➡

Best Places to Eat

➡ Little Goat (p533)
➡ Tucker's (p563)
➡ Old Fashioned (p587)
➡ Zingerman's Roadhouse (p572)
➡ Bryant-Lake Bowl (p597)

Best Places to Stay

➡ Inn on Ferry Street (p568)
➡ Acme Hotel (p529)
➡ Brewhouse Inn & Suites (p583)
➡ Cleveland Hostel (p553)
➡ Lighthouse B&B (p605)

Why Go?

Don't be fooled by all the corn. Behind it lurk surfing beaches and Tibetan temples, car-free islands and the green-draped night-lights of the aurora borealis. The Midwest takes its knocks for being middle-of-nowhere boring; so consider the moose-filled national parks, urban five-ways and Hemingway, Dylan and Vonnegut sites to be its little secret.

Roll call for the Midwest's cities starts with Chicago, which unfurls what is arguably the country's mightiest skyline. Milwaukee keeps the beer-and-Harley flame burning, while Minneapolis shines a hipster beacon out over the fields. Detroit rocks, plain and simple.

The Great Lakes themselves are huge, like inland seas, offering beaches, dunes, resort towns and lots of lighthouse-dotted scenery. Dairy farms and fruit orchards blanket the region, meaning that fresh pie and ice cream await road trippers.

When to Go

Chicago

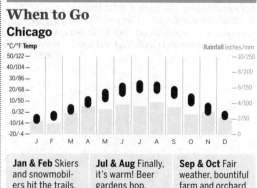

Jan & Feb Skiers and snowmobilers hit the trails.

Jul & Aug Finally, it's warm! Beer gardens hop, beaches splash, and festivals rock most weekends.

Sep & Oct Fair weather, bountiful farm and orchard harvests, and shoulder-season bargains.

Getting There & Around

Chicago's O'Hare International Airport (ORD) is the main air hub for the region. Detroit (DTW), Cleveland (CLE) and Minneapolis (MSP) also have busy airports.

A car is the easiest way to get around, especially if you want to head down Route 66 or dawdle on scenic backroads. Quarters and dollar bills are useful for tollways.

Greyhound (www.greyhound.com) connects many local cities and towns. Upstart **Megabus** (www.megabus.com/us) provides an efficient alternative between major Great Lakes cities; it has no terminals (drop-off and pick-up are at various street corners), and all purchases must be made in advance online (you cannot buy a ticket from the driver).

Amtrak's national rail network centers on Chicago. Trains depart at least once daily for San Francisco, Seattle, New York City, New Orleans and San Antonio. Regional trains chug to Milwaukee (seven daily) and Detroit (three daily).

The **Lake Express** (www.lake-express.com) car/passenger ferry provides a shortcut between Wisconsin and Michigan. It sails across Lake Michigan between Milwaukee and Muskegon.

DON'T MISS

Only in the Midwest can you fork into proper cheese curds (Wisconsin), deep-dish pizza (Chicago) and sugar cream pie (Indiana).

Fast Facts

➡ **Hub cities** Chicago (population 2.7 million), Minneapolis (population 393,000), Detroit (population 701,000)

➡ **Time zone** Eastern (IN, OH, MI), Central (IL, WI, MN)

➡ **Amount of cheese Wisconsin produces annually** 2.5 billion pounds (25% of America's hunks)

Did You Know?

The Great Lakes hold about 20% of the earth's and 95% of America's fresh water.

Resources

➡ **Chicago Reader** (www.chicagoreader.com) Arts and entertainment listings.

➡ **Great Lakes Information Network** (www.great-lakes.net) Environmental news.

➡ **Midwest Microbrews** (www.midwestmicrobrews.com) The sudsy lowdown.

PLANNING

A couple of things to know before you go: prebooking accommodation during summer is a good idea, especially in resort-orientated places such as Mackinac Island in Michigan, and the North Shore in Minnesota. It's also advised for festival-packed cities such as Milwaukee and Chicago.

Chowhounds who crave dinner at top-end restaurants such as Chicago's Alinea or Minneapolis' Butcher & the Boar should reserve in advance (for Alinea, start looking online a good two months prior).

Eyeing a nice beachfront campsite at one of the state parks? Better nab it early on; most parks take online reservations for a small fee.

Bring insect repellent, especially if you're heading to the Northwoods. The black flies in spring and mosquitoes in summer can be brutal.

Top Five Activity Hot Spots

➡ **Boundary Waters** (p605) Canoe where wolves and moose roam

➡ **Wisconsin's Rails to Trails** (p582) Pedal through cow-dotted farmland

➡ **Apostle Islands** (p591) Kayak through sea caves

➡ **New Buffalo** (p574) Learn to surf in Harbor Country

➡ **Isle Royale** (p580) Hike and camp in pristine backcountry

Great Lakes Highlights

1 Absorbing the skyscrapers, museums, festivals and foodie bounty of **Chicago** (p515).

2 Beach lounging, berry eating and surfing on Michigan's **western shore** (p574).

3 Slowing down for clip-clopping horses and buggies in **Amish Country** (p551).

4 Polka dancing at a Friday-night fish fry in **Milwaukee** (p581).

5 Paddling the **Boundary Waters** (p605) and sleeping under a blanket of stars.

6 Cycling along the river against the urban backdrop of **Detroit** (p564).

7 Taking the slowpoke, pie-filled route through Illinois on **Route 66** (p540).

History

The region's first residents included the Hopewell (around 200 BC) and Mississippi River mound builders (around AD 700). Both left behind mysterious piles of earth that were tombs for their leaders and possibly tributes to their deities. You can see remnants at Cahokia in southern Illinois, and Mound City in southeastern Ohio.

French voyageurs (fur traders) arrived in the early 17th century and established missions and forts. The British turned up soon after that, with the rivalry spilling over into the French and Indian War (Seven Years' War, 1754–61), after which Britain took control of all of the land east of the Mississippi. Following the Revolutionary War, the Great Lakes area became the new USA's Northwest Territory, which was soon divided into states and locked to the region after it developed its impressive canal and railroad network. But conflicts erupted between the newcomers and the Native Americans, including the 1811 Battle of Tippecanoe in Indiana; the bloody 1832 Black Hawk War in Wisconsin, Illinois and around, which forced indigenous people to move west of the Mississippi; and the 1862 Sioux uprising in Minnesota.

Throughout the late 19th and early 20th centuries, industries sprang up and grew quickly, fueled by resources of coal and iron, and cheap transport on the lakes. The work available brought huge influxes of immigrants from Ireland, Germany, Scandinavia and southern and eastern Europe. For decades after the Civil War a great number of African Americans also migrated to the region's urban centers from the South.

The area prospered during WWII and throughout the 1950s, but this was followed by 20 years of social turmoil and economic stagnation. Manufacturing industries declined, which walloped Rust Belt cities as Detroit and Cleveland with high unemployment and 'white flight' (ie white middleclass families who fled to the suburbs).

The 1980s and '90s brought urban revitalization. The region's population increased, notably with newcomers from Asia and Mexico. Growth in the service and high-tech sectors resulted in economic balance, although manufacturing industries such as car making and steel still played a big role, meaning that when the economic crisis hit in 2008, Great Lakes towns felt the pinch first and foremost.

Local Culture

The Great Lakes region – aka the Midwest – is the USA's solid, sensible heartland. It's no surprise that novelist Ernest Hemingway hailed from this part of the country, where words are seldom wasted.

If the Midwest had a mantra, it might be to work hard, go to church and stick to the straight and narrow...unless there's a sports game happening, and then it's OK to slather on the body paint and dye your hair purple (or whatever team colors dictate). Baseball, football, basketball and ice hockey are all hugely popular, with the big cities sponsoring pro teams for each sport.

Music has always been a big part of local culture. Muddy Waters and Chess Records spawned the electric blues in Chicago. Motown Records started the soul sound in Detroit. Alt rock shakes both cities (think Wilco in Chicago, White Stripes in Detroit) and has also come out of Minneapolis (the Replacements, Hüsker Dü) and Dayton, Ohio (Guided By Voices, the Breeders).

The region is more diverse than outsiders might expect. Immigrants from Mexico, Africa, the Middle East and Asia have established communities throughout the Midwest, mostly in the cities, where they are making welcomed contributions, especially to local dining scenes.

ILLINOIS

Chicago dominates the state with its sky-high architecture and superlative museums, restaurants and music clubs. But venturing further afield reveals Hemingway's hometown of 'wide lawns and narrow minds', scattered shrines to local hero Abe Lincoln, and a trail of corn dogs, pies and drive-in movie theaters down Route 66. A cypress swamp and a prehistoric World Heritage site make appearances in Illinois too.

ⓘ Information

Illinois Bureau of Tourism (www.enjoyillinois.com)

Illinois Highway Conditions (www.gettinga-roundillinois.com)

Illinois State Park Information (www.dnr.illinois.gov) State parks are free to visit. Campsites cost $6 to $35; some accept reservations (www.reserveamerica.com; booking fee $5).

Chicago

Loving Chicago is 'like loving a woman with a broken nose: you may well find lovelier lovelies, but never a lovely so real.' Writer Nelson Algren summed it up well in *Chicago: City on the Make*. There's something about this cloud-scraping city that bewitches. Well, maybe not during the six-month winter, when the 'Windy City' gets slapped by snowy blasts; however, come May, when the weather warms and everyone dashes for the outdoor festivals, ballparks, lakefront beaches and beer gardens – ah, nowhere tops Chicago (literally: some of the world's tallest buildings are here).

Beyond its mighty architecture, Chicago is a city of Mexican, Polish, Vietnamese and other ethnic neighborhoods in which to wander. It's a city of blues, jazz and rock clubs any night of the week. And it's a chowhound's town, where the queues for hot dogs equal those at North America's top restaurants.

Forgive us, but it has to be said: the Windy City will blow you away with its low-key, cultured awesomeness.

History

In the late 17th century the Potawatomi gave the name Checagou – meaning wild onions – to the once-swampy environs. The new city's pivotal moment happened on October 8, 1871, when (so the story goes) Mrs O'Leary's cow kicked over the lantern that started the Great Chicago Fire. It torched the entire inner city and left 90,000 people homeless.

'Damn,' said the city planners. 'Guess we shouldn't have built everything from wood. It's flammable.' So they rebuilt with steel and created space for bold new structures, such as the world's first skyscraper, which popped up in 1885.

Al Capone's gang more or less ran things during the 1920s and corrupted the city's political system. Local government has had issues ever since, with 31 city council members going to jail over the last four decades.

ILLINOIS FACTS

Nicknames Prairie State, Land of Lincoln

Population 12.9 million

Area 57,900 sq miles

Capital city Springfield (population 117,000)

Other cities Chicago (population 2.7 million)

Sales tax 6.25%

Birthplace of Author Ernest Hemingway (1899–1961), animator Walt Disney (1901–66), jazz musician Miles Davis (1926–91), actor Bill Murray (b 1950)

Home of Cornfields, Route 66 starting point

Politics Democratic in Chicago, Republican downstate

Famous for Skyscrapers, corn dogs, Abe Lincoln sights

Official snack food Popcorn

Driving distances Chicago to Milwaukee 92 miles, Chicago to Springfield 200 miles

Metro Chicago Area

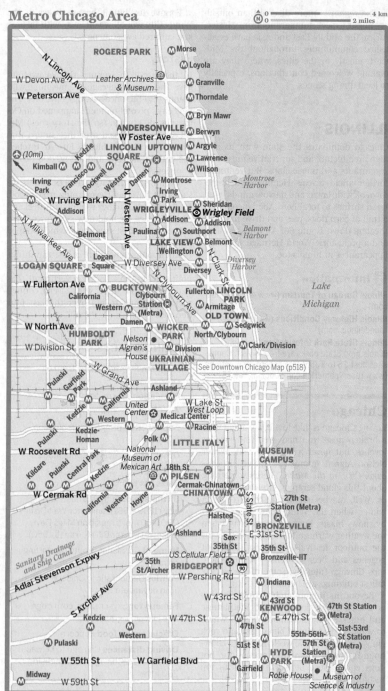

See Downtown Chicago Map (p518)

● Sights

Chicago's main attractions are found mostly in or near the city center, though visits to distant neighborhoods, such as Pilsen and Hyde Park, can also be rewarding. For more in-depth city explorations, pick up Lonely Planet's *Chicago* city guide.

● The Loop

The city center and financial district is named for the elevated train tracks that lasso its streets. It's busy all day, though not much happens at night other than in Millennium Park and the Theater District, near the intersection of N State and W Randolph Sts.

★**Millennium Park** PARK
(Map p518; ☑312-742-1168; www.millenniumpark.org; 201 E Randolph St; ◷6am-11pm; 🚻; Ⓜ Brown, Orange, Green, Purple or Pink Line to Randolph) FREE The city's showpiece is a trove of free and arty sights. It includes **Pritzker Pavilion** (Map p518; 201 E Randolph St), Frank Gehry's swooping silver band shell, hosting free concerts nightly in summer; Anish Kapoor's beloved silvery sculpture **Cloud Gate** (Map p518) (aka 'The Bean'); and Jaume Plensa's **Crown Fountain** (Map p518), a de facto water park that projects video images of locals spitting water, gargoyle style.

The **McCormick Tribune Ice Rink** fills with skaters in winter (and alfresco diners in summer). The hidden **Lurie Garden** blooms with prairie flowers and tranquility. The Gehry-designed **BP Bridge** spans Columbus Dr and offers great skyline views. And the **Nichols Bridgeway** arches from the park up to the Art Institute's 3rd-floor contemporary sculpture garden (free to view).

The pavilion concerts take place at lunchtime and at 6:30pm most nights. For the latter, bring a picnic and bottle of wine and tune in to indie rock and new music on Mondays, jazz and world music on Thursdays, and classical music on most other days. Each Saturday free exercise classes (yoga at 8am, Pilates at 9am and dance at 10am) take place on the Great Lawn. And the Family Fun Tent provides free kids' activities daily between 10am and 3pm. Free walking tours take place daily at 11:30am and 1pm; departure is from the Chicago Cultural Center Visitors Center, across the street from the park.

★**Art Institute of Chicago** MUSEUM
(Map p518; ☑312-443-3600; www.artic.edu; 111 S Michigan Ave; adult/child $23/free; ◷10:30am-5pm, to 8pm Thu; 🚻) The second-largest art museum in the country. The collection of impressionist and post-impressionist paintings is second only to those in France, and the number of surrealist works is tremendous. Download the free app for DIY tours. It offers 50 jaunts, everything from highlights (Grant Wood's *American Gothic*, Edward Hopper's *Nighthawks*) to a 'birthday-suit tour' of naked works.

Allow two hours to browse the museum's must-sees; art buffs should allocate much longer. The main entrance is on Michigan Ave, but you can also enter via the dazzling Modern Wing on Monroe St. Note that the 3rd-floor contemporary sculpture garden in this wing is free to peruse and provides

---

CHICAGO IN...

Two Days

On your first day, take an **architectural tour** and gaze up at the city's skyscrapers. Look down from the **John Hancock Center**, one of the world's tallest buildings. See 'The Bean' reflect the skyline, and splash with Crown Fountain's human gargoyles at **Millennium Park**. Chow down on a deep-dish pizza at **Giordano's**.

Make the second day a cultural one: explore the **Art Institute of Chicago** or **Field Museum of Natural History**. Grab a stylish dinner in the **West Loop**. Or listen to blues at **Buddy Guy's Legends**.

Four Days

Follow the two-day itinerary. On your third day, dip your toes in Lake Michigan at **North Avenue Beach** and saunter through leafy **Lincoln Park**. If it's baseball season, head to **Wrigley Field** for a Cubs game. In the evening yuck it up at **Second City**.

Pick a neighborhood on your fourth day: vintage boutiques and rock 'n' roll in **Wicker Park**, murals and mole sauce in **Pilsen**, pagodas and Vietnamese sandwiches in **Uptown**, or Obama sights and the Nuclear Energy sculpture in **Hyde Park**.

Downtown Chicago

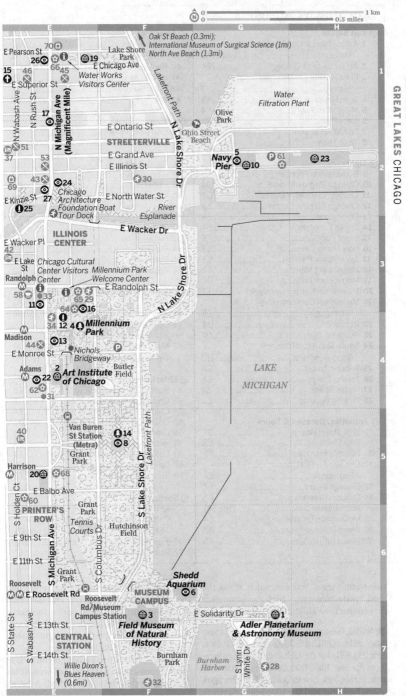

0 1 km
0 0.5 miles

E Pearson St
70
26
66 45
E Chicago Ave
19
Lake Shore Park
Water Works Visitors Center
15
46
E Superior St
17
N Michigan Ave (Magnificent Mile)
Oak St Beach (0.3mi);
International Museum of Surgical Science (1mi)
North Ave Beach (1.3mi)

Water Filtration Plant

Olive Park

E Ontario St

STREETERVILLE
E Grand Ave
E Illinois St
30

37
51
53
43
24
27
69
E Kinzie St
25

Chicago Architecture Foundation Boat Tour Dock

E North Water St

Ohio Street Beach

Navy Pier
5
10
61
23

River Esplanade

E Wacker Dr

E Wacker Pl
42
E Lake St
Randolph

ILLINOIS CENTER

Chicago Cultural Center Visitors Center
Millennium Park Welcome Center

58
33
65 29
11
64
16
E Randolph St

N Lake Shore Dr

LAKE MICHIGAN

34
12 4
Millennium Park

Madison
44
13
E Monroe St

Nichols Bridgeway

Butler Field

Adams
22
2
Art Institute of Chicago
62
31

Van Buren St Station (Metra)
14
8
Grant Park

Harrison
20
68
60

PRINTER'S ROW
E Balbo Ave

Grant Park

Tennis Courts

Hutchinson Field

E 9th St
E 11th St

S Michigan Ave
S Columbus Dr
S Lake Shore Dr
Lakefront Path

Grant Park

Roosevelt
E Roosevelt Rd

S State St
S Wabash Ave

Roosevelt Rd/Museum Campus Station
3
Field Museum of Natural History

MUSEUM CAMPUS

Shedd Aquarium
6

E Solidarity Dr
1
Adler Planetarium & Astronomy Museum

CENTRAL STATION
E 13th St
E 14th St

Willie Dixon's Blues Heaven (0.6mi)

Burnham Park

Burnham Harbor

S Lynn White Dr
28

32

Downtown Chicago

Top Sights
1 Adler Planetarium & Astronomy Museum ... G7
2 Art Institute of Chicago ... E4
3 Field Museum of Natural History ... F7
4 John Hancock Center ... E1
5 Millennium Park ... E4
6 Navy Pier ... G2
7 Shedd Aquarium ... F6
8 Willis Tower ... C4

Sights
9 Buckingham Fountain ... F5
10 Chicago Board of Trade ... D4
11 Chicago Children's Museum ... G2
12 Chicago Cultural Center ... E3
13 Cloud Gate ... E4
14 Crown Fountain ... E4
15 Grant Park ... F5
16 Holy Name Cathedral ... E1
17 Jay Pritzker Pavilion ... E3
18 Magnificent Mile ... E2
19 Monadnock Building ... D4
20 Museum of Contemporary Art ... E1
21 Museum of Contemporary Photography ... E5
22 Rookery ... D4
23 Route 66 Sign ... E4
24 Smith Museum of Stained Glass Windows ... H2
25 Tribune Tower ... E2
26 Trump Tower ... E2
27 Water Tower ... E1
28 Wrigley Building ... E2

Activities, Courses & Tours
29 12th Street Beach ... G7
30 Bike Chicago ... E3
31 Bobby's Bike Hike ... F2
32 Chicago Architecture Foundation ... E4
33 Chicago Bears ... F7
34 Chicago Greeter ... E3
InstaGreeter ... (see 34)
35 McCormick Tribune Ice Rink ... E4
36 Weird Chicago Tours ... D2
37 Windy City Rollers ... A5

Sleeping
38 Acme Hotel ... E2
39 Best Western River North ... D2
40 Buckingham Athletic Club Hotel ... D5
41 HI-Chicago ... E5
42 Hotel Burnham ... D4
43 Wit ... E3

Eating
44 Billy Goat Tavern ... E2
Cafecito ... (see 41)
45 Gage ... E4
46 Gino's East ... E1
47 Giordano's ... E1
48 Little Goat ... B3
49 Lou Malnati's ... D2
50 Lou Mitchell's ... C4
51 Mr Beef ... C1
52 Pizano's ... D1
53 Pizzeria Uno ... E2
54 Publican ... B3
55 Purple Pig ... E2
56 Xoco ... D2

Drinking & Nightlife
57 Aviary ... A3
58 Berghoff ... D4
59 Clark Street Ale House ... D1
60 Intelligentsia Coffee ... E3
61 Matchbox ... A1
Signature Lounge ... (see 4)

Entertainment
62 Buddy Guy's Legends ... E5
63 Chicago Shakespeare Theater ... G2
64 Chicago Symphony Orchestra ... E4
65 Goodman Theatre ... D3
66 Grant Park Orchestra ... E3
67 Hubbard Street Dance Chicago ... E3
68 Lookingglass Theatre Company ... E1
69 Lyric Opera Of Chicago ... C4
70 SummerDance ... E5

Shopping
American Girl Place ... (see 72)
Chicago Architecture Foundation Shop ... (see 32)
71 Jazz Record Mart ... E2
72 Water Tower Place ... E1

sweet city views. You can reach it via the mod, pedestrian-only Nichols Bridgeway that connects to Millennium Park.

★ **Willis Tower** TOWER
(Map p518; 312-875-9696; www.the-skydeck.com; 233 S Wacker Dr; adult/child $18/12; 9am-10pm Apr-Sep, 10am-8pm Oct-Mar; M Brown, Orange, Purple, Pink Line to Quincy) It's Chicago's tallest building, and the 103rd-floor Skydeck puts you 1454ft up into the heavens. Take the ear-popping 70-second elevator ride to the top, then step onto one of the glass-floored ledges jutting out in midair for a knee-buckling perspective straight down. The entrance is on Jackson Blvd.

Queues can be up to an hour on busy days (peak times are in summer, between 11am and 4pm Friday through Sunday). A bit of history: it was the Sears Tower until insurance broker Willis Group Holdings bought the naming rights in 2009. And it was the USA's tallest building until New York's One World Trade Center shot past it in 2013.

For those who prefer a drink with their vista, the Gold Coast's John Hancock Center is a better choice.

Chicago Cultural Center CULTURAL BUILDING
(Map p518; ☎ 312-744-6630; www.chicagoculturalcenter.org; 78 E Washington St; ⊗ 8am-7pm Mon-Thu, to 6pm Fri, 9am-6pm Sat, 10am-6pm Sun; Ⓜ Brown, Orange, Green, Purple or Pink Line to Randolph) **FREE** The block-long building houses ongoing art exhibitions and foreign films, as well as jazz, classical and electronic dance music concerts at lunchtime (12:15pm Monday to Friday). It also contains the world's largest Tiffany stained-glass dome, Chicago's main visitor center and StoryCorps' recording studio (where folks tell their tale, get a CD of it, and have it preserved in the Library of Congress). All free!

Grant Park PARK
(Map p518; Michigan Ave btwn 12th & Randolph Sts; ⊗ 6am-11pm) Grant Park hosts the city's mega-events, such as Taste of Chicago, Blues Fest and Lollapalooza. **Buckingham Fountain** (Map p518; cnr E Congress Pkwy & S Columbus Dr; Ⓜ Red Line to Harrison) is Grant's centerpiece. The fountain is one of the world's largest, with a 1.5-million-gallon capacity. It lets loose on the hour every hour between 9am and 11pm

mid-April to mid-October, accompanied at night by multicolored lights and music.

Route 66 Sign HISTORIC SITE
(Map p518; E Adams St btwn S Michigan & Wabash Aves; Ⓜ Brown, Orange, Green, Purple or Pink Line to Adams) Attention Route 66 buffs: the Mother Road's starting point is here. Look for the marker on Adams St's south side as you head west toward Wabash Ave.

⊙ South Loop

The South Loop, which includes the lower ends of downtown and Grant Park, bustles with the lakefront Museum Campus and gleaming new residential high-rises.

★ **Field Museum of Natural History** MUSEUM
(Map p518; ☎ 312-922-9410; www.fieldmuseum.org; 1400 S Lake Shore Dr; adult/child $15/10; ⊗ 9am-5pm; ⊕; ⊒ 146, 130) This museum houses everything but the kitchen sink: beetles, mummies, gemstones, Bushman the stuffed ape. The collection's rockstar is Sue, the largest *Tyrannosaurus rex* yet discovered. She even gets her own gift shop. Special exhibits, like the 3D movie, cost extra.

★ **Shedd Aquarium** AQUARIUM
(Map p518; ☎ 312-939-2438; www.sheddaquarium.org; 1200 S Lake Shore Dr; adult/child $29/20; ⊗ 9am-6pm Jun-Aug, to 5pm Sep-May; ⊕; ⊒ 146, 130) Top draws at the kiddie-mobbed Shedd Aquarium include the Oceanarium, with its beluga whales and frolicking white-sided

---

FAMOUS LOOP ARCHITECTURE

Ever since it presented the world with the first skyscraper, Chicago has thought big with its architecture and pushed the envelope of modern design. The Loop is a fantastic place to roam and gawk at these ambitious structures.

The Chicago Architecture Foundation (p528) runs tours that explain the following buildings and more:

Chicago Board of Trade (Map p518; 141 W Jackson Blvd; Ⓜ Brown, Orange, Purple, Pink Line to LaSalle) A 1930 art-deco gem. Inside, manic traders swap futures and options. Outside, check out the giant statue of Ceres, the goddess of agriculture, that tops the building.

Rookery (Map p518; www.gowright.org/rookery; 209 S LaSalle St; ⊗ 9:30am-5:30pm Mon-Fri; Ⓜ Brown, Orange, Purple, Pink Line to Quincy) The 1888 Rookery looks fortresslike outside, but the inside is light and airy thanks to Frank Lloyd Wright's atrium overhaul. Tours ($5 to $10) are available at noon weekdays. Pigeons used to roost here, hence the name.

Monadnock Building (Map p518; www.monadnockbuilding.com; 53 W Jackson Blvd; Ⓜ Blue Line to Jackson) Architectural pilgrims get weak-kneed when they see the Monadnock Building, which is two buildings in one. The north is the older, traditional design from 1891, while the south is the newer, mod half from 1893. See the difference? The Monadnock remains true to its original purpose as an office building.

dolphins, and the shark exhibit, where there's just 5in of Plexiglas between you and two dozen fierce-looking swimmers. The 4D theater, touch tanks and aquatic show cost extra (around $5 each).

★ **Adler Planetarium & Astronomy Museum** MUSEUM
(Map p518; ☑ 312-922-7827; www.adlerplanetarium.org; 1300 S Lake Shore Dr; adult/child $12/8; ☺ 9:30am-6pm Jun-Aug, 10am-4pm Sep-May; ⛟; ☐ 146, 130) Space enthusiasts will get a big bang (pun!) out of the Adler. There are public telescopes from which to view the stars, 3D lectures in which you can learn about supernovas, and the Planet Explorers exhibit where kids can 'launch' a rocket. The immersive digital films cost $10 extra. The Adler's front steps offer Chicago's primo skyline view.

Northerly Island PARK
(1400 S Lynn White Dr; ☐ 146 or 130) The prairie-grassed park has walking trails, fishing, bird-watching and an outdoor venue for big-name concerts (which you can hear from 12th Street Beach).

Museum of Contemporary Photography MUSEUM
(Map p518; ☑ 312-663-5554; www.mocp.org; Columbia College, 600 S Michigan Ave; ☺ 10am-5pm Mon-Wed, Fri & Sat, 10am-8pm Thu, noon-5pm Sun; ☒ Red Line to Harrison) **FREE** The small museum has intriguing exhibits worth a quick browse.

⊙ Near North

The Loop may be where Chicago fortunes are made, but the Near North is where those fortunes are spent. Shops, restaurants and amusements abound.

★ **Navy Pier** WATERFRONT
(Map p518; ☑ 312-595-7437; www.navypier.com; 600 E Grand Ave; ☺ 10am-10pm Sun-Thu, to midnight Fri & Sat; ⛟; ☒ Red Line to Grand, then trolley) **FREE** Half-mile-long Navy Pier is Chicago's most-visited attraction, sporting a 150ft Ferris wheel and other carnival rides ($5 to $6 each), an IMAX theater, a beer garden and gimmicky chain restaurants. Locals groan over its commercialization, but its lakefront view and cool breezes can't be beat. The fireworks dis-

---

CHICAGO FOR CHILDREN

Chicago is a kid's kind of town. **Chicago Parent** (www.chicagoparent.com) is a dandy resource. Top choices for toddlin' times include the following:

Chicago Children's Museum (Map p518; ☑ 312-527-1000; www.chicagochildrensmuseum.org; 700 E Grand Ave; admission $14; ☺ 10am-6pm Sun-Wed, to 8pm Thu-Sat; ⛟; ☒ Red Line to Grand, then trolley) Climb, dig and splash in this educational playland on Navy Pier; follow it with an expedition down the carnival-like wharf itself, including spins on the Ferris wheel and carousel.

Chicago Children's Theatre (☑ 773-227-0180; www.chicagochildrenstheatre.org) See a show by one the best kids' theater troupes in the country. Performances take place at venues around town.

American Girl Place (Map p518; www.americangirl.com; 835 N Michigan Ave; ☺ 10am-8pm Mon-Thu, 9am-9pm Fri & Sat, 9am-6pm Sun; ⛟; ☒ Red Line to Chicago) Young ladies sip tea and get new hair-dos with their dolls at this multistory, girl-power palace.

Chic-A-Go-Go (p523) Groove at a taping of this cable-access TV show that's like a kiddie version of Soul Train. Check the website for dates and locations.

Other kid-friendly offerings:

➡ North Ave Beach (p528)

➡ Field Museum of Natural History (p521)

➡ Shedd Aquarium (p521)

➡ Lincoln Park Zoo (p524)

➡ Art Institute of Chicago (p517)

➡ Museum of Science & Industry (p526)

OFFBEAT CHICAGO

Sure, your friends will listen politely as you describe your trip to the Willis Tower's tip, but you'll stop them mid-yawn when you unleash stories of how you boozed with roller babes and saw an iron lung. Chicago has a fine collection of unusual sights and activities to supplement its standard attractions.

International Museum of Surgical Science (312-642-6502; www.imss.org; 1524 N Lake Shore Dr; adult/child $15/7, Tue free; 10am-4pm Tue-Fri, to 5pm Sat & Sun; 151) Amputation saws, cadaver murals and a fine collection of 'stones' (as in kidney stones and gallstones) are among the offerings at this eerie museum. The antique hemorrhoid surgery toolkit serves as a reminder to eat lots of fiber. It's set in an old Gold Coast mansion, about a mile north of the Water Tower area.

Windy City Rollers (Map p518; www.windycityrollers.com; 525 S Racine Ave; tickets $20; Blue Line to Racine) The bang-'em-up sport of roller derby was born in Chicago in 1935, and the battlin' babes here will show you how it's played, bruises and all. Matches take place monthly at UIC Pavilion, west of the Loop.

Leather Archives & Museum (773-761-9200; www.leatherarchives.org; 6418 N Greenview Ave; admission $10; 11am-7pm Thu & Fri, to 5pm Sat & Sun; 22) The kinky museum holds all sorts of fetish and S&M exhibits, from the Red Spanking Bench to info on famous foot fetishists. It's 8 miles north of the Loop, and 1.5 miles north of Andersonville.

Chic-A-Go-Go (www.roctober.com/chicagogo) The cable access show's live dance audience isn't just kids: adults, too, can shake it on the dance floor with Miss Mia and Ratso.

plays on summer Wednesdays (9:30pm) and Saturdays (10:15pm) are a treat too.

The Chicago Children's Museum and Smith Museum of Stained Glass Windows are also on the pier, as are several boat-cruise operators. Try the Shoreline water taxi for a fun ride to the Museum Campus (adult/child $8/5).

Smith Museum of Stained Glass Windows   MUSEUM
(Map p518; 312-595-5024; 600 E Grand Ave; 10am-10pm Sun-Thu, to midnight Fri & Sat; Red Line to Grand, then trolley) FREE More than 150 gorgeous windows – including stained-glass Michael Jordan – hide along the lower-level terraces of Navy Pier's Festival Hall.

Magnificent Mile   STREET
(Map p518; www.themagnificentmile.com; N Michigan Ave) Spanning Michigan Ave between the river and Oak St, the Mag Mile is the much-touted upscale shopping strip, where Bloomingdales, Neiman's and Saks will lighten your wallet.

Tribune Tower   ARCHITECTURE
(Map p518; 435 N Michigan Ave; Red Line to Grand) Take a close look when passing by the Gothic tower to see chunks of the Taj Mahal, Parthenon and other famous structures embedded in the lower walls.

Trump Tower   TOWER
(Map p518; 401 N Wabash Ave; Red Line to Grand) Donald's 1360ft tower is Chicago's second-tallest building, though architecture critics have mocked its 'toothpick' look.

Wrigley Building   ARCHITECTURE
(Map p518; 400 N Michigan Ave; Red Line to Grand) Built by the chewing-gum maker; the white exterior glows as white as the Doublemint Twins' teeth.

Gold Coast

The Gold Coast has been the address of Chicago's wealthiest residents for more than 125 years.

★ **John Hancock Center**   ARCHITECTURE
(888-875-8439; www.jhochicago.com; 875 N Michigan Ave; adult/child $18/12; 9am-11pm; Red Line to Chicago) Get high in Chicago's third-tallest skyscraper. In many ways the view here surpasses the one at Willis Tower. Ascend to the 94th-floor observatory for the 'skywalk' (a screened-in porch that lets you feel the wind) and informative displays about the surrounding buildings. Or bypass the education and head up to the 96th-floor Signature Lounge, where the view is free if you buy a drink.

Museum of Contemporary Art   MUSEUM

(Map p518; ☎312-280-2660; www.mcachicago.org; 220 E Chicago Ave; adult/student $12/7; ◷10am-8pm Tue, to 5pm Wed-Sun; Ⓜ Red Line to Chicago) Consider it the Art Institute's brash, rebellious sibling, with especially strong minimalist, surrealist and arts collections, and permanent works by Franz Kline, René Magritte, Cindy Sherman and Andy Warhol.

Original Playboy Mansion   BUILDING

(1340 N State Pkwy; Ⓜ Red Line to Clark/Division) Hugh Hefner began wearing his all-day jammies here, when the rigors of magazine production and heavy partying prevented him from getting dressed. The building contains condos now, but a visit still allows you to boast that 'I've been to the Playboy Mansion.' Head east a block to Astor St and ogle more manors between the 1300 and 1500 blocks.

Water Tower   LANDMARK

(Map p518; 108 N Michigan Ave; Ⓜ Red Line to Chicago) The 154ft-tall turreted tower is a defining city landmark: it was the sole downtown survivor of the 1871 Great Fire.

◉ Lincoln Park & Old Town

Lincoln Park is Chicago's largest green space, an urban oasis spanning 1200 leafy acres along the lakefront. 'Lincoln Park' is also the name of the abutting neighborhood. Both are alive day and night with people jogging, walking dogs, pushing strollers and driving in circles looking for a place to park.

Old Town rests at the southwest foot of Lincoln Park. The intersection of North Ave and Wells St is the epicenter, with saucy restaurants, bars and the Second City improv club fanning out from here.

Lincoln Park Zoo   ZOO

(☎312-742-2000; www.lpzoo.org; 2200 N Cannon Dr; ◷10am-4:30pm Nov-Mar, to 5pm Apr-Oct, to 6:30pm Sat & Sun Jun-Aug; ♿; 🚌151) FREE A local family favorite, filled with gorillas, lions, tigers and other exotic creatures in the shadow of downtown. Check out the Regenstein African Journey, Ape House and Nature Boardwalk for the cream of the crop.

Lincoln Park Conservatory   GARDENS

(☎312-742-7736; www.lincolnparkconservancy.org; 2391 N Stockton Dr; ◷9am-5pm; 🚌151) FREE Near the zoo's north entrance, the magnificent 1891 hothouse coaxes palms, ferns and orchids to flourish. In winter, it becomes a soothing, 75°F escape from the icy winds raging outside.

Chicago History Museum   MUSEUM

(☎312-642-4600; www.chicagohistory.org; 1601 N Clark St; adult/child $14/free; ◷9:30am-4:30pm Mon-Sat, noon-5pm Sun; ♿; 🚌22) Multimedia displays cover it all, from the Great Fire to the 1968 Democratic Convention. President Lincoln's deathbed is here; so is the chance to 'become' a Chicago hot dog covered in condiments (in the kids' area, but adults are welcome for the photo op).

GANGSTER SITES

The city would rather not discuss its gangster past; consequently there are no brochures or exhibits about infamous sites. So you'll need to use your imagination when visiting the following as most are not designated as notorious.

Two murders took place near **Holy Name Cathedral** (Map p518; www.holynamecathedral.org; 735 N State St; ◷8:30am-8:30pm Mon-Sat, to 7pm Sun; Ⓜ Red Line to Chicago). In 1924 North Side boss Dion O'Banion was gunned down in his florist shop (738 N State St) after he crossed Al Capone. O'Banion's replacement, Hymie Weiss, fared no better. In 1926 he was killed on his way to church by bullets flying from a window at 740 N State St.

The **St Valentine's Day Massacre Site** (2122 N Clark St; 🚌22) is where Capone's goons, dressed as cops, lined up seven members of Bugs Moran's gang against the garage wall that used to be here and sprayed them with bullets. The garage was torn down in 1967; the site is now a parking lot.

In 1934, the 'lady in red' betrayed 'public enemy number one' John Dillinger at the **Biograph Theater** (2433 N Lincoln Ave). Dillinger was shot dead by the FBI in the alley beside the venue.

The speakeasy in the basement of the glamorous jazz bar Green Mill (p535) was a Capone favorite.

LOCAL KNOWLEDGE

BLUES FANS' PILGRIMAGE

From 1957 to 1967, the humble building at 2120 S Michigan Ave was Chess Records, the seminal electric blues label. Muddy Waters, Howlin' Wolf and Bo Diddley cut tracks here, and paved the way for rock 'n' roll with their sick licks and amped-up sound. Chuck Berry and the Rolling Stones arrived soon after. The studio is now called **Willie Dixon's Blues Heaven** (☎ 312-808-1286; www.bluesheaven.com; 2120 S Michigan Ave; tours $5-10; ◷ 11am-4pm Mon-Fri, noon-2pm Sat; ▢ 1), named for the bassist who wrote most of the Chess hits. Staff give tours of the premises. It's pretty ramshackle, with few original artifacts on display. Still, when Willie's grandson hauls out the bluesman's well-worn standup bass and lets you take a pluck, it's pretty cool. Free blues concerts rock the side garden on summer Thursdays at 6pm. The building is near Chinatown and about a mile south of the Museum Campus.

◉ Lake View & Wrigleyville

North of Lincoln Park, these neighborhoods can be enjoyed by ambling along Halsted St, Clark St, Belmont Ave or Southport Ave, which are well supplied with restaurants, bars and shops. The only real sight is ivy-covered **Wrigley Field** (www.cubs.com; 1060 W Addison St), named after the chewing-gum guy and home to the much-loved but perpetually losing Chicago Cubs. Ninety-minute tours ($25) of the iconic century-old ballpark are available. The area around the facility is getting a makeover with spiffed-up amenities for visitors.

◉ Andersonville & Uptown

These northern neighborhoods are good for a delicious browse. Andersonville is an old Swedish enclave centered on Clark St, where timeworn European-tinged businesses mix with new foodie restaurants, funky boutiques, vintage shops and gay and lesbian bars. Take the CTA Red Line to the Berwyn stop, and walk west for six blocks.

A short distance south, Uptown is a whole different scene. Take the Red Line to the Argyle stop, and you're in the heart of 'Little Saigon' and its pho-serving storefronts.

◉ Wicker Park, Bucktown & Ukrainian Village

West of Lincoln Park, these three neighborhoods – once havens for working-class central-European immigrants and bohemian writers – are hot property. Fashion boutiques, hipster record stores, thrift shops and cocktail lounges have shot up, especially near the intersection of Milwaukee and North Damen Aves. Division St is also prime wandering territory. It used to be called 'Polish Broadway' for all the polka bars that lined it, but now the requisite cafes and crafty businesses have taken over. There aren't many actual sights here, aside from **Nelson Algren's House** (1958 W Evergreen Ave; Ⓜ Blue Line to Damen), where he wrote several gritty, Chicago-based novels. Alas, it's a private residence, so you can only admire it from the sidewalk.

◉ Logan Square & Humboldt Park

When artists and hipsters got priced out of Wicker Park, they moved west to the Latino communities of Logan Sq and Humboldt Park. For visitors, these are places for small, cool-cat eateries, brewpubs and music clubs. Take the CTA Blue Line to Logan Sq or California.

◉ Near West Side & Pilsen

Just west of the Loop is, well, the **West Loop**. It's akin to New York City's Meatpacking District, with chic restaurants, clubs and galleries poking out between meat-processing plants. W Randolph St and W Fulton Market are the main veins. Nearby **Greektown** runs along S Halsted St near W Jackson Blvd. The areas are about 1.25 miles west of the Loop and easily reached by taxi.

Southwest lies the enclave of **Pilsen**, a festive mix of art galleries, Mexican bakeries, hipster cafes and murals on the buildings. The CTA Pink Line to 18th St drops you in the midst.

National Museum of Mexican Art MUSEUM (☎ 312-738-1503; www.nationalmuseumofmexicanart.org; 1852 W 19th St; ◷ 10am-5pm Tue-Sun; Ⓜ Pink Line to 18th St) **FREE** The largest Latino arts institution in the US. This museum's vivid permanent collection includes classical paintings, shining gold altars, skeleton-rich folk art and colorful beadwork.

Pilsen Mural Tours WALKING TOUR
(☑773-342-4191; per group 1½hr tour $125) Local artist Jose Guerrero leads the highly recommended tours, during which you can learn more about this traditional art form; call to arrange an excursion.

◉ Chinatown

Chicago's small but busy Chinatown is an easy 10-minute train ride from the Loop. Take the Red Line to the Cermak-Chinatown stop, which puts you between the neighborhood's two distinct parts: Chinatown Sq (an enormous bilevel strip mall) unfurls to the north along Archer Ave, while Old Chinatown (the traditional retail area) stretches along Wentworth Ave to the south. Either zone allows you to graze through bakeries, dine on steaming bowls of noodles and shop for exotic wares.

◉ Hyde Park & South Side

The South Side is the generic term applied to Chicago's myriad neighborhoods, including some of its most impoverished, that lie south of 25th St. Hyde Park and abutting Kenwood are the South Side's stars, catapulted into the spotlight by local boy Barack Obama. To get here, take the Metra Electric Line trains from Millennium Station downtown, or bus 6 from State St in the Loop. Several bicycle tours also cruise by the highlights.

University of Chicago UNIVERSITY
(www.uchicago.edu; 5801 S Ellis Ave; ☑6, MMetra to 55th-56th-57th) The campus is worth a stroll, offering grand Gothic architecture and free art and antiquities museums. It's also where the nuclear age began: Enrico Fermi and his Manhattan Project cronies built a reactor and carried out the world's first controlled atomic reaction on December 2, 1942. The **Nuclear Energy sculpture** (S Ellis Ave btwn E 56th & E 57th Sts), by Henry Moore, marks the spot where it blew its stack.

Museum of Science & Industry MUSEUM
(☑773-684-1414; www.msichicago.org; 5700 S Lake Shore Dr; adult/child $18/11; ⊙9:30am-5:30pm Jun-Aug, reduced hours Sep-May; ☒; ☑6, MMetra to 55th-56th-57th) Geek out at the largest science museum in the western hemisphere. Highlights include a WWII German U-boat nestled in an underground display ($8 extra

to tour it) and the 'Science Storms' exhibit with a mock tornado and tsunami. Kids will love the 'experiments' staff conduct in various galleries, like dropping things off the balcony and creating mini explosions.

Robie House ARCHITECTURE
(☑312-994-4000; www.gowright.org; 5757 S Woodlawn Ave; adult/child $15/12; ⊙11am-3pm Thu-Mon; ☑6, MMetra to 55th-56th-57th) Of the numerous buildings that Frank Lloyd Wright designed around Chicago, none is more famous or influential than Robie House. The resemblance of its horizontal lines to the flat landscape of the Midwestern prairie became known as the Prairie style. Inside are 174 stained-glass windows and doors, which you'll see on the hour-long tours (frequency varies by season).

Obama's House BUILDING
(5046 S Greenwood Ave) Hefty security means you can't get close to the president's abode, but you can stand across the street on Hyde Park Blvd and glimpse over the barricades at the redbrick Georgian-style manor.

Hyde Park Hair Salon BUILDING
(5234 S Blackstone Ave; ☑6, MMetra to 51st-53rd) Visit Obama's barber Zariff and the bulletproof glass–encased presidential barber chair. Staff don't mind if you come in and take a look.

🏃 Activities

Tucked away among Chicago's 580 parks are public golf courses, ice rinks, swimming pools and more. Activities are free or low cost, and the necessary equipment is usually available for rent. The **Chicago Park District** (www.chicagoparkdistrict.com) runs the show.

Cycling

Riding along the 18-mile lakefront path is a fantastic way to see the city. Bike rental companies listed here also offer two- to four-hour tours ($35 to $60, including bikes) that cover themes like the lakefront, beer and pizza munching, or South Side sights (highly recommended). Booking online saves money. The **Active Transportation Alliance** (www.activetrans.org) lists groovy bike events around town.

Bike Chicago CYCLING
(Map p518; ☑312-729-1000; www.bikechicago.com; 239 E Randolph St; bikes per hr/day from $10/35, tour adult/child from $39/25; ⊙6:30am-8pm Mon-Fri, from 8am Sat & Sun, closed Sat & Sun Nov-Mar;

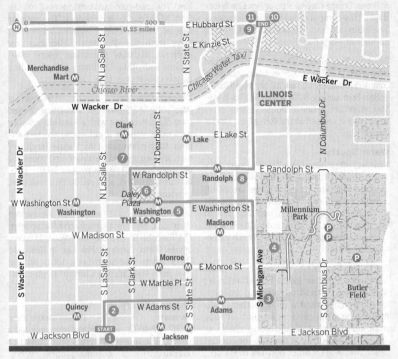

City Walk
The Loop

START CHICAGO BOARD OF TRADE
FINISH BILLY GOAT TAVERN
LENGTH 3 MILES; ABOUT TWO HOURS

This tour swoops through the Loop, highlighting Chicago's revered art and architecture, with a visit to Al Capone's dentist thrown in for good measure.

Start at the **1 Chicago Board of Trade** (p521), where guys in Technicolor coats swap corn (or something like that) inside a cool art-deco building. Step into the nearby **2 Rookery** (p521) to see Frank Lloyd Wright's handiwork in the atrium.

Head east on Adams St to the **3 Art Institute** (p517), one of the city's most-visited attractions. The lion statues out front make a classic keepsake photo. Walk a few blocks north to avant-garde **4 Millennium Park** (p517).

Leave the park and head west on Washington St to **5 Hotel Burnham** (p529). It's housed in the Reliance Building, which was the precursor to modern skyscraper design; Capone's dentist drilled teeth in what's now

room 809. Just west, Picasso's **6 Untitled** sculpture, created by Mr Abstract himself, is ensconced in Daley Plaza. Baboon, dog, woman? You decide. Then go north on Clark St to Jean Dubuffet's **7 Monument with Standing Beast**, another head-scratching sculpture.

Walk east on Randolph St through the theater district. Pop into the **8 Chicago Cultural Center** (p521) to see what free art exhibits or concerts are on. Now go north on Michigan Ave and cross the Chicago River. Just north of the bridge you'll pass the **9 Wrigley Building** (p523), shining bright and white, and the nearby Gothic, eye-popping **10 Tribune Tower** (p523).

To finish your tour, visit **11 Billy Goat Tavern** (p531), a vintage Chicago dive that spawned the Curse of the Cubs: the tavern's owner, Billy Sianis, once tried to enter Wrigley Field with his pet goat. The smelly creature was denied entry, so Sianis called down a mighty curse on the baseball team in retaliation. They've stunk ever since.

Ⓜ Brown, Orange, Green, Purple or Pink Line to Randolph) This company has multiple locations. The main one is at Millennium Park; there's another at Navy Pier.

Bobby's Bike Hike
CYCLING

(Map p518; ☑ 312-915-0995; www.bobbysbikehike. com; 465 N McClurg Ct; half/full day from $23/32; ☉ 8am-8pm Jun-Aug, 8:30am-7pm Sep-Nov & Mar-May; Ⓜ Red Line to Grand) Bobby's earns raves from riders; located at the River East Docks' Ogden Slip.

Water Sports

Visitors often don't realize Chicago is a beach town, thanks to mammoth Lake Michigan lapping its side. There are 24 official strands of sand patrolled by lifeguards in summer. Swimming is popular, though the water is pretty damn cold. Check www. cpdbeaches.com for water-quality advice before embarking.

North Ave Beach
BEACH

(www.cpdbeaches.com; 1600 N Lake Shore Dr; 🚻; 🚌 151) Chicago's most popular and amenity-laden stretch of sand wafts a southern California vibe. You can rent kayaks, jet skis, stand-up paddleboards and lounge chairs, as well as eat and drink at the party-orientated beach house. It's 2 miles north of the Loop.

Oak St Beach
BEACH

(www.cpdbeaches.com; 1000 N Lake Shore Dr; Ⓜ Red Line to Chicago) Packs in bodies beautiful at the edge of downtown.

12th Street Beach
BEACH

(Map p518; www.cpdbeaches.com; 1200 S Linn White Dr; 🚌 146, 130) A path runs from the Adler Planetarium to this handsome, secluded crescent of sand.

Ice Skating

Millennium Park's **McCormick Tribune Ice Rink** (Map p518; www.millenniumpark.org; 55 N Michigan Ave; skate rental $10; ☉ late Nov-late Feb) heats up when the temperature plummets.

☞ Tours

Many companies offer discounts if you book online. Outdoors-oriented tours operate from April to November only, unless otherwise specified.

Chicago Architecture Foundation
BOAT, WALKING TOURS

(CAF; Map p518; ☑ 312-922-3432; www.architecture.org; 224 S Michigan Ave; tours $10-40; Ⓜ Brown, Orange, Green, Purple or Pink Line to Ad-ams) The gold-standard boat tours ($40) sail from Michigan Ave's river dock. The popular Rise of the Skyscraper walking tours ($17) leave from the downtown Michigan Ave address. Weekday lunchtime tours ($10) explore individual landmark buildings. Buy tickets online or at CAF.

Chicago Greeter
WALKING TOUR

(Map p518; ☑ 312-945-4231; www.chicagogreeter. com) FREE Pairs you with a local city dweller who takes you on a personal two- to four-hour tour customized by theme (architecture, history, gay and lesbian, and more) or neighborhood. Travel is by foot and/or public transportation. Reserve 10 business days in advance.

InstaGreeter
WALKING TOUR

(Map p518; www.chicagogreeter.com/instagreeter; 77 E Randolph St; ☉ 10am-3pm Fri-Sun; Ⓜ Brown, Orange, Green, Purple or Pink Line to Randolph) FREE Offers one-hour Loop tours on the spot from the Chicago Cultural Center visitor center.

Chicago History Museum
CYCLING, WALKING TOURS

(☑ 312-642-4600; www.chicagohistory.org; tours $20-55) The museum counts pub crawls, El (elevated/subway system) jaunts, cycling routes and cemetery walks among its excellent tour arsenal. Departure points and times vary.

Weird Chicago Tours
BUS TOUR

(Map p518; ☑ 888-446-7859; www.weirdchicago. com; 600 N Clark St; 3hr tours $30; ☉ 7pm Fri & Sat, 3pm Sat; Ⓜ Red Line to Grand) Drives by ghost, gangster and red-light sites. Departs across from the Hard Rock Cafe.

Chicago Food Planet Tours
WALKING TOUR

(☑ 212-209-3370; www.chicagofoodplanet.com; 3hr tours $47-60) Go on a walkabout in Wicker Park, the Gold Coast or Chinatown, where you'll graze through seven neighborhood eateries. Departure points and times vary.

✹ Festivals & Events

Chicago has a full events calendar all year, but the biggies take place in the summer. The following events are held downtown on a weekend, unless noted otherwise.

St Patrick's Day Parade
CULTURAL

(www.chicagostpatsparade.com; ☉ mid-May) The local plumbers union dyes the Chicago River shamrock green; a big parade follows.

Blues Festival MUSIC

(www.chicagobluesfestival.us; ☺early Jul) The biggest free blues fest in the world, with four days of the music that made Chicago famous.

Taste of Chicago FOOD

(www.tasteofchicago.us; ☺mid-Jul) The free five-day bash in Grant Park includes bands and lots of food on a stick.

Pitchfork Music Festival MUSIC

(www.pitchforkmusicfestival.com; day pass $50; ☺mid-Jul) Indie bands strum for three days in Union Park.

Lollapalooza MUSIC

(www.lollapalooza.com; day pass $95; ☺early Aug) Around 130 bands spill off eight stages at Grant Park's three-day mega-gig.

Jazz Festival MUSIC

(www.chicagojazzfestival.us; ☺early Sep) Top names on the national jazz scene play over Labor Day weekend.

🛏 Sleeping

Chicago lodging doesn't come cheap. The best way to cut costs is to use a bidding site like Priceline or Hotwire (look for 'River North' or 'Mag Mile' locations). In summer and when the frequent big conventions trample through town, your options become much slimmer, so plan ahead to avoid unpleasant surprises. The prices we've listed are for the summer peak season. Taxes add 16.4%.

B&Bs give a nice bang for the midrange buck. Contact the Chicago Bed & Breakfast Association (www.chicago-bed-breakfast. com; r $125-250), which represents 18 guesthouses. Many properties have two- to three-night minimum stays. Vacation rentals in local apartments are also a good deal here. Try Vacation Rental By Owner (www.vrbo. com) or AirBnB (www.airbnb.com).

Hotels in the Loop are convenient to the museums, festival grounds and business district, but the area is pretty dead come nightfall. Accommodations in the Near North and Gold Coast are most popular, given their proximity to eating, shopping and entertainment venues. Rooms in Lincoln Park, Lake View and Wicker Park entice because they're often cheaper than rooms downtown; they are also near swingin' nightlife.

Wi-fi is free unless noted otherwise. You pay dearly for parking in Chicago; around $50 per night downtown, and $22 in outlying neighborhoods.

🛏 Loop & Near North

HI-Chicago HOSTEL $

(Map p518; ☎312-360-0300; www.hichicago.org; 24 E Congress Pkwy; dm incl breakfast $30-36; ⓟ❄@⏾; ⓜBrown, Orange, Purple or Pink Line to Library) Chicago's best hostel is immaculate, conveniently placed in the Loop, and offers bonuses like a staffed information desk, free volunteer-led tours and discount passes to museums and shows. The simple dorm rooms have six to 12 beds, and most have attached baths.

Buckingham Athletic Club Hotel BOUTIQUE HOTEL $$

(Map p518; ☎312-663-8910; www.bac-chicago. com; 440 S LaSalle St; r incl breakfast $169-209; ⓟ❄⏾⏾; ⓜBrown, Orange, Purple or Pink Line to LaSalle) Tucked into the 40th floor of the Chicago Stock Exchange building, this 21-room hotel is not easy to find. The benefit if you do? Elegant rooms so spacious they'd be considered suites elsewhere. There's also free access to the namesake gym with lap pool.

Best Western River North HOTEL $$

(Map p518; ☎800-780-7234, 312-467-0800; www. rivernorthhotel.com; 125 W Ohio St; r $169-249; ⓟ❄⏾⏾⏾; ⓜRed Line to Grand) The well-maintained rooms with maple veneer beds and desks, together with free parking (!), an indoor pool and sundeck overlooking the city, make this good Near North value.

★Acme Hotel BOUTIQUE HOTEL $$$

(Map p518; ☎312-894-0800; www.acmehotelcompany.com; 15 E Ohio St; r $179-309; ⓟ❄@⏾; ⓜRed Line to Grand) Urban bohemians are loving the Acme for its indie-cool style at (usually) affordable rates. The 130 rooms mix industrial fixtures with retro lamps, mid-century furniture and funky modern art. They're wired up with free wi-fi, good speakers, smart TVs and easy connections to stream your own music and movies. Graffiti, neon and lava lights decorate the common areas.

★Hotel Burnham BOUTIQUE HOTEL $$$

(Map p518; ☎312-782-1111; www.burnhamhotel.com; 1 W Washington St; r $269-399; ⓟ❄@⏾⏾; ⓜBlue Line to Washington) The proprietors brag that the Burnham has the highest guest return rates in Chicago; it's easy to see why. Housed in the landmark 1890s Reliance Building (precedent for the modern skyscraper), its slick decor woos architecture buffs. Mahogany writing desks and chaise lounges furnish the bright, butter-colored rooms. A free wine happy hour takes place each evening.

Wit   BOUTIQUE HOTEL $$$
(Map p518; ☑ 312-467-0200; www.thewithotel.com;
201 N State St; r $255-385; P ✳ @ 🛜; Ⓜ Brown,
Orange, Green, Purple or Pink Line to State/Lake)
Viewtastic rooms, a rooftop bar and an on-
site movie theater draw holidaying hipsters
and business travelers to the design-savvy,
green-glass Wit. Wi-fi is free in the lobby,
though there's a fee for in-room service.

Lake View & Wicker Park/Bucktown

★ **Urban Holiday Lofts**   HOSTEL $
(☑ 312-532-6949;   www.urbanholidaylofts.com;
2014 W Wabansia Ave; dm incl breakfast $30-45,
r from $100; ✳ @ 🛜; Ⓜ Blue Line to Damen) An
international crowd fills the mix of dorms
(with four to 10 beds) and private rooms
in this building of converted loft condos.
Exposed-brick walls, hardwood floors and
bunks with plump bedding are common to
all 25 rooms. It's close to the El (elevated/
subway system) and in the thick of Wicker
Park's nightlife.

Wrigley Hostel   HOSTEL $
(☑ 773-598-4471; www.wrigleyhostel.com; 3512 N
Sheffield Ave; dm incl breakfast $30; P ✳ @ 🛜;
Ⓜ Red Line to Addison) Opened in 2013, the
hostel sits in a brick three-flat building with-
in homerun distance of Wrigley Field and its
rowdy bar scene. The homey blue-and-green
rooms have an average of four beds (not
necessarily bunks). Some bathrooms have
vintage claw-foot tubs.

Willows Hotel   BOUTIQUE HOTEL $$
(☑ 773-528-8400;   www.willowshotelchicago.com;
555 W Surf St; r incl breakfast $149-265; P ✳ 🛜;
🖥 22) Small and stylish, the Willows wins an
architectural gold star. The chic little lobby
provides a swell refuge of overstuffed chairs
by the fireplace, while the 55 rooms, done
up in shades of peach, cream and soft green,
evoke a 19th-century French countryside
feel. It's a block north of the commercial
hub where Broadway, Clark and Diversey
Sts intersect.

Wicker Park Inn   B&B $$
(☑ 773-486-2743; www.wickerparkinn.com; 1329 N
Wicker Park Ave; r incl breakfast $149-199; ✳ 🛜;
Ⓜ Blue Line to Damen) This brick row house
is steps away from rockin' restaurants and
nightlife. The sunny rooms aren't huge, but
have hardwood floors, pastel colors and
small desk spaces. Across the street, two

apartments with kitchens provide a self-
contained experience. The inn is about a
half-mile southeast of the El stop.

Longman & Eagle   INN $$
(☑ 773-276-7110;   www.longmanandeagle.com;
2657 N Kedzie Ave; r $85-200; ✳ 🛜; Ⓜ Blue Line
to Logan Square) Check in at the Michelin-
starred gastropub downstairs, then head to
your wood-floored, vintage-stylish accommodation on the floor above. The six rooms
aren't particularly soundproofed, but after
using your whiskey tokens in the bar you
probably won't care. From the El stop, walk
a block north on Kedzie Ave.

Days Inn Lincoln Park North   HOTEL $$
(☑ 773-525-7010; www.daysinnchicago.net; 644
W Diversey Pkwy; r incl breakfast $125-185;
P ✳ @ 🛜; 🖥 22) This well-maintained chain
hotel in Lincoln Park is a favorite of both
families and touring indie bands, provid-
ing good service and perks including free
health-club access. It's an easy amble to
the lakefront's parks and beaches, and a
15-minute bus ride to downtown. It's right at
the hustle-bustle intersection of Broadway,
Clark and Diversey streets.

🍴 Eating

During the past decade Chicago has become
a gastronome's paradise. The beauty here is
that even the buzziest restaurants are acces-
sible: they're visionary yet traditional, pubby
at the core and decently priced. You can also
fork into a superb range of ethnic eats, es-
pecially if you break out of downtown and
head for neighborhoods such as Pilsen or
Uptown.

Need help deciding where to eat? LTH
Forum (www.lthforum.com) is a great local
resource.

The Loop & South Loop

Most Loop eateries are geared to lunch
crowds of office workers.

★ **Lou Mitchell's**   BREAKFAST $
(Map p518; ☑ www.loumitchellsrestaurant.com; 565
W Jackson Blvd; mains $6-11; ⊙ 5:30am-3pm Mon-
Sat, 7am-3pm Sun; 🚼; Ⓜ Blue Line to Clinton) A
relic of Route 66; Lou's old-school waitress-
es deliver double-yoked eggs and thick-cut
French toast just west of the Loop by Union
Station. There's usually a queue, but free
doughnut holes and Milk Duds help ease
the wait.

Cafecito CUBAN $

(Map p518; www.cafecitochicago.com; 26 E Congress Pkwy; sandwiches $5-7; ⊙7am-9pm Mon-Fri, 10am-6pm Sat & Sun; 🗟; Ⓜ Brown, Orange, Purple or Pink Line to Library) Attached to the HI-Chicago hostel and perfect for the hungry, thrifty traveler, Cafecito serves killer Cuban sandwiches layered with citrus-garlic-marinated roasted pork and ham. Strong coffee and hearty egg sandwiches make a fine breakfast.

Gage PUB $$$

(Map p518; ☎312-372-4243; www.thegagechicago. com; 24 S Michigan Ave; mains $17-36; ⊙11am-11pm, to midnight Fri; Ⓜ Brown, Orange, Green, Purple or Pink Line to Madison) This gastropub dishes up Irish-tinged grub with a fanciful twist, such as Guinness-battered fish and chips, and fries smothered in curry gravy. The booze rocks, too, including a solid whiskey list and small-batch beers that pair with the food.

🍴 Near North

This is where you'll find Chicago's mother lode of restaurants.

★**Billy Goat Tavern** BURGERS $

(Map p518; www.billygoattavern.com; lower level, 430 N Michigan Ave; burgers $4-6; ⊙6am-2am Mon-Fri, 10am-2am Sat & Sun; Ⓜ Red Line to Grand) *Tribune* and *Sun-Times* reporters have guzzled in the subterranean Billy Goat for decades. Order a 'cheezborger' and Schlitz, then look around at the newspapered walls to get the scoop on infamous local stories, such as the Cubs Curse.

Mr Beef SANDWICHES $

(Map p518; www.mrbeefonorleans.com; 666 N Orleans St; sandwiches $4-7; ⊙9am-5pm Mon-Fri, 10am-3pm Sat, plus 10:30pm-4am Fri & Sat; Ⓜ Brown or Purple Line to Chicago) A Chicago specialty, the Italian beef sandwich stacks up like this: thin-sliced, slow-cooked roast beef that's sopped in natural gravy and *giardiniera* (spicy, pickled vegetables), and then heaped on a hoagie roll. Mr Beef serves the best at its picnic-style tables.

Xoco MEXICAN $$

(Map p518; www.rickbayless.com; 449 N Clark St; mains $9-13; ⊙8am-9pm Tue-Thu, to 10pm Fri & Sat; Ⓜ Red Line to Grand) 🍴 Crunch into warm *churros* (spiraled dough fritters) for breakfast,

---

CHICAGO'S HOLY TRINITY OF SPECIALTIES

Chicago cooks up three beloved specialties. Foremost is deep-dish pizza, a hulking mass of crust that rises two or three inches above the plate and cradles a molten pile of toppings. One gooey piece is practically a meal. A large pizza averages $20 at the following places:

Pizzeria Uno (Map p518; www.unos.com; 29 E Ohio St; small pizzas from $13; ⊙11am-1am Mon-Fri, to 2am Sat, to 11pm Sun; Ⓜ Red Line to Grand) The deep-dish concept supposedly originated here in 1943.

Gino's East (Map p518; www.ginoseast.com; 162 E Superior St; small pizzas from $15; ⊙11am-9:30pm Mon-Sat, from noon Sun; Ⓜ Red Line to Chicago) Write on the walls while you wait for your pie.

Lou Malnati's (Map p518; www.loumalnatis.com; 439 N Wells St; small pizzas from $7; ⊙11am-11pm Mon-Thu, 11am-midnight Fri & Sat, noon-11pm Sun; Ⓜ Brown or Purple Line to Merchandise Mart) Famous for its butter crust.

Giordano's (Map p518; www.giordanos.com; 730 N Rush St; small pizzas from $15; ⊙11am-10:30pm Sun-Thu, to 11:30pm Fri & Sat; Ⓜ Red Line to Chicago) Perfectly tangy tomato sauce.

Pizano's (www.pizanoschicago.com; 864 N State St; 10in pizzas from $14; ⊙11am-2am Sun-Fri, to 3am Sat; Ⓜ Red Line to Chicago) Oprah's favorite.

No less iconic is the Chicago hot dog – a wiener that's been 'dragged through the garden' (ie topped with onions, tomatoes, shredded lettuce, bell peppers, pepperoncini and sweet relish, or variations thereof, but *never* ketchup), and then cushioned on a poppy-seed bun. Hot Doug's (p533) does it right.

The city is also revered for its spicy, drippy, only-in-Chicago Italian beef sandwiches. Mr Beef (p531) serves the gold standard.

ROLLING WITH FOOD TRUCKS

Until 2012 it was illegal to cook on a food truck in Chicago. But now food trucks are rolling en masse. They generally prowl office-worker-rich hot spots such as the Loop and Near North around lunchtime, and then Wicker Park and Lake View toward evening. Most trucks tweet their location; *Chicago Magazine* (@ChicagoMag/chicago-food-trucks) amalgamates them. Keep an eye out for the Tamale Spaceship!

meaty *tortas* (sandwiches) for lunch and rich *caldos* (soups) for dinner at celeb chef Rick Bayless' Mexican street-food joint. His upscale restaurants Frontera Grill and Topolobampo are next door, but you'll need reservations or a whole lot of patience to get in.

Purple Pig MEDITERRANEAN $$
(Map p518; ☑ 312-464-1744; www.thepurplepigchicago.com; 500 N Michigan Ave; small plates $8-16; ☺ 11:30am-midnight Sun-Thu, to 1am Fri & Sat; ☑; Ⓜ Red Line to Grand) The Pig's Magnificent Mile location, wide-ranging meat and veggie menu, long list of affordable vinos and late-night serving hours make it a crowd pleaser. Milk-braised pork shoulder is the hamtastic specialty.

✕ Lincoln Park & Old Town

Halsted, Lincoln and Clark Sts are the main veins teeming with restaurants and bars.

Wiener's Circle AMERICAN $
(☑ 773-477-7444; 2622 N Clark St; hot dogs $3-6; ☺ 10:30am-4am Sun-Thu, to 5am Fri & Sat; Ⓜ Brown or Purple Line to Diversey) As famous for its unruly, foul-mouthed ambiance as for its char-dogs and cheddar fries, the Wiener Circle is *the* place for drunken, late-night munchies.

★**Alinea** MODERN AMERICAN $$$
(☑ 312-867-0110; www.alinearestaurant.com; 1723 N Halsted St; multicourse menu $210-265; ☺ 5:30-9:30pm Wed-Sun; Ⓜ Red Line to North/Clybourn) Widely regarded as North America's best restaurant, Alinea brings on 20 courses of mind-bending molecular gastronomy. Dishes may emanate from a centrifuge or be pressed into a capsule, a la duck served with a 'pillow of lavender air.' There are no

reservations. Instead Alinea sells tickets two to three months in advance. Sign up at the website for details. Check the Twitter feed (@Alinea) for possible last-minute seats.

✕ Lake View & Wrigleyville

Clark, Halsted, Belmont and Southport are fertile grazing streets.

★**Crisp** ASIAN $
(www.crisponline.com; 2940 N Broadway; mains $7-12; ☺ 11:30am-9pm; Ⓜ Brown Line to Wellington) Music pours from the stereo, and cheap, delicious Korean fusions arrive from the kitchen at this cheerful cafe. The 'Bad Boy Buddha' bowl, a variation on *bi bim bop* (mixed vegetables with rice), is one of the best cheap lunches in town.

Mia Francesca ITALIAN $$
(☑ 773-281-3310; www.miafrancesca.com; 3311 N Clark St; mains $13-25; ☺ 5-10pm Mon-Thu, 5-11pm Fri, 10am-11pm Sat, 10am-10pm Sun; Ⓜ Red, Brown or Purple Line to Belmont) Local chain Mia's buzzes with regulars who come for the trattoria's Italian standards, such as seafood linguine, spinach ravioli and mushroom-sauced veal medallions, all prepared with simple flair.

✕ Andersonville & Uptown

For 'Little Saigon' take the CTA Red Line to Argyle. For the European cafes in Andersonville, go one stop further to Berwyn.

★**Hopleaf** EUROPEAN $$
(☑ 773-334-9851; www.hopleaf.com; 5148 N Clark St; mains $11-26; ☺ noon-11pm Mon-Thu, to midnight Fri & Sat, to 10pm Sun; Ⓜ Red Line to Berwyn) A cozy, European-style tavern, Hopleaf draws crowds for its Montreal-style smoked brisket, cashew-butter-and-fig-jam sandwich and the house specialty – *frites* and ale-soaked mussels. It also pours 200 types of brew, heavy on the Belgian ales.

Tank Noodle VIETNAMESE $$
(☑ 773-878-2253; www.tank-noodle.com; 4953 N Broadway; mains $8-14; ☺ 8:30am-10pm Mon, Tue & Thu-Sat, to 9pm Sun; Ⓜ Red Line to Argyle) The official name is Pho Xe Tang, but everyone just calls it Tank Noodle. The crowds come for *banh mi*, served on crunchy fresh baguette rolls, and the pho, which is widely regarded as the city's best.

✖ Wicker Park, Bucktown & Ukrainian Village

Trendy restaurants open almost every day in these 'hoods.

Big Star Taqueria   MEXICAN $
(www.bigstarchicago.com; 1531 N Damen Ave; tacos $3-4; ⊘11:30am-2am; M Blue Line to Damen) This honky-tonk gets packed, but damn, the tacos are worth the wait – pork belly in tomato-*guajillo* (chili) sauce and lamb shoulder with *queso fresco* (white cheese) accompany the specialty whiskey list. Cash only.

★Ruxbin   MODERN AMERICAN $$$
(☑312-624-8509; www.ruxbinchicago.com; 851 N Ashland Ave; mains $25-30; ⊘5:30-10pm Tue-Sat, to 9pm Sun; M Blue Line to Division) ✦ The passion of the brother-sister team who run Ruxbin is evident in everything from the warm decor made of found items to the artfully prepared flavors in dishes like the pork-belly salad with grapefruit, cornbread and blue cheese. It's a wee place of just 32 seats, and BYOB (bring your own bottle).

✖ Logan Square & Humboldt Park

Logan Sq has become a mecca for inventive, no-pretense chefs. Eats and drinks ring the intersection of Milwaukee, Logan and Kedzie Blvds.

★Hot Doug's   AMERICAN $
(☑773-279-9550; www.hotdougs.com; 3324 N California Ave; mains $3-9; ⊘10:30am-4pm Mon-Sat; M Blue Line to California or bus 52) Doug is the most famous weenie maker in town, and deservedly so. He serves multiple dog styles (Polish, bratwursts, Chicago) cooked multiple dog ways (char-grilled, deep-fried, steamed). Confused? He'll explain it all. Doug also makes gourmet 'haute dogs,' such as blue-cheese pork with cherry cream sauce. It's sublime, which is why there's always a queue. Cash only.

★Longman & Eagle   AMERICAN $$$
(☑773-276-7110; www.longmanandeagle.com; 2657 N Kedzie Ave; mains $17-29; ⊘9am-2am; M Blue Line to Logan Sq) Hard to say whether this shabby-chic tavern is best for eating or drinking. Let's say eating, since it earned a Michelin star for its beautifully cooked comfort foods like vanilla brioche French toast for breakfast, wild-boar sloppy joes for lunch and maple-braised pork shank for dinner. There's a whole menu of juicy small plates, too. Reservations not accepted.

✖ Near West Side & Pilsen

The West Loop booms with hot-chef restaurants. Stroll along Randolph and Fulton Market Sts and take your pick. Greektown extends along S Halsted St (take the Blue Line to UIC-Halsted). The Mexican Pilsen enclave has loads of eateries around W 18th St.

Don Pedro Carnitas   MEXICAN $
(1113 W 18th St; tacos $1.50-2; ⊘6am-6pm Mon-Fri, 5am-5pm Sat, 5am-3pm Sun; M Pink Line to 18th) At this no-frills Pilsen meat hive, a man with a machete salutes you at the front counter. He awaits your command to hack off pork pieces, and then wraps the thick chunks with onion and cilantro in a fresh tortilla. Cash only.

★Little Goat   DINER $$
(Map p518; www.littlegoatchicago.com; 820 W Randolph St; mains $8-12; ⊘7am-2am; 🛜🍴; M Green or Pink Line to Morgan) *Top Chef* winner Stephanie Izard opened this diner for the foodie masses across the street from her ever-booked main restaurant, Girl and the Goat. Sit on a vintage twirly stool and order from the all-day breakfast menu. Better yet, try lunchtime favorites like the goat sloppy joe with mashed potato tempura or the pork belly on scallion pancakes.

Publican   AMERICAN $$$
(Map p518; ☑312-733-9555; www.thepublican-restaurant.com; 837 W Fulton Market; mains $19-25; ⊘3:30-10:30pm Mon-Thu, 3:30-11:30pm Fri, 10am-11:30pm Sat & Sun; M Green or Pink Line to Morgan) ✦ Set up like a swanky beer hall, Publican specializes in oysters, hams and fine suds – all from small family farms and microbrewers.

♟ Drinking & Nightlife

During the long winters, Chicagoans count on bars for warmth. The usual closing time is 2am, but some places stay open until 4am. In summer many bars boast beer gardens.

Clubs in the Near North and West Loop tend to be cavernous and luxurious (with dress codes). Clubs in Wicker Park and Ukrainian Village are usually more casual.

The Loop & Near North

Restaurants such as the Gage, Billy Goat Tavern and Purple Pig (see Eating) make fine drinking destinations, too.

★ Signature Lounge   LOUNGE
(www.signatureroom.com; 875 N Michigan Ave; drinks $6-16; ⊙ from 11am; Ⓜ Red Line to Chicago) Have the Hancock Observatory view without the Hancock Observatory admission price. Grab the elevator up to the 96th floor and order a beverage while looking out over the city. Ladies: don't miss the bathroom view.

Berghoff   BAR
(Map p518; www.theberghoff.com; 17 W Adams St; ⊙ 11am-9pm Mon-Sat; Ⓜ Blue or Red Line to Jackson) The Berghoff was the first spot in town to serve a legal drink after Prohibition (ask to see the liquor license stamped '#1'). Little has changed around the antique wood bar since then. Belly up for frosty mugs of the house-brand beer and order *sauerbraten* from the adjoining German restaurant.

★ Clark Street Ale House   BAR
(Map p518; www.clarkstreetalehouse.com; 742 N Clark St; ⊙ from 4pm; Ⓜ Red Line to Chicago) Do as the retro sign advises and 'Stop & Drink Liquor.' Midwestern microbrews are the main draw; order a three-beer sampler for $6.

DON'T MISS

MIDWESTERN BEERS

The Midwest is ready to pour you a cold one thanks to its German heritage. Yes, Budweiser and Miller are based here, but that's not what we're talking about. Far more exciting is the region's cache of craft brewers. Keep an eye on the taps for these slurpable suds-makers, available throughout the area:

➜ Bell's (Kalamazoo, MI)

➜ Capital (Madison, WI)

➜ Founder's (Grand Rapids, MI)

➜ Great Lakes (Cleveland, OH)

➜ Lakefront (Milwaukee, WI)

➜ New Holland (Holland, MI)

➜ Summit (St Paul, MN)

➜ Surly (Minneapolis, MN)

➜ Three Floyds (Munster, IN)

➜ Two Brothers (Warrenville, IL)

Intelligentsia Coffee   CAFE
(Map p518; www.intelligentsiacoffee.com; 53 E Randolph St; ⊙ 6:30am-8pm Mon-Fri, 7am-9pm Sat, 7am-7pm Sun; Ⓜ Brown, Orange, Green, Purple or Pink Line to Randolph) The local chain roasts its own beans and percolates strong stuff. Staff recently won the US Barista Championship.

Old Town & Wrigleyville

★ Old Town Ale House   BAR
(www.theoldtownalehouse.com; 219 W North Ave; ⊙ 3pm-4am Mon-Fri, from noon Sat & Sun; Ⓜ Brown or Purple Line to Sedgwick) This unpretentious favorite lets you mingle with beautiful people and grizzled regulars, seated pint by pint under the nude-politician paintings. It's across the street from Second City.

★ Gingerman Tavern   BAR
(3740 N Clark St; ⊙ from 3pm Mon-Fri, from noon Sat & Sun; Ⓜ Red Line to Addison) The pool tables, the good beer selection and the pierced-and-tattooed patrons make Gingerman wonderfully different from the surrounding Wrigleyville sports bars.

Smart Bar   CLUB
(www.smartbarchicago.com; 3730 N Clark St; ⊙ 10pm-4am Wed-Sat; Ⓜ Red Line to Addison) A longstanding unpretentious favorite for dancing, attached to the Metro rock club.

Wicker Park, Bucktown & Ukrainian Village

Map Room   BAR
(www.maproom.com; 1949 N Hoyne Ave; ⊙ from 6:30am Mon-Fri, from 7:30am Sat, from 11am Sun; 🛜) At this map-and-globe-filled 'traveler tavern' artsy types sip coffee by day and suds from the 200-strong beer list by night.

Danny's   BAR
(1951 W Dickens Ave; ⊙ from 7pm; Ⓜ Blue Line to Damen) Danny's comfortably dim and dog-eared ambience is perfect for conversations over a pint. A poetry-reading series and occasional DJs add to the scruffy artiness.

Matchbox   COCKTAIL BAR
(Map p518; 770 N Milwaukee Ave; ⊙ from 4pm; Ⓜ Blue Line to Chicago) Lawyers, artists and bums all squeeze in for retro cocktails. It's small as – you got it – a matchbox, with about 10 barstools; everyone else stands against the back wall. Matchbox sits by its lonesome northwest of downtown.

Logan Square

Late Bar
CLUB

(www.latebarchicago.com; 3534 W Belmont Ave; ⊙from 10pm Tue-Sat; Ⓜ Blue Line to Belmont) Owned by a couple of DJs, Late Bar's weird, New Wave vibe draws fans of all stripes. It's off the beaten path in a forlorn stretch of Logan Sq, though easily reachable via the Blue Line train.

West Loop

Aviary
COCKTAIL BAR

(Map p518; www.theaviary.com; 955 W Fulton Market; ⊙from 6pm Tue-Sat; Ⓜ Green or Pink Line to Morgan) The Aviary won the James Beard Award for best cocktails in the nation. The ethereal drinks are like nothing you've laid lips on before. Some arrive with Bunsen burners, others with a slingshot you use to break the ice. They taste terrific, whatever the science involved. It's wise to make reservations online.

☆ Entertainment

Check the Reader (www.chicagoreader.com) for listings.

Blues & Jazz

Blues and jazz have deep roots in Chicago.

★ Green Mill
JAZZ

(www.greenmilljazz.com; 4802 N Broadway; cover charge $5-15; ⊙noon-4am Mon-Sat, from 11am Sun; Ⓜ Red Line to Lawrence) The timeless Green Mill earned its notoriety as Al Capone's favorite speakeasy (the tunnels where he hid the booze are still underneath the bar). Sit in one of the curved leather booths and feel his ghost urging you on to another martini. Local and national jazz artists perform nightly; Green Mill also hosts the nationally acclaimed poetry slam on Sundays.

★ Buddy Guy's Legends
BLUES

(Map p518; www.buddyguys.com; 700 S Wabash Ave; tickets Sun-Thu $10, Fri & Sat $20; ⊙from 5pm Mon & Tue, from 11am Wed-Fri, from noon Sat & Sun; Ⓜ Red Line to Harrison) Top local and national acts wail on the stage of local icon Buddy Guy. The man himself usually plugs in his axe for a series of shows in January. The venue hosts free, all-ages acoustic performances from noon to 2pm Wednesday through Sunday.

Kingston Mines
BLUES

(www.kingstonmines.com; 2548 N Halsted St; tickets $12-15; ⊙8pm-4am Mon-Thu, from 7pm Fri & Sat, from 6pm Sun; Ⓜ Brown or Purple, Red Line to

---

LOCAL KNOWLEDGE

HOW TO FIND A REAL CHICAGO BAR

Unfortunately, we can't list every watering hole in town, but we can give you the tools to go out and discover classic, character-filled bars on your own. Look for the following:

➡ an 'Old Style' beer sign swinging out front

➡ a well-worn dart board and/or pool table inside

➡ patrons wearing ballcaps with the logo of the Cubs, White Sox or Bears

➡ bottles of brew served in buckets of ice

➡ sports on TV

Fullerton) Two stages, seven nights a week, ensure somebody's always on. It's noisy, hot, sweaty, crowded and located in Lincoln Park.

BLUES
BLUES

(www.chicagobluesbar.com; 2519 N Halsted St; tickets $7-10; ⊙ from 8pm; Ⓜ Brown, Purple or Red Line to Fullerton) This veteran club draws a slightly older crowd that soaks up every crackling, electrified moment.

Rock & World Music

★ Hideout
LIVE MUSIC

(www.hideoutchicago.com; 1354 W Wabansia Ave; ⊙7pm-late Tue & Sat, from 4pm Wed-Fri, hours vary Sun & Mon; 🚌72) Hidden behind a factory at the edge of Bucktown, this two-room lodge of indie rock and alt-country is well worth seeking out. The owners have nursed an outsider, underground vibe, and the place feels like your grandma's downstairs rumpus room. Music and other events (bingo, literary readings etc) take place nightly.

SummerDance
MUSIC

(Map p518; ☎312-742-4007; www.chicago summerdance.org; 601 S Michigan Ave; ⊙6pm Thu-Sat, 4pm Sun late Jun–mid-Sep; Ⓜ Red Line to Harrison) FREE Boogie at the Spirit of Music Garden in Grant Park with a multi-ethnic mash-up of locals. Bands play rumba, samba and other world beats preceded by fun dance lessons – all free.

Empty Bottle
LIVE MUSIC

(www.emptybottle.com; 1035 N Western Ave; ⊙5pm-late Mon-Wed, from 3pm Thu & Fri, from 11am Sat & Sun; 🚌49) The scruffy, go-to club

GAY & LESBIAN CHICAGO

Chicago has a flourishing gay and lesbian scene. The **Windy City Times** (www.windycitymediagroup.com) and **Pink magazine** (www.pinkmag.com) provide the local lowdown.

The **Chicago Area Gay & Lesbian Chamber of Commerce** (www.glchamber.org) has an online tourism directory. Chicago Greeter (p528) offers personalized sightseeing trips.

The biggest concentration of bars and clubs is in Wrigleyville on N Halsted St between Belmont Ave and Grace St, an area known as Boystown. Andersonville is the other main area for GLBT nightlife; it's a more relaxed, less party-oriented scene. Top picks:

Big Chicks (www.bigchicks.com; 5024 N Sheridan Rd; ⊙ from 4pm Mon-Fri, from 9am Sat, from 10am Sun; 🐾; Ⓜ Red Line to Argyle) Despite the name, both men and women frequent Big Chicks, with its weekend DJs, art displays and next-door organic restaurant **Tweet** (www.tweet.biz; 5020 N Sheridan Rd; mains $7-12; ⊙ 9am-3pm; 🐾; Ⓜ Red Line to Argyle) 🐾, where weekend brunch packs 'em in.

Sidetrack (www.sidetrackchicago.com; 3349 N Halsted St; ⊙ from 3pm Mon-Fri, from 1pm Sat & Sun; Ⓜ Red, Brown or Purple Line to Belmont) Massive Sidetrack thumps dance music and show tunes and is prime for people-watching.

Hamburger Mary's (www.hamburgermarys.com/chicago; 5400 N Clark St; ⊙ from 11:30am Mon-Fri, from 10:30am Sat & Sun; Ⓜ Red Line to Berwyn) Cabaret, karaoke, burgers and a booze-soaked outdoor patio make for good times at this hot spot.

Chance's Dances (www.chancesdances.org) Organizes queer dance parties at clubs around town.

Pride Parade (http://chicagopride.gopride.com; ⊙ late Jun) Pride winds through Boystown and attracts more than 800,000 revelers.

North Halsted Street Market Days (www.northalsted.com; ⊙ early Aug) Another raucous event on the Boystown calendar, featuring a street fair and wild costumes.

for edgy indie rock and jazz; Monday's show is usually free (and there's $1.50 Pabst).

★ Metro　　　　　　　　　　　LIVE MUSIC
(www.metrochicago.com; 3730 N Clark St; Ⓜ Red Line to Addison) Local bands on the verge of stardom and national names looking for an 'intimate' venue turn up the volume at Metro.

Whistler　　　　　　　　　　　LIVE MUSIC
(☎ 773-227-3530; www.whistlerchicago.com; 2421 N Milwaukee Ave; ⊙ from 6pm Mon-Thu, from 5pm Fri-Sun; Ⓜ Blue Line to California) **FREE** Indie bands and jazz trios brood at this artsy little club in Logan Sq. There's never a cover charge.

Theater

Chicago's reputation for stage drama is well deserved. Many productions export to Broadway. The Theater District is a cluster of big, neon-lit venues at State and Randolph Sts. **Broadway in Chicago** (☎ 800-775-2000; www.broadwayinchicago.com) handles tickets for most.

Steppenwolf Theatre　　　　　THEATER
(☎ 312-335-1650; www.steppenwolf.org; 1650 N Halsted St; Ⓜ Red Line to North/Clybourn) Drama club of Malkovich, Sinise and other Hollywood stars; 2 miles north of the Loop in Lincoln Park.

Goodman Theatre　　　　　　　THEATER
(Map p518; ☎ 312-443-3800; www.goodmantheatre.org; 170 N Dearborn St; Ⓜ Brown, Orange, Green, Purple, Pink or Blue Line to Clark/Lake) The city's other powerhouse, known for new and classic American works.

Chicago Shakespeare Theater　THEATER
(Map p518; ☎ 312-595-5600; www.chicagoshakes.com; 800 E Grand Ave; Ⓜ Red Line to Grand, then trolley) The Bard's comedies and tragedies play at Navy Pier (and in local parks for free during summer).

Lookingglass Theatre Company　THEATER
(Map p518; ☎ 312-337-0665; www.lookingglasstheatre.org; 821 N Michigan Ave; Ⓜ Red Line to Chicago) Dreamy and magical literary productions in the old Water Works building.

Neo-Futurists
THEATER

([🔊] 773-275-5255; www.neofuturists.org; 5153 N Ashland Ave; [M] Red Line to Berwyn) Presents original works that make you ponder and laugh simultaneously.

Comedy

Improv comedy began in Chicago, and the city still nurtures the best in the business.

Second City
COMEDY

([🔊] 312-337-3992; www.secondcity.com; 1616 N Wells St; [M] Brown or Purple Line to Sedgwick) It's the cream of the crop, where Bill Murray, Stephen Colbert, Tina Fey and many more honed their wit. Bargain: turn up after the evening's last show (Friday excluded) and watch the comics improv a performance for free.

iO Theater
COMEDY

([🔊] 773-880-0199; www.ioimprov.com; 3541 N Clark St; [M] Red Line to Addison) Chicago's other major improv house. It's scheduled to move to new, larger digs at 1501 N Kingsbury St (in Lincoln Park) in late 2014.

Sports

Chicago Cubs
BASEBALL

(www.cubs.com; 1060 W Addison St; [M] Red Line to Addison) The Cubs last won the World Series in 1908, but that doesn't stop fans from coming out to see them. Part of the draw is atmospheric, ivy-walled Wrigley Field, which dates from 1914. The raucous bleacher seats are the most popular place to sit. No tickets? Peep through the 'knothole,' a garage-door-sized opening on Sheffield Ave, to watch the action for free.

Chicago White Sox
BASEBALL

(www.whitesox.com; 333 W 35th St; tickets $20-70; [M] Red Line to Sox-35th) The Sox are the Cubs' South Side rivals and play in the more modern 'Cell,' aka US Cellular Field. Tickets are usually cheaper and easier to get than at Wrigley Field; Monday is half-price night.

Chicago Bears
FOOTBALL

(Map p518; www.chicagobears.com; 1410 S Museum Campus Dr; [🚌] 146, 130) Da Bears, Chicago's NFL team, tackle at Soldier Field, recognizable by its classical-meets-flying-saucer architecture. Expect beery tailgate parties, sleet and snow.

Chicago Bulls
BASKETBALL

(www.nba.com/bulls; 1901 W Madison St; [🚌] 19, 20) Is Derrick Rose the new Michael Jordan? Find out at the United Center, where the Bulls shoot hoops. It's about 2 miles west of the Loop. CTA runs special buses (No 19) on game days; it's best not to walk here.

Chicago Blackhawks
HOCKEY

(www.chicagoblackhawks.com; 1901 W Madison St; [🚌] 19, 20) The 2010 and 2013 Stanley Cup winners skate in front of big crowds. They share the United Center with the Bulls.

Performing Arts

Grant Park Orchestra
CLASSICAL MUSIC

(Map p518; [🔊] 312-742-7638; www.grantparkmusicfestival.com; Pritzker Pavilion, Millennium Park; [🕐] 6:30pm Wed & Fri, 7:30pm Sat mid-Jun–mid-Aug; [M] Brown, Orange, Green, Purple or Pink Line to Randolph) **FREE** The beloved group puts on free classical concerts in Millennium Park throughout the summer.

Chicago Symphony Orchestra
CLASSICAL MUSIC

(Map p518; [🔊] 312-294-3000; www.cso.org; 220 S Michigan Ave; [M] Brown, Orange, Green, Purple or Pink Line to Adams) The CSO is one of America's best symphonies; it plays in the Daniel Burnham–designed Orchestra Hall.

Lyric Opera Of Chicago
OPERA

(Map p518; [🔊] 312-332-2244; www.lyricopera.org; 20 N Wacker Dr; [M] Brown, Orange, Purple or Pink Line to Washington) The renowned Lyric Opera hits high Cs in a chandeliered venue a few blocks west of the Loop.

Hubbard Street Dance Chicago
DANCE

(Map p518; [🔊] 312-850-9744; www.hubbardstreetdance.com; 205 E Randolph St; [M] Brown, Orange, Green, Purple or Pink Line to Randolph) Chicago's pre-eminent dance company performs at the Harris Theater for Music and Dance.

ⓘ DISCOUNT TICKETS

National ticket broker **Goldstar** (www.goldstar.com) sells half-price tickets to all sorts of Chicago entertainment, including theater performances, sports events and concerts. You'll fare best if you sign up at least three weeks ahead of time, as Goldstar typically releases its seats well in advance of shows.

For same-week theater seats at half price, try **Hot Tix** (www.hottix.org). You can buy them online or in person at the three downtown booths. The selection is best early in the week.

🛍 Shopping

A siren song for shoppers emanates from N Michigan Ave, along the Magnificent Mile. **Water Tower Place** (Map p518; www.shopwatertower.com; 835 N Michigan Ave; ⊙10am-9pm Mon-Sat, 11am-6pm Sun; Ⓜ Red Line to Chicago) is among the large vertical malls here. Moving onward, boutiques fill Wicker Park/ Bucktown (indie and vintage), Lincoln Park (posh), Lake View (countercultural) and Andersonville (all of the above).

Chicago Architecture Foundation Shop
SOUVENIRS

(Map p518; www.architecture.org/shop; 224 S Michigan Ave; ⊙9:30am-6pm; Ⓜ Brown, Orange, Green, Purple or Pink Line to Adams) Skyline posters, Frank Lloyd Wright note cards, skyscraper models and more for those with an edifice complex.

Strange Cargo
CLOTHING

(www.strangecargo.com; 3448 N Clark St; ⊙11am-6:45pm Mon-Sat, to 5:30pm Sun; Ⓜ Red Line to Addison) This retro store stocks kitschy iron-on T-shirts featuring Ditka, Obama and other renowned Chicagoans.

Jazz Record Mart
MUSIC

(Map p518; www.jazzmart.com; 27 E Illinois St; ⊙10am-8pm Mon-Sat, noon-5pm Sun; Ⓜ Red Line to Grand) One-stop shop for Chicago jazz and blues CDs and vinyl.

Quimby's
BOOKS

(www.quimbys.com; 1854 W North Ave; ⊙noon-9pm Mon-Thu, to 10pm Fri & Sat, to 7pm Sun; Ⓜ Blue Line to Damen) Ground Zero for comics, zines and underground culture; in Wicker Park.

ℹ Information

INTERNET ACCESS

Many bars and restaurants have free wi-fi, as does the Chicago Cultural Center.

Harold Washington Library Center (www.chipublib.org; 400 S State St; ⊙9am-9pm Mon-Thu, 9am-5pm Fri & Sat, 1-5pm Sun) A grand, art-filled building with free wi-fi throughout and 3rd-floor internet terminals (get a day pass at the counter).

MEDIA

Chicago Reader (www.chicagoreader.com) Free alternative newspaper with comprehensive arts and entertainment listings.

Chicago Sun-Times (www.suntimes.com) The daily tabloid-style newspaper.

Chicago Tribune (www.chicagotribune.com) The stalwart daily newspaper; its younger, trimmed-down, freebie version is *RedEye*.

MEDICAL SERVICES

Northwestern Memorial Hospital (☑312-926-5188; www.nmh.org; 251 E Erie St) Well-respected hospital downtown.

Stroger Cook County Hospital (☑312-864-1300; www.cchil.org; 1969 W Ogden Ave) Public hospital serving low-income patients; 2.5 miles west of the Loop.

Walgreens (☑312-664-8686; 757 N Michigan Ave; ⊙24hr; Ⓜ Red Line to Chicago) On the Mag Mile.

MONEY

ATMs are plentiful downtown, with many near Chicago and Michigan Aves. To change money, try Terminal 5 at O'Hare International Airport or the following places in the Loop:

Travelex (☑312-807-4941; www.travelex.com; 19 S LaSalle St; ⊙8am-6pm Mon-Fri, to 1pm Sat; Ⓜ Blue Line to Monroe)

World's Money Exchange (☑312-641-2151; www.wmeinc.com; 203 N LaSalle St; ⊙8:45am-4:45pm Mon-Fri; Ⓜ Brown, Orange, Green, Purple, Pink or Blue Line to Clark/Lake)

POST

Post office (Map p518; 540 N Dearborn St)

TOURIST INFORMATION

Choose Chicago (www.choosechicago.com) is the city's tourism bureau. It operates two visitor centers, each with a staffed information desk, CTA transit-card kiosk and free wi-fi:

Chicago Cultural Center Visitors Center (Map p518; www.choosechicago.com; 77 E Randolph St; ⊙9am-7pm Mon-Thu, 9am-6pm Fri & Sat, 10am-6pm Sun; 🛜; Ⓜ Brown, Orange, Green, Purple or Pink Line to Randolph) InstaGreeter and Millennium Park tours also depart from here.

Water Works Visitors Center (Map p518; www.choosechicago.com; 163 E Pearson St; ⊙9am-7pm Mon-Thu, 9am-6pm Fri & Sat, 10am-6pm Sun; 🛜; Ⓜ Red Line to Chicago) There's a Hot Tix booth inside.

WEBSITES

Chicagoist (www.chicagoist.com) Quirky take on food, arts and events.

Gapers Block (www.gapersblock.com) News and events site with Chicago attitude.

Huffington Post Chicago (www.huffingtonpost.com/chicago) Amalgamates news from major local sources.

ℹ Getting There & Away

AIR

Chicago Midway Airport (MDW; www.flychicago.com) The smaller airport used mostly by domestic carriers, such as Southwest; often has cheaper flights than from O'Hare.

O'Hare International Airport (ORD; www.flychicago.com) Chicago's larger airport, and among the world's busiest. Headquarters for United Airlines and a hub for American. Most non-US airlines and international flights use Terminal 5 (except Lufthansa and flights from Canada).

BUS

Greyhound (Map p518; ☎ 312-408-5800; www.greyhound.com; 630 W Harrison St; Ⓜ Blue Line to Clinton) Main station is two blocks southwest from the nearest CTA stop. Buses run frequently to Cleveland (7½ hours), Detroit (seven hours) and Minneapolis (nine hours), as well as to small towns throughout the USA.

Megabus (Map p518; www.megabus.com/us; Canal St & Jackson Blvd; ☎; Ⓜ Blue Line to Clinton) Travels only to major Midwestern cities. Prices are often less, and quality and efficiency are better than Greyhound on these routes. The bus stop is adjacent to Union Station.

TRAIN

Chicago's classic **Union Station** (www.chicagounionstation.com; 225 S Canal St) is the hub for **Amtrak** (☎ 800-872-7245; www.amtrak.com) national and regional service. Routes include the following:

Detroit (5½ hours, three trains daily)

Milwaukee (1½ hours, seven trains daily)

Minneapolis/St Paul (eight hours, one train daily)

New York (20½ hours, one train daily)

San Francisco (Emeryville; 53 hours, one train daily)

St Louis (5½ hours, five trains daily)

ⓘ Getting Around

TO/FROM THE AIRPORT

Chicago Midway Airport Eleven miles southwest of the Loop, connected via the CTA Orange Line ($3). Trains depart every 10 minutes or so; they reach downtown in 30 minutes. Shuttle vans cost $27, taxis cost $30 to $40.

O'Hare International Airport Seventeen miles northwest of the Loop. The CTA Blue Line train ($5) runs 24/7. Trains depart every 10 minutes or so; they reach downtown in 40 minutes. Airport Express shuttle vans cost $32, taxis around $50. They can take as long as the train, depending on traffic.

BICYCLE

Chicago is a cycling-savvy city with 200 miles of bike lanes and a bike-share program called **Divvy** (www.divvybikes.com). The **Department of Transportation** (www.chicagocompletestreets.org) provides free maps. Bike racks are plentiful. The biggest facility, with showers, is at the **McDonalds Cycle Center** (www.chicagobikestation.com; 239 E Randolph St) in Millennium Park.

CAR & MOTORCYCLE

Be warned: street and garage/lot parking is expensive. If you must, try **Millennium Park Garage** (www.millenniumgarages.com; 5 S Columbus Dr; per 3/24hr $23/30). Chicago's rush-hour traffic is abysmal.

PUBLIC TRANSPORTATION

The **Chicago Transit Authority** (CTA; www.transitchicago.com) operates the city's buses and the elevated/subway train system (aka the El).

➡ Two of the eight color-coded train lines – the Red Line, and the Blue Line to O'Hare airport – operate 24 hours a day. The other lines run from 4am to 1am daily. During the day, you shouldn't have to wait more than 15 minutes for a train. Get free maps at any station.

➡ CTA buses go everywhere from early morning until late evening.

➡ The standard fare per train is $3 (except from O'Hare, where it costs $5) and includes two transfers; per bus, it is $2.25.

➡ On the train, you must use a Ventra Ticket, which is sold from vending machines at train

ONLINE TICKETS & DISCOUNT CARDS

Most major sights, including the Art Institute of Chicago, Shedd Aquarium and Willis Tower, allow you to buy tickets online. The advantage is that you're assured entry and you get to skip the regular ticket lines. The disadvantage is that you have to pay a service fee of $1.50 to $4 per ticket (sometimes it's just per order), and at times the prepay line is almost as long as the regular one. Our suggestion: consider buying online in summer (especially for the Shedd Aquarium) and for big exhibits. Otherwise, there's no need.

Chicago offers a couple of discount cards that also let you skip the regular queues:

Go Chicago Card (www.gochicagocard.com) Allows you to visit an unlimited number of attractions for a flat fee; good for one, two, three, five or seven consecutive days.

CityPass (www.citypass.com) Gives access to five of the city's top draws, including Shedd Aquarium and Willis Tower, over nine days; a better option if you prefer a more leisurely sightseeing pace.

stations. You can also buy a Ventra Card, aka a rechargeable fare card, at stations. It has a one-time $5 fee that gets refunded once you register the card. It knocks 50¢ off the cost of each ride.

➡ On buses, you can use a Ventra Card or pay the driver with exact change.

➡ Unlimited ride passes (one-/three-day pass $10/20) are also available. Get them at rail stations and drug stores.

Metra commuter trains (www.metrarail.com; fares $2.75-$9.25, all-weekend pass $7) have 12 routes serving the suburbs from four terminals ringing the Loop: LaSalle St Station, Millennium Station, Union Station and Richard B Ogilvie Transportation Center (a few blocks north of Union Station).

PACE (www.pacebus.com) runs the suburban bus system that connects with city transport.

TAXI

Cabs are plentiful in the Loop, north to Andersonville and northwest to Wicker Park/Bucktown. Flagfall is $3.25, plus $1.80 per mile and $1 per extra passenger; a 15% tip is expected.

Flash Cab (☑773-561-1444; www.flashcab.com)

Yellow Cab (☑312-829-4222; www.yellowcab-chicago.com)

Around Chicago

Oak Park

Located 10 miles west of the Loop and easily reached via CTA train, Oak Park has two famous sons: novelist Ernest Hemingway was born here, and architect Frank Lloyd Wright lived and worked here from 1889 to 1909.

ROUTE 66: GET YOUR KICKS IN ILLINOIS

America's 'Mother Road' kicks off in Chicago on Adams St, just west of Michigan Ave. Before embarking, fuel up at Lou Mitchell's (p530) near Union Station. After all, it's 300 miles from here to the Missouri state line.

Sadly, most of the original Route 66 has been superseded by I-55 in Illinois, though the old road still exists in scattered sections, often paralleling the interstate. Keep an eye out for brown 'Historic Route 66' signs, which pop up at crucial junctions to mark the way.

Our first stop rises from the cornfields 60 miles south in Wilmington. Here the Gemini Giant – a 28ft fiberglass spaceman – stands guard outside the **Launching Pad Drive In** (810 E Baltimore St). The restaurant is now shuttered, but the statue remains a quintessential photo op. To reach it, exit I-55 at Joliet Rd, and follow it south as it becomes Hwy 53 into town.

Motor 45 miles onward to Pontiac and the tchotchke-and-photo-filled **Route 66 Hall of Fame** (☑815-844-4566; 110 W Howard St; ⊙9am-5pm Mon-Fri, 10am-4pm Sat & Sun) **FREE**. Cruise another 50 miles to Shirley and **Funk's Grove** (☑309-874-3360; www.funksmaplesirup.com; ⊙9am-5pm Mon-Fri, from 10am Sat, from noon Sun), a pretty 19th-century maple-syrup farm and nature preserve (exit 154 off I-55).

Ten miles later you'll reach the throwback hamlet of Atlanta. Pull up a chair at the **Palms Grill Cafe** (☑217-648-2233; www.thepalmsgrillcafe.com; 110 SW Arch St; pie slices $3; ⊙5am-8pm), where thick slabs of gooseberry, sour-cream raisin and other retro pies tempt from the glass case. Then walk across the street to snap a photo with **Tall Paul**, a sky-high statue of Paul Bunyan clutching a hot dog.

The state capital of Springfield, 50 miles further on, harbors a trio of sights: Shea's Gas Station Museum (p543), the Cozy Dog Drive In (p543) and Route 66 Drive In (p543).

Further south, a good section of old Route 66 parallels I-55 through Litchfield, where you can fork into chicken fried steak while chatting up locals at the 1924 **Ariston Cafe** (www.ariston-cafe.com; S Old Rte 66; mains $7-15; ⊙11am-9pm Tue-Fri, 4-10pm Sat, 11am-8pm Sun). Finally, before driving into Missouri, detour off I-270 at exit 3. Follow Hwy 3 (aka Lewis and Clark Blvd) south, turn right at the first stoplight and drive west to the 1929 **Chain of Rocks Bridge** (⊙9am-sunset). Only open to pedestrians and cyclists these days, the mile-long span over the Mississippi River has a 22-degree angled bend (cause of many a crash, hence the ban on cars).

For more information, visit the **Route 66 Association of Illinois** (www.il66assoc.org) or **Illinois Route 66 Scenic Byway** (www.illinoisroute66.org). Detailed driving directions are at www.historic66.com/illinois.

During Wright's 20 years in Oak Park, he designed many houses. Stop at the **visitor center** (☑ 888-625-7275; www.visitoakpark. com; 1010 W Lake St; ⊙10am-5pm) and buy an architectural site map ($4.25), which gives their locations. To actually get inside a Wright-designed dwelling, you'll need to visit the **Frank Lloyd Wright Home & Studio** (☑ 312-994-4000; www.gowright.org; 951 Chicago Ave; adult/child/camera $15/12/5; ⊙11am-4pm). Tour frequency varies, from every 20 minutes on summer weekends to every hour in winter. The studio also offers guided neighborhood walking tours, as well as a self-guided audio version.

Despite Hemingway calling Oak Park a 'village of wide lawns and narrow minds,' the town still pays homage to him at the **Ernest Hemingway Museum** (☑ 708-848-2222; www.ehfop.org; 200 N Oak Park Ave; adult/child $10/8; ⊙1-5pm Sun-Fri, from 10am Sat). Admission also includes access to **Hemingway's Birthplace** (339 N Oak Park Ave; ⊙1-5pm Sun-Fri, from 10am Sat) across the street.

From downtown Chicago, take the CTA Green Line to its terminus at the Harlem stop, which lands you a quarter-mile from the visitor center. The train traverses some bleak neighborhoods before emerging into Oak Park's wide-lawn splendor.

Evanston & North Shore

Evanston, 14 miles north of the Loop and reached via the CTA Purple Line, combines sprawling old houses with a compact downtown. It's home to Northwestern University.

Beyond are Chicago's northern lakeshore suburbs, which became popular with the wealthy in the late 19th century. A classic 30-mile drive follows Sheridan Rd through various well-off towns to the socioeconomic apex of Lake Forest. Attractions include the **Baha'i House of Worship** (www.bahai.us/bahai-temple; 100 Linden Ave; admission free; ⊙6am-10pm) **FREE**, a glistening white architectural marvel, and the **Chicago Botanic Garden** (☑847-835-5440; www.chicagobotanic.org; 1000 Lake Cook Rd; admission free; ⊙8am-sunset) **FREE**, with hiking trails, 255 bird species and weekend cooking demos by well-known chefs. Parking costs $20.

Inland lies the **Illinois Holocaust Museum** (☑847-967-4800; www.ilholocaustmuseum. org; 9603 Woods Dr; adult/child $12/6; ⊙10am-5pm Mon-Fri, to 8pm Thu, 11am-4pm Sat & Sun). Besides its excellent videos of survivors' stories from WWII, the museum contains thought-provoking art about genocides in Armenia, Rwanda, Cambodia and others.

Galena & Northern Illinois

The highlight of this region is the hilly northwest, where cottonwood trees, grazing horses and scenic byways fill the pocket around Galena.

En route is Union, where the **Illinois Railway Museum** (☑815-923-4000; www.irm.org; US 20 to Union Rd; adult $10-14, child $7-10; ⊙Apr-Oct, hours vary) sends trainspotters into fits of ecstasy with 200 acres of locomotives.

Galena

While it sometimes gets chided as a place for the 'newly wed and nearly dead,' thanks to all the tourist-oriented B&Bs, fudge and antique shops, there's no denying little Galena's beauty. It spreads across wooded hillsides near the Mississippi River, amid rolling, barn-dotted farmland. Red-brick mansions in Greek Revival, Gothic Revival and Queen Anne styles fill the streets, left over from the town's heyday in the mid-1800s, when local lead mines made it rich. Throw in cool kayak trips, horseback rides and winding backroad drives, and you've got a lovely slowpoke getaway.

◎ Sights & Activities

The **visitor center** (☑877-464-2536; www. galena.org; 101 Bouthillier St; ⊙9am-5pm), in the 1857 train depot as you enter from the east, is a good place to start. Get a map, leave your car in the lot ($5 per day) and explore on foot.

Elegant old Main St curves around the hillside and the historic heart of town. Among numerous sights is the **Ulysses S Grant Home** (☑815-777-3310; www.granthome. com; 500 Bouthillier St; adult/child $5/3; ⊙9am-4:45pm Wed-Sun Apr-Oct, reduced hours Nov-Mar), which was a gift from local Republicans to the victorious general at the Civil War's end. Grant lived here until he became the country's 18th president.

Outdoors enthusiasts should head to **Fever River Outfitters** (☑815-776-9425; www.feverriveroutfitters.com; 525 S Main St; ⊙10am-5pm, closed Tue-Thu early Sep-late May), which rents canoes, kayaks, stand-up paddleboards, bicycles and snowshoes. It also offers guided tours, such as two-hour kayak trips ($45 per person, equipment included) on the Mississippi River's backwaters. Or saddle up at **Shenandoah Riding Center** (☑ 815-777-2373; www.shenandoahridingcenter.com; 200 N Brodrecht Rd; 1hr ride $45). It leads trail rides through the valley for all levels of riders, including beginners. The stables are 8 miles east of town.

For a pretty drive mosey onto the **Stagecoach Trail**, a 26-mile ride on a narrow, twisty road en route to Warren. Pick it up by taking Main St northeast through downtown; at the second stop sign go right (you'll see a trail marker). And yes, it really was part of the old stagecoach route between Galena and Chicago

🍴 Sleeping & Eating

Galena brims with quilt-laden B&Bs. Most cost $100 to $200 nightly and fill up during weekends. The visitor center website provides contact information. Presidential types can be like Grant and Lincoln and stay in the well-furnished rooms at **DeSoto House Hotel** (☑ 815-777-0090; www.desotohouse.com; 230 S Main St; r $128-200; ❄ ❀ ☎) 🐾, which dates from 1855. **Grant Hills Motel** (☑ 877-421-0924; www.granthills.com; 9372 US 20; r $70-100; ❄ ❀ ☎) is a no-frills option 1.5 miles east of town, with countryside views and a horseshoe pitch.

111 Main (☑ 815-777-8030; www.oneelevenmain.com; 111 N Main St; mains $17-25; ☺ 4-9pm Mon-Thu, 11am-10pm Fri & Sat, 11am-9pm Sun) makes meatloaf, pork-and-mashed-potatoes and other Midwestern favorites using ingredients sourced from local farms. Dig into mussels with champagne sauce or maybe a tender schnitzel, at cozy French-German bistro **Fritz and Frites** (☑ 815-777-2004; www.fritzandfrites.com; 317 N Main St; mains $17-22; ☺ 4-9pm Tue & Wed, from 11:30am Thu-Sun). The **VFW Hall** (100 S Main St; ☺ from 4pm) provides a sublime opportunity to sip cheap beers and watch TV alongside veterans of long-ago wars. Don't be shy: as the sign out front says, the public is welcome.

Quad Cities

South of Galena along a pretty stretch of the **Great River Road** (www.greatriverroad-illinois.org) is scenic **Mississippi Palisades State Park** (☑ 815-273-2731), a popular rock-climbing, hiking and camping area; pick up trail maps at the north entrance park office.

Further downstream, the **Quad Cities** (www.visitquadcities.com) – Moline and Rock Island in Illinois, and Davenport and Bettendorf across the river in Iowa – make a surprisingly good stop. Rock Island has an appealing downtown (based at 2nd Ave and 18th St), with a couple of cafes and a lively pub and music scene. On the edge of town, **Black Hawk State Historic Site** (www.blackhawkpark.org; 1510 46th Ave; ☺ sunrise-10pm) is a huge park with trails by the Rock River. Its **Hauberg Indian Museum** (☑ 309-788-9536; Watch Tower Lodge; ☺ 9am-noon & 1-5pm Wed-Sun) **FREE** outlines the sorry story of Sauk leader Black Hawk and his people.

Out in the Mississippi River, the actual island of **Rock Island** once held a Civil War-era arsenal and POW camp. It now maintains the impressive **Rock Island Arsenal Museum** (☺ noon-4pm Tue-Sat) **FREE**, Civil War cemetery, national cemetery and visitor center for barge viewing. All are free, but bring photo ID as the island is still an active army facility.

Moline is the home of John Deere, the international farm machinery manufacturer. Downtown holds the **John Deere Pavilion** (www.johndeerepavilion.com; 1400 River Dr; ☺ 9am-5pm Mon-Fri, 10am-5pm Sat, noon-4pm Sun; ♿) **FREE**, which is a kiddie-beloved museum/showroom.

Springfield & Central Illinois

Abraham Lincoln and Route 66 sights are sprinkled liberally throughout central Illinois, which is otherwise farmland plain. East of Decatur, Arthur and Arcola are Amish centers.

Springfield

The small state capital has a serious obsession with Abraham Lincoln, who practiced law here from 1837 to 1861. Many of the attractions are walkable downtown and cost little or nothing.

🔵 Sights & Activities

Lincoln Home & Visitor Center HISTORIC SITE (☑ 217-492-4150; www.nps.gov/liho; 426 S 7th St; ☺ 8:30am-5pm) **FREE** Start at the National Park Service visitor center, where you must pick up a ticket to enter Lincoln's 12-room abode, located directly across the street. You can then walk through the house where Abe and Mary Lincoln lived from 1844 until they moved to the White House in 1861; rangers are stationed throughout to provide background information and answer questions.

Lincoln Presidential Library & Museum
MUSEUM
(☑217-558-8844; www.presidentlincoln.org; 212 N 6th St; adult/child $12/6; ⊙9am-5pm; ⊕) This museum contains the most complete Lincoln collection in the world. Real-deal artifacts like Abe's shaving mirror and briefcase join whiz-bang exhibits and Disneyesque holograms that keep the kids agog.

Lincoln's Tomb
CEMETERY
(www.lincolntomb.org; 1441 Monument Ave; ⊙9am-5pm, closed Sun & Mon Sep-May) FREE After his assassination, Lincoln's body was returned to Springfield, where it lies in an impressive tomb in Oak Ridge Cemetery, 1.5 miles north of downtown. The gleam on the nose of Lincoln's bust, created by visitors' light touches, indicates the numbers of those who pay their respects here. On summer Tuesdays at 7pm, infantry reenactors fire muskets and lower the flag.

Old State Capitol
HISTORIC SITE
(☑217-785-9363; cnr 6th & Adams Sts; ⊙9am-5pm, closed Sun & Mon Sep-May) Chatterbox docents will take you through the building and regale you with Lincoln stories, such as how he gave his famous 'House Divided' speech here in 1858. Suggested donation is $4.

Shea's Gas Station Museum
MUSEUM
(☑217-522-0475; 2075 Peoria Rd; ⊙by appointment) At the time of writing, the 91-year-old owner of this famed collection of Route 66 pumps and signs had finally stopped working. His family is trying to keep the museum afloat. Call for an appointment.

Route 66 Drive In
CINEMA
(☑217-698-0066; www.route66-drivein.com; 1700 Recreation Dr; adult/child $7/4; ⊙nightly Jun-Aug, Sat & Sun mid-Apr–May & Sep) Screens first-run flicks under the stars.

🛏 Sleeping & Eating

Statehouse Inn
HOTEL $$
(☑217-528-5100; www.thestatehouseinn.com; 101 E Adams St; r incl breakfast $95-155; P❄@🛜) It looks concrete-drab outside, but inside the Statehouse shows its style. Comfy beds and large baths fill the rooms; a retro bar fills the lobby.

Inn at 835
B&B $$
(☑217-523-4466; www.innat835.com; 835 S 2nd St; r incl breakfast $130-200; P❄🛜) The historic arts-and-crafts-style manor offers 11 rooms of the four-poster bed, claw-foot bathtub variety.

Cozy Dog Drive In
AMERICAN $
(www.cozydogdrivein.com; 2935 S 6th St; mains $2-4.50; ⊙8am-8pm Mon-Sat) This Route 66 legend – the reputed birthplace of the corn dog! – has memorabilia and souvenirs, and the deeply fried main course on a stick.

Norb Andy's Tabarin
PUB $
(www.norbandys.com; 518 E Capitol Ave; mains $7-10; ⊙from 11am Tue-Sat) A favorite with locals, Norb's is a dive bar-restaurant housed in the 1837 Hickox House downtown. It piles up Springfield's best 'horseshoe,' a local sandwich of fried meat on toasted bread, mounded with french fries and smothered in melted cheese.

❶ Information

Springfield Convention & Visitors Bureau (www.visitspringfieldillinois.com) Produces a useful visitors' guide.

❶ Getting There & Around

The downtown **Amtrak station** (☑217-753-2013; cnr 3rd & Washington Sts) has five trains daily to/from St Louis (two hours) and Chicago (3½ hours).

Petersburg

When Lincoln first arrived in Illinois in 1831, he worked variously as a clerk, storekeeper and postmaster in the frontier village of New Salem before studying law and moving to Springfield. In Petersburg, 20 miles northwest of Springfield, Lincoln's New Salem State Historic Site (☑217-632-4000; www.lincolnsnewsalem.com; Hwy 97; suggested donation adult/child $4/2; ⊙9am-5pm, closed Mon & Tue mid-Sep–mid-Apr) reconstructs the village with building replicas, historical displays and costumed performances – a pretty informative and entertaining package.

Southern Illinois

A surprise awaits near Collinsville, 8 miles east of East St Louis: classified as a Unesco World Heritage site with the likes of Stonehenge, the Acropolis and the Egyptian pyramids is Cahokia Mounds State Historic

Site (☎618-346-5160; www.cahokiamounds.org; Collinsville Rd; suggested donation adult/child $7/2; ☺visitor center 9am-5pm, grounds 8am-dusk). Cahokia protects the remnants of North America's largest prehistoric city (20,000 people, with suburbs), dating from AD 1200. While the 65 earthen mounds, including the enormous Monk's Mound and the 'Woodhenge' sun calendar, are not overwhelmingly impressive in themselves, the whole site is worth seeing. If you're approaching from the north, take exit 24 off I-255 S; if approaching from St Louis, take exit 6 off I-55/70.

A short distance north of St Louis, Hwy 100 between Grafton and Alton is perhaps the most scenic 15 miles of the entire Great River Rd. As you slip under windhewn bluffs, keep an eye out for the turnoff to itty-bitty Elsah (www.elsah.org), a hidden hamlet of 19th-century stone cottages, wood buggy shops and farmhouses.

An exception to the state's flat farmland is the green southernmost section, punctuated by rolling Shawnee National Forest (☎618-253-7114; www.fs.usda.gov/shawnee) and its rocky outcroppings. The area has numerous state parks and recreation areas good for hiking, climbing, swimming, fishing and canoeing, particularly around Little Grassy Lake and Devil's Kitchen. And who would think that Florida-like swampland, complete with bald cypress trees and croaking bullfrogs, would be here? But it is, at Cypress Creek National Wildlife Refuge (☎618-634-2231; www.fws.gov/midwest/cypresscreek).

Union County, near the state's southern tip, has wineries and orchards. Sample the wares on the 35-mile Shawnee Hills Wine Trail (www.shawneewinetrail.com), which connects 12 vineyards.

INDIANA

The state revs up around the Indy 500 race, but otherwise it's about slow-paced pleasures in corn-stubbled Indiana: pie-eating in Amish Country, meditating in Bloomington's Tibetan temples and admiring the big architecture in small Columbus. For the record, folks have called Indianans 'Hoosiers' since the 1830s, but the word's origin is unknown. One theory is that early settlers knocking on a door were met with 'Who's here?' which soon became 'Hoosier.' It's certainly something to discuss with locals, perhaps over a traditional pork tenderloin sandwich.

ℹ Information

Indiana Highway Conditions (☎800-261-7623; www.trafficwise.in.gov)
Indiana State Park Information (☎800-622-4931; www.in.gov/dnr/parklake) Park entry costs $2 per day by foot or bicycle, $7 to $10 by vehicle. Campsites cost $10 to $40; reservations accepted (☎866-622-6746; www.camp.in.gov).
Indiana Tourism (☎888-365-6946; www.visitindiana.com)

Indianapolis

Clean-cut Indy is the state capital and a perfectly pleasant place to ogle racing cars and take a spin around the renowned speedway. The art museum and White River State Park have their merits, as do the Mass Ave and Broad Ripple 'hoods for eating and drinking. And Kurt Vonnegut fans are in for a treat.

◉ Sights & Activities

Downtown's bulls-eye is Monument Circle. White River State Park and its many attractions lie about three-quarters of a mile west.

Indianapolis Motor Speedway   MUSEUM
(☎317-492-6784; www.indianapolismotorspeedway.com; 4790 W 16th St; adult/child $5/3; ☺9am-5pm Mar-Oct, 10am-4pm Nov-Feb) The Speedway, home of the Indianapolis 500 motor race, is Indy's supersight. The Hall of Fame Museum features 75 racing cars (including former winners), a 500lb Tiffany trophy and a track tour ($5 extra). OK, so you're on a bus for the latter and not even beginning to burn rubber at 37mph, but it's still fun to pretend.

The big race itself is held on the Sunday of Memorial Day weekend (late May) and attended by 450,000 crazed fans. Tickets (☎800-822-4639; www.imstix.com; $30-150) can be hard to come by. Try the prerace trials and practices for easier access and cheaper prices. The track is about 6 miles northwest of downtown.

White River State Park   PARK
(http://inwhiteriver.wrsp.in.gov) The expansive park, located at downtown's edge, contains several worthwhile sights. The adobe Eiteljorg Museum of American Indians & Western Art (☎317-636-9378; www.eiteljorg.org; 500 W Washington St; adult/child $10/6; ☺10am-5pm Mon-Sat, from noon Sun) features Native American basketry, pots and masks,

as well as several paintings by Frederic Remington and Georgia O'Keeffe. Other park highlights include an atmospheric minor-league baseball stadium, a zoo, a canal walk, gardens and a science museum.

The NCAA Hall of Champions (📞800-735-6222; www.ncaahallofchampions.org; 700 W Washington St; adult/child $5/3; ⏰10am-5pm Tue-Sat, from noon Sun) is also here, and reveals the country's fascination with college sports. Interactive exhibits let you shoot free throws or climb onto a swimming platform à la Michael Phelps.

Indianapolis Museum of Art
MUSEUM, GARDENS

(📞317-920-2660; www.imamuseum.org; 4000 Michigan Rd; ⏰11am-5pm Tue-Sat, 11am-9pm Thu & Fri, noon-5pm Sun) FREE The museum has a terrific collection of European art (especially Turner and post-impressionists), African tribal art, South Pacific art and Chinese works. The complex also includes Oldfields – Lilly House & Gardens, where you can tour the 22-room mansion and flowery grounds of the Lilly pharmaceutical family, and Fairbanks Art & Nature Park, with eye-popping mod sculptures set amid 100 acres of woodlands.

Kurt Vonnegut Memorial Library
MUSEUM

(www.vonnegutlibrary.org; 340 N Senate Ave; ⏰noon-5pm Thu-Tue) FREE Author Kurt Vonnegut was born and raised in Indy, and this humble museum pays homage with displays including his Pall Mall cigarettes, Purple Heart medal and box of hilarious rejection letters from publishers. The library also replicates his office, complete with checkerboard carpet, red-rooster lamp and blue Coronamatic typewriter. You're welcome to sit at the desk and type Kurt a note.

Rhythm! Discovery Center
MUSEUM

(www.rhythmdiscoverycenter.org; 110 W Washington St; adult/child $9/6; ⏰10am-5pm Mon-Sat, from noon Sun) Bang drums, gongs, xylophones and exotic percussive instruments from around the globe at this hidden gem downtown. Kids love the interactive whomping. Adults appreciate the exhibits of famous drummers' gear and the soundproof, drum-kitted studio where you can unleash (and record) your inner Neil Peart.

Monument Circle
MONUMENT, MUSEUM

(1 Monument Circle) At Monument Circle the city center is marked by the jaw-dropping 284ft Soldiers & Sailors Monument. For a

bizarre (and cramped) experience, take the elevator ($2) to the top. Beneath is the Civil War Museum (⏰10:30am-5:30pm Wed-Sun) FREE, which neatly outlines the conflict and Indiana's abolition position. A few blocks north, the World War Memorial (cnr Vermont & Meridian Sts) is another impressively beefy monument.

Sun King Brewing
BREWERY

(www.sunkingbrewing.com; 135 N College Ave; ⏰4-7pm Thu, noon-7pm Fri, 1-5pm Sat) FREE Join Indy's young and hip, slurping free beers at Sun King's unvarnished downtown warehouse. You get six tastings (about the equivalent of a pint overall) in plastic cups, including year-round brews such as Osiris Pale Ale and seasonals like a pepper-spiced amber ale.

Indiana Medical History Museum
MUSEUM

(📞317-635-7329; www.imhm.org; 3045 W Vermont St; adult/child $7/3; ⏰10am-3pm Thu-Sat) When you think 'horror movie insane asylum,' this century-old state psychiatric hospital is exactly what you envision. Guided tours roam the former pathology lab, from the cold-slabbed autopsy room to the eerie specimen room filled with brains in jars. It's a few miles west of White River park.

Bicycle Garage Indy
BICYCLE RENTAL

(www.bgindy.com; 222 E Market St; rental per hr/day $15/40) Cycling has really taken off in the city. Hop on the Cultural Trail in front of the shop; it eventually connects to the Monon Trail greenway. Rates include helmet, lock and map.

★ Festivals

The city celebrates the Indy 500 throughout May with the 500 Festival (www.500festival.com; tickets from $7). Events include a race-car drivers' parade and a community shindig at the racetrack.

🛏 Sleeping

Hotels cost more and are usually full during race weeks in May, July and August. Add 17% tax to the prices listed here. Look for low-cost motels off I-465, the freeway that circles Indianapolis.

Indy Hostel
HOSTEL $

(☎ 317-727-1696; www.indyhostel.us; 4903 Winthrop Ave; dm/r from $29/58; P ❄ @ 🛜) This small, friendly hostel has four dorm rooms in configurations from four to six beds. One room is for females only, while the others are mixed. There are also a couple of private rooms. The Monon Trail hiking/cycling path runs beside the property. It's located by Broad Ripple, so it's a bit of a haul from downtown (on bus 17).

Hilton Garden Inn
HOTEL $$

(☎ 317-955-9700; www.indianapolisdowntown.gardeninn.com; 10 E Market St; r incl breakfast $150-190; ❄ @ 🛜 🛜 ❄) The century-old neoclassical architecture, plush beds, free omelet-laden breakfast and downtown location right by Monument Circle make this a fine chain-hotel choice. Parking is $25.

Stone Soup
B&B $$

(☎ 866-639-9550; www.stonesoupinn.com; 1304 N Central Ave; r incl breakfast $85-145; P ❄ 🛜) The nine rooms sprawl throughout a rambling,

---

ⓘ

INDIANA FOODWAYS

Which restaurants serve the best pork tenderloin and sugar cream pie? Where are the local farmers markets and rib fests? What's the recipe for corn pudding? The Indiana Foodways Alliance (www.indianafoodways.com) is your one-stop shop for Hoosier cuisine info.

---

antique-filled house. It's a bit ramshackle, but it has its charm. The less-expensive rooms share a bath.

Alexander
HOTEL $$$

(☎ 317-624-8200; www.thealexander.com; 333 S Delaware St; r $160-280) Opened in 2013, the 209-room Alexander is all about art. Forty original works decorate the lobby; the Indianapolis Museum of Art curates the contemporary collection (the public is welcome to browse). The mod rooms have dark-wood floors and, of course, cool wall art. It's a block from the basketball arena, and it's where visiting teams typically stay. Parking is $27.

🍴 Eating

Massachusetts Ave (Mass Ave; www.discovermassave.com), by downtown, is bounteous when the stomach growls. Broad Ripple (www.discoverbroadripplevillage.com), 7 miles north, has pubs, cafes and ethnic eateries.

Mug 'N' Bun
AMERICAN $

(www.mug-n-bun.com; 5211 W 10th St; mains $3-5; ⏱ 10am-9pm Sun-Thu, to 10pm Fri & Sat) The mugs are frosted and filled with a wonderful home-brewed root beer. The buns contain burgers, chili dogs and juicy pork tenderloins. And don't forget the fried macaroni-and-cheese wedges. At this vintage drive-in near the Speedway, you are served – where else? – in your car.

City Market
MARKET $

(www.indycm.com; 222 E Market St; ⏱ 6am-9pm Mon-Fri, from 8am Sat; 🛜) A smattering of food stalls fill the city's old marketplace, which dates from 1886. The 2nd-floor bar pours 16 local brews; most other vendors close by 3pm.

Bazbeaux
PIZZERIA $$

(www.bazbeaux.com; 329 Massachusetts Ave; mains $8-12; ⏱ 11am-10pm Sun-Thu, to 11pm Fri & Sat) A local favorite, Bazbeaux offers an eclectic pizza selection, like the 'Tchoupitoulas,' topped with Cajun shrimp and andouille sausage. Muffaletta sandwiches, stromboli and Belgian beer are some of the other unusual offerings.

Shapiro's Deli
DELI $$

(☎ 317-631-4041; www.shapiros.com; 808 S Meridian St; mains $8-15; ⏱ 6am-8pm; 🛜) Chomp into a towering corned-beef or peppery pastrami sandwich on homemade bread, and then chase it with fat slices of chocolate cake or fruit pie.

🍸 Drinking & Entertainment

Downtown and Mass Ave have some good watering holes; Broad Ripple also has several.

Bars & Nightclubs

Slippery Noodle Inn — BAR
(www.slipperynoodle.com; 372 S Meridian St; ⊙from 11am Mon-Fri, from noon Sat, from 4pm Sun) Downtown's Noodle is the oldest bar in the state, and has seen action as a whorehouse, slaughterhouse, gangster hangout and Underground Railroad station; currently it's one of the best blues clubs in the country. There's live music nightly, and it's cheap.

Rathskeller — BEER HALL
(www.rathskeller.com; 401 E Michigan St; ⊙from 2pm Mon-Fri, from 11am Sat & Sun) Quaff German and local brews at the outdoor beer garden's picnic tables in summer, or at the deer-head-lined indoor beer hall once winter strikes. It is located in the historic Athenaeum building near Mass Ave.

Plump's Last Shot — BAR
(www.plumpslastshot.com; 6416 Cornell Ave; ⊙from 3pm Mon-Fri, from noon Sat & Sun; 🐾) Bobby Plump inspired the iconic movie *Hoosiers*. He's the kid who swished in the last-second shot, so his tiny school beat the 'big city' school in the 1950s state basketball championship. There's sports memorabilia everywhere. It's located in a big house in Broad Ripple – great for people-watching and sipping a cold one on the dog-friendly patio.

Sports

The motor races aren't the only coveted spectator events. The NFL's Colts win football games under a huge retractable roof at Lucas Oil Stadium (✆317-262-3389; www.colts.com; 500 S Capitol Ave). The NBA's Pacers shoot hoops at Bankers Life Fieldhouse (✆317-917-2500; www.pacers.com; 125 S Pennsylvania St).

🛍 Shopping

You could buy a speedway flag or Colts jersey as your Indy souvenir. Or you could purchase a bottle of mead made by a couple of enthusiastic former beekeepers at New Day Meadery (www.newdaymeadery.com; 1102 E Prospect St; ⊙2-9pm Tue-Fri, noon-9pm Sat, noon-6pm Sun). Sip the honeyed wares in the tasting room (six samples for $6) before making your selection.

WORTH A TRIP

GRAY BROTHERS CAFETERIA

Cafeterias are an Indiana tradition, but most have disappeared – except for Gray Brothers (www.graybrotherscatering.com; 555 S Indiana St; mains $4-8; ⊙11am-8:30pm Mon-Sat, from 10am Sun). Enter the time-warped dining room, grab a blue tray and behold a corridor of food that seems to stretch the length of a football field. Stack on plates of pan-fried chicken, meatloaf, mac 'n' cheese and sugar cream pie, then fork in with abandon. It's located in Mooresville, about 18 miles south of downtown Indianapolis en route to Bloomington.

ℹ Information

Gay Indy (www.gayindy.org) Gay and lesbian news and entertainment listings.

Indiana University Medical Center (✆317-274-4705; 550 N University Blvd)

Indianapolis Convention & Visitors Bureau (✆800-323-4639; www.visitindy.com) Download a free city app and print out coupons from the website.

Indianapolis Star (www.indystar.com) The city's daily newspaper.

Nuvo (www.nuvo.net) Free, weekly alternative paper with the arts and music low-down.

ℹ Getting There & Around

The fancy **Indianapolis International Airport** (IND; www.indianapolisairport.com; 7800 Col H Weir Cook Memorial Dr) is 16 miles southwest of town. The Washington bus (8) runs between the airport and downtown ($1.75, 50 minutes); the Go Green Airport van does it quicker ($10, 20 minutes). A cab to downtown costs about $35.

Greyhound (✆317-267-3076; www.greyhound.com) shares **Union Station** (350 S Illinois St) with Amtrak. Buses go frequently to Cincinnati (two hours) and Chicago (3½ hours). **Megabus** (www.megabus.com/us) stops at 200 E Washington St, and is often cheaper. Amtrak travels these routes but takes almost twice as long and (nonsensically) costs more.

IndyGo (www.indygo.net; fare $1.75) runs the local buses. Bus 17 goes to Broad Ripple. Service is minimal during weekends.

For a taxi, call **Yellow Cab** (✆317-487-7777).

Bloomington & Central Indiana

Bluegrass music, architectural hot spots, Tibetan temples and James Dean all furrow into the farmland around here.

Fairmount

This small town, north on Hwy 9, is the birthplace of James Dean, one of the original icons of cool. Fans should head directly to the **Fairmount Historical Museum** (☑765-948-4555; www.jamesdeanartifacts.com; 203 E Washington St; ☉10am-5pm Mon-Sat, from noon Sun Apr-Oct) **FREE** to see Dean's bongo drums, among other artifacts. This is also the place to pick up a free map that will guide you to the farmhouse where Jimmy grew up and his lipstick-kissed grave site, among other sights. The museum sells Dean posters, zippo lighters and other memorabilia, and sponsors the annual **James Dean Festival** (☉late Sep) **FREE**, when as many as 50,000 fans pour in for four days of music and revelry. The privately owned **James Dean Gallery** (☑765-948-3326; www.jamesdeangallery.com; 425 N Main St; ☉9am-6pm) **FREE** has more memorabilia a few blocks away.

Columbus

When you think of the USA's great architectural cities – Chicago, New York, Washington, DC – Columbus, Indiana, doesn't quite leap to mind, but it should. Located 40 miles south of Indianapolis on I-65, Columbus is a remarkable gallery of physical design. Since the 1940s the city and its leading corporations have commissioned some of the world's best architects, including Eero Saarinen, Richard Meier and IM Pei, to create both public and private buildings. Stop at the **visitor center** (☑812-378-2622; www.columbus.in.us; 506 5th St; ☉9am-5pm Mon-Sat year-round, noon-5pm Sun Mar-Nov, closed Sun Dec-Feb) to pick up a self-guided tour map ($3) or join a two-hour bus tour (adult/child $20/10) departing at 10am Monday to Friday, 10am and 2pm Saturday and 2:30pm Sunday. Over 70 notable buildings and pieces of public art are spread over a wide area (car required), but about 15 diverse works can be seen on foot downtown.

Hotel Indigo (☑812-375-9100; www.hotelindigo.com; 400 Brown St; r $135-180; ❋ 🛜 ✉ 🐾), downtown, offers the chain's trademark mod, cheery rooms, plus a fluffy white dog who works as the lobby ambassador (he even has his own email address). A few blocks away you can grab a counter stool, chat up the servers, and let the sugar buzz begin at retro, stained-glass-packed **Zaharakos** (www.zaharakos.com; 329 Washington St; ☉11am-8pm), a 1909 soda fountain.

Nashville

Gentrified and antique-filled, this 19th-century town west of Columbus on Hwy 46 is now a bustling tourist center, at its busiest in fall when leaf-peepers pour in. The **visitor center** (☑800-753-3255; www.browncounty.com; 10 N Van Buren St; ☉9am-6pm Mon-Thu, 9am-7pm Fri & Sat, 10am-5pm Sun; 🛜) provides maps and coupons.

Beyond gallery browsing, Nashville is the jump-off point to **Brown County State Park** (☑812-988-6406; tent & RV sites $12-36, cabins from $77), a 15,700-acre stand of oak, hickory and birch trees, where trails give hikers, mountain bikers and horseback riders access to the area's green hill country.

Among several B&Bs, central **Artists Colony Inn** (☑812-988-0600; www.artistscolonyinn.com; 105 S Van Buren St; r incl breakfast $112-180; 🛜) stands out for its spiffy Shaker-style rooms. The **dining room** (mains $9-17; ☉7:30am-8pm Sun-Thu, to 9pm Fri & Sat) offers traditional Hoosier fare, such as catfish and pork tenderloins.

As with Nashville Tennessee, Nashville Indiana enjoys country music, and bands play regularly at several venues. To shake a leg, mosey into **Mike's Music & Dance Barn** (☑812-988-8636; www.mikesmusicbarn.com; 2277 Hwy 46; ☉from 6:30pm Thu-Mon). The **Bill Monroe Museum** (☑812-988-6422; 5163 Rte 135 N; adult/child $4/free; ☉9am-5pm, closed Tue & Wed Nov-Apr), 5 miles north of town, hails the bluegrass hero.

Bloomington

Lively and lovely Bloomington, 53 miles south of Indianapolis via Hwy 37, is the home of Indiana University. The town centers on Courthouse Sq, surrounded by restaurants, bars, bookshops and the historic facade of Fountain Sq Mall. Nearly everything is walkable. The **Bloomington CVB** (www.visitbloomington.com) has a downloadable guide.

On the expansive university campus, the **Art Museum** (☑812-855-5445; www.indiana.edu/~iuam; 1133 E 7th St; ☉10am-5pm Tue-Sat, from noon Sun) FREE, designed by IM Pei, contains an excellent collection of African art, as well as European and US paintings.

The colorful, prayer-flag-covered Tibetan Mongolian Buddhist Cultural Center (☑812-336-6807; www.tmbcc.net; 3655 Snoddy Rd; ☉sunrise-sunset) FREE – founded by the Dalai Lama's brother – as well as the Dagom Gaden Tensung Ling Monastery (☑812-339-0857; www.dgtlmonastery.org; 102 Clubhouse Dr; ☉9am-6pm) FREE, indicate Bloomington's significant Tibetan presence. Both have intriguing shops and offer free teachings and meditation sessions; check the websites for weekly schedules.

If you arrive in mid-April and wonder why an extra 20,000 people are hanging out in town, it's for the Little 500 (www.iusf.indiana.edu; tickets $25; ☉mid-Apr). It's one of the coolest bike races you'll see, in which amateurs ride one-speed Schwinns for 200 laps around a quarter-mile track.

Look for cheap lodgings along N Walnut St near Hwy 46. Grant Street Inn (☑800-328-4350; www.grantsinn.com; 310 N Grant St; r incl breakfast $159-239; @☎) has 24 rooms in a Victorian house and annex near campus.

For a town of its size, Bloomington offers a mind-blowing array of ethnic restaurants – everything from Burmese to Eritrean to Mexican. Browse Kirkwood Ave and E 4th St. Anyetsang's Little Tibet (☑812-331-0122; www.anyetsangs.com; 415 E 4th St; mains $9-13; ☉11am-9:30pm Wed-Mon) offers specialties from the Himalayan homeland. Pubs on Kirkwood Ave, close to the university, cater to the student crowd. Nick's English Hut (www.nicksenglishhut.com; 423 E Kirkwood Ave; ☉from 11am) pours not only for students and professors, but has filled the cups of Kurt Vonnegut, Dylan Thomas and Barack Obama, as well.

Southern Indiana

The pretty hills, caves, rivers and utopian history of southern Indiana mark it as a completely different region from the flat and industrialized north.

Ohio River

The Indiana segment of the 981-mile Ohio River marks the state's southern border. From tiny Aurora, in the southeastern corner of the state, Hwys 56, 156, 62 and 66, known collectively as the Ohio River Scenic Route, wind through a varied landscape.

Coming from the east, a perfect place to stop is little Madison, a well-preserved river settlement from the mid-19th century where architectural beauties beckon genteelly from the streets. At the visitor center (☑812-265-2956; www.visitmadison.org; 601 W First St; ☉9am-5pm Mon-Fri, 9am-4pm Sat, 11am-5pm Sun), pick up a walking-tour brochure, which will lead you by notable landmarks.

Madison has motels around its edges, as well as several B&Bs. Main St lines up numerous places for a bite, interspersed with antique stores. Large, wooded Clifty Falls State Park (☑812-273-8885; tent & RV sites $12-36), off Hwy 56 and a couple of miles west of town, has camping, hiking trails, views and waterfalls.

In Clarksville, Falls of the Ohio State Park (☑812-280-9970; www.fallsoftheohio.org; 201 W Riverside Dr) has only rapids, no falls, but is of interest for its 386-million-year-old fossil beds. The interpretive center (adult/child $5/2; ☉9am-5pm Mon-Sat, from 1pm Sun) explains it all. Quench your thirst in adjacent New Albany, home to New Albanian Brewing Company (www.newalbanian.com; 3312 Plaza Dr; ☉11am-midnight Mon-Sat). Or cross the bridge to Louisville, Kentucky, where the tonsil-singeing native bourbon awaits...

Scenic Hwy 62 heads west and leads to the Lincoln Hills and southern Indiana's limestone caves. A plunge into Marengo Cave (☑812-365-2705; www.marengocave.com; ☉9am-6pm Jun-Aug, to 5pm Sep-May), north on Hwy 66, is highly recommended. It has a 40-minute tour (adult/child $14/8), 70-minute tour ($16/9) or combination tour ($24/13) walking past stalagmites and other ancient formations. The same group operates Cave Country Canoes (www.cavecountrycanoes.com; ☉May-Oct) in nearby Milltown, with half-day ($25), full-day ($28) or longer trips on the scenic Blue River; keep an eye out for river otters and rare hellbender salamanders.

Four miles south of Dale, off I-64, is the Lincoln Boyhood National Memorial (☑812-937-4541; www.nps.gov/libo; adult/child/family $3/free/$5; ☉8am-5pm), where young Abe lived from age seven to 21. This isolated site also includes admission to a working pioneer farm (☉8am-5pm late May-Aug).

New Harmony

In southwest Indiana, the Wabash River forms the border with Illinois. Beside it, south of I-64, captivating New Harmony is the site of two early communal-living experiments and is worth a visit. In the early 19th century a German Christian sect, the Harmonists, developed a sophisticated town here while awaiting the Second Coming. Later, the British utopian Robert Owen acquired the town. Learn more and pick up a walking-tour map at the angular Atheneum Visitors Center (☑812-682-4474; www.usi. edu/hnh; 401 N Arthur St; ☺9:30am-5pm).

Today New Harmony retains an air of contemplation, if not otherworldliness, which you can experience at its newer attractions, such as the templelike Roofless Church and the Labyrinth, a maze symbolizing the spirit's quest. The town has a couple of guesthouses and camping at Harmonie State Park (☑812-682-4821; campsites $12-29). Pop into Main Cafe (508 Main St; mains $4-7; ☺5:30am-1pm Mon-Fri) for a ham, bean and cornbread lunch, but save room for the coconut cream pie.

Northern Indiana

The truck-laden I-80/I-90 tollways cut across Indiana's northern section. Parallel US 20 is slower and cheaper, but not much more attractive.

Indiana Dunes

Hugely popular on summer days with sunbathers from Chicago and South Bend, the Indiana Dunes National Lakeshore (☑219-395-8914; www.nps.gov/indu; campsites $18; ☺Apr-Oct) stretches along 21 miles of Lake Michigan shoreline. In addition to its beaches, the area is noted for its plant variety: everything from cacti to pine trees sprouts here. Hiking trails crisscross the dunes and woodlands, winding by a peat bog, a still-operating 1870s farm and a blue-heron rookery, among other payoffs. Oddly, all this natural bounty lies smack-dab next to smoke-belching factories, which you'll also see at various vantage points. Stop at the Dorothy Buell Visitor Center (☑219-926-7561; Hwy 49; ☺8:30am-6:30pm Jun-Aug, to 4:30pm Sep-May) for beach details, a schedule of ranger-guided walks and activities, and to pick up hiking, biking and birding maps.

Or get guides in advance via the Porter County Convention & Visitors Bureau (www.indianadunes.com).

Indiana Dunes State Park (☑219-926-1952; www.dnr.in.gov/parklake; per car $10) is a 2100-acre shoreside pocket within the national lakeshore; it's located at the end of Hwy 49, near Chesterton. It has more amenities than the National Foreshore, but also more regulation and more crowds (plus the vehicle entry fee). Wintertime brings out the cross-country skiers; summertime brings out the hikers. Seven trails zigzag over the landscape; Trail 4 up Mt Tom rewards with Chicago skyline views.

Other than a couple of beachfront snack bars, you won't find much to eat in the parks, so stop at Great Lakes Cafe (201 Mississippi St; mains $6-9; ☺5am-3pm Mon-Fri, 6am-1pm Sat; ▣), the steelworkers' hearty favorite, at the Dunes' western edge in Gary.

The Dunes are an easy day trip from Chicago. Driving takes one hour. The South Shore Metra train (www.nictd.com) makes the journey from Millennium Station downtown, and it's about 1¼ hours to the Dune Park or Beverly Shores stops (both stations are a 1½-mile walk from the beach). Those who want to make a night of it can camp (national lakeshore campsites $18, state park tent & RV sites $19-36).

Near Illinois, the steel cities of Gary and East Chicago present some of the bleakest urban landscapes anywhere. Taking the train (Amtrak or South Shore line) through here will get you up close and personal with the industrial underbelly.

South Bend

South Bend is home to the University of Notre Dame. You know how some people say, 'football is a religion here'? They mean it at Notre Dame, where 'Touchdown Jesus' lords over the 80,000-capacity stadium (it's a mural of the resurrected Christ with arms raised, though the pose bears a striking resemblance to a referee signaling a touchdown).

Tours of the pretty campus, with its two lakes, Gothic-style architecture and iconic Golden Dome atop the main building, start at the visitor center (www.nd.edu/visitors; 111 Eck Center). Less visited but worth a stop is the Studebaker National Museum (☑574-235-9714; www.studebakermuseum.org; 201 S Chapin St; adult/child $8/5; ☺10am-5pm Mon-Sat, from noon Sun) near downtown, where you can gaze at a gorgeous 1956 Packard and other classic beauties that used to be built in South Bend.

Amish Country

East of South Bend, around Shipshewana and Middlebury, is the USA's third-largest Amish community. Horses and buggies clip-clop by, and long-bearded men hand-plow the tidy fields. Get situated with maps from the Elkhart County CVB (☎ 800-517-9739; www.amishcountry.org). Better yet, pick a back-road between the two towns and head down it. Often you'll see families selling beeswax candles, quilts and fresh produce on their porch, which beats the often-touristy shops and restaurants on the main roads. Note that most places close on Sunday.

Village Inn (☎ 574-825-2043; 105 S Main St; mains $3-7; ⏰ 5am-8pm Mon-Fri, 6am-2pm Sat; 🖥), in Middlebury, sells real-deal pies; bonneted women in pastel dresses come in at 4:30am to bake the flaky wares. Arrive before noon, or you'll be looking at crumbs.

Auburn

Just before reaching the Ohio border, classic car connoisseurs should dip south on I-69 to the town of Auburn, where the Cord Company produced the USA's favorite cars in the 1920s and '30s. The Auburn Cord Duesenberg Museum (☎ 260-925-1444; www.auto-mobilemuseum.org; 1600 S Wayne St; adult/child $12.50/7.50; ⏰ 10am-7pm Mon-Fri, to 5pm Sat & Sun) has a wonderful display of early roadsters in a beautiful art-deco setting. Next door are the vintage rigs of the National Automotive and Truck Museum (☎ 260-925-9100; www.natmus.org; 1000 Gordon Buehrig Pl; adult/child $7/4; ⏰ 9am-5pm).

OHIO

All right, time for your Ohio quiz. In the Buckeye State you can 1) watch butter churn on an Amish farm; 2) lose your stomach on one of the world's fastest roller coasters; 3) suck down a dreamy creamy milkshake fresh from a working dairy; or 4) examine a massive, mysterious snake sculpture built into the earth. And the answer is...all of these. It hurts locals' feelings when visitors think the only thing to do here is tip over cows, so c'mon, give Ohio a chance. Besides these activities, you can partake in a five-way in Cincinnati and rock out in Cleveland.

ℹ Information

Ohio Division of Travel and Tourism (☎ 800-282-5393; www.discoverohio.com)
Ohio Highway Conditions (www.ohgo.com)
Ohio State Park Information (☎ 614-265-6561; http://parks.ohiodnr.gov) State parks are free to visit; some have free wi-fi. Tent and RV sites cost $19 to $38; reservations accepted (☎ 866-644-6727; www.ohio.reserveworld.com; fee $8.25).

Cleveland

Does it or does it not rock? That is the question. Drawing from its roots as a working man's town, Cleveland has toiled hard in recent years to prove it does. Step one was to control the urban decay/river-on-fire thing – the Cuyahoga River was once so polluted that it actually burned. Check. Step two was to bring a worthy attraction to town, say the Rock and Roll Hall of Fame. Check. Step three was to get grub beyond steak-and-potatoes. Check. So can Cleveland finally wipe the sweat from its brow? More or less. Some of the downtown area remains bleak, though there are definite pockets of freshness.

OHIO FACTS

Nickname Buckeye State

Population 11.5 million

Area 44,825 sq miles

Capital city Columbus (population 810,000)

Other cities Cleveland (population 391,000), Cincinnati (population 297,000)

Sales tax 5.5%

Birthplace of Inventor Thomas Edison (1847–1931), author Toni Morrison (b 1931), entrepreneur Ted Turner (b 1938), filmmaker Steven Spielberg (b 1947)

Home of Cows, roller coasters, aviation pioneers the Wright Brothers

Politics Swing state

Famous for First airplane, first pro baseball team, birthplace of seven US presidents

State rock song 'Hang On Sloopy'

Driving distances Cleveland to Columbus 142 miles, Columbus to Cincinnati 108 miles

◉ Sights & Activities

Cleveland's center is Public Sq, dominated by the conspicuous Terminal Tower. It's bustling thanks to a ka-chinging new casino. Most attractions are downtown on the lakefront or at University Circle (the area around Case Western Reserve University, Cleveland Clinic and other institutions).

◉ Downtown

Rock and Roll Hall of Fame & Museum — MUSEUM

(☑ 216-781-7625; www.rockhall.com; 1 Key Plaza; adult/child $22/13; ⊙10am-5:30pm, to 9pm Wed year-round, to 9pm Sat Jun-Aug) Cleveland's top attraction is like an overstuffed attic bursting with groovy finds: Jimi Hendrix's Stratocaster, Keith Moon's platform shoes, John Lennon's Sgt Pepper suit and a 1966 piece of hate mail to the Rolling Stones from a cursive-writing Fijian. It's more than memorabilia, though. Multimedia exhibits trace the history and social context of rock music and the performers who created it.

Why is the museum in Cleveland? Because this is the hometown of Alan Freed, the disk jockey who popularized the term 'rock 'n' roll' in the early 1950s, and because the city lobbied hard and paid big. Be prepared for crowds (especially thick until 1pm or so).

Great Lakes Science Center — MUSEUM

(☑ 216-694-2000; www.glsc.org; 601 Erieside Ave; adult/child $14/12; ⊙10am-5pm; 🚻) One of 10 museums in the country with a NASA affiliation, Great Lakes goes deep in space with rockets, moon stones and the 1973 Apollo capsule, as well as exhibits on the lakes' environmental problems.

William G Mather — MUSEUM

(☑ 216-574-6262; www.glsc.org/mather_museum. php; 305 Mather Way; adult/child $8/6; ⊙11am-5pm Tue-Sun Jun-Aug, Fri-Sun only May, Sep & Oct, closed Nov-Apr) Take a self-guided walk on this humungous freighter incarnated as a steamship museum. It's docked beside the Great Lakes Science Center, which manages it.

USS Cod — MUSEUM

(☑ 216-566-8770; www.usscod.org; 1089 E 9th St; adult/child $10/6; ⊙10am-5pm May-Sep) The storied submarine USS Cod saw action in WWII. You're free to climb through it, tight spaces, ladders and all, while listening to audio stories about life on board.

The Flats — WATERFRONT

(www.flatseast.com) The Flats, an old industrial zone turned nightlife hub on the Cuyahoga River, has had a checkered life. After years of neglect, it's on the upswing once again. Developers poured $500 million into the East Bank for a waterfront boardwalk, restaurants, bars, an Aloft hotel and concert pavilion, all opened in 2013.

◉ Ohio City & Tremont

West Side Market — MARKET

(www.westsidemarket.org; cnr W 25th St & Lorain Ave; ⊙7am-4pm Mon & Wed, to 6pm Fri & Sat) The European-style market overflows with greengrocers and their fruit and vegetable pyramids, as well as purveyors of Hungarian sausage, Mexican flat breads and Polish pierogi.

Christmas Story House & Museum — MUSEUM

(☑ 216-298-4919; www.achristmasstoryhouse.com; 3159 W 11th St; adult/child $10/6; ⊙10am-5pm Thu-Sat, from noon Sun) Remember the beloved 1983 film A Christmas Story, in which Ralphie yearns for a Red Ryder BB gun? The original house sits in Tremont, complete with leg lamp. This attraction's for true fans only.

◉ University Circle

Several museums and attractions are within walking distance of each other at University Circle, 5 miles east of downtown. Carless? Take the HealthLine bus to Adelbert.

Cleveland Museum of Art — MUSEUM

(☑ 216-421-7340; www.clevelandart.org; 11150 East Blvd; ⊙10am-5pm Tue-Sun, to 9pm Wed & Fri) FREE Fresh off a whopping expansion, the art museum houses an excellent collection of European paintings, as well as African, Asian and American art. Head to the 2nd floor for rock-star works from impressionists, Picasso and surrealists. Interactive touch screens are stationed throughout the galleries and provide fun ways to learn more. There's also a neat-o free iPad app.

Cleveland Botanical Garden — GARDENS

(☑ 216-721-1600; www.cbgarden.org; 11030 East Blvd; adult/child $9.50/4; ⊙10am-5pm Tue-Sat, noon-5pm Sun, noon-9pm Wed) It has a Costa Rican cloud forest and Madagascan desert exhibits. An ice-skating rink opens nearby in winter; skate rentals cost $3. Parking costs $5 to $10 per day and gives access to all the museums here.

Museum of Contemporary Art Cleveland
MUSEUM

(MOCA; 🎧 audio tours 216-453-3960; www.moca-cleveland.org; 11400 Euclid Ave; adult/child $8/5; ☺ 11am-5pm Tue-Sun, to 9pm Thu) The shiny new building impresses, with four stories of geometric black steel, though there's not a lot to see inside. Floors 2 and 4 have the galleries; exhibits focus on an artist or two and change often. Call for an audio tour of the architecture and installations.

Lakeview Cemetery
CEMETERY

(🎧 216-421-2665; www.lakeviewcemetery.com; 12316 Euclid Ave; ☺ 7:30am-7:30pm) Beyond the circle further east, don't forget this eclectic 'outdoor museum' where President Garfield and John Rockefeller rest, or, more intriguingly, local comic-book hero Harvey Pekar and crime-fighter Eliot Ness.

🛏 Sleeping

Prices listed here are for summer, which is high season, and do not include the 16.25% tax. Modest motels are southwest of Cleveland's center, near the airport. The W 150th exit off I-71 (exit 240) has several options for less than $100.

Cleveland Hostel
HOSTEL $

(🎧 216-394-0616; www.theclevelandhostel.com; 2090 W 25th St; dm/r from $25/65) This new hostel in Ohio City, steps from an RTA stop and the West Side Market, is fantastic. There are 15 rooms, a mix of dorms and private chambers. All have fluffy beds, fresh paint in soothing hues and nifty antique decor. Add in the rooftop deck, free parking lot and cheap bike rentals (per day $15), and no wonder it's packed.

Holiday Inn Express
HOTEL $$

(🎧 216-443-1000; www.hiexpress.com; 629 Euclid Ave; r incl breakfast $130-190; P❄@✆) This goes way beyond the usual chain offering and is more like a true boutique hotel with large, nattily decorated rooms and lofty views. It's set in an old bank building that's conveniently located near the E 4th St entertainment strip. Parking costs $14.

Brownstone Inn
B&B $$

(🎧 216-426-1753; www.brownstoneinndowntown.com; 3649 Prospect Ave; r incl breakfast $89-139; P❄@✆) This Victorian townhouse B&B has a whole lotta personality. All five rooms have a private bath, and each comes equipped with robes to lounge in and an invitation for evening aperitifs. It's between downtown and University Circle, though it's in a bit of a no-man's-land for walking to entertainment.

Hilton Garden Inn
HOTEL $$

(🎧 216-658-6400; www.hiltongardeninn.com; 1100 Carnegie Ave; r $110-169; P❄@✆☀) While it's nothing fancy, the Hilton's rooms are good value with comfy beds, wi-fi–rigged workstations and mini refrigerators. It's right by the baseball park. Parking costs $16.

🍴 Eating

There's more range than you might expect in a Rust Belt town.

🍴 Downtown

The Warehouse District, between W 6th and W 9th Sts, jumps with trendy restaurants. Off the beaten path and east of the city center, Asiatown (bounded by Payne and St Clair Aves, and E 30th and 40th Sts) has several Chinese, Vietnamese and Korean eateries.

Noodlecat
NOODLES $$

(www.noodlecat.com; 234 Euclid Ave; mains $9-13; ☺ 11am-11pm) Hep-cat noodles fill bowls at this Japanese-American mash-up. Slurp mushroom udon, spicy octopus udon, beef-brisket ramen and fried-chicken ramen dishes. Lots of sake, craft beer and gluten-free options are available. There's another, smaller branch in the West Side Market.

Lola
MODERN AMERICAN $$$

(🎧 216-621-5652; www.lolabistro.com; 2058 E 4th St; mains $26-34; ☺ 11:30am-2:30pm Mon-Fri, 5-10pm Mon-Thu, 5-11pm Fri & Sat) Famous for his piercings, Food Channel TV appearances and multiple national awards, local boy Michael Symon has put Cleveland on the foodie map with Lola. The lower-priced lunch dishes are the most fun; say, coconut-and-lime-tinged scallop ceviche, or the showstopper: an egg-and-cheese-topped fried bologna sandwich.

Pura Vida
MODERN AMERICAN $$$

(🎧 216-987-0100; www.puravidabybrandt.com; 170 Euclid Ave; mains $23-29; ☺ 11:30am-2pm & 4-10pm Mon-Sat; 🎧) Pura Vida serves creative, locally sourced comfort foods in a bright, ubermodern space fronting Public Sq. The trout po' boy and duck-leg confit with buttermilk waffles win praise. Small plates let you sample a couple of dishes, or you can load up on a main.

Ohio City & Tremont

Ohio City and Tremont, which straddle I-90 south of downtown, are areas that have lots of new establishments popping up.

West Side Market Cafe   CAFE $
(☑216-579-6800; 1995 W 25th St; mains $6-9; ☺7am-3pm Mon-Thu, 6am-6pm Fri & Sat, 9am-3pm Sun) This is a smart stop if you're craving well-made breakfast and lunch fare, and cheap fish and chicken mains. The cafe is inside West Side Market itself, which overflows with prepared foods that are handy for picnicking or road-tripping.

South Side   AMERICAN $$
(☑216-937-2288; www.southsidecleveland.com; 2207 W 11 St; mains $14-20; ☺11am-2am; 🛜) Local athletes, blue-collar electricians and everyone in between piles into this sleek Tremont establishment to drink at the winding granite bar. They come for the late-night food too, like the grouper sandwich and bacon-cheddar burger.

Little Italy & Coventry

These two neighborhoods make prime stops for refueling after hanging out in University Circle. Little Italy is closest: it's along Mayfield Rd, near Lake View Cemetery (look out for the Rte 322 sign). Alternatively, relaxed Coventry Village is a bit further east off Mayfield Rd.

Presti's Bakery   BAKERY $
(www.prestisbakery.com; 12101 Mayfield Rd; items $2-6; ☺6am-9pm Mon-Thu, to 10pm Fri & Sat, to 6pm Sun) Try Presti's for its popular sandwiches, stromboli and divine pastries.

Tommy's   INTERNATIONAL $
(☑216-321-7757; www.tommyscoventry.com; 1823 Coventry Rd; mains $7-11; ☺9am-9pm Sun-Thu, 9am-10pm Fri, 7:30am-10pm Sat; 🛜🅿) Tofu, seitan and other old-school veggie dishes emerge from the kitchen, though carnivores have multiple options, too.

🍷 Drinking

The downtown action centers on the young, testosterone-fueled Warehouse District (around W 6th St), and around E 4th St's entertainment venues. Tremont is also chockablock with chic bars. Most places stay open until 2am.

Great Lakes Brewing Company   BREWERY
(www.greatlakesbrewing.com; 2516 Market Ave; ☺from 11:30am Mon-Sat) Great Lakes wins many prizes for its brewed-on-the-premises beers. Added historical bonus: Eliot Ness got into a shootout with criminals here; ask the bartender to show you the bullet holes.

Market Garden Brewery   BREWERY
(www.marketgardenbrewery.com; 1947 W 25th St; ☺4pm-2am Mon-Thu, 11am-2am Fri & Sat, 10am-3pm Sun) Since launching in 2011 this microbrewer has made a splash with its brown ale, though the other beers on tap are excellent, too. Sip indoors under the low-lit chandeliers, or outdoors at the communal wood tables striping the beer garden. It also distils small-batch whiskeys and rum, and shakes up beer cocktails.

Major Hoopples   BAR
(1930 Columbus Rd; ☺from 3pm Mon-Sat) Look over the bar for Cleveland's best skyline view from this friendly, eclectic watering hole. Films and sports games are projected on the bridge abutment out back.

☆ Entertainment

Gordon Square Arts District (www.gordonsquare.org) has a fine pocket of theaters, live-music venues and cafes along Detroit Ave between W 56th and W 69th Sts, a few miles west of downtown.

Live Music

Check *Scene* (www.clevescene.com) and Friday's *Plain Dealer* (www.cleveland.com) for listings.

★ Happy Dog   LIVE MUSIC
(www.happydogcleveland.com; 5801 Detroit Ave; ☺from 4pm Mon-Thu, from 11am Fri-Sun) Listen to scrappy bands while munching on a weenie, for which you can choose from among 50 toppings, from gourmet (black truffle) to, er, less gourmet (peanut butter and jelly); in the Gordon Sq district.

Grog Shop   LIVE MUSIC
(☑216-321-5588; www.grogshop.gs; 2785 Euclid Hts Blvd) Up-and-coming rockers thrash at Coventry's long-established music house.

Beachland Ballroom   LIVE MUSIC
(www.beachlandballroom.com; 15711 Waterloo Rd) Hip young bands play at this venue east of downtown.

Sports

Cleveland is a serious jock town with three modern downtown venues.

Progressive Field   BASEBALL
(www.indians.com; 2401 Ontario St) The Indians (aka 'the Tribe') hit here; great sightlines make it a good park to see a game.

Quicken Loans Arena   BASKETBALL
(www.nba.com/cavaliers; 1 Center Ct) The Cavaliers play basketball at 'the Q,' which doubles as an entertainment venue.

First Energy Stadium   FOOTBALL
(www.clevelandbrowns.com; 1085 W 3rd St) The NFL's Browns pass the football and score touchdowns on the lakefront.

Performing Arts

Severance Hall   CLASSICAL MUSIC
(216-231-1111;   www.clevelandorchestra.com; 11001 Euclid Ave) The acclaimed Cleveland Symphony Orchestra holds its season (August to May) at Severance Hall, located by the University Circle museums. The orchestra's summer home is Blossom Music Center in Cuyahoga Valley National Park, about 22 miles south.

Playhouse Square Center   THEATER
(216-771-4444; www.playhousesquare.org; 1501 Euclid Ave) This elegant center hosts theater, opera and ballet. Check the website for $10 'Smart Seats.'

ℹ Information

INTERNET ACCESS
Many of Cleveland's public places have free wi-fi, such as Tower City and University Circle.

MEDIA
Gay People's Chronicle (www.gaypeople-schronicle.com) Free weekly publication with entertainment listings.
Plain Dealer (www.cleveland.com) The city's daily newspaper.
Scene (www.clevescene.com) A weekly entertainment paper.

MEDICAL SERVICES
MetroHealth Medical Center (216-778-7800; 2500 MetroHealth Dr)

TOURIST INFORMATION
Cleveland Convention & Visitors Bureau (www.positivelycleveland.com) Official website; the Twitter feed lists daily deals.

Visitor center (216-875-6680; 334 Euclid Ave; ⊙ 8:30am-6:30pm Mon-Fri, from 10am Sat) Staff provide maps and reservation assistance.

WEBSITES
Cool Cleveland (www.coolcleveland.com) Hip arts and cultural happenings.
Ohio City (www.ohiocity.org) Eats and drinks in the neighborhood.
Tremont (www.tremontwest.org) Eats, drinks and gallery hops.

ℹ Getting There & Around

Eleven miles southwest of downtown, **Cleveland Hopkins International Airport** (CLE; www.clevelandairport.com; 5300 Riverside Dr) is linked by the Red Line train ($2.25). A cab to downtown costs about $30.

From downtown, **Greyhound** (216-781-0520; 1465 Chester Ave) offers frequent departures to Chicago (7½ hours) and New York City (13 hours). **Megabus** (www.megabus.com/us) also goes to Chicago, often for lower fares; check the website for the departure point.

Amtrak (216-696-5115; 200 Cleveland Memorial Shoreway) runs once daily to Chicago (seven hours) and New York City (13 hours).

The **Regional Transit Authority** (RTA; www.riderta.com; fare $2.25) operates the Red Line train that goes to both the airport and Ohio City. It also runs the HealthLine bus that motors along Euclid Ave from downtown to University Circle's museums. Day passes are $5.

For cab service, try phoning **Americab** (216-429-1111).

Around Cleveland

Sixty miles south of Cleveland, Canton is the birthplace of the NFL and home to the Pro Football Hall of Fame (330-456-8207; www.profootballhof.com; 2121 George Halas Dr; adult/child $22/16; ⊙ 9am-8pm, to 5pm Sep-May). The shrine for the gridiron-obsessed sports sweet new interactive exhibits since the museum's expansion. Look for the football-shaped tower off I-77.

West of Cleveland, attractive Oberlin is an old-fashioned college town, with noteworthy architecture by Cass Gilbert, Frank Lloyd Wright and Robert Venturi. Further west, just south of I-90, the tiny town of Milan is the birthplace of Thomas Edison. His home has been restored to its 1847 likeness and is now a small museum (419-499-2135;

www.tomedison.org; 9 Edison Dr; adult/child $7/4; ⊙10am-5pm Tue-Sat, from 1pm Sun, reduced hours winter, closed Jan) outlining his inventions, including the light bulb and phonograph.

Still further west, on US 20 and surrounded by farmland, is Clyde, which bills itself as the USA's most famous small town. It got that way when native son Sherwood Anderson published *Winesburg, Ohio* in 1919. It didn't take long for the unimpressed residents to figure out where the fictitious town really was. Stop at the Clyde Museum (☑419-547-7946; www.clydeheritageleague. org; 124 W Buckeye St; ⊙1-4pm Thu Apr-Sep & by appointment) FREE in the old church for Anderson tidbits or at the library, a few doors down.

Erie Lakeshore & Islands

In summer this good-time resort area is one of the busiest – and most expensive – places in Ohio. The season lasts from mid-May to mid-September, and then just about everything shuts down. Make sure you prebook your accommodations.

CEDAR POINT'S RAGING ROLLER COASTERS

Cedar Point Amusement Park (☑419-627-2350; www.cedarpoint. com; adult/child $55/30; ⊙10am-10pm, closed Nov–mid-May) regularly wins the 'world's best amusement park' award, chosen each year by the public, which goes wild for the venue's 16 adrenaline-pumping roller coasters. Stomach-droppers include the Top Thrill Dragster, one of the globe's tallest and fastest rides. It climbs 420ft into the air before plunging and whipping around at 120mph. Meanwhile, the winglike GateKeeper loops, corkscrews and dangles riders from the world's highest inversion (meaning you're upside down a *lot*). If those and the 14 other coasters aren't enough to keep you occupied, the surrounding area has a nice beach, a water park and a slew of old-fashioned, cotton-candy-fueled attractions. It's about 6 miles from Sandusky. Buying tickets in advance online saves money. Parking costs $15.

Sandusky, long a port, now serves as the jump-off point to the Erie Islands and a mighty group of roller coasters. The visitor center (☑419-625-2984; www.shoresandislands. com; 4424 Milan Rd; ⊙8am-7pm Mon-Fri, 9am-6pm Sat, 9am-4pm Sun) provides lodging and ferry information. Loads of chain motels line the highways heading into town.

Bass Islands

In 1812's Battle of Lake Erie, Admiral Perry met the enemy English fleet near South Bass Island. His victory ensured that all the lands south of the Great Lakes became US, not Canadian, territory. But history is all but forgotten on a summer weekend in packed Put In Bay, the island's main town and a party place full of boaters, restaurants and shops. Move beyond it and you'll find a winery and opportunities for camping, fishing, kayaking and swimming.

A singular attraction is the 352ft Doric column known as Perry's Victory and International Peace Memorial (www.nps.gov/ pevi; admission $3; ⊙10am-7pm). Climb to the observation deck for views of the battle site and, on a good day, Canada.

The Chamber of Commerce (☑419-285-2832; www.visitputinbay.com; 148 Delaware Ave; ⊙10am-4pm Mon-Fri, to 5pm Sat & Sun) has information on activities and lodging. Ashley's Island House (☑419-285-2844; www. ashleysislandhouse.com; 557 Catawba Ave; r with/ without bath from $100/70; ☒☎) is a 13-room B&B, where naval officers stayed in the late 1800s. The Beer Barrel Saloon (www. beerbarrelpib.com; Delaware Ave; ⊙11am-1am) has plenty of space for imbibing – its bar is 406ft long.

Cabs and tour buses serve the island, though cycling is a fine way to get around. Two ferry companies make the 20-minute trip regularly from the mainland. Jet Express (☑800-245-1538; www.jet-express.com) runs passenger-only boats direct to Put In Bay from Port Clinton (one way adult/child $15/2.50) almost hourly. It also departs from Sandusky ($19.50/5.50), stopping at Kelleys Island en route. Leave your car in the lot (per day $10) at either dock. Miller Boatline (☑800-500-2421; www.millerferry.com) operates a vehicle ferry that is the cheapest option, departing from further-flung Catawba (one way adult/child $7/1.50, car $15) every 30 minutes. It also cruises to Middle Bass Island, a good day trip from South Bass, offering nature and quiet.

Kelleys Island

Peaceful and green, Kelleys Island is a popular weekend escape, especially for families. It has pretty 19th-century buildings, Native American pictographs, a good beach and glacial grooves raked through its landscape. Even its old limestone quarries are scenic.

The Chamber of Commerce (☑419-746-2360; www.kelleysislandchamber.com; Seaway Marina Bldg; ⊙9:30am-4pm), by the ferry dock, has information on accommodations and activities – hiking, camping, kayaking and fishing are popular. The Village, the island's small commercial center, has places to eat, drink, shop and rent bicycles – the recommended way to sightsee.

Kelleys Island Ferry (☑419-798-9763; www.kelleysislandferry.com) departs from the wee village of Marblehead (one way adult/child $9.50/6, car $15). The crossing takes about 20 minutes and leaves hourly (more frequently in summer). Jet Express (☑800-245-1538; www.jet-express.com) departs from Sandusky (one way adult/child $15/4.50, no cars) and goes onward to Put In Bay on South Bass Island (island-hopping one way $22/6.50, no cars).

Pelee Island

Pelee, the largest Erie island, is a ridiculously green, quiet wine-producing and bird-watching destination that belongs to Canada. Pelee Island Transportation (☑800-661-2220; www.ontarioferries.com) runs a ferry (one way adult/child $13.75/6.75, car $30) from Sandusky to Pelee and onward to Ontario's mainland. Check www.pelee.org for lodging and trip-planning information.

Amish Country

Rural Wayne and Holmes counties are home to the USA's largest Amish community. They're only 80 miles south of Cleveland, but visiting here is like entering a pre-industrial time warp.

Descendants of conservative Dutch-Swiss religious factions who migrated to the USA during the 18th century, the Amish continue to follow the *ordnung* (way of life), in varying degrees. Many adhere to rules prohibiting the use of electricity, telephones and motorized vehicles. They wear traditional clothing, farm the land with plow and mule, and go to church in horse-drawn buggies. Others are not so strict.

Unfortunately, what would surely be a peaceful country scene is often disturbed by behemoth tour buses. Many Amish are happy to profit from this influx of outside dollars, but you shouldn't equate this with free photographic access – the Amish typically view photographs as taboo. Drive carefully as roads are narrow and curvy, and there's always the chance of pulling up on a slow-moving buggy just around the bend. Many places are closed Sunday.

◉ Sights & Activities

Kidron, on Rte 52, makes a good starting point. A short distance south, Berlin is the area's tchotchke-shop-filled core, while Millersburg is the region's largest town, more antique-y than Amish; US 62 connects these two 'busy' spots.

To get further off the beaten path, take Rte 557 or County Rd 70, both of which twist through the countryside to wee Charm, about 5 miles south of Berlin.

Lehman's   DEPARTMENT STORE
(www.lehmans.com; 4779 Kidron Rd, Kidron; ⊙8am-6pm Mon-Sat) Lehman's is an absolute must-see. It is the Amish community's main purveyor of modern-looking products that use no electricity, housed in a 32,000-sq-ft barn. Stroll through to ogle wind-up flashlights, wood-burning stoves and hand-cranked meat grinders.

Kidron Auction   MARKET
(www.kidronauction.com; 4885 Kidron Rd, Kidron; ⊙from 10am Thu) FREE If it's Thursday, follow the buggy line-up down the road from Lehman's to the livestock barn. Hay gets auctioned at 10am, cows at 11am and pigs at 1pm. A flea market rings the barn for folks seeking non-mooing merchandise. Similar auctions take place in Sugarcreek (Monday and Friday), Farmerstown (Tuesday) and Mt Hope (Wednesday).

Heini's Cheese Chalet   CHEESEMAKING FACTORY
(☑800-253-6636; www.heinis.com; 6005 Hwy 77, Berlin; tours free; ⊙8am-6pm Mon-Sat) Heini's whips up more than 70 cheeses. Learn how Amish farmers hand-milk their cows and spring-cool (versus machine-refrigerate) the output before delivering it each day. Then grab abundant samples and peruse the kitschy 'History of Cheesemaking' mural. To see the curd-cutting in action, come before 11am weekdays (except on Wednesday).

WORTH A TRIP

MALABAR FARM

What do Bogie, Bacall and Johnny Appleseed have in common? They've all spent time at Malabar Farm State Park (www.malabarfarm.org). There's a lot going on here: hiking and horse trails; pond fishing (ask for a free rod at the visitor center); tours of Pulitzer-winner Louis Bromfield's home (where Humphrey Bogart and Lauren Bacall got married); monthly barn dances; a farmhouse hostel (www.hiusa.org/lucas); and a fine restaurant (⊙11am-8pm Tue-Sun) that uses ingredients from the grounds. Malabar is 30 miles west of Millersburg via Hwy 39.

Hershberger's Farm & Bakery   FARM
(☑330-674-6096; 5452 Hwy 557, Millersburg; ⊙bakery 8am-5pm Mon-Sat year-round, farm from 10am mid-Apr–Oct; ⚑) Gorge on 25 kinds of pie, homemade ice-cream cones and seasonal produce from the market inside. Pet the farmyard animals (free) and take pony rides ($3) outside.

Yoder's Amish Home   FARM
(☑330-893-2541; www.yodersamishhome.com; 6050 Rte 515, Walnut Creek; tours adult/child $12/8; ⊙10am-5pm Mon-Sat mid-Apr–late Oct; ⚑) Peek into a local home and one-room schoolhouse, and take a buggy ride through a field at this Amish farm that's open to visitors.

🛏 Sleeping & Eating

Hotel Millersburg   HISTORIC HOTEL $$
(☑330-674-1457; www.hotelmillersburg.com; 35 W Jackson St, Millersburg; r $79-149; ✳🐾) Built in 1847 as a stagecoach inn, the property still provides lodging in its 26 casual rooms, which sit above a modern dining room and tavern (one of the few places you can get a beer in Amish Country).

Guggisberg Swiss Inn   HOTEL $$
(☑330-893-3600; www.guggisbergswissinn.com; 5025 Rte 557, Charm; r incl breakfast $110-160; ✳🐾) The 24 tidy, bright and compact rooms have quilts and light-wood furnishings. A cheesemaking facility and horseback riding stable are on the grounds, too.

Boyd & Wurthmann Restaurant   AMERICAN $
(☑330-893-3287; www.boydandwurthmann.com; Main St, Berlin; mains $6-11; ⊙5:30am-8pm Mon-Sat) Hubcap-sized pancakes, 23 pie flavors,

fat sandwiches and Amish specialties such as country-fried steak draw locals and tourists alike. Cash only.

❶ Information

Holmes County Chamber of Commerce (www.visitamishcountry.com)

Columbus

Ohio's capital city is like the blind date your mom arranges – average looking, restrained personality, but solid and affable. Better yet, she's easy on the wallet, an influence from Ohio State University's 55,000 students (the university is the nation's second largest). A substantial gay population has taken up residence in Columbus in recent years.

◉ Sights & Activities

German Village   NEIGHBORHOOD
(www.germanvillage.com) The remarkably large, all-brick German Village, a half-mile south of downtown, is a restored 19th-century neighborhood with beer halls, cobbled streets, arts-filled parks and Italianate and Queen Anne architecture.

Short North   NEIGHBORHOOD
(www.shortnorth.org) Just north of downtown, the browseworthy Short North is a redeveloped strip of High St that holds contemporary art galleries, restaurants and jazz bars.

Wexner Center for the Arts   ARTS CENTER
(☑614-292-3535; www.wexarts.org; cnr 15th & N High Sts; admission $8; ⊙11am-6pm Tue & Wed, 11am-8pm Thu & Fri, noon-7pm Sat, noon-4pm Sun) The campus arts center offers cutting-edge art exhibits, films and performances.

Columbus Food Tours   GUIDED TOUR
(www.columbusfoodadventures.com; tours $40-80) Foodie guides lead tours by neighborhood or theme (ie taco trucks, desserts, coffee), some by foot and others by van.

🛏 Sleeping & Eating

German Village and the Short North provide fertile grazing and guzzling grounds. The Arena District (www.arenadistrict.com) bursts with midrange chains and brewpubs. Around the university and along N High St from 15th Ave onward, you'll find everything from Mexican to Ethiopian to sushi.

Marriott Residence Inn HOTEL $$
(☎614-222-2610; www.marriott.com; 36 E Gay St; r incl breakfast $129-199; P ❄ @ 📶) A great location downtown, close to everything. All rooms are suites with a full kitchen. The cute breakfast buffet is served in the old bank vault each morning. Wi-fi is free; parking is $20.

Short North B&B B&B $$
(☎614-299-5050; www.columbus-bed-breakfast.com; 50 E Lincoln St; r incl breakfast $129-149; P ❄ 📶) The seven well-maintained rooms are steps away from the eponymous neighborhood's scene.

North Market MARKET $
(www.northmarket.com; 59 Spruce St; ⏲9am-5pm Mon, 9am-7pm Tue-Fri, 8am-5pm Sat, noon-5pm Sun) Local farmers' produce and prepared foods; renowned ice cream by Jeni.

Schmidt's GERMAN $$
(☎614-444-6808; www.schmidthaus.com; 240 E Kossuth St; mains $8-15; ⏲11am-9pm Sun & Mon, to 10pm Tue-Thu, to 11pm Fri & Sat) In German Village, shovel in Old Country staples like sausage and schnitzel, but save room for the whopping half-pound cream puffs. Oompah bands play Wednesday to Saturday.

Skillet AMERICAN $$
(☎614-443-2266; www.skilletruf.com; 410 E Whittier St; mains $12-16; ⏲11am-2:30pm & 5:30-9pm Wed-Fri, 8am-2pm Sat & Sun) A teeny restaurant in German Village serving rustic, locally sourced fare.

☆ Entertainment

Spectator sports rule the city.

Ohio Stadium FOOTBALL
(☎800-462-8257; www.ohiostatebuckeyes.com; 411 Woody Hayes Dr) The Ohio State Buckeyes pack a rabid crowd into legendary, horseshoe-shaped Ohio Stadium for their games, held on Saturdays in the fall. Expect 102,000 extra partiers in town.

Nationwide Arena HOCKEY
(☎614-246-2000; www.bluejackets.com; 200 W Nationwide Blvd) The pro Columbus Blue Jackets slap the puck at downtown's big arena.

Crew Stadium SOCCER
(☎614-447-2739; www.thecrew.com) The popular Columbus Crew pro soccer team kicks north off I-71 and 17th Ave, from March to October.

ℹ Information

Alive (www.columbusalive.com) Free weekly entertainment newspaper.

Columbus Convention & Visitors Bureau (☎866-397-2657; www.experiencecolumbus.com)

Columbus Dispatch (www.dispatch.com) The daily newspaper.

Outlook (www.outlookmedia.com) Monthly gay and lesbian publication.

ℹ Getting There & Away

The **Port Columbus Airport** (CMH; www.flycolumbus.com) is 10 miles east of town. A cab to downtown costs about $25.

Greyhound (☎614-221-4642; www.greyhound.com; 111 E Town St) buses run at least six times daily to Cincinnati (two hours) and Cleveland (2½ hours). Often cheaper, **Megabus** (www.megabus.com/us) runs a couple times daily to Cincinnati and Chicago. Check the website for locations.

Athens & Southeastern Ohio

Ohio's southeastern corner cradles most of its forested areas, as well as the rolling foothills of the Appalachian Mountains and scattered farms.

Around Lancaster, southeast of Columbus, the hills lead gently into **Hocking County**, a region of streams and waterfalls, sandstone cliffs and cavelike formations. It's splendid to explore in any season, with miles of trails for hiking and rivers for canoeing, as well as abundant campgrounds and cabins at **Hocking Hills State Park** (☎740-385-6165; www.hockinghills.com; 20160 Hwy 664; campsites/cottages from $24/130). **Old Man's Cave** is a scenic winner for hiking. **Hocking Valley Canoe Livery** (☎740-385-8685; www.hockinghillscanoeing.com; 31251 Chieftain Dr; 2hr tours $44; ⏲Apr-Oct) lets you paddle by moonlight and tiki torch from nearby Logan. **Earth-Water-Rock: Outdoor Adventures** (☎740-664-5220; www.ewroutdoors.com; half-day tour $85-110) provides thrills with guided rock climbing and rappelling trips; beginners are welcome.

Athens (www.athensohio.com) makes a lovely base for seeing the region. Situated where US 50 crosses US 33, it's set among wooded hills and built around the Ohio University campus (which comprises half the town). Student cafes and pubs line Court St,

Athens' main road. The Village Bakery & Cafe (www.dellazona.com; 268 E State St; mains $4-8; ⊙7:30am-8pm Tue-Sat, 9am-2pm Sun) uses organic veggies, grass-fed meat and farmstead cheeses in its pizzas, soups and sandwiches.

The area south of Columbus was a center for the fascinating ancient Hopewell people, who left behind huge geometric earthworks and burial mounds from around 200 BC to AD 600. For a fine introduction visit the Hopewell Culture National Historical Park (☑740-774-1126; www.nps.gov/hocu; Hwy 104 north of I-35; ⊙8:30am-6pm Jun-Aug, to 5pm Sep-May) FREE, 3 miles north of Chillicothe. Stop in the visitor center, and then wander about the variously shaped ceremonial mounds spread over 13-acre Mound City, a mysterious town of the dead. Serpent Mound (☑937-587-2796; www.ohiohistory.org; 3850 Hwy 73; per vehicle $7; ⊙10:30am-4pm Mon-Fri, from 9:30am Sat & Sun, reduced hours in winter), southwest of Chillicothe and 4 miles northwest of Locust Grove, is perhaps the most captivating site of all. The giant uncoiling snake stretches over a quarter of a mile and is the largest effigy mound in the USA.

Dayton & Yellow Springs

Dayton has the aviation sights, but little Yellow Springs (18 miles northeast on US 68) has much more to offer in terms of accommodations and places to eat.

◉ Sights & Activities

National Museum of the US Air Force   MUSEUM
(☑937-255-3286; www.nationalmuseum.af.mil; 1100 Spaatz St, Dayton; ⊙9am-5pm) FREE Located at the Wright-Patterson Air Force Base, 6 miles northeast of Dayton, the huu-uuge museum has everything from a Wright Brothers 1909 Flyer to a Sopwith Camel (WWI biplane) and the 'Little Boy' atomic bomb dropped on Hiroshima. The hangars hold miles of planes, rockets and aviation machines. Download the audio tour from the website before arriving. Plan on three or more hours here.

Wright Cycle Company   HISTORIC SITE
(☑937-225-7705; www.nps.gov/daav; 16 S Williams St, Dayton; ⊙8:30am-5pm) FREE Browse exhibits in the original building where Wilbur and Orville developed bikes and aviation ideas.

Huffman Prairie Flying Field   HISTORIC SITE
(Gate 16A off Rte 444, Dayton; ⊙8am-6pm Thu-Tue) FREE This peaceful patch of grass looks much as it did in 1904 when the Wright Brothers tested aircraft here. A one-mile walking trail loops around, marked with history-explaining placards. It's a 15-minute drive from the Air Force museum.

Carillon Historical Park   HISTORIC SITE
(☑937-293-2841; www.daytonhistory.org; 1000 Carillon Blvd, Dayton; adult/child $8/5; ⊙9:30am-5pm Mon-Sat, from noon Sun) The many heritage attractions include the 1905 Wright Flyer III biplane and a replica of the Wright workshop.

🛏 Sleeping & Eating

The following are located in artsy, beatnik Yellow Springs.

Morgan House   B&B $$
(☑937-767-1761; www.arthurmorganhouse.com; 120 W Limestone St, Yellow Springs; r incl breakfast $105-125; ✸🐾) The six comfy rooms have super-soft linens and private baths. Breakfasts are organic. It's walkable to the main business district.

★ Young's Jersey Dairy   AMERICAN $$
(☑937-325-0629; www.youngsdairy.com; 6880 Springfield-Xenia Rd, Yellow Springs; 🐾) Young's is a working dairy farm with two restaurants: the Golden Jersey Inn (mains $9-15; ⊙11am-8pm Mon-Thu, 11am-9pm Fri, 8am-9pm Sat, 8am-8pm Sun), serving dishes like buttermilk chicken; and the Dairy Store (sandwiches $3.50-6.50; ⊙7am-11pm Sun-Thu, to midnight Fri & Sat), serving sandwiches, dreamy ice cream and Ohio's best milkshakes. There's also mini-golf, batting cages, cheesemaking tours and opportunities to watch the cows get milked.

Winds Cafe   AMERICAN $$$
(☑937-767-1144; www.windscafe.com; 215 Xenia Ave, Yellow Springs; mains $18-25; ⊙11:30am-2pm & 5-10pm Tue-Sat, 10am-3pm Sun) A hippie co-op 30-plus years ago, the Winds has grown up to become a sophisticated foodie favorite plating seasonal dishes like fig-sauced asparagus crepes and rhubarb halibut.

Cincinnati

Cincinnati splashes up the Ohio River's banks. Its prettiness surprises, as do its neon troves, its twisting streets to hilltop Mt Adams, and the locals' unashamed ardor for a five-way. Amid all that action, don't forget to catch a baseball game, stroll the riverfront and visit the dummy museum.

Sights & Activities

Many attractions are closed on Monday.

Downtown

National Underground Railroad Freedom Center MUSEUM
(☑513-333-7500; www.freedomcenter.org; 50 E Freedom Way; adult/child $12/8; ⊙11am-5pm Tue-Sun) Cincinnati was a prominent stop on the Underground Railroad and a center for abolitionist activities led by residents such as Harriet Beecher Stowe. The Freedom Center tells their stories. Exhibits show how slaves escaped to the north, and the ways in which slavery still exists today. Download the free iPhone app for extra insight while touring.

Findlay Market MARKET
(www.findlaymarket.org; 1801 Race St; ⊙9am-6pm Tue-Fri, 8am-6pm Sat, 10am-4pm Sun) Indoor-outdoor Findlay Market greens the somewhat blighted area at downtown's northern edge. It's a good stop for fresh produce, meats, cheeses and baked goods. The Belgian waffle guy will wow your taste buds.

Rosenthal Center for Contemporary Arts MUSEUM
(☑513-721-0390; www.contemporaryartscenter.org; 44 E 6th St; adult/child $7.50/5.50, Mon evening free; ⊙10am-9pm Mon, 10am-6pm Wed-Fri, 11am-6pm Sat & Sun) This center displays modern art in an avant-garde building designed by Iraqi architect Zaha Hadid. The structure and its artworks are a pretty big deal for traditionalist Cincy.

Fountain Square PLAZA
(www.myfountainsquare.com; cnr 5th & Vine Sts; 🛜) Fountain Sq is the city's centerpiece, a public space with a seasonal ice rink, free wi-fi, concerts (7pm Tuesday to Saturday in summer), a Reds ticket kiosk and the fancy old 'Spirit of the Waters' fountain.

Roebling Suspension Bridge BRIDGE
(www.roeblingbridge.org) The elegant 1876 spanner was a forerunner of John Roebling's famous Brooklyn Bridge in New York. It's cool to walk across while passing cars make it 'sing' around you. It links to Covington, Kentucky.

Purple People Bridge BRIDGE
(www.purplepeoplebridge.com) This pedestrian-only bridge provides a unique crossing from Sawyer Point (a nifty park dotted by whimsical monuments and flying pigs) to Newport, Kentucky.

Covington & Newport

Covington and Newport, Kentucky, are sort of suburbs of Cincinnati, just over the river from downtown. Newport is to the east and known for its massive **Newport on the Levee** (www.newportonthelevee.com) restaurant and shopping complex. Covington lies to the west and its **MainStrasse** (www.mainstrasse.org) quarter is filled with funky restaurants and bars in the neighborhood's 19th-century brick row houses. Antebellum mansions fringe Riverside Dr, and old paddle-wheel boats tie up along the water's edge.

Newport Aquarium AQUARIUM
(☑859-491-3467; www.newportaquarium.com; 1 Aquarium Way; adult/child $23/15; ⊙9am-7pm Jun-Aug, 10am-6pm Sep-May; 🚼) Meet parading penguins, Sweet Pea the shark ray and lots of other razor-toothed fish at Newport's large, well-regarded facility.

OFF THE BEATEN TRACK

VENT HAVEN VENTRILOQUIST MUSEUM

Jeepers creepers! When you first glimpse the roomful of goggle-eyed wooden heads staring mutely into space, try not to run screaming for the door. (If you've seen the film *Magic*, you know what dummies are capable of.) Local William Shakespeare Berger started the **Vent Haven Museum** (☑859-341-0461; www.venthavenmuseum.com; 33 W Maple Ave; admission $5; ⊙by appointment May-Sep) after amassing a collection of some 700 dolls. Today Jacko the red-fezzed monkey, turtleneck-clad Woody DeForest and the rest of the crew sit silently throughout three buildings.

Lest you think this form of entertainment is history, stop by in July, when the annual conVENTion takes place and 400 ventriloquists arrive with their talkative wooden pals. The museum is located in Fort Mitchell, Kentucky, about 4 miles southwest of Covington off I-71/75.

Mt Adams

It might be a bit of a stretch to compare Mt Adams, immediately east of downtown, to Paris' Montmartre, but this hilly 19th-century enclave of narrow, twisting streets, Victorian town houses, galleries, bars and restaurants is certainly a pleasurable surprise. Most visitors ascend for a quick look around and a drink.

To get here, follow 7th St east of downtown to Gilbert Ave, bear northwest to Elsinore Ave, and head up the hill to reach the lakes, paths and cultural offerings in Eden Park. The yard at nearby Immacula Church (30 Guido St) is worth a stop for its killer views over the city.

Cincinnati Art Museum　　　　MUSEUM
(☎513-721-2787; www.cincinnatiartmuseum.org; 953 Eden Park Dr; ⊙11am-5pm Tue-Sun) `FREE` The collection spans 6000 years, with an emphasis on ancient Middle Eastern art and European old masters, plus a wing devoted to local works. Parking costs $4.

Krohn Conservatory　　　　GARDENS
(☎513-421-4086; www.cincinnatiparks.com/krohn; 1501 Eden Park Dr; adult/child $3/2; ⊙10am-5pm Tue-Sun) The greenhouse sprouts a rainforest, desert flora and glorious seasonal flower shows. Special exhibits cost extra.

West End

Cincinnati Museum Center　　　　MUSEUM
(☎513-287-7000; www.cincymuseum.org; 1301 Western Ave; adult/child $12.50/8.50; ⊙10am-5pm Mon-Sat, 11am-6pm Sun; ▣) Two miles northwest of downtown, this museum complex occupies the 1933 Union Terminal, an art-deco jewel still used by Amtrak. The interior has fantastic murals made of Rookwood tiles. The Museum of Natural History & Science is mostly geared to kids, but it does have a limestone cave with real bats inside. A history museum, children's museum and Omnimax theater round out the offerings; the admission fee provides entry to all. Parking costs $6.

American Sign Museum　　　　MUSEUM
(☎513-541-6366; www.signmuseum.org; 1330 Monmouth Ave; adult/child $15/10; ⊙10am-4pm Wed-Sat, from noon Sun) This museum stocks an awesome cache of flashing, lightbulb-studded beacons in an old parachute factory. You'll burn your retinas staring at vintage neon drive-in signs, hulking genies and the Frisch's Big Boy, among other nostalgic novelties. Guides lead tours at 11am and 2pm that also visit the on-site neon-sign-making shop. It's located in the Camp Washington neighborhood (near Northside); take exit 3 off I-75.

Tours

American Legacy Tours　　　　WALKING TOUR
(www.americanlegacytours.com; 1218 Vine St; 90min tours $20; ⊙Fri-Sun) Offers a variety of historical jaunts. The best is the Queen City Underground Tour that submerges into old lagering cellars deep beneath the Over-the-Rhine district.

Festivals & Events

Bunbury Music Festival　　　　MUSIC
(www.bunburyfestival.com; ⊙mid-Jul) Big-name indie bands rock the riverfront for three days; a day pass costs $55.

Oktoberfest　　　　FOOD
(www.oktoberfestzinzinnati.com; ⊙mid-Sep) German beer, brats and mania.

Sleeping

Hotel tax is cheaper on the Kentucky side at 11.3%, versus the 17% charged in Cincinnati. Tax is not included in the following prices.

Several midrange chain options line up on the Kentucky riverfront. You'll save money (less tax, free parking), but be prepared either to walk a few miles or take a short bus ride to reach downtown Cincy.

The Greater Cincinnati B&B Network (www.cincinnatibb.com) has links to Kentucky-side properties.

Holiday Inn Express　　　　HOTEL $$
(☎859-957-2320; www.hiexpress.com; 109 Landmark Dr; r incl breakfast $125-180; ▣❀@🛜🌊) A good pick among the riverfront chains; located about three-quarters of a mile east of Newport on the Levee.

Hotel 21c　　　　HOTEL $$$
(☎513-578-6600; www.21cmuseumhotels.com/cincinnati; 609 Walnut St; r $189-299; ▣❀@🛜) The second outpost of Louisville's popular art hotel opened in 2013, next door to the Center for Contemporary Arts. The mod rooms have accoutrements such as a Nespresso machine, free wi-fi, plush bedding and, of course, original art. The lobby is a public gallery, so feel free to ogle the trippy videos and nude sculptures. The on-site restaurant and rooftop bar draw crowds. Parking costs $28.

Residence Inn
Cincinnati Downtown
HOTEL $$$

(📱 513-651-1234; www.marriott.com; 506 E 4th St; r incl breakfast $199-299; 🅿 ❄ @ 🛜) All of the glistening rooms are suites with full kitchens. Parking costs $22.

✖ Eating

Vine St west of 12th St (in the Over-the-Rhine area) holds several hip new eateries. Restaurants also concentrate along the riverfront and in the Northside neighborhood (north of the intersection of I-74 and I-75, 5 miles north of downtown).

★ Tucker's
DINER $

(1637 Vine St; mains $4-9; 🕑9am-3pm Tue-Sat, 10am-2pm Sun; 🍴) Located in a tough neighborhood a few blocks from Findlay Market, Tucker's has been feeding locals – black, white, foodies, penniless – since 1946. It's an archetypal diner, serving shrimp and grits, biscuits and gravy, and other hulking breakfast dishes, along with wildly inventive vegetarian fare (like beet sliders) using ingredients sourced from the market.

Son Joe Tucker cooks; Ma Tucker, age 90-plus, still peels the veggies. Try the goetta (pronounced *get-uh*), an herb-spiced, pork-and-oats breakfast sausage that's found only in Cincinnati.

Graeter's Ice Cream
ICE CREAM $

(www.graeters.com; 511 Walnut St; scoops $2.50-5; 🕑6:30am-9pm Mon-Fri, 7am-9pm Sat, 11am-7pm Sun) A local delicacy, with scoop shops around the city. The flavors that mix in the gargantuan, chunky chocolate chips top the list.

Terry's Turf Club
BURGERS $$

(📱 513-533-4222; 4618 Eastern Ave; mains $10-15; 🕑11am-11pm Wed & Thu, to midnight Fri & Sat, to 9pm Sun) This 15-table beer-and-burger joint glows inside and out with owner Terry Carter's neon stash. A giant, waving Aunt Jemima beckons you in, where so many fluorescent beer and doughnut signs shine that no other interior lighting is needed. Terry grills a mean burgundy-mushroom-sauced burger to munch on while admiring the finery (the rosemary garlic and red curry ginger versions rock, too). Located 7 miles east of downtown via Columbia Pkwy.

Honey
AMERICAN $$

(📱 513-541-4300; www.honeynorthside.com; 4034 Hamilton Ave; mains $15-23; 🕑5-9pm Tue-Thu, 5-10pm Fri & Sat, 11am-2pm Sun; 🍴) Seasonal

comfort food – maybe Creole meatloaf or sweet pea ravioli – fills the plates on Honey's low-lit, sturdy wood tables. Brunch is a fan favorite, offering a special gift to herbivores: vegan goetta.

🍷 Drinking

Mt Adams and Northside are busy nightspots. The Banks, the riverfront area between the baseball and football stadiums, has several new hot spots.

Moerlein Lager House
BREWERY

(www.moerleinlagerhouse.com; 115 Joe Nuxall Way; 🕑from 11am) Copper kettles cook up the house beers (Moerlein is an age-old Cincy brand that was defunct until the new brewhouse revitalized it). The patio unfurls awesome views of the riverfront and Roebling bridge. It's a busy spot pre or post a Reds game, as it sits across the street from the stadium.

Blind Lemon
BAR

(www.theblindlemon.com; 936 Hatch St; 🕑from 5:30pm Mon-Fri, from 3pm Sat & Sun) Head down the passageway to enter this atmospheric old speakeasy in Mt Adams. It has an outdoor courtyard in summer, with a fire pit added in winter, and there's live music nightly.

Motr Pub
BAR

(www.motrpub.com; 1345 Main St; 🕑from 5pm Mon-Fri, from 2pm Sat, from 10am Sun) Located in the on-again, off-again – currently on-again –

gritty Over-the-Rhine neighborhood on downtown's northern edge, Motr lets arty types congregate around Hudepohls (local beer) and live rock bands.

☆ Entertainment

Scope for free publications like *CityBeat* for current listings.

Sports

Great American Ballpark BASEBALL
(☑ 513-765-7000; www.cincinnatireds.com; 100 Main St) Home to the Reds – pro baseball's first team – Cincy is a great place to catch a game thanks to its bells-and-whistles riverside ballpark.

Paul Brown Stadium FOOTBALL
(☑ 513-621-3550; www.bengals.com; 1 Paul Brown Stadium) The Bengals pro football team scrimmages a few blocks west of the ballpark.

Performing Arts

Music Hall CLASSICAL MUSIC
(☑ 513-721-8222; www.cincinnatiarts.org; 1241 Elm St) The acoustically pristine Music Hall is where the symphony orchestra, pops orchestra, opera and ballet hold their seasons. This is not the best neighborhood, so be cautious and park nearby.

Aronoff Center THEATER
(☑ 513-621-2787; www.cincinnatiarts.org; 650 Walnut St) The mod Aronoff hosts touring shows.

ℹ Information

Cincinnati Enquirer (www.cincinnati.com) Daily newspaper.

Cincinnati USA Regional Tourism Network (☑ 800-344-3445; www.cincinnatiusa.com) There's a visitor center on Fountain Sq.

CityBeat (www.citybeat.com) Free alternative weekly paper with good entertainment listings.

Rainbow Cincinnati (www.gaycincinnati.com) GLBT news and business listings.

ℹ Getting There & Around

The **Cincinnati/Northern Kentucky International Airport** (CVG; www.cvgairport.com) is actually in Kentucky, 13 miles south. To get downtown, take the TANK bus ($2) from near Terminal 3; a cab costs about $30.

Greyhound (☑ 513-352-6012; www.greyhound.com; 1005 Gilbert Ave) buses travel daily to Indianapolis (2½ hours) and Columbus (two hours). Often cheaper and quicker, **Megabus** (www.megabus.com/us) travels the same routes, and goes to Chicago (six hours). It departs from downtown Cincy at 4th and Race Sts.

Amtrak (☑ 513-651-3337; www.amtrak.com) choo-choos into **Union Terminal** (1301 Western Ave) thrice weekly en route to Chicago (9½ hours) and Washington, DC (14½ hours), departing in the middle of the night.

Metro (www.go-metro.com; fare $1.75) runs the local buses and links with the **Transit Authority of Northern Kentucky** (TANK; www.tankbus.org; fare $1-2).

MICHIGAN

More, more, more – Michigan is the Midwest state that cranks it up. It sports more beaches than the Atlantic seaboard. More than half the state is covered by forests. And more cherries and berries get shoveled into pies here than anywhere else in the USA. Plus its gritty city Detroit is the Midwest's rawest of all – and we mean that in a good way.

Michigan occupies prime real estate, surrounded by four of the five Great Lakes (Superior, Michigan, Huron and Erie). Islands (Mackinac, Beaver and Isle Royale) freckle its coast and make top touring destinations. Surfing beaches, colored sandstone cliffs and trekkable sand dunes also woo visitors.

The state consists of two parts split by water: the larger Lower Peninsula, shaped like a mitten; and the smaller, lightly populated Upper Peninsula, shaped like a slipper. They are linked by the gasp-worthy Mackinac Bridge, which spans the Straits of Mackinac (pronounced *mac*-in-aw).

ℹ Information

Michigan Highway Conditions (☑ 800-381-8477; www.michigan.gov/mdot)

Michigan State Park Information (☑ 800-447-2757; www.michigan.gov/stateparks) Park entry requires a vehicle permit (per day/year $9/31). Campsites cost $16 to $33; reservations accepted (www.midnrreservations.com; fee $8). Some parks have wi-fi.

Travel Michigan (☑ 800-644-2489; www.michigan.org)

Detroit

Tell any American that you're planning to visit Detroit, and then watch their eyebrows shoot up quizzically. They'll ask 'Why?' and warn you that the city is bankrupt, and has off-the-chart homicide rates, nearly 80,000 abandoned buildings and whoppingly high foreclosure rates, a place where homes sell for $1. 'Detroit's a crap-hole. You'll get killed there.'

While the city does have a bombed-out, apocalyptic vibe, these same qualities fuel a raw urban energy you won't find anywhere else. Artists, entrepreneurs and young people are moving in, and a DIY spirit pervades. They're converting vacant lots into urban farms and abandoned buildings into hostels and museums. Plus, they shred a mean guitar in 'the D.' Very mean.

History

French explorer Antoine de La Mothe Cadillac founded Detroit in 1701. Sweet fortune arrived in the 1920s, when Henry Ford began churning out cars. He didn't invent the automobile, as so many mistakenly believe, but he did perfect assembly-line manufacturing and mass-production techniques. The result was the Model T, the first car the USA's middle class could afford to own.

Detroit quickly became the motor capital of the world. General Motors (GM), Chrysler and Ford were all headquartered in or near Detroit (and still are). The 1950s were the city's heyday, when the population exceeded two million and Motown music hit the airwaves. But racial tensions in 1967 and Japanese car competitors in the 1970s shook the city and its industry. Detroit entered an era of deep decline, losing about two-thirds of its population.

In July 2013 Detroit filed the largest municipal bankruptcy claim in US history: $18 billion. Stay tuned to see how it plays out.

◉ Sights & Activities

Sights are commonly closed on Monday and Tuesday. And that's Canada across the Detroit River (Windsor, Canada, to be exact).

◉ Midtown & Cultural Center

★ **Detroit Institute of Arts** MUSEUM
(☑ 313-833-7900; www.dia.org; 5200 Woodward Ave; adult/child $8/4; ⊙ 9am-4pm Tue-Thu, 9am-10pm Fri, 10am-5pm Sat & Sun) The cream of the museum crop. The centerpiece is Diego Rivera's mural *Detroit Industry*, which fills an entire room and reflects the city's blue-collar labor history. Beyond it are Picassos, suits of armor, mod African American paintings, puppets and troves more.

★ **Museum of Contemporary Art Detroit** MUSEUM
(MOCAD; ☑ 313-832-6622; www.mocadetroit.org; 4454 Woodward Ave; suggested donation $5; ⊙ 11am-5pm Wed-Sun, to 8pm Thu & Fri) MOCAD is set in an abandoned, graffiti-slathered auto dealership. Heat lamps hang from the ceiling over peculiar exhibits that change every few months. Music and literary events take place regularly. The cafe hosts pop-up restaurants for Wednesday lunch and Sunday brunch.

◉ New Center

Motown Historical Museum MUSEUM
(☑ 313-875-2264; www.motownmuseum.org; 2648 W Grand Blvd; adult/child $10/8; ⊙ 10am-6pm Mon-Fri & 10am-8pm Sat Jul & Aug, 10am-6pm Tue-Sat Sep-Jun) In this row of modest houses Berry Gordy launched Motown Records – and the careers of Stevie Wonder, Diana Ross, Marvin Gaye and Michael Jackson – with an $800 loan in 1959. Gordy and Motown split for Los Angeles in 1972, but you can still step into humble Studio A and see where the famed names recorded their first hits.

MICHIGAN FACTS

Nicknames Great Lakes State, Wolverine State

Population 9.9 million

Area 96,720 sq miles

Capital city Lansing (population 114,000)

Other cities Detroit (population 701,000)

Sales tax 6%

Birthplace of Industrialist Henry Ford (1863–1947), filmmaker Francis Ford Coppola (b 1939), musician Stevie Wonder (b 1950), singer Madonna (b 1958), Google co-founder Larry Page (b 1973)

Home of Auto assembly plants, freshwater beaches

Politics Leans Democratic

Famous for Cars, cornflakes, tart cherries, Motown music

State reptile Painted turtle

Driving distances Detroit to Traverse City 255 miles, Detroit to Cleveland 168 miles

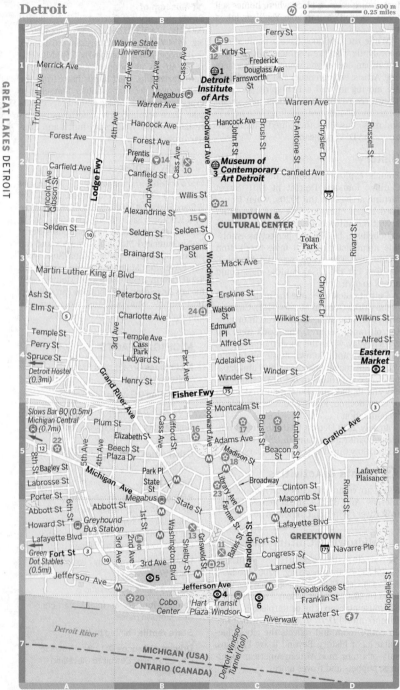

GREAT LAKES DETROIT

Wayne State University

Ferry St

9

12 Kirby St

Merrick Ave

1 Detroit Institute of Arts

Frederick Douglass Ave

Farnsworth St

Megabus

Warren Ave

Warren Ave

Hancock Ave

Hancock Ave

Forest Ave

Forest Ave

Prentis Ave 14

Carfield Ave

Canfield St

Museum of Contemporary Art Detroit 3

Canfield Ave

10

Willis St

Selden St

21

Alexandrine St

15

MIDTOWN & CULTURAL CENTER

Selden St

Selden St

Selden St

Brainard St

Parsens St

Tolan Park

Martin Luther King Jr Blvd

Mack Ave

Ash St

Peterboro St

Erskine St

Elm St 5

Temple St

Charlotte Ave

24

Watson St

Wilkins St

Wilkins St

Perry St

Temple Ave

Edmund Pl

Alfred St

Spruce St

Ledyard St

Adelaide St

Detroit Hostel (0.3mi)

Henry St

Winder St

Winder St

Eastern Market 2

Fisher Fwy

Slows Bar BQ (0.5mi)

Montcalm St

Michigan Central (0.7mi)

22

Plum St

Elizabeth St

16

17

19

Beech St

Adams Ave

Bagley St

Plaza Dr

Madison St

18

Labrosse St

Park Pl

Broadway

Lafayette Plaisance

Porter St

State St

23

Clinton St

Abbott St

Megabus

Macomb St

Howard St

Greyhound Bus Station

State St

Monroe St

Lafayette Blvd

GREEKTOWN

Lafayette Blvd

13

Fort St

Green Fort St

Dot Stables (0.5mi)

10

3

11

25

Congress St

Larned St

Navarre Ple

Jefferson Ave

5

Jefferson Ave

4

Woodbridge St

20

Cobo Center

Hart Plaza

Transit Windsor

6

Franklin St

Atwater St

7

Riverwalk

Detroit River

MICHIGAN (USA)

ONTARIO (CANADA)

Detroit Windsor Tunnel (toll)

0   500 m
0   0.25 miles

Detroit

A tour takes about 1½ hours, and consists mostly of looking at old photos and listening to guides' stories. The museum is 2 miles northwest of Midtown.

Model T Automotive Heritage Complex MUSEUM
(☏313-872-8759; www.tplex.org; 461 Piquette Ave; admission $10; ◎10am-4pm Wed-Fri, from 9am Sat, from noon Sun Apr-Oct) Henry Ford cranked out the first Model T in this landmark factory. Admission includes a detailed tour by enthusiastic docents, plus loads of shiny vehicles from 1904 onward. It's about 1 mile northeast of the Detroit Institute of Arts.

◎ Downtown & Around

Busy Greektown (centred on Monroe St) has restaurants, bakeries and a casino.

★Eastern Market MARKET
(www.detroiteasternmarket.com; Adelaide & Russell Sts) Produce, cheese, spice and flower vendors fill the large halls on Saturday, but you also can turn up Monday through Friday to browse the specialty shops (props to the peanut roaster), cafes, ethnic eats and occasional food trucks that flank the market on Russell and Market Sts.

Renaissance Center BUILDING
(RenCen; www.gmrencen.com; 330 E Jefferson Ave) GM's glossy, cloud-poking headquarters is a fine place to mooch off the free wi-fi, take a free hour-long tour (Monday through Friday at noon and 2pm) or embark on the riverfront walkway.

Hart Plaza PLAZA
(cnr Jefferson & Woodward Aves) This is the site of many free summer weekend festivals and concerts. While there, check out the sculpture of Joe Louis' mighty fist.

People Mover MONORAIL
(www.thepeoplemover.com; fare $0.75) As mass transit, the monorail's 3-mile loop on elevated tracks around downtown won't get you very far. As a tourist attraction, it's a sweet ride providing great views of the city and riverfront.

Heidelberg Project ART INSTALLATION
(www.heidelberg.org; 3600 Heidelberg St; ◎sunrise-sunset) FREE Polka-dotted streets, houses covered in Technicolor paint blobs, strange sculptures in yards – this is no acid trip, but rather a block-spanning neighborhood art installation. It's the brainchild of street artist Tyree Guyton, who wanted to beautify his run-down community. A 2013 fire burned much of the project, but Guyton has vowed to keep it open and turn what remains into art once again.

Get here by taking Gratiot Ave northwest to Heidelberg St; the project spans from Ellery to Mt Elliott Sts.

Riverwalk & Dequindre Cut WALKING, CYCLING
(www.detroitriverfront.org) The city's swell riverfront path runs for 3 miles along the churning Detroit River from Hart Plaza east to

DETROIT'S RUINS

More than 78,000 abandoned buildings blight Detroit's landscape. It has become popular among urban explorers to seek out the most spectacular 'ruins.' You can't go inside, obviously, but the exteriors make for striking photographs. Top of the list is Michigan Central Station (2405 W Vernor Hwy), the once-grand beaux-arts rail terminal now crumbling into oblivion within eyeshot of Corktown's main drag. The Packard Auto Plant (E Grand Blvd at Concord St) is another. Renowned architect Albert Kahn designed the 3.5-million-sq-ft factory, and it was a thing of beauty when it opened in 1903. Now it looks like something from a zombie movie. Stay tuned to see what happens to the structures. The city would like to demolish them, but it doesn't have the money. Detroiturbex (www.detroiturbex.com) provides good historical info on these and other ruins around town.

Mt Elliott St, passing several parks, outdoor theaters, riverboats and fishing spots en route. Eventually it will extend all the way to beachy Belle Isle (detour onto Jefferson Ave to get there now). About halfway along the Riverwalk, near Orleans St, the 1.5-mile Dequindre Cut Greenway path juts north, offering a convenient passageway to Eastern Market.

Wheelhouse Bikes   BICYCLE RENTAL
(☑ 313-656-2453;   www.wheelhousedetroit.com; 1340 E Atwater St; per 2hr $15; ⊘ 10am-8pm Mon-Sat, 11am-5pm Sun Jun-Aug, reduced hours Sep-May) Cycling is a great way to explore the city. Wheelhouse rents sturdy two-wheelers (helmet and lock included) on the Riverwalk at Rivard Plaza. Tours ($35 including bike rental) on weekends roll by various neighborhoods and architectural sites.

☞ Tours

Preservation Detroit   WALKING
(☑ 313-577-7674;   www.preservationdetroit.org; 2½hr tours $10-15; ⊘ 5:30pm Tue & 10am Sat May-Sep) Offers architectural walking tours through downtown, Midtown and other neighborhoods; departure points vary.

✷ Festivals & Events

North American
International Auto Show   CARS
(www.naias.com; tickets $13; ⊘ mid-Jan) It's autos galore for two weeks at the Cobo Center.

Movement Electronic
Music Festival   MUSIC
(www.movement.us; day pass $50; ⊘ late May) The world's largest electronic music festival congregates in Hart Plaza over Memorial Day weekend.

🛏 Sleeping

Add 9% to 15% tax (it varies by lodging size and location) to the rates listed here, unless stated otherwise.

Affordable motels abound in Detroit's suburbs. If you're arriving from Metro Airport, follow the signs for Merriman Rd when leaving the airport and take your pick.

Detroit Hostel   HOSTEL $
(☑ 313-451-0333;   www.hosteldetroit.com;   2700 Vermont St; dm $27-30, r $40-60; ℗ @ ⧄) Volunteers rehabbed this old building, gathered up recycled materials and donations for the patchwork furnishings, and opened it to the public in 2011. There's a 10-bed dorm, a couple of smaller dorms and a handful of private rooms; everyone shares the four bathrooms and three kitchens. Bookings are taken online only (and must be done at least 24 hours in advance).

Bike rentals costs $10 per day. The hostel is located in Corktown on a desolate street, but near several good bars and restaurants.

★ Inn on Ferry Street   INN $$
(☑ 313-871-6000; www.innonferrystreet.com; 84 E Ferry St; r incl breakfast from $159; ℗ ✳ @ ⧄) Forty guest rooms fill a row of Victorian mansions right by the art museum. Lower-cost rooms are small but have deliciously soft bedding; the larger rooms feature plenty of antique wood furnishings. The healthy hot breakfast and shuttle to downtown are nice touches.

Ft Shelby Doubletree Hotel   HOTEL $$
(☑ 800-222-8733, 313-963-5600; http://doubletree1.hilton.com; 525 W Lafayette Blvd; ste $126-189; ℗ ✳ @ ⧄) This newish hotel fills a historic beaux-arts building downtown. All rooms are suites, with both the sitting area and bedroom equipped with HDTV and free wi-fi. Parking costs $23, and there's free shuttle service around downtown.

✖ Eating

Two nearby suburbs also have caches of hip restaurants and bars: walkable, gay-oriented Ferndale at 9 Mile Rd and Woodward Ave, and Royal Oak just north of Ferndale between 12 and 13 Mile Rds.

✖ Midtown & Cultural Center

Good Girls Go to Paris Crepes   CREPERIE $
(☑877-727-4727; www.goodgirlsgotopariscrepes. com; 15 E Kirby St; mains $6-9; ⊙9am-4pm Mon-Wed, to 8pm Thu, to 10pm Fri & Sat, to 5pm Sun) This red-walled, French-style cafe transports diners across the pond via its sweet (Heath Bar and ricotta) and savory (goat's cheese and fig) pancakes.

Cass Cafe   CAFE $$
(☑313-831-1400; www.casscafe.com; 4620 Cass Ave; mains $8-15; ⊙11am-11pm Mon-Thu, 11am-1am Fri & Sat, 5-10pm Sun; 🕏🖉) The Cass is a bohemian art gallery fused with a bar and restaurant that serves soups, sandwiches and veggie beauties, like the lentil-walnut burger. Service can be fickle.

✖ Downtown

Lafayette Coney Island   AMERICAN $
(☑313-964-8198; 118 Lafayette Blvd; items $2.50-4; ⊙8am-4am) The 'coney' – a hot dog smothered with chili and onions – is a Detroit specialty. When the craving strikes (and it will), take care of business at Lafayette. The minimalist menu consists of burgers, fries and beer, in addition to the signature item. Cash only.

Foran's Grand Trunk Pub   PUB $$
(☑313-961-3043; www.grandtrunkpub.com; 612 Woodward Ave; mains $8-13; ⊙11am-midnight) If the high vaulted ceiling and long narrow space make you feel like you're in an old railroad ticket station, that's because you are. The food is pub grub – sandwiches, burgers and shepherd's pie – but made with local ingredients such as Avalon bread and Eastern Market produce. The taps pour 18 Michigan craft brews.

✖ Corktown & Mexicantown

Corktown, a bit west of downtown, shows the city's DIY spirit. Hipster joints slinging burgers, cocktails and artisanal coffee drinks line Michigan Ave. Mexicantown, along Bagley St 3 miles west of downtown, offers several inexpensive Mexican restaurants.

Green Dot Stables   BURGERS $
(www.greendotstables.com; 2200 W Lafayette Blvd; mains $2-3; ⊙11am-midnight Mon-Wed, 11am-1am Thu-Sat, noon-10pm Sun) It's a bit inconveniently located between downtown, Corktown and Mexicantown, but that doesn't deter young urbanites from flocking in to munch on 19 types of gourmet mini-burgers (say, wasabi-mayo tempeh or peanut-butter kimchi) with a side of poutine.

★**Slows Bar BQ**   BARBECUE $$
(☑313-962-9828; www.slowsbarbq.com; 2138 Michigan Ave; mains $10-19; ⊙11am-10pm Sun & Mon, to 11pm Tue-Thu, to midnight Fri & Sat; 🕏) Mmm, slow-cooked southern-style barbecue in Corktown. Carnivores can carve into the three-meat combo plate (brisket, pulled pork and chicken). Vegetarians have options from okra fritters to a faux-chicken sandwich. The taps yield 55 quality beers.

☕ Drinking

★**Bronx**   BAR
(4476 2nd Ave; ⊙from noon; 🕏) There's not much inside Detroit's best boozer besides a pool table, dim lighting and a couple of jukeboxes filled with ballsy rock and soul. But that's the way the hipsters, slackers and rockers (the White Stripes used to hang here) like their dive bars. They're also fond of the beefy burgers served late at night and the cheap beer selection.

Great Lakes Coffee Bar   CAFE
(www.greatlakescoffee.com; 3965 Woodward Ave; ⊙7am-11pm Mon-Thu, 7am-midnight Fri & Sat, 10am-6pm Sun) Roasts its own beans and serves them pour-over style. Locally sourced brewskis, vinos, cheeses and charcuterie are available too. The hep furnishings are made of wood reclaimed from razed houses nearby.

☆ Entertainment

Live Music

Cover charges hover between $5 and $15.

Magic Stick & Majestic Theater   LIVE MUSIC
(www.majesticdetroit.com; 4120-4140 Woodward Ave) The White Stripes and Von Bondies are rockers who've risen from the beer-splattered ranks at the Magic Stick. The Majestic Theater next door hosts larger shows. There's bowling, billiards, a pizza joint and cafe. Something cool rocks here nightly.

FROM MOTOWN TO ROCK CITY

Motown Records and soul music put Detroit on the map in the 1960s, while the thrashing punk rock of the Stooges and MC5 was the 1970s response to that smooth sound. By 1976, Detroit was dubbed 'Rock City' by a Kiss song (though – just Detroit's luck – the tune was eclipsed by its B-side, 'Beth'). In recent years it has been hard-edged rock – aka whiplash rock 'n' roll – that has pushed the city to the music-scene forefront. Homegrown stars include the White Stripes, Von Bondies and Dirtbombs. Rap (thank you, Eminem) and techno are Detroit's other renowned genres. Many music aficionados say the city's blight is what produces such a beautifully angry explosion of sound, and who's to argue? Scope free publications like the *Metro Times* and blogs like Motor City Rocks (www.motorcityrocks.com) for current show and club listings.

PJ's Lager House   LIVE MUSIC
(www.pjslagerhouse.com; 1254 Michigan Ave; ⊙from 11am) Scrappy bands or DJs play most nights at this small Corktown club. By day it serves surprisingly good grub with a New Orleans/vegan twist (like the tempeh po' boy on gluten-free bread).

Cliff Bell's Jazz Club   LIVE MUSIC
(www.cliffbells.com; 2030 Park Ave) With its dark wood, candlelight and art-deco decor, Bell's evokes 1930s elegance. Local jazz bands and poetry readings attract a diverse young audience nightly.

Performing Arts

**Puppet ART/Detroit
Puppet Theater**   THEATER
(☑313-961-7777; www.puppetart.org; 25 E Grand River Ave; adult/child $10/5; ⊛) Soviet-trained puppeteers perform beautiful shows in this 70-person theater; a small museum displays puppets from different cultures. Shows are typically held on Saturday afternoon.

Detroit Opera House   OPERA
(☑313-237-7464; www.motopera.com; 1526 Broadway Ave) Gorgeous interior, top-tier company and nurturer of many renowned African American performers.

Sports

Comerica Park   BASEBALL
(www.detroittigers.com; 2100 Woodward Ave; ⊛) The Detroit Tigers play pro baseball at Comerica, one of the league's most decked-out stadiums. The park is particularly kid friendly, with a small Ferris wheel and carousel inside (per ride $2).

Joe Louis Arena   HOCKEY
(www.detroitredwings.com; 600 Civic Center Dr) The much-loved Red Wings play pro ice hockey at this arena where, if you can wrangle tickets, you might witness the strange octopus-throwing custom.

Ford Field   FOOTBALL
(www.detroitlions.com; 2000 Brush St) The Lions toss the pigskin at this indoor stadium next to Comerica Park.

Palace of Auburn Hills   BASKETBALL
(www.nba.com/pistons; 5 Championship Dr) The Palace hosts the Pistons pro basketball team. It's about 30 miles northwest of downtown; take I-75 to exit 81.

🛍 Shopping

Pure Detroit   SOUVENIRS
(www.puredetroit.com; 500 Griswold St; ⊙10:30am-5:30pm Mon-Sat) Local artists create stylish products for Pure Detroit that celebrate the city's fast-cars-and-rock-music culture. Pick up handbags made from recycled seatbelts, groovy hoodies and local Pewabic pottery. Located in the landmark, mosaic-strewn Guardian Building (worth a peek in its own right).

People's Records   MUSIC
(3161 Woodward Ave; ⊙10am-6pm Mon-Sat) Calling all crate-diggers: DJ-owned People's Records is your vinyl Valhalla. Used 45s are the specialty, with more than 80,000 jazz, soul and R&B titles filling bins.

ℹ Information

The area between the sports arenas north to around Willis Rd is pretty deserted and best avoided on foot come nighttime.

EMERGENCY & MEDICAL SERVICES

Detroit Receiving Hospital (☑313-745-3000; 4201 St Antoine St)

INTERNET ACCESS

You'll find free wi-fi in many cafes and bars, as well as the Renaissance Center lobby.

MEDIA

Between the Lines (www.pridesource.com) Free weekly gay and lesbian paper.

Detroit Free Press (www.freep.com) Daily.

Detroit News (www.detnews.com) Daily.

Metro Times (www.metrotimes.com) Free alternative weekly that is the best guide to the entertainment scene.

TOURIST INFORMATION

Detroit Convention & Visitors Bureau (☑800-338-7648; www.visitdetroit.com)

WEBSITES

DetroitYES (www.detroityes.com) Images organized as 'tours' reveal the city's soul.

Model D (www.modeldmedia.com) Weekly e-zine about local developments and food/ entertainment options, broken down by neighborhood.

❶ Getting There & Around

Detroit Metro Airport (DTW; www.metroairport.com), a Delta Airlines hub, is about 20 miles southwest of Detroit. Transport options from the airport to the city are few: you can take a cab for about $45; or there's the 125 SMART bus ($2), but it takes one to 1½ hours to get downtown.

Greyhound (☑313-961-8005; 1001 Howard St) runs to various cities in Michigan and beyond. **Megabus** (www.megabus.com/us) runs to/from Chicago (5½ hours) daily; departures are from downtown (corner of Cass and Michigan) and Wayne State University (corner of Cass and Warren Aves).

Amtrak (☑313-873-3442; 11 W Baltimore Ave) trains go three times daily to Chicago (5½ hours). You can also head east – to New York (16½ hours) or destinations en route – but you'll first be bused to Toledo.

Transit Windsor (☑519-944-4111; www.city-windsor.ca/transitwindsor) operates the Tunnel Bus to Windsor, Canada. It costs $4 (American or Canadian) and departs by Mariner's Church (corner of Randolph St and Jefferson Ave) near the Detroit-Windsor Tunnel entrance, as well as other spots downtown. Bring your passport.

For taxi service, call **Checker Cab** (☑313-963-7000).

Around Detroit

Stunning Americana and good eatin' lie just down the road from Detroit.

Dearborn

Dearborn is 10 miles west of downtown Detroit and home to two of the USA's finest museums. The indoor Henry Ford Museum (☑313-982-6001; www.thehenryford.org; 20900 Oakwood Blvd; adult/child $17/12.50; ⊙9:30am-5pm) contains a fascinating wealth of American culture, such as the chair Lincoln was sitting in when he was assassinated, the presidential limo in which Kennedy was killed, the hot-dog-shaped Oscar Mayer Wienermobile (photo op!) and the bus on which Rosa Parks refused to give up her seat. Don't worry: you'll get your vintage

---

CLASSIC CARS IN MICHIGAN

More than sand dunes, beaches and Mackinac Island fudge, Michigan is synonymous with cars. While the connection hasn't been so positive in recent years, the state commemorates its glory days via several auto museums. The following fleets are within a few hours' drive of the Motor City.

Henry Ford Museum (p571) This Dearborn museum is loaded with vintage cars, including the first one Henry Ford ever built. In adjacent Greenfield Village you can ride in a Model T that rolled off the assembly line in 1923.

Automotive Hall of Fame (☑313-240-4000; www.automotivehalloffame.org; 21400 Oakwood Blvd; adult/child $8/4; ⊙9am-5pm Wed-Sun) Next door to the Henry Ford Museum, the interactive Auto Hall focuses on the people behind famed cars, such as Mr Ferdinand Porsche and Mr Soichiro Honda.

Gilmore Car Museum (☑269-671-5089; www.gilmorecarmuseum.org; 6865 Hickory Rd; adult/child $12/9; ⊙9am-5pm Mon-Fri, to 6pm Sat & Sun) North of Kalamazoo along Hwy 43, this museum complex offers 22 barns filled with 120 vintage autos, including 15 Rolls Royces dating back to a 1910 Silver Ghost.

RE Olds Transportation Museum (p573) Twenty vintage cars sit in the old Lansing City Bus Garage, including the first Oldsmobile, which was built in 1897.

car fix here, too. Parking is $5. The adjacent outdoor Greenfield Village (adult/child $24/17.50; ◷ 9:30am-5pm daily mid-Apr–Oct, Fri-Sun Nov & Dec) features historic buildings shipped in from all over the country, reconstructed and restored, such as Thomas Edison's laboratory from Menlo Park and the Wright Brothers' airplane workshop. Plus you can add on the Rouge Factory Tour (adult/child $15/11; ◷ 9:30am-3pm Mon-Sat) and see F-150 trucks roll off the assembly line where Ford first perfected his self-sufficient mass-production techniques.

The three attractions are separate, but you can get a combination ticket (adult/child $35/25.50) for Henry Ford and Greenfield Village. Plan on at least one very full day at the complex.

Dearborn has the nation's greatest concentration of people of Arab descent, so it's no surprise that the Arab American National Museum (☏ 313-582-2266; www.arabamericanmuseum.org; 13624 Michigan Ave; adult/child $8/4; ◷ 10am-6pm Wed-Sat, noon-5pm Sun) popped up here. It's a noble concept, located in a pretty, bright-tiled building, but it's not terribly exciting unless actor Jamie Farr's *M*A*S*H* TV-show script wows you. The Arabian eateries lining nearby Warren Ave provide a more engaging feel for the culture. Turquoise-roofed Hamido (www.hamidorestaurant.com; 13251 W Warren Ave; mains $5-12; ◷ 11am-midnight) serves hummus, chicken shwarma and other staples. The number of birds roasting on the spit show its popularity.

Ann Arbor

Forty-odd miles west of Detroit, liberal and bookish Ann Arbor is home to the University of Michigan. The walkable downtown, which abuts the campus, is loaded with free-trade coffee shops, bookstores and brewpubs. It's also a mecca for chowhounds; follow the drool trail toward anything named 'Zingerman's.'

◎ Sights & Activities

University of Michigan Museum of Art   MUSEUM
(☏ 734-764-0395; www.umma.umich.edu; 525 S State St; ◷ 11am-5pm Tue-Sat, from noon Sun) FREE The campus' bold art museum impresses with its collections of Asian ceramics, Tiffany glass and modern abstract works.

Ann Arbor Farmers Market   MARKET
(www.a2gov.org/market; 315 Detroit St; ◷ 7am-3pm Wed & Sat May-Dec, Sat only Jan-Apr) Given the surrounding bounty of orchards and farms, it's no surprise this place is stuffed to the rafters with everything from spicy pickles to cider to mushroom-growing kits; located downtown near Zingerman's Deli. On Sunday an artisan market with jewelry, ceramics and textiles takes over.

Zingerman's Bakehouse   COOKING COURSE
(www.bakewithzing.com; 3723 Plaza Dr) Part of Zingerman's epicurean empire, the Bakehouse offers popular 'bake-cations,' from two-hour cookie-making classes to week-long pastry courses.

✗ Eating & Drinking

Zingerman's Delicatessen   DELI $$
(☏ 734-663-3354; www.zingermansdeli.com; 422 Detroit St; sandwiches $11-17; ◷ 7am-10pm; ♿) The shop that launched the foodie frenzy, Z's piles local, organic and specialty ingredients onto towering sandwiches in a sprawling downtown complex that also includes a coffee shop and bakery.

Frita Batidos   CUBAN $$
(www.fritabatidos.com; 117 W Washington St; mains $8-13; ◷ 11am-11pm Sun-Wed, to midnight Thu-Sat) This mod take on Cuban street food is all the rage, offering burgers with tropical, citrusy toppings and booze-spiked milkshakes.

★ Zingerman's Roadhouse   AMERICAN $$$
(☏ 734-663-3663; www.zingermansroadhouse.com; 2501 Jackson Ave; mains $17-27; ◷ 7am-10pm Mon-Thu, 7am-11pm Fri, 9am-11pm Sat, 9am-9pm Sun) Two words: doughnut sundae. The bourbon-caramel-sauced dessert is pure genius, as are the traditional American dishes like Carolina grits, Iowa pork chops and Massachusetts oysters, all using sustainably produced ingredients. It's 2 miles west of downtown.

Jolly Pumpkin   BREWERY
(www.jollypumpkin.com; 311 S Main St; ◷ from 11am Mon-Fri, from 10am Sat & Sun) Known for its housemade sour beers (try the Bam Biere), rooftop patio, pizzas and truffle fries.

☆ Entertainment

If you happen to arrive on a fall weekend and wonder why 110,000 people – the size of Ann Arbor's entire population, more or less – are crowding into the school's stadium, the answer is football. Tickets are nearly impossible to purchase, especially when nemesis Ohio State is in town. You can try by contacting the U of M Ticket Office (☎734-764-0247; www.mgoblue.com/ticketoffice).

Blind Pig   LIVE MUSIC
(www.blindpigmusic.com; 208 S 1st St) Everyone from John Lennon to Nirvana to the Circle Jerks has rocked the storied stage.

Ark   LIVE MUSIC
(www.a2ark.org; 316 S Main St) The Ark hosts acoustic and folk-oriented tunesmiths.

ⓘ Information

There are several B&Bs within walking distance of downtown. Hotels tend to be about 5 miles out, with several clustered south on State St.
Ann Arbor Convention & Visitors Bureau (www.visitannarbor.org) Information on accommodations.

Lansing & Central Michigan

Michigan's heartland, plunked in the center of the Lower Peninsula, alternates between fertile farms and highway-crossed urban areas.

Lansing

Smallish Lansing is the state capital; a few miles east lies East Lansing, home of Michigan State University. The Greater Lansing CVB (www.lansing.org) has information on both.

Between Lansing's downtown and the university is the 8-mile River Trail (www.lansingrivertrail.org). The paved path is popular with cyclists and joggers, and links a number of attractions, including a children's museum, zoo and fish ladder.

On campus, the new Broad Museum of Art (www.broadmuseum.msu.edu; 547 E Circle Dr; ⊗10am-5pm Tue-Thu & Sat-Sun, noon-9pm Fri) FREE is a must-see. Renowned architect Zaha Hadid designed the wild-looking parallelogram of stainless steel and glass. It holds everything from Greek ceramics to Salvador Dali paintings. The RE Olds Transportation Museum (☎517-372-0529; www.reoldsmuseum.org; 240 Museum Dr; adult/child $6/4; ⊗10am-5pm Tue-Sat year-round, noon-5pm Sun Apr-Oct) will please car buffs.

Lansing's downtown hotels feed off politicians and lobbyists, so they're fairly expensive. It's best to head to East Lansing's Wild Goose Inn (☎517-333-3334; www.wildgooseinn.com; 512 Albert St; r incl breakfast $139-159; ☂), a six-room B&B one block from Michigan State's campus. All rooms have fireplaces and most have Jacuzzis.

Golden Harvest (☎517-485-3663; 1625 Turner St; mains $7-9; ⊗7am-2:30pm Mon-Fri, from 8am Sat & Sun) is a loud, punk-rock-meets-hippie diner serving the sausage-and-French-toast Bubba Sandwich and hearty omelets; cash only. Abundant restaurants, pubs and nightclubs also fill Michigan State's northern campus area.

Grand Rapids

The second-largest city in Michigan, Grand Rapids is known for office-furniture manufacturing and, more recently, beer tourism. Twenty craft breweries operate in the area. The Grand Rapids CVB (www.experiencegr.com) has maps and self-guided tour information online.

Let's cut to the chase: if you've only got time for one brewery, make it rock-and-roll Founders Brewing Company (www.foundersbrewing.com; 235 Grandville Ave SW; ⊗11am-2am Mon-Sat, noon-midnight Sun). The ruby-tinged Dirty Bastard Ale is good swillin', and there's meaty (or vegetable-y, for vegetarians) deli sandwiches to soak it up. Want to try one more? Head to Brewery Vivant (www.breweryvivant.com; 925 Cherry St SE; ⊗from 3pm Mon-Fri, from 11am Sat, from noon Sun), which specializes in Belgian-style beers. Set in an old chapel with stained glass and a vaulted ceiling, the atmospheric brewpub also serves locally sourced cheese plates and burgers at farmhouse-style communal tables.

For intriguing non-beer sights, the downtown Gerald R Ford Museum (☎616-254-0400; www.fordlibrarymuseum.gov; 303 Pearl St NW; adult/child $7/3; ⊗9am-5pm) is dedicated to Michigan's only president. Ford stepped into the Oval Office after Richard Nixon and his vice president, Spiro Agnew, resigned in disgrace. It's an intriguing period in US history, and the museum does an excellent job of covering it, down to displaying the burglary tools used in the Watergate break-in. Ford and wife Betty are buried in the museum's grounds.

The 118-acre Frederik Meijer Gardens (☎616-957-1580; www.meijergardens.org; 1000 E Beltline NE; adult/child $12/6; ⊗9am-5pm Mon-Sat, 9am-9pm Tue, 11am-5pm Sun) features impressive blooms and sculptures by Auguste

Rodin, Henry Moore and others. It is 5 miles east of downtown via I-196. There's a good art museum downtown, too.

At night, tuck in under bamboo sheets at the CityFlats Hotel (☑866-609-2489; www.cityflatshotel.com/grandrapids; 83 Monroe Center St NW; r $169-239; ▣☎) downtown; it's gold-certified by the LEED (Leadership in Energy and Environmental Design) program.

Lake Michigan Shore

They don't call it the Gold Coast for nothing. Michigan's 300-mile western shoreline features seemingly endless stretches of beaches, dunes, wineries, orchards and B&B-filled towns that boom during the summer – and shiver during the snow-packed winter. Note all state parks listed here take campsite reservations (☑800-447-2757; www.midnrreservations.com; fee $8) and require a vehicle permit (day/year $9/31), unless specified otherwise.

Harbor Country

Harbor Country refers to a group of eight small, lake-hugging towns just over the Michigan border (an easy day trip from Chicago). Yep, they've got your requisite beaches, wineries and antique shops; they've got a couple of big surprises too. The Harbor Country Chamber of Commerce (www.harborcountry.org) has the basics.

First up, surfing. Believe it, people: you can surf Lake Michigan, and the VW-bus-driving dudes at Third Coast Surf Shop (☑269-932-4575; www.thirdcoastsurfshop.com; 110-C N Whittaker St; ☉10am-6pm mid-May–late Sep) will show you how. They provide wetsuits and boards for surfing, skim boarding and paddleboarding (rentals per day $20 to $35). For novices, they offer 1½-hour lessons (including equipment $55 to $75) right on the public beach June through mid-September. The surf shop is in New Buffalo, Harbor Country's biggest town.

ⓘ WINE TRAIL

A dozen wineries cluster between New Buffalo and Saugatuck. The Lake Michigan Shore Wine Trail (www.lakemichiganshorewinetrail.com) provides a downloadable map of vineyards and tasting rooms. Most are signposted off the highway.

Three Oaks is the only Harbor community that's inland (6 miles in, via US 12). Here Green Acres meets Greenwich Village in a funky farm-and-arts blend. By day, rent bikes at Dewey Cannon Trading Company (☑269-756-3361; www.applecidercentury.com; 3 Dewey Cannon Ave; bike per day $20; ☉9am-5pm) and cycle lightly used rural roads past orchards and wineries. By eve, catch a provocative play or arthouse flick at Three Oaks' theaters.

Hungry? Get a wax-paper-wrapped cheeseburger, spicy curly fries and cold beer at Redamak's (www.redamaks.com; 616 E Buffalo St; burgers $5-10; ☉noon-10:30pm Mar-Oct) in New Buffalo.

Saugatuck & Douglas

Saugatuck is one of the Gold Coast's most popular resort areas, known for its strong arts community, numerous B&Bs and gay-friendly vibe. Douglas is its twin city a mile or so south, and they've pretty much sprawled into one. The Saugatuck/Douglas CVB (www.saugatuck.com) provides maps and more.

The best thing to do in Saugatuck is also the most affordable. Jump aboard the clackety Saugatuck Chain Ferry (foot of Mary St; one way $1; ☉9am-9pm late May-early Sep) and the operator will pull you across the Kalamazoo River. On the other side, walk to the dock's right and soon you'll come to Mt Baldhead, a 200ft-high sand dune. Huff up the stairs to see the grand view, and then race down the other side to beautiful Oval Beach.

Galleries and shops proliferate downtown on Water and Butler Sts. Antiquing prevails on the Blue Star Hwy running south for 20 miles. Blueberry U-pick farms share this stretch of road and make a juicy stop, too.

Several frilly B&Bs are tucked into the Saugatuck's century-old Victorian homes, with most ranging from $125 to $300 per night. Try the Bayside Inn (☑269-857-4321; www.baysideinn.net; 618 Water St; r incl breakfast $150-280; ☎), a 10-room former boathouse on Saugatuck's waterfront, or the retro-cool Pines Motorlodge (☑269-857-5211; www.thepinesmotorlodge.com; 56 Blue Star Hwy; r incl breakfast $139-199; ☎), with rooms amid the firs in Douglas.

For eats, Wicks Park Bar & Grill (☑269-857-2888; www.wickspark.com; 449 Water St; mains $11-25; ☉11:30am-9pm), by the chain ferry, gets props for its lake perch and live music.

Locals like to hang out and sip the house-made suds at **Saugatuck Brewing Company** (www.saugatuckbrewing.com; 2948 Blue Star Hwy; ☺11am-10pm Sun-Thu, to 11pm Fri & Sat). For dessert, buy a bulging slice at **Crane's Pie Pantry** (☑269-561-2297; www.cranespiepantry.com; 6054 124th Ave; pie slices $4; ☺9am-8pm Mon-Sat, from 11am Sun May-Oct, reduced hours Nov-Apr), or pick apples and peaches in the surrounding orchards. Crane's is in Fennville, 3 miles south on the Blue Star Hwy, then 4 miles inland on Hwy 89.

Muskegon & Ludington

The **Lake Express ferry** (☑866-914-1010; www.lake-express.com; ☺May-Oct) crosses between Muskegon and Milwaukee (one way adult/child/car from $83/26/87, 2½ hours), providing a substantial shortcut over driving the Michigan-to-Wisconsin route. The town isn't much, but the **Muskegon Luge & Sports Complex** (☑231-744-9629; www.msports.org; 442 Scenic Dr) kicks butt with its full-on luge track (usable during summer, too) and cross-country ski trails. To the north, lakeside **Ludington State Park** (☑231-843-8671; tent & RV sites $16-29, cabins $45) is one of Michigan's largest and most popular playlots. It has a top-notch trail system, a renovated lighthouse to visit (or live in, as a volunteer lighthouse keeper) and miles of beach.

Sleeping Bear Dunes National Lakeshore

This national park stretches from north of Frankfort to just before Leland, on the Leelanau Peninsula. Stop at the park's **visitor center** (☑231-326-5134; www.nps.gov/slbe; 9922 Front St; ☺8:30am-6pm Jun-Aug, to 4pm Sep-May) in Empire for information, trail maps and vehicle entry permits (week/year $10/20).

Attractions include the famous **dune climb** along Hwy 109, where you trudge up the 200ft-high dune and then run or roll down. Gluttons for leg-muscle punishment can keep slogging all the way to Lake Michigan, a strenuous 1½-hour trek one way; bring water. The **Sleeping Bear Heritage Trail** (www.sleepingbeartrail.org) paves 5 pretty miles from Glen Arbor to the Dune Climb; walkers and cyclists are all over it. It will stretch to Empire by summer 2014. Short on time or stamina? Take the 7-mile, one-lane, picnic-grove-studded **Pierce Stocking Scenic Drive**, perhaps the best way to absorb the stunning lake vistas.

GREAT LAKES LAKE MICHIGAN SHORE

WORTH A TRIP

MANITOU ISLANDS

If you're looking for a wilderness adventure, the Manitou Islands – part of Sleeping Bear Dunes National Lakeshore – deliver. **Manitou Island Transit** (☑231-256-9061; www.manitoutransit.com) can help plan overnight camping trips on North Manitou, or day trips to South Manitou. Kayaking and hiking are popular activities, especially the 7-mile trek to the Valley of the Giants, a mystical stand of cedar trees on South Manitou. Ferries (round trip adult/child $35/20, 1½ hours) sail from Leland two to seven times per week from May to mid-October.

After you leave the park, swing into little **Leland** (www.lelandmi.com). Grab a bite at a waterfront restaurant downtown, and poke around atmospheric Fishtown with its weatherbeaten shacks-cum-shops. Boats depart from here for the Manitou Islands.

Onward near Suttons Bay, **Tandem Ciders** (www.tandemciders.com; 2055 Setterbo Rd; ☺noon-6pm Mon-Sat, to 5pm Sun) pours delicious hard ciders in its small tasting room on the family farm.

Traverse City

Michigan's 'cherry capital' is the largest city in the northern half of the Lower Peninsula. It's got a bit of urban sprawl, but it's still a happenin' base from which to see the Sleeping Bear Dunes, Mission Peninsula wineries, U-pick orchards and other area attractions.

Stop at the downtown **visitor center** (☑231-947-1120; www.traversecity.com; 101 W Grandview Pkwy; ☺9am-6pm Mon-Sat, 11am-3pm Sun) for maps and the do-it-yourself foodie tour brochure (also available online; click 'Things to Do' on the website).

Road tripping out to the wineries is a must. Head north from Traverse City on Hwy 37 for 20 miles to the end of the grape- and cherry-planted Old Mission Peninsula. You'll be spoiled for choice: **Chateau Grand Traverse** (www.cgtwines.com; ☺10am-7pm Mon-Sat, to 6pm Sun) and **Chateau Chantal** (www.chateauchantal.com; ☺11am-8pm Mon-Sat, to 6pm Sun) pour crowd-pleasing Chardonnay and Pinot Noir. **Peninsula Cellars** (www.peninsulacellars.com; ⊙10am-6pm), in an old schoolhouse, makes fine whites and is often less crowded. Whatever bottle you buy, take it out to Lighthouse Park beach, at the peninsula's tip, and enjoy it with the waves chilling your toes. The wineries stay open year-round, with reduced hours in winter.

The town goes all Hollywood during the **Traverse City Film Festival** (www.traversecityfilmfest.org; ⊙late Jul), when founder (and native Michigander) Michael Moore comes in and unspools a six-day slate of documentaries, international flicks and 'just great movies.'

Dozens of beaches, resorts, motels and water-sports operators line US 31 around Traverse City. On weekends, lodgings are often full, and more expensive; the visitor center website has contact details. Most resorts overlooking the bay cost $150 to $250 per night. The Chantal and Grand Traverse wineries also double as B&Bs and fit into this price range.

Guests can rent jet skis and enjoy nightly bonfires at **Park Shore Resort** (☑877-349-8898; www.parkshoreresort.com; 1401 US 31 N; r incl breakfast from $199; ❋ ❡ ☲). Motels on the other side of US 31 (away from the water) are more moderately priced, such as **Mitchell Creek Inn** (☑231-947-9330; www.mitchellcreek.com; 894 Munson Ave; r/cottages from $60/125; ❡), near the state park beach.

After a day of fun in the sun, refresh with sandwiches at gastronome favorite **Folgarelli's** (☑231-941-7651; www.folgarellis.net; 424 W Front St; sandwiches $7-11; ⊙9:30am-6:30pm Mon-Fri, to 5:30pm Sat, 11am-4pm Sun) and Belgian and Michigan craft beers at **7 Monks Taproom** (www.7monkstap.com; 128 S Union St; ⊙noon-midnight).

Charlevoix & Petoskey

These two towns hold several Hemingway sights. They're also where Michigan's upper-crusters maintain summer homes. The downtown areas of both places have gourmet restaurants and high-class shops, and the marinas are filled with yachts.

In Petoskey, **Stafford's Perry Hotel** (☑231-347-4000; www.staffords.com; Bay at Lewis St; r $149-269; ❋ @ ❡) is a grand historic place in which to stay. **Petoskey State Park** (☑231-347-2311; 2475 Hwy 119; tent & RV sites $27-29) is north along Hwy 119 and has a beautiful beach. Look for indigenous Petoskey stones, which are honeycomb-patterned fragments of ancient coral. From here, Hwy 119 (aka the **Tunnel of Trees scenic route**) dips and curves through thick forest as it rolls north along a sublime bluff, en route to the Straits of Mackinac.

Straits of Mackinac

This region, between the Upper and Lower Peninsulas, features a long history of forts and fudge shops. Car-free Mackinac Island is Michigan's premier tourist draw.

One of the most spectacular sights in the area is the 5-mile-long **Mackinac Bridge** (known locally as 'Big Mac'), which spans the Straits of Mackinac. The $4 toll is worth every penny as the views from the bridge, which include two Great Lakes, two peninsulas and hundreds of islands, are second to none in Michigan.

And remember: despite the spelling, it's pronounced *mac*-in-aw.

Mackinaw City

At the south end of Mackinac Bridge, bordering I-75, is touristy Mackinaw City. It serves mainly as a jump-off point to Mackinac Island, but it does have a couple of interesting sights.

Next to the bridge (its visitor center is actually beneath the bridge) is **Colonial Michilimackinac** (☑231-436-5564; www.mackinacparks.com; adult/child $11/6.50; ⊙9:30am-7pm Jun-Aug, to 5pm May & Sep–mid-Oct). This National Historic Landmark features a reconstructed stockade first built in 1715 by the French. Some 3 miles southeast of the city on US 23 is **Historic Mill Creek** (☑231-436-4226; www.mackinacparks.com; adult/child

HEMINGWAY'S HAUNTS

A number of writers have ties to northwest Michigan, but none is as famous as Ernest Hemingway, who spent the summers of his youth at his family's cottage on Walloon Lake. Hemingway buffs often tour the area to view the places that made their way into his writing.

First up: Horton Bay. As you head north on US 31, past yacht-filled Charlevoix, look for Boyne City Rd veering off to the east. It skirts Lake Charlevoix and eventually arrives at the Horton Bay General Store (☑ 231-582-7827; www.hortonbaygeneralstore.com; 05115 Boyne City Rd; ⊙ 8am-2pm mid-May–mid-Oct). Hemingway fans will recognize the building, with its 'high false front,' from his short story 'Up in Michigan.' For the mother lode of Hemingway books and souvenirs, pop into the Red Fox Inn Bookstore (05156 Boyne City Rd; ⊙ late May–early Sep) next door.

Further up Hwy 31 in Petoskey, you can see the Hemingway collection at the Little Traverse History Museum (☑ 231-347-2620; www.petoskeymuseum.org; 100 Depot Ct; admission $3; ⊙ 10am-4pm Mon-Fri, from 1pm Sat late May–mid-Oct), including rare first-edition books that the author autographed for a friend when he visited in 1947. Afterward, toss back a drink at City Park Grill (☑ 231-347-0101; www.cityparkgrill.com; 432 E Lake St; ⊙ 11:30am-midnight), where Hemingway was a regular.

Tour Hemingway's Michigan (www.mihemingwaytour.org) provides further information for self-guided jaunts.

$8/4.75; ⊙ 9am-5pm Jun-Aug, to 4pm May & Sep–mid-Oct), which has an 18th-century sawmill, historic displays and nature trails. A combination ticket for both sights, along with Fort Mackinac, is available at a discount.

If you can't find lodging on Mackinac Island – which should be your first choice – motels line I-75 and US 23 in Mackinaw City. Most cost $100-plus per night. Try Days Inn (☑ 231-436-8961; www.daysinn.com; 206 N Nicolet St; r incl breakfast $115-170; ❄ 🐾 🐕).

St Ignace

At the north end of Mackinac Bridge is St Ignace, the other departure point for Mackinac Island and the second-oldest settlement in Michigan – Père Jacques Marquette founded a mission here in 1671. As soon as you've paid your bridge toll, you'll pass a huge visitor center (☑ 906-643-6979; I-75N; ⊙ 9am-5:30pm daily summer, Thu-Mon rest of year) which has racks of statewide information.

Mackinac Island

From either Mackinaw City or St Ignace you can catch a ferry to Mackinac Island. The island's location in the straits between Lake Michigan and Lake Huron made it a prized port in the North American fur trade, and a site the British and Americans battled over many times.

The most important date on this 3.8-sq-mile island was 1898 – the year cars were banned in order to encourage tourism. Today all travel is by horse or bicycle; even the police use bikes to patrol the town. The crowds of tourists – called Fudgies by the islanders – can be crushing at times, particularly during summer weekends. But when the last ferry leaves in the evening and clears out the day-trippers, Mackinac's real charm emerges and you drift back into another, slower era.

The visitor center (☑ 800-454-5227; www.mackinacisland.org; Main St; ⊙ 9am-5pm), by the Arnold Line ferry dock, has maps for hiking and cycling. Eighty percent of the island is state parkland. Not much stays open between November and April.

◎ Sights & Activities

Edging the island's shoreline is Hwy 185, the only Michigan highway that doesn't permit cars. The best way to view the incredible scenery along this 8-mile road is by bicycle; bring your own or rent one in town for $8 per hour at one of the many businesses. You can loop around the flat road in about an hour.

The two best attractions – Arch Rock (a huge limestone arch that sits 150ft above Lake Huron) and Fort Holmes (the island's other fort) – are both free. You can also ride past the Grand Hotel, which boasts a porch stretching halfway to Detroit. Unfortunately, if you're not staying at the Grand (minimum $240 per night per person), it costs $10 to stroll its long porch. Best to admire from afar.

Fort Mackinac   HISTORIC SITE

(☑906-847-3328; www.mackinacparks.com; adult/child $11/6.50; ☺9:30am-6pm Jun-Aug, 9:30am-4:30pm May & Sep–mid-Oct; ⊞) Fort Mackinac sits atop limestone cliffs near downtown. Built by the British in 1780, it's one of the best-preserved military forts in the country. Costumed interpreters and cannon and rifle firings (every half-hour) entertain the kids. Stop into the tearoom for a bite and million-dollar view of downtown and the Straits of Mackinac from the outdoor tables.

The fort admission price also allows you entry to five other museums in town along Market St, including the Dr Beaumont Museum (where the doctor performed his famous digestive tract experiments) and the Benjamin Blacksmith Shop. The Mackinac Art Museum (adult/child $5/3.50), housing Native American and other arts by the fort, is the newest member of the fold.

⌷ Sleeping

Rooms are booked far in advance during summer weekends; July to mid-August is peak season. The visitor center website has lodging contacts. Camping is not permitted anywhere on the island.

Most hotels and B&Bs charge at least $180 for two people. Exceptions (all are walkable from downtown) include the following.

Bogan Lane Inn   B&B $$

(☑906-847-3439; www.boganlaneinn.com; Bogan Lane; r incl breakfast $90-130) Four rooms, shared bath.

Cloghaun B&B   B&B $$

(☑906-847-3885; www.cloghaun.com; Market St; r incl breakfast $112-197; ☺mid-May–late Oct; ☎) Eleven rooms, some with shared bath.

Hart's B&B   B&B $$

(☑906-847-3854; www.hartsmackinac.com; Market St; r incl breakfast $150-190; ☺mid-May–late Oct; ⊞) Eight rooms, all with private bath.

✕ Eating & Drinking

Fudge shops are the island's best-known eateries; resistance is futile when they use fans to blow the aroma out onto Huron St. Hamburger and sandwich shops abound downtown.

JL Beanery Coffeehouse   CAFE $

(☑906-847-6533; Huron St; mains $6-13; ☺7am-7pm; ☎) Read the newspaper, sip a steaming cup of joe and gaze at the lake at this waterside cafe. It serves dandy breakfasts, sandwiches and soups.

Horn's Bar   BURGERS, MEXICAN $$

(☑906-847-6154; www.hornsbar.com; Main St; mains $10-19; ☺11am-2am) Horn's saloon serves American burgers and south-of-the-border fare, and there's live entertainment nightly.

Cawthorne's Village Inn   AMERICAN $$$

(☑906-847-3542; www.grandhotel.com; Hoban St; mains $18-27; ☺11am-2am) Planked whitefish, pan-fried perch and other fresh-from-the-lake fish, meat and pasta dishes stuff diners at this year-round local hang-out with a bar and outdoor seating. Operated by the Grand Hotel.

❶ Getting There & Around

Three ferry companies – **Arnold Line** (☑800-542-8528; www.arnoldline.com), **Shepler's** (☑800-828-6157; www.shoplersferry.com) and **Star Line** (☑800-638-9892; www.mackinac-ferry.com) – operate out of Mackinaw City and St Ignace, and charge the same rates: round-trip adult/child/bicycle $25/13/8. Book online and you'll save a few bucks. The ferries run several times daily from May to October; Arnold Line runs longer, weather permitting. The trip takes about 15 minutes; once on the island, horse-drawn cabs will take you anywhere, or you can rent a bicycle.

Upper Peninsula

Rugged and isolated, with hardwood forests blanketing 90% of its land, the Upper Peninsula (UP) is a Midwest highlight. Only 45 miles of interstate highway slice through the trees, punctuated by a handful of cities, of which Marquette (population 20,000) is the largest. Between the small towns lie miles of undeveloped shoreline on Lakes Huron, Michigan and Superior; scenic two-lane roads; and pasties, the local meat-and-vegetable pot pies brought over by Cornish miners 150 years ago.

You'll find it's a different world up north. Residents of the UP, aka 'Yoopers,' consider themselves distinct from the rest of the state – they've even threatened to secede in the past.

Sault Ste Marie & Tahquamenon Falls

Founded in 1668, Sault Ste Marie (Sault is pronounced 'soo') is Michigan's oldest city and the third oldest in the USA. The town is best known for its locks that raise and lower 1000ft-long freighters between the different lake levels. Soo Locks Park & Visitors Center (⊘9am-9pm mid-May–mid-Oct) FREE is on Portage Ave downtown (take exit 394 off I-75 and go left). It features displays, videos and observation decks from which you can watch the boats leap 21ft from Lake Superior to Lake Huron. Pubs and cafes line Portage Ave. The Sault CVB (www.saultstemarie.com) has all the lowdown.

An hour's drive west of Sault Ste Marie, via Hwy 28 and Hwy 123, is eastern UP's top attraction: lovely Tahquamenon Falls, with tea-colored waters tinted by upstream hemlock leaves. The Upper Falls in Tahquamenon Falls State Park (☑906-492-3415; per vehicle $9), 200ft across with a 50ft drop, wow onlookers – including Henry Wadsworth Longfellow, who mentioned them in his *Song of Hiawatha*. The Lower Falls are a series of small cascades that swirl around an island; many visitors rent a rowboat and paddle out to it. The large state park also has camping (tent & RV sites $16-23), great hiking and – bonus – a brewpub near the park entrance.

North of the park, beyond the little town of Paradise, is the fascinating Great Lakes Shipwreck Museum (☑888-492-3747; www.shipwreckmuseum.com; 18335 N Whitefish Point Rd; adult/child $13/9; ⊘10am-6pm May-Oct), where the intriguing displays include items trawled up from sunken ships. Dozens of vessels – including the *Edmund Fitzgerald* that Gordon Lightfoot crooned about – have sunk in the area's congested sea lanes and storm-tossed weather, earning it such nicknames as the 'Shipwreck Coast' and 'Graveyard of the Great Lakes.' The grounds also include a lighthouse that President Lincoln commissioned and a bird observatory that 300 species fly by. To have the foggy place to yourself, spend the night at Whitefish Point Light Station B&B (☑888-492-3747; r $150; ⊘May–Oct), which offers five rooms in the old Coast Guard crew quarters on site.

Pictured Rocks National Lakeshore

Stretching along prime Lake Superior real estate, Pictured Rocks National Lakeshore (www.nps.gov/piro) is a series of wild cliffs and caves where blue and green minerals have streaked the red and yellow sandstone into a kaleidoscope of color. Rte 58 (Alger County Rd) spans the park for 52 slow miles from Grand Marais in the east to Munising in the west. Top sights (from east to west) include Au Sable Point Lighthouse (reached via a 3-mile round-trip walk beside shipwreck skeletons), agate-strewn Twelvemile Beach, hike-rich Chapel Falls and view-worthy Miners Castle Overlook.

Several boat tours launch from Munising. Pictured Rock Cruises (☑906-387-2379; www.picturedrocks.com; 100 W City Park Dr; 2½hr tours adult/child $36/10; ⊘mid-May–mid-Oct) departs from the city pier downtown and glides along the shore to Miners Castle. Shipwreck Tours (☑906-387-4477; www.shipwrecktours.com; 1204 Commercial St; 2hr tours adult/child $32/12; ⊘late May–mid-Oct) sails in glass-bottom boats to see sunken schooners.

Grand Island (www.grandislandmi.com), part of Hiawatha National Forest, is also a quick jaunt from Munising. Hop aboard the Grand Island Ferry (☑906-387-3503; round-trip adult/child $15/10; ⊘late May–mid-Oct) to get there and rent a mountain bike (per day $30) to zip around. There's also a ferry/bus tour package ($22). The ferry dock is on Hwy 28, which is about 4 miles west of Munising.

Munising has lots of motels, such as tidy Alger Falls Motel (☑906-387-3536; www.algerfallsmotel.com; E9427 Hwy 28; r $60-90; ✳🐾🖥). Falling Rock Cafe & Bookstore (☑906-387-3008; www.fallingrockcafe.com; 104 E Munising Ave; mains $5-9; ⊘7am-10pm; 🖥) provides sandwiches and live music.

Staying in wee Grand Marais, on the park's east side, is also recommended. Turn in at Hilltop Cabins and Motel (☑906-494-2331; www.hilltopcabins.net; N14176 Ellen St; r & cabins $85-175; 🖥) after a meal of whitefish sandwiches and brewskis at rustic Lake Superior Brewing Company (☑906-494-2337; N14283 Lake Ave; mains $7-13; ⊘noon-11pm).

Marquette

From Munising, Hwy 28 heads west and hugs Lake Superior. This beautiful stretch of highway has lots of beaches, roadside parks and rest areas where you can pull over and enjoy the scenery. Within 45 miles you'll reach outdoorsy, oft-snowy Marquette.

Stop at the log-lodge visitor center (www.travelmarquettemichigan.com; 2201 US 41; ⊙9am-5pm) as you enter the city for brochures on local hiking trails and waterfalls.

The easy Sugarloaf Mountain Trail and the harder, wildernesslike Hogsback Mountain Trail offer panoramic views. Both are reached from County Rd 550, just north of Marquette. In the city, the high bluffs of Presque Isle Park make a great place to catch the sunset. The Noquemanon Trail Network (www.noquetrails.org) is highly recommended for mountain biking and cross-country skiing. Kayaking is awesome in the area; Downwind Sports (www.downwind-sports.com; 514 N Third St ; ⊙10am-7pm Mon-Fri, 10am-5pm Sat, 11am-3pm Sun) has the lowdown on it, as well as fly fishing, surfing, ice climbing and other adventures.

Marquette is the perfect place to stay put for a few days to explore the central UP. Budgeteers can bunk at Value Host Motor Inn (☑906-225-5000; www.valuehostmotorinn.com; 1101 US 41 W; r incl breakfast $55-70; ✳☎) a few miles west of town. Downtown's Landmark Inn (☑906-228-2580; www.thelandmarkinn.com; 230 N Front St; r $139-229; ✳☎) fills a historic lakefront building and has a couple of resident ghosts.

Sample the local meat-and-veggie pie specialty at Jean Kay's Pasties & Subs (www.jeankayspasties.com; 1635 Presque Isle Ave; items $4-7.50; ⊙11am-9pm Mon-Fri, to 8pm Sat & Sun).

DON'T MISS

DA YOOPERS TOURIST TRAP

Behold Big Gus, the world's largest chainsaw. And Big Ernie, the world's largest rifle. Kitsch runs rampant at Da Yoopers Tourist Trap and Museum (☑800-628-9978; www.dayoopers.com; ⊙9am-9pm Mon-Fri, to 8pm Sat, to 7pm Sun) FREE, 15 miles west of Marquette on Hwy 28/41, past Ishpeming. Browse the store for only-in-the-UP gifts like a polyester moose tie or beer-can wind chimes.

In a quonset hut at Main St's foot, Thill's Fish House (☑906-226-9851; 250 E Main St; items $4-9; ⊙8am-5:30pm Mon-Fri, to 4pm Sat) is Marquette's last commercial fishing operation, and it hauls in fat catches daily; try the smoked whitefish sausage. Hop-heads and mountain bikers hang out at Blackrocks Brewery (www.blackrocksbrewery.com; 424 N Third St; ⊙from 4pm), set in an cool refurbished house downtown.

Isle Royale National Park

Totally free of vehicles and roads, Isle Royale National Park (www.nps.gov/isro; per day $4; ⊙mid-May–Oct), a 210-sq-mile island in Lake Superior, is certainly the place to go for peace and quiet. It gets fewer visitors in a year than Yellowstone National Park gets in a day, which means the packs of wolves and moose creeping through the forest are all yours.

The island is laced with 165 miles of hiking trails that connect dozens of campgrounds along Superior and inland lakes. You must be totally prepared for this wilderness adventure, with a tent, camping stove, sleeping bags, food and water filter. Otherwise, be a softie and bunk at the Rock Harbor Lodge (☑906-337-4993; www.isleroyaleresort.com; r & cottages $237-271; ⊙late May-early Sep)

From the dock outside the park headquarters (800 E Lakeshore Dr) in Houghton, the Ranger III (☑906-482-0984) departs at 9am on Tuesday and Friday for the six-hour boat trip (round-trip adult/child $126/46) to Rock Harbor, at the east end of the island. Royale Air Service (☑877-359-4753; www.royaleairservice.com) offers a quicker trip, flying from Houghton County Airport to Rock Harbor in 30 minutes (round-trip $299). Or head 50 miles up the Keweenaw Peninsula to Copper Harbor (a beautiful drive) and jump on the Isle Royale Queen (☑906-289-4437; www.isleroyale.com) for the 8am three-hour crossing (round-trip adult/child $130/65). It usually runs daily during peak season from late July to mid-August. Bringing a kayak or canoe on the ferries costs an additional $50 round-trip; ensure you make reservations well in advance. You can also access Isle Royale from Grand Portage, Minnesota.

Porcupine Mountains Wilderness State Park

Michigan's largest state park, with 90 miles of trails, is another UP winner, and it's a heck of a lot easier to reach than Isle Royale. 'The

Porkies,' as they're called, are so rugged that loggers bypassed most of the range in the early 19th century, leaving the park with the largest tract of virgin forest between the Rocky Mountains and Adirondacks.

From Silver City, head west on Hwy 107 to reach the Porcupine Mountains Visitor Center (☑906-885-5275; www.porcupinemountains.com; 412 S Boundary Rd; ☺10am-6pm mid-May–mid-Oct), where you buy vehicle entry permits (per day/year $9/31) and backcountry permits (one to four people per night $14). Continue to the end of Hwy 107 and climb 300ft for the stunning view of Lake of the Clouds.

Winter is also a busy time at the Porkies, with downhill skiing (a 787ft vertical drop) and 26 miles of cross-country trails on offer; check with the ski area (☑906-289-4105; www.skitheporkies.com) for conditions and costs.

The park rents rustic cabins (☑906-885-5275; www.mi.gov/porkies; cabins $60) perfect for wilderness adventurers, as you have to hike in for 1 to 4 miles, boil your own water and use a privy. Sunshine Motel & Cabins (☑906-884-2187; www.ontonagon.net/sunshinemotel; 24077 Hwy 64; r $60, cabins $68-120; ☎🐾🐾), 3 miles west of Ontonagon, is another good base.

WISCONSIN

Wisconsin is cheesy and proud of it. The state pumps out 2.5 billion pounds of cheddar, Gouda and other smelly goodness – a quarter of America's hunks – from its cow-speckled farmland per year. Local license plates read 'The Dairy State' with udder dignity. Folks here even refer to themselves as 'cheeseheads' and emphasize it by wearing novelty foam-rubber cheese-wedge hats for special occasions (most notably during Green Bay Packers football games).

So embrace the cheese thing, because there's a good chance you'll be here for a while. Wisconsin has heaps to offer: exploring the craggy cliffs and lighthouses of Door County, kayaking through sea caves at Apostle Islands National Lakeshore, cow-chip throwing along US 12 and soaking up beer, art and festivals in Milwaukee and Madison.

ⓘ Information

Travel Green Wisconsin (www.travelgreenwisconsin.com) Certifies businesses as ecofriendly by grading them on waste reduction, energy efficiency and seven other categories.

> ### WISCONSIN FACTS
>
> **Nicknames** Badger State, America's Dairyland
>
> **Population** 5.7 million
>
> **Area** 65,500 sq miles
>
> **Capital city** Madison (population 240,000)
>
> **Other cities** Milwaukee (population 599,000)
>
> **Sales tax** 5%
>
> **Birthplace of** Author Laura Ingalls Wilder (1867–1957), architect Frank Lloyd Wright (1867–1959), painter Georgia O'Keeffe (1887–1986), actor Orson Welles (1915–85), guitar maker Les Paul (1915–2009)
>
> **Home of** 'Cheesehead' Packer fans, dairy farms, water parks
>
> **Politics** Leans Democratic
>
> **Famous for** Breweries, artisanal cheese, first state to legislate gay rights
>
> **Official dance** Polka
>
> **Driving distances** Milwaukee to Minneapolis 336 miles, Milwaukee to Madison 80 miles

Wisconsin B&B Association (www.wbba.org)
Wisconsin Department of Tourism (☑800-432-8747; www.travelwisconsin.com) Produces loads of free guides on subjects like birdwatching, biking, golf and rustic roads; also a free app.
Wisconsin Highway Conditions (☑511; www.511wi.gov)
Wisconsin Milk Marketing Board (www.eatwisconsincheese.com) Provides a free statewide map of cheesemakers titled *A Traveler's Guide to America's Dairyland*.
Wisconsin State Park Information (☑608-266-2181; www.wiparks.net) Park entry requires a vehicle permit (per day/year $10/35). Campsites cost from $14 to $25; reservations (☑888-947-2757; www.wisconsinstateparks.reserveamerica.com; fee $10) accepted.

Milwaukee

Here's the thing about Milwaukee: it's cool, but for some reason everyone refuses to admit it. Yes, the reputation lingers as a working man's town of brewskis, bowling alleys and polka halls. But attractions like the Calatrava-designed art museum, bad-ass Harley-Davidson Museum and stylish eating and shopping 'hoods have turned Wisconsin's largest city into a surprisingly groovy place. In summertime, festivals let loose with revelry by the lake almost every weekend. And where else on the planet will you see racing sausages?

History

Milwaukee was first settled by Germans in the 1840s. Many started small breweries, but a few decades later the introduction of bulk brewing technology turned beer production into a major industry here. Milwaukee earned its 'Brew City' and 'Nation's Watering Hole' nicknames in the 1880s when Pabst, Schlitz, Blatz, Miller and 80 other breweries made suds here. Today, only Miller and a few microbreweries remain.

◉ Sights & Activities

Lake Michigan sits to the east of the city, and is rimmed by parkland. The Riverwalk path runs along both sides of the Milwaukee River downtown.

Harley-Davidson Museum   MUSEUM

(☑ 877-436-8738; www.h-dmuseum.com; 400 W Canal St; adult/child $18/10; ◔ 9am-6pm Fri-Wed, to 8pm Thu May-Oct, reduced hours Nov-Apr) Hundreds of motorcycles show the styles through the decades, including the flashy rides of Elvis and Evel Knievel. You can sit in the saddle of various bikes (on the bottom floor, behind the Design Lab), as well

---

TWO-WHEELING WISCONSIN

Wisconsin has converted an impressive number of abandoned railroad lines into paved, bike-only paths. They go up hills, through old tunnels, over bridges and alongside pastures. Wherever you are in the state, there's likely a sweet ride nearby; check the Travel Wisconsin Bike Path Directory (www.travelwisconsin.com/things-to-do/outdoor-fun/biking/traffic-free-paved). The 400 State Trail (www.400statetrail.org) and Elroy-Sparta Trail (www.elroy-sparta-trail.com) top the list.

Bike rentals are available in gateway towns, and you can buy trail passes (per day/year $4/20) at area businesses or trailhead drop-boxes.

---

as get a mini lesson on how to ride (by the front entrance). Even nonbikers will enjoy the place.

It all started in 1903, when Milwaukee schoolmates William Harley and Arthur Davidson built and sold their first motorcycle. A century later the big bikes are a symbol of American manufacturing pride. The museum is located in a sprawling industrial building just south of downtown.

Harley-Davidson Plant   TOUR

(☑ 877-883-1450; www.harley-davidson.com/experience; W156 N9000 Pilgrim Rd; 30min tours free; ◔ 9am-2pm Mon) Hog-heads can get a fix at the plant where engines are built, in suburban Menomonee Falls. In addition to Monday's free tour, longer tours take place on Wednesday, Thursday and Friday, but only as part of a package deal you buy from the museum (per person $32, including tour, museum admission, and transport between the two venues).

Milwaukee Art Museum   MUSEUM

(☑ 414-224-3200; www.mam.org; 700 N Art Museum Dr; adult/child $15/12; ◔ 10am-5pm Tue, Wed & Fri-Sun, to 8pm Thu Sep-May) Even those who aren't usually museum-goers will be struck by this lakeside museum, which features a stunning winglike addition by Santiago Calatrava. It soars open and closed every day at 10am, noon and at closing time, which is wild to see. There are fabulous folk and outsider art galleries, and a sizeable collection of Georgia O'Keeffe paintings.

Miller Brewing Company   BREWERY

(☑ 414-931-2337; www.millercoors.com; 4251 W State St; ◔ 10:30am-3:30pm Mon-Sat, to 4:30pm summer) FREE Pabst and Schlitz have moved on, but Miller preserves Milwaukee's beer legacy. Join the legions of drinkers lined up for the free tours. Though the mass-produced beer may not be your favorite, the factory impresses with its sheer scale: you'll visit the packaging plant where 2000 cans are filled each minute, and the warehouse where a half-million cases await shipment. And then there's the generous tasting session at the tour's end, where you can down three full-size samples. Don't forget your ID.

Lakefront Brewery   BREWERY

(☑ 414-372-8800; www.lakefrontbrewery.com; 1872 N Commerce St; 1hr tours $7; ◔ 9am-4:30pm Mon-Thu, 9am-9pm Fri, 11am-4:30pm Sat, noon-4:30pm Sun) Well-loved Lakefront Brewery, across the river from Brady St, has afternoon tours, but the swellest time to visit is on Friday nights when there's a fish fry, 16 beers to try and a polka band letting loose. Tour times vary throughout the week, but there's usually at least a 2pm and 3pm walkthrough.

Discovery World at Pier Wisconsin MUSEUM
(☑414-765-9966; www.discoveryworld.org; 500 N Harbor Dr; adult/child $17/13; ☺9am-4pm Tue-Fri, 10am-5pm Sat & Sun; ☻) The city's lakefront science and technology museum is primarily a kid-pleaser, with freshwater and saltwater aquariums (where you can touch sharks and sturgeon) and a dockside, triple-masted Great Lakes schooner to climb aboard ($2 extra). Adults will appreciate the Les Paul exhibit, showcasing the Wisconsin native's pioneering guitars and sound equipment.

Lakefront Park PARK
The parkland edging Lake Michigan is prime for walking, cycling and in-line skating. Also here is Bradford Beach, which is good for swimming and lounging.

★ Festivals & Events

Summerfest MUSIC
(www.summerfest.com; day pass $17; ☺late Jun–early Jul) It's dubbed 'the world's largest music festival,' and indeed hundreds of rock, blues, jazz, country and alternative bands swarm its 10 stages over 11 days. The scene totally rocks; it is held at downtown's lakefront festival grounds.

Other popular parties, held downtown during various summer weekends, include **PrideFest** (www.pridefest.com; ☺mid-Jun), **Polish Fest** (www.polishfest.org; ☺late Jun), **German Fest** (www.germanfest.com; ☺late Jul) and **Irish Fest** (www.irishfest.com; ☺mid-Aug).

⌨ Sleeping

Rates in this section are for summer, the peak season, when you should book in advance. Tax (15.1%) is not included. For cheap chain lodging, try Howell Ave, south near the airport.

County Clare Irish Inn INN $$
(☑414-272-5273; www.countyclare-inn.com; 1234 N Astor St; r incl breakfast $129-179; P☀☎) A winner near the lakefront. Rooms have that snug Irish-cottage feel, with four-poster beds, white wainscot walls and whirlpool baths. There's free parking and an on-site Guinness-pouring pub, of course.

THE BRONZE FONZ

Rumor has it the Bronze Fonz (east side of Riverwalk), just south of Wells St downtown, is the most photographed sight in Milwaukee. The Fonz, aka Arthur Fonzarelli, was a character from the 1970s TV show *Happy Days*, which was set in the city. What do you think – do the blue pants get an 'Aaay' or 'Whoa!'?

Aloft HOTEL $$
(☑414-226-0122; www.aloftmilwaukeedowntown. com; 1230 Old World 3rd St; r $129-179; P☀☎) The chain's Milwaukee property has the usual compact, industrial-looking tone. It's inland near Old World 3rd St and Water St's bar action (thus a bit noisy). Parking costs $23.

Brewhouse Inn & Suites HOTEL $$$
(☑414-810-3350; www.brewhousesuites.com; 1215 N 10th St; r incl breakfast $189-229; ☀@☎) This 90-room hotel opened in 2013 in the exquisitely renovated old Pabst Brewery complex. Each of the large chambers has steampunk decor, a kitchenette and free wi-fi. It's at downtown's far west edge, about a half-mile walk from sausagey Old World 3rd St and a good 2 miles from the festival grounds. Parking costs $26.

Iron Horse Hotel HOTEL $$$
(☑888-543-4766; www.theironhorsehotel.com; 500 W Florida St; r $189-259; P☀☎) This boutique hotel near the Harley museum is geared toward motorcycle enthusiasts, with covered parking for bikes. Most of the loft-style rooms retain the post-and-beam, exposed-brick interior of what was once a bedding factory. Parking costs $25.

✗ Eating

Good places to scope for eats include Germanic Old World 3rd St downtown; hip, multi-ethnic Brady St by its intersection with N Farwell Ave; and the gastropub-filled Third Ward, anchored along N Milwaukee St south of I-94.

Milwaukee Public Market MARKET $
(www.milwaukeepublicmarket.org; 400 N Water St; ☺10am-8pm Mon-Fri, 8am-7pm Sat, 10am-6pm Sun; ☎) Located in the Third Ward, it stocks mostly prepared foods – cheese, chocolate, beer, tacos, frozen custard. Take them upstairs where there are tables, free wi-fi and $1 used books.

Leon's
ICE CREAM **$**

(www.leonsfrozencustard.us; 3131 S 27th St; items $1.30-4; ⊙11am-midnight) This 1950s-era neon-lit drive-in specializes in frozen custard, a local concoction that's like ice cream but smoother and richer. Cash only.

★ Comet Cafe
AMERICAN **$$**

(www.thecometcafe.com; 1947 N Farwell Ave; mains $8-12; ⊙10am-10pm Mon-Fri, from 9am Sat & Sun; 🖉) Students, young families, older couples and bearded, tattooed types pile in to the rock-and-roll Comet for gravy-smothered meatloaf, mac 'n' cheese, vegan gyros and hangover brunch dishes. It's a craft-beer-pouring bar on one side, and retro-boothed diner on the other. Be sure to try one of the giant cupcakes for dessert.

Distil
AMERICAN **$$**

(🖉414-220-9411; www.distilmilwaukee.com; 722 N Milwaukee St; mains $10-20; ⊙from 5pm Mon-Sat) It's all about artisanal fare at dark, coppery Distil. The menu focuses on cheese and charcuterie (burgers, too). Heck, the beef comes from the owner's cow. Mixologists stir up Corpse Revivers and Sidecars to accompany the food.

🍷 Drinking & Entertainment

Bars

Milwaukee has the second most bars per capita in the country (a hair behind New Orleans). Several pour around N Water and E State Sts downtown and in the Third Ward. Drinkeries stay open to 2am.

Best Place
BAR

(www.bestplacemilwaukee.com; 901 W Juneau Ave; ⊙noon-midnight Thu-Sat, to 6pm Sun) Join the locals knocking back beers and mas-

sive whiskey pours at this small tavern in the former Pabst Brewery headquarters. A fireplace warms the cozy, dark-wood room; original murals depicting Pabst's history adorn the walls. Staff give daily tours ($8, including a 16oz Pabst or Schlitz tap brew) that explore the building.

Uber Tap Room
BAR

(www.ubertaproom.com; 1048 N Old 3rd St; ⊙11am-8pm Sun-Wed, to 10pm Thu, to 11pm Fri & Sat) It's touristy, in the thick of Old World 3rd St and attached to the Wisconsin Cheese Mart, but it's a great place to sample local fare. Thirty Wisconsin beers flow from the taps, and cheese from the state's dairy bounty accompanies. Themed plates (spicy cheeses, stinky cheeses etc) cost $8 to $12.

Palm Tavern
BAR

(2989 S Kinnickinnic Ave; ⊙from 5pm Mon-Sat, from 7pm Sun) Located in the fresh southside neighborhood of Bay View, this warm, jazzy little bar has a mammoth selection of beer (heavy on the Belgians) and single-malt Scotches.

Kochanski's Concertina Beer Hall
BAR

(www.beer-hall.com; 1920 S 37th St; ⊙from 6pm Wed-Fri, from 1pm Sat & Sun; 🖉) Live polka music rules at kitschy Kochanski's, with beers from Schlitz to Polish drafts to Wisconsin craft labels. It's 5 miles southwest of downtown.

Sports

Miller Park
BASEBALL

(www.brewers.com; 1 Brewers Way) The Brewers play baseball at fab Miller Park, which has a retractable roof, real grass and racing sausages. It's located near S 46th St.

Bradley Center
BASKETBALL

(www.nba.com/bucks; 1001 N 4th St) The NBA's Milwaukee Bucks dunk here.

ⓘ Information

The East Side neighborhood near the University of Wisconsin-Milwaukee has several coffee shops with free wi-fi.

Froedtert Hospital (🖉414-805-3000; 9200 W Wisconsin Ave)

Milwaukee Convention & Visitors Bureau (🖉800-554-1448; www.visitmilwaukee.org) Tourist information.

Milwaukee Journal Sentinel (www.jsonline. com) The city's daily newspaper.

On Milwaukee (www.onmilwaukee.com) Traffic and weather updates, plus restaurant and entertainment reviews.

AMERICA'S BOWLING CAPITAL

You're in Milwaukee, so you probably should just do it: bowl. The city once had more than 200 bowling alleys, and many retro lanes still hide in timeworn dives. To get your game on try Landmark Lanes (www.landmarklanes.com; 2220 N Farwell Ave; per game $2.50-3.50; ⊙5pm-1:30am Mon-Thu, noon-1:30am Fri-Sun; 🖉), offering 16 beat-up alleys in the historic 1927 Oriental Theater. An arcade, three bars and butt-cheap beer round out the atmosphere.

Quest (www.quest-online.com) GLBT entertainment magazine.

Shepherd Express (www.expressmilwaukee.com) Free alternative weekly paper.

ℹ Getting There & Around

General Mitchell International Airport (MKE; www.mitchellairport.com) is 8 miles south of downtown. Take public bus 80 ($2.25) or a cab ($30).

The **Lake Express ferry** (☑ 866-914-1010; www.lake-express.com) sails from downtown (the terminal is located a few miles south of the city center) to Muskegon, Michigan, providing easy access to Michigan's beach-lined Gold Coast.

Greyhound (☑ 414-272-2156; 433 W St Paul Ave) runs frequent buses to Chicago (two hours) and Minneapolis (seven hours). **Badger Bus** (☑ 414-276-7490; www.badgerbus.com; 635 N James Lovell St) goes to Madison ($19, two hours). **Megabus** (www.megabus.com/us; 446 N 4th St) runs express to Chicago (two hours) and Minneapolis (six hours), often for lower fares than Greyhound.

Amtrak (☑ 414-271-0840; www.amtrakhiawatha.com; 433 W St Paul Ave) runs the *Hiawatha* train seven times a day to/from Chicago ($24, 1½ hours); catch it downtown (it shares the station with Greyhound) or at the airport.

The **Milwaukee County Transit System** (www.ridemcts.com; fare $2.25) provides the local bus service. Bus 31 goes to Miller Brewery; bus 90 goes to Miller Park.

For taxi service, try phoning **Yellow Cab** (☑ 414-271-1800).

Madison

Madison reaps a lot of kudos: most walkable city, best road-biking city, most vegetarian-friendly, gay-friendly, environmentally friendly and just plain all-round friendliest city in the USA. Ensconced on a narrow isthmus between Mendota and Monona Lakes, it's a pretty combination of small, grassy state capital and liberal, bookish college town. An impressive foodie/locavore scene has been cooking here for years.

◎ Sights & Activities

State St runs from the capitol west to the University of Wisconsin. The pedestrian-only avenue is lined with free-trade coffee shops, parked bicycles and incense-wafting stores selling hacky sacks and flowing Indian skirts.

RACING SAUSAGES

It's common to see strange things after too many stadium beers. But a group of giant sausages sprinting around Miller Park's perimeter – is that for *real*? It is if it's the middle of the 6th inning. That's when the famous 'Racing Sausages' (actually five people in costumes) waddle onto the field to give the fans a thrill. If you don't know your encased meats, that's Brat, Polish, Italian, Hot Dog and Chorizo vying for supremacy.

Chazen Museum of Art   MUSEUM
(www.chazen.wisc.edu; 750 University Ave; ◷ 9am-5pm Tue-Fri, 9am-9pm Thu, 11am-5pm Sat & Sun) **FREE** The university's art museum is huge and fabulous, fresh off an expansion and way beyond the norm for a campus collection. The 3rd floor holds most of the genre-spanning trove: everything from the old Dutch masters to Qing Dynasty porcelein vases, Picasso sculptures and Andy Warhol pop art. Free chamber-music concerts and arthouse films take place on Sundays from September to mid-May.

Monona Terrace   ARCHITECTURE
(www.mononaterrace.com; 1 John Nolen Dr; ◷ 8am-5pm) Frank Lloyd Wright designed the cool, white semicircular structure in 1938, though it wasn't completed until 1997. The one-hour tours ($3) explain why; they're offered daily at 1pm. The building serves as a community center, offering free lunchtime yoga classes and evening concerts; check the events schedule online. The rooftop garden and cafe offer sweeping lake views.

Dane County Farmers Market   MARKET
(www.dcfm.org; Capitol Sq; ◷ 6am-2pm Sat late Apr-early Nov) ✿ On Saturdays, a food bazaar takes over Capitol Sq. It's one of the nation's most expansive markets, famed for its artisanal cheeses and breads. In winter it moves indoors to varying locations.

State Capitol   BUILDING
(☑ 608-266-0382; ◷ 8am-6pm Mon-Fri, to 4pm Sat & Sun) **FREE** The X-shaped capitol is the largest outside Washington, DC, and marks the heart of downtown. Tours are available on the hour most days, or you can go up to the observation deck on your own for a view.

Museum of Contemporary Art MUSEUM
(☑608-257-0158; www.mmoca.org; 227 State St; ⊕noon-5pm Tue-Thu, noon-8pm Fri, 10am-8pm Sat, noon-5pm Sun) **FREE** It's worth popping into the angular glass building to see what's on the walls. Diego Rivera? Claes Oldenburg? Exhibits change every three months or so. The museum connects to the Overture Center for the Arts (www.overturecenter. com; 201 State St), home to jazz, opera, dance and other performing arts.

Arboretum GARDENS
(☑608-263-7888; http://uwarboretum.org; 1207 Seminole Hwy; ⊕7am-10pm) **FREE** The campus' 1260-acre arboretum is dense with lilac.

Machinery Row CYCLING
(☑608-442-5974; www.machineryrowbicycles. com; 601 Williamson St; rental per day $20; ⊕9am-9pm Mon-Fri, 9am-7pm Sat, 10am-7pm Sun) It'd be a shame to leave town without taking advantage of the city's 120 miles of bike trails. Get wheels and maps at this shop, located by various trailheads.

✦✦ Festivals & Events

World's Largest Brat Fest FOOD
(www.bratfest.com; ⊕late May) **FREE** More than 209,000 bratwursts go down the hatch; carnival rides and bands provide the backdrop.

Great Taste of the Midwest Beer Festival BEER
(www.greattaste.org; tickets $50; ⊕early Aug) Tickets sell out fast for this festival where 120 craft brewers pour their elixirs.

🛏 Sleeping

Moderately priced motels can be found off I-90/I-94 (about 6 miles from the town center), off Hwy 12/18 and also along Washington Ave.

HI Madison Hostel HOSTEL $
(☑608-441-0144; www.hiusa.org/madison; 141 S Butler St; dm $25-27, r $57-114; P@⊙) The brightly painted, 33-bed brick house is located on a quiet street a short walk from the State Capitol. Dorms are gender segregated;

WORTH A TRIP

ODDBALL US 12

Unusual sights huddle around US 12, all within an easy northerly day trip from Madison.

Heading west out of town (take University Ave), stop first at the National Mustard Museum (☑800-438-6878; www.mustardmuseum.com; 7477 Hubbard Ave; ⊕10am-5pm) **FREE** in suburban Middleton. Born of one man's ridiculously intense passion, the building houses 5200 mustards and kooky condiment memorabilia. Tongue-in-cheek humor abounds, especially if CMO (chief mustard officer) Barry Levenson is there to give you the shtick.

About 20 miles further on US 12 is the town of Prairie du Sac. It hosts the annual Cow Chip Throw (www.wiscowchip.com; ⊕1st weekend Sep) **FREE**, where 800 competitors fling dried manure patties as far as the eye can see; the record is 248ft.

Seven miles onward is Dr Evermor's Sculpture Park (www.worldofdrevermor.com; ⊕11am-5pm Thu-Mon) **FREE**. The doc welds old pipes, carburetors and other salvaged metal into a hallucinatory world of futuristic birds, dragons and other bizarre structures. The crowning glory is the giant, egg-domed Forevertron, once cited by *Guinness World Records* as the globe's largest scrap-metal sculpture. Finding the park entrance is tricky. Look for the Badger Army Ammunition Plant, and then a small sign leading you into a driveway across the street.

Baraboo, about 45 miles northwest of Madison, was once the winter home of the Ringling Brothers Circus. Circus World Museum (☑608-356-8341; circusworld.wisconsinhistory.org; 550 Water St; adult/child summer $18/8, winter $9/3.50; ⊕9am-6pm summer, reduced hours winter; ☒) preserves a nostalgic collection of wagons, posters and equipment from the touring big-top heyday. In summer, admission includes clowns, animals and acrobats doing the three-ring thing.

Continue north another 12 miles to the Wisconsin Dells (☑800-223-3557; www.wisdells. com; ☒), a megacenter of kitschy diversions, including 21 water parks, water-skiing thrill shows and mini-golf courses. It's a jolting contrast to the natural appeal of the area, with its scenic limestone formations carved by the Wisconsin River. To appreciate the original attraction, take a boat tour or walk the trails at Mirror Lake or Devil's Lake state parks.

FISH FRIES & SUPPER CLUBS

Wisconsin has two dining traditions that you'll likely encounter when visiting the state:

Fish Fry Friday is the hallowed day of the 'fish fry.' This communal meal of beer-battered cod, French fries and coleslaw came about years ago, providing locals with a cheap meal to socialize around and celebrate the workweek's end. The convention is still going strong at many bars and restaurants, including Lakefront Brewery (p582) in Milwaukee.

Supper Club This is a type of time-warped restaurant common in the upper Midwest. Supper clubs started in the 1930s, and most retain a retro vibe. Hallmarks include a woodsy location, a radish- and carrot-laden relish tray on the table, a surf-and-turf menu and a mile-long, unironic cocktail list. See www.wisconsinsupperclub.com for more information. The Old Fashioned (p587) in Madison is a modern take on the venue (it's named after the quintessential brandy-laced supper-club drink).

linens are free. There's a kitchen and common room with DVDs. Parking is $7.

★ **Arbor House** B&B $$
(☑608-238-2981; www.arbor-house.com; 3402 Monroe St; r incl breakfast $135-230; ⊚) Arbor House was a tavern back in the mid-1800s. Now it's a wind-powered, energy-efficient-appliance-using, vegetarian-breakfast-serving B&B. It's located about 3 miles southwest of the State Capitol but is accessible by public transportation. The owners will lend you mountain bikes, too.

University Inn HOTEL $$
(☑800-279-4881, 608-285-8040; www.universityinn.org; 441 N Frances St; r $99-129; P❂＠⊚) The rooms are fine, though flowery-bedspread dowdy; the inn's greatest asset is its handy location right by State St and university action. Rates are highest at weekends.

✗ Eating & Drinking

A global smorgasbord of restaurants peppers State St amid the pizza, sandwich and cheap-beer joints; many places have inviting patios. Cruising Williamson ('Willy') St turns up cafes, dumpling bars and Lao and Thai joints. Bars stay open to 2am. Isthmus (www.thedailypage.com) is the free entertainment paper.

Food Trucks INTERNATIONAL $
(mains $1-8; ☑) Madison's fleet impresses. The more traditional ones, serving barbecue, burritos, southwestern-style fare and Chinese food, ring the Capitol. Trucks ladling out more adventurous dishes – East African, Jamaican, Indonesian, vegan – huddle at the foot of State St by the campus.

★ **The Old Fashioned** AMERICAN $$
(☑608-310-4545; www.theoldfashioned.com; 23 N Pinckney St; mains $8-16; ⊗7:30am-10:30pm Mon & Tue, 7:30am-2am Wed-Fri, 9am-2am Sat, 9am-10pm Sun) With its dark, woodsy decor, the Old Fashioned evokes a supper club, a type of retro eatery that's common in this state. The menu is all Wisconsin specialties, including walleye, cheese soup and sausages. It's hard to choose among the 150 types of state-brewed suds in bottles, so opt for a sampler (four or eight little glasses) from the 30 Wisconsin tap beers. The restaurant also serves $5 breakfast dishes (pancakes, eggs and bacon etc) on weekdays.

Graze AMERICAN $$
(☑608-251-2700; www.grazemadison.com; 1 S Pinckney St; mains $11-21; ⊗7am-10pm Mon-Wed, 7am-11pm Thu-Sat, 9:30am-3pm Sun) ✔ Set in a glassy building with floor-to-ceiling windows and Capitol views, this green, cool-cat gastropub dishes up comfort foods such as fried chicken and waffles, mussels and *frites*, and burgers. Breakfast brings fresh-baked pastries, and lunch piles up fat sandwiches with vodka-battered cheese curds.

Himal Chuli ASIAN $$
(☑608-251-9225; 318 State St; mains $8-15; ⊗11am-9pm Mon-Thu, 11am-10pm Fri & Sat, noon-8pm Sun; ☑) Cheerful and cozy Himal Chuli serves up homemade Nepali fare, including lots of vegetarian dishes.

L'Etoile MODERN AMERICAN $$$
(☑608-251-0500; www.letoile-restaurant.com; 1 S Pinckney St; mains $36-44; ⊗from 5:30pm Mon-Fri, from 5pm Sat) ✔ L'Etoile started doing the farm-to-table thing more than three decades ago. It's still the best in the biz,

offering creative meat, fish and vegetable dishes, all sourced locally and served in a casually elegant room. Reserve in advance. The chef also runs Graze, the lower-priced, sustainably focused eatery that shares the building.

Memorial Union   PUB
(www.union.wisc.edu/venue-muterrace.htm; 800 Langdon St; ⊙ from 7am Mon-Fri, from 8am Sat & Sun; 🐾) The campus Union is Madison's gathering spot. The festive lakeside terrace pours microbrews and hosts free live music and free Monday-night films, while the indoor ice-cream shop scoops hulking cones from the university dairy.

🛍 Shopping

Fromagination   FOOD
(📞608-255-2430; www.fromagination.com; 12 S Carroll St; ⊙10am-6pm Mon-Fri, 8am-5pm Sat, 11am-4pm Sun) The state's best cheese shop specializes in small-batch and hard-to-find local hunks. Browse the basket of 'orphans' by the cash register, where you can buy small quantities for $2 to $5. The shop also sells sandwiches, beer and wine.

ℹ Information

Madison Convention & Visitors Bureau (www.visitmadison.com)

ℹ Getting There & Around

Badger Bus (www.badgerbus.com) uses Memorial Union as its pick-up/drop-off point for trips to Milwaukee ($19, two hours), as does **Megabus** (www.megabus.com/us) for trips to Chicago (four hours) and Minneapolis (4½ hours).

Taliesin & Southern Wisconsin

This part of Wisconsin has some of the prettiest landscapes in the state, particularly the hilly southwest. Architecture fans can be unleashed at Taliesin, the Frank Lloyd Wright ubersight, and Racine, where two of his other works stand. Dairies around here cut a lot of cheese.

Racine

Racine is an unremarkable industrial town 30 miles south of Milwaukee, but it has two key Frank Lloyd Wright sights, both of which offer tours that must be prebooked. The first, the Johnson Wax Company

Administration Building (📞262-260-2154; www.scjohnson.com/visit; 1525 Howe St; ⊙Fri & Sat) 🆓, dates from 1939 and is a magnificent space with tall, flared columns. There are three tour options, ranging from one hour to 3½ hours; departure times vary. The second is the lakeside Wingspread (📞262-681-3353; www.johnsonfdn.org; 33 E Four Mile Rd; ⊙9:30am-2:30pm Tue-Fri) 🆓, the last and largest of Wright's Prairie houses. Tours take 45 minutes.

Green County

This pastoral area holds the nation's greatest concentration of cheesemakers, and Green County Tourism (www.greencounty.org) will introduce you to them. Monroe is a fine place to start sniffing. Follow your nose to Roth Käse (657 2nd St; ⊙9am-6pm Mon-Fri, 10am-5pm Sat & Sun), a store and factory where you can watch cheesemakers in action from the observation deck (weekday mornings only) and delve into the 'bargain bin' for hunks. Bite into a fresh limburger-and-raw-onion sandwich at Baumgartner's (www.baumgartnercheese.com; 1023 16th Ave; sandwiches $4-7; ⊙8am-11pm), an old Swiss tavern on the town square. At night, catch a flick at the local drive-in movie theater, and then climb into bed at Inn Serendipity (📞608-329-7056; www.innserendipity.com; 7843 County Rd P; r incl breakfast $110-125), a two-room, wind-and-solar-powered B&B on a 5-acre organic farm in Browntown, about 10 miles west of Monroe.

For more on local dairy producers and plant tours, pick up, or download, A Traveler's Guide to America's Dairyland (www.eatwisconsincheese.com) map.

Spring Green

Forty miles west of Madison and 3 miles south of the small town of Spring Green, Taliesin was the home of Frank Lloyd Wright for most of his life and is the site of his architectural school. It's now a major pilgrimage destination for fans and followers. The house was built in 1903, the Hillside Home School in 1932, and the visitor center (📞608-588-7900; www.taliesinpreservation.org; Hwy 23; ⊙9am-5:30pm May-Oct) in 1953. A wide range of guided tours ($16 to $80) cover various parts of the complex; reserve in advance for the lengthier ones. The one-hour Hillside Tour ($16) provides a nice introduction to Wright's work.

A few miles south of Taliesin is the House on the Rock (☏608-935-3639; www.thehouseontherock.com; 5754 Hwy 23; adult/child $12.50/7.50; ☉9am-6pm May-Aug, to 5pm Aug–mid-Nov & mid-Mar–May, closed mid-Nov–mid-Mar), one of Wisconsin's busiest attractions. Alex Jordan built the structure atop a rock column in 1959 (some say as an 'up yours' to neighbor Frank Lloyd Wright). He then stuffed the house to mind-blowing proportions with wonderments, including the world's largest carousel, whirring music machines, freaky dolls and crazed folk art. The house is broken into three parts, each with its own tour. Visitors with stamina (and about four hours to kill) can experience the whole shebang for adult/child $28.50/15.50.

Spring Green has a B&B in town and six motels strung along Hwy 14, north of town. Small Usonian Inn (☏877-876-6426; www.usonianinn.com; E 5116 Hwy 14; r $85-135; ❋☎) was designed by a Wright student. Check www.springgreen.com for more options.

Chomp sandwiches or inventive specials like sweet-potato stew at Spring Green General Store (www.springgreengeneralstore.com; 137 S Albany St; mains $5-8; ☉9am-6pm Mon-Fri, 8am-6pm Sat, 8am-4pm Sun).

The American Players Theatre (☏608-588-2361; www.americanplayers.org) stages classical productions at an outdoor amphitheater by the Wisconsin River.

Along the Mississippi River

The Mississippi River forms most of Wisconsin's western border, and alongside it run some of the most scenic sections of the Great River Road (www.wigreatriverroad.org) – the designated route that follows Old Man River from Minnesota to the Gulf of Mexico.

From Madison, head west on US 18. You'll hit the River Rd (aka Hwy 35) at Prairie du Chien. North of town, the hilly riverside wends through the scene of the final battle in the bloody Black Hawk War. Historic markers tell part of the story, which finished at the Battle of Bad Ax when Native American men, women and children were massacred trying to flee across the Mississippi.

At Genoa, Hwy 56 leads inland for 20 miles to the trout-fishing mecca of Viroqua (www.viroquatourism.com), a pretty little town surrounded by organic farms and distinctive round barns. Pop into Viroqua Food Cooperative (www.viroquafood.coop; 609 Main

St; ☉7am-9pm) to meet farmers and munch their wares.

Back riverside and 18 miles upstream, La Crosse (www.explorelacrosse.com) has a historic center with restaurants and pubs. Grandad Bluff offers grand views of the river. It's east of town along Main St (which becomes Bliss Rd); follow Bliss Rd up the hill and then turn right on Grandad Bluff Rd. The World's Largest Six-Pack (3rd St S) is also in town. The 'cans' are actually storage tanks for City Brewery and hold enough beer to provide one person with a six-pack a day for 3351 years (or so the sign says).

Door County & Eastern Wisconsin

Rocky, lighthouse-dotted Door County draws crowds in summer, while Green Bay draws crazed football fans in the freakin' freezing winter.

Green Bay

Green Bay (www.greenbay.com) is a modest industrial town best known as the fabled 'frozen tundra' where the Green Bay Packers win Super Bowls. The franchise is unique as the only community-owned nonprofit team in the NFL; perhaps pride in ownership is what makes the fans so die-hard (and also makes them wear foam-rubber cheese wedges on their heads).

While tickets are nearly impossible to obtain, you can always get into the spirit by joining a pre-game tailgate party. The generous flow of alcohol has led to Green Bay's reputation as a 'drinking town with a football problem.' On nongame days, visit the Green Bay Packer Hall of Fame (☏920-569-7512; www.lambeaufield.com; adult/child $10/5; ☉9am-6pm Mon-Sat, 10am-5pm Sun) at Lambeau Field, which is indeed packed with memorabilia and movies that'll intrigue any pigskin fan.

The National Railroad Museum (☏920-437-7623; www.nationalrrmuseum.org; 2285 S Broadway; adult/child $9/6.50; ☉9am-5pm Mon-Sat, 11am-5pm Sun, closed Mon Jan-Mar) features some of the biggest locomotives ever to haul freight into Green Bay's vast yards; train rides ($2) are offered in summer.

Bare-bones Bay Motel (☏920-494-3441; www.baymotelgreenbay.com; 1301 S Military Ave; r $52-75; ☎) is located a mile from Lambeau Field. Hinterland (☏920-438-8050;

www.hinterlandbeer.com; 313 Dousman St; ⊗from 4pm Mon-Sat) gastropub brings a touch of rustic swankiness to beer drinkers.

Door County

With its rocky coastline, picturesque light-houses, cherry orchards and small 19th-century villages, you have to admit that Door County is pretty damn lovely. The area spreads across a narrow peninsula jutting 75 miles into Lake Michigan, and visitors usually loop around on the county's two highways. Hwy 57 runs beside Lake Michigan and goes through Jacksonport and Baileys Harbor; this is known as the more scenic 'quiet side.' Hwy 42 borders Green Bay and passes through (from south to north) Egg Harbor, Fish Creek, Ephraim and Sister Bay; this side is more action oriented. Only about half the businesses stay open from November to April.

◉ Sights & Activities

Parkland blankets the county. Bayside **Peninsula State Park** is the largest, with bluffside hiking and biking trails and Nicolet Beach for swimming, kayaking and sailing (equipment rentals available on site). In winter, cross-country skiers and snow-shoers take over the trails. On the lake side, secluded **Newport State Park** offers trails, backcountry camping and solitude. **Whitefish Dunes State Park** has sandscapes and

---

WORTH A TRIP

WASHINGTON ISLAND & ROCK ISLAND

From Door County's tip near Gills Rock, daily **ferries** (☑920-847-2546; www.wisferry.com; Northport Pier) go every half hour to **Washington Island** (round-trip adult/child/bike/car $13/7/4/26), which has 700 Scandinavian descendants, a couple of museums, beaches, bike rentals and carefree roads for cycling. Accommodations and camping are available. More remote is lovely **Rock Island**, a state park with no cars or bikes at all. It's a wonderful place for hiking, swimming and camping. Get there via the **Karfi ferry** (www.wisferry.com), which departs Jackson Harbor on Washington Island (round-trip adult/child $11/5).

---

a wide beach (beware of riptides). Adjacent **Cave Point Park** is known for its sea caves and kayaking.

Bay Shore Outfitters OUTDOORS
(☑920-854-9220; www.kayakdoorcounty.com; Sister Bay) Rents kayaks, stand-up paddleboards and winter gear and offers tours from locations in Sister Bay and Ephraim.

Nor Door Sport & Cyclery OUTDOORS
(☑920-868-2275; www.nordoorsports.com; Fish Creek) Nor Door rents bikes and snow shoes near the entrance to Peninsula State Park.

🛏 Sleeping & Eating

The bay side has the most lodgings. Prices listed are for July and August, the peak season; many places have minimum-stay requirements. Local restaurants often host a 'fish boil,' a regional specialty started by Scandinavian lumberjacks, in which whitefish, potatoes and onions are cooked in a fiery cauldron. Finish with Door's famous cherry pie.

Julie's Park Cafe and Motel MOTEL $
(☑920-868-2999; www.juliesmotel.com; Fish Creek; r $85-106; ❋⑦) A great low-cost option located beside Peninsula State Park.

Peninsula State Park CAMPGROUND $
(☑920-868-3258; Fish Creek; tent & RV sites $15-17) Holds nearly 500 amenity-laden campsites.

Egg Harbor Lodge INN $$
(☑920-868-3115; www.eggharborlodge.com; Egg Harbor; r $160-200; ❋⑦⛢) All rooms have a water view and free bike use.

Village Cafe AMERICAN $
(☑920-868-3342; www.villagecafe-doorcounty.com; Egg Harbor; mains $7-10; ⊗7am-8pm; 🖪) Delicious all-day breakfast dishes, plus sandwiches and burgers.

Wild Tomato PIZZERIA $$
(☑920-868-3095; www.wildtomatopizza.com; Fish Creek; mains $8-15; ⊗11am-10pm) Join the crowds indoors and out munching pizzas from the stone, wood-fired ovens. A lengthy list of craft beers help wash it down. It's extremely gluten-free friendly.

❶ Information

Door County Visitors Bureau (☑800-527-3529; www.doorcounty.com) Special-interest brochures on art galleries, cycling and lighthouses.

Apostle Islands & Northern Wisconsin

The north is a thinly populated region of forests and lakes, where folks paddle and fish in summer, and ski and snowmobile in winter. The windswept Apostle Islands steal the show.

Northwoods & Lakelands

Nicolet National Forest is a vast wooded district ideal for outdoor activities. The simple crossroads of Langlade is a center for white-water river adventures. Bear Paw Resort (☑715-882-3502; www.bearpawoutdoors.com; cabins $72-85; ☎) rents mountain bikes and kayaks, and provides full-day paddling lessons that include a trip on the river (per person $99). It also provides cozy cabins where you can dry off, get warm and celebrate your accomplishments in the on-site pub.

North on Hwy 13, folk artist and retired lumberjack Fred Smith's Concrete Park (www.friendsoffredsmith.org; ☉sunrise-sunset) FREE in Phillips is extraordinary, with 200-plus whimsical life-size sculptures.

West on Hwy 70, Chequamegon National Forest offers exceptional mountain biking with 300 miles of off-road trails. The Chequamegon Area Mountain Bike Association (www.cambatrails.org) has trail maps and bike rental information. The season culminates in mid-September with the Chequamegon Fat Tire Festival (www.cheqfattire.com), when 1700 strong-legged men and women pedal 40 grueling miles through the woods. The town of Hayward (www.haywardareachamber.com) makes a good base.

Apostle Islands

The 21 rugged Apostle Islands, floating in Lake Superior and freckling Wisconsin's northern tip, are a state highlight. Jump off from Bayfield (www.bayfield.org), a humming resort town with hilly streets, Victorian-era buildings, apple orchards and nary a fast-food restaurant in sight.

The Apostle Islands National Lakeshore visitors center (☑715-779-3397; www.nps.gov/apis; 410 Washington Ave; ☉8am-4:30pm daily Jun-Sep, Mon-Fri Oct-May) has camping permits (per night $10) and paddling and hiking information. The forested islands have no facilities, and walking is the only way to get around.

SCENIC DRIVE: HIGHWAY 13

After departing Bayfield, Hwy 13 takes a fine route around the Lake Superior shore, past the Ojibwa community of Red Cliff and the Apostle Islands' mainland segment, which has a beach. Tiny Cornucopia, looking every bit like a seaside village, has great sunsets. The road runs on through a timeless countryside of forest and farm, reaching US 2 for the final miles back to civilization at Superior.

Various companies offer seasonal boat trips around the islands, and kayaking is very popular. Try Living Adventure (☑715-779-9503; www.livingadventure.com; Hwy 13; half-/full-day tour $59/99; ☉Jun-Sep) for a guided paddle through arches and sea caves; beginners are welcome. If you prefer a motor to power your explorations, climb aboard a vessel with Apostle Islands Cruises (☑715-779-3925; www.apostleisland.com; ☉mid-May–mid-Oct). The 'grand tour' departs at 10am from Bayfield's City Dock for a three-hour narrated trip past sea caves and lighthouses (adult/child $40/24). A glass-bottom boat goes out to view shipwrecks at 2pm.

Inhabited Madeline Island (www.madelineisland.com), a fine day trip, is reached by a 20-minute ferry (☑715-747-2051; www.madferry.com) from Bayfield (round-trip adult/child/bicycle/car $13/7/7/24). Its walkable village of La Pointe has some mid-priced places to stay, and restaurants. Bus tours are available, and you can rent bikes and mopeds – everything is near the ferry dock. Big Bay State Park (☑715-747-6425; tent & RV sites $15-17, vehicle $10) has a beach and trails.

Back in Bayfield, there are loads of B&Bs and inns, but reserve ahead in summer; see www.bayfield.org for options. Most rooms at no-frills Seagull Bay Motel (☑715-779-5558; www.seagullbay.com; 325 S 7th St; r $75-105; ☎) have decks; ask for a lake view. Going upscale, Pinehurst Inn (☑877-499-7651; www.pinehurstinn.com; 83645 Hwy 13; r incl breakfast $139-229; ☎) is a carbon-neutral, solar-heated, eight-room B&B.

Ecoconscious Big Water Cafe (www.bigwatercoffee.com; 117 Rittenhouse Ave; mains $5-10; ☉6:30am-7pm summer, to 4pm winter) serves sandwiches, local farmstead cheeses and area microbrews. Kitschy, flamingo-themed

Maggie's (☎715-779-5641; www.maggies-bayfield.com; 257 Manypenny Ave; mains $7-16; ⊙11:30am-9pm Sun-Thu, to 10pm Fri & Sat) is the place to sample local lake trout and whitefish; there are pizza and burgers too.

The **Big Top Chautauqua** (☎888-244-8368; www.bigtop.org) is a major regional summer event that includes big-name concerts and musical theater.

MINNESOTA

Is Minnesota really the land of 10,000 lakes, as it's so often advertised? You betcha. Actually, in typically modest style, the state has undermarketed itself – there are 11,842 lakes. Which is great news for travelers. Intrepid outdoorsfolk can wet their paddles in the Boundary Waters, where nighttime brings a blanket of stars and the lullaby of wolf howls. Those wanting to get further off the beaten path can journey to Voyageurs National Park, where there's more water than roadway. If that all seems too far-flung, stick to the Twin Cities of Minneapolis and

---

MINNESOTA FACTS

Nicknames North Star State, Gopher State

Population 5.4 million

Area 86,940 sq miles

Capital city St Paul (population 291,000)

Other cities Minneapolis (population 393,000)

Sales tax 6.88%

Birthplace of Author F Scott Fitzgerald (1896–1940), songwriter Bob Dylan (b 1941), filmmakers Joel Coen (b 1954) and Ethan Coen (b 1957)

Home of Lumberjack legend Paul Bunyan, Spam, walleye fish, Hmong and Somali immigrants

Politics Leans Democratic

Famous for Niceness, funny accents, snowy weather, 10,000 lakes

Official muffin Blueberry

Driving distances Minneapolis to Duluth 153 miles, Minneapolis to Boundary Waters 245 miles

---

St Paul, where you can't swing a moose without hitting something cool or cultural. And for those looking for middle ground – a cross between the big city and big woods – the dramatic, freighter-filled port of Duluth beckons.

ℹ Information

Minnesota Highway Conditions (☎511; www.511mn.org)

Minnesota Office of Tourism (☎888-868-7476; www.exploreminnesota.com)

Minnesota State Park Information (☎888-646-6367; www.dnr.state.mn.us) Park entry requires a vehicle permit (per day/year $5/25). Campsites cost $12 to $28; reservations (☎866-857-2757; www.stayatmnparks.com; fee $8.50) accepted.

Minneapolis

Minneapolis is the biggest and artiest town on the prairie, with all the trimmings of progressive prosperity – swank art museums, rowdy rock clubs, organic and ethnic eateries and edgy theaters. It's always happenin', even in winter. But there's no attitude to go along with the abundance. It's the kind of place where homeless people are treated kindly at coffee shops, where the buses are kept immaculately clean, and where public workers tell everyone to 'Have a nice day' come rain or shine (or snow). The city is 'Minnesota Nice' in action.

History

Timber was the city's first boom industry, and water-powered sawmills rose along the Mississippi River in the mid-1800s. Wheat from the prairies also needed to be processed, so flour mills churned into the next big business. The population boomed in the late 19th century with mass immigration, especially from Scandinavia and Germany. Today Minneapolis' Nordic heritage is evident, whereas twin city St Paul is more German and Irish-Catholic.

◎ Sights & Activities

The Mississippi River flows northeast of downtown. Despite the name, Uptown is actually southwest of downtown, with Hennepin Ave as its main axis. Minneapolis' twin city, St Paul, is 10 miles east.

Most attractions are closed Monday; many stay open late on Thursday.

Downtown & Loring Park

Nicollet Mall STREET
Nicollet Mall is the pedestrian-friendly portion of Nicollet Ave in the heart of downtown, and is dense with stores, bars and restaurants. It's perhaps most famous as the spot where Mary Tyler Moore of '70s TV fame threw her hat into the air during the show's opening sequence. A cheesy MTM statue (7th St S & Nicollet Mall) depicts our girl doing just that. A farmers market (www.mplsfarmersmarket.com; ⊘6am-6pm) takes over the mall on Thursdays from May to November.

★Minneapolis Sculpture Garden GARDENS
(726 Vineland Pl; ⊘6am-midnight) FREE The 11-acre garden, studded with contemporary works such as the oft-photographed *Spoonbridge & Cherry* by Claes Oldenburg, sits beside the Walker Art Center. The Cowles Conservatory, abloom with exotic hothouse flowers, is also on the grounds. The garden connects to attractive Loring Park by a sculptural pedestrian bridge over I-94.

★Walker Art Center MUSEUM
(⌨612-375-7622; www.walkerart.org; 725 Vineland Pl; adult/child $12/free, Thu evening & 1st Sat of month admission free; ⊘11am-5pm Tue, Wed & Fri-Sun, to 9pm Thu) The first-class center has a strong permanent collection of 20th-century art and photography, including big-name US painters and great US pop art.

Riverfront District

At the north edge of downtown at the foot of Portland Ave is the St Anthony Falls Heritage Trail, a recommended 2-mile path that provides both interesting history (placards dot the route) and the city's best access to the banks of the Mississippi River. View the cascading St Anthony Falls from the car-free Stone Arch Bridge. On the north side of the river, Main St SE has a stretch of redeveloped buildings housing restaurants and bars. From here you can walk down to Water Power Park and feel the river's frothy spray. Pick up a free trail map at the Mill City Museum.

Definitely head next door to the cobalt-blue Guthrie Theater (p598) and make your way up to its Endless Bridge, a cantilevered walkway overlooking the river. You don't need a theater ticket, as it's intended as a public space – though see a show if you can as the Guthrie is one of the Mid-

west's finest companies. Gold Medal Park spirals next door.

Mill City Museum MUSEUM
(⌨612-341-7555; www.millcitymuseum.org; 704 2nd St S; adult/child $11/6; ⊘10am-5pm Tue-Sat, noon-5pm Sun, open daily Jul & Aug) The building is indeed a former mill, and highlights include a ride inside an eight-story grain elevator (the 'Flour Tower'), Betty Crocker exhibits and a baking lab. It's not terribly exciting unless you're really into milling history. The Mill City Farmer's Market (www.millcityfarmersmarket.org; ⊘8am-1pm Sat mid-May–late Oct) takes place in the museum's attached train shed; cooking demos fire up at 10am.

Northeast

Once a working-class Eastern European neighborhood, Northeast (so named because of its position to the river) is where urbanites and artists now work and play. They appreciate the dive bars pouring microbrews along with Pabst, and the boutiques selling ecogifts next to companies grinding sausage. Hundreds of craftsfolk and galleries fill historic industrial buildings. They fling open their doors the first Thursday of each month when the Northeast Minneapolis Arts Association (www.nemaa.org) sponsors a gallery walk. Heady streets include 4th St NE and 13th Ave NE.

University Area

The University of Minnesota, by the river southeast of Minneapolis' center, is one of the USA's largest campuses, with over 50,000 students. Most of the campus is in the East Bank neighborhood. Dinkytown, based at 14th Ave SE and 4th St SE, is dense with student cafes and bookshops. A small part of the university is on the West Bank of the Mississippi River, near the intersection of 4th St S and Riverside Ave. This area has a few restaurants, some student hang-outs and a big Somali community.

★Weisman Art Museum MUSEUM
(⌨612-625-9494; www.weisman.umn.edu; 333 E River Rd; ⊘10am-5pm Tue-Fri, to 8pm Wed, 11am-5pm Sat & Sun) FREE The Weisman, which occupies a swooping silver structure by architect Frank Gehry, is a uni (and city) highlight. It recently reopened with double the space and five new, airy galleries for American art, ceramics and works on paper.

Minneapolis

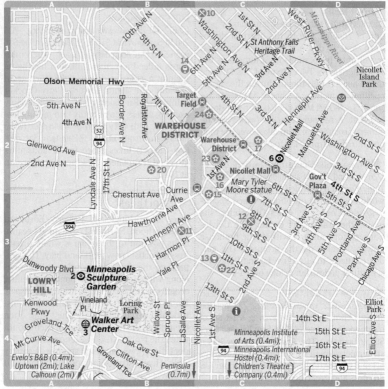

Minneapolis

Uptown, Lyn-Lake & Whittier

These three neighborhoods are south of downtown.

Uptown, based around the intersection of Hennepin Ave and Lake St, is a punk-yuppie collision of shops and restaurants that stays lively until late. Lyn-Lake abuts Uptown to the east and sports a similar urban-cool vibe; it's centered on Lyndale and Lake Sts. (Get the name?)

Uptown is a convenient jump-off point to the 'Chain of Lakes' – Lake Calhoun, Lake of the Isles, Lake Harriet, Cedar Lake and Brownie Lake. Paved cycling paths (which double as cross-country ski trails in winter) meander around the five lakes, where you can go boating in summer or ice skating in winter.

Lake Calhoun sits at the foot of Lake St, where there are amenities galore. Further around Lake Calhoun, Thomas Beach is popular for swimming. Cedar Lake's freewheeling Hidden Beach (aka East Cedar Beach) used to bring out the nudists, though it's mostly clothed folks lolling about these days.

Minneapolis Institute of Arts　MUSEUM
(☑612-870-3131; www.artsmia.org; 2400 3rd Ave S; ⊙10am-5pm Tue-Sat, 10am-9pm Thu, 11am-5pm Sun) FREE This museum is a huge treasure trove housing a veritable history of art. The modern and contemporary collections astonish, while the Prairie School and Asian galleries are also highlights. Brochures at the front desk can help you winnow it down to the must-sees if you're short on time. The museum is 1 mile due south of the convention center via 3rd Ave S.

Calhoun Rental　CYCLING
(☑612-827-8231;　www.calhounbikerental.com; 1622 W Lake St; per half/full day $25/35; ⊙10am-7pm Mon-Fri, 9am-8pm Sat, 10am-8pm Sun Apr-Oct) In Uptown, a couple blocks west of Lake

MINNEAPOLIS FOR CHILDREN

Note that many of the other top sights for wee ones are in St Paul, at the Mall of America and Fort Snelling.

Minnesota Zoo (☑952-431-9500; www.mnzoo.org; 13000 Zoo Blvd; adult/child $18/12; ☺9am-6pm summer, to 4pm winter; 🚼) You'll have to travel a way to get to the respected zoo in suburban Apple Valley, which is 20 miles south of town. It has naturalistic habitats for its 400-plus species, with an emphasis on cold-climate creatures. Parking is $7.

Valleyfair (☑952-445-7600; www.valleyfair.com; 1 Valleyfair Dr; adult/child $44/30; ☺from 10am daily mid-May–Aug, Sat & Sun only Sep & Oct, closing times vary; 🚼) If the rides at the Mall of America aren't enough, drive out to this full-scale amusement park 25 miles southwest in Shakopee. The animatronic dinosaur park ($5 extra) is a big hit. Save money by booking tickets online. Parking costs $12.

Children's Theatre Company (☑612-874-0400; www.childrenstheatre.org; 2400 3rd Ave S; 🚼) So good it won a Tony award for 'outstanding regional theater.'

Calhoun, this shop rents bikes (helmet, lock and bike map included); credit card and driver's license are required. It also offers two- to four-hour cycling tours ($39 to $49) around the water Friday through Sunday; reserve in advance.

Lake Calhoun Kiosk WATER SPORTS
(☑612-823-5765; base of Lake St; per hr $11-18; ☺10am-8pm daily late May-Aug, Sat & Sun only Sep & Oct) The kiosk, at the foot of Lake St, rents canoes, kayaks, bikes and pedal boats. It's a busy spot as there's also a patio restaurant and sailing school here.

🎉 Festivals & Events

Art-A-Whirl MUSIC
(www.nemaa.org; ☺mid-May) The Northeast's weekend-long, rock-and-roll gallery crawl heralds the arrival of spring.

Minneapolis Aquatennial CULTURAL
(www.aquatennial.com; ☺mid-Jul) Ten days celebrating the ubiquitous lakes via parades, beach bashes and fireworks.

Holidazzle CULTURAL
(www.holidazzle.com; ☺Dec) Parades, lights and lots of good cheer downtown throughout December.

🛏 Sleeping

B&Bs offer the best value – they have budget prices but are solidly midrange in quality. Tax adds 13.4% to prices.

Wales House B&B $
(☑612-331-3931; www.waleshouse.com; 1115 5th St SE; r incl breakfast $80, without bath $70; P❄🤙) This cheery 10-bedroom B&B often houses

scholars from the nearby University of Minnesota. Curl up with a book on the porch, or lounge by the fireplace. A two-night minimum stay is required.

Evelo's B&B B&B $
(☑612-374-9656; 2301 Bryant Ave S; r without bath incl breakfast $75-95; 🤙) Evelo's three rooms creak and charm in this polished-wood-filled Victorian home. They're close quartered, but the B&B's strategic location between the Walker Art Center and Uptown compensates.

Minneapolis International Hostel HOSTEL $
(☑612-522-5000; www.minneapolishostel.com; 2400 Stevens Ave S; dm $28-34, r from $60; ❄@🤙) A cool old building with antique furniture and wood floors, and the location beside the Minneapolis Institute of Arts is excellent. But it's also not very well tended. The rooms come in a variety of configurations, from a 15-bed male dorm to private rooms with en suite bath.

Aloft HOTEL $$
(☑612-455-8400; www.alofthotels.com/minneapolis; 900 Washington Ave S; r $139-189; P❄@🤙📶) Aloft's compact, efficiently designed, industrial-toned rooms draw a younger clientele. The clubby lobby has board games, a cocktail lounge and 24-hour snacks. There's a tiny pool and decent fitness room. Parking costs $15.

🍽 Eating

Minneapolis has ripened into a rich dining scene known for its many restaurants that use local, sustainable ingredients.

Downtown & Northeast

Nicollet Mall is loaded with eateries.

Hell's Kitchen
AMERICAN $$

(612-332-4700; www.hellskitcheninc.com; 80 9th St S; mains $10-20; 6:30am-10pm Mon-Fri, from 7:30am Sat & Sun;) Descend the stairs to Hell's devilish lair, where spirited waitstaff bring you uniquely Minnesotan foods, like the walleye bacon-lettuce-tomato sandwich, bison burger and lemon-ricotta hotcakes. It morphs from a restaurant into a club with DJs late on weekend nights. Upstairs there's a delicious bakery and coffee shop.

Butcher & the Boar
AMERICAN $$$

(612-238-8887; www.butcherandtheboar.com; 1121 Hennepin Ave; mains $25-32; 5pm-midnight;) The coppery, candlelit room is carnivore nirvana. Get your carving knife ready for wild-boar ham with country butter, rabbit pate with pickled cherries, chicken-fried veal sausage and many more house-crafted meats. Sampler plates are the way to go. The 30 taps flow with regional brews, backed up by a lengthy bourbon list. Reservations essential.

Bar La Grassa
ITALIAN $$$

(612-333-3837; www.barlagrassa.com; 800 Washington Ave N; pasta $12-24, mains $16-35; 5pm-midnight Mon-Thu, to 1am Fri & Sat, to 10pm Sun) Chef Isaac Becker won the 2011 James Beard award for 'best in the midwest,' so expect great things from the small plates menu of fresh pastas, bruschetta and *secondi*.

University Area

Low-priced eateries cluster in the campus area by Washington Ave and Oak St.

Al's Breakfast
BREAKFAST $

(612-331-9991; 413 14th Ave SE; mains $4-8; 6am-1pm Mon-Sat, 9am-1pm Sun) The ultimate hole in the wall: 14 stools at a tiny counter. Whenever a customer comes in, everyone picks up their plates and scoots down to make room for the newcomer. Fruit-full pancakes are the big crowd-pleaser. Cash only.

Uptown, Lyn-Lake & Whittier

Vietnamese, Greek, African and other ethnic restaurants line Nicollet Ave S between Franklin Ave (near the Minneapolis Institute of Arts) and 28th St – the stretch is known as 'Eat Street.' Lake St in Uptown is a rich vein for stylish bars and cafes.

★ Bryant-Lake Bowl
AMERICAN $$

(612-825-3737; www.bryantlakebowl.com; 810 W Lake St; mains $9-14; 8am-12:30am;) A workingman's bowling alley meets epicurean food at the BLB. Biscuit-and-gravy breakfasts, artisanal cheese plates, mock-duck rolls and cornmeal-crusted walleye strips melt in the mouth. A long list of local beers washes it all down. The on-site theater always has something intriguing and odd going on too.

Peninsula
ASIAN $$

(612-871-8282; www.peninsulamalaysiancuisine.com; 2608 Nicollet Ave S; mains $9-15; 11am-10pm Sun-Thu, to 11pm Fri & Sat;) Malaysian dishes – including *achat* (tangy vegetable salad in peanut dressing), red-curry hot pot, spicy crab and fish in banana leaves – rock the palate in this contemporary restaurant.

Drinking

Bars stay open until 2am. Happy hour typically lasts from 3pm to 6pm.

Brit's Pub
PUB

(www.britspub.com; 1110 Nicollet Mall; from 11am) A lawn-bowling green on the roof, plus Brit's sweeping selection of Scotch, port and beer, are sure to unleash skills you never knew you had.

TAP ROOM BOOM

In 2011 Minnesota passed a law that allowed brewers to open tap rooms on site, and since then the concept has exploded throughout the Twin Cities. Excellent ones to try for beer fresh from the tank:

Fulton Beer (www.fultonbeer.com; 414 6th Ave N; ⊘ 3-10pm Wed-Fri, noon-10pm Sat) There's usually a fab pale ale and red ale among the selection that you sip at communal picnic tables in the warehouse. It's a few blocks from the baseball stadium and fills up on game days. Food trucks hang out in front.

Dangerous Man Brewing (www.dangerousmanbrewing.com; 1300 2nd St NE; ⊘ 4-10pm Tue-Thu, 3pm-midnight Fri, noon-midnight Sat) Pours strong, European-style beers. You're welcome to bring in your own food. It's one of many tap rooms colonizing the Northeast neighborhood.

Surly Brewing (www.surlybrewing.com; Malcolm Ave & 5th St SE) One of the biggest brewers, and it's not kidding around: it hired the architects who designed the Guthrie Theater to build a huge brewery and bar in southeast Minneapolis' Prospect Park neighborhood. It's scheduled to open in 2014.

Grumpy's   BAR
(www.grumpys-bar.com/nordeast; 2200 4th St NE; ⊘ from 2pm Mon-Fri, from 11am Sat & Sun) Grumpy's is the Northeast's classic dive, with cheap (but good) beer and an outdoor patio. Sample the specialty 'hot dish' on Tuesdays for $1.

☆ Entertainment

With its large student population and thriving performing-arts scene, Minneapolis has an active nightlife. Check *Vita.MN* and *City Pages* for current goings on.

Live Music

Minneapolis rocks; everyone's in a band, it seems. Acts such as Prince and post-punkers Hüsker Dü and the Replacements cut their teeth here.

First Avenue & 7th St Entry   LIVE MUSIC
(www.first-avenue.com; 701 1st Ave N) This is the bedrock of Minneapolis's music scene, and it still pulls in top bands and big crowds. Check out the exterior stars; they're all bands that have graced the stage.

Nye's Polonaise Room   LIVE MUSIC
(www.nyespolonaise.com; 112 E Hennepin Ave) The World's Most Dangerous Polka Band lets loose Friday and Saturday. It's smashing fun, and enhanced if you find yourself an old-timer to twirl you around the room.

Triple Rock Social Club   LIVE MUSIC
(www.triplerocksocialclub.com; 629 Cedar Ave) Triple Rock is a popular punk-alternative club.

Lee's Liquor Lounge   LIVE MUSIC
(www.leesliquorlounge.com; 101 Glenwood Ave) Rockabilly and country-tinged alt bands twang here.

Theater & Performing Arts

The city hosts a vibrant theater scene. The neon-lit Hennepin Theater District (www.hennepintheatretrust.org) consists of several historic venues on Hennepin Ave between 6th and 10th Sts that host big touring shows.

Guthrie Theater   THEATER
(☏ 612-377-2224; www.guthrietheater.org; 818 2nd St S) This is Minneapolis' top-gun theater troupe, with the jumbo facility to prove it. Unsold 'rush' tickets go on sale 30 minutes before showtime for $15 to $35 (cash only). Download free audio tours from the website for self-guided jaunts around the funky building.

Brave New Workshop Theatre   THEATER
(☏ 612-332-6620; www.bravenewworkshop.com; 824 Hennepin Ave) An established venue for musical comedy, revue and satire.

Orchestra Hall   CLASSICAL
(☏ 612-371-5656; www.minnesotaorchestra.org; 1111 Nicollet Mall) Superb acoustics for concerts by the acclaimed Minnesota Symphony Orchestra.

Sports

Minnesotans love their sports teams. Note that ice hockey happens in St Paul.

Target Field   BASEBALL
(www.minnesotatwins.com; 3rd Ave N btwn 5th &
7th Sts N) The new stadium for the Twins pro
baseball team is notable for its beyond-the-
norm, locally focused food and drink.

Hubert H Humphrey Metrodome   FOOTBALL
(www.vikings.com; 900 5th St S) The Vikings pro
football team passes in the marshmallow-
like 'Dome.

Target Center   BASKETBALL
(www.nba.com/timberwolves; 600 1st Ave N) This
is where the Timberwolves pro basketball
team plays.

❶ Information

City Pages (www.citypages.com) Weekly
entertainment freebie.

**Fairview/University of Minnesota Medical
Center** (☑ 612-273-6402; 2450 Riverside Ave)

**Minneapolis Convention & Visitors Associa-
tion** (www.minneapolis.org) Coupons, maps,
guides and bike-route info online.

Minneapolis Public Library (www.hclib.org;
300 Nicollet Mall; ☺10am-8pm Tue & Thu,
10am-6pm Wed, Fri & Sat, noon-5pm Sun; ☎)
Mod facility with free internet and wi-fi (plus a
great used bookstore).

Pioneer Press (www.twincities.com) St Paul's
daily.

Star Tribune (www.startribune.com) Minneapolis' daily.

Vita.mn (www.vita.mn) The *Star Tribune*'s
weekly entertainment freebie.

❶ Getting There & Around

AIR

The **Minneapolis-St Paul International Airport**
(MSP; www.mspairport.com) is between the
two cities to the south. It's the home of Delta
Airlines, which operates several direct flights to/
from Europe.

The Blue Line light-rail service (regular/
rush-hour fare $1.75/2.25, 25 minutes) is the
cheapest way into Minneapolis. Bus 54 (regular/
rush-hour fare $1.75/2.25, 25 minutes) goes to
St Paul. Taxis cost around $45.

BICYCLE

Minneapolis hovers near the top of rankings for
best bike city in the US. The bicycle-share program **Nice Ride** (www.niceridemn.org; ☺Apr-
Oct) has 1500 bikes in 170 self-serve kiosks
around the Twin Cities. Users pay a subscription
(per day/year $6/65) online or at the kiosk, plus
a small fee per half-hour of use (with the first
half-hour free). Bikes can be returned to any
kiosk. Traditional rentals work better if you're

riding for recreation versus transportation purposes. See the **Minneapolis Bicycle Program**
(www.ci.minneapolis.mn.us/bicycles) for rental
shops and trail maps.

BUS

Greyhound (☑ 612-371-3325; 950 Hawthorne
Ave) runs frequent buses to Milwaukee (seven
hours), Chicago (nine hours) and Duluth (three
hours).

Megabus (www.megabus.com/us) runs
express to Milwaukee (six hours) and Chicago
(eight hours), often for lower fares than Greyhound. It departs from both downtown and the
university; check the website for exact locations.

PUBLIC TRANSPORTATION

Metro Transit (www.metrotransit.org; regular/
rush-hour fare $1.75/2.25) runs the excellent
Blue Line light-rail service between downtown
and the Mall of America. The new Green Line is
slated to begin running in mid-2014, connecting
downtown Minneapolis to downtown St Paul.
Until then, express bus 94 (regular/rush-hour
fare $2.25/3) plies the route between cities; it
departs from 6th St N's south side, just west of
Hennepin Ave. A day pass ($6) is available from
any rail station or bus driver.

TAXI

Call **Yellow Cab** (☑ 612-824-4444).

TRAIN

Amtrak chugs in to the newly restored **Union
Depot** (www.uniondepot.org; 214 E 4th St; ☎) in
St Paul. Trains go daily to Chicago (eight hours)
and Seattle (37 hours).

St Paul

Smaller and quieter than its twin city Minneapolis, St Paul has retained more of a
historic character. Walk through F Scott
Fitzgerald's old stomping grounds, trek the
trails along the mighty Mississippi River, or
slurp some Lao soup.

◉ Sights & Activities

Downtown and Cathedral Hill hold most
of the action. The latter features eccentric
shops, Gilded Age Victorian mansions and, of
course, the hulking church that gives the area
its name. Downtown has the museums. An
insider's tip: there's a shortcut between the
two areas, a footpath that starts on the Hill
House's west side and drops into downtown.

Revitalized **Harriet Island**, running
south off Wabasha St downtown, is a lovely
place to meander; it has a park, river walk,
concert stages and fishing dock.

F Scott Fitzgerald Sights & Summit Ave
STREET

The Great Gatsby author F Scott Fitzgerald is St Paul's most celebrated literary son. The Pullman-style apartment at 481 Laurel Ave is his birthplace. Four blocks away, Fitzgerald lived in the brownstone at 599 Summit Ave when he published *This Side of Paradise*. Both are private residences. From here stroll along Summit Ave toward the cathedral and gape at the Victorian homes rising from the street.

Literature buffs should grab the *Fitzgerald Homes and Haunts* map at the visitor center to see other footprints.

Landmark Center
MUSEUM

(www.landmarkcenter.org; 75 W 5th St; ⊙ 8am-5pm Mon-Fri, 8am-8pm Thu, 10am-5pm Sat, noon-5pm Sun) Downtown's turreted 1902 Landmark Center used to be the federal courthouse, where gangsters such as Alvin 'Creepy' Karpis were tried; plaques by the various rooms show who was brought to justice here. In addition to the city's visitor center, the building also contains a couple of small museums.

On the 2nd floor the Schubert Club Museum (☑651-292-3267; www.schubert.org; ⊙noon-4pm Sun-Fri) has a brilliant collection of old pianos and harpsichords – some tickled by the likes of Brahms and Mendelssohn – as well as old manuscripts and letters from famous composers. The club plays free chamber-music concerts Thursday at noon from October to April. A free wood-turning museum (it's a decorative form of woodworking) is also on the 2nd floor.

Mississippi River Visitors Center
INTERPRETIVE CENTER

(☑651-293-0200; www.nps.gov/miss; ⊙9:30am-5pm Sun-Thu, to 9pm Fri & Sat) FREE The National Park Service visitor center occupies an alcove in the science museum's lobby. Stop by to pick up trail maps and see what sort of free ranger-guided activities are going on. Most take place at 10am on Wednesday, Thursday and Saturday in summer. In winter the center hosts ice-fishing and snowshoeing jaunts.

Science Museum of Minnesota
MUSEUM

(☑651-221-9444; www.smm.org; 120 W Kellogg Blvd; adult/child $13/10; ⊙9:30am-9:30pm, reduced hours in winter) Has the usual hands-on kids' exhibits and Omnimax theater ($8 extra). Adults will be entertained by the wacky quackery of the 4th floor's 'questionable medical devices.'

Cathedral of St Paul
CHURCH

(www.cathedralsaintpaul.org; 239 Selby Ave; ⊙7am-7pm Sun-Fri, to 9pm Sat) Modeled on St Peter's Basilica in Rome, the cathedral presides over the city from its hilltop perch. Tours ($2) are available at 1pm weekdays.

James J Hill House
HISTORIC BUILDING

(☑651-297-2555; www.mnhs.org/hillhouse; 240 Summit Ave; adult/child $9/6; ⊙10am-3:30pm Wed-Sat, from 1pm Sun) Tour the palatial stone mansion of railroad magnate Hill. It's a Gilded Age beauty, with five floors and 22 fireplaces.

St Paul Curling Club
SNOW SPORTS

(www.stpaulcurlingclub.org; 470 Selby Ave; ⊙from 11am Oct-May) For those uninitiated in northern ways, curling is a winter sport that involves sliding a hubcap-sized 'puck' down the ice toward a bull's-eye. The friendly folks here don't mind if you stop in to watch the action. Heck, they might invite you to share a Labatt's from the upstairs bar.

☞ Tours

Down In History Tours
WALKING TOUR

(☑651-292-1220; www.wabashastreetcaves.com; 215 S Wabasha St; 45min tours $6; ⊙5pm Thu, 11am Sat & Sun) Explore St Paul's underground caves, which gangsters once used as a speakeasy. The fun ratchets up on Thursday nights, when a swing band plays in the caverns (admission $7).

✯✯ Festivals & Events

St Paul Winter Carnival
CULTURAL

(www.winter-carnival.com; ⊙late Jan) Ten days of ice sculptures, ice skating and ice fishing.

☷ Sleeping

You'll find a bigger selection of accommodations in Minneapolis.

Covington Inn
B&B $$

(☑651-292-1411; www.covingtoninn.com; 100 Harriet Island Rd; r incl breakfast $150-235; P ✳) This four-room Harriet Island B&B is on a tugboat in the Mississippi River; watch the river traffic glide by while sipping your morning coffee.

Holiday Inn
HOTEL $$

(☑651-225-1515; www.holiday-inn.com/stpaulmn; 175 W 7th St; r $99-169; P ✳ ☎ ☷) The rooms are the usual decent quality you expect from the Holiday Inn chain; the perks are the location adjacent to the RiverCentre (convention center), a small pool and an on-site Irish pub. Parking is $15.

Eating & Drinking

Grand Ave between Dale St and Lexington Pkwy is a worthy browse, with cafes, foodie shops and ethnic eats in close proximity. Selby Ave by the intersection of Western Ave N also holds a quirky line-up.

Mickey's Dining Car　DINER $
(www.mickeysdiningcar.com; 36 W 7th St; mains $4-9; ⊘24hr) Mickey's is a downtown classic, the kind of place where the friendly waitress calls you 'honey' and satisfied regulars line the bar with their coffee cups and newspapers. The food has timeless appeal, too: burgers, malts and apple pie.

Hmongtown Marketplace　ASIAN $
(www.hmongtownmarketplace.com; 217 Como Ave; mains $5-8; ⊘8am-8pm) The nation's largest enclave of Hmong immigrants lives in the Twin Cities, and this market delivers their favorite Vietnamese, Lao and Thai dishes at its humble food court. Find the West Building and head to the back where vendors ladle hot-spiced papaya salad, beef ribs, sticky rice and curry noodle soup. Then stroll the market, where you can fix your dentures or buy a cockatoo or brass gong.

WA Frost & Company　AMERICAN $$$
(☑651-224-5715; www.wafrost.com; 374 Selby Ave; mains $18-28; ⊘11am-1:30pm Mon-Fri, 10:30am-2pm Sat & Sun, 5-10pm daily) Frost's tree-shaded, ivy-covered, twinkling-light patio is right out of a Fitzgerald novel, perfect for a glass of wine, beer or gin. The restaurant locally sources many ingredients for dishes like the artisanal cheese plate, Moroccan-spiced roasted chicken and heirloom bean cassoulet.

Happy Gnome　PUB
(www.thehappygnome.com; 498 Selby Ave; ⊘from 11:30am; ☞) Seventy craft beers flow from the taps, best sipped on the fireplace-warmed outdoor patio. The pub sits across the parking lot from the St Paul Curling Club.

Entertainment

Fitzgerald Theater　THEATER
(☑651-290-1221; www.fitzgeraldtheater.org; 10 E Exchange St) Where Garrison Keillor tapes his radio show *A Prairie Home Companion*.

Ordway Center for Performing Arts　CLASSICAL MUSIC
(☑651-224-4222; www.ordway.org; 345 Washington St) Chamber music and the Minnesota Opera fill the hall here.

Xcel Energy Center　HOCKEY
(www.wild.com; 199 Kellogg Blvd) The Wild pro hockey team skates at Xcel.

Shopping

Common Good Books　BOOKS
(www.commongoodbooks.com; 38 S Snelling Ave; ⊘9am-9pm Mon-Sat, 10am-7pm Sun) Garrison Keillor owns this bright bookstore where statues of literary heroes stand guard over long shelves of tomes. It's west of downtown on the Macalester College campus.

ℹ Information

Visitor center (☑651-292-3225; www.visitsaintpaul.com; 75 W 5th St; ⊘10am-4pm Mon-Sat, from noon Sun) In the Landmark Center; makes a good first stop for maps and DIY walking tour info.

ℹ Getting There & Around

St Paul is served by the same transit systems as Minneapolis. See p599 for details. Union Depot (p599) is the hub for everything: Greyhound buses, city buses, the Green Line light-rail service and Amtrak trains.

Around Minneapolis–St Paul

◉ Sights

Mall of America　MALL, AMUSEMENT PARK
(www.mallofamerica.com; off I-494 at 24th Ave; ⊘10am-9:30pm Mon-Sat, 11am-7pm Sun; ⌘) The Mall of America, located in suburban Bloomington near the airport, is the USA's largest shopping center. Yes, it's just a mall, filled with the usual stores, movie theaters

---

DON'T MISS

BIG BALL O' TWINE

Behold the **World's Largest Ball of Twine** (1st St; admission free; ⊘24hr) **FREE** in Darwin, 62 miles west of Minneapolis on US 12. To be specific, it's the 'Largest Built by One Person' – Francis A Johnson wrapped the 17,400lb whopper on his farm over the course of 29 years. Gawk at it in the town gazebo. Better yet, visit the the **museum** (☑320-693-7544; ⊘by appointment) beside it and buy your own twine ball starter kit in the gift shop.

and eateries. But there's also a wedding chapel inside. And an 18-hole mini-golf course ($952-883-8777; 3rd fl; admission $8). And an amusement park, aka Nickelodeon Universe ($952-883-8600; www.nickelodeonuniverse.com), with 24 rides, including a couple of scream-inducing roller coasters. To walk through will cost you nothing; a one-day, unlimited ride wristband is $30; or you can pay for rides individually ($3 to $6). What's more, the state's largest aquarium, Minnesota Sea Life ($952-883-0202; www.visitsealife.com/minnesota; adult/child $24/16) – where children can touch sharks and stingrays – is in the mall too. Combination passes are available to save dough. The Blue Line light-rail runs to/from downtown Minneapolis. The mall is a 10-minute ride from the airport.

Fort Snelling HISTORIC SITE
($612-726-1171; www.historicfortsnelling.org; cnr Hwys 5 & 55; adult/child $11/6; ⊙10am-5pm Tue-Sat & noon-5pm Sun Jun-Aug, Sat only Sep & Oct; 🔄) East of the mall, Fort Snelling is the state's oldest structure, established in 1820 as a frontier outpost in the remote Northwest Territory. Guides in period dress show restored buildings and reenact pioneer life.

Southern Minnesota

Some of the scenic southeast can be seen on short drives from the Twin Cities. Better is a loop of a few days' duration, following the rivers and stopping in some of the historic towns and state parks.

DON'T MISS

SPAM MUSEUM

Sitting by its lonesome in Austin, near where I-35 and I-90 intersect in southern Minnesota, lies the Spam Museum ($800-588-7726; www.spam.com; 1101 N Main St; ⊙10am-5pm Mon-Sat, from noon Sun; 🔄) FREE, an entire institution devoted to the peculiar meat. It educates about how the blue tins have fed armies, become a Hawaiian food staple and inspired legions of haiku writers. What's more, you can chat up the staff (aka 'spambassadors'), indulge in free samples, and try your hand at canning the sweet pork magic.

Due east of St Paul, on Hwy 36, touristy Stillwater (www.discoverstillwater.com), on the lower St Croix River, is an old logging town with restored 19th-century buildings, river cruises and antique stores. It's also an official 'booktown,' an honor bestowed upon a few small towns worldwide that possess an extraordinary number of antiquarian bookshops. What's more, the town is filled with classy historic B&Bs.

Larger Red Wing, to the south on US 61, is a similar but less interesting restored town, though it does offer its famous Red Wing Shoes – actually more like sturdy boots – and salt-glaze pottery.

The prettiest part of the Mississippi Valley area begins south of here. To drive it and see the best bits, you'll need to flip-flop back and forth between Minnesota and Wisconsin on the Great River Road.

From Red Wing, cross the river on US 63. Before heading south along the water, though, make a cheesy detour. Go north on US 63 in Wisconsin for 12 miles until you hit US 10. Turn right and within a few miles you're in Ellsworth, the 'Cheese Curd Capital.' Pull into Ellsworth Cooperative Creamery ($715-273-4311; www.ellsworthcheesecurds.com; 232 N Wallace St; ⊙8am-6pm Mon-Fri, 9am-5pm Sat & Sun) – curd-maker for A&W and Dairy Queen – and savor squeaky goodness hot off the press (11am is prime time).

Back along the river on Wisconsin Hwy 35, a great stretch of road edges the bluffs beside Maiden Rock, Stockholm and Pepin. Follow your nose to local bakeries and cafes in the area.

Continuing south, cross back over the river to Wabasha in Minnesota, which has a historic downtown and large population of bald eagles that congregate in winter. To learn more, visit the National Eagle Center ($651-565-4989; www.nationaleaglecenter.org; 50 Pembroke Ave; adult/child $8/5; ⊙10am-5pm).

Inland and south, Bluff Country is dotted with limestone bluffs, southeast Minnesota's main geological feature. Lanesboro (www.lanesboro.com) is a gem for rails-to-trails cycling and canoeing. Seven miles westward on County Rd 8 (call for directions) is Old Barn Resort ($507-467-2512; www.barnresort.com; dm/r/ tent site/RV site $25/50/30/44; ⊙Apr–mid-Nov; 🔄), a pastoral hostel-campground-restaurant-outfitter. Harmony, south of Lanesboro, is the center of an Amish community and another welcoming town.

Duluth & Northern Minnesota

Northern Minnesota is where you come to 'do some fishing, do some drinking,' as one resident summed it up.

Duluth

At the Great Lakes' westernmost end, Duluth (with its neighbor, Superior, Wisconsin) is one of the busiest ports in the country. The town's dramatic location spliced into a cliff makes it a fab place to see changeable Lake Superior in action. The water, along with the area's trails and natural splendor, has earned Duluth a reputation as a hot spot for outdoors junkies.

◉ Sights & Activities

The waterfront area is distinctive. Mosey along the Lakewalk trail and around Canal Park, where most of the sights cluster. Look for the Aerial Lift Bridge, which rises to let ships into the port; about 1000 ships a year pass through here.

Maritime Visitors Center MUSEUM
(📞 218-720-5260; www.lsmma.com; 600 Lake Ave S; ⊘ 10am-9pm Jun-Aug, reduced hours Sep-May) **FREE** Check the computer screens inside to find out what time the big ships will be sailing through port. The first-rate center also has exhibits on Great Lakes shipping and shipwrecks.

William A Irvin MUSEUM
(📞 218-722-7876; www.williamairvin.com; 350 Harbor Dr; adult/child $10/8; ⊘ 9am-6pm Jun-Aug, 10am-4pm May, Sep & Oct) To continue the nautical theme, tour this mighty 610ft Great Lakes freighter.

Great Lakes Aquarium AQUARIUM
(📞 218-740-3474; www.glaquarium.org; 353 Harbor Dr; adult/child $16.50/10.50; ⊘ 10am-6pm; ⊕) One of the country's few freshwater aquariums; the highlights here include the daily stingray feedings at 2pm, and the otter tanks.

Leif Erikson Park PARK
(cnr London Rd & 14th Ave E) This is a lakefront sweet spot with a rose garden, replica of Leif's Viking ship and free outdoor movies each Friday night in summer. Take the Lakewalk from Canal Park (about 1½ miles) and you can say you hiked the Superior Trail, which traverses this stretch.

DYLAN IN DULUTH

While Hibbing and the Iron Range are most often associated with Bob Dylan, he was born in Duluth. You'll see brown-and-white signs on Superior and London Sts for **Bob Dylan Way** (www.bobdylanway.com), pointing out places associated with the legend (like the armory where he saw Buddy Holly in concert, and decided to become a musician). But you're on your own to find **Dylan's birthplace** (519 N 3rd Ave E), up a hill a few blocks northeast of downtown. Dylan lived on the top floor until age six, when his family moved inland to Hibbing. It's a private residence (and unmarked), so all you can do is stare from the street.

Enger Park PARK
(Skyline Pkwy) For a spectacular view of the city and harbor, climb the rock tower in Enger Park, located a couple miles southwest by the golf course.

Vista Fleet BOAT TOUR
(📞 218-722-6218; www.vistafleet.com; 323 Harbor Dr; adult/child $20/10; ⊘ mid-May–Oct) Ah, everyone loves a boat ride. Vista's two-hour harbor cruise is a favorite, departing from the dock beside the *William A Irvin* in Canal Park.

Spirit Mountain SKIING
(📞 218-628-2891; www.spiritmt.com; 9500 Spirit Mountain Pl; per day adult/child $35/28; ⊘ from 9am winter, from 10am summer) Skiing and snowboarding are big pastimes come winter; in summer there's a zip line, alpine slide and mini-golf. The mountain is 10 miles south of Duluth.

🛏 Sleeping

Duluth has several B&Bs; rooms cost at least $125 in the summer. Check **Duluth Historic Inns** (www.duluthbandb.com) for listings. The town's accommodations fill up fast in summer, which may mean you'll have to try your luck across the border in Superior, Wisconsin (where it's cheaper too).

Fitger's Inn HOTEL $$
(📞 218-722-8826; www.fitgers.com; 600 E Superior St; r incl breakfast $149-239; @ 🅰) Fitger's created its 62 large rooms, each with slightly varied decor, from an old brewery. Located

SCENIC DRIVE: HIGHWAY 61

Hwy 61 conjures a headful of images. Local boy Bob Dylan mythologized it in his angry 1965 album *Highway 61 Revisited*. It's the fabled 'Blues Hwy' clasping the Mississippi River en route to New Orleans. And in northern Minnesota it evokes red-tinged cliffs and forested beaches as it follows Lake Superior's shoreline.

But let's back up and get a few things straight. The Blues Hwy is actually US 61, and it starts just north of the Twin Cities. Hwy 61 is a state scenic road, and it starts in Duluth. To confuse matters more, there are two 61s between Duluth and Two Harbors: a four-lane expressway and a two-lane 'Old Hwy 61' (also called North Shore Scenic Drive, which morphs from London Rd in Duluth). Whatever the name, take it. After Two Harbors, it's one wondrous strip of pavement all the way to the Canadian border. For more information, check the North Shore Scenic Drive at www.superiorbyways.com.

on the Lakewalk, the pricier rooms have great water views. The free shuttle to local sights is handy.

Willard Munger Inn INN $$
(☑800-982-2453, 218-624-4814; www.mungerinn. com; 7408 Grand Ave; r incl breakfast $70-136; @🐾) Family-owned Munger Inn offers a fine variety of rooms (from budget to Jacuzzi suites), along with perks for outdoors enthusiasts, such as hiking and biking trails right outside the door, free use of bikes and canoes, and a fire pit. It's near Spirit Mountain.

🍴 Eating & Drinking

Most restaurants and bars reduce their hours in winter. The Canal Park waterfront area has eateries in all price ranges.

Duluth Grill AMERICAN $$
(www.duluthgrill.com; 118 S 27th Ave W; mains $8-16; ⊙7am-9pm; 🅿🏬) 🍃 The garden in the parking lot is the tip-off that this is a sustainable, hippie-vibed place. The diner-esque menu is huge, ranging from eggy breakfast skillets to curried polenta stew to bison burgers, with plenty of vegan and gluten-free options to boot. It's a couple miles southwest of Canal Park, near the bridge to Superior, Wisconsin.

DeWitt-Seitz Marketplace ASIAN, AMERICAN $$
(www.dewittseitz.com; 394 Lake Ave S) This building in Canal Park holds several eateries, including vegetarian-friendly Taste of Saigon (⊙11am-8:30pm Sun-Thu, to 9:30pm Fri & Sat; 🍽), hippie cafe Amazing Grace (⊙7am-10pm; 🍽) and Northern Waters Smokehaus (⊙10am-8pm Mon-Sat, to 6pm Sun), with sustainably harvested salmon and whitefish (primo for picnics).

Pizza Luce PIZZERIA $$
(☑218-727-7400; www.pizzaluce.com; 11 E Superior St; mains $10-20; ⊙8am-1:30am Sun-Thu, to 2:30am Fri & Sat; 🍽) 🍃 Cooks locally sourced breakfasts and gourmet pizzas. It's also plugged into the local music scene and hosts bands. Fully licensed.

★**Thirsty Pagan** BREWERY
(www.thirstypaganbrewing.com; 1623 Broadway St; ⊙from 11am) This one's a bit of a trek, over the bridge in Superior, Wisconsin (a 10-minute drive), but worth it for the aggressive, spicy beers to wash down hand-tossed pizzas.

Fitger's Brewhouse BREWERY
(www.fitgersbrewhouse.net; 600 E Superior St; ⊙from 11am) In the hotel complex, the Brewhouse rocks with live music and fresh brews. Try them via the seven-beer sampler (3oz glasses $8).

🛍 Shopping

Electric Fetus MUSIC
(☑218-722-9970; www.electricfetus.com; 12 E Superior St; ⊙9am-9pm Mon-Fri, 9am-8pm Sat, 11am-6pm Sun) Sells a whopping selection of CDs, vinyl and local arts and crafts, including Dylan tunes. It sits across the street from Pizza Luce.

ℹ Information

Duluth Visitors Center (☑800-438-5884; www.visitduluth.com; Harbor Dr; ⊙9:30am-7:30pm summer) Seasonal center, opposite the Vista dock.

ℹ Getting There & Around

Greyhound (☑218-722-5591; 4426 Grand Ave) has a couple of buses daily to Minneapolis (three hours).

North Shore

Hwy 61 is the main vein through the North Shore. It edges Lake Superior and passes numerous state parks, waterfalls, hiking trails and mom-and-pop towns en route to Canada. Lots of weekend, summer and fall traffic makes reservations essential.

Two Harbors (www.twoharborschamber.com) has a museum, lighthouse and B&B. Actually, the latter two are one and the same; the Lighthouse B&B (☑888-832-5606; www.lighthousebb.org; r incl breakfast $135-155) is a unique place to spend the night if you can snag one of its four rooms. Nearby, Betty's Pies (www.bettyspies.com; 1633 Hwy 61; sandwiches $5-9; ☺7am-9pm, reduced hours Oct-May) has a five-layer chocolate tinful among its rackful of wares.

Route highlights north of Two Harbors are Gooseberry Falls, Split Rock Lighthouse and Palisade Head. About 110 miles from Duluth, artsy little Grand Marais (www.grandmarais.com) makes an excellent base for exploring the Boundary Waters and environs. For Boundary permits and information, visit the Gunflint Ranger Station (☑218-387-1750; ☺8am-4:30pm May-Sep), just south of town.

Do-it-yourself enthusiasts can learn to build boats, tie flies or brew beer at the North House Folk School (☑218-387-9762; www.northhouse.org; 500 Hwy 61). The course list is phenomenal – as is the school's two-hour sailing trip aboard the Viking schooner *Hjordis* (per person $45). Reserve in advance.

Grand Marais' lodging options include camping, resorts and motels, like the Harbor Inn (☑218-387-1191; www.harborinnhotel.com; 207 Wisconsin St; r $115-135; ☎) in town or rustic, trail-encircled Naniboujou Lodge (☑218-387-2688; www.naniboujou.com; 20 Naniboujou Trail; r $95-115; ☺late May-late Oct), which is 14 miles northeast of town. Sven and Ole's (☑218-387-1713; www.svenandoles.com; 9 Wisconsin St; sandwiches $6-9; ☺11am-8pm, to 9pm Thu-Sat) is a classic for sandwiches and pizza; beer flows from the attached Pickled Herring Pub. Ecofriendly Angry Trout Cafe (☑218-387-1265; www.angrytroutcafe.com; 416 Hwy 61; mains $20-27; ☺11am-8:30pm May–mid-Oct) grills fresh-plucked lake fish in a converted fishing shanty.

Hwy 61 continues to Grand Portage National Monument (☑218-475-0123; www.nps.gov/grpo; ☺9am-5pm mid-May–mid-Oct) FREE, beside Canada, where the early voyageurs had to carry their canoes around the Pigeon River rapids. This was the center of a far-flung trading empire, and the reconstructed 1788 trading post and Ojibwe village is well worth seeing. Isle Royale National Park in Lake Superior is reached by daily ferries (☑218-475-0024; www.isleroyaleboats.com; day trip adult/child $58/32) from May to October. (The park is also accessible from Michigan).

Boundary Waters

From Two Harbors, Hwy 2 runs inland to the legendary Boundary Waters Canoe Area Wilderness (BWCAW). This pristine region has more than 1000 lakes and streams in which to dip a paddle. It's possible to go just for the day, but most people opt for at least one night of camping. If you're willing to dig in and canoe for a while, you'll lose the crowds. Camping then becomes a wonderfully remote experience: just you, the howling wolves, the moose who's nuzzling the tent and the aurora borealis' greenish light filling the night sky. Beginners are welcome, and everyone can get set up with gear from local lodges and outfitters.

Permits for camping (☑877-550-6777; www.recreation.gov; adult/child $16/8, plus reservation fee $6) are required for overnight stays. Day permits, though free, are also required; get them at BWCAW entry-point kiosks or ranger stations. Call Superior National Forest (☑218-626-4300; www.fs.usda.gov/attmain/superior/specialplaces) for details; the website

---

SUPERIOR HIKING TRAIL

The 290-mile Superior Hiking Trail (www.shta.org) follows the lake-hugging ridgeline between Duluth and the Canadian border. Along the way it passes dramatic red-rock overlooks and the occasional moose and black bear. Trailheads with parking lots pop up every 5 to 10 miles, making it ideal for day hikes. The Superior Shuttle (☑218-834-5511; www.superiorhikingshuttle.com; from $15; ☺Fri-Sun mid-May–mid-Oct) makes life even easier, picking up trekkers from 17 stops along the route. Overnight hikers will find 81 backcountry campsites and several lodges to cushion the body come nightfall; the trail website has details. The whole footpath is free, with no reservations or permits required.

has a useful trip planning guide. Try to plan ahead, as permits are quota restricted and sometimes run out.

Many argue the best BWCAW access is via the engaging town of Ely (www.ely.org), northeast of the Iron Range area, which has accommodations, restaurants and scores of outfitters. The International Wolf Center (☑218-365-4695; www.wolf.org; 1369 Hwy 169; adult/child $9.50/5.50; ⊙10am-5pm daily mid-May–mid-Oct, Fri & Sat only mid-Oct–mid-May) offers intriguing exhibits and wolf-viewing trips. Across the highway from the center, Kawishiwi Ranger Station (☑218-365-7600; 1393 Hwy 169; ⊙8am-4:30pm May-Sep) provides expert BWCAW camping and canoeing details, trip suggestions and required permits.

In winter, Ely gets mushy – it's a renowned dogsledding town. Outfitters such as Wintergreen Dogsled Lodge (☑218-365-6022; www.dogsledding.com; 4hr tour $125) offer numerous packages.

Iron Range District

An area of red-tinged scrubby hills rather than mountains, Minnesota's Iron Range District consists of the Mesabi and Vermilion Ranges, running north and south of Hwy 169 from roughly Grand Rapids northeast to Ely. Iron was discovered here in the 1850s, and at one time more than three-quarters of the nation's iron ore was extracted from these vast open-pit mines. Visitors can see working mines and the terrain's raw, sparse beauty all along Hwy 169.

In Calumet, a perfect introduction is the Hill Annex Mine State Park (☑218-247-7215; www.dnr.state.mn.us/hill_annex; 880 Gary St; tours adult/child $10/6; ⊙12:30pm & 3pm Fri & Sat), with its open-pit tours and exhibit center. Tours are held in summertime only, on Friday and Saturday; there's also a fossil tour both days at 10am.

An even bigger pit sprawls in Hibbing, where a must-see viewpoint (⊙9am-5pm mid-May–mid-Sep) FREE north of town overlooks the 3-mile Hull-Rust Mahoning Mine. Bob Dylan lived at 2425 E 7th Ave as a boy and teenager; the Hibbing Public Library (☑218-362-5959; www.hibbing.lib.mn.us; 2020 E 5th Ave; ⊙10am-7pm Mon-Thu, to 5pm Fri) has well-done Dylan displays and a free walking-tour map (available online, too) that takes you past various sites, like the place where Bobby had his bar mitzvah. Zimmy's (www.zimmys.com; 531 E Howard St; mains $14-20; ⊙11am-1am) has more memorabilia,

plus drinks and pub grub. For a bed, try Hibbing Park Hotel (☑218-262-3481; www.hibbingparkhotel.com; 1402 E Howard St; r $60-100; ✳ 🖥 ✉).

Soudan sports the area's only underground mine (www.dnr.state.mn.us/soudan; 1379 Stuntz Bay Rd; tours adult/child $12/7; ⊙10am-4pm late May-early Sep); wear warm clothes.

Voyageurs National Park

In the 17th century, French-Canadian fur traders (voyageurs) began exploring the Great Lakes and northern rivers by canoe. Voyageurs National Park (www.nps.gov/voya) covers part of their customary waterway, which became the border between the USA and Canada.

It's all about water up here. Most of the park is accessible only by hiking or motorboat – the waters are mostly too wide and too rough for canoeing, though kayaks are becoming popular. A few access roads lead to campgrounds and lodges on or near Lake Superior, but these are mostly used by people putting in their own boats.

The visitor centers are car accessible and good places to begin your visit. Twelve miles east of International Falls on Hwy 11 is Rainy Lake Visitors Center (☑218-286-5258; ⊙9am-5pm daily late May-Sep, Wed-Sun Sep-late May), the main park office. Ranger-guided walks and boat tours are available here. Seasonal visitor centers are at Ash River (☑218-374-3221; ⊙9am-5pm late May-Sep) and Kabetogama Lake (☑218-875-2111; ⊙9am-5pm late May-Sep). These areas have outfitters, rentals and services, plus some smaller bays for canoeing.

Houseboating is all the rage in the region. Outfitters such as Ebel's (☑888-883-2357; www.ebels.com; 10326 Ash River Trail) and Voyagaire Houseboats (☑800-882-6287; www.voyagaire.com; 7576 Gold Coast Rd) can set you up. Rentals range from $275 to $700 per day, depending on boat size. Novice boaters are welcome and receive instruction on how to operate the vessels.

Otherwise, for sleeping, your choices are pretty much camping or resorts. The 12-room, shared-bath Kettle Falls Hotel (☑218-240-1724; www.kettlefallshotel.com; r/cottage incl breakfast $80/180; ⊙May–mid-Oct) is an exception, located inside the park and accessible only by boat; make arrangements with the owners for pick-up (per person round-trip $45). Nelson's Resort (☑800-

433-0743; www.nelsonsresort.com; 7632 Nelson Rd; cabins from $180) at Crane Lake is a winner for hiking, fishing and relaxing under blue skies.

While this is certainly a remote and wild area, those seeking wildlife, canoeing and forest camping in all their glory are best off in the Boundary Waters.

Bemidji & Chippewa National Forest

This area is synonymous with outdoor activities and summer fun. Campsites and cottages abound, and almost everybody is fishing-crazy.

Itasca State Park (☎218-266-2100; www. dnr.state.mn.us/itasca; off Hwy 71 N; per vehicle $5, tent & RV sites $12-22) is an area highlight.

You can walk across the tiny headwaters of the mighty Mississippi River, rent canoes or bikes, hike the trails and camp. The log HI Mississippi Headwaters Hostel (☎218-266-3415; www.hiusa.org/parkrapids; dm $24-27, r $80-130; ❋🛜) is in the park; winter hours vary, so call ahead. Or if you want a little rustic luxury, try the venerable Douglas Lodge (☎866-857-2757; r $95-140; 🛜), run by the park, which also has cabins and a good restaurant.

On the western edge of the forest, about 30 miles from Itasca, tidy Bemidji is an old lumber town with a well-preserved downtown and a giant statue of logger Paul Bunyan and his faithful blue ox, Babe. The visitor center (www.visitbemidji.com; 300 Bemidji Ave N; ⊙8am-5pm, closed Sat & Sun Sep-May) displays Paul's toothbrush.

Understand
Eastern
USA

Eastern USA Today

Gun laws, health care, same-sex marriage and legalized marijuana remain hot topics across the landscape. A second term for Barack Obama has brought moments of self-reflection to both the Democrats – who achieved mixed results during the president's first term – and Republicans – who must evolve or face certain defeat in future elections. The two parties still can't seem to get along...

Best in Print

To Kill a Mockingbird (Harper Lee; 1960) Pulitzer winner about racism in Depression-era Alabama.

A Confederacy of Dunces (John Kennedy Toole; 1980) Pulitzer winner about a New Orleans misfit questing for a job.

Freedom (Jonathan Franzen; 2010) Follows a complex, troubled family living in modern-day Minnesota and New York City. London's *Guardian* deemed it 'the novel of the century.'

Bleeding Edge (Thomas Pynchon; 2013) Bold, labyrinthine story set in NYC during the terrorist attacks of September 11.

Best on Film

Gone with the Wind (directed by Victor Fleming; 1939) Civil War–era saga of the South.

Mr Smith Goes to Washington (directed by Frank Capra; 1939) Jimmy Stewart gets a crash course in DC politics and corruption.

The Untouchables (directed by Brian De Palma; 1987) Eliot Ness takes down Al Capone in gangster-era Chicago.

Lincoln (directed by Steven Spielberg; 2012) Historical drama about President Lincoln's efforts to abolish slavery.

Politics

President Obama won re-election in 2012, aided in large part by assembling the most ethnically and racially diverse coalition in American history. More than 90% of African Americans and nearly 70% of Latinos voted for him. In the eastern region, the Midwest, Northeast and Florida supported him (though the South did not).

The failure of Republicans to attract voters from different ethnic backgrounds has caused some soul-searching in the party. The party, perhaps in answer to this search for a new identity, has seen the rise of new faces from vastly different backgrounds. The young Florida senator and Cuban-American Marco Rubio is seen as one of the Republicans' rising stars – he'll be one to watch in the 2016 presidential elections.

Economy & Health Care

Although Democrats cheered his victory, Obama returned to the White House without quite the same hope and optimism that surrounded him the first time. When he took the Oath of Office in 2013, the unemployment rate – hovering around 8% – was about what it had been during his first inauguration back in 2009. While economic growth seems, at last, to be on a solid foundation in much of the country, it still lags in eastern pockets such as the manufacturing-heavy Midwest region around the Great Lakes (especially Illinois and Michigan).

Obama's ambitious plan to bring healthcare reform passed through Congress, becoming the most significant new healthcare expansion since the passage of Medicare and Medicaid in 1965. Despite challenges by Republicans who threatened to defund the *Affordable Care Act* (a major factor in the 16-day government shutdown in October 2013), and a close call by the Supreme Court (which narrowly ruled the act constitutional by a vote of five to four), the law is slated to go into effect in 2014. Whether it will be a success or failure continues to be hotly debated. It has become an issue of partisan politics and will play out in stark relief in states such as Florida, Georgia, North Carolina, Mississippi and Louisiana – which have some of the nation's highest uninsured rates (between 15% and 20%) as well as Republican-controlled state governments that actively oppose the law.

Gay Marriage & Marijuana

While Obama declared his support for same-sex marriage in 2012, Congress has remained opposed to it. Several states went ahead and set their own rules on the matter. By 2013, some 16 states (12 of them in the eastern US), as well as Washington, DC, had legalized same-sex marriage. A major breakthrough occurred in June 2013, when the Supreme Court ruled that the discriminatory *Defense of Marriage Act* – the law barring the federal government from recognizing same-sex marriages legalized by the states – was unconstitutional.

Meanwhile, the prevailing attitude about cannabis across the US is now one of relaxing restrictions on it. Some 20 states have supported the legalization of marijuana for medicinal use, and a handful of states have also decriminalized marijuana, making possession of small amounts of the substance a misdemeanor rather than a felony. All Northeastern states have one or the other of these laws in place.

Gun Violence

Mass shootings have been occurring with alarming frequency in recent years. Devastating incidents include the 2012 Newtown, Connecticut, massacre, where a heavily armed 20-year-old slaughtered 20 young children and six adults. The following year, a gunman killed 12 and wounded four in a rampage at the Navy Yard in Washington, DC. On average, 32 Americans are murdered by guns every day, and another 140 wounded.

Yet despite conclusive evidence (such as a 2013 study published in the prestigious *American Journal of Medicine*) that more guns equals more murders, and the fact that rates of death by firearms are rare in countries with strict gun laws (such as Australia and the UK), American legislators have been reluctant to enact even modest gun-control laws – such as reinstating the ban on assault weapons, which Congress failed to pass in 2013. One reason: gun lobbies such as the National Rifle Association wield incredible power, contributing over $16 million annually to state and national political campaigns.

US POPULATION: **317 MILLION**

US GDP: **$15.94 TRILLION**

US GDP PER CAPITA: **$50,700**

US UNEMPLOYMENT: **7.6%**

US ANNUAL INFLATION: **2.1%**

if USA were 100 people

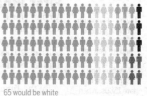

65 would be white
15 would be Hispanic
13 would be African American
4 would be Asian American
3 would be other

belief systems
(% of population)

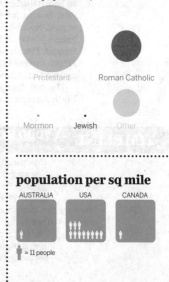

Protestant   Roman Catholic

Mormon   Jewish   Other

population per sq mile

AUSTRALIA   USA   CANADA

≈ 11 people

History

From its early days as an English colony to its rise to the forefront of the world stage in the 20th century, American history has been anything but dull. War against the British, westward expansion, slavery and its abolishment, Civil War and Reconstruction, the Great Depression, the postwar boom and more recent conflicts in the 21st century – they've all played a part in shaping the nation's complicated identity.

Before Jamestown or Plymouth Rock, a group of 116 British men and women set up a colony at Roanoke, North Carolina in the late 1580s. When a supply ship returned three years later, the settlers had disappeared. The fate of the 'Lost Colony' remains one of America's greatest mysteries.

First Inhabitants

Among North America's most significant prehistoric cultures were the Mound Builders, who inhabited the Ohio and Mississippi River valleys from around 3000 BC to AD 1200. In Illinois, Cahokia was once a metropolis of 20,000 people, the largest in pre-Columbian North America. Similar mounds rise up throughout the eastern USA, including several along the Natchez Trace in Mississippi.

By the time the first Europeans arrived, several different groups of Native Americans occupied the land, such as the Wampanoag in New England, the Calusa in southern Florida and the Shawnee in the Midwest. Two centuries later, they were all but gone. European explorers left diseases in their wake to which indigenous peoples had no immunity. More than any other factor – war, slavery or famine – disease epidemics devastated Native American populations by anywhere from 50% to 90%.

European Claims

In 1492 Italian explorer Christopher Columbus, backed by Spain, voyaged west looking for the East Indies. He found the Bahamas. With visions of gold, Spanish explorers quickly followed: Cortés conquered much of today's Mexico, Pizarro conquered Peru, and Ponce de León wandered through Florida looking for the fountain of youth. Not to be left out, the French explored Canada and the Midwest, while the Dutch and English cruised North America's eastern seaboard.

The first European-founded (and oldest continuously settled) city in North America was St Augustine, Florida, where the Spanish set up shop

TIMELINE	7000 BC–AD 100	1492	1607
	'Archaic period' marked by nomadic hunter-gatherer lifestyle. By the end of this period, corn, beans and squash (the agricultural 'three sisters') and permanent settlements are well established.	Italian explorer Christopher Columbus 'discovers' America. He names the indigenous inhabitants 'Indians,' mistakenly thinking he had sailed to India.	The Jamestown settlement, the first English colony in North America, is founded on marshland in present-day Virginia. The first few years are hard, with many dying from sickness and starvation.

in 1565. Up the coast in 1607, a group of English noblemen established that country's first permanent North American settlement at Jamestown. Earlier English settlements had ended badly, and Jamestown almost did, too: the noblemen chose a swamp, planted their crops late and died from disease and starvation. Local tribes gave the settlement enough aid to survive.

For Jamestown and America, 1619 proved a pivotal year: the colony established the House of Burgesses, a representative assembly of citizens to decide local laws, and it received its first boatload of 20 African slaves. The next year was equally momentous, as a group of radically religious Puritans pulled ashore at what would become Plymouth, Massachusetts. The Pilgrims were escaping religious persecution under the 'corrupt' Church of England, and in the New World they saw a divine opportunity to create a new society that would be a religious and moral beacon. The Pilgrims signed a 'Mayflower Compact,' one of the seminal texts of American democracy, to govern themselves by consensus.

Capitalism & Colonialism

For the next two centuries, European powers competed for position and territory in the New World, extending European politics into the Americas. As Britain's Royal Navy came to rule Atlantic seas, England increasingly profited from its colonies and eagerly consumed the fruits of their labors – tobacco from Virginia, sugar and coffee from the Caribbean. Over the 17th and 18th centuries, slavery in America was slowly legalized into a formal institution to support this plantation economy. By 1800, one out of every five persons was a slave.

Meanwhile, Britain mostly left the American colonists to govern themselves. Town meetings and representative assemblies, in which local citizens (that is, white men with property) debated community problems and voted on laws and taxes, became common. By the end of the Seven Years' War in 1763, Britain was feeling the strains of running an empire: it had been fighting France for a century and had colonies scattered all over the world. It was time to clean up bureaucracies and share financial burdens.

The colonies, however, resented English taxes and policies. Frustrations came to a head with the Boston Tea Party in 1773, after which Britain clamped down hard, shutting Boston's harbor and increasing its military presence. In 1774, representatives from 12 colonies convened the First Continental Congress in Philadelphia's Independence Hall to air complaints and prepare for the inevitable war ahead.

Revolution & the Republic

In April 1775, British troops skirmished with armed colonists in Massachusetts (who were prepared for the fight, thanks to Paul Revere's famous warning), and the Revolutionary War began. George Washington,

The New World (2005), directed by Terrence Malick, is a brutal but passionate film that retells the tragic story of the Jamestown colony and the pivotal peace-making role of Pocahontas, a Powhatan chief's daughter.

Famous Colonial Sights

Williamsburg, Virginia

Jamestown, Virginia

Plymouth, Massachusetts

North End, Boston

Philadelphia, Pennsylvania

Annapolis, Maryland

Charleston, South Carolina

1620	1675	1773	1775
The *Mayflower* lands at Plymouth with 102 English Pilgrims, who have come to the New World to escape religious persecution. The Wampanoag tribe saves them from starvation.	For decades, the Pilgrims and local tribes live fairly cooperatively, but deadly conflict erupts in 1675. King Philip's War lasts 14 months and kills over 5000 people (mostly Native Americans).	To protest a British tax on tea, Bostonians dress as Mohawks, board East India Company ships and toss their tea overboard – later named the Boston Tea Party.	Paul Revere rides from Boston to warn colonial fighters (Minutemen) that the British are coming. The next day, the 'shot heard round the world' is fired at Lexington, starting the Revolutionary War.

a wealthy Virginia farmer, was chosen to lead the American army. Trouble was, Washington lacked gunpowder and money (the colonists resisted taxes even for their own military), and his troops were a motley collection of poorly armed farmers, hunters and merchants, who regularly quit and returned to their farms due to lack of pay. On the other side, the British 'Redcoats' represented the world's most powerful military. The inexperienced General Washington had to improvise constantly, sometimes wisely retreating, sometimes engaging in 'ungentlemanly' sneak attacks. During the winter of 1777–78, the American army nearly starved at Valley Forge, Pennsylvania.

Meanwhile, the Second Continental Congress tried to articulate what exactly they were fighting for. In January 1776, Thomas Paine published the wildly popular *Common Sense,* which passionately argued for independence from England. Soon, independence seemed not just logical, but noble and necessary, and on July 4, 1776, the Declaration of Independence was finalized and signed. Largely written by Thomas Jefferson, it elevated the 13 colonies' particular gripes against the monarchy into a universal declaration of individual rights and republican government.

But to succeed, General Washington needed help, not just patriotic sentiment. In 1778, Benjamin Franklin persuaded France (always eager to trouble England) to ally with the revolutionaries, and they provided the troops, material and sea power that helped win the war. The British surrendered at Yorktown, Virginia, in 1781, and two years later the Treaty of Paris formally recognized the 'United States of America.' At first, the nation's loose confederation of fractious, squabbling states were hardly 'united.' So the founders gathered again in Philadelphia, and in 1787 drafted a new-and-improved Constitution: the US government was given a stronger federal center, with checks and balances between its three major branches, and to guard against the abuse of centralized power, a citizen's Bill of Rights was approved in 1791.

As radical as it was, though, the Constitution also preserved the economic and social status quo. Rich landholders kept their property, which included their slaves; Native Americans were excluded from the nation; and women were excluded from politics. These blatant discrepancies and injustices, which were widely noted, were the result of pragmatic compromise (eg to get slave-dependent Southern states on board) as well as widespread beliefs in the essential rightness of things as they were.

Louisiana Purchase & the Move West

As the 19th century dawned on the young nation, optimism was the mood of the day. Agriculture was industrialized, and US commerce surged. In 1803, Thomas Jefferson bought land from French leader Napoleon Bonaparte. The Louisiana Purchase included New Orleans and

Great History Museums

Henry Ford Museum/Greenfield Village, Detroit

National Civil Rights Museum, Memphis

New Bedford Whaling Museum, Massachusetts

National Museum of the American Indian, Washington, DC

The whaling industry thrived in New England in the 18th century, especially around Massachusetts. Buzzards Bay, Nantucket Island and New Bedford were all prominent centers. New Bedford eventually hosted a whaling fleet of over 300 ships, employing 10,000 people and earning over $12 million in profits.

1776	1787	1791	1803–06
On July 4, colonies sign the Declaration of Independence. Creators of the document include John Hancock, Samuel Adams, John Adams, Benjamin Franklin and Thomas Jefferson.	The Constitutional Convention in Philadelphia draws up the US Constitution. Federal power is balanced between the presidency, Congress and the judiciary.	Bill of Rights is adopted as 10 constitutional amendments articulating citizens' rights, including freedom of speech, a free press and the right to bear arms.	President Thomas Jefferson sends Meriwether Lewis and William Clark west. Guided by the Shoshone tribeswoman Sacajawea, they trailblaze from St Louis, Missouri, to the Pacific Ocean and back.

about 15 present-day states west of the Mississippi River. Expansion began in earnest.

Relations between the US and Britain – despite lively trade – remained tense, and in 1812 the US declared war on England again. The two-year conflict ended without much gain by either side, although the British abandoned their forts, and the US vowed to avoid Europe's 'entangling alliances.'

In the 1830s and 1840s, with growing nationalist fervor and dreams of continental expansion, many Americans came to believe it was 'Manifest Destiny' that all the land in North American should be theirs. The 1830 Indian Removal Act aimed to clear one obstacle by designating land west of the Mississippi as 'Indian territory.' Native Americans were meant to relocate themselves there, thus clearing fertile valleys in eastern states like Georgia and Alabama for white settlement. Many tribes resisted removal, including the Seminole in Florida, but the US government cajoled, threatened and bribed Native Americans to sign treaties and cooperate; when that failed, the government used guns.

Meanwhile, newly built railroads cleared another hurdle, linking midwestern and western lands with East Coast markets. As new states joined the USA, a troubling question loomed: would they be slave states or free states? The nation's future depended on the answer.

The Civil War

The US Constitution hadn't ended slavery, but it had given Congress the power to approve (or not) slavery in new states. Public debates raged constantly over the expansion of slavery, particularly since this shaped the balance of power between the industrial North and the agrarian South.

Since founding, Southern politicians had dominated government and defended slavery as 'natural and normal,' which an 1856 *New York Times* editorial called 'insanity.' The Southern proslavery lobby enraged Northern abolitionists – but even many Northern politicians feared that ending slavery with a pen-stroke would be ruinous. Limit slavery, they reasoned, and in the competition with industry and free labor, slavery would wither without inciting a violent slave revolt – a constantly feared possibility. Indeed, in 1859, radical abolitionist John Brown tried (unsuccessfully) to spark such an uprising at Harpers Ferry.

The economics of slavery were undeniable. In 1860, there were over four million slaves in the US, most held by Southern planters – who grew 75% of the world's cotton, accounting for over half of US exports. Thus, the Southern economy supported the nation's economy, and it required slaves. The 1860 presidential election became a referendum on this issue,

For 100-plus years, Tecumseh's Curse loomed over presidents elected in a year ending in zero (every 20 years). Tecumseh was a Shawnee warrior whom future president William Henry Harrison battled in 1811. Tecumseh hexed him as revenge. Harrison became president in 1840, but died a month later. Lincoln and Kennedy were also victims.

1812	1861–65	1870
The War of 1812 begins with battles against the British and Native Americans in the Great Lakes region. Even after the 1815 Treaty of Ghent, fighting continues along the Gulf Coast.	American Civil War erupts between North and South (delineated by the Mason–Dixon line). The war's end on April 9, 1865, is marred by President Lincoln's assassination five days later.	Freed black men are given the vote, but the South's segregationist 'Jim Crow' laws (which remain until the 1960s) effectively disenfranchise blacks from every meaningful sphere of daily life.

IN THIS TEMPLE
AS IN THE HEARTS OF THE PEOPLE
FOR WHOM HE SAVED THE UNION
THE MEMORY OF ABRAHAM LINCOLN
IS ENSHRINED FOREVER

NATHAN BLANEY / GETTY IMAGES ©

➡ Lincoln Memorial (p261)

and the election was won by a young politician from Illinois who favored limiting slavery: Abraham Lincoln.

In the South, even the threat of federal limits was too onerous to abide, and as President Lincoln took office, 11 states seceded from the union and formed the Confederate States of America. Lincoln faced the nation's greatest moment of crisis. He had two choices: let the southern states secede and dissolve the union, or wage war to keep the union intact. He chose the latter.

War began in April 1861, when the Confederacy attacked Fort Sumter in Charleston, South Carolina, and raged on for the next four years – in the most gruesome combat the world had ever known until that time. By the end, over 600,000 soldiers, nearly an entire generation of young men, were dead. Southern plantations and cities (most notably Atlanta) lay sacked and burned. The North's industrial might provided an advantage, but its victory was not preordained; it unfolded battle by bloody battle.

As fighting progressed, Lincoln recognized that if the war didn't end slavery outright, victory would be pointless. In 1863, his Emancipation Proclamation expanded the war's aims and freed all slaves. In April 1865, Confederate General Robert E Lee surrendered to Union General Ulysses S Grant in Appomattox, Virginia. The union had been preserved, but at a staggering cost.

Best Political Reads

Washington: A Life (2010), Ron Chernow

Thomas Jefferson: The Art of Power (2013), Jon Meacham

Team of Rivals: The Political Genius of Abraham Lincoln (2012), Doris Kearns Goodwin

The Great Depression, the New Deal & World War II

In October 1929, investors, worried over a gloomy global economy, started selling stocks – seeing others selling, everyone panicked until they'd sold everything. The stock market crashed, and the US economy collapsed like a house of cards.

Thus began the Great Depression. Frightened banks called in their dodgy loans, people couldn't pay, and the banks folded. Millions lost their homes, farms, businesses and savings, and as much as 33% of the American workforce became unemployed. Bread lines and shanty towns sprang up in cities; New York's Central Park held one of the biggest camps. In 1932, Democrat Franklin D Roosevelt was elected president on the promise of a 'New Deal' to rescue the US from its crisis, which he did with resounding success. When war once again broke out in Europe in 1939, the isolationist mood in America was as strong as ever. However, the extremely popular President Roosevelt, elected to an unprecedented third term in 1940, understood that the US couldn't sit by and allow victory for fascist, totalitarian regimes. Roosevelt sent aid to Britain and persuaded a skittish Congress to go along with it.

1880–1920	1896	1908	1917
Millions of immigrants flood in from Europe and Asia, fueling the age of cities. New York, Chicago and Philadelphia swell in size, becoming global centers of industry and commerce.	In *Plessy v Ferguson*, the US Supreme Court rules that 'separate but equal' public facilities for blacks and whites are legal, arguing that the Constitution addresses only political, not social, equality.	The first Model T (aka 'Tin Lizzie') car is built in Detroit, MI. Assembly-line innovator Henry Ford is soon selling one million automobiles annually.	President Woodrow Wilson enters US into WWI. The US mobilizes 4.7 million troops, and suffers around 110,000 of the war's nine million military deaths.

THE AFRICAN AMERICAN EXPERIENCE: THE STRUGGLE FOR EQUALITY

It's impossible to grasp American history without taking into account the great struggles and hard-won victories of African Americans from all spheres of life.

Slavery

From the early 1600s until the 1800s, an estimated 600,000 slaves were brought from Africa to America. Those who survived the horrific transport on crowded ships (which sometimes had 50% mortality rates) were sold in slave markets (African males cost $27 in 1638). The majority of slaves ended up in southern plantations where conditions were usually brutal – whipping and branding were commonplace.

All (White) Men Are Created Equal

Many of the founding fathers – George Washington, Thomas Jefferson and Benjamin Franklin – owned slaves, though they privately expressed condemnation for the abominable practice. The abolition movement, however, wouldn't appear until the 1830s, long after the appearance on the Declaration of Independence of the rousing but ultimately hollow words 'all men are created equal.'

Free at Last

While some revisionist historians describe the Civil War as being about states' rights, most scholars agree that the war was really about slavery. Following the Union victory at Antietam, Lincoln drafted the Emancipation Proclamation, which freed all blacks in occupied territories. African Americans joined the Union effort, with more than 180,000 serving by war's end.

Jim Crow Laws

During Reconstruction (1865–77), federal laws provided civil rights protection for newly freed blacks. Southern bitterness, however, coupled with centuries of prejudice, fueled a backlash. By the 1890s, the Jim Crow laws (named after a derogatory character in a minstrel show) appeared. African Americans were effectively disenfranchised, and America became a deeply segregated society.

The Civil Rights Movement

Beginning in the 1950s, a movement was underway in African American communities to fight for equality. Rosa Parks, who refused to give up her seat to a white passenger, inspired the Montgomery bus boycott. There were sit-ins at lunch counters where blacks were excluded; massive demonstrations led by Martin Luther King Jr in Washington, DC; and harrowing journeys by 'freedom riders' aiming to end bus segregation. The work of millions paid off: in 1964, President Johnson signed the Civil Rights Act, which banned discrimination and racial segregation.

1919	1920s	1933–38	1941–45
The temperance movement champions the 18th amendment, which bans alcohol. Prohibition is unsuccessful, leading to bootlegging and organized crime. The amendment is repealed in 1933.	Spurred by massive African American migration to northern cities, the Harlem Renaissance inspires an intellectual flowering of literature, art and music.	Roosevelt's New Deal establishes federal programs and legislation including Social Security, the Fair Labor Standards Act and the Civilian Conservation Corps to provide unemployment relief.	WWII: America deploys 16 million troops and suffers 400,000 deaths. (Overall, civilian deaths outpace military deaths two to one, and total 50 to 70 million people from over 50 countries.)

Then, on December 7, 1941, Japan launched a surprise attack on Hawaii's Pearl Harbor, killing over 2000 Americans and sinking several battleships. US isolationism transformed overnight into outrage, and Roosevelt suddenly had the support he needed. Germany also declared war on the US, and America joined the Allied fight against Hitler and the Axis powers. From that moment, the US put almost its entire will and industrial prowess into the war effort.

Fighting went on for over two years in both the Pacific and in Europe. The US finally dealt the fatal blow to Germany with its massive D-Day invasion of France on June 6, 1944. Germany surrendered in May 1945. Nevertheless, Japan continued fighting. Newly elected President Harry Truman – ostensibly worried that a US invasion of Japan would lead to unprecedented carnage – chose to drop experimental atomic bombs, created by the government's top-secret Manhattan Project, on Hiroshima and Nagasaki in August 1945. The bombs devastated both cities, killing over 200,000 people. Japan surrendered days later, and the nuclear age was born.

The Red Scare, Civil Rights & Vietnam War

The US enjoyed unprecedented prosperity in the decades after WWII but little peace. Formerly wartime allies, the communist Soviet Union and the capitalist USA soon engaged in a running competition to dominate the globe. The superpowers engaged in proxy wars – notably the Korean War (1950–53) and Vietnam War (1954–75) – with only the mutual threat of nuclear annihilation preventing direct war.

Meanwhile, with its continent unscarred and its industry bulked up by WWII, the American homeland entered an era of growing affluence. In the 1950s, a mass migration left the inner cities for the suburbs, where affordable single-family homes sprang up. Americans drove cheap cars using cheap gas over brand-new interstate highways. They relaxed with the comforts of modern technology, swooned over TV, and got busy, giving birth to a 'baby boom.' Middle-class whites did, anyway. African Americans remained segregated, poor and generally unwelcome at the party. Echoing 19th-century abolitionist Frederick Douglass, the Southern Christian Leadership Coalition (SCLC), led by African American preacher Martin Luther King Jr, aimed to end segregation and 'save America's soul': to realize color-blind justice, racial equality and fairness of economic opportunity for all.

Beginning in the 1950s, King preached and organized nonviolent resistance in the form of bus boycotts, marches and sit-ins, mainly in the South. White authorities often met these protests with water hoses and police batons, and demonstrations sometimes dissolved into riots, but with the 1964 Civil Rights Act, African Americans spurred a wave of

1948–51	1954	1963
The US-led Marshall Plan funnels $12 billion in material and financial aid to help Europe recover from WWII. The plan also aims to contain Soviet influence and reignite America's economy.	The Supreme Court rules that segregation in public schools is 'inherently unequal' and orders desegregation 'with all deliberate speed.' The fight to integrate schools spurs the civil rights movement.	On November 22, President John F Kennedy is publicly assassinated by Lee Harvey Oswald while riding in a motorcade through Dealey Plaza in Dallas, Texas.

➤ John F Kennedy

legislation that swept away racist laws and laid the groundwork for a more just and equal society.

Meanwhile, the 1960s saw further social upheavals: rock and roll spawned a youth rebellion and drugs sent Technicolor visions spinning in their heads. President John F Kennedy was assassinated in Dallas in 1963, followed by the assassinations in 1968 of his brother, Senator Robert Kennedy, and of Martin Luther King (in Memphis). Americans' faith in their leaders and government was further shocked by the bombings and brutalities of the Vietnam War, as seen on TV, which led to widespread student protests. Yet President Richard Nixon, elected in 1968 partly for promising an 'honorable end to the war,' instead escalated US involvement and secretly bombed Laos and Cambodia. Then, in 1972, the Watergate scandal broke: a burglary at Democratic Party offices in Washington was, through dogged journalism, tied to 'Tricky Dick,' who in 1974 became the first US president to resign from office.

The tumultuous 1960s and '70s also witnessed the sexual revolution, women's liberation and other events challenging the status quo. Milestones include the 1969 Stonewall riots in Greenwich Village, NYC, which galvanized the gay rights movement when patrons of a gay bar called the

NEW DEAL: RESCUING THE USA FROM ITS GREAT DEPRESSION

America reached its lowest point in history during the Great Depression. By 1932, nearly one third of all American workers were unemployed. National output fell by 50%, hundreds of banks were shuttered, and great swaths of the country seemed to disappear beneath enormous dust storms. Franklin Roosevelt easily won the 1932 election, and rather casually promised to give Americans a new deal. So began one of America's most progressive eras in history, under the rule of one of its most popular presidents.

Roosevelt wasted no time getting down to work. During his first 100 days, he completed the rescue of the ailing banking system with the creation of deposit insurance. He sent $500 million to states for direct relief and saved a fifth of all homeowners from foreclosure. He also sent people back to work on a grand scale. He created the Civilian Conservation Corps, which gave jobs to 250,000 young men to work in the parks and forests; they would go on to plant two billion trees. He also created the Works Progress Administration (WPA), which put another 600,000 to work on major projects across the country – building bridges, tunnels, dams, power plants, waterworks, highways, schools and town halls.

The New Deal wasn't just about infrastructure. Some 5000 artists (including famed Mexican painter Diego Rivera) were employed painting murals and creating sculptures in public buildings – many are still in existence today. Over 6000 writers were put to work crisscrossing the country, recording oral histories and folktales and compiling ethnographic studies.

1964	1965–75	1969	1973
Congress passes the Civil Rights Act, outlawing discrimination on basis of race, color, religion, sex or national origin. First proposed by Kennedy, it was one of President Johnson's crowning achievements.	US involvement in the Vietnam War tears the nation apart as 58,000 Americans die, along with four million Vietnamese and 1.5 million Laotians and Cambodians.	American astronauts land on the moon, fulfilling President Kennedy's unlikely 1961 promise to accomplish this feat within a decade and culminating the 'space race' between the US and USSR.	In *Roe v Wade*, the Supreme Court legalizes abortion. Even today this decision remains controversial and socially divisive, pitting 'right to choose' advocates against the 'right to life' anti-abortion lobby.

WOODSTOCK

Stonewall Inn fought back after a police raid, demanding equal rights and an end to persecution. A few months later, the Woodstock Festival defined the Vietnam era with its peace-love-and-flowers hippies swaying in the fields to rock music.

Reagan, Clinton & the Bushes

In 1980, California's Republican governor and former actor Ronald Reagan campaigned for president by promising to make Americans feel good about America again. The affable Reagan won easily, and his election marked a pronounced shift to the right in US politics. Military spending and tax cuts created enormous federal deficits, which hampered the presidency of Reagan's successor, George HW Bush. Despite winning the Gulf War – liberating Kuwait in 1991 after an Iraqi invasion – Bush was soundly defeated in the 1992 presidential election by Southern Democrat Bill Clinton. Clinton had the good fortune to catch the 1990s high-tech internet boom, which seemed to augur a 'new economy' based on white-collar telecommunications. The US economy erased its deficits and ran a surplus, and Clinton presided over one of America's longest economic booms.

In 2000 and 2004, George W Bush, the eldest son of George HW Bush, won the presidential elections so narrowly that the divided results seemed to epitomize an increasingly divided nation. 'Dubya' had the misfortune of being president when the high-tech bubble burst in 2000, but he nevertheless enacted tax cuts that returned federal deficits even greater than before. He also championed the right-wing conservative 'backlash' that had been building since Reagan.

On September 11, 2001, Islamic terrorists flew hijacked planes into New York's World Trade Center and the Pentagon in Washington, DC. This catastrophic attack united Americans behind their president as he vowed revenge and declared a 'war on terror.' Bush soon attacked Afghanistan in an unsuccessful hunt for Al-Qaeda terrorist cells, then attacked Iraq in 2003 and toppled its anti-US dictator, Saddam Hussein. Meanwhile, Iraq descended into civil war. Following scandals and failures – torture photos from the US military prison at Abu Ghraib, the federal response in the aftermath of Hurricane Katrina and the inability to bring the Iraq War to a close – Bush's approval ratings reached historic lows in the second half of his presidency.

Obama

In 2008, hungry for change, Americans elected political newcomer Barack Obama, America's first African American president. He certainly had his work cut out for him. These were, after all, unprecedented times economically, with the US in the largest financial crisis since the Great

Though the town of Woodstock, NY, lent its name to the mythic 1969 music fest, the event actually took place in the nearby hamlet of Bethel, where dairy farmer Max Yasgur rented his alfalfa field to organizers. Ticket price for the bash: $18 for a three-day pass ($24 at the gate).

1989	1990s	2001	2003
The 1960s-era Berlin Wall is torn down, marking the end of the Cold War between the US and the USSR (now Russia). The USA becomes the world's last remaining superpower.	The world wide web debuts in 1991. Silicon Valley, CA, leads a high-tech internet revolution, remaking communications and media; overvalued tech stocks drive the massive boom (and subsequent bust).	On September 11, Al-Qaeda terrorists hijack four commercial airplanes, flying two into NYC's twin towers and one into the Pentagon (the fourth crashes in Pennsylvania); nearly 3000 people are killed.	After citing evidence that Iraq possesses weapons of mass destruction, President George W Bush launches a preemptive war that will cost over 4000 American lives and some $3 trillion.

Depression. What had started as a collapse of the US housing bubble in 2007 had spread to the banking sector, with the meltdown of major financial institutions.

Wars in Afghanistan and Iraq, launched a decade prior, continued to simmer on the back burner of the ever-changing news cycle. In 2011, in a subterfuge operation vetted by President Obama, Navy Seals raided Osama bin Laden's Pakistan hideout and killed the Al-Qaeda leader, bringing an end to the search for America's greatest public enemy.

Following his sober announcement describing the raid, President Obama saw his approval ratings jump by 11%. The president, for his part, certainly needed a boost. The economy remained in bad shape, and the ambitious $800-billion stimulus package passed by Congress in 2009 hadn't borne much fruit in the eyes of many Americans – even though economists estimated that the stimulus did soften the blow of the recession, which would have been much worse without it. At the end of his first term, his approval ratings were around 49%.

With lost jobs, overvalued mortgages and little relief in sight, millions of Americans found themselves adrift. This was not a recession they could spend their way out of, as Obama's predecessor had suggested. People were upset and gathered in large numbers to voice their anger. This, in turn, gave birth to the Tea Party, a wing of politically conservative Republicans who believed that Obama was leaning too far to the left, and that government handouts would destroy the economy and, thus, America. High federal spending, government bailouts (of the banking and auto industries) and especially Obama's healthcare reform (derisively named 'Obamacare') particularly roused their ire.

For a heart-pounding take on national security operations, watch *Homeland*, an Emmy Award–winning cable TV series about a bipolar CIA officer (Claire Danes) playing a game of cat-and-mouse with a marine sergeant who may be an Al-Qaeda operative. It's one of President Obama's favorite shows.

Healthcare for All

For Democrats, however, Obama's healthcare bill, which became law in 2010, was a major victory in bringing healthcare coverage to more Americans, lowering the cost of care and closing loopholes that allowed insurance companies to deny coverage to individuals. Meanwhile, critics from both sides rained blows. From the right: 'This is socialism!' From the left: 'Where's the public option?' (That is, a government-backed plan, which would not force consumers to remain at the mercy of insurance companies.) Whether the new program achieves the lofty goals touted by Democrats (new coverage for 30 million uninsured Americans and lower premiums for all) – or wreaks havoc as per Republican predictions (busting budgets and causing staggering job losses) – remains to be seen.

2005	2008–09	2012	2013
On August 29, Hurricane Katrina hits the Mississippi and Louisiana coasts, rupturing poorly maintained levees and flooding New Orleans. More than 1800 people die, and cost estimates exceed $110 billion.	Barack Obama becomes the first African American president. The stock market crashes due to mismanagement by major American financial institutions. The crisis spreads worldwide.	Hurricane Sandy devastates the East Coast, becoming the second-costliest hurricane ($65 billion) in American history. More than 80 Americans die (plus 200 more in other countries). Obama wins re-election.	A huge scandal erupts when former NSA contractor Edward Snowden leaks classified information about a US intelligence program that monitors emails and conversations of American citizens and its allies.

The Way of Life

The eastern USA is a compelling mix of accents and rhythms, big-city financiers and small-town farmers, university students and sun-seeking retirees, Yankees and Southerners.

Multiculturalism

The US holds the world's second-largest Spanish-speaking population, behind Mexico and just ahead of Spain. Latinos are also the fastest-growing minority group in the nation. In the east, Florida, Illinois, New Jersey and New York have the largest Latino populations.

From the get-go, cities in the East were 'melting pots,' with a long and proud heritage of welcoming newcomers from all over the world. So it's no surprise that the region's diversity is vast.

In the Northeast, Irish and Italian communities have been well established in the urban areas since the 19th century. In Chicago, Latinos (mostly from Mexico) comprise roughly one-quarter of the population. The upper Great Lakes states are home to the nation's biggest enclaves of Somali and Hmong immigrants, a result of the area's long tradition of resettling refugees. In Florida, Cubans lead the multicultural pack. They began arriving in Miami in the 1960s following Castro's revolution and created a politically powerful community. Nicaraguans followed in the 1980s, fleeing war in their country, and now number over 100,000. The city's Little Haiti adds 70,000 Haitians to the mix. The South, more than any other region, is a culture unto itself; over half of all black Americans live here. These examples are just a fraction of the complex whole.

The East, like the rest of the country, can never quite decide if the continual influx of newcomers is its saving grace or what will eventually strain society to the breaking point. 'Immigration reform' has been a Washington buzzword for over a decade. Some people believe the nation's current system deals with illegal immigrants (there are 11 million of them, compared to 480,000 legal immigrants) too leniently – that the government should deport immigrants who are here unlawfully and fine employers who hire them. Other Americans think those rules are too harsh – that immigrants who have been here for years working, contributing to society and abiding by the law deserve amnesty. Despite several attempts, Congress has not been able to pass a comprehensive package addressing illegal immigration, though it has put through various measures to beef up enforcement.

Four million Americans tune in every week to Midwestern raconteur Garrison Keillor's old-timey radio show, *A Prairie Home Companion*. Listen to the live music, sketches and storytelling online at http://prairiehome.publicradio.org.

Religion

Separation of church and state has been the law of the land ever since the Pilgrims came ashore in Massachusetts in the early 1600s. Their faith – Protestant Christianity – continues to be the main one in the East.

Protestantism covers a wide swath of denominations. They fall under two main headings: evangelical Protestants, of which Baptists form the biggest contingent; and mainline Protestants, such as Lutherans, Methodists and Presbyterians. Evangelicals have the greater number of worshippers, and that number has grown in recent years: Baptists are their powerhouse, accounting for one-third of all Protestants and close to one-fifth of the USA's total adult population. Their numbers stack up in the South. In contrast, Lutherans (who are concentrated in Minnesota and Wisconsin, as well as the Dakotas) and the other mainline denominations have experienced declining figures.

Catholicism is the East's second-most-practiced faith. In fact, New England is the country's most Catholic zone, and the numbers trickle down to the Mid-Atlantic states. Massachusetts is the most Catholic state, with 45% of residents of that faith. Baltimore is the country's oldest archdiocese, established in 1789. States with large Latino populations, such as Florida and Illinois, also support big concentrations of Catholics.

Judaism has a significant presence in the eastern USA. Jews make up roughly 12% of the population in both south Florida and the New York metro area. The latter is a major center of Orthodox Judaism and home to more Jews than anywhere outside Tel Aviv.

Also in the East: Muslim Americans cluster in the New York, Chicago and Detroit metro areas. Hindu Americans bunch in New York and New Jersey, as well as big cities like Chicago, Washington, DC, and Atlanta.

Lifestyle

In general, the eastern USA has one of the world's highest standards of living, though there are some shocking variances by region. At the top end sits Maryland, with a median household income of $71,100 (based on 2011–12 census data). Mississippi dwells at the opposite end of the scale at $37,100. These amounts are the high/low not just for the region, but for the nation, upholding the pattern in which households in the Northeast earn the most, while those in the South earn the least. Wages also vary by ethnicity, with African Americans and Latinos earning less than whites and Asians ($33,300 and $39,000 respectively, versus $57,000 and $68,700).

TV shows like *The Biggest Loser* and Eric Schlosser's book and film *Fast Food Nation* shine a spotlight on the nation's deadly eating habits. Fast food, soft drinks and too much television have all been vilified in recent years.

Nearly 87% of Americans are high-school graduates, while some 30% go on to graduate from college with a four-year bachelor's degree. The university lifestyle (ie cafes, bookshops and progressive mindsets) is especially prevalent in the Northeast, home to the eight Ivy League schools as well as the 'Little Ivies' (a self-anointed collection of a dozen elite liberal-arts colleges) and the 'Seven Sisters' (top-tier women's colleges, founded in the days when the Ivy League was still a boys-only club). More than 50 institutions of higher learning range around Boston alone.

If you peeked in a house, you'd typically find a married couple with two kids occupying it. Both parents usually work, and 28% work more than 40 hours per week. Divorce is common – 40% of first marriages break up – but both divorce and marriage rates have declined over the last three decades. Single parents head 9% of households.

While many Americans hit the gym or walk, bike or jog regularly, over 50% don't exercise at all during their free time, according to the Centers for Disease Control and Prevention (CDC). Health researchers specu-

STATES & TRAITS

Regional US stereotypes now have solid data behind them, thanks to a study titled 'The Geography of Personality.' Researchers processed more than a half-million personality assessments collected from individual US citizens, then looked at where certain traits stacked up on the map. Turns out 'Minnesota nice' is for real – the most 'agreeable' states cluster in the Midwest, Great Plains and South. These places rank highest for friendliness and cooperation. The most neurotic states? They line up in the Northeast. But New York didn't place number one, as you might expect; that honor goes to West Virginia. Many of the most 'open' states lie out West. California, Nevada, Oregon and Washington all rate high for being receptive to new ideas – although they lag behind Washington, DC, and New York.

ICONIC SPORTING VENUES

Yankee Stadium, NYC The Bronx's fabled baseball field, steeped in history and the ghost of Babe Ruth.

Lambeau Field, Green Bay Stadium of the NFL's Packers; nicknamed 'the Frozen Tundra' for its insanely cold weather.

Fenway Park, Boston Baseball's oldest park (1912); home of the 'Green Monster' (aka the tall left-field wall).

Wrigley Field, Chicago Another vintage ballpark (1914), with ivy walls, a classic neon sign and good-time neighborhood bars all around.

Madison Square Garden, NYC Not only do the Knicks dribble at the 'mecca of basketball,' but Ali boxed here and Elvis rocked here.

Joe Louis Arena, Detroit The badass rink of pro hockey's Red Wings; witness the strange octopus-throwing custom.

Churchill Downs, Louisville Home of the Kentucky Derby: fine hats, mint juleps and the 'greatest two minutes in sports'.

Indianapolis Motor Speedway, Indianapolis Racecars scream by at 170 miles per hour at the hard-partying Indy 500.

late that this lack of exercise and Americans' fondness for sugary and fatty foods have led to rising obesity and diabetes rates. The South fares the worst: Mississippi, Alabama, West Virginia, Tennessee and Louisiana lead the obesity rankings, with the condition affecting one-third of residents.

About 26% of Americans volunteer their time to help others or help a cause, especially in the Midwest, followed by the West, South and Northeast, according to the Corporation for National and Community Service. Eco-consciousness has entered the mainstream: over 75% of Americans recycle at home, and most big chain grocery stores – including Wal-Mart – now sell organic foods.

Greenest Cities

Boston, MA

Minneapolis, MN

Cambridge, MA

Chicago, IL

Sports

What really draws Americans together (sometimes slathered in blue body paint or with foam-rubber cheese wedges on their heads) is sports. In spring and summer there's baseball nearly every day, in fall and winter there's football, and through the long nights of winter there's plenty of basketball to keep the adrenaline going – those are the big three sports. Car racing has revved up interest, especially in the South. Major League Soccer (MLS) is attracting an ever-increasing following. Ice hockey, once favored only in northern climes, has fans throughout the area.

Baseball

Despite high salaries and its biggest stars being dogged by steroid rumors, baseball remains America's favorite pastime. It may not command the same TV viewership (and subsequent advertising dollars) as football, but baseball has 162 games over a season versus 16 for football.

Besides, baseball is better live than on TV – being at the ballpark on a sunny day, sitting in the bleachers with a beer and hot dog, and indulging in the seventh-inning stretch, when the entire park erupts in a communal sing-along of 'Take Me Out to the Ballgame.' The playoffs, held every October, still deliver excitement and unexpected champions. The New York Yankees, Boston Red Sox and Chicago Cubs continue to be America's favorite teams, even when they're abysmal (the Cubs haven't won a World Series in more than 100 years).

Tickets are relatively inexpensive – seats average about $25 at most stadiums – and are easy to get for most games. Minor-league baseball games cost half as much, and can be even more fun, with lots of audience participation, stray chickens and dogs running across the field and wild throws from the pitcher's mound. For information, see www.milb.com.

Football

Football is big, physical, and rolling in dough. With the shortest season and least number of games of any of the major sports, every match takes on the emotion of an epic battle, where the results matter and an unfortunate injury can deal a lethal blow to a team's playoff chances.

It's also the toughest US sport, played in fall and winter in all manner of rain, sleet and snow – some of the most memorable matches have occurred at below-freezing temperatures. Green Bay Packers fans are in a class by themselves when it comes to severe weather. Their stadium in Wisconsin (Lambeau Field) was the site of the infamous Ice Bowl, a 1967 championship game against the Dallas Cowboys where the temperature plummeted to -13°F – mind you, that was with a wind-chill factor of -48°F.

The rabidly popular Super Bowl is pro football's championship match, held in late January or early February. The other 'bowl' games (such as the Sugar Bowl in New Orleans and Orange Bowl in Miami) are college football's title matches, held on and around New Year's Day.

Basketball

The teams bringing in the most fans these days include the Chicago Bulls (thanks to the lingering Michael Jordan effect), the Detroit Pistons (a rowdy crowd where riots have broken out), the Miami Heat (home of Lebron James, the league's most loved – and hated – player) and the New York Knicks (where Woody Allen and other celebrities sit courtside).

College basketball also draws millions of fans, especially every spring when the March Madness playoffs roll around; it culminates in the Final Four, when the remaining quartet of teams competes for a spot in the championship game. The Cinderella stories and unexpected outcomes rival the pro league for excitement. The games are widely televised and bet upon – this is when Las Vegas bookies earn their keep.

The Super Bowl costs America $800 million dollars in lost workplace productivity as employees gossip about the game, make bets and shop for new TVs online.

THE WAY OF LIFE SPORTS

Sport Websites

Baseball:
www.mlb.com

Basketball:
www.nba.com

Football:
www.nfl.com

Hockey:
www.nhl.com

Car racing:
www.nascar.com

Soccer:
www.mlssoccer.com

Regional Cuisine

The East's cuisine mixes myriad cultures, and each region has evolved its own unique flavor. From seafood in Maine to slow-cooked brisket in Mississippi, you're in for a treat. Tipplers will find the East to be the country's most spirited side. A booming microbrewery industry has brought artful beers to every corner of the region, while New York and Virginia give wine drinkers vintages to appreciate, and Kentucky pours on the bourbon.

Only three states in the nation have an official state pie, and they're all in the east: Indiana (sugar cream pie), Florida (key lime pie) and Vermont (apple pie). Maine lists blueberry pie as its 'state dessert,' while Delaware does the same for peach pie.

Local Flavors

NYC: Foodie Heaven

They say that you could eat at a different restaurant every night of your life in New York City and not exhaust the possibilities. Considering that there are more than 23,000 restaurants in the five boroughs, with scores of new ones opening each year, it's true. Owing to its huge immigrant population and an influx of over 50 million tourists annually, New York captures the title of America's greatest restaurant city. Its diverse neighborhoods serve up authentic Italian food and thin-crust pizza, all manner of Asian food, French *haute cuisine* and classic Jewish deli food, from bagels to piled-high pastrami on rye. More exotic cuisines are found here as well, from Ethiopian to Scandinavian.

Don't let NYC's image as expensive get to you: the *Zagat Guide* says the average cost of a meal – including drink, tax and tip – is $48.50. There may be no free lunch in New York, but compared to other world cities, eating here can be a bargain.

New England: Clambakes & Lobster Boils

New England claims to have the nation's best seafood, and who's to argue? The North Atlantic Ocean offers up clams, mussels, oysters and huge lobsters, along with shad, bluefish and cod. The bounty stirs into a mighty fine chowder (soup), for which every seafood shack up the coast has its own secret recipe, put to the test during summertime chowder fests and cook-offs. The clambake is another tradition, where shellfish are buried in a pit fire with foil-wrapped corn, chicken and sausages. Fried clam fritters and lobster rolls (lobster meat with may-

---

VEGETARIANS' DELIGHT

Vegetarian restaurants abound in major cities, though not always in rural areas. Here are our go-to favorites. To find more, browse www.happycow.net.

Angelica Kitchen (p98), New York City, NY

Café Zenith (p160), Pittsburgh, PA

Dandelion Communitea Café (p501), Orlando, FL

Green Elephant (p240), Portland, ME

Moosewood Restaurant (p121), Ithaca, NY

onnaise served in a bread bun) are served throughout the region.

Vermont makes excellent cheeses, Massachusetts harvests cranberries (a Thanksgiving staple), and New England's forests drip sweet maple syrup. Still hungry? Connecticut is famed for its thin-crust New Haven–style pizza (best topped with white clams); Boston specializes in baked beans and brown bread; and Rhode Islanders pour coffee syrup into milk and embrace traditional cornmeal johnnycakes.

Mid-Atlantic: Cheesesteaks, Crabcakes & Scrapple

From New York down through Virginia, the Mid-Atlantic states share a long coastline and a cornucopia of apple, pear and berry farms. New Jersey wins prizes for tomatoes and New York's Long Island for potatoes. Chesapeake Bay's blue crabs make diners swoon, as do Pennsylvania Dutch Country's heaped plates of chicken pot pie, noodles and meatloaf-like scrapple. In Philadelphia, you can gorge on 'Philly cheesesteaks', made with thin strips of sautéed beef, onions and melted cheese on a bun. Virginia serves its salt-cured 'country-style' ham with biscuits. New York's Finger Lakes, Hudson Valley and Long Island uncork highly regarded wines to accompany the region's well-set table.

The South: BBQ, Biscuits & Gumbo

No region is prouder of its food culture than the South, which has a long history of mingling Anglo, French, African, Spanish and Native American foods. Slow-cooked barbecue is one of the top stokers of regional pride; there are as many meaty and saucy variations as there are towns in the South. Southern fried chicken and catfish pop out of the pan crisp on the outside and moist inside. Fluffy hot biscuits, corn bread, sweet potatoes, collard greens, and – most passionately – grits (ground corn cooked to a cereal-like consistency) accompany Southern plates, all butter-smothered. Treasured dessert recipes tend to produce big layer cakes or pies made with pecans, bananas and citrus. Sweet iced tea (non alcoholic) or a cool mint julep cocktail (with bourbon) help wash it down.

For the region's crème de la crème, pull up a chair at Louisiana's tables. The state stands out for its two main cuisines – Cajun food is found in the bayou country and marries native spices like sassafras and chili peppers to provincial French cooking. Creole food is more urban and centered in New Orleans, where zippy dishes like shrimp remoulade, crabmeat ravigote and gumbo (a soupy stew of chicken, shellfish and/or sausage, and okra) have eaters dabbing their brow.

Midwest: Burgers, Bacon & Beer

Midwesterners eat big, and with gusto. Portions are huge – this is farm country, after all, where people need sustenance to get their work done. The region is tops for serving American classics like pot roast, meatloaf, steak and pork chops; add walleye,

January

The ice wine grape harvest takes place around the Finger Lakes, New York, and in northern Michigan. Sweet dessert drinks ensue.

March

In Vermont and Maine, it's sugaring season, when fresh maple syrup flows. Down south, crawfish ramps up: Louisiana harvests around 110 million pounds of the critters between now and May.

May

Georgia's peach harvest begins mid-month and goes until mid-August. To the north, Chesapeake Bay blue crabs hit the market through September.

July

Early in the month Michigan goes wild, picking tart cherries and hosting fruity festivities like the International Cherry Pit Spitting Championship in Eau Claire.

August

The action shifts to New England: the coast's lobster shacks and clambakes are in full swing, while Maine's wild blueberries get heaped into pies.

September & October

It's prime time to pick apples in New York and Michigan (the nation's second- and third-largest producers). Cider houses pour their wares. Meanwhile, it's cranberry season in Massachusetts and Wisconsin.

Lip-
Smacking
Festivals

*Crawfish Festival,
Breaux Bridge, LA*

*Kentucky Bourbon
Festival,
Bardstown, KY*

*Maine Lobster
Festival,
Rockland, ME*

*World's Largest
Brat Fest,
Madison, WI*

perch and other freshwater fish to menus in towns near the Great Lakes. Count on a nice cold beer to complement the wares. Chicago stands tall as the region's best place to pile a plate, with hole-in-the-wall ethnic eateries cooking alongside many of the country's most acclaimed restaurants. Another great place to sample Midwestern foods is at a county fair, which offers everything from bratwurst to fried dough to grilled corn on the cob. Elsewhere at diners and family restaurants, you'll taste the varied influences of Eastern European, Scandinavian, Latino and Asian immigrants, especially in the cities.

Habits & Customs

For breakfast Americans love their eggs and bacon, waffles and hash browns, and big glasses of orange juice. Most of all, they love a steaming cup of coffee. After a midmorning snack break, the lunch hour of most American workers affords time enough for just a sandwich, quick burger or hearty salad. While you may spot (rarely) diners drinking a glass of wine or beer with their noontime meal, the days of the 'three-martini lunch' are long gone. Early in the evening, people settle in to a more substantial weeknight dinner, which, given the workload of so many two-career families, might be takeout or prepackaged dishes.

Americans tend to eat dinner early, usually between 6pm and 8pm. In smaller towns, it may be hard to find anywhere to eat after 8:30pm or so. Dinner parties usually begin around 6:30pm or 7pm, with cocktails followed by a meal. If you're invited to dinner, it's polite to be prompt: ideally, you should plan to arrive within 15 minutes of the designated time. Americans are notoriously informal in their dining manners, although they will usually wait until everyone is served before eating.

Cooking Courses

Cooking schools that offer courses for enthusiastic amateur chefs include the following (though this list is by no means exhaustive):

Chopping Block Cooking School (www.thechoppingblock.net) Master knife skills or learn to make deep-dish pizza in Chicago.

International Culinary Center (www.internationalculinarycenter.com) Hosts the French Culinary Institute and Italian Culinary Academy in New York City.

Kitchen Window (www.kitchenwindow.com) Hosts market tours and restaurant crawls, plus classes on baking, outdoor grilling and world cuisine in Minneapolis.

Natural Gourmet Cookery School (www.naturalgourmetschool.com) Focuses on vegetarian and healthy 'flexitarian' cooking in NYC.

Zingerman's Bakehouse (p572) Offers popular 'bake-cations,' making bread or pastries in Ann Arbor.

Drinks
Beer

Classic
American
Diners

*Arcade,
Memphis, TN*

*Lou's,
Dartmouth, NH*

*Mickey's Dining
Car,
St Paul, MN*

*Miss Worcester
Diner,
Worcester, MA*

After founding the American beer industry in Milwaukee, 19th-century German immigrants developed ways to make beer in vast quantities and then deliver it all over America. Today about 80% of domestic beer still comes from the Midwest.

Despite their ubiquity, popular brands of American beer have long been the subject of ridicule abroad due to their low alcohol content and 'light' taste. Regardless of what critics say, sales indicate that American beer is more popular than ever – and now, with the meteoric rise of microbreweries and craft beer, even beer snobs admit that American beer has reinvented itself.

Today there are more than 2500 craft breweries in the USA, up from 1500 breweries in 2009. As of 2013, new breweries were coming online at a pace of roughly one per day. It has become possible to 'drink local' all over the region as microbreweries pop up in urban centers and unexpected small towns. Some restaurants now have beer 'sommeliers,' while others host beer dinners, where you can experience how small-batch brews pair with different foods.

Wine

About 20% of Americans drink wine on a regular basis. The West Coast states, predominately California, produce the majority of domestic vino. In the East, New York yields the most, enough to rank fourth nationwide when gauged by number of producers. The Finger Lakes region is the hot spot, awash in Riesling grapes and prime for sipping a good Chardonnay, Gewürztraminer or ice wine. Virginia is the fifth-biggest wine-producing state, with 192 vineyards within its borders, many located in the pretty hills around Charlottesville. Particularly notable is the Virginia Viognier, an exotic white grape. Michigan's west coast offers another vine-striped landscape; its winemakers are known for everything from lush Cabernet Franc to high-end sparkling wines. All of these bucolic regions have spawned entire industries of sip-tripping and bed-and-breakfast tourism.

In general, wine isn't cheap in the US, as it's considered a luxury rather than a staple (in contrast to some European countries). But it's possible to procure a perfectly drinkable bottle of American wine at a liquor or wine shop for around $10 to $12.

Spirits

The East is the cradle of the good stuff. Jack Daniels remains the most well-known brand of American whiskey around the world, and is also the oldest continually operating US distillery, going strong in Lynchburg, Tennessee, since 1870. Bourbon, made from corn, is the nation's only native spirit. Kentucky produces 95% of the world supply, most of which flows from seven distilleries in the state's central zone. The 225-mile loop between the booze-makers here is known as the Bourbon Trail, and road-tripping to visit the distilleries and sample their wares has become an offbeat version of California's Napa Valley.

Cocktails were invented in New Orleans, appropriately enough, before the Civil War. The first cocktail was the Sazerac – a mix of rye whiskey or brandy, simple syrup, bitters and a dash of absinthe. American cocktails created at bars in the late 19th and early 20th centuries include such long-standing classics as the Martini, the Manhattan and the Old-Fashioned.

Best Cocktail Bars

Aviary, Chicago

Drink, Boston

Franklin Mortgage & Investment Co, Philadelphia

Lantern's Keep, NYC

Maison Premier, NYC

Tonique, New Orleans

REGIONAL CUISINE DRINKS

BEST MICROBREWERIES

Microbreweries have exploded in popularity, and you'll never be far from a finely crafted pint. Careful though: craft beers can be stronger than mass-produced brands. Look for a brewery's 'session beer' if you want a lower alcohol content. Surprising towns such as Grand Rapids, Michigan, and Asheville, North Carolina, have become particularly famed for their suds. And for the record: Vermont boasts the most microbreweries per capita. As you travel around the region, keep an eye out for the following:

DC Brau (www.dcbrau.com; 3178B Bladensburg Rd) In Washington, DC.

Three Floyds (www.3floyds.com) In Munster, IN.

Magic Hat Brewery (p224) In Burlington, VT.

Bell's Brewery (www.bellsbeer.com) In Kalamazoo, MI.

Fullsteam Brewery (p341) In Durham NC.

The Vintage Cocktail Craze

Across US cities, it has become decidedly cool to party like it's 1929 by drinking retro cocktails from the days – less than a century ago – when alcohol was illegal. Good old Prohibition: instead of spawning a nation of teetotalers, it arguably only solidified a culture for which the forbidden became appealing – it felt good to be bad, and so-called respectable citizens congregated in secret 'speakeasies' to drink homemade moonshine and dance to hot jazz.

Fast forward to the 21st century. While Prohibition isn't in any danger of being reinstated, you'll find plenty of bars in the region where the spirit of the Roaring '20s and illicit 1930s lives on. Inspired by vintage recipes calling for natural and homemade elixirs, these cocktails – blending ingredients such as small-batch liqueurs, whipped egg whites, hand-chipped ice and fresh fruits – are lovingly concocted by nattily dressed bartenders who regard their profession as something between an art and a science.

Arts & Architecture

Jazz, blues, country and rock music all were born in the eastern USA, and their beats permeate clubs and juke joints from north to south. New York remains the dynamic heart of the theater and art worlds, while great literature finds its voice throughout the region. In the meantime, architects in New York and Chicago keep pushing ever higher.

Music

Blues

Willie Dixon said it best: 'The blues is the roots, and everything else is the fruits.' He meant that all US music starts with the blues. And the blues started in the South. That's where the genre developed out of the work songs, or 'shouts,' of black slaves and out of black spiritual songs and their call-and-response pattern, both of which were adaptations of African music.

By the 1920s, Delta blues typified the sound. Musicians from Memphis to Mississippi sung passionate, plaintive melodies accompanied by a lonely slide guitar. Traveling blues musicians, and particularly female blues singers, gained fame and employment across the South. Early pioneers included Robert Johnson, WC Handy, Ma Rainey, Huddie Ledbetter (aka Lead Belly) and Bessie Smith, who some consider the best blues singer who ever lived.

After WWII many musicians headed north to Chicago, which had become a hub for African American culture. And here the genre took a turn – it went electric. A new generation of players such as Muddy Waters, Buddy Guy, BB King and John Lee Hooker plugged in to amps, and their screaming guitars laid the groundwork for rock and roll.

Jazz

Down in New Orleans, Congo Sq, where slaves gathered to sing and dance from the late 18th century onward, is considered the birthplace of jazz. There ex-slaves adapted the reed, horn and string instruments used by the city's multiracial Creoles – who themselves preferred formal European music – to play their own African-influenced music. This fertile cross-pollination produced a steady stream of innovative sound.

The first variation was ragtime, so-called because of its 'ragged', syncopated African rhythms. Next came Dixieland jazz, centered on New Orleans' infamous Storyville red-light district. In 1917 Storyville shut down, and the musicians dispersed. Key player Louis Armstrong moved to Chicago to blow his trumpet, and set the tone for decades to come.

The 1920s and '30s are known as the Jazz Age, and New York City's Harlem was its hot spot, where Duke Ellington and Count Basie led their swingin' big bands. In the 1950s and '60s, Miles Davis, John Coltrane and others deconstructed the sound and made up a new one that was cool, free and avant-garde. NYC, New Orleans and Chicago remain the core of the scene today.

Shrines for Music Fans

Sun Studio, Memphis

Rock and Roll Hall of Fame, Cleveland

Preservation Hall, New Orleans

BB King Museum, Indianola, MS

Best Music Festivals

New Orleans Jazz Festival; April

Bonnaroo, Manchester, TN; June

Summerfest, Milwaukee; June/July

Newport Folk Festival, Rhode Island; July

Lollapalooza, Chicago; August

Country

Early Scottish, Irish and English immigrants brought their own instruments and folk music to America, and what emerged over time in the secluded Appalachian Mountains was fiddle-and-banjo hillbilly, or 'country,' music. In the Southwest, steel guitars and larger bands distinguished 'western' music. In the 1920s, these styles merged into 'country and western' and Nashville became its center, especially once the Grand Ole Opry began its radio broadcasts in 1925.

Something about the 'cry a tear in your beer' twanging clearly resonated with listeners, because country music is now big business. Singer-songwriters such as Blake Shelton, Tim McGraw and Taylor Swift have sold millions of albums. Subsequent riffs on the genre include bluegrass, rockabilly and alt-country. The South remains the genre's boot-wearin' stronghold.

Eastern
US Classic
Playlist

'Atlantic City,'
Bruce Springsteen

'Georgia on My
Mind,' Ray Charles

'No Sleep till
Brooklyn,' Beastie
Boys

'Sweet Home
Alabama,' Lynyrd
Skynyrd

Rock

Most say rock and roll was born in 1954 the day Elvis Presley walked into Sam Philips' Sun Studios and recorded 'That's All Right.' Initially, radio stations weren't sure why a white country boy was singing black music, or whether they should play him. It wasn't until 1956 that Presley scored his first big breakthrough with 'Heartbreak Hotel,' and in some ways, America never recovered from the rock-and-roll aftermath.

Musically, rock was a hybrid of guitar-driven blues, black rhythm and blues (R&B), and white country-and-western music. R&B evolved in the 1940s out of swing and the blues, and was then known as 'race music.' With rock and roll, white musicians (and some African American musicians) transformed 'race music' into something that white youths could embrace freely – and boy, did they.

Rock morphed into the psychedelic sounds of the Grateful Dead and Jefferson Airplane, and the electric wails of Janis Joplin, Jimi Hendrix, Bob Dylan and Patti Smith. Since then, rock has been about music and lifestyle, alternately torn between hedonism and seriousness, commercialism and authenticity. The Woodstock festival exemplified the scene in 1969, transforming a little patch of upstate New York into a legend.

Punk arrived in the late 1970s, led by the Ramones and the Dead Kennedys, as did the working-class rock of Bruce Springsteen, the pride of New Jersey. But it wasn't long before a new sound on the block took over the 'outlaw' mantle: rap. In the east, New York and Detroit became spawning grounds. Jay Z, Eminem and Chicago's Kanye West are its current frontmen.

Literature

Several famous
authors from
the eastern
USA wrote
books that have
been banned
at one time or
another, including Indianapolis'
Kurt Vonnegut
(Slaughterhouse-
Five), New York's
JD Salinger (The
Catcher in the
Rye) and Georgia-
born Alice Walker
(The Color
Purple).

The 'Great American Novel' has stirred the imagination for more than 150 years. Edgar Allan Poe told spooky short stories in the 1840s, and is credited with inventing the detective story, horror story and science fiction. Four decades later Samuel Clemens, aka Mark Twain, also made a literary splash. Twain wrote in the vernacular, loved 'tall tales' and reveled in absurdity, which endeared him to everyday readers. His novel *Huckleberry Finn* (1884) became the quintessential American narrative: compelled by a primal moment of rebellion against his father, Huck embarks on a search for authenticity through which he discovers himself. The Mississippi River provides the backdrop.

The 'Lost Generation' brought American literature into its own in the early 20th century. These writers lived as expatriates in post-WWI Europe and described a growing sense of alienation. Plain-speaking Midwesterner Ernest Hemingway exemplified the era with his spare, stylized realism. Minnesotan F Scott Fitzgerald eviscerated East Coast society life with his fiction. Back on home turf, William Faulkner examined the South's social rifts in dense, caustic prose, and African Americans such as poet Langston Hughes and novelist Zora Neale Hurston undermined racist stereotypes during New York's Harlem Renaissance.

After WWII, American writers began depicting regional and ethnic divides, experimented with style and often bashed middle-class society's values. The 1950s Beat Generation, with Jack Kerouac, Allen Ginsberg and William S Burroughs at the center, was particularly hardcore.

Today's literature reflects an ever more diverse panoply of voices. Toni Morrison, Amy Tan, Ana Castillo and Sherman Alexie have all written bestsellers and given voice to, respectively, African American, Asian American, Mexican American and Native American issues, among many others. Emerging novelists to watch out for include Junot Diaz, Gary Shyteyngart, Nicole Krauss and Jonathan Safran Foer (the latter two are husband and wife who live in Brooklyn).

Great American Novels

....

Beloved, Toni Morrison

....

The Great Gatsby, F Scott Fitzgerald

....

The Sound and the Fury, William Faulkner

....

The Sun Also Rises, Ernest Hemingway

ARTS & ARCHITECTURE FILM & TELEVISION

Film & Television

The studio system actually began in Manhattan, where Thomas Edison – inventor of the industry's earliest moving-picture technology – tried to create a monopoly with his patents. This drove many independents to move to a suburb of Los Angeles, where they could easily flee to Mexico in case of legal trouble – and ta-da, Hollywood was born.

While most of the movie magic still happens on the west coast, New York retains its fair share of film and TV studios. ABC, CBS, NBC, CNN, MTV and HBO are among the Big Apple's big shots, and many visitors come expressly to see David Letterman, Dr Oz or their other favorite talk shows taping. Many filmmakers and actors prefer New York to the west coast – Robert De Niro, Spike Lee and Woody Allen most famously – so keep an eye out on local streets. Other film-friendly cities include Miami and Chicago, and one you wouldn't normally think of: Wilmington, North Carolina, which hosts enough studios to earn the nickname 'Wilmywood.'

As YouTube, Hulu, Netflix and their ilk have entered the industry, the networks have responded by creating more edgy, long-narrative serial dramas, as well as cheap-to-produce, 'unscripted' reality TV: what *Survivor* started in 2000, the contestants and 'actors' of *American Idol, Duck Dynasty* and *The Voice* keep alive today, for better or for worse.

Theater

Eugene O'Neill put American drama on the map with his trilogy *Mourning Becomes Electra* (1931), which sets a tragic Greek myth in post–Civil War New England. O'Neill was the first major US playwright, and is still widely considered to be the best.

After WWII two playwrights dominated the stage: Arthur Miller, who famously married Marilyn Monroe and wrote about everything from middle-class male disillusionment (*Death of a Salesman,* 1949) to the mob mentality of the Salem witch trials (*The Crucible,* 1953); and Tennessee Williams, whose explosive works *The Glass Menagerie* (1945), *A Streetcar Named Desire* (1947) and *Cat on a Hot Tin Roof* (1955) dug deep into the Southern psyche.

Edward Albee gave the 1960s a healthy dose of absurdism, and David Mamet and Sam Shepard filled the '70s and '80s with rough-and-tough guys. These days Pulitzer Prize–winner Tracy Letts writes family dramas that are often compared to O'Neill, bringing the scene full circle.

Broadway is where shows get star treatment. The famed NYC district earns more than a billion dollars in revenue from ticket sales each year, with top shows pulling in a cool $2 million a week. Long-running classics such as *The Lion King* and *Wicked* continue to play before sold-out houses, while musicals such as *Les Miserables* get revamped and reopen to much fanfare

THE GOLDEN AGE OF AMERICAN TELEVISION

By the 21st century, cable TV was targeting all manner of niche audiences and producing sophisticated, complex dramas that surpassed most risk-averse Hollywood fare. The result? Some might say that the 2000s, not the mid-20th century, have proved to be the 'golden age' of American TV. Shows that give an eastern USA perspective include:

➡ *Dexter:* Can a serial killer have morals? A Miami police detective with a big secret proves that the answer just may be 'yes'.

➡ *Mad Men*: It follows the boozy antics of 1960s advertising execs in New York City.

➡ *Tremé:* New Orleans gets its close-up in this drama of the city's historic African American neighborhood trying to rebuild post-Katrina.

➡ *The Walking Dead*: Survivors of the apocalypse must fight off zombies in Atlanta and northern Georgia.

➡ *The Wire*: Politicians versus police versus drug dealers on the mean streets of Baltimore.

(as in 2014). But it's away from Broadway's bright lights, in regional theaters such as Chicago's Steppenwolf, Minneapolis' Guthrie and hundreds more, where new plays and playwrights emerge that keep the art vital.

Painting

In the wake of WWII, the USA developed its first truly original school of art: abstract expressionism. New York painters Jackson Pollock, Franz Kline, Mark Rothko and others explored freely created, nonrepresentational forms. Pollock, for example, made drip paintings by pouring and splattering pigments over large canvases.

Pop art followed, where artists drew inspiration from bright, cartoony consumer images; Andy Warhol was the king (or Pope of Pop, as he's sometimes called). Minimalism came next, and by the 1980s and '90s, the canvas was wide open – any and all styles could take their place at the arts table. New York remains the red-hot center of the art world, and its make-or-break influence shapes tastes across the nation and around the globe.

Architecture

In 1885, a group of designers in Chicago shot up the pioneering skyscraper. It didn't exactly poke the clouds, but its use of steel framing launched modern architecture.

Around the same time, another Chicago architect was doing radical things closer to the ground. Frank Lloyd Wright created a building style that abandoned historical elements and references, which had long been the tradition, and instead he went organic. He designed buildings in relation to the landscape, which in the Midwest were the low-slung, horizontal lines of the surrounding prairie. An entire movement grew up around Wright's Prairie Style.

European architects absorbed Wright's ideas, and that influence bounced back when the Bauhaus school left Nazi Germany and set up in the USA. Here it became known as the International Style, an early form of modernism. Ludwig Mies van der Rohe was the main man with the plan, and his boxy, metal-and-glass behemoths rose high on urban horizons, especially in Chicago and New York City. Postmodernism followed, reintroducing color and the decorative elements of art deco, beaux arts and other earlier styles to the region's sky-high designs.

Today's architects continue to break boundaries. Recent examples of visionary designs include Jeanne Gang's rippling Aqua Tower in Chicago – the world's tallest building designed by a woman. NYC's 1776ft-high One World Trade Center rose to become the USA's loftiest building in 2013.

Best Modern Art Museums

Museum of Modern Art, NYC

Whitney Museum of American Art, NYC

Salvador Dalí Museum, St Petersburg, FL

Andy Warhol Museum, Pittsburgh

Landscapes & Wildlife

Whether you've come to glimpse alligators, whales, manatees or moose, the eastern USA delivers. Its coasts, mountains, swamps and forests have heaps of habitat for wildlife spotting. The national parks are prime places to take it all in.

Landscapes

The eastern USA is a land of temperate, deciduous forests and contains the ancient Appalachian Mountains, a low range that parallels the Atlantic Ocean. Between the mountains and the coast lies the country's most populated, urbanized region, particularly in the corridor between Washington, DC, and Boston, MA.

To the north are the Great Lakes, which the USA shares with Canada. These five lakes, part of the Canadian Shield, are the greatest expanse of fresh water on the planet, constituting nearly 20% of the world's supply.

Going south along the East Coast, things get wetter and warmer till you reach the swamps of southern Florida and make the turn into the Gulf of Mexico, which provides the USA with a southern coastline.

West of the Appalachians are the vast interior plains, which lie flat all the way to the Rocky Mountains. The eastern plains are the nation's breadbasket, roughly divided into the northern 'corn belt' and the southern 'cotton belt.' The plains, an ancient sea bottom, are drained by the mighty Mississippi River, which together with the Missouri River forms the world's fourth-longest river system, surpassed only by the Nile, Amazon and Yangtze rivers.

Beyond the East, the Rocky Mountains and southwestern deserts eventually give way to the Pacific Ocean.

Plants & Trees

Displays of spring wildflowers and colorful autumn foliage are a New England specialty. Great Smoky Mountains National Park contains all five eastern-forest types – spruce fir, hemlock, pine-oak, and northern and cove hardwood – which support over 100 native species of trees.

In Florida, the Everglades is the last subtropical wilderness in the US. This vital, endangered habitat is a fresh- and saltwater world of marshes, sloughs and coastal prairies that support mangroves, cypresses, sea grasses, tropical plants, pines and hardwoods.

Land Mammals

Moose

Moose nibble on shrubs throughout the northern part of the region, specifically Maine, New Hampshire, Vermont, upstate New York and the Michigan-Minnesota-Wisconsin north woods. They're part of the deer family but are far more humungous, with skinny, ballerina-like legs that support a hulking body. Males weigh up to 1200lb, all put on by a vegetarian diet of twigs and leaves. Despite their odd shape, moose can move it: they run up to 35mph, and in water they can swim as fast as two men paddling a canoe.

Best Landscapes off the Beaten Path

....

Cypress Creek National Wildlife Refuge, IL: swamplands

....

Ouachita National Forest, AK: spring-fed mountains

....

Cape Henlopen State Park, DE: dunes, wetlands

....

Monongahela National Forest, WV: rivers

Geologists believe that roughly 460 million years ago the Appalachian Mountains were the highest mountains on earth – higher even than the Himalayas are today.

INFAMOUS NATURAL DISASTERS

Earthquakes, wildfires, tornadoes, hurricanes and blizzards – the US certainly has its share of natural disasters. A few of the more infamous events that have shaped the national conscience:

Hurricane Katrina August 29, 2005, is not a day easily forgotten in New Orleans. A massive hurricane swept across the Gulf of Mexico and slammed into Louisiana. As levees failed, floods inundated over 80% of the city. The death toll reached 1836, with over $100 billion in estimated damages – making it America's costliest natural disaster. Heartbreaking images of the destroyed city and anger over the government's bungled response still linger.

Hurricane Irene On August 27 and 28, 2011, a mammoth storm blew over the eastern seaboard, battering 15 states from Florida through to New England and as far inland as Pennsylvania. New York City evacuated many residents and took the unprecedented step of shutting down all public transit. More than 7.4 million homes lost electrical power, rivers ran wild, and at least 45 people died. The damage has been estimated to be $7 billion.

East Coast Earthquake On August 23, 2011, a rare earthquake rattled the Eastern USA. The 5.8 magnitude tremor had its epicenter located in Mineral, Virginia, but was felt from Maine right through to South Carolina, and was the area's strongest quake since 1897. There was no serious damage, though it did crack the Washington Monument and knock three spires off the National Cathedral in Washington, DC.

Hurricane Sandy On October 29, 2012, America suffered its second-costliest hurricane in US history (after Katrina). Sandy was the largest Atlantic hurricane ever recorded, with storm winds spanning over 1000 miles. The Jersey Shore and low-lying areas of New York City (such as Staten Island) were particularly hard hit. More than 80 people died in the USA, and estimated damages amounted to more than $65 billion.

Males grow a spectacular rack of antlers every summer, only to discard it in November. You'll spot moose foraging near lakes and streams. They generally are not aggressive, and often will pose for photographs. They can be unpredictable, though, so don't startle them. During mating season (September) the males can become belligerent, so keep your distance.

Moose have been dying at an alarming rate in many areas. Scientists think climate change may be partly to blame. In New Hampshire a longer fall with less snow has increased the number of winter ticks, parasites that prey on moose. In Minnesota it's the same story but with brain worms as the deadly parasite. In Maine, however, the population remains healthy.

Does it or exist or no? *Stalking the Ghost Bird: The Elusive Ivory-Billed Woodpecker in Louisiana* (2008), by Mike Steinberg, recounts what happened when kayakers claimed to have sighted the 'extinct' bird, igniting a frenzy in the bayou.

Black Bear

Despite a decline in numbers, black bears prowl most parts of the region, especially in the Adirondacks, the Great Smoky Mountains and the Midwest's north woods. Males can stand 7ft tall and weigh 550lb – but that depends on when you encounter them. In autumn they weigh up to 30% more than when they emerge from hibernation in the spring. Although they enjoy an occasional meaty snack, black bears usually fill their bellies with berries and other vegetation. They're opportunistic, adaptable and curious animals, and can survive on very small home ranges. As their forests diminish, they're occasionally seen traipsing through nearby populated areas.

Panther

A remnant population of panthers licks its chops in Everglades National Park, Florida. Before European contact, perhaps 1500 roamed the state. The first panther bounty ($5 a scalp) was passed in 1832, and over the next 130 years they were hunted relentlessly. Though hunting was stopped in 1958, it was too late for panthers to survive on their own. Without a captive breeding program, begun in 1991, the Florida panther would now be extinct, and with only some 120 known to exist, they're not out of the swamp yet.

Wolf & Coyote

Wolves are rare in the Eastern USA. Those that are here wander mostly in northern Minnesota, particularly the Boundary Waters. The area's cold, boreal forest is prime territory, as well as home to the **International Wolf Center** (www.wolfcenter.org) in Ely, Minnesota. Another small pack lives in Michigan's Isle Royale National Park. The wolf can be every bit as fierce and cunning as is portrayed in fairy tales, although it rarely attacks humans. If you're out in the wilderness, you may hear them howling at the moon.

The coyote looks similar to the wolf but is about half the size, ranging from 15lb to 45lb. An icon of the Southwest, coyotes are found all over the Eastern region too, even in cities – Chicago recently had one that loped into a sandwich shop during the lunchtime rush.

Deer

The white-tailed deer can be found everywhere in the region, from top to bottom. Endemic to the Florida Keys are Key deer, a Honey-I-Shrunk-the-Ungulate subspecies: less than 3ft tall and lighter than a 10-year-old boy, they live mostly on Big Pine Key.

Reptiles

Alligator & Crocodile

American alligators slither throughout the southeast's wetlands, mostly in Florida and Louisiana. With snout, eyeballs and pebbled back so still they hardly ripple the water's surface, alligators have watched over the swamps for more than 200 million years.

Louisiana has close to two million gators, and Florida counts 1.5 million among the state's lakes, rivers and golf courses, mostly in the central and southern zones. The Everglades are perhaps the best place to find them lurking. Alligators are alpha predators who keep the rest of the food chain in check, and their 'gator holes' become vital water cups in the dry season and during droughts, aiding the entire wetlands ecosystem. They live about 30 years, can grow up to 14ft long and weigh 1000lb. No longer officially endangered, alligators remain protected because they resemble the still-endangered American crocodile.

South Florida is home to the only North American population of American crocodiles, around 1500 of them. They prefer saltwater, and to distinguish them from gators, check their smile – a croc's snout is more tapered and its teeth stick out.

Sea Turtles

Florida is the hot spot for sea-turtle nesting in the continental US. Three main species create over 80,000 nests annually, mostly on southern Atlantic Coast beaches, but extending to all Gulf Coast beaches, too. Loggerheads comprise the vast majority, followed by green and leatherback turtles and, historically, hawksbill and Kemp's ridley as well; all five species are endangered or threatened. The leatherback is the largest, bulking up to 10ft and 2000lb.

During the May-to-October nesting season, sea turtles deposit from 80 to 120 eggs in each nest. The eggs incubate for about two months, and then the hatchlings emerge all at once and make for the ocean. Contrary to myth, hatchlings don't need the moon to find their way.

LANDSCAPES & WILDLIFE REPTILES

In addition to its national parks, the Eastern USA holds eight national seashores (including Cape Cod in Massachusetts), four national lakeshores (including Sleeping Bear Dunes in Michigan) and 10 national rivers (including New River Gorge in West Virginia). The National Park Service (www.nps.gov) has the lowdown.

EASTERN USA'S NATIONAL PARKS

NAME	STATE	FEATURES	ACTIVITIES	BEST TIMES
Acadia National Park	ME	1530ft Cadillac Mountain, rocky coastline, islands	hiking, cycling	May–Oct
Biscayne National Park	FL	coral reefs, manatees, dolphins, sea turtles	kayaking, snorkeling, diving, glass-bottom boat tours	mid-Dec–mid-Apr
Congaree National Park	SC	moss-draped cypresses, swamp, owls	fishing, canoeing	spring & autumn
Cuyahoga Valley National Park	OH	rivers, waterfalls, canal tow path	hiking, cycling, scenic train ride	May–Oct
Dry Tortugas National Park	FL	remote islands, Civil War fort, 300 bird species, sea turtles	snorkeling, diving, bird watching	Dec–Apr
Everglades National Park	FL	grasslands, swamp, alligators, panthers, manatees	cycling, canoeing, kayaking, hiking	Dec–Apr
Great Smoky Mountains National Park	NC, TN	mountains, woodlands, wildflowers, black bears, elk	hiking, horseback riding, fishing	mid-Apr–Oct
Hot Springs National Park	AK	thermal waters, historic buildings	spa soaking, hiking	Sep–Feb
Isle Royale National Park	MI	huge isolated island, thick forest, lakes, moose, wolves	kayaking, hiking, back-country camping	mid-May–Oct
Mammoth Cave National Park	KY	never-ending caves, underground rivers, bats	hiking, spelunking	year-round
Shenandoah National Park	VA	Blue Ridge Mountains, waterfalls, deer, bobcats	hiking, camping	Apr–Oct
Voyageurs National Park	MN	thick forest, islands, lakes, wolves, aurora borealis	boating, snowmobiling	May–late Sep

Snakes

First, here's the bad news: there are four species of rattlesnake found east of the Mississippi – the diamondback, pygmy, canebrake and timber. At 7ft long, the diamondback is the biggest and the most aggressive. Copperheads, cottonmouths and coral snakes are other poisonous types in the region. All of them slither primarily through the mid-Atlantic and South.

Now the good news: running into a poisonous snake is uncommon. Need proof? Great Smoky Mountains National Park, with more than 9.5 million visitors per year, has never recorded a snakebite fatality in its 70-plus-year history.

A particularly virulent strain of red algae killed more than 240 manatees in 2013. The algae produces toxins that are absorbed by the sea grass, which manatees eat. It's unknown why the outbreak was so severe for the year.

Marine Mammals & Fish

For stunning coral reefs and vibrant tropical fish, the Florida Keys are place to go.

Whales & Dolphins

The eastern USA's top spot to whale-watch is off Massachusetts' coast at Stellwagen Bank National Marine Sanctuary, a summer feeding ground for humpbacks. These awesome creatures average 49ft and 36 tons – serious heft to be launching up and out of the water for their playful breaching. They also come surprisingly close to boats, offering great photo ops. Many of the 300 remaining North Atlantic right whales, the world's most endangered leviathan, frequent the same waters.

Cruises depart from Boston, Plymouth, Provincetown and Gloucester, Massachusetts.

The waters off the coast of Florida are home to several dolphin species. By far the most common species is the bottlenose dolphin, which is highly social, extremely intelligent and frequently encountered around the entire peninsula. Bottlenose dolphins are the species most often seen in captivity.

Manatees

Florida's coast is home to the unusual, gentle manatee, which moves between freshwater rivers and the ocean. Around 10ft long and weighing on average 1000lb, these agile, expressive creatures don't do much, spending most of each day resting and eating 10% of their body weight. In winter they seek out Florida's warm-water springs and power-plant discharge canals. In summer they migrate back to the ocean and can be spotted in the coastal waters of Alabama, Georgia and South Carolina, in addition to Florida.

Manatees have been under some form of protection since 1893, and they were included in the first federal endangered species list in 1967. They were once hunted for their meat – finer than filet mignon, allegedly – but collisions with boats are now a leading cause of manatee deaths, accounting for over 20% annually. Manatees number more than 4000 today.

Birds

The bald eagle, the USA's national symbol since 1782, is the only eagle unique to North America. Its wingspan can reach more than 6.5ft across. Good wintertime viewing sites are along the Mississippi River in Minnesota, Wisconsin and Illinois; in summer, eagles are common throughout Florida, wherever there's fish-rich water for chowing alongside tall trees for nesting. The eagle has come off the endangered species list, having made a remarkable comeback from a low of 417 breeding pairs in 1963 to more than 9750 pairs today (that's in the lower 48 states; another 30,000-plus live in Alaska).

White pelicans, which are among the region's largest birds, arrive in winter (October to April), while brown pelicans, the only kind to dive for their food, live here year-round. They're found around the Gulf Coast and throughout Florida.

In a program to introduce endangered whooping cranes to the east, naturalists use ultralight aircraft to lead young cranes from their breeding ground in central Wisconsin to a winter habitat along Florida's Gulf Coast. Once the birds learn the route, they can retrace it unaided. Follow them at http://www.ustream.tv/migratingcranes.

Survival
Guide

Directory A–Z

Accommodations

For all but the cheapest places and the slowest seasons, reservations are advised. In high-season tourist hot spots, hotels can book up months ahead.

Seasons

➡ Peak season is summer, generally May to September, when prices are highest.

➡ Exceptions include Florida and the northern ski areas, when winter is the busiest and costliest time to visit.

Amenities

➡ Most properties offer in-room wi-fi. It's typically free in budget and midrange lodgings, while top-end hotels often charge a fee (typically $10 to $15 per day).

➡ Many smaller properties, especially B&Bs, ban smoking. Marriott and Westin hotels are 100% smoke free. All other properties have rooms set aside for nonsmokers.

➡ Air-conditioning is standard at most places.

Discounts

Check hotel websites for special online rates. The usual suspects also offer discounted room prices:

Expedia (www.expedia.com)

Hotels.com (www.hotels.com)

Hotwire (www.hotwire.com)

Priceline (www.priceline.com)

Travelocity (www.travelocity.com)

B&Bs & Inns

These accommodations vary from small, comfy houses with shared bathrooms (least expensive) to romantic, antique-filled historic homes and mansions with private baths (most expensive). Those focusing on upscale romance may discourage children. Also, inns and B&Bs often require a minimum stay of two or three days on weekends, and reservations are essential. Always call ahead to confirm policies (ie regarding kids, pets, smoking) and bathroom arrangements.

B&B agencies:

Bed & Breakfast Inns Online (www.bbonline.com)

BedandBreakfast.com (www.bedandbreakfast.com)

BnB Finder (www.bnbfinder.com)

Select Registry (www.selectregistry.com)

Camping

Campsites at national and state parks typically come in three types:

Primitive Free to $10 per night, no facilities.

Basic $10 to $20, with toilets, drinking water, fire pits and picnic tables.

Developed $20 to $45, with more amenities such as showers, barbecue grills, RV sites with hookups etc.

Make reservations for national parks and other federal lands through **Recreation.gov** (☏518-885-3639, 877-444-6777; www.recreation.gov). Camping is usually limited to 14 days and can be reserved up to six months in advance. For some state park campgrounds, you can make bookings through **Reserve America** (www.reserveamerica.com).

Most privately owned campgrounds are geared to RVs (motor homes), but will also have a small section

---

SLEEPING PRICE RANGES

Rates listed are based on double occupancy for high season and do not include taxes, which can add 10% to 15%, or even more, to the rate. When booking, ask for the rate including taxes.

$ less than $100

$$ $100 to $200

$$$ more than $200

available for tent campers. Expect lots of amenities, like swimming pools, laundry facilities, convenience stores and bars. **Kampgrounds of America** (KOA; ☎406-248-7444; www.koa.com) is a national network of private campgrounds; their Kamping Kabins have air-con and kitchens.

Hostels

Hostelling International USA (HI-USA; ☎301-495-1240; www.hiusa.org; annual membership adult/child/senior $28/free/$18) runs several hostels in the eastern US. Most have gender-segregated dorms, a few private rooms, shared baths and a communal kitchen. Overnight fees for dorm beds range from $23 to $54 (NYC being the priciest). You don't have to be a member to stay, but you pay a slightly higher rate. Reservations are accepted.

The region also has many independent hostels not affiliated with HI-USA. Browse listings at the following:

Hostels.com (www.hostels.com)

Hostelworld.com (www.hostelworld.com)

Hostelz.com (www.hostelz.com)

Hotels

Hotels in all categories typically include in-room phones, cable TV, internet access, private baths and a simple continental breakfast. Many midrange properties provide minibars, microwaves, hairdryers and swimming pools, while top-end hotels add concierge services, fitness and business centers, spas, restaurants and bars.

We try to highlight independently owned hotels, but in some towns, chain hotels are the best – and sometimes the only – option. Common chains:

Best Western (☎800-780-7234; www.bestwestern.com)

Comfort Inn (☎877-424-6423; www.comfortinn.com)

Hampton Inn (☎toll free 800 426 7866; www.hampton-inn.com)

Hilton (☎800-445-8667; www.hilton.com)

Holiday Inn (☎toll free 800 465 4329; www.holiday-inn.com)

Marriott (☎888-236-2427; www.marriott.com)

Super 8 (☎800-800-8000; www.super8.com)

House & Apartment Rentals

To rent a house or apartment from locals, visit **Airbnb** (www.airbnb.com), which has thousands of listings across the country. Budget travelers can also rent a room; it's a great way to connect with locals if you don't mind sharing facilities.

Motels

Motels – distinguishable from hotels by having rooms that open onto a parking lot – tend to cluster around interstate exits and along main routes into town. Many are inexpensive 'mom-and-pop' operations; breakfast is rarely included; and amenities might top out at a phone and TV (maybe with cable). Although most motel rooms won't win any style awards, they can be clean and comfortable and offer good value. Ask to see a room first if you're unsure.

Resorts

Florida, in particular, has behemoth resorts. Facilities can include all manner of fitness and sports, pools, spas, restaurants and bars, and so on. Many also have on-site babysitting services. However, some also tack an extra 'resort fee' onto rates, so always ask.

Customs Regulations

For a complete list of US customs regulations, go online to **US Customs and Border Protection** (www.cbp.gov).

Duty-free allowance per person is as follows:

➡ 1L of liquor (provided you are at least 21 years old)

➡ 100 cigars and 200 cigarettes (if you're at least 18)

➡ $200 worth of gifts and purchases ($800 if a returning US citizen)

➡ If you arrive with $10,000 or more in US or foreign currency, it must be declared.

There are heavy penalties for attempting to import illegal drugs. Forbidden items include drug paraphernalia, items with fake brand names, and most goods made in Cuba, Iran, Myanmar (Burma) and Sudan. Fruit, vegetables and other food must be declared (whereby you'll undergo a time-consuming search) or left in the bins in the arrival area.

Discount Cards

The following cards can net savings (usually about 10%) on museums, accommodations and some transport (including Amtrak):

American Association of Retired Persons (AARP; www.aarp.org) For US travelers age 50 and older.

American Automobile Association (AAA; ☎800-874-7532; www.aaa.com) For members of AAA or reciprocal clubs in Europe and Australia.

BOOK YOUR STAY ONLINE

For more accommodations reviews by Lonely Planet authors, check out http://lonelyplanet.com/hotels/. You'll find independent reviews, as well as recommendations on the best places to stay. Best of all, you can book online.

International Student Identity Card (ISIC; www. isic.org) For students any age. There's also a card for non-students under age 26.

Student Advantage Card (www.studentadvantage.com) For US and foreign travelers.

Electricity

120V/60Hz

120V/60Hz

Embassies & Consulates

In addition to the following embassies in Washington, DC (see www.embassy.org for a complete list), most countries have an embassy for the UN in New York City. Some countries have consulates in other large cities.

Australian Embassy (☎20 2-797-3000; www.usa.embassy. gov.au; 1601 Massachusetts Ave NW)

Canadian Embassy (☎20 2-682-1740; www.canadainternational.gc.ca; 501 Pennsylvania Ave NW)

French Embassy (☎20 2-644-6000; www.info-france-usa.org; 4101 Reservoir Rd NW)

German Embassy (☎20 2-298-4000; www.germany. info; 2300 M St NW)

Irish Embassy (☎202-462-3939; www.embassyofireland. org; 2234 Massachusetts Ave NW)

Mexican Embassy (☎20 2-728-1600; http://embamex. sre.gob.mx/eua; 1911 Pennsylvania Ave NW)

Netherlands Embassy (☎877-388-2443; http:// dc.the-netherlands.org; 4200 Linnean Ave NW)

New Zealand Embassy (☎202-328-4800; www.nzembassy.com/usa; 37 Observatory Circle NW)

UK Embassy (☎20 2-588-6500; www.gov.uk/ government/world/usa; 3100 Massachusetts Ave NW)

Food

See p626 for everything you need to know about eating and drinking in the region.

Gay & Lesbian Travelers

In general, the Northeast is the most tolerant region in the eastern USA, and the South the least so, though big cities in all of the regions have long-standing gay communities.

Hot Spots

Manhattan has loads of great gay bars and clubs, especially in Hell's Kitchen, Chelsea and the West Village. A few hours away (by train and ferry) is Fire Island, the sandy gay mecca on Long Island. Other East Coast cities with gay and lesbian scenes are Boston, Philadelphia, Washington, DC, Massachusetts' Provincetown (on Cape Cod) and Delaware's Rehoboth Beach. Even Maine has a gay beach destination: Ogunquit.

In the South, there's always steamy 'Hotlanta.' In Florida, Miami and the 'Conch Republic' of Key West support thriving gay communities, though Fort Lauderdale attracts bronzed boys and girls, too. Of course, everyone gets their funk on in New Orleans. In the Midwest, seek out Chicago and Minneapolis.

Attitudes

Most major US cities have a visible and open GLBT community that is easy to connect with.

The level of public acceptance varies nationwide. In some places, there is absolutely no tolerance whatsoever, and in others acceptance is predicated on GLBT people not 'flaunting' their sexual orientation or identity. Be aware that bigotry still exists here. In rural areas and conservative enclaves, it's unwise to be openly out, as verbal abuse and even violence can sometimes occur. When in doubt, assume that locals follow a 'don't ask, don't tell' policy. Following a Supreme Court ruling in 2013, same-sex marriage is now legally recognized at the federal level, and 16 states (including many in the Northeast) have so far legalized same-sex marriages.

Resources

The Queerest Places: A Guide to Gay and Lesbian

Historic Sites, by Paula Martinac, is full of juicy details and history, and covers the country. Visit her blog at queerestplaces.wordpress.com.

Advocate (www.advocate.com) Gay-oriented news website reports on business, politics, arts, entertainment and travel.

Damron (www.damron.com) Publishes the classic gay travel guides, but they're advertiser-driven and sometimes outdated.

Gay Travel (www.gaytravel.com) Online guides to dozens of US destinations.

Gay Yellow Network (www.gayyellow.com) Yellow-page listings for over 30 US cities.

Out Traveler (www.outtraveler.com) Has useful online city guides and travel articles to various US and foreign destinations.

Purple Roofs (www.purpleroofs.com) Lists gay-owned and gay-friendly B&Bs and hotels.

Health

The eastern region, like the rest of the USA, has a high level of hygiene, so infectious diseases are not a significant problem. There are no required vaccines, and tap water is safe to drink.

Bring any medications you may need in their original containers, clearly labeled. Having a signed, dated letter from your physician that describes all of your medical conditions and medications (including generic names) is also a good idea.

Health Insurance

The United States offers possibly the finest health care in the world – the problem is that it can be prohibitively expensive. It's essential to purchase travel health insurance if your home policy doesn't cover you for medical expenses abroad. Check the Insurance section of the **Lonely Planet** (lonelyplanet.com/travel-insurance) website for more information.

Find out in advance if your insurance plan will make payments directly to providers or reimburse you later for overseas health expenditures.

Health Care Availability

➡ If you have a medical emergency, go to the emergency room of the nearest hospital.

➡ If the problem isn't urgent, call a nearby hospital and ask for a referral to a local physician; this is usually cheaper than a trip to the emergency room.

➡ Stand-alone, for-profit, urgent-care centers provide good service, but can be the most expensive option.

➡ Pharmacies are abundantly supplied. However, some medications that are available over the counter in other countries require a prescription in the US.

➡ If you don't have insurance to cover the cost of prescriptions, they can be shockingly expensive.

Infectious Diseases

Most infectious diseases are acquired by mosquito or tick bites or through environmental exposure. The **Centers for Disease Control** (www.cdc.gov) has further details.

Giardiasis Intestinal infection. Avoid drinking directly from lakes, ponds, streams and rivers.

Lyme Disease Occurs mostly in the Northeast. Transmitted by deer ticks in late spring and summer. Perform a tick check after you've been outdoors.

West Nile Virus Mosquito-transmitted in late summer and early fall. Prevent by keeping covered (wear long sleeves, long pants, hats, and shoes rather than sandals) and apply a good insect repellent, preferably one containing DEET, to exposed skin and clothing.

Environmental Hazards

Cold exposure This can be a problem, especially in the northern regions. Keep all body surfaces covered, including the head and neck. Watch out for the 'Umbles' – stumbles, mumbles, fumbles and grumbles – which are signs of impending hypothermia.

Heat exhaustion Dehydration is the main contributor. Symptoms include feeling weak, headache, nausea and sweaty skin. Lay the victim flat with their legs raised, apply cool, wet cloths to the skin, and rehydrate.

Insurance

It's expensive to get sick, crash a car or have things stolen from you in the US. Make sure to have adequate coverage before arriving. To insure yourself for items that may be stolen from your car, consult your homeowner's (or renter's) insurance policy or consider investing in travel insurance.

Worldwide travel insurance is available at the Insurance section of the **Lonely Planet** (lonelyplanet.com/travel-insurance) website. You can buy, extend and claim online at any time – even if you're already on the road.

GOVERNMENT TRAVEL ADVICE

Australia (www.smartraveller.gov.au)

Canada (www.voyage.gc.ca)

New Zealand (www.safetravel.govt.nz)

UK (www.fco.gov.uk)

Internet Access

➡ Travelers will have few problems staying connected in the tech-savvy USA. This guide uses an internet icon (@) when a place has a net-connected computer for public use and the wi-fi icon (📶) when it offers wireless internet access, whether free or fee-based.

➡ Big cities have a few internet cafes but in smaller towns, you may have to head to the public library or a copy center to get online if you're not packing a laptop or other web-accessible device. Most libraries have public terminals (though they have time limits) and wi-fi.

➡ Wi-fi is widely available. Most lodgings have it (in room, with decent speed), as do many restaurants, bars and coffee shops (such as Starbucks). Some towns even have wi-fi-connected parks and plazas.

➡ If you're not from the US, remember that you may need an AC adapter for your laptop (if it's not 110/220 dual-voltage), plus a plug adapter for US sockets; both are available at large electronics shops, such as Best Buy.

➡ For a list of wi-fi hotspots, visit www.wififreespot.com or http://v4.jiwire.com.

Legal Matters

Note that, if you are stopped by the police, there is no system of paying traffic tickets or other fines on the spot. The officer will explain your options to you; there is usu-ally a 30-day period to pay fines by mail.

If you are arrested, never walk away from an officer. You are allowed to remain silent, and you are entitled to have access to an attorney. The legal system presumes you're innocent until proven guilty. All persons who are arrested have the right to make one phone call. If you don't have a lawyer or family member to help you, call your embassy or consulate. The police will give you the number on request.

Drugs & Alcohol

➡ In most places it's illegal to walk with an open alcoholic drink on the street. New Orleans and Memphis' Beale St are notable exceptions.

➡ Being 'carded' (ie asked to show photo ID to prove you're of legal drinking age, which is 21 years old) is standard practice everywhere.

➡ Some states, especially in the South, have 'dry' counties where liquor sales are banned altogether.

➡ In all states, the blood alcohol limit is 0.08%. Driving under the influence of alcohol or drugs is a serious offense, subject to stiff fines and even imprisonment.

➡ Twenty states – including most from New York on through the Northeast – treat possession of small amounts of marijuana as a misdemeanor (generally punishable with a fine of around $100 or $200 for the first offense).

➡ Aside from marijuana, recreational drugs are prohibited by law. Possession of any illicit drug, including cocaine, ecstasy, LSD, heroin, hashish or more than an ounce of pot, is a felony potentially punishable by lengthy jail sentences.

Money

Most locals do not carry large amounts of cash for everyday use, relying instead on credit cards, debit cards and ATMs. Don't, however, plan to rely exclusively on credit cards, as some machines (notably at many gas stations) won't accept foreign cards. Smaller businesses may refuse to accept bills over $20.

ATMs

➡ ATMs are available 24/7 at most banks and in shopping centers, airports, grocery stores and convenience shops.

➡ Most ATMs charge a service fee of $2.50 or more per transaction and your home bank may impose additional charges.

➡ For foreign visitors, ask your bank for exact information about using its cards in stateside ATMs. The exchange rate is usually as good as you'll get anywhere.

Credit Cards

Major credit cards are almost universally accepted. In fact, it's next to impossible to rent a car or make phone reservations without one. Visa and MasterCard are the most widely accepted. Contact the issuing company for lost or stolen cards:

American Express (☎800-528-4800; www.americanex-press.com)

MasterCard (☎800-627-8372; www.mastercard.com)

Visa (☎800-847-2911; www.visa.com)

Currency Exchange

➡ Banks are usually the best places to exchange foreign currencies. Most large city banks offer the service, but banks in rural areas may not.

➡ Currency-exchange counters at the airport and in tourist centers typically have the worst rates; ask about fees and surcharges first.

➡ **Travelex** (☏877-414-6359; www.travelex.com) is a major currency-exchange company, but **American Express** (☏800-528-4800; www.americanexpress.com) travel offices may offer better rates.

Taxes

➡ Sales tax varies by state and county, and ranges from 5% to 9%. Most prices you see advertised will exclude tax, which is calculated upon purchase.

➡ Hotel taxes vary by city from around 10% to over 18% (in NYC).

Tipping

Tipping is *not* optional; only withhold tips in cases of outrageously bad service.

Airport & hotel porters $2 per bag, minimum $5 per cart

Bartenders 10% to 15% per round, minimum $1 per drink

Hotel maids $2 to $4 daily, left under the card provided

Restaurant servers 15% to 20%, unless a gratuity is already charged on the bill

Taxi drivers 10% to 15%, rounded up to the next dollar

Valet parking attendants At least $2 when handed back your car keys

Opening Hours

Typical normal opening times are as follows:

Banks 8:30am to 4:30pm Monday to Friday (and possibly 9am to noon Saturday)

Bars 5pm to midnight Sunday to Thursday, to 2am Friday and Saturday

Nightclubs 10pm to 3am Thursday to Saturday

Post offices 9am to 5pm Monday to Friday

Shopping malls 9am to 9pm

Stores 9am to 6pm Monday to Saturday, noon to 5pm Sunday

Supermarkets 8am to 8pm, some open 24 hours

Post

➡ The **US Postal Service** (USPS; ☏800-275-8777; www.usps.com) is reliable and inexpensive. The postal rates for 1st-class mail within the USA are 46¢ for letters weighing up to 1oz (20¢ for each additional ounce) and 33¢ for postcards.

➡ International airmail rates are $1.10 for a 1oz letter or postcard.

Public Holidays

On the following national public holidays, banks, schools and government offices (including post offices) are closed, and transportation, museums and other services operate on a Sunday schedule. Holidays falling on a weekend are usually observed the following Monday.

New Year's Day January 1

Martin Luther King Jr Day Third Monday in January

Presidents' Day Third Monday in February

Memorial Day Last Monday in May

Independence Day July 4

PRACTICALITIES

Newspapers & Magazines

➡ Regional newspapers: *Washington Post, Boston Globe, Miami Herald, Chicago Tribune*

➡ National newspapers: *New York Times, Wall Street Journal, USA Today*

➡ Mainstream news magazines: *Time, Newsweek, US News & World Report*

Radio & TV

➡ Radio news: National Public Radio (NPR), lower end of FM dial

➡ Broadcast TV: ABC, CBS, NBC, FOX, PBS (public broadcasting)

➡ Major cable channels: CNN (news), ESPN (sports), HBO (movies), Weather Channel

Video Systems

➡ NTSC standard (incompatible with PAL or SECAM)

➡ DVDs coded for Region 1 (US and Canada only)

Weights & Measures

➡ Weight: ounces (oz), pounds (lb), tons

➡ Liquid: oz, pints, quarts, gallons (gal)

➡ Distance: feet (ft), yards (yd), miles (mi)

Smoking

As of 2013, about half the eastern states, the District of Columbia and many municipalities across the region were entirely smoke-free in restaurants, bars and workplaces.

Labor Day First Monday in September

Columbus Day Second Monday in October

Veterans' Day November 11

Thanksgiving Fourth Thursday in November

Christmas Day December 25

Safe Travel

Hurricane season along the Atlantic seaboard and Gulf of Mexico extends from June through November, but the peak season is late August through October. Relatively speaking, very few storms become East Coast hurricanes, but the devastation they wreak when they do can be enormous. Travelers should take all hurricane alerts, warnings and evacuation orders seriously.

Inland in the Midwest and South, tornado season is roughly from March to July. Again, the chances you'll encounter one are slim.

When natural disasters do threaten, listen to radio and TV news reports. For more information on storms and preparedness, contact the **National Weather Service** (www.nws.noaa.gov).

Telephone

The US phone system mixes regional service providers, competing long-distance carriers and several cell-phone companies. Overall, the system is efficient. Calls from a regular landline or cell phone are usually cheaper than a hotel phone or pay phone. Services such as **Skype** (www.skype.com) and **Google Voice** (www.google.com/voice) can make calling quite cheap. Check the websites for details.

Cell Phones

Most of the USA's mobile-phone systems are incompatible with the GSM 900/1800 standard used throughout Europe and Asia (though some convertible phones will work). G3 phones such as iPhones will work fine – but beware of roaming costs, especially for data. Check with your service provider about using your phone here.

It might be cheaper to buy a prepaid SIM card for the USA, like those sold by AT&T or T-Mobile, which you can insert into your international mobile phone to get a local phone number and voicemail. **Planet Omni** (www.planetomni.com) and **Telestial** (www.telestial.com) offer these services, as well as cell-phone rentals.

You can also buy inexpensive, no-contract (pre-paid) phones with a local number and a set number of minutes, which can be topped up at will. Virgin Mobile, T-Mobile, AT&T and other providers offer phones starting at $20, with a package of minutes starting at around $40 for 400 minutes. Electronics store chain **Best Buy** (www.bestbuy.com) sells these phones, as well as international SIM cards.

Rural swaths of the East, especially in the mountains and various national parklands, don't pick up a signal. Check your provider's coverage map.

Dialing Codes

➡ All phone numbers within the USA consist of a three-digit area code followed by a seven-digit local number.

➡ If you are calling long-distance, dial 🗹1 + the area code + the phone number. For local calls, you can sometimes dial just the seven-digit local number. If you're not sure whether the number is local or long distance (new area codes are added all the time, confusing even residents), try it one way, and if it's wrong, usually a recorded voice will correct you.

➡ Always dial 🗹1 before toll-free numbers (which start with 800, 888, 877, 866).

Most toll-free numbers only work within the USA.

➡ Dial the international country code for the USA (🗹1) if calling from abroad.

➡ To make an international call from the USA, dial 🗹011, followed by the country code, area code and phone number. Canada is the exception, for which you just dial 1 plus the area code and number.

➡ Dial 🗹00 for assistance making international calls.

➡ Dial 🗹411 for directory assistance nationwide.

➡ Dial 🗹1-800-555-1212 for directory assistance for toll-free numbers.

Pay Phones

Pay phones are an endangered species in the ever-expanding mobile-phone world. Local calls cost 35¢ to 50¢ for the first few minutes; talking longer costs more.

Phone Cards

Private prepaid phone cards are a good solution for travelers on a budget. They are available from convenience stores, supermarkets and pharmacies. AT&T sells a reliable phone card that is widely available.

Time

The eastern region is split between the Eastern and Central time zones, which are an hour apart. The demarcation line slices through Indiana, Kentucky, Tennessee and Florida. When it's noon Eastern time, it is 11am Central time (and 5pm Greenwich Mean Time).

The region, as well as most of the country, observes Daylight Saving Time (DST). On the second Sunday in March, clocks are set one hour ahead ('spring ahead'). Then, on the first Sunday of November, clocks are turned back one hour ('fall back').

And FYI: the US date system is written as month/day/year. Thus, the 8th of June, 2015, becomes 6/8/15.

Tourist Information

The official tourism website of the USA is www.discover america.com. It has links to every US state tourism office and website, plus loads of ideas for itinerary planning.

Most cities and towns have some sort of tourist center that provides local information, typically operated by the convention and visitor bureau (CVB) or chamber of commerce. These entities tend to list only the businesses that are bureau/chamber members, so not all of the town's hotels and restaurants receive coverage – keep in mind that good, independent options may be missing.

A couple of websites to get you started:

New York State Tourism (www.iloveny.com)

Visit Florida (www.visit florida.com)

Washington, DC (www. washington.org)

Travelers with Disabilities

Travel in the region is relatively accommodating.

➡ Most public buildings are wheelchair-accessible and have appropriate restroom facilities.

➡ All major airlines, Greyhound buses and Amtrak trains will assist travelers with disabilities; just describe your needs when making reservations at least 48 hours in advance.

➡ Some car-rental agencies, such as Budget and Hertz, offer hand-controlled vehicles and vans with wheelchair lifts at no extra charge, but you must reserve them well in advance

➡ Most cities have taxi companies with at least one accessible van, though you'll have to call ahead.

➡ Cities with underground transport have elevators for passengers needing assistance. Washington, DC, has the best network (every station has an elevator); NYC's elevators are few and far between.

➡ Many national and some state parks and recreation areas have wheelchair-accessible paved, graded dirt or boardwalk trails.

A number of organizations specialize in the needs of disabled travelers:

Access-Able Travel Source (www.access-able. com) General travel website with useful tips and links.

Flying Wheels Travel (☎877-451-5006, 507-451-5005; www.flyingwheelstravel. com) A full-service travel agency, highly recommended for those with mobility issues or chronic illness.

Mobility International USA (☎541-343 1284; www. miusa.org) Advises disabled travelers on mobility issues and runs educational exchange programs.

Wheelchair Getaways (☎800-642-2042; www. wheelchairgetaways.com) Rents accessible vans throughout the USA.

Visas

Admission requirements are subject to rapid change. The **US State Department** (http://travel.state.gov) has the latest information, or check with a US consulate in your home country.

Visa Waiver Program & ESTA

➡ Under the US visa-waiver program, visas are not required for citizens of 36 countries – including most EU members, Japan, Australia, New Zealand and the UK – for visits of up to 90 days (no extensions allowed), as long as you can present a machine-readable passport and are approved under the **Electronic System for Travel Authorization** (ESTA; www.cbp.gov/esta). Note: you must register at least 72 hours before arrival and there's a $14 fee for processing and authorization (payable online).

➡ In essence, ESTA requires that you register specific information online (name, address, passport info, etc) prior to entering the US. You will receive one of three responses: 'Authorization Approved' (this usually comes within minutes; most applicants can expect to receive this response); 'Authorization Pending,' in which case you can go back online to check the status within roughly 72 hours; or 'Travel not Authorized,' meaning your application is not approved and you will need to apply for a visa.

➡ Once approved, registration is valid for two years, but note that if you renew your passport or change your name, you will need to re-register. The entire process is stored electronically and linked to your passport, but it is recommended that you bring a printout of the ESTA approval just to be safe.

➡ Canadians are exempt from the process. They do not need visas, though they do need a passport or document approved by the **Western Hemisphere Travel Initiative** (www. getyouhome.gov).

➡ Those who need a visa should apply at the US consulate in their home country.

Visiting Canada

It's temptingly easy to make trips across the border to Canada from the eastern USA, but upon return, non-Americans will be subject to the full immigration procedure. Always take your passport when you cross the border.

Citizens of most Western countries will not need a visa to visit Canada, so it's really not a problem to cross to the Canadian side of Niagara Falls or detour up to Québec. Travelers entering the USA by bus from Canada may be closely scrutinized.

Volunteering

Volunteering opportunities abound in the eastern USA, providing a memorable chance to interact with locals and the land in ways you never would when just passing through.

Casual, drop-in volunteer work is plentiful in the big cities. Check weekly alternative newspapers for calendar listings or browse the free classified ads online at **Craigslist** (www.craigslist. org). The public website **Serve.gov** (www.serve.gov) and private websites **Idealist.org** (www.idealist.org) and **VolunteerMatch** (www. volunteermatch.org) offer free searchable databases of short- and long-term volunteer opportunities nationwide.

More formal volunteer programs, especially those designed for international travelers, typically charge a fee of $250 to $1000, depending on the length of the program and what amenities are included (eg housing, meals). None cover travel expenses.

Recommended volunteer organizations:

Green Project (☏504-945-0240; www.thegreenproject. org) Working to improve battered communities in New Orleans in sustainable, green ways.

Habitat for Humanity (☏800-422-4828; www. habitat.org) Focuses on building affordable housing for those in need.

Sierra Club (☏415-977-5522; www.sierraclub.org) 'Volunteer

vacations' restore wilderness areas and maintain trails, including in national parks and nature preserves.

Volunteers for Peace (☏802-540-3060; www.vfp. org) Grassroots, multiweek volunteer projects emphasize manual labor and international exchange.

Wilderness Volunteers (☏801-949-3099; www.wildernessvolunteers.org) Week-long trips helping maintain national parklands and outdoor recreation areas.

World Wide Opportunities on Organic Farms USA (☏415-621-3276; www. wwoofusa.org) Represents more than 1500 organic farms in all 50 states that host volunteer workers in exchange for meals and accommodation, with opportunities for both short- and long-term stays.

Women Travelers

➡ Women traveling by themselves or in a group should encounter no particular problems unique to the eastern USA. Simply use the same common sense as you would at home.

➡ In bars and nightclubs solo women can attract a lot of attention, but if you don't want company, most men will respect a firm 'no, thank you.'

➡ Physical attack is unlikely, but if you are assaulted, consider calling a rape-crisis hotline before calling the police, unless you are in immediate danger, in which case you should call ☏911. The 24-hour **National Sexual Assault Hotline** (☏800-656-4673; www.rainn. org) can help.

➡ The community website www.journeywoman. com facilitates women exchanging travel tips, with links to resources. The

Canadian government also publishes the booklet 'Her Own Way,' filled with useful general travel advice; click to http://travel.gc.ca/travelling/publications to access it.

Work

Seasonal service jobs in tourist beach towns, theme parks and ski areas are common and often easy to get, if low-paying.

If you are a foreigner in the USA with a standard nonimmigrant visitors visa, you are expressly forbidden to take paid work in the USA and will be deported if you're caught working illegally. In addition, employers are required to establish the bona fides of their employees or face fines. In particular, South Florida is notorious for large numbers of foreigners working illegally, and immigration officers are vigilant.

To work legally, foreigners need to apply for a work visa before leaving home. Student exchange visitors need a J1 visa, which the following organizations will help arrange.

For nonstudent jobs, temporary or permanent, you need to be sponsored by a US employer (who will arrange an H-category visa). These are not easy to obtain.

American Institute for Foreign Study (☏866-906-2437; www.aifs.com)

BUNAC (☏020-7251-3472; www.bunac.org)

Camp America (☏in the UK 020-7581-7373; www.campamerica.co.uk)

Council on International Educational Exchange (☏207-553-4000; www.ciee. org)

InterExchange (☏212-924-0446; www.interexchange.org) Camp and au-pair programs.

Transportation

GETTING THERE & AWAY

Flights, tours and rental cars can be booked online at www.lonelyplanet.com/bookings.

Entering the Country

Entering the USA is pretty straightforward.

➡ If you are flying, the first airport that you land in is where you must go through immigration and customs, even if you are continuing on the flight to another destination.

➡ As of 2013, the arrival/departure record (form I-94) that was once required of all foreign visitors is no longer used. Instead, you'll be asked to fill out only the US customs declaration, which is usually handed out on the plane. Have it completed before you approach the immigration desk. For the question, 'US Street Address,' give the address where you will spend the first night (a hotel address is fine).

➡ The immigration officer will look at your passport and have you register with the Department of Homeland Security's Office of Biometric Identity Management. For most visitors (excluding, for now, most Canadian and some Mexican citizens), registration consists of having a digital photo and electronic (inkless) fingerprints taken; the process takes less than a minute.

➡ The immigration officer may ask about your plans and whether you have sufficient funds. It's a good idea to list an itinerary, produce an onward or round-trip ticket and have at least one major credit card.

➡ Once you go through immigration, you collect your baggage and pass through customs. If you have nothing to declare, you'll probably clear customs without a baggage search, but don't assume this.

➡ For information on visa requirements for visiting the USA – including the Electronic System for Travel Authorization (ESTA) now required before arrival for citizens of Visa Waiver Program (VWP) countries – see p649.

➡ Remember: your passport should be valid for at least six months longer than your intended stay in the US.

Air

Airports

Atlanta is the busiest airport, followed by Chicago. The main international gateways in the eastern USA include:

CLIMATE CHANGE & TRAVEL

Every form of transport that relies on carbon-based fuel generates CO_2, the main cause of human-induced climate change. Modern travel is dependent on airplanes, which might use less fuel per kilometer per person than most cars but travel much greater distances. The altitude at which aircraft emit gases (including CO_2) and particles also contributes to their climate change impact. Many websites offer 'carbon calculators' that allow people to estimate the carbon emissions generated by their journey and, for those who wish to do so, to offset the impact of the greenhouse gases emitted with contributions to portfolios of climate-friendly initiatives throughout the world. Lonely Planet offsets the carbon footprint of all staff and author travel.

Atlanta Airport (Hartsfield-Jackson International; ATL; www.atlanta-airport.com)

Boston Airport (Logan International; ☎800-235-6426; www.massport.com/logan)

Chicago Airport (O'Hare International; ORD; www.flychicago.com)

Charlotte Airport (Charlotte/Douglas International; CLT; www.charmeck.org/departments/airport)

Miami Airport (Miami International; MIA; www.miami-airport.com)

Minneapolis-St Paul Airport (Minneapolis-St Paul International; MSP; www.mspairport.com)

New York Airport (John F Kennedy International; JFK; www.panynj.gov)

Newark Airport (Liberty International; EWR; www.panynj.gov)

Orlando Airport (Orlando International; MCO; www.orlandoairports.net)

Washington, DC Airport (Dulles International; www.metwashairports.com/dulles)

Tickets

Flying midweek (especially Tuesday and Wednesday) is typically less expensive. Also, keep in mind your entire itinerary when booking. Some deals for travel within the USA can only be purchased overseas in conjunction with an international air ticket, or you may get discounts for booking flights and car rental together.

Land

Border Crossings

The eastern USA has more than 20 official border crossings with Canada, accessed via Maine, New Hampshire, Vermont, New York, Michigan and Minnesota. It is relatively easy to cross into Canada; it's crossing *back* that can pose problems if you haven't brought all your documents. **US Customs and Border Protection** (http://apps.cbp.gov/bwt) tracks current wait times at the main border crossings. Some borders are open 24 hours, but most are not.

In general, waits rarely exceed 30 minutes, except during peak times (ie weekends and holidays, more so in summer). Some entry points are especially busy:

➡ Detroit, MI, to Windsor, Ontario

➡ Buffalo, NY, to Niagara Falls, Ontario

➡ Calais, ME, to St Stephen, New Brunswick

As always, have your papers in order, act polite and don't make jokes or casual conversation with US border officials.

Bus

Greyhound (www.greyhound.com) and its Canadian equivalent, **Greyhound Canada** (www.greyhound.ca), operate the largest bus network in North America. There are direct connections between main cities in the USA and Canada, but you usually have to transfer to a different bus at the border (where it takes a good hour for all passengers to clear customs and immigration). Most international buses have free wi-fi on board.

Megabus (www.megabus.com) also has international routes between Toronto and eastern cities including New York City, Philadelphia and Washington, DC. They are often cheaper than Greyhound. Tickets can be purchased online only.

Car & Motorcycle

➡ To drive across the US–Canadian border, you'll need the vehicle's registration papers, proof of liability insurance and your home driver's license.

➡ Rental cars can usually be driven across the border either way, but make sure your rental agreement says so in case you are questioned by border officials.

➡ If your papers are in order, border crossing is usually fast and easy, but occasionally the authorities of either country decide to search a car *thoroughly*.

Train

Amtrak (☎800-872-7245; www.amtrak.com) and **VIA Rail Canada** (www.viarail.ca) run daily services between Montreal and New York (11 hours), and Toronto and New York via Niagara Falls (13 hours total). Customs inspections happen at the border, not upon boarding.

Sea

Several cities on the East Coast are cruise-ship hubs, including New York City, Boston, New Orleans and Charleston, SC. Florida's ports harbor the most ships of all, particularly Miami, followed by Port Canaveral and Port Everglades (Fort Lauderdale).

You can also travel to and from the eastern USA on a freighter. These vessels usually carry between three and 12 passengers and, though considerably less luxurious

GREYHOUND INTERNATIONAL BUS ROUTES & FARES

ROUTE	APPROX FARE ($)	DURATION (HR)	FREQUENCY (PER DAY)
Boston–Montréal	80	7–9½	7
Detroit–Toronto	60	5–6	5
New York–Montréal	90	8–9	5

than cruise ships, give a salty taste of life at sea.

For more information on the ever-changing routes:

Cruise & Freighter Travel Association (☎800-872-8584; www.travltips.com)

Maris (www.freightercruises. com)

GETTING AROUND

Air

Flying is usually more expensive than traveling by bus, train or car, but it's the way to go when you're in a hurry.

Airlines in the Eastern USA

Overall, air travel in the USA is very safe (much safer than driving out on the nation's highways). For comprehensive details by carrier, check out **Airsafe.com** (www. airsafe.com).

The main domestic carriers:

AirTran Airways (☎800-247-8726; www.airtran.com) Atlanta-based airline; primarily serves the South, Midwest and eastern US.

American Airlines (☎800-433-7300; www.aa.com) Nationwide service.

Delta Air Lines (☎800-221-1212; www.delta.com) Nationwide service.

Frontier Airlines (☎800-432-1359; www.flyfrontier. com) Denver-based airline with nationwide service.

JetBlue Airways (☎800-538-2583; www.jetblue.com) Nonstop connections between eastern and western US cities, plus Florida and New Orleans.

Southwest Airlines (☎800-435-9792; www.southwest. com) Service across the continental USA.

Spirit Airlines (☎801-401-2200; www.spiritair.com) Florida-based airline; serves many US gateway cities.

TRAVELING TO CANADA

It's easy to journey across the border to Canada from the Eastern USA and quite common to do so, especially at Niagara Falls. Here are a few things to keep in mind:

➧ You will have to show your passport. The exception is US citizens at land and sea borders, who have other options besides using a passport, such as an enhanced driver's license or passport card. See the **Western Hemisphere Travel Initiative** (www.getyouhome.gov) for approved identification documents.

➧ Citizens of the USA, most Western European nations, Australia, New Zealand and Japan do not need a visa to enter Canada for stays of up to 180 days, but some nationalities do. **Citizenship and Immigration Canada** (CIC; www.cic.gc.ca) has the details.

➧ Upon return to the USA, non-Americans will be subject to the full immigration procedure.

➧ For the lowdown on where to go, what to do and all things north of the border, check out Lonely Planet's *Canada* or *Discover Canada* guides.

United Airlines (☎800-864-8331; www.united.com) Nationwide service.

US Airways (☎800-428-4322; www.usairways.com) Nationwide service.

Virgin America (☎877-359-8474; www.virginamerica.com) Flights between East and West Coast cities and Las Vegas.

There are also smaller regional services:

Cape Air (☎866-227-3247; www.flycapeair.com) Flights to several New England destinations, including Martha's Vineyard and Nantucket; also runs a popular Florida route between Fort Myers and Key West.

Royale Air Service (☎877-359-4753; www.royaleairservice.com) Flights to Rock Harbor in Isle Royale National Park from Houghton County Airport in Michigan's Upper Peninsula.

Air Passes

International travelers who plan on doing a lot of flying might consider buying a North American air pass. Passes are normally available only to non–North American citizens, and they must be purchased in conjunction with an international ticket. Conditions and cost structures can be complicated, but all passes include a certain number of domestic flights (from two to 10) that typically must be used within a 60-day period. Two of the biggest airline networks offering air passes are **Star Alliance** (www.staralliance. com) and **One World** (www. oneworld.com).

Bicycle

Regional bicycle touring is popular: winding back roads and scenic coastlines make for great itineraries. Many cities (including New York City, Chicago, Minneapolis and Boston) also have designated bike routes. Renting a bicycle is easy throughout the eastern USA. Some things to keep in mind:

➧ Cyclists must follow the same rules of the road as vehicles, but don't expect drivers to always respect your right of way.

➝ Helmets are mandatory for cyclists in some states and towns (though there is no federal law that requires it). It usually applies to children under age 18. The **Bicycle Helmet Safety Institute** (www.bhsi.org/mandator.htm) has a thorough, state-by-state list of local rules.

➝ The **Better World Club** (📞866-238-1137; www.betterworldclub.com) provides emergency roadside assistance for cyclists. Membership costs $40 per year, plus a $12 enrollment fee, and entitles you to two free pick-ups.

➝ The **League of American Bicyclists** (www.bikeleague.org) offers general tips, plus lists of local bike clubs and repair shops.

Transportation

If you're bringing your own wheels, call around to check oversize luggage prices and restrictions. Bikes are considered checked luggage on airplanes, but often must be boxed and fees can be high (over $200). Amtrak trains and Greyhound buses will transport bikes within the USA, typically for much less.

Rental

Outfitters renting bicycles exist in most tourist towns. Rentals typically cost between $20 and $30 per day, including a helmet and lock. Most companies require a credit-card security deposit of $200 or so.

Purchase

Buying a bike is easy, as is reselling it before you leave. Specialist bike shops have the best selection and advice for new bikes, but general sporting-goods stores and big-box retailers may have lower prices. Better yet, buy a used bike. To sniff out the best bargains, scour flea markets, garage sales and thrift shops, or browse the free classified ads at **Craigslist** (www.craigslist.org).

Boat

Several ferry services provide efficient, scenic links in the East. Most transport cars too, but you must make reservations well in advance. Popular services across the region:

Northeast

Bay State Cruise Company (📞877-783-3779; www.boston-ptown.com) Ferries between Boston and Provincetown.

Block Island Ferry (📞401-783-7996; www.blockislandferry.com) Ferries to Block Island from Narragansett and Newport, RI.

Lake Champlain Ferries (📞802-864-9804; www.ferries.com) Ferries between Burlington, VT, and Port Kent, NY.

Staten Island Ferry (📞718-876-8441; www.siferry.com) Commuter boats between Staten Island and Manhattan, NY.

Steamship Authority (📞508-477-8600; www.steamshipauthority.com) Ferries to Martha's Vineyard and Nantucket from Cape Cod, MA.

Great Lakes

To reach Mackinac Island, MI, three passenger ferry companies – **Arnold Line** (📞800-542-8528; www.arnoldline.com), **Shepler's** (📞800-828-6157; www.sheplersferry.com) and **Star Line** (📞800-638-9892; www.mackinacferry.com) – operate out of both Mackinaw City and St Ignace, MI.

Lake Express (www.lake-express.com) crosses Lake Michigan between Milwaukee, WI, and Muskegon, MI.

South

North Carolina Ferry System (📞800-293-3779; www.outer-banks.com/ferry) runs ferries throughout the Outer Banks.

Bus

Greyhound (📞800-231-2222; www.greyhound.com) is the major long-distance carrier, plowing along an extensive network throughout the USA, as well as to/from Canada. As a rule, buses are reliable, clean(ish) and comfortable, with air-conditioning, barely reclining seats, onboard lavatories and a no-smoking policy. Several buses have wi-fi. While some shorter-route buses run express, most stop every 50 to 100 miles to pick up passengers, and long-distance buses stop for meal breaks and driver changes.

Other carriers (most with wi-fi and power outlets on board):

Bolt Bus (📞877-265-8287; www.boltbus.com) Fast, cheap routes between major northeast cities, including NYC, Boston, Philadelphia, Baltimore, Newark and Washington, DC.

DC2NY (📞202-332-2691; www.dc2ny.com) Cheap fares between the nation's capital and NYC.

Go Buses (www.gobuses.com) Plies the Boston-to-NYC route.

Megabus (📞877-462-6342; www.megabus.com) Bolt Bus' main competitor, with routes between main cities in the Northeast and also the Midwest, radiating from hubs in NYC or Chicago. Fares can be quite low; tickets booked online only.

Peter Pan Buslines (📞800-343-9999; www.peterpanbus.com) Serves 54 destinations in the Northeast, as far north as Concord, NH, and as far south as Washington, DC.

Trailways (📞703-691-3052; www.trailways.com) Mostly in the Midwest and Mid-Atlantic states; may not be as useful as Greyhound for long trips, but fares can be competitive on shorter routes.

Yo! Bus (www.yobus.com) Some six buses per day between Boston, NYC's Chinatown and Philadelphia.

Costs

➡ In general, the earlier you book, the lower the fare.

➡ On Bolt Bus, Megabus and some of the smaller companies, the first tickets sold for a route cost $1.

➡ For lower fares on Greyhound, purchase tickets at least seven days in advance (purchasing 14 days in advance will save even more).

➡ If you're traveling with family or friends, Greyhound's companion fares let up to two additional travelers get 50% off with a minimum three-day advance purchase.

Reservations

Greyhound and Bolt Bus tickets can be bought over the phone or online, as well as at terminals. For Megabus, Go Bus and most of the smaller companies, tickets can only be purchased online in advance. Seating is normally first-come, first-served. Greyhound recommends arriving an hour before departure to get a seat.

Car & Motorcycle

For maximum flexibility and convenience, and to explore outside of the cities, a car is essential.

Automobile Associations

➡ The **American Automobile Association** (AAA; ☎800-874-7532; www. aaa.com) has reciprocal membership agreements with several international auto clubs (check with AAA and bring your membership card from home). For its members, AAA offers travel insurance, tour bookings, diagnostic centers for used-car buyers and a wide-ranging network of regional offices. AAA advocates politically for the auto industry.

➡ A more ecofriendly alternative, the **Better World Club** (☎866-238-1137; www. betterworldclub.com) donates 1% of revenue to assist environmental cleanup, offers ecologically sensitive choices for every service it provides and advocates politically for environmental causes.

➡ For either organization, the primary member benefit is 24-hour emergency roadside assistance anywhere in the USA. Both also offer trip planning, free travel maps, travel-agency services, car insurance and a range of travel discounts (eg on hotels, car rentals and attractions).

Bring Your Own Vehicle

Unless you're moving to the USA, don't even think about freighting your car.

Driver's License

Foreign visitors can legally drive a car in the USA for up to 12 months using their home driver's license. However, an International Driving Permit (IDP) will have more credibility with US traffic police, especially if your home license doesn't have a photo or isn't in English. Your automobile association at home can issue an IDP, valid for one year, for a small fee. Always carry your home license together with the IDP.

To drive a motorcycle in the USA, you will need either a valid US state motorcycle license or an IDP specially endorsed for motorcycles.

Fuel

Gas stations are ubiquitous and many are open 24 hours a day. Small-town stations may be open only from 7am to 8pm or 9pm. Plan on spending roughly $4 per US gallon. At many stations, you must pay before you pump.

Insurance

Insurance is legally required. Without it, you risk legal consequences and possible financial ruin if there's an accident.

➡ Car-rental agencies offer liability insurance, which covers other people and property involved in an accident.

➡ Collision Damage Waivers (CDW) reduce or eliminate the amount you'll have to reimburse the rental company if there's damage to the car itself.

➡ Paying extra for all of this insurance increases the cost of a rental car by as much as $10 to $30 a day.

➡ Some credit cards cover CDW for a certain rental period (usually less than 15 days), if you use the card to pay for the rental, and decline the policy offered by the rental company. Always check with your card issuer to see what coverage they offer in the USA.

Rental
CAR

To rent a car in the USA you generally need to be at least 25 years old, hold a valid driver's license and have a major credit card.

GREYHOUND DOMESTIC BUS ROUTES & FARES

ROUTE	APPROX FARE ($)	DURATION (HR)	FREQUENCY (PER DAY)
Boston–Philadelphia	57	7	10
Chicago–New Orleans	149	24	3
New York–Chicago	119	18–22	5
Washington, DC–Miami	155	25	5

→ Some companies will rent to drivers between the ages of 21 and 24 for an additional charge.

→ You should be able to get an economy-sized vehicle for about $30 to $75 per day. Child safety seats are compulsory (reserve them when you book) and cost about $13 per day.

→ Some national companies, including Avis, Budget and Hertz, offer 'green' fleets of hybrid rental cars (eg Toyota Priuses, Honda Civics), although you'll usually have to pay a lot extra to rent a more fuel-efficient vehicle.

→ Online, **Car Rental Express** (www.carrentalexpress.com) rates and compares independent agencies in US cities; it's particularly useful for searching out cheaper long-term rentals.

Major national car-rental companies:

Alamo (☏877-222-9075; www.alamo.com)

Avis (☏800-230-4898; www.avis.com)

Budget (☏800-527-0700; www.budget.com)

Dollar (☏800-800-3665; www.dollar.com)

Enterprise (☏800-261-7331; www.enterprise.com)

Hertz (☏800-654-3131; www.hertz.com)

National (☏877-222-9058; www.nationalcar.com)

Rent-a-Wreck (☏877-877-0700; www.rentawreck.com)

Thrifty (☏800-847-4389; www.thrifty.com)

MOTORCYCLE & RECREATIONAL VEHICLE (RV)

If you dream of riding a Harley, **EagleRider** (☏888-900-9901; www.eaglerider.com) has offices in major cities nationwide and rents other kinds of adventure vehicles, too. Beware that motorcycle rental and insurance are expensive.

Companies specializing in RV and camper rentals:

Adventures on Wheels (☏800-943-3579; www.wheels9.com)

Cruise America (☏800-671-8042; www.cruiseamerica.com)

Recreational Vehicle Rental Association (www.rvra.org) Good resource for RV information and advice, and helps find rental locations.

Road Conditions & Hazards

Road conditions are generally very good, but keep in mind:

→ Winter travel in general can be hazardous due to heavy snow and ice, which may cause roads and bridges to close periodically. The **Federal Highway Administration** (www.fhwa.dot.gov/trafficinfo/index.htm) provides links to road conditions and construction zones for each state.

→ If you're driving in winter or in remote areas, make sure your vehicle is equipped with four-season radial or snow tires, and emergency supplies in case you're stranded.

→ Where deer and other wild animals frequently appear roadside, you'll see signs with the silhouette of a leaping deer. Take these signs seriously, particularly at night.

Road Rules

If you're new to US roads, here are some basics:

→ Drive on the right-hand side of the road. On highways, pass in the left-hand lane.

→ The maximum speed limit on most interstates is 65mph or 70mph; a couple of eastern states go up to 75mph. It then drops to around 55mph in urban areas. Pay attention to the posted signs. City street speed limits vary between 15mph and 45mph.

→ The use of seat belts and child safety seats is required in every state. In some states, motorcyclists are required to wear helmets.

→ Unless signs prohibit it, you may turn right at a red light after first coming to a full stop (note that NYC is an exception, where it's illegal to turn right on a red).

→ At four-way stop signs, the car that reaches the intersection first has right of way. In a tie, the car on the right has right of way.

→ When emergency vehicles (ie police, fire or ambulance) approach from either direction, pull over safely and get out of the way.

→ In an increasing number of states, it is illegal to talk (or text) on a handheld cell phone while driving; use a hands-free device or pull over to take your call.

→ The blood-alcohol limit for drivers is 0.08%. Penalties are very severe for 'DUI' – Driving Under the Influence of alcohol and/or drugs.

→ In some states it is illegal to carry 'open containers' of alcohol in a vehicle, even if they are empty.

Hitchhiking

Hitchhiking in the USA is potentially dangerous and definitely not recommended. Indeed, drivers have heard so many lurid reports they tend to be just as afraid of those with their thumbs out. Hitchhiking on freeways is prohibited.

Local Transportation

Except in large cities, public transportation is rarely the most convenient option for travelers. However, it is usually cheap, safe and reliable. In addition, more than half the states in the nation have adopted 📞511 as an all-purpose local-transportation help line.

Bicycle

Some cities are more friendly to bicycles than others, but most have at least a few dedicated bike lanes and paths, and bikes usually can be carried on public transportation. Many big cities – New York, Chicago, Boston and Washington, DC, among them – have bike-share programs.

Bus

Most cities and larger towns have dependable local bus systems, though they are often designed for commuters and provide limited service in the evening and on weekends. Costs range from free to between $1 and $3 per ride.

Subway & Train

The largest systems are in New York, Chicago, Boston, Philadelphia, Washington, DC, and Chicago. Other cities may have small, one- or two-line rail systems that mainly serve downtown.

Taxi

Taxis are metered, with flagfall charges of around $2.50, plus $2 to $3 per mile. They charge extra for waiting and handling baggage, and drivers expect a 10% to 15% tip. Taxis cruise the busiest areas in large cities; otherwise, it's easiest to phone and order one.

Tours

Hundreds of companies offer all kinds of organized tours of the USA; most focus on either cities or regions.

Reputable tour companies:

Backroads (📞800-462-2848, 510-527-1555; www.backroads.com) Designs a range of active, multisport and outdoor-oriented trips for all abilities and budgets.

Contiki (📞866-266-8454; www.contiki.com) Party-hardy

sightseeing tour-bus vacations for 18- to 35-year-olds.

Gray Line (📞800-966-8125; www.grayline.com) For those short on time, Gray Line offers a comprehensive range of standard sightseeing tours across the country.

Green Tortoise (📞800-867-8647, 415-956-7500; www.greentortoise.com) Offering budget adventures for independent travelers, Green Tortoise is famous for its sleeping-bunk buses. Most trips leave from San Francisco, traipsing through the West and nationwide.

Road Scholar (📞800-454-5768; www.roadscholar.org) For those aged 55 and older, this venerable nonprofit offers 'learning adventures' in all 50 states.

Trek America (📞in North America 800-873-5872, in the UK 0844-576-1400; www.trekamerica.com) For active outdoor adventures; group sizes are kept small.

Train

Amtrak (📞800-872-7245; www.amtrak.com) has an extensive rail system throughout the USA, with several long-distance lines traversing the nation east to west, and even more running north to south. These link all of America's biggest cities and many of its smaller ones. In some places, Amtrak's Thruway buses provide connections to and from the rail network.

➡ Compared with other modes of travel, trains are rarely the quickest, cheapest

or most convenient option, but they turn the journey into a relaxing, social and scenic all-American experience.

➡ Rail services are busiest in the northeast corridor, where high-speed Acela Express trains run from Boston, MA, to Washington, DC (via New York City, Philadelphia and Baltimore).

➡ Other busy routes include NYC to Niagara Falls, Chicago to Milwaukee and Chicago to St Louis.

➡ Free wi-fi is available on many, but not all, trains. The wi-fi speed is fine for email and web browsing, but not suitable for streaming videos or music.

➡ Smoking is prohibited on all trains.

➡ Many big cities, such as NYC, Chicago and Miami, also have their own commuter rail networks. These trains provide faster, more frequent services on shorter routes.

Classes

➡ Coach Class buys you a basic, if indeed quite comfortable, reclining seat with a headrest. On some routes you can reserve seats.

➡ Business Class is available on many trains, especially on shorter routes in the northeast. Seats are more spacious and have outlets for plugging in laptops. You also get reserved seating and access to quiet cars (no cell-phone usage etc).

AMTRAK SAMPLE FARES

ROUTE	ONE-WAY FARE ($)	DURATION (HR)	FREQUENCY (PER DAY)
Chicago–New Orleans	127	20	1
New York–Chicago	101	19	1
Washington, DC–Miami	179	23	2
Boston–New York	100	3½–4	11–19

➡ First Class is available on Acela Express trains only, and adds an at-seat meal to the mix.

➡ Sleeper Class is available on overnight routes. Sleeping cars include simple bunks (called 'roomettes'), bedrooms with en-suite facilities and suites sleeping four with two bathrooms. Sleeping-car rates include meals in the dining car, which offers everyone sit-down meal service (pricey if not included).

➡ Food service on commuter lines, when it exists, consists of sandwich and snack bars. Bringing your own food and drink is recommended on all trains.

Costs

Various one-way, round-trip and touring fares are available from Amtrak, with the usual discounts available to seniors (15%), students ($20 or so) and children (50% when accompanied by a paying adult). AAA members get 10% off. Web-only 'Weekly Specials' offer good discounts on certain under-sold routes.

Generally, the earlier you book, the lower the price. To get many of the standard discounts, you need to re-serve at least three days in advance. If you want to take a high-speed Acela Express train, avoid peak commute times and aim for weekends.

Amtrak Vacations (☑800-268-7252; www.amtrak-vacations.com) offers vacation packages that include rental cars, hotels, tours and at-tractions. Air-Rail packages let you travel by train in one direction, then return by plane in the other.

Reservations

Reservations can be made any time from 11 months in advance up to the day of departure. Space on most trains is limited, and certain routes can be crowded, especially during summer and holiday periods, so it's a good idea to book as far in advance as you can; this also gives you the best chance of fare discounts.

Train Passes

➡ Amtrak's USA Rail Pass offers coach-class travel for 15 ($439), 30 ($669) or

45 ($859) days, with travel limited to eight, 12 or 18 one-way 'segments,' respectively.

➡ A segment is *not* the same as a one-way trip. If reaching your destination requires riding more than one train (for example, getting from New York to Miami with a transfer in Washington, DC) that one-way trip will actually use two segments of your pass.

➡ Reservations should be made by phone (call ☑800-872-7245, or +1-215-856-7953 from outside the USA) as far in advance as possible. Each segment of the journey must be booked.

➡ Present your pass at an Amtrak office to pick up your ticket(s) for each trip.

➡ All travel must be completed within 180 days of purchasing your pass.

➡ Passes are not valid on the Acela Express, Auto Train, Thruway motorcoach connections or the Canadian portion of Amtrak routes operated jointly with Via Rail Canada.

Behind the Scenes

SEND US YOUR FEEDBACK

We love to hear from travelers – your comments keep us on our toes and help make our books better. Our well-traveled team reads every word on what you loved or loathed about this book. Although we cannot reply individually to postal submissions, we always guarantee that your feedback goes straight to the appropriate authors, in time for the next edition. Each person who sends us information is thanked in the next edition – the most useful submissions are rewarded with a selection of digital PDF chapters.

Visit **lonelyplanet.com/contact** to submit your updates and suggestions or to ask for help. Our award-winning website also features inspirational travel stories, news and discussions.

Note: We may edit, reproduce and incorporate your comments in Lonely Planet products such as guidebooks, websites and digital products, so let us know if you don't want your comments reproduced or your name acknowledged. For a copy of our privacy policy visit lonelyplanet.com/privacy.

OUR READERS

Many thanks to the travelers who used the last edition and wrote to us with helpful hints, useful advice and interesting anecdotes: Jiaying Zhu, Leslie Oxley and Rex Jewell

AUTHOR THANKS

Karla Zimmerman

Many thanks to Carrie Biolo, Lisa DiChiera, Lea Dooley, Jim DuFresne, Ruggero Fatica, Mark Fornek, Jonathan Hayes, April Ingle, Julie Lange, Kari Lydersen, Melissa McCarville, Betsy Riley and Neil Anderson, Susan Hayes Stephan, Andrea and Greg Thomson, Sara Zimmerman and Karen and Don Zimmerman. Thanks most to Eric Markowitz, the world's best partner-for-life, who indulges all my hare-brained, pie-filled road trips. Sorry about the bug bites.

Amy C Balfour

Big thanks to my friends and experts in the Carolinas: Mike Stokes, Jay Bender, Dan Oden, Lori Bauswell, Jeff Otto, Paul Stephen, Josh Lucas, Barry Radcliffe, Patricia Robison, Lacy Davidson, Deborah Wright, Amy Marks, Paige Abbitt Schoenauer, Barbara Blue, Anna Schleunes, David Kimball, Noell and Jack Kimball and Jennifer Pharr Davis. In the Southwest, kudos to BLM maestro Chris Rose for his invaluable insights and knowledge; Justin Shephard, Tracer Finn, Jim Christian, Alex Amato, Mike Roe, Catrien van Assendelft, Lewis Pipkin, Sara Benson, Dan Westermeyer; fellow adventurers Sandee McGlaun, Lisa McGlaun, Paul Hanstedt and Karen Schneider.

Gregor Clark

Thanks to all the generous fellow Vermonters who helped with this project, especially John McCright, Sarah Pope, Namik Sevlic, Saba Rizvi, Sarah Shepherd, Sue Heim and David Alles. Love and thanks as well to Gaen, for sharing my excitement about exploring that next side road, to Meigan for giving me hugs at deadline time and to Chloe, whose infectious love of climbing Mt Mansfield barefoot always makes me smile.

Ned Friary

Thanks to all the people I met along the way who shared their tips, including the helpful folks staffing the counters at the local tourist offices. A special thanks to the rangers at the Cape Cod National Seashore and to Bob Prescott of the Massachusetts Audubon Society for sharing their one-of-a-kind insights.

Michael Grosberg

Special thanks to Carly Neidorf, my sometime trip and otherwise helpful companion; my parents, Sheldon and Judy for advice; to Kristin Mitchell and Claire Shubik on Pittsburgh; Darrah Feldman on Milford; Rebbecca Steffan for

Adirondacks help; Gregory Henderson in the Catskills; Julie Donovan in the Laurel Highlands; Nina Kelly in the Brandywine Valley; and Terri Dennison for Route 6 insight.

Paula Hardy

I'd like to thank the following for sharing the best of Connecticut and Rhode Island: Anne McAndrews, Dave Fairty, Pat and Wayne Brubaker, Rick Walker, Sanjeev Seereeram, Cinta Burgos, David King, Dave Helgerson, Harry Schwartz, Elizabeth MacAlister and the Preservation Society of Newport. Thanks also to the super Jennye Garibaldi and Mara Vorhees. Finally, thanks to Rob Smith for the laughs and letting me bring home Baggo.

Adam Karlin

Thank you to the Lonely Planet crew: Regis St Louis, Michael Grosberg, the fabulous in-house team of Suki Gear, Bruce Evans, Alison Lyall, Emily Wolman and Jennye Garibaldi. Thanks to Mom and Dad for raising me the way they did, and to Rachel Houge, my wife, greatest fan and best friend. And finally, thank you Lonely Planet. You let me wander the world and write about it. That's a blessedly exciting and rewarding way to make a living.

Mariella Krause

Thanks to Suki Gear for an amazing year full of Lonely Planet goodness, and to Jay Cooke for getting me involved in the first place. And thanks to all the amazing people I met on the road who served as a constant reminder of what traveling is all about.

Caroline Sieg

Thanks to everyone who shared their tips with me and for the friendly conversations at lobster shacks, ski resorts and brewpubs. A very special thank you to the Schmidt family who keep me coming back to New England year after year.

Adam Skolnick

Thanks to Stephanie Greene, Dana McMahan, Carla Carlton, Phoebe Lipkis, Kristin Schofield and Louisville Basketball in Louisville; Jennifer Bohler and Shanna Henderson in Nashville; Nealy Dozier, Walter Thompson, Chloe Friedman, Lydia Hardy and Chi Bui in Atlanta; and Keith, Peggy and Melissa in Natchez. My love and appreciation go out to best Savannah buds Alicia Magee, Anna Cypris Jaubert, and (by proxy) Joe Bush. Thanks also to Suki Gear, Regis St Louis and the whole Lonely Planet team. It's a joy and privilege to work with and know you all!

Mara Vorhees

My heart goes out to all the victims of the Boston Marathon bombings, all of the runners and the city as a whole. Patriots' Day has always been about facing challenges with courage – it's now true more than ever. Bostonians love their city. Love will prevail.

ACKNOWLEDGMENTS

Climate Map Data Climate map data adapted from Peel MC, Finlayson BL & McMahon TA (2007) 'Updated World Map of the Köppen-Geiger Climate Classification', Hydrology and Earth System Sciences, 11, 1633¬44.

Illustrations pp78-9, pp258-9 by Javier Martinez Zarracina.

Cover photograph: Curtis Island Lighthouse, Maine, Daniel Dempster Photography/Alamy

THIS BOOK

This 2nd edition of *Eastern USA* was coordinated by Karla Zimmerman. The content was researched and written by Karla, along with Amy C Balfour, Gregor Clark, Ned Friary, Michael Grosberg, Paula Hardy, Adam Karlin, Mariella Krause, Caroline Sieg, Adam Skolnick and Mara Vorhees. The previous edition was written by Karla Zimmerman along with Glenda Bendure, Jeff Campbell, Ned Friary, Michael Grosberg, Emily Matchar and Regis St Louis. This guidebook was commissioned in Lonely Planet's Oakland office, and produced by the following:

Commissioning Editors Jennye Garibaldi, Katie O'Connell

Coordinating Editors Ali Lemer, Martine Power

Senior Cartographer Alison Lyall

Book Designers Virginia Moreno, Wendy Wright

Associate Product Directors Sasha Baskett, Angela Tinson

Senior Editors Catherine Naghten, Karyn Noble

Assisting Editor Kate James

Assisting Cartographer Rachel Imeson

Cover Research Naomi Parker

Thanks to Brendan Dempsey, Lauren Egan, Ryan Evans, Larissa Frost, Briohny Hooper, Genesys India, Jouve India, Indra Kilfoyle, Chad Parkhill, Trent Paton, Alison Ridgway, Dianne Schallmeiner, Luna Soo, John Taufa, Juan Winata

Index

Map Legend

Sights

- Beach
- Bird Sanctuary
- Buddhist
- Castle/Palace
- Christian
- Confucian
- Hindu
- Islamic
- Jain
- Jewish
- Monument
- Museum/Gallery/Historic Building
- Ruin
- Sento Hot Baths/Onsen
- Shinto
- Sikh
- Taoist
- Winery/Vineyard
- Zoo/Wildlife Sanctuary
- Other Sight

Activities, Courses & Tours

- Bodysurfing
- Diving
- Canoeing/Kayaking
- Course/Tour
- Skiing
- Snorkeling
- Surfing
- Swimming/Pool
- Walking
- Windsurfing
- Other Activity

Sleeping

- Sleeping
- Camping

Eating

- Eating

Drinking & Nightlife

- Drinking & Nightlife
- Cafe

Entertainment

- Entertainment

Shopping

- Shopping

Information

- Bank
- Embassy/Consulate
- Hospital/Medical
- Internet
- Police
- Post Office
- Telephone
- Toilet
- Tourist Information
- Other Information

Geographic

- Beach
- Hut/Shelter
- Lighthouse
- Lookout
- Mountain/Volcano
- Oasis
- Park
- Pass
- Picnic Area
- Waterfall

Population

- Capital (National)
- Capital (State/Province)
- City/Large Town
- Town/Village

Transport

- Airport
- BART station
- Border crossing
- Boston T station
- Bus
- Cable car/Funicular
- Cycling
- Ferry
- Metro/Muni station
- Monorail
- Parking
- Petrol station
- Subway/SkyTrain station
- Taxi
- Train station/Railway
- Tram
- Underground station
- Other Transport

Note: Not all symbols displayed above appear on the maps in this book

Routes

- Tollway
- Freeway
- Primary
- Secondary
- Tertiary
- Lane
- Unsealed road
- Road under construction
- Plaza/Mall
- Steps
- Tunnel
- Pedestrian overpass
- Walking Tour
- Walking Tour detour
- Path/Walking Trail

Boundaries

- International
- State/Province
- Disputed
- Regional/Suburb
- Marine Park
- Cliff
- Wall

Hydrography

- River, Creek
- Intermittent River
- Canal
- Water
- Dry/Salt/Intermittent Lake
- Reef

Areas

- Airport/Runway
- Beach/Desert
- Cemetery (Christian)
- Cemetery (Other)
- Glacier
- Mudflat
- Park/Forest
- Sight (Building)
- Sportsground
- Swamp/Mangrove